COMPANION ENCYCLOPEDIA
OF THEOLOGY

COMPANION ENCYCLOPEDIA OF THEOLOGY

EDITED BY

*PETER BYRNE AND
LESLIE HOULDEN*

London and New York

First published in 1995
by Routledge
11 New Fetter Lane, London EC4P 4EE
29 West 35th Street, New York, NY 10001

© 1995 Routledge

Phototypeset in 10½ pt Ehrhardt by Intype, London
Printed in Great Britain by Clays Ltd, St. Ives PLC

Printed on acid-free paper

British Library Cataloguing in Publication Data

A catalogue record for this book is available from the British Library.

Library of Congress Cataloging-in-Publication Data

A catalog record for this book is available on request.

ISBN 0–415–06447–3

CONTENTS

General Introduction   ix
Leslie Houlden and Peter Byrne
The contributors   xiii

PART I: THE BIBLE

Introduction   3
Leslie Houlden

1. The Hebrew Bible: formation and character   7
John Barton

2. The Hebrew Bible: role in Judaism   28
Gary Gilbert and Alan F. Segal

3. The Christian adoption of the Old Testament   47
G. R. Evans

4. The Old Testament: historical study and new roles   64
John Rogerson

5. The New Testament: content and character   85
Leslie Houlden

6. The New Testament: the tradition of interpretation   102
John Muddiman

7. The New Testament in theology   122
Heikki Räisänen

8. The Bible as holy book   142
Stephen Prickett

PART II: THE TRADITION

Introduction   163
Leslie Houlden

9. Jesus in history and belief   168
Leslie Houlden

10. The triune God of the Bible and the emergence of orthodoxy   187
Robert L. Wilken

11. Christendom: medieval Christianity 206
    David d'Avray
12. The transition to modernity 230
    Alister McGrath
13. The Enlightenment 251
    John Kent
14. Theology now 272
    Keith Clements
15. Christian theology and other faiths 291
    Gavin D'Costa
16. Christian theology's dialogue with culture 314
    Frank Burch Brown

PART III: PHILOSOPHY
    Introduction 337
    Peter Byrne
17. The concept of God 342
    Keith Ward
18. The idea of reason 367
    Terence Penelhum
19. Natural theology 388
    David A. Pailin
20. Religious language 413
    Mark Wynn
21. Theology and scientific understanding 433
    Peter Byrne
22. Theological anthropology 453
    Roger Trigg
23. Evil and theology 472
    Stewart Sutherland
24. Feminism in the philosophy of religion 490
    Grace Jantzen

PART IV: SPIRITUALITY
    Introduction 511
    Leslie Houlden
25. Spirituality and theology 514
    Philip Sheldrake
26. Patristic spirituality 536
    Anthony Meredith
27. Mysticism and devotion in the Middle Ages 558
    Benedicta Ward
28. Religious experience in the era of reform 576
    Rowan Williams

29. Theology and spirituality in the nineteenth and
    twentieth centuries   594
    Terry Tastard
30. Religious experience and language   620
    William J. Wainwright
31. Spirituality and liberation   642
    Kenneth Leech
32. Spirituality and liturgy   665
    Gordon S. Wakefield

PART V: PRACTICAL THEOLOGY
    Introduction   687
    Peter Byrne
33. The idea of Christian ethics   691
    James M. Gustafson
34. Violence, warfare and peace   716
    Barrie Paskins
35. Ethics and the personal life   738
    Helen Oppenheimer
36. Theology, wealth and social justice   759
    Jack Mahoney
37. Power and the State   777
    Edward Norman
38. The pastoral experience   794
    Jack Dominian
39. Theology, medicine and health   817
    John Morgan
40. Environmental ethics   843
    Stephen Clark

PART VI: CHRISTIAN THEOLOGY: SCENE AND PROSPECT
    Introduction   871
    Leslie Houlden
41. The character and possibility of Christian theology today 875
    John Kent
42. Making sense of God   895
    Theodore Jennings
43. The figure of Jesus Christ in contemporary Christianity   917
    John Macquarrie
44. The Trinity in modern theology   937
    Colin Gunton
45. Theology in the narrative mode   958
    Brian Horne

46. Theology in the dogmatic mode   976
     Paul Avis
47. Theology as praxis   1001
     Dan Cohn-Sherbok
48. Theology and the future of the Church   1017
     Walter Hollenweger

Index   1036

GENERAL INTRODUCTION

Leslie Houlden and Peter Byrne

The aim of this *Companion Encyclopedia* is to provide as comprehensive a guide as possible to the present state of Christian theology in its Western academic manifestations and in the setting of the modern world. To understand the present, especially in the case of a long-standing phenomenon like Christianity, it is necessary to be aware of the past. So here there is much history as well as contemporary reflection and assessment.

The contributors are drawn from many different traditions of belief and thought, but all reflect broadly the assumptions and methods of the modern Western academy, and write as analysts rather than propagandists. No attempt has been made to seek or impose a single viewpoint, and readers will sometimes find themselves presented with different angles on the same material. Inevitably, too, some features of the scene will recur, most notably the eighteenth-century Enlightenment: readers will at least become convinced of the cruciality of this episode, greater, from a modern standpoint, in many ways than even the early period or the Reformation. At the same time, however far-reaching the developments or the applications which it undergoes, Christian theology never loses sight of the originating impulse given by Jesus of Nazareth. Behind and beneath all the ideas and all the books, it rests on the story that centres on him.

Modern Christian theology (and everything in this book is 'modern' in standpoint even when it examines writings and ideas of the distant past) is far from being a unified phenomenon. In the first place, there are significant differences of theological agenda, ethos, priority and content between the various Christian Churches, from the largest to the smallest; and, especially in the case of the great Churches, there are also significant internal differences, traceable both to history and to contemporary movements of thought and life. Thus, the Anglican Communion contains strong 'Catholic', 'Protestant' and 'liberal' elements, and the Roman Catholic Church includes both traditionalists and reformists.

Second, theology involves different styles and emphases according to the location of its practitioners: whether, for example, they operate in the context of church life, schools or universities. In the first, there is likely to be a note of authority and commitment and a tendency towards construction and synthesis that would usually seem inappropriate in the academy. Matters of church order and discipline (one has only to cite the question of the ordination of women, often scarcely intelligible as problematic to people outside the Churches) are likely to figure prominently in church theology, and often the posture is dogmatic rather than critical.

In school theology, on the other hand, the agenda tends to be formed by society at large; hence the interest in the world faiths and what they have in common, and in currently pressing ethical issues. Here there is often a felt need to respond to urgent social demands, fuelled perhaps by government or parent power.

When we turn to university theology, which this book chiefly and essentially reflects, we find a third situation, quite distinct from the other two, even though individual theologians may well feel loyalty to the Church or sensitivity to the needs of the school. Here, the dominant atmosphere is provided by the secular university as a whole, as it has developed in the West, where, despite regional variations, there is much homogeneity. While there may often be unadmitted ideology (sometimes erupting violently as in the literary world), the public stance is deeply antipathetic to anything that smacks of sectionalism or propaganda: in these respects the Churches' tarnished past is often hard to forget and theology's attempts to present itself as a reformed character are not always trusted. The emphasis is on openness, the critical assessment of all ideas, however venerable or (it may sometimes appear) trivial. More nobly, the quest for truth, by its very nature never concluded and certainly inimical to other authorities, is pre-eminent.

There can be no doubt that, despite setbacks and failures to penetrate beyond the academy as widely as may be wished or expected, this style of theology has done much to reduce bigotry and to foster human understanding. One may point, for example, to the shaming of anti-Semitism, attributable, at least in part, to developments in New Testament studies as conducted in the modern academy, giving us a more balanced picture of the Judaism that Jesus knew and inhabited; and to the ecumenical movement, where Christians of long-warring traditions have sought to let greater comprehension of one another's historical positions bring about better relations in the present.

But if we look at the university from within, then theology's situation is undeniably complex for it owes allegiance in several different, even conflicting, directions. (It is worth noting that even the numerous confessional higher educational institutions, whose teachers are usually trained in universities, are often sensitive to the complexity, even if not as strongly.) Theology owes allegiance first to the modern secular academy in which it is placed and which is its paymaster. This 'parent' may indeed be in many ways beneficent, as has been indicated, but it may also be subversive or corrosive, for the secular university has no interest whatsoever in the claims concerning God or 'the Other' which are the lively centre of theology's interest and, many would say, the single mainspring of its whole life. Theology, in other words, however dispassionate and critical it may be, can never reduce itself to purely secularist terms – to the 'study of religion' as a phenomenon in human life (alongside, for instance, sport or work). It is aware of itself, bluntly, as concerned with the holy – not only as a major presence in the world but also as a factor whose claims (whether true or false) are unique in kind and scale. *Christian* theology has its own distinctive features, of course, but here is the nub of the matter, and the source of theology's strange mixture of ease and unease in the modern university – a situation of which, despite its wide tolerance, the university itself occasionally, though perhaps surprisingly rarely, takes cogniz-ance. To put the matter at a more personal level, there is something both hard and peculiar in engaging in the study of God as if he were an object in one's hand, while knowing of him also as the one in whose hands one exists (whether as idea or as reality). However, Christian theology's own bringing together of God as mystery and yet as involving himself radically with the world suggests ways of resolving the difficulty.

All this is a way of saying that theology owes allegiance not only to the university but also to the Christian tradition, even perhaps, in some settings, to that tradition as currently instantiated in a Church. But most of that tradition was formed and expressed in conditions far removed from the modern post-Enlightenment academy, breathing authority and often even com-pulsion for the enforcement of its teaching. Not only is this a legacy still sometimes hard to live down (e.g. when a church seminary asks for accredit-ation by a university; though either side may well blur the issues at stake – corporate memory is often weaker than one might expect!); it is also bound to mark the study of the Bible and the tradition, and to rub off, perhaps quite subtly, on critical scholarship in general.

This book is about 'thought' rather than 'life'; so, though the distinction cannot be absolute without artificiality, this is not a survey of Christianity and the Churches as social phenomena – their distribution, worship, organization, and so forth. The book reflects the various intellectual disciplines which have grown up over the centuries to investigate and consider aspects of theology. It makes abundantly plain what a rich and diverse field this now is – and indeed long has been.

Some of the forty-eight chapters that make up the book are largely descrip-tive, whether of a period of past thought or of the current state of scholarship. Others are more ambitious and deliberately sketch out new ways of considering the matter in hand, pointing to possible and even desirable future develop-ments. But all through, every effort has been made to transcend the merely informative. Even though, naturally, a great deal of essential information is given, there could be no attempt at completeness, and contributors have sought to stimulate as well as to instruct, to suggest patterns of comprehension rather than to burden the reader with raw data.

The book falls into six Parts. The first three deal with major foundational aspects of Christian theological reflection: the Bible, the tradition, and the contribution of philosophy, especially in the modern period. Though there can be no rigid division, the other three Parts are more concerned with application: in relation to spirituality and to contemporary ethics, and, finally, issues in and aspects of present-day theological construction.

The editors acknowledge with gratitude the work of those who have contributed to this book and the collaboration they have enjoyed with their publishers, in particular Jonathan Price, who initiated the idea which now reaches fruition, Seth Denbo and Colville Wemyss.

THE CONTRIBUTORS

PAUL AVIS is an Anglican parish priest and a Prebendary of Exeter Cathedral. He was educated in London and Cambridge, gaining his doctorate from the University of London in 1976. He is a member of the Church of England's General Synod, Doctrine Commission and Faith and Order Advisory Group, an Inspector and Examiner of theological colleges and courses, and Honorary Research Fellow and part-time lecturer in the Department of Theology of the University of Exeter. His publications include *Anglicanism and the Christian Church: Theological Resources in Historical Perspective* (1989), *Christians in Communion* (1990) and *Authority, Leadership and Conflict in the Church* (1992). He has edited a collection of essays on the Resurrection (1993) and is now working on a fundamental theology in several volumes under the general title *Christian Theology in the Modern World*.

JOHN BARTON is Oriel and Laing Professor of the Interpretation of Holy Scripture and Fellow of Oriel College, Oxford. After a Junior Research Fellowship at Merton College, Oxford, in 1974 he became University Lecturer in Theology (Old Testament) and Official Fellow of St Cross College, Oxford. He was Reader in Biblical Studies at the University of Oxford from 1989 until 1991, when he assumed his current position. He is the author of *Amos's Oracles against the Nations* (1980), *Reading the Old Testament: Method in Biblical Study* (1984), *Oracles of God: Perceptions of Ancient Prophecy in Israel after the Exile* (1986), *People of the Book?: The Authority of the Bible in Christianity* (1988) and *What is the Bible?* (1991). His study guide on Isaiah 1–39 is in press, and he is completing a book on the biblical canon. He is joint editor with John Muddiman of *The Oxford Bible Commentary*, to be published in 1998.

FRANK BURCH BROWN has been Frederick Doyle Kershner Professor of Religion and the Arts at the Christian Theological Seminary, Indianapolis, since 1994. He gained his Ph.D. from the University of Chicago in 1979, and was Professor of Religion and the Humanities at the Virginia Polytechnic Institute and State University from 1979 to 1994. His publications include

Transfiguration (1983), *The Evolution of Darwin's Religious Views* (1986) and *Religious Aesthetics* (1989); he is Area Editor in Religion, Arts, Culture and Media for the fourth edition of *Die Religion in Geschichte und Gegenwart*. He is also a composer, keyboard instrumentalist and choir director.

PETER BYRNE has been a lecturer/senior lecturer in the philosophy of religion at King's College, London, since 1975. He read philosophy at the University of York and obtained a B.Phil. in philosophy at the University of Oxford. He has published widely in the philosophy of religion and ethics. He has edited a series of five books on medical ethics, and is the author of *Natural Religion and the Nature of Religion* (1989), *The Philosophical and Theological Foundations of Ethics* (1992) and *Religion Defined and Explained* (1993, with Peter B. Clarke). He is co-editor of the journal *Religious Studies*.

STEPHEN CLARK is Professor of Philosophy at Liverpool University. His publications include *Aristotle's Man*, *The Moral Status of Animals*, *The Nature of the Beast*, *From Athens to Jerusalem*, *The Mysteries of Religion*, three volumes of *Limits and Renewals: Civil Peace and Sacred Order*, *A Parliament of Souls*, *God's World and the Great Awakening*, and *How to Think about the Earth*. He is editor of *Berkeley: Money, Obedience and Affection*, and co-editor of the *Journal of Applied Philosophy*.

KEITH CLEMENTS is a Baptist minister, and since 1990 he has been Coordinating Secretary for International Affairs of the Council of Churches for Britain and Ireland. From 1977 to 1990 he was a tutor at Bristol Baptist College and part-time lecturer in the Department of Theology and Religious Studies at the University of Bristol. His publications include *Faith* (1980), *A Patriotism for Today: Love of Country in Dialogue with the Witness of Dietrich Bonhoeffer* (1986), *The Theology of Ronald Gregor Smith* (1986), *Friedrich Schleiermacher* (1987) and *Lovers of Discord: Twentieth-Century Theological Controversies in England* (1988). He is currently working on a biography of J. H. Oldham.

DAN COHN-SHERBOK teaches at the University of Kent and is a Visiting Professor at the University of Middlesex. He has been a Visiting Professor at the University of Essex, Visiting Fellow at Wolfson College, Cambridge, and Visiting Scholar at Mansfield College, Oxford, and the Oxford Centre for Hebrew and Jewish Studies. He is a rabbi and the author or editor of over forty books, including *The Jewish Heritage* (1988), *Religion in Public Life* (1992) and *Judaism and Other Faiths* (1993).

DAVID D'AVRAY is Reader in Medieval History at University College London, where he has taught since 1977. He studied at the Universities of Cambridge, Oxford and Munich. His publications include *The Preaching of the*

Friars: Sermons Diffused from Paris Before 1300 (1985) and *Death and the Prince: Memorial Preaching Before 1350* (1994).

GAVIN D'COSTA is Senior Lecturer in Theology in the Department of Theology and Religious Studies at the University of Bristol. He was educated at the Unversities of Birmingham and Cambridge. An Indian Roman Catholic, he is involved in interfaith dialogue, is adviser to the Catholic Bishops of England and Wales and is a consultant to the Pontifical Commission for Interreligious Dialogue. His publications include *Theology and Religious Pluralism* (1986), *John Hick's Theology of Religions* (1987) and *Christian Uniqueness Reconsidered* (editor, 1990). He is currently writing a book on the Trinity and religious pluralism.

JACK DOMINIAN is a consultant psychiatrist with special interest in personal relationships and marriage. He was educated in Athens, Bombay, Stamford as well as in England, at Cambridge University, Oxford University, and the Institute of Psychiatry, the Maudsley Hospital, London. He has been involved in pastoral counselling and is the author of several books on marriage, sexuality and ethical issues, including *Christian Marriage* (1968), *Depression* (1976) and *God, Sex and Love* (1989). He is Director of One Plus One Marriage and Partnership Research, London. In 1994 he received the MBE for his work on marriage.

G. R. EVANS has lectured at the Universties of Reading, Bristol and Cambridge, and was British Academy Research Reader in Theology from 1986 to 1988. She serves on the Faith and Order Advisory Group of the Church of England. Her publications include *Anselm and Talking about God* (1978), *Anselm and a New Generation* (1980), *Old Arts and New Theology* (1980), *Augustine on Evil* (1983), *The Language and Logic of the Bible: The Earlier Middle Ages* and *The Road to Reformation* (1984–85), *Problems of Authority in the Reformation Debates* (1992) and *Philosophy and Theology in the Middle Ages* (1993).

GARY GILBERT obtained his Ph.D. at Columbia Univesity, New York, for work on pagan involvement with the world of Judaism in Roman antiquity. He has taught at the University of Pittsburgh and elsewhere, and now works for the Association of Theological Schools. He is currently working on a project that examines the influence of Roman imperial propaganda on early Jewish and Christian thought.

COLIN GUNTON has been a minister of the United Reformed Church since 1972. He holds degrees in Classics and Theology from the University of Oxford, and in 1993 he was awarded a Doctorate of Divinity from the University of London. He was appointed as a Lecturer in the Philosophy of

Religion at King's College, London, in 1969, and Professor of Christian Doctrine in 1984. In 1992 he was Bampton Lecturer at the Universitiy of Oxford, and in 1993 Warfield Lecturer at Princeton Theological Seminary. His publications include *The Actuality of Atonement* (1989), *The Promise of Trinitarian Theology* (1991), *The One, the Three and the Many: God, Creation and the Culture of Modernity (The 1992 Bampton Lectures)* (1993).

JAMES M. GUSTAFSON is Henry R. Luce Professor of Humanities and Comparative Studies at Emory University, Atlanta. He was educated at North Park Junior College, Northwestern University (B.S., 1948), Chicago Theological Seminary and the University of Chicago (B.D., 1951) and Yale University (Ph.D., 1955). From 1955 to 1972 he was a member of faculty at Yale University, where he became Professor of Christian Ethics in the Divinity School and the Department of Religious Studies. From 1972 to 1988 he was University Professor of Theological Ethics in the Divinity School and served on the Committee on Social Thought at the University of Chicago. His publications include *Treasure in Earthen Vessels: The Church as a Human Community, Christ and the Moral Life, Can Ethics be Christian?, Protestant and Roman Catholic Ethics: Prospects for Rapprochement* and *Ethics from a Theocentric Perspective*. He is an ordained minister in the United Church of Christ.

WALTER HOLLENWEGER was ordained in the Swiss Reformed Church in 1961. He gained his doctorate in theology from the University of Zurich in 1966. From 1965 to 1971 he was Executive Secretary of the World Council of Churches in Geneva, and from 1971 to 1989 he was Professor of Mission at the University of Birmingham. His books include *Evangelism Today: Good News or Bone of Contention?* (1976), *Erfahrungen der Leibhaftigkeit: Interkulturelle Theologie 1* (1979, 2nd edn 1980), *Umgang mit Mythen: Interkulturelle Theologie 2* (1982, 2nd edn 1992), *Geist und Materie: Interkulturelle Theologie 3* (1988) and *The Pentecostals* (2 vols, 1988 and 1995). His articles include: 'Towards an Intercultural History of Christianity' in *International Review of Mission* (October 1987); 'Interaction between Black and White in Theological Education' (September 1987), 'Healing Through Prayer: Superstition or Forgotten Christian Tradition' (May 1989) and 'Music in the Service of Reconciliation' (July 1989) in *Theology*; 'The Critical Roots of Pentecostalism' in *Journal for Pentecostal Theology* (1992); and 'Verheißung und Verhängnis der Pfingstbewegung' in *Evangelische Theologie* (1993). He has also written plays, musicals and choreographies.

BRIAN HORNE is Lecturer in Systematic Theology in the Department of Theology and Religious Studies at King's College, London. He was educated in South Africa, the United Kingdom and the United States, gaining degrees from the Universities of Natal, Durham and London, and the General Theological Seminary, New York. His publications include *A World to Gain* and several articles and essays on literary and theological subjects.

LESLIE HOULDEN is Emeritus Professor of Theology at King's College, London, and is a Fellow of the College. Earlier he taught theology in Oxford, where he was Fellow and Chaplain of Trinity College. His publications include *Paul's Letters from Prison* (1970), *The Johannine Epistles* (1973), *Connections* (1986), and *Ethics and the New Testament* (1973); he edited (with R. J. Coggins) *A Dictionary of Biblical Interpretation* (1990). He is a priest of the Church of England.

GRACE JANTZEN is John Rylands Senior Research Fellow in the Department of Religions and Theology at the University of Manchester. Formerly Reader at King's College, London. She holds a doctorate in Philosophy from the University of Calgary and a doctorate in Theology from the University of Oxford. Her special interests are in mysticism, feminism and theorizing religion in (post-) modernity. She has written several books, including *Power, Gender and Christian Mysticism* (1995) and *Julian of Norwich* (1987), and published many articles on mysticism in journals including *Relgious Studies* and *Modern Theology*. In 1989 she was appointed to a Canadian Royal Commission on New Reproductive Technologies, whose final report, *Proceed with Care*, was published in 1993. She is a member of the Religious Society of Friends.

THEODORE JENNINGS is Professor of Constructive Theology at the Chicago Theological Seminary and a United Methodist minister. He is a graduate of Duke University (B.A., 1964), the Candler School of Theology (B.D., 1967) and Emory University (Ph.D., 1971). He has taught at the Candler School of Theology of Emory University and, as a United Methodist missionary, at the Seminario Metodista de Mexico in Mexico City. His publications include *Introduction to Theology* (1976), *Beyond Theism* (1986), *Loyalty to God* (1992) and many articles on themes as diverse as Wesley, the study of ritual, pastoral care, homosexuality and social ethics.

JOHN KENT is Emeritus Professor of Theology at Bristol University. His publications include *The End of the Line: The Development of Christian Theology since 1700* (1982), *The Unacceptable Face: The Modern Church in the Eyes of the Historian* (1987), *William Temple: Church, State and Society in Britain 1880–1950* (1992) and 'Religion and Science 1850–1914' in *Nineteenth Century Religious Thought in the West* (ed. N. Smart, 1985).

KENNETH LEECH is M. B. Reckitt Urban Fellow at St Botolph's Church, Aldgate, East London. Ordained in 1964, he has spent most of his ministry in the East End of London. He built up a ministry among homeless youth and heroin users in Soho in the 1960s, founding the Soho Drugs Group in 1967 and Centrepoint Night Shelter in 1969. He was Rector of St Matthew's, Bethnal Green, from 1974 to 1980, Race Relations Field Officer of the Church of England Board for Social Responsibility from 1981 to 1987, and Director of the Runnymede Trust from 1987 to 1990. His publications include *Soul Friend* (1977, rev. edn 1994), *Care and Conflict* (1992) and *The Eye of the Storm: Spiritual Resources for the Pursuit of Justice* (1993).

ALISTER McGRATH is Research Lecturer in Theology at the University of Oxford, Research Professor of Systematic Theology at Regent College, Vancouver, and Lecturer in Historical and Systematic Theology at Wycliffe Hall, Oxford. His publications relating to the Renaissance and Reformation include *Luther's Theology of the Cross* (1985), *The Intellectual Origins of the Reformation* (1987) and *A Life of John Calvin* (1990).

JOHN MACQUARRIE was Professor at Union Theological Seminary, New York, and latterly Lady Margaret Profesor of Divinity and Canon of Christ Church, Oxford. His many publications include *Principles of Christian Theology* (1966), *God-Talk* (1967) and *Jesus Christ in Modern Thought* (1990).

JACK MAHONEY has been Dixons Professor of Business Ethics and Social Responsibility at the London Business School since 1993. He was educated at the University of Glasgow and the Pontifical Gregorian University, Rome. He is a Jesuit priest and former Principal of Heythrop College, London. From 1986 to 1993 he was F. D. Maurice Professor of Moral and Social Theology at King's College, London, where he was also founding Director of King's College Business Ethics Research Centre. His publications include *Bioethics and Belief: Religion and Medicine in Dialogue* (1984), *The Making of Moral Theology: A Study of the Roman Catholic Tradition* (1987) and *Teaching Business Ethics in the UK, Europe and the USA: A Comparative Study.* He is founding editor of the quarterly *Business Ethics: A European Review,* which has been published since 1992.

ANTHONY MEREDITH entered the Society of Jesus in 1954 and was ordained in 1968. He studied philosophy and theology at Heythrop, Oxford-shire, and classics in Oxford. After ordination, he gained a D.Phil. at Oxford with a thesis on Gregory of Nyssa; since then he has been mainly engaged in teaching Early Christian Doctrine in Oxford and at Heythrop College, London. Most of his publications have been on the relationship between Early Christianity and its Classical background.

JOHN MORGAN is a Canon Residentiary of St John's Cathedral, Brisbane, and Warden of St John's College, University of Queensland, where he is also Director of the Australian Institute of Ethics and the Professions. He graduated from the Universities of Melbourne and Oxford, where he served as Chaplain of Oriel College. He is an Academic Fellow of the Faculty of Medicine at the University of Queensland, and teaches both medical and business ethics as well as theological ethics. He has been a lecturer in the United Faculty of Theology, Melbourne, and is a Fellow Commoner of Peterhouse, Cambridge. He is a former member of the Medical Research Ethics Committee of the National Health and Medical Research Council of Australia.

JOHN MUDDIMAN is the George Caird Fellow in New Testament Studies at Mansfield College, Oxford, and a lecturer in the Faculty of Theology. He studied at the Universities of Oxford, Cambridge and Louvain. His publications include *The Bible, Fountain and Well of Truth* (1983) and contributions to *The Religion of the Incarnation* (edited by Robert Morgan, 1989) and *A Dictionary of Biblical Interpretation* (edited by R. J. Coggins and J. L. Houlden, 1990). He is a member of the Anglican–Roman Catholic International Commission.

EDWARD NORMAN is Chaplain of Christ Church College of Higher Education, Canterbury. He is an Anglican priest, and has written and broadcast extensively about issues in the relationship of Church and State in many parts of the world. He is a Fellow of the Royal Historical Society and of the Royal Society of Arts, and Emeritus Fellow of Peterhouse, Cambridge. His publications include *Church and Society in England* (1976), *Christianity and the World Order* (1979) and *Entering the Darkness* (1991).

HELEN OPPENHEIMER was educated at Lady Margaret Hall, Oxford, where she obtained a B.Phil. She taught ethics at Cuddesdon Theological College from 1964 to 1969. She has served on various Church of England commissions and groups, especially on marriage and divorce, and on the Inter-Anglican Theological and Doctrinal Commission. She was President of the Society for the Study of Christian Ethics from 1989 to 1991, and was awarded the Lambeth Doctorate of Divinity in 1993. Her publications include *Incarnation and Immanence* (1973), *The Character of Christian Morality* (1974), *The Hope of Happiness: A Sketch for a Christian Humanism* (1983), *Looking Before and After* (1988), *Marriage* (1990), *Finding and Following* (1994) and numerous articles in journals and books.

DAVID A. PAILIN is Professor of Philosophy of Religion and Head of the Department of Philosophy at the University of Manchester, where he has taught the philosophy of religion and philosophical theology since 1966. He studied at Trinity College, Cambridge, Perkins School of Theology in Southern Methodist University, Dallas, and the University of Manchester. His publications include *The Way to Faith, Attitudes to Other Religions, Groundwork of Philosophy of Religion, God and the Processes of Reality, The Anthropological*

Character of Theology, A Gentle Touch: From a Theology of Handicap to a Theology of Human Being and *Probing the Foundations: A Study in Theistic Reconstruction*, as well as numerous contributions to books and journals. He is at present working on a study provisionally entitled *Understanding and Truth: The Formation of Theological Interpretation of Reality* and on a six-volume collection of texts on faith and reason in the seventeenth and eighteenth centuries. When these are completed he intends to explore further the debates about faith and reason in the seventeenth and eighteenth centuries.

BARRIE PASKINS has been a Lecturer in the Department of War Studies at King's College, London, since 1971. He trained as a philosopher at Trinity College, Cambridge. His research interests include literature as well as general ethics and ethics of war. His publications include *The Ethics of War* (1979, with M. Dockrill) and *Ethics and European Security* (1986).

TERENCE PENELHUM is Professor Emeritus of Religious Studies at the University of Calgary. He was educated at the University of Edinburgh and Oriel College, Oxford. He has taught at the Universities of Alberta and Calgary, and has held many visiting positions in universities in the United States. At Calgary he has been Professor of Philosophy, Dean of Arts and Science and Director of the Humanities Institute. In 1988 he was awarded the Canada Council Molson Prize in Humanities. His publications include *Survival and Disembodied Existence* (1970), *Religion and Rationality* (1971), *Problems of Religious Knowledge* (1971), *Hume* (1975), *God and Skepticism* (1983), *Butler* (1985) and *David Hume: An Introduction to his Philosophical System* (1992).

STEPHEN PRICKETT is Regius Professor of English Language and Literature at the University of Glasgow. Until 1990 he held the Chair of English at the Australian National University in Canberra, and, before that, teaching posts at the University of Sussex, the University of Minnesota and Smith College, Massachusetts. He is Chairman of the UK Higher Education Foundation and President of the European Society for the Study of Literature and Theology. His publications include *Romanticism and Religion: The Tradition of Coleridge and Wordsworth in the Victorian Church* (1976), *Words and the Word: Languager, Poetics and Biblical Interpretation* (1986) and (with Robert Barnes) *The Bible* (part of the Landmarks of World Literature series). He also edited *Reading the Text: Biblical Criticism and Literary Theory* (1991). He has recently prepared an introduction and notes for a new Oxford World's Classics edition of the Bible and is currently preparing a book on literary appropriation and its historical consequences.

HEIKKI RÄISÄNEN has been Professor of New Testament Exegesis at the University of Helsinki since 1975; from 1984 to 1994 he was Distinguished

Research Professor at the Academy of Finland. His publications include *Die Mutter Jesu im Neuen Testament* (1969), *The Idea of Divine Hardening* (1972), *Paul and the Law* (1983), *The 'Messianic Secret' in Mark's Gospel* (1990), *Beyond New Testament Theology* (1990) and *Jesus, Paul and Torah* (1992). In 1990 he received the honorary degree of Doctor of Theology from the University of Edinburgh.

JOHN ROGERSON has been Professor and Head of the Department of Biblical Studies at the University of Sheffield since 1979, and is an Honorary Canon of Sheffield Cathedral. From 1964 to 1979 he taught in the Department of Theology at the University of Durham. His publications include *Myth in Old Testament Interpretation* (1974), *Anthropology and the Old Testament* (1978), *Old Testament Criticism in the 19th Century: England and Germany* (1984), *W. M. L. de Wette: Founder of Modern Biblical Criticism* (1992) and (with P. R. Davies) *The Old Testament World* (1989); his *Atlas of the Bible* (1985) has been translated into six languages. He retired in 1995 to concentrate on writing a Theology of the Old Testament.

ALAN F. SEGAL is Professor of Religion at Barnard College, Columbia University, New York. He was educated at Worcester Academy, Amherst College, Brandeis University, Hebrew Union College–Jewish Institute of Religion, and Yale Unversity; and taught at Princeton University and the University of Toronto. He has held fellowships from the Woodrow Wilson Foundation, the American Council of Learned Societies, the National Endowment for the Humanities and the J. S. Guggenheim Foundation. His publications include *Jews and Arabs: A Teaching Guide, Two Powers in Heaven, Deus Ex Machina: Computers in the Humanities, Rebecca's Children: Judaism and Christianity in the Roman World, The Other Judaisms of Late Antiquity* and *Paul the Convert: The Apostolate of Saul of Tarsus.*

PHILIP SHELDRAKE is Director of Pastoral Studies at Westcott House, teaches Church History in the Cambridge Theological Federation and is a member of the Faculty of Divinity, University of Cambridge. From 1984 to 1992 he was Co-Director of the Institute of Spirituality, Heythrop College, University of London. He was co-editor, then general editor, of the spirituality journal *The Way* and its supplements from 1981 to 1994. He is a member of several editorial committees including that of the Society for the Study of Christian Spirituality (associated with the American Academy of Religion). He is the author of several books, including *Spirituality and History: Questions of Interpretations and Method* (1991).

STEWART SUTHERLAND is Principal and Vice-Chancellor of the University of Edinburgh. He taught at the University College of North Wales, Bangor, from 1965 to 1968, and at the University of Stirling from 1968 to

1977. He was Professor of the History and Philosophy of Religion at King's College, London from 1977 to 1994, Principal of King's College from 1985 to 1990, and Vice-Chancellor of the University of London from 1990 to 1994. He was editor of the journal *Religious Studies* from 1984 to 1990. His publications include *Atheism and the Rejection of God* (1977), *God, Jesus and Belief* (1984), *Faith and Ambiguity* (1984) and many articles and edited books. He is currently working on the nature of integrity, and the interface between ethics and religion.

TERRY TASTARD is a Catholic priest in the Diocese of Westminster. He is a graduate of Rhodes University, Grahamstown, and of the Universities of London and Birmingham, and has taught philosophy of religion at King's College, London, and at Birkbeck College Centre for Extra-Mural Studies, London. He is the author of *The Spark in the Soul: Spirituality and Social Justice* and has contributed to two other books as well as to theological journals.

ROGER TRIGG has been Professor of Philosophy at the University of Warwick since 1987, where he has been Lecturer, Senior Lecturer and Reader in Philosophy since 1966. He was educated at New College, Oxford, where he gained his M.A. and D.Phil. He was Visiting Fellow at St Cross College, Oxford, from 1986 to 1987 and from 1991 to 1992. In 1993 he was elected as the first President of the British Society for the Philosophy of Religion. His publications include *Pain and Emotion* (1970), *Reason and Commitment* (1973), *The Shaping of Man: Philosophical Aspects of Sociobiology* (1982), *Understanding Social Science* (1985), *Ideas of Human Nature* (1988), *Reality at Risk: A Defence of Realism in Philosophy and the Sciences* (2nd edn, 1989) and *Rationality and Science: Can Science Explain Everything?* (1993). His current interests include the relationship between theology and science, and he is writing a book on Rationality and Religion.

WILLIAM J. WAINWRIGHT is a Professor at the University of Wisconsin-Milwaukee. He was educated at Kenyon College, Ohio, gaining his B.A. in 1957, and at the University of Michigan, gaining his M.A. in 1959 and his Ph.D. in 1961. He was an instructor at Dartmouth College, New Hampshire, from 1960 to 1962, then Instructor and Assistant Professor at the University of Illinois at Urbana-Champaign from 1962 to 1968. He then became Associate Professor at the University of Wisconsin-Milwaukee, where he is now a full Professor. His publications include *Philosophy of Religion: An Annotated Bibliography* (1978), *Mysticism* (1981), *Philosophy of Religion* (1988) and over thirty articles. He has recently completed a book on the role of passion in religious reasoning entitled *Reason and the Heart*, which is to appear in 1995 or 1996.

GORDON S. WAKEFIELD was ordained to the Methodist ministry in 1947. He was educated at the Universities of Cambridge, where he read the Theological Tripos, and Oxford, gaining his B.Litt in Ecclesiastical History in 1954. He was Fernley-Hartley Lecturer in 1957, and became Connexional Editor in 1963. After a period as Chairman of the Manchester and Stockport District, during which he edited Sir Edwyn Hoskyns' incomplete *Crucifixion-Resurrection* with a biographical introduction, he was made Principal of the ecumenical Queen's College, Birmingham, and Recognized Lecturer in Liturgiology at Birmingham University. He was editor of *A Dictionary of Christian Spirituality* (1983); his most recent publication is *John Bunyan the Christian* (1992). He was awarded the Lambeth Doctorate of Divinity in 1986.

BENEDICTA WARD teaches for the Theology Faculty of the University of Oxford. She has been a member of the Anglican Religious Community of the Sisters of the Love of God since 1955. Her first degree was in History at the University of Manchester, and her doctorate was taken at Oxford. In addition to five books on the early traditions of Christian monasticism, she has written exclusively on the Middle Ages, including a translation of the Prayers and Meditations of St Anselm of Canterbury and a monograph on the Venerable Bede, and her collected essays have recently been published as as a *Variorum* monograph. She is at present engaged in a study of the cult of relics in the Middle Ages.

KEITH WARD has been Regius Professor of Divinity at the University of Oxford since 1991. He has lectured in Logic and Philosophy at the Universities of Glasgow, St Andrews and London. He was Fellow and Dean of Trinity Hall, Cambridge, from 1976 to 1983; at the University of London, he was Professor of Moral Theology from 1983 to 1986 and Professor of the History and Philosophy of Religion from 1986 to 1991. His publications include *Ethics and Chrstianity* (1970), *Kant's View of Ethics* (1972), *The Concept of God* (1974), *Rational Theology and the Creativity of God* (1982), *Images of Eternity* (1992), *A Vision to Pursue* (1992) and *Religion and Revelation* (1994). At present he is particularly interested in the restatement and development of theological beliefs in the context of new scientific knowledge and of a positive conversation between difference belief-systems.

ROBERT L. WILKEN is William R Kenan Jr Professor of the History of Christianity at the University of Virginia, Charlottesville. His publications include *The Land Called Holy: Palestine in Christian History and Thought* (1992).

ROWAN WILLIAMS has been Bishop of Monmouth since 1992. He was educated at Christ's College, Cambridge, and Wadham College, Oxford. From 1986 to 1992 he was Lady Margaret Professor of Divinity at the University of Oxford. He has carried out research in Eastern Orthodox thought, and has published on the history of doctrine and spirituality. His recent publications include *Teresa of Avila* (1991) and *Arius* (1987).

MARK WYNN is a lecturer in the School of Religion and Philosophy at the Brisbane Campus of the Australian Catholic University. He studied at the University of Oxford from 1982 to 1986 and from 1987 to 1991; he then taught the philosophy of religion at King's College, London, from 1991 to 1993. His interests include the rationality of religious belief and the concept of God.

I

THE BIBLE

INTRODUCTION

Leslie Houlden

There can be useful argument whether a treatment of Christian thought should begin with the Bible or with the tradition. The issue is commonly and sometimes crudely thought of as that which fundamentally divides the Protestant element in the Christian world on the one hand from the Catholic and Eastern Orthodox elements on the other. It is of course not as simple as that: no Christian community considers itself to be other than dependent on the authority and pervasive influence of Scripture or to be independent of what it conceives to be authentic tradition. The fact that, with this common basis, they can disagree so profoundly merely shows how varied is the interpretation to which both Scripture and tradition are susceptible. These massive entities, the one in literary bulk, the other in temporal, conceptual and human expanse, cannot reasonably be expected to yield simple and clear directives to those who would base themselves upon them.

What is undeniable is that there has always been a complex interaction between the Bible and tradition. From one point of view, the Bible as Christians have received it is itself the product of tradition, one (albeit towering) element in the Christian story. Though much of it (the Old Testament) was inherited from Judaism, those books were arranged – in early Christian tradition – in a Christianly significant order rather than a Jewish order, and the original Christian writings (the New Testament) were as much deposits of, as formative of, early Christianity, that is they were a fruit of the tradition. In that basic sense, tradition has priority.

But from another point of view, Scripture has occupied a normative place in Christianity that has been unrivalled. In realistic terms, it is arguable that the creeds or the eucharistic liturgies, both of them succinct and, by their repeated use, deeply influential embodiments and formers of faith, have, as it were, largely carried Christianity along on the tide of history. But, despite the tenacious reverence accorded to these formulas by most Christian communities, they have never received the deference and devotion given to the Bible. In however strange (to us) or partial the manner of its use, Scripture

3

has been the court of appeal to which upholders of doctrine have turned and the source from which they have reckoned to derive their tenets. It has been Scripture whose terms have had to be met and it has been to Scripture that, directly or obliquely, Christians have chiefly turned for religious nourishment and guidance.

Here in our present context, however, it is not only the massive, public and 'up-front' role played by the Bible in Christianity as a matter of sheer fact that leads to its appearing first in this volume. Nor does that position reflect a decision between the Bible and tradition as claimants to primacy in authority: such a decision would, in the constraints of this brief chapter, be rash or crude, and in any case is inappropriate in an academic work such as this. What is involved is more straightforwardly the plain historical datum that the Bible, in the shape of the Old Testament, is the primary surviving bond linking Christianity to its ancient Jewish antecedents and, indeed, its ever-present Jewish contemporaries, with whom its relationship has been always so complex, problematic, and often so tumultuous or catastrophically scandalous. In that perspective at the very least, the Bible pushes itself to the front in any orderly survey of Christian thought.

In part, it is also an obstacle to be circumnavigated, or at any rate treated with caution. For much else in Christian thought has been couched so commonly (and so early, and even when Scripture was ostensibly the source) in abstract or philosophical patterns that, whatever the claims and appearances, the Bible, with its quite different idioms, chiefly narrative and poetry, has been left far behind, as far as its own thought worlds are concerned. Historical approaches to the Bible, developed in recent centuries, have made that so utterly plain that the Bible has become, despite the profligate and even fanatical use of it in many Christian circles, in many ways an alien work – all too clearly mishandled when too readily handled, yet often also in practice treated like a precious icon, revered from afar but not closely examined, lest its native language should prove largely beyond our capactiy to absorb and use, even when understood intellectually.

It is in this perspective that the chapters that follow should be read. They begin with an account of the make-up of the Hebrew Bible in the complicated and drawn-out context of its assemblage as a normative body of sacred writings. But John Barton provides more than this. In drawing attention to the vast range and diversity of the background of this literature, he draws our attention implicitly to its alienness as far as all subsequent readers and users are concerned – all those, that is, who, in whatever precise spirit, lump it together as a canonical whole and make it authoritative, as God-given words. We cannot help but feel the (unwitting) audacity of that step.

It is a step which two major inheritors have taken, or rather a step which is at the start of two different paths. The second chapter traces the movement, from the beginnings that Barton described, down the initial stretches of the Jewish path, that is, in the period when Judaism and Christianity, both reckoning Scripture as their major authority and each unabashedly confident in their favoured way of interpreting it, were establishing the camps from which they would henceforward stare at each other, from time to time launching missiles – and, until very recently, being largely without comprehension of or even respect for each other's readings of their common sacred literary inheritance. 'Neutral' academic scholarship has in recent years at least given some Jews and some Christians a fruitful common land.

The third chapter outlines the parallel Christian development in patristic and medieval times, so different from mainline Jewish scriptural interpretation, but, paradoxically, owing much to the Philonic strain in first-century Alexandrian Judaism which Judaism itself so soon lost, ignored or forswore, thus losing the major possibility of a common language in which the two faiths might conceivably (hope against hope) have interpreted their shared writings.

Modern (i.e. post-Enlightenment) historical study of the Old Testament, whose story is told in the fourth chapter, has, in part, operated as a boomerang. It has made available the knowledge of Scripture's past and especially its origins, which the earlier chapters have described. In doing so, it has sabotaged the traditional theological purposes to which both Christians and Jews have put the Scriptures, showing those uses up as anachronistic, arbitrary or, at any rate by historical standards, unjustifiable – for all their ingenious learning. John Rogerson's chapter shows equally, however, that these inevitable challenges to traditional ways of regarding the Old Testament have not led Christian scholars to abandon this literature to the Jews or, more neutrally, to the historical limbo of its own original times. No, Christian scholars have, by a variety of strategies, risen to the challenges and found in the Old Testament a renewed source of edification or formation, whether seeing it in its own right or as giving shape to themes whose further destiny lay ahead in the career of Jesus and early Christian reflection on him. Both the theological thrusts of the Old Testament and its irresistible historical character have given major contributions to Christian thought, recalling it to a neglected Hebrew inheritance.

The next three chapters attend to various aspects of the New Testament, partly in tandem with the treatment already given to the Old Testament writings. The fifth chapter highlights the essential gap, not immediately apparent to the reader of the Bible as a single book, between the two Testaments. At one level, it is a gap of time – that which scholarship labels 'the intertestamental period', a time whose Jewish literary deposit, so far as it has survived, at Qumran or elsewhere, never achieved canonical, i.e. biblical status; yet, historically, it contributed to the world of thought in which Christianity arose, so that to ignore it is to distort the picture of that world. What is involved is the culture of first-century Judaism – including not only its literary possessions but its methods for interpreting them. This volume, being concerned with the biblical texts, can do no more than draw attention to this factor, so important from a historical point of view.

More importantly, there is a profound conceptual gap. Not only do the New Testament writings fail to follow those of the Old in immediate and uninterrupted temporal sequence; they also arise by what we may describe as a quite different mechanism. From one point of view they are indeed, within their far narrower time-scale, the record of the history, beliefs and practices of a community of faith, just as is the Old Testament. But more significantly, they are, in their diverse literary forms, all responses to and reflections on the figure of Jesus, seen as the decisive and all-embracing agent of God for human salvation. This dominating personal presence and force has no counterpart in the Old Testament – which indeed he was also quickly seen to dominate, for it foreshadowed him and he fulfilled it. In Christian perception, he is more than one character in a long story: he colonizes all of it, from start to finish. More modestly, we may say that the terms and images of the Old Testament, suitably adapted and developed, alone made him intelligible: in the first years, there was no other resource.

In the sixth chapter, John Muddiman shows how richly and diversely the writings of the New Testament served as the 'proofs' for Christian beliefs about God and Christ as they developed, with increasing sophistication, chiefly of a philosophical kind, in the subsequent period – expressed as they were in conceptual idioms that were as foreign to most, if not all, of the New Testament as to the Old.

This process, once brought unavoidably to our attention by candid historical investigation and the use of historicality of imagination, raises questions of great urgency for standard Christian theology, some of whose tenets and much of whose idiom seem undermined by an awareness of its traditional pedigree in New Testament terms and proof texts. These issues, still scarcely absorbed in much of the theological and ecclesiastical establishment, are raised in one dimension by Heikki Räisänen in chapter seven and in a more persistently biblical and literary way by Stephen Prickett's concluding chapter. Here we read of some of the profound questions posed by the presence of a 'holy book', now that we know so much about it and about its functioning.

Thus we end without a closure, with pointers towards a future which theological reflection had better not refuse, for its own health and integrity. As many of these chapters indicate, it is a future in which, on the one hand, the Bible is a fast disappearing cultural force in society at large and even in practice in some major parts of the Christian world; while on the other hand, in the academy it is read and studied by both believers and unbelievers, with unprecedented fertility, as new methods and approaches continually arrive on the scene, some more theological in their bearing than others. It is a perplexing state for the Bible to be in.

1

THE HEBREW BIBLE: FORMATION AND CHARACTER

John Barton

This chapter is divided into two sections. The first deals with the growth of Hebrew literature and its gradual formation into the canon of the Hebrew Bible. The second discusses the matrix from which Hebrew Scripture came, and especially its roots in the social life of ancient Israel.

THE FORMATION OF THE HEBREW SCRIPTURES

The Hebrew Bible is the product of two processes, distinct yet interacting at many points. One is the growth of the national literature of Israel, built up as the sayings of sages, the hymns and poems of singers, narratives of early historians, oracles of prophets, and the judgements of lawyers were written down and shaped by many subsequent generations of scribes. The other process, which began as early as the time of the Babylonian Exile (586–532 BCE), is the selection and codification of the core of these disparate works to form the official literature of the nation. Before the Exile only the first process was clearly at work, though some legal materials already had an authoritative status from the seventh century, perhaps even earlier. After about the second century BCE the second process was virtually complete, with only marginal disputes about the scriptural status of a few books possibly continuing down into the Christian era. But between these dates 'sacred writings' were still being produced even though other, more ancient ones were already fixed and settled as the core of Holy Scripture. Once some books were already regarded as 'holy', that had an effect on how other books were written: pastiche of earlier biblical books became common. Later books of the Bible thus have a complex relationship with earlier ones, and this will be explored below by examining first, the growth of Israel's national literature; second, its acceptance as Scripture; and finally, the interaction of the two processes (Sanders 1992).

GROWTH OF THE LITERATURE

The bulk of the Hebrew Bible was composed between the early days of the monarchy (tenth century BCE) and the period of Persian dominance (fifth century BCE). Most of the books we now have are the result of a long process of reworking and rewriting, in which editors introduced new material, either composed for the purpose or taken from existing documents. Hardly any of the major books of the Bible seems to derive from a single author in the modern sense, and the few that may do so (e.g. Jonah, Ruth) are generally from a somewhat later time, perhaps the Hellenistic age (fourth century and later). For theology, this aspect of the way the national literature of Israel was formed raises questions about inspiration, revelation, and authority, and also about the relation of religious content to literary form (Barr 1983). Six broad types of literature will be examined: narrative, law, wisdom, poetry, prophecy and psalmody.

Narrative

Unusually in the ancient world, even the earliest fragments of Israelite story-telling or historical narration are in prose (Alter 1981). In the Pentateuch, Genesis contains stories about the 'patriarchs' (Abraham, Isaac, Jacob, and Jacob's twelve sons), and Exodus about Moses and the escape of the Israelites from Egypt, which may derive from a source document ('J') written perhaps as early as the tenth century, and based on yet older materials. Other narrative books also contain what seem to have been originally independent legends or folk memories – stories about prophets, for example, in the books of Samuel and Kings (see 1 Sam. 9–10; 1 Kgs. 13, 18–22; 2 Kgs. 1–2). It was not until the fifth century that all the disparate materials in the Pentateuch came together to form the five books as we now have them, and much that was then included was certainly later than the early sections just mentioned. In the meanwhile, Israelite historiography had developed to a degree of sophistication unparalleled among the other nations in the ancient Near East. It is usual to single out the account of David's monarchy in its middle and later years (including his affair with Bathsheba, the near loss of his throne to his son Absalom, and the eventual succession of Solomon) as a separate 'Court History' or 'Succession Narrative', comprising 2 Samuel 9–20 and 1 Kings 1–2 (Whybray 1968). But the whole of 1 and 2 Samuel exhibit much the same skill in narration, and may show that such literary skills were already developing well before the monarchies of Israel and Judah went into terminal decline in the eighth century (Gunn 1978, 1980). The greatest work of compilation and editing can be found in the single 'history' running from Joshua through Judges and Samuel and ending with Kings (thus incorporating the already existing Succession Narrative), which was probably put together from older materials, or reworked from earlier editions, during the Exile in

the sixth century BCE (Noth 1981). This massive narrative work is traditionally known as the 'Former Prophets' but in modern scholarship as the 'Deuteronomistic History', since it is an interpretation of the history of Israel
down to the Exile according to criteria in part derived from the book of
Deuteronomy.

All Israel's narrative literature is interpretative – narration necessarily interprets what it narrates. But a comparison of the finished Deuteronomistic
History with its underlying sources, and with narratives in the Pentateuch,
brings out two characteristic features of the interpretation of history in Hebrew
literature. First, from the earliest times for which we have any evidence the
narrators interpreted the history of the nation in religious terms. Israel's God
is involved in what happens to the Israelites. This may be true at a local level,
when a prophet or patriarch experiences the events that befall him as a contact
with the divine; or it may be at a national or even international level, with
events being interpreted as part of an unfolding divine purpose for the whole
people of Israel, or even for the whole world. But second – and perhaps
surprisingly – the divine element in human history tends to be heightened as
Israelite historiography develops. Modern readers may expect that the earlier
a story is, the more 'supernatural' it will be, but, if anything, the reverse is
the case. It is in the Succession Narrative that the most 'secular' accounts of
human events are to be found; the Deuteronomistic History tends to heighten
the divine control of history, and includes more miraculous elements. The
trend continued after the Exile, with Chronicles to some extent rewriting the
events recorded by the Deuteronomistic Historian to make them reveal
the hand of God more explicitly. Thus the development of Israel's historio-
graphical tradition manifests an increasing 'sacralization' or 'theologization'.
As we shall see, this is equally characteristic of other branches of the national
literature.

Law

Israelite law developed in its early days along lines familiar from other cultures
of the area, with similarities to the law codes of ancient Mesopotamia, such
as the famous Code of Hammurabi (Greengus 1992). The early law codes in
the Hebrew Bible may have been taken over from the indigenous Canaanite
population of Palestine. The earliest, the 'Book of the Covenant' (Exod. 21–4),
concentrates on providing the rules needed for life in a fairly simple society,
regulating tenure of land and ownership of property, and seeking to maintain
the peace through rules for dealing with murder, theft, and personal injury.
'Law' in this context means something similar to what it means today, and is
not a religious term as it was to become later in Judaism.

However, even at this early stage (at the beginning of the monarchic
period or even earlier) there were some distinctive features of Israelite law. It
presupposed a less stratified society than did most Mesopotamian law, with

few laws differentiating between people of different social status – perhaps because Israelite society was as yet less 'advanced' than the city states of Mesopotamia. And it cast the law in forms less commonly found outside Israel, in particular the 'apodeictic' form, where the law is a simple imperative, either positive or (more often) negative, e.g. 'You shall not commit adultery'. (The theory of Alt (1967) that apodeictic law was actually *unique* to Israel cannot be sustained.) Most ancient Near Eastern law (including much in the Hebrew Bible) takes the form 'if x, then y': 'If a man steals an ox or a sheep, and kills it or sells it, he shall pay five oxen for an ox, and four sheep for a sheep' (Exod. 22:1; Hebrew 21:37) (Gilmer 1975; Sonsino 1992). Thus even at the earliest stages we can recognize a tendency to couch law in the form of teaching. It addresses the potential criminal, rather than simply providing a code to which judges can refer when sentencing, and accords protection to all human beings just because they are human, not because they have a particular status in society. But the codes still remain primarily legal documents in the normal sense.

Later legal texts, by contrast, developed some of these peculiar features to a point where the term 'law' becomes rather questionable. Deuteronomy, edited probably in the seventh century BCE from earlier materials (including the Book of the Covenant), envisages a society which is perhaps more ideal than real – with something approaching equality between the sexes, even in the case of slaves (Deut. 15:12–18), and even the king himself brought under the rule of law (Deut. 17:14–20). Deuteronomy also includes long sections of comment on the law and encouragement to keep it (e.g. Deut. 11:1–25) – hardly in place in an actual code, but fitting for a book which was meant to be read (probably aloud) in a religious setting, and to change society rather than merely regulating it.

Much the same is true of the (perhaps slightly later) 'Holiness Code' (Lev. 16–26). Both these works add a clear theological rationale to the more commonsensical approach of the Book of the Covenant, maintaining that the laws come from God and are the terms and conditions of his special relationship ('covenant') with his people (Lev. 26:3–20; Deut. 29:2–9 (Hebrew 29:1–8)). This laid the foundation for the fresh understanding of the law which developed in post-exilic times, in contents where Jews could no longer regulate their own affairs. In law as in historiography we can see a steady theologizing of originally pragmatic material. All commandments are attributed to God as their author – thus classically in the Ten Commandments or Decalogue (Exod. 20:1–17; Deut. 5:6–21), a digest of the essential core of the law which traces all legislation back to the God of the Exodus, Israel's covenant-lord.

Wisdom

Just as the roots of Hebrew law go down into a common ancient Near Eastern soil, so do those of 'wisdom' (Crenshaw 1981). The only clear example of wisdom literature in the Hebrew Scriptures is the book of Proverbs, and this manifests all the defining characteristics of the genre as found throughout the ancient Near East and, indeed, further west in the classical world (Hesiod's *Works and Days* is a Greek example). Typically a wisdom book is a collection of aphorisms or 'sentences', often only one or two lines long, though sometimes collected into groups with a common theme. In other works there are short paragraphs evidently composed to have a genuine progression of thought. Alongside the 'sentence literature', this 'instruction literature' occurs in the wisdom books of both Mesopotamia and Egypt, where it is typically attributed to a high court official, giving advice to his son (see the examples in Pritchard 1969: 412–25). The Hebrew tradition preserves this form, though whether Hebrew wisdom was really rooted in the royal court, it is hard to say (see below). Wisdom also includes riddles (as in Prov. 30:15), questions (Prov. 30:4), and paradoxes (Prov. 30:24–8).

Scholars have long debated the extent to which Hebrew wisdom is religious. In the sentence collections proverbs referring to God mingle freely with those that do not mention him, as is the case also in Egyptian wisdom. Sometimes it is argued that Israel's wisdom was distinctive from the very beginning, and always rested on the experience of Israel's special God, even where he is not mentioned (von Rad 1972). Others think, perhaps more plausibly, that teachers of wisdom, though indeed they were hardly atheists, did not take God and his ways in the world as their primary topic of interest (McKane 1970: 10–22). They were concerned to observe and comment primarily on human behaviour, in a more pragmatic spirit. What is certain, however, is that we possess no example of a purely secular wisdom document, and some of the most frequent statements in Hebrew wisdom are theological: 'The fear of the Lord is the beginning of wisdom' (or some variant of this) occurs more often than any other sentence in the Hebrew Bible.

But it is important to see that the style of theology in Proverbs differs markedly from that in many other books, approaching at times what in Christian thought is called 'natural theology' (Barr 1993). Wisdom is interested in observation of the human and natural worlds, rather than in divine revelation. It refers hardly at all to the national history, or to other Hebrew literature. It seems to be a self-contained system. This is still true in the book of Job, a work from the Persian period (possibly the fifth century), which most scholars assign to 'wisdom'. This work reflects on the human experience of suffering and especially the lack of correspondence between reward and desert, but it does so entirely without reference to the law, the prophets, or the history of Israel.

The later post-exilic period saw a sharp shift of emphasis. The books of

Ecclesiasticus (Ben Sira) and the Wisdom of Solomon are recognizably wisdom, but they presuppose a knowledge of and a commitment to the rest of Israel's national literature in its post-exilic form. Wisdom is being, as it were, contaminated by other traditions within Israel's literary heritage, and the theology of wisdom increasingly comes into line with those traditions. This is part of the way in which older parts of the canon of Scripture came to affect later parts, which will be examined in the section 'Interaction between the canonization of old texts and the composition of new ones'.

Poetry

It is hard to know how much of the literature of ancient Israel has survived in the Hebrew Bible, and how much has been lost to us; but at least in the case of poetry, it seems quite clear that there were once far more texts than we now have. There are references to books of poems, now lost, in Numbers 20:14, Joshua 10:13, and 2 Samuel 1:18; and these may have contained appropriate poems for various types of occasion, by no means all of which need have been religious in character. But the major collection in the Hebrew Bible is the book of Psalms, which contains only religious verse. A few of the Psalms are more like wisdom instructions, reflecting on good and evil, prosperity and adversity (Pss. 37; 49). But most seem to be intended for address to God. Some speak in the plural (e.g. Ps. 80), some in the singular (Ps. 88), and this might suggest a rough and ready division into liturgical texts meant for corporate worship, and private prayers to be uttered by an individual. Studies of ancient Israelite worship have argued persuasively, however, that almost all the extant Psalms could have had a liturgical function, since the 'I' who speaks may on many occasions be taken as a collective – the community represented, perhaps, by a single singer or reciter. (Note the change of number, for example, in Ps. 81.)

Most scholars now think that the majority of the Psalms originated before the Exile, and had a place in the worship of the Solomonic Temple (Mowinckel 1962; Kraus 1966; Day 1990). They characteristically express either praise or lament/petition, much as do the prayers of many religions. But some may also have been used in private devotion – even those couched in 'corporate' language. The Psalter is rather like a Christian hymn book: the poems may have originated as hymns, or as private lyric poems, but in their present context all are meant for public worship. Yet an individual may well use any or all of them for private prayer. The actual formation of the Psalter as a fixed collection may owe something to both motives, the desire to collect together common liturgical texts and the desire to produce a book for private devotion – though the latter term might imply a more widespread literacy than it is reasonable to assume for the pre- and early post-exilic periods.

The Psalter must have been formed through a number of stages. As it stands it is divided into five 'books' (1–41; 42–72; 73–89; 90–106; 107–50), perhaps on the analogy of the Pentateuch; but within the books (and some-times even cutting across them) are indications of earlier small collections, such as the Psalms of Asaph (50, 73–83) or the Psalms of 'Ascents' (120–34). Most scholars assume that groups of priests or other Temple officials were responsible for these collections. When and how they were made remains wholly in the realm of conjecture. (For what can be known, see Day 1990: 109–22.) There are hymns and prayers from neighbouring cultures, but no compendium of psalmody that offers any close analogy to the Psalter.

The oscillation between corporate and individual piety in the Psalms, indeed the practical impossibility of knowing for sure which we are dealing with, make it harder to write a literary history of Israel, but throw much light on its religious thought. Yahweh, the God of the nation, is also seen as the protector and helper of the individual Israelite. Israel did not acknowledge (at least not officially) the pattern of thought common in other ancient cultures, where there were 'guardian' gods for the individual who were distinct from, and could act as intercessors with, the greater gods of the pantheon. From at least the time of the great prophets (eighth century BCE) it was claimed that one and the same God was both ruler of the universe, rightly worshipped in hymns and liturgies, and the friend of the individual – especially the afflicted or persecuted individual. As a finished collection, the Psalter reflects this religious tradition, which distinguished ancient Israel rather sharply from most of its neighbours.

Prophecy

The prophets after whom books are named – Isaiah, Jeremiah, Hosea, and so on – were once called 'the writing prophets', on the assumption that each actually wrote the book that bears his name. There is no impossibility in supposing the prophets to have been literate; but the present form of their books is difficult to explain, if they composed these books themselves. Even the most orderly of the prophetic books (Ezekiel) strikes the modern reader as rather jumbled, in comparison with books familiar today, while Hosea or Isaiah present a quite bewildering variety and disorder. To cope with this, modern scholarship has proposed that each book contains a core of authentic oracles by the prophet in question, which he probably delivered orally but did not write down, but that the remainder of the book (usually the greater part) derives from later writers.

There is a division of opinion over who these later writers may have been (see the discussion in Sawyer 1987: 24–38). Some think of them as the prophets' disciples, who composed additional oracles in the prophets' name (rather like the disciples of rabbis in later times), and who were then in turn followed by their own disciples, until it makes sense to speak of a 'school' of this or that prophet lasting as long as several centuries. The book of Isaiah, for example, contains material from the eighth century, but probably also from as late as the fifth or fourth. Others hold that the prophet commissioned the writing down of his oracles – Jeremiah tells us the name of his secretary, Baruch – and once these were in written form, they were reworked by successive generations of scribes, in much the same manner as the historical books or the wisdom collections. (For a discussion of these issues see, for example, Clements 1982.) On either model the picture we receive from a prophetic book is far removed from the realities of the prophet's own day, and the 'message' of the book may differ widely from that of the prophet himself. Simplifying greatly, we may say that the general trend in editing the prophetic books was to make what the prophet had said in his own day relevant either to the specific situation of a later time, or to the circumstances of all times. As we shall see, this had the effect of enabling the prophetic books to serve as models for the 'apocalyptic' books of later times, in which both these features are strongly apparent.

By the time of the Exile there must already have been early editions of Amos, Hosea, Micah, Isaiah, and Jeremiah. It is widely thought that these books, whatever their transmission down to this point, were subjected to a reworking during the Exile by the same school of scribes as the Deuteronomistic History. By this means all these books became theological interpretations of the pre-exilic history of the kingdoms of Israel and Judah. Historiography and prophecy came to present a united understanding of why the nation had fallen, and how any revived Israel could avoid suffering the same fate again. Amos and, probably, Hosea were little revised thereafter, but the exilic edition of Isaiah received further massive additions, the collections known as 'Deutero-Isaiah' (40–55) and 'Trito-Isaiah' (56–66). It is hard to say at what point such re-edited works came to be seen as 'Scripture'. There must have been a stage at which they were felt to be holy or inspired enough for there to be some advantage in adding oracles to them, rather than issuing those oracles separately; and yet not so holy or inspired that nothing legitimately could be added to them, as was the case by the last pre-Christian centuries. Few books seem to have become 'canonical' in Judaism without passing through an intermediate phase of this kind.

ACCEPTANCE OF THE HEBREW WRITINGS AS SCRIPTURE

As just indicated in the case of the prophets, it is not easy to say at exactly which point in their development the writings that now form the Hebrew Bible became 'Scripture'. Canonization, in the technical sense of inclusion in a fixed list with absolute boundaries, can hardly be spoken of before the first century BCE, perhaps not even then (Barr 1983; Sanders 1992). But already by the early post-exilic age all the types of literature discussed above were acquiring a high status and authority – greater than any newly written work could claim – as the literary deposit of a revered past. Once this has happened, it makes sense to speak of the existence of 'Scripture'. Again this can be illustrated in detail by concentrating on different genres of literature.

Narrative + Law

When the Pentateuch was edited into its present shape, probably in the late sixth or early fifth century BCE, the legal material surveyed on pp. 9–10 above was placed in its 'correct' historical context. The Book of the Covenant and the Holiness Code were presented as part of the divine revelation given to Moses at Sinai, the Deuteronomic law as part of his final address to the Israelites in the plains of Moab, just before they were to cross the Jordan into the Promised Land. This had the effect of integrating law and narrative in a way that has been critically important for Judaism ever since. The finished Pentateuch itself came to be called the Torah or Law, as though all of it – not just the legal portions – had the function of 'law' (or guidance) for Jewish life. The historical narrative thereby took on the character of moral instruction, beginning the tendency to treat historical incidents primarily as moral examples which has been common in both Judaism and Christianity (Barton 1986: 154–78). (This is the ancestor of the 'moral sense' in medieval biblical interpretation.) On the other hand, law (in the literal sense) was anchored firmly to the foundation narrative of the Jewish people, so that it could not be treated as a human construction but must be accepted as divine revelation given through Moses, the greatest lawgiver and prophet Israel had ever known.

The fixing of the Pentateuch also established that the formative period for Israel should be seen as ending when the revelation of the Torah ended – with the death of Moses. From now on the Pentateuch, which before had perhaps run on without a break into Joshua and the subsequent histories, formed a separate entity – an account of the classic age of Israel's origins. One feature that may strike the modern reader as odd about this is that this age then ends before the conquest of Canaan, for at the end of Deuteronomy the Israelites are about to enter the land; it is not until Joshua that the entry actually occurs. It has been plausibly suggested (Sanders 1972) that this is theologically significant, and reflects the experience of the generation that compiled the Pentateuch. Living in exile, no more able than Moses himself to enter the promised Land, the compilers deliberately left the Torah as an open-ended work, addressed to readers who might indeed hope to return to the land, but had certainly not yet done so. One consequence was to make the occupation of Canaan the beginning of the second great block of narrative, the Deuteronomistic History, which lost its original connection with Pentateuchal materials and came to begin with the book of Joshua.

For the early post-exilic generation both the Pentateuchal and Deuteronomistic historical narratives belonged firmly in the past. They were accounts of the first and second epochs in the Israelite story, both of which had ended. The profound sense of discontinuity between *then* and *now* is a highly characteristic element in the post-exilic view of reality, which both encourages and is encouraged by the recognition of these writings no longer just as national records but as the community's Scripture, closed to all possibility of correction or supplementation (cf. Barton 1986: 115–16). Much later, Josephus will say that no scriptural book was written 'from the death of Artaxerxes to our own time' (*Against Apion* 1:37–43) – which means in practice after the time of Ezra, whose work marked the decisive inauguration of the Second Commonwealth of Israel in the fifth century BCE. That belief was not yet present when the Pentateuch was being edited, probably somewhat before the work of Ezra; but its spirit is quite close to that of the early post-exilic community. Revelation, whether of law or of history, lay for them in the past. Such an attitude was an essential part of the acceptance of ancient writings as 'Scripture'. It also, as we shall see, affected what sorts of new writing could be produced.

Wisdom

Whereas the Pentateuch and Former Prophets (Deuteronomistic History) were clearly regarded as 'scriptural' by the middle of the Persian period, the wisdom literature seems to have retained a less official status right down into the Hellenistic age. Evidence that it is beginning to be seen as part of sacred literature can be found in the attempt of editors to make the rather sceptical and critical wisdom books, Job and Ecclesiastes, yield an orthodox message. In the case of Job this may be found in features of the narrative framework (Job 1; 2; 42:7–17), the introduction of the pious utterances of Elihu (32–7), and, above all, the repentance of Job (42:1–6) – if we assume, as do many but not all scholars, that these passages are interpolations into an originally far less orthodox work. Where Ecclesiastes is concerned, it is well established that a work strongly critical of established religion and of accepted wisdom teaching has been 'improved' by the addition of such passages as 2:26 and 12:13–14, which in effect reverse the book's original teaching and bring it into line with what wisdom teachers had always said anyway (Whybray 1980). Thus Job and Ecclesiastes edge their way towards becoming 'Scripture'. Whether Proverbs received, or needed, such reworking is a moot point. Some scholars think that all the sayings in it which mention God are part of a post-exilic retouching (McKane 1970). But the majority view is probably that they were always an integral part of the work, and that its canonization did not necessitate any radical rewriting.

Psalmody

It is not clear how early the book of Psalms became 'canonical' in its present form. The presence among the Dead Sea Scrolls of Psalter manuscripts differing in arrangement from our Psalter may indicate that the order of the

Psalms was still not fixed in the first century BCE, though some scholars argue that these manuscripts are selections, arranged for liturgical use, from a book that was already fixed (see the discussion in Sanders 1992: 842–3). In either case it is likely that most Jewish communities by this time would have recognized 'the Psalms', with whatever variations of detail, as Scripture. Probably this had been so for several centuries. The Psalter is often described as 'the hymnbook of the second temple', and it seems from 1 Chronicles 16 that excerpts from it were already a familiar part of worship in the fifth century. Just as all law was attributed to Moses, and all wisdom to Solomon, so psalmody came to be ascribed to David; and this had the effect (or was the result) of placing the composition of Psalms firmly in the past – just like law and wisdom.

By New Testament times the Psalms had become a book of religious teaching, their character as address to God submerged under the idea that they were God's address to his people. Thus, in the New Testament, Psalm texts can be read in the same way as prophecy (Acts 2:25–8), while Philo uses them as teaching about the spiritual life. Thus the Psalms became one of the 'foundation documents' of Judaism – no longer a collection which could be added to freely, but a complete and self-contained work from a past age. The book contained 150 Psalms, and it is interesting that though these are counted differently in the Hebrew, Greek, and Latin traditions, care is taken to ensure that the total remains the same, by combining and/or subdividing various Psalms. (The LXX's Ps. 151 is a later text which never formed part of the collection.)

Prophecy

We have already seen that the prophetic books grew by a complex process, in which old oracles were updated and new ones added. At what stage in this process any given prophetic book came to be seen as 'Scripture' is hard to say. Presumably (see above) a book is not yet scriptural if its contents can be freely reworked. But there are some prophetic books (Isaiah is the classic case) which were expanded by the addition of complete blocks of material at the end, perhaps after the work of interpolation into the original book was complete, and here it might make sense to say that the original book was being seen as already a complete – and hence arguably 'scriptural' – text. On the whole, however, it may be better to think of the prophets as becoming 'canonical' only at the point where all further work on the text had ceased. In that case few of the books were Scripture until at least the fifth century, and some not until a couple of centuries later still.

An interesting phenomenon is the 'Book of the Twelve', seen as a unit by Ben Sira (Ecclus. 48:10). This obviously postdates the latest of the individual books of the minor prophets (Malachi), though some think there were earlier collections – a 'Book of the Six' (or two such books), or a 'Book of the Nine'.

Whatever the details, the collection witnesses to a way of seeing the prophets comparable to what we have already observed for the Torah and the Psalms. Their individuality is lost beneath a perception of their works as a collection of divine oracles, all of much the same kind.

INTERACTION BETWEEN THE CANONIZATION OF OLD TEXTS AND THE COMPOSITION OF NEW ONES

A major concern of this chapter has been to show that the formation of the Hebrew Bible did not take place in neat, discrete stages. It is not the case that all the texts were written 'in their own right', then were all 'canonized', and then began to be interpreted. Some books were still as yet unwritten when others were already seen as authoritative. And the way in which books already scriptural were understood influenced the writing of later books, which would in due course become scriptural themselves. The processes are complicated even further by the fact that different types of writing seemed to have acquired scriptural status at different relative dates: the law, for example, became 'official' very early (as is the nature of law), and the narratives associated with it in the Pentateuch likewise; while new prophecy was still being written well into the post-exilic age. Older works which were already held in great reverence could thus affect newer works, which for later generations would appear to be on the same level, but which at the time were really quite secondary and derivative in style or content. This can again be illustrated briefly for different genres of writing.

Narrative

The interaction between texts that were well on the way to being Scripture, and new texts that would eventually become so, can be seen most clearly in the books of Chronicles. Though there may be some independent sources lying behind Chronicles, it is clear that for the most part these books are a reworking of the books of Samuel and Kings – parts of the Deuteronomistic History. Chronicles describes the history of Judah as it would have been, if history conformed to more regular patterns of cause and effect, merit and reward. To this end the author has to rewrite Samuel–Kings extensively. But it is not as though Samuel–Kings itself had provided an objective account of events, while Chronicles gives us pure fantasy. The Deuteronomistic History is already far from neutral, and often reshapes the events it describes; while Chronicles clearly feels bound by the constraints of 'what really happened' to a much greater degree than if it were a work of pure fiction.

For example, in Chronicles David rather than Solomon takes most of the credit for the Temple: he plans it, collects the materials, appoints the builders (1 Chr. 28–9). This accords with the Chronicler's depiction of David as the originator of all Israel's sacred institutions. Yet it is still Solomon who actually inaugurates the building: evidently this was regarded as an unalterable fact. The Deuteronomistic version is pulled into a new shape, embellished, curtailed, rewritten; but it is not, strictly speaking, contradicted. For the Chronicler, it seems, the books of Samuel and Kings had a high – more or less a 'scriptural' – status, so that any retelling of the history must be in close reliance on them and not openly at odds with them. On the other hand, it was still apparently open to writers to produce an original retelling of the story, not just a commentary on the existing one.

And yet this retelling was like the original in conception and in style. It was a kind of pastiche, and skilful enough that the reader of the English Bible, faced with Samuel–Kings and Chronicles both rendered into the same 'biblical English', does not immediately see that one is an imitation of the other, but reads both alike as scriptural narrative. The text conceals the fact that there was a time (perhaps in the fifth century) when Samuel–Kings was already Scripture, and Chronicles was just another newly written work, with no authority but that of its author(s).

Wisdom

At least some law acquired an authoritative status before the Exile; and the Deuteronomistic History was in some sense 'Scripture' by the time the Chronicler began his work. But the authority of wisdom literature, which never claimed a divine origin, seems to have been accepted later than that of either law or narrative. We do not know when Proverbs came to seem unalterable and divinely inspired. We may guess that the attribution to Solomon helped in this, as it probably did also for Ecclesiastes and the Song of Songs. Books ostensibly so ancient, and written by so revered a figure, did in due course come to seem of divine origin. It is interesting that none of these books appears to be a conscious imitation of any other, and the same is true of Job. Pastiche did perhaps eventually occur, for Ecclesiasticus is clearly a Proverbs-type book. But here it may be simply that the tradition of wisdom writings continued to exist and to develop, rather than that Ben Sira deliberately modelled his work on the earlier book. The Hellenistic book called *The Wisdom of Solomon*, produced in the first century BCE in Alexandria, and written in Greek, owes little to biblical models. So in wisdom, probably a late arrival in canonical Scripture, we have little of the 'contamination' of new writings by old ones which is so marked a feature in other genres.

Prophecy and Apocalyptic

As we have seen, the prophetic books are among the most complicated cases of the development from freely composed literature to fixed Scripture. Even the latest books, composed well after some others were already more or less 'canonical', show signs of having passed through several stages of redaction (e.g. Haggai and Zechariah); and some books, such as Isaiah, span several centuries. From about the third century a new kind of literature, 'apocalyptic', is generally held to have developed, as prophecy ceased to be written or even reworked (Rowland 1982).

This literature expresses a generally more deterministic and dualistic attitude towards the events of human history than the prophets had done, and though it is attributed to ancient sages and seers, it does not really derive from them as the prophetic books do (at least in their inner core). In a work such as Daniel – the only apocalyptic book usually recognized in the canon – predictions are attributed to Daniel, a figure said to have lived in the sixth century, a contemporary of Ezekiel. These predictions, however, do not concern the sixth century but the second, and it is clear that the book was in fact written during the Maccabean crisis around 165 BCE.

What is happening here is thus similar to the attribution of the Psalms to David, or of the Pentateuch to Moses. It could be said that Daniel is the only kind of prophetic book that could be written, once it had been decided that true prophecy derived from the time before Ezra. In early post-Ezra times this idea could be respected by adding new oracles to existing prophetic books; but by the second century these books existed as finished wholes, and the only available expedient was to invent a new 'ancient' prophet and write a fresh book, as a pastiche of those that already existed. This does not imply that the corpus of the prophetic books was closed in the time of 'Daniel' – perhaps the reverse, since if it had been, there would have been no point in the false attribution to a venerable figure from the past. What it does imply is that existing books could no longer be supplemented, and also that (avowedly) new prophecy was not credible – it must be attributed to an ancient figure.

The sense that all revelation, and hence all Scripture, lies in the past, was very strong in Judaism in the last pre-Christian centuries, and the development of apocalyptic literature is strong evidence for it. There are important theological questions here that must be faced by any religion that acknowledges a written holy book. Why should it be thought that revelation ceased at a given point in the past? And how, if it did, can God still communicate with the community and with individuals? Judaism and Christianity have both had to grapple with these issues, and the very form the canon has makes it possible to trace the stages by which such ideas developed.

THE MATRIX OF THE HEBREW SCRIPTURES

The Hebrew Bible has its roots in a wide national literature that contained not only religious but also secular documents. With few exceptions, however, it is only religious texts that survived as part of the Scripture recognized by Jews in the last pre-Christian centuries. The Hebrew Bible is not just a national literature but a national *religious* literature – a religious literature that was to be the mainstay of Judaism after it had lost any geographical homeland or political independence. Nevertheless the diverse origins of these texts need to be kept in mind, if they are not to be seen in a rather two-dimensional way as parts of an undifferentiated 'Holy Scripture'. The texts in the Hebrew Bible are rooted not only in worship (in Temple or synagogue), but also in day-to-day social life; not only in piety, but in the conduct of business, commercial and legal. This makes these books a very different kind of foundation document from the New Testament, which is a far more narrowly 'religious' work.

Much depends here on our starting point. If we approach the Hebrew Bible from our experience of modern, secular literature, we shall of course be struck by how 'religious' it is. But if we turn to it after reading the New Testament or later works in the Christian tradition, it is likely to seem to connect with religion intermittently at best. Many of the narrative texts are political history rather than 'ecclesiastical' history; many of the proverbs are wise advice rather than religious teaching; and many of the laws legislate for situations that arise in any society, religious or secular, rather than reflecting the concerns of a religious community of believers, as is the case in the New Testament. It is not surprising that people wanting guidance from the Bible on social and political questions have usually turned to the Old Testament in preference to the New. The New Testament has much on the ordering of the Christian community, but far less than the Old Testament on anything to do with secular institutions and daily life in society.

The increasing selection and codification of Israelite writings as 'Scripture' were accompanied, not surprisingly, by a tendency to increase their religious content. This was done either by editing out texts or portions of text which were felt to be too secular, or by adding overtly religious passages, and thus moving texts away from their original secular setting. But it is still sometimes possible to reconstruct the original social contexts within which Israelite literature was produced, and to speculate on the kinds of material that were increasingly lost as the 'sacralization' of the national literature advanced.

Narrative

Is it possible to say anything about the original social context of Hebrew narrative? All the texts that we now possess are the product of scribes, and presuppose a literate society in which written narratives could be collected and revised. How early such a society existed in Israel is disputed, but it will hardly have been before the early monarchy (tenth century BCE). Where the underlying sources of the finished narrative texts are concerned, we have to look in two very different directions. Kings contains many references to archival sources, the 'books of the chronicles of the kings of Israel and Judah', and some of the Deuteronomistic editors' more dry and factual information may well come from such works. Books of annals and other official records were kept in the royal chancelleries of the Hebrew kingdoms, just like their counterparts at the courts of Mesopotamia. On the other hand, almost all scholars think that many stories in the narrative books rest ultimately on oral tradition: folk-tale, legend, local memories. Despite the work of Old Testament form critics, there is still little agreement about how such material was transmitted in Israel or other ancient cultures, how much real historical information it may conceivably have conveyed (or did in fact convey), or who were the principal transmitters of such oral materials.

It is clear that some of the stories in the Hebrew Bible had a 'secular' origin, in the sense that they were not religious texts: tales about the rise of David to power (1 Sam. 16–2 Sam. 8), or the deeds of heroes like Samson (Judg. 14–16), were not originally remembered because they had a religious 'message'; and accordingly we might have to look outside the religious circles (about which we are relatively better informed) to find those responsible for handing them on. Still, in many ancient societies religious ceremonies provided the occasions when tales were told and memories stirred; and it is surprisingly difficult to isolate a non-religious core in many Hebrew narratives, where God is often one of the actors in the drama. Certainly the revisions and collections of old tales that produced the Pentateuch, the Deuteronomistic History, and the books of Chronicles, sprang from highly religious motives and (as we have seen) tended, as time went on, to heighten the theological content of the narratives. No-one knows who the 'Deuteronomists' were – except that they were presumably 'scribes', since they wrote books. But they must have had some relation to both prophets and priests, and were certainly not 'secular' officials.

Law

The original setting for Hebrew law is not mysterious. Legal disputes were decided and criminals sentenced by the council of elders who met just inside the gate of Israelite cities: such a system is still implied in the story of Naboth's vineyard (1 Kgs. 21), in the ninth century BCE. It is in that context that we must look for the first codifications of the principles of criminal and civil law in Israel. With the advent of the monarchy there seems to have developed a system of higher courts, perhaps with royal judges travelling on circuit. But the stories of Samuel may suggest that such an institution, serviced by a religious 'judge', pre-existed the monarchy (1 Sam. 7:15–8:3), and this may mean that here, too, the distinction between sacred and secular is hard to maintain. Even within the Hebrew Bible's legal sections the interplay of sacred and secular jurisdiction can be observed. In the Book of the Covenant, difficult cases, which the elders cannot settle, have to be taken to the local sanctuary for resolution (Exod. 22:8, 10–11).

It is hard to know how far later law codes were rooted in forensic reality at all. Certainly the whole Torah functioned as a code of practical law in

Jewish communities both in Palestine and elsewhere in the late post-exilic age; but much of the material in them is quite ill-fitted to be used as a code, as can be seen from the very complex interpretative frameworks that had to be provided in the course of time, if the material was to be legally 'workable'. (The Mishnah, from *c.*200 CE, is a first codification of these.) Deuteronomy in particular seems much more an ideal blueprint for an imaginary Israel than a real code of law. The social function of much of the material in the Priestly Code, in Exodus 25–30 and Leviticus, is also unclear. Detailed as it seems to the average modern reader, it would nevertheless not be sufficient if it were used to instruct temple personnel in carrying out the rituals it describes. It seems more probable that it is a digest of the rituals, written with the layman in mind, and serving the purpose more of admonition than of legislation.

Wisdom

The origins of wisdom are hotly disputed. The basic disagreement is over the respective importance of 'folk' and 'court' wisdom. Folk wisdom would mean the kind of reflection on life and its meaning that goes on in all communities everywhere, and which in traditional cultures is often transmitted by local 'wise men/women'. In a sense, no doubt, all 'wisdom' (indeed, all human ideas of whatever kind) must ultimately go back to such a setting. But some scholars think that the wisdom we encounter in the Hebrew Bible, though it may appear to spring from the 'folk', actually reflects a more developed form of the phenomenon, which had its home especially in the royal courts of the ancient Near East (see the discussion in Whybray 1974). The proverbs in the book of Proverbs may seem like commonplace sayings, but their careful poetic form reveals them to be the products of a sophisticated type of 'wisdom' which was linked, in the ancient world, to professional counsellors at the courts of kings. One interesting corollary of this, if it is true, might be that the 'secular' aspects of wisdom should be stressed more strongly than scholars are apt to do in more 'theological' accounts of the genre. After all, royal counsellors were the sort of people the Hebrew prophets regarded as being 'wise in their own eyes', but not in the sight of God (e.g. Isa. 5:21), and thus as lacking in the 'fear of the Lord'. However, courtly wisdom in other cultures (especially Egypt) could be quite religious in content (see Schmid 1966); so the 'religious versus secular' problem in interpreting Old Testament wisdom probably cannot be resolved by theories concerning its social background, any more than by an analysis of its 'message'.

A further complication is that there are those who would link wisdom closely to the Israelite educational system, arguing that the literate and literary classes who wrote wisdom books were probably those engaged in educating young professional Israelites as scribes (Lemaire 1992). In some cases the aim might be to produce royal counsellors, but well-trained scribes would enter the civil service, of which the king's own counsellors formed only the very upper echelons: there were plenty of other officials in more modest grades. A good deal is known about the education system in ancient Egypt, which was closely connected to the civil service (Brunner 1957), and the Hebrew material can be fitted into a similar pattern; though all the evidence is circumstantial, since no biblical author (before Ben Sira) refers to a school or a civil service. None the less, Hebrew wisdom could have a 'learned' origin. What is agreed by all, including defenders of the 'folk wisdom' theory, is that wisdom teachers were not religious officials, and did not draw on national traditions about what the national God had done or said; and this is equally true of the parallels in other ancient Near Eastern cultures.

Poetry

Almost all extant Hebrew poetry is religious, and most is probably liturgical (see above). Some fragmentary poems in the Hebrew Bible, however, look as though they originally had a secular setting: take, for example, Numbers 21: 14–15, 17–18, 27–30. There are funeral dirges (2 Sam. 1:19–27; cf. Jer. 22:18–19), and we know from texts in the prophets that Israelite society had professional lament-singers who could be employed to use such poems on behalf of the mourners (see Jer. 9:17–22, and cf. 2 Chr. 35:25). Like wisdom, of course, songs go deep into any nation's soil, and it is hard to imagine a culture without them. Perhaps the most surprising large-scale evidence for secular songs in Israel is the Song of Songs, which may be an epithalamion (song for a marriage), though marriage is never mentioned in it, and its extended treatment of sexual intimacy is perhaps too explicit for public marriage celebrations. Its importance for the historian of Hebrew literature is that it clearly demonstrates the existence of sophisticated non-liturgical and non-sacred poetry. When textbooks class it with the wisdom literature, this is sometimes merely a counsel of despair, trying to avoid treating it as unclassifiable; but at the same time the circles that could produce such a work must surely be close to those that could produce the nicely turned epigrams of Proverbs or the clever dialogues of Job. At this point, therefore, wisdom and poetry do meet.

The setting of the great bulk of Hebrew poetry remains the liturgy, first of the Temple (Solomon's and its post-exilic successor), then of the synagogue. Form critics have suggested likely occasions for the various types of Psalm in the biblical Psalter (Mowinckel 1962; cf. Day 1990). Anyone can see that some of these suggestions are likely to be correct: for example, Psalm 65 is obviously a harvest thanksgiving psalm, Psalm 21 a psalm for some celebration in time of war, Psalm 114 for a festival commemorating the Exodus (probably the Passover), and so on. Just how the Psalms were used in practice is harder to decide – we ought not to assume that they were sung congregationally in unison, like hymns in a modern Western church. Once again, our evidence is nearly all circumstantial – it consists of the texts of the Psalms themselves.

Nowhere is their use described in detail – the nearest to this is 1 Chronicles 16.

Prophecy

The prophetic books, for all their complexity, are tied more overtly to a particular social setting than any other form of Hebrew literature. The historical books record how prophets lived and died, how they were consulted for guidance and how, sometimes, they gave warnings or reprimands or predictions even unasked. It is true that we have very few 'oracles' from the prophets whose lives are related in the histories, and equally few details of the lives of the prophets whose utterances appear in the books named after them. Consequently there is not much mutual illumination between narrative and prophetic books. Nevertheless even the oracles themselves, as we find them in Amos or Isaiah or Ezekiel, imply a social context – a gathering of Israelites for worship or business, into which the prophetic word erupted, contradicting people's expectations and confounding their assurance of enjoying divine favour.

It is clear that the oracles of the 'classical' (or 'writing') prophets were precisely designed with the known thoughts of their intended audience in mind. But it is also clear that the form of these utterances often cleverly exploited the audience's expectations. On the one hand, they used expected prophetic forms, but filled them with unexpected content: 'Thus says the LORD' was a perfectly standard opening which created an expectation of helpfulness or blessing, but more often than not was followed by denunciation and words of doom (see Westermann 1967). On the other hand, for much of the time the classical prophets did not use 'proper' prophetic forms at all, but adopted speech forms from other spheres, speaking as if they were (for example) a priest or a singer. Through that vehicle they were able to communicate a harsh message to people caught off their guard. (See Amos 5:2, where the prophet uses the form of a funeral lament; Amos 5:4–5, where he parodies a priestly call to worship; and Isaiah 5:1–7, where an oracle of judgement is cast in the form of a popular song.) Thus, paradoxically, these most 'theological' of books preserve some of our best evidence for the secular forms of everyday Israelite life. We should know hardly anything about popular songs in Israel without Isaiah! The process of canonization effectively smoothed out the prophetic books, made them timeless, and detached them from any real social anchorage. Source- and form-critical work has made it possible to re-establish the place of the prophets in the community, and in the process to follow up hints in the text that restore the environing culture within which alone they made sense.

REFERENCES

Alt, A. (1967) 'The Origins of Israelite Law', in *Essays on Old Testament History and Religion*, New York; trans. from *Die Ursprünge des israelitischen Rechts*, Leipzig (1934).

Alter, R. (1981) *The Art of Biblical Narrative*, New York: Basic Books.

Barr, J. (1983) *Holy Scripture: Canon, Authority, Criticism*, Oxford: Oxford University Press.

—— (1993) *Biblical Faith and Natural Theology*, Oxford: Clarendon Press.

Barton, J. (1986) *Oracles of God: Perceptions of Ancient Prophecy in Israel after the Exile*, London: Darton, Longman and Todd.

Brunner, H. (1957) *Altägyptische Erziehung*, Wiesbaden.

Clements, R. E. (1982) 'The Ezekiel Tradition: Prophecy in a Time of Crisis', in R. Coggins, A. Phillips and M. Knibb (eds) *Israel's Prophetic Tradition*, Cambridge: Cambridge University Press.

Crenshaw, J. L. (1981) *Old Testament Wisdom*, London.

Day, J. (1990) *Psalms*, Sheffield.

Gilmer, H. W. (1975) *The If-You Form in Israelite Law*, Missoula, Montana.

Greengus, S. (1992) 'Law: Biblical and Ancient Near Eastern Law', in D. N. Freedman and G. A. Herion *et al.* (eds) *Anchor Bible Dictionary* iv:242–52.

Gunn, D. M. (1978) *The Story of King David*, Sheffield.

—— (1980) *The Fate of King Saul*, Sheffield.

Kraus, H. J. (1966) *Worship in Israel*, Oxford.

Lemaire, A. (1992) 'Education (Ancient Israel)', in D. N. Freedman, G. A. Herion et al. (eds) *Anchor Bible Dictionary* ii:305–12.

McKane, W. (1970) *Proverbs*, London.

Mowinckel, S. (1962) *The Psalms in Israel's Worship*, Oxford: Blackwell.

Noth, M. (1981) *The Deuteronomistic History*, Sheffield; trans. of *Überlieferungsgeschichtliche Studien* i, Tübingen: 1st edn (1943):43–266, 2nd edn (1957):1–110.

Pritchard, J. B. (ed.) (1969) *Ancient Near Eastern Texts* (3rd edn), Princeton: Princeton University Press.

von Rad, G. (1972) *Wisdom in Israel*, London; trans. of *Weisheit in Israel*, Neukirchen-Vluyn (1970).

Rowland, C. (1982) *The Open Heaven*, London.

Sanders, J. A. (1972) *Torah and Canon*, Philadelphia: Fortress Press.

—— (1992) 'Canon: Hebrew Bible', in D. N. Freedman, G. A. Herion et al. (eds) *Anchor Bible Dictionary* i:837–52.

Sawyer, J. F. A. (1987) *Prophecy and the Prophets of the Old Testament*, Oxford: Oxford University Press.

Schmid, H. H. (1966) *Wesen und Geschichte der Weisheit*, Berlin.

Sonsino, R. (1992) 'Law: Forms of Biblical Law', in D. N. Freedman and G. A. Herion *et al.* (eds) *Anchor Bible Dictionary* iv:252–4.

Westermann, C. (1967) *Basic Forms of Prophetic Speech*, London; trans. of *Grundformen prophetischer Rede*, Munich (1964).

Whybray, R. N. (1968) *The Succession Narrative*, London.

—— (1974) *The Intellectual Tradition in the Old Testament*, Berlin: Walter De Gruyter.

—— (1980) 'The Identification and Use of Quotations in Ecclesiastes', in J. A. Emerton (ed.) *Congress Volume, Vienna 1980*, Supplements to *Vetus Testamentum* 32.

FURTHER READING

Ackroyd, P. R. and Evans, C. F. (eds) (1970) *The Cambridge History of the Bible* i, Cambridge: Cambridge University Press.

Beckwith, R. T. (1987) *The Old Testament Canon of the New Testament Church*, London.

Charlesworth, J. H. (ed.) (1983 and 1985) *The Old Testament Pseudepigrapha*, 2 vols, London.

Kermode, F. and Alter, R. (eds) (1987) *The Literary Guide to the Bible*, London: HarperCollins.

Sundberg, A. C. (1964) *The Old Testament of the Early Church*, Cambridge, Mass. and London.

See also chapters 2, 3, 4, 8.

2

THE HEBREW BIBLE: ROLE IN JUDAISM

Gary Gilbert and Alan F. Segal

FORMING THE BIBLE

From the time of the Babylonian Exile to the compilation of the Babylonian Talmud over a millennium later, Judaism underwent a tremendous change. Developments in political and religious leadership, conceptions about the divine world, the locations and practices of worship, and relations with non-Jews helped to mould Judaism in this formative period. The changing religious landscape also influenced the shaping and interpretation of Judaism's sacred texts. Although containing earlier traditions, the Hebrew Bible is essentially a product of the Second Temple period (515 BCE–70 CE). At that time the final editing of the Pentateuchal and major prophetic texts took place. Likewise, several other biblical works including Third Isaiah (Isa. 56–66), Haggai, Zechariah, Malachi, Ecclesiastes, Ruth, Daniel, Ezra, Nehemiah, Chronicles, and possibly Job were composed. In addition to the biblical texts, scores of other writings narrated stories about Israelite heroes, recounted important events in Jewish history, offered praises to God, recorded visions of the heavenly world, or extolled the ethical values of Judaism.

Centuries of literary activity produced an abundance of documents, many of them articulating important Jewish themes or concepts. This burgeoning output brought with it attempts to distinguish between those texts that possessed distinctive value and authority from those that did not. The formation of the canon, that is, a fixed list of books whose texts are immutable and held to be authoritative for all Jews, did not happen all at once. The Hebrew Bible as we have it is the result of a process lasting centuries. The first collection of texts was the Torah, or Law. The five books of Genesis, Exodus, Leviticus, Numbers, and Deuteronomy achieved this recognition by 400 BCE. Authorship of the Torah was ascribed to Moses, although only Deuteronomy identifies the lawgiver as narrator or author. The next major body of generally accepted texts were the Prophets. This grouping, which appears to have been fixed by 200 BCE, contained the books of Joshua, Judges, Samuel, and Kings, as well as the four scrolls containing words attributed to Isaiah, Jeremiah, Ezekiel, and twelve 'minor' prophets.

In addition to the Law and the Prophets, other works were considered to be deserving of recognition as sacred texts. Josephus, the first-century Jewish historian, noted that the Jews possessed twenty-two divine books. These include the five books of Moses, thirteen books of prophets, and four books containing hymns to God and precepts for the conduct of human life (*Against Apion* 1.8, sec. 38–41). Josephus' conception of Scripture notwithstanding, the precise boundaries separating sacred texts from profane continued to be debated as late as the third or fourth century CE. Some Jews incorporated in their collections not only the texts identified by Josephus, but several others including 1 and 2 Maccabees, Ben Sira (Ecclesiasticus), Wisdom of Solomon, and Tobit. These writings, often referred to as apocrypha, are included in the major Greek translation of the Bible, the Septuagint, but not the Hebrew Bible. There also existed a surfeit of lesser known works. Some of them appear to have held a degree of authority possibly rivalling that of the canonical texts. Sectarian documents found at Qumran, such as the *Manual of Discipline* or the *Temple Scroll*, and diverse works collectively referred to under the broad title of pseudepigrapha, such as the apocalyptic visions of *1 Enoch* or *Jubilees* (a work that rewrites narrative portions of the Torah), cast doubt on the notion that a closed canon existed in the Second Temple period. Clearly the notion of what constituted the definitive canon of Jewish Scriptures was far from settled in the first century.

Tradition states that the rabbis at Yavneh in about 90 CE put an end to this situation by deciding on the status of a third portion of the Hebrew canon, the Sacred Writings. Books were supposed to be in Hebrew, and pre-exilic or close to it. The second-century BCE apocalypse Daniel was accepted because it outwardly appeared to have these characteristics, whereas the more straightforward history of the same period in the books of the Maccabees was seen as ineligible. The legend possesses dubious historical value but reflects the attitude that a distinct body of sacred literature was of immense value. The result of this lengthy process is the Hebrew Bible, known also among Jews as the *Tanak*, an acronym for the three Scriptural divisions – Torah (Law), Nebi'im (Prophets), and Ketuvim (Writings).

The formation of the Hebrew Bible marked a significant development in the history of Judaism. It established the authoritative texts, the canon, for the entire Jewish community. Not only did the texts reflect the values of Jewish society, but they also played a critical role in defining the shape of that society. By privileging some texts and not others, the canon's world-view endorsed particular ideas and practices while pushing others to its margins or removing them altogether. With most of the Pentateuch occupied with legal material and the dearth of mystical experiences anywhere in the canon, the Hebrew Bible facilitated the growth of certain forms of Judaism, including the authority of the rabbinic community.

TRANSLATING THE BIBLE

The books of the Hebrew Bible, with a few exceptions, were written in Hebrew. Beginning in the Second Temple period and continuing after its destruction in 70 CE, fewer and fewer Jews could understand their ancestral language. The earliest indication that Hebrew no longer served the entire Jewish populace comes in the fifth century. As Ezra, a priest, scribe, and leader of a reform movement in fifth-century BCE Judea, publicly read the law in Jerusalem, he enlisted persons to translate and help the people understand what was being said (Neh. 8:7–8). This trend progressed as Jews came into more frequent and more substantive contact with non-Hebraic cultures. The translation of the Hebrew texts into Greek was an early attempt to meet the needs of Jews living in the Mediterranean regions, particularly the large Jewish community of Alexandria. Following the conquests of the famous Macedonian leader Alexander in the late fourth century BCE, Jews came into much more direct contact with Hellenistic culture. Hellenization, the process of mixing Greek and indigenous cultures, began on a promising note, including the adoption of the Greek language by many of the indigenous populations of the eastern Mediterranean basin. Jews also incorporated many aspects of Hellenistic society. Greek names, styles of architecture, and dress all contributed to the changing dimensions of Judaism. Greek culture and the spread of trade made a new world perception necessary and eroded the automatic assent of Judeans to the religion of their ancestors. The religion had to explain itself in new ways and had to evolve new forms of expressing and understanding itself in a Greek environment.

The translation of the Bible into Greek represents a notable moment in the Hellenization of Judaism. According to one legend, seventy scholars, working independently, by a miracle produced identical translations of the Torah for Ptolemy, King of Egypt in the third century BCE. These texts formed the core of what eventually became a Greek Bible called the Septuagint (abbreviated LXX). Though the story is only a fable, it gives the translation a place of authority and respect. The miracle authenticates it as religiously authoritative, on a par with the original Hebrew texts.

By the first century the Septuagint had become accepted as the legitimate translation for Greek-speaking Jews. Christians also consulted the Bible, and those who did so in Greek, therefore, turned to the Septuagint. This version of the Hebrew Bible evolved into the Christian Old Testament. As the Septuagint became increasingly identified as a Christian text, Jews were moved to produce other Greek versions. The result was two new Greek versions, one attributed to Aquila, a convert to Judaism, and the second to Theodotion. Both translations were composed in the second century CE and attempt a reading of the original Hebrew more literal than the Septuagint.

Apart from Greek, Aramaic served as the primary means of communication for many Jews in the Land of Israel and regions of the eastern diaspora.

Aramaic, a Semitic language closely akin to Hebrew, had gained prominence in the Near East through the conquests of the Persian empire in the sixth century BCE. Even after the collapse of Persia in the late fourth century, Aramaic remained an important method of communication among Jews and non-Jews alike. As with their Greek-speaking counterparts, many of these Jews eventually required the biblical texts be made accessible to them in a language they could understand. The Aramaic versions are designated by the term *targum* (plural, *targumim*). Some of the more complete and important *targumim* include Onkelos, Pseudo-Jonathan, and Neofiti on the Pentateuch and Jonathan on the Prophets. Individual *targumim* also exist for all the Writings, except those with substantial portions in Aramaic – Ezra, Nehemiah, and Daniel. *Targumim* themselves varied from those, such as Onkelos, that provided a relatively straightforward translation to others than inserted into the Hebrew text numerous phrases, sentences, and sometimes even full paragraphs. The *targum* of Pseudo-Jonathan, about twice the length of the Hebrew Bible it claims to translate, is an example of how some *targumim* significantly expanded the biblical accounts. As one example, Pseudo-Jonathan takes the extremely terse narration of Cain's murder of Abel, and uses it to explain ambiguous portions of Genesis and to express related theological ideas.

> Cain said to Abel his brother, 'Let us go out to the field.' And when they were in the field, Cain rose up against his brother Abel, and killed him.
>
> (Gen. 4:8)

> Cain said to Abel his brother, 'Come, let us both go out into the field.' And it came to pass, when they had gone out, both of them, into the field, that Cain answered and said to Abel, 'I see that the world has been created through mercy, but it is not ordered according to the fruit of good deeds; and that there is partiality in judgement. Otherwise why was your offering accepted with favour, whereas my offering was not accepted from me with favour?' Abel answered and said to Cain, 'The world has been created through mercy, and it is ordered according to the fruit of good deeds, and there is no partiality in judgement. It is because the fruit of my deeds was better than yours and preferable to yours that my offering was accepted with favour.' Cain answered and said to Abel, 'There is no judgement, no judge, no other world; there is no fair reward given to the righteous nor punishment exacted from the wicked.' Abel answered and said to Cain, 'There is judgement, there is a judge, and another world; there is a fair reward given to the righteous and punishment exacted from the wicked.' On account of these matters they were quarrelling in the open field, and Cain rose up against Abel his brother, drove a stone into his forehead, and killed him.
>
> (Pseudo-Jonathan)

This example demonstrates how a *targum* could be much more than a translation. The *targumim*, therefore, inform us not only about the Aramaic competence of many Jews, but also how the biblical texts were interpreted in these communities, and the theological ideals they valued. Despite the service that these versions provided for Aramaic-speaking Jews, no *targum* achieved universal acceptance as the standard Aramaic translation for any given biblical text.

INTERPRETING THE BIBLE

The growing importance of the biblical texts in the life of Jewish communities coupled with their often enigmatic language spawned a host of interpretations. The translations discussed above are themselves one form of interpretation. In addition, the Second Temple and early rabbinic periods were inundated with far more expressive and imaginative examples. While diffuse in method, each one attempted to infuse the ancient texts with new meaning, and thus allow them to speak to a contemporary audience. The rewriting of biblical stories functioned as an early and enduring form of interpretation. The *Biblical Antiquities* of Pseudo-Philo, *Genesis Apocryphon* from Qumran, and Josephus' *Jewish Antiquities* rework the accounts of creation, the ancestral narratives, the Exodus from Egypt, and other biblical stories. The results are not so much paraphrases as new versions, with significant expansions and deletions of the original. Many other works developed around minor biblical characters. Several documents describe the heavenly journeys of Enoch, the obscure antediluvian figure who, according to Genesis 5:22, 'walked with God'. Another impetus for rewriting the Bible was to explain an obscure passage or remove something problematic about the text. Joseph's Egyptian wife, Aseneth, whom Genesis mentions in only two verses (Gen. 41:45; 46:20), becomes the central figure in a romance usually entitled *Joseph and Aseneth*. In the story, Aseneth converts to Judaism, thus eliminating the theologically embarrassing situation of having the biblical hero marry a foreign woman. In these and many other examples, the language, literary style, and thought are heavily influenced by the effects of non-Jewish cultures, especially Hellenization.

Other types of interpretation were more sophisticated in their method. In the Dead Sea Scrolls appear several examples of a method referred to as *pesher*, from the Hebrew meaning, 'to interpret'. The structure of these documents follows a typical form. The work cites a brief biblical passage, no more than a few verses, and follows with its explanation, often indicating the significance of the passage for the author's contemporary situation. The commentary on Habakkuk offers a clear example of how *pesher* worked. The biblical text (Hab. 1:5) reads: 'Behold the nations and see, marvel and be astonished; for I accomplish a deed in your days but you will not believe it when told.' About this verse, the author of the commentary writes:

> [Interpreted, this concerns] those who were unfaithful together with the Liar, in that they [did] not [listen to the word received by] the Teacher of Righteousness from the mouth of God. And it concerns the unfaithful of the New [Covenant] in that they have not believed in the covenant of God [and have profaned] his holy name. And likewise, this saying is to be interpreted [as concerning those who] will

be unfaithful at the end of days. They, the men of violence and the breakers of the covenant, will not believe when they hear all that [is to happen to] the final generation from the priest [in whose heart] God set [understanding] that he might interpret all the words of his servants the prophets, through whom he foretold all that would happen to his people and [his land].

(1QpHab 2:2–10)

Understanding this method of interpretation requires that we suspend our rationalist assumption that the words of the late seventh-century prophet could have nothing to do with circumstances that arose 450 years later. For the author, and for the way *pesher* functioned generally at Qumran, prophecy first and foremost relates to the time and context of the community. The members of the community regarded these interpretations not as guesswork or idiosyncratic readings, but the result of a God-given ability that helped to explain the community's history and validated its ideology.

One of the more complicated forms of interpretation comes from the allegorical writings of Philo of Alexandria. Philo was an Alexandrian Jewish philosopher and a great intellectual of his day. Though he was hardly representative of the majority of Jews, his opinions give hints about a large group of Hellenized Jews whose beliefs would otherwise be mostly unknown. A product of first-century Alexandria, roughly contemporary with Jesus and Paul, Philo's literary purpose was to show that Scripture and Greek philosophy were in complete harmony, and that Jewish ethics and morality were superior. Since this agreement is not evident from a literal reading of Scripture, he had to adopt a systematic method of interpretation, allegory, which had been developed by the Greeks in order to understand the Homeric epics and hymns. By allegory, Philo means the use of a story to symbolize the development of the soul's moral virtues. Abraham's journey from Ur to Canaan, for instance, is interpreted by him as the soul's migration towards the more perfect realms of being. For Philo, stories like that of the Garden of Eden and the other creation accounts are allegorically but not literally true. The story properly understood reveals how God created the world of ideas before he created the material world and other parts of the cosmos. In his interpretation of Jewish law, Philo explains the higher truths embodied by the physical practices. Circumcision, for instance, accomplishes not only the cutting of the flesh, but the excision of harmful passions. Understanding the spiritual dimensions of the law, however, does not obviate the need for physical observance. While circumcision and other physical acts have a higher, more spiritual meaning, Philo insists that all the laws in the Bible are to be carried out as they were written.

The various translations, expansions, *pesharim*, and allegories provide us with a wealth of information on how the Hebrew Bible was read and understood in this period of formative Judaism. By far, however, the greatest amount of interpretive material was generated in the rabbinic communities. The rabbis devoted innumerable hours to the explanation of the biblical texts, and

33

produced a vast literature known as *midrash*. The term itself refers not only to the specific comments or commentaries, but more generally to the exegetical approach characteristic of this literature. The rabbis believed the Bible to be a perfect and unified revelation from God, containing nothing that was irrelevant, repetitious, or superfluous. Every verse, word, letter, even parts of letters had potential meaning, in most instances more than one. The rabbis also believed that a verse from one book could justifiably be brought into service to explain another verse from a completely different text. At times, the resulting *midrash* appears capricious. Even at its most playful, the interpretation of the Bible was one of the most fundamental and reverential types of religious activity.

As with Jews of other periods, the rabbis created their *midrash* in an attempt to relate the Bible to the issues and concerns of their time. To accomplish this goal the rabbis employed various interpretive techniques. Some, such as *qal vahomer* (argument from lighter to heavier), have parallels in Greek and Roman literature, revealing intellectual connections between the rabbinic and Graeco-Roman worlds. These rules (*middoth*) of interpretation would eventually be compiled into lists that were credited to illustrious figures such as the first-century sage Hillel.

The early midrashic commentaries were line-by-line interpretations of the Bible. Several of the earlier works concentrate on the Pentateuchal legal material. These books – the *Mekhilta* for Exodus, *Sifra* for Leviticus and *Sifre* for Numbers and Deuteronomy – describe rabbinic visions of how Jewish life should be conducted. Occasionally we can also catch a glimpse of how Jewish life in the Land of Israel was actually practised in the second and third centuries. Distinguishing historical reality from rabbinic idealization, however, is often a difficult task. Other collections, the homiletical *midrashim*, are mostly later in time and contain a great many discussions which appear to have been generated in rabbinic homilies and sermons. The major collection is *Midrash Rabba*, which includes rabbinic interpretations of the Pentateuch and the five scrolls (Ruth, Ecclesiastes, Song of Songs, Lamentations, and Esther).

Rabbinic *midrash* was an open-ended process that permitted biblical texts to speak to different situations and viewpoints. It allowed for multiple interpretations of what the rabbis refer to as the written Torah. The rabbis also speak of a second Torah and this is the oral Torah. The rabbis conceived that, in addition to the five books traditionally ascribed to Moses, there was another body of precedent and interpretation that had been passed down from Moses in a direct line of oral tradition. The rabbis were the heirs to this great chain of transmission, and thus the authentic arbiters of custom, practice, and thought. According to later rabbinic traditions, *midrash* forms one part of a triad of the oral Torah. The two remaining segments are law (*halakha*) and legend (*haggada*).

As the name indicates, these rabbinic laws, interpretations, and stories were transmitted orally from teacher to student. Not until the third century did large portions of these rabbinic traditions come to be written down. Even then, the rabbis preferred learning the oral law apart from any written text. Rabbis regularly committed large portions of it to memory. In order to facilitate the memorization of immense amounts of material the rabbis employed various mnemonic devices.

The oral law was uniquely suited for rabbinic purposes. Highly legal and highly technical by comparison to apocalyptic or early Christian writing, the oral law gained adherents as the rabbis gained respect. Its principles were derived from experience, reason, and precedent. The rabbis often describe their rulings as coming from God. In practice, however, they were made by the majority. The rabbis sensed the tension between tradition and their creative and often innovative enterprise.

> Rabbi Eliezer used every argument to substantiate his opinion, but they [the other rabbis] would not accept them. He said, 'If the law is as I have argued, may this carob tree argue for me.' The carob tree uprooted itself and moved a hundred cubits from its place. Some say it moved four hundred cubits. They said, 'From a tree no proof can be brought.' Then he said, 'May the canal prove it.' The water of the canal flowed backwards. They said, 'From a canal no proof may be brought.' Then the walls of the house bent inwards, as if they were about to fall. Rabbi Joshua rebuked the walls, and said to them, 'If the learned dispute about the law, what has that to do with you?' So, to honour Rabbi Joshua, the walls did not fall down, but to honour Rabbi Eliezer, they did not become straight again. Then Rabbi Eliezer said, 'If I am right, may the heavens prove it.' Then a heavenly voice said, 'What have you against Rabbi Eliezer? The law is always with him.' Then Rabbi Joshua got up and said, 'It is not in heaven [Deut. 30:12].' What did he mean by this? Rabbi Jeremiah said, 'The Torah was given to us at Sinai. We do not attend to this heavenly voice. For it was already written in the Torah at Mt Sinai that, 'By the majority you are to decide [Exod. 23:2].' Rabbi Nathan met Elijah and asked him what God did in that hour. Elijah replied, 'He laughed and said, "My children have defeated me." '
>
> (B. Baba Metzia 59b)

The story displays folkloric motifs, but also strongly held rabbinic values. The playful, even humorous narration of Rabbi Eliezer's miracles is emphasized by the meeting of Rabbi Nathan with the prophet Elijah, which exposes even God's amusement. But the moral of the story is serious. It demonstrates rabbinic suspicion of all sources of authority dependent on charismatic or miraculous claims, whether they be outside of the rabbinic movement or even, as here, within it. The story of Rabbi Eliezer is meant to illustrate how to andle conflict with people claiming miraculous support for their religious opinions. The claims of such people, including Christians as well as rabbis, are to be evaluated by the rules of legal discourse and decided by vote. The rule of the majority, not miraculous actions, was to be the basic system for power brokerage.

The classic rabbinic writings were edited in the third century CE and later. They were edited in an atmosphere of confident, albeit incomplete, control by the rabbis of the Jewish community. That sense of control was projected backward to traditions that had been laid down in totally different circumstances, some when Pharisaism was merely a sectarian movement in Judaism. By the second century it was taken for granted that the rabbinic movement had always been the majority movement in Judaism. In reality, however, rabbinic authority took hold only gradually. While the oral law hypothetically applied to all Jews, priests, landowners, and even lay people as late as the third and fourth centuries turned to the rabbis only for a limited range of issues.

The earliest collection of rabbinic legal traditions (*halakha*) was the Mishnah, codified around the year 200 CE. The Mishnah ('repetition' or 'teaching') was written in Hebrew and contains the legal opinions of over 100 named scholars and many more anonymous ones. It is divided into six orders – Seeds, Holy Seasons, Damages, Women, Holy Things, and Purities. Each of the orders is divided into tractates, sixty-three in all, that cover the major heads of the legal system that the rabbis administered. Under Seeds, for instance, are listed rules of agricultural life but also, surprisingly, prayer. Though the Mishnah makes no attempt to record all disputes, it makes critical distinctions and argues crucial cases. As a code of community procedures, it presents principles and exemplars for cases.

One surprising feature of the Mishnah is its reluctance (in some respects its refusal) to have its authority derived from Scripture. The Mishnah pays scant attention to the written law, and rarely attempts to justify its prescriptive rulings on the basis of Scripture. The authority of the Mishnah derived not from Scripture, but from the rabbis themselves, and its thematic organization reflects their interests. The rabbis recognized the often tenuous connection between Scripture and oral law. 'The [rabbinic] laws of the sabbath, of festival offerings, and of sacrilege are as mountains hanging by a hair; Scripture is scanty but the laws are many' (*m. Hag* 1:8).

Over the first few centuries of rabbinic Judaism, traditions developed on various subjects. The earliest stages involved the codification of laws dealing with the Sabbath, purity, and tithing. Marriage and divorce were also issues of primary interest to the early rabbis, for along with matters of ritual purity these rules of personal status defined membership in the Jewish community. The deliberations involving the sphere of personal status combined in the Mishnah with an enormous effort to discuss and record matters of the defunct sacrificial system in the Temple, and purity issues that had depended upon the Temple. As it turned out, this whole enterprise was theoretical, for the failure of the Bar Kokhba revolt (132–135 CE) made it painfully clear that the Temple would not soon be rebuilt. Yet the rabbinic commentary on Temple law continued, serving as a model for an idealized temple populated by idealized assemblies of priests and rabbis, when God should choose to accomplish it in the messianic age.

The period of rabbinic activity surrounding Rabbi Judah the Prince (Judah ha-Nasi), about 200 CE, is crucial for understanding rabbinism. It took a century and a half to go from Pharisaic sectarianism and the destruction of the Temple to the Mishnah of Rabbi Judah the Prince as the first canonical, analytically organized codification of law outside the Bible. By 200 CE, the formerly open and growing body of interpretation that the rabbis had rationalized as coming orally from Moses had, like the Bible, become a fixed text. And, like the Bible, the Mishnah of Rabbi Judah would become the subject of intense scrutiny and passage by passage commentary. The structure of the Mishnah in its six orders, subdivided into its sixty-three tractates, would come to serve as the skeleton of this body of expansion, a large collection known as the Talmud.

There is one Mishnah. It is no bigger than a desk dictionary. There are two different Talmuds, each close to the size of a multi-volume encyclopedia. Each Talmud consists of the Hebrew Mishnah of Rabbi Judah plus one of the two bodies of commentary, known as a *gemara*. One *gemara* is from the Jewish community living in the Land of Israel, the other from the Jewish community living in Babylonia. The Mishnah and the Palestinian *gemara* form the Palestinian Talmud, also referred to as the Jerusalem Talmud, though it was most likely not produced there. The same Mishnah together with the *gemara* produced in Babylonia form the Babylonian Talmud.

In the course of time, the Babylonian Talmud became the more substantial and extensive of the two and would come to be considered the more definitive. This came about because life became increasingly difficult for the Jews of the Land of Israel as compared with those in Babylonia. A deteriorating economic situation, and greater restrictions placed on the Jewish communities in the Land of Israel by the later Roman and Byzantine empires contributed to this situation. In approximately 425 CE, the Christian Emperor Thoedosius II abolished the office of the patriarch, the head of the leading Palestinian academy. Meanwhile in Babylonia, where the ruling Sasanian Persians were more tolerant of Jews, the Jewish community rose in importance and became the centre of Jewish life. Its Talmud thus became the authoritative one for the Jewish community.

Since the text of the Mishnah, the core of the Talmud, is a document of law, a considerable amount of the *gemara* is strictly prescriptive. Jews speak of such prescriptive discussion as *halakha*, the study of the proper legal procedure for living life. But there is another style of expansion that is more anecdotal; it is referred to as *haggadah*, or in Aramaic, *agada*, meaning narrative. *Halakha* makes its directives by explicit statement; *agada* will indicate its preferences by telling a story usually with a moral.

The *gemara* recorded discussions of over 2,000 sages, arguing over specific ways to resolve a plethora of complex issues. Typically, the text of the Talmud gives a passage (the length of a few scriptural verses, or a short paragraph) from the Mishnah and then follows that with the text of the related *gemara*, which could be many times the length of the Mishnah text to which it was attached. The *gemara* often functions as a commentary on a passage from the Mishnah, but more often than not pursues its own wide-ranging agenda. In printed editions this material is in a column occupying the entire centre of the page, while the columns on either side carry later commentaries and helpful notations. References to the Talmud conventionally follow the pagination of an earlier printed edition, produced in Venice in 1520–3. Thus, for instance, 'b. Suk. 52a' would mean Babylonian Talmud, tractate Sukkah, folio 52, side a.

TRANSFORMING BIBLICAL IDEAS

As biblical interpretation of the written law and the rabbinic oral law developed, so did Jewish thought. Developments occurred in a wide array of subjects, including conceptions of God, prayer, charity, the family, and relations with non-Jews. To understand Judaism in the first century and the emergence of Christianity, the areas of ritual actions and notions of purity, eschatology and the afterlife, and the messiah deserve particular attention.

Ritual actions are typical of much of the world's religious practice. Particularly complex are the messages implicit in concepts of purity prevalent among the Pharisees and rabbis. Purity laws have been viewed in modern times as a kind of primitive hygiene, because societies tend to make taboo harmful or noxious substances such as corpses or human excreta. However, cultures often identify as being taboo completely harmless substances, while harmful ones are sometimes central to ritual events. Biblical and rabbinic rules, similarly, do not always have obvious medical value.

Israelite society, like many non-Western societies, had a series of food taboos, of which meat from pigs is the best known. Others included not eating blood, a kid seethed in its mother's milk, nor any of the birds and mammals that themselves violate these rules in their activity as predators. Rabbinic authorities greatly expanded these ordinances, directing that the slaughter off all *kosher*, 'ritually acceptable', animals be done in a humane way, and that meat and milk be kept strictly separate, as a safeguard against violating the biblical rules. The Bible says not to eat a young goat boiled in its mother's milk; it says nothing about keeping separate utensils for meat and milk or about not eating a fowl, which provides no milk for its young, at the same meal as cheese. Yet as the rules were interpreted, poultry was treated like meat and cheese was treated like milk, so that combining these too became forbidden. The rabbinic expression of these rules illustrates what the rabbis called 'making a fence around the Torah', setting up rules that prevented the inadvertent violations of Torah statutes.

Biblical texts, especially Leviticus, describe a complex network of laws concerning ritual purity. Coming into contact with the dead or experiencing certain bodily fluids, such as menstrual blood or semen, would render a person impure. These laws had the practical effect of regulating an individual's participation in the Temple. Priests were required to maintain a high degree of purity while performing their official duties. In addition, anyone who wished to make a sacrifice, which could only be performed at the Temple, was to be free from impurity. Most forms of impurity were easily removed through immersion in water and/or the passage of time. These laws became the focus of attention for several Jewish groups in the Second Temple period, especially the Pharisees and Essenes. Their basic objective was to observe the laws of purity even when not interacting with the Temple. For them and for the rabbis who also devoted considerable attention to this subject, purity laws provided boundary markers for the areas of Jewish life that were to be held sacrosanct.

While much of the rabbinic corpus seeks to explain the correct practices to observe in this world, thoughts about life after death and the end of time often receive considerable attention. In discussing Jewish ideas about the end of time, we have to distinguish between projections of what might be the fate of the nation or the world at the end of this age, on the one hand, and the destiny of the individual at the end of this existence, on the other. Biblical literature abounds with examples of the first, but we come up practically empty-handed when looking for the second.

The doctrine of the events at the end of the age is termed 'eschatology', from the Greek word for the end. A genre of Jewish literature that developed in the later prophetic books and flourished in the Hellenistic era is termed 'apocalyptic', from the Greek word for unveiling. Most apocalyptic literature is eschatological, but that is not its only characteristic. The genre is visionary in its presentation; whereas the prophets had said, 'Thus says Yahweh,' the apocalyptists more often wrote, 'I saw, and behold.' The visions offered a form of coded symbolic representation. A human figure can represent a divine one, a beast a dynasty, a horn on that beast one of its rulers. Sometimes the code is explained for the reader, as in the sequence of visions in the first six chapters of Zechariah. Other times, it is left undeciphered, offering a wide field for reinterpretation and innovative application in later centuries. By and large, the evident concern of these texts is the corporate fate of Israel, or of a particularly faithful subgroup.

While people in biblical Israel may have formulated ideas about what happens to someone after death, scarcely anything in their literature antici-pated the post-biblical ideas of paradise or resurrection as a reward for a righteous life. The original solution to the problem of where personality goes after death was Sheol, a place like the Greek Hades, where the person resides in greatly attenuated form. Sheol certainly is not equivalent to heaven or hell. It is a pit, a place of weakness and estrangement from God, from which the spirits of the dead issue on the rare occasions when they can be seen on the earth.

On the whole, ancient Israelite society was hardly preoccupied with the question of whether there is life after death. Whenever the question is raised as a direct issue, the answer seems to be no. Consider Ecclesiastes 3:19:

> For the fate of the son of man and the fate of the beasts is the same; as one dies, so dies the other. They all have the same breath, and man has no advantage over the beasts, for all is vanity.

The book of Job (14:14) asks directly whether people live again after they die: 'If a man die, shall he live again?' Job's answer (14:20–2) appears to be that people grow old and die, and there is nothing else:

> Thou prevailest forever against him, and he passes; thou changest his countenance, and sendest him away. His sons come to honour, and he does not know it; they are brought low, and he perceives it not. He feels only the pain of his own body, and he mourns only for himself.

In another passage that has suffered in transmission, Job's death is not clearly stated, though his death and resurrection have often been understood (19:25–7):

> For I know that my redeemer lives, and that at last he will stand upon the earth; and after my skin has been thus destroyed, then from my flesh I shall see God, whom I shall see on my side, and my eyes shall behold, and not another.

Although this passage is often read as a prediction of Job's resurrection, it appears only to affirm that Job wants to be vindicated while still alive, in a heavenly court by a heavenly vindicator or lawyer, as the logical outcome of his challenge to the justice of God. The original context for these statements must be extrapolated from ancient Near Eastern mythology, where the high god was pictured as a judge or king in a heavenly courtroom. The passage does not suggest there is life after death. Rather, it portrays a man seeking redress from God in God's own heavenly court. The book of Job almost seems to argue explicitly against any simple pietistic belief in immortality, in direct contradiction to the way the book is often understood.

Nothing in the Hebrew Bible describes the expectation of a literal resurrection. The metaphor of resurrection is explicitly interpreted in Isaiah and Ezekiel as a description of the people when they begin to live again under prophetic influence. Even the stirring phrases in Isaiah 26:19 which have contributed to the sophisticated doctrine of resurrection in later Judaism, appear to mean more than they do in fact: 'Thy dead shall live, their bodies shall rise. O dwellers in the dusk, awake and sing for joy! For thy dew is a dew of light, and on the land of the shades thou wilt let it fall.' This has been taken as a literal statement of resurrection. But like the vision of the dry bones in Ezekiel 37, Isaiah is speaking of the end of spiritual death and actual poverty that the nation was experiencing. These references were to be creatively re-understood in the first and second centuries when the note of resurrection was clearly sounded within the society.

The first indubitable reference to resurrection in biblical literature comes from the visions of the book of Daniel, which date to the years of oppression that engendered the Maccabean revolt, not to the earlier Babylonian period, as the book purports. Daniel 12:2 states:

> And many of those who sleep in the dust of the earth shall awake, some to everlasting life, and some to shame and everlasting contempt. And those who are wise shall shine like the brightness of the firmament; and those who turn many to righteousness, like the stars for ever and ever.

No general theory of immortality is articulated here, only the resurrection of the 'many', which satisfies the Hebrew concept of justice. Those who suffered and died in remaining true to God's Torah will be vindicated. The reference to the saved as 'sleepers in the dust' may be a reinterpretation of Isaiah 26:19. Those who persecuted the righteous of Yahweh will also be resurrected so that they can be punished. The doctrine of resurrection, therefore, arose in response to the problem of righteous suffering and martyr-dom. Immortality becomes a special reward for martyrs in Judaism, just as it was in Greek mythology for the heroes like Hercules and Perseus who accomplished superhuman tasks. The story of the seven martyred sons in 2 Maccabees 7 exemplifies this idea. A mother watches as her seven sons are tortured and put to death because they will not eat pork. The approach of death evokes the hope of being transported to heaven as an eternal reward after the short period of pain and suffering on earth.

Another important aspect of Jewish speculation dealing with the afterlife concerns the journey to heaven. In most cases a journey to heaven is assumed to take place at death, for paradise and hell were both thought to be located in one of the several heavens. No matter how the journey is viewed to have been made, the texts are unanimous in understanding the power of the voyage to be due to God's own desire for the adept to pay a visit. Once a credible prophet is actually said to have visited heaven and seen the ultimate rewards there, the proleptic experiences of eternal life and compensation after death are demonstrated vividly to the community in his writings. Great personages or mystics could undertake heavenly ascent during life by means of ecstatic trance or other extracorporeal experiences. *1 Enoch* and other apocalyptic texts report the fabulous journeys of well-known biblical heroes. The resulting heavenly journey serves to verify the eschatological beliefs of the community. Reports of rabbis ascending to the heavenly world are preserved in *merkavah* (chariot) traditions, an image adapted from the opening vision in the book of Ezekiel. Many rabbis, however, worried about possible dangers associated with these experiences, and therefore restricted study of mystical texts to persons of sufficient age and discretion.

By the first century, Judaism had developed ideas about numerous divine agents – angels, sons of God, magicians, and others. The messiah, however, ranks first because of its importance for understanding the development of Judaism and Christianity. Jews and especially Christians often have an impression that the concept was rooted in the time of the Israelite monarchy. What creates that impression is that an older vocabulary and older texts were pressed into service by Jews and Christians in the Hellenistic period. The Hebrew word *mashiah*, rendered in English as 'messiah', means 'an anointed one'. The ritual of anointing consisted of pouring oil over someone's head to inaugurate that person into a divinely sanctioned official position. In ancient Israelite society, principally kings but also prophets and sometimes priests were appointed to office by anointing. In the Hebrew Bible, the term *mashiah* is associated characteristically with the currently reigning king, not with some future king. Sometimes it appears in reference to priests, and twice in reference to the patriarchs. Saul's shield is once described as 'anointed', showing that the process of ordaining something for special service is more basic than the royal meaning of the word. Once it refers to Cyrus, the Persian king (Isa. 45:1).

The pre-exilic prophets sometimes express the expectation that God will raise up a king who will rule with justice and righteousness. Experience with less than perfect kings, as well as with foreign domination of the country, probably stimulated the belief in an ideal future kingship. The idea was greatly augmented when the last heir to the Davidic throne disappeared without historical trace during the Persian period. Since 2 Samuel 7 had promised that Israel should never fail to have a king of the Davidic line, there was a basis to hope for its restoration. Yet idealized future kings are not described in the time of the Israelite kingdoms by the term 'messiah'. The expected king is sometimes called the son of David (Isa. 11; Ezek. 34; Mic. 5); or he is called the branch, ostensibly a 'new shoot of the Davidic family tree' (Jer. 23). The concept of messiah would not have been self-evident or even comprehensible to an Israelite of the First Temple period. The explicit concept of a messianic hope does not develop until well after the Babylonian Exile.

Beginning in the Hellenistic period, the idea develops of a future anointed king, a messiah, who will lead Israel to victory against iniquitous foreign rulers. In the *Psalms of Solomon*, dated variously to the first century BCE or CE, the theme of the victorious battles of the messiah is extended to all those Gentile nations who have harmed Jerusalem, and the messiah himself is seen as a blameless ruler (17:41, 37, 44):

> And he himself [will be] pure from sin, so that he may rule a great people. He will rebuke rulers, and remove sinners by the might of his word. His hope will be in the Lord; who then can prevail against him? [He will be] mighty in his works, and strong in the fear of God, [He will be] shepherding the flock of the Lord faithfully and righteously.

The messiah is not an absolutely necessary feature of Jewish eschatology of this period. Even in apocalyptic literature, many descriptions of the end of time do not include a messiah. The important characters of God's redemption tend to be either the leaders of the people or the angels, though the leaders may become angels in the end. In other words, the presence of the messiah is not a *sine qua non* for the redemption.

At Qumran, the concept of the messiah was tailored to fit the community's expectation of the last days. The generic term 'messiah' was used to describe both priestly and royal anointed leaders who would lead the community in the final days and preside at its eschatological banquet. In Alexandria, Philo also refers in a very veiled way to the messiah. He thinks of an actual future victory over evil and unjust rulers (*On Rewards*: 115–19). He does not, however, make explicit his criticism of the present political order or his hope for the pre-eminent role of the Jewish people in the coming revolution.

The most profound development in messianic thinking comes with Christianity. For most Jews, the coming of the messiah was an anticipated event whose fulfilment lay in the future. For Christians, and possibly Jesus himself, the messiah predicted in Scripture had arrived. Because Christianity originated within the broad spectrum of the varieties of Judaism in the first century CE, Christians were familiar with the biblical texts and their interpretive possibilities. Jesus' followers naturally chose to describe his life and death using the language of Scripture.

The fundamental distinction that separates Jewish and Christian conceptions of the messiah is the latter's faith in Jesus as the crucified messiah. Nowhere before the start of Christianity had there been any evidence that the messiah would suffer. The righteous might suffer, and the messiah in his rule might end the suffering of the righteous by finally implementing divine justice. Jewish texts do not reflect any evidence that the messiah was expected to die for humanity's sins. In the literature of the prophets the messiah is never viewed as weak or suffering. As the Lord's anointed, he is, according to Isaiah 11:3–4, the strong vindicator who will carry out God's vengeance against the unjust enemies of Israel:

> He shall not judge by what his eyes see, or decide by what his ears hear; but with righteousness he shall judge the poor, and decide with equity for the meek of the earth; and he shall smite the earth with the rod of his mouth, and with the breath of his lips he shall slay the wicked.

Jesus' failure to redeem his people, at least not in the visible manner expected of the messiah, along with his ignominious death on the cross appeared to disprove any messianic pretensions. Christians, therefore, had to reconcile the apparent contradiction between the expectation of what the messiah should be and do with the reality of Jesus' life and death. The result was a combination of reshaping messianic expectations and constructing stories about Jesus using scriptural references as inspiration or models. In other words, biblical exegesis served as the primary means by which early Christians made sense of Jesus' life and death.

Christians applied numerous biblical passages, many of which had been read without any messianic connotations, to Jesus as proof that he was and is the messiah. This process demonstrated that Jesus' death was not the scandal and folly that many perceived, but was actually foretold in Scripture. Paul writes to the Christian community in Corinth:

> For I delivered to you as of first importance what I also received, that Christ died for our sins in accordance with the Scriptures, that he was buried, that he rose on the third day in accordance with the Scriptures, and that he appeared to Cephas, then to the twelve.

> (1 Cor. 15:3–4)

Not only Jesus' death and resurrection, but his birth, preaching and miraculous deeds also came to be understood in connection with biblical texts. Luke, for instance, reports how Jesus read from Isaiah in a synagogue in Nazareth, and proclaimed to those assembled that he was the fulfilment of that prophecy (4:16–30). The formula, 'this was to fulfil what was spoken', and similar expressions appear often in the canonical Gospels, especially Matthew, as demonstrative proof of the claim that Jesus is the messiah. Various scriptural images took on new life as they became the basis for understanding Jesus' identity. Titles applied to Jesus, such as 'Son of David', 'Son of Man', 'Son of God' and 'Lord', had their origins in biblical traditions. Descriptions of Jesus sitting at the right hand of God were adopted from biblical passages such as Psalm 110. The entire Bible became fair game for all sorts of christological exegesis. The interpretive methods employed by early Christians were indistinguishable from those of their Jewish contemporaries. The results, however, were very different. Christianity read the Bible through the lens of Jesus, and as a result united otherwise disparate biblical traditions and in an entirely new fashion.

The developing christological interpretation of Scripture ultimately resulted in the rift between Judaism and Christianity. Most Jews rejected the claims made by Christians that Jesus was the messiah and that his identity was confirmed by Scripture. For Christians the refusal by most Jews to accept Jesus as the messiah was indicative of their failure to comprehend Scripture. This latter idea is most vividly portrayed by Paul in 2 Corinthians. In chapter three he recalls Moses' ascent of Mt Sinai. The story in Exodus reports how Moses upon descending to rejoin the Israelites wore a veil. Paul interprets the covering as Moses' attempt to hide the fading splendour. In the same way, Paul explains, whenever Jews turn to Scripture they are masked by a veil that obscures the true meaning of the text. By having faith in Jesus, however, the veil is removed and one gains a proper understanding. The image of Jews as readers who lack the proper comprehension of Scripture was extremely durable. Medieval Christian art commonly portrayed the Synagogue in feminine persona wearing the very blindfold Paul describes.

Having begun as a sect of Judaism, Christianity soon established itself as a separate religious community. Although divided, Jews and Christians shared a common biblical tradition and many of the same methods for interpreting these texts. They differed, however, in the fundamental assumptions that each community brought to the exegetical process. Jews could not imagine Jesus as the messiah. Christians could not conceive of Jesus as anything else. These differences ultimately brought about the separation of Judaism and Christianity. The breach, bitter at first, turned malicious and in all too many instances lethal, especially after Christianity became the sanctioned religion of the Roman empire. The level of animosity is in part a reflection of this shared biblical heritage.

CONCLUSION

From the time of the Israelite monarchy to the early rabbis, Judaism had been transformed from a cultic religion centring on sacrificial practices to a religion of the book. The reading, study, and interpretation of the Hebrew Bible had replaced the Temple as the central focus of the religion. Differences persisted in terms of the language, method, sophistication, and genre in the interpretations. Nevertheless, they all shared the basic goal of providing new understandings to ancient texts. As these understandings evolved, so did the nature of Judaism. Jews drew from their own religious and cultural experiences in the process of interpretation, and in turn the interpretations helped to foster developments in Jewish thought and practice. The history of the Hebrew Bible in the Second Temple and early rabbinic periods reflects an attempt to make the laws and legends of Scripture more applicable to the society of those times. In so doing, Jews were able to keep the text of the Bible as a living and valuable tradition and from not becoming authoritative by itself.

FURTHER READING

Bloch, R., (1978) 'Midrash', in W. S. Green (ed.) *Approaches to Ancient Judaism*, Missoula: Scholars.

Charlesworth, J. H. (ed.) (1983, 1985) *The Old Testament Pseudepigrapha*, Garden City: Doubleday.

Horgan, M. P. (1979) *Pesharim: Qumran Interpretations of Biblical Books* (Catholic Biblical Quarterly Monograph Series 8), Washington: Catholic Biblical Association.

Juel, D. (1988) *Messianic Exegesis: Christological Interpretation of the Old Testament in Early Christianity*, Philadelphia: Fortress.

Kugel, J. L. and Greer, R. A. (1986) *Early Biblical Interpretation*, Philadelphia: Westminster.

Mulder, J. (ed.) (1988) *Mikra: Text, Translation, Reading and Interpretation of the Hebrew Bible in Ancient Judaism and Early Christianity* (Corpus Rerum Iudaicarum ad Novum Testamentum II, 1), Assen/Maastricht-Philadelphia: Van Gorcum-Fortress.

Neusner, J. (1981) *Judaism: The Evidence of the Mishnah*, Chicago: University Press.

Porten, G. G. (1985) *Understanding Rabbinic Midrash*, Hoboken: KTAV.

Runia, D. T. (1986) *Philo of Alexandria and the Timaeus of Plato*, Leiden: Brill.

Sanders, E. P. (1992) *Judaism: Practice and Belief 63 BCE–66 CE*, London-Philadelphia: SCM-Trinity.

Schürer, E. (1973–87) *The History of the Jewish People in the Age of Jesus Christ*, rev. and ed. Geza Vermes, Fergus Millar, *et al.*, Edinburgh: T. & T. Clark.

Strack, H. L. and Stemberger, G. (1991) *Introduction to the Talmud and Midrash*, Edinburgh: T. & T. Clark.

Winston, D. (1981) *Philo of Alexandria: The Contemplative Life, The Giants and Selections*, New York-Toronto: Paulist Press.

See also chapters 1, 3, 4, 8.

3

THE CHRISTIAN ADOPTION OF THE OLD TESTAMENT

G. R. Evans

CHRISTIAN USE OF THE OLD TESTAMENT IN THE NEW

The writers of the books which eventually made up the New Testament take the Old Testament to be the Word of God and a constitutive part of the tradition of Christianity itself. In Acts 4:25, for example, the Holy Spirit is said to have spoken through the mouth of David. The foretelling of the life, death and resurrection of Christ in the Old Testament is a constant theme running through the New. Micah 5:2, for instance, speaks of the birth at Bethlehem; Hosea 11:1 of the coming from (after a flight into) Egypt of the Son of God (cf. Matt. 2:15); Psalm 41:9 of the betrayal. In both the Gospel and the Epistles Old Testament authors speak as authorities: 'David said . . .' (Mark 12:36); 'Moses said . . .'; 'Moses wrote . . .' (Mark 7:10; 12:19); 'Isaiah prophesied . . .'; 'Isaiah cried . . .'; 'Isaiah says . . .' (Mark 7:6; Rom. 9:27; 10:20). As well as this direct citation, we find a weaving of words and phrases and images and echoes from the Old Testament into the very texture of the New Testament's language. 1 Peter 2:1–10 and Acts 7, where Stephen makes his speech, are particularly rich examples. In these ways the Old Testament forms in part the very stuff of which the New Testament is made.

All this is perhaps to be expected in authors whose upbringing and tradition had thus provided them with an intimate knowledge of the Old Testament texts. It is much the same phenomenon as is to be found in the work of certain medieval Christian authors who are so familiar with Scripture that they can scarcely frame a sentence which is not full of it, such as St Bernard of Clairvaux in the twelfth century. But it also reflects a number of conscious or semi-conscious assumptions about the Old Testament text and its authority, which carry over with some modifications into the Christian tradition.

The first is the dual assumption that the text is divinely inspired and at the same time the work of men of God who are worthy of respect in their own right. The Jewish apologist, Philo of Alexandria (c.20 BCE–c.50 CE) wrote a Life of Moses in which that point is strongly made (II.11). The second follows from the first. Even in Jewish exegesis of the Old Testament, and certainly in early and medieval Christian exegesis, every word, phrase or passage is regarded as capable of being used as proof of a point in its own right, and as available for comparison with any other without regard to its context.

This extreme respect for and attentiveness to the text extended as fully to translations into the Greek (in the case of the Septuagint) and into the Latin as to the text in the original language or its composition. Yet there is talk as early as Jerome of the *Hebraica veritas*, the 'truth' of the Hebrew text, and during the Middle Ages a few scholars made a special effort to understand and use the Old Testament through the Hebrew. Andrew of St Victor in Paris in the mid-twelfth century talked to local Jews and asked their advice on the meaning of key words, as well as making use of Josephus and the help to be had in Jerome. Among his successors in the later Middle Ages and the Reformation was Johannes Reuchlin (1455–1522), who produced a textbook on *The Rudiments of Hebrew* (1506) and an edition of the seven penitential Psalms in Hebrew with a Latin translation (1512), with a later work (1518) on Hebrews accents and spelling. He was one of the pioneers on the Hebrew side of the return 'to the sources' (*ad fontes*) of the Renaissance and Reformation. Where the scholars of Andrew of St Victor's day had been content on the whole to elucidate specific difficulties over words and thus to provide themselves with a deeper understanding of the sense of the Latin, their late fifteenth- and early sixteenth-century successors were seeking to equip themselves to read the whole in the original language. It is of some significance here that, even among the reformers, the Latin of Jerome's Vulgate was slow to lose ground as a text to be weighed as minutely as the Hebrew or Greek and was used as a source for proof texts alongside them.

A number of features of the Old Testament proved to be especially useful to Christian writers from the New Testament period onwards. Jewish rabbis placed a strong emphasis on the Old Testament texts as a source of rules for right living, and the habit continued into Christianity. The New Testament reflects the concerns raised by the question whether or not Christians should continue to be subject to the Law; this issue, as we shall see, was especially painful to Paul, and the problem of what was to be done about circumcision of new converts remained a pressing problem for some time. The general dilemma was resolved in roughly these terms: the Law is God-given and therefore good; Christians should still be subject to its moral principles; but they are not to be bound to detailed observation of its ceremonial aspects, which they should read allegorically and not as literally binding upon them. This allegorical approach is apparent in the First Epistle of Clement, thought to have been bishop of Rome at the end of the first century. He gives Old Testament examples of good and bad behaviour in individuals who are seen as 'types'.

Various Old Testament rules for right living are taken up in the New Testament, some to be adopted for Christians, and others seen in a new light.

In a discussion on helping the poor in 2 Corinthians 8:15 there is reference to Exodus 16:18, with approval of the precedent it sets. Jesus himself used an Old Testament reference to show the Pharisees their error when his disciples picked ears of corn on the Sabbath; he reminded them that when he and his men were hungry, David had gone into the Temple and eaten the very bread of the offering (Mark 2:23–8; 1 Sam. 21:1–6). The principle was thus established of finding in the Old Testament itself a warrant for a new Christian freedom. The problems raised for Christians as to whether they were free to eat unclean foods, or foods sacrificed to idols, were in part resolved by the declaration in Psalm 24:1 that all things belong to God (cf. 1 Cor. 10:26). The shift in emphasis could go either way. In the discussion of the laws of marriage and divorce in Mark 10:2–12, for example, Jesus points to the inner meaning of the Mosaic principles and advocates a stricter practice than the Law itself. But in the debate on the admission of the Gentiles, the Christian community decided against circumcision and the requirement of obedience to the Judaic Law.

A second important area of borrowing and adjustment from Old Testament to New is eschatology. New Testament writers generally believed themselves to be living in the Last Time. In the very early *Didache* we hear the cry, 'Come Lord' with imminent expectation of Christ's return. Here the Old Testament prophecies, to which we shall return, had a direct reference to the coming of the messiah. But even in the Second Epistle of Peter there is a sign of a change of emphasis. The author encourages those who are beginning to complain at the delay to take a long-term view. A day is as a thousand years in God's sight (Ps. 90:4). The second coming may be not yet, but still it is sure. With this new view came the possibility of using the Old Testament's descriptions of a world at peace and flourishing as glimpses of the perfection to come. Irenaeus in the second century and Origen a generation or so later were influential here.

But by far the most important theme of the New Testament's borrowing from the Old is the evidence that the Old Testament Law and Prophets foretold the birth, life and death of Christ and that they are fulfilled in him. Jesus himself underlined the point when he read in the synagogue at Nazareth from Isaiah 61:1 ff., 'The Spirit of the Lord is upon me . . .' (Luke 4:18ff.). It was above all from the common consent of the Christian community on this point from the first that there arose the pattern of interpretation of the Old by the New which came to be most characteristic of Christian exegesis from the first centuries to the Reformation and beyond: the use of figurative readings.

CHRISTIAN UNDERSTANDING OF THE RELATIONSHIP OF THE OLD TESTAMENT TO THE NEW

The relationship of the Old Testament to the New came to be described in a series of analogies – it was like the outside to the inside; before to after;

shadow to substance; figure to truth; letter to spirit; prophecy to its realization. These are all comparisons to the disadvantage of the Old Testament, but they all make it an indispensable member of the pair. The Old Testament is the root, trunk and leaves of the tree whose fruit is the New Testament. The Gospel comes through the Law. From Old Testament to New is (in Augustine's words) a *transitus ad Christum*, 'a journey to Christ'. As Gregory the Great put it in the sixth century, 'The Catholic church receives the New Testament without rejecting the Old; she venerates the Old in such a way that in the Spirit she understands the New in the very sacrifices of the flesh.' 'Thus no Christian should think himself an outsider in Israel', says Augustine.

There is a tension in all this between seeing the two Testaments as succeeding one another and seeing them as in some measure opposed, or at any rate, deeply differentiated. As a result, much is characteristically made in the patristic and medieval period of the unity of Scripture, in an attempt to ensure that the Old Testament is in no way set aside. Jerome insists that the whole Bible is linked by one Spirit. 'All Holy Scripture is one book', says Hugh of St Victor in the twelfth century, 'for all Holy Scripture speaks of Christ and all Holy Scripture is fulfilled in Christ.' Other exegetes speak of the two Testaments as 'brothers' or as two wings in flight.

The most usual way of understanding the relationship between the two Testaments is to regard the message of the Old as 'veiled' and that of the New as removing the veil (cf. 2 Cor. 3). This notion is intimately connected with the ancient Christian view of Christ as the bringer of light. Tertullian (*c*.160–*c*.220) speaks of Christ as 'illuminator'. In the twelfth century Bernard of Clairvaux elaborates the idea to make Christ the Word the opener of his own Book. Peter of Celle, a little later, sees the Bible as a reading of the very mind of God by its authors. He discusses the sealing of the 'great book', which is the divine mind, in Isaiah 29:11 and Revelation 5:1, and the understanding of it in Ezekiel. This general notion of illumination is commonly employed to describe the unveiling of the Old Testament by and in the New. 'In the Old Testament is the hiding of the New (*occultatio*) and in the New the manifestation of the Old', says Augustine. Augustine allows that the Old Testament writers sometimes lifted the veil in part, but the veil is removed completely only in the New Testament, where the 'truth of the Holy Spirit now shines without any veil of the Old Testament', as Isidore puts it. Bede found the shift from shadow to light as he moved from Old Testament to New a startling and sudden one, and the same sense of dramatic change is expressed by others (for example, Peter Lombard).

The New Testament is the truth (*veritas*) of the Old Testament figure, the spirit which gives life where the Old Testament letter, or literal sense, 'kills'. With these ideas we come to the use of figurative interpretation.

FIGURATIVE INTERPRETATION

Figurative interpretation was by no means a Christian innovation. It was recognized even in pagan antiquity that inspired utterance will often be obscure. Oracles required interpretation. Philo was anxious to show that Moses had anticipated the best in Greek thought, and he himself used allegorical interpretation for the purpose. But Christian interpreters developed the figurative rendering to unprecedented heights of sophistication under the stimulus of the need to show the harmony of Old Testament and New where a literal reading would make them incompatible.

The central idea of all figurative interpretation is that it is possible to come to an understanding (at least in some measure) of that which cannot be directly grasped, by making a comparison with something which is relatively easy to understand. The 'similitude' provides a stepping stone or a pointer. Many early and later Christian authors argued that God must be unknowable in any other way, and that he himself has therefore provided in his mercy for the needs of his people, by giving them such analogies and pointers, both in creation and in his revealed Word. In the late twelfth century, Peter of Celle contrasts the angelic condition with our own: 'The angels have the truth; you have a likeness.' But he reassures us that it is possible to proceed from an understanding of the likeness to grasp the truth itself.

Genesis 1:26, with its reference to man's creation in the 'image and likeness' of God, provided a convenient scriptural point of departure for many commentators. Man can be seen as designed to make the necessary shift in his understanding from likeness to reality, from what he can grasp more or less straightforwardly by the light of natural reason, to glimpse the higher and deeper spiritual realities which are ultimately beyond his creaturely nature but which he is created to desire to know. Figures are thus seen as part of God's plan in revelation, and especially in the revelation in Scripture. On this basis, it can confidently be expected that there will be a literal and a spiritual, an outward and an inner sense in Scripture, like the book written 'inside' and 'outside' of Revelation 5:1 (cf. Ezek. 2:9–10).

Christian enthusiasm for figurative interpretation was mixed at first. At Antioch in the fourth century the preference was for keeping to the literal sense. But the 'Alexandrian' system developed by the apologists of the second century, and their successors Clement of Alexandria and Origen, became dominant; although there remained some concern that they were indulging in 'pagan allegorizing' like the Gnostics. Origen, the most adventurous of them, wrote copious scriptural commentaries, and took a particular interest in the Old Testament. He composed a *Hexapla*, an edition of the Old Testament with the Hebrew text in both Hebrew and Greek characters, and four Greek versions. He placed a high value on the spiritual sense, putting it above the literal, and sometimes denying that a given passage had a literal sense at all. In the Western tradition one of the most influential proponents of figurative

interpretation was Tyconius the Donatist. He proposed seven rules for interpreting the Scriptures, with particular emphasis upon finding pointers to
Christ in the Old Testament. Augustine of Hippo forgave him his Donatism
so far as to make substantial use of his rules in his own *De Doctrina Christiana*,
and so from the fifth century Tyconius' pattern became familiar in Latin
exegesis.

Augustine himself suggested several ways of subdividing or classifying
figurative interpretations; but it was his contemporary John Cassian who drew
from Clement of Alexandria the fourfold division which became standard
throughout the Middle Ages. This took the literal or historical sense as the
base, 'which speaks of things as they happened' as Guibert of Nogent puts
it, giving the stock definition. The allegorical sense, strictly speaking (although
the term may be used more generally to cover all the spiritual or figurative
senses), is that 'in which one thing is understood by another'. The tropological
or moral interpretation draws lessons for the living of a good Christian life.
The anagogical sense is that through which the reader is led upwards in his
understanding so that he glimpses the highest spiritual truths; it is also the
'prophetic' sense. This pattern is used by Gregory the Great, and it was he
who made it familiar through the considerable medieval popularity of his
exegetical writings, especially the *Moralia* on the book of Job.

In the medieval West, although the figurative senses continued to be
regarded as superior, the literal was not despised or neglected. On the contrary,
as Hugh of St Victor insists in the twelfth century, it is the foundation on
which all the others rest. It may, like the foundations of a house, consist of
rough-hewn stones and even rubble, but the next layer of the construction,
and all the superstructure, is cut to fit into it, and that is how the building
is made strong and stable (cf. de Lubac (1959) on architectural images of
Scripture's structure). There was a fine balance to be struck here, however,
as Hermannus Judaeus, a converted Jew of Hugh's time, acknowledges in
speaking about his own conversion. He looks back in amazement to his
obstinacy as a Jew in insisting upon keeping to the literal sense, the mere
husks of the meaning, when he could have been eating the sweet kernel with
the Christians.

Figurative interpretation had another significant element from patristic
times. The emphasis of the education of the late antique world was upon the
acquisition of rhetorical skills, and no educated man in the Eastern or Western
halves of the Roman Empire read without a consciousness of the stylistic
devices which were being employed in the text. Augustine of Hippo, as a
young man, found this a barrier to his becoming a Christian because he could
not but despise the rude style in which the Scriptures then appeared to him
to be written. In maturity, however, he composed the *De Doctrina Christiana*
(On Christian Doctrine) in an effort, first to understand what function signs,
symbols and figures serve epistemologically speaking, and second, to give
advice to Christian preachers about the proper use of figurative language in

their own discourse and exegesis. He was able to find many examples of the use of rhetorical figures in Scripture, and others after him were quick to use this device as a means of explaining away difficulties in the text especially of the Old Testament. Hugh of St Victor asks why Satan is called a serpent in Genesis. He thinks that this is a way of speaking one might use, for example, of a thief who dressed up as a monk in order to steal from a monastery; when he is caught in the act his captors might call him a 'monk' in derision. Such mocking or ironical usages may conveniently turn an unacceptable literal meaning on its head.

Systematic treatment of the types of figures (*schemata*) and tropes or 'ways of speaking' was attempted by Isidore in the sixth century and by Bede in the seventh, with a more sophisticated and technically demanding attempt by Peter the Chanter at the end of the twelfth century (when much more was understood about modes of equivocation). Bede's work was influential in helping to make sense of many Old Testament passages. He finds a *prolēpsis* in Psalm 86:1–2, which speaks of 'foundations' and only later explains whose they are; a variety of *translationes* or metaphors: Psalm 2:1, where 'the people' are described as roaring in the way lions do; Zechariah 11:1, where a personified Lebanon is called to 'open' its 'gates'; transferences from inanimate to animate in the withering of the peak of Carmel in Amos 1:2 and from animate to inanimate in Ezekiel 11:19, where there is reference to removing a heart of stone; Psalm 103:26 contains a *metalēpsis*, which gradually insinuates its meaning; Genesis 24:20 refers to the pouring out of water-jars, with the container being referred to instead of that which it contains; there is *antonomasia* in 1 Kings 17:4, where Goliath is not called a giant in so many words, but we are told that he is six and a half cubits high. There are New Testament examples in Bede, too, but the Old Testament cases are often the most testing.

One particular aspect of this complex system of figurative interpretation almost always involves the pairing of the Old Testament and the New. The 'types' are found not by looking into the language for its hidden meanings or special usages, but by examining actual persons and events in history and finding in them correspondences with the later persons and events of the New Testament. Christ himself gave the lead here, by speaking of Jonah as a type of his resurrection (Matt. 12:39–41). St Paul thought baptism typified by the crossing of the Red Sea by the Israelites (1 Cor. 10:1–6) and in Hebrews, Melchizedek is a type of Christ. Similarly, the sacrifice of Isaac is a type of Jesus' Crucifixion, and the Tower of Babel is a type of Pentecost. The inference could always be drawn that, as Guibert of Nogent puts it, 'there are applications of the Old Testament in the New which make the listeners more attentive'; that

> there is nothing in the prophetic and apostolic books which does not build up faith, for when we read carefully of God speaking in many and varied ways to the prophets of old, we discover beyond doubt the mysteries of the time of Christ foretold there.

It is on these firm assumptions that everything in the Old Testament can be taken to be as true as everything in the New, the very concords attesting to the truth.

PROPHECY AND HISTORIOGRAPHY

In 1 Corinthians 14:21 St Paul quotes Isaiah 28:11–12, with its acknowledgement that unintelligible speaking in tongues has the disadvantage that it does not instruct those who already believe, but only calls to 'strangers'. He wants to encourage the Corinthians to 'prophesy' instead. The question at issue here is whether there can be any place for prophecy in the Old Testament sense when the promised Messiah has come and all prophecy is fulfilled in him; and with it the cognate question whether the gift of prophecy given to certain individuals in Old Testament times is given in the same way in the Christian era. Paul seems to have meant something like 'preaching the Gospel' when he spoke of prophecy to the Corinthians. But he implied for Christian readers after him some continuity of the prophetic tradition into the new Christian dispensation. That implication was taken up in the patristic period and the Middle Ages by a series of authors anxious to demonstrate the working out of God's providential plan in history.

A foundation text here is the Genesis account of the six days of creation. These could be interpreted to refer to the six ages of the world, with the consummation of all things in eternity forming the seventh day of rest. This theme was taken up by Augustine, and it helped to give rise to a lively debate about the beginnings and endings of these 'days', and the periods of history to which they referred. It encouraged early historians of the Christian era, such as Eusebius (*c.*260–*c.*340) in his *Chronicle*, Orosius, a contemporary of Augustine, in his *History against the Pagans*, Gregory of Tours in the sixth century, and numerous medieval chroniclers after them, to begin at the beginning of God's work in the world and to see recent history as a direct continuation and unfolding of that work.

Another pattern of interpretation of history as prophecy unfolding was introduced on the basis of Daniel 7. Three beasts rise from the sea, a lion, a bear and a leopard with four heads. A fourth beast comes and eats the other three. It has ten horns, but an eleventh horn, with the eyes of a man and a boasting mouth, rises up among them and begins to destroy, and so on. Out of this were fashioned identifications with four world monarchies rising and falling in the course of history, with the eleventh horn of the beast seen as Antichrist. Christians were, of course, the first to use the term Antichrist (1 John 4:3), but the idea he represents is nascent in Old Testament prophecies and in Jewish Apocalypses. Out of this text in Daniel a schema of interpretation of history in four ages was thus devised, with, alongside it, another, also attested to in Daniel (4:1–25). A great tree falls, but it is not uprooted. It is a fallen king. Seven 'times' or ages will pass while it lies there. These are the seven ages of the world which Augustine had found in the six days of creation and God's day of rest at the end.

Yet a third prophetic division of history became popular from the twelfth century. Rupert of Deutz wrote a biblical commentary, *On the Holy Spirit and his Works*, at the beginning of the century, in which he works his way through Scripture in order, pointing to the seven days of creation as the age and work of God the Father; the seven ages of the world from the Fall to Christ's passion as the age and work of the Son; the seven gifts of the Spirit at work in the period from the Incarnation to the last Judgement during the age of the Holy Spirit. This schema of three *status* or ages reappears with fresh interpretations in the work of Joachim of Fiore at the end of the twelfth century and the beginning of the thirteenth. In Joachim's scheme, the age of the Father covers the period during which mankind lived under the Law, that is, the Old Testament era; then began the age of the Son, lived under grace, to last as Joachim thought for forty-two generations, each of about thirty years. The third age, of the Holy Spirit, was then to begin, in which there would be spiritual life and contemplation. Joachim prophesied that this would start about 1260. His was seen by the ecclesiastical authorities as a dangerous doctrine, because it put great influence into the hands of the spiritual Franciscans and others who were leading movements in the Church which were seen by some to be threatening to the status quo. Moreover, it brought prophecy into the present day and encouraged speculation about the end of the world and the last world Emperor which also had political repercussions. Joachim had an enormous and lasting influence, and did a good deal to begin the habit of identifying the Pope with Antichrist which was to last into the Reformation and beyond.

All these periodizations of history had, then, a prophetic content, and they proved remarkably durable historiographically. Jean Bodin in his *Method of History* as late as 1566 thought himself to be taking a bold step in abandoning the four-monarchy system; the debate about the place of prophecy and miracle in the interpretation of history continued into the nineteenth century.

Particular motifs were important in their own right in this connection. The image of Babylon as archetype of an evil regime could be applied equally readily to the Roman *imperium* and to the Church by the enemies of state or Church establishment. The Old Testament prophets were immensely rich in images with considerable potential for interpretation in such political ways.

A logicians' paradox, a version of the 'Cretan liar' paradox, provided an amusing but not unserious theme in the later Middle Ages. Amos says 'I am not a prophet' (Amos 7:14). Yet unless he is a prophet, he cannot prophesy that truthfully. The issue raised was of some interpretative significance because it made it necessary to ask whether the prophets prophesy under inspiration in everything they say in the Old Testament, or whether a prophet may be a prophet at certain times and not others. This was prompted in part by Gregory the Great's widely used account of prophets and prophecy in his

Homilies on Ezekiel. That had raised the related question whether a prophet always knows the meaning of what he is saying if he is a true prophet. In the thirteenth century, Hugh of St Cher, a Dominican in Paris, pressed the view that prophecy must involve knowledge. He cites Job 13:1: 'My eye has seen all this and my ear has heard and I have understood.' Hugh thought that God first put the message into the prophet's mind, then told him what it meant, before the prophet delivered it. But there are problems. Jonah's prophecy was unfulfilled. Here there seems to be a prophet who was not given understanding of what he was saying. That is what Gregory the Great believed, arguing that sometimes even true prophets speak without the Spirit's prompting and cannot tell the difference between their own ideas and those put into their minds by God. Then again there is the case of Amos' saying *propheta non sum*, 'I am not a prophet' (7:14). This is more than a paradox; it is a challenge to the principle that the prophet is simply the Lord's mouthpiece. All these difficulties have to do with the theory of prophetic inspiration, on the basis of which Christian exegesis understood Old Testament prophecy to be the Word of God.

A further set of issues came into play in the fourteenth century, although they were by no means new. Aristotle's discussion of conditional futurity in the *De Interpretatione* had given rise to a considerable literature among Christian scholars, because of its bearing on the theology of predestination. It was also relevant to prophecy. A prophet could only truly prophesy if the future was determined. The issue of the tenses used in Scripture also has a bearing here. Augustine had discussed the problem that since God is eternal no tense of the verb used in Scripture can be strictly limited as to the time to which it refers. The same matter was taken up by Anselm of Canterbury and others. It is still current in the fourteenth century, when Wyclif looks at Matthew 9:9–10, 'I say to you that he is a prophet and more than a prophet.' Wyclif explains that Moses prophesied about the past when he wrote (as it was then believed he did) the account in Genesis of the creation of the world. Elizabeth prophesied about the present when Mary the mother of Jesus came to her (Luke 1:39–56). Prophecies about the future in Scripture are legion. The tense is not important. In such a manner one might get over the difficulty about conditional futurity, by suggesting that there is no such thing as futurity, of past or present, with God. William of Ockham's view, which was widely adopted in the fourteenth century, was that it is essential to distinguish between the verbal difference of tense and a real difference of time referred to, which he said could apply in Scripture; but Wyclif could not find that satisfactory.

Wyclif also addressed the problem whether God is the author of a lie in those prophets whose prophecies have not been fulfilled. He is sure that the prophets were fully shown all those things which have to do with the Christian faith. He is also certain that Scripture is wholly true in everything it says. He explains the unfulfilled prophecies as using language in a figurative way, or as warnings or threats. He concedes that prophecies can have no certitude if they are conditional expressions about the future. But if Christ himself is to be seen as the *propheta maximus*, it must be possible for prophecy to see the future truly and perfectly, and for this prophet at least to understand fully what he foretells.

LAW AND GRACE

The relationship between the Law of the Old Testament and the operation of grace in the New is a strong Pauline theme in Scripture itself. It became topical in Augustine's time because of his battle with the Pelagians. Pelagius, a society preacher in Rome at the end of the fourth century, had argued that the Christian was responsible for his own actions and not necessarily dependent upon grace to be good. Augustine wrote a good deal on the issues Pelagius' teaching raised, both pastorally and theologically. In *De Gratia Christi* he tried to clarify the relationship between keeping the Law and depending upon grace. Pelagius was prepared to accept that grace illuminates the mind and shows Christians what to do, but he did not believe that it gives us a power to act well which we would not have without it. Augustine argues that since there is no sin where there is no law (Rom. 4:15), the Law is not only unprofitable, but even prejudicial without the assistance of grace. That would mean that Law was positively undesirable. He identifies the utility of the Law as consisting in the compelling of sinners to ask for grace to help them keep it. Law makes demands, but it does not assist the sinner to meet them; it points to sickness of the soul but it does not heal it; indeed, it makes it worse and the cure grace can give is thereby desired the more. No-one can be justified by keeping the Law. Righteousness comes from God not from the Law, he claims, citing Romans 3:19–21. Nevertheless, the Law cannot be counted for nothing, for it is God's Law. Augustine sees its value as lying in making it clear to us that we need grace.

Thomas Aquinas addressed the question of the place of the Old Testament Law in the context of the various concerns of the thirteenth century. In the *Summa Theologiae* (II^{i}q. 98–109) he asks whether the Old Law was good, and answers that because it accorded with reason, it was certainly a good thing; nevertheless, it could not confer that grace which only Christ can give. The Law was given by Moses; grace and truth by Christ (John 1:17). Thus the Law was good, but it brought nothing to perfection (Heb. 7:19). The Old Law was given by God through the angels. It was given to the Jews alone and only they were bound to obey it. Aquinas distinguishes moral and ceremonial precepts in the Law, and also judicial precepts; the first are dictated by natural law; the second are to do with patterns of worship; the third settle the rules for the maintenance of justice among men. He argues that the moral precepts remain indispensable, but that the moral precepts of the Old Law did not justify men in the sight of God. The ceremonial precepts also did not justify; they ceased at Christ's coming and it is sin to obey them since. The judicial precepts had to do with man's conduct towards his neighbour, but these too ceased at Christ's coming.

Aquinas then moves on to consider the New Law of the Gospel. The New Law is written in the heart; it is not, like the Old Law, merely a written law. He has to defend its late introduction against the accusation that it ought, if it is the better law, to have been introduced at the beginning. He explains that this New Law consists chiefly in grace, the gift of the Spirit, and it was not proper for grace to abound until Christ had done his redeeming work; that a perfect Law had to be developed through a due succession of events in time, the Old Law coming first to teach mankind and prepare the human heart for the reception of the New. In this way, through experience of sin under the Old Law, mankind might learn his own weakness and need of grace. The New Law is distinct from the Old; it fulfils it; it is less burdensome than the Old. Aquinas completes his treatment of the theme in a series of questions on grace in which he stresses the need for grace to help if the Law is to be kept. He also discusses the relation of the New Testament of grace to the Old Testament of Law.

This theme was of the first importance in the debates of the Reformation. Two aspects of Paul's discussion were given particular prominence: first, the notion that it is the Law which gives sin its power by defining it and making it apparent to the sinner (Gal. 2:17ff.; 1 Cor. 15:56; Rom. 5:20; 5:13 etc.); and second, Paul's stress on Christ's liberation of his people from the implications of the old legal system (Gal. 3:10–13; 5:2–4; 4:8–11; 5:1; 5:13–4 etc.). Luther's particular concern was with the role in the salvation of the individual of the good works which keeping the Law involves. In his discussion of the Decalogue in the *Large Catechism*, he explains that the Ten Commandments show what God wills that mankind shall do and not do, in order to please him. But they do not give the means of keeping the Law. Luther holds that the Law is necessary to the Christian life, because it is in Scripture, and because the Commandments can be reduced to the two New Testament commands to love God and one's neighbour. They all, he believes, derive from the first commandment of faith in God, with the other nine amounting to fruits, or effects of justifying faith. These are not, for that reason, necessary to salvation. He makes a distinction between inward and outward obedience, the keeping of the Law by formal observance or even legal tricks; and the obedience of the heart to which the ninth and tenth Commandments point. His position in sum is that the Christian is bound to keep the Law in the same way that a living tree is bound to bring forth good fruit. The Law is at the least a check upon the activities of the unrepentant non-believer who hardens his heart. For those predestined to life it performs the function for which it was designed. It shows them their sinfulness, terrifies the conscience and prepares the heart for the Word of God to work in it.

Not all reforming parties held so positive a view of the value of the works done in observance of the Law, and there were those who said that works done by those without saving faith in Christ were not only of no value for salvation, but so far do they fail to please God that they may be viewed as sins. This is a position reflected in Article Thirteen of the Church of England's Thirty-Nine Articles. The debate about the place of works in the economy of salvation is only partly concerned with the question of the relationship of Old Testament Law to New Testament grace, however, and not perhaps ultimately dependent on it, so is not our direct concern here.

ART AND ICONOGRAPHY

The first Christian plastic images are found about 200 CE. Catacomb paintings include such Old Testament scenes as Adam and Eve separated by the tree with the serpent upon it; Noah and the Ark; Daniel in the lions' den; the story of Jonah in episodes. Here there was perhaps some dependence upon an existing Jewish tradition of pictorial representation of Old Testament figures and events. The synagogue at Dura had pictures of the Lion of Judah; of Moses leading the chosen people across the Red Sea; of the resurrection of the dead before Ezekiel; of the Ark and the Temple. Christian art could build on such examples, representations of Old Testament themes which could be seen to have strong symbolism for Christians: the ascension of Elijah, for example, or the three visitors grouped round Abraham's table (Gen. 18) seen as figures of the Trinity.

By the fifth or sixth centuries Old Testament and New Testament images appear in cycles of scenes in sequence, not necessarily paired as yet as they were later to be, so as to show how the Old Testament pointed forward to the New. Abraham, Moses, Jonah, for example, may be seen as representing stages in the salvation story. Manuscripts such as the Vienna Genesis provided Old Testament models and the experiment with New Testament additions to the repertoire is found for instance in S. Maria Maggiore in Rome. The concords between Old and New Testament, however, proved irresistible to artists. Benedict Biscop brought back from his fourth trip to Rome late in the seventh century a collection of symbolic images to illustrate the agreement of the two. There were strong incentives to pair images, the New Testament fulfilment of a prophecy with the Old Testament prophecy itself; Isaiah with the Virgin and Child; wonders worked by Moses with the miracles of Christ. These tie in closely with the typological parallels being developed in literature by the Fathers, especially Origen, Tertullian, Gregory of Nyssa, Ambrose, and Augustine.

By the twelfth century, the influence of liturgical drama is increasingly apparent. For example, in Easter week Christ's meeting the disciples on the road to Emmaus would be acted out, with Christ dressed as a pilgrim with a staff and a shepherd's scrip, in a way which closely parallels representations in art. Abbot Suger of St Denis in northern France was especially important in leading fashions in iconographical design, and in his iconographical largeness of vision. The 'Tree of Jesse' window with the Kings of Judah, which he developed, was further elaborated upon at Chartres in the window there. The Virgin is enthroned above the Kings, with God above her, and on either side of the tree the Prophets are placed one above another. At St Denis the Old Testament Kings stand on either side of the door. At Dijon the Queen of Sheba with the feet of a goose or ass stands facing Solomon across the doorway.

For iconographical conventions to serve their purpose of making a story or a message immediately comprehensible, and telling truths both narrative and symbolic in pictures for the edification of the illiterate, there must be some more or less settled agreement about the interpretation of the biblical scenes which are being portrayed. By the twelfth century that had been more or less arrived at, at least for the purposes of pairing Old Testament with New or relating the history of God's plan for the world from the beginning. In the central bay of the north portal at Chartres cathedral ten statues of patriarchs and prophets both foretell Christ and tell in outline the history of the world. Melchizedek, Abraham, Isaac represent the age when men lived according to the law of circumcision; Moses, Samuel and David the age of the Law; Isaiah, Jeremiah, Simeon and John the Baptist the prophetic age. In scenes around the Crucifixion in windows at Bourges, Chartres, le Mans, Tours, parallels are drawn between the rock smitten by Moses from which a spring leapt forth and the water and blood issuing from Christ's side when he was 'smitten' by the 'rod' of the Cross. The crowd who complained while they waited for the miracle are the people who do not rest content with the Law but come to quench their thirst at the New Testament's living spring (Exod. 17:1–7; Num. 20:1–13). The brazen serpent raised by Moses to heal the people is a figure for the elevation of Christ on the Cross. Abel is a prototype of Christ because he is the just man who is slain; Cain is the ancient people of God who slew him, just as the Jews killed Christ.

In most cases such visually depicted parallels can readily be found in writing in the standard gloss which had evolved by the end of the twelfth century (the *glossa ordinaria*); or are commonplaces of patristic exegesis. Iconography followed scholarship and attempted nothing new in terms of interpretation. It was of its essence that it should not, if it was to be theology in pictures for ordinary people.

A serious drawback to iconographical method was the difficulty of rendering many ideas and principles graphically or in sculpture. The bitter waters of Mara, changed into sweet when Moses threw in a piece of wood (Exod. 15:23–5), can readily be understood to represent the Church's work of producing living water for God's people, but the parallel is not easily conveyed fully in a picture. Still less can the finer conceptual points of doctrine be treated in this way with any hope of doing it accurately, or of making them intelligible to the unlettered. The real strengths of iconography lay in its symbolic and story-telling powers. The *Protevangelium of James* tells of many legendary events connected with the birth of Christ which entered into the iconographic 'canon'. The power of Old Testament iconography, then, always lay in the making of links with the New Testament, the underlining of the success of prophecies emptied out into fulfilment in Christ. It could also say something about God's care for the world by reminding the 'reader' of God's providential intervention in such episodes as those of the Ark, the burning bush, or the sending of manna. Perhaps above all, it has something to say about the nature of revelation, by putting before the eyes God's 'showing' of himself and his purposes.

SPECIAL STUDIES

Throughout Christian history until the Enlightenment, Christian authors made particular studies of individual Old Testament books or episodes or themes. The *Hexaemeron* was especially attractive, at first because it was important for Christians to take a view of the differences between the Bible's account of creation and that of late antique philosophers; and later because there always remained (and still remain) important differences from the current scientific understanding. At first it was important to defend the belief that God made matter and a material world, against Gnostic teaching. It was also necessary to establish the Christian principle that God made both matter and form and created everything from nothing, against the version of the *Timaeus* of Plato, which imputes eternal existence to matter and form. Basil of Caesarea (*c.*330–79) was influential here on Ambrose of Milan, whose own sermons on the *Hexaemeron* were heard by the young Augustine of Hippo in Milan. Jerome also praised Basil's *Hexaemeron* and it was translated into Latin about 440. Augustine's own appreciation of a Genesis which had previously seemed to him to tell a crude story was greatly enhanced by hearing Ambrose. In later writings he was firm that God created all things from nothing. Isidore; Bede; Walafrid Strabo and Rabanus Maurus among the Carolingians; Thierry of Chartres; William of Conches and Honorius of Autun in the twelfth century; Robert Grosseteste in the thirteenth, all contributed to the body of Hexaemeral literature, which by the late Middle Ages had become a series of pegs upon which to hang treatises on subjects of scientific interest. (God is seen as creating light and thus the very subject of the science of optics, and so on.) Much of the newly rediscovered corpus of Aristotelian science could thus be respectably studied in the West, though not without controversy.

The Fall and its aftermath were of course central to the Christian story, and the motif of Christ as the new Adam was always significant in Christian thought (cf. Rom. 5:12–21). It became important from the second century to insist that evil was not, as the Gnostics claimed, an independent divine power, but had come into the world through the sin of Adam. That sin was increasingly seen as having wrought a permanent change in human nature. Athanasius (*c*.296–373) put it in terms of a fall from a state of grace, in which it was possible for man to be in God's image, to a 'natural' condition. Other Greek Fathers argued for some transmission of the damage done by sin from one generation to another; the Latin Fathers from Tertullian were increasingly clear that it constituted a mark or deficiency in all human nature since Adam, a sinfulness bred in the bone. Augustine formulated the doctrine of original sin more fully than any before him, and made the point (which remained controversial), that one of its effects was to damage the will, so that no-one can will the good at all without the aid of grace.

The figure of Satan was often shadowy in all this, because the thrust of the enquiry had to do with the alteration caused in man's relationship to God, and not with his seducer. But Anselm of Canterbury in the late eleventh century asked how it had been possible for Satan to fall, if he was an angelic spirit created to gaze on god. His answer was in terms of a desire on the part of Satan for a good which was beyond the measure of his nature. Satan was culpable in reaching for it, he argued, becuase he had not accepted the perseverance in rightness of will which God offered to all his angels. Medieval liturgical drama kept the person of Satan before the popular imagination. Milton's Satan in the seventeenth century is a psychologically altogether more sophisticated figure, but still in every way a personal Devil, working for evil in the world and for the downfall of human souls. Old Testament warrant for this view came largely from the book of Job (1:6–12; 2:1–7), and 1 Chronicles 21:1.

The book of Job as a whole was the subject of a detailed 'moral' or tropological interpretation by Gregory the Great (the *Moralia*), which became immensely popular throughout the Middle Ages and later. It contained a vast array of cross-matched images, theories about the significances of numbers and links with other parts of Scripture, presented with a vividness and simplicity which gave the material an appeal to readers who might have found it difficult to draw on theologically more demanding treatments.

The Psalms were always a popular subject of commentary. They lent themselves to detailed discovery of allusion and correspondence and to elaborate figurative renderings. Because they were heavily used liturgically and formed the backbone of the round of monastic offices throughout the Middle Ages, they were perhaps the most familiar texts of the Old Testament. Here Augustine's *Enarrationes* on the Psalms provided a key text for later Western readers and exegetes, though almost every medieval scholar who attempted scriptural commentary addressed himself to the Psalms.

The book of Ezekiel was seen as a special challenge because of its difficulty. Gregory the Great preached on it, with a strong sense of the imminence of danger from the hordes pressing upon the city even as he spoke; Peter Abelard took it as a display piece when he wanted to show that he, a newcomer to theology though a consummately skilled logician, could lecture on the Bible as well as the famous master Anselm of Laon; for Richard of St Victor a generation or so later in the middle of the twelfth century, it set a puzzle, as he tried to work out how, architecturally speaking, the design for the Temple could be made to work and produce a building which would stand up. In Isaiah, Alan of Lille focused on the six wings of the cherubim (Isa. 6:2), to produce an allegory. In these and similar ways Christian scholars and poets to the end of the Middle Ages and later found in Old Testament episodes source material for a wide range of writing and a spur to theological, philosophical and scientific investigation.

As late as Milton the classic patterns of interpretation were still strongly influential. In Books XI and XII of *Paradise Lost*, the archangel Michael reveals the future to Adam while Eve sleeps. First he shows him Cain murdering Abel, so that Adam learns of death. Then Adam sees groups of Cain's descendants, including sensual women who lead men astray, and Adam learns about sin. Then there are wars, Noah and the Flood, with God's promise not to destroy mankind. Book XII continues with the history of the Jews after the Flood, Nimrod, the Tower of Babel, Abraham's journey to the Promised Land, slavery in Egypt, Moses and Aaron, the Plagues, the crossing of the Red Sea, the wilderness, and the Ark of the Covenant. The moral is drawn that God has still a land of promise for his people. Then Michael explains the way in which salvation will come. Sin makes law necessary, although the Law cannot cure sin. There is to be a New Covenant (that is why Joshua, not Moses the Lawgiver, leads the entry into Canaan). Then the royal line of David will produce the Son, and Old Testament history and prophecy will empty out into hope fulfilled and redemption accomplished.

FURTHER READING

Beckwith, R. (1985) *The Old Testament Canon of the New Testament*, London: SPCK.
Cassirer, H. W. (1988) *Grace and Law*, Grand Rapids, Mich.: Eerdmans.
De Lubac, H. (1959) *Exégèse médiévale*, Paris: du Cerf.
Ellis, E. E. (1957) *Paul's Use of the Old Testament*, Edinburgh: Oliver and Boyd.
Smalley, B. (1983) *The Study of the Bible in the Middle Ages*, (3rd edn) Oxford: Basil Blackwell.
Steneck, N. (1976) *Science and Creation in the Middle Ages*, Notre Dame: Notre Dame University Press.
Sullivan, D. J. (1952) *The Summa Theologica of Saint Thomas Aquinas*, (rev. edn) Chicago/London/Toronto: William Benton.
Walter, C. (1977) *Studies in Byzantine Iconography*, London: Variorum.
See also chapters 2, 4, 6, 7, 8, 11.

4

THE OLD TESTAMENT: HISTORICAL STUDY AND NEW ROLES

John Rogerson

THE ENLIGHTENMENT

In the seventeenth and eighteenth centuries a fundamental change took place in Europe in the way in which thinking people understood the world and the place of the human race within it. This change is usually called the Enlightenment; and it can be defined for our purposes as a move from seeing humanity as part of a divinely ordered universe, to understanding the universe in terms of human reason, experience and discovery. These broad generalizations need to be qualified, of course. If thinking people, whose views were propagated by their books, articles and reviews, began to see the world differently, this was not necessarily the case with the largely rural and agricultural populations of Western Europe who could not or did not read learned literature. Also, the pace of the Enlightenment varied from country to country, and in some cases, opposition to Enlightenment thought led to reactions against it. Thus, in Britain, the Enlightenment flourished in the period roughly 1680–1750, after which there was a period of reaction that lasted until the 1860s. At the moment of Britain's 'decline', the Enlightenment came of age in Germany, from the 1750s onwards.

The Enlightenment began what is usually called the modern period, or modernism, for short. In the present century, and particularly in the past twenty years, there have been attacks upon the Enlightenment in Western Europe and North America. A movement called post-modernism has emerged, although it is a movement more united in its opposition to modernism than in having a coherent set of aims. How modernism and post-modernism have affected the use of the Old Testament as a theological resource is the subject of the present chapter.

Before the Enlightenment, Old Testament scholars had dealt in a scholarly and critical way with textual, translational, historical and sociological problems of the text for well over a thousand years. They had done this, however, in the context of an agenda that set clear and explicit limits to their work.

According to this agenda the Old Testament was completed by, and looked forward to, the New Testament. Old Testament prophecies were principally forecasts of the birth, death and resurrection of Jesus, of the spread of the Gospel among the nations. Old Testament sacrifices pointed to the sacrifice of Jesus on the cross. Psalms such as Psalm 22 also described the passion of Jesus, while the great characters of the Old Testament were models of virtuous living, to be imitated by Christians. If these characters seemed to do immoral things, such as slaughtering whole populations, having many wives, or committing adultery, there were ways of justifying such actions without, however, recommending them for imitation.

The Enlightenment swept away the various devices for excusing wicked behaviour. These had included justifying Joshua for slaughtering whole populations by saying that the Canaanites were grossly immoral and deserved to be punished, and by distinguishing between people acting in their capacity as holders of an office, and acting as private individuals. In this way, Samson and David could be upheld as a model judge and a model king respectively. The former's amours with foreign women and the latter's adultery with Bathsheba and the indirect murder of her husband Uriah, were the actions of private individuals.

Enlightenment thinkers were more inclined to believe that God commanded things because they were good than that whatever God commanded was good by definition. In effect, they put to the Old Testament the question asked by Abraham of God in Genesis 18:25: shall not the Judge of all the earth do what is just? If the answer was yes, then there was no way of justifying human behaviour and divine commands in the Old Testament that offended the Enlightenment's moral sensitivity. The Old Testament was not, therefore, a collection of examples of pious living worthy of imitation by Christians; it contained stories of Israelites who lived in barbaric times when human life was valued cheaply, and when belief in God was sufficiently primitive for people to believe that he could legitimately command immoral acts.

This new emphasis upon the Old Testament as the product of a small Semitic people living in the ancient world snapped its link with the New Testament and with the various dogmatic theological agendas that had used both Testaments as an arsenal of infallible proof texts to support Catholic or (various) Protestant doctrines. It would not have been surprising if the Old Testament had ceased to be used as a theological resource among Christians; it is a testimony to its varied and enduring content that new ways were found, and continue to be found, for its theological use.

POLITICAL READINGS IN THE SEVENTEENTH AND EIGHTEENTH CENTURIES

The first examples to be considered here are what can be called political theological uses of the Old Testament; and they are an interesting anticipation of the liberation theologies of the twentieth century. They did not begin with the Enlightenment; indeed, we find Josephus in the first century CE using the Old Testament to make political points. These political readings show, however, what uses could be made of the Old Testament under the Enlightenment (Rogerson 1992b). Holland was a part of Europe where free expression of thought emerged very early, and in 1617 Petrus Cunaeus (1586–1638), a professor of law, published a book entitled *De republica Hebraeorum* (Cunaeus 1653). This is a reading of the history and sociology of the Old Testament whose purpose is to commend the equality of humankind and to condemn the acquisition and accumulation of power, whether this is done by kings, land-owners or clergy. Cunaeus' ideal is the Jubilee law described in Leviticus 25, which prescribes that all debts must be cancelled, all slaves must be freed and all land must revert to the original owners every fifty years. This ideal, that 'the wealth of some might not tend to the oppression of the rest' (ibid.: 14), was constantly ignored or frustrated in Israel, according to Cunaeus, by bad kings such as Jeroboam, who led the revolt of the northern tribes after the death of Solomon (931 BCE), and by the Levites, who seized power after the return of the Jews from exile in Babylon (539 BCE). The Old Testament is seen to contain a series of object lessons pertinent to the ordering of society in Cunaeus' day and situation, exemplifying the principle that 'by concord a small Estate is raised, and the greatest is by discord overthrown' (ibid.: preface).

In Moses Lowman's *Dissertation on the Civil Government of the Hebrews* (Lowman 1745) we have the same agenda applied to the political situation of eighteenth-century England, where the Stuart rebellion against the Protestant revolution of 1688 saw the forces of Prince Charles Edward reach as far south as Derby in 1745. Lowman (1680–1752) argues that, in ancient Israel, the authority of the king rested upon the consent of the people. When Saul condemned his son Jonathan to death for violating an oath that Saul and the people had taken in Jonathan's absence (1 Sam. 14:24), it was the people, according to Lowman, who determined that Jonathan should live (cf. 1 Sam. 14:45), exercising their rights as an assembly that had powers that could overrule the king. Thus, kings have no absolute power over their subjects.

Given that England's Protestant succession had been secured by a revolution and was threatened by a counter-revolution, it is noteworthy that Lowman discussed incidents in the Old Testament that involved rebellions against kings. Treason, according to Lowman, was rebellion against the God of Israel and the wish to substitute other gods. Any king who sought to do this could legitimately be deposed; and thus it was right for prophets to have foretold the downfall of the houses of Jeroboam, Baasha and Omri, and to have anointed Jehu to overthrow the son of Ahab. Lowman drew an explicit analogy between this prophetically inspired rebellion, and the incidents that had resulted in the deposition of the Roman Catholic James II in 1688. Protestantism and Catholicism were, for the dissenting clergyman Lowman, analogous to the true worship of the God of Israel and idolatry respectively.

The political–theological use of the Old Testament by Cunaeus and Lowman was possible precisely because of the Old Testament's content. Unlike the New Testament, the Old Testament is the history of a nation, its laws and its political fortunes. In this, and in other matters, it had much to offer that was absent from the New Testament.

RATIONALISM AND ROMANTICISM IN THE EIGHTEENTH CENTURY

The next two examples come from Germany in the late eighteenth century, and concern scholars who, whole not producing a coherent theological reading of the Old Testament, adumbrated opposing principles that laid down two lines of approach that have been followed many times. They are Johann Philip Gabler (1753–1826) and Johann Gottfried Herder (1744–1803).

In 1787 Gabler delivered an inaugural address at the University of Altdorf, near Nuremberg. This address, on how to discover a pure biblical theology, has been regarded as a watershed in the development of the discipline of biblical theology (Gabler 1831). Gabler was concerned at the way in which historical–critical study of the Bible was producing results that differed increasingly from the use of the Bible in the dogmatic formularies of the various churches. He was also concerned that a truly 'scientific' study of the Bible should yield agreed results, in opposition to the divergent and mutually exclusive claims made in the dogmatic formularies. Gabler proposed that the study of the Bible should be separated from dogmatic theology. The biblical authors were to be studied within their historical settings, with the aid of philological and grammatical methods. The aim of this would be to identify what truths and principles they had maintained. A further aim would be to separate what had been disclosed from God from what was human opinion. In this way, a series of universal truths or principles would be arrived at, which would represent pure biblical theology. This could then become the basis for dogmatic theologies.

Gabler never worked this programme up into an actual biblical theology; but he is usually credited with having established that biblical theology must be a 'scientific' discipline practised independently of ecclesiastical dogmatic agendas. Whether it would be possible to carry out his programme is to be doubted. How does one distinguish between what is divine and thus universal, and what is human and thus appropriate only to specific times and circumstances? The answer can only be by using human reason. Thus biblical theology depends upon philosophy; and it is not unreasonable to see behind Gabler's enterprise a philosophical problem that has been called an 'ugly ditch' (Brett 1991). This refers to a distinction that was common in the eighteenth century between necessary truths of reason and contingent truths (i.e. truths limited to specific times and circumstances) of history. Given that a good deal of the Old Testament consists of historical narrative, how could it contain necessary truths that would have universal application? Gabler attempted to answer this question by suggesting that an initial historical treatment of texts could isolate truths which, by God's providence, were of universal application.

A quite different approach is evident in the writings of Herder. If Gabler wishes to study the Old Testament historically in order to isolate intellectual truths, Herder wants to proceed in the same way in order to experience something primal. For Herder, religion is aroused by human appreciation of nature, among other things. Nature awakes feelings of awe, wonder and beauty in the human soul, and these feelings are expressed most profoundly in poetry. In the Old Testament, the Hebrew language and its use in poetry expressed vividly and dramatically the Israelites' encounter with God through nature. Further, God used the processes of nature to educate and guide human reason (Herder 1993).

Herder applied historical criticism to texts in a way quite different from Gabler. Gabler belonged to a 'mythical school' of scholars who believed that, in handling biblical texts, the supernatural trappings should be stripped away because they resulted from the naive and pre-scientific way in which the early human race had conceptualized natural events. Thus, in Genesis 3, the talking serpent, the tree that made Adam and Eve aware of sexual difference and the divine decree banishing the couple from the Garden of Eden were the result of the naive conceptualizing of Adam and Eve and the narrator. The reality was that a serpent had eaten some fruit without being harmed, the couple had imitated the serpent but discovered that the fruit was mildly poisonous, and a thunderstorm had driven the couple from the garden. Although Herder sometimes rationalized narratives he also insisted that biblical narratives had to be read as the products of an ancient society quite different from our own. Thus the interpreter should enter with sympathy and imagination into the language and world of the biblical writers in order to grasp or sense the experience of nature or God that the text was expressing. To be sure, a philosophy lay behind Herder's approach just as much as behind that of Gabler. It was the philosophy of Spinoza, suitably purified (Bell 1984), that enabled Herder to see God as the life and energy of the processes of the natural world; a God speaking to human souls and educating them in countless ways in natural processes vast and minute. But we can also say of Herder's approach that it respected the text much more than Gabler's method.

The differing approaches of Gabler and Herder exemplify the rationalist and the romantic method of interpretation. The first uses the scientific knowledge of today as the criterion for distinguishing between what is of permanent value in the Old Testament and what is not. The second questions whether contemporary knowledge has a monopoly on the truth and looks for insights in ancient and exotic cultures. The first runs the danger of reductionism; the second runs the danger of making the gulf between contemporary Western culture and ancient or so-called primitive cultures so wide that it becomes difficult to see how there can be any translation of ideas from the one to the other.

PHILOSOPHICAL CONCERNS IN THE NINETEENTH CENTURY

The next scholar to be considered was taught by both Gabler and Herder, and combined something of the spirit of both. He is W. M. L. de Wette (1780–1849) and two works of his will be considered; his 'Beytrag zur Charakteristik des Hebraismus' (de Wette 1807) and his book *Über die Religion* (de Wette 1828). De Wette had gained from Herder a love of literature and from the philosophy of his colleague in Heidelberg, J. F. Fries (1773–1843), a way of understanding types of literature as means of grappling with the tragedies and vicissitudes of life. His sensitivity to the tragic dimension of life had been greatly sharpened by the death of his wife in childbirth in 1806. When de Wette studied the Old Testament Psalms, on which he was to publish a remarkable commentary in 1811, he noticed that a large proportion of them were laments expressing the despair of the psalmists over their sufferings or the injustices that they saw in the world. In spite of his recent personal loss, de Wette believed that reality was ultimately harmonious and purposeful, and that the task of religion was to enable people to grasp this essential goodness at the heart of things. Literature was one of the ways in which the apparent contradictions between the ultimate goodness of reality and the sufferings experienced by individuals could be explored and resolved. This was one of the functions of the Psalms. The same was true of the book of Job which, together with Psalms and Ecclesiastes, were the main Old Testament books discussed in the 'Beytrag' (Rogerson 1992a: 66–9). There is no rational explanation of why the innocent suffer and Job does not attempt to give one. But the matter is explored at great length, and, at the end of the book, Job has an experience of the majesty of God that resolves the problem. Job does not find an intellectual answer but, by discovering his weakness and frailty, accepts that God does not need to justify himself nor to be justified in the matter of why innocent people suffer. The third text discussed by de Wette, Ecclesiastes, is a book which is outspoken in proclaiming that much of life seems to be without purpose, and that human endeavour is often futile. Yet, according to de Wette, the writer of Ecclesiastes does not abandon faith in God; and the value of the book lies in its honest expression of doubt as the writer perceives a contradiction between a sensed harmony at the heart of reality and his experience of frustration.

De Wette's task in his article was to sketch the characteristic features of Hebrew religion, and this he did by comparing the Hebrew nation to a child that had never been young, and that reflected much on its inner life. Because it sensed that reality was ultimately free from injustice and disorder, it longed for a coming messianic age of justice and truth. Meanwhile, through its literature it explored, and came to terms with, the disorder of the world that it perceived so clearly. This was the soil in which Christianity was planted, Christ being the fulfilment of Old Testament hopes for a new order. Thus de Wette saw the Old Testament as preparatory to the New Testament, and in his treatment of the Psalms, Job and Ecclesiastes was engaging in historical–critical exegesis. But it is clear that he did not limit the value of these texts to their historical setting. They could help modern readers to explore their own perplexities in the face of injustice and suffering, and embolden them to have faith in the goodness of the world.

At first sight, de Wette's position might seem to be anti-rational; but this is not the case. His friend Fries, a follower and, as he believed, an improver of the philosophy of Kant, was trying to develop a philosophy that did justice to the aesthetic and moral experience of the human race as well as to its scientific experience. He linked religion to aesthetics, and held that through art, architecture, music, literature and experiences of the sublime in nature, the human spirit could grasp and imperfectly express the ultimate harmony and purposefulness of reality. De Wette's position tried to do justice to a philosophy that could only regard the attitude of someone like Gabler as dealing with a single part of human reason, while ignoring the rest.

De Wette's treatment of the Old Testament in his mature work *Über die Religion* also builds upon the philosophy of Fries; but it is noteworthy in that it considers the Old Testament in the context of a historical study of the development of religion, including the major world religions (Rogerson 1992a: 217–25). For de Wette, one of the major achievements of the philosophy of his day was the distinction between reason (*Vernunft*) and understanding (*Verstand*), together with an analysis of the part played by each of these in religion. Understanding (*Verstand*) was concerned with the empirical experience of human beings, with their response to the world as mediated by sense impressions. Reason (*Vernunft*) was knowledge that humans gained independently of sense impressions by reflection on inner experience. The knowledge gained included moral imperatives such as duty; and religion was also knowledge gained by inner reflection. In the case of religion, (as well as moral imperatives) the knowledge gained was a revelation from God, and all human beings were capable of receiving this revelation.

The history of religion was the history of the development of human self-understanding, guided by the divine revelation granted to the reason (*Vernunft*) of each human being. Thus, all religions contained some truth in as much as they were responses to an intuition of the divine granted to reason (*Vernunft*). But religions were not all equally true, and it was only in Christian (German) Protestantism that religion had reached its fullest expression. The task of a history of religion was to discover what was true and what was false in religion; and it was here that understanding played its part. If religion was sensed by reason, it had to be expressed and lived out in the world as people understood it; and if a people's understanding of the world was deficient, then their religious expression would be deficient. For example, the Greeks had a highly developed sense of moral virtue, disclosed to them by reason. But in their religion they identified the virtues with different gods. Understanding made it clear to modern humanity that the Greek gods had never existed. Thus reason was able to identify what was true in religion, while understanding indicated what was false in its articulation.

The distinction between reason and understanding enabled de Wette to be a radical biblical critic (such criticism belonged to the sphere of understanding) while at the same time recognizing through reason what was true in biblical religion. In the context of his view of religion as a whole, de Wette was able to praise Hebrew religion for its belief in the transcendence and yet approachability of God, for its cult freed from idolatry, nature worship or superstition, for its theocratic state based upon moral principles, and for its personal piety as exhibited in the Psalms and prophetic writings. No doubt we can detect in de Wette's agenda the persistence of the 'ugly ditch' between necessary truths of reason and contingent truths of history. In his case, it is reason that provides necessary truths, and understanding that shows how the expressions of these truths in particular circumstances are inadequate. But what is important about de Wette's contribution is that it addresses fundamental questions about what it means to be human, and how religion functions in human society. Few thinkers reflecting on how to use the Old Testament theologically have addressed these questions as directly as de Wette, and most have largely ignored them.

One of the thinkers who emulated de Wette's concern to place the Old Testament within a general theory of religion, and who were indebted in many ways to de Wette, was (Johann Karl) Wilhelm Vatke (1806–82) whose *Biblical Theology* was published in 1835 (Vatke 1835; see Rogerson 1984: 69–78). It is usually asserted that Vatke's work was heavily influenced by the philosophy of Hegel, and implicit in this assertion is a criticism. Vatke did indeed study under Hegel among others in Berlin, and his work certainly owes something to Hegel. Whether this was a bad thing is arguable. This chapter has indicated so far that, in the post-Enlightenment period, after the Old Testament was freed from its subservience to a New Testament or Christian dogmatic agenda, it was handled in the light of various philosophical agendas. In this regard, Vatke was no different from those who preceded or followed him, and his treatment of the Old Testament wrestled with questions that were genuinely raised by the text. He did not simply impose Hegelian philosophy upon the text.

Vatke's view of the history of religion was that it was the story of gradual development from religion that found the divine immanent in nature to religion in which the spirituality of the individual acknowledged the transcendence of God. This development from lower to higher religion was the work of God through natural and historical processes. These enlarged the capacity of the people to receive new ideas and insights, and hence to move to higher forms of religion. In one respect, Vatke's view of Israelite religion differed from that of de Wette. The latter saw the destruction of Jerusalem in 587/6 BCE and the subsequent Babylonian exile as a turning point after which Hebrew religion declined into the legalism of Judaism. Vatke could admit of no such degeneration; the history was one of continuing progress. In other respects, Vatke followed de Wette in seeing Old Testament religion in the context of the religions of the world, especially of those of the ancient Near East. Vatke paid particular attention to the ways in which outside religious influences had affected the development of Israelite religion. These influences included the following: the religion of Egypt at the time of the Exodus, the sun worship introduced when a Phoenician architect built Solomon's temple, the religions of Assyria and Babylon during the ascendancy of those empires over Israel and Judah in the eighth to the sixth centuries, the idolatry of the non-Israelite population of Israel and the Persian religion mediated by Judah's absorption into the Persian empire from 539–333 BCE. Vatke saw the Persian period as the high point of Old Testament religion, with the disappearance of idolatry, the introduction of detailed laws to regulate the cultic and civic life of the community, and the development of personal prayer and piety. Thus, God had been at work in multifarious ways, guiding the people towards their maturest understanding and practice of their religion.

REACTIONS TO CONFESSIONAL ORTHODOXY IN THE NINETEENTH CENTURY

By the time that Vatke's *Biblical Theology* was published, the theological mood in Germany was moving strongly against the type of criticism represented by him and de Wette, criticism that resulted in radical reconstructions of the history of Israelite religion that were at variance with the picture presented in the Old Testament itself. The reunion of Lutheran and Reformed Churches in some parts of Germany occasioned by the defeat of Napoleon, and the 300th anniversary of the Reformation (1817) and the Augsburg Confession (1830) focused attention on Christian doctrine. In some quarters reunion was opposed and a Lutheran Old Prussian Union was formed. At the same time, a revival movement was gaining strength that emphasized the traditional doctrines of the fall of mankind, redemption only by the vicarious sacrifice of Christ, and the need for personal acceptance of salvation. The net result of these tendencies was that the all-encompassing approach of theologians such as de Wette was replaced by a return to seeing the Old Testament as a key element in dogmatic theology. It was the Old Testament, after all, that narrated the Fall of the human race in Genesis 3 (de Wette had denied the historicity of the Fall); and it was the Old Testament (according to the new orthodox piety) that foretold the atoning death of the messiah that was fulfilled in Jesus Christ.

The ascendancy of confessional orthodoxy in Germany from roughly 1830 to 1865 put the theological use of the Old Testament back to where it had been in Germany a hundred years earlier; and yet, even within this confessional orthodoxy there were theologians moving in new directions. One of these was Johannes Christian Konrad von Hofmann (1810–77) who was a professor at Erlangen from 1845 until his death (Rogerson 1984: 104–11). As a student in Berlin, Hofmann had studied history under Ranke, and had gained a lifelong interest in what causes events in history and how events are connected. He had also, directly or indirectly, been influenced by the later philosophy of Schelling. The combination of his historical, philosophical and theological interests resulted in an interpretation of the Bible in terms of *Heilsgeschichte* (salvation history).

Hofmann believed that the purpose of the creation was to enable the eternal Trinity to have fellowship with the human race. This desire was consummated in the Incarnation and the new possibilities of divine/human fellowship which the Incarnation initiated. History was the process through which God created and sought fellowship with the human race. If God had not wished to create a human race and to have fellowship with it there would be no history. Although Hofmann owed something to Schelling's later philosophy for his understanding of why creation had happened and what history was, he believed that it was only the Bible that contained the record of the divine search for human fellowship. Further, the Bible could only be properly understood by those who had experienced new birth in Christ. They had entered into the fellowship with God which was the purpose of creation, and they could read the Bible as the record of a progressive series of events that had reached its goal in the fellowship that faith in Christ made possible.

This position entailed the following approach to the Old Testament. First, Hofmann accepted and used historical criticism in order to understand and illuminate each historical period described in the Old Testament. Second, he did not allow historical criticism to question the accuracy of the Old Testament record. If it was the account of God's successive actions in history which climaxed in the Incarnation, then it was privileged and beyond criticism. *Heilsgeschichte* was God's history, and could not be questioned. Third, Hofmann broke with traditional orthodoxy in a number of ways. He did not accept that prophecies in the Old Testament predicted the coming of Christ. Prophets spoke to the people of their own times (Hofmann's historical interests are foremost here). It was Scripture as a whole that was prophetic, as each stage in the divine direction of history led to the next stage, culminating in the coming of Christ. For orthodox scholars, this historical interpretation of prophecies put Hofmann into the company of the 'rationalists'. He was also non-orthodox in his view of the Fall and the atonement. The Fall did not occasion the Incarnation as a remedy for it, and the purpose of the atonement was to assist the human race to overcome its self-alienation which prevented it from receiving what God offered.

Hofmann was criticized by his contemporaries for virtually denying free will to the human race. If Old Testament history was entirely driven by God's reaching out to the human race, where did human choice come in? Also, by regarding the Old Testament as containing a series of stages, each of which was preparatory to the next until the climax was reached in Christ, Hofmann in effect made the Old Testament little more than proof that there had been a goal attained. The Old Testament was virtually obsolete. However, it is easier to condemn Hofmann from the point of view of hindsight than to appreciate that he was attempting a synthesis of the dominating critical, philosophical and theological concerns of his day.

A contemporary and friend of Hofmann, Franz Delitzsch (1813–90), attempted a similar synthesis, albeit with much more orthodox results (Rogerson 1984: 111–20). Once again it was the speculative and idealist philosophy of that period that provided the general context for Delitzsch's scholarship. Delitzsch relied upon the work of Anton Günther, a Catholic priest, who attempted to use speculative philosophy as a foundation for articulating theology. His work was greeted with suspicion by his church, and in 1857 it was condemned.

There are some similarities between Günther's position and that which Hofmann adopted. The creation was an act of love on the part of God the Holy Trinity and the aim was to establish fellowship with the human race. Humans were also a trinity in unity – spirit, nature and humanity. However, Günther's view of Old Testament history was much more realistic than that of Hofmann. It was a dialectic between human misuse of freedom and divine attempts to win over the human race to responsible behaviour. The giving of the law, the provision of a sacrificial system and the establishment of the Hebrew theocracy were the institutional framework in which the divine/human dialectic was worked out.

This thoroughly orthodox-looking position enabled Delitzsch to produce a series of commentaries that are still not without value for their thoroughness and insights. However, his dependence on Günther led to his most singular work, his *System of Biblical Psychology* (Delitzsch 1855). This maintained that the Bible (especially the Old Testament) reveals truths about the nature of God and about the physical, spiritual and emotional constitutions of humans. In itself, this is an unexceptional claim; but as worked out by Delitzsch it takes some strange forms. Thus, an examination of Hebrew words describing God's glory showed that God was threefold in his self-revealing nature, while the account of the creation of humanity in Genesis 2:7 reveals how, in a human being, the divine spirit relates to human emotions and energies. To modern readers the book seems distinctly odd; but it is making a claim that is similar to a claim that would be made by the 'biblical theology' movement of the twentieth century. This was that the Hebrew language and the way that it described the nature of God and of humanity were a privileged source of knowledge about reality; that it was divine revelation about reality and not simply the culturally shaped understanding of reality of a small ancient people.

LIBERAL THOUGHT IN NINETEENTH-CENTURY BRITAIN

In Britain in the middle of the nineteenth century a creative use of the Old Testament is to be found among so-called liberal Anglicans, men such as Thomas Arnold (1795–1842) and Frederick Denison Maurice (1805–72). While they rejected the theories of verbal inspiration that characterized British theology, they were not biblical critics in the German sense (Rogerson 1984: 188–92). Their view of the Old Testament was that its history was by and large accurate if not infallible, and it had considerable relevance for modern readers. As a famous headmaster of Rugby School, Arnold was concerned to inculcate in his pupils a high sense of moral responsibility; and he used the Old Testament accordingly. He did not deny that it contained moral crudities that could not be accepted by nineteenth-century Christians, and he explained this by saying that the human race had passed through successive stages of development, in each of which God had adapted his revelation to the particular point of development that each stage had reached. Yet at each stage there had been a conflict between good and evil, and those involved had been faced with a moral choice. Thus even though the slaughter of the Canaanites by Joshua could not be regarded as civilized behaviour, the accounts of the slaughter could be pressed into service to show the need today for humans to be on the side of morality and virtue.

Maurice, too, was an educationalist; but he had deep social concerns, and for him the Old Testament had much to say about how a nineteenth-century Christian country should be ordered. His overall view of the Bible can be summed up in his own words: 'It is throughout, the history of an actual government, – throughout, the history of an actual education; a government of voluntary creatures to teach them subjection; – an education of voluntary creatures to make them free' (Maurice 1855: 63). The account of this education was the story of God's dealings with Israel; but the Old Testament showed that God was the creator of the whole human race. Just as he continually reached out to Israel in spite of its people's continual backsliding, so he reaches out to the whole human race. This is not apparent when the general history of the human race is considered, but it is made clear in the Bible. Old Testament history thus becomes the key to understanding all history as God's progressive education of the human race.

Two other themes that are important in Maurice are sacrifice and the hallowing of every part of human activity. Maurice saw in the Old Testament sacrificial system the principle that, in order to restore the disorder brought about by human self-will, sacrifice, i.e. surrender of self-will, was necessary. In contemporary Christianity this meant the surrender of self-will in the service of God. The Old Testament was also important to Maurice because

it concerned a people who, as a whole, were a chosen nation. It was the whole
nation that was a 'priestly kingdom and a holy nation' (Exod. 19:6) not just
its priests and Levites. Maurice held that this was as true for Britain as for
Israel and appealed to the Old Testament to argue that the Church of England
and its clergy existed to show that the whole of life in Britain was of concern
to God – its modes of government, its commerce and its industry. If these
were of concern to God, then any injustice or wrong that was found in them
stood under God's judgement.

THE IMPACT OF THE NATURAL SCIENCES IN THE LATE NINETEENTH CENTURY

In the nineteenth century, until around 1870, it was possible for scholars to
use the Old Testament as a resource for theological insights that applied
to their contemporary situation. From around 1870 the picture changed
radically. There were several reasons for this. First, the rise of the natural
sciences as subjects in their own right, and backed by professional associations,
led to the demise in Germany of idealistic and speculative philosophy. Further,
the new social sciences such as economics and sociology looked for material
explanations of how societies worked and had developed. In Britain in the
late nineteenth century there was a flourishing of a neo-Hegelian idealist
philosophy; but this, in alliance with social Darwinism, saw the history of
humanity as one of progress brought about by human achievement. The Old
Testament was fitted into a developmental theory of the history of religion,
and became little more than evidence for the religion of an ancient people.

Within this context it was still possible for people to have a high regard
for the Old Testament; but this high regard was for an achievement in the
past rather than something that could inspire the present. Thus, the German
scholar Hermann Gunkel (1862–1927), who pioneered the comparative study
of Israelite and ancient Near Eastern creation and other myths, could defend
the way in which the distinctive faith of Israel had shaped their version and
use of these stories; but this was still an admiration for a past achievement.

A particularly interesting figure of this period is William Robertson Smith
(1846–94), who became professor of Arabic in Cambridge after a career that
saw him dismissed from his chair of Old Testament at the Free Church
College in Aberdeen. He also worked as editor of the ninth edition of the
Encyclopaedia Britannica. Scotland was much more open to influences from
the continent of Europe than England was in the 1860s, and thus it was that
Smith studied philosophy under Hermann Lotze in Göttingen in 1869. Lotze
is an almost totally neglected figure today; but in his day he was regarded as
one of Germany's greatest philosophers, and his particular contribution was
the way in which he combined idealist and materialist perspectives in accounting for the history and development of the human race (Lotze 1892).

By adopting Lotze's philosophy, Smith was able to study the Old Testament sociologically. He emphasized that, in the ancient world, religion was a corporate thing first and an individual thing second. Religion was an element in all aspects of life. It bound kinship groups together, and found communal expression at local and national festivals. Its sacrifices were occasions of rejoicing, when groups believed themselves to be in communion with God through the eating of a sacrificial animal or plant. Smith is often regarded as one of the founders of the sociological study of religion; and in Britain he championed the controversial theory of the history of Israelite religion given classical expression in Wellhausen's *Prolegomena to the History of Israel* (1883). Wellhausen's position owed much (as he readily admitted) to de Wette, and maintained that the high point of Hebrew religion was that of the prophets of the eighth and seventh centuries. Josiah's reformation in 622 BCE began a process of degeneration which culminated in the priestly religion of the post-exilic period with its emphasis on sacrifice as atonement.

Unlike de Wette, Wellhausen was mainly interested in reconstructing what had happened. He had no philosophical theological interest in applying his results to his own day. Robertson Smith, on the other hand, was able to combine his sociological interests and his championship of Wellhausen's position with the sincere and fervent evangelical faith that he owed to the Free Church of Scotland. He saw the history of Israelite religion as reconstructed by modern scholarship as a history of grace. It was the story of God dealing graciously with his people; and it could inspire modern readers to trust and hope in that same gracious God. In order to maintain his position, Smith not only reconstructed the sacred history; he privileged that part of it that was most congenial to his own theology. Thus he argued that the high point of Israelite religion had been that time before and during the early monarchy when families and villages had enjoyed easy access to God in their own celebrations and at local sanctuaries. The reform of Josiah, which resulted in Jerusalem becoming the only place where God could legitimately be worshipped, was a betrayal of all that had been spontaneous and joyous in Israel's religion (Smith 1892).

OLD TESTAMENT HISTORY VERSUS SCHOLARLY HISTORY

The rise of historical criticism, and especially the era initiated by the work of de Wette, raised a fundamental question for the theological use of the Old Testament. If scholars were correct in arguing that the picture of the history of Old Testament religion present in the Old Testament itself differed radically from what had actually happened, how could the Old Testament be used theologically? If all that Moses had instituted at the *beginning* of Israel's history (according to the Old Testament) was in fact a product of the *latest* stage of Israel's religion, after the exile, where did this leave readers?

De Wette had worked ahistorically; that is, he had regarded the Old Testament as essentially the literature of a people wrestling with ultimate questions about meaning and purpose. The value of the Old Testament lay in its literary–aesthetic grappling with these questions. Vatke had seen in Israel's history, as reconstructed by critical scholarship, the outworking of a dialectic of education between the divine and the human. For Robertson Smith also, the critically reconstructed history of Israel could be used positively, as a history of grace. Hofmann, Delitzsch, Arnold and Maurice, on the other hand, accepted Old Testament history at its face value, Hofmann particularly so, because he believed that it was the history of God's involvement in human affairs.

In the twentieth century, all creative theological use of the Old Testament had to accept the new 'ugly ditch' that de Wette had discovered, between the actual (scholarly critical) and the recorded (Old Testament) history of Israel's religion. Responses were as follows.

In his *Theology of the Old Testament* published in the 1930s, Walther Eichrodt (1890–1978) proceeded ahistorically by seeing the covenant between God and Israel as that which determined everything (Eichrodt 1933–9). The covenant resulted from God's irruption into human history, and it was an anticipation of the kingdom of God. It shaped the whole of Israel's life and institutions which were considered by Eichrodt in great detail. The value of the Old Testament was therefore its indication of how the divine–human relationship had affected the life and institutions of an ancient people. For contemporary believers in Israel's God as further revealed in the New Testament, this was of considerable interest.

If Eichrodt worked ahistorically, G. von Rad (1901–71) fully accepted the consequences of de Wette's 'ugly ditch' (von Rad 1957–61). Working on the basis of the various histories within the Old Testament as isolated by the scholarship of the 1950s, von Rad described the theology of the Jahwist, the Deuteronomists, the Priestly school and the Prophets in his Old Testament Theology. Yet this was not just description of past beliefs. Von Rad invoked the notion of *kerygma* (proclamation) in order to characterize what was going on in the various histories within the Old Testament. Thus, the *kerygma* of the Jahwist was a witness to faith expressed in a historical account of God's workings in Israel. Even if modern scholarship could not always accept the accuracy of the Jahwist's version of what had happened (it was, after all, written at a time when historical research and writing as we know them did not exist), what could not be denied was the Jahwist's faith in what God had done and was doing. This faith had shaped and sustained Israel through many crises, and had had to be recast in the light of these crises. Von Rad thus provided a dynamic picture of a people of faith living out their faith in a real and difficult world, a world where it was possible for modern readers to relate to many problems.

Another view that took history as the main avenue of approach to the Old Testament is to be found in the school of the American W. F. Albright (1891–1971). Albright and his students, especially G. E. Wright, used archaeology to try to defend the basic historicity of the Old Testament. Their purpose in so doing was to speak of acts of God in history, in which the divine had objectively set something in motion in human affairs, to which the faith of Israel as expressed in the Old Testament was a witness (Rogerson 1988: 143–4). Their position differed from that of von Rad in that they regarded events such as the Exodus as mighty acts of God, whereas von Rad held that we could know little of what happened at the Exodus, and that the prime datum was not the event itself but Israel's faith about the event.

Closely bound up with the approach of the Albright school was the biblical theology movement. This assumed that divine action in Israel's history had produced a distinctive Hebrew world-view that not only contrasted with the world-views of Israel's neighbours, but which could be a source of contemporary knowledge about God. According to this approach, the Canaanite world-view was magical, cyclical and mythical, whereas the Hebrew understanding of reality saw the world as the creation of a God who was directing history lineally towards an ultimate goal. The distinctive understanding of God implied in Hebrew language and culture (as opposed particularly to that of the Greeks) was that God was dynamic rather than abstract, was the object of trust rather than assent and whose righteousness was not an attribute but an activity of delivering those in need. Biblical theology was able to produce books on the biblical view of man (*sic*) or work or on key biblical attributes of God such as his *hesed* (unfailing love). In its way, biblical theology is reminiscent of Delitzsch's biblical psychology.

LIBERATION AND FEMINIST THEOLOGIES

In the 1970s and 1980s a quite new agenda for using the Old Testament was set by social materialist, liberation and feminist theologies. Social materialist scholars used a refined form of historical criticism to study the social background of Israelite society; they were also informed by Marxist theories about the development of societies and were sympathetic to left-wing political aspirations. A major contribution in this field was N. K. Gottwald's *The Tribes of Yahweh: The Sociology of Liberated Israel 1250–1050 BCE* (Gottwald 1979). This massive study of the sociology of Israel's origins argued that, in the thirteenth century BCE, Israel had come into existence when peasant farmers had rebelled against the Canaanite city states in ancient Palestine, and had formed an egalitarian society. This social revolution had, at the same time, produced faith in Yahweh as a God of liberation. For Gottwald, this ancient egalitarian stage was the high point of Israelite religion after which the advent of kingship had introduced oppressive structures against which the people had to struggle. Seen in this way, the Old Testament was an encouragement to the establishment of a society where power was shared among the people, and a call to oppose oppressive structures.

Gottwald was still working within the methodology of biblical criticism as it had been produced by the Enlightenment, even if he was criticizing many of its received ideas; he was still within modernism. In liberation theology we find hints of post-modernism, that is, a challenge to the Enlightenment belief in the existence of universal norms of reason. Liberation theologians challenged the situation in which the interpretation of the Old Testament had become the prerogative of academics working within the Western academic tradition. Being located among the poor and under-privileged of South America, they asserted that the Old Testament was originally written not for Western academics but for the poor and oppressed in ancient Israel; that if one wished to hear the authentic message of the Old Testament this was possible only if it was heard from the perspective of the poor and oppressed.

In liberation theology generally, the Old Testament came into its own because its understanding of concepts such as salvation, righteousness and steadfast love has a concrete and practical side as well as a spiritual side. For the Hebrew slaves in Egypt, salvation was not a sense of being valued that enabled them to endure their slavery more patiently, nor was it a promise of better life after this one. It was an experience of actual liberation from bondage. Righteousness meant God actively bringing about justice where there was none; God's steadfast love was expressed in the covenant relationship which he established with his people, a relationship which required that justice and compassion were shown in action to the poor and needy.

Feminist theologians have also addressed the Old Testament in new ways. For many of them, their motivation was that the Old Testament had been used in theology and the Church to maintain and defend the subordination of women to men; and passages such as Genesis 2, which suggests that woman was created to be a helper for man, and Genesis 3 which seems to envisage a predominantly child-bearing role for women, have received much attention (Rogerson 1991: 35–41). Some feminist treatments of the Old Testament have assumed a 'hermeneutics of rejection'; that is, they have maintained that the Old Testament is too much the product of a patriarchal society for it to be applicable to a modern world which accepts the right of women to set their own agendas for their roles and aspirations. (A similar view is taken by some liberation theologians on the ground that the Old Testament was writtten by, and reflects the outlook of, a ruling elite.)

Our understanding of the resources available from the Old Testament for theological reflection has been greatly enriched by liberation and feminist approaches. Even those that embrace a 'hermeneutics of rejection' alert people in the opposite camps to the need for great sensitivity, and for reconsidering much that had been taken for granted. Two very simple examples will indicate this. First, scholars have long been concerned to identify the mysterious 'servant of God' who is mentioned in general in Isaiah 40–55 and in particular in the four poems of 42:1–4; 49:1–6; 50:4–9 and 52:13–53:12. But it has been generally overlooked that a female character, the daughter of Sion (i.e. Jerusalem personified as a young woman), also appears in passages such as 49:

14–26; 52:1–3; 54:1–10 as well as in chapters 56–66. This character is also deserving of close study (Sawyer 1989).

The other example is a translation matter. In Psalm 22:9 the traditional English translation is 'But thou art he that took me out of the womb.' This is found, with insignificant variations, from the Authorized Version to the Revised Standard Version and the Revised English Bible. Grammatically it is correct; but it is arguable that the translation, by insisting on the 'he', obscures the fact that the Psalmist has used the female image of God as midwife. The New Revised Standard Version has 'Yet it was you who took me from the womb.'

ECOLOGICAL MATTERS

The final instance of theological use of the Old Testament is taken from the context of renewed general concern about the environment, and the rise of so-called creation spiritualities. The passage in Genesis 1:26–30, with its command to the humans to fill the earth, subdue it and have dominion over it, has brought the accusation that the Judeo-Christian tradition, obedient to this passage, is responsible for the current ecological crisis in the world. This is, of course, nonsense; and the main culprits are Stalinist-type socialism in the East and a type of capitalism in the West that is concerned only with profiteering. But the accusation has made scholars examine the meaning of the Hebrew verbs translated as 'subdue' and 'have dominion', and it has been argued that the latter has a primary 'shepherding' sense, while the former should be understood to mean to take legal possession of the earth by setting foot on it (Rogerson 1991: 19–20).

Whether or not Genesis 1:26–30 can be 'rescued' in this way, there is no doubt that the Old Testament can contribute to the debate about whether we need a spirituality that will enable people to 'get close' to nature. According to the Old Testament, the Canaanites tried to be close to nature by using sacred prostitution to imitate and stimulate the cycle of fertility. Further, Canaanite kings, and Israelite kings who imitated them, were not afraid to exercise their power for their own advantage. Perhaps they had noticed that, in the natural world, bigger and stronger animals generally prey on smaller and weaker ones.

Prophetic religion in particular opposed the abuse of power by rulers; and in the laws of Exodus and Deuteronomy we can see how Israel's belief in a God of liberation shaped their view of what society should be like and how that should affect the natural order also. Thus in Exodus 23:9–13, Israel's existence as a collection of homeless aliens before the Exodus is invoked as the reason why they must not oppress homeless aliens in Israel. There follow regulations about leaving fields, vineyards and olive trees 'fallow' every seventh year. This is not an agricultural necessity; vineyards and olives do not need to be fallowed, and fields had to be fallowed on a two- to three-year cycle in

Iron Age Israel. The produce of the fallowed items are to be for the poor and needy and also for the wild animals. The next regulation is a version of the sabbath commandment and the main beneficiaries are the oxen and donkeys, the domesticated beasts of burden that could so easily be worked for seven days a week. Thus we see that the Old Testament expected ancient Israel to adopt a spirituality for ordering society and dealing with nature. It was rooted in the redemptive work of God, and in response to that redemption sought to bring graciousness to bear on all dealings between humans and between humans and the natural world.

CONCLUSION

Some readers who have reached the end of this chapter may be surprised that the Old Testament has continued to command so much attention from interpreters. After all, did not the Enlightenment expose the Old Testament for what it is – the annals of a small and unimportant barbaric Semitic tribe? That the Old Testament contains crudities that can make no claims upon today's readers cannot be denied; but the Old Testament has suffered too much from selective reading and selective judgements. If passages can be found that describe an angry and irrational God, there are also passages that liken God to a lover who is constantly seeking to win back a beloved who has spurned his love (e.g. Ezek. 16). If there are passages that concentrate upon the nationalistic interests of ancient Israel there are also passages that credit non-Israelites with more faithfulness to God and their neighbours than is found among Israelites (e.g. the Moabitess Ruth in the book of Ruth). If there are bland statements about the prosperity of the righteous and the punishment of the wicked there are books such as Job and Ecclesiastes that call into question any simplistic view of a moral universe. The prophets are people called to undertake missions that mostly result in their being misunderstood, opposed and, in some cases, persecuted by the Israelites to whom they are sent. If there are laws in the Old Testament that fall below what we regard as appropriate in a civilized society (e.g. the death penalty for adultery), there are other laws, such as those regulating the Jubilee in Leviticus 25, that are based upon the view that human dignity is superior to economic necessity.

Thus it comes about that the Old Testament has a continuing appeal not only for the Jewish and Christian communities that regard it as Scripture. Anyone who becomes really familiar with its contents (and few do outside professional circles) will be struck by the power of that content. At the very least, it contains great literature, and therefore has the power that all great literature possesses to excite and to stimulate the imagination. But it also contains some of the greatest religious writings of the world, and where that religion is at its most personal, for example, in the Psalms or Job or Isaiah 53, it is unrivalled in its honesty, passion and poignancy. Approaches to the Old Testament since the Enlightenment have had their agendas set by the changing philosophical and theological concerns of each generation; but they have found that the Old Testament has the resources to engage with these concerns and to shed new light on them. The Enlightenment passed judgement on the Old Testament too hastily. Modern readers will be well advised not to make the same mistake.

REFERENCES

Bell, D. (1984) *Spinoza in Germany from 1679 to the Age of Goethe*, London: Bithell series of Dissertations.

Brett, M. G. (1991) *Biblical Criticism in Crisis: The Impact of the Canonical Approach on Old Testament Studies*, Cambridge: Cambridge University Press.

Cunaeus, P. (1653) *On the Republic of the Hebrews*, London; transl. of *De republica Hebraeorum*, Leyden (1617).

Delitzsch, F. (1855) *System der biblischen Psychologie*, Leipzig; transl. *System of Biblical Psychology*, Edinburgh (1875).

De Wette, W. M. L. (1807) 'Beytrag zur Charakteristik des Hebraismus', in C. Daub and F. Creuzer, (eds) *Studien* 3.2, Heidelberg.

—— (1828) *Über die Religion: Ihr Wesen, ihre Erscheinungsformen und ihr Einfluß auf das Leben*, Berlin.

Eichrodt, W. (1933–9) *Theologie des Alten Testaments*, Leipzig: Hinrichs; transl. *Theology of the Old Testament*, London: SCM Press.

Gabler, J. P. (1831) 'De iusto discrimine theologiae biblicae et dogmaticae regundisque recte utriusque finibus', in *Kleinere theologische Schriften*, vol II, Ulm, 179–98, translation in J. Sandys-Wunsch and L. Eldrege (1980) 'J. P. Gabler and the Distinction between Biblical and Dogmatic Theology: Translation, Commentary, and Discussion of his Originality', *Scottish Journal of Theology* 33: 133–58.

Gottwald, N. K. (1979) *The Tribes of Yahweh: The Sociology of Liberated Israel 1250–1050 BCE*, London: SCM Press.

Herder, J. G. (1993) *Against Pure Reason: Writings on Religion, Language and History*, ed. and transl. by M. Bunge, Minneapolis: Fortress Press.

Lotze, H. (1892) *Microcosmos: An Essay Concerning Man and his Relation to the World*, transl. E. Hamilton and E. E. C. Jones, Edinburgh.

Lowman, M. (1745) *Dissertation on the Civil Government of the Hebrews*, London.

Maurice, F. D. (1855) *Patriarchs and Lawgivers of the Old Testament*, 2nd edn London.

Rad, G. von (1957–61) *Theologie des Alten Testaments, I Die Theologie der geschichtlichen Überlieferungen Israels, II Die Theologie der prophetischen Überlieferungen Israels*, Munich: Kaiser; transl. *Old Testament Theology*, Edinburgh: Oliver & Boyd (1962–5).

Rogerson, J. W. (1984) *Old Testament Criticism in the Nineteenth Century: England and Germany*, London: SPCK.

—— (1988) 'The Old Testament', in J. Rogerson, C. Rowland, B. Lindars, *The Study and Use of the Bible*, vol. 2 of *The History of Christian Theology*, ed. P. Avis, Basingstoke: Marshall Pickering.

—— (1991) *Genesis 1–11*, Old Testament Guides, Sheffield: Sheffield Academic Press.

—— (1992a) 'W. M. L. de Wette. Founder of Modern Biblical Criticism: An Intellectual Biography', *Journal for the Study of the Old Testament* Supplement Series 126, Sheffield: Sheffield Academic Press.

—— (1992b) 'Writing the History of Israel in the 17th and 18th Centuries', in F. G. Martinez *et al. The Scriptures and the Scrolls: Studies in Honour of A. S. van der*

Woude on the Occasion of his 65th Birthday, Supplements to Vetus Testamentum 49, Leiden: E. J. Brill, 217–27.

Sawyer, J. F. A. (1989) 'Daughter of Zion and Servant of the Lord in Isaiah: A Comparison', in *Journal for the Study of the Old Testament* 44: 89–107.

Smith, W. R. (1892) *The Old Testament in the Jewish Church*, 2nd edn Edinburgh.

Vatke, W. (1835) *Die biblische Theologie wissenschaftlich dargestellt, 1 Die Religion des Alten Testamentes*, Berlin (there was no vol. 2).

FURTHER READING

Arnold, T. (1845) *Sermons Chiefly on the Interpretation of Scripture*, London.

Black, J. S. and Chrystal, G. (1912) *The Life of William Robertson Smith*, London: A. & C. Black.

Gutierrez, G. (1974) *A Theology of Liberation*, London: SCM Press.

Hofmann, J. C. K. von (1841–4) *Weissagung und Erfüllung im alten und im neuen Testament*, Nördlingen.

Reventlow, H. Graf (1984) *The Authority of the Bible and the Rise of the Modern World*, London: SCM Press.

Rogerson, J. W. (1974) *Myth in Old Testament Interpretation*, Beihefte zur Zeitschrift für die alttestamentliche Wissenschaft 134, Berlin: de Gruyter.

—— (1978) *Anthropology and the Old Testament*, Oxford: Basil Blackwell.

Smend, R. (1989) *Deutsche Alttestamentler in drei Jahrhunderten*, Göttingen: Vandenhoeck & Ruprecht.

—— (1991) *Epochen der Bibelkritik*, Gesammelte Studien Band 3, Munich: Kaiser.

See also chapters 3, 6, 7, 8, 12, 13, 41, 45.

5

THE NEW TESTAMENT: CONTENT AND CHARACTER

Leslie Houlden

THE EMERGENCE OF THE CANON

Apart from familiar church buildings, the New Testament is surely the feature of the Christian religion most taken for granted. It is read in every church service and its language colours prayers and hymns. Even in secularized Western countries, it plays a part in school education and figures in many current idioms of speech. Judges and lawyers reach for it when they want to insist on adherence to oaths (even though the New Testament itself is against oath-taking!). Scarcely ever is it thought of as other than a single unit, even more so than the Bible as a whole, and it might as well have existed from the furthest reaches of time.

Yet sharp historically minded critics will point out that for the first four centuries of Christianity's existence this 'unit' did not exist as the accepted ('canonical') whole we are familiar with and that for the last four it has been subject to a creeping process of disintegration, in the form of historical and literary analysis, examining and describing it part by part, bit by bit. Other elements in scholarly opinion will rebut this striking revisionism, pointing to the role of something very close to the New Testament from early days and to its very substantial unities of theme and message. No doubt it is judicious to seek truth somewhere between these two extremes. Plainly, much depends on how close the observer stands to the history and the documents themselves and on the roles they are being asked to play in any particular context.

This chapter concerns the origins of the New Testament. Inevitably, there-fore, it moves from the parts to the whole. Equally, because it focuses on matters that are in themselves small and detailed, it works by way of distinc-tions and diversities. That is the dominant modern manner and virtually imposes itself. It will emerge in other chapters that in other periods Christ-ianity has had much more of any eye for homogeneity and synthesis in its view of the New Testament – as this section began by noting in relation to its everyday use.

It has to be said at the outset that much in any analysis of Christian origins remains obscure, and this subject is no exception. The evidence is meagre and even where it seems relatively abundant, it is hard to interpret and to set in context. So it is a study where there is much controversy, even among the learned, and much diversity of opinion. There is no need to be deterred from forming pictures and there is such a thing as the balance of probability, but certainty is hard to come by. Now we turn to the various kinds of early Christian writing (Aune 1987).

KINDS OF WRITING

The oldest type of Christian writing to survive is the epistle. Though this word derives from the ordinary Greek term for a letter, there is some advantage in keeping the traditional name. For among the many letters that have survived from different levels of society in the ancient world, these early Christian communications have their own characteristics and have become something of an independent genre. They are neither upper-class literary products, such as were written in many cases with an eye to publication, nor mere notes about day-to-day matters like travel and business affairs: though they have something in common with both. On the one hand, there are signs that some of them were intended to be read by more than one Christian group to which they are addressed (Col. 4:16); on the other hand, they do contain, along with material of much more serious import, remarks about local crises and problems (e.g. 1 Cor.) and about movements from one place to another (e.g. Rom. 15:22; 16:1–2). But chiefly, in a manner established (so far as our evidence goes) by the apostle Paul, they contain attempts to state and commend central features of Christian belief and behaviour, often, naturally, in response to challenge or misunderstanding. Local and occasional as they are, they do therefore have the possibility of wider significance, even if not the timelessness with which they have often been credited (Stowers 1986).

The chief letters of Paul (as well as others, some of them eventually appearing in the New Testament, others not) certainly fit this description: notably, 1 Thessalonians, 1 and 2 Corinthians, Galatians, Romans, Philippians (to give a likely historical sequence of the apostle's most probably authentic works). The genuine but ephemeral Letter to Philemon is something of a puzzle: perhaps its survival is owed to its mattering very much to some individual or group of importance at the time of the letters' collection, probably around 100 CE.

It has already been indicated that the survival of the great epistles should be ascribed to the intrinsic importance of their contents: they were worth pondering again and again, and worth turning to for guidance and authority in dealing with recurring difficulties, or even with problems other than those originally addressed. No doubt their position derived also from the significance of their author: when the weight of the Church shifted, in the final years of the first century, from Palestine to Asia Minor, Greece and Rome, and from Jewish to Gentile membership, it is not surprising that Paul's pioneering efforts in at least some of those areas gave a major boost to his posthumous position and so to the value and dominance of his writings. Time and again, as the years went by, it seems that these two factors – intrinsic value and relevance on the one hand and apostolic authority (genuine or not) on the other – combined to bring certain books to prominence in the life of the Church. A dual process was therefore under way: first, the Church itself, in various places and operating in a variety of ways, ascribed value to writings which it found useful or impressive. Partly they imposed themselves (e.g. they were by Paul); partly they chimed in with existing convictions about Jesus or church life, or else met certain needs. Second, the writings came to form Christian life and belief – as it were, they returned the compliment which the churches had conferred on them: in other words, they became authoritative (Metzger 1987).

An additional factor is present from the start. Reception of an epistle means interpretation – and a communication may be 'heard' in other senses than that in which it is 'spoken'. And the process of interpretation, once begun, is continuous and unstoppable, with constant diversity. Hence, whatever the authority ascribed to a writing, the life of those who read it continues to affect the way they read – and the way they think and act on the basis of it. They are not automata, not blank sheets on which the writing impresses itself. These matters are of course of the utmost importance for the whole continuing process of the reception and use of Scripture, not only in the early period but always; not only with regard to epistles but equally with regard to all writings accepted as authoritative.

It is generally supposed that Paul lived and died (in the later 60s of the first century) before even the first of the Gospels (probably that of Mark) was written. This cannot be established with certainty: there may have been earlier pioneering attempts to write down information about Jesus' life and teaching which have simply disappeared or found some role in the Gospels that have survived. However that may be, it is worth reflecting that in all probability Christians first put pen to papyrus not in order to make a record of Jesus whom they revered and were beginning to worship as well as obey, but in order to deal with pressing practical problems of belief and behaviour. To realize that is to gain a certain perspective: Christianity is in its origins a living and present faith before it is a society of adherents of the memory of Jesus of Nazareth. It would of course be wrong to press this distinction, and much may well depend (even if we are right about the relative lateness of writings about Jesus) on the special character of Paul, so much the dominant surviving voice from those first days – who had never known Jesus in his lifetime and seems, perhaps unusually, to have been much less interested in

Jesus' deeds and teaching than in his present lordship. All the same, the writing of the Gospels represents a move towards recapturing knowledge of Jesus, embedding Christianity in that foundation, and perhaps countering tendencies away towards speculative religion that was losing touch with the founder. In that sense, the writing of the Gospels is itself a move towards the formation of an authoritative Christian Scripture in a way that the writing of epistles, at least those of Paul, with their immediacy of concern, was not.

However, this way of looking at the matter must immediately be countered by pointing out that the Gospel writers did not start from scratch. The books themselves, probably written in the order Mark, Matthew, Luke (with the Acts of the Apostles as a sequel), John, may come from the last three decades of the first century; as, perhaps, did the Gospel of Thomas and some other writings about Jesus which have survived only in fragments and which did not achieve authoritative, canonical status. But they surely used traditions about Jesus, both his deeds and his teaching and above all his death and resurrection, that had long been current in the Christian congregations. This is not to deny that there was a process of embellishment, invention and certainly re-application of stories and sayings of Jesus – the differences between the Gospels are tangible evidence of that; and what was said earlier about the continuous and inevitable nature of interpretation still applies.

Meanwhile, it may suffice to describe the Gospels, each with its own outlook and programme, as fusions of history and belief, each using the other as its medium. In many ways, the Gospels are in this way not unlike 'lives' of famous figures written in the same period: only the stakes are higher, the belief-claims more intense – and the colouring (and legitimating) of the story of Jesus by depicting him as the fulfilment of already accepted Jewish Scripture adds a unique feature which may have a distorting as well as an illuminating role. The relative parts played by oral tradition and creative writing in the making of the Gospels are a matter of much dispute and do not lend themselves to dogmatizing. What is of interest is that the two phases are different in their implications – certain kinds of fluidity have been closed off by the act of writing; and that writing does not bring oral development to an end – people continue to tell stories and repeat teaching, and, especially in such circles as the early Christian groups, it is likely that writing did not preclude re-writing, so that it may be inappropriate to entertain the idea of 'the original manuscript' of a Gospel after the manner of a modern book (Stanton 1989).

There is a third mode of early Christian writing to survive – apocalypse or 'revelation'. Represented by only one complete book in the New Testament (apart from the letters in chapters 2 and 3), the Revelation of John, it nevertheless typifies much in first-century Christian mentality; and it plays a not inconspicuous part in the Gospels (Mark 13; Matt. 24; Luke 17, 21). It adopts, as a natural mode of communication, a genre established in Judaism from the mid-second century BCE: 'apocalyptic' or revelatory writing works in a quasi-poetic and ecstatic manner with a code of imagery with deep roots in Jewish literature (cf. the Old Testament books of Ezekiel and Zechariah), and presents a picture of the inside of heaven and the future course of history, focused on God's faithful ones and their enemies, soon to be vanquished. This riotous (to us) way of expressing other-worldly hope for this world tells us something of the proportions of the minds of many early Christians. However, the Revelation of John did not have an easy passage into the formal collections of authorized Christian writings and, except in certain limited circles, has remained somewhat on the margins. It was more important in what it reflected of the time of its writing than for its continuing role as Scripture at the centre of the Church's use (Rowland 1982).

The first Christians were already equipped with authoritative books in the shape of the great collection of central Jewish writings which in due course they characterized as 'the Old Testament'. These gave the Church a firm rooting not only in a venerable past but also in God's purposes – once they were interpreted in the light of Jesus, seen as their fulfilment. But there is nothing surprising in the fact that Christians came to adopt their own sup-plementary collection of authorized and normative writings; and as we have seen, that role was, in various ways, virtually implicit in the earliest use or even, in some cases, the actual making of those writings from the start (Lindars 1961). However, the process received a considerable fillip and a certain formalization in the second century when the maverick Marcion propa-gated a version of Christianity which displaced from redemptive usefulness the Jewish heritage, the Jewish God (as he saw him) and the Scriptures that spoke of him and issued from him. Christianity was already a 'bookish' religion: so its own new books (a 'new testament') came to the fore in their own right and soon became the standard by which all else, including the Jewish writings, retained by most Christians, was to be interpreted and to which it led. The process of deciding exactly what the list of those books should be was not concluded much before the last years of the fourth century, but in essentials it was in place by the latter part of the second. Use of, above all, Paul's letters and the Gospels became generally settled in both liturgy and teaching. They were one of the chief rocks on which Christians could endeavour to rest amid the continuing swirl of interpretation and speculation to which the books themselves, in part, gave rise.

READING THE NEW TESTAMENT NOW

It is one thing to try to form a picture of how the New Testament came together in the early Christian centuries, another to decide how best to read it today. Over the past two or three hundred years, numerous approaches have been adopted to the text, mostly literary or historical in character – in line with general cultural and academic trends. Though usually conducted by religious people, these enquiries have tended to move attention from the New Testament writings as essentially having their role within present-day religion.

Measured by literary or historical methods, they become documents of their time of origin, to be assessed and analysed in their original contexts, so far as those can be identified. While there need be no denial or even neglect of their religious and theological significance, that too comes to be viewed in its first-century setting, and 'significance for us' is mediated through a first-century prism. In certain respects of course, 'significance for us' has come to seem problematic in the light of the original home of these writings in such distant and alien times and places (Morgan and Barton 1988).

Ever since critical study of the New Testament in the modern way began, it has concentrated overwhelmingly on discovering (and imagining) various aspects of the contexts in which the writings arose. The last two or three centuries have seen phase after phase of this historical picture-making (Tuckett 1987). Each phase has brought its own kind of question to the text, but always with an eye on its origins. For instance: who was the author, the one to whom the work is ascribed, or some other? And if we cannot know his (alas, unlikely to be 'her') name, can we outline his mind-set, his education, perhaps his religious or social provenance? Where did the writing take place, given what we know of the geographical spread of early Christianity? And again, where the text itself gives information, is it to be taken at face value? Given that some at least of our texts (especially the Gospels) surely have a pre-history, in the shape of traditions about Jesus or collections of his teachings, can we get at them by penetrating the skin of the finished products? Adding what we may know from other sources, from Judaism and Hellenistic writings, can we construct a viable picture and, if possible, story of Jesus (Meier 1991)?

Taking another line, can we imagine the circumstances in early Christianity in which it would have been desirable to preserve the various kinds of material? Assuming that the early Churches were not given to appointing full-time archivists and remembered what remained useful, what activities, such as preaching, decision-making or worship, led to the using and the writing of books like the Gospels and the epistles?

This catalogue of questions, coming in turn upon the scene, covers the greater part of scholarly activity down to the middle of this century. Notice that while there has certainly been analysis of the text itself, most of this work goes behind the text, in order to imagine (with both the strengths and the weaknesses implied by that word) what lies there – the early Christian world and its activities or the life of Jesus. The text has been a door: and where only the text is in our hands, is it surprising that it seems to open, in its various parts, on to any number of different scenes, some complementary, but some at odds with one another? And is it surprising that sometimes scholars are modest enough to sprinkle their work lavishly with 'perhaps' or 'possibly', or (less modestly) 'probably'?

In recent years, that historical orientation has continued to flourish and to express itself, it seems, ever more sharply. Two trends are promising. One of them means crediting the writers of the Gospels, and not just those of the epistles (where the fact is obvious), with strong religious and theological interests – ideas with which they have been ready to impregnate their books from end to end. Whatever traditions, whatever older documentary sources (e.g. Matthew and Luke using Mark) they have adopted, they have put their individual stamp on the work as a whole (Perrin 1970). That word, 'whole', comes to the fore. We move away from traditions, stories and sayings, playing their individual part in early church life and being modified by various pressures, and instead we contemplate finished products – still, certainly, in imagined historical settings, but as wholes, totalities.

The second trend leads off from the first, but takes the step of bringing modern sociological angles of vision to bear on these ancient religious texts. More obviously than any of the other approaches that have been used, this one blatantly asks of the original writers and their readers questions that would dumbfound them. Paul thought he was writing transcendental truth about Jesus and the hopes of his followers: ah yes, but he was also constructing a new symbolic universe, expressing deep concerns with the distribution of power, and inventing devices to deal with unrealized hopes (e.g. for the triumphant return of Jesus). Such treatment of the documents, again usually viewing them holistically, is subversive, and certainly seems to place barriers between the text and those who wish to use it devotionally: they are not forbidden but they are given a douche before they go about their business (Kee 1980).

Treating texts as wholes has, however, provided the setting for another, quite different development. All along, and not surprisingly, the various kinds of enquiry addressed to the New Testament writings have been in tune with interests current in other kinds of study and in the culture at large. In different periods, different kinds of enquiry seem to impose themselves – only to fade later into the background. So some of the purer insights of modern literary criticism have come to be applied to our texts. With ascetic radicalism, there has been in some circles a banishing of all historical interest: the text is what we have, and to the text alone we must attend (and indeed, because it is all we have, it is only to the text that it is sensible to attend) (Moore 1989). Of course it does not please: people will not cease to ask about the history behind the text, and even if they have begun to learn that definite answers are often not available, many have begun to feel an interest in discovering the frames within which the truth about Christian origins, including Jesus' life, is likely to lie. While it may be possible to combine the best of various approaches, there is, all the same, no doubt that a purely literary enquiry into the books (a Gospel's structure, patterns of words and themes, repetitions and echoes), with historical matters simply put aside, can give unsuspected light – and even make some of the old historical questions and their answers look crass. Is it more important to fidget about the precise historicity of Jesus' passion or to grasp meaning in the various tellings of the story?

DIFFERENT CHRISTIANITIES

The identification of the various 'belief-pictures' discernible in the New Testament writings, each author, each book having its own 'world' of ideas and communication, has dominated recent scholarship. It has also revolution-ized many intuitive and long-held assumptions about Christianity. For instance: to begin with it was pure, clear and unified ('one faith, one church, one Lord'), and only later did human weakness (and diabolical manoeuvre) produce diversity and error. Or, to be a little more sophisticated, early Christianity was in agreement on certain fundamentals – about basic facts of Jesus' career, like his death and resurrection; about his status in God's purpose as universal saving agent; about certain moral priorities such as the centrality of love, the renunciation of family and property ties, monogamous marriage and no divorce. There might well be differences of emphasis and of custom, but they concerned only peripheral matters (perhaps the details of worship or baptismal practice). The central message was clear and went back either to Jesus himself or to his immediate apostolic circle.

It appears that these optimistic pictures were full of oversimplification or even downright falsehood. Of course a good deal depends on how closely you examine the phenomena: viewed from the air, little local features merge into the environment. All the same, give historical enquiry its head (and given an inch it will always take a mile), and it seems that early Christianity was richly diverse, often at loggerheads, even over quite fundamental matters, and forever correcting predecessors and neighbours. It is not so much that old certainties (once again) dissolve as that the inevitable consequences of human vitality, especially in the early days of a new movement, simply must be recognized. Not only did the early Church not appoint archivists, it also did not possess recognized and smoothly running organs of authority. Treating the various New Testament books in their own individual right and going realistically behind the (in terms of origins) pseudo-unity of the canon, we see a plethora of ideas and practices, all expressing allegiance to Jesus in one way or another – and, where they were not deliberately controverting other views, frequently oblivious, surely, to what was being believed or done in other Christian circles (Dunn 1977).

Nowhere has this diversity become clearer than in relation to the Gospels. Of course it has always been noted that they differed in vocabulary and content and it has been recognized that John was more 'theological' than the others. But the overwhelming tendency has been to seek to harmonize them, easing or explaining discrepancies, on the assumption that they must all contribute to a single consistent and historically accurate picture. Or else it is as if the four evangelists all dipped into a pool of information about Jesus and each, to an extent at least, fished out different material.

But now, whether they are viewed theologically or literarily, it is evident that such an approach does scant justice to the realities of the evangelists' achievement. While, in a literary way, the first three at least are, in some way which is still not fully elucidated, closely related, having much in common, it now seems that this similarity of wording and content can be a decoy: it has for too long blinded us to the distinctive vision of each book. But once we notice the different overall framework within which each is set and the deliberate alterations made by successors to predecessors, then we begin to see how rich was the range of reaction to the figure of Jesus (Sanders and Davies 1989). We see too how pervasive was the thought-dimension in early Christianity. It will not do to say that the Gospels give us the facts and the epistles the doctrine which is to be derived from them. Rather, we have in all cases, Gospels and epistles alike, though in quite different modes, history interpreted and events theologized – with, again in all cases, the enmeshed contribution of the thought, personality and setting of the particular writer.

This perception has led to some startling reversals in the fortunes of New Testament books. For example, over the greater part of Christian history the Gospel of Mark was neglected: it was briefer than Matthew which shared much of the same material and it was less useful for teaching, and, though it might contain memories from Peter, it did not bear an apostle's name. In the nineteenth century it stepped forward, seeming early, simple, and usefully biographical. Now, however, while the fact that it is the earliest of the Gospels is generally agreed, its supposed simplicity has gone to the winds. Instead it is widely interpreted as a work of great subtlety and mystery, focusing with astonishing candour on that prime scandal, Jesus' death, and, while drawing attention to it constantly, doing nothing to justify easy or comforting ideas about its meaning (Hooker 1983). This insistence on Jesus' death as the key to his significance had already been apparent in Paul (see 1 Cor. 1:23; 11:23–6), but along with his resurrection – which Mark, in his refusal, it seems, of alleviation, scarcely deals with at all (16:1–8) (9–20 are a later addition).

The Gospel of Matthew, reproducing most of Mark, nevertheless rewrote it, often with hardly perceptible changes – yet in the interests of a contrasting way of belief. Mystery largely disappears, to be replaced by impressive clarity and authoritative argument from accepted (Old Testament) Scripture: see, for example, the opening chapters telling of Jesus' origins and birth and the explicit details of his resurrection (Houlden 1987). Jesus gains in unmistakeable charismatic power, though his messianic reality is, for the time being, veiled by 'lowliness'; and soon public manifestation will supervene (Matt. 11:28–30; 28:16–20). And ample guidance is given for Christian life, in Jesus' long discourses (chapters 5–7; 10; 13; 18; 24–5). All in all, we are in a more reassuring and dependable Christian 'world'. So Matthew respected ('canonized') Mark enough to use him extensively but not enough to refrain from altering his sense (Stanton 1992).

Luke–Acts is generally seen as most intelligible if taken as a single work, or at any rate two related products of a single mind and a single set of needs and interests. Acts, so long treated as more or less plain history, has, in most quarters, come to be seen in the dominant theological perspective: even here identifiable pressures and assumptions have dictated not only the selection of material but also its detailed presentation. Thus, this writer sees Jesus in the setting of a dual relationship with Judaism: it both formed him and, in its leadership, rejected him. So he grows out of it, including its great symbolic institutions, temple and Scripture (chapters 1–2; 4:16–30), and yet is its lord, inaugurating a new, universal scope for God's saving purpose. The historical sweep (going back to Adam, Luke 3:38) and the geographical sweep, reaching right on from Jerusalem, via Syria, Asia Minor and Greece, to Rome itself (Acts 1–28), colour this writer's religious outlook to a greater degree than that of Mark (especially) or Matthew; as also do social concerns – to provide a framework in which Jewish and non-Jewish Christians (Acts 10; 15), rich and poor Christians (Luke 4:16–30) can interrelate harmoniously and above all sit at table (Acts 2:42) with one another (a crucial symbolic requirement in Luke's understanding of Jesus' legacy (cf. Luke 24:13–35) (Talbert 1990).

More insistently than the others, and with great economy of vocabulary, the Gospel of John sees Jesus against a cosmic background (1:1–14). His human origins are eclipsed by his existence from 'the beginning' with the Father and his eternal roots in him. Even his time here 'below' does nothing to obscure that 'true' level of his life. Though certainly he dies a genuine death at his human enemies' hands, that death has a steady significance which is described, daringly, as 'glorious' – it reveals the true splendour of God himself (13:31). So such a saviour draws his followers into a tight community around himself, guaranteed a kind of immunity at the point of ultimacy (chapters 13–17). What matters here is above all the bonding which Jesus creates between his followers, with 'love one another' as their sole instruction for life – in one sense obscure, in another all the more compelling for standing alone (Ashton 1991).

It will be apparent that allowing each writer to be seen in his own right (and we have concentrated only on the evangelists – the same could be done for the rest) lends a certain clarity: each voice makes itself heard, with its own character and quality. It may, undeniably, share this or that feature with others, but listing such shared properties is a way of hearing no single voice at all. Moreover, it obscures the fact that a given whole is more than a collection of separable features. In this light, the powerful impulse to identify what was common to (most) early Christians is misleading, though it may be comforting for those who are alarmed by diversity.

The impulse to unify, to homogenize, became very strong from the second century onwards, and with varyingly (though on the whole increasingly) effective pressure from church authorities, often with political back-up. It meant reading the New Testament writers with assumptions of unified witness and ultimate harmony, and in the light of agreed creeds and other doctrinal norms. In that way, as we now think, it meant doing injustice both to the documents themselves and to the specific intentions of their authors. But (and here modern literary theory and, implicitly, ecclesiastical power join hands), authors have no monopoly on the interpretation of their work!

While modern study of the New Testament writings, whether of a historical or literary kind, has focused attention on the distinctiveness of each writer, that does not wholly silence the question about common ground and about a possible centre of gravity in the New Testament as a whole. After all, this collection of early Christian writings has lived happily together between a single pair of covers for many centuries, and it would be absurd to think that phenomenon to be unintelligible or purely misguided! Further, surely it is partly because this set of works is both so small and so important, and has therefore received such minute examination, that the individuality of the various writings has come to be highlighted.

CENTRE OF GRAVITY

It seems the merest truism to announce that Jesus of Nazareth is the uniting element in these diverse works from the early Christian movement. It is a statement which, nevertheless, requires some refining. For example, the Letter of James notoriously lacks all reference to Jesus apart from the formal opening greeting and one single passing remark (2:1). The Third Letter of John makes no reference to Jesus whatsoever, and some other epistles coming from the latter part of the period (i.e. the late first or early second century) can scarcely be said to be consumed with interest in him and many of their statements about him seem largely formal (e.g. 2 Timothy and Jude). Moreover, certain early Christian writings which did not find acceptance in the canon, such as the Gospel of Thomas and the Epistles of Ignatius have much to say that relates to the understanding of Jesus in the early Church and is in some ways different from anything in the canonical writings. We may be left with the rather banal statement that the New Testament writings centre on Jesus in the sense that their impulse in every case ultimately springs from him and the movement that derived from him. That is of course a 'lowest common denominator' way of putting it: the central writings are full of imaginative, often brilliant perceptions of Jesus and attempts to articulate his supreme importance.

That leads to the further reflection that if Jesus is put forward as the centre of gravity in the New Testament, then it is Jesus as (however it is expressed) saviour. None of these writers is interested in him in a spirit of historical detachment. As we have seen, even the most historical-looking books, to the modern observer, the Gospels and the Acts of the Apostles, are theological writings through and through, whatever use they make of historical remi-niscence or tradition. In that sense, Jesus the figure of history is hidden behind, quite as much as he is disclosed within, the central New Testament writings. If he is the source of the Christian tradition, then he is its concealed source, visible only indirectly through the testimony of those who wrote about him and gave accounts of their beliefs about him. For an understanding of the character of the New Testament and indeed of the Christian religion, it is of profound importance that Jesus the founder left behind no writings of his own whatsoever: that in itself gives an undeniably indirect quality to the New Testament's role in Christianity, however great the importance that may be ascribed to it. Christian faith cannot appeal to the direct legacy of the founder, with its potentiality for claims to fixity of belief and teaching. Of course, our current sensitivity to the apparently infinite capacity of interpretation to shift and develop would still apply, but 'the words of the founder' would nevertheless carry enormous weight and put a burden of proof on those who would wish to point to the role of interpretation, with its propensity to change from one time and place to another according to need and cultural circumstances. True, many still act as if the Gospels did indeed give us a complete compendium of the ideas of Jesus and as if their record had the directness of a tape-recording of his words or a film of his actions; but it is not hard to show that selectivity has been at work and that the evangelist inevitably acts as a screen or a filter between the life of Jesus and our perception of it.

The realization of this secondariness of even the Gospels (it is easier to see in relation to the other New Testament books) leads to the promotion of another candidate for the position of centre of gravity or unifying factor in the New Testament; that is, the life and mission of the early Church. Again, there is an element of mere truism: where else would anyone suppose these books to have had their origin? But it draws attention to their character as products of a specific community or set of communities making up the early Christian movement. At the very least we are surely right to suppose that none of them stems from the reflection of some isolated sage considering the meaning of Jesus from afar. This is not to say that they are necessarily to be seen as 'community products' – quite the contrary: we see more clearly than ever the coherence and power of many of the individual minds that produced these works. All the same, they are the minds of people deeply involved in particular (and very diverse) Christian groups, aware of their needs and subject to specific pressures of a local and transient kind.

Think for example of the prologue of the Gospel of John. Every reader is struck by the contrast between the sublimity of the greater part of John 1:1–18 and the seemingly intrusive fussiness of the references to John the Baptist (verses 6–8, 15). There are various ways of demonstrating that these verses are integral to the flow of the whole passage, but the initial impression lingers. Without these verses, one could well embark on this Gospel in the conviction that it was the product of detached contemplation of the significance of Jesus, far removed from the everyday life and concerns of any such thing as a Christian church. But the references to John the Baptist give pause to such a view. Whatever the reason – perhaps controversy over the role of John the Baptist in relation to Jesus, perhaps unclear relations between surviving followers of John the Baptist and the Christians involved in the writing of this Gospel – it seems that 'real life' impinges, even in this most reflective of the early Christian writings.

Similarly, the Letter to the Hebrews consists to a large degree of highly wrought and interwoven analogies between leading figures in the Hebrew Scriptures and Jesus, and there can be little doubt that the author revels in the working out of his patterns of fulfilment – he has an ingenious mind. Yet from time to time he turns aside from his intellectual pattern-weaving to utter moral exhortations that surely have specific situations in view (e.g. 5:11–6:12). The Revelation of John too, chiefly devoted to elaborate literary textures formed out of visionary material in the books of Ezekiel, Daniel and Zechariah (chiefly), comes right down to earth in the seven letters to the churches which come near the beginning (chapters 2–3) and whose situations seem to represent the actual occasion for the book. And in this perspective the writings which scored badly as significant testifiers to the centrality of Jesus come fully into view. Even if the Letter of James is not greatly concerned with Jesus, it is much concerned with the Christian mission and Christian community life, including the difficulty of uniting rich and poor and adopting a moral policy with regard to wealth. Looking at the matter in this way, we may even say that though of course the strong impulse of Jesus' life, death and resurrection was the main driving force in the Church's life, there were circles and occasions towards the end of the first century when the Church could function on its own momentum and deal with its own concerns without always turning to Jesus, either as living lord or as traditional teacher.

Neither of these possible centres of gravity in the New Testament (Jesus as saviour and the life of the Church) in fact applies exclusively to the writings which achieved canonical status. The other surviving early Christian writings (Staniforth and Louth 1968), some of which have been referred to, can be assessed under precisely the same headings. And if what we seek in a scriptural canon is the literary deposit of earliest Christianity, then the actual collection in the New Testament needs to be fortified by the works usually referred to as the Apostolic Fathers and the Gospel of Thomas.

If we ask why the twenty-seven books of the eventual New Testament attained a status denied to the others, there appear to be two likely answers, as suggested earlier: supposed authorship by or association with an apostle, and actual reception and use in sufficiently wide areas of the Church. It is now generally supposed that the beliefs of second- and third-century Christians (i.e. in the crucial formative period of the canon) about the former matter were mostly mistaken, just as their determination to father as many of their institutions as possible on immediate followers of Jesus led them into much legend-making.

It is likely that widespread use (itself partly dependent on believed apostolic source but also on usefulness) was perhaps the most powerful practical factor in determining the eventual bounds of the canonical collection. In that way, the life and mission of the Church as the unifying centre of the New Testament come into play in another way. However, it is important not to overstate the role of the Church in the sense that this suggests. It is not the case that only writings that were congenial or agreed with developed Christian ideas survived and uncomfortable documents were laid aside. Though they might strive to arrive at acceptable interpretations of them, Christians quite soon came to feel under the sway of their Scriptures. Not all Christians found the strenuous Gospel teaching about the renunciation of property and family particularly congenial, and in the settled circumstances of congregational life after the lifetime of Jesus, it was virtually unworkable. Nevertheless, Christian teachers set about finding ways of doing some justice to it, either easing it or applying it with uncomfortable rigour to the regulation of Christian marriage. They did not feel free simply to abandon books which said hard things.

It has already been hinted that something of this process was already at work in the period of the writing of the New Testament books themselves. Matthew's Gospel is, in part, an adoption yet, at the same time, an amending of the Gospel of Mark; and the Pastoral Epistles (1 and 2 Timothy and Titus) and Ephesians combine reverence for Paul with a readiness to adapt his teaching to changed circumstances.

OUTSTANDING PROBLEMS

The New Testament was formed as a collection of writings at a time when its sheer verbal content was uppermost in people's minds. Whatever the importance of apostolic authorship, real or supposed, and whatever the degree of a writing's usefulness for Christian devotion or guidance, it was the actual words that counted. So it has continued to be through most of Christian history. While academic interest in some questions of context and history has arisen from early times, the words have generally been viewed without reference to setting and background. The imagination has focused on the writing before the eyes rather than on the churches, human beings and situations that lay behind them. And of course the New Testament is still widely used in this way, with teaching and edification its chief purpose, and direct verbal authority the chief means to its attainment.

But the growth in the past two or three centuries of awareness of the historical context of the writings, that is, of what lies behind them, so that they are significant as windows opening on to early Christian life, produces some uncertainty about the scriptural canon. As we have seen, the more it is taken in this way, the more arbitrary and incomplete it seems as the way to achieve the end in view: other writings also offer us glimpses of the early Church in at any rate the later part of the period of the New Testament's origin. Whether it is often felt or not, the duality of perspective on these canonical writings creates a tension that deserves more attention, especially in the Church's use of them, where the two attitudes often sit uneasily side by side.

There are also unresolved matters with regard to the figure of Paul (Sanders 1985; 1991). In the preceding section, he was not put forward as a possible centre of gravity of the New Testament as a whole, but he might have been, without too much forcing of the evidence. For while, clearly, Paul saw himself as but the agent of Jesus for the furthering of the Gospel concerning him, it is a particular way of looking at Jesus that Pauls puts forward – and that way dominates the canonical collection as does that of no other figure, both in Paul's own writings and, with modifications, in those of Christians dependent on him and admiring of his work. Not only the undoubted writings but also the letters pseudonymously ascribed to him, signifying, in the practice of the time, the intention of continuing in his tradition, witness to his importance: from the earliest stage in the formation of a collection of Christian writings, these works, or most of them, formed its core. In addition, the writer of Luke–Acts was plainly a devotee of Paul, one who saw him as central in the Church's early expansion, and so perhaps (if certain similarities of thought are any guide) were the authors of the Gospel of Mark, of the First Epistle of Peter and even of the Gospel of John. In sheer bulk of writing, Paul dominates the New Testament, one way or another.

Recognizing that the Gospels present Jesus only indirectly, we may then say that Paul has left behind in the New Testament both more of a direct picture of his mind than did Jesus himself and testimony to a widespread influence. Undoubtedly the reason for this prominence of Paul is related to the removal of Palestine from centrality in early Christianity after the fall of Jerusalem in 70 CE and the consequent shift of weight to the churches of Asia Minor, Greece and Rome, precisely the sphere of Paul's activity and import-ance. It is thus probable that he loomed larger in the period following his death than he did in his lifetime. It may also be that in his lifetime he was less prominent than he now appears in relation to other early Christian missionaries and leaders, and perhaps atypical in his style of thought and presentation of Christian belief. The very fact that he often argues against formidable opposition, admittedly much of it relating to the Jewish Christ-ianity prominent in the first decades, suggests that he was, at that stage, less of a mainstream Christian thinker than he subsequently came to appear.

If Paul himself is, in these ways, something of an enigma within the New Testament, so is the issue with which many of his struggles and indeed his whole Christian identity were concerned: the relation between Christian faith and Judaism from which it derived. In the books of the New Testament we can see examples of almost every possible relationship between the two: Christianity within Judaism (but could it still qualify?) but open to non-Jews on the basis of adherence to Jesus as God's universal agent and with the letting go of the necessity for basic Jewish observances and marks of identity – as in Paul; Christianity as the continuator and fulfilment of Judaism, which remained in certain ways essential in its heritage – as in Luke–Acts; Christianity as retaining Jewish observance, it seems, but with the Jews' rejection of Jesus as the great apostasy – as in Matthew. With this variety, the matter is not resolved within the New Testament – and it is arguable that it has never yet been resolved. Does Jesus represent, theologically, a brand-new start, with Judaism no more than the factual historical antecedent (as Marcion's doctrine was to suggest), or is he the (even a) crown of a deep-laid redemptive process, or else one important development among a number of such processes to be experienced in the religions of the human race? While it scarcely considers (at least in anything like the modern way) the last of these possibilities, the New Testament contains examples of the other tendencies, and, for those wishing to use it in this way, can be held to authorize a variety of policies towards Christianity's own mission and its relations with Judaism and with other faiths.

Finally, the elusiveness of Jesus, who comes before us vividly but only through the testimony of those who write about him, so expressing their response to him in their distinctive ways, seems strangely juxtaposed with his utter pervasiveness in most of the New Testament books. The Gospels in particular force the question – how important is historical knowledge about Jesus? And if important, how possible, given the distance of time and the indirectness of these writings in relation to him? Once more, we swing between seeing Christianity as continually and essentially marked by Jesus and recognizing that, with the partial obscurity of Jesus and the continuing flux of interpretation of him, the life of the Church and, now partially independent of the Church, the work of scholarship have their own independence, and even self-sufficiency. Yet the enigmatic quality of Jesus may be seen as the essential condition of his continuing and fertile influence, whether through the New Testament or through other channels.

In more positive vein, it is possible to see the New Testament canon as representing in early, perhaps pristine form a picture of the gamut of legitimate faithful human responses to God's initiative through Jesus; a picture too of the range of styles of Christian thought and devotion in relation to a number of vital matters, not least the place of Jesus in the whole history of human relations with God, but also the relationship of morals with faith, the balance of this- and other-worldliness, and the proper understanding of our relation with the material order. On these and other matters, it is possible to see the canon representing both a general unity and a range of tendencies which may prove suggestive and fruitful both inside and outside the tradition of which the New Testament is one of the earliest tangible expressions.

REFERENCES

Ashton, J. (1991) *Understanding the Fourth Gospel*, Oxford: Clarendon Press.

Aune, D. E. (1987) *The New Testament in its Literary Environment*, Cambridge: James Clarke.

Dunn, J. D. G. (1977) *Unity and Diversity in the New Testament*, London: SCM Press.

Hooker, M. D. (1983) *The Message of Mark*, London: Epworth Press.

Houlden, J. L. (1987) *Backward into Light*, London: SCM Press.

Kee, H. C. (1980) *Christian Origins in Sociological Perspective*, London: SCM Press.

Lindars, B. (1961) *New Testament Apologetic*, London: SCM Press.

Meier, J. P. (1991) *A Marginal Jew*, London and New York: Doubleday.

Metzger, B. M. (1987) *The Canon of the New Testament*, Oxford: Clarendon Press.

Moore, S. D. (1989) *Literary Criticism and the Gospels*, New Haven and London: Yale University Press.

Morgan, R. and Barton, J. (1988) *Biblical Interpretation*, Oxford: Oxford University Press.

Perrin, N. (1970) *What is Redaction Criticism?*, Philadelphia: Fortress Press.

Rowland, C. (1982) *The Open Heaven*, London: SPCK.

Sanders, E. P. (1985) *Paul, the Law and the Jewish People*, Philadelphia: Fortress Press.

—— (1991) *Paul*, Oxford: Oxford University Press.

—— and Davies, M. (1989) *Studying the Synoptic Gospels*, London: SCM Press.

Staniforth, M. and Louth, A. (eds) (1968) *Early Christian Writings*, Harmondsworth: Penguin Books.

Stanton, G. N. (1989) *The Gospels and Jesus*, Oxford: Oxford University Press.

—— (1992) *A Gospel for a New People: Studies in Matthew*, Edinburgh: T. & T. Clark.

Stowers, S. K. (1986) *Letter Writing in Greco-Roman Antiquity*, Philadelphia: Westminster Press.

Talbert, C. H. (1990) *Reading Luke*, London: SPCK.

Tuckett, C. (1987) *Reading the New Testament: Methods of Interpretation*, London: SPCK.

FURTHER READING

Ackroyd, P. R. and Evans, C. F. (eds) (1970) *The Cambridge History of the Bible*, vol. I, chapters 9–12, Cambridge: Cambridge University Press.

Barton, J. (1988) *People of the Book?*, London: SPCK.

Burridge, R. A. (1994) *Four Gospels, One Jesus?*, London: SPCK.

Carroll, R. P. (1991) *Wolf in the Sheepfold: The Bible as a Problem for Christianity*, London: SPCK.

Evans, C. F. (1971) *Is 'Holy Scripture' Christian?*, London: SCM Press.

Houlden, J. L. (1991) *Bible and Belief*, London: SPCK.

Neill, S. and Wright, T. (1988) *The Interpretation of the New Testament, 1861–1986*, Oxford: Oxford University Press.

See also chapters 6, 7, 8, 9, 41, 43.

6

THE NEW TESTAMENT: THE TRADITION OF INTERPRETATION

John Muddiman

Traditional interpretation of the New Testament is discussed in this chapter in both its loose and its strict senses. Loosely, it refers to interpretations which precede the rise of biblical criticism in the eighteenth century or which thereafter, reject or continue in blissful ignorance of it. Strictly, it is interpretation according to tradition, that is, according to the system of belief and practice of the Christian religion handed on within living communities. Even when, as at the Reformation, a contrast was drawn between the teaching of the New Testament and contemporary ecclesiastical tradition, the use of Scripture remained traditional in this latter sense. It is only in the modern period that attempts have been made to interpret the New Testament in a purely historical way, without regard for, or even in conscious opposition to, the beliefs and practices of the communities that claim it as their title deeds.

The precise character of the 'shift to modernity' at the Enlightenment is itself a subject of intense research and debate. It is, for instance, possible to describe it as a move from fragmentation to synthesis, from the New Testament as a repository of proof texts to the New Testament as documentary evidence for historical reconstruction. But the method of extracting proofs from authoritative text did not exist in isolation, either in Medieval Scholasticism or Protestant neo-Scholasticism; it was always accompanied by other types of reading that emphasized context and integration. The two types of Jewish exegesis, *halakah* and *haggadah* (see Chapter 2) function in this way, and they have had their counterparts in Christian exegesis; in medieval terms, for instance, *sacra pagina* (Scripture studied in the Schools) and *lectio divina* (devotional reading). Doctrinal, often figurative, interpretations of individual texts were underpinned by a single, integrating biblical narrative, the history of salvation from Creation to the Second Coming. Thus, it is equally possible to characterize the advent of modern biblical criticism (with Hans Frei 1974) as the exact opposite, a movement from synthesis to disintegration, dividing up the text into its component elements and treating it as the residue of contingent history, with no necessary relation to the timeless truths of reason.

It is not our present concern to describe the causes of the transition from traditional to modern interpretation, or evaluate them. But one result did emerge clearly from the change. The study of the New Testament was displaced from its former, central place in Christian theology and was seen to provide at best only historical prolegomena, and, at worst, a sharp historical criterion which threw into question the legitimacy of all subsequent developments. Historical–critical study drove a wedge between the original meaning of the New Testament and the uses and abuses it had suffered at the hands of the Church. With the truth of the foundational, literal scheme of salvation history under critical attack, the allegorical interpretations, constructed upon it, stood out even more blatantly as arbitrary and absurd. New Testament scholarship, in Germany first and then elsewhere, broke with its own past and started over again, with a narrower focus on the texts themselves, their dates, authenticity, inter-relationships and pre-literary sources, as evidence for the life of the historical Jesus and the beliefs of his first followers. Like revolutionaries in other spheres, critical New Testament scholars became obsessed with the story of their own recent liberation, and were glad to pass the study of traditional, now discredited, interpretation over to others, patristic and medieval historians, systematic theologians and sociologists of religion.

However, recent changes in New Testament study are beginning to modify the account New Testament scholars give of their own discipline, and to re-establish certain points of continuity with the aims and methods of traditional interpretation. In the following sections I shall first describe some of the distinctive characteristics of traditional interpretation; then, I shall review some of the ways in which it typically distorts the meaning of the text; and lastly, I shall attempt to assess the reasons for, and possible hazards in any move back towards the traditional use of the New Testament.

FOUR DISTINCTIVE FEATURES

The history of biblical interpretation is a massive subject; even when the scope of the enquiry is limited to its inner developments and major contributors, it fills three great volumes of *The Cambridge History of the Bible* (Greenslade 1963; Lampe 1969; Ackroyd and Evans 1970). The following discussion selects four distinctive features, which may be said to characterize traditional interpretation as a whole, though they will be described in relation to particular periods in order to offset the impression of gross generalization.

Second-century interpretation

In pre-modern exegesis, doctrine and ethics appear to be deduced straight from the text, and prescribed for the reader's assent and action. By contrast, critical interpretation typically affects a tone of neutral description. In both cases, what is actually going on is much more subtle and complex.

It was by no means clear, during the course of the second century, that the documents we know as the New Testament would emerge as Christian Scripture. The early Fathers afforded higher authority to apostolic testimony passed on in the Church. Papias, quoted by Eusebius (*Eccl. Hist.* 3.39.4) 'considered that what was in books would not benefit me so much as what came from the living and continuing voice'. And this view had the added advantage of avoiding arguments over words with contentious Jewish Christians: hence the statement of Ignatius of Antioch (*Phil.* 8.2) that the true 'archives' for a Christian are not books, but the person and work of Christ and the faith that came through him. Practice reflects this principle. Clement of Rome (47.1) and Ignatius (*Eph.* 12.2) refer explicitly to Paul's epistles, but more because of his status as apostle to the Gentiles and as their own predecessor in letter-writing, than for anything particularly striking that he said. Allusions to the Gospels in the Apostolic Fathers are even less frequent and exact; the material is often freely rearranged (as at *Didache* 1:3–4; cf. Matt. 5:44, 46, 47, 39, 48, 40, 41); or even corrected and counterbalanced (as at *Didache* 1:6; cf. Matt. 6:3) in a way that strongly suggests the use of continuing oral tradition rather than consultation of the text. Neither the popular style nor the genres of the New Testament documents ('memoirs' of the life of Jesus or ephemeral letters from the first generation missionaries) naturally commended them for canonization as Scripture.

For the earliest Church, then, Scripture was not the New Testament but the Greek Old Testament, treated as divine prophecy of the coming of Christ, who died and rose again 'according to the Scriptures' (1 Cor. 15:3f.); the Prophets and the Law prophesied until John the Baptist (Matt. 11:13) but now a totally new, non-scriptural reality, the immediate advent of the Kingdom of God, takes their place. 'In the past, God had spoken in many and varied ways through the Prophets, but in these last days he has spoken to us in his Son' (Heb. 1:1–2).

The conflict between Christianity and the Judaism of Pharisaic scribes over the Law provided another reason for the subordination of the 'letter that kills' to 'the Spirit that gives life' (2 Cor. 3:6). In order to resist the demand for the circumcision of Gentiles, Paul attempted to reinterpret that commandment as fulfilled spiritually in the heart of the believer (Rom. 2:29) or allegorically in the crucifixion of Christ (Col. 2:11), but in the end he was also obliged to oppose the plain sense of Scripture by relegating the law of circumcision to a now superseded period of salvation-history (Gal. 3:24).

Other social factors may also have played a part. For instance, Christian congregations were less well organized than the synagogue to equip their members with the basics of literacy. And above all, the bookish learning of the educated elite ran the risk of dangerous, deviant opinion. Marcion doctored the Gospel of Luke and the letters of Paul to produce a coherent anti-Jewish substitute for the Old Testament which would serve him as 'Scripture'. The gnostic Gospel of Thomas makes salvation depend on the 'correct' interpretation of sayings of Jesus, ignoring altogether his death and resurrection. And Heracleon, a follower of the Gnostic Valentinus, produced the first New Testament commentary (on the Fourth Gospel). Thus, canon, interpretation, commentary – the apparatus of biblical scholarship – were the innovations of heretics. To combat them, the Church was faced with a stark choice, either populist anti-intellectualism (which some would have preferred) or to use the deviants' own methods against them.

From this strange sequence of events one enduring principle of traditional interpretation emerged, articulated most clearly by Irenaeus, namely that the text of the New Testament is not as such the final authority, until it is interpreted correctly according to the Rule of Faith or Rule of Truth, that is, the teaching of the apostles faithfully preserved in the Church (e.g. *Against Heresies* 4, 33, 8). The very notion of the New Testament as Scripture, though clearly established by the end of the second century, when it is quoted on a par with the Old, nevertheless retains this ambiguity, for the ultimate revelation of God is not mediated by mere words or text; it is direct and immediate, the Word of God incarnate in Christ.

It would be wrong to restrict or objectify the notion of a Rule of Faith. It is not a 'canon outside the canon', the Church's creeds and conciliar definitions imposed upon the text; nor a reduced essence, a 'canon within the canon' like justification by faith, or the love of God and neighbour. It is the whole revelation, transcendent yet immanent, faithfully transmitted through, and behind and along with the apostolic writings.

Alexandrian and Antiochene interpretation

Patristic use of typology and allegory in interpreting the Old Testament is described elsewhere in this volume. It was a neat way of coping with apparent factual and moral difficulties in texts deemed to have authority, and even more of reading the whole Old Testament in a consistently Christian manner. The range of actual quotations from the Old Testament used by the New Testament writers is surprisingly limited and hardly sufficient to justify the immense effort of copying and disseminating the Jewish Scriptures in the Church, and explaining their obscurities. In order to make this worthwhile, the Christian relevance of all of it had somehow to be demonstrated, and this was the task which the exegetical school at Alexandria set itself, with Origen as its commanding genius.

Naturally these methods of Old Testament interpretation came to influence the treatment of the New Testament. First, allegory was available to clear up oddities and conflicts, such as the date of the Cleansing of the Temple in John, or Matthew's account of the Triumphal Entry, where Jesus rides on two donkeys; these were explained as signs and pointers to deeper truths – the 'Temple' in John 2 is the sanctuary of the human intellect needing to be cleansed from philosophical arrogance; and in Matthew 21, Jesus as the Word of God is carried into Jerusalem by the two Testaments (Lindars, in Rogerson *et al.* 1988: 265). Origen did not doubt the literal, historical occurrence of either incident, of course; that was established sufficiently by the other versions in the Gospels. But his method enables him to retain as deeply significant even minor variations in wording and order which his perceptive eye had noticed. And he is not just wriggling out of the problems by any means however arbitrary. The general drift of his comments is often extraordinarily apposite as here: that John's Gospel is the purification of reason by faith; and that Matthew's intention was to get Jesus to Jerusalem on the back of Scripture.

Sometimes Origen adopts a different tactic: he supposes for example that the variation in the words of John the Baptist about 'carrying' (Matt. 3:11) or 'untying' (the Mark, John and Luke parallels) the sandals of the One to come, show that they were spoken on two different occasions – sayings bear repetition, after all, but dramatic actions would lose their impact if repeated. But then he proceeds to allegorize both versions, since Origen had had no more success than modern commentators in tracking down precise parallels for these metaphors for humble service (Wiles in Ackroyd and Evans 1970: 471, 479).

Second, and more important than such details is the use of the 'more than literal' sense to defend the unity and orthodoxy of Scripture. The New Testament as well as the Old Testament was involved here, because of the interpretations of the Gnostics. They took up with enthusiasm Jesus' injunction that the allegory of the sower was to be the model for understanding all the parables (Mark 4:13), and it is their heterodox interpretations that set the agenda for refutation by the Church Fathers. So, for instance, the astonishing treatment of the parable of the Good Samaritan, from Irenaeus through Origen to Augustine, in which the whole creed and half the catechism are squeezed into its innocent details is an answer to the very different understanding of the Fall, christology, the Church and morality proposed on the same textual basis by the Gnostics (Hanson in Ackroyd and Evans 1970: 416ff.). To appeal instead to a common sense and the simple moral lesson of the story was probably not a real option in the circumstances of the time.

Third, the deeper meanings of Scripture correspond to the way the Bible was being used for spiritual nurture. Most of Origen's exegetical works were delivered, we should remember, as homilies for the edification of the faithful, and this also sets a peculiar agenda, in relation to progress in the Christian life. A parallel is thus drawn between the human person, made up of body, soul and spirit, and the threefold meanings of Scripture, literal, moral and spiritual. In any passage he is on the look-out, like any preacher, for lessons to be drawn for ethics and spirituality.

Origen had immense influence, before his belated posthumous condemnation in the mid-sixth century, even more in the West, through Augustine, than in the East. But his fanciful speculations also provoked opposition, particularly in Antioch – a rival centre of biblical learning in the third century, which flowered in the work of John Chrysostom and Theodore of Mopsuestia in the fourth. The Antiochenes were in close touch with Jewish scholarship and were able to offer satisfactory explanations of the literal sense of many passages which the Alexandrians could only understand allegorically. At the same time, they were determined to refute Jewish opponents on their own terms and find in the Old Testament prophecies of the Messiah which could be shown to be intended by their authors and not just hidden by some special divine inspiration unbeknown to them. The moderate, dissenting voice of Antiochene interpretation, with its genuine feel for the historical distance of the text, fell under suspicion of heresy in the aftermath of the Arian controversy. In particular, its realistic exegesis of the human life of Jesus was open to the charge, however unjustly, of Nestorianism. The Alexandrian and Antiochene approaches, despite the rhetoric of mutual condemnation, are not incompatible; for it is possible to focus at one level on the conscious intention of the author and yet at another to acknowledge that these same texts, when reapplied in Christian contemplation and worship and interpreted together in a unifying way, can take on new and deeper meanings.

Medieval interpretation

After the christological debates of the fourth and fifth centuries, the East adopted a more settled stance on biblical interpretation, repeating and amplifying the commentaries of the orthodox fathers. In the West also the patristic legacy was preserved through the writings of Augustine and the clarifications of exegetical method promoted by Pope Gregory the Great in the sixth century, in particular the theory of the four senses of Scripture: the literal relating to history; the allegorical to doctrine; the tropological to moral duty; and the anagogical to future hope. With the help of this scheme, the Latin Church classified and preserved the views of earlier writers in the form of a systematic cumulative commentary, the Gloss, similar to and no doubt influenced by contemporary elaboration of the Code of Roman civil law. The intention was to provide for the training of the clergy in cathedral schools, and later in the universities. In class, quotations from the Bible were presented in topics or 'questions' to which answers, 'sentences', would be provided by the lecturer and carefully copied by the student, which is still the standard form of lecturing in higher education. The Medieval Schools are often accused of creating a separation between biblical exegesis and theology (e.g. Grant 1965: 92; Smalley in Lampe 1969: 198f.) with disastrous consequences for both: biblical texts were handled without regard for context and revealed theology was reduced to a series of intellectual propositions. But the charge is somewhat unsympathetic (see Evans 1984), for analytical, even mechanical procedures are a necessary stage in the process of learning. Furthermore, the Schoolmen saw the danger themselves; Hugh of St Victor in the twelfth century, for example, set out to hold analysis and synthesis, text and context together.

The medieval period also saw the re-affirmation of the priority of the literal sense, and imposed restraint on the excesses of allegorism, especially through the work of Albert the Great and Thomas Aquinas. The literal (i.e. intended, including metaphorical) sense was alone admissible in theological debate. But there were also problems caused by literalism, when it became a weapon to attack the Church, from St Francis to Joachim of Fiore.

The one feature that runs through medieval interpretation, in all its varied forms, is the central place of the Bible in society; its truth is public truth, a matter of serious concern and strenuous debate, whether the topic is the poverty of Christ or the powers of the papacy. It is symbolized in the great cathedrals and abbeys, which could be described as visual commentaries on the Bible. In illustration of this point, we refer to the work of John Wycliffe, who pioneered English biblical translation in the fourteenth century. For all his concern to give the people direct access to the source of salvation in Scripture, free from the corruption and tyranny of the contemporary Church, Wycliffe did not retreat into pious individualism, but attempted to mobilize popular support for a programme of public reform, as his other largely political writings make clear. Barnabas Lindars writes: 'Wycliffe saw the New Testament as the revelation of God's Law. He took the idea of the Kingdom of God quite literally, and wanted to see all secular rulers model their statecraft on the Gospel' (Lindars, in Rogerson 1988: 291).

Reformation interpretation

In several respects, the interpretation of the New Testament in the sixteenth century Reformation anticipates modern critical study: its appeal to the original Greek, its search for ancient manuscripts, its sense of the distance of the past, its emphasis on authorial intention, its eye to the plausible in explaining textual problems and so forth. The Reformers confidently disposed of the great accumulation of medieval glosses and commentaries and enjoyed a sudden feeling of intellectual freedom.

It may seem doubly ironic, then, to include Reformation exegesis in a chapter on traditional interpretation since the Reformers opposed Scripture to tradition and argued from Scripture alone. But the tradition that they rejected was, as it were, recent tradition, including the claim of the Pope to be the ultimate arbiter of interpretation. Luther and Calvin regularly quote from selected earlier commentators, like Augustine and Bernard; and they share the patristic focus on christology and Trinity. They were very aware of the problem, exemplified in the radical wing of the movement, that no consensus, and therefore no real reform, was possible, if every individual Christian simply interpreted the text according to his own views. Some control was necessary and this was provided by the notion of the clarity, or perspicuity of Scripture. Scripture has clarity in two senses, according to Luther: it has a clear, verbal meaning discerned by philology and scholarship; and it has a clear, basic message: all the sacred books 'preach Christ', which for Luther means free grace and justifying faith. Calvin's answer to the problem of ensuring that religious freedom did not lapse into public anarchy was very similar. He wrote commentaries on all the books of the New Testament, attempting to provide the plain, grammatical sense of the authors' original intention. And Calvin also appeals to a hermeneutical principle to bring clarity to the text, namely the internal testimony of the Holy Spirit.

The Reformers' emphasis on brevity, simplicity and clarity reflects no doubt the recovery of these aesthetic ideals from classical antiquity; but, more importantly, it answers a religious need, which is a constantly recurring motif in traditional interpretation, to find consistency and a basic unity in Scripture. Just as vernacular translations came off the printing presses in the sixteenth century to be placed in the hands of ordinary people, so also the Gospel itself had to be made religiously accessible; the profound mystery of God and the complexities of biblical science had to be counterbalanced by a simple living truth that could grasp the heart and move the will.

A detailed history of the development of New Testament exegesis up to the eighteenth century would have revealed many discontinuities and a confusion of disputes and new directions. For example, emphasis on the literal or allegorical senses appears to come in a pattern of alternating waves through the history of New Testament interpretation. But if one stands far enough back from the detail, points of family resemblance in what we are calling traditional interpretation do appear, which come to the surface at particular periods but are latent throughout. Among them are the four to which we have drawn particular attention.

First, the rule of faith as guide to correct interpretation – the principle that the ultimate revelation of God is not textual but historical, the person and work of Jesus Christ and the apostolic testimony to him. This is not to say that the meaning of the New Testament is determined by the imposition of an external standard of apostolicity, for the New Testament is itself, after the end of the second century, the sole source of knowledge of apostolic teaching. It is rather that the interpreter approaches the text and copes with any gaps or apparent contradictions on the assumptions of its unity and coherence. Implicit in these assumptions are the notions of its finality and maturity. The New Testament is not evidence for some kind of 'primitive Christianity' at the beginning of a long history of evolution; it is the witness to 'pristine Christianity'; when interpreted according to faith, it contains a full and normative form of Christian doctrine.

Second and correlatively, the New Testament no less than the Old is an inspired book. The Holy Spirit who spoke through the prophets did not leave the apostles and evangelists to rely on their own unaided human faculties in recording the significance of Christ; he invested their words with a certain kind of deeper meaning. Preservation from historical or scientific error was not the main issue here; indeed, the occasional slip of that kind might be a deliberate ploy to alert the attentive reader to the deeper meaning. Rather, the activity of the Spirit in producing by means of the text repentance and faith, understanding, love and hope is the presupposition on which it is prescribed for solemn reading in the liturgy, expounded in sermons and pored over minutely in private devotion and study. Even those who most vigorously rejected the allegorical method, like the Antiochenes, St Thomas and the Reformers, did not contemplate the rejection of the spiritual sense, so defined.

Third, the New Testament rightly belongs in the domain of public truth. Its influence is to be felt and its teaching applied in every sphere of life. Its authority does not depend on the acceptance of it by any individual; it is a given. In a Christian society, most obviously the medieval West but equally the Byzantine Empire or Calvin's Geneva or Philip II's Spain, all its leaders, clerical and lay, were expected to take it into account. The breadth of traditional interpretation is apparent here. Its use in public debate makes it a contemporary authority, relevant to the present and not just a record of the past.

Finally, and again in correlation to the preceding point, the teaching of the New Testament is not just for the learned and powerful, but for the common people, and as such its basic message must be fundamentally simple and of universal application. The Reformers were not introducing a novel idea in their emphasis on the clarity of Scripture; it is a factor that keeps coming to the surface through the history of interpretation, cutting through the complexities and subtleties of exegetes, and assented to in principle even by the most eruditie.

These characteristics, the normativeness, inspiration, public relevance and basic simplicity of the New Testament are as typical of traditional interpretation as they are untypical, in each case, of modern critical interpretation.

DISTORTIONS IN TRADITIONAL INTERPRETATION

For all that may be said in defence of traditional interpretation, its distortions of the New Testament must also be frankly acknowledged.

The title of the New Testament

We might begin with the very title of the collection, known from the time of Tertullian onwards as the New Covenant (Latin *Testamentum*). Like the word Gospel, it had evolved from reference to the reality of salvation in Christ to the form of its written representation. The basis for such a title is decidedly thin in the New Testament itself. Apart from some versions of the words of Jesus at the Last Supper, it does not figure in the Gospels at all. Paul occasionally exploits the two senses of the word, covenant, as God's contract with Israel and as last will and testament, to show the theological necessity for the death of Christ. It appears in Hebrews as part of the author's demonstration that the Old Testament itself points forward to its fulfilment in Christ (Heb. 9:15). In general, it has the sense of God's original covenant, now renewed, as Jeremiah prophesied (Jer. 31:31). In later Christian usage, however, the emphasis falls on the newness rather than the renewal, the beginning of a new religion, rather than the consummation of the faith of Israel. The title of a book is an important factor in the interpretation of its contents, and the title of this book tends to support the traditional assumption of a radical divide between two competing religions.

Genres

By the end of the second century, as we have seen, the New Testament had become the chief source book for Christian doctrine, but the varied character of its contents does not naturally equip it for that function and leads to distortions. That there are four Gospels, despite Paul's assertion that there could only ever be one Gospel (Gal. 1:6) already constitutes a difficulty. Marcion selected and expurgated Luke's Gospel. Tatian ran them all together into a composite narrative, the *Diatessaron*. Gnostic sects took their cue from the plurality, and composed even more of their own. Irenaeus defended the traditional four by, among other arguments, finding the evangelists in disguise as the four beasts around the throne of God in the book of Revelation (Rev. 4:6–8). There was some hesitation about which beast represented which evangelist, but they made a complete set, perfectly complementary with each other; they were full of insight (with eyes inside and out) and, suspended in mid-heaven, contemplated only the worship of God. But the Gospels are generically more varied than this theory suggests. Matthew was probably a revised and expanded version of Mark which was intended to replace its predecessor. Luke's Gospel is only one half of a two-volume work, Luke–Acts. John prefaces his narrative of the Passion with a selection of signs and discourses that may not have been intended or received by its first audience simply as historical reportage. John may therefore lend itself more to doctrinal and devotional reading, as Clement of Alexandria recognized when he dubbed it 'the spiritual Gospel'. But the Synoptics are more biographical in form, narratives interspersed with wisdom and apocalyptic teaching; and this genre is not particularly conducive to doctrinal construction. They are unified by the narrative flow, not by theological consistency. And it is very difficult to extract theory from narrative without severely injuring it. In any case, several different theories can be deduced from the same story: for example, the various episodes in the Passion, the parable of the wicked tenants, the words at the Last Supper, the prayer in Gethsemane and the cry of Dereliction each invite very different understandings of the Atonement. Traditional interpretation, by contrast, has ignored differences, and worked on the principle that

111

the Gospels are all the same kind of thing and their contents all doctrinally homogeneous.

The epistles of Paul and others and the account of the early missionary preaching in Acts are in some ways easier to use for the purposes of Christian doctrine, since they address theological and moral issues explicitly. But in another sense they are even more problematic since they include material highly specific to particular situations, and are less generalized than the Gospels.

Marginal interests

There are several ideas which are marginal or unrepresentative in the New Testament, which become central or even controlling features of later Christian doctrine. Some cannot be found at all except by reading them into the text. Many of these became topics of heated controversy at the Reformation such as prayers for the dead and the doctrine of Purgatory, or Mariology and the cult of the saints. But it is open to question whether accretions like these are necessarily distortions. The impression of fairness and generosity in the New Testament picture of divine Judgement might be argued as justifying the former; and its distinct interest (rare among Jewish writings of the first century) in contemporary heroic personalities (see the Acts of the Apostles) lays the ground for the latter. More central to the edifice of Christian doctrine, however, is something like the doctrine of Original Sin. It is well known that the New Testament basis for the Augustinian doctrine is meagre, namely Romans 5:12 in the Vulgate translation, and a great deal even then has to be assumed. One might have expected the Reformers to point this out, but they were not prepared to discard the Western account of the human plight on which the call to repentance and the offer of forgiveness rested. The Fall of Adam sets the whole stage for the redemption wrought by Christ. It is less often acknowledged that the Fall story itself is marginal in the New Testament, even in the letters of Paul. Apart from Romans 5, the New Testament ignores it and prefers the view current in first-century Judaism that there is not one single catastrophic event which brought about the corrupt state of the human race, but a cumulative history of moral decline, exacerbated by malign demonic forces. It was the fall of the 'sons of God', the rebellious angels of Genesis 6, producing hordes of unclean spirits, that was the really crucial event for soteriology.

Central omissions

Conversely, there are some points of doctrine deeply rooted in the New Testament, which are muted or neglected in orthodox doctrine. To take the most obvious example, the Synoptic Gospels' teaching of Jesus on the kingdom is not even mentioned in the second paragraph of the Creed. One might reply that its content, the Fatherhood and Sovereignty of God have simply been transferred to the first paragraph, but to move straight from the virginal conception to the crucifixion is a distortion of the Gospel narratives. Of course, the parables and sayings of Jesus have been immensely influential in spiritual reading and in moral preaching on the Gospels, but their impact on doctrine has been slight, because they seem out of tune with classical christology.

Other neglected features, like the emphasis in the New Testament on evil spirits, the gifts of miracles and speaking in tongues, and imminent expectation of the End fail to find a place or are sidelined in constructive theologies, only then to be 'rediscovered' and made central by radical dissenting groups. In each of these cases the problem arises, at least in part, from the ambiguity of the New Testament itself. For example, the voluntarist analysis of sin as deliberate disobedience is accompanied by a determinist element in which sin is a demonic force beyond human control or responsibility. Both of these are found, alongside each other, in the Jesus tradition and in Paul. Similarly, miracles are both used to prove the messiahship of Jesus and denied any probative value; speaking in tongues is commended and also relativized by Paul. Hope for the imminent coming of the Son of Man is counterbalanced by the injunction to patient agnosticism about the timing of its arrival, and the assertion of the presence already of the powers of the Age to Come. The imperious demand for logic and consistency in doctrine has made traditional interpretation unwilling, by and large, to admit the possibility that truth may sometimes be expressed in the form of a dialectic.

Polemics

One of the causes of internal Christian division down the centuries has probably been the New Testament itself. I do not mean this in the sense propounded by some modern critics that the New Testament contains a variety of conflicting views. For traditional interpretation has been blind to such differences, possibly justifiably. The extent of the conflicts may well have been exaggerated by modern criticism: the New Testament is theologically much more 'compact' and unanimous than, say, the Old Testament. But the New Testament is a collection of highly polemical writings. In almost every book, warnings about deviants within the community are issued. Christians are put on the alert for 'false apostles', 'antichrists', 'grievous wolves' and so forth. Even the attacks on 'the Jews' and 'the scribes and Pharisees' are taken, on the principle of the continuing relevance of Scripture, to be symbolic for later heretics, contaminated by Jewish unbelief. The atmosphere of suspicion and inquisition thus engendered has had a lasting effect, and dramatically raised the stakes in later theological controversies in the Church.

Traditional interpretation, nevertheless, regularly fails to draw the appropriate conclusion from the polemical side to the New Testament, namely that its doctrine may sometimes be intended as the correction of an alternative, rather than the balanced statement of the case, and that other less polemical ways of making the point should be given preference. The interpretation of Galatians and Romans is one illustration of this. Paul's exaggerated attacks on the Law, bringing only condemnation, a curse, death and provocation to sinful desire, should not have been taken as calm statements of the Christian position and allowed to override the rest of the New Testament. The effect of this has been to make opposition to Jewish legalism, so-called, practically constitutive of Christian orthodoxy and to plant the theoretical seed for centuries of Christian anti-Semitism in Europe.

Mistranslation

Traditional interpretation has often inadvertently mistranslated the New Testament, not only in the medieval West by using the Latin as its starting point, but even when it has turned back to the original Greek. For translation is not simply a matter of language but also of cultural presuppositions and context. Out of a vast array of possibilities, two examples may suffice. The whole debate about the doctrine of grace, whether conducted in Greek or in Latin, could be said to be built on such a mistranslation. For grace in the New Testament (*charis, gratia*) takes its sense from the Jewish tradition; it is the elective favour of God, essentially corporate and historical. It has little or nothing to do with individual conversion or sanctification, with 'means of grace' or divine assistance for the frailty of the human will. When and if such ideas appear, they are denoted by 'the Holy Spirit poured into the heart', which is spoken of far more frequently in the New Testament in this way than as a separate person of the Godhead.

To take a more precise example. At Ephesians 5:32 the author comments on the 'two shall become one flesh' of Genesis 2:24 as follows 'This is a great mystery (Latin *sacramentum*) and I take it to mean Christ and the Church, but let husbands love their wives.' This text is the main basis for the doctrine of the sacramentality of marriage, a doctrine with wide-ranging implications. If marriage is a sacrament, then it comes under direct hierarchical control like other sacraments, i.e. under canon, not civil, law; and its significance is promoted above all practical considerations, despite the very practical tone of the New Testament on the subject, this passage included. Furthermore, the sacramentality of marriage and the sacramentality of holy orders are treated as parallel and mutually exclusive; one either marries a wife, or becomes a priest (or a nun) and marries the Church. The Reformers rejected clerical celibacy and the sacramentality of marriage; and took the 'mystery' in this text to refer to the Church as the bride of Christ, indeed, to the pure, reformed and invisible Church in opposition to the corrupt, sacerdotal, visible institution. Both interpretations are probably based on mistranslations; the 'great puzzle' is neither marriage nor the Church but the text of Genesis!

Trinity and christology

We have left until last the two issues that most preoccupy traditional interpretation, in Patristic, Scholastic and Reformation periods alike, namely Trinity
and christology, that God is three persons in one substance and that Christ
has two natures, the human and the divine. Traditional interpreters were well
aware that the varied terminology in which they discussed these issues was
not drawn from Scripture itself but from philosophy and law, but they believed
that this was necessary to contradict heresy and safeguard the truth of the
doctrine implied less formally in the New Testament. That is not an unreasonable defence. But to summarize the doctrine of the New Testament as consisting principally in belief in the threefold Godhead and the divinity of Christ
is a distortion of emphasis. Triadic formulae do occur in the New Testament,
such as the Great Commission of Matthew 28:19 or the doxology of 2
Corinthians 13:14. And it is possible to claim that this is but the tip of an
iceberg, and that the Gospel and epistle writers would not have dissented
from the doctrine. But while the Fathers were concerned to defend the idea
of three and only three divine persons, the New Testament writers were more
concerned, against Jewish emphasis on the singularity of God, to establish
the 'plurifocal' divine activity. Thus, binitarian formulae, as in the opening
greetings of most New Testament letters, are much more common and achieve
this end equally well. The book of Revelation speaks of the One on the
Throne and of the Lamb but adds the seven spirits of God and the Bride,
the Heavenly Jerusalem to its pantheon. Mark 13:32 refers to the Father, the
Son and the angels in similar vein. Furthermore, while the Fathers, especially
the Cappadocians and Augustine, dwelt on the 'substantive Trinity' – God in
himself in the communion between the three persons – the emphasis in the
New Testament, and the Bible generally, is on the 'economy' of God,
the diverse forms of the divine activity in Creation and Salvation. When the
hieroglyph of the Trinity replaces the vivid sense of a loving, forgiving
personal God, as it does in classical doctrine, if not in Christian spirituality,
it distorts the emphasis of the New Testament.

In the same way, the New Testament contains explicit assertions of the
divinity of Christ (John 1:1; 20:28, and even perhaps Rom. 9:5), but overall
it rests content with less provocative claims, that Jesus is Lord, Son of God
and Christ. In fact the latter, by far the most frequent designation in the
New Testament, receives scant attention in traditional interpretation. The *fact*
of Jesus' messiahship, refuting Jewish denials, is emphasized frequently
enough; but the *content* of the title and role, relating as it does to the destiny
of Israel in the purposes of God, is almost entirely ignored. This is a further
example, in addition to those we have already mentioned, Covenant and Law,
of the way traditional interpretation, so anxious to fit the Old Testament in
with the New, is reluctant to admit the relation works also the other way
round.

Second, when the 'two natures' doctrine is not merely maintained as the logical outworking of the implications of the Gospel, but is applied as an hermeneutical principle in reading the Gospels, its effect is thoroughly distortive. When he is attributed with divine omnipotence and omniscience, impassibility and foreknowledge, the human reality of Jesus' life and death are eclipsed; incarnation becomes a form of theatrical accommodation, or disintegrates into intolerable paradoxes. That the Jesus of the Gospels, not least the fourth Gospel, who is so single-minded to do the will of the Father, should be supposed to have possessed two wills, one human and the other divine, illustrates the main pitfall of traditional exegesis, that the pressure of the doctrinal system may override the evidence of the text and even common sense.

THE MODERN RELEVANCE OF TRADITIONAL INTERPRETATION

After such a catalogue of complaints, it may seem strange to end with a section on the modern relevance of traditional interpretation. And there can be no question of a return to the sort of errors and distortions we have just mentioned. But there are, on the other hand, signs that it is no longer to be dismissed summarily, as though predicated on totally false premises, like pre-Copernican astronomy. Research into the work of pre-critical exegetes and commentators is now accepted as a legitimate department of biblical scholarship, and closer study of the past normally elicits a certain affection and respect for its positive achievements. Even the basic aims and methods of traditional interpretation, suitably qualified, are being rehabilitated to scholarly respectability, from a number of different directions. (In popular preaching and bible study, of course, they have always remained the norm.)

Textual criticism

We may begin with an uncontroversial point, but one whose full significance is not always appreciated even by critical scholars. We do not have direct access to the New Testament documents, we can only read them in later copies. Although important papyrus discoveries over the last hundred years have pushed our knowledge of part of the textual tradition back to about 200 CE, the variety of readings does not diminish in the earlier period. And the other sources of knowledge about the text, the early Latin, Syriac and Coptic versions, and the citations of the Church Fathers, remain vital. New Testament textual criticism, a discipline which spans the divide between traditional and modern interpretation and can claim Origen and Erasmus among its illustrious exponents, is the foundation of all scholarly work. But it is based on the history of interpretation, on the part of scribes, translators and commentators, in the pre-modern period. There is no pure text of the New Testament; it reaches us only via the work of its traditional interpreters.

The historical–critical method

New Testament scholars once confidently believed that the historical–critical method would deliver the original meaning of the text, the meaning which the author intended to convey to his original readers/hearers. While pre-critical interpreters read their own later concerns into the text, the modern biblical critic was objectively reading meaning out of the text. There are both moderate and radical reasons for questioning this confidence.

First, meaning depends on context, including issues like place, date and authorship. For the Gospels we know nothing from the texts themselves about these issues; their authors effectively hide themselves behind the stories they tell. For the epistles, some are pseudonymous works, in which date, authorship and even place may be part of the fictional disguise. And for those that are genuine letters – such is the nature of the genre – the crucial context is assumed by the parties to the correspondence, only one side of which are we privileged to overhear. It has dawned on many critics, therefore, that we may be asking questions of the text which it is now quite simply impossible for it to answer, because the context is unavailable.

Furthermore, the methods of source, form and redaction criticism, so industriously pursued this century have yet failed to produce consensus among the experts. If we do not know whether Mark was using Matthew or vice versa, or whether John was dependent on the Synoptics or not, we cannot evaluate the evangelists' own contributions. Redaction criticism started with a sharp distinction between the evangelists' editing and earlier traditions, but it has eroded its own starting point by attributing more and more to authorial creativity and leaving less and less to be accounted for by the tradition. Form-critics were once certain that the Synoptic Gospels were popular literature made up of independently circulating units, whose transmission history could be traced back through the oral period. But both the assumptions and the categories of the method have been reopened to scrutiny and doubt. There is a real possibility that the Synoptic evangelists themselves created episodic, apparently disjointed narrative for literary and social reasons of their own, and that this feature is not necessarily evidence for their use of fragmentary, popular oral tradition.

The historical–critical method had hoped to be able to provide a complete history of earliest Christianity from Jesus of Nazareth to the immediate post-apostolic period, fitting all the documents and the pre-documentary traditions into a coherent developmental scheme. That programme now appears to be much too ambitious. Paradoxically, at the same time as this radical questioning of historical criticism, there has been a sudden revival of 'Jesus of history' research, perhaps because, with the method in doubt, scholars have been

117

encouraged to trust to intuition, with a little help from Jewish background studies and sociological theory.

Narrative criticism

It is not surprising in view of the insolubility of the questions posed by historical criticism, that some scholars have recently abandoned the attempt to go behind the text of the Gospels and have begun to concentrate instead on their final form, using the literary technique known as narrative criticism. This method concentrates solely on the story world of the text and asks how the implied author achieves rhetorical effect on the implied audience by means of plot, setting and characterization. It refuses to take account of the pre-literary history of the text in the process of interpretation, a position which would once have been condemned as pre-critical.

This method strives to appear ultra-modern. For that reason it does not draw upon the resources that traditional exegesis could provide for narrative critical readings. But there is a strong affinity between them. To give one example: Origen commenting on Matthew 13:36, where Jesus takes his disciples 'into the house' to expound to them the deeper meaning of the parables, suggests that the house signifies the mind and soul of those who wish to be interpreters of the hidden truths of Scripture. Maurice Wiles (in Ackroyd and Evans 1970: 486) remarks wryly: 'Such an answer is the delight of the pious and the despair of critical scholars.' But modern narrative critics, on the contrary, are also quite prepared (see Malbon 1986) to take the house as a symbol representing Christian fellowship and esoteric instruction.

Following the lead of secular literary critics, this method can even abandon authorial intention as a control on meaning and focus instead on the response of the competent reader to the text. It comes very close then to the notion of *plenior sensus* used in traditional interpretation. The content of the deeper meaning in each case may be different; aesthetic appreciation and theological significance, respectively. But the method is strikingly similar; and many would consider narrative criticism's main deficiency to be its indifference to theology.

The presuppositions of the exegete

Modern criticism once believed that it had solved the problem of the subjectivity of the interpreter by the objectivity of its method. It has been attacked from many sides for this presumption and accused of several latent prejudices, such as anti-Semitism, patriarchalism and political quietism. The alternative approach adopted now by different forms of liberation exegesis (political, feminist, psychological) is to make explicit from the start the presuppositions and current agenda of the interpreter. Just as pure text and pure authorial intention have had to be treated as unattainable abstractions, so also, it is alleged, the purely neutral interpreter does not exist in the real world. Traditional exegesis did not pretend to neutrality either, and although it sometimes provided scriptural justification for the oppression of women, Jews and the poor it has also been the source of a radical critique of contemporary society and an instrument of social change. The history of the pre-modern interpretation of the book of Revelation is particularly interesting in this respect.

On the other hand there are certain disadvantages in inviting interpreters to parade their prejudices like this. It focuses attention on the prior commitments of the writer rather than on the transforming effect of his or her encounter with Scripture; and it reinforces modern notions of relativity and pluralism. In both respects it parts company with traditional interpretation. That the exegete should be 'open and laid bare' before the 'sharp piercing word' (Heb. 4:12f.) may be impossible in practice, but it is an ideal towards which to strive.

The rehabilitation of allegory

It was one of the assured results of critical study that the parables of Jesus were not allegories. It was demonstrable that the allegorical interpretations of the sower (Mark 4:13–20) and the wheat and the tares (Matt. 13:36–43), and added features in many others, were the work of the evangelists or earlier Christian preachers; and that the original parables of Jesus were simple, single-point analogies, immediately understandable without assistance, and that they referred to the coming of the Kingdom of God. This consensus has now collapsed, attacked from different directions – Jewish background, literary study of the forms of Jesus' teaching and redaction criticism. Whatever view is taken now about the authenticity of the allegorical parables, there is a new appreciation for the method. It is not necessarily arid, esoteric, artificial or dishonest. Allegory is an extended form of metaphorical speech, and as such has a kind of indeterminacy. There is not one single correct interpretation of a poetic image; the reader is invited to explore as deeply as may be the evocativeness and reverberations of the figure in his or her own experience.

Just how much of the language of the New Testament, in addition to the sayings of Jesus, is poetic and open to fuller meanings is a matter of current debate. Rhetorical analysis of the epistles is revealing the hitherto unsuspected presence of non-literal discourse. Pre-critical interpretation used to be dismissed, in some respects unfairly, as insufficiently concerned with the literal, intended sense. But the more it is recognized that the intended meaning is in fact metaphorical, the more this defect in traditional exegesis will come to be seen as its strength.

The history of influence

Critical scholars commenting on a book of the New Testament have been prepared to quote the Fathers occasionally on textual or philological points, or for some short, striking phrase. We are beginning to see commentaries (e.g. Luz 1990: 95–9) which devote much more space to tracing the history of influence (*Wirkungsgeschichte*) of the text beyond its original time and setting. This development is a recognition of the fact that those who consult New Testament commentaries include many who have developed an interest in the text flowing not from academic theology so much as from the study of Western literature, history and philosophy, and who want to know, certainly, what the text originally meant, but also how on earth it came to mean what it has since. The availability of computer databases of patristic and later commentaries is making a complete historical survey of the way New Testament texts came to be understood more of a possibility. To avoid a computer-aided equivalent of the medieval Gloss, however, it will be necessary amid the mass of data to provide also a focus of attention on the present influence of the New Testament among those for whom it remains influential.

In conclusion, distinctions between periods in history are always to some extent arbitrary and open to revision in the light of later developments. The great pre-Enlightenment/post-Enlightenment divide may eventually come to be seen more like an interlude, before the tradition of New Testament interpretation (now chastened, and 'post-critical') resumes its primary objective, to expound the New Testament not merely as source documents for the early history of Christianity but as the treasury of faith and of the knowledge of God.

REFERENCES

Ackroyd, P. R. and Evans, C. F. (eds) (1970) *The Cambridge History of the Bible 1: From the Beginnings to Jerome*, Cambridge: Cambridge University Press.

Evans, G. R. (1984) *The Language and Logic of the Bible*, vol. 1, *The Earlier Middle Ages*, Cambridge: Cambridge University Press.

Frei, H. (1974) *The Eclipse of Biblical Narrative: A study in 18th and 19th century Hermeneutics*, New Haven: Yale University Press.

Grant, R. M. (1965) *A Short History of the Interpretation of the Bible*, London: A. & C. Black.

Greenslade, S. L. (ed.) (1963) *The Cambridge History of the Bible 3: The West from the Reformation to the Present Day*, Cambridge: Cambridge University Press.

Lampe, G. W. H. (ed.) (1969) *The Cambridge History of the Bible 2: The West from the Fathers to the Reformation*, Cambridge: Cambridge University Press.

Luz, U. (1990) *Matthew 1–7*, Edinburgh: T. & T. Clark.

Malbon, E. (1986) *Narrative Space and Mythic Meaning in Mark*, New York: Harper & Row.

Rogerson, J., Rowland C. and Lindars, B. (1988) *The Study and Use of the Bible*, vol. 2 of *The History of Christian Theology*, ed. P. Avis, Basingstoke: Marshall Pickering.

FURTHER READING

Barr, J. (1961) *The Semantics of Biblical Language*, London: SCM Press.
—— (1983) *Holy Scripture: Canon, Authority, Criticism*, London: SCM Press.
Caird, G. B. (1980) *The Language and Imagery of the Bible*, London: Duckworth.
Childs, B. S. (1984) *The New Testament as Canon: An Introduction*, London: SCM Press.
Coggins, R. J. and Houlden, J. L. (eds) (1990) *A Dictionary of Biblical Interpretation*, London: SCM Press.
Drury, J. (1985) *The Parables in the Gospels*, London: SCM Press.
Evans, G. R. (1983) *The Language and Logic of the Bible*, vol. 2, *The Road to Reformation*, Cambridge: Cambridge University Press.
Kelsey, D. (1975) *The Uses of Scripture in Recent Theology*, London: SCM Press.
Kümmel, W. G. (1973) *The New Testament: a History of the Investigation of its Problems*, London: SCM Press.
Louth, A. (1983) *Discerning the Mystery*, Oxford: Clarendon Press.
McKnight, E. V. (1988) *Post-Modern Use of the Bible: The Emergence of Reader-Oriented Criticism*, Nashville: Abingdon.
Powell, M. (1993) *What is Narrative Criticism?*, London: SPCK.
See also chapters 5, 7, 8, 9.

7

THE NEW TESTAMENT IN THEOLOGY

Heikki Räisänen

TRADITIONAL USES OF THE BIBLE BECOME UNVIABLE

The late eighteenth and especially the nineteenth century saw a paradigm shift in theology, in particular as regards the role of biblical study. From divine revelation, usable as a string of proof texts for doctrines, the Bible was turned into materials for historical reconstruction. Since then, scholars have developed a set of historical–critical techniques, each of which has produced remarkable results.

Source criticism showed for example that the Fourth Gospel could no longer be assessed as an historical account of the life of Jesus (though bits of historical information are dispersed in it). To this day, the significance of this step has not been fully recognized; it has severed the link which traditional christology was supposed to have with the Jesus of history. In our century, form criticism made the supposedly solid Synoptic sources (Matthew, Mark and Luke) for the history of Jesus evaporate into a fluid oral tradition. Redaction criticism demonstrated that the Gospels were not innocent collections of traditions, but tendentious constructions by their authors, even the Synoptics differing markedly among themselves in scope and content. The Gospel authors could now be seen to be in competition with each other.

New methods informed by social sciences have sharpened the focus, but they have not really changed the paradigm. Scholars are learning to pay increased attention to the different social contexts in which New Testament authors operate. The net effect has been to emphasize the cultural gap which separates our societies from those in which the New Testament writings arose.

The direct impact of this development on theology may seem negative. For it seems obvious that if biblical studies are taken really seriously, traditional ways of using the Bible in theology, even in modified forms, become unviable. This is due to the recognition by biblical scholarship of the wide diversity of beliefs within the New Testament itself, the non-historicity of crucial 'events' and of the inherently problematic nature of many New Testament beliefs which presuppose an antiquated world-view.

It does not take exegetical training to perceive such problematic points. One needs only some common sense to realize that, for example, what is said about prayer in the Sermon on the Mount (Matt. 7:7–11: whatever you ask will be given to you) is unrealistic, or that the 'God who acts', glorified by an influential school of 'biblical theology' a generation ago, becomes a problem, if few or none of the events celebrated as God's mighty acts ever took place in real history. Problems connected with world-view likewise impose themselves on any attentive reader. The contribution of exegetical study is to sharpen the focus in locating the texts in their socio-historical contexts, and in providing the investigator with the linguistic and other tools necessary for a closer study of the problems.

Contrary to a common prejudice, mainstream exegesis has no esoteric doctrines to which only initiates could have access. There have been some major shortcomings, to be sure, but these are of a different kind. The canonical New Testament is a tiny body of texts for a 'guild' of thousands of specialist scholars to cover again and again. One result has been that people have tried to reconstruct the New Testament world with much greater accuracy than is really possible on the basis of the extant sources. This has led to attempts to refine to an extreme degree methods which are in themselves sound. Abuse, however, does not annul proper use. Thus, the uneven and disjointed character of many Gospel texts strongly indicates that many texts have a pre-history. Different traditions or different sources have been conflated, for some of the seams still show. This general fact, true of many of the biblical books, in itself casts light on the nature of the Bible which is important to theology. It is another question, however, to what extent the materials used in the making of a Gospel can still be retrieved; too much energy and ingenuity have indeed been devoted to the construction of possible sources which are impossible to verify. Probably the exegetes should cast their nets much wider, abandoning the distinction between biblical exegesis and early Church history which, from a scientific point of view, is artificial anyway.

Another inherent problem has been the intertwining of exegesis with religious proclamation which has in some schools of thought given to a supposedly exegetical exposition a pronouncedly theological–philosophical slant. A case in point is Rudolf Bultmann's explication of Paul's teaching about the human condition. This problem has followed the historical study of the Bible throughout its history, for it did not start as unbiased reconstruction of the past, but as an attempt to glean from the biblical record whatever was useful for modern thought. In the Enlightenment when it all began, it was hoped to distinguish the eternal moral–religious truths of the Bible from its time-bound notions; in a slightly different guise the same concern has been operative till Bultmann and beyond. Today there seems to exist a methodological gap between 'everyday exegesis' and theological syntheses ('New

Testament theologies') or programmatic statements on what the discipline is all about. (Relatively) unbiased history is the (of course, unattainable) ideal in the former area, but presentations belonging to the latter category incline to harmonization and proclamation (witness the difference of tone between Bultmann's *History of the Synoptic Tradition* and his *Theology of the New Testament*). Theology would gain from a distinction between historical exegesis and contemporizing theological interpretation; otherwise it runs the risk of only getting back from exegesis what it has first put into it.

It is seldom realized how vast a difference it would make if critical points made by common sense and careful exegesis were really taken seriously. Biblical scholars themselves are to be blamed: they have seldom tried hard enough to make themselves heard in their own terms. It is questionable whether very many scholars have drawn even for themselves adequate conclusions from their own work. Exegetes have acted also as systematic theologians, as if their historical findings were relatively easy to translate into viable present-day theological idiom. This has tended to water down many of their findings at the outset.

The New Testament has turned out to be filled with theological contradictions, many of them by no means peripheral. There are different expectations of the future and different notions of salvation. For some parts of the New Testament, Jesus' death, interpreted in vicarious terms, is an indispensable part of God's plan for human salvation; to others, it is the typical fate of a prophet brought about by men's iniquity but not invested with soteriological significance. There are different perceptions of the person and work of Christ. Some regard his divine sonship as based on the raising by God of the man Jesus from the dead, others on his eternal pre-existence.

It takes no 'radical', but only a 'moderately critical' reading of the New Testament to reach such conclusions. Ernst Käsemann's dictum that 'the New Testament canon does not, as such, constitute the foundation of the unity of the Church', but 'the basis for the multiplicity of the confessions' (Käsemann 1964: 103) is explicitly endorsed by James Dunn (Dunn 1990: 376f.), though the latter pays lip service to unity by never using the word 'contradiction' (only 'diversity': Dunn 1990: xxi). Of course there are also constant features (many of which, like monotheism, are not 'specifically Christian') but they are not very impressive. Thus, what Dunn finds to be the unifying factor between all the different writings and strands is the conviction of the 'unity between the historical Jesus and the exalted Christ' – a thin and elusive bond and moreover hardly in harmony with Dunn's own findings. For his claim that the 'adoptionist' christology of the early Jerusalem Church is 'ultimately one and the same' as John's incarnational theology stretches the reader's imagination to the breaking point: to hold that Jesus received his high status after his death is different from the belief that it was his from all eternity.

Exegesis discloses the contradictory diversity of the New Testament. It is bound to end up by pointing out that the New Testament lacks that uniqueness on which some generations of biblical scholars used to put a lot of stress. In the words of Gerd Theissen, historical–critical scholarship shows

> that the religious traditions were made by humans, that historically everything hangs together with everything, that Christianity was a somewhat blown-up heresy of Judaism and that Judaism was an outstanding phenomenon of the history of oriental religion. In other words, there are no isolated events.

He continues, 'In short, historical–critical study shows, independently of the aims of individual scholars, that religious traditions are very earthly, very relative, very questionable.' Theissen rightly deems this 'an irreversible insight' (Theissen 1978: 3f.).

All this should have consequences for notions of 'revelation', 'inspiration' or 'word of God'. Add the discontinuity of large segments of the New Testament with much of the (supposed) Old Testament 'revelation', most palpable in Paul's comments on the Torah: at times, this (in classical biblical terms) divine gift to Israel is even relegated to the status of a demonic trap designed to mislead (cf. Gal. 4:1–3; 8–11). Where such contradictions are involved, talk of 'revelation' seems empty of content.

Rather than try once again to find some 'method' of applying the Bible, the simplest and most plausible solution is to admit that there is no direct path from historical study to present-day application.

CHALLENGES TO THE HISTORICAL APPROACH?

Not surprisingly, such an outcome of the reign of the historical method has been detrimental in the eyes of many. Where people have looked to biblical scholarship for spiritual guidance, disappointment has been unavoidable. Predictably, the dominant position of the historical approach has been challenged from various quarters: conservative theology, pastoral psychology, contextual theology, and literary criticism.

Conservative theologians have stressed the alleged theological unity of the two Testaments and striven towards a canonical, pan-biblical theology (Childs 1992; Stuhlmacher 1992). The enterprise has required them to iron out obvious differences not only between the Testaments but also within each one. Stuhlmacher demands that 'agreement' with the text be included among the guiding principles of historical criticism, but such a requirement runs counter to the rules of sound scholarship which must never let its hands be bound in advance. It is absurd to require that one should always 'agree' with the text one is treating. None of those who make such claims for the study of the Bible would plead for the same programme, say, in the study of the Koran, nor would they apply it to all books of the Bible itself (say, Leviticus).

An attempt to set a 'new paradigm' for biblical study was made in the 1970s by Walter Wink who opened his programmatic booklet with the claim that 'historical biblical criticism is bankrupt' (Wink 1973: 1). This statement is often quoted out of context. Wink used 'bankrupt' in the exact sense of the term, making it clear that we are 'not holding a wake'. A bankrupt business 'is not valueless, nor incapable of producing useful products'. The only thing wrong is 'that it is no longer able to accomplish its avowed purpose for existence'. Historical criticism of the Bible is, Wink claims, 'incapable of achieving what most of its practitioners considered its purpose to be: so to interpret the Scriptures that the past becomes alive and illumines our present with new possibilities for personal and social transformation'. But it is precisely the issue, whether this should be considered the purpose of historical study of the Bible (rather than, say, the purpose of some branch of practical theology). If one practises exegesis 'seeking insights about living', one is likely to be disappointed.

Wink intentionally blends the historical task of exegesis with that of contemporary application in sermons and workshops. His Jungian approach is a valuable tool in therapeutic group work. But it transcends the realm which exegesis may meaningfully inhabit to ask (in connection with Mark 2), Who is the 'paralytic' in you? (Answers: 'It is the way I've been over-academized', 'the suppressed power I have as a woman', etc.; Wink 1973: 56.) These are valuable applications, but it is hard to see what the gain would be if historical exegesis were replaced by this kind of internalizing. By contrast, there is no reason why work with the Bible should necessarily stop at the historical level. But a division of labour between the historian and the pastor (who need not be two different persons) would clarify the task of each. It is not the task of historical exegesis any more than it can be the task of Church history to 'enable personal and social transformation' (ibid.: 61), though exegesis can well serve as an incentive for such transformation. Still, it is quite possible that insights reached at the level of application will in turn enrich the historical work in that they suggest questions to be asked and possibilities of interpretation to be explored. These questions, however, can also imply criticisms of the texts. It is not just that the texts can enable transformation; personal transformation may also presuppose a liberation from the grip of some texts through a critical confrontation with them, say, in a therapeutic group.

Many biblical interpreters in the Third World find likewise that historical exegesis does not answer their questions. High expectations are indeed directed to exegesis, if 'the quest for the historical Jesus lies not only in finding the truth about the man of Nazareth, but also in fighting for the truth that will liberate mankind' (Sugirtharajah 1991b: 436). But the problematic nature of such expectations is pointedly disclosed when the same interpreter states: 'The primary concern of an interpreter lies not only in transforming social inequalities . . . but also in bringing racial and religious harmony among peoples of different faiths' (Sugirtharajah 1991a: 363). These goals are admirable, but, ironically, it is very hard to find the ideal of inter-religious harmony in the Bible which is rather militant with regard to non-biblical faiths. Moreover, in trying to demonstrate the liberating character of Jesus' mission, Third World theologians easily fall into the old trap of Christian triumphalism, painting the Jewish society of Jesus' time in very dark colours as the 'background' against which the liberating message shines forth. The consequences to which this approach has led in history should by now ring a warning bell.

The Asian theologian S. J. Samartha who makes a strong plea for interfaith dialogue also criticizes traditional attempts to establish a direct correspondence between our situation and the situations of biblical writers speaking of other religions. Such assumptions, he says, forget the gap between past and present (Samartha 1991: 43). This is an interesting criticism, for it runs counter to the assertions of Third World theologians like Sugirtharajah who see in the postulation of such a gap the original sin of historical method (Sugirtharajah 1991b: 436). Yet when it comes to a fair assessment of non-Christian religions, it is Asian theologians themselves who point out the gap and in the interest of an earnest dialogue in effect relativize the biblical message which seems, on this issue, to be based on too limited experience of life (Samartha 1991: 43). It would seem quite helpful to distinguish between historical elucidation of the Bible and contemporary theological attempts to relate Christian experience to non-Christian experience. The same, of course, applies to feminist theology: being a thoroughly patriarchal book, the Bible offers little that is directly of help to feminist concerns; feminists are bound to read the texts with a critical eye, among other things by locating them as closely as possible in their social settings. In this, historical criticism with a social-scientific flavour is indispensable.

Though some liberation theologians tend to establish straightforward analogies between ancient and modern situations, others find them problematic. Clodovis Boff (1991: 33) frankly states that the relationship with Scripture 'ought to tend more to the acquisition of a hermeneutic *habitus* than to immediate practical applications', in effect approximating a division of labour between historical work and present-day application.

Liberation theology, however, would be impossible without historical criticism of the Bible. It is precisely a historical–critical interpretation, to be sure an interpretation informed by a certain kind of social-scientific analysis (Norman Gottwald's interpretation of the origins of Israel), on which it is built. For it is clear – the point is made by many liberation theologians themselves – that not all of the Bible is liberationist, though parts of it are. An additional problem is that the historicity of the main 'liberating' events praised in the Old Testament has become very suspect; this kind of contextual theology then faces problems similar to those which eventually undermined the once-popular 'biblical theology' of the 'God who acts' type. What liberation theology needs is a selective attitude to the Bible, though some of its exponents are reluctant to admit this. Again, it is hard to see what is gained by fusing the historical task with the application; distinguishing between the two levels of interpretation would seem very helpful precisely from the point of view of contextual theology.

Perhaps the most formidable challenge to the historical approach comes from the side of literary criticism. Under this umbrella a rich variety of approaches can be assembled, such as structuralist analysis, rhetorical criticism, narrative criticism, reader-response criticism, even deconstructionist criticism. Their growth is often perceived as a paradigm shift designed to render the historical approach obsolete. Others feel that they should be accommodated to the old paradigm to sharpen its focus yet again. If it turns out that these new approaches cannot be integrated with the historical paradigm, the outcome can hardly be the death of the latter. Rather, one would then have to reckon with two (or more) quite different approaches to the biblical texts, each legitimate in itself, each capable of handling one type of question and incapable of handling others. They would not be in competition with each other, because they would fulfil different functions.

The new methods are not without inherent problems of their own, though. In their 'holistic passion' (Malbon 1992: 35) they tend to assume *a priori* that texts like the Gospels are coherent wholes of 'one cloth'. Their practitioners are also inclined towards an uncritical admiration of the literary accomplishment of the evangelists. They duplicate the exaggerations of some redaction critics on a slightly different level: whereas the former saw Mark as a very subtle and sophisticated theologian, literary critics tend to conceive of him as a masterly story-teller. Narrative critics are, as any interpreter should be, often eager to know as much as possible about the cultural contexts of the texts; yet they claim to be wary of 'interpretations based on elements external to the narrative' (Malbon 1992: 28). It is not at all clear how these two aims could be served at the same time, and, in fact, narrative critics do resort to 'external' elements, often in an uncritical modernizing manner at that (for instances see Räisänen 1990b: 14–37, especially 34f.). Moreover, the enthusiasm for 'rhetorical persuasion' covers up the possibility that all kinds of ends can be reached through efficient rhetoric; rhetorical skill does not remove but enhances the need for a critical scrutiny of the message.

If ahistorical readings avoid such shortcomings, they are fine as far as they go; yet they do not go very far. If one sticks to story worlds, one will end up with a dozen or more New Testament story worlds. Yet 'nagging questions about the truth and value of realities envisaged in the Bible, refined as they are by sensitive readings, rightly continue to haunt the reader' (Davies 1990: 405). With respect to the relation between exegesis and theology, the replacement of the historical method through a set of ahistorical ones would not solve anything, for Christian theology has been fundamentally concerned with historical matters. It is in this area that many of its burning problems lie and it will not help simply to brush the issues aside. It is possible (and in my view, desirable) that historical issues may eventually be found to be insignificant, but this amounts to such a major shift in theology itself that it should not take place without a thorough wrestling with the issues.

From the point of view of theology, then, literary criticism tends to confirm the pluralistic picture already painted by redaction criticism. For instance, Matthew can be seen as a 'resisting reader' of Mark's Gospel; 'the Gospels are far more in competition with each other than is commonly suspected' (Fowler 1992: 79, 81). These insights of reader-response criticism – actually a new version of the insights of redaction criticism – may still be of some direct help in preaching, for a preacher can concentrate on one text – and thus on one narrative world – at a time. He or she can be greatly stimulated by studying Matthew's way of wrestling with Mark's text. Theology, by contrast, is concerned with the question of how the different text worlds hang – or do not hang – together. Separate narrative worlds may well be juxtaposed in 'Introductions' to the books that together make up the New Testament. But they will not answer questions about the religious and theological convictions which lie behind the different narratives, and it is these that are the ultimate concern of theology. 'Worlds' other than the narrative world are at least as relevant for the task of the interpreter: the 'real world' in which the author lived, and both his own and his community's 'symbolic world' (the shared values, ideals and convictions that gave coherence to their world-view and are in many ways reflected also in the narrative world; see Syreeni 1990: 126–32).

It is hard to avoid the suspicion that ahistorical approaches are sometimes cherished because one wishes to get rid of problems connected with the foundations of a religion which claims to be firmly grounded in history. Some narrative critics may choose an ahistorical approach because of a religiously based fear of such critical issues, while others may find theological questions simply uninteresting. Ahistorical work may, paradoxically, offer a ground on which fundamentalists and secularists can meet, the price paid being that it fails to ask the questions most pressing to those who stand somewhere in-between.

There is one challenge, however, that will undoubtedly stay: that of ideological criticism. It asks about the interests behind the texts which are viewed as ideological documents that serve some particular group. While such a criticism is not new in itself, 'what is new is the emphasis on the partisanship of every text' and

> on the demand to press beyond mere description of the ideology of the texts to a critique of it. This orientation to the texts has both a historical and an ahistorical dimension, and so may represent a new alliance between the historical and the literary approaches to biblical studies.
>
> (Clines 1993: 84).

This kind of criticism has so far been more practised in Old Testament study, but it should prove fruitful in New Testament studies as well. It has been applied to the New Testament in the form of feminist criticism. It can be applied to other issues as well. Philip Esler's studies on 'legitimation' as a Lukan concern could serve as an example: Luke legitimates Jewish–Gentile table-fellowship by radically re-writing the history of early Christianity relating to this subject (Esler 1987: 107). In other New Testament books too, strategies used to legitimate practical decisions can be found. Paul's complex discussions of the law can be seen as attempts to account for the decision to abandon the concrete demands of the Torah while simultaneously trying to uphold some continuity with it. A sound interpretation must not adopt Paul's position *a priori*, but must try to do justice to different positions (such as those of his more conservative critics) as well (see Räisänen 1992a: 267–77).

The net effect of an ideological–critical approach will be 'to relativize the biblical text and make it less malleable to theological reconstruction' to a greater degree than mere historical criticism has been able to do.

> When the partisan character of the biblical texts is more extensively uncovered . . . theology is going to have to come to terms with a Bible far different from the confessional document preserved by 'believing communities' and then by the church . . . It is going to have to busy itself with a tendentious document that says what it says not because it is true but because it paid to say so. And the Bible may become, under those conditions, what it always should have been – the object of theological (or ideological) scrutiny rather than, in some sense, its source or guide.
>
> (Clines 1993: 85f.)

It could well be that

> the most interesting prospects for biblical studies lie precisely in reading against the grain of the texts, in bringing to bear on our texts our own cultural and historical and personal positions, and in evaluating the texts against the hundred and one yardsticks that the pluralist world of international biblical scholarship will inevitably suggest.
>
> (Ibid.: 87)

The challenges to the historical approach, then, do not endanger the relevance of the historical approach to the New Testament nor do they allow theology to circumvent that approach in considering what to do with the Bible. Study of religion must be distinguished from the acting out of religion. Assessed realistically, historical–biblical scholarship may be able to sketch a picture of 'how it all began'. Knowing from where we come may aid us in orienting ourselves to where we are now, but the yield is bound to be very indirect.

But it is not the case that exegetes should act as new popes who determine which application of the Bible is right and which is wrong. It might be claimed that the exegete only has 'the right of veto', the right to protest if an application seems to distance itself too much from the range of possible original meanings. Ideological criticism adds the possibility of a moral veto, opening up a wide range of possibilities for constructive theology in critical confrontation with the texts.

COSMIC ESCHATOLOGY AS A TEST CASE

Let us consider cosmic eschatology as a test case for the actual treatment of exegetical findings in recent theology. A number of New Testament writers expect a cosmic reversal, preceded by signs and portents, to take place in a not very distant future. This reversal includes the destruction and re-creation of the world, the return of Christ, the resurrection of the dead and the great judgement. This is indeed the dominant view, though there are strands which imply a more spiritual notion of post-mortem existence: an individual moves immediately after death to paradise (or to a place of punishment), as in Luke 16: 22ff.; 23:43). The juxtaposition of these two views is a problem in itself; another problem is the question of the plausibility of the cosmic view (either view, for that matter) today.

If one adopts a literal reading of the texts, one has to choose one of the options and play down the other (unless, of course, one discards both). In Western theological thought the cosmic view has tended to dissolve into images and symbols. By contrast, in Third World theologies it is the spiritualized view which is under attack.

As an example of a non-literal reading of cosmic eschatology we may consider its reduction to 'a vision of a global community' by Paul Hanson, a leading authority on apocalyptic prophecies. Hanson first gives a sympathetic account of the historical setting of cosmic apocalyptic eschatology, starting with the Syrian persecution in Palestine under Antiochus Epiphanes in the mid-second century BCE. When it comes to the application of the apocalyptic message today, he suggests that 'we can take this part of our scriptural legacy as an invitation to engage our own imaginations, using the idioms and images of our own time to describe a world reconciled, living in peace and harmony' (Hanson 1988: 134).

> The vision of God's universal reign . . . becomes the means by which the faithful recognize signs of the new creation, wherever groups are dedicated to the cause of justice and peace and wherever individuals are committed to placing compassion at the center of all their thoughts, actions, and relationships.
>
> (Ibid.: 120)

Apocalyptic texts have offered and still offer encouragement for the oppressed, warnings for the oppressors and awakening for the sleeping. They aid modern readers seeking their course between facile optimism and dire pessimism.

In this reinterpretation, the texts offer no new 'knowledge', for surely one need not know Daniel or Revelation to become committed to the cause of peace and justice. What these biblical books do offer is food for the imagination, support from the tradition for those among the global visionaries who happen to have a Christian background.

Hanson makes the point that the 'interpretation of a specific apocalyptic text must relate positively to the message of Scripture as a whole' (Hanson 1988: 57); on which count modern apocalyptic works like those by Hal Lindsey (e.g. *Late Great Planet Earth*) are seen as failures, especially because of their pervading spirit of hatred. Hanson thus exercises justified ideological criticism of the modern interpretation of the biblical texts. But as his own construction shows, the envisaged totality of Scripture is an elusive thing. It is a dictate of the modern interpreter, based on a selective reading, that 'the message of Scripture as a whole' discourages a spirit of hatred. It does not. Whether it pleases us or not, in Scripture itself, suspicion and even hatred of the 'others' is one conspicuous theme, running from Old Testament narratives and Psalms all the way through to the book of Revelation which indulges in feelings of revenge when celebrating the anticipated fall of 'Babylon' (and, contrary to most textbooks, does not seem to belong to a setting of grave persecution at all). Actually Hanson has not come up with 'the' message of Scripture 'as a whole'; implicitly he has applied ideological criticism to the texts and has thus produced a selective re-reading. There is nothing wrong with this, but one should be aware of what is actually taking place.

A related attempt to do justice to the totality of Scripture when interpreting apocalyptic eschatology is made by some systematic theologians. We shall consider the work of Medard Kehl, a pupil of Karl Rahner.

Kehl opts for a 'cautious demythologization' of scriptural notions. The really important thing in the imminent expectation of the end is not the future, but the present. Faith is aware that God acts in a liberating way, now. The point of imminent expectation is that the present is seen as an absolutely serious moment of conversion and decision before God who comes towards us. Since God's salvation is greater than any human views of it, an expectation which trusts in God can never fail. Imminent expectation cannot fail, because it can be realized in any number of ways – in whatever way Yahweh's will of justice and peace reaches its goal (Kehl 1986: 112f.).

This is a version of the classic method of relieving cognitive dissonance by reinterpreting the issue to the point of complete vagueness. An expectation which cannot be falsified by any contrary evidence whatsoever runs the risk of being empty of content. On this account there never was any failed expectation of the millennium in any Christian or quasi-Christian group.

Kehl solves the problem of unfulfilled eschatological expectation by eliminating the temporal element altogether. He excludes the possibility that God might intervene in the course of history in a visible manner. No historical–cosmic 'eschatological events' are to be expected. Kehl points out that we have long since given up the three-storeyed world-view of apocalyptic messages and that it would be inconsistent to cling to a view of history rooted in that very apocalypse. The kind of fulfilment we can hope for takes place in the death of each individual. This is what the apocalyptic talk of the resurrection of the dead 'really' means. The return of the Son of Man has already begun in the resurrection of Jesus, and it is happening all the time in the celebration of the Eucharist.

Kehl thus preserves the 'language game' of eschatological fulfilment, while thoroughly reinterpreting the content of cosmic eschatology. He realizes that his view may seem too spiritualizing, anticipating objections by noting that there is no alternative theory in view which would be able to combine the diverse viewpoints of Christian hope even as well as his model does (Kehl 1986: 279). It is an awkward combination, though, as one of the two points to be combined is completely devoured by the other.

Kehl's trust that there is something we can hope for is ultimately based on the conviction that God has already acted in a decisive way in Jesus. God has shown his faithfulness and love in the resurrection of Jesus. But how well-grounded is such trust if the apocalyptic view of history is dismissed along with other time-bound notions of the apocalyptic world-view?

How is it at all possible to speak of God's unique, once-and-for-all acting 'in Jesus', except precisely in the framework of an apocalyptic view of history? The first Christians interpreted the significance of Jesus in unique terms just because their apocalyptic world-view led them to expect that unique events would take place. Ideological criticism will note that the attempts to solve pressing problems and to make sense of overwhelming experiences (the Easter visions and other charismatic phenomena) led to vast generalizations on the intellectual level. The limited experiences of a group (the perception of living in the eschatological era, the significance given to specific events, such as the appearances of Jesus after his death) were perceived to be matters absolutely central for the history of the world at large, a history that transcended any mundane limits.

Though Kehl rejects millenarianism, he still wants to cling to a certain kind of Christian utopianism connected with it. He finds the millenarian notion of an earthly 'interim reign' before the final fulfilment justified to a degree: already in this history some anticipatory signs of God's reign – a reign of justice and peace for the poor and oppressed – ought to be visible. It is liberation theologians in particular who provide the framework for such partial 'real–symbolic' realization of 'God's reign'. At this point Kehl comes close to Hanson.

Decisive for Kehl's construction is the wish to reconcile the very divergent Christian – New Testament and other – viewpoints of eschatological hope; it was this wish that led him to opt for a spiritualized, internalized view of cosmic eschatology. Not every interpreter, however, is prepared to let the apocalyptic cargo go. Christopher Rowland for one takes sides for an 'apocalyptic' view even in the present, following Latin American theologies of liberation. For Rowland, 'continuity with the biblical revelation demands' that one reckons even today with realistic eschatology 'as the central pillar of Christian doctrine'. The book of Revelation 'is much nearer to the centre of early Christian belief than is often allowed' (Rowland 1987: 117). In the Lord's Prayer, the petition 'your kingdom come' envisages a concrete kingdom on earth. The spiritualization of this earthly hope, its removal to a transcendent heavenly realm, is the great error of early Christianity. However, Rowland later gives a far too unitary account of 'early Christian eschatologies'. It is simply not the case that these eschatologies 'fairly consistently down to the time of Irenaeus in the second century looked for the consummation of all things in this world, when Christ would reign' (Rowland and Corner 1991: 92, cf. 118, 123) – though many did. He also completely neglects the morally problematic sides of the book of Revelation; nor does he make clear how the problems connected with the antiquated world-view are to be avoided in modern versions of the apocalypse. Ideological criticism is applied to part of the material only.

Clearly, Rowland's position is diametrically opposite to that of Kehl; it reflects the opposition of liberation theology to the spiritualizing mainstream view (once established by Augustine). The point of the present discussion is that both views can appeal to the New Testament, i.e., to some segments in it. In the New Testament we find both an apocalyptic, realistic, earthly view, and a spiritualized view which locates the 'kingdom' beyond this earth. The distinction roughly corresponds to that between the 'Jewish' view of the resurrection of the body and the 'Greek' view of the immortality of the soul (though the latter had in New Testament times penetrated many Jewish circles as well).

The distinction is elaborated by Nikolaus Walter in an article on 'Hellenistic eschatology in the New Testament'. At its close he takes sides for pluriformity (Walter 1985: 355–6). We should not reject either alternative to the advantage of the other. But neither should we try to construct an overall compromise which seeks to accommodate the contradictory views within a single larger framework, to 'combine in one "system" what is structurally incompatible'. On the contrary, precisely the plurality of the eschatological language should 'stimulate us to ever new contemporizations'.

In this very central case the New Testament contains at least two divergent lines of thought which can only be deemed incompatible, if they are perceived as 'teachings'. On another level, with respect to social contexts, the contradictory views can be seen as alternative answers to a common dilemma: in human life, injustice and meaninglessness reign. To this dilemma different solutions, each dependent on the group's tradition and thought world, are sought. The problem is, by and large, common; the solutions vary. (Of course there are differences even in sensing the problem: freedom fighters in Roman Palestine conceived the plight of the world in terms different from those of many Diaspora Jews.)

The New Testament thus presents us with a problem which has not lost its urgency during the past two millennia. It also presents us with a number of people struggling with the problem and looking for solutions in different directions. A natural thing to do would be to recognize ourselves as one more link in a long chain of people struggling with basically similar problems. Different groups have always tried to deal with the dilemma with the help of their respective traditions, interpreted in the light of their respective experiences. This applies to us as well. We too have to deal with the seeming absurdity of life with the help of our tradition in the light of our experience which includes world wars, nuclear bombs and holocausts.

Thus, the New Testament in itself tends to nurture variety, even pluralism. There is no point in simply appealing to 'the New Testament', much less to 'the Bible'. The 'Scripture' one appeals to is never Scripture 'as such', but is always construed in some special way (for examples see Kelsey 1975: 14–119). The least one can do is to spell out on which part of Scripture one wishes to found one's claims – and which parts, by implication at least, are dropped.

That is the least one can do, but one should do more. Having discussed eschatological expectation and also the appropriation of the traditions of and about Israel, Leslie Houlden notes that these two 'vital elements in the first Christians' symbolic universe' are 'wholly problematic', 'a tangle of confused notions and unsatisfactory answers' (Houlden 1986: 90).

The expectation of the End as expressed in the Synoptic apocalypse (Mark 13 and parallels) or in Revelation was the way in which those Christians 'sought identity and intelligibility for themselves'. But 'in truth, all they really knew and had, at the factual level, was "Jesus" – whose impact was the basis of their distinctive experience and institutional existence', and 'all they knew and had that was distinctive at the theological level was belief about him in the light of their already existing belief in God'. The ideas about the End were 'wholly conditioned by time and circumstance', 'not "hard" doctrine, but simply attempts to solve pressing problems in the only terms then available' (Houlden 1986: 90). Those terms, the existing beliefs, had been decisively shaped by the ancient Israelite conviction that Yahweh was the victorious helper of the nation in its battles and the inviolability of Zion. The former attitude was based on old stories about Exodus, in reality a very minor event, if it ever took place at all; the latter went back to Canaanite beliefs. As history had defied these convictions, they had been projected onto the screen of the eschatological future. What a tenuous basis this would be for salvation–historical constructions in a world which has experienced Auschwitz and Hiroshima. It is questionable if a 'harder' core exists on any other point either.

A FORMAL MODEL FOR THEOLOGY

Houlden proceeds to ask the following question:

Is there not then freedom for other Christians, receiving the impact of Jesus in their own time and place, to form their own identity by seeing past and future, and indeed the wider present, in terms drawn naturally from present circumstances?
(Houlden 1986: 90)

The answer can only be yes. The contribution of historical study to theology could well consist in liberating the religious quest from false expectations concerning the Bible.

Indeed, biblical criticism may provide a formal model for theology. It shows that the formation of biblical (as of any other) tradition can be viewed as a process of interaction between tradition, experience and reinterpretation. Here especially the redaction–critical and sociological approaches are helpful. The New Testament is full of traces of experiences, not all of them 'religious'; social experience actually looms large in the development of Christian thought, e.g. the experience of being rejected by the majority of the Jewish community. These experiences have been interpreted and reinterpreted in the light of the tradition of the interpreter (see Räisänen 1990a: 122–36). This process has always been going on: before, in and after the Bible. One has of course not always been conscious of it; one has pretended simply to exegete the Bible when one has in fact presented a strong reinterpretation. This should encourage theologians to engage in conscious and admitted reinterpretation of their theological tradition in the light of their experience as modern persons. Hanson and Kehl are not necessarily wrong in interpreting eschatology, but it should be admitted that their constructions are far less 'biblical' than they themselves suggest. There should be no pressure necessarily to agree with this or that biblical strand; one should, in fact, feel free, in the spirit of ideological criticism, to decide against all biblical options, if need be. A modern attitude to the New Testament might perhaps resemble the attitude taken by early Christians like Paul towards the Old Testament – with the significant difference that the radical re-application of Scripture should take place consciously, not in a hidden or unreflective manner. We might then take the New Testament in a radically typological sense: we use its words and symbols, but we use them as foreshadowings of something new which is demanded by our very different global situation.

The diversity will remain, and has to be respected or even appreciated – made canonical, if you like. The New Testament could be seen as a discussion in the style of Talmud: open-ended, introducing endless debates. Christians should learn to read the canon of the New Testament 'in a living conversation with all the writings in all their diversity and divergence' (Johnson 1986: 548).

In the process of selective and conscious reinterpretation, biblical ideas and concepts may well turn into 'symbols' (a more elusive notion). Whether or not 'kingdom of God' was, for Jesus, a 'tensive symbol' as Norman Perrin (1976: 29–32) held, it can be interpreted as such a symbol for us. 'Kingdom of God', 'resurrection', 'redemption', even 'Christ' and 'God' may be thoroughly problematic as concepts or ideas, but can still serve as evocative and challenging symbols (we recall how Kehl wants to retain the 'millennium' as a 'real-symbol' with an ethical meaning and hortatory force). Symbols, values and stories can be freely moulded and used by theologians in the light of their experience and sense of reality and responsibility. Reflecting on the history of a central Christian doctrine, Maurice Wiles comments:

> If what held Christians together were seen as the use of the same myths rather than the holding of the same beliefs, it might be easier for Christians to accept the measure of variety that there both should and will be between them.
>
> (Wiles 1977: 164)

An impressive early example of a 'symbolic' theology is provided by Johannes Weiss (1892). He realized that the kingdom of God as proclaimed by Jesus (a supramundane future reality) was quite different from the 'kingdom' as interpreted by Ritschl (a community of morally acting people). Still, he found the notion as used by Ritschlians theologically helpful. The point is that he knew what he was doing in using the concept (we might say: the symbol) in a different sense than it had been used in the beginning.

Originally, Christianity is not a 'biblical' religion in the sense that its doctrines were based directly on the Bible (Carroll 1991: 68ff.). In this sense, freedom with regard to the Bible is nothing very novel (it is more like a return to pre-Reformation Christianity). But of course there is no return to a non-biblical authoritarian theology either. Critical study of the Bible has alerted scholars with ears to hear to use the same canons of criticism in the study of any documents, including formulations of doctrines. Experience gained in biblical studies does not tend to produce trust in set doctrines.

This approach appeals to imagination. Conceivably the literary–rhetorical methods, whose contribution to historical issues is of limited value, could help here, on the level of application, at least when particular texts are being applied. Biblical study could, then, provide theology with stimuli and challenges, with symbols and values. Or, in the words of liberation theologian Clodovis Boff (1991: 30), it could offer 'something like orientations, models, types, directives, principles, inspirations', 'not a what, but a how – a manner, a style, a spirit'.

The experience–reinterpretation model is of some ecumenical relevance: it allows everybody to start where he or she stands, working with his or her own tradition. It should be helpful to recognize for example that not only both Catholics and Protestants can appeal to certain strands respectively in the New Testament, and that certain parts are difficult to both, but that the same also applies to the 'conservatives' and the 'liberals' of the various confessions. The New Testament itself amounts to a story of an ongoing battle between 'conservatives' and 'liberals' in the early Church. Contextual hermeneutics becomes all the more relevant.

The model is also of inter-religious relevance. The realization that many early Christian theological statements have functioned as legitimating strategies in a battle with non-Christian Jews over a common biblical heritage helps one not to absolutize them. It is easy to understand that mainstream Judaism emphasized other experiences and other interpretations of the biblical tradition than did the emerging Church. Significantly, some of the difficulties Jews and Muslims have had with Christian doctrine are today shared by many biblical scholars and Christian theologians (witness the debate on the myth of incarnation).

The proposed model is a purely formal one. Exegesis cannot provide theology with criteria that could determine the content of contemporary theological affirmations. It can of course establish which are majority views in the New Testament, but this information is of historical interest only. The content and meaning given to the inherited symbols must depend on extra-biblical (philosophical, theological and ethical) criteria for which the theologian himself or herself must take responsibility. Systematic theologian Gordon Kaufman makes the point well:

> However important biblical and historical materials are to the reflection of the theologian, they never can function as final authorities. In every generation it is the theologian herself or himself who makes the final decision about what con-tours the notion of God will have on the pages being written.
>
> (Kaufman 1981: 273f.)

The model implies that propositional theology in the old style will be discouraged. Theology can be understood as an attempt to make sense of our experience of reality with the aid of our tradition (which includes a strong religious, partly biblical element) as our starting point, and as making sense of our tradition in the light of our interpreted experience of reality. This kind of theology does not presuppose any predetermined results. What is encouraged is theology as 'seeing as . . .', as a sort of poetry. John Hick makes the point well in connection with incarnation (1977: ix): the (later) conception of Jesus 'as God Incarnate, the Second Person of the Holy Trinity living a human life, is a mythological or poetic way of expressing his significance for us' (though it must be kept in mind that this was probably not the intention of those who created the doctrines of trinity and incarnation; it is a conscious reinterpretation of our own which, in this case, comes closer to the earlier strata than the established doctrines do). The preponderance of ethics and action over dogmatics seems a natural consequence too.

Is such a model not highly subjective? Of course; but then theology always was a subjective undertaking, though this was seldom admitted. Kaufman makes it clear that theology 'can no longer take it for granted that there is a fixed body of belief which is simply to be interpreted and explained'. He continues:

> On the contrary, the central task of theology in the present situation is to ascertain just what beliefs or concepts inherited from the tradition are still viable, and to determine in what ways they should be reconstructed so that they will continue to serve human intellectual and religious needs.
>
> (Kaufman 1981: 179f.)

The inevitable subjectivism can be reduced, however, by paying attention to the rule that a tree will be known by its fruits. An appreciation of the effects of the New Testament on the lives of women and men could serve as an important link between historical analysis and theological contemporization. As assessment of these effects from the point of view of ideological criticism could lead to an ethical criticism of the New Testament itself. Unfortunately, the actual 'effective history' of the Bible (which is not identical with the history of its exegetical interpretation) has not yet been the subject of systematic study; here a vast area of research awaits workers (Räisänen 1992b). What effects has the Bible had as Scripture? Obviously it has had both salutary and detrimental effects, and these should be carefully sorted out. An unbiased 'effective history' of the Bible, coupled with ideological criticism, could function as a realistic prelude to a reflective use of the Bible in theology. It does set one thinking that some of the darkest sides of the biblical influence are linked with quite central points of traditional Christian faith: precisely the notion of the absoluteness of Christ has contributed to the annihilation of those who disagreed, trusting their own traditions.

> The critical reading of the Bible has often been seen as hostile to theology. On the contrary, it is perhaps the first stage in the development of a seriously critical theology. If criticism and theology appear to be at loggerheads it can only be because theology is trying to shore up pre-scientific ways of doing theology by utilizing uncritical methods of reading the Bible . . . If half the energy which some theologians devote to reconciling (integrating?) modern science with religion were put to integrating biblical criticism and theology, intelligent critical theology might be in better shape today . . . Both [i.e. theology and Bible] would have to make serious concessions to each other, and the developing consensus – if such were possible – would probably look nothing like earlier and more traditional forms of theology.
>
> (Carroll 1991: 145f.)

REFERENCES

Boff, C. (1991) 'Hermeneutics: Constitution of Theological Pertinency', in R. S. Sugirtharajah (ed.) *Voices From the Margin: Interpreting the Bible in the Third World*, London: SPCK.

Bultmann, R. (1952 and 1955) *Theology of the New Testament*, London: SCM Press.

Carroll, R. P. (1991) *Wolf in the Sheepfold: The Bible as a Problem for Christianity*, London: SPCK.

Childs, B. S. (1992) *Biblical Theology of the Old and New Testaments*, London: SCM Press.

Clines, D. J. A. (1993) 'Possibilities and Priorities of Biblical Interpretation in an International Perspective', *Biblical Interpretation* 1: 67–87.

Davies, M. (1990) 'Literary Criticism', in R. J. Coggins and J. L. Houlden (eds) *A Dictionary of Biblical Interpretation*, London: SCM Press.

Dunn, J. D. G. (1990) *Unity and Diversity in the New Testament*, London: SCM Press.

Esler, P. F. (1987) *Community and Gospel in Luke–Acts: The Social and Political Motivations of Lucan Theology*, Cambridge: Cambridge University Press.

Fowler, R. M. (1992) 'Reader-Response Criticism', in J. C. Anderson and S. D. Moore (eds) *Mark and Method: New Approaches in Biblical Studies*, Minneapolis: Fortress.

Gottwald, N. (1979) *The Tribes of Yahweh*, London: SCM Press.

Hanson, P. D. (1988) *Old Testament Apocalyptic*, Nashville: Abingdon.

Hick, J. (1977) (ed.) 'Preface', in *The Myth of God Incarnate*, London: SCM Press.

Houlden, J. L. (1986) *Connections: The Integration of Theology and Faith*, London: SCM Press.

Johnson, L. T. (1986) *The Writings of the New Testament*, Philadelphia: Fortress.

Käsemann, E. (1964) *Essays on New Testament Themes*, London: SCM Press.

Kaufman, G. D. (1981) *The Theological Imagination: Constructing the Concept of God*, Philadelphia: Fortress.

Kehl, M. (1986) *Eschatologie*, Würzburg: Echter.

Kelsey, D. H. (1975) *The Uses of Scripture in Recent Theology*, London: SCM Press.

Malbon, E. (1992) 'Narrative Criticism', in J. C. Anderson and S. D. Moore *Mark and Method: New Approaches in Biblical Studies*, Minneapolis: Fortress.

Perrin, N. (1976) *Jesus and the Language of the Kingdom*, Philadelphia: Fortress.

Räisänen, H. (1990a) *Beyond New Testament Theology*, London: SCM Press.

—— (1990b) *The 'Messianic Secret' in Mark*, Edinburgh: T. & T. Clark.

—— (1992a) *Jesus, Paul and Torah*, Sheffield: Sheffield Academic Press.

—— (1992b) 'The "Effective History" of the Bible: A Challenge to Biblical Scholarship?', *Scottish Journal of Theology* 45: 303–24.

Rowland, C. (1987) *Christian Origins*, London: SPCK.

Rowland, C. and Corner, M. (1991) *Liberating Exegesis: The Challenge of Liberation Theology to Biblical Studies*, London: SPCK.

Samartha, S. J. (1991) 'The Asian Context: Sources and Trends', in R. S. Sugirtharajah (ed.) *Voices From the Margin: Interpreting the Bible in the Third World*, London: SPCK.

Stuhlmacher, P. (1992) *Biblische Theologie des Neuen Testaments 1*, Göttingen: Vandenhoeck & Ruprecht.

Sugirtharajah, R. S. (1991a) 'Inter-faith Hermeneutics', in R. S. Sugirtharajah (ed.) *Voices From the Margin: Interpreting the Bible in the Third World*, London: SPCK.

—— (1991b) 'Postscript', in R. S. Sugirtharajah (ed.) *Voices From the Margin: Interpreting the Bible in the Third World*, London: SPCK.

Syreeni, K. (1990) 'Matthew, Luke and the Law. A Study in Hermeneutical Exegesis', in T. Veijola (ed.) *The Law in the Bible and in its Environment*, The Finnish Exegetical Society, Helsinki-Göttingen: Vandenhoeck & Ruprecht.

Theissen, G. (1978) *Argumente für einen kritischen Glauben*, München: Chr. Kaiser; trans., *On Having a Critical Faith*, London: SCM Press (1979).

Walter, N. (1985) ' "Hellenistische Eschatologie" im Neuen Testament', in E. Grässer and O. Merk (eds) *Glaube und Eschatologie*, Festschrift W. G. Kümmel, Tübingen: J. C. B. Mohr.

Weiss, J. (1892) *Die Predigt Jesu vom Reiche Gottes*, Göttingen: Vandenhoeck & Ruprecht; trans., Philadelphia: Fortress (1971).

Wiles, M. (1977) 'Myth in Theology', in J. Hick (ed.) *The Myth of God Incarnate*, London: SCM Press.

Wink, W. (1973) *The Bible in Human Transformation: Toward a New Paradigm for Biblical Study*, Philadelphia: Fortress.

FURTHER READING

Bowden, J. (1988) *Jesus: The Unanswered Questions*, London: SCM Press.
Casey, M. (1991) *From Jewish Prophet to Gentile God*, Cambridge: James Clarke.
Teeple, H. M. (1992) *How Did Christianity Really Begin?*, Evanston: Religion and Ethics Institute.
See also chapters 5, 6, 8, 9, 41, 45.

8

THE BIBLE AS HOLY BOOK

Stephen Prickett

The concept of the Bible as a holy book contains special pitfalls. Even the apparently simple question of definition raises acute problems of circularity and question-begging. Conventional academic methodology would presumably begin with defining what is a 'holy book' and then proceeding to enquire in what ways the Bible might or might not be held to conform to this genre. Yet even the most cursory inspection of the historical material reveals how much our idea of a holy book is rooted in, and stems directly from, the Bible. The result has produced a curious paradox: because our word for 'book' has a common semantic root with the title by which our own holy book is known, there is a sense in which the idea of a book, *any* book, has become 'holy' in Western thought; at the same time, the Bible itself has acquired – and it is important to recognize that it is a historical acquisition rather than an innate right – a unique and exclusive status. Books are symbols of spiritual power. As Heine in the nineteenth century prophetically remarked, 'Wherever books are burned men also, in the end, are burned.' Film clips from the 1930s of Nazis ceremonially burning books is a twentieth-century illustration of the awesome power, and therefore potential danger, attributed to the status of a book by at least one secular modern European state – however disturbed and irrational an example Hitler's Germany might be. The uneasiness aroused by the sight of the same thing being done before television cameras in Bradford in the 1980s is not merely a reflection of inhibitions in our own collective psyche stemming from the consequences of Hitler's Third Reich, but also, indirectly, of the complex relationship that seems to exist between two self-defined holy books. If we needed an example of the degree to which our notion of the category is essentially singular and exclusive, we need only look at the difficulty Western Christendom has had, since at least the Crusades, in coming to terms with the existence of that other holy book, the Koran.

The depth of this cultural clash between Christianity and Islam immediately suggests a further hidden agenda to the whole question of definition. If, on the one hand, we can all freely acknowledge that there are many examples of holy books to be found in the various major religions – past and present – it may on the other hand also be true, to a greater degree than we are consciously prepared to recognize, that, deep down for us in what might be called our cultural psyche, the category is totally exclusive. There may be many books in the world that have been reverenced as 'holy' by the adherents of particular religions: other cultures, Buddist, Hindu, Zoroastrian or even ancient Egyptian, may indeed have allowed for a plurality of such works; but, if the category is to have an internalized as distinct from simply a formal meaning for us, in the last resort we, as Christians (or Jews, or Muslims, as the case may be), know that there is, and can be, only one genuine holy book – the rest can safely be assigned to a spectrum of categories ranging from 'possessing some divine insight or even inspiration' through to 'blasphemous nonsense'. At least for Jews, Christians and Muslims, the various 'people of the book', that last noun can only be in the singular. The 'People of the books' would be a meaningless Babel.

THE FORMATION OF 'THE BIBLE'

This curious ambiguity between implied pluralism and effective singularity is as typical of the Bible structurally as it is historically. Our English word 'Bible' is derived, via the French word *bible*, from the late Latin *biblia*, a feminine singular noun that meant simply 'the book'. In its older Latin form, however, *biblia* was not read as the feminine singular, but as the (identical) neuter plural form, which was, in turn, derived from the Greek *ta biblia*, which meant 'the books' – essentially no more than a collection of individual works. This shift in meaning reflects the changing physical conditions of the book (or books) themselves. Before the invention of the codex, or bound manuscript volume, the biblical texts were held as individual scrolls stored together in a wooden chest or cupboard. Under such conditions the question of the precise canon of what works did, or did not constitute the 'holy book', or the exact order in which the constituent works should occur, though it might have been a matter of doctrinal debate, was not an immediately practical question. Just as today, one would rarely read from more than one section at once, and the individual scrolls (representing what we would now call the biblical 'books') could (in theory at least) be assembled in more or less whatever order one chose. With the invention of the codex, however, with its immediate practical advantages of compactness and ease of handling and storage, that potential flexibility of sequence was lost. From then on the books had to come in a specific order – and it is significant that the final decisions both as to what constituted the canon of the Hebrew Bible and of the New Testament coincide historically with the widespread introduction of the codex form. What began as 'the books' had, literally and physically, become 'the book'.

As was to happen again later with the invention of printing, that change in physical conditions with the production of the codex was to have incalculable consequences on the meaning and reception of the Bible as a holy book. To begin with, as we have just seen, this loose collection of very different kinds of material composed over a period of almost nine hundred years – including in the Old Testament, history, prophecy, law, devotional verse, proverbs, and even love poetry and fiction, as well as, in the New, letters from named individuals – all had to be placed in a specific order. Juxtaposition always has implied meaning. The ordering necessary for the codex revealed that there were, in effect, not one but several Bibles – and the relationship between the various canons is extremely complex. Indeed, it is a moot point whether we can say the Hebrew Bible is actually older than the Christian one. The work of creating the Hebrew canon did not really begin until after the destruction of Jerusalem in 70 CE – by which time certainly some of the New Testament books (Paul's letters, for example) were already in existence. Anyone who doubts the political nature of the creation of these rival canons, Hebrew or Christian, needs only to look in detail to see the reasons why they were found necessary and how the final choices were made. It is significant that the first known list of Christian books – in effect a putative New Testament – was made by a second-century heretic, Marcion. That we now so label him is an indication that he was the loser in just one of the many political struggles of the period – as is the fact that all his works were subsequently destroyed. Nevertheless, we know of the Marcion canon from the attacks that were made upon it: it consisted of one Gospel (Luke's) and some of Paul's letters. Marcion also took the quite logical step of dropping the Hebrew Scriptures altogether from the Christian canon. It was in response to Marcion that the early Church, led by the redoubtable Irenaeus, then had to define orthodoxy by making its own canon and declaring it to be a single, sacred and unalterable corpus. It is true that, as Robert Carroll has remarked, 'Canons are about struggle and community conflict . . . Much persecution helped to create the illusion of uniformity, and the arrow of time allowed the mythology of the victors to write the history books' (Carroll, 1991: 7) – but it is also true that these 'victories' were not always as clear cut and decisive as such political theories of history might suggest. The process of canon-formation was accompanied by intense and often acrimonious debate, and only finally completed (though still not quite in its present form) by Eusebius after the Council of Nicaea – which had been summoned by the Emperor Constantine with an interest in formulating Christian doctrine and defining heresy not altogether unconnected with the political objective of defining the role the Emperor was to play in the new Christian state (Romer 1988: 196–7).

It is hardly surprising therefore that the arrangement of the Old Testament as it emerged from various councils, including finally that of Nicaea, is significantly different from that of the Hebrew Bible, from which all its constituents are taken. The latter is divided into three sections: the Torah (the five books of Moses corresponding to what Christians have traditionally called the Pentateuch); the Prophets (traditionally sub-divided into the 'Former Prophets', or what Christians know as the 'histories' from Joshua to Kings, excluding Ruth, Esther, Chronicles, and Ezra–Nehemiah, and the 'Latter Prophets', comprising the books also known as the Prophets in the Christian Bible); and a final grouping known simply as Writings, which includes the Psalms, Proverbs, Job, the five Megilloth (or 'Scrolls': Song of Songs, Ruth. Lamentations, Ecclesiastes, and Esther), and Daniel, ending with Ezra–Nehemiah and Chronicles. In contrast, the Christian Old Testament is commonly divided into four sections: the Pentateuch, the Histories (which include Joshua to Kings, with Ruth following Judges, Chronicles, Ezra, Nehemiah, and Esther); the Poetical Books (Job, Psalms, Proverbs, Ecclesiastes, and the Song of Songs); and the Prophets (including Daniel). The difference implied by this rearrangement is striking.

For Jews, the Torah is the foundational document which defines who they are as a people; the histories from Joshua to the fall of the monarchy are combined with the prophetic texts as historical illustrations of God's promises or threats to his people; while the Writings are a more open-ended group of texts, relating to the practice of the Jewish religion after the Babylonian exile. The effect is at once timeless and open. The ending of the Torah, for instance, with the death of Moses outside the Promised Land, rather than including the book of Joshua and the triumphant conquest of Canaan, can be seen as a clear signal as to how the whole Hebrew Scriptures are to be read. It points not least to the pattern of perpetual exile and questioning that has now characterized the Jewish people for thousands of years. The Christian rearrangement of the Hebrew Scriptures to form the Old Testament, on the other hand, is a polemical and even a doctrinal pointer to what is to follow it in the New. All the historical books are now put together, as if to place the history of Israel firmly in the past; the poetical books occupy a kind of timeless space reserved for prayer and meditation; while the prophets come last, pointing to the future and the coming fulfilment in the New Testament. It suggests a dynamic and purposeful sequence, rather than an open quest.

It also means that among the political moves that underlay the formation of the Christian Bible was the emerging idea of the Bible itself as a holy book of a quite new kind. As re-created from the Hebrew Scriptures, it encompassed the history of the world from its creation, through the Fall and redemption of mankind, to the final judgement. Given the implied completeness of this grand sweep, it is difficult to imagine what else another holy book, in addition to or complementary to itself, might contain. The exclusiveness of the Bible was thus a direct concomitant of the exclusiveness of Christianity. For Irenaeus and those like him there could be no compromise with paganism – and, unlike the first generations of Christians, that meant no compromise either with the local penumbra of gnostic sects or with Jews. Unity was an essential ingredient of the formula, not an extra. Yet the mere fact that the unity of this exclusive holy book was composed of such a wide range of apparently miscellaneous parts necessarily meant that right from the first formations of the Christian canon our sense of the Bible has, as we have seen, involved an inherent tension between singularity and pluralism, unity and diversity. The traditional phrase 'the Book of Books', contained an ambiguity that implied both that its contents somehow contributed to a mysterious and God-given unity greater than its constituent parts, and, at the same time, as has already been suggested, that it was *the* pre-eminent and superlative book: as it were, the class-definer, the book by which all other books were to be known as *books*. Historically it is not so much that the Bible is a member of an exclusive sub-species of book – the 'holy book' – as that all books are in some sense 'holy' in that they belong to the same category of objects as the Bible.

A BIBLICAL CULTURE

As a result our culture has become 'biblical' in ways that at first sight seem far removed from the Bible's Hebrew origins or the Eusebian canon. To begin with, we have acquired from it, directly and indirectly, a very particular set of literary expectations. Because it is taken for granted in the Bible that there is a meaning to the whole cycle of human existence, both individual and collective, and that every event, however seemingly trivial, has a figurative, typological, or, as we would now say, symbolic relation to the whole, we have learned in other areas of our existence to look for narrative, with a pattern of hidden meaning, rather than a mere chronicle of events. This expectation runs very deep in Western society, affecting not merely fiction, but biography, history, and, of course, science – that distinctive product of a belief in a rational and stable universe where every part has its meaning in relation to the grand 'story' of the whole. It is a paradox still too rarely appreciated (especially by those puzzled by Newton's obsessive interest in biblical history and prophecy) that the scientific revolution of the seventeenth century probably owed more to Hebrew mysticism than to Greek rationality.

Second, and following directly from this, our idea of what constitutes a book includes within itself that notion of unity with diversity. Our concept of narrative assumes the possibility of many parallel stories – sometimes apparently unrelated; we take for granted sub-plot and main plot; stories within stories; parallel, complementary, and even contradictory stories that may link thematically rather than by direct influence. It is no accident, for instance, that many of the foundational works of English literature: Malory's *Le Morte d'Arthur*, Chaucer's *The Canterbury Tales*, or Spencer's *The Faerie Queene* are also, in effect, collections of stories relating in various ways to a single common theme. The same kinds of structures were used by Boccaccio in Italy and Rabelais in France. Similarly, the frequency of two or more thematically related plots in Elizabethan drama – and most notably in Shakespeare's plays – emphasizes the origins of English drama in the biblical models provided by the medieval Miracle Plays. Again, popular drama had similar origins on the continent – in Italy, France, and Germany; it was only later that the French court, as ever, leading a francophile Europe, initiated a taste for the more austere and concentrated classical forms.

BIBLE AS INTERPRETATION

Above all, whether in the French or English tradition, we are accustomed to the idea that a book is, by its very nature, interpretative. Here the Christian Bible differs in degree but not essentially in kind from the Jewish one. As we have seen, right from the start the problem of creating the Christian canon came up against the problem of translating and re-interpreting its Hebrew past. The process of translating the Jewish Scriptures for Christian purposes also inevitably involved a massive re-interpretation of their contents. Some of this turns on what Ernst Fuchs and Klaus Ebeling have called *Neuheitserlebnis* or the experience of radical novelty, where the existing cultic language of Judaism was given new life by being redeployed with reference to Jesus as its paradigm example (Ernst 1979: 34). The re-orientation of the Old Testament idea of sacrifice in relation to Jesus' crucifixion would be just one example. What we see happening right at the dawn of the Christian era is thus, in effect, a two- or even arguably three-fold process of translation and appropriation. Thus, when the Hebrew, Aramaic, and Greek of the Christian Bible were translated into Latin, the very terms of the translation were also being transformed with radically new meanings. By identifying Jesus with the sacrificial Passover lamb of Jewish ritual, not merely was the idea of sacrifice being given a new focal point and meaning, but in addition a rich vein of figurative pastoral typology was simultaneously being opened up and appropriated from the Hebrew Scriptures to link with similar imagery in the New Testament – as the many popular translations of the twenty-third Psalm bear witness.

Many of the books of the Hebrew canon, however, involved prescriptions for Jewish cultic rituals which had little or no relevance to the practices or beliefs of the new Hellenistic Christian communities scattered around the eastern Mediterranean. In many cases their narratives, laws, and even ethical teachings actually seemed to contradict those of the New Testament. Marcion's open dismissal of the Hebrew Scriptures was one response, if a blunt one, to the obvious difficulty. For those like Irenaeus and Eusebius who believed the Hebrew writings to be nevertheless divinely inspired, some method had to be found to harmonize them with what was now believed to be their fulfilment. Jewish interpreters had already shown with their allegorizing of the Song of Songs how texts could be given other meanings apart from their obvious literal one, and this existing tradition was now reinforced and made more easily acceptable by the adoption of similar Greek methods of exegesis. In the first century CE, Philo, a Hellenized Jew, foreshadowed the later Christian synthesis of Hebrew and Greek traditions by claiming that not only were the Hebrew Scriptures compatible with Greek philosophy but that in many cases the latter had been influenced by them. In so doing he showed how Greek allegorical methods could be used on other Hebrew scriptural books. Soon the general claim that Christianity was the key to understanding the Hebrew Scriptures – the message of Philip to the Ethiopian in Acts 8 – was supported by an increasingly elaborate system of figurative and allegorical interpretation. Later critics, such as Origen and Augustine, were to lay the foundations of a system of exegesis so complex and polysemous that by the Middle Ages the literal meaning of even such writings as Paul's letters took second place to figurative meanings. The interpretation of texts was thus not so much an incidental activity of the new religion as an integral part of its foundation and subsequent development. From the recorded sayings of Jesus onwards, Christianity in effect constituted a new critical theory.

Yet just because Christianity began with a special sense that it differed from the world that preceded it, and that its own heritage had now to be thought of differently from the way in which it had been previously understood, the interpretative function of narrative was uniquely central to its development. It is said that Herodotus visiting Thebes in Egypt, gazed in awe at the 300 generations of high priests of the temple recorded on its walls, as he realized that such a list went back for thousands of years before the dawn of Greek history. Recounting this anecdote, J. H. Plumb argues that it was precisely this sense of the past as a problem that made Herodotus the first real historian – and he contrasts this with the untroubled and uncritical approach of the ancient Chinese chroniclers, for whom there was no threatening earlier civilization, and for whom the succession of one emperor after another for upwards of five thousand years was simply an extension of time (Plumb 1969: 111). In contrast with the Chinese, the compilers of the New Testament, like Herodotus, approached the past not as a sequence of time, but as a problem with a meaning that had to be explained.

This sense of the past as a problem was compounded rather than relieved by the first few centuries of the Christian era. One reason, perhaps, why Christianity, rather than its many rivals, was able to ride out the destruction of the Roman Empire was that its own literature prefigured models not merely for the destruction of great empires, but for a meaningful pattern to their rise and fall. The biblical world was never a self-sufficient culture isolated from surrounding societies. It had clung rather to a marginal existence at the intersection of the spheres of influence of greater powers, and Jewish political and cultural life had only flowered in the brief intervals between the waning and waxing of the imperial ambitions of others – Egyptians, Assyrians, Babylonians, Persians, Greeks, and Romans. Moreover, if the arguments of Albright, Damrosch and others are correct that the origins of the Bible do lie in the 'problem' presented to the ancient Hebrews by the older literature and cultures of surrounding Near Eastern peoples (Damrosch 1987), then it is also true that this quality of having a multiple, even a 'translated' past which must then be appropriated, was in some sense already present even in Old Testament times. The section in which that past is most clearly acknowledged is, of course, the pre-Patriarchal part of Genesis, but it is also true that the Bible as a whole is permeated with an awareness of other hostile and inimical cultures that threaten not merely the political existence of Israel, but much more fundamentally, its own unique culture.

BIBLE AS TRANSLATION

This brings us to one of the most important qualities of the Bible – and one that marks it out as being peculiarly different from, say, its great rival in exclusivity, the Koran. For Europe the Bible has always been a translated book. More than that: it is a book whose translated, and therefore foreign, status has always been a conspicuous part of our whole civilization's historical identity – in a social, literary, and even religious sense. Almost every line of its text serves to remind us that it is about the people of another time and place who belonged to other kinds of societies from our own and who spoke different languages from ourselves. We have grown so accustomed to this curious fact that it is worth pausing for a moment to call attention to the obvious. Whatever its degree of borrowing from the Bible and other earlier writings, the Koran is mediated to the Islamic world in the same Arabic in which it was written by the prophet Muhammad. A Muslim, whether in Glasgow, Mecca, Samarkand, or Jakarta, is obliged to pray in the original and therefore sacred language dictated to the founder of his faith, it is said, by the Archangel Gabriel for that purpose – and for that reason there must be no tampering with the word of God. Three-quarters of the Christian Bible, by contrast, is acknowledged even by its most fundamentalist adherents to be originally the Scriptures of another religion and written in a language never spoken by any Christian community. Moreover, even that section, originally the Hebrew Bible, was not at any stage a linguistically homogenous whole. It is only when we contrast these basic assumptions about origins with the doctrine of the verbal stability of the Koran that we begin to realize just how great is the gulf separating Christianity and Islam in their unconscious preconceptions about the nature of a text. In spite of a strong fundamentalist tradition in certain parts of evangelical Protestantism, Christianity, by the very appropriative eclecticism of its origins, has always been at least dimly conscious of its own distance from its sacred writings. In other words, the problem of its own origins has always warranted a theory of reading, a hermeneutic system of interpretation – even if, as in some cases, that appears to be largely in the form of an insistence on the inspired nature of the King James Version. In contrast, though English-language versions of the Koran are, of course, now available, it is nevertheless clearly understood by Muslims that these are not translations; they do not, and cannot carry the force of the original inspired Arabic wording. Moreover, whatever earlier sources or degrees of appropriation modern scholars may detect behind the various Surahs of the Koran, there is, officially at least, no counternancing of the idea that the way in which we understand the past might be conditioned by the cultural circumstances of the present. This has, of course, been made easier by the fact that for contingent historical reasons, until large-scale migration of Islamic communities to Europe and North America began in this century, it was possible for most of the Muslim world not to feel any problematic or disturbing cultural gap between itself and its sacred texts. Though it had spread outward from the countries of its origin in the Arabian peninsula, unlike Christianity, Islam had never been forced to decamp from its own geographical heartland.

But if the Bible is essentially a book in exile from its original context, we should note that this has always been true of it. As other chapters in this volume will make clear, recent scholarship has repeatedly stressed the eclectic and diverse nature of its origins. Though what non-Jews now call the Old Testament was mostly written in Hebrew, substantial parts of the canon are translations or paraphrases from yet other earlier sacred texts – Canaanite, Mesopotamian or Egyptian, for instance. If it is true that much of it appears to have originated as a critical and often hostile commentary on those earlier religious writings, there is a very real sense in which the Bible can be said to owe its very origins to intertextuality. There are, for instance, many well-documented earlier external sources for biblical stories. The Flood narrative of Genesis is remarkably similar to that written in Hurrian, the language of a tribe which seems to have entered the ancient Near East from north India around 1600 BCE. The name of its hero, Nahmizuli, contains the (vowelless) Hebrew word for Noah, *Nhm*, and his ark also comes to rest on Mount Ararat – which, though it is some way from Canaan, happens to have been right in the heart of the ancient Hurrian Empire. But whereas that story ends with the goddess Ishtar pledging a marvellous necklace, 'the Jewels of Heaven', that she will save humanity from the god Enlil's wrath in future, the biblical account ends with the covenant between man and God, with the rainbow as its sign (Romer 1988: 30–2).

Indeed the resemblances between some of the early Genesis stories and the Mesopotamian *Atrahasis Epic* and the *Epic of Gilgamesh* have led some critics to argue for the existence of a genre of creation-to-flood epics in the ancient Near East (Romer 1988: 30–2). Similarly, if Albright's hypothesized large-scale 'Ugaritic epics' have as yet inconveniently failed to turn up quite as predicted, there is plenty of undeniably Ugaritic and Canaanite material that has – not least in the apparent origins of the 'historical' or 'history-like' events narrated in Exodus. Many biblical terms for household items, including clothing, furniture, and perfumes are demonstrably Ugaritic in origin. There are, for instance, clear parallels in the use of metaphors between David's lament for Jonathan and Ugaritic lyrics; and where Psalm 137 reads 'If I forget thee, O Jerusalem, let my right hand forget her cunning', an earlier Ugaritic text has 'If I forget thee, O Jerusalem, let my right hand wither.' There are also strong Egyptian influences on parts of the Old Testament. Psalm 104, for example, bears a striking similarity to the 'Hymn to Aten', reputedly written by the heretical monotheistic Pharaoh, Akhenaten, in about 1345 BCE. Similarly the story of Joseph and Potiphar's wife (Gen. 39) first occurs in an Egyptian story called the 'Tale of Two Brothers' dating from at least 1200 BCE. Even more interesting are stories which seem to bear the marks of at least two external sources. Thus, although the name 'Moses' is an authentic Egyptian one, the story of the baby in a floating reed basket caulked with pitch is also told of King Sargon, who, by the Bible's own dating, lived more than a thousand years earlier than Moses around 2500 BCE. Pitch, moreover, does not occur in Egypt, but was a common material in Sargon's Mesopotamia (Romer 1988: 51–2; 52–3; 55).

There had almost certainly been strong Mesopotamian influences in Israel before the Captivity, but more than fifty years of exile in Babylon completed the cultural cross-fertilization. It was in this period too that the Jews in captivity came into close contact with the much older monotheistic religion of the Persians, Zoroastrianism. The post-exile court of Zerubbabel and his descendants even spoke Aramaic, the common language of the Persian Empire, not Hebrew. There are ironies here that are still the centre of controversy. As G. B. Caird has noted:

> The language of Haran, whence Abraham is said to have come, was Aramaic ... Hebrew was the language of Canaan (Isa. 19:18) and was taken over by Israel from the Canaanites, along with their knowledge of agriculture and the pertinent sacrificial rites ... When during the last three centuries B.C. Hebrew gradually fell into disuse and was supplanted by Aramaic as the vernacular of the Palestinian Jews, this was reversion rather than innovation.
>
> (Caird 1980: 35)

Certainly by the time Ezra returned to Jerusalem, some eighty years after Zerubbabel and the first wave of exiles, and the bulk of the writings that now compose the Old Testament were either written or put into their present form, there is a lot of evidence to suggest that Hebrew was no longer the normal language of these Jews. As we shall see, it is not an aberration but actually a recurring characteristic of the Bible that it is written in a language at some remove from that spoken by its readers. When the New Testament came to be written during the first century CE, Hebrew was so unfamiliar to the Palestinian Jews that, even in the synagogues, the Hebrew Scriptures had to be read either by means of paraphrases into Aramaic, called Targums, or, in Greek-speaking areas, by the Greek translation called the Septuagint.

If we assume that Jesus and his immediate circle were themselves Aramaic-speakers, we have to note also the fact, so easily passed over, that the written accounts of his life and sayings are themselves, even in their earliest known forms, translations – since the remaining section of our Bible was written in a different language altogether: *koinē* Greek, a non-literary low-status form of the language spoken mostly by traders and non-Greeks throughout Asia Minor in the early years of the Christian era. This was a sign of the times, for within only a generation or so the early Christians had lost almost all contact with both Hebrew and Aramaic and were using either the Septuagint or the Old Latin and then the Vulgate versions. Thus what was in effect the first truly unified monoglot version of the Bible was already itself not merely a translation, but a translation of translations. Nor was this the end of the long process of textual accommodation. The English King James Authorized Version was, in turn, a political as well as a religious undertaking in which the Protestant appropriation and alteration of the Catholic Vulgate paralleled the earlier Christian appropriation and alteration of the Jewish Scriptures.

These origins of the Christian Bible in a tradition of multi-layered and polysemous readings has left it with a very particular, even peculiar, cultural flavour. It is easy to assume, for instance, that the Reformation meant a shift back to a literal reading of the Bible, but figurative readings were in fact to persist well into the nineteenth century – and are by no means extinct today. Indeed, the idea of a literal reading is itself not unproblematic. More to the point, however, is the fact that just as its openly translated and appropriated quality is more than just part of the 'givenness' of the Bible, but seems to flaunt itself as somehow intrinsic to the way we are expected to read it, so too does a continued sense of it as meaning something more and other than what it appears to say. As has already been suggested, it is possible that the origins of the Hebrew Scriptures themselves lie not so much in a particular revelation as in a critical commentary on yet earlier texts or even unwritten traditions of neighbouring societies. A text that, in this sense, gives evidence within itself of the existence of other, prior, texts already also implicitly suggests multi-layered ways of reading. It may also help to account for a curious contradiction in our attitude to the Bible that has had a profound effect on the development of many modern European languages – not least upon English.

BIBLE AS PROBLEMATIC

Though historically European Christian communities may have had little difficulty in accepting the Bible's general relevance to their immediate situation, they have always been simultaneously aware that in some very profound sense it was nevertheless an alien book. That such a statement immediately sounds as if it is flying in the face of two millennia of often highly rhetorical and emotional polemic to the contrary is an indication of the tensions behind all discussions of the 'relevance' of the Bible. Ricoeur's claim that the letters of St Paul were no less addressed to him than to the Romans, the Galatians, and the Corinthians (Ricoeur 1981: 191), is a modern and deliberately paradoxical restatement of an argument that in origins goes back at least to the days of the Church Fathers. Nevertheless, in spite of the way in which the traditional culture of many European Protestant societies has centred on particular translations of the Bible, it has never been possible for them to lose sight altogether of the immense cultural distance separating them from the worlds of both the Old and New Testaments. The immense weight of traditional moralistic and devotional rhetoric urging people to see it as pointing directly to themselves merely serves to illustrate the almost intractable scale of the original problem.

As might be expected, the result has been a polarization of reactions. On the one hand the tradition of medieval stained-glass windows and illuminated manuscripts where the Patriarchs or apostles are performing their typological roles in contemporary dress and setting has been continued with increasing personal emphasis into the post-Reformation world. We are familiar with the corresponding deployment of biblical metaphor and typology not merely in religious and moral polemics but in the parallel contemporary discourses of politics, of trade, medicine, and everyday life. The *Sarum Antiphoner*, a late fourteenth-century manuscript at Ranworth Church, near Norwich, shows Jonah, dressed much as a local parson, being swallowed by a great fish from the nearby Broad. A panel of thirteenth-century stained glass in Canterbury Cathedral shows Jesus raising Jairus's daughter in a curiously perspectived medieval merchant's house. To James I of England, thundering against the filthy habit of smoking, it seemed entirely natural to compare the perverted lusts of smokers to the Children of Israel 'lusting in the wilderness after quails'. To Oliver Cromwell, fighting against Catholics in Ireland, it seemed no less appropriate to justify the brutal obliteration of Catholic society and, if necessary, the massacre of his opponents, by supporting the Protestant Plantation in Ulster with images of the Israelites occupying Canaan appropriated from the book of Joshua. To the Catholic Gaelic Irish of the same period – and later – it seemed equally obvious to compare their sufferings with 'the children of Israel in Egypt under the oppression of the enemies of God' – a reciprocity of images that has prompted Conor Cruise O'Brien to comment that one could say Ireland was inhabited not really by Protestants and Catholics but by two sets of imaginary Jews (O'Brien 1972: 309).

On the other hand, it has prompted an equally fierce resistance to the Bible's traditional status as a holy book. One example must stand for many. In September 1791 the Revolutionary French National Assembly was formally presented by its Secretary, the former aristocrat Constantin-François de Volney, with a short monograph entitled *Les Ruines, ou méditation sur les révolutions des empires*. The enigmatic title gave little clue to its real thesis, which concerned the origins of religion, and in particular of Christianity. According to Volney, not merely all Indo-European and Semitic religion but even astrology as well could be traced back to a common origin in ancient Egypt at least seventeen thousand years ago. All modern forms of supernatural and revealed religion were, he claimed, in reality nothing more than the misplaced products of primitive nature-worship, time, and the accidents of historical diffusion. Thus the gods of Egypt had been appropriated by the Aryans into their own pantheon before being eventually reduced to a single deity in Persia in the sixth century BCE. This new syncretistic monotheism had in turn been adopted by the Israelites when released from the Babylonian captivity by the Persians, transmitted to the Christians and thence eventually to Muhammad and the Bedouin tribesmen of the Arabian desert: 'Jews, Christians, Mahometans, howsoever lofty may be your pretensions, you are in your spiritual and immaterial system, only the blundering followers of Zoroaster' (Volney 1881: 83). In keeping with the uniformitarian assumptions of the Enlightenment, miracles were attributed to the power of imagination, the gods to their origins in the forces of nature and the regulation of human society to the operation of natural law and self-love (ibid.: 14–15, 93) Volney supported this argument by a dazzling and a curious range of erudition ranging from Hindu cosmology to the esoteric doctrines of the Essenes (ibid.: 83, 84–5). That, together with its strongly revolutionary and anti-clerical context, was sufficient to account for the book's immediate popularity both inside and outside France. At least three English translations had appeared by the end of the 1790s, and it was still being reprinted by freethinking and radical groups in Britain as late as the 1880s.

If Volney's thesis appears to have lost something of its shock value today – not least because later biblical scholarship has confirmed so much of his evidence – we only need to recall just how devastating in the long term his radical and relativistic historicism was to prove for nineteenth-century Christianity. Though we are more likely to associate the impact of such a methodology in Victorian Britain with later names like those of Hennell, Feuerbach, Strauss, and Renan, this is more because Volney's association with the French Revolution effectively served to discredit his scholarship among the clergy and the world of the Anglican establishment than because his arguments were themselves ineffective. Volney remains a key figure in the history of interpretative theory, and, as the number of translations suggests, he had a considerable direct impact on English radicals at the end of the eighteenth and beginning of the nineteenth centuries (Thompson 1965: 107–8). The book was a major influence on Tom Paine. Thomas Spence published lengthy extracts from *The Ruins* in his journal *Pig's Meat or Universal School of Man's Rights* (McCalman 1988: 24). It was also extensively summarized in the *Freethinking Christian's Magazine* and in the strongly anti-Christian *Theological Enquirer*, as well as in other pamphlets by its editor, George Cannon, an ex-Spencean turned (among other things) pornographer, who published a number of eruditely ironic pseudo-theological works under the pen-name of the Reverend Erasmus Perkins (McCalman 1988: 74). One of the contributors to Cannon's *Enquirer* was the young poet Percy Bysshe Shelley, who allowed him to publish extracts from both his 'Refutation of Deism' and 'Queen Mab' in the first issue of March 1815. If 'Queen Mab', which was to become one of the classic texts of early nineteenth-century radicalism, shows unmistakable evidence of Volney's influence, the same is equally true of his now better-known poem of 1817, 'Ozymandias'. After all, Ramses II (Ozymandias is the Greek form of the name) was, of course, not merely an earthly tyrant, but also a god. Like Blake – who also knew Volney's book – Shelley was quick to see the connections between earthly and spiritual tyranny. That same year, 1817, Mary Shelley, the poet's wife, was to give the *Ruins of Empire* further mythopoeic status by putting it on her Monster's reading list in *Frankenstein*.

Though there was little in the general thesis of Volney's syncretistic and diffusionist argument that was specifically new, and that had not appeared in the writings of, say, Vico, Holbach, Sir William Jones's studies of classical Indian languages and religion, or in such eighteenth-century German historical critics of the Bible as Eichhorn, Reimarus and Lessing, it was perhaps the first time that a polemical work of this kind had caught the popular imagination to this degree. Nor was its refusal to make clear separation between Christianity and other Near Eastern religions the most shocking of its conclusions. Worse, perhaps, was its claim that the Bible had antecedents that might extend back over a period of up to seventeen thousand years. Standard biblical commentaries of the eighteenth century were often in the habit of including not merely the dates BCE of particular events, but also the date of those events after the Creation of the world – which as everyone knew, following the famous calculations of Archbishop Ussher, had occurred in 4004 BCE. Even this implied attack on conventional biblical dating was, however, probably less disturbing for many orthodox Christians than another implicit suggestion of Volney's: that the Old Testament – and in particular the book of Genesis – was not the earliest known written text.

For many contemporary scholars the authority of the Bible was bound up with the belief that Hebrew was the oldest known language – containing at least elements of the original unfallen Adamic language where words stood in an essential rather than a contingent and arbitrary relationship to the things they described (Aarsleff 1982: 58–60). Thus even Johann Gottfried Herder, in his great literary study of the Old Testament, *The Spirit of Hebrew Poetry*, published only shortly before in 1782–3, had done no more than sum up conventional wisdom when he took it for granted that Hebrew poetry 'expresses the earliest perceptions, the simplest forms, by which the human soul expressed its thoughts, the most uncorrupted affections that bound and guided it'. But Herder had still been a clergyman – however unorthodox a one. The idea that there might be behind Genesis a nexus of yet older literary texts, and that the first book of the Bible, so far from being in every sense the beginning of written human experience, the fount and origin of all history, was in some sense a re-writing or a commentary on those texts, constituted for many as great a challenge to contemporary thought as the sixteenth-century substitution of the Copernican for the Ptolemaic astronomical system, or Darwin's placing of Man within the chain of evolutionary biology. Far from being the foundation document of Christian civilization, laid down by divine fiat, it now seemed possible, to those prepared to consider the iconoclastic arguments of Volney and his successors, that the Bible in some sense had begun as an appropriation of the mythological and historical writings of other earlier civilizations.

BIBLE AS DURABLE

Nevertheless, those who believed that the status of the Bible could not survive either the evidence of its syncretistic origins or the historicist critique mounted against it by its more destructive critics were, like so many prophets of its demise, proved wrong. Similarly, reports of the death of Christianity, like those of the death of God, seem on the whole to have been greatly exaggerated. But one effect of the Higher Criticism and the French Revolution was to drive a wedge between the status of the Bible, and belief in the religion whose holy book it was supposed to be. 'The Jewish poets deserve a better fate', wrote the arch-radical and Deist, Tom Paine, 'than that of being bound up, as they are now with the trash that accompanies them, under the abused name of the word of God.' Certainly it would have been difficult to predict in 1700, at the height of neo-classicism, that a hundred years later, with the advent of Romanticism, the literary and aesthetic prestige of the Bible would be at a new zenith. Many biblical critics, both then and later, have failed to understand the significance of this, believing that if the historical authority of the Bible was undermined, then its authority was of only residual aesthetic rather than religious significance. Yet, as we have seen, the peculiar nature of the concept of the holy book as it has evolved within Western civilization has always resisted this kind of compartmentalization. The separation of biblical from literary criticism in fact only dates from the end of the eighteenth century (Prickett 1986: 1–2). In the 1770s, Robert Lowth, the greatest English biblical critic of the century, in massive notes to his *New Translation of Isaiah*, was still following conventional aesthetics when he described Aristotle's *Poetics* as 'the Great Code of Criticism' (Lowth 1807: lxxviii); twenty years later William Blake was consciously to echo and challenge Lowth's formulation when he wrote that 'the Old and New Testaments are the Great Code of Art'. Ironically, that is not a view that Shelley would have disagreed with. The same English radicals, such as Paine, who were avidly reading Volney in the 1790s, even while they were rejecting the ecclesio-political authority claimed for the Bible by the *ancien régime*, were nevertheless turning to its apocalyptic prophecies in search of an appropriate language of change to describe the permanent transformation they had rightly perceived in the structure of European politics (Mee 1992). For Blake the new scholarship also offered something more: a way of escaping the repression and mystification often associated with the established notion of a holy book. His own prophetic works (which he printed and coloured himself) are unique among printed books in their refusal to create a single univocal text. To the despair of modern editors, each is subtly different from the next in the position of the words, or the arrangement and colouring of illustrations – thus preventing any one version establishing itself as final or definitive. For Blake, the power of the Bible lay not in its unchanging truth, but its dynamism and fluidity. As had so often happened in the past, by offering a new way of reading it, Volney and his fellow critics did not in the end so much destroy the power of the Bible, as give it a new lease of life – not least by calling attention to the fact that there had been many such re-readings before.

Extremes meet. In so far as the conventional fideistic readings of the Bible had stressed its special meaning in the individual personal circumstances of each believer, what they were also stressing, in spite of an accompanying rhetoric of unchanging permanence, was its polysemous responsiveness to change. In so far as the radicals stressed its constant re-writing of history to meet the changing circumstances of different societies, they were also tacitly admitting, in spite of an accompanying rhetoric of its essential primitivism and fluidity of meaning, the Bible's astonishing durability from age to age. What in the end differentiates the Bible from other holy books is not its incorporation of much primitive, legendary or miraculous material, nor its eclectic and diverse origins, but the way in which this material is incorporated. Each layer of appropriation is inevitably accompanied by a new hermeneutic theory. Thus, if we are to accept the postulates of the German Higher Critics, those shadowy first Hebrew scribes and redactors differed from those of the surrounding tribes not so much in the actual legends they were re-telling as in the way those legends were now made to serve the new creed of monotheism. The Church Fathers did not alter the words of the Hebrew Bible to create the Old Testament (those were divinely inspired); they altered the order of the books, concluding the Old Testament with Malachi, in order to point to the coming of Christ and the ultimate fulfilment of their messianic prophecies in the New. In turn, the Reformers of the sixteenth century did not alter the wording of the Vulgate, they translated it, consigning the deutero-canonical books of the Old Testament to the Apocrypha, and insisting that Paul's Epistles should be read not typologically, but as theological argumentation. The Higher Critics and the Romantics, whether pro- or anti-Christian, by historicizing the canon, opened the way for yet another radical re-reading not merely of the text, but also of the idea of a holy book itself.

In human affairs, as in physics, there are no fixed points. Inevitably, it was not just the Bible that was transformed by such radical appropriations. The Vulgate, a single authoritative monolingual text for the entire Western Church, was the instrument of the new Imperial power of the Roman Church. Luther's translation of the Bible was to change the German language forever; his commentary on Romans to set the agenda of theological debate for centuries. Tyndale's translation of the New Testament, on which the Authorized Version was to be so closely modelled, did the same if not more for English. Typically, in defending his translation he turned naturally to the imagery of previous biblical appropriation – comparing contemporary Catholics to the Jews who had rejected Jesus:

> because the kingdom of heaven, which is the scripture and word of God, may be so locked up, that he which readeth or heareth it, cannot understand it; as Christ testifieth how that the scribes and Pharisees had so shut it up (Matt. 23) and had taken away the key of knowledge (Luke 11) that their Jews which thought themselves within, were yet locked out, and are to this day that they can understand no sentence of the scripture unto their salvation, though they can rehearse the texts everywhere and dispute thereof as subtly as the popish doctors of dunce's dark learning, which with their sophistry, served us, as the Pharisees did the Jews.
>
> (Tyndale 1989: 3)

Enlightenment criticism and historicization, together with the Romantic reaction, gave to the Age of Revolution a new vocabulary and rhetoric – even in some cases a new agenda. Each changed reading in the light of new circumstances took as its text an earlier change – in what we are now beginning to realize is a tradition with no visible first point. The Bible is apparently a holy book without an ur-text, instead there are only endless layers of appropriation.

We return finally to the evasion with which we began: if the Bible is a holy book, how are we to define that term? If it were not cumbersome to the point of defeating its purpose, one of the most effective ways would be to tell its history – not, that is, biblical history, but the history of the Bible. That story alone is sufficient to establish its categorical uniqueness. Beyond the barest tautology we are into exclusive territory: a class of one whose full meaning we have yet to understand.

REFERENCES

Aarsleff, H. (1982) *From Locke to Saussure: Essays on the Study of Intellectual History,* Minneapolis: University of Minnesota Press.

Caird, G. B. (1980) *The Language and Imagery of the Bible,* London: Duckworth.

Carroll, R. P. (1991) *Wolf in the Sheepfold: The Bible as a Problem for Christianity,* London: SPCK.

Damrosch, D. (1987) *The Narrtive Covenant: Transformations of Genre in the Growth of Biblical Literature,* San Francisco: Harper & Row.

Ernst, C. (1974) 'World Religions and Christian Theology', *Multiple Echo: Explorations in Theology,* London: Darton, Longman and Todd.

Herder, J. G. (1879–80) *The Spirit of Hebrew Poetry,* Berlin: Weidmannsche.

Lowth, R. (1807) *Isaiah: A New Translation,* 5th edn, 2 vols, Edinburgh, vol. 1.

McCalman, I. (1988) *Radical Underworld: Prophets, Revolutionaries and Pornographers in London, 1745–1840,* Cambridge: Cambridge University Press.

Mee, J. (1992) *Dangerous Enthusiasms: William Blake and the Culture of Radicalism in the 1790s,* Oxford: Clarendon Press.

O'Brien, C. C. (1972) *States of Ireland,* London: Hutchinson.

Plumb, J. H. (1969) *The Death of the Past,* London: Macmillan.

Prickett, S. (1986) *Words and the Word: Language, Poetics and Biblical Interpretation*, Cambridge: Cambridge University Press.

Ricoeur, P. (1981) 'Appropriation', *Hermeneutics and the Human Sciences*, ed., trans. and introduced by J. B. Thompson, Cambridge: Cambridge University Press.

Romer, J. (1988) *Testament*, London: Michael O'Mara Books.

Thompson, E. P. (1965) *The Making of the English Working Class*, London: Gollancz.

Tyndale, W. (1989) 'W.T. Unto the Reader', *Tyndale's New Testament*, ed. D. Daniell, New Haven: Yale University Press.

Volney, C.-F. de (1881) *The Ruins: or a Survey of the Revolutions of Empires*, Introduction by C. Bradlaugh, London: Freethought Publishing Co.

FURTHER READING

Barton, J. (1986) *Oracles of God*, London: DLT.

Bright, J. (1980) *The Authority of the Old Testament*, Grand Rapids, Mich.: Baker Book House.

von Campenhausen, H. (1972) *The Formation of the Christian Bible*, London: A. & C. Black.

Cross, F. M. (1973) *Canaanite Muth and Hebrew Epic*, Cambridge, Mass.: Harvard University Press.

Evans, C. F. (1971) *Is 'Holy Scripture' Christian?* London: SCM Press.

Frye, N. (1982) *The Great Code*, London: Routledge & Kegan Paul.

Hill, C. (1993) *The English Bible and the Seventeenth Century Revolution*, London: Allen Lane.

Prickett, S. (ed.) (1991) *Reading the Text: Biblical Criticism and Literary Theory*, Oxford: Basil Blackwell.

Sawyer, J. F. A. (1991) 'Combating Prejudices about the Bible and Judaism', in *Theology*, 94: 269–78.

Wiles, M. F. (1994) *A Shared Search*, London: SCM Press.

See also chapters 1, 2, 3, 4, 5, 6, 7.

II

THE TRADITION

INTRODUCTION

Leslie Houlden

Looked at from the side of theological thought, the Christian tradition is a sustained process of reflection on the significance and implications of Jesus of Nazareth in the light of the being of God. The process has two other fundamental features. First, it did not start from scratch, but (as Part 1 demonstrates) arose as a development within and out of the already long tradition of the religion of Israel, crystallized above all in the Hebrew Bible. Second, in this process belief about God himself came to be profoundly modified as a result of the phenomenon of Jesus and of thought concerning him: in various ways, God came to be seen as 'Jesus-like'.

It is possible to see this process as a continuous, living whole, involving change certainly, but by way of intellectual growth and development that have been so organic, so free from jolts and re-starts as almost to compel the belief in their being providential. (That is, of course, on the question-begging and rarely questioned assumption that God himself favours the straight and unbroken line and that his followers can and should therefore strive to do the same!)

The process can, however, seem to be more like a chain made up of connected but discrete links: a series of episodes, each drawing on what precedes and contributing to what succeeds, but best understood in its own unique context of culture, sensibility and indeed political and social life. Churches and those who speak for them have almost always had a tendency to maximize continuity, even to see it as unchangingness; while more independent observers bring out rather the movement and the discontinuity.

It depends partly on what counts as 'the tradition'. If the focus is on 'the winners' in a particular episode or period, in effect those who turned out to be the bearers of continuity, then others ('the losers') are likely to fade to the margins and to be discounted. And, given the will they almost certainly possess, the winners are likely to insist on defining their ideas in such a way as to demonstrate continuity. Old ideas are not abjured but, it is alleged, reframed in more serviceable terms.

163

If, however, one insists on a rounded and comprehensive view of particular times and places, resisting hindsight and aiming to look at them in their own right, then a much more complex picture of the tradition will emerge, a much more adventitious sense of the story as a whole. Each part, however defined, will then seem to be most fairly and helpfully assessed on its own terms, and 'tradition' will be a concept both broader and looser.

Tradition functions not only as an unfolding story, like the history of a nation or a college, but as a locus of authority. In this capacity, it exercises what many institutions feel as the *weight* of tradition. In so far as the tradition (or elements within it) has come to be seen as the vehicle of theological truth, arrived at by divine gift perhaps, though bestowed by way of human instruments, then its deliverances will seem to be binding on successors. It is an accumulating body of beliefs and insights, passed on from generation to generation, able to be added to by way of elucidation and coherent provision for new needs or predicaments, but never reduced by the discarding of what critics or protesters come to see as obsolete or plain false. At best, such elements may be reinterpreted. Then the outsider may discern some kind of evasion, and perhaps attribute it to the familiar inertia and power-consciousness of all institutions, here decked out with divine sanction. Only in rare moments is the authoritative tradition in a position to accept that charge or even to comprehend it. The Second Vatican Council has been controversial for seeming to be one such moment, impelled by Pope John XXIII.

A tradition is by definition something handed down. The very notion conveys the sense of continuity of culture. A break in culture would seem to threaten the possibility of genuine continuity and thus authentic tradition. The very word, that is, is biased towards the organic rather than the chain model. And plainly, a strong case can be made, even in these days of detached observation and historical candour, for the organic model. Whatever the shifts of interest, perspective and conviction, the Christian theological tradition has never lost the sense of the God-given character of the created order, the centrality of Jesus' person and teaching, and the sense of an ultimate hope in relation to God – to mention three basic tenets.

Yet it is equally undeniable that we must recognize the discontinuities which 'tradition' masks. In its very first decades, the Christian movement left (and largely lost) its original Palestinian, Aramaic-speaking milieu for the Greek-speaking world of the Roman Empire. And (to leap to recent centuries) it has come to find itself addressing and inhabiting virtually every people, every culture, every language under the sun – with a growing consciousness of the challenge to discern the proper limits of adaptability. The very missionary success of the great Churches in particular brought them agonizing problems which have become all the more acute as cultural self-awareness and sophistication have spread across the globe. Even those Churches most authoritarian in structure and most firmly wedded to ideas of theological identity can scarcely shut their eyes to the situation. It is apparent that everybody has the right to exist!

In some ways, the most significant intellectual change in this regard began to arise in the sixteenth century, when many, at first within Christianity itself, came to test the tradition against various yardsticks: initially against a biblically derived picture of Christian origins and the early Church, as in classical Protestantism, and then against more abstract criteria of rationality, historical evidence (now with its independent measures of truth), or even common sense. All these forces have tended to compel a sense of Christianity as a mobile tradition, involving numerous shifts in beliefs and attitudes, despite the undoubted continuities of faith, institution and concern.

Tradition has its points of crystallization. Creeds, liturgies, the decrees of councils and synods, great leaders and teachers or great books, all will epitomize the tradition in a particular context and add to its illuminative power, often for centuries to come, even, it seems, world without end. Innovations, like new liturgies, are best 'sold' as re-presentations of very old ones, though of course the cultural setting of their use is as new as could be.

Tradition dances in a peculiarly complex pattern with Scripture – in one sense an early product of Christian tradition, and in another a partner whose voice must always be listened to, but (and this is crucial) the interpretation of which is a task for the tradition, embodied in the living Church. This is true as much for those who acknowledge this interpretative role for tradition in relation to Scripture as for those who claim to be taking Scripture in its plain sense as their sole guide.

In order to form a view of whether tradition is better pictured as moving in a continuous line or as jerking and even lurching its way along its path through time and place, it is necessary to be conscious of one's vantage point; whether as a historian observing the course of events and endeavouring to discern intelligible patterns, or as a theologian seeking to identify the various articulations of Christian belief. The days of the blinkered propagandist will no doubt never come to an end: so there are accounts of the Christian tradition that seem wilfully to exclude large parts of the available evidence, in order to further some sectional cause. They may seek to commend a particular strand in the tradition or to demonstrate the falsity of the tradition in part or whole. In the past, such procedures have indeed been the norm. Nowadays, though widely differing accounts can still be offered, even by those innocent of crudely sectarian interests, especially of major episodes like the Reform of the sixteenth century, the characteristic stance of the modern academic describing the tradition combines detachment with sympathy; enough detachment to deal justly with the evidence, and enough sympathy to enter into the aims and achievements of those whose lives and work are being described. This tone certainly marks the chapters in this Part.

The chapters are not all of the same kind. Thus, the first seeks to imprint on the reader's mind both the fundamental and pervasive role of Jesus in

Christian tradition and something of the complexity that is inescapably associated with that role. It is partly a question of disentangling the historical facts about Jesus from the plethora of ideas that have been associated with him, and partly a matter of recognizing the changing tones of those ideas as they have come on the scene down the centuries.

The five following chapters trace the tradition chronologically, dealing with the major phases in its development (see also the parallel chapters in Part 4 on Spirituality). In the first phase, the early centuries, it is a matter of seeing how, with a minimum of organization, the Church succeeded in forging both the idea of orthodox faith and a more or less agreed content for that orthodoxy – at the expense of relegating dissident beliefs to the penumbra of heresy. Nowhere more than in this period is the modern theologian, lacking the machinery and probably the inclination to distinguish so sharply between legitimate and illegitimate features of the tradition, compelled to consider how far to applaud the undoubted clarification produced in this period, even though the idiom of thought was so different from the earliest Christian thought forms found in the New Testament.

At the end of his chapter, Robert Wilken throws out a bridge towards the medieval period, which was in so many ways the closely related heir of the patristic period. Yet in how different a world! David d'Avray tells the tale of the movement of the tradition through a period and a society where Christianity was no longer precarious, no longer one option among others, a process begun in the fourth century but long in gestation, and occurring differently in Eastern and Western Christianity. Indeed, the burden of this chapter is that it took most of the so-called age of faith to produce the maximally integrated Christian society of the West – and no sooner was it in existence, with papal authority at its most extensive, than it began to disintegrate, as the Reformation loomed – in this perspective, itself the product of late medieval Christianity in the West.

The fragmentation of the Christian tradition in the sixteenth century, chiefly in Northern Europe (then with its eventual diffusion across the colonial territories of America, Africa and the Far East), is the subject of Alister McGrath's chapter, which itself points forward to the more modern intellectual movements which have their roots in this period. John Kent outlines the profound problems created for traditional ways of discussing Christian belief by the movements of thought that go under the name of the Enlightenment. These centre on the greatly increased sense that it was possible, even mandatory, to think about the sources and content of Christianity as if from outside, from a position of 'honest' impartiality. It was therefore both a philosophical and a historical movement, and it was decisive for all subsequent developments. It was accompanied in due course by profound political changes which resulted in the secularization – in ethos even when not in official stance – of many Western societies, thus creating a quite novel context in which the Christian tradition must live.

This it has done with varying degrees of realism and success, as Keith Clements's chapter indicates. It also shows some of the ways in which the Christian tradition has 'bounced back' in answer to the challenges of modernity, producing fresh responses to fresh situations, notably in the liberation theology that addresses the grievous ills of parts of the Third World.

Gavin D'Costa's chapter examines the ways in which the Christian tradition may relate to another aspect of the modern world which impinges with undeniable force: the realization that, whether it takes an exclusive view of its truth-claims or seeks greater accommodation, Christianity must recognize itself as only one of the mature great faiths of the world. The European perspective of 'Christendom', fortified in the long colonial era, is no longer adequate. But how can the Christian tradition adapt itself to the new light, and how far ought it to do so?

All through history, the Christian tradition has been embodied in and expressed through the phenomena of human culture, across a great spectrum of forms and activities. No wonder it has been, inevitably, such a diverse, even chameleon-like tradition. The final chapter draws attention eloquently to this multi-coloured factor in the whole story, something that has run like a subterranean river below all the chapters.

Organism or chain? The different styles inevitably displayed by the various writers of the chapters that follow tend both to exemplify and to enhance the latter view. But they also show the many points of continuity and the underlying singleness of commitment and devotion that the first chapter of this Part sought to bring out.

9

JESUS IN HISTORY AND BELIEF

Leslie Houlden

JESUS IN CHRISTIANITY

If it is reasonable to say that Jesus is the centre of Christianity, that is not a statement beyond challenge and correction. First, it is not beyond challenge. Christianity has often been at pains to assert its position as a monotheistic faith, whether in the early centuries, in the face of the polytheism of Graeco-Roman paganism, or in recent times, in the context of the diverse religions and belief-systems of the modern world.

Today, in a religio–cultural or inter-faith perspective, it is common to stress the common ground and shared heritage of Judaism, Christianity and Islam. Of course, the voices asserting distinction are far from silent, and observers have to consider whether to place the weight more on differences or similarities, and much will depend on the context in which judgement is made; but it is undeniable that these three faiths (at least) have a certain family likeness, as well as actual historical connections.

Further, on the premise that worship is the heart of any religion, then, though there has been Christian prayer to Jesus from earliest times, its most characteristic formulation has always been that it is addressed to God the Father – 'through Jesus Christ our Lord'. And though much mainstream Trinitarian thought has emphasized the thorough mutuality of Father, Son and Holy Spirit, and so the inherently 'social' character of Deity, equally commonly (and certainly in everyday Christian understanding) the Father appears as the fount of divinity, so that distinction from other monotheistic faiths is felt (however incorrectly) to turn more on the position of Jesus than on division about 'God' at the deepest level. In that sense, Jesus seems to be, however crucial, nevertheless secondary in the Christian religion's scheme of things.

A plain biblical reading seems to confirm such a view. If Scripture as a whole is to be our authoritative guide, then most of it is about God before ever Jesus appears on the scene: in Charles Wesley's words, 'Late in time behold him come'. Far more of the Bible is (if one wishes to put it in these terms) 'the word of God' than 'the word of Jesus'. This plain approach is not greatly discouraged by its traditional Christian qualification by way of the pattern of 'prophecy and fulfilment'. There again, though the picture of the overall thrust and direction of the Bible cannot commend itself except to Christians, the monotheistic assumption of the Old Testament forms the solid foundation on which attitudes to Jesus and convictions about him are built. Putting it crudely, it is the one God who is in charge of the whole biblical operation: creation itself, the foretelling of Jesus and the bringing about of prophecy's fulfilment in his life, death and victory.

It is no wonder that, from the first century onwards, Christians have (sometimes inconsistently with the pattern just outlined) favoured other models, which give greater prominence to Jesus, from the beginning of everything to the end. Thus, Paul, the earliest Christian writer known to us, already identifies Jesus with 'wisdom', which, from being an attribute of God, had long been the subject of personifying or mythologizing tendencies in Judaism (Prov. 8:22ff.; 1 Cor. 1:24). And the Gospel of John identifies him with God's 'word', a term which had developed in Judaism along similar lines to 'wisdom' (Ps. 33:6; Isa. 55:10–11; John 1:1–14). Both ideas carried with them the notion of heavenly existence from 'the beginning', and, when applied to Jesus, implied a leap forward in the way he was perceived – and at least some modification of his subordinate role as an agent of God at a specific time in the course of history, one element (albeit decisive) in a God-centred universe and a God-centred temporal process. It was one thing to apply the language of 'pre-existence', as it were poetically, to an attribute of God, viewed somewhat anthropomorphically; it was, in its implications and consequences, quite another thing to apply it to a man of known time and place, whose historical identity was subject to scrutiny and assessment. But, in their conviction of Jesus' comprehensive function and of his having revolutionized human relations with God in all possible dimensions, Christians speedily took this audacious step. It led them to read even the old Jewish Scriptures (the 'Old Testament') in their own new way: not only as foretelling Jesus' physical arrival and subsequent career, but also as recording his presence and interventions in Israel's (indeed, the world's) whole story, from creation onwards, often incognito and disguised as God's angel; so that the Old Testament was, when rightly interpreted, a thoroughly Christian and Jesus-centred book. Thus, when in Genesis 1:26, God says, 'Let us make man in our own image', it was the pre-existent Christ who was being included in that momentous decision.

This brilliant and innovative move, creating a revolutionary picture both of Deity and of Jesus, was only eroded as, in recent centuries, historical study compelled (and made natural) a more realistic understanding of the Old Testament in the light of its own assumptions and its historical origins. Its authors came necessarily to be seen as people of their time and Scripture as the expression of concepts appropriate to the period of writing. Christians may still read the Old Testament with Christian priorities and values in mind, as a comparison with Jewish ways of reading it soon demonstrates (e.g. the Christian tendency to emphasize the Psalms and the prophetic books and to ignore the Law, which is central to Judaism), but they are less inclined than formerly to see Jesus as speaking in its pages; though old liturgical forms working with the old picture are still in use (e.g. 'by whom all things were made', with reference to Jesus, is the Nicene Creed). In so far as that picture has become unconvincing, then the centrality of Jesus has, implicitly, been reduced in favour of a seemingly monotheistic pattern, with Jesus in a crucial but subordinate role. Historical criticism of the Old Testament may be said to have had this as perhaps its most far-reaching practical effect on Christian belief – one wholly unacknowledged by public ecclesiastical authority (though absorbed in practice by many who exercise it) and, where discerned, sometimes still denied.

It is not only monotheism which may offer a challenge to the apparent truism that Jesus is the centre of Christianity and the heart of its distinctiveness as a faith. From a number of points of view, chiefly of a historical or institutional character, it seems that the Church is the truly central element. Sometimes this is said in a spirit of hostility or cynicism. Christians may claim allegiance to Jesus, but, as deeds speak louder than words (especially pious words), their actions show them much more concerned with the aggrandizement, enrichment and preservation of the Church. It is not hard to point to profound contradictions between the life-style and teaching of Jesus and those of the overwhelming majority of his followers, particularly in their corporate and institutional capacity. And this applies not just to their mediocre achievement (which may be readily understandable) but also to their avowed policies. Even where individual sanctity abounds, the interests of the Church may stultify its impact and be less amenable to the display of Jesus-like qualities. Indeed, it seems that a major feature of Jesus' behaviour was a freedom from those trammels which seem inseparable from the life of organized and long-term institutions.

Similar points may be made from the point of view of objective historical realism. Like any other human phenomenon, Christianity is embodied in time and space, and so in the constant flow of history and cultural circumstance. Whatever its allegiance to Jesus and however great the acclaim it gives to him, it can only view him from its own diverse and incessantly changing settings. Moreover, it must continually reckon with and accommodate itself to the social and cultural contexts in which it exists – and whether it does it by hostility or separation or easy conformity (or some mixture of all three), the principle of context-relatedness is in operation. From this angle too, therefore, the Church, as, in its various manifestations, the 'location' of Christianity, is its true centre. In this perspective, the claim to overriding allegiance to Jesus invites at the least a measure of caution and self-scrutiny, even a recognition of when it is appropriate for the bluff to be called. At all events, the historian is likely to see Jesus as the initiator of a process which has taken a multitude of turns, many of them involving surprising (if understandable) ways of expressing that commitment to him which they all share.

It seems then that the claim to the centrality of Jesus in Christianity is at the very least open to correction. Developed historical awareness makes more and more obvious the astonishing diversity of even contradictory ways in which he has been seen – mostly, with equal and unbounded devotion. Jesus may be central, at least in the sense that Christianity is chiefly differentiated from other faiths by the unique place it gives to him; but the style, character and degree of that uniqueness are subject to immense variety, so that, not surprisingly, the question is raised from time to time whether a particular expression of belief is adequate or permissible. There is room for the ironic reflection that such protests often dwell on matters of belief (e.g. about the manner of Jesus' birth or the historicity of the resurrection), while blatant departures from Jesus' teaching (e.g. about the renunciation of wealth and family) attract no comparable censure and even merit Christian applause (Houlden 1992).

Correction may be offered and plain departures from Jesus' teaching may reasonably be justified by a sober understanding of the nature of institutions-through-history, and so of the inevitability of change, not only in matters where self-interest or practical convenience may incline people to welcome it (the rejection or re-vamping of Jesus' radical ideas on family and property) but also in matters of belief – where there is usually no such intimate threat and both traditionalist and radical tendencies can be indulged freely, even irresponsibly. Or, more theologically, correction may be seen in terms of an understanding of the life of the Christian community (the Church – but in which of its manifestations?) which sees it as itself involved in the redemptive process and as having a God-given contemporary role that goes well beyond its being the mere perpetuator of Jesus' memory and Jesus' teaching and moves in the direction of its being the extension of his work and the God-guided scene of its development, not only in practical activity but also at the level of thought and concept. Here the challenge of the Church to Jesus' position of centrality finds its more judicious and religiously authentic statement: Jesus is to be viewed from within this live tradition available in the Church in the here and now. Commitment to him in that context gives the framework in which change can be theologically legitimated.

This encouraging picture is of course darkened by the difficulty not only of deciding where precisely 'the Church' is located for the due performance of this great task, but also that of knowing what is to be done when it shows itself immobile and far from capable of responding to what seems to many the manifest truth, of eradicating manifest evil and striving for urgent good. It may often seem, in its official organs at least, to belie any claim to a monopoly of discernment.

If the nature of the place of Jesus in relation to Christianity proves on reflection to be a subject surrounded by complexity, one route to clarification is surely a grasp of the facts about Jesus as a historical figure. Even if the elucidation of this matter can only be a preliminary to judging and deciding about beliefs concerning Jesus, it is widely and almost intuitively felt to be an essential piece of ground-clearing or foundation-laying. It is at least a matter of interest to discover how well beliefs fare in the light of knowledge of the history.

JESUS IN HISTORY

Given the historical orientation of modern scholarship, it is not surprising that a vast amount of learned effort has been – and still is – applied to the identifying of the history behind the Gospels and the historical context of Jesus' life (Schweitzer 1910). That over the years so many quite different and even contradictory accounts of these matters have been put forward is due in part to the sparseness and uncertainty of evidence concerning the ancient world, partly to the large faith-investment of many investigators that has often coloured their judgement, and partly to legitimate differences of opinion about the extent to which the Gospels are conditioned by the time of their writing as well as by good tradition about the lifetime of Jesus itself. However, though on many matters wide differences of view remain, recent years have seen considerable narrowing of the limits within which the truth is likely to lie – and some elimination of confessionalism in determining the line to be taken. Differences of view are less likely now than formerly to be dictated by a scholar's background in Judaism or in Catholic or Protestant Christianity.

It would of course be erroneous to suppose that those who at the beginning and indeed down the centuries have come to faith in Jesus have done so after the dispassionate consideration of the evidence, now the object of such attention. The absence of that kind of consideration may deter modern people from taking their testimony seriously and making the effort to look at the matter in their way – and perhaps lead to a dismissal of them as the victims of credulity or superstition, however sublime or heroic the expression of their faith may have been. But the point for us is that, at least in present-day Western society, such consideration is widely felt to be mandatory, at any rate as a step in the right direction. Belief may or may not follow, but at least this essential hurdle must be surmounted. While many now find some such feeling to be inevitable and desirable, we should recognize that in the past it has played little part. Once we have seen this, we may be less surprised by some of the styles of faith that have been held and refrain from blaming those holding them for wilfully ignoring 'the facts' or viewing them through distorting lenses. It may be another matter now when publicly available evidence or angles of vision are neglected and ignored when found threatening or inconvenient.

A preliminary step is to acquire as clear a picture as possible of the Palestine of Jesus' lifetime – and indeed of the wider Roman and Hellenistic context of which Palestine was a small part. Such a picture provides a framework of institutions and social and economic realities within which Jesus belonged (Theissen 1986; Freyne 1988). It would prevent the ascription to him of ideas and modes of action which were simply not then available and reveal the likely influences and reactions to various groups and opinions then active. For example, archaeological discovery and the reappraisal of various literary sources have confirmed that in the period before the fall of Jerusalem in 70 CE, the failure of the Jewish revolt against Roman power, and the subsequent establishing of a tighter rabbinic hegemony over Judaism, Hellenistic culture and Greek language had made considerable inroads into Palestine, especially in urban life. This is clear from the prevalence of inscriptions on burial urns and elsewhere in Greek, and from the remains of Greek-style theatres in towns like Sepphoris, a few miles from the village of Nazareth, the home of Jesus. (The town is, incidentally, never referred to in the Gospels, revealing how patchy is our most direct source of evidence for Jesus and how subject to the vagaries of surviving tradition where there was no particular interest in mere biographical completeness.) Even letters probably from the hand of Bar Kokhba, leader of the later Jewish rebellion (132–5 CE), are written in Greek, which he apparently found a more congenial medium for writing than Aramaic or Hebrew, the native Semitic tongues (Meyers and Strange 1981).

More than any other single influence, the discovery (and then gradual publication) of the Dead Sea Scrolls in the years following the Second World War have given a fillip to the whole subject of the Judaism of the turn of the eras (Vermes 1977). Everything seemed to go into the melting pot, for here was the literary fruit of a virtually unknown, but plainly highly significant Jewish group, belonging to but in sharp reaction against the world of the Jerusalem Temple and its ruling priesthood. Against this background, other groups like the Pharisees needed to be reassessed (who exactly were they and what precisely did they stand for?), and the movement around Jesus came up for comparison. It became customary not only to look for points of similarity and distinction, but to see earliest Christianity as a reform movement within Judaism – and so to debate the criteria for identifying its becoming detached from Judaism: thus raising in another form our earlier question of Jesus' real innovatory role (Dunn 1992).

While this increase of information about first-century Palestine is greatly to be welcomed, as is the sharper and more confident understanding which it makes possible, our knowledge remains relatively meagre and there can be disagreement about quite central matters, for example, what precisely were the Pharisees' main tenets or how economically deprived and then how discontented were the peasants of Galilee in Jesus' day? A judgement on these matters can have a major influence on our ability to 'place' Jesus: for example with regard to controversy with groups like the Pharisees (Sanders 1985) or in relation to a possible political or socially revolutionary thrust to his teaching (Bammel and Moule 1984).

Uncertainty about aspects of the historical setting combines with uncertainty about the degree to which the Gospels reflect the circumstances of their writing, as well as those of Jesus himself, to surround the quest for 'the facts' about Jesus with difficulty. This does not deter many scholars and others from entering on the task of writing lives of Jesus or accounts of his teaching and significance. Each will adopt a policy which seems promising to the author concerned, and many are likely to achieve a measure of success. A feature of recent years has been the degree of convergence despite different starting points and methods.

For example, on the basis of knowledge of the social and religious possibilities in first-century Palestine, Jesus may be put in the category of 'apocalyptic prophet'. Leaving aside later doctrinal formulations and the then fashionable appreciations of Jesus as a sublime moral teacher, a number of writers turned to this identification at the beginning of this century (Schweitzer 1910), and increased knowledge of the Jewish setting has not undermined its fundamental correctness. Jesus was a figure preaching an imminent cosmic crisis, God's supreme intervention to save his own, called by Jesus to rally to God's cause. That was the heart of his purpose and remained the best assessment of him, whatever view was taken of other, more timeless elements in the teaching ascribed to him and whatever reconstruction was made of his fatal relations with authority. That teaching might be seen as moral provision for the interim period before the crisis, or as evidence that Jesus bore also the character of a traditional teacher of 'wisdom' and saw no discrepancy with his more urgent message, or indeed as owing less to Jesus than to the creative activity of the later first-century churches for whom the sense of imminent crisis had faded and who needed guidance (as from the Master's lips) for their everyday problems.

Jesus' death has been seen as the unsurprising result of his own political agenda: he was something of a religious freedom-fighter, moved by the acute poverty of the Galilean peasantry, anticipating some aspects of the later Jewish rebellion against the Romans in 66 CE (Brandon 1967). Or else, more convincingly, as evidence of the extreme nervousness of Jewish and Roman authorities, acting in collusion to neutralize all possible powder kegs, and so fearing Jesus' forthright message (Rivkin 1984). Or, in particular, as provoked by his demonstration in the Temple (Mark 11:15–19) – whatever precisely it signified, the various evangelists interpret it differently – rather than, as the Gospels seem to imply, by his challenges to the Jewish Law, by sabbath healings especially. Here Jesus' behaviour and teaching seem not to be beyond the range of contemporary Jewish debate, and certainly not grounds for a death sentence, and their presentation may well be coloured by the rift between Church and synagogue by the time of the Gospels' writing (Sanders 1985).

A modification of the 'apocalyptic prophet' identification of Jesus draws on sociological analysis: he was a charismatic figure, in the technical sense of one who revolutionizes existing values and thought-patterns, bringing about the rejection of accepted life-styles and institutions (Hengel 1981). This approach focuses on traditions such as Jesus' injunction to a would-be follower to abandon family responsibility even to the extent of neglecting the fundamental duty to bury his father – so urgent is the call of God (Matt. 8:21–2); and on the strong theme that discipleship involves the quitting of both family and property (Mark 10:17–31). It is generally felt that the authenticity of this material is assured by the speedy abandonment of insistence on such requirements in the developing churches: especially in urban centres, householders of some affluence were virtually a necessity for the establishment and support of church life (Theissen 1982); and emphasis soon came to be laid on the fostering of the Christian family (Eph. 5:22–6:4).

Another (and broader) way of building on knowledge of the first-century setting is to use it to establish the boundaries within which the historical truth about Jesus is likely to lie (Harvey 1982). It is a matter of constructing a profile of Jesus by way of congruity with Jewish customs, legal procedures, messianic beliefs and other religious ideas. Along these lines it may be possible to claim a high degree of accuracy for the Gospel record, without denying the obvious effects of later reflection. Or else attention may concentrate on the persistence and frequency with which particular sayings and themes are to be found in the tradition about Jesus, whether in the Gospels or other early Christian literature, and this may help us to see the main thrusts of Jesus' teaching (Crossan 1992) – for example his openness to the outcast and marginalized of his society and in his espousing of accessible table-fellowship, pushing aside conventional frontiers of race, gender and social type.

It is possible to set Jesus so naturally in the context of his times that, whatever the subsequent effect of his life, he merges into his background – perhaps as a typical 'holy man' of the period (Vermes 1977). Valuable as this approach is, it can leave a hard historical question: how then was Jesus' legacy so utterly different from any of his Jewish contemporary teachers? It is scarcely credible that belief in his resurrection can be made to account for all of it, with his life and teaching not particularly remarkable. It was after all the resurrection of Jesus that was involved, that of a person with memorable characteristics which, with whatever development, were religiously significant in their own right.

FROM HISTORY TO FAITH

Jesus preached the kingdom of God: the Church preached Jesus. Some such formulation often comes to expression as a way of summing up a crucial (and perhaps discomfiting) transition at the roots of Christianity. Like most such succinct statements, this one is as problematic as it is illuminating. It is true that if we concentrate on the first three Gospels (called 'synoptic' because of the amount of material they share, in one combination or another), Jesus' preaching centres on what can best be summed up as 'the kingdom of God' – that is, God's overwhelming sovereignty and its impending realization in a reformed and rejuvenated world. The expression itself and the theme dominate, for example, the tradition of Jesus' parables (Mark 4 etc.). In this respect at any rate, it is generally agreed that these Gospels are more true to Jesus' life than the Gospel of John, where this phrase scarcely occurs (3:3, 5), and where attention focuses on Jesus' own person, albeit as himself pointing to God, with whom he is seen as identified in will and purpose (1:1; 5:17; 10:30).

The move from the first three Gospels to that of John seems in this respect to typify emerging attention on Jesus himself as the centre of Christian devotion and Christian claims. On the other hand, even if the first three Gospels depict a Jesus who preaches God's rule over the world and the urgency of God's call, there can be no doubting that Jesus is the subject of their story, the impulse for their writing and a figure whose person is a matter of some measure of definition. He is, for example, called 'messiah' (Greek, *christos* = anointed one), a term used in Judaism to designate a leader chosen by God, but now aligned to the character of Jesus' own activity and disposition. He is also called Son of God, again indicating a role as God's special agent in the world; and Son of man, chiefly eliciting apocalyptic associations but again signifying (putting it in general terms) 'agent of God for the purpose of salvation'. Each of these (and other) expressions has a pedigree in Jewish usage which contributes to its application to Jesus and helps to explain why it was felt by his followers to be appropriate. Equally, however, application to Jesus produces a shift in the sense of the expression itself – at least in the general way that usage always involves re-interpretation; and the very concentration of these expressions (and the symbols they evoke) on Jesus brings about a certain merging of their sense. At all events, their prevalence in the Gospels goes to show that the evangelists see Jesus not simply as pointing to God but as a person playing a clear and prominent role on God's behalf – and (especially given the use by Jesus alone of 'Son of man') as not reluctant to articulate that role. To that degree, it may be held that Jesus preached not only the kingdom of God but also his own place within the reality to which it pointed. He was no mere anonymous signpost (see Hahn 1969; Hengel 1976; Lindars 1983; Houlden 1992).

There is, as might be expected, a difficulty in being sure how much of this self-referring material in the first three Gospels is, like a great deal of that in the Gospel of John by general agreement, the result of subsequent church development affecting the way older material was put or the way older terms were understood. On that there is a wide variety of opinion. But it would be hard to maintain that Jesus had no ideas about his own role in his mission: as at least some kind of prophet or messianic figure, however (as especially in

Matthew's and Mark's portrayal of him) self-effacing (Mark 5:43; Matt. 12: 15–21; 21:4–5).

This account of the Gospels, though important for clarifying the dictum that 'Jesus preached the kingdom of God: the Church preached Jesus', is misleading in one major respect. Before ever the Gospels were written, the letters of Paul show an overwhelming concentration on 'preaching Jesus' (e.g. 1 Cor. 1:23). There is no question of denying the priority of God ('to the glory of God the Father', Phil. 2:11), but novelty and significance for salvation lie squarely with Jesus, his fully authorized and empowered agent (Ziesler 1983) (Gal. 4: 4; 2 Cor. 5: 17–21; Phil. 2: 6–11). Belief about Jesus, fully formed and articulate christology, is there from the start – or at least from the time of the earliest Christianity observable to us. At the same time, these writings show no sign whatsoever of Jesus having pointed away from himself to 'the kingdom of God', and indeed show little interest in Jesus' own message and teaching. There is an imminent new dispensation but Jesus will be at its heart, even if it is taken for granted that God is its initiator (1 Thess. 4:13–17). Though we do not know how fully Paul's way of looking at the matter dominated the Christian scene in the later first century, when the Gospels were being written (as he came to dominate the finished collection of early Christian writings put together rather later into the New Testament), it may be a general confirmation of the first three Gospels' faithfulness to the true proportion of things that, despite the impulse to concentrate all claims on Jesus, they portray him pointing away from himself – preaching the kingdom of God (Mark 1:14–15).

Yet, whether by direct statements about him or by the very character of the Gospels, Jesus is the subject of early Christian preaching. From earliest times (1 Cor. 15:3–5) that preaching emphasized above all the concluding aspects of Jesus' earthly career – his death and his victory (whether that was, as most commonly, seen in terms of his resurrection, albeit variously identified, or in terms of his heavenly exaltation) (Evans 1970). The instinct was right – if the concern was to home in on Christianity's most striking and distinctive claim. Most elements in Jesus' teaching could be paralleled, more or less, in much Jewish or Hellenistic (or indeed other) moral teaching, and his healing and other activity were not strikingly unique – though its implications with regard to the nature of salvation and the emphases which it displayed were certainly distinctive, especially when subsumed into the great climax to which they led. But it was the ending which rightly came to dominate the Christian picture, as most strikingly demonstrating what Jesus stood for and as achieving what he came to do.

It may be that much of this concentration on Jesus' death and triumph, and especially the former, was due not so much to the desire to proclaim as to the necessity to explain. It was not easy to tell others – or to tell oneself – that an obscure death by the ignominious judicial act of crucifixion was demonstrative of God's saving love and the key to his purposes for the human race. Here is another reason why, whether it came to the fore or (as in Paul's letters) did not, the actual human reality of Jesus, his teaching and behaviour, were crucial to his 'survival' as a major object of devotion and faith. This was no faceless person to whom cross and resurrection as it were fortuitously happened – thereby compelling the highest of claims for his importance. That account is scarcely credible. Again, it is the death and resurrection not of anyone but of Jesus of Nazareth with which we are concerned; and in that sense the transition is smooth between what Jesus stood for and what so soon came to be believed and preached about him. Indeed, it was surely the impact of his life which, in part at least, stimulated the determination of his followers not to permit his effect to cease and to give an account of his death that was consonant with his mission.

The 'resurrection' came to be seen in no single light, indeed there was soon difference of view on precisely what it was. Did it centre on post-death appearances of Jesus to his followers (1 Cor. 15:5–8; Luke 24; John 20–1), or on the emptiness of his tomb (Mark 16:1–8), or on his physicality (Luke 24:42–3; John 20:26–9)? Emphases and even actual beliefs seem to have differed even to the point of contradiction. Some of these ways of looking at the matter had important links with other, more central beliefs (e.g. about divine action through Jesus), others were more related to dispelling incredulity (e.g. the stress on physicality).

In any case, there is a question whether the resurrection belief was at the start itself subordinate to the conviction that God had vindicated Jesus by taking him to heaven and associating him with his own universal rule and its future completion: thus we find references not only to the kingdom of God but also to the kingdom of Christ (1 Cor. 15:21–8; Matt. 16:28); God had brought about the climax to which Jesus' whole life had always pointed. Psalm 110:1 ('Yahweh said to my lord: sit at my right hand, until I make your enemies your footstool') is the most widely quoted scriptural text in the New Testament: eloquently it legitimated and assured both Jesus' triumph and the future cosmic consummation to which he had always looked.

Whether it be seen in terms of resurrection from the tomb or appearances to followers or, less physically, heavenly vindication, it is impossible, given the lateness and disparateness of the evidence available to us, to tell exactly what lay at the root of this faith. Explanations of a modernizing kind are put forward: there were hallucinations to people in a state of shock; some modern religious or political movements whose basis has been shattered bounce back to life when, in rational terms, they should dissolve; the disciples embarked on a deliberate process of deception. But here too the distance of time and the nature of the material make it impossible to confirm or deny. What is clear is the broad character of the conviction that Jesus was in authority in heaven, in touch with his followers (cf. 'the Spirit' in John 14–16; Acts 2; 9), and thus a figure of the present and not just of the past.

In the movement of Christianity into the position of a faith, the death of

Jesus was in many ways, given the world-picture and the assumptions of the time (where heavenly exaltation was an 'available' idea), harder to handle than its sequel (Lindars 1961). We know how widely it became a matter of derision and incomprehension as people encountered the Christian faith (Wilken 1984). It was therefore vital that it received positive explanation, that it was shown to be no unfortunate happening but an essential element in God's design, and even characteristic of the profundities of God's dealings with humankind. It was not an embarrassment at all but an outcome wholly to be expected by the discerning, and wholly welcome to those conscious of their deepest needs, for release from sin, futility and death.

In this matter, it is no surprise that Christians turned to their major authoritative resource, the Scriptures: in part those writings came to the rescue in a situation that was potentially one of disillusion and failure; in part, if certain passages (Pss. 22; 69; and, a little later, Isa. 53) were highlighted, they made possible a path of reflection already present as an ingredient in Judaism – concerning the redemptive value of suffering itself. It was indeed a pattern embedded in Israel's history as a people, with its constant memory of liberation from captivity in Egypt and Babylon. So passages such as these, and symbols such as the figure of Isaac in Genesis 22, not withheld from death by his father (cf. Rom. 8: 32), and the lamb of Passover (John 19: 37), could illuminate the death of Jesus, give it positive meaning and indeed render it exactly what ought to have been expected all along. The Gospels show precisely that expectation (Mark 8: 31; 10: 32–45), and it is impossible to know how far it is a case of prophecy after the event and how far Jesus, aware of prophetic destiny, did indeed see himself as meant for a martyr's death: there would be nothing surprising in that. It did not necessarily mean that his actual death was much easier to absorb; but it would have meant that the process of understanding and assimilation had already begun in his lifetime, and the development of profound explanation along a number of different lines, apparent so early in Paul and no doubt even antedating him, was already launched.

Though we have, somewhat neutrally, described Jesus as God's agent for salvation, and seen how his death and resurrection were brought within an understanding of that role, it is also to be noted that the particular colour given to belief in Jesus as a result of his death was not without effect on belief in God. Here is an important further aspect of the Christian monotheism that was discussed at the start of this chapter, and it affects the matter of Christianity's position alongside other monotheistic faiths. Those faiths may indeed share belief in the one God, but their perception of him can still differ a great deal. In Christianity from the start, God was now seen as 'the God and Father of our Lord Jesus Christ' (1 Peter 1:3): in effect, God was such that he showed his hand most characteristically in the suffering of Jesus, not in 'permitting' it but rather in achieving his saving purpose by means of it.

It is not exactly, at that time, that it was seen as throwing light on what has come to be seen as 'the problem of suffering', so that, whatever the difficulties, we can say that God has been alongside us there – however encouraging such a way of looking at the matter may have come to be. It is more that appeal was made to the idea, deeply embedded in Judaism (as indeed elsewhere), of the saving efficacy of the offering of sacrificial animal victims for human sins and ills. That and other imagery enabled Jesus' death to be seen as, and God to be involved in, the possibility of transition from darkness to light, death to life, sin to forgiveness.

The sense of God as involved in human suffering, even suffering alongside us, has not always been equally congenial to Christian patterns of belief – it has been particularly problematic when, as in the patristic period following on from New Testament times, God's transcendence and immunity to change were basic data of belief; but there have also been times, like the present, when it has been much to the fore, and indeed helped to commend Christianity as a faith facing human life realistically (Moltmann 1974).

FROM FAITH TO RELIGION

It is neither easy nor, perhaps, necessary to define the criteria whereby a faith, a way of devotion and commitment, such as the followers of Jesus gave to him in his lifetime and afterwards, turns into a religion. Such a question has institutional as well as conceptual aspects, and there is a difference between things as they saw them and our perception in the light of history. But a crucial moment must be Jesus' becoming an object of worship and prayer. The indications are that this preceded by some way the development of concepts that might give it formal validity. That is to say: if worship is something properly given only to the divine, then either to worship Jesus was implicitly to affirm his divinity or that which was offered to him before he was seen as divine was not truly worship; but the early stages of Christianity seem not to have observed these tidy distinctions.

Prayer to Jesus is evidenced very early – it is found in the language of Palestinian Christianity, Aramaic: *maranatha*, our Lord, come (1 Cor. 16:22). The belief in Jesus' exaltation to God's 'right hand' (Psa. 110:1; Acts 2:34–6) surely hastened the process: a heavenly, right-hand figure has a status of supreme mediatorship when it is a matter of approaching God. It is, however, often felt to be a revolutionary step when Jesus comes explicitly to be called 'God' – as he is most clearly of all within the New Testament in John 1:1, 18; 20:28; but compare Philippians 2:6–11 for an intermediate step. In one sense, this judgement is correct: Judaism affords no clear parallel to such exalted claims, certainly not with regard to someone who had so recently walked the earth and about whom memories and stories abounded (not to speak of his all too human suffering and death). It is here indeed that Judaism has seen, from the first century onwards, the blasphemy inherent in Christianity, surfacing already in the Gospel of John (e.g. John 5:18).

Yet once again the picture is less clear than has often been thought. Judaism's unambiguous monotheism, which came to stamp on all ideas that might seem to dilute it, was itself partly in reaction against Christianity's intolerable assertion of Jesus' divinity. The Judaism of the turn of the eras was in fact densely populated with heavenly mediators between God and the human race – not indeed divine, but conveyors of divine power, divine gifts and divine will. Angels, great figures of Israel's past now in heaven, like Enoch, Moses and Elijah, personified attributes of God like 'wisdom' and 'word' – all these, depicted vividly in the Jewish literature of the period, provided a basis for that small yet revolutionary and decisive shift which occurred in the case of Jesus – to identification as himself 'God'. It took conceptual elaboration in the terms of Greek philosophy to give anything like coherence to this way of thinking of Jesus – and the more Christianity advanced down that road, from the second century onwards, the more it was moving away from Jewish roots and developing its own independent terminology, making mutual comprehension with Judaism virtually impossible from then on. But in the immediate setting of Christianity's beginnings, communication, or at any rate common ground, was by no means lacking, and the factor that made the decisive difference was the extreme character of the devotion, amounting to worship, accorded to the human figure of Jesus, whose death and vindication were seen in the ways that have been described.

The development of divine language about him was aided too by the common Jewish understanding of the virtual identity brought about when a person bestows authority on an agent or a son who can serve as his plenipotentiary. It was probably in this framework that Jewish writers sometimes referred to a hero like Moses as 'God' or 'second God' (cf. Exod. 7: 1 as a biblical basis). The Gospel of John shows clear evidence of this style of thinking, using it as the dominant model for Jesus' relation to God – and indeed for Jesus' followers' relation to himself (John 13:16; 20:21). It seems that this framework goes a long way to showing how this writer saw Jesus as 'God'. Certainly it would be anachronistic to attribute to him anything like the later Platonist framework in the light of which his words came to be read. In John it is one strand in the unprecedented concentration of terms and images used to describe the supreme role of Jesus – and that is where the innovative character of the book's achievement is to be located. So concentrated and pervasive is the supremacy of Jesus that there is indeed ground for seeing here a new religion; and the writer himself is not slow to recognize its incompatibility with the religion of 'the Jews' (John 9:22; 16:2) (Hurtado 1988; Borgen 1986).

THE MARGINALIZING OF HISTORY

It has already been suggested that the history surrounding Jesus, which it now seems so important to get as clear as possible, even if as ground-clearing en route to belief, was not seen in that way by Christians of the first century. Where we might feel it to be honest and clear-sighted to establish 'the facts', and then move on to the task of deciding what interpretations they might justify, and where we might write first of the one and then of the other, they drew no such distinction. Even in their narrative writings (the Gospels and Acts), events and a particular theological view of the events are thoroughly intertwined – and in such a way that not only are 'events' seen in the light of belief about them but stories are surely created, in whole or part, out of belief, often with the aid of the Old Testament texts now seen as fulfilled. The most striking instance of this procedure is in the stories of Jesus' birth (Matt. 1–2), but a detail like the sharing out of Jesus' clothing at the crucifixion may be owed to the effect of Psa. 22:18, a psalm read in the early Church as a prophecy of (and commentary on) the death of Jesus, rather than to straight historical reminiscence.

We have already seen that from the second century a philosophical mentality gradually came to dominate the formulation of Christian belief and its concepts owed more to Platonism than to any other source. There could scarcely have been an idiom of thought more inimical to a religion built on historical foundations and imbued with the interpretation of events. To non-Christian Platonists of the period, Christians, even sophisticated ones like Origen, could seem absurdly attached to sordid factuality and wretched happenings like the suffering and death of Jesus. Yet from a modern point of view, they often seem to view Jesus through a haze of abstraction and speculation that renders their grasp on historical realities tenuous. Flesh and blood seem to have dissolved into aspects of mental and spiritual perception, and where the historical or physical nature of Jesus is insisted on (often in opposition to dissident Christians who virtually denied it) it is done in such a way that it finds few echoes of sympathy in modern ways of imagining events and people of the past. For them, Jesus certainly did what the Gospels said he did and died the death recorded of him, but he walked the earth as the divine one from heaven whose ways were not as our ways.

THE RETURN TO HISTORY

The history of beliefs about Jesus in as long a period as the last seven hundred years may be viewed, with a strong dose of hindsight, as a laborious and many-faceted reclamation of a sense of historical realism with regard to Jesus. The twelfth century saw the beginnings of natural portrayals of Jesus and Gospel episodes, which came to clearest fruition in Renaissance art. Crucifixes that depicted Christ suffering, as the Gospel story told, superseded stylized crucifixes where Jesus was robed and crowned with head erect, triumphing in his cross: then, doctrinal considerations had obliterated the realities of the story, and painting and sculpture had served symbolic at the expense of emotional purposes.

Similarly, devotion to Jesus came to involve the heart much more obviously, as imaginative meditation on Gospel events was encouraged. Popular devotion was directed to the crib placed in churches at Christmas; to the stations of the cross, showing the various agonized stages in Jesus' progress from his trial to his death and burial; to Mary in the meditations on the rosary and emotional hymns like the *Stabat mater*, where the worshipper could identify with the mother of Jesus at the foot of the cross on which her son was dying. The depth of emotional response along these lines finds extended literary form in, for example, the fourteenth-century *Revelations of Divine Love* by Julian of Norwich (Jantzen 1987; Houlden 1992).

But in all this, perhaps to the surprise of the modern observer, there is no question of historical research or a neutral attempt to discover what actually happened. Rather, the established doctrinal pattern, with its abstract concepts, remained in place; only now it found new channels of expression. Not until post-Reformation times did independent research come to be applied to the Bible and so to the career of Jesus as recorded in Scripture, a process fostered both by the break-up of the old single authoritative Western Christendom and by the development of independent rational criteria applied both to ideas and to historical evidence (Scholder 1990; Kümmel 1973). As that took place, so the analytical standpoint described in this chapter, and indeed represented in its very writing, took hold – and in Western culture every belief about Jesus and every line of his story has had (to put it dramatically) to fight for its life. As we have seen, much of it may well survive, though all of it will look and feel different in the light of kinds of investigation that are far removed from the outlook and conscious intentions of the New Testament writers. Some of it will be identified as typical religious legend, and some will be debated in the context of philosophical discussion of the miraculous rather than strictly historical weighing of evidence. Often indeed 'We do not know' is the honest modern alternative to the old confidence in the pure historical accuracy of the Gospels (which minimized contradictions and difficulties and failed to appreciate the theological character of the narratives).

FROM HISTORY TO FAITH – AGAIN?

So the question arises: has the advent of historical criticism then been all loss from a religious point of view, and has Jesus disappeared behind a screen of obscurity or positive distortion? And has belief about him become disjointed from history, incapable of being connected plausibly to things that once happened in Palestine? The questions are inescapable, for it would be a strange (if not wholly impossible) sort of Christianity which was indifferent to the career of Jesus and its historical veracity and was content to be a free-floating piety going its meandering way through a welter of different cultural settings. That is indeed too close to much of the truth, too near the bone, to be lightly dismissed. But is it the case that the tradition, whose course is to be described in the following chapters, is now something belonging effectively only to the past, having reached a terminus? Have its roots in Jesus been so rotted that, while the tree may seem to survive, for a time, in reality it is doomed? And does the sheer awareness of other world faiths not tend to a further marginalizing of Jesus (as well as his being a bone of contention)?

An alternative view is that the jolt administered at this fundamental level by modern study of Jesus and Christian origins is on a par with other jolts which the Christian tradition has undergone down the centuries, just one more among the many intellectual and cultural changes to which it has been subject. If this less alarming line commends itself, then the question is whether there is anything more 'authentic' or 'healthy' about this change than those of the past. After all, those of the past have taken place without the self-consciousness, the historical reflectivity about the whole sweep of Christian history, which now imposes itself. Those who were part of them had a naive belief (as it may now seem) that they were simply telling it and seeing it 'as it is'. In that case, there is a certain purity and rigour about modernity which is difficult to live with but is bracing and gratifying to the survivors.

But perhaps we can be less ascetic than that. After all, though there is an element of delusion in our imaginative reconstruction of the past and what we see is always from our point of view, at the same time a self-effacing (so far as may be) effort to 'get inside' the thoughts of past writers and the circumstances in which they lived and wrote has its rewards. At the very least, we have learnt to refrain from compelling writers of the past to sing our tunes and to be content to listen to theirs.

Above all, we are made to attend to the inescapable realities of being in a tradition, whether that be a religious faith, with its relatively strong cohesiveness and claims to identity through time, or a nation or a culture, with perhaps looser demands for loyalty and more hazy means of identifying itself. Always there is a combination of recognition of the familiar combined with uncertainty about what will come next. And in periods of rapid change – and strong awareness of it – the sense of uncertainty will be prominent, whether it is felt in an adventurous or a timid spirit. Except by the brute fiat of authority (but it had better have adequate sanctions if it is to be effective!), there is no way of being certain what will pass as legitimate development and what as travesty, nor any way of securing unanimity (Chadwick 1957).

The historical roots of a tradition, excavated with as much rigour and honesty as possible, may at least have the purpose of warning against travesty. Christian perception of Jesus will take new forms as quite new human standpoints are adopted: but it should be possible to rebut false claims to be faithful to Jesus – if that is what people reckon to be doing – and point them in more authentic directions. Not that they will necessarily be able to follow them; but they may think and act more knowingly. Perhaps that is as much as historical enquiry can hope to achieve when applied to a religious tradition that reckons to be involved with a living God not limited by those origins that are now found so interesting and that we now have the means to investigate with unprecedented and demanding efficiency.

REFERENCES

Bammel, E. and Moule C. F. D. (1984) *Jesus and the Politics of his Day*, Cambridge: Cambridge University Press.

Borgen, P. (1986), in J. Ashton (ed.) *The Interpretation of John*, ch. 4, London: SPCK.

Brandon, S. G. (1967) *Jesus and the Zealots*, Manchester: Manchester University Press.

Chadwick, O. (1957) *From Bossuet to Newman*, Cambridge: Cambridge University Press.

Crossan, J. D. (1992) *The Historical Jesus*, Edinburgh: T. & T. Clark.

Dunn, J. D. G. (1992) *The Partings of the Ways Between Christianity and Judaism and their Significance for the Character of Christianity*, London: SCM Press.

Evans, C. F. (1970) *Resurrection and the New Testament*, London: SCM Press.

Freyne, S. (1988) *Galilee, Jesus and the Gospels*, Dublin: Gill & Macmillan.

Hahn, F. (1969) *The Titles of Jesus in Christology*, London: Lutterworth.

Harvey, A. E. (1982) *Jesus and the Constraints of History*, London: Duckworth.

Hengel, M. (1976) *Son of God*, London: SCM Press.

—— (1981) *The Charismatic Leader and his Followers*, Edinburgh: T. & T. Clark.

Houlden, J. L. (1992) *Jesus, A Question of Identity*, London: SPCK.

Hurtado, L. W. (1988) *One God, One Lord*, London: SCM Press.

Jantzen, G. M. (1987) *Julian of Norwich*, London: SPCK.

Kümmel, W. G. (1973) *The New Testament: The History of the Investigation of its Problems*, London: SCM Press.

Lindars, B. (1961) *New Testament Apologetics*, London: SCM Press.

—— (1983) *Jesus Son of Man*, London: SPCK.

Meyers, E. M. and Strange, J. F. (1981) *Archaeology, the Rabbis and Early Christianity*, London: SCM Press.

Moltmann, J. (1974) *The Crucified God*, London: SCM Press.

Rivkin, E. (1984) *What Crucified Jesus?*, London: SCM Press.

Sanders, E. P. (1985) *Jesus and Judaism*, London: SCM Press.

Scholder, K. (1990) *The Birth of Modern Critical Theology*, London: SCM Press.

Schweitzer, A. (1910) *The Quest of the Historical Jesus*, London: A. & C. Black.

Theissen, G. (1982) *The Social Setting of Pauline Christianity*, Edinburgh: T. & T. Clark.

—— (1986) *The Shadow of the Galilean*, London: SCM Press.

Vermes, G. (1977) *The Dead Sea Scrolls: Qumran in Perspective*, London: Collins.

Wilken, R. L. (1984) *The Christians as the Romans Saw Them*, New Haven and London: Yale University Press.

Ziesler, J. A. (1983) *Pauline Christianity*, Oxford: Oxford University Press.

FURTHER READING

Ashton, J. (1991) *Understanding the Fourth Gospel*, Oxford: The Clarendon Press.

Barton, S. and Stanton, G. (eds) (1994) *Resurrection*, London: SPCK.

Coggins, R. J. and Houlden, J. L. (1990) *A Dictionary of Biblical Interpretation*, London: SCM Press.

Harvey, A. E. (1990) *Strenuous Commands*, London: SCM Press.

Houlden, J. L. (1977) *Patterns of Faith*, London: SCM Press.

Knox, J. (1967) *The Humanity and Divinity of Christ*, Cambridge: Cambridge University Press.

Meier, J. P. (1991) *A Marginal Jew*, London and New York: Doubleday.

Page, R. (1991) *The Incarnation of Freedom and Love*, London: SCM Press.

Schürer, E., revised and ed. G. Vermes and F. Millar (1973) *The History of the Jewish People in the Age of Jesus Christ*, vols 1–3, Edinburgh: T. & T. Clark.

Tatum, W. B. (1982) *In Quest of Jesus*, London: SCM Press.

See also chapters 5, 6, 7, 43.

10

THE TRIUNE GOD OF THE BIBLE AND THE EMERGENCE OF ORTHODOXY

Robert L. Wilken

Christians confess God as Father, Son and Holy Spirit. The classical statement of belief in the Triune God was adopted at the Council of Nicaea in 325 CE and reaffirmed and expanded at the Council of Constantinople in 381 CE. This creed, with its tripartite structure ('We believe in one God the Father Almighty, maker of heaven and earth ... and in one Lord Jesus Christ, the only son of God, begotten of the Father before all worlds ... and in the Holy Spirit the Lord and Lifegiver'), is used to this day by millions of Christians throughout the world when they celebrate the Eucharist. It is the most ancient authoritative summary of Christian teaching and the mark of orthodox Christian faith.

To many Christians, however, the doctrine of the Trinity appears as a theological construct, useful perhaps as a way of explaining the manifold ways God is known to us, but not a necessary teaching of the Christian faith. In the early nineteenth century when Friedrich Schleiermacher organized his dogmatics, *The Christian Faith*, he relegated the doctrine of the Trinity to an appendix. He acknowledged that the doctrine expressed a fundamental truth about the union of the divine and human, but he considered it a means of defending something else, an effort at theological explanation of more fundamental truths, not a teaching in its own right. The doctrine of the Trinity, he wrote, is not 'an immediate utterance concerning the Christian self-consciousness'. In his view there are only two immediate utterances, that the being of God is present in Christ, and that the divine unites itself with human nature in the Spirit who animates the Church. Neither of these affirmations requires that one posit a triune God.

Schleiermacher's approach to the problem was not new. Already in the early Church Sabellius had taught that the various terms, Father, Son, and Holy Spirit, were simply names that Christians give to the ways we know and experience God's activity and presence, the modes by which God is known. In calling God Father, Son, and Holy Spirit, it was argued, we are only speaking about how God manifests himself to us; we are not saying anything about the nature of God. The questions raised centuries ago by Sabellius, and echoed by later critics of the doctrine of the Trinity during the Church's history, can be stated as follows: if we take it as axiomatic that God is one, is there any reason, on the basis of the several ways God is known to us, to project the plurality of our experience of God into the life of God? Why should the manifestations of God be thought to designate distinctions within the Godhead?

Sabellius was not the only Christian thinker to raise questions about the emerging doctrine of the Trinity. Almost from the beginning some Christians had reservations about confessing God as 'triune'. Although the terms Father, Son and Holy Spirit were used in the Bible and in Christian worship, not all agreed on how this language was to be understood. To speak of God as Father, Son and Holy Spirit seemed to compromise belief in the one God. During the early centuries these matters were debated as Christian thinkers sought to express what they had come to know through the revelation of God in Jesus Christ. In time differing views began to coalesce around a centre, and it was this centre, expressed in the Nicaeno-Constantinopolitan Creed, which came to define orthodox Christian faith. It is historically and theologically important to understand how this came to be, and in the pages that follow I discuss several of the factors, the Bible, the Resurrection of Jesus, and the Church's liturgical life, that contributed to the formation of the Trinitarian faith.

THE TRIUNE GOD OF THE BIBLE

The first Christians were Jews who recited the ancient words of the Shema in their daily prayers: 'Hear, O Israel: The Lord our God is one Lord; and you shall love the Lord your God with all your soul, and with all your might' (Deut. 6:4). Jesus quoted the words of the Shema in answer to the question, 'Which commandment is the first of all?' and the earliest Christians affirmed their belief in the one God. 'We have one God the Father from whom are all things' (1 Cor. 8:6). The first commandment, according to the second-century work, the Shepherd of Hermas, is, 'Believe that God is one, who created and completed all things and made all that is from that which is not . . .' (Herm, Man. 1:1). The first article of the creed is 'we believe in one God'.

Though the earliest Christians were in agreement with their fellow Jews in confessing one God, from the beginning Christianity set itself apart from Judaism by the veneration it gave to Christ. This is apparent in the exalted language to describe Christ in the New Testament, son of God, image of the invisible God, the eternal word who is with God, the one in whom the 'fullness of the Godhead dwells', 'the express image of God's very being'; in hymns in honour of Christ, e.g. 'God highly exalted him and gave him the name that is above every name' (Phil. 2); in the baptismal formula which joked Christ, a human being, with God the Creator of all things; and in the early Christian Eucharist where Christ was celebrated as alive and present in the breaking of bread. As early as the second decade of the second century an outside observer, Pliny, the Roman governor of Bithynia, reported that Christians were in the habit of meeting on a fixed day before it was light to 'recite a hymn to Christ as to god'.

One of the ways to reconcile the apparent conflict between worshipping Christ as God and venerating the one God, i.e. to offer rational justification for the shape of Christian language and practice, was to draw directly on the Greek philosophical tradition. Because of the influence of Christianity and Judaism on Western thought we are inclined to think of the divine as a category that has only one member (the one supreme God), but in antiquity the divine was a broad and expansive category of existence which included many different members. Within this tradition the most obvious way to deal with the 'divinity' of Christ and the Holy Spirit was to conceive of a hierarchy of divine beings. One could acknowledge the existence of the one high God, while also venerating lesser deities, who, though they did not rule over the whole universe as did the one high God, were nevertheless considered divine. 'The person who worships several gods, because he worships some one of those which belong to the great God, even by this very action does that which is loved by him', wrote Celsus the second-century pagan philosopher.

Influenced by this understanding of the divine, some early Christian apologists thought that in the polytheistic world of ancient Rome it was a shrewd strategy to accentuate the pluralistic character of Christian conceptions of the divine. Athenagoras, an apologist born in Athens who wrote in the latter part of the second century, informs his critics, with barely concealed glee at his cleverness in trumping an adversary:

> Who . . . would not be amazed if he heard that folks who are called atheists bring forth God the Father, God the Son, and the Holy Spirit . . . Nor does our teaching concerning the Godhead stop there, but we also say that there is a host of angels and ministers whom God . . . set in their places . . .

How can we be called atheists, implies Athenagoras, when we confess not one God but three gods and many lesser divine beings who are associated with these three? In Graeco-Roman society the pluralism of Christian theology was not an embarrassment; for some it was a valuable selling point of the new movement.

Other apologists used similar language. Justin Martyr, for example, said that Christians honour Jesus Christ as the 'son of the true God himself, and hold him to be in the second rank and the prophetic spirit in the third rank'. Origen of Alexandria even went so far as to use the term 'second God' with reference to the Son. In a discussion with a Christian bishop from Arabia, he said, 'we are not afraid to speak in one sense of two Gods, and in another sense of one God'. As a temporary solution these ideas about the plurality of gods helped early Christian thinkers to explain how Christ and the Holy Spirit could be divine while retaining the belief that God is one, but under closer examination such formulations proved unsatisfying and were eventually discarded. For they seemed to make the Son and the Holy Spirit into 'assistants' to God, not 'associates'. Plurality with respect to God, however, had impressed itself on Christian thinkers from the very beginning.

Nevertheless when some in the churches heard theologians talk about a second God or different ranks of deity they believed that something had gone awry. After all, in becoming Christians they had been delivered from the worship of many gods to serve the one true God. Wasn't this talk of several gods a reversion to the life they had left behind? At the beginning of the third century, Tertullian of Carthage in North Africa, the first Christian thinker to write in Latin, said that the rank and file among Christians (he called them the 'simple folk') believed that in preaching 'two or even three Gods' the Church's belief in one God was compromised. They say, 'We hold to the monarchy', the one single God who rules all things. Because they held to the belief that there was one sole ruler, such Christians were called 'monarchians', that is, adherents of belief in the single (*monos*) rule (*archē*) of God.

As one examines the writings of the criticism of monarchianism by the Church's leading thinkers, e.g. Irenaeus, Tertullian, or Origen in the early period, it is evident that something deep within Christian tradition was propelling Christian thinkers to move beyond received conceptions of God's oneness and unity. One of the sources for this ferment was of course the Bible itself, not simply the New Testament, but also the Greek version of the Old Testament, the Septuagint. Within some Jewish circles prior to the advent of Christianity, 'wisdom' (*sophia*) was pictured not simply as a divine attribute displaying God's activity in the world, e.g. in creation, but also as a 'divine agent', carrying out God's purposes for humankind. In time 'wisdom', though closely associated with God and identified with God, came to be conceived of as having a kind of independent existence in the heavenly realm. An important text is Wisdom of Solomon 7:

> For wisdom is more mobile than any motion; because of her pureness she pervades and penetrates all things. For she is a breath of the power of God, and a pure emanation of the glory of the Almighty; therefore nothing defiled gains entrance into her. For she is a reflection (*apaugasma*) of eternal light, a spotless mirror of the working of God, and an image of his goodness.

> (7:24–6)

In the Wisdom of Solomon wisdom is called 'the fashioner of all things' (7:22), 'an associate in [God's] works' (8:4), a member of God's heavenly council who exists from eternity (24:9).

The New Testament identifies Christ with Wisdom: 'Christ the power of God and the wisdom of God' (1 Cor. 1:24). Hence one of the tasks of early

Christian thinkers was to draw out the implications of identifying Christ with the figure of Wisdom as a divine agent portrayed in books such as the Wisdom of Solomon and Proverbs. Of course, the New Testament had pointed the way. For example, the opening sentences of the book of Hebrews use an expression that echoes the book of Wisdom: Christ is the 'reflection (*apaugasma*) of God's glory and the exact imprint of God's very being' (Heb. 1:3). In his treatise *On First Principles* Origen calls attention to the correspondence between such texts in the New Testament and passages from the Septuagint (besides the Wisdom of Solomon, also Prov. 8:22–5), as well as other passages in the New Testament that speak of Christ as the image of God, e.g. 'image of the invisible God' in Colossians (1:15). From these texts, he concluded that the 'wisdom of God has her subsistence nowhere else but in him who is the beginning of all things'. Because Christ is the Wisdom of God, argues Origen, he is rightfully called God. He is also called the 'only-son' of God, the one whose origin is to be found in God. To say, then, that Christ is the 'image of God' means that he shares God's nature in the way that a child shares the nature of his parents.

Origen realized that the term 'wisdom' was normally used adjectivally as in the phrase 'wise man', that is, 'wisdom' referred to a quality or attribute or characteristic of a person. In conventional usage wisdom did not designate something that acted as an agent or existed independently of something else. Applied to the doctrine of God, the question was whether wisdom (i.e. Christ) was to be understood as having its own proper existence, or whether wisdom was a way of talking about a mode of God's existence in relation to human beings. In technical theological language the question was whether the figure of wisdom was to be 'hypostasized', i.e. understood as an independent entity, albeit within God, what later theology would call 'person'.

The presence of passages in the Septuagint that spoke of Wisdom as a divine agent, indeed as the pre-eminent divine agent, helped Christians understand the language of the New Testament and gave them an initial conceptual framework to express, on the one hand, the belief that Christ is God, and on the other, that he is not simply a divine attribute or emanation but had his own proper existence. Wisdom, however, was only one 'title' for Christ in the New Testament and only as it was interpreted in light of other biblical titles, notably 'son of God' and 'Word (*logos*) of God', were Christian thinkers able to do justice to the reality that they had come to know in Christ. In his Commentary on the Gospel of John, Origen discussed these and other titles at length, e.g., light, door, way, shepherd, king, life, *et al.*, but it was these three, 'wisdom', 'son', and 'word', that were most important in formulating the Church's doctrine of the Trinity.

Already in Origen's day the meaning of the term *logos* had become a matter of dispute within the Christian community. The question was asked whether 'word' was to be taken in its conventional sense to mean something which has no existence apart from the one who speaks the word, or whether when used of Christ it had a different sense. The term *logos* occurs in the LXX version of Psalm 45:2 (44:2) which reads: 'My heart uttered a good word.' The 'word' mentioned here and the 'word' in the prologue of the Gospel of St John were taken to be the same, and some Christians thought the meaning of the term was plain. 'Word' was to be taken in its usual sense, hence it designated 'an utterance occurring in syllables', i.e. a sound that disappears as soon as it is heard. Applied to Christ this meant that he had no existence apart from the Father.

Origen admits that it is difficult to understand how one can speak of a 'word' in the same way that one can speak of a 'son'. Hence the term word should be interpreted in conjunction with the title 'son', a term that implies 'having life in itself'. Though a son receives life from his mother he exists as a human being independent of her. If the terms word and son are taken together it is clear that 'the word is distinct from God (the Father) and has its own existence'. Origen reminds his reader that in reading the Bible one must discern the 'sense' of the terms used; when one reads the term 'door' or 'vine' or 'way' no-one thinks that Christ is an actual door or a vine or a path. These terms must be taken as intended, i.e. to refer to something spiritual that is like a door or a vine. The word of God, then, must be understood as something that is like a human word, but is not a human word. The 'word of God', writes Origen, has its own 'individuality, i.e. has life in itself', and in this way is to be distinguished from word or reason in human beings, 'which has no individuality apart from us'. The Scriptures teach, says Origen, that the 'Son is other than the Father', i.e. has his own proper existence.

Tertullian had come to a similar conclusion though his reasoning is some-what different. Like Origen he argued that the title in the Scriptures should not be taken in isolation; no one title could be taken as definitive in and of itself, not word, not son, not wisdom. The Scriptures speak of the same 'power . . . now with the name of wisdom, now with the designation word'. The several titles complemented each other. Hence in answer to those who took Psalm 45 ('My heart has uttered a good word') to imply no distinction between God and his 'word', Tertullian cites other texts applied to Christ that speak of Christ as the 'son'. If one argues that the word spoken by the Father cannot be distinguished from the Father, it would seem that the son in Psalm 2:7, 'You are my son, this day have I begotten you', must be the same as the Father, which is absurd.

Equally significant is Tertullian's analysis of the term 'word' or 'reason', *logos* in Greek, *ratio* in Latin. He argues that there is a sense in which reason in human beings, and hence in God, can be understood to have its own existence. Consider, says Tertullian, that as a human being made in the image and likeness of God

you have reason within yourself . . . Consider how when you deliberate silently

192

within yourself by reason, this same action takes place within you [that takes place in God], while reason accompanied by discourse (*sermo*) meets you at every moment of your thought, at every impression of your consciousness; your every thought is discourse, your every consciousness is reason; you must perforce speak it in your mind, and while you speak it you experience as a partner in conversation (*conlocutorem*) that discourse which has in it this very reason by which you speak when you think in company of that [discourse] in speaking by means of which you think.

Tertullian is making a simple but profound point. As human beings we think of ourselves as a single person, with our own individual consciousness, and we look at the world from the perspective of our unique and distinctive 'ego'. Yet it is the universal experience of human beings, because they are rational creatures, that they have within themselves the power of reasoning. Reasoning is always dialectical, i.e. it involves questioning, saying yes and then saying no, a back and forth in the mind as words, ideas and concepts challenge, criticize, or confirm each other. This silent dialogue takes place within the mind without speaking a word. In thinking we become aware of an other within ourselves. This other of course takes many different forms depending on the topic and the purpose of our deliberations, whether we are thinking alone or in discussion with someone else. Yet the other is always present in the form of a question, an alternative, a doubt, a contrary proposal or complementary thought. The very term 'deliberation' suggests that thinking is a form of debate that goes on inside the self.

Because of the dialectical character of human reasoning, it is plausible, argues Tertullian, to speak of a kind of second 'person' within us. 'So in a sort of way you have in you a second discourse by means of which you speak by thinking and by means of which you think by speaking: discourse itself is another [than you].' Tertullian is not interested in establishing a truth about human psychology, though he wrote a large book dealing with the human soul, but in drawing an analogy between the human mind and the nature of God as God. Human beings were made in the 'image and likeness of God'. If it is the case that one can speak of a 'partner in conversation' in the human mind, an 'associate' if you will, 'how much more completely ... does this action take place in God, whose image and similitude you are authoritatively declared to be, that even while silent he has in himself reason, and in [that] reason discourse'. Therefore it is not unreasonable to say that God is not a solitary monad.

> So I have been able without rashness to conclude that even then, before the establishment of the universe, God was not alone, seeing he continually had in himself Reason, and in Reason Discourse, which he made another beside himself by activity within himself.

NOT A SOLITARY GOD

The interpretation of the biblical titles of Wisdom, Word and Son took place in conjunction with the account of Christ's life as recorded in the Gospels. The New Testament presents Christ as a human being born of a woman, who lived the life of a child, grew to maturity, taught and worked miracles in the villages and towns of Galilee, was crucified in Jerusalem, executed on a cross, and three days after the his death rose to new life. This portrait was indelibly part of Christian thought and experience. Hence when Christians used phrases such the 'wisdom of God' or 'word of God', or said that in Christ 'the fullness of God dwelled bodily', they had reference to a concrete historical person as well as a divine being who existed in intimate fellowship with God. What they knew of God's Wisdom or Word was disclosed to them not only through the Scriptures but also by the life of Christ, i.e. by what had happened in history. The several titles were complementary and had to be interpreted in relation to one another. God's Wisdom may have been known through reading the Septuagint, but the Son could not be clearly discerned in the Septuagint without first knowing the Son who lived on this earth. As St Irenaeus put it at the end of the second century: 'according to the *economy* of our redemption there is a father and a son'.

Irenaeus uses the term 'economy', an expression that is puzzling to modern readers, but essential for understanding the Christian doctrine of the Trinity. In Christian theology the term 'economy' designates God's ordered self-disclosure in creation, in the history of Israel and pre-eminently in the life, death, and resurrection of Christ. Hence the term was used as a shorthand way of referring to the Incarnation and the events that had followed from God's descent into human affairs, i.e. to the evangelical history. More than any other term it captured what was unique to Christianity, and that in the words of Ignatius of Antioch (early second century) was the suffering and death of Christ: 'Now the Gospel has something distinctive; the coming of the Saviour, our Lord Jesus Christ, his suffering and resurrection.'

Tertullian's chief argument against the 'monarchians' is that in claiming to safeguard belief in the one God, they ignore the economy, i.e. the evangelical history. They do not understand that 'while they must believe in one God only, yet they must believe in him along with his economy'. In his view, and in the view of all early Christian thinkers, thinking about God has to begin with history, specifically the appearance of God in the person of Christ. Reasoning about God had to proceed differently now than it had before the coming of Christ. The rank and file, whom Tertullian condescendingly calls the 'simple folk' (*simpliciores*), fail to see this and 'take fright at the economy'.

The difficulty with the 'monarchians' is that they steadfastly hold to conceptions of God that were formed before the coming of Christ. Of course, it should be acknowledged that the critics of monarchianism also suffered from a kind of theological inertia. On certain points, e.g. notions of divine impassibility and immutability, they too clung to older conceptions of the divine. Origen, for example, said that as a result of 'God's descent to human affairs', i.e. the economy, we 'have been able to perceive clearly the true conception of God's nature'. Yet when he states what has been learned, he uses conventional Greek categories: God is 'incorruptible, simple, uncompounded, and indivisible'. Tertullian was one thinker who realized that the 'economy' required a more radical critique of earlier philosophical notions of God than that provided by his contemporaries. But all agreed that thinking about God had to begin with the economy, God's ordered self-disclosure in history. 'The human mind', writes Gregory of Nyssa, 'can only speak about God as it is instructed by God's works', i.e. what is disclosed in the economy. The economy is the engine that drives Trinitarian thinking.

How important the 'economy' was in forcing Christians to revise their ideas of God can be seen in a passage from the fourth-century Latin theologian, Hilary of Poitiers, sometimes called the Athanasius of the West because, like the latter, his contemporary, he spent most of his life, which spanned the fourth century (he was born about 300 CE and died in 367), defending the decrees of the Council of Nicaea (325 CE). He was also a biblical interpreter from whom we have a commentary on the Gospel of Matthew and a Commentary on the Psalms (covering about fifty psalms). But his greatest achievement was a large work, *On the Trinity*, written at the height of the Arian controversy. In this work Hilary not only shows he has mastered the arguments of earlier writers but that he was able to rework them with great originality. Hilary writes: 'We cannot as true believers assert that God is one, if we mean by it that he is alone . . .'. If God were solitary and alone, that would give no place for his Word. If, on the other hand, we simply assert that the Son is a second God alongside of the supreme God, we deny that God is one. We must, says Hilary, confess: 'though he is one he is not solitary'.

That Hilary would frame the issue in this way is significant. The Arians had argued that the Son was not wholly divine. The Scriptures, for example, called him the 'first born of all creation' (Col. 1:15) and other passages (e.g. Prov. 8:22) suggested that he should be ranked as the highest of created beings. In their response, the defenders of the Nicene formula ('of one substance with the Father'), Athanasius and others, tried to show, by an exegesis of disputed texts from the Scriptures, that Christ was fully God. The question raised by the Arians concerned the status of the Son, not the nature of God. Hilary, of course, joined other Nicene thinkers in defending the full divinity of the Son; but in the passage I have just cited he moves the debate into new territory by making it a discussion of the nature of God.

His argument runs as follows. The first Christians were Jews and as Jews they recited each day the ancient prayer of the Jews, the Shema, 'Hear, O Israel, the Lord your God is one.' Since this is so, asks Hilary, what are we to make of Thomas' confession, 'My Lord and my God'? How could Thomas have confessed Jesus, a human being, as 'my God' and at the same time pray the Shema? How could a faithful Jew and apostle forget the divine command to recite the Shema and make a new confession, that Christ is God, when he knew that his very life depended on the confession that God is one? Thomas had often heard Jesus say things such as 'I and the Father are one', and 'all things that the Father has are mine', as we know from the Gospel of John.

What is striking about Hilary's argument is that it is so consciously historical. He explains that the facts of history, i.e. the 'economy', forced a rethinking of the traditional way of conceiving God. Hilary envisions a time at the very beginning of Christianity when all Christians were Jews and continued to observe Jewish traditions. His comments indicate that he had asked himself a question that I am sure many have asked, especially when reading St Paul. How could a faithful Jew, formed by Jewish tradition and accustomed to Jewish rites and prayers, for whom the most fundamental article of faith was that God is one, how could Paul use such exalted language about Christ and employ on occasion formulas of greeting that link Christ with God, e.g.: 'the grace of our Lord Jesus Christ, the love of God, and the fellowship of the Holy Spirit be with you all' (2 Cor. 13:13)?

Hilary's answer is that everything was transformed with the resurrection of Christ, and Thomas was the first to grasp the nature of the change. Once Jesus was raised, Thomas 'understood the whole mystery of the faith through the power of the resurrection'. For 'no nature is able to rise from death to life by its own power except God's nature'. Now, i.e. in light of the resurrection, Thomas was able to confess Christ as God 'without rupturing his loyalty to the one God', for he saw that his confession was not the 'acknowledgement of a second God, nor a betrayal of the unity of the divine nature'. The resurrection of Christ teaches us, says Hilary, that God is not a 'lonely God' or an 'isolated God' (*in solitudine*), yet at the same time it does not teach us that there are two Gods.

For Hilary, the resurrection of Jesus was the basis for rejecting a strictly monistic view of God. One cannot exaggerate the significance of this reasoning for the development of the Christian doctrine of the Trinity. The economy not only reveals God's purposes for humankind; it also discloses the inner life of God. In the words of a contemporary theologian, Wolfhart Pannenberg: 'As God reveals himself, so he is in his eternal deity' (Pannenberg 1991: 300). Though God is ineffable and his ways beyond finding out, the Scriptures teach that in Christ we come to know not only the 'face' of God but are able to look within God. A striking text in this regard was Colossians 1:19, 'In [Christ] all the fullness of God was pleased to dwell.' With characteristic boldness, Origen took this passage to mean that through God's revelation in Christ we become 'spectators' of the 'depth of God'.

Hilary, then, has reason to say that through Christ's resurrection the apostles learned something of God that was not evident prior to the 'economy'. He expresses what is implicit in early Christian discussions of the Trinity and states the reasoning that was at work in early Christian thinking about God. The event in Christ's life that was decisive in God's self-disclosure, the event that sealed and completed his mission, was the resurrection from the dead. Through the resurrection Christ's unique relation to God was made apparent. In the words of St Paul: Christ 'was declared to be the Son of God with power according to the spirit of holiness by resurrection from the dead' (Rom. 1:3).

THE SON NEVER ACTS ALONE

What had been disclosed in the economy gave early Christian thinkers the confidence to explore the nature of God afresh, guided of course by the Scriptures. Thinking about God could no longer be carried on independently of what had occurred in the evangelical history. Of course, in the strict sense of the term, the argument that God was not a 'solitary God' was not concerned with the doctrine of the Trinity. The debate focused on the status of the Son and whether the Son or Word is an emanation from the Father or whether he has his own proper identity.

Christian language, however, is resolutely tripartite. This is most evident in the formula used at Baptism: 'in the name of the Father and of the Son and of the Holy Spirit'. But there were also expressions within the Bible, e.g. the greeting in 2 Corinthians 13:13 quoted above, or the opening words of 1 Peter: 'To the exiles . . . who have been chosen and destined by God the Father and sanctified by the Spirit to be obedient to Jesus Christ and to be sprinkled with his blood' (1 Pet. 1:2). Of these passages J. N. D. Kelly wrote in *Early Christian Creeds*:

> In all of them there is no trace of fixity so far as their wording is concerned, and none of them constitutes a creed in any ordinary sense of the term. Nevertheless the Trinitarian ground-plan obtrudes itself obstinately throughout, and its presence is all the more striking because more often than not there is nothing in the context to necessitate it. The impression inevitably conveyed is that the conception of the threefold manifestation of the Godhead was embedded deeply in Christian thinking from the start . . .
>
> (Kelly 1950: 23)

Although the Church's language was 'tripartite', it would take time for the doctrine of the Holy Spirit to be subjected to theological analysis. In the fifth century Augustine wrote:

> There has not been as yet, on the part of learned and distinguished investigators of the Scriptures, a discussion [of the Holy Spirit] full enough or careful enough to make it possible for us to obtain an intelligent conception of what also constitutes his special individuality (*proprium*) . . .

By the end of the fourth century, as the teaching concerning the Son was being given its definitive form, the same thinkers who had written works dealing with the status of the Son began to address the topic of the Holy

Spirit. Though their arguments deal with the distinctive work of the Holy Spirit, their reasoning is not dissimilar to that used to discuss the doctrine of the Son. That is, they argued for the divinity of the Holy Spirit from the economy, e.g. the role of the Spirit in the work of Christ, as well as from the gifts of the Spirit to the Church. History, as recorded in the Scriptures, and experience, especially liturgical experience, were seen as complementary, each serving to illuminate the other.

The reality of the Holy Spirit was evident in the Church's life. In the central prayer in the Christian liturgy, the prayer said over the bread and wine in the Eucharist (the *anaphora*), the bishop besought the Holy Spirit to descend on the gifts. In a third-century Roman example of the prayer, after reciting the narration of the institution of the Eucharist, and bringing to memory the saving death and resurrection of Christ, he continued:

> And we pray that you would send your Holy Spirit upon the offerings of your holy church; that gathering them into one, you would grant to all your saints who partake of them to be filled with the Holy Spirit . . .

Likewise when a new bishop was consecrated, the other bishops laid hands on the candidate and prayed:

> Pour forth now that power which is yours of your royal Spirit which you gave to your beloved servant Jesus Christ which he bestowed on his holy apostles . . . And by the Spirit of high-priesthood give him authority to remit sins according to your commandments . . .

Catechumens were baptized in the name of the Father and of the Son and of the Holy Spirit and trinitarian doxologies were sprinkled throughout Christian worship.

For the Christian doctrine of the Trinity these 'experiences' were foundational. They were certain evidence that God's presence among his people was not restricted to the time of Christ's sojourn on earth. The Scriptures taught that after Christ's departure the Spirit would be sent on his followers: 'When the Spirit of truth comes, he will guide you into all the truth . . .' (John 16:9; 14:16 and 15:26). Beginning with the outpouring of the Holy Spirit on Pentecost and continued in the spiritual gifts in the life of the Church, these promises had been confirmed. 'Having received the promise of the Holy Spirit, he had poured out this that you both see (!) and hear' (Acts 2:33). Just as Christ had given evidence of who he was when he dwelled on earth, so the Spirit gave evidence of his presence in the sacraments, in the witness of the martyrs and the lives of holy men and women, in the bishops. The latter was no less certain than the former. Gregory of Nazianzus writes: 'The Spirit dwells among us, offering us a most clear display of himself.'

The opponents of the developing Trinitarian theology, however, argued that the Nicene theologians 'bring in a strange God [the Holy Spirit] of whom Scripture is silent'. Everyone knew of course that the Spirit was mentioned in the Scriptures, in, for example, the baptismal formula in Matthew 28 or the triadic greeting at the end of 2 Corinthians as well as in many other places. At issue was whether the work of redemption was solely the work of God in Christ or was accompanied and completed by the work of the Holy Spirit. In response to this challenge Christian thinkers pointed to those passages that link specific actions in Christ's life with the work of the Spirit. 'Consider the following', writes Gregory of Nazianzus in his theological oration on the Holy Spirit:

> Christ is born, the Spirit is his forerunner (Luke 1:35); Christ is baptized, the Spirit bears witness (Luke 3:21–2); Christ is tempted, the Spirit leads him up (Luke 4:2, 14); [Christ] works miracles, the Spirit accompanies him (Matt. 12:28); Christ ascends, the Spirit takes his place (Acts 1:8–9).

In the Scriptures Christ's works are not presented as activities of the Son alone. God's revelation in Christ is made possible through the presence of the Holy Spirit. The tripartite nature of God is evident in the way Father, Son and Spirit relate to each other in the events of revelation.

Gregory of Nyssa writes:

> With regard to the divine nature . . . we do not learn [from the Scriptures] that the Father does something on his own, in which the Son does not co-operate, or that the Son acts on his own without the Spirit. Rather every operation which extends from God to creation and is designated according to our different conceptions of it has its origin in the Father, proceeds through the Son, and reaches its completion by the Holy Spirit.

It is sometimes said that the doctrine of the divinity of the Holy Spirit is a deduction based on the logic of Christian thinking about the status of the Son. There is some truth to this view, but it does not do justice to the explicit statements in the Scriptures about the work of the Spirit in the economy. For example, Romans 8:11:

> If the Spirit of Him who raised Jesus from the dead [note that Father, Son and Spirit are involved in a single activity] dwells in you, he who raised Christ from the dead will give life to your mortal bodies also through his Spirit that dwells in you.

Athanasius of Alexandria cites this passage in his first Letter to Serapion, an important document from Christian antiquity in which biblical texts on the Holy Spirit are expounded. In the same letter he also cites 1 John 4:12–13. 'If we love one another, God lives in us, and his love is perfected in us. By this we know that we abide in him and he in us, because he has given of us his Spirit', glossing that verse with the words from the Gospel, 'Those who love me will keep my word, and my Father will love them, and we will come to them and make our home with them' (John 14:23). From these and other passages, Athanasius concludes that through the gift of the Holy Spirit we share in God's life and become heirs of God with Christ. 'The Spirit', writes Athanasius, 'is no stranger to the Son.'

The Son always acts in conjunction with the Holy Spirit, never on his own. On that point the Scriptures were clear. To be sure the Bible does not make explicit statements about the divine status of the Holy Spirit; but neither does it say explicitly that Christ is 'God' without qualifier. In the Scriptures, however, the Spirit is called a gift of living water (John 7:39) that brings life to those who receive it. He is the one who 'gives life' to our mortal bodies (Rom. 8:11). Unlike creatures who receive life from someone other than themselves, the Holy Spirit bestows life and sanctification. Commenting on the phrase in John 1:13, 'begotten of God', Cyril of Alexandria wrote: 'Those who have been reborn by the Spirit through faith are called and indeed are begotten of God.' When the Spirit dwells in us we become 'temples of God' (1 Cor. 3:16; 2 Cor. 6:16). Only God could rise from death to life, and only God can bestow life. Again and again Christian thinkers argue that in the Scriptures the activity of the Spirit is the work of God, a point echoed in our century by Karl Barth. 'According to these statements [in the Scriptures] the work of the Holy Spirit in revelation is a work which can be ascribed only to God and which is thus expressly ascribed to God' (Barth 1936: 467).

The Fathers also observed that in some passages the biblical writers speak not only of the work of the Spirit in the economy, but also of the Spirit's life within God. An important text is 1 Corinthians 2:10:

> The Spirit searches everything, even the depths of God. For what human being knows what is truly human except the human spirit that is within? So also no one truly comprehends what is truly God's except the Spirit of God.

In his book on the Holy Spirit, written in the late fourth century, Basil interpreted this text (he cites it twice) along lines similar to those that Tertullian had pursued in his discussion of the term 'word'. He writes: 'But the greatest proof that the Spirit is one with the Father and the Son is that He is said to have the same relationship to God as the spirit within us has to us.' As God is revealed, so is the internal life of God.

BIBLICAL LANGUAGE AND DIVINE KINSHIP

The shape of the classical doctrine of the Trinity was given by the Holy Scriptures. The Church Fathers insisted that the Scriptures held a privileged place in Christian thinking. Consequently they were chary of efforts to 'translate' its terms and concepts into a conceptual idiom that was thought to be more intelligible. To be sure, some thinkers, for example Gregory of Nyssa, drew on philosophical terms and concepts to aid in expounding the Bible. Yet even Gregory believed that the biblical language was irreplaceable. This is apparent in a fascinating exchange between Gregory of Nyssa and a fellow bishop who was sharply critical of the creed adopted at Nicaea. The question had arisen whether the biblical terms, 'Father', 'Son', 'Holy Spirit', could be replaced by other terms that were more precise philosophically. In place of the Father, Son and Holy Spirit, Eunomius had substituted what he considered more appropriate expressions: 'the highest and most authentic being' to designate the Father; 'the one who exists because of that being and after that being has supremacy over all the rest' for the Son; and a 'third . . . subject to the one because of causation and to the other because of the activity by which it exists' for the Holy Spirit.

The difficulty with Eunomius' proposal, says Gregory, is that in the name of precision and accuracy, he ignores the scriptural names of Father, Son and Holy Spirit, which have been used by Christians in all parts of the world since they were first handed on by the earliest Christian communities. It is neither 'pious nor safe to alter the text of the creed [or the Bible] in this new direction', says Gregory.

Now one might reply that Gregory, by appealing to the authority of Scripture and tradition, ignores the real issue, i.e. how is the language of the Scripture to be adapted, and perhaps reformulated, so that it becomes intelligible to people who have been formed in a Hellenistic culture? Eunomius' translation of the scriptural language was based on a judgement as to what was philosophically intelligible within Graeco-Roman culture. The language of the Bible, as interpreted by Christian tradition, cut against the grain of what were considered well-grounded conceptions of the nature of divinity.

Gregory was of course as much aware of the philosophical difficulties of traditional conceptions of the divine as was Eunomius. Yet he defends the scriptural language and offers arguments as to why it should be preserved and more, why it is to be preferred over the terms proposed by Eunomius. The words one uses, argues Gregory, cannot be indiscriminately exchanged, as though what they designate will remain the same no matter what the vehicle. Words carry connotations and associations, they are not referential. They bear dimensions of meaning that would be lost if they are replaced by other terms. This is particularly true of metaphorical words such as Father and Son. The term Father, for example, is quite different from 'supreme and absolute being', and Son from 'one existing after the other', because when the words Father and Son are spoken, the listener recognizes at once 'the proper and natural relationship to one another' that the terms imply. These terms signify a relationship that the others do not. By abandoning the terms 'Father' and 'Son' Eunomius does not simply jettison the biblical language, he also abandons 'the idea of relationship which enters the ear with the words'.

The point important for our consideration is that the terms Father and Son, in contrast for example to words such as Logos or Wisdom, are directly related to the revelation of God in Christ, i.e. to the economy. The term 'father' is seldom used in the Old Testament to speak of God. It occurs in some key passages, e.g. in the oracle to David, transmitted by the prophet Nathan, that God will establish an everlasting kingdom in which he will be a 'Father' to the house of Israel (2 Sam. 7:14). It also also occurs occasionally in the prophets, but it only appears eleven times in the Old Testament with respect to God, whereas in the New Testament Jesus invokes God as 'Father' over 170 times. The New Testament intensifies the identification of God as Father. Gregory realized that the terms Father and Son, which came into general use among Christians because of God's appearance in Christ, imply a 'kinship' between Father and Son that is at the heart of the Trinitarian theology. By abandoning the terms Father, Son and Holy Spirit, Eunomius is forced to jettison the very thing that is most distinctive of God.

The idea of kinship suggested that 'relation' is a primary characteristic of the divine life. The term 'father', for example, does not designate God's 'nature' but an internal relation within God. Likewise other terms that were used in Trinitarian theology, for example 'unbegotten' (*agen[n]ētos*) and 'Begotten (*gen[n]ētos*), were not abstract terms to speak of what is characteristic of divinity; 'unbegotten' (the term used for God as the source of all things) is a relative term like the word Father. It names the 'relation in which the Father stands to the Son, and the Son to the Father', writes Gregory of Nazianzus. The profound truth, learned from the economy, that the Son (or Wisdom or Word) was not simply an emanation from God but must be conceived as an 'other', a 'co-speaker', or associate, gave 'relation' a primary role in conceiving of God. As Robert Jenson writes: 'The original point of trinitarian dialectics is to make the relations between the identities . . . and therewith the temporal structures of evangelical history, constitutive in God' (Jenson 1982: 119). God's works, as presented in the Scriptures, are never the activities of a solitary God.

How this truth, that relations between the 'persons' of the Trinity were constitutive of God, was lived and experienced by Christians is most evident, as already noted, in the Church's Liturgy, preeminently in the *anaphora*, the great prayer said over the gifts of bread and wine, and in the rite of baptism. But it also took root in Christian spirituality and speculative theology as can be seen in a book written by Richard of St Victor, a twelfth-century Latin theologian. If we agree, he says, that God is love, as we learn from the First Epistle of John, then we can say that this love is exhibited first and foremost in the love between the Father and the Son. Of course, some would say that the primary form of love that is found in the Scriptures is the love God has 'toward his own creation'. But such love, responds Richard, can hardly be called 'supreme love', for how could God love one supremely who is not deserving of supreme love?

Richard is an earlier scholastic, and in the fashion of medieval theology, he presents his argument, not in the fashion of the Church Fathers, i.e. by citing scriptural texts (except as a starting point), but by drawing inferences from what is already known. Hence he says in order that 'fullness of love might have a place within God', it was necessary that a divine person have a relation with an 'equally worthy person', and such a person would, perforce, have to be divine. For just as love demands a plurality of persons, for one cannot love unless there is an other, someone to receive the love, so 'supreme love demands equality of persons'.

By making love the central feature of the relation of the persons, and not the analogy of the mind as Augustine had (he had explored the possibilities of a trinity of love in his *De Trinitate*), Richard was able to accent not only the plurality of persons but also the distinctive character of the relations within God. That is, he found a way that made 'plurality' or 'associates' within God necessary, for in giving the Holy Spirit an equal place in the divine life, he helped make Christian theology genuinely trinitarian, not simply binitarian.

In a remarkable passage that could only be written by someone who loved God but had also known human love, Richard wrote:

Where equal benevolence exists in either person it is necessary that each with equal desire and for a similar reason should seek out a sharer of his excellent joy. For when two persons who mutually love embrace each other with supreme longing and take supreme delight in each other's love, then the supreme joy of the first is in intimate love of the second, and conversely the excellent joy of the second is in love of the first.

But then he adds:

As long as the first is loved by the second, he alone seems to possess the delights of his excellent sweetness. Similarly, as long as the second does not have someone who shares in love for a third, he lacks the sharing of excellent joy. In order that both may be able to share delights of that kind, it is necessary for them to have someone who shares in love for a third.

In Augustine the Spirit was the love that binds the Father and the Son, in Richard love was a third person without whom the love of the Father and the Son for each other was incomplete.

ASSOCIATORS

The Muslims use a very distinctive term to apply to the Christians. They call them 'associators'. The word first occurs in Christian literature in St John of Damascus who was born a generation after the Muslim conquest of the Middle East (675 CE). His father was the chief representative of the Christians to the Caliph who resided in Damascus and John who spoke Arabic had contact with Muslim thinkers. In his monumental work the *Fount of Wisdom*, written when he was a monk at the monastery of Mar Saba in Palestine, he includes a long chapter on Islam, one of the first efforts of a Christian thinker to respond to the challenge of the new religion that had arisen in Arabia several generations earlier. '[The Muslims] call us Associators', he writes, 'because, they say, we introduce beside God an associate to Him by saying that Christ is the Son of God and God.' John was not simply passing on something he had heard from Muslim critics in Damascus or Palestine. He had studied the Koran and knew that the charge could be found in the sacred book of the Muslims. In Surah 3, The House of Imram, it reads:

> Say, 'People of the book! Come now to a word common between us and you, that we serve none but God, and that we associate nothing with Him, and do not some of us take others as Lords, apart from God.'
>
> (Koran 3:54)

In the same treatise John of Damascus alludes to an even more explicit passage from the Koran dealing with the deficiencies of the Christian doctrine of God. Muhammad, says John, said that there is one God 'who was neither begotten nor has he begotten'. The reference here is to Surah 112 which in its entirety reads: 'In the Name of God, the Merciful, the Compassionate. Say: "He is God, One, God, the Everlasting Refuge, who has not begotten, and has not been begotten, and no one is equal to Him." ' It is clear from this Surah that Muhammad was familiar with the Christian doctrine of the Trinity, indeed the Koran gives an Arabic translation of two of the technical terms used in Trinitarian theology, begotten and unbegotten, *gen[n]ētos* and *agen[n]ētos*.

The Muslim critics were correct. The Christians were associators. Because of the economy, they found it necessary to say that God the Father had associates. What is more, in response to the Muslims, Christian thinkers urged that such a way of conceiving God was preferable not simply because it was reasonable, but because it was found in the biblical tradition that Muslims shared with Christians and Jews and that was evident in the Koran. In discussion with Muslims, John of Damascus does not begin with arguments about the nature of God in general. The Koran, he notes, speaks of the 'Word' and also of the 'Spirit'. In saying that the Word and the Spirit are 'outside of God', and hence in 'trying to avoid making associates of God', Muslim thinkers have 'mutilated God'. He continues:

> It would be better to say that God has an associate than to mutilate God and deal with him as if he were a stone, or wood, or any of the inanimate objects. Therefore you accuse us falsely by calling us Associators; we, however, call you Mutilators of God.

St Hilary's phrase 'not a solitary God' was felicitous. In its original setting it was a tentative effort to find a way of explaining that after the coming of Christ it was not possible to conceive of God as a solitary monad. Though God was still confessed as one, God was not alone. But it led to more. If God is not solitary and exists always in relation, there can be no talk of God that does not involve love. Love unites Father, Son and Holy Spirit, love brings God into relation with the world, and by love human beings cleave to God and to one another.

REFERENCES

Barth, K. (1936) *The Doctrine of the Word of God: Prolegomena to Church Dogmatics*, vol. 1, Part 1, Edinburgh: T. & T. Clark.

Jenson, R. (1982), *The Triune Identity*, Philadelphia: Fortress Press.

Kelly, J. N. D. (1950) *Early Christian Creeds*, London: Longmans.

Pannenberg, W. (1991) *Systematic Theology*, Grand Rapids, Mich.: Eerdmans, 1: 259–336.

FURTHER READING

Basil, St (1980) *St Basil the Great on the Holy Spirit*, Crestwood, New York: St Vladimir's Seminary Press.

Gregory of Nyssa (n.d.) 'Contra Eunomium', in *A Select Library of Nicene and Post-Nicene Fathers of the Christian Church*, second series, vol. 5. Grand Rapids, Mich.: Eerdmans.

Hanson, R. P. C. (1988) *The Search for the Christian Doctrine of God*, Edinburgh: T. & T. Clark.

Hilary of Poitiers (n.d.) 'De Trinitate', in *A Select Library of Nicene and Post-Nicene Fathers of the Christian Church*, second series, vol. 9. Grand Rapids, Mich.: Eerdmans.

Hurtado, L. W. (1988) *One God, One Lord: Early Christian Devotion and Ancient Jewish Monotheism*, London: SCM Press.

Kelly, J. N. D. (1958) *Early Christian Doctrines*, London: A. & C. Black.

Kimel, A. F. Jr. (1992) *Speaking the Christian God: The Holy Trinity and the Challenge of Feminism*, Grand Rapids, Mich.: Eerdmans.

Norris, F. W., Wickham, L. and Williams, F. (1991) *Faith Gives Fullness to Reasoning: The Five Theological Orations of Gregory Nazianzen*, Leiden: Brill.

Oden, T. C. (1987) *The Living God: Systematic Theology*, vol. 1, San Francisco 181–225.

Origen (1966) *On First Principles*, trans. G. W. Butterworth, New York: Harper & Row.

Richard of St Victor (1979) *The Twelve Patriarchs, The Mystical Ark, Book Three of the Trinity*, trans. by G. A. Zinn, New York: Paulist Press.

Stylianopoulos, T. (1982) 'The Biblical Background of the Article on the Holy Spirit in the Constantinopolitan Creed', *La Signification et l'actualité du IIe Concile Oecuménique pour le Monde Chrétien d'aujourdhui*, Geneva, 155–73.

Tertullian (1948) *Tertullian's Treatise Against Praxeas*, ed., trans. E. Evans, London: SPCK.

See also chapters 9, 11, 12, 13, 26, 27, 43, 44.

11

CHRISTENDOM: MEDIEVAL CHRISTIANITY

David d'Avray

THE LATE DEVELOPMENT OF CHRISTENDOM

The term 'medieval Christendom' is normally applied to the Latin West, and tends to call to mind an 'Age of Faith' beginning with the conversion of the barbarian conquerors of the Western Roman Empire, reaching its apogee under papal leadership between the late eleventh and the early thirteenth century, then sliding into the decline which would in the end provoke the Reformation. That schema is not particularly accurate. Only from the beginning of the thirteenth century did Greek Christianity become separated unambiguously from Latin 'Christendom', although the drastic transformation of the Western Church from the mid-eleventh century – the battle for a celibate clergy independent of the laity, the crusades, new religious orders, and close papal government – had widened the gap between the two sectors. For all the religious energy of the period beginning *circa* 1050, it is unclear whether an articulate version of Christianity was available to the laity *en masse* before the mid-thirteenth century if not later, so one cannot straightforwardly describe the whole period as an Age of Faith (even if one leaves aside the history of dissidence and unbelief). Moreover, the strong papacy which had orchestrated religious change from the eleventh century did not degenerate into a merely political institution in the last medieval centuries. Except perhaps during the Great Schism from 1378 to 1417 the institution remained close to the mainstream of theological development and religious enthusiasm. In a sense, therefore, Christendom only really came into being in the later stages of the period covered by this chapter. One may, of course, use 'Christendom' as a term of convenience for the medieval period in its religious aspect, provided one bears in mind the foregoing qualifications, as also the more obvious point that the period from the fall of the Roman Empire in the West to the Protestant Reformation of the sixteenth century does not have much meaning as a unit in the history of Greek Christianity.

'CHURCH' AND 'STATE' IN THE MIDDLE AGES

Even for the West the limits of the period cannot be drawn sharply. In the West, as in the East, some of the characteristics acquired by Christianity under the Christian Empire before c.400 were carried over into the succeeding period: notably the interestingly ambiguous relation between religion on the one hand and secular culture and government on the other. In many (if not most) religions, there is no real distinction between Church and State, religion and culture, except in modern times when it has been unconsciously and widely implanted by Western influence. Christianity, however, grew up out of a Jewish tradition quite distinct from (even if influenced by) the dominant rhetorical culture of the Roman Empire. More important still, perhaps, the Church's own structures of hierarchical authority were well developed before the Empire turned Christian. In its formative phase, Christianity had faced the indifference or hostility of classical culture, and imperial authority; thus to regard them as essential and intrinsic aspects of the religion would involve an almost unthinkable *volte face*. On the other hand, classical culture was almost irresistibly attractive and the conversion of the Empire seemed like a miracle. Greek philosophy had supplied conceptual weapons to Christian apologists from St Paul onwards, and the legitimacy of imperial authority *per se* had some scriptural authority behind it (Rom. 13). The outcome was an attitude of mind which sought to distinguish, but not separate, secular and sacred (with respect both to culture and to government). In any case, there was never any practical possibility of popes controlling Europe politically, even in the thirteenth century. Conversely, the papacy provided a counter-weight to royal and imperial domination of religious affairs in the West, especially in relation to the post-Carolingian German Empire between c.1100 and c.1300, but also to a real if varying extent outside these limits. Even the Eastern Emperor's control of his church was to some degree hemmed in, during the early Middle Ages (notably during the Acacian schism and the Iconoclastic controversy) by the tendency of his opponents to look to Rome. In the later Middle Ages, on the other hand, Greek Emperors pushing for union with Rome faced fierce opposition from monks and many others in the East. Although the Byzantine Emperors legislated for the church in their territory, and exercised enormous influence over religious affairs, they were not thought to possess overriding authority in this sphere. The Patriarch of Constantinople was by no means necessarily a tool of the Emperor: witness the opposition to the fourth marriage of the Emperor Leo VI, or the strong patriarchs of the thirteenth and fourteenth centuries.

EAST AND WEST IN THE EARLY MIDDLE AGES

The Eastern and Western halves of the Christian world obviously had much in common apart from their attitude to the secular: notably monasticism, the structuring of the day for monks (at least) by prayers consisting largely of psalms, the arrangement of the year to commemorate the birth of Christ, his death and resurrection, etc., not to mention fundamental things such as the mass and the doctrines of the Three, Father, Son and Holy Spirit, in one God, and two natures in Christ. None of these things, obviously, are universal in the history of Christianity when viewed as a whole.

In the fifth and sixth centuries, moreover, close connections were maintained between the two worlds. Both were centred on the Mediterranean. Popes were drawn deeply into otherwise principally Eastern disputes about what the union of natures in Christ implied. Except when pitted against an emperor, popes were only too eager to remain under imperial protection, in the tradition of the Christian Empire. In the sixth century, Justinian actually reconquered Italy, though it was soon lost to the Lombards.

The failure of Byzantine emperors to find the means to protect Rome from the Lombard threat must slowly have diminished papal anxiety to stay within the imperial fold. Because of the astonishing conquests of the Arabs, the Mediterranean ceased to be a Christian lake by the end of the seventh century. In the meantime, papal preoccupations were being drawn northwards to England, where the mission sent by Gregory the Great at the end of the sixth century had taken root, after initial reverses. Together with Irish monks (who were with time won over to Roman ways) this mission created a church where it was possible to appeal to Rome in a manner that anticipates the central Middle Ages. The close links between England and Rome had far-reaching consequences, for it was missionaries from England, above all St Boniface, who were able to convert the pagan parts of Germany in the eighth century, and they worked closely and deferentially with the popes.

THE WESTERN AND EASTERN EMPIRES

Both the English missionaries and the Popes received protection from the Carolingian dynasty which had, by the mid-eighth century, become supreme *de facto* in the realm of the Franks. When the Lombards seemed finally to be on the point of engulfing Rome, the papal call for help was answered by the Carolingian Pepin, who crushed them. Shortly after that, in 751, the Pope duly agreed that the last Merovingian king should lose his royal office (which had long been purely nominal) to Pepin. This was at a time when the Emperor in Byzantium was attacking the use of religious images, which made him heretical in papal eyes. Thus a combination of things had shifted papal orientation decisively to the West by the mid-eighth century. Finally, on Christmas day 800, another Pope crowned Pepin's son Charlemagne as Emperor, a ritual which has been variously interpreted but which marks at least symbolically the end of the papacy's (admittedly stormy) love affair with the imperial power in Constantinople.

Nonetheless the Eastern and Western halves of the Christian world remained more or less united. The ninth-century conflict between Pope Nicholas I and Photius was a messy but temporary interlude. The evidence for some other alleged manifestations of division does not stand up to close examination. Thus for instance it has been maintained that Patriarch Sisinnios II (996–8) brought out the anti-Roman encyclicals of Photius, which had fallen into oblivion, under his own name. Although these encyclicals can be found attributed to Sisinnios in later manuscripts, other manuscripts attribute them to men who could not possibly have held the views they contain: in short, there is no trusting these late attributions (Beck 1980: 127).

The course of a dispute over the fourth marriage of the Byzantine Emperor Leo IV shows the continued desire of the Greeks for communion even in strained circumstances. Greek Christianity frowned on re-marriage after a spouse's death, and Emperor Basil I, Leon VI's father, went so far as to declare a fourth marriage not only forbidden but invalid. The mortality rate of Leo VI's wives was high, however, and in 906 he married for the fourth time; so the Patriarch Nikolaos Mystikos banned the Emperor from participation in the liturgy. The Emperor put the question of the possibility of a fourth marriage to the Pope and the Eastern Patriarchs. The papal legates who subsequently arrived decided in favour of the Emperor. The dispute rumbled on for a long time, well after the death of Leo. Though leading Byzantine churchmen were at odds during this time, there was at least a consensus, reaffirmed by a synodal decision in 920, that fourth marriages should not be permitted. Nikolaos wrote twice after this decision to try and persuade the Pope to join the Byzantine consensus, but the papacy appeared to have maintained a diplomatic silence – perhaps because of genuine disagreement between Western and Eastern thinking on this issue. Finally Nikolaos made overtures for reconciliation without any conditions, and this time the Pope responded. This episode left unresolved the question of how genuine differences of principle between the Churches should be settled. It was evident that the two halves of the Christian world were moving towards substantially different conceptions of marriage, and a decision by a synod of Greek bishops was not likely to command obedience from their Western counterparts. In the short term, however, the episode shows how reluctant the two sectors were to lose contact with one another. The efforts of the Patriarch, above all, would seem to show a remarkably eirenic spirit.

If one abstracts from obvious social and political differences between the Byzantine empire and the West, moreover, these two great sectors of Christianity continued to look in some ways quite similar. Tenth-century German and English kings had an often decisive influence on episcopal appointments. Their control over and generally good relations with the episcopate were an important power base. It did not amount to the 'Caesaropapism' sometimes associated with Byzantium, but then as we have seen, there were definite limits to the influence even of Byzantine Emperors over the Church in their territory. Both Greek and Latin missionaries were active and successful in

Eastern Europe in the ninth and tenth centuries. In both East and West this was a great period in the history of monasticism. The order of Cluny in the West and Mount Athos in the East, most notably, exercised an incalculable influence on the spirituality of their respective societies. Admittedly the two sorts of monasticism were very different. One peculiarity of the West was the remarkable concentration by religious communities on the liturgical *memoria* (i.e. commemoration) of the absent living and the absent dead – a preoccupation which can already be found in the eighth century but which was carried in the tenth to astonishing lengths. The essential idea seems to have been to let absent individuals participate in the community of those present.

Contrasts in the styles of spiritual life need not have affected relations between Eastern and Western Christianity. It was possible for Otto II, the Western Emperor, to marry a Byzantine princess, and their son Otto III, who was deeply imbued with Byzantine culture, was due to follow this precedent when he died in 1002. The serious breach of 1054, when Leo IX was Pope and Michael Cerularius was Patriarch, arose in part out of the high-handed insensitivity of the papal envoy Humbert. Imbued with the idea that a strong interventionist papacy was a key to reform in the Church that he knew, he brought to Constantinople an abrasive attitude which had predictable results. Although the dispute can scarcely be regarded as, at the time, a formal schism, the spirit of intolerance shown by both sides, notably on matters of ritual and the introduction into the dispute of the dogmatic 'Filioque' issue (i.e., whether the words 'and the Son' should be included in the third part of the Nicene Creed, concerning the Holy Spirit), boded ill for further relations between the two traditions.

Military intervention from the West to protect the Eastern Christians from the Turks at first seemed to offer the likelihood of genuine *rapprochement*. The fiery reforming Pope Gregory VII proposed the plan to Emperor Michael VII, who liked it, and though it came to nothing then, Pope Urban II had managed by the end of the eleventh century to launch the first Crusade, at least one aim of which was to save the Greeks from Islam. However, direct contact between Frankish knights and Byzantium generated dislike and distrust on both sides, in both this and subsequent crusades.

Moreover, the religious transformation in the West, of which the crusading movement was a part, tended to increase the distance between Latin and Greek Christianity to a point where mutual comprehension would not be at all easy, especially since many of the changes were bound up with a rapid growth of papal *dirigisme*: fierce and dramatic initiatives, then rapidly expanding bureaucratic intervention, which made Rome seem quite different from that remote final court of appeal that Byzantine churchmen had at times seemed happy to accept.

It would be futile to look for a single cause for the religious transformation of the West. In the case of the crusading movement one might single out (at the cost of oversimplification) the popularity of pilgrimage and religious attempts to limit violence by the 'Truce of God' movement, and a papal idea of channelling this violence into a defence of Eastern Christians.

WESTERN DEVELOPMENTS

One can, however, single out certain significant changes which took place in the West which accelerated the division of the Church between East and West.

Simony and investitures

A major theme in the religious upheaval is the struggle against Simony (the purchase of Church office), which broadened into a general conflict between Popes and Kings for control of the episcopate. It had for a long time been perfectly normal for strong rulers to choose bishops and abbots, though it would be wrong to regard this as a formal ideological or administrative system or assume that the power could always be exercised successfully. Bishops and abbots controlled great economic, and therefore also political and military power, however, so it was natural for rulers to want men who would work with them. It could also be in their interest to enhance episcopal and abbatial power, since bishops and abbots did not have sons. A grant to a lay noble, on the other hand, might be rewarded by loyalty for one generation, but then by opposition from the heirs and successors. With ecclesiastical offices the ruler had the chance to exercise patronage every time the holder died. Moreover, prospective bishops and abbots might be expected to give the ruler a financial sweetener in return for their promotion.

It is possible that the cash aspect was relatively new in the eleventh century. It has been plausibly linked with the rapid expansion of the money economy. At any rate the reformers thought it outrageous. They came to feel that the whole system of lay control in the Church was improper, furthermore, and to push for the election of bishops by the clergy of the cathedral. A system of this kind was introduced for the papacy itself by the Lateran synod's election decree of 1059 (previously either German Emperors or Roman noble families had tended to control the choice of Popes). The same synod decided that no cleric or priest should obtain a 'a church' at lay hands either gratis or for payment. This was a very general programme, apparently aimed at all appointments by laymen, not only those tainted by simony. Indeed, it would seem to have included the appointment of parish priests, which was commonly in the hands of a powerful local layman.

In the last part of the eleventh and the early twelfth century the conflict over lay control focused on the question of investitures – the conferring of symbols of office on the bishop by the Emperor or King. The compromise solution eventually reached by the Pope and the Emperor was to embody a conceptual distinction between the religious and the temporal power of the bishops in the inauguration rituals: the King or the Emperor ceased to confer the ring and staff which symbolized spiritual power, but did confer secular power through his sceptre. At the same time the problem of episcopal appointment was settled, rather to the Emperor's disadvantage, by the rule that the cathedral clergy should elect bishops. In Germany they should do so in the Emperor's presence (so they would be unlikely to ignore his wishes), but not so in Italy, where the Emperor had hitherto exercised real power (in part of course precisely by controlling episcopal appointments). Similar solutions had been reached earlier elsewhere in Christendom, notably in England.

The system of appointment by cathedral clergy led to numerous disputed elections, not only because of intervention by secular rulers but also because there was no clear rule that the numerical majority should prevail. The upshot was frequently an appeal to the Pope, who might well then appoint someone entirely different. Although the reformed papacy did not at this stage aim to control episcopal appointments, the system began, in effect, to evolve in that direction. In the meantime the appeals contributed to the expansion of papal bureaucracy and judicial activity.

Papal government and law

From the twelfth century onwards in particular, many other kinds of disputes ended with an appeal to the Roman curia. Papal successes against secular rulers meant that increasingly the Pope, rather than the King or Emperor, became the supreme court of the Church. It was a period when litigation generally was increased by a quantum leap. It was not inevitable that so many lawsuits should go to the Pope. Bernard of Clairvaux thought it was bad for the papacy. A king like Henry II of England would have been glad to hear ecclesiastical cases himself. For instance, he settled the dispute between the Abbey of Battle and the Bishop of Chichester over the abbey's exemption from episcopal authority. This was before the death in 1170 of Thomas Becket (at the time of the Battle Abbey dispute, indeed, royal chancellor and a king's man). After Becket's *volte face* on becoming Archbishop, appeals to the Pope were among the issues which stood between him and the King. Becket's murder and Henry II's penance put an end to his opposition on this score. Throughout the middle and later decades of the twelfth century more and more litigants took their cases to Rome. The papacy coped by *ad hoc* delegation of its supreme judicial authority for the duration of a given case to local men whom it trusted. Papal judgements set precedents and collections of them were made, at first informally, for future reference.

In part as a result of the expansion of papal justice, Church law became an academic discipline in the course of the twelfth century. It was studied with the help of two techniques typical of the intellectual life of the age. First, there was interpretative commentary on an accepted textbook (for Church law it was the *Decretum* of Gratian). The other technique (used skilfully by Gratian in this work) was to confront and reconcile authoritative texts which seemed incompatible. Universities developed out of schools in which these techniques were practised as a means of teaching Church law (or 'Canon Law') and other subjects.

Scholasticism and universities

Arguably the most successful application of these techniques was to theology. Here Peter Abelard's *Sic et non* – in which he juxtaposed the apparently contradictory authorities without providing the solution – provided a sharp stimulus. Peter Lombard's *Sentences* (which owed a lot to Abelard) would eventually become the theological counterpart of Gratian's *Decretum*: the standard textbook for creative commentary. Schools in Northern French cathedral towns, between which scholars and students could move freely, were the main institutional setting, and took the intellectual initiative away from the monasteries. Paris (where Abelard among others had taught and where the Lombard became permanently established) became the dominant school of theology and of 'Arts' (which consisted, above all, of philosophy), as Bologna was of law. In the thirteenth century they can both be called universities. Others were also establishing themselves, notably Oxford, where the fascinating intellectual maverick Robert Grosseteste (d. 1253) mixed science with theology in interesting ways. He stands outside the problem-solving tradition, which may be called 'scholasticism', that can be traced from Abelard, through the Lombard, to great thirteenth-century scholastics like Thomas Aquinas. (It should be added that both Aquinas, the problem-solver and synthesizer, and Grosseteste, with his 'provincial mind' and individualistic genius, made major contributions to the assimilation of Aristotle into Christian thought – Grosseteste by translating the *Nicomachaean Ethics*, and Aquinas by working the pagan philosopher's newly discovered ideas into the fabric of his theological system.)

The rapid growth of academic centres like Paris may have been fostered indirectly by the outcome of the reformer's war on simony. Once money had ceased to be an easy means of getting a good church benefice, other roads to promotion became attractive. The successful study of theology or Church law was an obvious one. No doubt it brought a man into a network of recommendations and of friendships between the talented that could only advance a career. It was probably also assumed (then as now) that academic study brought with it 'transferable skills' which were sought after in the administrators, counsellors and diplomats of up-to-date rulers. In consequence many civil servants were 'clerics' (cf. the modern 'clerk') and unmarried. In England this remained true until at least the second half of the fourteenth century. *A fortiori* it was necessary to remain unmarried and a cleric if one wished to make a career as an academic theologian. As for canon lawyers, in Italian universities it was possible for a married layman to achieve eminence in the discipline, but north of the Alps, marriage was out.

Clerical celibacy

Commitment to celibacy had become in practice *de rigueur* for professional academics of all kinds in Northern Europe even before it had become a strong moral imperative for, say, cathedral canons. It may have been because of the convention of academic celibacy that the self-sacrificing Heloise was at first unwilling to marry Abelard: she feared to ruin his career.

Outside academe clerical marriage was still socially respectable at the time of their affair, but attitudes were changing. Since the eleventh century reformers had been campaigning against the marriage of priests, which had long been forbidden in theory but normal in practice. Together with the attack on simony, it had been a principal plank in their platform. The papal synod of 1139 struck a blow against the social respectability of the status quo by saying that it did not deem such unions, which were contracted in violation of Church law, to be valid marriages. This applied to subdeacons, deacons, and priests (as well as to bishops, of course, for whom marriage had never been admissable). To say that the unions were copulation rather than marriage must have been a serious deterrent to a respectable girl interested in, say, a cathedral canon. If such unions were sinful, but valid, one would be a wife in the end (and sins could be forgiven). To be a mistress was a different matter. Clerical marriage became clerical concubinage. Here we have a sharp contrast with the Eastern Church, where the norm was for parish priests to be married (though bishops had to be celibate, with the result that they would normally be recruited from monks). The Western reform movement of the central Middle Ages, even if only partially successful, accentuated this difference between the two traditions.

One of the ways in which the papacy tried to promote clerical celibacy seems to have been to encourage the clergy to live in communities. At the Lateran synod of 1059 a fierce clause against clerical concubinage is followed by a clause telling chaste priests to share a common table and dormitory at the churches they served. They are urged to strive to live 'the apostolic, that is the common life' (clause 4).

Religious movements before Innocent III

The 'apostolic life' ideal was clearly the slogan for its age: the idea spread like wildfire. It seems unlikely that this was due to papal propaganda alone. A possible explanation is that feasts of the apostles had enjoyed an especially prominent place in the liturgical calendar since at least the tenth century. Their holy days were also holidays from work – a rare privilege in the early Middle Ages, despite a vague idea current among scholars that days like these were common. With every allowance made for areas too remote for the Church's structuring of the year to impinge on lay consciousness, and for all kinds of mental confusion, a high proportion of the laity must have grasped that apostles had a special status among saints. Perhaps the papacy only activated a latent assumption.

The multiplication of communities of 'regular' or Augustinian canons doubtless owed much to the conception of the common life as the life of the apostles. Otherwise it is hard to generalize about this loosely defined 'order', except that it was rather more flexible than the forms of monastic life available at the time. Throughout the Middle Ages Popes were able to use it as a broad institutional framework for quite different forms of religious life. Premonstratensians, Dominicans, and the later Canons of Windesheim were all at least theoretically attached to it. However, there were other forms of the apostolic life ideal which took on a life of their own and threatened the papacy itself. People reflected that the apostles had lived lives of extreme poverty and that they had been sent out to preach by Christ. To imitate the apostles one must abandon one's goods and go out to preach. Thus in the late twelfth century a merchant of Lyons gave away his wealth and began to evangelize together with some followers. They went to the papacy for approval of their way of life, but permission to preach was made dependent on local episcopal approval, which was denied. So the group broke away and became the Waldensian movement, which exists to this day.

The ideals of poverty and preaching proved transferable even to the Cathars, whose fundamental beliefs may not have been Christian in origin (they thought for instance that everything material or physical was evil). Their leaders were poor preachers who doubtless looked a lot more like apostles than did the Catholic parish clergy. These leaders were the 'perfect ones' whose reception of the sacrament called *Consolamentum* had committed them to living out the logic of dualist principles by abstention from all sex and all foods resulting from it. In the twelfth century the Catholic Church seemed to be losing ground steadily to the Cathars, who were strong in northern Italy and virtually dominant in southern France.

The only orthodox preachers that could be found to combat them whose spiritual stature seemed comparable to the Cathar 'perfect ones' were Cistercians. The Cistercian order, a product of the early twelfth century, was a revival, not so much of the life of the apostles, as of the primitive Benedictine ideal, as they understood it: manual labour, a big role for lay brothers, less involvement in administration of manors, simpler liturgy and rural and deserted locations. One may note, however, that in at least one important respect the Cistercians departed from ancient Benedictine tradition, by discontinuing the practice of admitting child 'oblates' into the order. The general trend away from this practice in other orders in the twelfth century may perhaps be attributed to the massive influence of the Cistercians, who were the most dramatically successful of the many orders – whose forms of life varied from the eremitical (e.g. the Carthusians) to the military (e.g. the Templars) – which appeared between the Gregorian Reform and the Fourth Lateran Council of 1215. The Cistercian order took off due to the religious prestige of Bernard of Clairvaux, who diffused within it and outside it a style of affective spirituality that would colour the piety of the West for centuries.

Since a major point of the Cistercian life was to pray and work away from the rest of the world, they were not an obvious choice for the task of anti-heretical preaching. No doubt they were chosen because of the admiration that their austere life aroused (though this very austerity, combined with a religious dedication to work, was to bring the order immense corporate wealth which left observers less impressed). In any case, the Cathars seemed more powerful than ever by the start of the thirteenth century, as did the Waldensians and other heretical groups imbued with 'apostolic' ideals.

The friars

One may reasonably think that the crisis facing the authorities of the medieval Church by *c.*1200 might have exploded with a force comparable to that of the Reformation of the sixteenth century. It was skilfully defused by Pope Innocent III, whose evident policy it was to bring apostolic movements within the fold as religious orders. A section of the Waldensians and a movement known as the *Humiliati* were incorporated in this way into the Church's structure. So too were the Franciscans, though St Francis himself was so committed to the idea of ecclesiastical obedience that one should avoid the temptation to present him as a heretical leader *manqué*: he remained cooperative even when he thought his movement was not turning out as he had wanted. At about the same time, St Dominic was starting a movement consciously designed to combat heresy. It would show that the orthodox could live the apostolic life of poverty and preaching better than the heretics. Its members would also acquire the intellectual equipment whereby to win conviction by undergoing a thorough theological training.

Not everyone can have approved of Innocent III's policy of creating new religious orders, and the Fourth Lateran Council of 1215 ruled that the process should stop; but the Franciscans had already been given approval and the Dominicans were categorized as Augustinian Canons, so the two orders survived and rapidly established themselves in most of the towns of Europe. The same Lateran Council had hoped to establish a system of preachers to assist the bishops. They never materialized in the form envisaged, but the friars did the preaching instead, especially in towns but also in areas accessible from them. They were also much in demand to hear confessions, especially since the Council of 1215 had made annual confession obligatory for all the faithful. Some critics said that preaching and hearing confessions were the task of the bishop and parish priests, and that religious orders should stick to prayer, etc. The papacy overrode the criticisms.

Some Paris university masters had taken a high profile in what amounted to a debate about the structure of the Church and the Pope's power to transform the system. These men had a more immediate and local problem with the friars. The Dominicans, and (less predictably) the Franciscans, had rapidly come to dominate academic theology at Paris university and elsewhere, putting the other professors (or 'masters') in the shade. The two most famous theologians of the thirteenth century were a Franciscan and a Dominican: Bonaventure and Aquinas. The sheer intellectual merit of the friars and strong papal backing left their academic opponents without any cards in their hands.

Popes had great confidence in the capacities of the friars, and used them in a variety of ways, notably for the preaching of crusades and as inquisitors. The inquisition in this period was not so much an institutional organ as a series of *ad hoc* commissions, so that its destructive effect varied enormously. Although it was a principle of medieval theology, and indeed papal teaching, that nobody could be compelled to accept the faith in the first place, heretics were generally regarded indiscriminately as persons who had understood and accepted Catholicism in its entirety and abandoned it out of moral perversity. This unsophisticated psychology of religious conviction could lead to savage repression. In fourteenth-century Bohemia, for instance, a great many Waldensians paid for their beliefs with their lives.

Popes also used friars to control or direct the communities of religious women which had appeared in large numbers, above all apparently in the Low Countries and the Rhineland, by the first half of the thirteenth century. Some communities belonged to religious orders proper – it should be noted that both the Dominican and the Franciscan orders had female branches – but there were other communities which did not fit so easily into familiar ecclesiastical categories. Popes had to provide priests to hear their confessions, preach to them, and generally guide their spiritual lives. The friars seemed natural candidates though they did not necessarily always want the job. One friar who preached to religious communities was Meister Eckhart. In the context of this work he developed ideas about spiritual perfection and the extinction of individual personality which have much in common with Buddhist and Hindu principles. It is likely enough that he felt that women like the ones he was directing had a greater likelihood than most of the Church, even than ascetics, Popes and prelates, or Franciscans who had abandoned any kind of material ownership, to reach the ranks of God's elite; and we need not assume that these women felt inferior to anyone.

It has been plausibly argued that the spirituality which developed in female communities under the influence of Eckhart was another, if rather special form of the 'apostolic life' ideal. The apostles were absolutely poor. Women could not perhaps imitate them by abandoning all property and begging on the streets. They could however achieve spiritual poverty by abandoning their individuality.

The apostolic ideal, which could take so many forms, was thus a powerful and unpredictable force (rather like the ideas of 'liberty' and 'equality' in more recent times), and Innocent III probably changed history by channelling much of the force into the Franciscan and Dominican Orders. The impetus would even take them to China, for missionary work was an important part of their understanding of the ideal. For a time there was a Franciscan archbishop of Peking. The Dominican William of Rubruck tells a rather self-congratulatory but charming story of how he convinced a Muslim, a Hindu and a Nestorian Christian in a four-cornered debate at the court of the Great Khan of the Mongols. Within Europe itself it was the persuasive skills of the friars, as well as the Inquisition, which recaptured religious initiative from heretical movements.

The Albigensian Crusade and the Fourth Crusade

From the early thirteenth century on the Cathars, in particular, lost ground rapidly. The spirituality of Christ's physical humanity – as a baby, on the cross – to which Francis of Assisi brought a special intensity, was diametrically opposed to the Cathar denial of all value to the body. Each had their attractions but religious public opinion was turning towards a positive evaluation of the body. This is reflected, for instance, in the marriage preaching of the mendicant orders, in which marriage is presented as holy if difficult. This attitude was poles apart from that of mainstream Catharism, for which marriage was evil (though permitted, paradoxically, in the amoral world of those who had not received the *Consolamentum* and become perfect). Even before Franciscan and Dominican propaganda could have had much effect, the Cathars suffered a crippling blow from a crusade of (principally) Northern French knights, launched by Innocent III after the murder of a papal legate, when the situation in Southern France seemed about to slip right out of orthodox control. This is known as the Albigensian Crusade (the southern French city of Albi was a Cathar stronghold). It is not counted among his successes by most modern writers, for it was soon out of his own (apparently well-meaning) control and turned into what came close to being a political conquest of the south by the north.

The Fourth Crusade of 1204 had followed a somewhat similar pattern. Sent to defend the Latin East, it was diverted to the conquest of Constantinople from the Greeks. The commercial interests of the Venetians and their financial hold on the Crusade, together with a high degree of anti-Greek prejudice, built up over the preceding century, seem to have brought this about, and Innocent III was presented with a *fait accompli*. The Latin Empire and Patriarchate that resulted would not last nearly so long as the resentment felt by Greek Christians, which echoes to this day.

Development of doctrine: practice and theory

A significant spin-off in the West of the tension and conflict with Greek Christians was the articulation by the papacy of ideas about issues on which it might not otherwise have uttered. Papal inerrancy was one such issue. At a time when canonists and theologians did not apply Luke 22:32 to Peter's successors, so far as is known, Innocent III does so in a letter of 12 November 1199 to the Patriarch of Constantinople. Here Innocent says that in praying that Peter's faith should not fail, etc., Christ was signifying clearly that his successors would at no time ever deviate from the faith (Haluscynskyi 1944: 189). Innocent may have been influenced by a letter which would have been an obvious precedent, written by his predecessor Leo IX in 1053 to another Patriarch of Constantinople, Michael Cerularius (cf. Migne 1882:744–69).

The doctrine of purgatory is a rather different case. Although its origins go back to before the Middle Ages, its place in the religious life of the West was transformed out of all recognition in the twelfth century, without, however, any explicit papal approval (except perhaps indirectly through the growth of indulgences). But in the thirteenth century papal approval was given first by Innocent IV, and then at the second Council of Lyons in 1274, when the doctrine was included in the profession of faith of the Greek Emperor Michael VIII Palaeologus. In both cases the context was an effort on both sides to achieve the reunion of Greek and Latin Churches.

This was achieved in 1274. Though the political exigencies of the Byzantines have been stressed in the historiography of the subject, close examination of the negotiations preceding this outcome suggests that it was not a matter of simple expediency. The Greek Emperor and Pope Gregory X (d. 1276) seem to have made genuine efforts at mutual understanding. The offensive heavy-handedness of Gregory's successors worked to destroy all this. The influence of the King of Sicily and Naples, who aimed to conquer Constantinople, on a Pope whom he had helped to get elected, Martin IV, seems to have been the decisive negative influence on the Latin side. A leading modern authority has judged that the Union was 'wilfully and irresponsibly broken off by the pope' (Beck 1980: 202).

It could be argued that in accepting the doctrine of purgatory and other Latin developments, Michael Palaeologus and the Greek Christians who agreed with him in 1274 were implicitly accepting too that the formulation of belief was not static, but incremental. Whether or not they would have put it that way, it should be noted that this was a period in which the development of doctrine not only occurred (the coining of the term 'transubstantiation' and its adoption by the Council of 1215 had been another case) but was recognized as a concept. Its occurrence in the *Summa Theologica* of Thomas Aquinas is well known (2a 2ae q I a 10; Mirbt 1934, no. 262, 200–1). He argued that the Pope could, as it were, update the creed by deciding questions as they arose.

A considerably earlier articulation of the idea of development arose out of the papal settlement of a practical question about the permanence of marriage. It is an example of the interesting overlap between theological doctrine and canon law in the period. Pope Alexander III (d. 1181) ruled that a marriage could be dissolved by entry into a religious order if marriage had not yet been consummated (*Corpus Juris Canonici*, Decretal. Gregor. IX. Lib III. Tit. XXXII Cap. II, Friedberg (ed.) 1881: col. 579). Sometime later a leading Paris theologian, Stephen Langton (later Archbishop of Canterbury) commented that until that decision had been made, no-one would have believed that it was within the Pope's power to take it (Powick 1928: 140). In other words, the papal judgement had drawn the boundaries of indissolubility in an unexpected way. This went far beyond the idea of annulment on grounds of impotence, where the Church's view was that a marriage had never existed in reality. Alexander III's decision related to genuine marriages where consummation was possible but had not yet occurred. Incidentally this decision could be regarded as part of a general tendency within orthodox Catholicism of the time to put a positive emphasis on sex within marriage (though pleasure as the motive for rather than side-effect of sex was widely regarded as a venial sin).

In the early fourteenth century the Dominican theologian John of Naples raised the analogous question of whether entry to sacred orders did, or did not, dissolve a previous marriage. He concluded that since there was nothing explicit on this point in the Law (of the Church) a Decretal or constitution on this matter was to be devised (John of Naples 1618: Quaestio XL, Punctum II, 343). A papal decision did in fact follow, ruling that even if the marriage had not been consummated, it was not dissolved by Holy Orders, unless the man were to enter a religious order (*Corpus Juris Canonici*, Extravag. Ioann. XXII. Tit. VI.i, Friedberg (ed.) 1881: 1212–13.) The question of whether the Pope could in principle alter the rule so that Holy Orders dissolved a prior unconsummated marriage is perhaps left open by this decision. Here we are in the border territory between canon law and doctrine.

The papal judgement begins with language reminiscent of two other documents relevant to the idea of development from early fourteenth-century Popes in that it proposes to put an end to *Concertatio*, dispute or disagreement. The first of the two documents in question is by Pope John XXII, who was also responsible for the ruling on Holy Orders after marriage. John seems to have been imbued with the idea that it was a role of the papacy first to encourage a fairly free intellectual debate on major religious issues, and then finally to settle the matter by a papal decision. It is possible that he had in mind the model of an academic disputation, in which the participants debated freely until the master, who had listened to all their arguments, gave his *determinatio* at the end. At any rate it has been plausibly argued that John XXII aimed to shift the theological centre of gravity from Paris to the papal court at Avignon.

The debate which he settled in 1322 (Mirbt 1934, no. 379: 219), 'wishing to put an end to this dispute' (*concertationi*), had by no means been argued out in an atmosphere of academic calm, however, and his decision was not to be followed by a tranquil consensus. The dispute was about the poverty of Christ and the apostles. It should be distinguished from a dispute which he had decided immediately before, leaving much bitterness, between the 'Spiritual' and 'Conventual' wings of the Franciscan order. The Spirituals believed that the order had let slip the original Franciscan ideal by watering down in practice the poverty they were committed to. The Spirituals were also attracted by the prophetic ideas of Joachim of Fiore (d. 1202), who was understood by some to have announced an age of the Holy Spirit, to follow on the ages of the Father (Old Testament) and the Son (Christ onwards), in which New Spiritual Men – the Spiritual Franciscans themselves – would take over the religious leadership of the Church. Popes who opposed them risked being characterized as the imminently awaited Antichrist. John XXII came down firmly against these Spirituals.

Whatever the differences between Spirituals and Conventuals about the practical implications of their poverty principle, however, they tended to agree that the order legally owned nothing even as a corporation, and that in this they were closer to Christ and the apostles than any other order. To make this theory work, the Pope had to be the legal owner of all their buildings, books, and everything else they had. Not everyone in the Church agreed that absolute corporate poverty was a supreme ideal in itself, however, or that Christ and the apostles did not even collectively possess anything. Thomas Aquinas, for instance, argued firmly against the idea. In his eyes the ideal religious order would own some things collectively, though individual members would be absolutely poor. John XXII was an admirer of the Dominican Thomas, and may have been influenced by his thought when he officially decided against the Franciscan understanding of apostolic poverty. Unlike the conflict between 'Spirituals' and 'Conventuals' within the Franciscan order, which had seemed to be destabilizing the Church, this was a decision which he might well have been able to avoid. So far as the circumstances are understood today, there was nothing to prevent him from staying on the sidelines of the debate between Franciscans and Dominicans. He seemed to have wanted to bring the problem into focus, and to have himself stirred up a debate which inevitably became charged with passionate emotion, especially on the Franciscan side. He makes it clear, however, that he is not crystallizing an existing belief of the Church. He stresses the previous lack of consensus among academics (*viros scholasticos*). Furthermore he goes on to say that the view he is condemning should be judged erroneous and heretical henceforth (*deinceps*).

The word *deinceps* is used in a similar manner (in 1336) by John XXII's successor Benedict XII, when he settled the debate about the Beatific Vision by declaring that the saints and those who had completed their penance in purgatory did not have to wait until the resurrection of the body before they saw God face to face (Mirbt 1934, no. 382: 221-2). For Benedict XII it was particularly important to emphasize that the binding character of his statement was new, since his predecessor (John XXII again) had held the contrary as a private theologian, and stirred up a fierce controversy. Though the whole business had been a propaganda present to John's opponents on the question of apostolic poverty, one may surmise that John had been pursuing the idea that doctrinal progress should be pushed forward by lively debate on unsettled issues which should finally be decided, to be sure, by a papal *determinatio*. Benedict XII emphasized that John had not lived to give his *determinatio* as Pope, and painted a picture of a flux of mutually contradictory theological views. This state of affairs was harmful to souls, he said, so by his apostolic authority he would give a definition 'by this constitution which will be valid for ever'. On the one hand, then, Benedict XII did not claim to be stating officially what most Catholics would have said already. On the other hand, his new formulation was meant to last forever.

A Byzantine development: Palamism and Hesychast spirituality

This notion of development is itself an interesting development, and its legitimation in terms of papal succession from St Peter is distinctive among the forms of Christianity, but the practice of doctrinal dispute settlement by a *magisterium* is not in itself unusual, however that *magisterium* was constituted. In the case of the later medieval Byzantine Church the *magisterium* took the form of a sort of permanent synod of the Patriarch of Constantinople and the bishops around him, supplemented now and again by special assemblies to which representatives came from farther afield.

It was an assembly such as this which in 1351 finally endorsed the theology of Gregorios Palamas (1296–1359), the theological theorist of Hesychast spirituality. Hesychasm was a method of prayer. The idea was to put oneself in a state of readiness to receive the grace of God by repeatedly reciting a brief prayer while holding one's breath. Palamas developed his theology in response to an attack on Hesychasm. On the one hand, he believed that a direct experience of God is possible to Christians, of a kind quite different from that accessible to pagan philosophers (his opponent tended to play down the difference). On the other hand, he distinguished sharply between God's unknowable essence and his energy or energies. It was the latter which could be experienced.

The close connection between theological system-building and spirituality is a salient feature of Palamism, whose history sufficiently refutes any notion that Byzantine religious and intellectual life was static in the later Middle Ages. Another symptom of its remarkable vitality is the growing curiosity about Latin theology in some quarters around the middle of the fourteenth century. The *Summma contra Gentiles* of Thomas Aquinas was translated by Demetrios Kydones, to be followed by large parts of the *Summa Theologica*.

Demetrios Kydones also conducted a vigorous controversy over the method of Thomas with his former teacher Meilos Kabasilas.

Late medieval Western academic and pastoral theology

In the West the theology and philosophy of Thomas must have seemed rather old-fashioned to many intellectuals by this time, though Dominicans kept up the tradition. William of Ockham tried to cut away what he viewed as the metaphysical fat of earlier theological systems, including the idea of general essences, which were reduced in his system to concrete mental signs in a person's mind. (This is usually called Nominalism.) He and other fourteenth-century theologians also moved away from synthesis to more specific investigations, and showed a particular interest in questions about the absolute power of God. A hundred years ago the limited interest felt in Thomistic theology by the fourteenth-century academics on the cutting-edge might have been presented in an article like the present one as symptomatic of the general decline of the medieval Church. Such a view would be misleading. Though it ceased to be normal for the best minds to devote themselves to vast theological syntheses, the research of the last half-century or so has produced plenty of evidence of theological creativity. Perhaps the most important reason for avoiding generalizations about decline is that a vast amount of the evidence for late medieval thought remains unexplored. The manuscripts are on the whole a tougher proposition than their twelfth- or thirteenth-century counterparts and the theology can get highly technical, but as it comes to be better understood there may be exciting surprises for historians of ideas.

As for the thought of Thomas Aquinas, it may have seemed *passé* to many academic theologians on the cutting-edge, but its influence was enormous at the level of pastoral popularization. John of Freiburg's popular handbook for priests hearing confessions draws heavily on Thomas, whose ideas were thus brought into contact with the consciences of ordinary people. Furthermore, preliminary soundings suggest that his theology also infiltrated popular preaching in the fifteenth century. (In Thomas' own time academic theology of this systematic kind seems not to have been much used in preaching to the laity or even indeed in preaching to the university clergy.) The decline of Thomistic theology has thus been exaggerated, perhaps in reaction to the unscholarly assumption that his thought enjoyed the same status in the Middle Ages as it would do in the Catholic Church from the last decades of the nineteenth century.

This spread of what one might call 'pastoral Thomism' is one aspect of a wider trend – the fast-rising standard of religious education among the lower clergy and the laity. The friars had already made a big impact in the thirteenth century and continued to do so in the fourteenth and fifteenth centuries (indeed, in the fifteenth-century preachers like Bernardino of Siena led dramatic religious revivals). This 'competition' was probably in itself an incentive to parish priests to improve themselves – there was room for it since, in the absence of seminaries or theological colleges, the normal method of training seems to have been an informal kind of apprenticeship. At the beginning of the fourteenth century Boniface VIII made it easier for parish priests to get time off to study at university, without their parish being left unmanned, and even before this the situation had been changing by a stream of 'self-help' handbooks, designed to assist priests to teach themselves the art of pastoral care. This literature was designed to equip the lower clergy to carry out all aspects of their job, including preaching the basics of the faith to the laity. In parishes far from towns, out of reach of the preaching of the friars, the possession of one of these manuals by a parish priest might make all the difference to the lay parishioners' grasp of their religion.

Lay piety

Meanwhile 'pious and literate' laymen and women were becoming more common in the upper reaches of society. Vernacular works of edification (which could be combined with fictional entertainment, as in Wolfram von Eschenbach's *Parzifal* or in the anonymous *Sir Gawain and the Green Knight*) were widely available. Lay people could write as well as read. In the mid-fourteenth century a duke of Lancaster wrote an edifying *Book of Holy Medicines* in Norman French, and Dante could of course write fluent literary Latin, as well as Italian (though this sort of mastery of Latin by laymen would not be common outside Italy in Dante's time). Lay prayer books became plentiful in the late Middle Ages. Books of 'Hours' were the most usual sort, and more of them than of any other kind of manuscript book survive from the medieval period. They are in effect a simplified adaptation of the monastic liturgical office for private lay use. Psalms constitute a large proportion of the text, which is commonly accompanied by pictures. One may speculate that the real function of the books was to encourage attentive meditation on the life of Christ and the Virgin, and on Death: the pictures would stimulate the religious imagination and the muttered words of psalms could have served as a sort of mantra to ward off distraction and focus the mind.

The slow process by which Christianity penetrated Western society had thus gone quite far by the late Middle Ages, so that, as was suggested above, phrases like 'the Age of Faith' are probably more applicable to the end of the period covered by this chapter than to any earlier age of post-Roman Western history. Whether or not late medieval religion was in a healthy state depends on the clinician's criteria, but it was certainly not moribund. In fact the work of Protestant reformers in the sixteenth century may have been made easier by the generally high level of commitment: it was easy to interest people in religious ideas, and more people were more shocked by abuses in the high levels of the Church. The reforms of the Counter-Reformation papacy and the Council of Trent in the sixteenth century would be a commentary on these abuses.

The papacy and religious movements before the Reformation

Even though many historians would now hesitate to speak of a general deterioration of medieval religion, most would still agree that the papacy had declined, been corrupted and become politicized. It has been regarded as little more than an aggressive Italian Renaissance state, competing for territory with other powers in the peninsula. A common interpretation of papal history from the thirteenth century goes something like this. By the mid-thirteenth century, the papacy had again lost the moral high ground, which Innocent III had briefly recaptured by backing the Franciscans and winning over heretical groups. A long-drawn-out conflict with the imperial Hohenstaufen dynasty involved the papacy deeply in high politics, thus weakening it as a religious institution. In any case, victory over the Hohenstaufen was followed less than half a century later (1303) by the humiliation of Pope Boniface VIII at the hands of forces of the French king Philip IV and the Colonna clan. Not long afterwards the papacy, which could not control its own lands in Italy, moved to Avignon (not in but close to the French king's domain), which remained the papal base for many decades while periodic and expensive efforts were made to regain control of Rome and the papal state. Though much weaker in the arena of high politics than in the thirteenth century, the hold of the papal power over the clergy of Christendom and their incomes was consolidated; but nevertheless contact had been lost with the forces of true religious feeling. Then, in 1378, two years after the final return to Rome, a disputed papal election produced a schism which lasted until 1417, when it was finally resolved at the Council of Constance. During the 'Great Schism' the rival lines of popes were very dependent on their respective adherents among the rulers of Europe, and desperate for money, with consequences for the way in which indulgences were administered. Attempts to resolve the Schism encouraged the construction, with the help of materials available in earlier writings by canon lawyers, of theories which distinguished the authority of the Pope from that of a general council of the Church, and invested supreme authority (even over a Pope) in the latter. This body of theory survived the end of the Schism, and became the animating ideology of the Council of Basle (1431–49), which broke with and took on the papacy.

Success of reunion negotiations with the Greek Church (at the papally directed Council of Florence, 1438–45) helped tip the balance of opinion away from the Council of Basle and towards the then Pope Eugenius IV (even though the Byzantine empire would be overwhelmed not long after, in 1453). Although it survived the Schism and the challenge of the 'Conciliar' movement, however, the papacy was only a shadow of its high medieval self: just another Italian principality struggling for survival and jostling for quite local territorial gains. The moral atmosphere at the papal court deteriorated, and the patronage of humanists and artists, which gives the fifteenth-century papacy an honourable place in the history of Renaissance culture, could not compensate for the institution's alienation from the religious forces of the age. Consequence: the Reformation.

Not much of this picture is actually false. The Schism, in particular, was a ruinous episode. Nevertheless the omissions from the preceding sketch are such that it lacks all proportion. The papacy was not in fact 'out of touch with the religious feeling of the age'. Much of the religious feeling of the age, for instance, was channelled into the system of indulgences. Simply to classify this with post-Reformation hindsight, under 'superstition', is hard to justify, unless the word can be used for any religious practice found unsympathetic. If one defines superstition as a fragmentary belief unsupported by the structure of a system, then indulgences need another label, for belief in indulgences was intimately related to some of the fundamental ideas of medieval Christianity: penance, vicarious atonement, purgatory, sanctity, and the mystical body of Christ. No doubt a lot of people did not understand these connections and simply thought they could pay to reduce time in purgatory, but it would be unduly cynical to assume that misunderstanding was the norm.

There are curious forgeries which would seem to indicate, in the minds of the people at whom they were aimed, a connection between indulgences, the papacy and spirituality. This we find in MS. British Library Add. 37,787 an indulgence supposedly granted by Pope John XXII for a set of 'Hours' which he had allegedly composed. It is interesting that someone thought he would tap a market by inventing a link between this tough Pope and that favourite form of devotion.

The charismatic female mystics who are prominent in late fourteenth-century Church History, above all Catherine of Siena, do not seem to have had a mass popular following, but were rather docilely accepted by the papacy even when they were attacking abuses. Catherine afterwards received the ultimate compliment of canonization (1461), as did Bridget of Sweden (1391).

The 'Modern Devotion' movement, of which *The Imitation of Christ* by Thomas à Kempis is the best-known product, was handled by the papacy in a manner reminiscent of Innocent III's treatment of the Franciscans. The Windesheim Congregation, which came out of the Modern Devotion, received approval from Boniface IX in 1395 and in 1425 from Martin V. As with the Franciscans, the papal attitude tended to 'domesticate' an originally unconventional movement.

In the later fifteenth century when the papacy had supposedly been reduced to the status of a Renaissance principality, papal religious prestige may in one way at least have been higher than ever before. Books of model sermons to help popular preachers must have been reaching a wider audience after the invention of printing, and these popularized for a mass public the ideology of papal authority. No-one has yet succeeded in finding a similar degree of emphasis on papal authority in sermons for the laity available in the period when papal authority is supposed to have been at its height.

Thus a simple picture of rise and decline is not really appropriate for the history of the medieval papacy, any more than for Christendom as a whole. Nor should such a picture be necessary to explain the Reformation. As already suggested above, religious vitality worked to the advantage of both conventional Catholic belief and its opponents. In the fifteenth century this was already evident, for Lollardy in England and Hussitism in Bohemia in many ways anticipate sixteenth-century Protestantism. John Wycliffe (whose ideas were grasped by the Lollards much more accurately than used to be thought) foreshadows sixteenth-century Reformers, especially in his rejection of transubstantiation and in his emphasis on predestination, and on the authority of the Bible alone. Jan Hus was influenced by Wycliffe, but did not depart so far from the orthodox line. The movement he inspired broke up into competing factions, some very radical indeed. The Lollards were suppressed by force; the Hussites, after a long and at times remarkably successful struggle, were defeated but not crushed. It was only in the sixteenth century that a religious dissident was protected by a prince from forcible repression for long enough for his movement to become an established church. Luther's new church was soon followed by many others.

Continuities from the early Middle Ages

The Protestant Reformation is the natural place at which to end the history of medieval Christendom. In suggesting that its real beginning is most usefully dated only a few centuries earlier, there is a risk of underestimating the importance of the early medieval period in the history of Christianity. It should therefore be stressed that the origins of 'Christendom' as understood here can be traced far back into the early medieval past, so that there is something to be said for a sort of 'Whig interpretation' of Christendom's history as a progress (in terms of the system's own rationality, which the historian does not have to like personally) from adumbrations and anticipations to institutional and ideological realization. Four such long-term developing continuities may be singled out from the complexities in the body of the article. One, obviously, was papal authority. The papacy's high profile in the last four or five medieval centuries is foreshadowed by its role in the theological disputes of the Greek East in the early Middle Ages, and in the organization of missions to England and Germany. In the early Middle Ages the papacy was imperceptible as a factor in everyday religious life, but periodic episodes anticipate what would later become the routine exercise of religious sovereignty. Second, there was the effort to Christianize the mass of the population; for although it is possible that the majority of people had only the haziest grasp of their religion before the later thirteenth century, the programme of instruction which we find in Charlemagne's 'General Admonition' of 789 makes the same clear, simple, articulate statement of fundamental beliefs which we meet much later in thirteenth-century synodal legislation and priests' manuals. It is even possible that baptism ritual and the instruction of godparents kept some understanding of the creed and Lord's Prayer alive between the Carolingian reforms and the central Middle Ages. Third, early medieval society was a 'society orientated towards death', to borrow a phrase associated with the waning of the Middle Ages. One may trace a line from massive commemorations of the dead in the eighth century and after to the chantries and multiplication of masses for the dead in the later Middle Ages. Finally, the apostolic ideal which informed the spirituality of both dissident and orthodox religious movements in the central and later Middle Ages may well have grown out of the quite special prominence given to feasts of the apostles in the early medieval liturgy, from the tenth century if not before. Even supposing that most lay people never heard an extended verbal explanation of Christian beliefs in the early Middle Ages, they would have known that apostles were something special, if their feasts were celebrated by holidays from work.

This last suggestion may be broadened out into a more general consideration. The structure of the liturgical year, with its imprecise but powerful messages about Christianity, was a common factor linking the different periods of medieval religion, but it was not exclusive to the medieval period. In its main lines it goes back to the Roman period, and much of it survived in Protestantism (in the Lutheran Church and the Church of England at any rate). Deep currents of liturgical practice and sentiment flow beneath the tides and waves of religious history.

REFERENCES

Beck, H.-G. (1980) *Geschichte der orthodoxen Kirche im Byzantinischen, Die Kirche in ihrer Geschichte*, Bd 1, Lieferung D 1; Göttingen: Vandenhoeck & Ruprecht.

Friedberg, A. (1881) *Corpus Iuris Canonici*, ii, Leipzig: B. Tauchnitz.

Haluscynskyj, T. (ed.) (1944) *Acta Innocentii PP. III (1198–1216)*, Pontificia Commissio ad Redigendum Codicem Iuris Canonici Orientalis, Fontes, series III, vol. II; Vatican City: Typis Polyglottis Vaticanis.

John of Naples (1618) *Quaestiones Variae Parisiis Disputatae*, Naples.

Migne, J. P. (1882) *Patrologia Latina*, 143, Paris: Garnier.

Mirbt, C. (1934) *Quellen zur Geschichte des Papsttums und des römischen Katholizismus*, 5th edn., Tübingen: Verlag von J. C. B. Mohr (Paul Siebeck).

Powicke, F. M. (1928) *Stephen Langton*, Oxford: Clarendon Press.

FURTHER READING

Beck, H.-G. *et al.* (1980) *From the High Middle Ages to the Eve of the Reformation*, in H. Jedin and J. Dolan (eds) *History of the Church*, vol. iv, London: Burns & Oates.

Hamilton, B. (1986) *Religion in the Medieval West*, London: E. Arnold.

Herrin, J. (1987) *The Formation of Christendom*, Oxford: Basil Blackwell.

Hussey, J. M. (1986) *The Orthodox Church in the Byzantine Empire*, Oxford: Clarendon Press.

Knowles, D. and Obolensky, D. (1969) *The Middle Ages*, vol. ii of *The Christian Centuries*, London: Darton, Longman and Todd.

Livingstone, E. A. (ed.) (1977) *The Concise Oxford Dictionary of the Christian Church*, Oxford: Oxford University Press.

Lynch, J. H. (1992) *The Medieval Church: A Brief History*, London: Longman.

Morris, C. (1989) *The Papal Monarchy: The Western Church from 1050 to 1250*, Oxford: Clarendon Press.

Ozment, S. (1980) *The Age of Reform, 1250–1550: An Intellectual and Religious History of Late Medieval and Reformation Europe*, New Haven: Yale University Press.

Richards, J. (1979) *The Popes and the Papacy in the Early Middle Ages, 476–752*, London: Routledge & Kegan Paul.

Schimmelpfennig, B. (1992) *The Papacy*, trans., New York: Columbia University Press.

Southern, R. W. (1970) *Western Society and the Church in the Middle Ages*, Harmondsworth: Penguin.

See also chapters 10, 12, 27, 28, 32.

12

THE TRANSITION TO MODERNITY

Alister McGrath

BASES FOR MODERN THEOLOGICAL METHOD

This chapter aims to survey the theological developments over the period 1400–1750, which did so much to lay the foundations for the modern period in theology. In many ways, the period may be regarded as witnessing a series of developments which prepared the ground for modern theological methods, particularly in relation to three areas:

1 The dawn of a historical perspective.
2 The development of a critical approach to Scripture.
3 The shift in meaning of the word 'Church'.

1 The dawn of a historical perspective

Many medieval writers appear to have been unaware of the radical differences between their own period, and classical antiquity. This lack of awareness fostered the belief that past ideas, values and methods could continue to be employed in the present, without the need for modification (Burke 1986). The Renaissance witnessed the birth of both artistic and historical perspective, raising a series of issues concerning the authority of the past in present theological debates. The need for criteria by which the past could be interpreted and appropriated became of increasingly pressing importance. The Renaissance itself tended to use aesthetic criteria, where the Reformers would develop theological criteria. Gradually, the potential of reason as such a criterion can be seen emerging. Yet with this development, the authority of the past was itself undermined, in that a present resource was assigned priority over past authorities (McGrath 1990). The transition from reliance on past authorities to an emphasis on reason had taken place.

2 The development of a critical approach to Scripture

Much medieval theology was based upon Scripture, specifically the Vulgate Latin translation (Evans 1985). Largely due to the literary and philological programme of the Renaissance, Scripture came to be regarded in a different light. It was seen as the literary embodiment of an experience, which could be, at least in part, recreated through appropriate interpretative manners (McGrath 1987). The debate over the extent of the canon, which became especially significant in the 1520s, led to the introduction in reforming circles of the category of 'apocryphal' works, of lower theological status than the canonical works. The term 'Scripture' thus underwent a significant change in the period under study; initially, it was generally regarded as meaning 'the Vulgate'; by the end of the sixteenth century, there was conflict between the Renaissance and Reformation approaches, which identified Scripture with 'the canonical biblical texts in their original languages', whereas Roman Catholic theology, following the decision of the Council of Trent, regarded Scripture as both the text and translation of the Vulgate.

3 The shift in meaning of the word 'Church'

Other terms changed meaning over the period; the term 'religion', for example, gradually divested itself of its specifically Christian associations, and came to refer to a wider body of beliefs (Bossy 1987). However, the term 'Church' also undergoes a significant change in meaning. The term was originally understood to refer to the Church, on the assumption, inherent to the notion of Christendom, that there was only one Catholic Church. With the eviction of the reforming faction at Wittenberg in the 1520s, and the rapid growth of evangelicalism in German and Swiss cities in the following decade, this notion became problematical. The term developed competing associations, which would eventually lead to the emergence of the denominational mindset characteristic of modern Western culture.

This is not to say that the period witnessed the espousal of consistently modern attitudes; it was a period of transition, with recognizable continuity with both the medieval period and the modern period. Thus Ernst Troeltsch drew attention to the medieval character of aspects of Melanchthon's thought, whereas Quentin Skinner stressed the modernity of aspects of the political thought of sixteenth-century Calvinism. Like a bridge, the period in question links up with both the eras which it separates. Our concern is not with Church history, but with the manner in which theology functioned during this era and the period can be broken down into four main sections:

1 Late Medieval Scholasticism.
2 Renaissance Humanism.
3 The Reformation.
4 The post-Reformation period.

1 LATE MEDIEVAL SCHOLASTICISM

The term 'scholasticism', along with a group of related terms, owes its origins to the agenda of the later Renaissance. Humanist writers, concerned to undermine the intellectual and cultural credibility of the period still known as 'The Middle Ages', developed a vocabulary designed to discredit it. The term 'Middle Ages' begins to emerge in the early sixteenth century, in writers such as Vadian (Joachim von Watt) and Beatus Rhenanus. The term is intended to imply that the 'Middle Ages' is to be viewed as little more than an interval between the intellectual and cultural glories of classical antiquity and those of the Renaissance.

Definition of scholasticism

'Scholasticism' is an elusive term, which is resistant to precise definition. The polemical origins of the term are partly to blame for this imprecision; however, the intellectual diversity within the movement is also a contributing cause of importance. Despite these difficulties, the following general characteristics are sufficient to define a general 'family resemblance' of the various components of the movement, as it is encountered in the fifteenth and sixteenth centuries.

Scholasticism was concerned with the rational justification of Christian belief, particularly in relation to the demonstration of the inherent rationality of theology. It is generally thought that this aspect of the movement is seen at its best in the later writings of Thomas Aquinas, especially the *Summa Theologica*. Even William of Ockham, concerned to emphasize the distinction between *ratio* (reason) and *fides* (faith), made extensive use of reason in matters of theology (Gilson 1978).

In its earlier phase, the movement made extensive use of Aristotelianism. This trend can be seen especially clearly in the writings of Dominican theologians of the late thirteenth century. However, Aristotelianism was treated in this manner on account of a belief that it represented a mature and universally valid set of rational assumptions, to which any intellectual discipline (*scientia*) should conform. During the fifteenth century, a significant internal debate developed within scholasticism concerning the intellectual credentials of Aristotelianism, as growing evidence of intra- and extra-systemic inconsistency emerged, not least on account of the development of the still nascent natural sciences. By the early sixteenth century, there was a growing recognition of the shortcomings of Aristotle.

Scholasticism was also concerned with the systematization of Christian theology. Earlier works of theology were often occasional, written in response to controversies or debates, and hence limited by the specific shape of the polemical stimulus. The anti-Pelagian writings of Augustine, upon which the Reformation drew with such enthusiasm, are an excellent example of this form of limitation. Scholasticism was concerned to develop a proactive, rather than reactive, approach to theology, by anticipating possible questions or objections to existing doctrines.

This systematic approach to theology was encouraged by the publication of Peter Lombard's *Sententiarum libri quattuor* during the twelfth century, which offered a comprehensive framework for the discussion of the central questions of theology. These 'four books of the sentences' (that is, quotations from the writings of the patristic era, especially from the writings of Augustine) were systematically arranged, thus bringing an order to the material which was generally lacking in their original contexts. The proliferation of commentaries upon these *Sentences*, not to mention the formal importance of such a commentary as a qualification for the advanced teaching of theology, ensured that the scholastic mind-set was characterized by a conviction of the propriety and necessity of such systematization.

Types of scholasticism

Scholasticism was a heterogeneous movement. Even during the thirteenth century, significant divergences became evident within the movement, as may be seen by comparing the writings of Aquinas, Bonaventure and Duns Scotus, representing the characteristic approaches of the early Dominican school, the early Franciscan school and the later Franciscan school respectively.

By the late medieval period, at least nine major schools had developed within the movement, reflecting considerable diversity in relation to both methods and doctrines. Two schools of thought are of especial importance in relation to the late medieval situation: the *via moderna*, which designates the school of thought deriving from William of Ockham, whose leading late medieval representative was the Tübingen theologian Gabriel Biel; and a loose body of opinion or theological tendency, which cannot be regarded as a 'school' in the strict sense of the word, which favoured more radically Augustinian approaches to the doctrines of justification and predestination. This tendency, sometimes referred to as the *schola Augustiniana moderna*, is associated with writers such as Gregory of Rimini. However, it occurs in a number of different forms which are not readily susceptible to categorization.

Important issues in scholasticism

Four issues may be discerned as being of particular importance to scholasticism during the late medieval period, as follows:

(a) The debate between realism and terminism.
(b) The debate over logico-critical and historico-critical approaches to theology.
(c) The tension between intellectualism and voluntarism.
(d) Tensions relating to the doctrine of justification.

(a) The debate between realism and terminism

Writers of the earlier medieval period (including Aquinas and Scotus) were committed to a position which has come to be known as 'realism'. This position, which is clearly influenced by Platonism, acknowledged the existence of 'universal qualities' (such as a universal human nature, which is instantiated in individual human beings). The fourteenth century witnessed the development of a rival position, initially through the influence of William of Ockham, which is generally referred to as 'terminism' or 'nominalism'. This approach, which became of major importance during the fifteenth century, entailed the rejection of such 'universal qualities'. There is no such thing as a 'universal human nature'; the term 'humanity' designates individual humans, not a universal quality which lies behind such individuals. (It should be stressed that the term 'nominalism' should only be used to refer to this terminist position. Its use in earlier secondary sources to designate the allegedly Pelagian theological views of writers such as William of Ockham or Gabriel Biel is seriously misleading.) By the time of the Reformation, terminism had gained considerable influence, and can be seen echoed in the writings of Luther and others.

(b) The debate over logico-critical and historico-critical approaches to theology

In its earlier period, scholasticism tended to assume that theology proceeded by the rational analysis of foundational texts – such as the writings of Augustine. By increased precision of definition of central terms (such as *gratia*), order could be brought to what at first sight seemed an occasionally inconsistent set of beliefs. In the later medieval period, especially due to the influence of Ockham, increased use came to be made of the logical tool of the 'dialectic between the two powers of God' to clarify such points of interpretation. This approach involved a distinction between the *potentia absoluta Dei*, the 'absolute power of God', whereby God was able to do anything subject to the limitation of non-contradiction; and the *potentia ordinata Dei*, the 'ordained power of God', designating a self-imposed limitation upon the power of God as a consequence of the divine decision to act in certain stipulated manners. This decision, by its very nature, eliminated other hypothetical possibilities which, although remaining logically possible, were nonetheless excluded by the divine decision to act in other manners.

However, this approach came to be regarded with suspicion by some, who argued that the only appropriate way of dealing with these difficulties was by gaining access to the full text of writers such as Augustine (instead of the isolated extracts of the *Sentences*), and interpreting them within their historical context. This latter consideration was one of the factors which fuelled the production of critical editions of the works of Augustine and others, and may be regarded as having made a major contribution both to the origins of the

Reformation and to the development of source-critical methods in theology subsequently.

(c) The tension between intellectualism and voluntarism

Earlier scholastic writers, such as Aquinas and Bonaventure, had stressed the priority of the divine intellect over the will. Thus, in the case of human merit, the divine intellect recognizes the morality of a human act, and informs the divine will to reward it accordingly. In other words, the intrinsic moral value of the human act is the foundation of its meritorious value. From Scotus onwards, the emphasis came to be placed upon the divine will. In the case of merit, the divine will determines the value to be placed upon the human moral action, and rewards it accordingly. In other words, the meritorious value of a human action is determined by the will of God, which imposes a value upon it which need not bear any relation to the intrinsic moral value of that act. The intellectualist position is rejected, as making God dependent upon created entities.

This new emphasis upon the priority of the divine will can also be discerned in the increasing sympathy evident for more predestinarian modes of thought, such as those associated with Augustinian writers such as Gregory of Rimini or Hugolino of Orvieto, on the eve of the Reformation. Calvin is an excellent example of a sixteenth-century theologian who appears to have been deeply influenced by this new trend towards voluntarism, evident in his discussion of the grounds of the merit of Christ and his doctrine of predestination.

(d) Tensions relating to the doctrine of justification

Perhaps the most important debate within scholasticism to relate to the Reformation concerns the manner in which human beings find acceptance in the sight of God (McGrath 1986). Two radically different approaches may be discerned. Writers of the *via moderna*, such as Gabriel Biel, developed many of the ideas of the later Franciscan school, laying emphasis upon the positive human contribution to justification (Oberman 1963). Human beings were able to make the foundational response to the divine offer of grace, by which they were accepted into the divine favour. This view, which finds its expression in the early writings of Martin Luther, is diametrically opposed to the view of writers such as Gregory of Rimini; this view stresses the total priority and absolute necessity of grace at every stage in justification.

Luther eventually came to regard the views of the *via moderna* as Pelagian. His *Disputatio contra scholasticam theologiam* of 1517 is actually a sustained diatribe against the views, not of scholastic theology in general, but against the teachings of one scholastic theologian in particular (Gabriel Biel), chiefly as they concern the doctrine of justification. However, it is not clear whether Luther's new respect for Augustinianism reflects an acquaintance with writings of scholastic authors sympathetic to this viewpoint, or whether it emerged from a direct engagement with the anti-Pelagian writings of Augustine, which became readily available in the closing years of the first decade of the sixteenth century (Oberman 1981).

The Renaissance and Reformation attitudes towards scholasticism

The predominant attitude within both the Renaissance and early Reformation towards scholasticism can perhaps best be described as a studied indifference. This attitude treats the movement as something which is not worthy of being taken seriously. Reformers sympathetic to the Renaissance outlook – such as Melanchthon, Zwingli and Vadian – are generally dismissive of the petty views of the *scholastici*. However, others, including both Luther and Calvin, deemed the movement worthy of criticism, recognizing its intellectual credentials and its potentially destabilizing impact upon the Reformation. Luther's four main criticisms of late medieval scholasticism are primarily methodological (Janz 1989), and may be summarized as follows.

(a) The movement fails to do justice to human experience. Its excessively rational character fails to engage with the experiential aspects of the Christian faith. Luther's existential approach to faith contrasts sharply with the more detached and analytic approach of scholasticism.

(b) Scholasticism places excessive emphasis upon the role of human reason. Luther occasionally suggests a parallel between the scholastic emphasis upon reason, and the confidence in human soteriological resources associated with the *via moderna*.

(c) A related criticism concerns the priority given to Aristotelianism. For Luther, the scholastics have allowed Aristotle to dominate theology with unbiblical assumptions and outlooks. In part, this reflects Luther's deep suspicion of Aristotle's ethics, which he regarded as severely detrimental to a right understanding of the doctrine of justification.

(d) Scholasticism has failed to do justice to Scripture. This criticism is echoed throughout the Reformation, and parallels the humanist determination to return *ad fontes*. Luther argues that scholasticism has detached the Christian faith from its roots in Scripture by interposing successive layers of interpretative glosses, hermeneutical devices, and philosophical assumptions between the text and its readers. The task of theology is to return directly to the scriptural text.

2 RENAISSANCE HUMANISM

The second great theme to be surveyed in this chapter is the movement known as 'humanism', which is closely linked with the northern European Renaissance of the fourteenth and fifteenth centuries (Burke 1986). A central component of the world-view of the Italian Renaissance is a return to the cultural glories of antiquity, and a marginalization of the intellectual achievements of the Middle Ages (Kristeller 1979). Renaissance writers had scant regard for these, regarding them as outweighed by the greater achievements of antiquity. What was true of culture in general was also true of theology: they regarded the late classical period as totally overshadowing the theological writings of the Middle Ages, both in substance and in style.

Definition of humanism

The term 'humanism' is difficult to define, not least on account of the strongly secular overtones which the term now possesses. In modern use, the term has come to designate a world-view which denies the existence or relevance of God, or which is committed to a purely secular outlook. This is not what the word meant at the time of the Renaissance. Most humanists of the period were religious, and concerned to purify and renew Christianity, rather than eliminate it. In any case, intensive study of humanist writings uncovered the disquieting fact that 'humanism' was remarkably heterogeneous. For example, many humanist writers did indeed favour Platonism – but others favoured Aristotelianism. Some Italian humanists did indeed display what seemed to be anti-religious attitudes – but most Italian humanists were profoundly religious.

In short, it became increasingly clear that 'humanism' seemed to lack any coherent philosophy. No single philosophical or political idea dominated or characterized the movement. It seemed to many that the term 'humanism' would have to be dropped from the vocabulary of historians, because it had no meaningful content. Designating a writer as a 'humanist' actually conveys little hard information concerning his or her philosophical, political or religious views.

A more realistic approach, which has gained widespread acceptance in scholarly circles, is to view humanism as a cultural and educational movement, primarily concerned with the promotion of eloquence in its various forms (Kristeller 1979). Its interest in morals, philosophy and politics is of secondary importance. To be a humanist is to be concerned with eloquence first and foremost, and with other matters incidentally. Humanism was essentially a cultural programme, which appealed to classical antiquity as a model of eloquence. In art and architecture, as in the written and spoken word, antiquity was seen as a cultural resource, which could be appropriated by the Renaissance. Humanism was thus concerned with how ideas were obtained and expressed, rather than with the actual substance of those ideas. A humanist might be a Platonist or an Aristotelian – but in both cases, the ideas involved derived from antiquity. A humanist might be a sceptic or a believer – but both attitudes could be defended from antiquity.

Northern European humanism

The form of 'humanism' which proved to be of especial importance theologically is primarily *northern European* humanism rather than *Italian* humanism. We must therefore consider what form this northern European movement took, and how it developed. It is becoming increasingly clear that northern European humanism was decisively influenced by Italian humanism at every stage of its development.

Although there are major variations within northern European humanism, two ideals seem to have achieved widespread acceptance throughout the movement. First, we find the same concern for *bonae litterae* – written and spoken eloquence, after the fashion of the classical period – as in the Italian Reformation. Second, we find a religious programme directed towards the corporate revival of the Christian Church. The Latin slogan *Christianismus renascens*, 'Christianity being born again', summarizes the aims of this programme, and indicates its relation to the 'rebirth' of letters associated with the Renaissance.

The theological impact of humanism

The impact of humanism upon the theology of the early sixteenth century was considerable, and may be illustrated by considering its implications for biblical scholarship. The literary and cultural programme of humanism can be summarized in the slogan *ad fontes* – back to the original sources. The squalor of the medieval period is bypassed, in order to recover the intellectual and artistic glories of the classical period. In much the same way, the 'filter' of medieval biblical commentaries was abandoned, in order to engage directly with the original texts. Applied to the Christian Church, the slogan *ad fontes* meant a direct return to the title deeds of Christianity – to the patristic writers, and supremely to the Bible, studied in its original languages. This necessitated direct access to the Greek text of the New Testament.

The first printed Greek New Testament was produced by Erasmus in 1516. Erasmus' text was not as reliable as it ought to have been as Erasmus had access to a mere four manuscripts for most of the New Testament, and only one for its final part, the book of Revelation. As it happened, that manuscript left out five verses, which Erasmus himself had to translate into Greek from the Latin of the Vulgate. Nevertheless, it proved to be a literary milestone. For the first time, theologians had the opportunity of comparing the original Greek text of the New Testament with the later Vulgate translation into Latin.

Drawing on work carried out earlier by the Italian humanist Lorenzo Valla, Erasmus showed that the Vulgate translation of a number of major New Testament texts could not be justified. As a number of medieval Church practices and beliefs were based upon these texts, Erasmus' allegations were viewed with something approaching panic by many conservative Catholics (who wanted to retain these practices and beliefs) and with equally great delight by the reformers (who wanted to eliminate them). Three classic examples of translation errors will indicate the relevance of Erasmus' biblical scholarship.

(a) Much medieval theology justified the inclusion of matrimony in the list of sacraments on the basis of a New Testament text which – at least, as in the Vulgate translation – spoke of marriage being a *sacramentum* (Eph. 5:31–2). Erasmus pointed out that the Greek word (*musterion*) here translated as 'sacrament' simply meant 'mystery'. There was no reference whatsoever to marriage being a 'sacrament'. One of the classic proof texts used by medieval theologians to justify the inclusion of matrimony in the list of sacraments was thus rendered virtually useless.

(b) The Vulgate translated the opening words of Jesus' ministry (Matt. 4:17) as 'do penance, for the Kingdom of heaven is at hand'. This translation suggested that the coming of the kingdom of heaven had a direct connection with the sacrament of penance. Erasmus, again following Valla, pointed out that the Greek should be translated as 'repent, for the Kingdom of heaven is at hand'. In other words, where the Vulgate seemed to refer to an outward practice (the sacrament of penance), Erasmus insisted that the reference was to an inward psychological attitude – that of 'being repentant'. Once more, an important justification of the sacramental system of the medieval church was challenged.

(c) According to the Vulgate, Gabriel greeted Mary as 'the one who is full of grace (*gratia plena*)' (Luke 1:28), thus suggesting the image of a reservoir full of grace, which could be drawn upon at time of need. But, as Erasmus pointed out, the Greek simply meant 'favoured one', or 'one who has found favour' (a translation which was eventually adopted by the Jerusalem Bible in the 1960s). Once more, an important feature of medieval theology seemed to be contradicted by humanist New Testament scholarship.

These developments undermined the credibility of the Vulgate translation, and thus opened the way to theological revision on the basis of a better understanding of the biblical text. It also demonstrated the importance of biblical scholarship in relation to theology. Theology could not be permitted to base itself upon translation mistakes, even when hallowed by centuries of tradition. The recognition of the vitally important role of biblical scholarship in relation to the foundational texts of Christian theology thus dates from the second decade of the sixteenth century. It also led to the theological concerns of the Reformation, to which we now turn.

3 THE REFORMATION

The Reformation was primarily a Western European movement, centring upon individuals such as Martin Luther, Huldrych Zwingli, and John Calvin. For reasons which are only partly understood, the movement had considerable appeal to the cities of the region. Initially, up to about 1525, the Reformation may be regarded as centring upon Martin Luther and the University of Wittenberg, in modern-day north-eastern Germany. However, the movement also gained strength, initially independently, in the Swiss city of Zurich. Through a complex series of developments, the Zurich Reformation gradually underwent a series of political and theological developments, eventually coming to be associated primarily with the city of Geneva (now part of modern-day Switzerland, although then an independent city-state) and John Calvin.

Definition of Reformation

The Reformation movement was complex and heterogeneous, and concerned an agenda far broader than the reform of the doctrine of the Church. It addressed fundamental social, political and economic issues, too complex to be discussed in any detail here. The agenda of the Reformation varied from one country to another, with the theological issues which played major roles in one country (for example, Germany) often having relatively little impact elsewhere (for example, in England). The issue of indulgences, which played a significant role in the origins of the Wittenberg reformation, had no comparable role in Geneva, Strasbourg, or Zurich. Similarly, the authority of the Pope to annul royal marriages, which proved to be of importance in relation to the political initiation of the English Reformation (although its impact upon the theological substance of the Reformation was somewhat slight), was of little interest in Germany or Switzerland. Local conditions led to local reformations.

In response to the Reformation, the Catholic Church moved to put its own house in order. Prevented from calling a reforming council in the 1530s on account of political instability in Europe resulting from tensions between France and Germany, the then pope was eventually able to convene the Council of Trent in 1545. This set itself the task of clarifying and defending Catholic thought and practice against its evangelical opponents.

The term 'Reformation' is used in a number of senses, and it is helpful to distinguish them. Four elements may be involved in its definition:

(a) The Lutheran Reformation.
(b) The Calvinist Reformation (the Reformed Churches).
(c) The radical Reformation (Anabaptism).
(d) The Catholic Reformation (the Counter Reformation).

In its broadest sense, the term 'Reformation' is used to refer to all four movements. The term is also used in a somewhat more restricted sense, meaning 'the Protestant Reformation', excluding the Catholic Reformation. In this sense, it refers to the three Protestant movements noted above. In many scholarly works, however, the term 'Reformation' is used to refer to what is sometimes known as the 'magisterial Reformation', or the 'mainstream Reformation' – in other words, that linked with the Lutheran and Reformed Churches (including Anglicanism), and excluding the Anabaptists.

(a) The Lutheran Reformation

The Lutheran Reformation is particularly associated with the German territories and the pervasive personal influence of one charismatic individual – Martin Luther. Luther was particularly concerned with the doctrine of justification, which formed the central point of his religious thought. The Lutheran Reformation was initially an academic movement, concerned primarily with reforming the teaching of theology at the University of Wittenberg. Wittenberg was an unimportant university, and the reforms introduced by Luther and his colleagues within the theology faculty attracted little attention. It was Luther's personal activities – such as his posting of the famous Ninety-Five Theses (31 October 1517) – which attracted considerable interest, and brought the ideas in circulation at Wittenberg to the attention of a wider audience.

Strictly speaking, the Lutheran Reformation only began in 1522, when Luther returned to Wittenberg from his enforced isolation in the Wartburg. Luther was condemned by the Diet of Worms in 1521. Fearing for his life, certain well-placed supporters removed him in secrecy to the castle known as the 'Wartburg', until the threat to his safety was over. In his absence, Andreas Bodenstein von Karlstadt, one of Luther's academic colleagues at Wittenberg, began a programme of reform at Wittenberg which seemed to degenerate into chaos. Convinced that he was needed if the Reformation was to survive Karlstadt's ineptitude, Luther emerged from his place of safety, and returned to Wittenberg.

At this point, Luther's programme of academic reform changed into a programme of reform of Church and society. No longer was Luther's forum of activity the university world of ideas – he now found himself regarded as the leader of a religious, social and political reforming movement which seemed to some contemporary observers to open the way to a new social and religious order in Europe. In fact, Luther's programme of reform was much more conservative than that associated with his Reformed colleagues, such as Huldrych Zwingli.

(b) The Calvinist Reformation

The origins of Calvinist Reformation, which brought the Reformed Churches (such as the Presbyterians) into being, lie with developments in certain leading cities (especially Zurich, Berne and Basle) within the Swiss Confederation. Subsequently, the city of Geneva came to play a prominent role in relation to the Reformed Churches. Geneva, it should be noted, was not part of the Swiss Confederation at this stage, but was a fiercely independent city-state which sought to ensure its independence through military and economic alliances with nearby Swiss cities. Whereas the Lutheran Reformation had its origins in an academic context, the Reformed Church owed its origins to a series of attempts to reform the morals and worship of the Church (but not necessarily its doctrine) according to a more biblical pattern. It must be emphasized that although Calvin gave this style of Reformation its definitive form, its origins can be traced back to earlier reformers, such as Huldrych Zwingli and Heinrich Bullinger, based in the leading Swiss city of Zurich.

Although most of the early Reformed theologians – such as Zwingli – had an academic background, their reforming programmes were not academic in nature. They were directed towards the Church, as they found it in certain Swiss cities, such as Zurich, Berne and Basle. Whereas Luther was convinced that the doctrine of justification was of central significance to his programme of social and religious reform, the early Reformed thinkers had relatively little interest in doctrine, let alone one specific doctrine. Their reforming programme was institutional, social and ethical, in many ways similar to the demands for reform emanating from the humanist movement.

The consolidation of the Reformed Church is generally thought to begin with the stabilization of the Zurich reformation after Zwingli's death in battle (1531) under his successor, Heinrich Bullinger, and to end with the emergence of Geneva as its power base, and John Calvin as its leading spokesman, in the 1550s. The gradual shift in power within the Reformed Church (initially from Zurich to Berne, and subsequently from Berne to Geneva) took place over the period 1520–60, eventually establishing the city of Geneva, its political system (republicanism) and its religious thinkers (initially Calvin, and after his death, Theodore Beza) as predominant within the Reformed Church. This development was consolidated through the establishment of the Genevan Academy (founded in 1559), at which Reformed pastors were trained.

(c) The radical Reformation (Anabaptism)

The term 'Anabaptist' owes its origins to Zwingli (the word literally means 'rebaptizers', and refers to what was perhaps the most distinctive aspect of Anabaptist practice – the insistence that only those adults who had made a personal public profession of faith should be baptized). Anabaptism seems to have first arisen around Zurich, in the aftermath of Zwingli's reforms within the city in the early 1520s. It centred on a group of individuals (among whom we may note Conrad Grebel) who argued that Zwingli was not being faithful to his own reforming principles. He preached one thing, and practised another.

Although Zwingli professed faithfulness to the *sola scriptura*, 'by Scripture alone', principle, Grebel argued that he retained a number of practices – including infant baptism, the close link between Church and magistracy, and the participation of Christians in warfare – which were not sanctioned or ordained by Scripture. In the hands of such thinkers, the *sola scriptura* principle would be radicalized; reformed Christians must believe and practise only those things explicitly taught in Scripture. Zwingli was alarmed by this, seeing it as a destabilizing development which threatened to cut the Reformed Church at Zurich off from its historical roots and its continuity with the Christian tradition of the past.

A number of common elements can be discerned within the various strands of the Anabaptist movement: a general distrust of external authority; the rejection of infant baptism in favour of the baptism of adult believers; the common ownership of property, and an emphasis upon pacifism and non-resistance. To take up one of these points: in 1527, the governments of Zurich, Berne and St Gallen accused the Anabaptists of believing 'that no true Christian can either give or receive interest or income on a sum of capital; that all temporal goods are free and common, and that all can have full property rights to them'. It is for this reason that 'Anabaptism' is often referred to as the 'left wing of the Reformation' (Roland H. Bainton) or the 'radical Reformation' (George Hunston Williams). For Williams, the 'radical Reformation' was to be contrasted with the 'magisterial Reformation', which he broadly identified with the Lutheran and Reformed movements (Williams 1992).

(d) The Catholic Reformation

This term is often used to refer to the revival within Roman Catholicism in the period following the opening of the Council of Trent (1545). In older scholarly works, the movement is often designated the 'Counter Reformation'. As the term suggests, the Roman Catholic Church developed means of combating the Protestant Reformation, in order to limit its influence. It is, however, becoming increasingly clear that the Roman Catholic Church countered the Reformation partly by reforming itself from within, in order to remove the grounds of Protestant criticism. In this sense, the movement was a reformation of the Roman Catholic Church, as much as it was a reaction against the Protestant Reformation.

The same concerns underlying the Protestant Reformation in northern Europe were channelled into the renewal of the Catholic Church, particularly in Spain and Italy. The Council of Trent, the foremost component of the Catholic Reformation, clarified Catholic teaching on a number of confusing matters, and introduced much-needed reforms in relation to the conduct of the clergy, ecclesiastical discipline, religious education and missionary activity. The movement for reform within the Church was greatly stimulated by the reformation of many of the older religious orders, and the establishment of new orders (such as the Jesuits). As a result of the Catholic Reformation, many of the abuses which originally lay behind the demands for reform – whether these came from humanists or Protestants – were removed.

243

The theological agenda of the Reformation

As will be clear from the analysis thus far, the Reformation was a complex movement, with a very broad agenda. In part, the debate centred upon the sources of Christian theology; in part, upon the doctrines which resulted from the application of those sources. We shall consider these matters individually.

(a) The sources of theology

The mainstream Reformation was not concerned with establishing a new Christian tradition, but with the renewal and correction of an existing tradition. On the basis of their assertion that Christian theology was ultimately grounded in Scripture, reformers such as Luther and Calvin argued for the need to return to Scripture as the primary and critical source of Christian theology. The slogan 'by Scripture alone (*sola scriptura*)' became characteristic of the reformers, expressing their basic belief that Scripture was the sole necessary and sufficient source of Christian theology. However, as we shall see later, this did not mean that they denied the importance of tradition.

This new emphasis upon Scripture had a number of direct consequences. Beliefs which could not be demonstrated to be grounded in Scripture were either to be rejected, or to be declared as binding on none. For example, the reformers had little time for the doctrine of the Immaculate Conception of Mary (that is, the belief that Mary, as the mother of Jesus, was conceived without any taint from sin). They regarded this as lacking in scriptural basis, and thus discarded it. A new emphasis also came to be placed upon the public status of Scripture within the Church. The expository sermon, the biblical commentary and works of biblical theology (such as Calvin's *Institutes*) came to be characteristic of the Reformation.

(b) The doctrine of grace

The first period of the Reformation is dominated by the personal agenda of Martin Luther. Convinced that the Church had lapsed into an unwitting Pelagianism, Luther proclaimed the doctrine of justification by faith to whoever would listen to him. The question 'How can I find a gracious God?' and the slogan 'by faith alone (*sola fide*)' resonated throughout much of Western Europe, and earned him a hearing throughout a substantial section of the Church.

(c) The doctrine of the sacraments

By the 1520s, the view had become well established within reforming circles that the sacraments were outward signs of the invisible grace of God. This forging of a link between the sacraments and the doctrine of justification (a development especially associated with Luther and his colleague at Wittenberg, Philip Melanchthon) led to a new interest in the sacraments. It was not long before this area of theology became the subject of considerable controversy, with the reformers disagreeing with their Catholic opponents over the number and nature of the sacraments, and Luther and Zwingli arguing furiously over whether, and in what sense, Christ was really present at communion services. Luther's position, often referred to as 'consubstantiation' (though he himself did not use this term), retained many aspects of traditional Catholic teaching on the matter. Zwingli's position, often designated 'memorialism' (though it is in fact a form of 'transsignification') represented a radical departure from the traditional teaching, asserting that Christ was remembered at the Lord's Supper in his absence.

(d) The doctrine of the Church

If the first generation of reformers were preoccupied with the question of grace, the second generation turned to address the question of the Church. It must be appreciated that Luther's conception of 'reformation' was initially that of reforming the Church from within. He envisaged his supporters as a reforming presence inside the Church, not a breakaway faction. Luther did not choose to separate from the medieval Church; he was forced to undertake a programme of reform from outside that Church. Even as late as 1519, well after his discovery of the 'righteousness of God' and the posting of the Ninety-Five Theses, Luther wrote:

> If, unfortunately, there are things in Rome which cannot be improved, there is not – nor can there be! – any reason for tearing oneself away from the church in schism. Rather, the worse things become, the more one should help her and stand by her, for by schism and contempt nothing can be mended.

Schism was forced upon, not chosen by, Luther.

By the 1540s, however, it was clear that there was likely to be permanent schism between the evangelical factions and the Catholic Church. Having broken away from the mainstream of the Catholic Church over the doctrine of grace, the reformers came under increasing pressure to develop a coherent theory of the Church which would justify this break, and give a basis for the new evangelical churches springing up in the cities of Western Europe. Where Luther is especially linked with the doctrine of grace, it is Martin Bucer and John Calvin who made the decisive contributions to the development of Protestant understanding of the Church.

The essential development is the reformulation of the identifying characteristics of the Church. For Calvin, two such defining characteristics existed: the true preaching of the Gospel, and the authentic administration of the sacraments. Bucer wished to add the maintenance of proper church discipline as a third element. Calvin, while stressing the importance of such discipline (for example, through the establishment of the Genevan Consistory), did not regard it as of essential importance to the definition of the Church. On the basis of this approach, Calvin argued that historical continuity with the apostolic Church was not of foundational importance to evangelicals. As he argued in his *Reply to Sadoleto*, doctrinal continuity with the early Church was of greater importance than historical continuity with its institutions. It was preferable to teach what Augustine taught than maintain links with a body which had historical continuity with Augustine, but had, in his view, suppressed his theology.

4 THE POST-REFORMATION PERIOD

It seems to be a general rule of history that periods of enormous creativity are followed by eras of stagnation. The Reformation is no exception. Perhaps through a desire to preserve the insights of the Reformation, the post-Reformation period witnessed the development of a strongly scholastic approach to theology. The insights of the reformers were codified and perpetuated through the development of a series of systematic presentations of Christian theology.

In the period after Calvin's death a new concern for method – that is, the systematic organization and coherent deduction of ideas – gained momentum. Reformed theologians found themselves having to defend their ideas against both Lutheran and Roman Catholic opponents. Aristotelianism, hitherto regarded with a certain degree of suspicion by Calvin, was now seized upon as an ally. It became increasingly important to demonstrate the internal consistency and coherence of Calvinism. As a result, many Calvinist writers turned to Aristotle, in the hope that his writings on method might offer hints as to how their theology might be placed upon a firmer rational foundation. The following developments are of especial importance during this period.

(a) A new concern for method. Reformers such as Luther and Calvin had relatively little interest in questions of method. For them, theology was primarily concerned with the exposition of Scripture. Indeed, Calvin's *Institutes* may be regarded as a work of 'biblical theology', bringing together the basic ideas of Scripture into an orderly presentation. However, in the writings of Theodore Beza, Calvin's successor as director of the Genevan Academy (a training institute for Calvinist pastors throughout Europe), there was a new concern for questions of method. The logical arrangement of material, and its grounding in first principles, come to assume paramount importance. The impact of this development is perhaps most obvious in the way in which Beza handles the doctrine of predestination, to be noted later.

(b) The development of works of systematic theology. The rise of scholasticism within Lutheran, Calvinist and Roman Catholic theological circles led to the appearance of vast works of systematic theology, comparable in many ways to

Thomas Aquinas's *Summa Theologiae*. These works aimed to present sophisticated and comprehensive accounts of Christian theology, demonstrating the strengths of their positions and the weaknesses of their opponents.

Thus Theodore Beza (1519–1605), a noted Calvinist writer who served as professor of theology at the Genevan Academy from 1559–99, produced three volumes of his *Tractationes Theologicae* (1570–82). These volumes represent a rationally coherent account of the main elements of reformed theology, using Aristotelian logic. The result is a tightly argued and rationally defensible account of Calvin's theology, in which some of the unresolved tensions of that theology (chiefly relating to the doctrines of predestination and atonement) are clarified. Some writers have suggested that Beza's concern for logical clarity leads him to misrepresent Calvin in a number of critical points; others have argued that Beza merely streamlined Calvin's theology, tidying up some loose ends. The starting point of Reformed theology thus came to be general principles, not a specific historical event. The contrast with Calvin will be clear. For Calvin, theology centres on and derives from the event of Jesus Christ, as this is witnessed to by Scripture.

Confessionalization and the concern for right doctrine

Lutheranism and Calvinism were, in many respects, very similar. Both claimed to be evangelical, and rejected more or less the same central aspects of medieval Catholicism. But they needed to be distinguished. And doctrine proved to be the most reliable way of distinguishing two otherwise very similar bodies. At most points of doctrine, Lutherans and Calvinists were in broad agreement. Yet there was one matter – the doctrine of predestination – upon which they were radically divided. The emphasis placed upon the doctrine of predestination by Calvinists in the period 1559–1662 partly reflects the fact that this doctrine distinguished them from their Lutheran colleagues.

The importance of this point can easily be appreciated by comparing the German situation with that of England. The sixteenth-century English Reformation under Henry VIII (1509–47) bore little relation to its German equivalent. In Germany, there was a protracted struggle between Lutheran and Roman Catholic, as each attempted to gain influence in a disputed region. In England, Henry VIII simply declared that there would only be one national church within his realm. By royal command, there would only be one Christian body within England. The reformed English Church was under no pressure to define itself in relation to any other Christian body in the region. The manner in which the English Reformation initially proceeded demanded no doctrinal self-definition, in that the Church in England was defined socially in precisely the same way before the Reformation as after, whatever political alterations may have been introduced. This is not to say that no theological debates took place in England at the time of the Reformation; it is noteworthy that they were not seen as being of decisive importance. They were not regarded as identity-giving (McGrath 1990).

The Lutheran Church in Germany was obliged to define and defend its existence and boundaries by doctrine because it had broken away from the medieval Catholic Church. That church continued to exist in Lutheran regions, forcing Lutheranism to carry on justifying its existence. The Henrician church in England, however, regarded itself as continuous with the medieval Church. The English Church was sufficiently well defined as a social unit to require no further definition at the doctrinal level. The various formularies of faith issued during the reign of Henry VIII suggested a definite move away from traditional Catholicism towards an acceptance of at least some aspects of Protestantism, a process continued under Edward VI, suppressed under Mary Tudor, and subtly redirected under Elizabeth I. Yet the fundamental principle remained intact: whatever its theological identity might be, there was only one English Church, and it was continuous with the pre-Reformation Church.

The 'Elizabethan Settlement' (1559) laid down that there would only be one Christian Church in England – the Church of England, which retained the monopoly of the pre-Reformation Church, while replacing it with a church which recognized royal, rather than papal, authority. There was thus no particular reason for the Church of England to concern itself with doctrinal questions. Elizabeth ensured that it had no rivals within England. One of the purposes of doctrine is to divide – and there was nothing for the Church of England to divide itself from. England was insulated from the factors which made doctrine so significant a matter on the mainland of Europe in the Reformation and immediate post-Reformation periods.

The rise of rationalism

A point of major importance here concerns the political situation in Europe, especially Germany, in the later sixteenth century. In the 1550s, Lutheranism and Roman Catholicism were well established in different regions of Germany. A religious stalemate had developed, in which further expansion into Roman Catholic regions by Lutheranism was no longer possible. Lutheran writers therefore concentrated upon defending Lutheranism at the academic level, by demonstrating its internal consistency and faithfulness to Scripture.

If Lutheranism could be shown to be intellectually respectable, it was believed that it might well prove attractive to Roman Catholics, disillusioned with their own system of beliefs. But this was not to be the case. Roman Catholic writers responded with increasingly sophisticated works of systematic theology, drawing on the writings of Thomas Aquinas. Johannes Capreolus established the Spanish city of Salamanca as a centre of Thomist studies, and established the now widely accepted principle of basing an understanding of Thomism upon the *Summa Theologica*, rather than the earlier *Commentary on the Sentences*. The Society of Jesus (founded in 1534) rapidly established itself as a leading intellectual force within the Roman Catholic Church. Its leading writers, such as Roberto Bellarmine and Francisco de Suarez, made major contributions to the intellectual defence of Roman Catholicism.

The situation in Germany became even more complicated during the 1560s and 1570s, as Calvinism began to make major inroads into previously Lutheran territory. Three major Christian denominations were now firmly established, often in the same geographical area – Lutheranism, Calvinism, and Roman Catholicism. All three were under major pressure to identify themselves. Lutherans were obliged to explain how they differed from Calvinists on the one hand, and Roman Catholics on the other. And doctrine proved the most reliable way of identifying and explaining these differences: 'we believe this, but they believe that'. The period 1559–1622, characterized by its new emphasis upon doctrine, is generally referred to as the 'Period of Orthodoxy'. A new form of scholasticism began to develop within both Protestant and Roman Catholic theological circles, as both sought to demonstrate the rationality and sophistication of their systems.

The result was, perhaps inevitably, the gradual rise of rationalism in Western European theology; in that agreement could not be reached on the identity and priority of theological sources, the debate shifted to the rationality of the resulting doctrines (Fox 1987). From the late 1500s onwards, reason came to play an increasingly prominent role in both Protestant Orthodoxy and its Roman Catholic counterpart. This approach can be seen at its zenith in the works of leading seventeenth-century Lutheran and Reformed dogmaticians.

However, this trend served to foster the view that reason was a resource, independent of the particularities of religious tradition, which could serve as an adequate foundation for a mediating theology. The Thirty Years War, ended by the Peace of Westphalia (1648), was initiated and sustained by religious issues; by its end, there was a certain weariness in Western Europe over matters of religion, which received a further impetus through a reaction against the religious excesses of the Puritan Commonwealth in England.

A general appreciation of the virtues of religious toleration gave momentum to the rise of Latitudinarian ideals. The rise of rationalism is observable, initially in its Lockean forms, in England, and subsequently in more pronounced forms within the movement loosely known as 'Deism'. By the end of the period surveyed in this chapter, the transition to modernity is unmistakeable. Wars of religion seemed to many to be little more than the military counterpart of an underlying theological argument. A new orientation seemed eminently in order. The new emphasis on reason seemed to offer the only way ahead. A cultural climate thus emerged, sympathetic to the rationalist world-view which would be characteristic of the Enlightenment.

REFERENCES

Bossy, J. (1987) *Christianity in the West, 1400–1700*, Oxford: Oxford University Press.

Burke, P. (1986) *The Italian Renaissance: Culture and Society in Italy*, Cambridge: Polity Press.

Evans, G. R. (1985) *The Language and Logic of the Bible*, Cambridge: Cambridge University Press.

Fox, A. (1987) 'The Intellectual Consequences of the Sixteenth-Century Religious Upheaval and the Coming of a Rational World View', *Sixteenth Century Journal* 18: 63–80.

Gilson, E. (1978) *History of Christian Philosophy in the Middle Ages*, London: Sheed & Ward.

Janz, D. R. (1989) *Luther on Thomas Aquinas*, Stuttgart: Franz Steiner.

Kristeller, P. O. (1979) *Renaissance Thought and its Sources*, New York: Columbia University Press.

McGrath, A. E. (1986) *Iustitia Dei: A History of the Christian Doctrine of Justification*, 2 vols, Cambridge: Cambridge University Press.

—— (1987) *The Intellectual Origins of the European Reformation*, Oxford: Basil Blackwell.

—— (1990) *The Genesis of Doctrine*, Oxford: Basil Blackwell.

Oberman, H. A. (1963) *The Harvest of Late Medieval Theology*, Cambridge, Mass.: Harvard University Press.

—— (1981) *Masters of the Reformation: The Emergence of a New Intellectual Climate in Europe*, Cambridge: Cambridge University Press.

Williams, G. H. (1992) *The Radical Reformation*, 3rd edn, Kirksville, Mo: Sixteenth Century Journal Publishers.

FURTHER READING

Dickens, A. G. and Tonkin, J. M. (1985) *The Reformation in Historical Perspective*, Cambridge, Mass.: Harvard University Press.

Nauert, C. G. (1973) 'The Clash of Humanists and Scholastics', *Sixteenth Century Journal* 4: 1–18.

Overfeld, J. (1976) 'Scholastic Opposition to Humanism in Pre-Reformation Germany', *Viator* 7: 391–420.

Pelikan, J. (1984) *The Christian Tradition: A History of the Development of Doctrine. 4. Reformation of Church and Dogma, 1300–1700*, Chicago: University of Chicago Press.

Pieper, J. A. (1960) *Scholasticism: Personalities and Problems of Medieval Philosophy*, London: Faber.

Steinmetz, D. C. (1980) *Luther and Steinmetz: An Essay in the Intellectual Origins of the Protestant Reformation*, Durham, NC: Duke University Press.

See also chapters 11, 16, 27, 28, 32.

13

THE ENLIGHTENMENT

John Kent

CHARACTERISTICS OF 'ENLIGHTENMENT'

When one talks about 'the Enlightenment', 'les Lumières', or 'die Aufklärung', one is thinking of a period of European cultural change which lies between the early seventeenth century and the first French Revolution, and doing so from the point of view of a series of radical thinkers – thinkers such as Locke, Montesquieu, Voltaire, Diderot, Beccaria, Hume and Lessing – for whom intellectual experiment was to be valued rather than resisted. The Tridentine form of Roman Catholic theology and the world-views which went with it had reached a natural limit of usefulness by the mid-seventeenth century, although the system as a whole was still heavily backed by state power; ecclesiastical Protestantism, despite its divisions, was no less dogmatic in intention and often socially repressive. The gradual revolt of a section of Europe's cultural elites against the hegemony of Christian world-views was not so much a sinful function of human pride, whose errors would be clearly revealed in the fate of the so-called 'Enlightenment-project', as a natural development as the late-medieval world-order, already weakened in the sixteenth century, fell apart.

The conviction, which spread through the educated elites of Europe in the course of the eighteenth century, that one had a new, superior, rational and historical insight into what had happened in the past and into what was happening in the present (which is the basic meaning of 'being enlightened' and so 'a member of this enlightened age') did not in itself necessarily lead on to specific intellectual, social or religious radicalism. It had many roots, for the social chaos, the constant warfare, the religious persecution which had characterized the period between 1500 and 1714, together with the expanding contact of Europeans with other societies and religions, especially in the Far East, all produced their own reactions. There was also an educated elite which resented its exclusion from politics by baroque absolutism.

Arguably, what many eighteenth-century radicals wanted was a culture which was less dogmatically Christian, less superstitious (in the straightforward sense of burning women on the ground that they were witches), certainly less clerical, but without being less religious. Professor Stephen Toulmin has suggested as the opening gambit of 'modern' philosophy Montaigne's (1533–92) restatement of classical scepticism in the *Apology of Raimond Sebond* 'Unless some one thing is found of which we are completely certain, we can be certain about nothing' (Toulmin 1990: 42). No such final certainty could be found, even in Descartes' treatment of the individual's mental activity as the only indubitable fact of experience, and as Christian systematic theology lost its hold, Newtonian science, which described the universe as subject to immutable natural laws, seemed to offer greater certainty. Politically, the nation-state extended its grip on society, and would soon seek to establish its own cult and its own ethic.

One of the difficulties of understanding this transformation from a theological point of view has been that almost as soon as the eighteenth-century French Revolution began, conservative religious thinkers, including Roman Catholics like de Maistre and Montalembert, began to interpret eighteenth-century radicalism as a disastrous process which had inevitably produced Jacobin politics and Kantian philosophy, the roots of a godless totalitarianism. 'The Enlightenment' became a codeword for everything in modern European history which had militated against the intellectual, social and political authority of Christianity, and in this rebellion, as it was felt to have been, more recent writers have discovered the origins of the sad record of the twentieth century. A dismissal of alleged 'Enlightenment-attitudes' is not uncommon among present-day theologians as well as among some of the most distinguished modern conservative political thinkers, such as the American scholar, Leo Strauss, and the British conservative, Michael Oakeshott.

It is also true, however, that writers like Beccaria, Hume, Kant, Lessing and Voltaire criticized superstition and religious intolerance; they hoped that a rational analysis of problems would advance human happiness, and they protested against the habit of judicial cruelty which still characterized Western culture. They supported freedom of thought and publication against the preference of governments as well as Churches for censorship. They valued social order, but not necessarily the baroque politico-religious order which had been set up since the sixteenth century, and which was still liable to carry out religious cleansing, as when the Protestant minority was expelled from Salzburg by the Catholic Archbishop in 1731/2. Yet their expectations of political change were modest: they were not Jacobins before the event. Although they rejected the theological politics which based absolute power on a religious foundation, whether Catholic or Protestant, they were tempted by the possibilities of authoritarian government should it also be 'enlightened'.

THE EARLY RADICALS: THE ENGLISH DEISTS AND JOHN LOCKE

Examined against its actual historical background the verbal violence and intellectual sang-froid with which some of the English Deists and mid-eighteenth century French *philosophes* often attacked Christianity was a measure both of the shift of mood which was taking place and of the power which the Churches still had to resist it. To argue that the Deists were not 'men of the Enlightenment' is to think too much in terms of a movement with a specific programme: they were an essential part of a shift of feeling and thinking which spread out across the eighteenth century. In societies which, even after 1700, were still recovering from religious war, the rhetoric of the English Deists seemed like a threat to social stability. The Deists have also been reproached on the ground that they failed to appreciate the existential value of what they were attacking: their criticisms of the historical basis of Christianity (John Toland and Matthew Tindal), of the plausibility of the New Testament miracles (Thomas Woolston), of the traditional argument in favour of Christianity from the alleged fulfilment of Old Testament prophecy in the time of Jesus (Anthony Collins), disregarded (it is said) the functional value of Christian belief and practice in the individual life. The Deists' preference, on the ground of greater certainty and rational clarity, for a 'natural religion' which combined the ideas of a distant Creator and a demanding moral system, ignored (it is argued) and could not equal the personal experience of Christian holiness.

Eighteenth-century theological orthodoxy reacted to Deist criticism by presenting Christianity as a 'religion of the heart', in which repentance, faith and the work of the Holy Spirit enabled the believer to 'know' Jesus as crucified personal saviour and Lord. There was a deep eighteenth-century disagreement, however, between Christian and non-Christian about the value of such experiences, because there was a prior disagreement about the proper description of human nature. Some eighteenth-century thinkers rejected the idea of the Fall of Man both at a literal–historical and at a symbolic level, holding that belief in the idea did the individual and society more harm than good. There was a move to disentangle the concept of human nature from Christian theological presuppositions. Although at the close of the century Immanuel Kant restated the view that human nature was evil, he nevertheless argued that it was on good life-conduct rather than on faith in a vicarious atonement that one should rely for salvation (Kant 1934: 105–14).

Freedom to reject publicly the core of Christian orthodoxy was a major issue for the Deists. Anthony Collins (1676–1729), for example, wrote that

> the subjects of which men are denied the right to think by the enemies of free-thinking, are of all others those of which men not only have a right to think, but of which they are obliged in duty to think; viz. such as of the nature and attributes of the Eternal Being or God, of the truth and authority of books esteemed

sacred, and of the sense and meaning of those books; or in one word, of Religious Questions.

(Collins 1965: 32)

The assertion was not acceptable, nor did the situation alter quickly: in 1784 Immanuel Kant said that the motto of the Aufklärung was: 'Dare to know: have the courage to make use of your own intellect' (Kant 1964: 169), but this attitude led him into deep trouble with his own Prussian monarchy in 1792–4, when he was seeking to publish *Religion within the Limits of Reason Alone*. Kant was officially accused of using his philosophy to undermine the fundamental doctrines of Christianity, and he abstained from making fresh public statements about religion until the King of Prussia died in 1797.

Nevertheless, the partial intellectual displacement of Christianity started well before the *philosophes* of the great French *Encyclopédie* (published between 1751 and 1780) first met. It is possible, for example, to present John Locke, as does Bernard Cottret, in *Le Christ des Lumières* (Cottret 1990: 43), as christocentric, but difficult to make him more than a very Latitudinarian Christian. He was privately sympathetic to unitarian views and reluctant to give Jesus the status of membership of the Godhead (Byrne 1989: 44). His dismissal of innate ideas horrified those of his Anglican contemporaries who preferred to believe that people were born with an innate knowledge of God and of a divinely grounded ethical system. In modern terms, Locke was disputing the idea that knowledge of God comes from personal encounter with him in the risen Christ. He did not deny in so many words that God could enlighten the understanding by a ray darted immediately into the mind from 'the fountain of light' (Locke 1823: 150), but he said that any claims to such enlightenment had to be tested against the principles of reason as well as the guaranteed revelation of Scripture.

> It is not the strength of our private persuasion within ourselves that can warrant it to be a light or motion from heaven; nothing can do that but the written word of God without us, or that standard of reason which is common to us with all men.
>
> (Locke 1823: 158)

Locke argued, in *The Reasonableness of Christianity as delivered in the Scriptures* (1695), that the status of Jesus as Messiah was the only article of faith that one had to hold in order to be accepted as a Christian. Nevertheless, Jesus was not only the Messiah, but also the ultimate clarifier of the moral ideas of humanity, and God therefore also required, not, it was true, perfect obedience to the moral law of the Gospel, but that one obey to the best of one's ability. Cottret regards this emphasis on the role of Jesus as legislator as the germ of an eighteenth-century 'secularization' of the person of Jesus (Cottret 1990: 56–7), but 'humanization' would be a better term: the image of Jesus as the visible bearer of the perfect moral will of the Divine still appealed in the late eighteenth century to Rousseau's imagination, in the image of the Vicaire Savoyard; it was also the root of the humanizing nineteenth-century 'lives of Jesus'. On the orthodox side, despite, or even because of, the efforts of such different figures as John Wesley (1703–91) and the Northern Italian Catholic, Paul Danei (1694–1745, founder of the Passionist Order), the image of Jesus was gradually imprisoned within the bounds of a static, impersonal 'crucified Christ'. Nevertheless, it can be argued that what enabled the Churches to survive was their ability to engender what people accepted as religious experience. This river ran on, through the devotions of the Passionists in Italy, the holiness movement of the early Wesleyans, and the determination with which French women (much more than men) defended Catholic worship against the Revolution after 1789.

There was nothing new in Locke's making a distinction between essential and inessential doctrines in Christianity in order to define a small core which had to be believed. Erasmus had used the Creed in this way to argue for the 'essential' good faith of Luther, and Hooker, as an Anglican, had tried to make the distinction a way of meeting the Presbyterian position in England in the late sixteenth century. One consequence of the Reformation, however, was a wave of confessional statements from the emerging Protestant bodies which redefined the boundaries of orthodoxy, while Trent performed a similar function for Roman Catholicism. The English Civil War had been fought by groups who differed religiously as well as politically, and the Restoration had produced further conflict between Catholic and Protestant. Locke gave intellectual support to the idea that governments should give up the attempt to prescribe the total content of religion, but should instead enforce mutual toleration between competing religious bodies. The radical view was expressed by David Hume, who said:

> Is there any maxim in politics more certain and infallible, than that both the number and the authority of priests should be confined within very narrow limits, and that the civil magistrate ought, forever, to keep his *fasces* and *axes* from such dangerous hands?

> (Hume 1980: 199)

He (or Philo, who seems to represent Hume's position in the *Dialogues Concerning Natural Religion*) thought that the wisest maxim was to 'give indulgence to several sects', while preserving 'a very philosophical indifference to all of them' (ibid.: 199), and carefully restraining the pretensions of the prevailing sect.

The view that in practice the best interests of both the state and the ordinary citizen were served by limiting the influence of religious groups became widespread in the later eighteenth century. The radicals threw more emphasis on ethical behaviour than on 'theological' belief, and so favoured the formation of what in England has been called the 'Hanoverian civic religion', which was more concerned with the ethical style of society as a whole than with the individual's belief in Christian doctrine. Orthodox Christian opinion saw this shift as disastrous, but compulsory clerical subscription to the Anglican Articles was attacked as illiberal in the unsuccessful Feathers Tavern Petition of 1772. This was the logical direction of Locke's thought, but it was as long afterwards as 1975 that the Church of England stopped requiring ordinands and holders of benefices to give general assent to the Articles.

A RADICAL CRITIQUE OF CHRISTIAN RELIGIOUS EXPERIENCE

At the heart, then, of the religious attitudes of what may be collectively called 'the Enlightenment' lay a scepticism about the value of the dogmatic systems of Roman Catholicism and Protestantism together with the world-views which these theologies supported, and the religious experience which they engendered. Nothing was more characteristic than Goethe's decision, when he arrived in Assisi in 1786, to go and look at the almost unaltered portico of the surviving Roman temple which was now a Catholic church, but to ignore the medieval Franciscan basilica and the myths which had created it. This, however, was the late sophistication of the self-assured intellectual: English Deists such as Collins, John Toland, Thomas Chubb, and Matthew Tindal, were less confident. Nevertheless, they already felt the same intolerance of what seemed to them, as to Goethe, a wilful theological obfuscation of the relations between God and humanity. Toland, for example, whose philosophical materialism was to appeal to Diderot, editor of the great *Encyclopaedia*, struck the common note when he published *Christianity not Mysterious* in 1696, and his *Letters to Serena* (1704) were an anticlerical attack on the Church for having brought mystery back. For the early Deists the Christian Churches seemed monstrous survivors from a wrongheaded past in which people had been misled into making insufficient use of their own reason: the weakness of early Deist writing was this impatience with the very existence of both Catholicism and Protestantism.

Another example of the changing mood was the ironic work of Shaftesbury, another of Locke's friends, whose 'Letter Concerning Enthusiasm' (1707) was an attempt to rescue the word 'enthusiasm' from its associations with the achievement of ecstatic states of the religious consciousness. He wrote, 'Inspiration is a real feeling of the Divine Presence, and enthusiasm a false one – but the passion they raise is much alike' (Shaftesbury, 1900: 37). Shaftesbury and Locke were living at a time when Protestant and Catholic theologians had elaborated, on the basis of a close examination of individual Christian experience, whole vocabularies, often Augustinian in ethos, intended to describe intuitive, non-intellectual, but allegedly religious sensations in terms of 'taste' and 'relish', 'illumination' and 'heart', 'holy affections' and 'gracious dispositions'.

The conviction that one had been personally illuminated by the Holy Spirit had been reduced to farce for Shaftesbury by the refugee French Protestant 'prophets' whose ecstasies bewildered London in 1707 and whose tradition still affected John Wesley in the 1730s (Shaftesbury 1900: 20–2). Locke's successors, including Hume, who in the chapter on miracles in *An Enquiry Concerning Human Understanding* used the 'miracles' worked at the tomb of a Jansenist Abbé in Paris in 1731 as a basis for his criticism, did not deny that people often honestly reported subjective experiences, but they did not accept such statements as self-authenticating 'encounters with God'.

> What have we to oppose to such a cloud of witnesses, but the absolute impossibility or miraculous nature of the events, which they relate? And this surely, in the eyes of all reasonable people, will alone be regarded as a sufficient refutation.
>
> (Hume 1936: 125)

This critical philosophical reaction against the claims to religious experience helps to explain why many people in England, including, significantly, Bishop Butler, dismissed as 'enthusiasm' John Wesley's assertion that some of his followers had received through 'faith' the gift of perfect holiness. Wesley claimed that they had as clear an inward witness that they were fully renewed as they had formerly had of their justification by faith. In the *Dialogues* Hume specifically said that

> even though superstition or enthusiasm should not put itself in direct opposition to morality, the very diverting of the attention, the raising up a new and frivolous species of merit, the preposterous distribution which it makes of praise and blame, must have the most pernicious consequences, and weaken extremely men's attachment to the natural motives of justice and humanity.
>
> (Hume 1963: 198)

The struggle between the two attitudes went unresolved, and in the 1790s Kant, for example, wrote that 'whenever, over and above good life-conduct, man fancies that he can do to become well-pleasing to God is mere religious illusion and pseudo-service of God' (Kant 1934: 158).

THE 'ENLIGHTENED' ATTITUDE TO HISTORY AND BIBLICAL EXEGESIS

At the heart of Locke's *The Reasonableness of Christianity*, moreover, lay a historicization of the New Testament. Locke's free approach to the text offered a historical interpretation of its purpose rather than a theological exposition of a 'revelation'. His approach is not unlike that of the Jewish philosopher, Spinoza (1632–77), who said that in biblical exegesis one was concerned not with the truth of a passage but with its meaning, and that one should not distort the meaning in order to make it fit some idea which one already held to be 'true'. One should treat the Scriptures as ancient historical documents, to which one applied judgement and learned scholarship. This link between freedom of thought, the critical reason and historical thinking also expressed itself through the work of eighteenth-century historians like

Montesquieu (1689–1755), Gibbon (1737–94), and Hume who, perhaps influenced to some extent by Newtonian cosmology, abandoned the assumption that human history was directly under divine control, both in the immediate detail of events and in its final consummation. Scholars and scientists increasingly became tired of a theological time-scale heavily dependent on the book of Daniel, in which 'modern' history occupied a regularly extended 'fourth monarchy', an abstraction which had no meaning except as an interim before the supernatural Last Judgement, an event which no longer commanded the serious assent of the imagination of these historians.

The same attitude is marked by the publication of the first volume of Buffon's *Natural History* in 1749. That the planet was far older than the theological system suggested, and that its life-forms had not been fixed in their present form at the Creation, was realized by many of the educated elite in the course of the eighteenth century. Philo, in David Hume's *Dialogues Concerning Natural Religion*, thought that the most plausible system was one which 'ascribes an eternal, inherent principle of order to the world, though attended with great and continual revolutions and alterations' (Hume 1963: 148), a neatly ironical resolution of the problems which were beginning to emerge. As Norman Hampson wrote:

> The twentieth-century reader is most acutely aware of the limitations of eighteenth-century science, of its ignorance of basic processes and of the presuppositions of earlier ages which led it still to think in terms of the Fall, of the original creation of species as they now exist and of degeneration from a distant Golden Age. What was more significant at the time was men's emancipation from an Old Testament chronology that made human and natural prehistory unintelligible . . . This immense widening of men's intellectual horizons was bound to influence the way in which they now began to consider their own past.
>
> (Hampson 1968: 231–2)

The new historians quietly dropped the notion of supernatural intervention. They began to think of the past, not as a source of precepts and heroic examples, but as a mass of evidence which could be sorted out so as to reveal inner social relationships which might combine to offer this-worldly explanations of what had happened. Montesquieu said, in *Considerations on the Causes of the Greatness of the Romans and their Decay* (1734), a book whose title itself was an example of changing historical attitudes, that

> there are general causes, whether moral or physical, which act in every society to prosper, maintain or destroy it . . . and if the chance of one battle – that is, a particular cause – has brought a state to ruin, there was a general cause which made it inevitable that the state perish through a single battle . . . In a word, the main trend brings with it all particular accidents.
>
> (Montesquieu 1951: 173)

Montesquieu's interest, which he developed further in *De l'esprit des lois* (1748), in the effect of climate and geography on the long-term success or failure of societies was an example of a new awareness of the inter-relatedness of events in time and space, and this kind of historical analysis implied a new conception of politics as a conscious attempt to alter the future shape of a society.

HISTORY AND THE IMAGE OF JESUS

Once this historical attitude spread it was inevitable that it should be applied to the biblical documents and to the life of Jesus. Writing the history of the Jewish and Christian religions became, not simply a study of the background of Revelation, but the description of a social process. Hume was already writing *The Natural History of Religion* between 1749 and 1751. What happened took two forms. There was the more polemical writing about the Bible produced by writers in the Deist tradition, among them John Toland, Anthony Collins, Thomas Chubb and William Woolston, by French radicals such as Jean Meslier (1664–1729), Voltaire and d'Holbach, and in Germany especially by Hermann Reimarus (1694–1768). These writers may be distinguished from an academic school of biblical criticism, which built up slowly through the work of men like Ernesti, Semler, Michaelis and Lessing.

Bernard Cottret makes an important point here:

> France, more than any other country, witnessed a confrontation between religion and philosophy. This division ['cette fracture'] has still not disappeared from our culture: whether one likes or deplores it, it has had a lasting effect on our attitudes. This confrontation over the image of Christ lasted throughout the eighteenth century: Newton and Locke, each in their own way, produced a new image of Jesus: they made him either a wise teacher ['sage'] or a visionary; they removed him from the dogmatic framework in order to take him over. French anticlericalism, on the other hand, was always more jarring ['grinçant']: Meslier and Voltaire were hysterically fascinated by blasphemy.
>
> (Cottret 1990: 170)

For Jean Meslier, a local village priest in the Ardennes who concealed his materialism and atheism from his parish during his lifetime, there was no question of portraying Jesus in a favourable light. Meslier was not a Parisian intellectual but a man who experienced at first hand the misery to which a militaristic monarchy allied to a complacent Church had reduced the French countryside. He left the *Testament* of his real opinions to be found after his death, which happened in 1729. Voltaire knew of the manuscript's existence by the mid-1730s, but when he published part of it in 1762 as a weapon in his campaign against the French Catholic Church he implied that Meslier was a Deist, ignored his philosophical materialism and egalitarian politics and concentrated on his fierce attacks on the Scriptures and the Church.

Meslier, however, was responding to a deeper current of emotional and political change. At heart he rejected the religious option altogether. He denied the alleged spiritual value of suffering; he dismissed the late seventeenth-century Catholic cult of ascetic practices, and the morality which

259

went with them, as unnatural. He said that Christianity had not 'redeemed' the world, that there was no evidence that more people were saved or damned (if one believed in such categories) than had been the case before the time of Jesus. On the contrary, evil seemed to increase and multiply every day, which meant that the so-called miracles of the New Testament had failed in their object, and this in turn reflected on the wisdom of the 'God' who was supposed to have performed them (Meslier 1970: 192). But what else would you have expected, Meslier asked his former parishioners? Jesus was a poor man, the son of a carpenter; most people thought he was mad and he was finally hanged. Yet Jesus himself imagined that he was the great and powerful liberator who had so often been promised to the Jews. 'Are these not obviously the thoughts and imaginings of a fanatic? Did Don Quixote, the notorious fanatic and knight errant, ever have anything like them?' (Meslier 1970: 397). Quixote claimed to be interpreting ancient texts, and if one interpreted Cervantes in the same way as the Christians interpreted the Bible (Meslier said) one could produce an equally marvellous theological system.

The polemical writers desperately wanted to shake the position of the Christian Churches in European society. Marie-Hélène Cotoni has written: 'For Voltaire as for d'Holbach, biblical criticism, not out of technical incompetence but as a matter of practical effect, was centred on a defence of experimental science against magic, and of happiness, sometimes confused with bourgeois comfort, against illusion' (Cotoni 84: 217). The German eighteenth-century academics, on the other hand, were often at least as interested in the use of historical method as in theological polemic. Johann David Michaelis (1717–91), for example, ceased to treat the New Testament as a 'unity' but worked instead in terms of separate 'books' and 'parties' for the purposes of historical criticism. Johann Salomon Semler (1725–91) historicized the formation of the biblical canon in his *Abhandlung von freier Untersuchung des Kanon* (1771–5) by showing that the received canon was the product of a centuries-long process involving rival traditions and ecclesiastical compromises. Hermann Samuel Reimarus of Wolffenbüttel (1694–1768), whose bitterly anti-Christian New Testament work was published posthumously by Lessing between 1774 and 1778, deeply affected later New Testament scholarship because he demonstrated that in the New Testament there might be not only different literary levels superimposed one upon the other, but also levels which were aimed at quite different audiences. He suggested that the text could be read as having a double meaning: that, first, Jesus' own target was immediate political power based on a revival of the Jewish faith, but that, second, after his death his followers substituted the idea that he would return triumphantly from Heaven to bring about universal redemption. They failed, however, to remove from the biblical texts which survive all traces of the original intentions of Jesus.

Exegesis was beginning to free itself from the specifically dogmatic restrictions set by Christian theology: the division between 'New Testament scholars' and 'systematic theologians' has remained to the present day. The Pietist world (including the Wesleyans and Anglican Evangelicals) simply rejected the academic historical–critical approach to the Bible altogether; so did Rome, which had the temporary advantage of having always appealed to tradition as well as Scripture as an authority for Christian truth. For a romantic conservative like Coleridge in the early nineteenth century, what mattered was the possession of a living tradition of faith, collective and individual, which could, if necessary, cope even with the disappearance of the written record of the Scriptures.

THE STATUS OF REVELATION: JOSEPH BUTLER AND DAVID HUME

To eighteenth-century theologians, however, biblical criticism seemed less threatening that the question of the status – as supernatural revelation or human imagining – of the biblical text which was being criticized. The orthodox Christian world-view was losing its grip on the Western imagination. This may be seen in the way that Bishop Butler (1692–1752), the most distinguished eighteenth-century defender of revelation, dealt with these issues in *The Analogy of Religion* (1736). His views may be contrasted briefly with those of David Hume (1711–76), whose *Dialogues Concerning Natural Religion*, which appeared in 1779, clearly took account of Butler's views among others.

Like the Deists, Butler assumed God's existence. Reason and external revelation had initially made available 'natural religion', which implied a divine moral government of the world and the inevitability of a future state of rewards and punishments. The answer to Deism, and here Butler's argument was powerful, was that natural religion was not enough. If one looked at the world realistically, it seemed to be 'in a state of ruin' which natural religion did not repair, and this ruin was 'the very ground of the Christian dispensation' (Butler 1874: 213). It was all very well for the Deists (and Locke must have been in Butler's mind at this point) to insist on 'the efficacy of repentance . . . in opposition to Christianity' (ibid.: 212), but the notion that repentance alone was sufficient to expiate guilt 'appears to be contrary to the general sense of mankind' (ibid.: 213), for propitiatory sacrifices were generally prevalent (Butler claimed) across the heathen world. The creation had to be restored by a Divine Person, the Messiah, and Jesus had carried out this divine mission. Now, the Holy Spirit gave 'ordinary assistance' to 'good men'. Butler, sketching the biblical history of mankind on the basis of a six-thousand-year period, said that

> its chronology, its account of the time when the earth . . . was first peopled with human creatures, is no way contradicted, but is really confirmed, by the natural and civil history of the world, collected from common historians, from the state of the earth, and from the late invention of arts and sciences.
>
> (ibid.: 280–1)

Here Butler's position was weak because both the scientists and the historians of the eighteenth century were abandoning this pattern.

In his general argument, therefore, Butler tried to turn the 'wretched state of the world' (ibid.: 198), and even what he described as our ignorance of exactly how the death of Christ redeems us, to Christianity's advantage: the New Testament confirmed our desperate situation, and provided a solution which unaided reason could not have expected. Much of his argument, however, remained dependent on the traditional appeal to attestative miracles: those recorded in the Scriptures, together with the 'miraculous' spread of the Church, and the fulfilment of Old Testament prophecy in the New. Christianity, he said, was originally received as true in terms of miracles – 'the generality of the first converts to Christianity must have believed them', and 'their testimony is the same kind of evidence for those miracles, as if they had put it in writing and these writings had come down us' (ibid.: 257). Moreover, the survival of a dispersed Judaism was a 'standing miracle' (ibid.: 285), a fulfilment of prophecy and confirmation of the truth of the Christian revelation.

Butler made a dual appeal, first, to the assumption, common to many of the Deists as well, that reason showed that the world was subject to a divine purposive and moral direction, and second, to the concept of supernatural intervention or visible miracle. The radical position on miracle seems to be put by Hume, who said that

> it is no miracle that a man, seemingly in good health, should die on a sudden: because such a kind of death, though more unusual that any other, has yet been frequently observed to happen. But it is a miracle that a dead man should come to life, because that has never been observed in any age or country.
>
> (Hume 1936: 115).

He concluded 'that the Christian Religion not only was at first attended with miracles, but even at this day cannot be believed by any reasonable person without one' (ibid.: 131).

Orthodox Christian theology, as Butler described it, rested on the assumptions of God's existence, the ruined state of humanity, and the need for a special act of redemption which only God in Jesus could perform. At the end of the *Dialogues*, Hume allowed Philo to deny that such a theological system gave an accurate account of how things are. He said that natural theology reduced itself to one simple, though somewhat ambiguous proposition, 'that the cause or causes of order in the universe probably bear some remote analogy to the human intelligence'. But even that analogy, 'imperfect as it is, can be carried no farther than to the human intelligence and cannot be transferred, with any appearance of probability, to the qualities of the mind' (Hume 1963: 203). It followed that even if one accepted that the observable evidence suggested that the universe could not have existed without some designing intelligence, the evidence did not oblige one to believe that such an intelligence was moral at all. And in that situation, one should not, as Butler did, take any 'orthodox' God's existence for granted, nor should one assume that any particular relationship could be shown between the human 'moral sense' and the 'religious hypothesis'. The Christian system itself was morally unconvincing.

> Punishment, according to our conception, should bear some proportion to the offence. Why then eternal punishment for the temporary offences of so frail a creature as man? . . . Heaven and Hell suppose two distinct species of men, the good and the bad; but the greatest part of mankind float betwixt vice and virtue . . . Nature has rendered human infancy peculiarly frail and mortal, as it were on purpose to refute the notion of a probationary state; the half of mankind die before they are rational creatures.
>
> (ibid.: 266–7)

At the end of the essay on immortality Hume said ironically that 'nothing could set in fuller light the infinite obligations which mankind have to Divine revelation, since we find that no other medium could ascertain this great and important truth' (ibid.: 270).

Hume exposed the problem which 'enlightened' and academic theologians were hoping to solve: was there a case for revelation apart from the assertion that it was self-authenticating? Neither Locke, Hume nor Kant was impressed by the appeal to religious experience. At the time, however, Hume had little influence, because the pressure of censorship on him was almost as great as it had been on the earlier Deist writers: the essay on immortality was not published in England until after his death in 1776, though a French translation, attributed to d'Holbach, appeared in Paris in 1770. His scepticism, which recalls Montaigne, was not even typical of 'enlightened' attitudes.

'ENLIGHTENMENT' AND SOCIETY: THE IDEA OF PROGRESS

A different, more widespread element in 'enlightened' attitudes was a belief that visible progress in civilization was possible. This was progress in a limited sense, relatively uninfluenced by utopianism (which had its own marginal revival in the eighteenth century), but it involved faith in the possibility of human happiness. This attitude emerged as both a religious and a political alternative to the social theories of mainstream Christianity, Protestant as well as Catholic, in which society was still analysed in terms of the revealed doctrine of the Fall of man. The 'fourth kingdom' and man's fallen state remained as a theological backcloth but they had less and less influence on what was happening centre-stage in the eighteenth century. There was a turning away in many quarters from the ascetic Christian denial of the world as a proper form of human behaviour, and a fresh attachment to human happiness in this world. One important aspect of 'enlightenment' was a feeling that Christian piety put too much stress on self-negation, not just in its view of human nature, but also in its method of pursuing holiness. One could now abandon this whole attitude and technique, rise from one's knees and study the passions, the affections, reason, the moral sense and so on, learning to seek one's own and the general good in a different, more secular sense, with confidence that the deity supported virtue rather than vice. The position was sound to the extent that it concentrated on the aim of doing what was both individually and socially possible and useful: it was not so much a matter of complacently ignoring sin and misery as of assuming that the relevant reaction to life was practical, that one should do what one could, and rather more perhaps than cultivating one's garden. This new optimism was often expressed in terms of 'improvement', including, in England (for example), the improvement of industry, commerce and agriculture.

It was at the level of daily life that the hegemony of the Churches suffered most from the new mood. One consequence was that the exclusion of the Church from political power became a steadily more important aim of the radicals, especially in France: in the *Encyclopédie*, for example, the important article 'Législateur' (1765) by Saint-Lambert (1716–1803), asserted that the state should not make use of religion as a principal part of the machinery of government, because this only encouraged religious fanaticism and politically ambitious priests. This contradicted the universal view of European rulers that atheism, not religion, was the enemy of social harmony. The characteristic note of the *Encyclopédie*'s articles on religion was a demand for religious toleration. As recently as 1746 Diderot had been imprisoned for publishing his *Pensées philosophiques*, in which he cast doubt on the idea of resurrection. It is not surprising that it was now increasingly asserted that a properly 'enlightened' attitude required that state and Church discontinue the centuries-old policy of restricting freedom of religious publication to what was allegedly neither heretical nor blasphemous. It is significant that one of the sources of French Deism, and therefore of the break with traditional religious thinking, seems to have been a revulsion against Louis XIV's religious persecution of the French Protestants: the 'Militaire Philosophe', who wrote against Christianity in about 1710, had taken part in the Dragonnades and had clearly never forgiven himself for doing so. By the later eighteenth century opinion shifted far enough for the Habsburg Emperor Joseph II to try to enforce toleration in his dominions.

TWENTIETH-CENTURY CRITICISM OF 'THE ENLIGHTENMENT': KARL BARTH

The effect of these changes has been seen as disastrous. A modern German historian, Gerhard Benecke, wrote that 'the *Aufklärung* was the most serious political mistake any generation of German politicians and intellectuals could possibly have made' (Benecke 1979: 79): between 1770 and 1800 they destroyed the stability, partly religious in origin, of an older federal German Reich.

'They provided as an alternative the secular practice of citizens' rights and eventually nation-state pretensions that soon fragmented into a new kind of bourgeois nationalist individualism copied from a more economically and politically advanced western Europe' (ibid.: 82). This was a more secular form of the Swiss Protestant theologian Karl Barth's influential attack on 'enlightened' theology in his *Protestant Theology in the Nineteenth Century* (originally written in 1932/3). Barth believed that from the eighteenth to the twentieth century the essential theological choice in Protestantism lay between a saving, scriptural Reformation orthodoxy (as he understood it) and a humanizing rationalistic theology which had developed steadily after 1700, reducing Christianity to the equivalent of a natural religion, whose tenents were belief in God, human freedom, morality and immortality. He even doubted the Enlightenment theology's claim to rational foundations, quoting Karl Aner's assertion that one could not understand the German Enlightenment 'if one characterises it in a purely intellectualistic way; its criticism of dogma is not born of reason, but of ethical and personal needs' (Barth 1972: 164). As late as 1960, in *The Humanity of God*, Barth argued that nineteenth-century theologians, still governed by the principles of the Aufklärung, assumed that they must come to terms with the world-views of their contemporaries, so that theologians became philosophers of religion and thought of Christianity as one religion among others.

> Theology was still being penalised for accepting the Renaissance discovery that man was the measure of all things, including Christian things. On this ground the testimony of the Christian faith, however honest, and however richly endowed with Biblical and Reformation recollections, could only exist like a fish out of water.
>
> (Barth 1961: 25)

Convinced of the unique truth of the Christian religion as the Gospel of Jesus Christ as heard in Holy Scripture, Barth could not attach a positive theological value to the history of human ideas about religion, still less accept that the orthodox Christian idea of revelation was a product of it. Yet eighteenth-century Christian theologians and their intellectual opponents both shared an intellectual life which did not totally depend on politics or on the bourgeois discovery of the self which foreshadowed Romanticism, or on the state of the economic base of Western culture, or, in more Barthian terms, on the pride of the human will. By the late eighteenth century it was no longer possible to restrict all theologians, let alone all intellectuals, to an unquestioning acceptance of orthodox dogma as laid down by Church authority on the basis of a verbally inspired and therefore flawless Scripture, all parts of which spoke equally of Christ. As a Protestant theologian, Semler, for example, abandoned the idea of the apostolic purity of the primitive Church: he reasserted the divinity of Jesus but argued that his teaching needed to be freed from the Jewish thought-forms to which he had accommodated it.

God's revelation is now seen as expansive, as a function of human development, embodied, in a sense, in history itself and marked out by certain definite periods in which man's moral awareness broke the bounds of the temporal forms of historical religion.

(P. H. Reill 1975: 169)

The problem of primitive Christian history, a problem which in its eighteenth-century form the Deists had formulated, changed. It was no longer a question of the relationship between the contingent and the eternal in the origins of the Christian Church, expressed as a conflict around the orthodox emphasis on the apodictic value of miracles. Once the expansion of the early Church was no longer thought of as an end in itself, as miraculous evidence of the truth of revelation, Church history could be reinterpreted in idealistic terms as part of a general process.

CHRISTIANITY AND RELIGION: LESSING AND ROUSSEAU

This approach was facilitated by the growth of the perception that Christianity was only one religion among others, a secular view quite different from the Deist attempt to dissolve Christianity into 'natural religion'. There had for long been a Western perception of the rest of the world as having developed differently, but this had been understood as a mystery of Providence. God had simply chosen not to redeem the Chinese – a familiar presence to the eighteenth-century West – before the arrival of the Europeans, rather late in Chinese history, with the offer of salvation in Christ. What happened in the eighteenth century, through secular and religious contact, was the partial invalidation of that older perspective, a putting of the West, religion and all, on the same level as other cultural centres of the race.

Lessing consolidated this transition, from doubt about Christianity's claim to be both a historical religion and finally true to the conviction that the history of the human race was itself the medium through which truth would be finally grasped, because an inner rationality determined humanity's arrival at moral perfection. He wrote in 1777:

> If I have no historical grounds on which to object to the statement that Christ resurrected a dead man, must I therefore hold it true that God has a son who shares his essence? . . . If I have no historical grounds on which to deny that Christ rose from the dead, must I therefore consider it true that this resurrected Christ was the son of God?

(Lessing 1970: 48)

Semler had conceived of Christianity as a changing, developing religion, but he had not really doubted its uniqueness. In *The Education of the Human Race* (1781) (Pelters 1972) Lessing drew his own consequence from the historical nature of Christianity, that its doctrines could only be relatively true. He could then defend orthodox doctrines like original sin on the ground that they were historically conditioned: they contained an element of the ultimate truth but they would certainly be transcended. Men like Jesus could be interpreted as having been so far ahead of their contemporaries as to seem divine, perhaps even to themselves. There was no question of human history being transformed by the intervention of revelation; instead, revelation was in history, and the gradual education of humanity would end in universal enlightenment (Allison 1966).

Lessing's plea for toleration was quite different from the violent Jacobin attempt to wipe the past slate clean and invent society all over again. The Jacobins dissolved the links between the French state and the Catholic Church, executed numbers of priests, drove many others into exile, and tried to set up their own religious institutions. This revolutionary tradition continued into the nineteenth century, especially in the Marxist view that violence was part of the historical dialectic. Later eighteenth-century 'enlightened' writers, however, thought in gentler terms of social amelioration, of change through education, of monarchs who allowed their subjects freedom of religion, speech and publication. Christian dogma might be tolerated, but only if the dogmatic institutions were themselves tolerant.

One misinterprets 'enlightenment' if one sees it chiefly as a revolt against religion, as distinct from a revolt against some Christian doctrines and institutions. The real challenge to the Churches came from the gradual emergence of a religious alternative which did not look for its authority in Christian sources, as, for example, the Unitarian tradition had done since the sixteenth century, but which combined morality and emotion more successfully than had been the case in early Deism. Kant contributed to this movement of feeling, by his renewed criticism of Christian worship and his philosophical defence of moral conviction, but it was Rousseau more especially who released religious aspirations in people who had decided that the Christian vocabulary and symbolism did not fit or extend their experience, and who did not respond to the view of the human being as a sinful creature separated utterly from a transcendent God, who, when approached through Christ in fear and trembling, offered grace.

Rousseau did not draw the religious opinions which he put in the mouth of the Savoyard Vicar in *Émile, ou de l'éducation* (1762) from the New Testament. He believed that one should turn away from both Christian metaphysics and philosophical materialism to an inner principle of justice and virtue, the light of conscience, assent to whose promptings enabled one to pursue justice and the eternal order. His image of Jesus, which had vast influence in the nineteenth century, was of someone whose reason and conscience had been purified of the influence of the passions and schooled to the highest possible point. 'If the life and death of Socrates are those of a philosopher, the life and death of Christ are those of a God', he wrote in the *Lettre à Mgr de Beaumont* (1763), the Archbishop of Paris, who had publicly condemned *Émile* as heretical and dangerous and forbidden his flock either to read or to own it (Grimsley 1970: 297). Rousseau meant that Jesus was a sublime spirit who invented a sublime morality. In the *Lettre* Rousseau rejected both New Testament and eighteenth-century miracles, giving as his example of the latter the miracles which allegedly took place in 1731 at the tomb of a pious Jansenist in Paris. For Rousseau, neither the Church nor the Bible could claim absolute authority over the conscience: authority was within, and on that basis he dismissed the doctrines of the Trinity, original sin and eternal punishment in hell (Cotini 1984: 256).

Rousseau shared Lessing's passion for toleration. Religion was too important as a social binding force to be left at the mercy of radical critics like Diderot and d'Holbach, or in the hands of the Churches, which had either substituted or accepted social oppression for social creation. Hence the provision of a civil religion at the end of the *Contrat social*, a religion whose primary aim was to underwrite social morality, and show, indirectly, that it was not necessary to use Christianity as the civil religion. What Locke, the Deists, Voltaire and his friends, and Rousseau all shared was their recoil both from the idea of an interventionist deity in the orthodox tradition, and from the secular equivalent, the intolerant, intervening state. There was therefore no question of supernatural grace because there was no need for an externally produced transformation in a human being who was endowed with reason and liberty and able to give an internal assent. This was the other face of the denial of the miraculous in the New Testament.

CONCLUSION: AN UNBRIDGED GAP

Not everyone reacted in this way. The early Wesleyan holiness movement, for example, which lasted from about 1740 to about 1760, reverted to a more rigorous, inward-looking holiness technique, so that some Protestants thought of it as a regression to Catholicism. But in the perspective of the period one sees that there was a relationship between Wesley's idea of holiness and the subjectivism of the nascent Romantic movement. Wesleyan women, for example, benefited as much in terms of personal freedom as of religious development. There is also a parallel with Jean-Jacques Rousseau, because although he encouraged his readers to withdraw into themselves and discover, not a fallen nature which had to be 'regenerated', but an essential being which was in harmony with a rational, spiritual universe, Rousseau was also celebrating ecstatic states of consciousness which were not so different in kind, whatever the myths employed for description, from those described by Wesley's itinerants when they gave an account of their, usually brief, experiences of holiness. Humanity's natural goodness was sufficient (as Rousseau saw it) for salvation, which could be achieved by freeing oneself from the ideology of a corrupt contemporary 'civilization'. Modern Christian theologians tend to interpret the apparent disorder of human existence as evidence of the truth of the Christian understanding of human nature in terms of sin, and so convict such eighteenth-century thinking of naive optimism, of an 'Enlightenment-project' which has failed utterly. Eighteenth-century critics of

Christianity, on the other hand, started from the view that the Christian-project had failed, accepted visible disorder as the price of existence, and did not think that Christianity was the only possible religious option. Some human experience of the divine might conceivably be possible, but at the end of the century Kant, well aware of the nature of German Pietism, set intellectual limits to any appeal to religious experience:

> we cannot, by any token, recognise a supersensible object in experience, still less can we exercise an influence upon it to draw it down to us; though to be sure, at times there do arise stirrings of the heart making for morality, movements which we cannot explain and regarding which we must confess our ignorance . . . to wish to observe such heavenly influences in ourselves is a kind of madness, in which there can, no doubt, be method (since those supposed inner revelations must always be attached to moral, and hence to rational, ideas), but which nonetheless remains a self-deception prejudicial to religion. To believe that there may be works of grace and that perhaps these may even be necessary to supplement the incompleteness of our struggle towards virtue, that is all we can say on this subject; beyond this we are incapable of determining anything concerning their distinctive marks and still less are we able to do anything to produce them.
>
> (Kant 1934: 162)

Kant's strictures on religious experience never carried much weight outside a narrow philosophical field, and had no effect on Protestant theology. Some scholars date 'modern theology', by which they mean the liberal Protestant theology which was a characteristic element of the period 1789–1914, from Schleiermacher (1768–1834), on the ground that his use of the concept of the 'religious consciousness', in which the human and the divine could encounter one another, marked a fundamental breach with Christian ortho-doxy, but it is equally arguable that Schleiermacher was simply finding a way to set orthodoxy itself free from 'enlightenment' control, and that what he found in his consciousness was good Lutheran teaching. Central to the experi-ence of 'enlightenment' had been a different subjectivity which did not necessarily interpret human emotions, including both sexual and religious emotions, in terms of a traditional Christian supernaturalism. The element in Rousseau's religiosity which struck the deepest chord with his contemporaries was his description of his own subjective response to natural phenomena as mediating an experience of the divine.

Theologically speaking, therefore, eighteenth-century 'enlightened' thinkers expressed, rather than created, a growing dissatisfaction with the social, spiri-tual and intellectual authority of the Christian Churches. This reaction could take forms as distinct from one another as Diderot's materialism and Robespi-erre's cult of the Supreme Being, but had at its centre a developing historical perspective which relativized what humanity had so far experienced, and helped to clear a path for twentieth-century religious pluralism, as opposed to religious fundamentalism.

REFERENCES

Allison, H. (1966) *Lessing and the Enlightenment*, Ann Arbor: University of Michigan Press.

Barth, K. (1961) *The Humanity of God*, London: Collins.

—— (1965) *The German Conflict*, London: Lutterworth Press.

—— (1972) *Protestant Theology in the Nineteenth Century*, London: SCM Press.

Benecke, G. (1979) 'The German Reichskirche', in W. J. Callahan (ed.) *Church and Society in Catholic Europe of the Eighteenth Century*, Cambridge: Cambridge University Press.

Butler, J. (1874) *The Analogy of Religion*, Oxford: Clarendon Press.

Byrne, P. (1989) *Natural Religion and the Nature of Religion: The Legacy of Deism*, London: Routledge & Kegan Paul.

Collins, A. (1965) *A Discourse of Freethinking*, G. Gawlick, (ed.) Stuttgart: Kohlhammer.

Cotoni, M.-H. (1984) *L'Exégèse du Nouveau Testament dans la philosophie française du dix-huitième siècle*, Oxford: Voltaire Foundation, Taylor Institution.

Cottret, B. (1990) *Le Christ des Lumières*, Paris: Éditions du Cerf.

Diderot, D. (1746) *Pensées philosophiques*, in J. Assézat, M. Tourneaux (eds) *Œuvres complètes*, Paris: Garnier Frères.

Grimsley, R. (ed.) (1970) *Rousseau: Religious Writings*, Oxford: Clarendon Press.

Hampson, N. (1968) *The Enlightenment*, Harmondsworth: Penguin.

Harrison, P. (1990) *'Religion' and Religions in the English Enlightenment*, Cambridge: Cambridge University Press.

Hume, D. (1936) *Hume's Enquiries*, ed. L. A. Selby-Bigge, Oxford: Clarendon Press.

—— (1963) *Hume on Religion*, ed. R. Wollheim, London: Collins.

—— (1976) *The Natural History of Religion*, ed. A. W. Colver and J. V. Price, Oxford: Oxford University Press.

—— (1980) *Dialogues Concerning Natural Religion*, ed. N. Kemp Smith, Indianapolis: Bobbs Merrill.

Kant, I. (1934) *Religion within the Limits of Reason Alone*, trans. T. Green and H. Hudson, Indiana: Open Court.

—— (1964) 'Beantwortung der Frage: Was ist Aufklärung?', in W. Weischadel (ed.) *Werke*, vol. vi, Frankfurt: Indel Verlag.

Lessing, G. E. (1970) 'Über den Beweis des Geistes und der Kraft', in L. Zscharnack (ed.) *Werke*, vol. xxiii, Hildesheim/New York: G. Olms.

Locke, J. (1823) *The Reasonableness of Christianity*, in *Works of John Locke*, vol. vi, London: Rivingson.

—— (1975) *An Essay Concerning Human Understanding*, ed. P. H. Nidditch, Oxford: Oxford University Press.

Mauzi, R. and Menant, S. (1977) *Le Dixième siècle 1750–1778*, Paris: Arthaud.

Meslier, J. (1970) *Œuvres Complètes*, vol. i, ed R. Desne, Paris: Éditions Anthropos.

Montesquieu, C. de Secondat, Baron (1951) 'Considérations sur les causes de la grandeur des Romains et de leur décadence', in *Œuvres complètes*, vol. ii, ed. R. Caillois, Paris: Gallimard.

—— (1989) *The Spirit of the Laws*, ed. A. Cohler, B. Miller, H. Stone, Cambridge: Cambridge University Press.

O'Higgins, J. (1970) *Anthony Collins: The Man and his Works*, The Hague: Martinus Nijhoff.

Pelters, W. (1972) *Lessings Standort: Sinndeutung der Geschichte als Kern seines Denkens*, Heidelberg: Stiehm.

Reill, P. H. (1975) *The German Enlightenment and the Rise of Historicism*, Berkeley: University of California Press.

Rousseau, J.-J. (1926a) *Lettre à Mgr de Beaumont, in Classiques Garnier: J.-J. Rousseau,* Paris: Garnier Frères.
—— (1926b) *Du contrat social,* Paris: Garnier Frères.
Semler, J. S. (1771–75) *Abhandlung von freier Untersuchung des Canons,* 4 parts, Halle.
Shaftesbury, A. (1900) *Characteristics,* ed. J. M. Robertson, London: Grant Richards.
Toulmin, S. (1990) *Cosmopolis,* New York: Free Press.

FURTHER READING

Batley, E. M. (1990) *Catalyst of Enlightenment: G. E. Lessing,* Bern: P. Lang.
Burns, R. M. (1982) *The Great Debate on Miracles from Joseph Glanvil to David Hume,* London and Toronto: Associated University Presses.
Chadwick, O. (1981) *The Popes and European Revolution,* Oxford: Clarendon Press.
Cranston, M. (1988) *Rousseau, Selections,* London: Macmillan.
Drury, J. (ed.) (1989) *Critics of the Bible, 1724–1873,* Cambridge: Cambridge University Press.
Furbank, P. N. (1992) *Diderot: A Critical Biography,* London: Secker and Warburg.
Gay, P. (1964) *The Party of Humanity: Studies in the French Enlightenment,* London: Weidenfeld and Nicholson.
Mason, H. (1981) *Voltaire: A Biography,* London: Granada.
Porter, R. and Teich, M. (1981) *The Enlightenment in National Context,* Cambridge: Cambridge University Press.
Scholder, K. (1990) *The Birth of Modern Critical Theology,* London: SCM Press.
Ugrinsky, A. (ed.) (1986) *Lessing and the Enlightenment,* London: Greenwood.
Venturi, F. (1972) *Italy and the Enlightenment,* London: Longman.
Wade, L. O. *The Structure and Form of the French Enlightenment,* 2 vols, New Jersey: Princeton University Press.
Yolton, J. W. (1985) *Locke: An Introduction,* Oxford: Basil Blackwell.
See also chapters 12, 14, 16, 18, 29, 41.

14

THEOLOGY NOW

Keith Clements

The very title 'Theology Now' suggests that theology, far from being a static body of knowledge, moves on. At least as much as other intellectual disciplines, theology is a dynamic enterprise, interacting with circumstance and changing through time. Even those theologies which claim to be maintaining fixed positions of traditional doctrine, and to be resistant to passing philosophical and cultural fashions, are able to do so only by developing new forms of argument to counter new criticisms of their position. Theology has been likened to a bird on the wing, and therefore to give an account of 'theology now' – particularly when there are in fact a number of birds, not all flying in the same direction or at similar speeds – is a far from easy undertaking. In order to do justice to the historical dynamism of theology, rather than attempt to describe a multiplicity of present 'positions' it is more important to indicate the most important directions in which various types of theology are moving, and the motivating forces behind them. Clearly in a chapter of this size a broad picture must suffice, and certain limits of scope must be drawn.

By 'theology' in this chapter is meant what is broadly called systematic theology, which has the task of interpreting Scripture and the doctrinal tradition for the believing community – and as always, this takes place in a particular historical situation. By 'now' is meant, more or less, the last two decades of the twentieth century. Of course a specific 'here' should also be added which in the case of the author means Britain, or perhaps Europe or 'the West', but with certain global dimensions to theology fully recognized.

Even the 'now' of theology, however, cannot be described in isolation from the 'then' which has preceded it. To say that theology is a dynamic, developing enterprise does not mean that in every period it starts anew from scratch. The significance of the 'now' lies in the way it receives and develops the legacy of the past, both recent and historically distant, and continues in dialogue with it. This chapter will therefore first outline the recent historical legacy to which theology now is indebted in the West, and will illustrate how a good deal of contemporary Christian thought is still in recognizable continuity with the theology and philosophy of the immediate post-Enlightenment world. It will then examine how contemporary theologies take different approaches to the central question bequeathed by the Enlightenment to this century: that of defining the relationship of theology itself to the total intellectual, religious and cultural world of its time. Finally, it will attempt a survey of how, for much contemporary theology, a most critical question is the necessity, or peril, of relating itself to a quite specific context within this total world milieu in which it is set. Indeed, as will be shown, it is the highly self-conscious approach to contextuality which is perhaps the chief distinguishing feature of theology now. It is certainly one of the most controversial aspects of theology today, especially when 'context' is defined in social and political terms.

THEOLOGY NOW: ITS INHERITANCE

Theology now, as in every historical context, has a sense of the legacy bequeathed by the past. A peculiar mark of Western theology in the last two decades is that as the twenty-first century approaches, so its appreciation of the nineteenth seems to increase. Writing from prison in 1944, Dietrich Bonhoeffer, one of the most seminal influences on theology in the second half of the century, commented:

> There are so few people now who want to have any intimate spiritual association with the eighteenth and nineteenth centuries . . . [Who] bothers at all now about the work and achievements of our grandfathers, and how much of what they knew have we already forgotten? I believe that people will one day be quite amazed by what was achieved in that period, which is now so disregarded and so little known.
> (Bonhoeffer 1971: 227)

Perhaps now that prophecy is being fulfilled. Far from the previous century being left behind and outgrown, much of its religious and philosophical thought has returned to question and haunt the present generation, which is increasingly in dialogue with those who brought the Enlightenment to its critical climax and who pioneered theological responses to it. A sketch of how much of theology now sees the main features of that past is therefore vital to understanding the current scene.

There is widespread agreement that in summing up the Enlightenment and in pointing beyond it, Immanuel Kant (1724–1804) redefined the human intellectual task, in both theology and philosophy, in such a way as to provide a continuing challenge down to the present. While Kant believed with the Enlightenment in human reason as the key to knowledge, he radically redefined the scope and role of that reason: it is capable of dealing only with the sensible, empirical world. It does so by applying to the 'phenomena' perceived by the senses the innate or *a priori* categories with which the human mind operates. Human knowledge is thus a synthesis of the mind working upon sensory data, and thereby contains an irreducibly subjective element. There is no completely 'objective' knowledge of 'things-in-themselves', that is, totally independent of the knowing mind. Along with much else, the traditional metaphysical systems in which the doctrine of God, and the proofs of God's existence, had been framed, collapsed. From Kant onwards, human awareness, subjectivity and feeling became central in Western understanding of 'truth'. Illustrative of this was Kant's own argument for God's existence, based on the human inward *moral* sense from which the existence of the divine Giver of the moral law could be inferred.

On the Continent, response to the critical situation posited by Kant took several forms. Friedrich Schleiermacher (1768–1834) gave a fresh and long-lasting impulse to Protestant theology by identifying the essence of religion as lying not in knowledge, whether of a scientific or metaphysical kind, nor in the moral sense, but in a specifically religious emotion, the feeling of absolute dependence. G. F. W. Hegel (1770–1831) grappled with Kant in a singularly contrasting way. If, as Kant had argued, knowledge is limited to the scope of reason, then one may as well say that there is nothing outside reason, and therefore reason is itself the basis of reality. On this idealistic premise, therefore, the whole of human, historical reality, and indeed nature as well, was interpreted as the out-working of absolute Spirit or mind in the conditions of finitude, becoming self-conscious in the human mind. Later in the century 'Liberal Protestantism' led by Albrecht Ritschl (1822–89) returned to the ethical emphasis which Kant himself had made so primary, seeing the kingdom of God as the progressive realization of the ethical ideals of human brotherhood as promulgated and exemplified in Jesus.

Amid this diversity of response, one issue stood central: history in general, and in particular the history of Jesus and the Christian movement which somehow flowed from him. For such as Schleiermacher the historical Jesus was important as the definitive example and imparter of the uniquely full consciousness of God. For Hegel and the idealists the figure of Jesus – or at least the doctrines that had been subsequently created about him – had the significance of demonstrating in a particular way the eternal truths of spiritual reality. For Liberal Protestants like Ritschl, and still more so for the celebrated Church historian Adolf von Harnack (1851–1931), it became crucially important to recover the actual 'Jesus of history' as distinct from the Christ of later dogma, so that the specific nature of his ethical teaching could be identified. But at the same time, the element of subjectivity could not be kept out of historical knowledge any more than other areas of human understanding. Is 'objective' historical knowledge of the past, beyond the frames of reference and experiential background of the historian, possible at all? This was the question first explored in depth by Wilhelm Dilthey (1833–1911). And in reconstructing the past could we get behind the subjectivities and synthetic creations of those who themselves compiled the earliest records? In the Christian case, could we get behind the 'Christ of faith' of the early Church to the 'historical Jesus'? This last question was posed by Martin Kähler (1835–1912) as one of the most important enquiries which nineteenth-century New Testament scholarship asked itself, just as Søren Kierkegaard (1813–55) threatened to undermine the whole rationalist and idealist presuppositions with his agonizing recognition that 'truth is subjectivity'.

Perhaps the figure who best sums up the nineteenth century and brings it right into the twentieth is Ernst Troeltsch (1855–1923), in whom elements of the Kantian, idealist and Liberal Protestant approaches can all be seen, within the framework of the most thorough-going historical perspective. For Troeltsch, all human religions are an integral part of the ultimate wholeness of human history. This means that religion is an ineluctable feature of human existence, and that no one religion can claim absolute significance or truth-value over all the others. Christianity can claim to be the one most nearly approaching the absolute, and indeed is the normative one for Western culture. But the absolute can never be wholly manifest within history itself.

In Britain, too, the tendency to emphasize the inwardness of faith and its affinity with moral sensibility, and the divine as an immanent process within nature and human history rather than an external deity controlling from afar or from above, were marked features of nineteenth-century thought, as was the wrestling with the implications of an unqualified commitment to historical (as distinct from purely dogmatic) understanding of religious truth. This can be seen in the explorations of Samuel Taylor Coleridge, in the enquiries of John Henry Newman into the development of dogma and the nature of religious authority, in the authors of *Essays and Reviews* (1860), and the later High Church Anglicans of the *Lux Mundi* school (1889).

The fact is that for much of theology now, that century of thought remains deeply significant, and in some ways increasingly so. It is evidenced in the increasing scholarly attention being paid to it by theologians and historians alike. The fundamental reason lies in the fact that the questions being faced then are recognized as the questions still requiring answers now.

CONTINUITIES AND DISTURBANCES

A theologian of the turn of the century being reincarnated in the West (certainly the British part of it) of the present decade would find a good deal of congeniality. Much that has caused controversy in the past twenty years has represented intellectual values and approaches highly reminiscent of both the idealistically-based theology characteristic of much Anglicanism, and of Liberal Protestantism, of that earlier generation. In the writings of Maurice Wiles, for example, one sees a concern to do justice to a notion of God as ultimate reality relating to the world in a loving way – but whose 'actions' can be spoken of only as symbols and parables of his purpose. The cross of Jesus is the supreme parable of a loving, living God engaged with evil. Wiles, like many of his contemporaries, prefers the language of 'spirit' in reference to God, conveying as it does the nature of a quasi-personal reality existing only in relation to others. Wiles articulates the concern of many of his generation in stating the conception of God which he is attempting to articulate:

> [It] must be a profoundly personal concept, yet one that bursts the bounds of what it is to be an individual person as we know that in our finite human experience. And secondly it is God in relation to us with which we have to do, for any knowledge of God that we have is so inextricably bound up with our particular experience of him that what we say about him can never be wholly separated out from the limiting and distorting prism of that contingent experience.
>
> (Wiles 1982: 120)

So too there is a re-routing of historical theology, behind the heavily incarnational, dogmatic formulae of the ecumenical councils, to 'Jesus as he was' in his first-century Palestinian context, as found for example in the essays in *The Myth of God Incarnate* (Hick 1977). The argument of John Hick, for instance, that what was primary in the first Christian community was an overwhelming experience of acceptance by God in Jesus, which later found expression in credal formulae, is strongly reminiscent of Harnack's view of early Christian history, as a steady decline from the religious consciousness of Jesus himself, and those of his first disciples, into Hellenizing, Catholic orthodoxy. Both views are based on a certain historical presupposition.

No less striking is the very close affinity between the views of John Hick in his study *God and the Universe of Faiths* (1973) and the thought of Ernst Troeltsch. For both, religion is a universal phenomenon. For both, God alone is the absolute to which the historical religions all point and of which they have apprehended some truth. No one religion can claim to be the centre, any more than any one planet can claim to be the hub of the solar system. Hick, one might say, has continued Troeltsch's thought into the contemporary context where the need for a full recognition of the multi-faith nature of the world has become urgent and unavoidable.

In the case of the English theologian who has excited most controversy since 1980, Don Cupitt, the debt to the nineteenth century is overtly paid at many key points. Cupitt's rejection of 'realist' or 'objective' theism, in deference to a view of all God-language as symbolic and unifying of our own spiritual and moral ideals, is explicitly based on a reading of the post-Kantian situation, reinforced by such as Kierkegaard and Feuerbach, which denies the possibility of any knowledge of transcendence beyond our human subjectivity. Here is the logical end of subjective idealism: God is 'only human'.

On the other hand, by the same token, religious language and symbolism are being taken much more seriously by contemporary theology than was the case during the period, roughly speaking the 1960s, when secularization was the dominant theme. Based on a certain reading of Bonhoeffer's prison writings, particularly his emphasis on human autonomy or the 'coming of age' of the world, together with the sociological approach of such theologians as Harvey Cox in the United States and A. T. van Leeuwen on the Continent, 'secular theology' (often aided by the demythologizing programme set in motion by Rudolf Bultmann) saw a need for a stripping away of traditional symbolism and metaphor from Christian belief if the Gospel was to be re-appropriated by contemporary Western society. Paul van Buren's *The Secular Meaning of the Gospel* (1963) attempted to translate the Gospel entirely into a matter of the contagiousness of Jesus' life-for-others existence, on the grounds that such a translation accorded far more with contemporary empiricist understanding of reality. For secular theology, in order to preserve the reality of faith the language had to be drastically changed. By contrast, for much contemporary radical theology the reality lies precisely in the language – symbolically and metaphorically understood. Liturgy is less in need of modernizing, indeed, it may perform far less well its function of integrating and motivating life for spiritual values if it is denuded of mystery and symbolism. Does this mean that the secularization thesis was wrong, both as a description of what was happening in Western (and Western-dominated) society, and as a prescription for the biblical message for today? Certainly it is clear that 'religion' as a phenomenon is far from over, not only in the societies where radical Islam and other Eastern faiths are reasserting themselves, but also in the Western world where highly conservative and even fundamentalist forms of Christianity are increasingly powerful. In an important sense, however, at least one aspect of the secularization thesis – as far as Western society is concerned – is in fact borne out by these developments. This is, that no one religious authority now dominates society. Society is increasingly autonomous and self-directing. Or perhaps one should say that now there are increasingly autonomous societies within any one 'society', each pursuing a self-chosen life-style and set of values. The freedom of secularity includes among its options the freedom to be 'religious', which in turn can take a very conservative (that is, self-enclosed) form, especially given the appeal that such versions may have for people in an age of uncertainty, looking for strong, authoritarian leadership and clear sets of rules for daily living. Or, that freedom may be expressed in those who choose a religious and liturgical life with which to identify, not as denoting 'objective reality' but because it does indeed, in Cupitt's sense, provide them with a framework of unity, community and spiritual aspiration, a meaning that can be found nowhere else.

We may therefore once again cite Maurice Wiles as speaking for a whole generation of contemporary theology, as well as furthering his own particular argument for wishing to speak of God as spirit, when he writes:

> On the religious side the image needs supplementing by other symbols and images. The primary advantage that I have been claiming for the image of God is its fruitfulness as a co-ordinating concept at a comparatively formal level of understanding. It is . . . not without value in terms of material content for the articulation of faith also. But other images which are less comprehensive in the range of their

application may prove to have a far richer imaginative content for the furtherance of the life of faith.

(Wiles 1982: 125)

This conveys well what is essentially a pragmatic approach to the assessment of theological languages: their utility and fruitfulness 'for the furtherance of the life of faith'. It is this perception of the purpose of theology by contemporary liberal or radical theologians which sets them apart from conservatives and traditionalists, quite as much as any disagreements over the 'content' of belief.

One factor in the contemporary theological interest in the nature of the language of faith, has been the impact – if uneven – of the neo-orthodox theology associated particularly with Karl Barth and Emil Brunner in the mid-century, which if nothing else raised acutely the whole question of how, if at all, human language may speak about the transcendent God. That theology, in reaction to the dominant liberal trends preceding the First World War, manifested a determination to reassert the distinctiveness of the Christian tradition of revelation in Scripture, as interpreted in the classic creeds, while at the same time recognizing that if God is indeed 'wholly other' even in his self-revelation to humankind, a sheer reiteration of that tradition is inadequate. God is more than the words we use about God. A further factor in the contemporary theological scene is therefore a continuing attention to the Christian doctrinal tradition – as material to be interpreted for the present. Vital here has also been the continuing impact of the Second Vatican Council with its recognition of the dynamic, historical nature of revelation and of the need for continual examination of Scripture and tradition.

To be concerned with 'tradition' is not necessarily in itself therefore a sign of 'conservatism' or 'traditionalism'. This fact in itself is one sign that classification of current theology and theologies is far from straightforward. It is, however, a necessary exercise and a brief look at two recent attempts at such analysis, namely those of Dorothee Sölle and Hans Frei, is illuminating.

Dorothee Sölle: 'orthodox', 'liberal' and 'radical'

The German theologian Dorothee Sölle proposes that contemporary theology can broadly be classified according to three main paradigms: orthodox, liberal and radical (Sölle 1990). Orthodox, or 'right-believing', theology starts with the Bible and the dogmatic tradition as conveying revealed truth. It is essentially conservative both theologically and politically, being blind to its own cultural provisos. True, under the influence of Karl Barth Protestant orthodoxy, or neo-orthodoxy, enabled the German Confessing Church with the Barmen Declaration of 1934 to take a prophetic stand against the Nazification of Christianity. But aside from this particular historical context, orthodoxy – whether in its Protestant or Catholic, ancient or more recent forms – tends towards conservatism and indeed, at the present time, to fundamentalism.

The paradigm of orthodoxy was fundamentally shaken by the Enlightenment, and ever since has been in intellectual and cultural retreat.

Liberal theology, by contrast, accepted much of the understanding of the world opened by the Enlightenment, especially in the fields of natural science and historical study, and saw the need for belief to be expressed in ways which did not contradict such knowledge. Closely allied to its belief in the historicity of all religions, and its recognition that no one religion can claim absolute status of truth and authority, is the central value it places on tolerance, and, moreover, the separation of Church and state. Its weakness is that it has tended to accept too readily an identification of Christianity with a certain culture, and to leave politics to the politicians – with disastrous results when those politicians are dictators, as in Nazi Germany or certain countries of Latin America. Like orthodoxy, liberal theology is essentially a theology of and for the bourgeoisie, as seen in its individualism.

In contrast to both orthodox and liberal theologies, the theology of liberation begins in the experience of the poor, oppressed and marginalized people, especially in the Third World. 'For liberation theology, the one Word of God is the messianic praxis of Jesus and his followers' (Sölle 1990: 19), a praxis discovered through committed action by the poor themselves as they take steps for their own liberation from oppression. God is with and for the poor in his 'preferential option' for them.

Sölle's threefold analysis of the contemporary theological scene certainly corresponds to some broad perceptions at the popular level. There is indeed dispute between 'conservatives' and 'liberals' in Western Christian theological circles, and certainly a challenge is being felt from the perspective of doing 'theology from below', especially in Third World contexts. But the use of just three paradigms is somewhat too simplistic and does not do justice to the connections, interplay and dynamics in the contemporary theological scene. It implies, for instance, that all three approaches are mutually exclusive and self-sufficient, whereas, for example, there are many liberation theologians who are grateful for the historico-critical methods of liberal theology and equally for the interpretation of Scripture and tradition provided by 'orthodox' theology. Karl Barth has been read and utilized by radicals in South Africa as well as by conservative ecclesiastical restorationists in Europe. Where, on this analysis, would one place a theologian such as Jürgen Moltmann who has dealt deeply with the doctrinal, trinitarian tradition yet has also chosen the political and social context as the frame of reference for its interpretation, so creating a fruitful link between the two (as for example in the social model of the Trinity as counteractive to a hierarchical view both of God and of human society)? Or Wolfhart Pannenberg, who likewise stays firmly within the orthodox trinitarian tradition yet also sets his theology within a universal context of anthropology and history? Are such theologians conservatives, liberals or something else?

Moreover, an analysis of this kind itself reflects very much a Western,

Protestant approach with its implication that to be conservative, liberal or radical are options which one can select from a detached vantage point. But for some, to be attached to the tradition of doctrine is not so much an option as a fundamental feature of one's basic identity in faith within the confessional family. It is in effect the house one inhabits. The question then becomes that of one's relation to this tradition, whether it is to be one of unexamined acceptance, or of continual, critical reflection and interpretation. In the Roman Catholic Church, for example, the theological endeavour of Karl Rahner (1904–84) was 'to retrace, rethink and restate the truths Christians are called to believe' (Kelly 1992: 31) by rigorous study of 'the intricate nature of credal statements and his church's dogmatic pronouncements in their historical–critical setting and in their philosophical, anthropological and spiritual foundations', 'an articulation of what must be affirmed as perennial truth under the ever-changing garments of history, culture and language' (Kelly 1992: 32). To classify this theological vision as 'orthodox' because of its attachment to tradition would be insulting, if it means placing Rahner alongside fundamentalists. And to call him a liberal simply because of his affirmation of the necessity for free enquiry would be no less misleading. Similarly, space must be found in any scheme of classification for such a creative thinker from the Orthodox Church as John Zizioulas who identifies the crucial question lying between the Bible and Greek-based thought, from the patristic times to our own, as: 'How can a Christian hold to the idea that truth operates in history and creation when the ultimate character of truth, and its uniqueness, seem irreconcilable with the change and decay to which history and creation are subject?' (Zizioulas 1985: 70). To state the question in this way is to recognize, no less than the liberals do, the force of historicity. Yet, for Zizioulas, light on the question can be shed from Greek patristic thought itself. Rahner and Zizioulas both represent ways of looking at theology which defy conventional classification simply because they insist on keeping an open dialogue between the tradition and contemporary culture. A more revealing analysis would therefore attempt to analyse how various theologies in fact understand and work out this relationship between themselves and the wider intellectual, religious, cultural and social context.

Hans Frei: five types of theology

Hans Frei (1922–88) has proposed that any theology can be analysed in terms of how far it is first, an exercise in internal self-description by the Christian community, and second, a function of the wider and general religious or philosophical activity of its cultural context. By taking these two poles as possible reference-points, five main types of theology may be identified, both historically and in the present (Frei 1992).

First, theology may be considered simply to be a branch of philosophy, i.e. the emphasis falls entirely on the second pole to the exclusion of the first pole, above. The task of theology in the modern Western world of intellectual discourse, where ultimate meaning is searched for, is to explore and clarify the function of the term 'God'. Two such functions emerge: to indicate a limitation to the concept 'world', and to refer to the humanizing possibilities that can be brought to the world. This is the approach of a thinker such as Gordon Kaufman. 'The images or symbols of specific religious traditions become imaginative representations whose meaning is their paraphrasing . . . of the metaphysical, conceptual master construct' (Frei 1992: 29). If theology is an activity of the Christian community itself, then it has significance only as exemplifying this wider cultural–philosophical activity. In itself, it brings nothing that cannot be produced elsewhere. Christianity is one expression of a universal and inalienable human capacity or necessity, and like every other religion 'its message is a republication of the natural and universal quest', and theology is but part of a general intellectual–cultural enquiry. In some respects the radical subjectivism of contemporary British theologians such as Don Cupitt could be classified under this heading. Its basic assumption is that religious and theological discourse is one imaginative and symbolic way of expressing the universal spiritual quest and insights. Christianity and its theological expressions have no unique contribution to make to it.

Second, theology is seen as a philosophical discipline, but one within which Christianity does have a very specific contribution to make. Theology is therefore a kind of synthesis of external philosophical reflection and Christian self-description. The American David Tracy is a definitive contemporary example of this theological model which he formulates thus: 'Contemporary Christian theology is best understood as philosophical reflection upon the meanings present in common human experience and the meanings present in the Christian tradition.' Philosophical reflection upon experience points to limit-experiences of crisis and ecstasy in which the ordinary is transcended. The specifically Christian contribution is found in the parabolic language of the New Testament which discloses, in its own limit-language, that a certain way of being in the world, through faith and love, is possible. Theology therefore seeks certain correlations between the philosophically perceived generalities about human existence and the offers of particular possibilities disclosed in the Gospel. In a way, of course, this model has an honourable tradition – it can be seen as heir to the medieval synthesis of nature and grace, reason and faith, as well as to Paul Tillich's method of correlating culture's questions and Christianity's answers, or to Rudolf Bultmann's use of the existential philosophy of Martin Heidegger to describe the condition of human existence to which the New Testament makes the offer of authentic existence through the Gospel. A contemporary British exemplar of this model is John Macquarrie, who utilizes the phenomenological approach to uncover those features of human existence and experience within which discourse about God, grace, sin, sacraments etc. take on significance, and which in turn are further illuminated by the theological language. Many would wish to place

Wolfhart Pannenberg in this category in so far as he wishes to locate an exposition of the specifically Christian doctrinal tradition within a universal anthropological horizon of meaning, especially that of history.

For his third model Frei takes as the classic exemplar Friedrich Schleiermacher, for whom religion, centred on the inner emotion of the feeling of dependence, was entirely distinct from knowledge (whether scientific or metaphysical) and therefore for whom philosophy and theology were entirely autonomous. But though autonomous, theology and the disciplines of science, philosophy, history etc. require to be correlated to the extent that they need to be seen as at least compatible – for example, the theological understanding of miracle (as of God's activity in the world in general) has to be shown not to contradict the scientific understanding of the interconnectedness of natural cause and effect. Its contemporary counterpart is found in the widespread 'liberal' view that 'religion' and 'science' represent quite distinct yet equally legitimate understandings of the world. A particular affinity is found between Schleiermacher's understanding of providence as relating to our religious consciousness and Maurice Wiles's suggestion (see above) that God's action is recognized as that which evokes a personal response of commitment from us.

Fourth, more unequivocally than in any of the previous models, theology is a function of self-description by the believing Christian community, yet, in the responsible freedom of being true to the reality which it is setting forth, theology can and will utilize whatever philosophical, anthropological or other tools it perceives as appropriate – not according to any general theory or principle of knowledge but simply in accordance with the particular task in hand at any given moment. Here the great role-model is Karl Barth who, despite his rigorous diatribe against natural theology and all pretence that there exists any *a priori* point of departure for the knowledge of God in fallen human nature, recognized the need for theology, as rational discourse, to have a formal or technical philosophical vocabulary, and whose *Church Dogmatics* include dialogue with philosophers as much as other theologians. Philosophers no less than the apostles and prophets deal with humankind, God's elect creatures, and may at times be in line with the word of God, even serving the word of God, in their insights into human nature. The relation between internal Christian self-description and external philosophical and cultural discourse therefore remains *ad hoc* – almost one might say utilitarian, from the theological side. It is undoubtedly true that while the precise extent of Barth's direct influence since his death in 1968 is debatable, his legacy is still apparent in the confidence with which many in the present generation, both Catholics and Protestants, have been able to combine exposition of the Christian doctrinal tradition with deep and wide anthropological, cultural and political interest going far beyond the bounds of the purely ecclesiastical (cf. the work of e.g. Jürgen Moltmann, Hans Küng, T. F. Torrance, and J. Lochman).

Fifth and finally, Frei cites the British philosopher of religion D. Z. Phillips as exemplifying one for whom theology is not only autonomous, but a discipline from which philosophy is rigorously barred since Christian discourse can only be a matter of Christian self-description. 'God' cannot even be remotely 'understood' from outside the religious community of faith and discourse. A completely different logic applies to this reality, distinct from any other logic which philosophy may analyse. Theology is internal to religion, and religion and its rule of discourse are of a quite different order from all other activities involving knowledge-claims. Not only this, but it is not clear what place there can be even for theological reflection (as distinct from reassertion of first-order utterances of belief). As well as being a radical philosophical position, round the back it meets a kind of fundamentalist assertion that 'This is the truth' which brooks no argument or questioning. Here is where modern, open, pluralist society ironically sees one of its products in the autonomy of completely closed communities beset by internal conservatism and which, paradoxically, now have more freedom to be conservative if they so wish, than ever before.

Frei's analysis takes us further than Sölle's does into the dynamics of theology now, in its wider cultural and intellectual context. It does not, however, address what is for many today the crucial issue of that wider context: the world of different faiths. To talk about Christian theology's context being that of 'the West', and to talk about 'Western culture' as if it was a homogeneous entity is on the one hand to deny the worldwide, multicultural scope of present-day Christianity. It is also seriously to underestimate the multifaith nature even of 'the West' today. In the light of this, the first model may be extended to view the universal human quest for meaning as embracing that of all the non-Christian faiths as well. Christian theology is but one element in that wider religious quest – and it is that wider religious quest which should therefore be the real object of theology. In this respect the approaches of John Hick and Wilfred Cantwell Smith towards a 'global theology' would belong. This, however, is not the only option on offer. Gavin D'Costa argues that what is crucial is simply the recognition that the context for systematic theology today is now, for example, Hinduism and Buddhism, with their critical questions to the theistic tradition, as much as it has been natural science and atheistical thought in Europe for the past two centuries or more (D'Costa 1992: 332). This does not mean a direct attempt at an universal theology which all faiths can find acceptable, so much as establishing a dialogue where mutual encounter, including that of mutual criticism, becomes possible. This can be expected to be one of the critical debating points of 'theology now'.

THEOLOGY AS RELATED TO COMMUNAL IDENTITY-CONSCIOUSNESS

However, even such a wide-ranging and subtle analysis of theological types as the above fails to do justice to one of the most outstanding features of theology over the past two and a half decades, namely, the tendency for certain groups in society, marked by a realization of their marginalization, oppression or exploitation, to claim a specific perspective on, and a methodology for, theology. For such, the notion of theology as self-description by the Christian community has proved too general and abstract. The question has to be, which section or group within that 'community' has the most claim to be heard in its self-description? The answer is, those people who are struggling for justice, liberation or even simply recognition. It is those who are reflecting on their struggles, whose self-description of faith will be the most pertinent for the understanding of the Gospel at the present time. Three examples can be mentioned here, namely, black theology, liberation theology and feminist theology.

1 Black theology emerged in the later 1960s and 1970s in the United States, in the context of the civil rights and black power movements, which involved a challenge to white supremacist attitudes in the mainstream churches no less than in secular political and social life. Its central premise is summed up by one of its leading advocates, James Cone, thus:

> Christian theology is a theology of liberation. It is a rational study of the being of God in the world in the light of the existential situation of an oppressed community, relating the forces of liberation to the essence of the gospel, which is Jesus Christ.
> (Cone 1970: 17)

2 Liberation theology as a term originated in Latin America during the 1960s and 1970s in the context of the struggles of the poor from economic exploitation and dependence. Central to its thesis is that the poor are agents of their own liberation, which involves at root the liberation of their mind through 'conscientization' and the realization of new possibilities for their communities. This perspective leads to a fresh reading of the biblical witness, where 'liberation' has in the past all too often been spiritualized and privatized at the expense of its social, political and cultural dimensions.

3 Feminist theology, which largely arose in the United States at the end of the 1960s but is now a vital theological impulse in many parts of the world, is the project of criticizing and reconstructing the Christian theological tradition from the perspective of women, who have not only been to a great extent excluded from the leadership of the churches but whose experience has typically been ignored in doctrine, worship and theology generally.

The mutual affinities of such theologies are signalled by the rather slippery terminology and blurred lines of categorization. Thus black and feminist theologies often see themselves as cases of 'liberation theology' in general, where liberation is seen as the challenge of the Gospel to all forms of domination, whether of blacks by whites, poor and powerless by rich and powerful, or women by men. In turn, however, 'liberation' theology is sometimes used almost interchangeably with 'political theology', while in Southern

Africa the struggle for both racial and political equality has given rise to 'contextual theology' (most notably expressed in the *Kairos Document* of 1985). Equally, there can be particular combinations within the broader categories, as for example in black feminist theologies. What they all have in common is the negative social experience of a particular category of membership of church and society as a prior and essential ingredient in their critique of the prevailing theological tradition. This has led to the familiar accusation that such theologies are simply baptizing a fashionable sociological trend of the day with Christian terminology, and thereby seeking to justify a quest for power (in a way parallel to the attempts of earlier theologians to make a respectable marriage with a prevailing school of contemporary philosophy, idealism or existentialism for example, for the sake of acquiring respectability in the eyes of the world). Vital to these theologies, therefore, is their argument that within both Church and society an unjust power structure already exists, and that this already receives powerful legitimation, indeed sanctification, from much traditional theology: God has ordained the status quo for everyone's benefit, if not everyone's immediate happiness; the state is God's servant and always to be obeyed; men were created to rule (and of course look after) women; and so on. Crucial to all such theologies therefore is the exposure of how relationships of power actually operate in Church and society, between social and economic groups, races and the sexes. Directly or indirectly, they also draw on those sociologies of knowledge which, ever since Marx in the last century, and the Frankfurt School in this, have seen knowledge as sociologically determined. The argument that theologies of liberation are substituting sociology for theology is therefore countered by the claim that much conventional and traditional theology in the Church is already sociologically determined, contextualized and politicized – but in the interests of the dominant and powerful who disguise their control with a supposed 'neutrality' in socio-political matters.

Such theologies, as part of the process of strengthening the identity and support of the social group seeking liberation, characteristically seek a new historical identity as well. A new history of black, poor or women Christians is recovered, from within the Bible as well as from later tradition and Church history. 'Our heritage is our power.' This has been a particular, and controversial, feature of much feminist theology, for instance in Elisabeth Schüssler Fiorenza's reconstruction of the place of women within the biblical narratives (Fiorenza 1983).

Contemporary theology is thus marked by a particular set of cross-currents, which are not simply between 'liberal' and 'orthodox' theologies, as between quite different understandings of which features of the contemporary cultural context theology should relate to, or which intellectual endeavours it should be part of. As stated earlier, for much of the modern period, the issue has been of the relationship between theology and philosophy. Now, it is much more a matter of the relation between theology and socio–political analysis.

But the issue lies still deeper. What is emerging in the debates about black, liberation and feminist theology, is the question of who owns theology in the Christian community, and by whom and for whom it is to be done. Hitherto it has been assumed that it is an activity to be carried on in academic objectivity for the eventual enlightenment of the whole Christian community. But that, state the various theologians of liberation, is to beg the question of whether there ever can or should be such detached objectivity, since present claims for it in fact mask a concern for power of control both in Church and society. It is now half a century since Dietrich Bonhoeffer in his prison writings raised the question of 'who Christ is, for us today'. In so doing he released a new stream of discussion on an interpretation of Christ, God, the Church, ethics etc. which might be relevant for 'modern society'. Only relatively recently, however, has the significance of the 'for us' in his question been recognized. Does the 'us' refer to a generalized 'Western society', as much post-Bonhoeffer theologizing has assumed, not least the secular theology of the 1960s? Or does it refer much more specifically to those whom Bonhoeffer described as having seen 'the view from below', who have seen 'the great events of world history . . . from the perspective of the outcast, the suspects, the maltreated, the powerless, the oppressed, the reviled – in short, from the perspective of those who suffer' (Bonhoeffer 1971: 17). It may well be that only now is theology starting to appreciate the full depth of Bonhoeffer's question, with its implication that it is especially the marginalized, the alienated and the forgotten who have the title deeds to theology based on the suffering Christ.

LIMITS TO CONTEXTUALITY?

Contextuality, however, is unlikely by itself to be able to provide a totally secure anchorage for theology in the modern, or post-modern, age. In the first place, Christian theology springs not solely from a social context, but from the engagement of the scriptural and doctrinal tradition with the questions and challenges of the context. That is well understood by liberation theologians such as Gustavo Gutiérrez, Jose Miguez-Bonino and Clodovis Boff, and by feminist theologians like Elisabeth Schüssler Fiorenza and Rosemary Radford Ruether – provided of course debate is allowed on precisely what 'the tradition' is! But it is also the case that 'context' itself always has to be held open to examination. In certain important respects, liberation or contextual theology shares the critical stance of the Marxist or post-Marxist 'hermeneutics of suspicion': claims to absolute truth harbour agendas of social control and dominance (or, at least, defensive self-justification) and should therefore be exposed for what they are. However, once the dynamics of suspicion are set in play, who is to say when they should be halted? Revolutions have a habit of being devoured by their own children. Should liberation, contextual and feminist theologies themselves be beyond suspicion in this respect? Have they identified their 'context' accurately enough – and who is to be arbiter on this question? As a black South African theologian, Itumeleng Mosala, observes in a critical comment on self-styled 'contextual theology': '[All] theology is contextual theology. The real question is . . . what is the socio-political context out of which a particular theology emerges and which it serves' (Mosala 1985: 103f.). That question has to be put even to those theologies claiming to be 'from below' in their perspective. No such claims can enjoy immunity from inspection. While indeed they are consciously seeking to speak from a certain context, other contextual elements apart from those of which they are aware may also be at work. European and North American 'radicals' may, to their Third World readers, appear to be European and North American in their presuppositions at least as much as 'siding with the oppressed'.

There is a clear danger in the emphasis on the contextual, of Christian theology committing itself to a process of fragmentation, resulting in a multiplicity of peculiar theologies unable to communicate with each other, and each tending to claim the absoluteness of the significance of its contextual and cultural setting over all others. This danger is being clearly recognized in current ecumenical theology where, precisely because of the global and international (as well as inter-confessional) nature of ecumenical relationships, the diversity of expression of Christian belief is becoming starkly apparent. This emerged clearly at the Seventh Assembly of the World Council of Churches in Canberra, Australia, in 1991 (see WCC 1991). There, the claims by some Third World theologians that the Gospel must be radically inculturated in the thought-forms of particular contexts – including the forms of traditional indigenous religions – provoked strong reactions from more conservative Western Protestants as well as Orthodox representatives. It was in particular the Korean theologian Chung Hyun Kyung who sparked controversy. Concluding her presentation on the Holy Spirit, she stated:

> For me the image of the Holy Spirit comes from the image of *Kwan In*. She is venerated as the goddess of compassion and wisdom by East Asian women's popular religiosity. She is a *bodhissattva*, enlightened being. She can go into nirvana any time she wants to, but refuses to go into nirvana by herself. Her compassion for all suffering beings makes her stay in this world enabling other living beings to achieve enlightenment. Her compassionate wisdom heals all forms of life and empowers them to swim to the shore of nirvana. She waits and waits until the whole universe, people, trees, birds, mountains, air, water, become enlightened. They can then go to nirvana together where they can live collectively in eternal wisdom and compassion. Perhaps this might also be a feminine image of the Christ who is the first-born among us, one who goes before and brings others with her.

(WCC 1991: 46)

This passage focuses, as few others could, one of the critical challenges of contemporary theology, set as it is in the context of global pluralism on the one hand, while acting as trustee for the particularity of the Christian tradition on the other.

Within ecumenism, the issue is also becoming central within the Faith and

Order movement in particular. As one recent ecumenical study document states:

> Diversity used to be considered acceptable and containable because there was a universal framework of theological understanding acknowledged by the whole Church. Now the universal framework itself is under radical attack. In the absence of clarity about what is to be believed 'at all times, everywhere, and by all' (Vincent of Lerins), local variety looks quite different and raises questions which cause great difficulty.
>
> (WCC 1993a: 19)

At the Fifth World Conference on Faith and Order at Santiago de Compostela, Spain, in 1993 the relationship of diversity to unity in the faith, the boundaries between legitimate and illegitimate diversity, the relation between the Gospel and different cultures, were all recognized to be crucial challenges of the hour (see WCC 1993b). The extent to which the contextual tide will run should not, however, be exaggerated in advance. Even when it comes to speaking on social issues, which one would imagine would encourage the greatest possible contextual perspective in different regions of the world, there is a surprising degree of consensus irrespective of geographical and cultural location (Ellingsen 1993: 20).

Questions about the unity of Christian belief, and the essence around which that unity coheres, are therefore as much a part of contemporary theological debate as they were in previous generations. The theological debate, however, has generated a new question: just how important is theology itself, for defining the acceptable limits of belief in the Christian community? Or, put another way, is doctrinal and theological precision the only means by which the integrity of the believing community can be assured? In part, the question has emerged (or re-emerged) in the last quarter-century because of the resurgence in Western Christianity of a new interest in spirituality, or what is traditionally called in Orthodox circles *mystical theology*. This puts a premium on prayer rather than on theological formulation, on an integrated wholeness of living rather than exact intellectual consistency and uniformity of belief. An Anglican theologian, Stephen Sykes, has challenged the assumed rights of theology, by itself, to determine the boundaries of the community and its unifying beliefs, and indeed suggests that conflict is necessarily inherent within the Christian tradition. 'Christians do discuss their doctrines, and they must do so in a sensitive way; but Christianity is also a community of worshippers, and this fact makes for a decisive difference' (Sykes 1984: 261). It is worship, rather than theology or doctrine, which is the crucial organizational context for the community.

> Rituals . . . have the function of restoring a system of meaning by constant repetition and committal to memory, and by the reabsorption of individuals into the common fabric. They are the counterpoint to the detachment of rational thought, and are the appropriate means for the expression of profound commitment.
>
> (ibid.: 281)

This is by no means to detract from the task of theology which, like any human enterprise, fails if it attempts just too much.

It is in fact at this point that, for all the conflicts and divergences, one can detect a significant convergence in theology now. Theology is perhaps more aware than ever before of the metaphorical and parabolic nature of its language. The recovery of orthodoxy as right-worship rather than simply right-believing (*pace* Sölle, above), and the liberation theologians' emphasis upon ortho-praxis (right-doing), have both contributed to this new perspective. So too, from otherwise contrasting approaches, has the neo-orthodox stress on the transcendence of God on the one hand, and the radical 'non-realist' view of the symbolic nature of religious language on the other. 'The time when people could be told everything by means of words, whether theological or pious, is over . . .' (Bonhoeffer 1971: 279). Theology has always been wont to quote poetry. If earlier generations had a fondness for Robert Browning and Francis Thompson, it is perhaps still T. S. Eliot who expresses the hope no less than the frustrations of theology now:

> Words strain,
> Crack and sometimes break, under the burden,
> Under the tension, slip, slide, perish,
> Will not stay still.

CONCLUSION

Theology now is at least as alive as in any previous decade – or century. As always, it is engendering debate and controversy, especially between those on the one hand who see the prime responsibility of theology to preserve intact the cohesion of the received tradition, and those on the other who perceive the necessity of bringing that tradition into engagement with the contemporary context of thought and culture. But this latter approach itself breeds vital differences within itself. There are those who see the most important 'culture' as that of contemporary philosophy, others the multi-faith world of the global village. For others, it is in the particular contextuality of socio-economic, racial or sexual oppression and the struggles for liberation from these, which define the wider locus of theology. Whether this degree of diversity can, or should, be seen as contributing to a creative tension within an ultimate unity of aim in theology, or whether there are irreconcilable divergences, is perhaps the most serious challenge of theology now as it looks towards its future.

REFERENCES

Barth, K. (1936–69) *Church Dogmatics*, Edinburgh: T. & T. Clark.
Bonhoeffer, D. (1971) *Letters and Papers From Prison*, London: SCM Press.
Cone, J. (1970) *A Black Theology of Liberation*, Philadelphia: Lippincott.
Cupitt, D. (1980) *Taking Leave of God*, London: SCM Press.
—— (1985) *Only Human*, London: SCM Press.

D'Costa, G. (1992) 'The End of Systematic Theology', *Theology* XCV: 324–34.
Ellingsen, M. (1993) *The Cutting Edge: How Churches Speak on Social Issues*, Geneva: WCC Publications and Grand Rapids, Mich.: Eerdmans.
Fiorenza, E. Schüssler (1983) *In Memory of Her: A Feminist Theological Reconstruction of Christian Origins*, London: SCM Press.
Frei, H. W. (1992) *Types of Christian Theology*, Yale and London: Yale University Press.
Gore, C. (ed.) (1889) *Lux Mundi*, London: John Murray.
Hick, J. 1973) *God and the Universe of Faiths*, London: Macmillan.
—— (ed.) (1977) *The Myth of God Incarnate*, London: SCM Press.
The Kairos Theologians (1985) *The Kairos Document: Challenge to the Church*, London: Catholic Institute for International Relations and British Council of Churches.
Kelly, G. (1992) *Karl Rahner: Theologian of the Graced Search for Meaning*, Minneapolis: Fortress Press.
Mosala, I. (1985) 'African Independent Churches: A Study in Sociological Protest', in C. Villa-Vicencio and J. de Guchy (eds) *Resistance and Hope: South African essays in honour of Beyers Naudé*, Cape Town: David Philip, and Grand Rapids, Mich.: Eerdmans.
Sölle, D. (1990) *Thinking About God: An Introduction to Theology*, London: SCM Press.
Sykes, S. (1984) *The Identity of Christianity*, London: SPCK.
Van Buren, P. (1963) *The Secular Meaning of the Gospel*, London: SCM Press.
WCC [World Council of Churches] (1991) *Signs of the spirit: Official Report of the Seventh Assembly*, (ed.) M. Kinnamon, Geneva: WCC Publications, and Grand Rapids, Mich.: Eerdmans.
—— (1993a) *Costly Unity*, Geneva: WCC.
—— (1993b) *Fifth World Conference on Faith and Order: Message, Section Reports, Discussion Document*, Geneva: WCC Publications.
Wiles, M. (1982) *Faith and The Mystery of God*, London: SCM Press.
Zizioulas, J. D. (1985) *Being as Communion: Studies in Personhood and the Church*, London: Darton, Longman and Todd.

FURTHER READING

Clements, K. W. (1988) *Lovers of Discord: Twentieth Century Theological Controversies in England*, London: SPCK.
Coakley, S. (1988) *Christ Without Absolutes: A Study of the Christology of Ernst Troeltsch*, Oxford: Clarendon Press.
Edwards, D. L. (1989) *Tradition and Truth: A Critical Examination of England's Radical Theologians 1962–1989*, London: Hodder & Stoughton.
McFague, S. (1987) *Models of God: Theology for an Ecological, Nuclear Age*, Philadelphia: Fortress Press.
Macquarrie, J. (1990) *Jesus Christ in Modern Thought*, London: SCM Press.
Russell, L. M. (1993) *Church in the Round: Feminist Interpretation of the Church*, Louisville: Westminster Press.
Schillebeeckx, E. (1980) *Christ: The Christian Experience in the Modern World*, London: SCM Press.
See also chapters 13, 15, 29, 41, 45, 46, 47, 48.

15

CHRISTIAN THEOLOGY AND OTHER FAITHS

Gavin D'Costa

In the modern world Christians cannot ignore the existence of other religions. Global communications, extensive travel, migration, colonialism, and international trade are all factors that have brought the religions closer to each other in both destructive and creative ways. While statistics are difficult to interpret and their accuracy is open to question, the changing situation is clearly depicted in a comparison between 1491 and 1991. In 1491 roughly 19 per cent of the world's population was Christian and while 2 per cent of the non-Christian world was in contact with Christianity, 79 per cent remained entirely ignorant of its existence. Some 93 per cent of all Christians were white Europeans. Compare these figures with 1991 where 33 per cent of the global population were Christians, with 44 per cent of the non-Christian world being aware of Christianity, while only 23 per cent had no contact with Christians and the Gospel. The ethnic basis of Christianity has also radically shifted so that from a position of white European dominance, the largest Christian community is now to be found in Latin America, followed by Europe, with Africa third (and growing much faster than Europe), followed by North America and then South Asia. Statistically, the majority of Christians are non-European although it would still be fair to say that the power base of most mainline Christian communities lies within the European orbit.

To complement this overview, it will be helpful to survey briefly the figures for 1991 regarding the numerical strengths of world religions. After Christians (roughly 1 billion), Muslims are the largest religious group (962 million), followed by Hindus (721 million), with Buddhists forming less than half the number of Hindus (327 million). New religions, notoriously difficult to classify, number some 119 million, followed by another amorphous classification, tribal religions which constitute roughly 99 million. Finally, and in Western consciousness far more prominent, come Sikhs with nearly 19 million and Jews, with nearly 18 million (Barrett 1991: 72–3).

From these statistics it is safe to say two things. First, Christians cannot ignore the existence of other religions. Second, with the awareness of their existence a host of theological, philosophical, methodological and practical questions are raised. Should, for example, Buddhist meditation groups be allowed the use of church halls?; how should religious education be taught?; what kind of social and political co-operation or opposition is appropriate with people of other faiths? There are also fundamental theological issues at stake. If salvation is possible outside Christ/Christianity, is the uniqueness of Christ and the universal mission of the Church called into question? Or if salvation is not possible outside Christ/Christianity, is it credible that a loving God would consign the majority of humankind to perdition, often through no fault of their own? Can Christians learn from other faiths? Can they be enriched rather than diluted or polluted from this encounter? Clearly, other religions in varying degrees have also undergone their own self-questioning in the light of religious pluralism, but that is altogether another subject. (See for example: Jung *et al.* 1963; McKain 1964; Coward 1985; Hick and Askari 1985; D'Costa 1988; Küng & Moltmann 1990; Griffiths 1991; Braybrooke 1992; Cohn-Sherbok 1992).

There have been many different Christian responses to the world religions in the modern age. Equally, there are many different motives behind these attitudes involving theological, political, social and economic factors. For Christians living in the twentieth century there is also the recent history of colonialism and imperialism in which many large parts of the non-Christian world have been subjugated by white Christian powers. The history of internal carnage is equally shocking: two world wars, and the destruction of nearly a third of Jewry within a culture deeply nourished by Christianity. This chequered history has caused a crisis in confidence both within Christianity and also in its relation to world faiths.

No set of categories is adequate to analyse and deal with the complexity of the topic, but it may help to label three types of theological response to other religions for heuristic purposes. There are, of course, considerable differences between theologians belonging to the same 'camp' and many features of overlap between different approaches. I shall use the following terms for these approaches:

1 Pluralism = all religions are equal and valid paths to the one divine reality and Christ is one revelation among many equally important revelations.
2 Exclusivism = only those who hear the Gospel proclaimed and explicitly confess Christ are saved.
3 Inclusivism = Christ is the normative revelation of God, although salvation is possible outside of the explicit Christian Church, but this salvation is always from Christ.

Various presuppositions undergird each approach, often revolving around christology and the doctrine of God and the doctrine of human beings.

A GENERAL THEOLOGY OF RELIGIONS

1 Pluralism

Pluralist theologies have been developed most forcefully in the modern period, although traces are present in earlier Christian history. There are important differences among pluralists. Some argue that all religions have a common core or essence that can be historically identified, often within the mystical traditions of the world religions (see for example Radhakrishnan 1927; Huxley 1945; James 1977). A variation on this argument is that a straightforward historical comparison of the religions will not show this common essence, but rather within the different traditions the 'esoteric' believers who have penetrated in depth their own tradition will discover the non-duality of God and the soul, a unity that transcends all formulations. 'Exoteric' believers, on the other hand, absolutize their symbols and creeds and fail to penetrate to the transcendent unity of religions. To exoteric believers Christ and/or the Church become the only way to salvation (Schuon 1975). Another form of pluralism begins from a consideration of historical relativity and it is argued that all traditions are relative and cannot claim superiority over other equally limited and relative ways to salvation (Toynbee 1957; Troeltsch 1972). A variation of this is the argument that while the histories of religions are diverse, the common element in all is 'faith' in the transcendent (Smith 1978). Yet again, others argue that all religions have important and substantial historical differences and the view of a common essence is in danger of compromising the integrity of each particular tradition by emphasizing only one aspect of that tradition. The real unity of religions is found not in doctrine or mystical experiences but in the common experience of salvation or liberation. Some (Knitter 1985, 1987a, 1987b; Pieris 1989) develop this insight in dialogue with liberation theology. Others, such as John Hick, have developed their position in dialogue with traditional Western philosophy. It will be instructive to look in detail at John Hick, who combines strengths of all the above approaches while trying to avoid their weaknesses.

Initially, Hick argued that the *solus Christus* assumption (that salvation is only through Christ) held by exclusivists is incompatible with the Christian teaching of a God who desires to save all people. There are many millions who have never heard of Christ through no fault of their own, before and after New Testament times – the invincibly ignorant. So it is therefore un-Christian to think that God would have 'ordained that men must be saved in such a way that only a small minority can in fact receive this salvation' (Hick 1977: 122). Hick therefore proposed a theocentric revolution away from a Christocentric or ecclesiocentric position that has dominated Christian history. Hence, it is God, and not Christianity or Christ, towards whom all religions move, and from whom they gain their salvific efficacy. He argued that the doctrine of the incarnation should be understood mythically – as an expression of devotion and commitment by Christians, not as an ontological claim that here and here alone God has been fully revealed (ibid.: 165–79). Hick stressed the doctrine of an all-loving God over that of the *solus Christus* principle.

An important recent development in Hick's position came in response to the criticism that his theological revolution was still theocentric and thereby excluded non-theistic religions. I have noted these developments within Hick's position as they indicate the kind of issues and problems encountered by a full-blown pluralism. Hick, in response to these criticisms, makes a Kantian-type distinction between a divine noumenal reality 'that exists independently and outside man's perception of it' which he calls the 'Eternal One', and the phenomenal world, 'which is that world as it appears to our human conscious-ness', in effect, the various human responses to the Eternal One (Hick 1988: 233–52). These responses are then seen as both theistic and non-theistic (e.g. God, Allah, Nirvana, Brahman). In this way Hick tries to overcome any underlying theistic essentialism.

The above arguments cumulatively suggest that Christians can fruitfully view the history of religions as a history of God's/the Eternal One's activity without making any special claims for Christianity. Christian attitudes to other religions need not be characterized by a desire to convert, or claims to superiority, but a will to learn and grow together towards the truth. Mission should be jointly carried out to the secular world by the religions, rather than towards each other. Hick suggests that exclusivism and inclusivism cannot provide such fruitful conditions for inter-religious dialogue.

There have been a number of objections to Hick's thesis, some of which indicate more general problems with pluralism. (For critical debate on Hick, see D'Costa 1986: 22–51; 1987; Carruthers 1990; Loughlin 1990, 1991; and Hick responding to his critics in Hick 1990, 1991.) First, there are objections to the way in which the centrality of Christ within Christianity seems to be bypassed. It is argued that Hick's initial theocentric revolution is based on a shaky premise. He rejects the *solus Christus* for he thinks it leads to the *a priori* damnation of non-Christians. Theologically, this is not necessarily the case as we shall see in the outlines of exclusivism and inclusivism below. Furthermore, when Hick proposes a theocentric revolution away from Christocentricism he is in danger of severing christology from ontology and introducing a free-floating God divorced from any particular revelation. The theistic religions, including Christianity, centre on revelatory paradigms for their discourse and practice. Hick's theocentricism pays little attention to the importance of historical particularity. In fact, the theological basis of his proposal (that of an all-loving God) is undermined if Hick cannot give normative ontological status to the revelatory event upon which this axiom is grounded – originally for Hick, that of the revelation of God in Christ. Christology is important precisely because it is through Jesus that Christians claim that God has revealed himself in a unique (although not necessarily exclusive) manner. A theocentricism without a Christocentricism is in danger of leading towards a reductionist abstract common denominator God. Pluralist approaches are in danger of relativizing or denigrating particularity, so central to the historical religions. Hick's response to this type of criticism is to note that an all-loving God is to be found in many religions such as Judaism, Christianity, Islam and Hinduism and is not solely based on Christian revelation. Furthermore, within Christianity (as with the others cited) there have been periods when 'God' was understood as a tyrant, a cruel and vengeful ruler, a favourer of only men, and so on. Hence, it cannot be claimed that the God of love stands commandingly and unclouded in these religions or in Christianity alone. Rather, the discerning pluralist must recognize and affirm what is best within each religion.

Another objection to pluralist theologies concerns the doctrine of God. In Hick's context, this relates to his attempt to overcome his initial theistic bias. If the meaning of 'God' lacked specificity in Hick's theocentrism, it seems further relativized in his more recent works for 'God' is seen as one aspect of the 'Eternal One' that apparently can also be characterized by opposite non-theistic predicates. As all such predicates are from the human side they are thereby not properly applicable to the Eternal One. Hence, 'God' cannot be said to be personal or loving in a proper ontological sense. The Kantian noumenon encountered a similar problem in not providing for a correspondence between phenomena and things-in-themselves. Hick seems to be close to a transcendental agnosticism (i.e. affirming a transcendence without any qualities). Despite his stress on soteriocentrism, the liberated life-style, can he properly address the question of the nature of God/the Eternal One who actually saves and liberates people, or is his doctrine of 'God' in danger of avoiding all particularities so as to accommodate every particularity? Again, Hick's response is along the lines of that we can never properly describe the Eternal One 'in himself', only in 'relation to us'. Clearly, the outcome of these debates remain unresolved, but such questions highlight the theological centrality of christology and the doctrine of God in the discussion about other faiths.

Hick's philosophical approach to religious pluralism could be contrasted with the very pragmatic approach taken by those deeply influenced by liberation theology, such as Paul Knitter. Knitter does not begin with any assumption of commonality, thereby overcoming the danger of essentialism and foundationalism. Rather, he argues that all religions are to be judged as to their truthfulness, their real responsiveness to God, in so much as they promote the 'kingdom'. The kingdom is a life-style characterized by justice, peace, and goodness in both personal relations and social and economic structures. Hence, when religions promote the oppression of women in whatever way, they are to be judged as being against the kingdom. When they tackle the marginalization and exploitation of the poor and weak they promote the kingdom and in this context can be seen to be responding to the one true God. Hence, no religion is better than another except by these criteria, and under these criteria they are all in need of reform and mutual help (Knitter 1987b).

Knitter's attempt to bypass problems of Christocentricism, theocentricism and ecclesiocentricism are admirably motivated by a desire for justice and righteousness. However, critics have argued that Knitter cannot really address the question of liberation without the categories of Christ, God and the Church (Küng 1986: 123; D'Costa 1990b; Milbank 1990). It is precisely in Christ and the trinitarian revelation therein, that the decisive meaning of liberation is to be found. The further Knitter tries to get away from such specification the closer he gets to another but unstated set of assumptions. From where does he derive the meaning of 'kingdom'? Why should such a meaning be privileged and exalted above all religions and used as a judge of them? Is this not a form of liberal imperialism? ('kingdom' is a favourite category in liberal Christian thought.) And is Knitter not in danger of simply promoting a vague meaning of liberation which has no real cutting edge as it is not grounded in the praxis of any real community, but in a reified ideal type? From a more Protestant angle, Knitter's vision has been criticized as a betrayal of the *sola fide* principle and an implicit adoption of salvation by works, for he assumes that works and human action are determinative for salvation. Knitter responds that his is an 'imperialism' with the poor and disempowered on its side and he is emphatic that within all religions there are resources that support such a vision. (See also Küng and Moltmann 1986; Pieris 1989; Braybrooke 1992; Cohn-Sherbok 1992 for further exploration of this type of approach.) Clearly, within this political perspective, one can see a role for a type of feminist theology of religions which focuses specifically on the question of the liberation of women within the world religions – and such an approach is open to the same kinds of question as those posed to Knitter (see Sharma 1987; O'Neill 1990).

What is clear is that the debate is far from resolved, but what is also clear is that at the heart of the debate lie questions regarding the nature of the Church, Christ, God and humankind. All these factors are construed quite differently in exclusivism.

2 Exclusivism

The rape of cultures and civilizations has often been justified in the name of Christianity armed with an exclusivist missionary theology (Morris 1973). Furthermore, racism and colonial imperialism are often closely identified with Christian mission. While this aspect cannot be ignored, it also needs to be said that some scholars have argued that much missionary work was not pursued in tandem with empire building, but actually resisted it (Stanley 1990), and others have defended the rich cultural contributions made by missionaries and criticized the 'Western guilt complex' in relation to mission work (Sanneh 1987).

I have highlighted these issues to show the ways in which theological attitudes have often been translated into practice. Nevertheless, there are serious theological issues underlying exclusivism. The exclusivist position (most often found in Lutheran and Calvinist circles) is fundamentally concerned to affirm two central insights. The first is that God has sent his Son, Jesus Christ, to bring salvation into the world and that this salvation is both judgement and mercy to all human beings who are deeply estranged from God. Second, this salvation won by Christ is only available through explicit faith in Christ which comes from hearing the Gospel preached (*fides ex auditu*) and requires repentance, baptism and the embracing of a new life in Christ. Concerning the first principle, most exclusivists regard human nature as fallen and sinful. Hence, men and women are only capable of idolatry, for all their attempts to reach God are precisely that: human attempts at capturing the living God (Barth 1970: s.17). Herein lies the judgement of God upon all acts of idolatry for all human actions ultimately, subtly and not so subtly, usurp God's power in disclosing to themselves gods of their own making. Human beings in their best moments are capable of great wonder, art, discipline, and even intellectual speculation about the divine. However, all these are the products of fallen persons, who in their very attempt to reach out and upwards, compound their own situation for they blind themselves to the way in which God has reached down and inward to humanity in the person of Christ in a totally gratuitous act. In fact, the extent of sinfulness is such that human beings are incapable of truly recognizing their own situation of radical fallenness and it is only in the light of Christ that sin is seen most clearly and fully for what it really is (Barth 1956: s.60).

Given the predicament of humankind, the logic of this theology requires that salvation is a freely received gift which is offered to men and women through no merit of their own. Humans certainly do not deserve salvation, but God in his infinite mercy comes to fallen and sinful men and women. Rather than be indignant at God's particularity, as is the pluralist, the exclusivist theologian is instead awed and grateful at God's graciousness. His mercy and redemption are not something merited and they are also universal in import, so that the exclusivist can only humbly proclaim this truth rather than question it. The *sola fide* principle is paramount, for anything less compromises the incarnation and atonement and God's salvific action towards his creatures (Lindsell 1949; Fernando 1987). The sensitive exclusivist does not wish that all non-Christians be lost, but rather simply proclaims that the heart of the Christian message requires that *sola fide* be maintained. In response to the 'problem' of non-Christians, many an exclusivist will emphasize the urgency and necessity of world-wide evangelization, rather than spend time and energy on improper speculation about the possibility of salvation occurring in the non-Christian religions. However, the salvation of all non-Christians is addressed in the following statement taken from the proclamation of the Chicago Congress on World Mission in 1960:

In the years since the war, more than one billion souls have passed into eternity and more than half of these went to the torment of hell fire without even hearing of Jesus Christ, who He was, or why He died on the cross of Calvary.
(Percy 1961: 9; see also Frankfurt Declaration 1970; Lausanne Statement 1975)

This type of exclusivism faces a number of theological objections. First, Hick has criticized this position for being incompatible with the God of love disclosed at the heart of Christianity. Quoting the statement of the Congress on World Mission (see above), Hick argues that such an outcome is theologically unacceptable especially when one considers the invincibly ignorant (Hick 1977: 121–2). There are two important points in the exclusivist response. First, for some exclusivists Hick presumes too much in questioning the ways of God as being unjust! Rather, given human sinfulness, we should start from being amazed that God saves anyone at all. Clearly, here the issue concerns human nature. Second, a number of exclusivists have taken seriously the problem of those who through no fault of their own have never heard the Gospel. This group is increasingly large among exclusivists and a number of strategies is employed regarding the invincibly ignorant. The first is to suggest that we cannot know the fate of non-Christians and must simply trust in the mercy and justice of God (Newbigin 1981: 20; Stott 1988: 327). Hence, such exclusivists are willing to acknowledge that salvation may be offered to the invincibly ignorant, although they refuse to speculate further about how this will happen. Second, some have gone further and suggested that there will be a 'time' after death in which the non-Christian may come to faith in Christ. Perhaps the boldest and most carefully spelt out proposal comes from a Roman Catholic theologian who utilizes the doctrine of purgatory to allow for this possibility (DiNoia 1992). DiNoia develops critically the theological insights of his mentor, Lindbeck (1984; see also Pinnock 1976). A third and somewhat novel strategy has been suggested whereby reincarnation is posited to solve the problem so that the invincibly ignorant will have a chance to hear the Gospel at least once before they 'properly' die (Jathanna 1981). These responses go some way to address the prime weakness regarding the invincibly ignorant, although further criticisms may follow regarding the specific options outlined or regarding other theological tenets within exclusivism. It is to the latter we turn now.

Another criticism aimed at exclusivists is that grace, within the Christian tradition, is not limited purely to an explicit confrontation with Christ (D'Costa 1986: 52–79). This contention is based on a number of arguments. In traditional Christian theology, Judaism up to the time of Christ was certainly accorded revelatory status. Hence, a Christian exclusivist who denied any revelation outside Christ would be hard-pressed to explain the use of the Old Testament as part of Christian Scripture. In fact, Marcion (second century) was deemed heretical for just such an exclusion of the Old Testament. Besides the history of Israel testifying to salvific grace outside the particular event of the historical Jesus, there are also a number of passages within the

New Testament that highlight the importance of right living. If for instance, a person's courageous self-sacrificing love is due to certain demands within his or her religion, can these acts of responding to grace be divorced from the mediators of such grace? Or, can the humanist's self-sacrificial love for another, so powerfully portrayed in Camus' *The Plague*, have nothing to do with Jesus' implied teaching that 'as you did it to one of the least of my brethren, you did it to me' (Matt. 25:40)?

The exclusivist may respond in a number of ways. First, by pointing out that the revelation Israel received was always directed towards Christ and was not properly salvific. Hence, the real question here is whether implicit faith in Christ is sufficient for salvation. Furthermore, if salvific grace is available through creation and history, apart from explicit faith, does this not call into question the necessity of Jesus Christ for salvation? Exclusivists are also likely to suggest that any resort to argument from virtuous actions is to depart from the *sola fide* principle, and concede to Pelagianism. Clearly, the arguments have no clear-cut conclusion, but again we find the central questions revolving around christology, God, human nature and the Church. We will find that this is true of the final position to which we now turn, and here again there is a differing construal of these central issues.

3 Inclusivism

Inclusivism has a venerable pedigree in the Christian tradition. Quite a number of Roman Catholics share this approach with varying differences. The main concern of inclusivists is to balance the two central axioms in this debate: *solus Christus* and the universal salvific will of God. Many maintain that while Christ brings salvation into the world, God's grace is not absent in his creation and in history. However, the various intimations of God's grace find their source and completion in grace made flesh: in the incarnation of Jesus Christ. Hence, inclusivism has often been related to theologies of fulfilment, drawing on the ancient tradition of a *praeparatio evangelica*. The main division within inclusivism is between those who argue that the grace of Christ is available within the non-Christian religions and therefore the non-Christian religions have a certain salvific status (Rahner 1966), and those who argue that while the grace of Christ is available to non-Christians, one cannot confidently attribute the mediation of this grace to the non-Christian religions (van Straelen 1966; Ruokanen 1992). Within Catholic circles, both these groups claim the support of Vatican II for their position, and this indicates the ambivalent nature of the main document of that council on other religions: *Nostra Aetate* (1963). However, both groups are united in affirming that Christ's saving grace is available to the invincibly ignorant and therefore question a rigorous and literalist application of the ancient axiom: 'no salvation outside the Church' (*extra ecclesiam nulla salus*) (see D'Costa 1990a). It is a well-known irony that Fr Leonard Feeney SJ was excommunicated from the

Catholic Church in the mid-1950s for teaching that there was no salvation outside the Catholic Church.

Karl Rahner, a German Jesuit, is probably the most influential inclusivist theologian of the twentieth century. Rahner's theological anthropology shapes his form of inclusivism. He argues that the precondition of finite (categorial) knowledge is an unconditional openness to being (*Vorgriff*), which is an unthematic, pre-reflective awareness of God – who is infinite being. Our transcendental openness to being constitutes the hiddenness of grace. Men and women therefore search in history for a categorial disclosure of this hidden grace. In Jesus' total abandonment to God, his total 'Yes' through his life, death and resurrection, he is established as the culmination and prime mediator of grace. Therefore Christian revelation is the explicit expression of grace which men and women experience implicitly in the depths of their being when, for example, they reach out through the power of grace in trusting love and self-sacrifice, or in acts of hope and charity.

Rahner (1966, 1978) attempts to balance the *solus Christus* principle with that regarding the universal salvific will of God, so as to maintain that Christ is the sole cause of salvation in the world, but that this salvific grace may be mediated within history without an explicit confrontation with Christ. Such is the case with the history of Israel. If with Israel, may it not in principle be the case with other religions of the world? Rahner argues that christology and the doctrine of God should not be separated from the Church in which they are found, and Rahner therefore maintains that Christ is historically mediated through the Church. This means that Rahner must reconcile membership of the the Church as a means of salvation and the possibility that salvific grace is mediated outside the historically tangible borders of the Church. He does this along the lines of the traditional Catholic teachings regarding the *votum ecclesiae* (a wish to belong to the Church), and the related notion of implicit desire. (See the beginnings of Rahner's thought on this matter in relation to Pius XII's *Mystici Corporis Christi*: Rahner 1963: 1–89).

Rahner argues that if salvific grace exists outside the visible Church, as he believes it does in the history of Israel, and in creation and through conscience, then this grace is causally related both to Christ (always and everywhere – as prime mediator) and to his Church. Furthermore, given the socio-historical nature of men and women, grace must be mediated historically and socially. The incarnation is paradigmatic in suggesting this. Hence, if and when non-Christians respond to grace, then this grace must be mediated through the non-Christian's religion, however imperfectly. Rahner thus coins the term 'anonymous Christian' and 'anonymous Christianity' (Rahner 1966: ch. 5; 1969: chs. 16, 2; 1972: ch. 9; 1974: ch. 9; 1976: ch. 17; 1979: chs. 4, 13; 1980: ch. 5). The first refers to the source of saving grace that is responded to (Christ) and the second refers to its dynamic orientation towards its definitive historical and social expression (the Church).

Because God has already been active within the non-Christian religions, the Christian can be open to learning about God through a non-Christian partner. Furthermore, the Christian is also free to engage in active social and political co-operation when appropriate. Hence, the inclusivist has a firm theological basis for fruitful dialogue. Given Rahner's notion the grace must seek to objectivize itself, mission is clearly important. Hence, Rahner is able to affirm that Christianity is the one true religion, while at the same time holding that other religions may have a provisional salvific status.

Rahner has been criticized by both pluralists and exclusivists. Pluralists have argued that the term 'anonymous Christian' is deeply offensive to non-Christians and creates a stalemate in dialogue, with each side calling the other names (anonymous Hindus, anonymous Muslims and so on) (Hick 1977: 131–2; Race 1983: 45–62). Hans Küng, a fellow Roman Catholic, has accused Rahner of creating a terminological distinction to sweep a resistant non-Christian humanity into the Christian church through the back door (Küng 1976: 77–8). Rahner has made it very clear that his theory is for internal Christian consumption only, i.e. it is a question within dogmatic theology and not a reflection meant for interfaith dialogue. He is simply reflecting on the possibility that the non-Christian may already have encountered God and that if this is so, then 'God' must be the same God as disclosed by Christ. Pluralists have also criticized the way in which Rahner wants to secure all grace as christologically mediated when he in fact acknowledges that it is mediated within other religions where Christ is not known. Rahner would respond that his argument is one regarding ontological causality, not particular historical mediation.

Rahner has also faced severe criticism from those who oppose pluralism and see in his work certain pluralist tendencies. For instance, it is argued that Rahner compromises the *solus Christus* principle in a fundamental manner. Salvation is made possible without surrender to Christ, thereby rendering Christ unnecessary in the economy of salvation (van Straelen 1966; Lindbeck 1974, 1984; DiNoia 1992). If salvation requires no explicit faith at all then this dangerously obscures the way in which the Church claims to form and nourish genuine faith within a historical–social community. Furthermore, Lindbeck accuses Rahner of operating with a very defective view of the relationship between experience and interpretation such that experience is given priority, followed by interpretation of it. Hence, Christianity is seen as just a better interpretation of the same experience had by different religions. But surely, Lindbeck argues, Christian faith is more than this? It is a matter of the person's being shaped in a specific 'Christoformic' fashion by involvement within the specific community of the Church. Hence, the question posed to Rahner: what would the difference be between an anonymous and explicit Christian in terms of faith? Rahner's invisible Church, it is claimed, is unbiblical and also detracts from the importance of explicit confession as a criterion for membership (Lindbeck 1974, 1984: 30–46). The very foundations of Rahner's theology have also been called into question by his Roman Catholic colleague, Hans urs von Balthasar, who has seen in Rahner's transcendental anthropology the danger of the conflation of nature and grace (von Balthasar 1969; Williams 1986). Balthasar is concerned that by viewing supernatural grace as being part of the very nature of men and women, Rahner minimizes the character of sin and of tragedy, and consequently has an impoverished theology of the cross.

Rahner has responded to these criticisms and one cannot follow the complex debate here, except to say briefly that he has maintained against his more conservative critics that there is no compromise on the basic tenet (shared with exclusivists) that salvation comes exclusively through faith in Christ; and that Christ's life, death and resurrection have ontologically (not chronologically) brought salvation irrevocably into the world. Rahner claims he is simply offering one explanation of a teaching maintained by the Church that salvation is available to invincibly ignorant non-Christians and he is not unconditionally giving theological endorsement to the value of non-Christian religions *per se*. Once again, christology, God, human nature and the Church are the central questions which determine the attitude to non-Christian religions.

ALTERNATIVES TO THE THREEFOLD TYPOLOGY

Before leaving this particular debate it will be appropriate to note those who have either claimed a fourth option or those who are unhappy with this threefold classification altogether (and, therefore, also with any fourth option). Regarding those who propose a fourth option (DiNoia 1992; Ogden 1992), I can only briefly register some reservations. In DiNoia's case, he restricts the definition of exclusivism to stipulating that only those who explicitly confess Christ in this life will be saved. Hence, his purgatorial option allegedly constitutes a fourth option. In Ogden's case his fourth option rests on the distinction that pluralists claim that other religions *are* salvific means, while he wishes to claim that they *may be* salvific means. Ogden claims this to be a new fourth option between inclusivism and pluralism, but it rests on a very shaky definition of pluralism, for not all pluralists are committed to an *a priori* affirmation of other religions as salvific means. Ogden's representative atonement theology places him firmly in the pluralist camp. However, readers must judge for themselves on this matter.

Challenges to the whole approach have been put forward most forcefully by Kenneth Surin and John Milbank, both primarily reacting against pluralism but finding problems with the entire project (Milbank 1990; Surin 1990). Surin's criticism is essentially political and genealogical (deriving from Michel Foucault), suggesting that rather than serve up theories about religious unity in an abstract, ahistorical and apolitical fashion, real attention should be paid to the social, political and power relationships between religions in their particular locality, rather than reified global speculation. Theological talk has usually served to obscure rather than identify the real terrain of importance. If anything, it perpetuates the existing status quo by distracting attention away from the real problems. While Surin's criticisms are powerful and incisive, there is a danger that he redescribes the territory so radically that there are no valid theological questions left, only political–sociological questions. While this materialist reductionism is insightful, ultimately it surrenders theology entirely into the hands of social and political theorists, reducing all theological discourse to genealogical origins. Milbank, while sharing much with Surin, proposes a quite different role for theology. Milbank is deeply suspicious of the notion of 'religion', as well as the belief that dialogue provides a privileged access to truth. Rather, he urges that Christianity simply proclaim its vision and practice, for there is no intrinsic theological rationale for 'dialogue', while there is regarding mission. While Milbank's essay is taunting and polemical in places, it raises significant questions. It seems that while he has offered a devastating criticism of pluralism, despite his claims, he has not really attended to the different approaches within the theology of religions and cannot therefore be justified in calling for 'The End of Dialogue'. What both Surin and Milbank do so clearly is alert us to the fact that all theology is also tied up within a political and social nexus. We shall return to this point in what follows.

CHRISTIANITY AND THE SPECIFIC ENCOUNTERS

Having looked at a theology of religions, we now turn to the question of the different theologies for the meeting with each specific religion. Questions of mission and indigenization/inculturation are obviously central, but they in turn depend on doctrines regarding God, Christ, the Church and humankind. When Christianity meets Judaism, the questions are very different from when Christianity meets Hinduism; and this occurs not only because of the historical differences between Judaism and Hinduism, but also because of the differing social and political contexts of the meetings of these religions. I cannot possibly deal with even a brief outline of Christianity's relationship to the four major religions (let alone the many others), so I will offer two brief case studies, so that some contours of this particular map become evident. First, I will briefly examine Christianity's encounter with Judaism, perhaps the most intimate, destructive and painful of all relationships.

Christianity and Judaism

In this section I wish to make two points. First, in encountering Judaism, Christianity has so often demonized Judaism while being in politically more powerful positions that one must ask (polemically) whether Christianity has really encounted Judaism or whether it has encounted a heresy of its own making. Second, and relatedly, how intrinsic is anti-Judaism to Christian theology, or more specifically to christology? Rosemary Ruether has uncompromisingly charged traditional christology with being intrinsically anti-Jewish (Ruether 1974).

It must be said that at the beginning of 'Christian' history it would have been very difficult to distinguish Christianity from Judaism. Recent scholarship (Sanders 1977, 1985; Vermes 1983) has emphasized the Jewishness of Jesus, the Jewishness of his first followers, and subsequently the Jewish sectarian nature of early Christianity. There is growing consensus on this point. The difficulty is in locating the moments of separation and distinction, whereby Christianity becomes transformed from a Jewish sectarian group into a non-Jewish world religion. At this point the internal sectarian squabble is turned into an inter-religious dispute with great emotional power at its heart. Jews are charged with deicide (murdering God – in Christ) and some explanation must be found for their rejection of the fulfilment of their own religious tradition (hard-heartedness, sin, God's purpose).

A number of Christian (and Jewish) scholars have begun to investigate the many areas of Christian theology and history related to Christian anti-Judaism. These explorations have excavated the possible anti-Judaism in the New Testament itself (Baum 1965; Maccoby 1986), and in pre-Christian culture (Gager 1983). This has been accompanied by an examination of the *Adversus Judaeos* tradition in early Church history (Williams 1935; Isaac 1964; Simon 1986), up to the present day (Flannery 1985). New Testament theologies and modern theology in this century and the last have been critically reviewed for the negative and stereotypical assessment of Judaism and the Jewish people (Saunders 1977; Klein 1978), as have the doctrinal and liturgical aspects of contemporary theology (Pawlikowski 1982). There have also been numerous studies of the church's involvement with Nazi Germany during the war (Littel and Locke 1974) and of ecclesiastical documents after the war (Croner 1977, 1985). All this research has not resulted in consensus on fine details of the overall landscape, but concurs on the acknowledgement of varying degrees of anti-Judaism throughout Christian history, with some putting the guilt of the Holocaust squarely on the shoulders of Christianity.

I do not wish to offer a survey of the various debates and topics (Pawlikowski 1980, 1982). Here, to continue my examination of common themes, I want to show how a christological issue lies at the heart of the problem of Christian anti-Judaism. The problem can be summarized as follows: for nearly two thousand years Christianity has defined itself as the fulfilment of Judaism. The 'new covenant' and 'new Israel' were formed with the coming of the Messiah Jesus and the Church that he established. Israel's history reached its fulfilment in these messianic events. Judaism should have flowered into Christianity – but (and here there are some variations) through ignorance or hard-heartedness the Jews rejected their true destiny. Hence, for most of Christian history Judaism has been seen as an anachronism. Some argue that this theology of fulfilment implicitly requires the theological extinction of Judaism and the subsequent attempts at historically liquidating the Jews were an inevitable corollary (Ruether 1974).

Some theologians have therefore argued for what is called a 'dual covenant' position. Christianity should view the Jewish and Christian traditions as two distinct yet complementary covenants. Jews, in remaining Jews rather than becoming Christians, are being faithful to their covenant with God – the same God who forged a further complementary covenant into which the Gentiles were grafted. Neither negates the other. The fulfilment model should be abandoned as should mission towards the Jewish people (Parkes 1960; Rylaarsdam 1972; Ruether 1974). The upshot of this is that mission to the Jewish people is inappropriate. However, some theologians argue that Christian attitudes to Judaism should catalytically reorient Christianity's attitude to other religions, so that the Christian

> message of hope does not imply that people are called to become Christians out of the great world religions. The church's claim to be the unique source of saving truth is a judgement on the systems of the world, not on the great world religions.
> (Baum 1977: 113)

This is the equivalent of pluralism, but argued for initially on very specific Jewish–Christian grounds. While some theologians extend the principles of this particular case to the other world religions, others feel that such an extension is illegitimate. Those who do extend it argue that colonialist imperialism bears analogy to the anti-Judaism fostered by theological supersessionism. Blindness to the many revelations in the world religions bears analogy to the theological obliteration of post-Second Temple Judaism (Ruether 1974; Baum 1977). In contrast, others argue that while there is no legitimate place for mission to the Jews, mission is valid to the other world religions as these religions are not analogous to Judaism (Küng 1981: 132–50). Indigenization is a very complex and controversial question in this area, for most groups of messianic Jews and Hebrew Christians (Jews who accept Jesus as Messiah and remain Jews) are often regarded with deep suspicion by both Jewish and Christian communities (Schonfield 1936; Juster 1986).

Once again, at the heart of the Christian anti-Jewish question lies the issue of christology and its perceived socio-political implications. In opposition to this view, some critics have sorrowfully acknowledged Christian guilt and complicity in anti-Judaism. But they have defended the position that the affirmation of Jesus as the Messiah is precisely what the early Church was proclaiming and it is impossible to properly understand Jesus divorced from this Jewish messianic context. Similarly, such critics have questioned whether theological negation leads to socio-political liquidation, for 'negation' must be combined with affirmation – which is precisely the relationship to Judaism that Jesus enjoyed (D'Costa 1990c). What is at stake here is whether traditional christological proclamation actually intrinsically entails such socio-political consequences, and Christian history is too full of examples of anti-Judaism to be complacent on this point. The debate will go on, but all sides are at least agreed that all forms of anti-Jewishness within the Christian churches must be fully and unambiguously resisted. Furthermore, all sides in the debate tend to be in agreement that the portrayal of Judaism in Christian history is highly questionable, so that one can genuinely wonder whether real encounter has flourished between the two religions. Christianity's relationship to Judaism sharply highlights social and political factors that so dramatically affect theological reflection. When we turn to Islam, the picture is no less problematic.

Christianity and Islam

As with Judaism, it is possible to venture the claim that Christianity has rarely encounted Islam in a situation free of misperception and political hostility. The latter has hardly diminished today, despite there being no formal Christian or Ottoman empire. Furthermore, this misperception is also partly related to christology in so much as, if Islamic claims about the prophet Muhammad are taken as true, then the Christian claims about Jesus could not be true – and vice versa. Hence, to some extent, the self-identity of each is closely tied up with the denial of the other. As with Christianity's fratricidal relationship to the Jews, its relationship to Islam has also been incestuous in that both have shared (different versions of) common Scripture – the 'Old Testament', both have profound respect for Abraham, the Patriarchs, Mary, and Jesus too. Furthermore, Jesus is found in the Koran as are various references to Christian teaching (Robinson 1991). Hence, we have the volatile combination of common ancestry and common traditions, which makes the issue of self-definition so problematic. This is perhaps one reason why inculturation and indigenization have featured more prominently in relation to Hinduism and Buddhism, than with Judaism and Islam.

The history of the production of Islam for Western consumption has been widely documented, (Daniel 1960, 1975; Southern 1962; Said 1978, 1981). Here, however, it is only relevant to highlight two main features noted by most commentaries. First, the economic and military might of Islam and its proximity to the West have always been (and often still are) central factors in the portrayal of Islam. These factors also need to be located in the imperial conquests by Western powers and their fear of competitors. The main tradition of Islam's portrayal by Europe began with the context that, by the end of World War I, Europe had colonized 85 per cent of the earth. Second, Oriental study was initially conducted by predominantly Christian scholars whose religious concerns further skewed the production of Islam that was then carried over into more recent secular scholarship built on earlier Orientalist foundations.

For example, one of the foundation texts of the Orientalist tradition was Barthélemy d'Herbelot's massive, learned and influential dictionary *Bibliothèque orientale* (1697) which after supplying the Prophet's names, notes:

This is the famous impostor Mohomet, Author and Founder of a heresy, which has taken on the name of religion, which we call Mohammedan ... The interpreters of the Alcoran and other Doctors of Muslim or Mohammedan Law have applied to this false prophet all the praises which the Arians, Paulicians or Paulinists, and other Heretics have attributed to Jesus Christ, while stripping him of his Divinity.

(cited in Said 1978: 66)

Note the following – the charge that Muhammad was an impostor relates to his rival status to Jesus. He follows Jesus and is the last of the great prophets, thereby making Jesus into a John the Baptist. If, however, he is an impostor, the supersessionist chain is broken. Hence, Islam becomes a form of Christian heresy, a second-rate Arianism. As Rana Kabani notes, 'For a thousand years Muhammad was described by a long line of Christian detractors as a lustful and profligate false prophet, an anti-Christ, an idolater, a "Mahound" ' (Kabani 1989: 27). The concentration on Muhammad skews Islam into a religion of the founder (an impostor), rather than placing emphasis on the Koran (a book whose credentials are also thereby questioned). The 'Quran was seen as the product of the events of the life of the Prophet, but rather as a deliberate contrivance than as God's revelation in response to particular needs' (Daniel 1975: 231). Daniel continues that Christians did not then realize that their hermeneutic strategies applied to Islam would eventually be turned upon themselves; but that is another story.

This leads on to a further point. After the decline of Christianity in the West, the 'latent' images of Islam were not fundamentally altered, but only their 'manifestations'. I refer to Said's terminology, whereby 'latent' means the deep, underlying, 'almost unconscious' representations of the Orient's 'eccentricity, its backwardness, its silent indifference, its feminine penetrability, its supine malleability', among other characteristics (Said 1978: 206). By 'manifest' is meant the various styles in which this representation is perpetuated. Hence, from the eighteenth century, the development of Orientalism was different only in its methods (such as philology), 'which in turn were naturalized, modernized, and laicized substitutes for (or versions of) Christian supernaturalism' (Said 1978: 122). Said's thesis has been deeply influential in alerting us to the portrayal of Islam in the West. Taken with Daniel, Southern and others, it presents a complicated, consistent, though not unbroken, picture of the misportrayal and misrepresentation of Islam for political and religious purposes.

One should remember that this brief sketch constitutes a massive generalization, and Watt has recently criticized Said's 'bias', giving an interesting history of perception and misperception from both the Muslim and the Christian sides (Watt 1991). Young, on the other hand, has presented a devastating epistemological criticism of Said which calls into question the basis (rather than the outcome) of Said's project (Young 1991: 119–56). As with Judaism, the christological issues are central, as noted above, but with Islam they revolve more acutely around the trinitarian confession of faith in orthodox christology, as opposed to the Muslim insistence on the oneness of Allah and the sin of *shirk* (associating God with that which is not God: i.e. a human). Muslim–Christian dialogue has gone some distance in exploring the difficult issues involved here and there is less historical pressure (in comparison with the context of the Holocaust) to arrive at clear resolutions. Nevertheless, there are similar tendencies operating as within Jewish–Christian relations. For instance, Hick's contribution to Jewish–Muslim–Christian dialogue has been to remove the stumbling block of christology for many Jews and Muslims, by proclaiming the mythological character of Christian belief in Christ as God incarnate, in keeping with the pluralism he espouses, as outlined earlier. However, in so doing he has incurred severe criticism from Christian quarters. Others have not felt called to deny traditional Christian claims, but to explore points of contact and difference, finding that there is much more room for exploration before one arrives at unresolvable differences – while not denying that this may well be the outcome (see for example Cragg 1959, 1965; Samartha and Taylor 1973).

I am unable to pursue this theme of political–social contexts and christological underpinnings contributing to the misperception of different religious traditions, but would draw the readers's attention to various literature which throws more light on either pole of this duality. For example, for Christianity's encounter with Hinduism, see Hacker 1978: 580–608; Schwab 1984; Halbfass 1988. For Christianity's encounter with Buddhism see Almond 1988. For an excellent bibliography of Christianity's encounter with specific religions and for a general theology of religions, see Sherida 1977; Hick and Hebblethwaite 1980: 239–50; Amato 1992.

CONCLUSION

If the reader now has a sense of the theological, historical, socio-political and methodological issues involved when considering the relationship between Christianity and other religions generally and specifically, then this chapter will have served some purpose.

There are two particular questions which I have left untouched but which are perhaps vital to this topic. I can only raise them rather than indicate possible answers. First, what is the relationship of theology of religions to systematic theology or dogmatic theology? Some have suggested that it should be located at the centre of systematic theology and not seen as a partial specialism (Smart and Konstantine 1991; D'Costa 1992), while others have argued that a global or world theology is required, which is a far more radical proposal (Smith 1981; Hick 1988; Swidler 1990). Others would disagree with both groups. Second, is a theology of religions very different from the question of what kind of relationship Christianity has to culture? The way in which this is answered will also determine the way in which the first question is answered; and again one can only indicate that there are different perspectives on this point, as will be expected. It is hoped that other chapters within this Encyclopedia will help clarify some of these issues and also alert readers to the interrelationship between these different questions facing modern Christian theology.

REFERENCES

Almond, P. (1988) *The British Discovery of Buddhism*, Cambridge: Cambridge University Press.

Amato, A. (1992) 'Jesus Christ, Lord and Saviour, and the Encounter with Religions: A Bibliography', *Bulletin*, 27(2): 217–61.

Barrett, D. (1991) 'The Status of the Christian World Mission in the 1990's', In G. Anderson *et al., Mission in the Nineteenth Nineties*, Grand Rapids, Mich.: Eerdmans.

Barth, K. (1956) *Church Dogmatics*, vol. 4/1, Edinburgh: T. & T. Clark.

—— (1970) *Church Dogmatics*, vol. 1/2, Edinburgh: T. & T. Clark.

Baum, G. (1965) *Is the New Testament Anti-Semitic?*, New York: Paulist Press.

—— (1977) 'Rethinking the Church's Misson After Auschwitz', in E. Fleischner (ed.) *Auschwitz: Beginning of a New Era?*, New York: KTAV.

Braybrooke, M. (1992) *Stepping Stones to a Global Ethic*, London: SCM Press.

Carruthers, G. (1990) *The Uniqueness of Jesus Christ in the Theocentric Model of the Christian Theology of World Religions: An Elaboration and Evaluation of the Position of John Hick*, Lanham: University Press of America.

Cohn-Sherbok, D. (ed.) (1992) *World Religions and Human Liberation*, New York: Orbis.

Coward, H. (1985) *Pluralism: Challenge to World Religions*, New York: Orbis.

Cragg, K. (1959) *Sandals at the Mosque*, London: SCM Press.

—— (1965) *The Call of the Minaret*, New York: Oxford University Press.

Croner, H. (ed.) (1977) *Stepping Stones to Further Jewish–Christian Relations*, New York: Paulist Press.

—— (ed.) (1985) *More Stepping Stones to Jewish–Christian Relations*, New York: Paulist Press.

Daniel, N. (1960) *Islam and the West: The Making of an Image*, Edinburgh: University Press.

—— (1975) *The Arabs and Medieval Europe*, London: Longmans, Green & Co.

D'Costa, G. (1986) *Theology and Religious Pluralism*, Oxford: Basil Blackwell.

—— (1987) *John Hick's Theology of Religions: A Critical Evaluation*, Lanham/London: University Press of America.

—— (ed.) (1988) *Faith meets Faith*, London: BFSS.

—— (1990a) ' "Extra ecclesiam nulla salus" revisited', in I. Hamnett (ed.) *Religious Pluralism and Unbelief: Studies Critical and Comparative*, London: Routledge.

—— (1990b) 'The Reign of God and a Trinitarian Ecclesiology: An Analysis of Soteriocentricism', in P. Mojzes and L. Swidler (eds) *Christian Mission and Interreligious Dialogue*, New York: Edwin Mellen Press.

—— (1990c) 'One Covenant or Many Covenants? Towards a Theology of Christian—Jewish Relations', *Journal of Ecumenical Studies*, 27(3): 441–52.

—— (ed.) (1990d) *Christian Uniqueness Reconsidered: The Myth of a Pluralistic Theology of Religions*, New York: Orbis.

—— (1991) 'John Hick and Religious Pluralism: Yet Another Revolution', in H. Hewitt (ed.) *Problems in the Philosophy of John Hick*, Basingstoke: Macmillan.

—— (1992) 'The End of Systematic Theology', *Theology*, 767: 324–34.

de Bary, W. (ed.) (1958) *Sources of Indian Tradition*, vol. II, New York: Columbia University Press.

DiNoia, J. (1992) *The Diversity of Religions: A Christian Perspective*, Washington DC: The Catholic University Press of America.

Fernando, A. (1987) *The Christian's Attitude Towards World Religions*, Wheaton: Tyndale.

Flannery, E, (1985) *The Anguish of the Jews: Twenty-Three Centuries of Antisemitism*, New York: Paulist Press.

Frankfurt Declaration (1970) 'Frankfurt Declaration', *Christianity Today*, 19 June, 844–6.

Gager, J. (1983) *The Origins of Anti-Semitism: Attitudes towards Judaism in Pagan and Christian Antiquity*, Oxford: Oxford University Press.

Griffiths, P. (ed.) (1991) *Christianity through Non-Christian Eyes*, New York: Orbis.

Hacker, P. (1978) *Kleine Schriften*, Wiesbaden: Franz Steiner Verlag.

Halbfass, H. (1988) *India and Europe*, New York: State University of New York.

Hewitt, H. (ed.) (1991) *Problems in the Philosophy of John Hick: Critical Studies of the Work of John Hick*, Basingstoke: Macmillan.

Hick, J. (1977) *God and the Universe of Faiths*, London: Collins.

—— (1988) *An Interpretation of Religion*, Basingstoke: Macmillan.

—— (1990) 'Straightening the Record: Some Responses to Criticism', *Modern Theology*, 6(2): 187–95.

—— (1991) 'Reponses', in H. Hewitt (ed.) *Problems in the Philosophy of John Hick*, London: Macmillan.

Hick, J. and Askari, H. (eds) (1985) *The Experience of Religious Diversity*, Aldershot: Gower.

Hick, J. and Hebblethwaite, B. (eds) (1980) *Christianity and Other Religions*, Glasgow: Collins.

Huxley, A. (1945) *The Perennial Philosophy*, New York: Harper & Brothers.

Issac, J. (1964) *The Teaching of Contempt*, New York: Holt, Rinehart & Winston.

James, W. (1977) *The Varieties of Religious Experience*, London: Collins.

Jathanna, O. (1981) *The Decisiveness of the Christ Event and the Universality of Christianity in a World of Religious Plurality*, Berne: P. Lang.

Jung, M. *et al.* (eds) (1963) *Relations among Religions Today*, Leiden: E. J. Brill.

Juster, D. (1986) *Jewish Roots: A Foundation of Biblical Theology for Messianic Judaism*, Rockville: DAVR.

Kabani, R. (1989) 'Words for Rushdie', *New Statesman and Society*, 31 March, 27.

Klein, C. (1978) *Anti-Judaism in Christian Theology*, Philadelphia: Fortress Press.

Knitter, P. (1985) *No Other Name?: A Critical Study of Christian Attitudes Towards the World Religions*, London: SCM Press.

—— (1987a) 'Towards a Liberation Theology of Religions', in J. Hick and P. Knitter (eds) *The Myth of Christian Uniqueness*, London: SCM Press.

—— (1987b) 'Dialogue and Liberation', *Drew Gateway*, 58(1): 1–53.

Küng, H. (1976) *On Being a Christian*, London: Collins.

—— (1981) *The Church*, London: Search Press.

—— (1986) 'Towards an Ecumenical Theology of Religions: Some Reflections', in H. Küng and J. Moltmann (eds) *Christianity Among the World Religions: Concilium*, Edinburgh: T. & T. Clark, 119–25.

Küng, H. and Moltmann, J. (eds) (1986) *Christianity Among the World Religions: Concilium*, Edinburgh: T. & T. Clark.

—— (eds) (1990) *The Ethics of World Religions and Human Rights: Concilium*, Edinburgh: T. &. T. Clark.

Lausanne Statement (1975) 'The Lausanne Covenant', in G. Anderson and T. Stransky (eds) *Mission Trends Number 2: Evangelization*, New York: Paulist Press, 239–52.

—— (1980) *Christian Witness to the Jewish People*, Illinois: Lausanne Committee for World Evangelization.

Lindbeck, G. (1974) 'Fides ex auditu and the salvation of non-Christians', in V. Vajta (ed.) *The Gospel and the Ambiguity of the Church*, Philadelphia: Fortress Press.

—— (1984) *The Nature of Doctrine: Religion and Theology in a Post Liberal Age*, London: SPCK.

Lindsell, H. (1949) *A Christian Philosophy of Religion*, Wheaton: Van Kampen Press.

Littel, F. and Locke, H. (eds) (1974) *The German Church Struggle and the Holocaust*, Detroit: Wayne State University Press.

Loughlin, G. (1990) 'Prefacing Pluralism: John Hick and the Mastery of Religion', *Modern Theology*, 7(1): 29–57.

—— (1991) 'Squares and Circles: John Hick and the Doctrine of the Incarnation', in H. Hewitt (ed) *Problems in the Philosophy of John Hick*, London: Macmillan.

Maccoby, H. (1986) *The Mythmaker: Paul and the Invention of Christianity*, London: Weidenfeld & Nicholson.

McKain, D. (ed.) (1964) *Christianity: Some Non-Christian Approaches*, London: Greenwood Press.

Milbank, J. (1990) 'The End of Dialogue', in G. D'Costa (ed). *Christian Uniqueness Reconsidered*, New York: Orbis.

Morris, J. (1973) *Heaven's Command: An Imperial Progress*, London: Faber & Faber.

Newbigin, L. (1981) 'The basis, purpose and manner of inter-faith dialogue', in R. Rousseau (ed.) *Interreligious Dialogue*, Montrose: Ridge Row.

Ogden, S. (1992) *Is There Only One True Religion or Are There Many?*, Dallas: Southern Methodist University Press.

O'Neill, M. (1990) *Women Speaking, Women Listening: Women in Interreligious Dialogue*, New York: Orbis.

Parkes, J. (1960) *The Theological Foundations of Judaism and Christianity*, London: Vallentine-Mitchell.

Pawlikowski, J. (1980) *What are They Saying about Jewish–Christian Relations?* New York: Paulist Press.

—— (1982) *Christ in the Light of the Christian–Jewish Dialogue*, New York: Paulist Press.

Percy, J. (ed.) (1961) *Facing the Unfinished Task: Messages Delivered at the Congress on World Mission*, Grand Rapids, Mich.: Eerdmans.

Pieris, A. (1989) *An Asian Theology of Liberation*, New York: Orbis.

Pinnock, C. (1976) 'Why is Jesus the Only Way?', *Eternity*, December, 14–34.

Race, A. (1983) *Christians and Religious Pluralism*, London: SCM Press.

Radhakrishnan, S. (1927) *A Hindu View of Life*, London: Allen & Unwin.

Rahner, K. (1963) *Theological Investigations*, vol. 1, London: Darton, Longman and Todd.

—— (1966) 'Christianity and the non-Christian Religions', *Theological Investigations*, vol. 5, London: Darton, Longman and Todd.

—— (1969) *Theological Investigations*, vol. 6, London: Darton, Longman and Todd.

—— (1972) *Theological Investigations*, vol. 9, London: Darton, Longman and Todd.

—— (1974) *Theological Investigations*, vol. 12, London: Darton, Longman and Todd.

—— (1976) *Theological Investigations*, vol. 14, London: Darton, Longman and Todd.

—— (1978) *Foundations of Christian Faith*, London: Darton, Longman and Todd.

—— (1979) *Theological Investigations*, vol. 16, London: Darton, Longman and Todd.

—— (1980) *Theological Investigations*, vol. 17, London: Darton, Longman and Todd.

Robinson, N. (1991) *Christ in Islam and Christianity: The Representation of Jesus in the Quran and the Classical Muslim Commentaries*, Basingstoke: Macmillan.

Ruether, R. (1974) *Faith and Fraticide: The Theological Roots of Anti-Semtism*, New York: Seabury Press.

Ruokanen, M. (1992) *The Catholic Doctrine of Non-Christian Religions According to the Second Vatican Council*, Leiden: E. J. Brill.

Rylaarsdam, J. (1972) 'Jewish–Christian Relationship: The Two Covenants and the Dilemmas of Christology', *Journal of Ecumenical Studies*, 9: 249–70.

Said, E. (1978) *Orientalism*, New York: Pantheon Books.

—— (1981) *Covering Islam: How the Media and the Experts Determine How We See the Rest of the World*, London: Routledge & Kegan Paul.

Samartha, S. and Taylor, J. (eds) (1973) *Christian–Muslim Dialogue (Broumana Consultation, 1972)*, Geneva: World Council of Churches.

Sanneh, L. (1987) 'Christian Mission and the Western Guilt Complex', *Christian Century*, 8 April, 330–4.

Saunders, E. (1977) *Paul and Palestinian Judaism*, London: SCM Press.

—— (1985) *Jesus and Judaism*, London: SCM Press.

Schonfield, H. (1936) *The History of Jewish Christianity*, London: Duckworth.

Schuon, F. (1975) *The Transcendent Unity of Religions*, New York: Harper & Row.

Schwab, R. (1984) *Oriental Renaissance: Europe's Rediscovery of India and the East*, New York: Columbia University Press.

Sharma, A. (ed.) (1987) *Women in the World Religions*, New York: State University Press of New York.

Sherida, J. (1977) 'Bibliography on the Theology of Religions in Relation to Dialogue with Non-Christians', *Bulletin*, 12: 65–79.

Simon, M. (1986) *Versus Israel: A Study of the Relationship between Christians and Jews in the Roman Empire (135–425)*, Oxford: Oxford University Press.

Smart, N. and Konstantine, S. (1991) *Christian Systematic Theology in a World Context*, Minneapolis: Fortress Press.

Smith, W. C. (1978) *The Meaning and End of Religion: A New Approach to the Religious Traditions of Mankind*, London: Sheldon.

—— (1981) *Towards A World Theology*, Philadelphia: Westminster Press.

Southern, R. (1962) *Western Views of Islam in the Middle Ages*, Massachusetts: Harvard University Press.

Stanley, B. (1990) *The Bible and the Flag*, Leicester: Apollos.

Stott, J. (1988) 'Reponse to D. L. Edwards', in D. Edwards (ed.) *Evangelical Essentials: A Liberal–Evangelical Dialogue*, Illinois: IVP.

Surin, K. (1990) 'A Politics of Speech: Religious Pluralism in the Age of the Macdonald's Hamburger', in G. D'Costa (ed.) *Christian Uniqueness Reconsidered*, New York: Orbis.

Swidler, L. (1990) *After the Absolute: The Dialogical Future of Religious Reflection*, Philadelphia: Fortress Press.

Toynbee, A. (1957) *Christianity Among the Religions of the World*, New York: Scribners.

Troeltsch, E. (1972) *The Absoluteness of Christianity and the History of Religions*, London: SCM Press.

van Straelen, H. (1966) *The Catholic Encounter with World Religions*, London: Burns & Oates.

Vatican II (1975) *Nostra Aetate (Declaration on the Relation of the Church to Non-Christian Religions*, in A. Flannery (ed.) *Vatican Council II: The Conciliar and Post Conciliar Documents*, Dublin: Dominican Publications.

Vermes, G. (1983) *Jesus the Jew*, London: SCM Press.

von Balthasar, H. (1969) *The Moment of Christian Witness*, New York: Newman Press.

Watt, M. (1991) *Muslim–Christian Encounters: Perceptions and Misperceptions*, London: Routledge.

Williams, A. (1935) *Adversus Judaeos: A Bird's Eye View of Christian Apologiae until the Renaissance*, Cambridge: Cambridge University Press.

Williams, R. (1986) 'Balthasar and Rahner', in J. Riches (ed.) *The Analogy of Beauty*, Edinburgh: T. & T. Clark.

Young, R. (1991) *White Mythologies: Writing History and the West*, London: Routledge.
See also chapters 31, 41, 42, 43, 44, 47, 48.

16

CHRISTIAN THEOLOGY'S DIALOGUE WITH CULTURE

Frank Burch Brown

THE STUDY OF CULTURE WITHIN THE STUDY OF THEOLOGY

Apart from culture there could be no religion. Although religious faith may seek to transform culture, a religion can take shape for the faithful only as it develops some kind of cultural 'body' consisting in distinctive patterns of language, thought, art, ritual, and social organization. Thus every religion necessarily participates in culture by making and transmitting its own kind of cultural tradition, which may vary from place to place and time to time. Furthermore, every religion must respond to forms of culture it has neither made nor claimed for itself. As a religion develops, it must orient itself both in relation to the culture of its origins and in relation to the contemporary cultures it encounters – each of which presents alternative possibilities that a religion may reject, modify, or eventually adopt.

It follows that if theology is to reflect deeply and broadly on the religious life and faith of Christians, it needs to consider the role of culture in human existence and the specific ways in which Christianity has been culturally embodied. It must also analyse how culture that is identified as Christian relates to culture that is identified as something other than Christian. In other words, Christian theology is called on to engage in cultural history, hermeneutics, and criticism. This can be done in terms of culture as a whole or in terms of specific cultures and specific spheres within culture.

Whatever the approach, any effort to understand or further theological dialogue with culture must consider the meaning of the term 'culture', which is remarkably elastic. At one time this term referred primarily to the cultivation of crops and the raising of livestock. Early in the modern era its meaning was extended to encompass the cultivation of the human mind (Williams 1982:10). 'Culture' has since come to refer also to the general process of making a distinctly human world or, especially when used in the plural, to denote the patterns in which different peoples live and interpret their lives (Geertz 1973:4–5). The term has likewise been used widely to refer to the attainment of a high level of education and sophistication, particularly in the arts and humanities, though secondarily in science. When in 1799 Friedrich Schleiermacher wrote his famous speeches to the 'cultured despisers of religion', he was explicitly addressing people who had, in his words, 'raised themselves above the herd' by means of their cultivation in the areas of philosophy, science, artistry, and sensibility (Schleiermacher 1988:77). 'Culture' can denote, too, the products and objects of such cultivation, as when Matthew Arnold spoke of culture as 'the best which has been thought and said in the world' (Arnold 1960: xi).

In our own time still other pertinent meanings of 'culture' are associated with the burgeoning of an area of scholarship commonly called cultural studies, which is an outgrowth of the social sciences as well as of the academic study of literature (see Easthope 1991: 162–81). Cultural studies as an area of inquiry and criticism are concerned not merely with elite culture but also with popular media, diverse forms of material culture, and a wide range of modes of discourse and social practice, especially as these have a bearing on issues of gender, class, race, politics, and economics. In the self-consciously postmodern context of cultural studies today, religion often appears in a distinctly negative light, as an image or agent of patriarchy, social oppression, and authoritarian ideology. Yet, particularly in recent feminist and liberationist theologies, postmodern approaches contribute as well to constructive theological proposals regarding ways to re-imagine God and God's purposes for the world and society.

The nature of theology's dialogue with culture, complex as it is, can best be analysed and illustrated in a chapter of limited scope by focusing primarily on one sphere of culture. Here the focus will be on the arts; for the arts are intimately connected not only with religion but also with culture in virtually all of its manifestations. In approaching art theologically, however, it will be important also to consider various theological viewpoints on culture as a whole. For this kind of analysis the framework offered by H. Richard Niebuhr's classic study *Christ and Culture* (1951) has become virtually indispensable.

CONTRASTING THEOLOGIES OF CULTURE

Culture in the widest sense obviously encompasses a great deal – everything from science and technology to social customs and fine art. Indeed, it comprises whatever human beings create and cultivate beyond the sphere of biological necessity, including artifacts, practices, and symbol systems, along with their attendant meanings and values. Culture in this broad sense arises in the human space between nature and divinity. Wherever nature or God touches the human, culture becomes a factor. From a theological standpoint it can be said that, in the degree to which religious truths or realities accommodate themselves to human expression, they are precisely to that extent 'incultured'.

This is not to suggest that Christian theologians have all conceived of the connection between religion and culture in the same way. As Niebuhr shows in *Christ and Culture*, theologians have differed widely in their estimate of the whole sphere of human productivity, meaning, and value. Niebuhr's analysis highlights five types of theological viewpoint on culture, which he terms Christ against culture, Christ of (within) culture, Christ above culture, Christ and culture in paradoxical tension, and Christ the transformer of culture.

Without being exhaustive, Niebuhr's typology provides a means of surveying the range of options available within Christian theologies of culture as a whole. The first of Niebuhr's types constitutes an essentially antagonistic conception of the relation between Christ and culture. It is the sort of outlook implicit in Tertullian's famous rhetorical question: 'What has Athens to do with Jerusalem, the Academy with the Church?' In Tertullian's case – and in the case of many other Church Fathers – suspicion of Classical culture was accompanied by a deep suspicion of the arts associated with it, such as literature, theatre, and music.

In contemporary theology a variation on the theme of Christ against culture can be found in the work of certain 'postliberal' theologians. Stanley Hauerwas, for instance, argues that Christian identity and character are formed in relation to the particular narrative generated and transmitted by the Christian community. Seen from this standpoint, Christians and the Church properly exist as aliens in the midst of other communities which, having been formed by different stories, make up 'the world'. To this world Christian culture as such is neither indebted nor accountable (Hauerwas 1991: 23–44). Among postliberal theologians, there is no denying that the Christian story is itself in some sense cultural; but its values are seen as independent of, and often contrary to, those of culture at large.

The second approach discussed by Niebuhr is one of cultural accommodation, identifying Christ with the best that culture already produces. This outlook pervaded Enlightenment Christianity of the sort represented by Matthew Tindal (1730), who was inclined to identify the 'reasonableness' of Christianity with rational moral principles that could be formulated and defended apart from any special revelation or specific event in religious history. While Niebuhr does not say so, it appears to be consistent with the Enlightenment's theological accommodation to secular norms that much church music in this era of Mozart and Haydn exhibited affinities with opera.

In a theology of cultural accommodation it is always possible that Christian values, doctrines, and institutions may be subordinated to, or supplanted by, cultural substitutes. In the Victorian era, for instance, Matthew Arnold argued that, more and more, poetry could and would take the place of religious institutions and dogma, interpreting life and consoling and sustaining us. With Walter Pater the aestheticism of religion became still more pronounced.

He wrote:

> If there is no other world, art in its own interest must cherish such characteristics as beautiful [religious] spectacles ... Religious belief, the craving for objects of belief, may be refined out of our hearts, but they must leave their sacred perfume, their spiritual sweetness, behind.
>
> (Fraser 1986: 212)

From such a perspective it appears that Christ serves only to enhance culture and beauty.

Niebuhr's third type is exemplified by the mediating approach of Thomas Aquinas. Placing Christ 'above' culture, Thomas in his synthesis of pagan, Jewish, Muslim, and Christian insights nonetheless affirmed both Christ and culture, not as indistinguishable but as fitted to one another. As Thomas saw the matter, grace perfects and completes human nature as expressed in the artifacts of reason and culture; the natural, temporal goals of human existence are good in their way and, when attained, yield happiness of a sort; but, as intelligent reflection shows, these temporal goods are insufficient for perfect happiness. Such happiness can be attained only in a supernatural and eternal vision of God, made possible by God's mercy bestowed through Jesus Christ.

In the realm of the arts, we can find a similar theology of culture embodied in Gothic architecture. For the medieval Gothic cathedral typically signified and employed virtually all the human arts and sciences, which it blessed and sanctified by constituting, in its totality, a visible image of the Heavenly Jerusalem and a setting for Holy Communion. Something of this outlook toward culture reappeared in the Oxford Movement of the mid-nineteenth century, with its revival of medieval forms of art and liturgy. It was no less evident in the thought of John Henry Newman after his conversion to Catholicism. Taking pains to distance himself from sheer aestheticism, Newman nevertheless averred that the very being of the Catholic Church – her psalms, her arts, her ceremonies, even her logic – is in the highest sense 'poetical'.

According to Niebuhr, those who advocate the fourth of his alternatives, viewing Christ and culture in paradoxical relationship, likewise seek a middle path, inasmuch as they regard culture and Christ as both necessary. But in the interpretation offered by these Christians – represented by theologians such as Martin Luther and Søren Kierkegaard and (it would appear) by Karl Barth in the twentieth century – the culture and religion that human beings themselves fabricate on the basis of their own desires must be overturned through encounter with the judging yet gracious God revealed in Christ. Instead of expecting grace to raise or complete cultural accomplishment, those who take this approach conclude that they must, rather, surrender themselves and their human culture as worthless in their present, sinful condition. Only then, miraculously, does God allow human activity and creativity to work (in largely hidden ways) for God's ultimate glory.

The paradoxical character of such a theology of culture does not prevent it from manifesting itself at a practical level in Christian art and worship. Luther scorned the idea that human beings have anything of their own to offer God, yet (paradoxically) he felt free to adopt appealing secular tunes for church use. And he praised music, which of course he understood to require human artistry and effort, as a gift of God second only to theology itself (Blume 1974: 5–14, 30). The paradoxical approach to theology and culture has recently been carried to the limit in certain deconstructive strategies, which seek to undermine any notion of a secure foundation, whether in Christ or in culture. While rejecting theism, these forms of deconstruction are not simply atheistic. Rather, they provide an 'a/theology' of culture, both avoiding and approaching theology – specifically, negative theology. Deconstructive a/ theologies of culture disseminate radical, yet almost jubilant, scepticism regarding the capacity of any cultural sign – religious or secular – to produce a stable meaning and so to convey the presence of whatever it is taken to signify (Hart 1992: 202; Taylor 1992: 141–2, 310–19).

The fifth and last option that Niebuhr examines is also the one he favours: Christ as transformer or converter of cultural values and achievements. The conversionist, maintaining what Niebuhr describes as a 'radical distinction between God's work in Christ and man's work in culture' (Niebuhr 1951: 190), nevertheless believes that human culture has never been without God's ordering action and that its spiritual worth is not a sheer paradox. Augustine enunciates the conversionist motif when he depicts human culture as perverted good, not as intrinsically evil. Calvinists show a conversionist impulse as well, despite a profoundly negative estimate of human nature in its fallen state. For they typically express exceptional confidence that cultural institutions, particularly government, can be transformed here and now in such a way as to glorify God.

We can deduce that a conversionist attitude towards the arts would include the expectation that, when properly cultivated, genres such as tragedy, comedy, or satire would not only show the human condition as impoverished but also, in so doing, prepare for its transformation. Calvin himself was very fearful of artistic idolatry and therefore banished most arts from houses of worship; yet he counted on the singing of Psalms to move and transform the will and heart. Similarly, Calvin's Puritan descendants were hardly patrons of the theatre or various other worldly arts, but they promoted music and sometimes even dance under carefully controlled conditions. In the twentieth century, Dutch neo-Calvinist theologians have placed great emphasis on artistic beauty as integral to the harmonious transformation of life and society in accordance with the sovereign will of God (Begbie 1991: 81–163).

Niebuhr acknowledges that, even though the views of culture he examines are mutually exclusive at an abstract level, in practice they tend to overlap or coexist, sometimes even in the work of a single theologian. This is evident if one reflects on the case of Paul Tillich, who, while omitted from Niebuhr's historically oriented work, warrants special consideration here, since he stands as one of the twentieth century's most influential theologians of culture.

Tillich affirms the religious character of human culture in its 'depth' dimension (1959: 40–51; 1987: 139–57). He asserts repeatedly that 'religion is the substance of culture and culture is the form of religion' (Tillich 1957: 57). In explaining this point, Tillich claims that, however varied in immediate content, the forms of culture fundamentally express ultimate concern, or faith, which finally is religious in import. For this reason there is no deep cultural expression, and certainly no deep art, that is not in some sense religious. Nor is there any religion without cultural forms. God is the ground of being and likewise of culture, without which religion could not exist. Yet culture is often only dimly aware of its religious depth. In all this, Tillich stresses a continuity between cultural aspiration and religious meaning; at the same time, without embracing supernaturalism, he symbolizes ultimate reality as transcending mundane culture – grounding culture from below instead of completing it from above. In these respects his theology of culture relates at least marginally to Niebuhr's 'Christ above culture' type, which for Tillich would have to be rephrased, 'Christ as ground of culture'.

Tillich's work actually conforms more fully, however, to the 'Christ of culture' type, because Tillich declares that culture is inherently religious, not merely potentially so. Tillich does not, to be sure, see culture as *uniformly* religious, even if its religious character is inherent. In the sphere of art, for example, he attributes to expressionist styles the greatest religious potential because of their capacity to break through the surface of finite forms. He declares, moreover, that some forms of culture are autonomous, which is to say that they consciously try to resist religious claims. Other forms of culture he regards as overtly heteronomous in character, by which he means that they reflect an attempt to acquiesce to religious values that are regarded as supernaturally revealed and that function as externally imposed absolutes. Only a theonomous culture, in Tillich's view, allows for the full interpenetration of religion and culture; and theonomy is always fragmentary in its realization. Nevertheless, Tillich argues, an adequate and theonomous analysis of culture sees the theonomous basis of all culture whatsoever, so that from this point of view 'no cultural creation can hide its religious ground' (Tillich 1957: 57).

It appears, then, that Tillich's theology at different moments displays and highlights elements of two different theological types, designated by Niebuhr as 'Christ above culture' and 'Christ of culture'. Yet Tillich's thought – especially in the middle decades of the twentieth century – develops other emphases as well, including the necessity for a prophetic criticism of culture growing out of what he calls the Protestant principle, which insists on the fallibility of all cultural forms. Tillich's famous 'method of correlation' in fact sees culture as raising ultimate questions that theology alone can adequately address (Tillich 1951: I: 59–66). Tillich goes on to argue that it is culture that provides the matrix of the theological response itself, which is necessarily framed in symbolic – and therefore cultural – terms; but from this he concludes not that some part of culture (the Christian part) is to be embraced uncritically but, rather, that even theology's answers cannot be absolutized. Here one finds more than a hint of Niebuhr's 'Christ and culture in paradox', together with a strong emphasis on the conversion of culture. Culture is at once relativized as penultimate, and affirmed as susceptible to transformation in spite of human estrangement and fallibility.

In the end it must be said that even when one mixes Niebuhr's theological types, the resulting pattern does not exactly match Tillich's thought. Whereas Niebuhr makes 'Christ' the key term, Tillich's reflections on culture do not centre explicitly on Christ, who is depicted in Tillich's systematics as the paradigm and historical manifestation of the (more fundamental) New Being that overcomes the estrangement evident in existence. Indeed, the present-day author whose analysis of culture is in many ways closest to Tillich's is not Christian but Jewish (though unorthodox). There is a definite Tillichian trajectory, at any rate, to the literary and cultural criticism of George Steiner when he draws together Jewish and Christian symbols in an attempt to point out the ultimately metaphysical or religious basis of all meaningful cultural expression (Steiner 1989: 134–232).

The fact that Tillich's theology of culture does not conform precisely to any of Niebuhr's types shows not only the tensions in Tillich's thought but also the limitations of Niebuhr's typology, which, like any scheme, is bound to simplify. The more serious limitation, however, has to do not with Niebuhr's typology itself but with the generality of the kind of theology of culture studied and undertaken in *Christ and Culture*. Like many other theologians, Niebuhr tries in this work to appraise the merits and deficiencies of culture as whole – or, in traditional terms, to discern the relationship between human nature and grace. Whatever its value, such a general approach does not allow the theologian to differentiate carefully among specific human cultures, to reckon with their diversity, or to examine particular cultural ideologies and dynamics (of race and gender, for instance). Nor does it encourage close scrutiny of particular spheres of culture, such as science, politics, and art – as is indicated by the fact that few of the comments on art in the preceding discussion derive from Niebuhr himself.

The importance of greater specificity in a theology of culture is underscored by newer understandings of how cultural meaning is constituted. Few theologians would argue that Christians need to abandon altogether their interest in distinguishing in a general way between the standards of Christ and the standards of culture, and similarly in distinguishing between what God does for and through human beings and what human beings do for themselves. But, especially in recent times, it is not uncommon for theologians to accept some form of the premise that revelation itself (in or apart from Christ) always requires cultural forms – social, political, aesthetic, linguistic. Accordingly, whatever 'Christ' means, this meaning is necessarily pointed to, or made available by, something cultural. Starting from this premise, the theologian may well be less interested in distinguishing Christ from culture *per se* than in discerning, for example, exactly how that which has been accepted as Christian, and perhaps as divinely revealed, actually communicates culturally, how it is transmitted into action, and how a particular religious message is conditioned by the modes of communication in which it is embedded. In attending thus to the medium as well as the message, and so to the ways in which meaning is socially and linguistically encoded, theology can also attend to specifically artistic and aesthetic features of culture.

THEOLOGICALLY SIGNIFICANT ART

In modern European languages the word 'art' and its equivalents can be used to refer to an ability or skill, such as that shown by a potter; or to a process, such as the act of making pottery; or (most often) to a product, such as an earthenware communion cup. There are several things that together distinguish the work of art from other objects and products. Normally it is made or shaped by human beings; its making exhibits skill, know-how, or inspiration; it has a publicly recognizable (though possibly tenuous) connection with practices or institutions associated with the art world; and its appreciation depends to a large extent on aesthetic features – that is, features of sensory form and/or imaginative invention which we customarily identify as expressive, beautiful, or intrinsically interesting. No single configuration of these traits serves to identify all art; and avant-garde art, by definition, resists conforming to certain conventional ideas of art. Nevertheless, the features described above generally mark off what we think of as art and suggest where it fits into culture.

It should be noted, however, that the concept of art sketched here, being relatively modern, was not fully shared by many of the peoples whose products we now regard as remarkable artistic accomplishments. Nor was it shared by many of the finest theologians in history. Prior to the eighteenth century, Christian theologians and their peers rarely thought of 'art' generically or of 'the arts' collectively; they discussed this art or that, thought more about beauty than expression, claimed to prize non-sensuous, intellectual beauty above anything sensory, and often held in low esteem the actual making of art, this being the work of mere 'artisans'.

In any case, most modern students of the theological aesthetics would agree that nothing about the identifying traits of art guarantees a relation to theology. Some superb art is theologically uninteresting, just as some excellent theology is artistically inconsequential. What invites – or even requires – various kinds of theological dialogue is the fact that in actuality much that is associated with art reflects and affects matters of religion and faith.

From art's very inception the things we call artistic and aesthetic have played a major part in religious practice and experience. This is clear from the apparent ritual uses of the palaeolithic cave paintings and of the megaliths created thousands of years later. As for the place of the arts in Christian traditions, it is not insignificant that large portions of the Bible are comprised of poetry and of artistic narrative and that Jesus, with his parables and sayings, engaged in a kind of verbal artistry.

The Church from the start made extensive use of psalms, canticles and hymns, probably sung unaccompanied and often antiphonally. We now know that visual art played a part as well. Scholars have concluded, partly on the basis of artwork found in a synagogue and a church both excavated at a third-century site at Dura-Europos (in modern Syria), that neither Jews nor Christians consistently interpreted the second commandment of the Decalogue as prohibiting images of all kinds. As for the Christian art and architecture that began to pervade the Roman world following the Edict of Milan in 313, one can safely say that it was a major part of a revolution wherein Christianity became a new spiritual force as well as a very public and popular movement with political influence and social prestige.

Architecture became an especially important means by which Christians reinterpreted their identity in relation to the pagan world of classical antiquity. For their places of worship Christians widely adopted (and adapted) not the pagan temple but the Roman basilica – a rectangular civic building that when turned ninety degrees on its axis would not only accommodate many worshippers but would orient them towards a focal point, this being at the east end, the direction of prayer and the locus of the eucharistic altar table. Here Christians built an apse, inserting a triumphal arch at the termination of the interior hall and erecting immediately beyond it a semi-circular structure roofed by a half dome typically decorated with luminescent mosaics depicting Christ, either enthroned or ascending into heaven. When transepts were added, the cruciform shape further Christianized the whole design.

From the third to the sixth centuries, Christians developed a multifaceted visual christology, interpreting Christ not only as Ruler of the universe (and hence as the one true Emperor) but also as an alternative to any earthly emperor. In early Christian art, Christ is sometimes seen as an anti-emperor who triumphs in humility, entering Jerusalem on a donkey; or as a worker of magic and miracles; as the Good Shepherd; as the new Orpheus who restores life; as the new Asclepius with boundless powers of healing; as the infinitely wise philosopher conversing with his inquiring disciples; as androgyne in whom opposite sexes are reconciled and united; or as the unique human whose halo and golden garments identify him as nothing less than also truly God – possibly in refutation of Arianism. In all these instances, the art makes visible some significant feature of Christ that will at once dissociate him from merely pagan expectations while associating him with powers, functions, and realities that a pagan world could learn to recognize and worship. In this way the art functions to shape and vivify early Christian christology (see Miles 1985: 41–62; Mathews 1993).

In subsequent centuries Christianity became one of the world's greatest (and most ambivalent) patrons of the arts. The arts in turn not only illustrated its tenets but gave them imaginative life, nurturing and challenging faith in a fashion unavailable to doctrine alone – and sometimes in tension with official dogma. Such diverse art products as the sculptures of Chartres Cathedral, the epics of Dante and John Milton, and spiritual songs of African Americans all in their own way interpret the despair and hope of human experience while enlivening a sense of God's involvement with human history. The intellectually complex metaphysical poems of George Herbert's *The Temple* (1941) and the erotically tinged, fervent lyrics of the Spanish mystic St John of the Cross undeniably probe the mysteries of sin and salvation. Rembrandt's distinctively Protestant art gives at times a palpable expression to the need for reliance on grace alone. At the level of devotional art, countless crucifixes and painted altarpieces, whether or not conforming to the criteria of fine art, serve as objects before which, and because of which, prayer has continually transpired. In the sphere of secular culture art can still animate religious perceptions and ideas. Thus Mozart's treatment of the theme of human forgiveness in *The Marriage of Figaro* and other operas bestows on it an ineffable graciousness that hints at divine grace as well.

Various kinds of art have also helped define particular traditions within Christianity. Eastern Orthodox worship has been distinguished and enabled to a considerable degree by the veneration of icons, which are prominently displayed in processions and on the iconostasis separating the sanctuary from the nave of the church. By contrast, Protestantism has been known for its preaching, Bible reading, and vigorous congregational singing – coupled with a sharp reduction in, or elimination of, visual images and ceremony.

The examples given above indicate that art has often had a religious vocation. They also suggest that the religious vocation of art differs with the character and context of the artwork. Some art serves as prayer or praise; other art serves an overtly didactic purpose, informing the viewer about the Bible or the teachings of the Church. Some art serves primarily to beautify the place and moment of worship; other art motivates action in the world. Some art celebrates and plays with creation itself; other art agonizes and questions. There is sacred art, which is dedicated explicitly to church use; there is broadly religious art, which may be presented in a gallery or in the theatre or on a concert stage; and there is art that, despite its ostensibly secular character, nonetheless has religious or theological significance because of the depth of its soundings or because of the sense of transcendence that it generates. In addition there are arts that a given religious tradition prohibits. In the history of Christianity, forbidden arts have at one time or another included drama, dance, instrumental music, organ playing, harmonized singing, sculpture, and visual imagery *per se*. The exclusion of certain arts or styles, when it occurs, establishes perceptible boundaries for a tradition's identity.

Repeatedly throughout history theologians and Church leaders have attempted to set forth more-or-less universal guidelines for sacred art. Favourite *desiderata* for such art include: simplicity, dignity, order, restraint, beauty, harmony, sincerity, truthfulness. Nevertheless, much sacred art has been created with other aims in mind, especially when commissioned for special religious occasions and uses. Donors, patrons, and artists themselves have frequently aimed at an art of splendour, glory, exuberance, magnitude, awe-inspiring complexity, animated surfaces and rhythms. In point of fact, sacred art tends to bifurcate into an art of 'less' and an art of 'more'. This split is exemplified by the striking contrast one finds between the beautifully severe and ascetic Cistercian monastery churches of medieval France and the grander, more elaborate Benedictine pilgrimage churches. There is no less a contrast between a Rococo church in Bavaria, with its dizzying, lavishly ornamented interior surfaces, and an 'auditory church' in England designed by Christopher Wren a half-century earlier, featuring geometrical clarity.

This aesthetic divergence between the ways of 'less' and 'more' is intermittently accompanied by a theological explication and defence of one approach over the other. In a famous rebuke directed partly at the Benedictine monastery of Cluny and its dependencies, Bernard of Clairvaux in the year 1125 set a very high spiritual value on artistic austerity, although he acknowledged that where the church serves more worldly people its art may need to make a stronger appeal to the senses (Bernard 1990: 10–12). At the opposite pole, Bernard's contemporary Abbot Suger of St Denis defended the spiritual merits of aesthetic brilliance and splendour – a mark of the Gothic style inaugurated by renovations to Suger's abbey church (Suger 1979: 41–81).

Whatever theologians have supposed at one time or another, the opposition between aesthetic spareness and abundance, or between emptiness and plenitude, has not necessarily been equivalent to the opposition between spirituality and worldliness. The sonic exuberance of the *Sanctus* from Bach's Baroque *Mass in B Minor* is far from 'worldly', conveying instead a sense of the convergence of heaven and earth, both filled with divine glory. Conversely, the often plaintive or rough-hewn quality of the Appalachian tunes published in *Southern Harmony* in 1835 creates an impression that their Gospel message, far from being ethereal in its spirituality, is rooted in the soil of daily experience. It would therefore seem that, just as negative and positive theology both have legitimacy in Christian thought, so the art of privation and the art of superfluity can each aspire to religious authenticity.

ART AND THE VARIETIES OF RELIGIOUS EXPERIENCE

The plurality of Christian religious styles naturally goes well beyond anything suggested by the simple distinction between the arts of 'more' and 'less'. The wider spectrum of Christian aesthetic expression becomes visible if one observes that contrasting kinds of art potentially mediate a sense of divine transcendence, and do so in at least four different modes: negative, radical, proximate, and immanent (see Brown 1989: 115–30).

As regards the first mode, it can be said that certain works of holocaust literature, for instance, raise the question of God's sustaining presence so painfully and powerfully that they convey to Jewish and Christian readers alike a sense of what Martin Buber terms the 'eclipse of God' – a sense of terrifying yet holy absence (Buber 1952: 23–4). For many listeners, overtones of negative transcendence are also produced by Arnold Schoenberg's opera *Moses and Aaron*, left unfinished at his death in 1951. This work, which demonstrates the full expressive range of Schoenberg's twelve-tone technique, revolves around the desperate struggle of Moses to be the prophet of the utterly inexpressible, infinite, incomprehensible God. Whereas the efforts of Moses to give voice to the unutterable truth manifest themselves in a far from ingratiating *Sprechgesang* (midway between speech and song), Aaron adapts to the needs of the people by singing in a lyrical tenor voice; but in the very act of trying to make the Holy Word accessible, Aaron propagates idolatry, adulterating the very truth he professes. Hence what the opera discloses is the profound hiddenness of the one God, whose omnipresence is unmanifest.

A different kind of art is allied with what can be called radical transcendence. This is art that creates a sense of the profound Otherness of a God who nevertheless can at any moment reach across infinite distance to address, judge, and transform human life. In musical art, radical transcendence resonates today in the contemplative spiritual minimalism of Arvo Pärt, as heard for instance in the quiet intensity and occasionally hair-raising outbursts of his *Te Deum* (1986). The radical character of God's transcendence is expressed in another but related way by the interiors of early New England Puritan meeting houses. By their conspicuous plainness they show that they were not meant to be temples, because nothing made by human hands can become the habitation of the Almighty God who wills nevertheless to enter the hearts of the Elect.

Proximate transcendence starts from a point nearer to the world of human reality and enters it more completely. One thinks of the warmly radiant frescoes that Fra Angelico, in the quattrocento, painted for the friars at San Marco in Florence – one of the scenes being a vibrant *Annunciation* in which angel and virgin lean towards one another in mutual acknowledgment and anticipation. The alternately tender and invigorating melodies and rhythms of African American spirituals likewise give aesthetic body to a transcendence that readily comes near, both sharing in human suffering and liberating life from oppression and captivity. For many listeners, today's popular 'praise choruses' tend to mediate a sense of proximate transcendence as well – but transmuted into a feeling of casual closeness to God.

Last, there is an art of what, speaking paradoxically, we can term immanent transcendence. It is not surprising that, in the modern era, the sense of immanence exists alongside the widespread denial of any transcendence at all. It is a thin, though significant, line that separates an entirely sacred world from a world emptied of all sacrality. But certainly from the perspective that embraces immanent transcendence, which is sacramentalism pushed to the limit, all human life and indeed all creation is envisioned as holy. This is a vision sometimes re-created and celebrated, for instance, in the poems of William Wordsworth and Gerard Manley Hopkins. The motif of immanence appears, too, in contemporary hymnody concerned with social justice and liberation, conceived of as harbingers of the reign of God on earth. Immanence has a close connection with ecological spirituality as well. This is plainly audible in the blend of Franciscan and 'New Age' spirituality pervading the *Missa Gaia (Earth Mass)* that was presented and recorded in 1981 by Paul Winter and his Consort. In the final portion of this work, the text of the 'Canticle' of Saint Francis is woven into a musical fabric that incorporates the voices of whales and wolves, together with a song paraphrasing the scriptural passage in which Job is instructed to learn from the beasts and birds and fish. Here no clear distinction is made between God and world; or, if there is a distinction, it is panentheistic in nature, seeing the world as God's body and therefore as inseparable from God.

Although tensions clearly exist between the four basic types of religious aesthetic experience examined above, none need be accorded a position of absolute priority in Christian theology and spirituality. Whereas Paul Tillich gave a privileged position to expressionist art, as compared with naturalistic or idealistic styles, the present analysis is consonant with a more pluralistic approach. This is not to say that, in the realm of theology, all artistic styles are to be affirmed uncritically; nor is it to say that the various kinds of religiously significant art lead in different ways to the same goal: a common, unitary vision of God and of human transformation. It is rather to say in aesthetic terms what theologians have increasingly recognized – namely, that Christian experience is genuinely varied, however common its primary elements. Christian spirituality therefore elicits and depends on various aesthetic styles, each of which becomes integral to a particular sense of divine transcendence and of human possibility.

It would be misleading, however, to conceive of the import of a particular style or work as something static and invariable. Just as religious significance is not directly correlated with religious subject matter, neither is it inevitably correlated with a particular style. Many factors enter into the impact of a work of art, including the context in which it is received and perceived. A given work of art can thus have many kinds of religious import, or none at all.

ON CREATING ART RELIGIOUSLY: THE ROLE OF THE ARTIST

It is not only the work of art as such that can become religiously significant and a bearer of transcendent meaning. Advocates of art as a spiritual discipline are well aware, for instance, that the very act of singing Gregorian chant in a dedicated group and at prescribed hours can function as a spiritual exercise aside from any purely musical outcome. Even when the artwork can be valued for its own sake, the process of creating the work can transform the creator, who is thus worked on spiritually in the act of working. Michelangelo in his later years meditated long on the themes of judgement and grace as he laboured irregularly on his final two *Pietà*s. The first of these – the Florentine *Pietà* – he reportedly intended for his own tomb. The second, known as the *Rondanini Pietà* (Milan), he worked on until six days before his death in 1564. He completed neither one. Surviving letters and reports suggest that, indirectly influenced by the Reformation, the deeply troubled artist turned during this time from pride in his artistic accomplishment to trust in the mercy of God alone. It is not implausible to see the last *Pietà*s, poignant and compassionate, as protracted prayers worked out in stone, yet unfinished as art.

With a celebrated artist like Michelangelo, it becomes clear that the very person of the artistic creator can at times embody and signify spiritual values transcending matters of mere personality. In European civilization, the view that the artist potentially has a sacred vocation or divinely bestowed gift goes back at least as far as the ancient Greeks, with their notion of the inspired madness of the poet-singer. In the late Middle Ages and the Renaissance the cult of the artist grew in relation to larger-than-life figures such as Dante and Michelangelo, later expanding in the eighteenth century to include the 'genius' of a writer like Goethe, and in the nineteenth, to include such 'titans' as Beethoven and Wagner. Eventually the Romantic cult of the artist led to the modern apotheosis of a very different kind of figure, such as the sensitive and tortured writer Franz Kafka and the vulnerable, psychologically exposed poet Sylvia Plath.

The theological question remains as to whether, and when, the artist and the religious figure (prophet, priest, apostle, or saint) can be said to coalesce. Despite the artistry of his own theological essays, Søren Kierkegaard scorned the idea that the roles of the apostle and the creative genius can ever be united (Kierkegaard 1955: 104–5). By contrast, William Blake wrote: 'The Whole Business of Man is the Arts.... A Poet, a Painter, a Musician, an Architect: the Man or Woman who is not one of these is not a Christian' (Blake 1953: 328). Between these extremes, the theologian can say that the role of artist can at times be religious, and in a unique way. This is true when aesthetic imagination and artistic creativity disclose the particular qualities of human fault, finitude, and possibility, or when (as we have seen) the artist's work is able to generate an awareness of transcendence in one of its authentic modes. Beyond that, some theologians have argued convincingly that there is an oblique religious significance to artistry when the artist is able to produce something delightful in itself or aesthetically captivating; for this can contribute to 'shalom', the peaceable flourishing and communal harmony that God ordains for earthly existence at its fullest (Wolterstorff 1980: 169). Undertaken with such ends in mind, the making of art can be (broadly speaking) a religious calling.

At about the same time in modern history that art began to establish a large measure of independence from religion and morality, the secular institutions of art began to cultivate and capitalize on the widespread quasi-religious veneration of the artist. Concert halls and museums began to foster an attitude of what can only be called reverence, often becoming places of pilgrimage and spiritual renewal. Modern artists themselves have at times consciously assumed the posture of the shaman or prophet or sage – an image only enhanced by the unconventionality of many artists' lives.

The cult of the artist is not confined, of course, to high culture. Popular musicians and media stars with worldwide followings can become not merely purveyors of entertainment but also the makers of powerful dreams and symbols that articulate basic attitudes towards life. In the confusion of the media marketplace it is seldom clear what religious needs are being met or possibly distorted at the level of popular culture – or, for that matter, in the contemporary museum or classical concert hall. What is clear is that artists in both popular and elite culture participate in the formation and transformation of cultural ideals and moral values. It is also clear that, outside the Church, modern and possibly postmodern religious sensibilities are shaped to a large extent by the same conflicting forces (economic and spiritual) that together shape artists themselves.

THEOLOGY IN DIALOGUE WITH ART: PROBLEMS AND PROSPECTS

If theology, as classically conceived, is the pre-eminent means by which Christian faith seeks to understand itself, and if the arts afford insights and experiences significant to Christian life and faith, then it might stand to reason that the fullest Christian understanding of the arts would be found above all in the works of professional theologians. In actuality, however, the arts have been marginal to the study and practice of formal theology. This does not change the fact that some sort of dialogue has continued throughout the history of Christianity. But it means that, if one is to understand the peculiarities of theology's dialogue with art, one must pay attention to several factors that until recently have tended to keep the arts out of the mainstream of theological discussion.

One obstacle to dialogue is simply that theology and art rarely speak the same language. A large part of theology – academic theology – is highly conceptual in nature, striving to keep aesthetic imagination at a safe distance, or at least under careful control. It is true that theology has its own rhetorical and aesthetic features. In the eleventh century Anselm of Canterbury deemed it fitting that his theological treatise *Cur deus homo* be beautifully crafted; at points he even compared his efforts to those of a painter. Even so, for the purposes of rigorous and intricate argumentation, he could never have been content with pictures.

The arts, by contrast, tend to be low in logical, conceptual clarity and high in sensory and imaginative qualities, thriving on the particularity of images and on the evocative power of symbols and stories. These give form to the life of feeling as well as to ideas, constructing overt fictions and entertaining new possibilities. Thus, as Immanuel Kant recognized, the thinking that transpires through aesthetic symbols lacks intellectual precision; yet it glimpses more than concepts can encompass, thereby challenging thought to transcend itself (Kant 1987: 181–6). This being the case, it appears that neither art nor theology can fully comprehend or translate the language of the other, although each can be transformed in response to the other.

The second deterrent to theological dialogue with art is this: academic theological education belongs to a long tradition of learning which assumes that the highest and most complete form of understanding is intellectual and rational. The liberal arts of the medieval university were not the ones that eventually came to be called 'fine arts'; nor did the medieval university cultivate the criticism and interpretation of such arts. Although music appeared in the medieval university curriculum, it did so not in its audible form but in its theoretical guise, as a mathematical art related to astronomy, arithmetic, and geometry. Literary art was approached only as part of the study of grammar and rhetoric, or in later times as a historical document. Arts such as painting or sculpture had no place, being manual and 'servile'.

It is only in modern times that arts other than classical literature have been given concentrated attention in institutions of higher education. Even then, there has often been a question as to exactly what the study of literature and the arts might contribute to the 'life of the mind'. John Henry Newman, writing in the middle of the nineteenth century, felt it necessary to explain and defend the importance of literature within university education, basing his defence on the plausible premise that literature is a major means by which human beings can gain insight into themselves, their history, their moral and social nature, and the texture of their lives (Newman 1982: 173–4). (The more playful or potentially subversive side of literature was something he could not afford to emphasize.) Soon, however, the major apologists for literature and the arts would take a different tack, misapplying Kant in order to argue that art properly occupies its own sphere – the aesthetic – which is supposedly divorced from anything moral, cognitive, or religious. In being thus liberated, art was also isolated and could therefore hardly be expected to occupy a central place in the life of learning, whether humanistic or theological.

There has been a third hindrance to theological dialogue with art. Christian theology has in varying degrees been influenced from the beginning by Platonic and Gnostic ontologies that depict the sensory, material, and bodily world as at best inferior to the world of the intellect and incorporeal spirit. From this point of view, things that are sensory and material are either corrupt and seductive or, if essentially good, are nonetheless transitory and subject to decay. The most that one can hope from them, therefore, is that they will provide a first step on the spiritual path. This does not bode well for art, which is sensuous even in its appeal to the mind and imagination.

Christianity, despite its Jewish heritage, has imbibed a good deal of this attitude. Thus Augustine in Book Ten of his *Confessions* worried that the music of the hymns he sang in church, though previously it had moved him to tears, might distract him from the truth of what was being sung. And he congratulated himself on having arrived at a state of spiritual maturity in which he was in fact moved not by the chant or by anything sensory but by the words, with their eternal, non-sensuous truth (Augustine 1991: 10. 33 [207–8]). Echoes of this line of thought can be heard in every century of Christian history, creating a profound suspicion of things artistic.

The deprecation of the senses is not always cancelled out when beauty is celebrated by theologians, as it is by Pseudo-Dionysius, Thomas Aquinas, Jonathan Edwards, John Henry Newman, or Hans Urs von Balthasar. As is well known, certain of these theologians go so far as to declare Beauty to be one of the names of God. In doing so, however, the theologian (particularly in the past) has typically urged the lover of sensuous beauty to ascend towards the non-sensuous, invisible Beauty that alone is eternal and true. It is less common for the theologian to linger with things of this world or to regard them as imbued with beauty transcending anything that the intellect alone could contemplate. It is true that, as Balthasar has amply demonstrated, theology has made extensive use of aesthetic categories to carry out its work (see Balthasar 1982–91). Under the influence of Romanticism, theology has even been known to conflate the religious and the aesthetic, thereby obliterating distinctions that it might have done better to qualify and refine. Nevertheless, art and sensuous beauty have by and large been treated with great theological ambivalence.

Visual art in particular has often been relegated to the level of the spiritually immature or illiterate. Thus the Western Church, taking its cue from Gregory the Great, has most often justified visual arts as a Bible for the poor and uneducated. At other times these arts have simply been banished. Karl Barth spoke for one major part of the Protestant tradition when he declared that images and symbols 'have no place at all in a building designed for Protestant worship' (Barth 1965: 93). Even the Eastern Orthodox tradition, when in the eighth century it ultimately gave approval to the use of icons, offered theological justifications that had little to do with specifically artistic values. The iconodules argued that the veneration given to the image would transfer to the invisible, spiritual prototype behind the image. And they claimed that the Incarnation showed the spiritual worth of material things, including material images of Christ. While this line of thought resulted in a sacramental view of sacred images, it said nothing about the special power of the images as art. Moreover, the principle of sacramentality was applied selectively. It did not extend equally to sculpture or dance (or indeed to instrumental music). In fact the use of the arts in the Eastern Church, however rich and intense, has been tightly governed by theology and tradition.

Finally, it must be said that Christian reservations about art have not been only theological in a narrow sense. The sheer costliness of much art and architecture, for example, has added fuel to the periodic fires of iconoclasm and asceticism. The concern over cost has been moral as well as pragmatic. Over the centuries there has been a recurrent tension between giving to the causes of art and giving to the poor – a tension only partly mitigated by the joy and spiritual satisfaction that the poor have been able at times to derive from impressive churches and sacred art.

Having spelled out reasons for art's historically marginal status in the realm of theology, it may be necessary to reiterate that, in practice, the Church has made much of the arts. Equally important, it has become clear that, ever since the beginning of the Romantic era, the bases for much of the theological neglect and suspicion of art have gradually (though by no means steadily) eroded.

For one thing, within constructive or fundamental theology there has occurred a significant shift in ideas of epistemology and language. Many – perhaps most – leading theologians today have rejected foundationalism, whether in the form of rationalism or positivist empiricism or religious dogmatism. Like some of their nineteenth-century predecessors, such theologians now tend to see understanding (theological and otherwise) as something always in process, relying at crucial points on metaphor and hypothesis, and inevitably retaining degrees of ambiguity and incoherence.

Over the last fifty years or more, in the world of thought outside theology *per se*, considerable support has built up for such a shift. Whether one turns to Martin Heidegger, Alfred North Whitehead, Hans-Georg Gadamer, Paul Ricoeur, Jacques Derrida, Thomas Kuhn, Michael Polanyi, Richard Rorty, or indeed to scientists studying the hemispheres of the brain, one finds in these quite heterogeneous and often antagonistic sources a shared emphasis on the role of the hypothetical, the figurative, the narrative, the poetic, the tacit, or the truly ambiguous in making thought possible, and thus in constructing any fabric of meaning or framework of interpretation.

Specifically in the realm of aesthetics and hermeneutics, most theorists have jettisoned the modernist purism that has seen art as most fully itself when completely autonomous and hence free of moral, cognitive, or religious associations. Theorists now readily acknowledge that art, for all its fictive, affective, and playful qualities, can affect and reflect larger patterns of thought, discourse, and discernment.

Related shifts in orientation have occurred in other fields within or adjacent to theology. The artistic and literary features of Scripture itself, which have long been recognized in some degree, have more and more captured the attention of biblical scholars and theologians. In historical studies of the

Church and doctrine, greater attention is now given to the place of story and art in the formation of faith and of Christian identity – including its diversity. As a result, certain historians see artworks as having become, for many Christians, significant religious classics – sometimes in opposition to a verbally articulate dominant tradition. Practical theologians, for their part, now widely reject any sharp split between theory and practice, or between body and spirit, and have set aside the dualistic hierarchy in which things having to do with the body and the senses are relegated to an essentially inferior rank. Finally, specialized programmes in the study of religion and various arts (particularly literature and the visual arts) have enjoyed at least intermittent success in universities and theological schools – especially in North America, but now also in Great Britain and in continental Europe. So it is that dialogue with the arts begins to seem increasingly integral to the practice of theology in many of its modes.

Even apart from such developments, however, the dialogue between theology and the arts is unlikely to abate. It occurs throughout history in theologically reflective art (such as T. S. Eliot's *Four Quartets*) and in artistically creative theology (such as the visionary writings of Hildegard of Bingen). It occurs when a work of secular art affects the perceptions of the theologian and when a religious idea affects the perspective of the secular artist. Finally, and most significantly, the dialogue between theology and art occurs informally and spontaneously in the experience of people who are not them- selves either certified artists or accredited theologians – people whose lives are touched by art and by religion and who daily approach the world in aesthetic and religious ways, and frequently in both ways together. That this commonly happens in human life provides, finally, the best warrant for theology's more formal dialogues with art and culture.

REFERENCES

Augustine (1991) *Confessions*, trans. H. Chadwick, Oxford: Oxford University Press.

Arnold, M. (1960) *Culture and Anarchy*, Cambridge: Cambridge University Press.

Balthasar, H. U. von (1982–91), *The Glory of the Lord: A Theological Aesthetics*, 7 vols, Edinburgh: T. & T. Clark.

Barth, K. (1965) 'The Architectural Problem of Protestant Places of Worship', in *Architecture in Worship: The Christian Place of Worship*, ed. A. Bieler, Edinburgh: Oliver & Boyd.

Begbie, J. S. (1991) *Voicing Creation's Praise: Towards a Theology of the Arts*, Edinburgh: T. & T. Clark.

Bernard of Clairvaux (1990) *Apologia*, trans. C. Rudolph in *The 'Things of Greater Importance': Bernard of Clairvaux's* Apologia *and the Medieval Attitude Toward Art*, Philadelphia: University of Pennsylvania Press.

Blake, W. (1953) *Selected Poetry and Prose*, ed. N. Frye, New York: Modern Library.

Blume, F. (1974) *Protestant Church Music*, Part One, trans. F. Ellsworth Peterson, New York: W. W. Norton.

332

Brown, F. B. (1990) *Religious Aesthetics: A Theological Study of Making and Meaning*, London: Macmillan Press.

Buber, M. (1952) *Eclipse of God*, New York: Harper & Row.

Easthope, A. (1991) *Literary into Cultural Studies*, London: Routledge.

Fraser, H. (1986) *Beauty and Belief: Aesthetics and Religion in Victorian Literature*, Cambridge: Cambridge University Press.

Geertz, C. (1973) *The Interpretation of Cultures*, New York: Basic Books.

Hart, K. (1992) *The Trespass of the Sign: Deconstruction, Philosophy and Theology*, Cambridge: Cambridge University Press.

Hauerwas, S. (1991) *After Christendom?: How the Church Is to Behave If Freedom, Justice, and a Christian Nation Are Bad Ideas*, Nashville: Abingdon Press.

Herbert, G. (1941) *The Works of George Herbert*, ed. F. E. Hutchinson, Oxford: Oxford University Press.

Kant, I. (1987) *Critique of Judgment*, trans. W. S. Pluhar, Indianapolis: Hackett.

Kierkegaard, S. (1955) *On Authority and Revelation: The Book on Adler, or a Cycle of Ethico-Religious Essays*, trans. W. Lowrie, Princeton, NJ: Princeton University Press.

Mathews, T. F. (1993) *The Clash of Gods: A Reinterpretation of Early Christian Art*, Princeton, NJ: Princeton University Press.

Miles, M. R. (1985) *Image as Insight: Visual Understanding in Western Christianity and Secular Culture*, Boston: Beacon Press.

Newman, J. H. (1982) *The Idea of a University*, ed. M. J. Svaglic, Notre Dame, Ind.: University of Notre Dame Press.

Niebuhr, H. R. (1951) *Christ and Culture*, New York: Harper & Row.

Schleiermacher, F. (1988) *On Religion: Speeches to its Cultured Despisers*, ed. R. Crouter, Cambridge: Cambridge University Press.

Steiner, G. (1989) *Real Presences*, London: Faber and Faber.

Suger, (1979) *Abbot Sugar on the Abbey Church of St.-Denis and its Art Treasures*, 2nd edn, ed. and trans. E. Panofsky, Princeton, NJ: Princeton University Press.

Taylor, M. C. (1992) *Disfiguring: Art, Architecture, Religion*, Chicago: University of Chicago Press.

Tillich, P. (1951–63) *Systematic Theology*, 3 vols., Chicago: University of Chicago Press.

—— (1957) *The Protestant Era*, trans. J. L. Adams, abridged edn, Chicago: University of Chicago Press.

—— (1959) *Theology of Culture*, New York: Oxford University Press.

—— (1987) *On Art and Architecture*, ed. J. Dillenberger and J. Dillenberger, New York: Crossroad.

Tindal, M. (1730) *Christianity as Old as the Creation*, London.

Williams, R. (1958) *Culture and Society, 1780–1950*, New York: Columbia University Press.

—— (1982) *The Sociology of Culture*, New York: Schocken.

Wolterstorff, N. (1980) *Art in Action: Toward a Christian Aesthetic*, Grand Rapids, Mich.: Eerdmans.

FURTHER READING

Dillenberger, J. (1986) *A Theology of Artistic Sensibilities: The Visual Arts and the Church*, New York: Crossroad.

Dixon, J. W., Jr. (1978) *Art and the Theological Imagination*, New York: Crossroad-Seabury.

Gunn, G. (1987) *The Culture of Criticism and the Criticism of Culture*, New York and Oxford: Oxford University Press.

Jasper, D. (1989) *The Study of Literature and Religion: An Introduction*, London: Macmillan Press.

Jeffrey, D. L. (1992) *A Dictionary of Biblical Tradition in English Literature*, Grand Rapids, Mich.: Eerdmans.

Krautheimer, R. (1986) *Early Christian and Byzantine Architecture*, 4th edn, New Haven: Yale University Press.

Leeuw, G. van der (1963) *Sacred and Profane Beauty: The Holy in Art*, New York: Holt, Rinehart & Winston.

Lipsey, R. (1989) *An Art of Our Own: The Spiritual in Twentieth Century Art*, Boston: Shambhala.

Pattison, G. (1991) *Art, Modernity and Faith: Towards a Theology of Art*, London; Macmillan.

Scott, N. A., Jr. (1971) *The Wild Prayer of Longing: Poetry and the Sacred*, New Haven: Yale University Press.

Tracy, D. (1981) *The Analogical Imagination: Christian Theology and the Culture of Pluralism*, New York: Crossroad.

Wienandt, E. A. (1980) *Choral Music of the Church*, New York: Da Capo.

See also chapters 11, 13, 14, 30, 32, 45, 48.

III

PHILOSOPHY

INTRODUCTION

Peter Byrne

Throughout its history Christian theology has displayed an equivocal attitude to philosophical reflection. It has been viewed from the earliest beginnings of theology as a hostile source of rival ideas to the Gospel. Christianity played a part in the closure of the philosophical academies of the ancient world. St Augustine, in *The City of God*, saves some of his harshest polemics for the follies and pretensions of pagan philosophy. There has hardly ever been a time in the history of theology when the call to escape the false snares of philosophy in order to return to the purity of the Gospel has not been powerful.

Yet, also from the earliest times, Christian theology has felt the need to draw upon philosophical ideas to support and articulate its claims. Augustine, and other Fathers before him, employed Platonic ideas in their accounts of the nature of the soul and of God. In the medieval period, Aristotelian ideas formed the basis for a number of grand theological syntheses, the most famous being that of Aquinas. The Reformers were not free of philosophical influences. Subsequently, phases of theological construction reflected the passing dominance of natural law, Kantian and Hegelian and other schemes of thought.

This mixture of hostility and dependence towards philosophy is natural once we reflect that Christianity cannot be a philosophy and yet must be dependent on one. It cannot be a philosophy pure and simple, because it is a Gospel. A Gospel is something with a unique starting point and disclosure; a proclamation which cannot be separated from its proclaimer; a message irredeemably bound up with a particular origin in history and geography. A philosophy is not so bound up with its origins. Its content and basis are separate from whomever happened to first proclaim it. In these respects it aims to be universal and timeless, as opposed to particular and historical. Turn Christianity into a philosophy and the connection between Christianity and its founder becomes contingent: it ceases to be a message about Jesus but only one that happens to have been taught by him.

Yet a Gospel can make little headway without a philosophy. For folk to be persuaded that a Gospel offers news that is genuinely liberating, they must be convinced that it contains a real wisdom. But that requires showing that it confirms and extends truths already taught and known. Moreover, if a Gospel contains genuine insight, general conclusions about the nature of reality and human nature should flow from it. So it will require philosophical support to establish its credentials and to work out its implications. Hence the reason why, virtually from the beginning, patristic apologists and theologians drew upon pagan wisdom even as they attacked its pretensions.

What theology ideally requires is live and fruitful sources of philosophical reflection which are not at the same time autonomous of theological presuppositions and control. Ever since the end of the Christian centuries and the emergence of the modern secularization of learning, that ideal has been unattainable. Philosophy as regained the autonomy it had in pagan times. So the modern period has exhibited the natural consequence – rough relations between theology and philosophy. These rough relations have, at various times since the Enlightenment, exhibited philosophy pretending to act as the gatekeeper to faith and its contents. That is to say, philosophy has seen its job in relation to theology as consisting in acting as the custodian of a set of criteria of rationality to which theology must conform if it is to be acceptable as a branch of reflection.

In English-speaking philosophy since the Second World War, the gatekeeper role of philosophy in relation to theology has been paramount. This philosophy has been dominated by empiricist ways of thinking. Empiricism has made the relations with theology rougher still. First it brought puritanical conceptions of reason with it – making the gate through which theology had to pass narrower still. Second it lacked, necessarily, any grand, synthetic metaphysical vision which might have been apt as a framework for the articulating of theological insights. Up and till the 1970s, the result of the forces which shaped dominant trends in analytical philosophy was that philosophy of religion was left with a narrow syllabus, leaving it with little input into theology. The 'rationality of religious belief' was its dominant topic. Such positive case as could be mustered in favour of that rationality was the business of natural theology. In this, prominence tended to be given to arguments from world to God with some kind of empirical starting point – *a priori* proofs like the ontological being treated primarily as exercises to show undergraduates the folly of trying to argue from concepts to reality. The negative case, against theology's rationality, was in part dependent on treatment of such age-old pieces of natural atheology as the problem of evil. More direct critiques of theology's pretensions and faith's rational acceptability were concentrated on debates about the meaningfulness of religious language. Particularly as these were reflected in matters to do with verifiability and falsifiability, they provided the occasion of bringing empiricist ideas directly to bear on theology. The character of this empiricist critique is clearly displayed in Mark Wynn's chapter.

It was unlikely that this puritanical conception of philosophy and philosophy's role in relation to religion would enable much positive dialogue between philosophy and theology to take place. The details of theological enquiry did not matter to philosophy, and theology was suspiciously 'metaphysical' in any event. Theologians could find little in philosophy that was constructive or ambitious enough to help in the development of theological ideas – though some attempts were made to unite 'religionless' and 'demythologized' Christianity with the practice-oriented redescriptions of religious beliefs by the empiricists described by Wynn.

In the last two decades of the century there has been nothing less than a sea change in the stance analytic philosophy has taken towards religion, and with that the engagement with theology has been transformed. The key to this change has been the collapse of narrow empiricist paradigms and, with them, both the suspicion of metaphysics and narrow notions of the rational.

Wynn's commentary on the objections to verificationist criteria of meaning illustrates some of the difficulties which forced the abandonment of the empiricist paradigms. The re-emergence of metaphysics as respectable was also helped by developments elsewhere in philosophy. One upshot of this re-emergence has been a renewed interest in the concept of God, with philosophers of the last two decades adding to the age-old concern of philosophy to shape the key concept of theistic belief. Philosophy has in this respect returned to a path trodden by earlier metaphysicians. In this way, a new interest has been awakened in, for example, medieval philosophy and theology as relevant to contemporary enquiry in the philosophy of religion. So a greater sense of continuity between present and past philosophy of religion has arisen. Twentieth-century metaphysical systems, such as process thought, have likewise received greater attention and respectability in this revival of metaphysics. The grand sweep of Keith Ward's survey of philosophical thinking on the concept of God brings all these points home clearly.

A nodal point in the demise of puritanical empiricism is the collapse of its evidentialist view of reason and justification. It is this view which allowed religious assent and theological claim to be permissible only if they were backed by evidences matching the putative universal standards of adequacy whose purity it was the job of philosophy to preserve. Terence Penelhum's chapter on the idea of reason gives a penetrating survey of the rise and fall of philosophical evidentialism. As he explains, it currently faces the challenge of epistemologies which contend that a substantive belief system, such as Christianity, can be justifiably embraced and held without resting upon supposedly more fundamental starting points for reason. In other words, Christian beliefs could be properly basic. If rational belief in a world-view does not wait on evidence independent of it, it does not wait upon philosophy to adjudicate upon it. The questioning of the ideas of a universal reason and a universal rationality has led to the demise of philosophy's role as gatekeeper to faith. The persuasiveness of these trends, while it complicates, to say the least, epistemology and its application to religious belief, still leaves open the question of whether there are any universal, theory-neutral elements to rationality at all. If there are none, then relativism of course threatens. Penelhum's argument will be seen to suggest the conclusion that the abandonment of all universality and neutrality leads to a disquieting conclusion for religious belief and theology in what is after all a religiously ambiguous universe.

With the arrival of doubts about philosophy's role as the adjudicator of the permissibility of faith, the interest in natural theology changes. It need not be seen as of importance merely to philosophical apologetics. David Pailin's chapter brings out not only the history of natural theology, but also renewed interest in it as a source of a range of widely shared experiences which has informed faith down the centuries. In this light, it complements sources of faith in revelation and spirituality. Indeed, Pailin's chapter makes a case for regarding these distinctions as not hard and fast, but rather as ways of dividing up a continuum.

The lesser role given to the business of philosophical apologetics can also help to shift the tone and focus of discussions of the problem of evil. Stewart Sutherland's chapter shows plainly how the problem of evil has functioned as a piece – the chief piece – of natural a-theology through many centuries. yet his main emphasis falls in the end upon the means that possible theological responses to evil provide for reflection on the moral bearings of theology. Seen in this light, the problem of evil is not so much the first stage in an attempted decisive disproof of the existence of God. It is more a way of asking theology to articulate to an audience of the faithful and non-faithful alike how its vision of the economy of good and evil remains morally worthy of respect in the light of the actual state of the world.

The re-emergence of the respectability of metaphysics has not only had implications for the new, constructive attempts to explore the concept of God. It has also made it possible to discuss in detail the relations between religion and science. In the days of the dominance of the radical empiricist paradigm, it was rather taken for granted that theological construction had nothing to contribute to the character of thinking about the foundations of science. The history of the relations between science and religion was viewed as a simple matter of science gaining its liberty from the shackles of dogma. Now, both the present and the past of theology's relation to science are debated afresh. Peter Byrne's chapter shows the variety of models for understanding this relation which is now actively discussed. It explores in detail the bold attempts now made to argue that theological understanding is in fact a necessary underpinning of the scientific enterprise. The relation between theological understanding and the social and human sciences is the concern of Roger Trigg's chapter. He brings out the extent to which dominant determinist and relativist accounts of human nature challenge and are challenged by the legacy of religious teaching on human responsibility and immortality.

The empiricist paradigm of reason and clarity which once dominated English-speaking philosophy of religion was one evident legacy of the Enlightenment. Its challenge by fresh ideas about justification, meaning and the like marks ways in which the Enlightenment's legacy has come to be questioned in philosophy of religion. A yet more radical challenge and questioning of that legacy has arisen with varieties of post-modernist thought. Grace Jantzen's essay on feminism and the philosophy of religion brings out with clarity and force the character and attractiveness of aspects of post-modernism. Her chapter, read as the conclusion to this Part, will bring home the extent to which philosophy promises in the next decades to offer a variety of developing lines of enquiry for the construction of theological insight.

17

THE CONCEPT OF GOD

Keith Ward

THE BIBLICAL SOURCES

The Christian concept of God naturally originates with the Bible, as a source
of revelation. Scholars have claimed to see a development of the idea of God
within the Old Testament (the Jewish Bible). There are passages which seem
to suggest the existence of many gods, with Yahweh as the tribal deity of the
Hebrews, one god among the many gods of the surrounding peoples: 'God
has taken his place in the divine council; in the midst of the gods he holds
judgement' (Ps. 82:1). Yet there is no doubt that, even if there was a development of this sort, God is primarily seen in the Bible as the 'creator of heaven
and earth'. So the first chapter of Genesis stresses that God created both
heaven and earth – the sun, stars and all living things. There is no room for
any other God, where there is one creator: 'To the Lord your God belong
heaven and the heaven of heavens, the earth with all that is in it' (Deut.
10:14).

God is a perfectly just God, and the eighth-century BCE prophets insist
upon his justice and upon the judgement that is coming upon evil: 'The Lord
will come in fire, and his chariots like the storm wind, to render his anger in
fury' (Isa. 66:15). At the same time, he is a God of mercy, ready to forgive:
'He will again have compassion upon us, he will tread our iniquities under
foot' (Mic. 7:19). He is a God of steadfast love: 'To thee, O Lord, belongs
steadfast love' (Ps. 62:12).

The idea of God is not systematically worked out in the Old Testament.
However, there is a clear idea of a creator God who works out his purpose
in history by calling the Jewish people to a special vocation: 'I will give you
[Israel] as a light to the nations, that my salvation may reach to the end of
the earth' (Isa. 49:6). Moreover, his power is unlimited; God is omnipotent:
'I know that thou canst do all things' (Job 42:2). His knowledge is unlimited;
God is omniscient: 'Thou searchest out my path and my lying down, and art
acquainted with all my ways' (Ps. 139:3). The God of the Old Testament is

one unique creator, limitless in power, in knowledge, in justice, mercy and in steadfast love. There is no suggestion that this idea develops by any sort of rational argument from the nature of the observed world. Rather, it is founded on the experience of the prophets as they find themselves and their people encountering a presence which demands justice, promises mercy and calls to obedience throughout their tumultuous history.

God is spoken of throughout the Old Testament in very picturesque, metaphorical ways. In Habakkuk 3:3–15, God is said to ride a burning chariot through the sky, firing arrows at his enemies and shaking the mountains. God is said to enjoy the smell of sacrifices; he is pictured as walking in the garden of Eden or eating with Abraham. He is pictured as sitting on a throne above the heavens, or as rolling up the stars at Judgement Day. It is important to note the prevalence of these poetic forms of speech, since a major theological task is to distinguish imagery used about God from more straightforward truth-asserting statements. As we shall see, some theologians deny any such distinction can be made, while others insist upon it; and that leads to crucial differences in ideas of God.

The New Testament accepts the Old Testament idea of God, but introduces the idea of Jesus as the Son of God and of the Spirit as sent to lead the Church into all truth (John 16:13). Especially in John's Gospel, Jesus is identified in a special way with God: 'In the beginning was the Word, and the Word was with God, and the Word was God' (John 1:1). Over the first three centuries of the Church's existence, this Johannine vision developed into the doctrine of the Trinity, defined at the Council of Nicaea, in 325 CE. There are various interpretations of the doctrine, but the basic point is that God is not conceived as totally 'beyond' or distinct from creation. For God 'assumes' or unites human nature with himself in Jesus, thus establishing a form of union between finite and infinite. Moreover, the Christian hope for redemption (or atonement) comes to be conceived as a form of sharing in the being of God, as humans are incorporated in Christ through the Spirit. The Christian concept of God is thus, at least to some extent, one which relates Divine and human, eternal and temporal, in a rather different way from that pictured in the Old Testament. It is still basically an idea of one omnipotent, omniscient, perfectly good creator; but the relation of God to creation is now seen as involving the transformation of the finite into the infinite life of God.

THE GREEK TRADITION

Early Christian theology was dominated by the interaction of concepts from the Hebrew tradition and from a basically Platonic tradition, which was found very suitable to the development of a doctrine of Incarnation. In particular, the idea of the utter mystery, or ineffability, of God, played a major role. Jewish tradition had always stressed that no images could be made of God; that 'no man could see God and live'. With the development of the idea of

God as Trinity, as three-in-one, it became even more evident that God could simply not be pictured or conceived by ordinary uses of human concepts. In Plato's *Republic*, this sensory world is seen as a realm of half-reality and opinion. It participates in an intelligible realm, the world of Forms or Essential Natures, which has true, unchanging reality. At the apex of the world of Forms is the supreme Form of the Good, from which all other Forms flow. It is so remote from ordinary human perception, however, that it is said to be even 'beyond Being itself' (6. 503–7. 521; Plato 1955: 300–25). In the *Timaeus*, a Demiurge, or world-shaper, is introduced, who uses the Forms as a pattern to shape a world of independent matter as well as he can. Plato's view swings between regarding the ultimate principle of being as an impersonal and wholly transcendent Form of the Good and an uneasy triad of Designer, Forms and matter. It also swings between regarding the material world as merely half-real, to be transcended by the enlightened soul, and as being a positive living and dynamic image of the eternal world, 'the moving image of Eternity' (37; Plato 1965: 50).

Plato's philosophy was developed more systematically in a number of ways by pagan philosophers, especially by Plotinus (210–70 CE). He saw the ultimate principle of Being as a Triad, consisting of 'the One', beyond all comprehension; the Mind or *Nous*, which emanates from it, and contains all intelligible Forms; and the World-Soul, a further emanation which shapes the material world. From this Triad the whole universe necessarily emanates, radiating outwards in descending degrees of reality, so that evil is caused by the lack of being at the periphery of the cosmos. The process of emanation is inevitable, and the religious quest is to return from plurality and evil to the One Source, in a 'liberation from the alien that besets us here, a life taking no pleasure in the things of earth, the passing of solitary to solitary' (6, 9; Plotinus 1991: 549).

Christian theologians, especially in Alexandria and in Cappadocia (in modern Turkey), also used Plato's thought to develop a more systematic doctrine of God. Believing in Incarnation, they could not say that the material world is illusory, or only half-real. Believing in resurrection, they could not see the ultimate destiny of the soul as escape from matter. Believing in Divine freedom, they could not see the world as a necessary emanation from God. They could, however, see God as supreme Goodness, beyond all human description. They identified the Forms with the *Logos*, the Eternal Word or Son of God. They saw Jesus as the *eikon*, the image, of the invisible God. The whole material universe was seen as a sacrament, or temporal expression, of Eternity, and thus given a much more positive role than in Plato himself. The key move made by Christian theologians was to place the Forms in the mind of God, the supreme One, and to see the material world as a free and purposive creation out of nothing (i.e. not out of independently existing stuff) to be a temporal image of the eternal Forms. This unified Platonism in a coherent way and created an attractive framework for the doctrine of Incarnation, seen as the manifestation of the Eternal (the *Logos*) in the world of time (in Jesus).

Augustine (354–430 CE) is the best-known theologian of the Western tradition whose doctrine of God was basically Platonist. In *The City of God*, he stated in a classical form what was to become the standard doctrine of creation (Book 11; Augustine 1945: 314–17). He assumes, with the Platonic tradition, that no changing being can be perfect. Since time is the measure of change, a perfect immutable reality will be eternal, in the sense of timeless. How can a timeless reality, God, freely create a temporal, changing world? It obviously cannot first of all wonder whether to create a world, then wonder which world to create, then decide to create it. All these processes assume that time exists, that God is in time. If God is not in time, he cannot go through such processes; God cannot do one thing after another; God cannot even be in different states. Thus whatever God does is done timelessly. Creation is therefore not bringing the universe into existence at a point in time. It must be: bringing the whole of time, from beginning to end, into existence – in a timeless sense.

This is Augustine's doctrine of creation. Every moment of space–time has the same essential relation to God, a relation of depending wholly for its existence upon a timeless reality. It is important to see that God is not in time. For Augustine, it is silly to say that God started the universe at the beginning, and then let it proceed on its own. For creation is the relation of space–time as a whole to God. According to such a view, there is no problem with omnipotence and omniscience. In one timeless act, God by sheer willing brings about everything that ever exists. God does not have to peer into some unknown future, for God creates what is future to us in the very same act as that by which he creates our past and present. God immediately knows every time, past, present and future, and God causes every time to be just what it is.

The main problems of Augustine's view relate to Divine and human freedom. If God creates every human act, including those that are future to us, in one Divine act, how can humans have any real freedom? The future already exists, as far as God is concerned; God has already decided it, without any reference to what creatures decide (since God did not wait to see what they would decide before creating the next part of the future). How can our choices be free, if they have been already decided by God? Augustine does believe in human freedom; but he has to interpret it as action not determined by any past temporal state. It will, however, be determined by Divine decree, and one might wonder whether this really allows for full human responsibility.

There is a related problem with Divine freedom. God is supposed to be free to create any universe, or none. Normally, if *P* is free to do *A* or *B*, one envisages a time when a decision has not yet been made, followed by a time when it has. If there was no time when the issue was not decided, it is hard to see how one can speak of a 'decision' at all. Yet God, being timeless, can never have been in a state when it was not already decided to create world *A* (this world). How does such a 'decision' differ from something that necessarily follows from God's changeless nature? Of course, God can be free in that God is not compelled by any other power to do what God does, that God always acts in accordance with Divine desires. Such a sense of freedom, however, is clearly compatible with the ascription of absolute necessity to God; and that seems to be the consequence of Augustine's view. It is perhaps partly for this reason that the problem of evil is not seen as being too serious by Augustine. If God necessarily (and freely) creates this universe, God has no alternative, and cannot be blamed for what exists in it. If one sees that God's own being is supremely perfect, and that this world is inevitable in every detail, there is no contradiction between Divine goodness and the existence of evil. It is possible to obtain a coherent Augustinian view; but for some it will leave a feeling of uneasiness or outrage to think that the damnation of many human souls is freely willed by a perfect God.

MEDIEVAL DEVELOPMENTS

There are many fascinating theologians of the early Middle Ages, but the doctrine of God remained basically Platonic. It found a particularly clear expression in the work of Anselm (1033–1109), whose ontological argument is considered elsewhere. In the course of that argument he propounded a definition of God as 'that than which nothing greater can be conceived' (2; Anselm 1965: 117). He added that God is in fact 'a greater than anything that can be conceived' (15; ibid.: 137). This is an elegant definition of God's perfection. It proposes that the most adequate way for humans to think of God is to think of all the properties that it is better to have than not (such as power, knowledge, happiness and wisdom). Then think of them in their maximal possible degree (omnipotence, omniscience, supreme happiness and perfect wisdom). Think of the largest compossible set of the most valuable possible properties, enlarged to the maximal degree, united in one supreme reality. Finally, posit that God is infinitely more valuable than this being, which is the most valuable humans can think of.

This definition of God combines the 'way of eminence' (the cataphatic way) and the 'way of negation' (the apophatic way) which were important in early medieval theology, and are found expressed in the influential but unknown writer who called himself Dionysius (c.500). By the former, one ascribes all positive perfections to God. By the latter, one denies all properties of God, in the sense in which we understand them. Thus Dionysius calls God 'super-just' and 'super-wise', but insists that the essence of God remains wholly unknown. The philosopher may wonder whether the concept of a being which possesses all perfections is coherent, since many of them may be incompatible. Perhaps perfections (valuable properties) are results of merely subjective preference, so there can be nothing which all would agree on as a perfect being. Perhaps there is no maximal degree of most perfections (like happiness). Perhaps the negative way, denying all properties of God, is simply vacuous. The Anselmian definition is not without its problems. Perhaps, however, there could be something which is so perfect in being that the greatest being we can conceive would be far less perfect than it, but would at least point in its direction. If so, theists would at least wish to assert that it must be identical with the God of Christian worship.

Meanwhile, the works of Aristotle, which rejected Plato's distinction of the intelligible and material worlds, were influential among Islamic theologians like Avicenna (Ibn Sina, 980–1037) and Averroes (Ibn Rushd, 1126–1198). The idea of God found in Aristotle's *Metaphysics*, Book 12, represents God as *noesis noeseos*, 'thought thinking itself'. For Aristotle, God is the 'prime mover', or 'unchanging cause of all change', an eternal and immovable substance which moves the outer sphere of the fixed stars, and so indirectly moves all things. It will live a life 'such as the noblest and happiest that we can live', so it will always be engaged in contemplative thought. Since it must changelessly think of what is best, and since the best possible thing is the Divine intellect itself, its object of thought must be itself. The activity of the prime mover consists in the contemplation and love of its own perfect essence. The outer sphere of the fixed stars is moved into an eternal circular motion by its love of the perfection of the prime mover; so 'the final cause moves by being loved, while all other things that move do so by being moved'. Aristotle's idea of a self-sufficient, self-contemplating unchanged first cause, which draws all finite things to itself by love, became very influential in Muslim, Jewish and later Christian theology.

Aristotle's God does not actively cause the world and does not even seem to know it directly. It knows and loves only itself, though the world is drawn to imitate it by love. The Muslim philosophers and Maimonides (1135–1204), the greatest Jewish medieval philosopher, naturally sought to modify this concept to allow for a doctrine of creation, of Divine knowledge and providence, with varying degrees of success. When Aristotle's works were translated from Arabic into Latin in the twelfth century many Christians also attempted to integrate their faith with this newly discovered system of metaphysics. The best known is Thomas Aquinas (1225–74), whose theology, although resisted at first, soon became a normative philosophical theology for the Roman Catholic Church.

In the *Summa Theologiae*, questions 3–11, Aquinas sets out his doctrine of God, beginning with the assertion that 'we cannot know what God is, but only what he is not'. A main reason for this is that God is absolutely simple. He is not composed of extended parts, and is therefore neither in time nor in space. He is not composed of form and matter, and is therefore 'pure form', an essence or intelligible nature which is self-subsistent. God's nature is identical with God's existence, therefore God is *'esse suum subsistens'*, or Being-itself, not a particular thing which partakes of existence. Finally, being simple, God is totally different from any finite, composite thing, and nothing finite can be part of the unlimited reality of God. One might say that God is an 'unlimited ocean of being'. When humans try to think of God, they naturally think of a particular individual, entering into relations with finite things. All such thoughts fail to grasp the Divine infinity by making God finite. We cannot know what God is, because human concepts are not adequate to comprehend infinite being.

It may seem that nothing at all can be said of God. Yet Aquinas holds that some statements about God (e.g. 'God is good') are literally true. They are, however, analogically true. Such terms as 'good' apply to God, but not in the sense in which we understand them. This is because all perfections exist in God in a higher manner. 'Effects obviously pre-exist potentially in their causes' (Part 1a, Question 4, Article 2; Aquinas 1964: 53), and God, as first cause, contains the perfections of everything, though in a simple, undivided way. To say that God is perfect is to say that God is purely actual, containing no merely potential being, having in himself the actuality of all things in an unlimited way.

As achieved and unlimited actuality, God is supremely desirable, and so can properly be called good. Indeed, God alone is supremely good, 'as being the first source of every perfection things desire' (Part 1a, Question 6, Article 2; Aquinas 1964: 85). God is omnipresent, since all things exist solely by his substance, power and presence, and agents are present wherever they are active. God is immutable, since supreme perfection does not allow of increase or decrease, and since pure actuality excludes any potentiality in God. God is eternal, 'the instantaneously whole and perfect possession of unending life' (Part 1a, Question 10, Article 1; Aquinas 1964: 135), since any existence of past, present and future in God would contradict his simplicity and infinity. God is one, since there cannot be two actually infinite sources of all being.

Aquinas' concept of God is that of an infinite reality, purely actual, with no element of potentiality, yet containing in itself, in an incomprehensible way, the perfections of all possible things, as their cause. This is about as far as one can get from an anthropomorphic idea of God as a disembodied person who is constantly interacting with, or intervening in, the world in response to prayers and new crises. A major philosophical problem is that the concept may be vacuous. An unkind critic may suggest that the idea of 'Existence itself' existing is simply a nonsensical and ungrammatical construction, like saying that nobody in particular runs, but there is such a thing as 'Running itself' which runs. There is also a tension, to say the least, between saying that we cannot know what God is, and saying that God is an all-perfect cause of the universe. If God is the cause of the universe, must he not be, in some sense, an individual (a substance), which Aquinas denies? Moreover, to claim that 'God is good' is literally true, but that the word 'good' does not mean what we think, is not very illuminating. If it does not mean what we think, what is the point of saying it?

As well as problems of internal coherence, there are problems about how such a God can relate to the created universe. It has been noted that Aristotle's God neither knows nor creates the universe. Can Aquinas' God do either? Aquinas says that 'Things other than himself [God] sees not in themselves but in himself' (Part 1a, Question 14, Article 5; Aquinas 1964: 19). This must be so, if God, being immutable, cannot be changed by knowledge of what is other than himself. God is simple, however, so that in knowing himself, God knows his essential nature, which cannot change. It looks as though all things are wholly determined to be what they are by the Divine will, which is identical with the Divine nature. God being what he is, other things cannot but be what they are. God could have created a different universe only if his nature (which is identical with his existence) had been different. That is, God could have created a different universe only if he had been a different God. If this is so (and of course Aquinas would seek to deny that it is), this God can only create this universe – which contradicts a dogma of the Catholic faith.

The problems are even worse with the Christian doctrines of Incarnation and Trinity. If God is utterly simple, how can there be three *hypostases* in God? If no finite thing can be part of God, because of his absolute infinity, how can the human nature of Jesus be identical with the eternal Word? If God is completely unchanged by what happens in the world, how can he suffer on the cross, respond to prayer or act in believers through the Spirit? I do not suppose that such questions are unanswerable, but they do pose great difficulties for Aquinas' account. The most basic question is whether God is to be conceived as a personal individual who enters into real causal relations with the universe, or as a purely actual, simple and infinite unity of all perfections, bearing no real relation to anything outside itself (Part 1a, Question 6, Article 2; Aquinas 1964: 87), yet being the pattern, source and goal of all finite realities. It is the latter conception which characterizes the classical Christian tradition – though, surprisingly, it does not seem to be well known outside philosophical circles.

The late medieval period was rich in philosophical disputation. William of Ockham (1290–1349) is often taken to be the major exponent of 'nominalism', the school that denies that universals or Forms are real. Taken to its logical conclusion, this makes a Platonic concept of God as Pure Form impossible, though William did not go so far. He did, however, insist that God is not subject to any necessity, even of his own nature. By sheer fiat, God directly wills individuals to exist; the whole universe, including its natural and moral laws, could have been quite different. God is pure omnipotent will, and is not subject to any logical or moral constraints. God cannot therefore be criticized or assessed on philosophical or moral grounds. This is an idea that appealed to some of the sixteenth-century reformation theologians, who rejected all philosophical approaches to the question of God, and insisted on simply accepting the Bible as final.

THE SEPARATION OF REVELATION AND REASON

John Calvin (1509–64), while not being especially interested in philosophical issues about the concept of God, holds that God is self-existent and eternal. God's essence is incomprehensible, but he relates to us in loving kindness, judgement and righteousness. He is omniscient, in that 'to his knowledge there is no past or future' (Book 3, Ch. 21, 5; Calvin 1989: 206). This omniscience follows from the more basic fact that 'God by his eternal and immutable counsel determined once for all those whom it was his pleasure one day to admit to salvation, and those whom, on the other hand, it was his pleasure to doom to destruction' (ibid. 1989: 210). Calvin argues that God's sheer will and pleasure determine humans to Heaven or Hell; yet they deserve Hell because of the corruption of their natures, so that God is both just and merciful. Given that one cannot morally assess God, there is not much one can say to this. One might doubt whether a God whose pleasure it is to torture sentient beings forever can consistently be called perfectly good. However, Calvin argues that God sets the standard of goodness by his mere willing, too; so he is good if he says he is. To say 'God is good' is simply to say that God is what he is, and call it good. Calvin here expresses a strain of anti-philosophical thought about God which has existed in Christianity since Tertullian, who asked, 'What has Athens to do with Jerusalem?' If revelation is simply to be accepted without rational justification, then reason is powerless against its claims. The unrepentant philosopher might ask, however, how one is to decide which revelation to accept, and how to decide between competing interpretations of it. It is perhaps not obvious, after all, that the Bible portrays the omnipotent undetermined will of which Calvin writes, or that the Bible is to be accepted in precisely the way Calvin thinks.

If Calvin and some of his Reformation colleagues divorced revelation from philosophy in a radical way, the philosophers responded by bidding farewell to revelation. In England, Lord Herbert of Cherbury (1583–1648) argued that five ideas are common to all religions, forming a 'natural religion':

1 There is a God.
2 God ought to be worshipped.
3 Virtue is the chief form of worship.
4 Repentance is a duty.
5 There is life after death.

He was the forerunner of Deism, whose adherents hold that revelation is not needed for knowledge of God, and that God does not interfere in the workings of creation. The idea that it would show bad workmanship if the Creator had to interfere in his creation to put it right or adjust it in any way gained strength after the scientific discoveries of Isaac Newton (1642–1727). Newton himself believed in miraculous intervention by God. However, the view of nature as a vast mechanism, running in accordance with immutable mathematical laws, which seemed to many to follow from Newtonian mechanics, made Divine interference seem to many superfluous or even impossible and derogatory to the Divine wisdom. A Deistic view of God became popular in France, with Voltaire and Rousseau, and was later accepted by Immanuel Kant.

The fathers of modern secular philosophy, Descartes, Leibniz and Spinoza, developed a purely rational concept of God without any appeal to the Bible. They defined God as the supreme substance, existing without dependence on any other and containing all perfections in itself. Spinoza (1632–77) argues in his *Ethics* that there could be only one true substance, which would include all things, and have infinite perfections to an infinite degree. This substance is necessary in every respect, and we know only two of its attributes, thought and extended matter. Because Spinoza's God is the all-inclusive substance, he has been seen as a pantheist (identifying God with the universe), though clearly God is much more than the material cosmos we see. Perhaps his most interesting conceptual move is to interpret 'infinity' (unlimitedness) as necessarily excluding (and so being limited by) nothing, i.e. as including all things. For Aquinas, infinity was different in kind from all finite things, and could not mix with them. For Spinoza, infinity is the unlimited whole of which all finite things are part. A better term for this is panentheism, a term coined by K. Krause (1781–1832).

Leibniz (1646–1716), in his *Monadology*, held that the universe consists of an infinite number of substances, or monads. God is the highest possible substance, necessarily existent, from which all other monads proceed. Leibniz famously argued that God must (morally must) create the 'best of all possible worlds', a position effectively satirized by Voltaire in *Candide*. This is because God, surveying all possible worlds, and being perfectly good, must create the best world he can. Since he is omnipotent, he can create the best possible world; and so his moral nature dictates that he must do so. The success of this argument depends upon there being one best of all possible worlds, which entails that all possible worlds must be locatable on one common scale of increasing intensity, which is not infinite (or there would be no 'best'). It is not obvious that this is so.

In opposition to these Rationalist philosophers, the British Empiricists held that all knowledge must be based on sense-experience; or, in its extreme form, that knowledge must be confined to possible sense-experience. This led David Hume (1711–76) to deny (sometimes) that there are any necessities in nature, that the concept of a pure Spirit is coherent, and that God can be inferred from the world. The German philosopher Immanuel Kant (1724–1804), in his *Critique of Pure Reason* (1781), tried to mediate between the Rationalists and the Empiricists. He argued that all theoretical knowledge is confined to experience, so one cannot have such knowledge of God. His definition of God remained the Rationalist idea of a supreme substance containing all perfections, an *Ens Realissimum*. This idea becomes a regulative ideal for thought and action. We need to think that God exists, Kant argues, as a presupposition of scientific activity, which assumes that the world is wholly intelligible. The idea of God is also, he argues, a presupposition of rational moral commitment, which must assume that rational moral activity aims at a state of happiness-in-accordance-with-virtue (the *Summum Bonum*), which only God can guarantee. In general, reason postulates three main ideas, those of God, freedom and immortality, on moral grounds. One must postulate that one is free, to account for moral responsibility. One must postulate that one is immortal, if the supreme purpose of our moral commitment is to be achieved. One must postulate there is a God, who can ensure this purpose can be achieved.

None of these postulates, for Kant, gives any theoretical knowledge. They are postulates of Reason. One must therefore act on the assumption that they are true. Yet they cannot be given any content in the phenomenal world of sense-perception. The noumenal world, or the world of things-in-themselves, is completely unknowable, so they cannot be given any content there either. The postulates are thus necessary but purely regulative Ideas of Reason: 'this idea is thus valid only in respect of the employment of our reason in reference to the world' (Kant 1952: 316). It is in this sense that Kant sees himself as restricting Reason to the phenomenal world, 'to deny knowledge in order to make room for faith' (ibid.: 22). Faith, here, consists in the acceptance of the postulates of God, freedom and immortality, without claiming knowledge of them, on the basis of a practical commitment to specific forms of moral action.

Kant sees the concept of God as playing a regulative role in making possible certain forms of human action, but as having no constitutive (theoretical) role. We can have no knowledge of reality-in-itself, but we must think of it as though God exists as its ultimate ground, while admitting that it cannot really be just as we suppose. Kant's account hovers between pragmatism (the view that concepts of God are used because they are useful for certain human purposes) and an extremely apophatic rationalism (the view that Reason compels us to believe in God, but forbids us from thinking we can know theoretically what God is). The pragmatic account is prominent in *Religion within the Limits of Reason Alone*, in which concepts such as that of Hell are recommended solely on the ground of their moral efficacy. Critics will protest that Reason does not compel us to think the idea of an *Ens Realissimum*; that the belief that there is a noumenal world which is the cause of the phenomenal world, but of which we can say nothing, is self-referentially incoherent; and that pragmatic considerations are not sufficient for asserting the existence of anything. Kant's notion of God as regulative Ideal is deeply problematic. It is, however, the forerunner of more recent views which see God as a regulative concept making possible a religious form of life, but not entailing any statements of empirical fact.

ROMANTICISM AND IDEALISM

Kant's view of God was Deistic. That is, God is the supremely wise and powerful creator, but does not act providentially within the natural order, and is not a possible object of human experience. He seems a remote and intellectual absentee God, though Kant finds it necessary to postulate his existence as a support to scientific investigation and moral commitment. Reacting to this austere doctrine, Schleiermacher (1768–1834) argued that religion is based on feeling, not intellect or moral practice. He defined religion, in the *Speeches on Religion* (1799), as 'a sense and taste for the infinite'; 'To be one with the infinite in the midst of the finite and to be eternal in a moment, that is the immortality of religion' (Schleiermacher 1988: 140). He was often accused of pantheism, because he often spoke of faith as lying in 'intuition of the universe'. In his later work, *The Christian Faith* (1821), he redefined religion as 'the feeling of absolute dependence', making it clear that the universe was absolutely dependent on a timeless, simple, immutable reality beyond itself.

Schleiermacher denied speculative force to reflection about the Divine attributes, holding that 'they are only meant to explain the feeling of absolute dependence' (Schleiermacher 1989: 198). He holds that 'everything for which there is a causality in God happens and becomes real' (ibid.: 21), so that, in willing himself, God wills the world. Moreover, God 'thinks of nothing else save what he actually produces' (ibid.: 225). The influence of Spinoza is clear; this universe, all that is, is co-incident with all that can be; and it necessarily flows from God in one timeless causality.

Critics point out that it is unlikely that these doctrines really explain or derive solely from a feeling or human experience. They seem much too intellectual and detailed for that. It is more likely that the 'feeling' is being described, ironically, in terms of a Rationalist form of classical theism. Schleiermacher's stress on religious experience as a source of doctrine has been influential in Protestant theology, especially on the work of Rudolf Otto (1869–1937) and Paul Tillich (1886–1965). Otto coined the term 'numinous' to refer to a core experience underlying all religion. In *The Idea of the Holy* (1917), Otto expounded numinous feeling as '*mysterium tremendum et fascinans*', a non-rational feeling of mystery, dread and fascination. This is later rationalized and moralized to produce intellectual concepts such as that of God as moral cause of nature. According to such views, God is an immediate object of a unique sort of feeling, intuition or experience. It does not seem very likely that such human experiences could justifiably ground belief that there exists an omnipotent creator of the whole universe. Yet basic human feelings or attitudes (including so-called 'mystical experience') may be an important element in the development of ideas of God, which the Rationalism of Kant and of the later Scholastic philosophers ignored.

In addition to the Romantic reaction of Schleiermacher against Kantian

Rationalism, Kant's view of the phenomenal world as in some sense a construction of mind led to the development of philosophical Idealism, by Schleiermacher's contemporary, Hegel (1770–1831). Hegel rejected the appeal to feeling, insisting that Reason is competent to discern the nature of reality. In fact, he took the view that the whole of physical reality is a product of Absolute Reason or Spirit (*Geist*). His reaction to Kant was to abolish the noumenal realm, which was supposed to be beyond the grasp of theoretical knowledge, and hold that the temporal universe is the self-realization of Absolute Spirit, first objectifying itself in matter and then coming to know itself and thus being reconciled to itself in and through finite minds. Absolute Spirit is thus Trinitarian in form, moving from existence 'in itself', to an objectified and alienated existence 'for itself', and finally achieving a state in which it exists 'in and for itself'. 'There are three moments to be distinguished: Essential Being; explicit Self-existence, which is the express otherness of essential Being, and for which that Being is object; and Self-existence or Self-knowledge in that other' (Hegel 1931: 767). Time and history have an important part to play, and indeed are essential to the realization of Spirit. Time is 'the necessity compelling Spirit to . . . make manifest what is inherent' (ibid.: 800). Hegel himself saw this as a deeply Christian philosophy, for which Pure Spirit incarnates in time and then reconciles all time to itself in an eternal consummation. He saw the Christian dogmas of Incarnation, Atonement and the Trinity as pictorial expressions of deeper and more universal philosophical truths. Accepting Spinoza's interpretation of the infinite as all-inclusive, he included temporality and development in the Divine Being in a way impossible for Thomas Aquinas. Although Hegel's system is obscure and ambiguous, most interpreters see the process of history as completed in a timeless realized existence of Spirit, which therefore remains above, though inclusive of, all temporal processes. 'The essential Being is inherently and from the start reconciled with itself' (ibid.: 780). God is not actually a developing reality. Rather, temporal development manifests what is timelessly true of Being's own self-knowing and realizing unity.

Hegel's concept of a temporally self-realizing Spirit has been influential in most subsequent German theology, which can hardly be understood without it. Important to his methodology is the idea of dialectic, according to which ideas pass over into their opposites in the historical process, and then swing back on a higher level, which includes (sublates) the other two. The 'dialectical theology' of Karl Barth (1886–1968) exemplifies such a methodology, swinging from the idea of God as the 'Wholly Other' to the contrasting idea of the humanity of God. Barth, of course, replaces 'Reason' by 'Revelation', which Hegel would never have done (see below). For both, however, the truth lies beyond the grasp of concepts of understanding, which always divide up reality in partial and more or less abstract ways. Reason grasps that truth only by undergoing the dialectical process of Understanding or conceptual thought. So although Hegel holds that 'the Real is the Rational and the Rational is the Real', it is important to see that he did not think the rational can be stated in precise unambiguous concepts. It must be grasped by a higher, though fully rational, mental faculty, beyond the opposition of concepts.

THE ROAD TO NON-REALISM

Though Hegel's philosophy has been influential, there has been a general reaction against claims that pure Reason can discern the ultimate nature of Reality, against claims to discern wide-ranging patterns of spiritual development in history, and against the view that Reality is somehow mind-constituted or mind-dependent. These reactions have given rise to diverse forms of post-Hegelian thought, which has often been atheistic. Those who reject the pretensions of Reason to disclose a coherent truth about Reality have sometimes insisted upon a rigorous empiricism. The philosophers who comprised the Vienna Circle in the early twentieth century – most notably Schlick and Carnap – inaugurated the radically anti-metaphysical school of Logical Positivism. This school of thought is Positivist, insisting that all meaningful assertions must in the end refer to 'positive' facts, states of affairs which are subject to testing by observation. It is Logical, propounding a theory of meaning according to which no statement is meaningful unless it is verifiable or falsifiable by sense-observation. Statements like 'God is love' or 'The Absolute manifests itself in history' are declared to be senseless, because they are unverifiable. Such philosophers assert that they do not deny the existence of God. They simply point out that statements about God, like statements about round squares, are senseless and so not worth philosophical consideration. The basis of these Positivist views about God is explored fully in chapter 20. There the reader will also find set out the connections between positivism and re-interpretations of conceptions of God which stress the links between, on the one hand, the sense of the idea of God and, on the other, human practice and the ethical requirements upon it. Such re-interpretations, in the hands of thinkers like R. B. Braithwaite, eschew the idea that 'God' is the name for a metaphysical reality beyond the universe. The particularly Wittgensteinian version of this last thought in the writings of D. Z. Phillips is the net effect of all these departures from a metaphysically-based theism (however great the differences between them may be) to exclude much that has been characteristic of theological ideas of God.

Such views of God are at odds with most Christian tradition. They entail that God does not literally answer prayer, raise the dead or judge the world. They raise the question of why one should adopt a Christian way of life, when so many alternatives are available. And they seem to many to eliminate any cognitive element in religion, thereby devaluing the mystical traditions of prayer in the Church. Ian Ramsey, in *Religious Language* (1957), attempted a more cognitive analysis. He roots religious language in experiences of a special character, 'disclosure situations' of cosmic discernment and total commitment.

One discerns a 'depth' in things, when one sees the empirical and something more that cannot be described. There is a sort of verification here, and so a cognitive element, though it is admittedly 'odd', in that the experience is indescribable. 'Miracle' marks such a moment of disclosure, though it does not contravene the laws of nature. The way of life which one commits oneself to is not arbitrarily chosen, but is a response to a discernment which cannot be guaranteed, but which may be evoked by the use of God language. On such a view, the word 'God' is used to express and evoke a depth disclosure which re-orients one's life. All talk of God is symbolic, taken from contexts in which disclosures occur and used to evoke them in others, not to describe the ineffable.

Ramsey's view is similar in many ways to that of Paul Tillich, who insists, in *Systematic Theology* (1951–63) that God is not 'a being', one individual to be set over against others. Rather, God is 'Being-itself', beyond subject–object duality, the abyss and ground of all beings. This 'God beyond god' is the ultimate reality in which the world is rooted, but it is not an individual. It is known in 'ecstatic experience', when one perceives the depth and power of being in and through all beings. For Tillich, all talk of God is symbolic, except for the sentence, 'God is Being-itself', which is itself primarily apophatic. He holds that any 'literal' talk about Divine omnipotence and omniscience (about a being who can do anything and knows everything) must be abandoned. One must speak instead of 'the power of being which resists non-being . . . and is manifest in the creative process' (Tillich 1968: vol. 1, 303), and of the fact that 'nothing falls outside the *logos* structure of being' (ibid.: vol. 1, 309).

I think it would be fair to regard both Ramsey and Tillich as holding that the concept 'God' does refer to facts, but not in the same way as ordinary empirical discourse. In this, of course, they agree with the classical tradition of philosophical theism, both in its Thomist and Hegelian forms. They differ from the tradition in denying that God has particular causal effects in the world, that God ever contravenes the laws of nature, and that God will ensure a literal life after death – 'participation in eternity' is not 'life hereafter' (ibid.: vol. 3, 437). They differ, in other words, about the empirical features of Christian belief. It is obvious that Positivists would simply discard all talk of 'Being-itself' or of 'cosmic depth' as vacuous. Since Logical Positivism, however, both as a theory of meaning and as an account of the basis of all knowledge in the apprehension of sense-data, has been fairly thoroughly refuted, this is hardly decisive. More difficult questions are whether empirical and causal elements can be eliminated from the concept of God, whether the idea does not essentially embody metaphysical claims, and whether the idea of objective truth (of 'realism') is not more important than such accounts imply.

The classical tradition based its concept of God on a key metaphysical insight – either into the necessity of the causal principle, in Aquinas, or into the rational structure of Reality, in Hegel. Tillich retains a Hegelian tendency, though he also tends to select appropriate symbols for God because of their efficacy in promoting the New Being in Christ. Ramsey more explicitly selects models for God because of their moral or salvific efficacy. In this respect, a pragmatic element becomes dominant in much twentieth-century theology. John Hick, in *An Interpretation of Religion* (1989), returns to the Kantian view that Reality in itself is wholly unknowable. He then selects as authentic symbols for this reality those which are salvifically effective, which bring joy, compassion and wisdom to human persons. The Christian God is one of these authentic symbols. Like Ramsey and Tillich, he is reluctant to abandon truth-claims about Reality altogether. He holds, however, that since the noumenal Real is unknowable, apparently contradictory concepts – of God and Nirvana, for example – can both be true of the phenomenal world. The hold on reality, now being divorced from any possibility of empirical testing, has become very tenuous, and it is the pragmatic test that is doing all the work. Thus he holds that 'the truth [of religious concepts] lies in their soteriological effectiveness' (Hick 1989: 373), their ability to lead one from self-centredness to altruism and happiness.

Pragmatist theories of truth tend to oscillate between saying that 'X is true' means that X produces happiness, and saying that 'X is true' is to be accepted because it produces happiness. The objection to the former interpretation is that many truths make one very unhappy. The objection to the latter is that it is hard to distinguish rational belief from mere wish-fulfilment. However, one may be able to defend a more complex view that human language exists to serve basic human interests and dispositions, which may indeed conflict and cause unhappiness. In religion, the proper question to ask may not be, 'Does it correspond to reality?' – which is uncheckable – but 'What interests does it serve?' What is sometimes called 'post-modern theology' works with such a generally pragmatic view of truth, and of language in general. If one cannot check for correspondence with reality, one can examine the forms of life which such language supports. There is a tendency to see particular language-games as stratagems for supporting particular power structures. Various forms of liberation theology, black and feminist theology, practise the 'hermeneutic of suspicion', to reveal the hidden power plays which concepts of God may express. For example, the idea of God as a (male) omnipotent monarch many legitimate partriarchal and hierarchical social structures. Such theologies seek to uncover the social agenda of language-games. One criterion of choice among concepts of God, for Christians, might then be to ask which concepts support the poor and oppressed? Which legitimate oppression and control?

At this point there is often a link between such functionalist analyses of God and Marxism, which is another form of reaction to Hegel. Marx famously said that he turned Hegel on his head. Hegel had seen all history as the self-realization of Spirit, but was unclear about whether Spirit had any existence independently of history. Marx adopted the Hegelian philosophy wholesale, except that he subsumed Spirit completely into the material order, and saw history as a dialectical process moving from a material basis towards a society of free creative spirits. Spirit becomes wholly immanent in the material, and is the dynamic progress towards a just society. It is 'materialistic', only in the sense that the bases of all causal change are the economic and social structures which are inevitably developing dialectically towards the goal of the classless society. Classical Marxism was atheistic, in denying the existence of a substantial personal being who could give life after death as a compensation for life's injustices. However, it retains the idea of a purposive movement towards a moral goal, announced by the 'prophet' Marx, and aimed at the liberation of humanity from slavery and oppression.

Liberation theology has been influenced by a 'soft' version of Marxism, playing down the violence and elements of class-conflict which are central to political Marxism. The link with functionalist accounts is that 'truth' is an expression of certain social and economic circumstances, and the 'final truth' means only that, when a truly just society exists, all will agree in their basic judgements. However, there is a central paradox in this view: if Marxist analysis is itself true, that cannot be simply a matter of agreement, since very few people agree with it! But if it is just one view among others, why should one not reject it on the good pragmatic ground that it produces suffering and hatred in practice? Or simply that one prefers a hierarchical and ordered society?

For classical Marxists, God is a symbol of oppressive social structures, to be overcome. It is possible, however, from a generally Marxist base, to see God as a symbol of liberation from oppression, as the 'eschatalogical future', which calls the present towards itself. This is a view taken by Jürgen Moltmann, who tries, for instance in *History and the Triune God* (1991), to interpret the Trinity as a paradigm of an egalitarian society of free and creative persons. It does seem, however, as if Moltmann is making a claim about truth – i.e. that history actually will end in a certain way, whether or not anyone thinks that it will. How can a functionalist account of truth contain this possibility, if truth is something like agreement? In the end, to make 'God' a key concept in one language-game among many others seems very hard to reconcile with the claim that God is the creator of all things, and would exist even if there were no language-users. It looks as though the language-game which contains the word 'God' carries, as part of its internal grammar, the claim that God exists outside of all language-games. This makes a purely functionalist or pragmatic account of 'God' very difficult to sustain.

EXISTENTIALISM

Another form of revolt against Hegel is the rejection of any attempt to discern a universal pattern in history, or to speak in general terms about the nature of human existence. Existentialism is a form of philosophy which attempts to examine human life as it is lived, in concrete detail, not in terms of abstract theorizing. Reacting against the apparent subordination of the individual to the Absolute Spirit, in Hegel, it makes the individual the centre of its investigations. Since it is in principle anti-systematic, it is difficult to say much in general about it; and it finds some of its best expressions in the novels and plays of J.-P. Sartre (1905–80). The movement has its roots in the work of Nietzsche (1844–1900), who advocated rejection of the 'weak' morality of Christianity in favour of the will to power, a severe and pitiless, though aesthetically cultivated and disciplined life. God was seen by him as a force of repression. His famous statement that 'God is dead' was meant as a liberation from the rule of a powerful, though wholly imaginary, tyrant into the freedom of human creativity. Sartre's idea of God follows that of Nietzsche, and they both regard it as necessary to reject God in order to be truly free. They also accept that with the death of God any sense of an objective meaning or purpose in human existence disappears. Humans must invent their own meaning. To do this, they must escape from the tyranny of convention, confront the absurdity of human existence, and create a personal meaning, or 'authentic' life, which will take full responsibility for its own future.

It may seem that existentialist philosophers must be atheists. In fact, however, Kierkegaard (1813–55), who first used the word 'existentialism', was a Christian. He attacked the established Church of Denmark and what he saw as the systematic pretensions of Hegel. He wrote that 'truth is subjectivity', meaning that in religion truth must be a matter of personal engagement, not correct theoretical belief. He defended the religious life as at a higher level than the aesthetic and the ethical (by which he meant conventional and rule-bound). In true religion, as opposed to the hypocrisy of the churches, one freely chooses to commit oneself, risking everything in acceptance of the 'Absolute Paradox' that in Christ, the Eternal has entered time. Obviously, Kierkegaard does not reject God, though he rejects philosophical ideas of God and all attempts at rational systematization in theology. Authenticity lies in personal choice; but that choice is a response to the non-rational, overtly paradoxical, demand of faith. There is a meaning in human existence, though it can only be grasped by commitment, not by Reason. The ideas of the ultimacy and irreducibility of paradox, of the non-rational basis of faith and of the need to subordinate reason to revelation figure largely in the work of the Protestant theologian Karl Barth.

Another important figure in the existentialist movement (though he denied being an 'existentialist') is Heidegger (1889–1976). Heidegger does not speak of God, but of 'das Nichts', the reality of non-being, of that which is not a particular being and threatens to annihilate all beings. This notion is reminiscent of the mystical idea of God as the nameless infinite (in Meister Eckhart, for example), which both threatens all finite beings and yet gives them the power of being. Before it one comes to feel an existential anxiety which throws one out of the world of convention into the necessity of living an authentic, personally chosen life. Heidegger has been influential upon the Protestant theologians Paul Tillich (who speaks of God as 'the power of being beyond all beings'), and Rudolf Bultmann (1884–1976).

Bultmann interpreted the Gospel as calling humans to be free from the past and open to the future in an authentic, chosen, life. His concept of God is philosophically undeveloped, but is based on the notion of God as the demand for authentic living, as providing the possibility of authentic life and enabling such a life, through the proclamation of the Gospel. Such ideas of God converge upon the non-realist ideas of the empiricist school, and also upon post-Marxist liberation theology, with its emphasis on the primacy of the practical. However, opposition to 'system' can be an excuse for intellectual sloppiness. One must ask how far such views of God really escape metaphysical implications. Talk of 'demand', 'possibility' and 'liberating power' seems to entail talk of a morally authoritative and powerful Reality. Is one making the claim that there is such a being or not? Is it different from the biblical idea of a powerful, knowing creator or not? Further, is one not claiming that there is such a being, whether or not it furthers human interests or seems agreeable to us? Or is one recommending a particular set of human possibilities, of ways of being-in-the-world? If one recommends one way as 'authentic', is one not making a realist claim that it is the way one ought to live, whether or not one believes one ought? In my view, questions of the rationality and truth of theistic belief have not been dissolved by non-realist, existentialist or post-modern approaches to the concept of God. However, this is a fundamental question of basic theology and philosophy that needs to be addressed with full seriousness.

The three movements just mentioned (non-realism, pragmatism and existentialism) can be construed as reactions to Hegel's Idealism, Rationalism and metaphysical confidence. If metaphysical schemes of cosmic proportions are rejected, one may go on to reject human reason itself as a reliable source of truth. Such a view is most fully expressed by Karl Barth, whose *Church Dogmatics* rejects any appeal to reason as justifying faith. The Bible is to be accepted on faith, as defining the grammar of faith, and any doctrine of God must be taken solely from the Bible.

In two volumes of the *Church Dogmatics*, he expounds the doctrine of God as solely and truly known in his self-revelation in Christ. God makes himself known as perfect love and freedom, creating fellowship between humans and the Divine. All the properties of God are interpreted by Barth within this scheme. He is particularly critical of philosophical views of God as an 'impersonal absolute', or of God as in panentheistic symbiosis with creation. He insists that God is a person, a knowing, willing Subject, and indeed the only true person, and that God is wholly other than the universe. God is free in the sense of being unmoved by anything other than himself, and loving in a way which is not dependent on the character or actions of those who are loved. All this can be known solely on the basis of revelation; reason can only lead to arrogance and idolatry. Many critics feel that this approach leaves the rationality of revelation itself in doubt, and in any case question whether Barth's account is quite so free of philosophy as he claims. What is often seen as Barthian fideism can seem rather arbitrary in a world in which so many different alleged revelations compete for human allegiance.

PROCESS THEOLOGY

In complete contrast to Barth's approach, an important strand in twentieth-century thinking about God, especially in the United States, is process theology. It represents a development from a Hegelian view, together with new insights derived from mathematical physics. Its originator was A. N. Whitehead (1861–1947), a mathematical physicist who wrote *Principia Mathematica* with Bertrand Russell. Among theologians, the work of Charles Hartshorne and David Griffin is representative of the school.

Process theology begins by rejecting the notion of substance, as a permanent substratum of changing properties. Reality is composed of 'events' or 'actual occasions', linked together in a temporal process which is without beginning or end. Each actual occasion 'prehends', or is causally affected by, every other actual occasion in its immediate past. It organizes all these data from its own point of view, and in an act of creative synthesis, it continues the temporal pattern they form into the immediate future. As it does so, it perishes, giving rise to a new set of actual occasions in the process. This scheme derives from Leibniz's *Monadology*, with its infinite monads all reflecting the others from their own viewpoint. It differs from Leibniz by the stress laid on the transient and instantaneous nature of the actual occasions, and on the creativity of the temporal flow. Whereas Leibniz saw monads as substances, containing all their possible properties, and only appearing to be temporal, Whitehead reduced them to events and made temporality their essential property.

For Whitehead, actual occasions are layered in hierarchies of greater and less complexity. More complex actual occasions 'include' less complex ones – as the human mind includes all the actual occasions which make up the cells of the body, for instance. God is defined as the all-inclusive actual occasion, or infinite process of all actual occasions, forming one organic unity. Thus God includes all reality within his own being. God literally prehends every actual occasion, and so knows everything that any being can know. However, God does not know the future, since it is yet to come into being, as a result of an infinite number of creative acts by actual occasions. Since these acts are truly creative, and are not determined by the past or by God or existent in some supra-temporal sense, even God cannot know what will happen in future.

Similarly, God is not omnipotent, in the sense that God can do anything, or that he is the ultimate cause of everything that happens. On the contrary, the actual occasions are the real causes of what happens, and God must simply prehend their activity; he cannot compel it. According to this view, God is not an all-determining monarch; he is 'the fellow-sufferer who understands' (Whitehead 1929: 532). He literally shares all experiences. Like all other beings, he is in continual temporal process. Yet God, unlike all other beings, is not wholly confined to the temporal process.

A crucial doctrine of process thought is that God is dipolar; he has a twofold nature. First, he has a 'primordial nature', which is, says Whitehead, abstract, without consciousness and 'deficiently actual' (ibid.: 521). It is a sort of sum total of all possibilities or 'abstract objects', always deficient inasmuch as it contains a 'yearning after concrete fact – no particular facts, but after some actuality' (ibid.: 50). God is, in a sense, the realm of Platonic Forms, 'the ultimate conceptual realisation of the absolute wealth of potentiality' (ibid.: 521). In that respect, God is changeless and eternal. But he is also lacking in concrete reality, for the real must be the concrete and particular, not just the abstract and universal.

This primordial nature of God contains all possible futures. The second pole of the Divine nature is the 'consequential nature', by which God prehends all actual occasions, including their experiences, at every time. At any particular time, God prehends what is the case. From his primordial nature, he then provides each actual occasion with an 'initial aim', which is its best, most creative, possibility. In this sense, he is 'the lure for feeling, the eternal urge of desire', 'the poet of the world' (ibid.: 522). He does not compel things to happen; but he persuades, by his primordial nature, towards the best. However, actual occasions may not be persuaded; and God must simply prehend whatever they freely decide to do. Whatever they do, however, God, who is infinitely patient, is finally able to harmonize their choices into the all-inclusive harmony of his own experience. Thereby things obtain an 'objective immortality' (not conceived as a real, independently enduring existence) by being taken into the unitary experience of God. In this sense, 'God is completed by the individual, fluent satisfactions of finite fact, and the temporal occasions are completed by their everlasting union with their transformed selves, purged into conformation with the eternal order' (ibid.: 527).

God necessarily seeks some concrete temporal expression of his primordial nature; so the world is necessary to God. The world is a real temporal order in which creativity is an essential feature, which even God cannot obliterate. God can, however, 'lure' actual occasions towards the good. Having endless time at his disposal, he will in the end increase the beauty and harmony of the world. In any case, the experience of God will be completed by taking the temporal process into his own being and giving it there, in an ever-extending creative pattern, an eternal satisfaction.

Whitehead's philosophy picks up many elements of Hegelian thought – the stress on the necessity of the world; the stress on temporality; the idea of God as including all finite reality. He develops from it, however, a radically new metaphysical system, in which God has an important place. God is not, however, the impassible, non-temporal, simple Infinite of Thomism. Being dipolar, God does have such a nature, a primordial nature. But that nature is necessarily expressed in his consequential nature, which introduces possibility, temporality and complexity into the Divine Being. To put it bluntly, the process God is not omnipotent or omniscient, and cannot ensure that his purposes will be realized, since he is limited to persuasion. He is a temporal God, who shares in the travails of the world, seeks to lure it towards greater good, and includes it, as so far completed, in the eternal memory of his own awareness.

Building on Whitehead's scheme, there are many possible variants of process theology, but they all share the general features of attributing to God dipolarity, all-inclusive infinity, temporality, creativity and persuasive action. They usually deny or re-interpret the notions of omnipotence and omniscience. They tend to see creation, not as a freely willed act of God, but as a necessary concretization of the abstract primordial nature of God, which endlessly proceeds by the free creative acts of many 'atomic' acts of actual occasions, not by direct Divine ordinance. Process philosophy is a difficult, ambitious and total metaphysical system, which is enough to make it suspect for many. Its stress on Divine temporality, possibility and persuasive action has influenced many theologians who might be suspicious of its general claims. In these respects it seems to show more affinity with the God of ordinary Christian belief than with the God of classical theism, who is never affected by the world and who therefore never really responds to free creaturely actions or is able to do anything radically new. The idea that God becomes human, suffers on the cross, responds creatively to prayer and seeks to persuade by love seems to fit quite well with the idea of an incarnate God. However, most theologians have difficulty with limiting the Divine power and knowledge, with accepting that God can never create a perfect heaven and earth by his own free decision, and with the denial of individual resurrection or life after death.

Creativity and sensitivity are often thought to be qualities a perfect being should have; but it is not so clear that a perfect being should be conceived as being essentially dependent upon the world for actuality, as being limited in power and knowledge, or as being constantly developing and improving. The process concept of God remains controversial among theologians. It has, however, raised a challenge to the classical theistic position on a number of fronts. It is possible that the basic idea of Divine dipolarity, with its associated place for temporality and possibility in God, may survive dissociation from general process metaphysics, and may contribute to further discussion of the proper attributes of a being 'than which no greater can be conceived'.

PERSONALISM

If Hegelian metaphysics has transmuted into process theology, and the reaction against it is found in non-realist and post-modern theologies, there is a sort of 'middle way' which has become popular among some twentieth-century theologians. Refusing either to give up metaphysics altogether or to subscribe to an all-embracing and visionary metaphysics, it concentrates its resources on constructing a realist and personalist concept of God. It regards experience as important evidence for God, when supplemented by evidence from the nature of the universe as ordered and contingent and by revelation, usually interpreted as encounter between God and authoritative experients. In opposition both to Thomist notions of God as 'Self-subsistent Being' and to Romantic ideas of God as 'the all-inclusive Infinite', it construes God as, in Richard Swinburne's words, 'A person without a body who is eternal, free, able to do anything, knows everything, is perfectly good, is the proper object of human worship and obedience, the creator and sustainer of the universe' (Swinburne 1977: 1).

Personalism views God as primarily a disembodied mind or person, who relates to humans as one person, albeit a supreme person, to others. In the works of John Oman, H. H. Farmer, John Baillie and Vincent Brümmer this concept of God assumes prominence. It is sometimes explicitly opposed to the allegedly 'impersonal' concept of Thomism, with its concomitant doctrines of grace and sacramental life which seem to its opponents to operate automatically and almost mechanically. Personalists stress that grace is God's personal love, that faith is trust in God's promises, and that it is in direct encounter with God as ultimate demand and final succour (in Farmer's words) that one comes to theistic belief.

The Thomist doctrine of analogy is not needed for such a concept of God, since it is straightforwardly true that God is a personal being who knows and has abilities. One may have to stretch ordinary usage a little, but not out of all recognition (in contrast to Aquinas, for whom words applied to God do not mean what we understand by them). A great deal of philosophical work has been done to defend this concept of God. One of the most extended defences is Swinburne's *The Coherence of Theism* (1977). Many philosophers regard the idea of God as incoherent, however, and among forceful attacks on this idea of God, especially important are Richard Gale, *On the Existence and Nature of God* (1991), and J. L. Mackie, *The Miracle of Theism* (1982).

Attacks tend to concentrate on the incoherence of such ideas as the existence of a disembodied person; on the idea of a being who can do anything (including preventing itself doing something?); on the idea of a being who knows everything, without being in time (including what time it is now?); and on the idea of a being who is both free and necessary, in some sense. Obvious problems are also pointed out concerning consistency between the existence of a perfectly good and all-powerful God and the existence of innocent suffering; Divine omnipotence and human responsibility; and Divine foreknowledge and human freedom. Personalists usually try to resolve these problems by making God temporal and passible, and giving creatures a great degree of freedom. Divine–human relationship is seen as more a personal partnership than a relation of finite and Infinite being.

As far as Christian theism is concerned, the idea of God as a person is hard to square with a doctrine of God as Trinity (as three *hypostases* of one nature). It seems to make a doctrine of Incarnation especially difficult. Either the Divine or the human person will have to disappear in Jesus; whereas on the classical account, a union of finite and Infinite in Jesus allows the human person to be a manifestation of the Infinite Word. And it seems much more anthropomorphic than either the biblical or classical traditions. Is it adequate to regard God as one person among others, however superior he may be?

CONCLUSION

At the time of writing, four main concepts of God are strongly supported by different schools of philosophers and theologians. Thomism, especially in its more apophatic interpretations, has experienced a strong revival. Process theology and personalism are the subjects of vigorous debate. Varieties of non-realism or of what is sometimes called 'post-metaphysical thought' are current among more radical theologians. A fifth concept, Hegelian Idealism, is suffering something of an eclipse, though it has greatly influenced most European theologians. The influence of some currents of thought in the sciences and growing interest in Indian and Asian religious thought may yet give it a new lease of life.

It is difficult to see any possibility of gaining agreement among proponents of such diverse strands of thoughts. Since concepts of God inevitably affect all other theological ideas, it seems that theology will remain an internally pluralistic discipline for the foreseeable future. The basic biblical sources for a doctrine of God allow, with degrees of plausibility which are variously assessed, all these interpretations. In such a situation, one important task for the theologian is to be aware of the range of possible interpretations and their history, and to be aware of the fundamental decisions which are implied in advocating a particular concept of God. Such knowledge inevitably brings a sense of the severe limitations of human thought on these matters, and the absurdity of easy or definitive solutions. It may thus also lead to a sense of the importance of human encounter with the ultimate mystery of being, towards which concepts of God inadequately point.

REFERENCES

Anselm (1965) *Proslogion*, trans. M. J. Charlesworth, Oxford: Oxford University Press.
Aquinas, T. (1964) *Summa Theologiae*, trans. T. McDermott and T. Fornall, London: Eyre and Spottiswoode.
Aristotle (1928) *Metaphysics*, trans. W. D. Ross, Oxford: Oxford University Press.
Augustine (1945) *City of God*, trans. J. Healey, Letchworth: J. M. Dent.

Barth, K. (1957) *Church Dogmatics*, ed. G. W. Bromiley and T. F. Torrance, Edinburgh: T. & T. Clark.

Calvin, J. (1989) *Institutes of the Christian Religion*, trans. H. Beveridge, Grand Rapid, Mich.: Eerdmans.

Gale, R. (1991) *On the Existence and Nature of God*, Cambridge: Cambridge University Press.

Hegel, G. W. F. (1931) *Phenomenology of Mind*, trans. Sir J. Baillie, London: Allen and Unwin.

Hick, J. (1989) *An Interpretation of Religion*, London: Macmillan.

Kant, I. (1952) *Critique of Pure Reason*, trans. N. Kemp Smith, London: Macmillan.

Mackie, J. L. (1982) *The Miracle of Theism*, Oxford: Clarendon Press.

Moltmann, J. (1991) *History and the Triune God*, London: SCM Press.

Otto, R. (1958) *The Idea of the Holy*, trans. J. Harvey, Harmondsworth: Penguin.

Plato (1955) *The Republic*, trans. D. Lee, Harmondsworth: Penguin.

—— (1965) *Timaeus*, trans. D. Lee, Harmondsworth: Penguin.

Plotinus (1991) *Enneads*, trans. S. MacKenna, Harmondsworth: Penguin.

Ramsey, I. T. (1957) *Religious Language*, London: SCM Press.

Schleiermacher, F. E. D. (1988) *Speeches on Religion*, trans. Richard Crouter, Cambridge University Press.

—— (1989) *The Christian Faith*, ed. H. R. MacKintosh and J. S. Stewart, Edinburgh: T. & T. Clark.

Swinburne, R. (1977) *The Coherence of Theism*, Oxford: Clarendon Press.

Tillich, P. (1968) *Systematic Theology*, Welwyn: Nisbet.

Whitehead, A. N. (1929) *Process and Reality*, Cambridge: Cambridge University Press.

FURTHER READING

Cobb, J. B. and Griffin, D. (1976) *Process Theology*, Louisville: Westminster Press.

Fiddes, P. (1988) *The Creative Suffering of God*, Oxford: Clarendon Press.

Helm, P. (1988) *Eternal God*, Oxford: Clarendon Press.

Macquarrie, J. (1984) *In Search of Deity*, London: SCM Press.

Mascall, E. L. (1945) *He Who Is*, London: Longmans.

Morris, T. (1987) *Anselmian Explorations*, Notre Dame: University of Notre Dame Press.

Plantinga, A. (1974) *God, Freedom and Evil*, London: Allen & Unwin.

Swinburne, R. (1979) *The Existence of God*, Oxford: Clarendon Press.

Ward, K. (1974) *The Concept of God*, Oxford: Basil Blackwell.

—— (1982) *Rational Theology and the Creativity of God*, Oxford: Basil Blackwell.

See also chapters 18, 19, 20, 21, 23, 42.

18

THE IDEA OF REASON

Terence Penelhum

The relationship between philosophy and religious faith has never been an easy one. Philosophers deem it to be peculiarly their business to assess the rationality of others' activities and attitudes. In modern times, most of them have considered the rationality of faith to be at least problematic, and many have judged that it does not meet the standards of rationality they have applied to it.

There have always been those on the side of faith who have thought this presumptuous. Some of them have thought this because they consider faith has no obligation to be rational (a view known as fideism). Others have thought it because they consider the criteria of rationality philosophers have applied to faith are the wrong ones. In our day this latter opinion has been gaining influence among Christian philosophers, because of a change in the self-understanding of philosophy. Many philosophers, Christians or not, have come to abandon a perception of their role that has dominated modern philosophical thought since Descartes. It has been called a foundationalist conception of philosophy; and some contemporary Christian philosophers argue that if this conception of philosophy is abandoned, the rationality of faith ceases to be problematic, and the defender of faith does not have to adopt a fideist stance in apologetics.

The purpose of this chapter is to explain this view, and the philosophical history behind it; and to assess its strengths and weaknesses.

FAITH AND REASON BEFORE DESCARTES

Debates about faith and reason often proceed without analysis of what reason is. It has been a philosophical commonplace since Aristotle to distinguish between theoretical and practical reason: between the use of our intellectual powers to gain truth, and their use to guide our conduct. Someone noteworthy for success in the first has been said to show theoretical wisdom, and someone successful in the second has been said to show practical wisdom, or prudence.

Theoretical reason is commonly divided into pure reason, which proceeds wholly *a priori*, and inductive or empirical reason, which proceeds with the guidance of sensory or other forms of experience. Theoretical and practical reason are thought of as species of one genus because each has to proceed according to principles that it is the business of the logician to examine; so that a person can be judged irrational if his or her beliefs are incoherent or confused, and equally if his or her conduct is inconsistent or self-defeating.

Debates about the rationality of faith are most commonly about its relationship to theoretical reason: about the extent to which the beliefs that the man or woman of faith adheres to can be established by pure or inductive reasoning, or cohere with truths learned through reasoning in either of its forms, or are internally consistent with one another. But they may also be about the extent to which the believer is pursuing a form of life that is prudent or self-fulfilling, or frustrating or immature; and such questions are questions about the practical, rather than the theoretical, rationality of faith. There is a third range of questions that seems to straddle this division: philosophers have often said that considerations of prudence or obligation arise not only for our conduct but also for our beliefs. It is said that we have certain duties that we must carry out if we are to attain to truth – to believe only on good evidence, for example. Let us call these doxastic duties. Some critics of faith have suggested that those who have it neglect some of these duties. Contemporary debates about the impact of the decline of foundationalism in philosophy have raised questions about what doxastic duties we have, and whether faith satisfies them. These questions have become prominent because foundationalism is based on assumptions about such duties that are now under attack.

Parallel questions can be raised about beliefs that are not the core of faith, such as those of secular common sense or natural science. Philosophical reasoning can be used to question the achievements of reason itself. This questioning is the essence of the Sceptical tradition, and the foundationalism that we owe to Descartes is in part an attempt to respond to it. It is important to note that those who see faith and reason as enemies may judge Scepticism to be an ally of faith, in spite of appearances to the contrary.

Whatever the effects of foundationalism on debates about the status of faith, Descartes and his successors did not begin such debates; so it is not likely, on the face of it, that self-conscious freedom from foundationalist assumptions can resolve more than some of them. The debates are as old as theological thought itself. They arose because Christianity spread in a culture that had already attained the highest level of philosophical sophistication, but had achieved it without seeing any need to integrate philosophical understanding and religious devotion (Gilson 1941; Mascall 1949: ch. 1). Philosophy seemed unnecessary and religiously hazardous to many Christians, yet its conceptual resources were indispensable for responding to pagan critics and for distinguishing orthodoxy from heresy. In these disputes it became clear that some pagan philosophical traditions, especially those deriving from Plato, were rich sources of theological nourishment, whose availability looked providential. Hence the protracted controversies about the relation between reason and faith in the medieval period (Gilson 1938).

Two major positions in these debates have had great influence. The first is that of Augustine and Anselm, which holds that the understanding the metaphysician seeks is not a condition of faith, but is one of its rewards; indeed that faith is required for it. As Anselm says in his address to God in the *Proslogion*, he does not seek to understand so that he may believe, but he believes in order to understand. The Augustinian position is hard to square with the actual use of argument in faith's service (Hopkins 1972; Wolterstorff 1986).

The most systematic and influential resolution of the problem of faith and reason is that found in Aquinas. It is a system that forges an alliance between Aristotelian philosophy and Christian revelation as found in the Scriptures and interpreted by the Church, while recognizing the separate provenance and integrity of each (Wicksteed 1920; Aquinas 1955: I, 1–12, III, 1–63; Aquinas 1963: Ia, Qu. 1,2).

Aquinas believes that the ultimate good for human nature is the enjoyment of the vision of God. But such fulfilment is not possible for us in this life, since our minds must always begin from what is supplied to them by the senses. We can move beyond the limitations of the senses, however, in ways that other creatures cannot. This movement, which can point us towards the vision that constitutes our ultimate satisfaction, is possible in two ways. Our reason can abstract from the sensory and recognize the existence of a higher realm, while remaining incapable of penetrating the nature of the supernatural reality it can show us exists. Some divine truths, therefore, are accessible to us through philosophical reflection. The second way in which we can be pointed towards the vision of God is a way that is available both to those who can engage in philosophical reasoning and to those who cannot; this is the way of revelation. Revelation provides us with a body of truths about God, our nature, and our salvation. It is to be found in the Scriptures and the doctrinal pronouncements of the Church, especially the creeds. The faith the Christian proclaims in reciting the creeds is primarily a matter of accepting these truths. Such acceptance entails no more than a very dim and partial understanding of the realities which these doctrines tell us, since these realities transcend the capacities of our finite intellects. But in spite of this, it is not foolish (or irrational) to accept them. On the contrary, good reasons can be given for doing so. Some of them (such as the existence of God and the providential governance of the world) can be proved by reason, so that the spheres of reasoning and of revelation overlap. Those that reason cannot prove (such as the triune nature of God) complement those that can. And the revelation of those truths that are beyond reason's power to prove is accompanied by signs of its divine source: miracles, the fulfilment of prophecies, and the workings of the Spirit in the growth of the Church itself. Such evidence attests the divine source of the revelation we are called on to accept. We can, therefore, also assume that when the truths of revelation seem to contradict reason (as, for example, the doctrine of Incarnation has been held to do), this appearance must be illusory and can be dispelled by careful argument and reflection.

Faith, then, is rational in three ways. First, some of the truths proclaimed in revelation can be proved independently, in what came to be known as natural theology. Second, those that cannot be so proved, or even understood, by reason, are attested by evidence that makes it fully reasonable to assent to them as coming from God. Third, the appearance of contradiction in revealed doctrine, or of its conflict with natural knowledge, can always be shown to be the result of misunderstanding or of sophistry. The gift of revelation carries us beyond, but does not contradict, the knowledge and satisfaction that the natural exercise of reason gives to us, just as the supernatural virtues of faith, hope, and charity are gifts that supervene upon the natural virtues we can develop for ourselves. Grace does not replace nature, but perfects it.

If we ask, from a standpoint determined by later philosophical concerns, whether or not Aquinas thought he was providing philosophical foundations for faith, the answer has to be negative. The faith does not need the philosopher to legitimize it or establish its credentials. Nevertheless, he argues that it is not 'foolishness' to assent to the truths of revelation, and that it is 'fitting' that those truths about God that reason can discover should also be made available in the Scriptures for those who do not have the training or opportunity to learn them through philosophy; and the fact that he argues these things shows that he sees philosophical argument (and few thinkers in history have penned so much of it) has critical apologetic functions for him (Wicksteed 1920: 176–96).

DESCARTES, FOUNDATIONALISM AND MODERN PHILOSOPHY

The centrality of epistemology in modern philosophy is clearly due to Descartes. He himself tells us he is seeking to start from the foundations in order to build a firm and lasting structure in the sciences. Whatever the precise order of priorities in his mind, he certainly had two key objectives. One was to free scientific enquiry, once and for all, from the criticisms of Pyrrhonian scepticism, recently fashionable through the rediscovery of the writings of Sextus Empiricus (Descartes 1966; Curley 1978; Popkin 1979; Burnyeat 1982). Another was to free scientific enquiry, once and for all, from the theological suspicion and interference typified by the condemnation of Galileo.

To refute Pyrrhonian scepticism, Descartes carries some of its arguments further than they had been carried by its classical proponents, to whom Pyrrhonism was a practical stance that yielded peace of mind by generating suspense of judgement and the avoidance of dogma. Descartes raises sceptical doubts about the senses, and then about reason, as purely theoretical exercises that it would be absurd to take seriously in practice, but which he insists must be refuted if true certainty and assurance are to be found. Assuming, as an argumentative procedure, that any proposition that can be questioned is false, he finds there are two truths that he cannot question however resolutely he doubts: the fact of his own existence as a thinking being, and the fact that even if his thoughts and perceptions do not correspond to any outer reality, he cannot be in error about what his mental contents themselves are: the fact, as he expresses it, that mind is more certainly known than body. The Pyrrhonian sceptic had rested with appearances and suspended judgement about whether a non-evident reality lay behind them. This sceptic is replaced in Cartesian thought by a doubter who must accept he has knowledge of his own conscious states but needs reassurance about the very existence of a physical world beyond them, and even about the existence of other conscious subjects like himself. He confronts what has been called the Egocentric Predicament – the supposed challenge of solipsism. He wrestles with a radical form of doubt that no-one feels in practice, where the classical sceptic had embraced conventional opinion in the absence of anything demonstrably better. The Pyrrhonian did not query the existence of an outer reality, or that of a community of perceivers; he suspended judgement on whether he and other members of that community perceived it as it is. The truth he doubted his ability to attain was truth about a reality he assumed to be there. The Cartesian sceptic sees a way towards certainty by holding that his very doubts entail real knowledge of himself and his mental states, and seeking to use them to move outward.

It is well known that Descartes' attempt to move outward depends on the doctrine of clear and distinct ideas, whose veracity is guaranteed by proof of God's existence. This proof notoriously depends on the claim that the idea of God is one that, uniquely, could not be present in the mind if there were no being without to correspond to it. The so-called Cartesian circle is commonly thought to result from the fact that the demonstration of God's reality relies on the very rational processes God's perfection guarantees. Whether or not Descartes is guilty of this circularity is not our present concern (for discussion, see Hookway 1990: chs 3 and 4). What is of concern is that the 'foundationalism' of modern epistemology derives from the manner in which Descartes seeks to refute scepticism, and has two key components: first, the belief that the certainty of all real knowledge depends on the derivation of the propositions we claim to know from propositions of a privileged class that are beyond doubt; second, the belief that the propositions in this class are propositions that are uniquely accessible to, because they are in some sense within, the subject's consciousness – such as self-evident truths (for Descartes himself and his rationalist successors) or sensory experiences (for Locke and his empiricist followers).

But in seeking to establish the foundations of the sciences, Descartes was not only attempting to meet the challenge of scepticism. He was also seeking to create an accommodation between the scientist and Church authorities that would fend off the sort of interference that had humiliated Galileo. This required a sound base in theory for non-interference. Galileo's condemnation had arisen because he was unwilling to accept the supposedly conciliatory suggestion that his astronomical claims were mere convenient devices for predicting celestial phenomena (de Santillana 1955). Descartes wanted science to have the unquestionable underpinning that shows it tells us how the material reality of the outer world is. The foundations on which science is based show it to be the source of truth. But the truth science yields is truth about the material world: the Cartesian separation of the mental and the physical provides for the separation of the spheres of science and theology. In spite of the intractable difficulties of Cartesian dualism, which became obvious at once, it was a major cause of the nearly universal cultural assumption of our age that science and theology can have nothing to say to one another. Instead of Aquinas' view of human knowledge, in which secular learning and theological truth are continuous, we have a metaphysic designed to ensure their separation. The provision of a metaphysical and epistemological guarantee of the autonomy of science was an assumed objective of all the major systems of thought that succeeded that of Descartes, with the possible exception of Berkeley's (Warnock 1953; Bracken 1974).

It is widely agreed that the assumption of the autonomy of science has been the most important cultural factor in the secularization of modern Western society. As this secularization has deepened, the orientation of philosophical discussions of faith and reason has shifted. In Aquinas, their relationship was articulated in order to resolve debates about the proper place of secular science in a culture assumed to be Christian. While this is still nominally the assumption of Descartes and his successors, it is increasingly obvious that their relationship is now examined in order to determine whether a culture dominated by natural science can remain Christian.

Cartesianism, therefore, defined the role of the philosopher as the entrenchment of science in the face of an imaginary challenge from scepticism. Yet this challenge was not one that prevented scientific advance. When Kant came to state the problem of epistemology in the second edition of *The Critique of Pure Reason* in 1787, he said that the philosopher cannot question the reality of mathematics and natural science, but only explore what makes them possible; but this investigation is one that may well show metaphysics to be an activity that is quite unable to yield knowledge, even though the inclination to engage in it is deeply rooted in our intellectual natures (Kant 1929: 56–7). He assumes theology to be a part of metaphysics. The scientist is conceded the right to proceed without waiting for the epistemologist's seal of approval; but the theologian may have to be headed off before he begins.

Naturally enough, the discharge of the philosopher's duty, thus understood, is commonly thought to depend on the success or failure of the enterprise of natural theology. Even though it did not owe its existence and practice to the

Cartesian view of the philosopher's function, the discharge of that function, once assumed, was thought to depend on how far natural theology could demonstrate the reality of God and the credentials of revelation in the way Aquinas had claimed. How else, after all, could the philosopher show that theology even has a subject matter?

Inevitably there were those who rejected philosophy's pretensions to adjudicate the claims of revelation. They were apologists who questioned the foundationalist objective of epistemology, and saw scepticism as the friend of faith, not its enemy. The foundationalist tradition has been paralleled by the tradition of sceptical fideism, which has seen natural theology as 'the sustained attempt to replace conversion by argument' (MacIntyre 1957: 210). Let us now examine the two traditions.

FOUNDATIONALISM, NATURAL THEOLOGY, AND REVELATION

Descartes himself, although he uses proofs of God to cement the structure of his intellectual foundation of human knowledge, does not involve himself with any implications his epistemological programme might have for theology. His anxiety to remain a loyal son of the church while establishing the bases of science, precludes such an extension of his programme. It fell to those who followed him to discern these implications. They were radical. The first was the severance of the two key parts of the traditional philosophical supports of faith inherited from St Thomas Aquinas: instead of seeing natural theology as providing grounds for judging it rational for us to accept the claims of revelation, many thinkers who still practised it decided that it undermined those claims, and that revealed religion should yield to natural religion. The second was a progressive scepticism about the possibility of natural theology itself.

Proofs of God's existence abounded. Descartes, Spinoza and Leibniz use the ontological proof; Descartes and Leibniz use the cosmological argument, which receives its best expression in the work of Samuel Clarke (1738). In an era when the establishment of the credentials of science was the core of philosophical systems, however, the popularity of the argument from design became greater and greater. It was inevitably changed from the teleological form it had taken in Aquinas' Fifth Way; while Kant could still call it the physico-teleological proof, it did not presuppose the Aristotelian natural philosophy, but came to represent a theistic inference from Newtonian physics. Its most famous version is that found in Paley's *Natural Theology*, where it is argued that it is as unlikely that the world's order, in particular the biological adaptation within it, is accidental as it is that the workings of a watch I find on the ground have come to be there without human contrivance (Paley 1838: vol. 1). The design argument only claims to establish intelligent design, not creation *ex nihilo*, but this limitation was commonly ignored. It is also merely probabilistic, but this was not seen as a limitation either, for two reasons: it is based on an inference that mimics the inductive procedure of natural science, and therefore attracts empiricist thinkers who question the *a priori* demonstrations; and the probability it established was considered to be over-whelmingly great. Indeed, it was the supposed power of the design argument that most of all fed the widespread consensus that atheism was intellectually unthinkable.

But it was natural religion, so-called, not revealed religion, that was the major beneficiary of this consensus (Byrne 1989). For the inherited supports for the rationality of revealed religion were the fulfilment of prophecies and the occurrence of miracles, and both these manifestations of the presence of an interventionist deity seem to contradict the mechanical uniformity on which the most popular case for God's reality now depended. As Pascal had foreseen in Descartes' own day, it was deism, not Christianity, that was the likely product of natural theology in the age of science (Pascal 1966: fragment 449).

We can see the shift to deism in the progress from Locke to his successors. In the concluding chapters of the *Essay Concerning Human Understanding*, Locke seeks to show that faith can be saved from 'enthusiasm' by being shown to be conformable to reason: a thesis which he argues at length in his last work, *The Reasonableness of Christianity*. He distinguishes in the *Essay* between propositions that are according to reason, which are those that can be inferred from the ideas of sensation and reflection or through 'natural deduction'; propositions that are above reason, because they cannot be derived in these ways yet are nevertheless fit to be accepted; and propositions that are contrary to reason, which are 'inconsistent with or irreconcilable to our clear and distinct ideas'. 'Thus the existence of one God is according to reason; the existence of more than one God, contrary to reason; the resurrection of the dead, above reason' (Locke 1894: vol. 2, 412–13). He specifically adds that the latter two categories contrast not only with rational certainty, but with probability. The implication here is that it may be rational to accept the improbable as a part of one's faith, without falling into enthusiasm:

> But since God, in giving us the light of reason, has not thereby tied up his own hands from affording us, when he thinks fit, the light of revelation in any of those matters wherein our natural faculties are able to give a probable determination; revelation, where God has been pleased to give it, must carry it against the probable conjectures of reason.
>
> (ibid.: 423–4)

But if we ask how this can be, we find Locke presenting us with his version of the traditional apologetic of prophecies and miracles. He insists that 'it still belongs to reason to judge of the truth of its being a revelation' (ibid.: 424); this means that revelation cannot contain what is contrary to reason, and that if it contains what is above reason, this must be discernible through more than the inner light of the enthusiast:

Thus we see the holy men of old, who had revelations from God, had something else besides that internal light of assurance ... They were not left to their own persuasions alone, that those persuasions were from God, but had outward signs to convince them of the Author of those revelations.

(ibid.: 439)

The assent of faith, then, is rational for Locke, if we are able to supply it with what he refers to in picturesquely foundationalist language, in *The Conduct of the Understanding*, as 'bottoming' (Locke 1823: vol. III, 283). Faith, he tells us in chapter XVIII of the *Essay,* is

the assent to any proposition, not thus made out by the deductions of reason, but upon the credit of the proposer, as coming from God, in some extraordinary way of communication. This way of discovering truths to men, we call revelation.

This credit is something that can be vouched for by the fulfilment of prophecies and by miracles. Both are treated in *The Reasonableness of Christianity* and *A Discourse of Miracles* (Locke 1958). The authority of Jesus' preaching is attested by the fulfilment of prophecies that show him to have been the Messiah; and his authority is shown by the miracles he wrought (ibid: 83).

Locke was notoriously conservative in the number of Christian doctrines he thought to be authenticated in this way; but he does not depart from his position in the *Essay* that some of these are above reason, since this is what makes it needful to authenticate their acceptance by rational hearers. But Locke still insists that it is reason itself that determines what is above it, since 'reason must be our last judge and guide in everything' (Locke 1894: vol 2, 438). It is a small step from this to the view of his deistic successors that there is no place for mysteries above reason at all. The most famous treatises arguing this view were John Toland's *Christianity not Mysterious* (1696), and Matthew Tindal's *Christianity as Old as the Creation* (1730). Toland's work had as its subtitle: 'a Treatise Shewing that there is nothing in the Gospel Contrary to Reason, nor above it: and that no Christian Doctrine can be properly call'd a Mystery' (see Toland 1964; Daniel 1984). Tindal tells us that 'whatever is confused and perplexed, can never come from the clear fountain of all knowledge; nor that which is obscure from the father of inexhaustible light' (Tindal 1978: 105). In the deists we find the view that the rational order that is the most striking evidence of the reality of God is an order that is inconsistent with the disruptive interventions that Aquinas and Locke had appealed to as grounds for the acceptance of mysteries. Mystery, therefore, becomes the obfuscatory product of 'priestcraft'; and if revelation retains a place at all, it is as a folkloric representation of moral lessons that the educated reason can discern in nature without it. Something similar had been maintained earlier by Spinoza, in his attack on Jewish orthodoxy in the *Tractatus Theologico-Politicus*, published in 1670 (Spinoza 1883). But the deists said these things in a nominally Christian context, and based them on an understanding of the nature of God that they claimed to support by the post-Newtonian version of the design argument.

The deists met their match in Joseph Butler, who argued in *The Analogy of Religion* (1736) that just as there are obscurities in nature that the design argument shows us must have a place in God's plan, so there may be a place in that plan for miracle and revelation: that the deist has no warrant for confidence when he tells us what God would not include in his governance (Butler 1900). This was an effective reply to the deists, but of course shared their premise that the design argument places God's governance beyond reasonable doubt. The second stage of disintegration of the post-Cartesian consensus on the rationality of faith was the rejection of that premise.

The main agent of this disintegration was Hume. While he is still more immediately recognized as the last of the great critics of belief in miracles, there can be no reasonable question that his greatest contributions to philosophical reflection on religion come in his destructive criticisms of the design argument and his introduction of the study of comparative religion. The design argument is shown wanting in the *Dialogues Concerning Natural Religion*, the main burden of which is the weakness of the popular inference from natural order to designing intelligence: the existence of God cannot be represented as a hypothesis confirmed by evidence (Hume 1947). In *The Natural History of Religion*, Hume offers a pioneering study in religious anthropology, in which he represents belief in God as a development from primitive religious forms that originate in humanity's fearful encounter with unpredictable natural forces. Actual religion, therefore, is the psychological product of a way of perceiving the natural world that is quite opposite to the supposed orderliness on which the design argument depends (Hume 1957). While acknowledging Hume's destructive criticisms of the design argument, Kant produces the classic refutations (or supposed refutations) of the ontological and cosmological proofs in the Dialectic of the *Critique of Pure Reason*, in which he represents natural theology as an illegitimate extension of intellectual activity beyond the realm of possible experience (Kant 1929).

The Humean and Kantian criticisms of natural theology, especially when combined with the development of biblical criticism that had been stimulated by the work of Spinoza and the deists, left the claims of revelation without the 'bottoming' that Locke had claimed to offer. Although the import of their criticisms was not fully recognized by apologists (Paley, for example, being satisfied to elaborate the design argument in detail without acknowledging the Humean criticisms of it – see Paley 1838: vol. 1), the progressive secularization of our culture, and the impact of Darwinism in particular, served to entrench a widespread perception that faith has no rational basis. This, indeed, had been asserted all along by some apologists.

THE TRADITION OF SCEPTICAL FIDEISM

One reason for the popularity of the Pyrrhonism that Descartes tried to refute was its tactical value in the battle between Catholicism and Protestantism. Catholic apologists had seized upon the Pyrrhonist abandonment of argument and acquiescence in tradition to recommend a similar conservatism in matters of faith. Religion became, in their hands, what it had been for Sextus: a matter of conformity with the subject's own communal observance, unencumbered by dogmatic assertion. This is the position nominally adopted by Montaigne, and Erasmus' apparent sympathy for it roused the ire of Luther (Popkin 1979; Penelhum 1983).

Sceptical fideism has taken two forms (Penelhum 1983: ch. 1). In the first, found in Montaigne and Bayle, the serenity consequent on faith is identified with the *ataraxia*, or unperturbedness, that the Greek sceptics said followed on the cessation of belief, and faith itself is seen as the subject's acquiescence in tradition. In the second, found in Pascal and Kierkegaard, the sceptic is held rather to be faith's unwitting ally: in exposing the pretensions of reason to arrive at saving truth, the sceptic has paved the way for grace to fill the vacuum thus created. This second form of fideism, unlike the first, is not shy of dogma and is impatient of sceptic detachment. Both forms hinge on the abandonment of the attempt to use reason as a ground for faith.

It is only possible to characterize this apologetic tradition here very briefly. It involves, first, a rejection of attempts to prove the existence of God by reason. Pascal, with a particular eye to the design argument, insists that such proof can only yield a facilely optimistic deism, not a real faith (Pascal 1966: fragment 449). It further involves an insistence that reason is powerless to support the beliefs on which common sense and science depend, so that daily life requires a secular faith that parallels the religious (ibid.: fragments 110, 131). Its third contention is that even if faith provides those who have it with the sort of illumination that Augustine and Anselm attribute to it (as Pascal seems to think), faith is not intelligible to the unregenerate reason. Bayle insists in many places (Bayle 1965) that application of the Cartesian criteria of clarity and distinctness to Christian doctrines shows them to involve irresoluble paradoxes (hence the common belief that he is seeking to undermine them). Kierkegaard insists not only that the incarnation is a paradox, but that to suppose Christ to be the bearer of teachings that the philosopher has the right to adjudicate is to reject, from the start, the need for submission that is the only proper response to God's entry into history: that to require the satisfaction of rational preambles to faith is to try to domesticate, and thus to refuse, the Paradox (Kierkegaard 1985: 37–54). Aquinas had said that assent to revelation was not foolishness; the sceptical fideist claims it must be.

We can best summarize the stance of sceptical fideism in Hume's words: 'To be a philosophical sceptic is . . . the first and most essential step towards being a sound believing Christian' (Hume 1947: 228). The omitted phrase is 'in a man of letters' and Hume of course was parodying the fideists. But if we change the tone of voice the parody vanishes.

PRUDENTIAL THEISM

There is one famous argument from the sceptical fideist tradition that takes the debate on faith and reason into another dimension. This is the argument known as Pascal's Wager. It depends on the sceptical premise that theoretical reason cannot determine whether God exists or not. In these circumstances it is appropriate for prudence to determine what one believes. If God does exist, and one has not believed, one forfeits eternal bliss; if he does not, and one has believed, one merely forfeits a few trivial wordly advantages; so it is manifestly the wiser bet to believe than not to believe. But Pascal recognizes that if one has no theoretical grounds for preferring belief to unbelief, one will not be able to have the belief it is better to have. In such circumstances the prudent gambler will induce belief in himself by acting as if he believed already: by doing those things that believers do from belief, he will perhaps bring about in this own soul the belief they have (Pascal 1966: fragment 418; Rescher 1985).

Pascal's argument has not had many admirers. Its many hostile critics have seldom sought to understand it or its context in his work. He does not suggest, as some assume, that the person who acts as though he believes has faith. One the contrary, faith is what this person hopes will issue from this course of action. Pascal never suggests that faith itself comes about through anything other than divine grace; the prudent wagerer seeks to open himself to it, not to pre-empt it. Even more importantly, Pascal does not seek to undermine the intellectual autonomy of the rational enquirer. The Wager presupposes that enquiry has produced a sceptical equipoise, so that considerations of evidential weight are no longer pertinent.

Two apologetic writings that echo the Wager have been very influential. One is the defence of revelation against the deists in Butler's *The Analogy of Religion* (1736). The other is William James's lecture, 'The Will to Believe', first published in 1896. Butler, telling us that for finite intellects like ours, 'probability is the very guide of life', argues that it is sometimes prudent to act upon propositions that have a low degree of likelihood, provided it is a real one, when the risks attendant on a wrong decision are very great. He then stresses that our knowledge of God's existence is accompanied by great ignorance of his detailed intentions, and in these circumstances it is wise to pay careful heed to what the Church says God has revealed, and to act as though the commands of conscience, which he assumes to be coincident with those of the New Testament, come from him. He stops short, however, of recommending his readers to adopt psychological inducements to induce belief, perhaps assuming that careful heed will always be enough (Butler 1900; Penelhum 1985, 1992).

William James argues against the claim of W. K. Clifford that we have a doxastic duty to avoid believing anything upon insufficient evidence. We find ourselves in matters of religion facing the choice between two hypotheses; this option, says James, is 'live' (since each hypothesis 'makes some appeal'), 'forced' (since, as Pascal had emphasized, suspending judgement is equivalent to a negative decision), and 'momentous' (since the choice one makes is unique and irreversible). In this situation our 'passional nature', says James, must decide when the choice cannot be made on intellectual grounds; the decision to run the risk of believing falsely rather than risk losing the truth is the only rational course (James 1979). It has seemed to most of James's readers that, in spite of his expressed distaste for Pascal's argument, his own does not greatly differ from it, and it does not tell us clearly, as Pascal does, what the seeker for truth must do if the passion for truth is to be satisfied. A prudential argument should issue in a plan; and James's argument does not.

FAITH AND RATIONALITY AFTER FOUNDATIONALISM

The decline in the influence of foundationalism in recent years has many sources. These cannot be evaluated here, but some, at least, require mention for the arguments of post-foundationalist apologetic to be fully intelligible. In the first instance, the circularity that besets Descartes' epistemology does not seem to be correctable. Sceptical doubts about reason, once admitted, cannot be resolved by argument; and in the absence of intellectual demonstration of the reality of an external world, scepticism of the senses, once admitted, cannot be refuted by an appeal to experience. Also, the supposedly certain starting points of the Cartesian tradition are commonly dismissed as illusory. For me to know that I have certain conscious states, these must not merely occur, but occur to a subject who can identify them. But the concepts needful for this, it is commonly held, are only available to language users; and language is a communal rule-governed activity that presupposes the very environment that the egocentric predicament requires us to question. Another argument is that the Cartesian tradition equates rational justification with the presence of inferences from indubitable starting points. The epistemic status of a belief is a function of the calibre of the inference from those beginnings. Since Wittgenstein, it has been increasingly recognized that this model of justification is at odds with the actual practice of human reason in the sciences, at the common-sense level, and in practical affairs. While the Enlightenment's equation of human dignity with rationality is still influential, the equation of rationality with derivation from certain foundations is discredited. There are many distinct and autonomous forms of rationality, and it is arbitrary to suppose that the standards of one must apply within another (Winch 1967).

It has become commonplace to maintain that we have an irreducible plurality of doxastic practices, and that scepticism about any one of them is inarticulable within it, and arbitrary and chauvinistic if advanced from outside it (Wittgenstein 1969; Alston 1991: 162).

The influence of Wittgenstein has been felt in philosophy of religion in three distinct, and incompatible, ways. There have been those who have claimed that the religious form of life is incoherent (Flew 1955; MacIntyre 1964). There have been those, most notably D. Z. Phillips, who have argued, in a mode more reminiscent of the apparent views of Wittgenstein himself, that the religious form of life is coherent, but can only be seen to be if it is given a non-realist analysis in which questions of dogma and its justification do not arise (Phillips 1965, 1970, 1988; Keightley 1976; Cupitt 1980). Both these perceptions of religion are motivated by an overriding concern with problems of meaning. In the 1970s and 1980s, however, analytical philosophers of religion have been more concerned with the epistemology of religion; the result of this concern has been the appearance of several influential versions of what I shall call the Basic Belief Apologetic (Plantinga 1979, 1983b, 1993a, b; Wolterstorff 1983a, b; Alston 1991).

While it is important not to ignore individual differences, it seems fair to venture the following characterization of the stance that is common to those who adopt this apologetic position. Its essence is the rejection of the view that the rationality of religious belief depends on the possibility of inferring all or part of its content from prior non-religious beliefs. This view is commonly referred to as 'evidentialism', and Locke is most commonly identified as its classical exponent. It is not denied that there may be evidence in favour of religious beliefs; it is denied that such evidence must be forthcoming if religious belief is to be rational, or justified.

This position has important affinities with sceptical fideist claims, but also key verbal differences. The sceptic fideist denies that reason can establish the reality of the external world or the existence of God and tells us to abandon the search for rational justification for either; the Basic Belief Apologetic, while commonly accepting the analogy between the commitments of common sense and those of faith, retains our conviction in the reasonableness of both, by denying something the Cartesian sceptic has assumed: that reasonableness depends on derivation from starting points that are certain. The assertion that it does so depend is an assertion that is not, itself, either beyond doubt or deducible from other assertions that are (Plantinga 1979). To insist on external support for the propositions of faith, while not insisting on such support for propositions of secular common sense or science (a common position) is to be guilty of what Alston calls epistemic chauvinism (Alston 1991). Once this chauvinism is abandoned, it is possible to recognize that belief in God can be rationally held as a basic belief. A basic belief is one that is not held because it is inferred from another belief. Such beliefs, on this view, are *prima facie* justified: justified, that is, unless one finds evidence that defeats, or refutes, them. In these circumstances, the apologist is best advised to concentrate on showing that potential 'defeaters', such as the problem of evil, do not undermine the faith, rather than labouring to find external grounds for adopting it.

It is natural for critics to respond to this apologetic by accusing it of being a defence of arbitrary or groundless believing. This has been answered through an important distinction between the ground or occasion of religious beliefs, and evidence for them. To say that religious beliefs are not based upon others (in the manner of traditional natural theology) is not to say they are groundless (Plantinga 1983b); for they may be grounded in religious experience, or the reading of Scripture. Such grounds, however, are not the sources of premises from which religious beliefs are inferred (as they were, for example, in the traditional 'argument from religious experience'). They are, rather, the proper occasions for them, as sensory experiences are the proper occasions for the onset of perceptual beliefs about our environment (rather than the source of premises from which we infer propositions about that environment). Alston has argued at length (Alston 1991) that 'Christian mystical experience' in fact provides a source of nurture and testing for Christian beliefs, as sensory observation provides such a source for secular common-sense beliefs about the physical world. In both cases, however, the demand for external justification is a vain and self-defeating one, and the justification of the doxastic practice of the perceiver and the Christian does not depend on the completion of the foundationalist enterprise of providing it.

Plantinga has lately argued that Christian beliefs may well have warrant, which is his term for that 'elusive quality or quantity enough of which, together with truth and belief, is sufficient for knowledge' (Plantinga 1993b: vi). Warranted beliefs are those that are the product of cognitive faculties that are functioning as they should in their proper environment, and follow a design plan aimed at truth (rather than at survival or happiness). This epistemology permits us to ascribe warrant not only to the beliefs favoured by classical foundationalism, but also to sensory beliefs, beliefs based on testimony, inductively grounded beliefs, and many others. Each type, if generated appropriately, is properly basic. He plans to argue that Christian beliefs also have warrant, as they too derive from such a cognitive faculty: one that disposes us to accept beliefs about God.

The basic belief apologetic has rapidly become a received wisdom. It has become so because its proponents have, rightly, challenged a fundamental assumption of an earlier received wisdom that has perhaps run its course. In doing so they have shown that religious beliefs can be accommodated within the purview of an understanding of the powers and limitations of human reason that envisages a wide variety of rational forms of life, each with standards of its own that are independent of the judicial processes to which philosophers have sought to subject it. It is important to concede that such an understanding is not intrinsically anti-religious (or, for that matter, anti-metaphysical). But it is also important to recognize that the catholicity of its ascription of rationality extends to many forms of life that are hostile to Christianity, and also to many forms of religion that appear incompatible with it.

There seems no case for denying the qualification of rationality to religious faith, merely because one supposes it to lack external justification – unless one is willing to follow the sceptic in denying this qualification to common-sense perceptual judgements, or to natural science. For the doxastic practices that are a part of faith are discernible, capable of discriminating justified from unjustified constituent beliefs, and of responding to external criticisms. It is also possible, from within the doxastic framework of the faith, to provide systematic criticism of competing belief-systems, and of explaining the inclination of the adherents of those competing systems to embrace and sustain them. The faith can provide plausible explanations for evils; it can discriminate between genuine and bogus spiritual manifestations; and it can offer a critical understanding of the secular mind and the mind of other faiths.

But the very parity that makes it needful to classify the faith as rational makes it needful to classify competing belief-systems as rational also. There are many of them, and it is a striking cultural phenomenon of our time that we understand them, and how they view one another, better than it has been possible to understand them before. It is not merely that Christianity and atheistic naturalism confront one another, each armed with its arguments and insights to answer and expose the other, although this confrontation is real and familiar. It is also a feature of our cultural scene that there are a wide variety of apparently competing religious belief-forms that are live options to many thousands; and there are a wide variety of competing naturalistic systems of thought that contend for the conversion of their adherents' personalities in a manner that used to be thought unique to religion. What John Hick has called the religious ambiguity of the universe (the fact that it is rational to accept both a religious and a naturalistic understanding of our situation) is a multi-faceted ambiguity, in which the rationality of an indefinite number of sophisticated and unsophisticated systems of thought, each equipped with transforming experiences and ways of life, presses itself upon us (Hick 1989). The situation is one that seems tailor-made for the classical sceptic's suspense of judgement, for he did not deny, but emphasized, that the systems between which he declined to make a selection were all supported with reasons, which seemed to balance one another. In Plantinga's most recent terminology, many systems rest on convictions that seem to their adherents to have warrant; and since the factors that yield warrant only turn true beliefs into knowledge and not false ones, one cannot ascribe warrant without making a judgement of truth first.

It is clear, and denied by no-one, that a belief can be *prima facie* justified, or properly basic, yet turn out to be mistaken, or unjustified ultimately. Although apologists are right to question the pretensions of philosophers who insist on adjudicating the faith before permitting the rational person to adhere to it, they cannot fail to recognize that the faith they defend in this way makes uncompromisingly 'realist' claims to truth: it does not offer itself as a mere viable option for the rational seeker, but as the key to an authentic relationship with God.

It might be that the one true faith is surrounded with comparably rational alternatives between which one merely has to do one's best to choose, just as it might be that, as John Hick and Wilfred Cantwell Smith have argued, there is reason not to regard the religious world-views as competitors in the way they appear to be (Smith 1981; Hick 1989). But it is a highly questionable understanding of rationality that does not admit that the fact of such an embarrassing richness of alternative world-views, and the existence of the supportive experiences and intellectual resources of the alternatives to one's own option, create a rational difficulty for that preferred option – especially when the demand of the faith is not for the sort of adherence proportionate to the relative weighting of a preferred alternative among many, but for a total commitment.

In these circumstances it is important to look again at what the arguments of traditional natural theology were thought to establish. They were thought to establish not merely that the faith was rational, but that some key elements within it could be proved to be true. This implied not merely that it was rational to believe the propositions of the faith, but that it is irrational not to believe those that were proved. It was this, indeed, that helped to make it intellectually necessary that the faith be seen not to contradict reason in those areas where it might seem at first sight to do so – for if God is a proven reality, intellectual difficulties in acknowledging him *must* have a solution.

This should suggest that the abandonment of a foundationalist view of the role of philosophy does not show that a successful natural theology, or a successful pursuit of religious evidences, is not of apologetic importance. (It is noteworthy that Plantinga himself argues that his epistemology points to a theistic metaphysics, while insisting that warrant does not depend upon it. See Plantinga 1993b: 216–37.) I conclude with some explicit suggestions of how these forms of philosophical activity could fulfil vital apologetic roles.

Believers rarely, now, reject the cultural assumption that it is to science we must turn if we are to learn the workings of our world. They differ from their naturalist fellows in insisting it is necessary to add to what science tells us in order to recognize our place within the cosmos. While no natural theologian has maintained that all the details of the Christian, or any other theistic, world-view can be established by his arguments, some forms of such argument, beginning with (say) cosmological theories acceptable to both, have been said to show that the early development of the universe required benignly intelligent direction (Leslie 1989, 1990; Van Inwagen 1993), or that evolutionary explanations of adaptive human and animal behaviour cannot account for the emergence of conscious mental life (Swinburne 1986: ch. 10). I offer no assessment of these arguments here; but if they were successful, they would serve to lessen the degree of ambiguity that otherwise besets us, by showing that commonly recognized evidence requires the sort of explanation that only theistic cosmic schemes can provide.

It is common among defenders of the faith to maintain that the primary obstacle to faith is our unwillingness to accept our own need for it; and it was Kierkegaard's great contribution to discern the role such unwillingness plays in the philosophical debates about faith's rationality. It is, however, also true that in our secular and pluralistic age, the abundance of rational alternatives is also a motive that makes many hesitate. In such circumstances the continued pursuit of the objectives of natural theology has a clear function, and defeatism about its feasibility can have no theological justification. A successful natural theology would not stand in the way of human obstinacy; people could refuse to believe as easily as now. But a successful natural theology would demonstrate that only obstinacy, not rational puzzlement, stood in their way.

CONCLUSION

We have taken foundationalism to be the thesis that a belief is only to be judged rational if it is a belief of an epistemically favoured class, or is validly inferred from a belief of that favoured class. Its theological counterpart is the thesis that belief in God, or beliefs that presuppose the existence of God, are only rational if they are inferred from other beliefs that do not presuppose the existence of God. Natural theology is the attempt to infer God's existence, or doctrines that entail it, from premises that do not presuppose it; so the decline of foundationalism in contemporary thought has led to the claim that the rationality of belief in God does not depend on the success of natural theology. This claim can be accepted, however, without the apologetic significance of natural theology being much affected. For the rationality thus conceded to one religious faith must be conceded to other religious faiths, and to many of their secular competitors. To regard the apologetic role of philosophy as exhausted by this is to accept as ultimate a huge plurality of apparently exclusive world-views and associated doxastic practices, and to acquiesce in a fashionable relativism that denies the choice between them to be subject to rational evaluation. What natural theology, if successful, would show, is that one's faith is indeed rationally defensible by criteria not wholly internal to it. The search for this sort of justification is something the Christian philosopher should only abandon for the very strongest of reasons. The apparent demise of foundationalism does not, of itself, provide any such reason.

REFERENCES

Alston, W. P. (1989) *Epistemic Justification: Essays in the Theory of Knowledge*, Ithaca: Cornell University Press.
—— (1991) *Perceiving God: The Epistemology of Religious Experience*, Ithaca: Cornell University Press.
Anselm, St (1962) *Basic Writings*, trans. S. N. Deane, 2nd edn, La Salle, Ill.: Open Court.
Aquinas, St Thomas (1955–7) *Summa Contra Gentiles*, trans. as *On the Truth of the Catholic Faith*, by A. C. Pegis *et al.* 5 vols, Garden City, New York: Doubleday.
—— (1963) *Summa Theologiae*, Dominican translation ed. T. Gilby, 60 vols, London: Eyre and Spottiswoode.
Bayle, P. (1965) *Historical and Critical Dictionary: Selections*, trans. and ed. R. H. Popkin, Indianapolis: Bobbs-Merrill.
Bracken, H. (1974) *Berkeley*, London: Macmillan.
Burnyeat, M. (1982) 'Idealism and Greek Philosophy: What Descartes Saw and Berkeley Missed', *Philosophical Review* 91: 3–40.
Butler, J. (1900) *The Analogy of Religion*, in J. H. Bernard (ed.) *The Works of Joseph Butler*, vol. II, London: Macmillan.
Byrne, P. (1989) *Natural Religion and the Nature of Religion: The Legacy of Deism*, London: Routledge.
Clarke, S. (1978) *A Demonstration of the Being and Attributes of God*, in vol. 2 of *The Works of Samuel Clarke*, 4 vols, New York: Garland Publishing.
Cupitt, D. (1980) *Taking Leave of God*, London: SCM Press.
Curley, E. M. (1978) *Descartes Against the Skeptics*, Oxford: Basil Blackwell.
Daniel, S. H. (1984) *John Toland: His Methods, Manners and Mind*, Kingston and Montreal: McGill-Queen's University Press.
de Santillana, G. (1955) *The Crime of Galileo*, Chicago: University of Chicago Press.
Descartes, R. (1966) *Philosophical Writings*, trans. and ed. E. Anscombe and P. Geach, London: Nelson.
Flew, A. (1955) 'Theology and Falsification', in A. Flew and A. MacIntyre (eds) *New Essays in Philosophical Theology*, London: SCM Press.
—— (1976) *The Presumption of Atheism*, London: Pemberton Publishing Co.
Gilson, E. (1938) *Reason and Revelation in the Middle Ages*, New York: Charles Scribner's Sons.
—— (1941) *God and Philosophy*, New Haven: Yale University Press.
Hick, J. (1989) *An Interpretation of Religion: Human Responses to the Transcendent*, London: Macmillan Press.
Hookway, C. (1990) *Scepticism*, London: Routledge.
Hopkins, J. (1972) *A Companion to the Study of St. Anselm*, Minneapolis: University of Minnesota Press.
Hume, D. (1947) *Dialogues Concerning Natural Religion*, ed. N. Kemp Smith, Edinburgh: Thomas Nelson.
—— (1957) *The Natural History of Religion*, ed. H. E. Root, London: Adam and Charles Black.
James, W. (1979) *The Will to Believe and Other Essays in Popular Philosophy*, Cambridge, Mass. and London: Harvard University Press.
Kant, I. (1929) *Critique of Pure Reason*, trans. N. Kemp Smith, London: Macmillan.
Keightley, A. (1976) *Wittgenstein, Grammar, and God*, London: Epworth Press.
Kenny, A. (1992) *What is Faith?: Essays in the Philosophy of Religion*, Oxford: Oxford University Press.
Kierkegaard, S. (1985) *Philsophical Fragments*, trans. H. Hong and E. Hong, Princeton, I: Princeton University Press.

Leslie, J. (1989) *Universes*, London: Routledge.
—— (1990) (ed.) *Physical Cosmology and Philosophy*, New York: Macmillan.
Locke, J. (1823) *The Conduct of the Understanding*, in *The Works of John Locke*, London: Thomas Tegg *et al.*, vol. 3.
—— (1894) *Essay Concerning Human Understanding*, ed. A. C. Fraser, 2 vols, Oxford: Oxford University Press.
—— (1958) *The Reasonableness of Christianity (with A Discourse on Miracles and part of A Third Letter Concerning Toleration)*, ed. I. T. Ramsey, London: Adam and Charles Black.
MacIntyre, A. (1957) 'The Logical Status of Religious Belief', in A. MacIntyre (ed.) *Metaphysical Beliefs*, London: SCM Press.
—— (1964) 'Is Understanding Religion Compatible with Believing?', In J. Hick (ed.) *Faith and the Philosophers*, London: Macmillan.
Mascall, E. L. (1949) *Existence and Analogy*, London: Longmans Green.
—— (1963) 'Faith and Reason: Anselm and Aquinas', *Journal of Theological Studies* 14, 67–90.
Paley, W. (1838) *The Works of William Paley*, 4 vols, London: Longman.
Pascal, B. (1966) *Pensées*, trans. A. J. Krailsheimer, Harmondsworth: Penguin.
Penelhum, T. (1983) *God and Skepticism*, Dordrecht: Reidel.
—— (1985) *Butler*, London: Routledge.
—— (1992) 'Butler and Human Ignorance', in C. Cunliffe (ed.) *Joseph Butler's Moral and Religious Thought*, Oxford: Clarendon Press.
Phillips, D. Z. (1965) *The Concept of Prayer*, London: Routledge.
—— (1970) *Faith and Philosophical Enquiry*, London: Routledge.
—— (1988) *Faith After Foundationalism*, London: Routledge.
Plantinga, A. (1979) 'Is Belief in God Rational?', in C. F. Delaney (ed.) *Rationality and Religious Belief*, Notre Dame: Notre Dame University Press.
—— (1981) 'Is Belief in God Properly Basic?', *Nous* 15, 41–51.
—— (1983a) 'The Reformed Objection to Natural Theology', in H. Hart, J. van der Hoeven and N. Wolterstorff (eds) *Rationality in the Calvinian Tradition*, Lanham, Md: University Press of America.
—— (1983b) 'Reason and Belief in God', in A. Plantinga and N. Wolterstorff (eds) *Faith and Rationality*, Notre Dame: Notre Dame University Press.
—— (1993a) *Warrant: The Current Debate*, New York: Oxford University Press.
—— (1993b) *Warrant and Proper Function*, New York: Oxford University Press.
Popkin, R. (1979) *The History of Scepticism from Erasmus to Spinoza*, Berkeley: University of California Press.
—— (1980) *The High Road to Pyrrhonism*, San Diego: Austin Hill Press.
Rescher, N. (1985) *Pascal's Wager*, Notre Dame: Notre Dame University Press.
Smith, W. C. (1981) *Towards a World Theology: Faith and the Comparative Study of Religion*, London: Macmillan Press.
Spinoza, B. de (1883) *A Theologico-Political Treatise*, trans. R. H. M. Elwes,, London: G. Bell & Sons.
Swinburne, R. (1981) *Faith and Reason*, Oxford: Clarendon Press.
—— (1986) *The Evolution of the Soul*, Oxford: Clarendon Press.
Tindal, M. (1978) *Christianity as Old as the Creation*, New York: Garland Publishing Company.
Toland, J. (1964) *Christianity Not Mysterious*, ed. G. Gawlick, Stuttgart-Bad Cannstatt: Friedrich Frommann.
Van Inwagen, P. (1993) 'Review of *Universes*, by J. Leslie', in *Faith and Philosophy* vol. 10, 439–43.
Warnock, G. J. (1953) *Berkeley*, Harmondsworth: Penguin.

Wicksteed, P. H. (1920) *The Relation Between Dogma and Philosophy, Illustrated from the Works of S. Thomas Aquinas*, London: Williams and Norgate.

Winch, P. (1967) 'Understanding a Primitive Society', in D. Z. Phillips (ed.) *Religion and Understanding*, Oxford: Basil Blackwell.

Wittgenstein, L. (1969) *On Certainty*, ed. G. E. M. Anscombe and G. H. von Wright, trans. D. Paul and G. E. M. Anscombe, Oxford: Basil Blackwell.

Wolterstorff, N. (1983a) 'Can Belief in God be Rational if It has No Foundations?', in A. Plantinga and N. Wolterstorff (eds) *Faith and Rationality*, Notre Dame: University of Notre Dame Press.

—— (1983b) 'Thomas Reid on Rationality', in H. Hart, J. Van der Hoeven and N. Wolterstorff (eds) *Rationality in the Calvinian Tradition*, Lanham, Md: University Press of America.

—— (1986) 'The Migration of the Theistic Arguments: from Natural Theology to Evidentialist Apologetics', in R. Audi and W. J. Wainright (eds) *Rationality, Religious Belief and Moral Commitment: New Essays in the Philosophy of Religion*, Ithaca: Cornell University Press.

FURTHER READING

Gale, R. M. (1991) *On the Nature and Existence of God*, Cambridge: Cambridge University Press.

Loades, A. and Rue, L. D. (eds) (1991) *Contemporary Classics in Philosophy of Religion*, La Salle, Ill.: Open Court.

Mavrodes, G. (1988) *Revelation in Religious Belief*, Philadelphia: Temple University Press.

Mitchell, B. (1973) *The Justification of Religious Belief*, London: Macmillan.

Penelhum, T. (ed.) (1989) *Faith*, New York: Macmillan Publishing Co.

Schellenberg, J. L. (1993) *Divine Hiddenness and Human Reason*, Ithaca: Cornell University Press.

Swinburne, R. (1979) *The Existence of God*, Oxford: Clarendon Press.

—— (1992) *Revelation: From Metaphor to Analogy*, Oxford: Clarendon Press.

See also chapters 13, 19, 21, 24.

19

NATURAL THEOLOGY

David A. Pailin

Since the word 'nature' has many connotations and since theologians do not agree about what is meant by 'theology', it is not surprising to find that the expression 'natural theology' is used to refer to a variety of forms of theological understanding. 'Natural theology' may, for example, connote a theology *of* nature in the sense of a theology that seeks to identify divine purposes and correlative values that apply to the non-human world. Those who develop such a natural theology may seek to challenge the anthropocentric and patriarchal attitudes that have traditionally tended to restrict theology to a study of 'me and my God' that ignores 'our relationship – and God's relationship – with the natural world' (Clatworthy 1992: 4) and to replace those attitudes with a theology that appreciates the proper dignity of each component of the natural order, respecting 'every entity for its intrinsic value as well as for its instrumental value to others' (Birch and Cobb 1981: 152). Where such a natural theology reaches theistic conclusions, God may be held to have ecological concerns for the well-being of all the members of the commonwealth of the natural order throughout the cosmos (McFague 1993).

A different use of 'natural theology' is to refer to attempts to discern the basic character of reality through examining the natural order, with the intention of prescribing therefrom principles of conduct whereby human beings will be able to worship, think and act in satisfying harmony with the ultimate and all-embracing character of what is. Such a theology may properly be deemed theistic if it holds that the basic character of reality is most adequately conceived as grounded in a personal mode of being. An example of this form of 'natural theology' may be seen in the basic understanding of that 'natural religion' which, according to William Wollaston, seeks to conform to the will of 'the Author' of humankind through 'the pursuit of happiness by the practice of reason and truth' (Wollaston 1726: 52; see 40).

Another use of 'natural theology' is to identify attempts to justify claims about the reality and will of the God by reference to the natural order alone. Such a form of natural theology may, for example, cite instances of what are held to be evidences of design and purpose in the natural order to warrant the conclusion that 'there must be something in the world more than what we see, ... an intelligent mind concerned in its production, order, and support' which is properly to be venerated (Paley 1837: IV, 356).

A fourth use of 'natural theology' is to denominate theological understanding that is allegedly common (and in this sense 'natural') to all humankind or at least to all those who are held to apprehend 'correctly' their human situation. Some hold that this theology is 'natural' because it expresses a recognition of truths that God, in creating human beings, implanted in them (Herbert of Cherbury 1937: 118, 121). Others maintain that these truths have their origin in divine revelation but that the universal availability of this revelation in principle means that they are 'natural' to all humankind (Ellis 1747: 39f.; 1757: 5). A third variety of this view of 'natural theology' claims that the universality of the acknowledgement of its contents arises from the fact that they are the product of rational reflection on evidence where both the logic and the evidence are available to and accepted by all people.

A fifth view of natural theology identifies itself more by its rejection of revealed insights than by any particular affirmations. Here natural theology is seen as that theological understanding which is independent of any reference to supposed acts of divine self-revelation. William Temple thus points out that while the doctrines of a natural theology and the doctrines of a theology which derives its insights from revelation may be the same, the grounds for holding those beliefs are radically distinct: 'so far as any doctrine is accepted on authority only, such acceptance lies beyond the frontier of Natural Theology, and all conclusions drawn from the belief so accepted must be excluded from its sphere' (Temple 1934: 6f.). A more positive expression of this view of natural theology presents it as theological understanding which results from the attempt to determine truths about the reality and will of God by means of rational reflection upon the character of the world, human experience and the intrinsic demands of reason itself (Campbell 1957: 5). Thus Terence Penelhum summarizes what is meant by 'the concept of natural theology' as 'an attempt to fuse the metaphysical search for a comprehensive explanation of the world with the religious search for an adequate object of worship' in which 'the object of each search is identified with that of the other' (Penelhum 1971: 4). Theologians who promote such natural theology but also see themselves as expounding a particular confession of faith generally maintain that natural theology on its own is unable to discern all the truths essential to that confession. Natural theology is hence seen as limited to certain important but propaedeutic tasks which, as John Macquarrie puts it, allow 'theological discourse to get started' (Macquarrie 1966: 41).

This fifth use of the phrase 'natural theology' is the most common way of understanding the expression and provides the prime object of consideration in this chapter. As so understood, however, natural theology has provoked, as Emil Brunner experienced in debate with Karl Barth, 'varied and passionate controversies' (Brunner 1949: 132; see Brunner and Barth 1946). Some theologians deny even its possibility as an authentic way of theological understanding. For example, while Barth describes 'natural theology' as 'a science of God, of the relations in which the world stands to Him and of the human ethics and morality resulting from the knowledge of Him' that 'is to be constructed independently of all historical religions and religious bodies as a strict natural science . . . apart from any special and supernatural revelation', he is 'convinced that so far as it [i.e. natural theology] has existed and still exists, it owes its existence to a radical error' (Barth 1938: 3–5). Authentic knowledge of God, the world and humanity is 'founded on the Word of God alone, on God's revelation in Jesus Christ, as it is attested in the Scripture, and on faith in that Word' (Barth 1938: 8f; for a sustained criticism of Barth's attack on natural theology in relation to the Bible, see Barr 1993).

Nevertheless, while some object to the principle of natural theology, and while others who accept that natural theology may be legitimate in principle challenge the rational justifiability of conclusions that are claimed to be reached therein, there is a long tradition of natural theology within theological understanding. We shall illustrate how it has been understood in practice by critically reviewing some of its more famous examples from the Middle Ages to the present day.

NATURAL THEOLOGY IN THE MIDDLE AGES

At the close of the invocatory first chapter of his *Proslogion* Anselm (Anselm 1962: 7) echoes Augustine (see Augustine, *On John*: 40, §9: 1874: 26; cf. 40, §10; 28; 27, §9; Augustine 1873: 387) in using the phrase '*credo ut intelligam*' ('I believe in order that I may understand'). This remark has commonly been interpreted as stating the theological approach used in this work. Examination of Anselm's argument, however, indicates that it is not based upon faith (*credere*), as might be expected, but upon what are put forward as self-authenticating reasons. The basic premise of Anselm's argument is the definition of 'God' as 'that than which nothing greater can be conceived' (Anselm 1962: ch. 2, 7). On this basis Anselm argues that it is incoherent to hold that God as so defined does not exist (and hence that God must exist), and that God must exist as one who, as the highest of all beings, is 'whatever it is better to be than not to be' (ibid.: ch. 5, 11). The details of Anselm's argument need not detain us here. What is important to note is that what he intends to put forward is an *a priori* argument that demonstrates, by unpacking the implications of a supposedly self-evident premise (namely, what is meant by 'God') by incontrovertible reasoning, both that God exists and that God basically has the attributes traditionally ascribed to the divine.

The validity of Anselm's so-called 'ontological argument' for the existence of God has been the subject of wide-ranging debates (Hartshorne 1965), while his deduction of the attributes of God has also been challenged. For instance, his assumption that God as 'the supreme Good' (Anselm 1962: ch. 5, 11) must, among other attributes, be 'passionless' (and hence 'affected by no sympathy for wretchedness' – ibid.: ch. 8, 13f.) arguably shows that what in one cultural era are regarded as the highest qualities of being are not necessarily deemed to be such in another era. Nevertheless, whatever logical defects and cultural prejudices may be identified in his argument, Anselm presents in *Proslogion* a classical *a priori* form of natural theology. The conclusions which he reaches are supposed to depend upon nothing other than a premise and inferences which are intuitively recognized to be correct.

Thomas Aquinas is not convinced by the *a priori* kind of argument presented by Anselm. In his judgement, that God exists is known by God to be self-evidently true since God is aware of the nature of God's own being, but it is not so knowable by us 'because we are not able to conceive in our minds that which God is' (*Summa Contra Gentiles* I, 11, 2 – Aquinas 1975: 81). There are, however, other arguments that, in his judgement, demonstrate *that* God is and *what* are some of the attributes of God (*SCG* I, 13ff. – ibid.: 85–304; *Summa Theologica* I, 2, 3 – Aquinas 1947: 11–48). These arguments, and especially the five 'ways' by which Aquinas claims to demonstrate the existence of God (namely, the arguments for the first mover, the first efficient cause, the being having its own necessity that is the cause of all others, the perfect being, and the being which gives intelligent order to the world (*SCG* I, 13 – Aquinas 1975: 85–96; *ST* I, 2, 3 – Aquinas 1947: 13f.), have had a major influence on the development of natural theology. A great deal of the subsequent work in the subject can be regarded as providing either footnotes and amendments to what Aquinas discerned, or criticisms of his kinds of argument.

Because of his influence on natural theology, it is important to note how Aquinas himself understood the significance of such reasoning. He holds that while some truths about God are beyond the competence of human reason and can only be apprehended through revelation, 'there are some truths which the natural reason also is able to reach' and which 'have been proved demonstratively by the philosophers, guided by the light of the natural reason' (*Summa Contra Gentiles*, I, 3, 2 – Aquinas 1975: 63). He goes on to point out that the truths discerned by reason and those manifested by revelation cannot conflict because both are 'true' and because what God makes us able to know naturally cannot conflict with what God makes known to us by revelation (*SCG* I: 7 – Aquinas 1975: 74f.). Furthermore there are, in his opinion, 'fitting arguments' which give good reasons for assenting to revealed truths (see *SCG* I: 6 – Aquinas 1975: 71). Nevertheless, in spite of these remarks, Aquinas' confidence in the power of human reason to discern and to establish truths about God is significantly limited. He considers it important that God makes known by revelation even those truths which in principle can be grasped by human reason. This is because not all people have the time, competence and disposition to reach these truths, because such knowledge can only be reached after long training and reflection, and because human reasoning is known to be liable to err. The limitations of human reason in practice thus make it 'necessary that the unshakeable certitude and pure truth concerning divine things' should be revealed. Divine providence meets this need. It instructs us 'to hold by faith even those truths that the human reason is able to investigate' in order that all may 'have a share in the knowledge of God, and this without uncertainty and error' (*SCG* I: 4 – Aquinas 1975: 68).

The most important developments in natural theology in the centuries after Aquinas did not consist of further extensions of his arguments nor of the formulation of novel ones, but in increasing questions about the competence of this approach to theological understanding. Investigations into the character of the reasoning involved in natural theology were held by some to show that it can at best provide only a very limited foundation for theistic belief, and possibly no significant foundation for it at all.

One major contributor to these developments was Duns Scotus. For example, he concludes his *De Primo Principio* by pointing out that while natural reason can prove 'the metaphysical attributes' of God (as 'the first efficient cause, the ultimate end, supreme in perfection, transcending all things'), it cannot demonstrate such doctrines as that God is 'omnipotent, immense, omnipresent, just yet merciful, provident of all creatures but looking after intellectual ones in a special way'. These attributes of God are matters of belief, not of reason. As such, in Duns Scotus' judgement, they 'are the more certain since they rest firmly upon your [*sc* God's] own most solid truth and not upon our intellect which is blind and weak in many things' (4. 84–6 – Duns Scotus 1966: 142–6; cf. Duns Scotus 1962: 162).

Another thinker in this period noted for learning and ingenuity is William of Ockham. According to Etienne Gilson he 'always maintained that absolutely nothing could be proved about God in the light of natural reason, not even his existence. To him . . . what reason can say concerning theological matters never goes beyond the order of mere dialectical probability' (Gilson 1938: 87f). Ockham's subtle distinctions lead him in his *Quodlibeta Septem*, for instance, to conclude on the one hand that it is possible to demonstrate that there must be only one God if by 'God' is understood 'some thing more noble and more perfect than anything else besides him', but that it is not possible to demonstrate that such a being exists. On the other hand, if by 'God' is meant 'that than which nothing is more noble and more perfect', it is possible to demonstrate that such a being exists but not that there is only one such being (I, q. i in Ockham 1957: 125f., see V, q. i in ibid.: 100). Unfortunately for natural theology, the latter way of understanding what is meant by 'God' is a theologically inadequate concept of the divine. According to Ockham, the fundamental truths about God are to be held as articles of faith, and not as the conclusions of rational reflection. Furthermore, where the declarations of faith and the findings of reason contradict each other, one must hold what faith lays down rather than what reason claims to show (Ockham 1957: 133f.; cf. Ockham 1969: 34–70).

NATURAL THEOLOGY IN THE REFORMATION

This view of the relationship between faith and reason is shared by many of the Reformers. According to Martin Luther scholastic theologians deal 'in mere imaginings derived from human reason' whereas the Bible, as 'the basis and source of faith', is not to be criticized, explained or judged by 'our mere reason' but 'diligently' searched and obeyed under the direction of the Holy Spirit (Luther 1848: 2–4). While John Calvin accepts that 'there exists in the human mind, and indeed by natural instinct, some sense of Deity', he holds that human sinfulness, on the one hand, suppresses the effects and perverts the contents of this implanted knowledge of God and, on the other hand, renders people incapable of recognizing God through the created order. As a result, 'since the human mind, through its weakness, was altogether unable to come to God' by its own powers, 'God has given the assistance of his Word to all whom he has ever been pleased to instruct effectually' (Calvin 1953: I, 43, 66f.; cf. I, 46–63). Even the humanistic Philip Melanchthon holds that although some rational knowledge of God is available through natural understanding, it is subject to doubt and corruption and, in any case, is insufficient for salvation. Consequently 'we are to seek knowledge of God in his revelations and his clearly expressed words' in the 'divine Scripture' (Melanchthon 1965: 5–7).

Nevertheless, whatever the views of the Reformers and their opponents, the theological controversies which they provoked in the sixteenth and seventeenth centuries led to renewed interest in the question of natural theology. This was because of the need to find some way of resolving disputes when both parties claim that the final court of appeal is to (their own interpretation of) the Scriptures. Some responded to the fact of clashing interpretations by accepting that the principle of *sola scriptura* needs to be modified by assertions of the authority of Scripture and of the Church as its interpreter. They soon discovered, however, that the problem of identifying true doctrine was not overcome but aggravated by this modification. Disputes about what Scripture means were compounded by differences about who or what may constitute 'the Church' that is properly authorized as its interpreter.

The failure to resolve disputes about what the Bible taught (cf. Anthony Collins, *Discourse of Free-Thinking*, 1713: 45–61) led a few to be sceptical about the authority of the Bible (cf. Pierre Bayle's *Historical and Critical Dictionary* – e.g., the article on David, and Voltaire's *Philosophical Dictionary* – e.g., the article on Abraham), some to urge toleration for different interpretations (cf. Jeremy Taylor 1647: 73), and others to resort to violence to impose their interpretations. A fourth option which gained increasing support appealed to reason as the way to determine belief and settle conflicts. For some this appeal is limited to finding reasons to justify claims about the identity and meaning of divine revelation, especially as contained in the Bible. Others, however, extended it to include basic beliefs about the reality and will of God. The complex, sometimes lively, and unfinished story of the arguments used in attempts to show that it is possible by rational reflection to determine various fundamental truths about the reality of God is the story of natural theology in modern thought.

NATURAL THEOLOGY IN THE SEVENTEENTH AND EIGHTEENTH CENTURIES

In the first half of the seventeenth century, Edward Herbert, first Baron Herbert of Cherbury, looked to reason to find a credible alternative to fanaticism and scepticism. According to his *De Veritate*, certain 'common notions' that express fundamental truths have been planted in humankind by divine providence. All people, therefore, recognize them to be true once they become aware of them. They provide the foundation and touchstone for all true understanding (Herbert of Cherbury 1937: 116–18). The five 'common notions concerning religion' identified by Herbert hold that there is 'a supreme God' who 'ought to be worshipped', that virtue is the most important characteristic of piety, that wickedness is 'expiated by repentance', and that 'there is reward or Punishment after this life' (ibid.: 291–303). In later works, *De Religione Gentilium* and *A Dialogue between a Tutor and his Pupil*, Herbert attempts to rebut charges that empirical evidence falsifies the claim that these common notions are universally acknowledged. He does this by holding that either the evidence about other religions has been misinterpreted or the true 'catholic' religion which accords with the common notions has been corrupted by priestcraft.

René Descartes, a younger contemporary of Herbert of Cherbury, developed several arguments for the reality of God that were not so obviously subject to threats of empirical falsification arising from increasing knowledge of the world's religions. One of these arguments applies to the idea of God the principle that a cause must contain at least the qualities of its effect. On this basis he argues that since the idea of God is the idea of a perfect being, the idea must be caused by a being with at least that degree of reality. This cannot be Descartes himself (since his doubt and ignorance show that he is not perfect). Hence the idea of God must come from and be evidence of a perfect being that is independent of Descartes, namely God (Descartes 1931: I, 170f.). Descartes also uses the causal principle and the supposed incoherence of infinite regression to produce various forms of the cosmological argument. For example, he argues that our coming to be and our continuation in being is not within our own power but must finally derive from God who 'has so much power that He can conserve us out of Himself' but does 'not require to be conserved by any other' (ibid.: I, 228; cf. I, 169). Another form of this kind of argument holds that in recognizing their limitations human beings show that they are not self-caused but that there is 'necessarily some other more perfect Being' from which they acquire their qualities (ibid.: I, 102f.). A third kind of argument presents versions of the ontological proof. Holding that God is to be defined as essentially perfect, and so as having all possible attributes, Descartes argues that the predicate 'exists' cannot not be given to God. Hence the idea of God shows that it must be necessarily true that God exists (ibid.: I, 224f.).

In England the Cambridge Platonists affirmed the important place of reason, and in particular reason's reflection on its own insights, for reaching theological understanding. Although many of their contemporaries were content to bombard each other with biblical texts, the Cambridge Platonists held that reason is 'the candle of the Lord' by which, as Nathanael Culverwel puts it, people can discover (*invenire*), not make (*facere, ferre*), the 'Law of Nature' which God gives for the proper direction of their lives (Culverwel 1661: 56). According to John Smith, another of this group of thinkers, God has given many indications of the divine nature in the characteristics of 'this conspicable & sensible world' in general but the 'most clear and distinct copy' of it is provided by the character of human being. By 'the contemplation of our owne Souls', then, 'we may rise up to . . . the true knowledge of the Divine Nature and Attributes' (Smith 1660: 125f., 140).

The view that reason is the enlightening candle of the Lord within every person may be interpreted, however, as endorsing various forms of inner intuition. Because of this, the sober appeal to 'reason' presented by the Cambridge Platonists could be adopted and adapted by illuminaries such as those found in the Quaker movement. This was a disturbing conclusion for those who looked to reason to bridle such 'enthusiasts'. It also had to be recognized that another – and major – problem for those who affirmed in principle the canon of reason is that people may differ greatly over what they consider to be warranted thereby. John Locke accordingly set out to determine the character and limits of human understanding. In his *Essay Concerning Human Understanding*, he lays down, both as a principle of understanding and as a matter of obedience to the will of God in creating human beings as rational, that a person 'governs his Assent right and places it as he should, who in any Case or Matter whatsoever, believes or disbelieves, according as Reason directs him' (Locke 1979: 688).

In the *Essay* Locke examines the case for the existence of God. Using a form of the cosmological argument, he concludes, on the basis of our knowledge of 'our own Existence' and of our 'intuitive Certainty' that 'bare nothing' cannot produce any real being, that we can 'more certainly know that there is a GOD, than that there is any thing else without us' (ibid.: 619–21). Later he considers the status of revelation: duly authenticated claims to revealed knowledge are to be given assent so long as they do not contradict, even though they may go beyond, what reason itself establishes to be the case concerning the nature and will of God. He seeks to justify the fundamental principle that 'reason must be our last Judge and Guide in every Thing' by holding that when God

> would have us assent to the Truth of any proposition, he either evidences that Truth by the usual Methods of natural Reason, or else makes it known to be a Truth . . . by some Marks which Reason cannot be mistaken in.
>
> (ibid.: 704; cf. 688–706)

Although a number of critics judged the 'reasonable' form of Christian belief that emerges from Locke's application of the canon of reason to be seriously defective, the canon itself was widely considered to be unquestionable. The problem was how to satisfy it by producing a rationally justified natural theology that may serve as the foundation for Christian belief.

After Locke's death one of the most able thinkers in England was Samuel Clarke. In his Boyle Lectures he claims to present 'One clear and plain Series of Propositions necessarily connected' that demonstrates 'the Certainty of the Being of God' and 'the Necessary Attributes of his Nature, so far as by our Finite Reason we are enabled to discover and apprehend them' (Clarke 1732: 8). What he provides is, as far as possible, an *a priori* argument for the reality of God that starts by asserting that it is 'Absolutely and Undeniably certain, that *Something has existed from all Eternity*' and goes on to argue that this eternal 'Something' must be immutable, independent, self-existing, necessarily existing and one (ibid.: 8; cf. 8–50). In order, however, to demonstrate that this 'Self-existent Being' satisfies the notion of God, Clarke has to show that it is not 'a Blind and *Unintelligent* Necessity' but 'an *Intelligent* and *Knowing* Cause' acting 'with *Liberty* and Choice'. To do this he introduces *a posteriori* arguments from the character of the world (ibid.: 51, 63). By combining *a priori* and *a posteriori* considerations he reaches the conclusion that this God must necessarily be '*The Supreme Cause and Author of all Things*' who is infinitely powerful, wise, good, just and true, and has 'all other *Moral Perfections*' (ibid.: 109, 116; cf. 73–126). On this foundation, Clarke proceeds in the second series of his lectures to demonstrate both 'the *unalterable Obligations of Natural Religion*, and the certainty of *Divine Revelation*' that makes known those matters necessary for salvation that human reason cannot determine by its own powers (ibid.: 149; cf. 128).

While Clarke sought as far as possible to present a natural theology based on *a priori* reasoning, many of those who attempted to develop such a theology in this period preferred to concentrate on *a posteriori* arguments. Theologians who develop this form of natural theology plunder the latest observations of scientific study for illustrations of the reality, power and benevolence of the Creator. John Ray, for example, finds the 'Majesty, Wisdom, and Power of God' displayed in such various matter as the provision of the wind 'to dissipate noisom and contagious Vapours', 'the *Magnet* for Navigation', the structure of the tongue and the windpipe, and the form of the camel's foot (Ray 1722: 176, 90, 160; see 268–71, 343).

Similar arguments are presented by William Derham. In his Boyle Lectures for 1711 and 1712, *Physico-Theology: Or, A Demonstration of the Being and Attributes of God from His Works of Creation*, he holds, for example, that if there were no other evidence than that of the five senses in 'Sensitive Creatures', it would be 'abundantly sufficient to evince' the admirable character of the Creator (Derham 1723: 85). He adduces, however, much more evidence, including the 'sagacity' of birds and insects in knowing where to place their eggs (ibid.: 246f., 373f.) and 'the great Variety throughout the World of Mens Faces, Voices, and Handwriting' which prevents mistaken identity and fraud (ibid. 308f.)! In another work, *Astro-Theology: Or, A Demonstration of the Being and Attributes of God from a Survey of the Heavens*, Derham takes up recent advances in astronomy. He argues that the size, contents, distribution, movements, shape and relationship of the components of the universe, together with the provision of light and heat, manifest the '*Indulgence*', '*Care*' and '*Kindness*' of their 'CONTRIVER and MAKER' (Derham 1738: 214).

The arguments for natural theology are, however, also subject to various and in some cases trenchant criticisms on religious, theological and philosophical grounds. It is argued, for instance, from a religious perspective that attempts to establish the rational justification of belief subvert the all-sufficiency of its biblical basis. They are condemned for trying to replace faith in God by trust in the powers of human reasoning (Edwards 1692: Preface (i) and, for a modern version, Bultmann 1969: 313). A fundamental theological objection to natural theology is that human thought using human experience can never establish an adequate understanding of the divine. According to John Ellis, for example, it is not possible to reach the infinite and perfect through reflection on our experience of finite and imperfect objects (Ellis 1743: 32). Nevertheless, 'what Nature could not do, Grace and Mercy have supplied . . . by Revelation, Inspiration, and Instruction' (Ellis 1747: 438)

The most formidable challenges to natural theology in the eighteenth century, however, were the philosophical criticisms of its arguments presented by David Hume and Immanuel Kant. While it seems that each of the criticisms which Hume makes in his *Dialogues Concerning Natural Religion* had been expressed in the theological debates of the previous half-century, his clearly presented and wide-ranging combination of them has justifiably been considered by many to indicate the basic unsatisfactoriness of previous attempts to establish a natural theology on either *a priori* or *a posteriori* grounds. In his judgement, it follows from 'a just sense of the imperfections of natural reason' that the appropriate position to adopt in these matters is one of philosophical scepticism (Hume 1935: 282).

Kant's determination of the proper limits of pure reason in the *Critique of Pure Reason*, his exposure of the antinomies which arise when attempts are made to demonstrate transcendental truths, and his criticisms of the ontological, cosmological and teleological arguments were judged by many to drive further nails into the coffin of natural theology, especially so far as it claimed to demonstrate the truth of basic theistic beliefs. Although some might find comfort in his conclusion that one could and should be 'morally certain' about 'belief in a God and in another world', others were deeply troubled by his argument that no longer can any one claim to 'know' these things (Kant 1933: 650). Theistic belief did not seem properly credible when its rational foundations had apparently been so thoroughly undermined.

NATURAL THEOLOGY IN THE NINETEENTH AND TWENTIETH CENTURIES

Not everyone, however, was persuaded that it was time to write the obituary for natural theology. In spite of criticisms, the argument from the observed character of the natural order remained for many decades a popular and, seemingly for numbers of people, a convincing case for the reality of God. Probably the most famous example of this argument is William Paley's *Natural Theology*, published in 1802. Starting from the evidence that a watch gives of its being the product of 'an artificer or artificers who formed it for the purpose which we find it actually to answer' (Paley 1837: IV, 2), Paley holds that the structures of animals and vegetables provide an analogous argument for the being and attributes of God. Implicitly responding to some of Hume's criticisms of earlier (and generally cruder) forms of the argument, he maintains that the argument from artefact to artisan is not overturned by our ignorance of how certain things are made and of what some things are for, nor by what seem to us to be imperfections in the artefacts, nor by the ability of artefacts to reproduce themselves. On the grounds that the works of nature show to 'a degree that exceeds all computation' all the characteristics of 'contrivance' and 'design' that are found in human artefacts and are combined in a connected system, Paley concludes that everything has been planned by one 'stupendous Being' on whom our happiness as well as our existence depends. Nevertheless, although 'Natural Theology' can show a great deal about God, it does not rule out revealed disclosures of further aspects of the divine. Instead it facilitates them by providing reasonable grounds for accepting them (ibid: 12, 355f.).

In 1829 the Earl of Bridgewater bequeathed eight thousand pounds for treatises to be written on

> the Power, Wisdom, and Goodness of God, as manifested in the Creation; illustrating such work by all reasonable arguments, as for instance the variety and formation of God's creatures in the animal, vegetable, and mineral kingdoms; the effect of digestion, and thereby of conversion; the construction of the hand of man, and an infinite variety of other arguments.

The eight Bridgewater Treatises, published between 1833 and 1840, present, however, a way of justifying natural theology that had soon to be modified significantly, even if not wholly abandoned. The publication of Charles Darwin's study of the evolution of species meant that particular structures and adaptations could no longer be convincingly regarded as evidence for the reality of a powerful, wise and benevolent creator.

In 1885 Adam Gifford made a will in which he left funds to the four Scottish universities for lectureships promoting, as was mentioned earlier, 'the study of Natural Theology'. The universities were to appoint people who would treat the knowledge of God and God's relationship to the world 'as a strictly natural science . . . without reference to or reliance upon any supposed special exceptional or so-called miraculous revelation' (Jaki 1986: 72, 74). The first Gifford Lectures were given in 1888 and the series has continued ever since. Among the more important treatments of natural theology that have been given as Gifford Lectures are William Ritchie Sorley's *Moral Values and the Idea of God* (1913–15), Samuel Alexander's *Space, Time, and Deity* (1916–18), Alfred Edward Taylor's *The Faith of a Moralist* (1926–8), Alfred North Whitehead's *Process and Reality* (1927–8), William Temple's *Nature, Man and God* (1932–4), John Macmurray's *The Self as Agent* and *Persons in Relation* (1952–4), Charles Arthur Campbell's *On Selfhood and Godhood* (1953–5), Henry Habberley Price's *Belief* (1960–2), John Baillie's *The Sense of the Presence of God* (1961–2 – given posthumously), and Ian Barbour's *Religion in an Age of Science* and *Ethics in an Age of Technology* (1989–91).

Since the Enlightenment, then, in spite of justifiable criticisms of earlier arguments and an often unsympathetic intellectual environment, attempts to develop a rationally credible and theistically significant form of natural theology have continued to be made. Some of them have explored relatively fresh lines of thought. For example, one early challenge to both the eighteenth-century approach to natural theology and to its critics is made by Friedrich Daniel Ernst Schleiermacher's *On Religion: Speeches to Its Cultured Despisers* and his later, more systematic *The Christian Faith*. Schleiermacher considers that those who seek to develop natural theology as a kind of metaphysical knowledge or, with Kant, as kind of moral understanding fundamentally misapprehend the nature of religion. Religion preserves its integrity 'only by completely removing itself from the sphere and character of speculation as well as from that of praxis' and by understanding itself as a third, 'necessary and indispensable' dimension of human being (Schleiermacher 1988: 102). 'God' is 'the co-determinant' of what Schleiermacher identifies and analyses as 'the feeling of absolute dependence'. Thus 'to feel oneself absolutely dependent and to be conscious of being in relation with God are one and the same thing'. What are regarded as attributes of God are correlates of this feeling (Schleiermacher 1928: 17; cf. 194). It is a mistake, however, to consider that Schleiermacher's location of religion in self-consciousness reduces it to the self's consciousness of its own isolated subjectivity. The consciousness to which he refers involves an awareness of that to which the self thereby discerns itself to be fundamentally related. Schleiermacher thus implies the possibility of a kind of natural theology that bases religion on and looks to the knowledge of God in a distinct mode of human intuition. It is a line of enquiry that has been pursued in very different ways – as is illustrated, for example, by the studies of religious experience presented by William James, Rudolf Otto, Martin Buber and John Baillie – and that raises critical questions about how far some such mode of intuition or experience can reasonably be claimed to provide reliable information about the ground of being, whether theistic or not (see Hepburn 1958; Davis 1989).

Since the time of Kant, and particularly between the end of the nineteenth century and the middle of the twentieth, one aspect of the argument from experience has attracted considerable attention and a variety of forms. This argument attempts to derive a natural theology from moral experience. Kant himself holds that the reality of God, together with that of freedom and immortality, is a 'postulate' that is necessarily required for the coherence of the categorical demand of the practical (i.e., moral) reason (see Kant 1909: 226f.). Among other forms of the argument from morality to the reality of God are Sorley's argument that the reality of the world of nature can only be harmonized with the moral order in an intelligible way through 'the acknowledgement of the Supreme Mind or God as the ground of all reality' (Sorley 1924: 504); Hastings Rashdall's idealist argument that the existence of God is 'essential to the logical justification of that idea of objective validity which is implicit in the moral consciousness' (Rashdall 1924: 2, 250); and Taylor's arguments that the 'complete unification of personality in ourselves, the very goal of all . . . moral effort', is only real if God is real as 'the concrete unity of all good in its one source' (Taylor 1932: I, 101), and that conscience's witness to the authoritative demand of right and wrong is factual evidence of 'the active reality of the living God' (Taylor 1961: 135; see 133). The significance of the demand of morality has, however, declined as psychological and sociological studies have drawn increasing attention to conditioning factors that are considered to relativize not just particular moral judgements but also the notion of morality itself.

Awareness of earlier criticisms has not prevented some twentieth-century thinkers from attempting to develop forms of the teleological, cosmological and ontological arguments. Frederick Robert Tennant, for example, seeks in his *Philosophical Theology* to construct 'a philosophy of the soul, the world, and God' through 'a sustained application of the empirical method' (Tennant 1956: II, 247). Recognizing that evolutionary theory has fatally flawed arguments from specific 'cases of adaptedness in the world', he argues that the strength of a teleological interpretation 'consists rather in the conspiration of innumerable causes to produce . . . and to maintain, a general order of Nature' (ibid: 79). He particularly draws attention to five factors: 'the mutual adaptation of thought and things', the 'directivity in the process and plan in the primary collocations' of the evolutionary process, 'the continuity of apparent purposiveness' between the inorganic and the organic realms, the fact that 'the world is a bearer of values' and so shows affinity with beings that appreciate beauty, and the way in which 'the whole process of Nature is capable of being regarded as instrumental to the development of intelligent and moral creatures' (ibid.: 81–103). His case is that when these factors are put together, the most reasonable hypothesis for understanding the fundamental character of the world as we observe it empirically is the theistic one.

In the final decades of the twentieth century some theologians have interpreted certain current theories in physics about cosmogenesis as indicating that the world is fundamentally a product of intelligent, deliberate and divine design. While those who pursue this line of argument do not deny that the processes of cosmological development in the first jiffies after the hot big bang are the result of chance interactions within the structure of certain necessary conditions imposed by the cosmic constants, they are impressed by what seems to be the immense unlikelihood that an evolutionary cosmos would emerge from what happened in those very first jiffies. For example, Ian Barbour in his Gifford Lectures cites various considerations that have led some physicists to suggest that there may be 'evidence of design in the early universe' (Barbour 1990: 135f.). While, however, these results are intriguing and while David Bartholomew, for instance, argues that stochastic considerations show that the chance-character of the physical order could nevertheless be known to have a generally predictable outcome (Bartholomew 1984), the kind of divine 'design' indicated by them is so hugely remote from justifying claims about a benevolent God interacting with the world in which people exist that it is debatable whether it could provide the foundation for a religiously satisfying natural theology.

A modern version of the traditional cosmological argument from contingency to the necessary existence of God is presented by Eric Lionel Mascall in *He Who Is*. Starting from the question of why things continue in being rather than 'collapse into non-existence', he argues that the contingent nature of finite things presents us with the dilemma that either we consider the series of contemporary contingent dependencies to be inexplicable, or we 'admit the existence of a Cause which does not require a cause for itself' (Mascall 1943: 46; see 72f.). Mascall's view is that to 'perceive finite beings as they actually are' (i.e, to have a proper appreciation of their finitude) brings us to 'perceive them as creatures of God': hence 'in perceiving them' we 'recognize the existence of God whom we cannot perceive' (ibid.: 74). It is a conclusion that rests upon considering the continuing existence of contingent things to be a problem. Is it, however, problematic?. In a debate with Frederick Copleston SJ, Bertrand Russell maintains that it is not. He is content to 'say that the universe is just there' and to regard 'the notion of the world having an explanation' as 'a mistake' (Russell 1975: 140f.). Furthermore, it may be held that the argument from contingency begs the question. This is on the grounds that it is only possible to consider the contingent nature of things as posing a problem by presupposing the existence of a necessary being – and so by presupposing what the argument is intended to show.

In the middle of the twentieth century, studies by Norman Malcolm and Charles Hartshorne drew attention to a modal form of the ontological argument, claiming it to be immune from standard challenges to that argument. This modal form of the argument uses the distinction between necessary existence and contingent existence to maintain that the definition of God as 'that than which a greater cannot be conceived' entails that God's existence must be considered to be necessary rather than contingent (for necessary existence is intuitively recognized to be superior to contingent existence). From this the conclusion is reached that since God has necessary existence, God must exist (see Hartshorne 1965: 301; Pailin 1968: 109ff.). This modal form of the ontological argument (as is also the case with other forms of the argument) is, however, subject to the fundamental objection that the reality of something cannot validly be inferred simply from the concept of it. This applies to the concept of the divine as to that of anything else. What the modal form of the ontological shows is that *if* God exists, *then* God must exist as one whose mode of existence is that of necessary rather than that of contingent existence.

Hartshorne's major contribution to theological understanding, however, is his independent development of ideas also put forward by Whitehead. In *Process and Reality: An Essay in Cosmology* and other writings, Whitehead seeks to apprehend the fundamental and universal nature of actuality as temporal and social. God is conceived as the ground of its processes. What Whitehead calls the 'primordial nature' of God is the source of all novelty, the 'consequent nature' preserves all that occurs, and the 'superjective nature' draws the processes of reality towards the actualization of further and valuatively richer experiences. He also develops a concept of God which rejects the notion of God as 'the ruling Caesar, or the ruthless moralist, or the unmoved moved' in favour of the notion of one who saves the world by leading it in 'tender patience . . . by his vision of truth, beauty and goodness' (Whitehead 1978: 342f., 346).

Hartshorne's especial insight has been to identify and analyse the 'dipolar' nature of the theistic concept of God and thereby to solve fundamental problems concerning its coherence. According to the dipolar understanding, it is possible to speak coherently of the material attributes of God as absolute, necessary and unchanging in certain respects, and as relative, contingent and changing in other respects (see Pailin 1989: ch. 4). On this basis Hartshorne has developed a 'panentheistic' understanding of the relationship between God and the world which, without denying the relative autonomy of the divine and the non-divine, considers that all that occurs contributes to God's experience (cf. ibid: ch. 5). The resulting understanding of reality as 'creative synthesis' (Hartshorne 1970) provides the basis for Hartshorne's understanding of a 'natural theology for our time' (Hartshorne 1967).

Although the views of God advanced by 'process theologians' (see Cobb 1965 and Ogden 1967) are often hotly disputed by the supporters of classical concepts of deity (e.g., as timeless, unchanging, and impassible), they do indicate that it may be rationally justifiable to speak of the divine as properly ultimate, sympathetically aware and intentionally active in relation to the world, and to overcome the traditional understanding of the distinction between God and the world that makes any significant relationships between them impossible. In this respect process theology offers an understanding of theistic faith that suggests that natural theology may at least be possible in principle as a way of understanding the relationship between the world in which we find ourselves and the God who, as transcendent and immanent, is both internally and externally related to the world and is to be worshipped as the proper object of religious faith.

THE CONTEMPORARY DEBATE ABOUT NATURAL THEOLOGY

While, however, attempts continue to be made to establish a natural theology on more or less traditional lines by revising and reformulating the arguments for the reality of God in order to avoid particular criticisms, objections have been made in principle to any kind of natural theology. Some of these objections have taken the form of radical re-interpretations of what is meant by 'God' that claim to show that the proper reference of the concept is non-theistic. Ludwig Feuerbach, for example, holds that 'God' is an objectifying projection by human beings of the qualities of their species (Feuerbach 1957: 12). It is a basic error to consider that theology is about a divine reality which is ontologically independent of the human. A similar root-and-branch demolition of theism is put forward by Sigmund Freud. He interprets religious beliefs psychologically as illusions which arise from infantile responses to the demands of life. Beliefs in the reality of 'a God who created the world and was a benevolent Providence, and . . . a moral order in the universe and an after-life' indicate what people think 'would be very nice' (Freud 1962: 29); they do not tell us what mature people in a scientific age realistically ought to recognize to be the case. While, however, those who put forward such interpretations imply that natural theology rests upon a total misreading of what is meant by references to 'God', theists may reply that what they show is not the utter untenability of theism but the character of certain factors which are likely to influence and distort thought about God. These analyses thus indicate the importance of recognizing how beliefs are conditioned (see Pailin 1990), and of seeking as far as possible to take account of that conditioning in evaluating the significance of theistic claims.

Others criticize natural theology on the grounds that it is either incompatible with or unable as such to produce authentic faith. Søren Kierkegaard, for example, holds that the approach to belief in God underlying natural theology makes the fundamental mistake of considering that faith is like entertaining the conclusion of a successful argument. In his *Philosophical Fragments* he argues that reason is necessarily incapable of conceiving, let alone showing the reality of, 'the Unknown', the 'absolutely different' which it encounters as its 'limit' (Kierkegaard 1936: 35). In any case, the notion of proving is such that 'as long as I . . . continue to demonstrate' God's existence, 'the existence does not come out, if for no other reason than that I am engaged in proving it'. It is only there when 'I let the proof go' and 'leap' into relationship with God (ibid.: 34; see Kierkegaard 1941: 116). So far as human existence is concerned, truth and faith have the same definition – 'an objective uncertainty held fast in an appropriation-process of the most passionate inwardness'. Since, then, 'without risk there is no faith', it follows that 'if I am capable of grasping God objectively, I do not believe, but precisely because I cannot do this I must believe' (Kierkegaard 1941: 182). In reply it may be maintained that while, as Newman puts it, a conclusion is essentially 'conditional' in that, *qua* conclusion, it depends upon its antecedent argument whereas faith is unconditional assent (Newman 1870), theistic believers may legitimately ask themselves and be asked by others to show that they have sound warrants for believing that the object in which, as believers, they put their trust does actually exist. In that case, while natural theology may never by itself produce faith, it may be held to provide a crucial preamble to the commitment of faith.

All forms of natural theology presuppose the reliability and authority of human rationality in general, and in matters concerning the ultimate and sacred in particular. Doubts about the warrantability of this confidence provide a third basis for questioning the possibility of natural theology in principle as well as in practice. Although this challenge may be ignored as self-destructive where it purports to show by reason that the conclusions of all forms of reasoning are fatally flawed, it carries weight when it does not deny reason itself but rather provides significant grounds for concluding that rational examination of reason shows its incompetence to determine truth about the reality and will of God. It is a case which has many facets. Examination of the principles of rational understanding as well as of the fundamental difficulties which arise when attempts are made to determine the ultimate nature of reality leads Kant, for instance, to conclude that reason 'stretches its wings in vain in thus attempting to soar above the world of sense by the mere power of speculation' (Kant 1933: 500).

Although idealist philosophy, following Georg Wilhelm Friedrich Hegel in holding that what is real is rational and what is rational is real (Hegel 1892: 10, 258f., 383f.), attempts to work out a synthesis of thought and reality, other movements and thinkers in the two centuries since Kant emphasize the relativity of rational thinking. Marxist and sociological analyses draw attention to the ways in which the social and political context of a thinker moulds her or his thought. Recent feminist and racial studies claim that gender and race as well as culture and upbringing are other prejudicing factors. Since the publication of Edwin Hatch's Hibbert Lectures for 1888 on *The Influence of Greek Ideas and Usages upon the Christian Church* and Adolf Harnack's *History of Dogma*, critically self-aware theologians have been seeking to come to terms with the cultural relativity of their source materials and of their own conclusions. In studies of the nature of rational thought generally, the demise of the crude logical positivist attempt to 'eliminate' metaphysical thought (cf. the title of the first chapter of Alfred Jules Ayer's seminal *Language, Truth and Logic*) by the application of the 'verification principle' has been followed by a more subtle challenge to reason in the form of linguistic philosophy's insights into the ways that the use of language to identify and to draw inferences from what is being thought conceptually conditions it.

In the last quarter of the twentieth century self-styled 'postliberal', 'deconstructionist', 'antifoundationalist' and 'postmodernist' positions have drawn attention to ways in which reflection on rational thinking challenges the authority of reason, the validity of traditional (and perhaps of all) notions of truth, and the credibility of rational ways of determining what is true. A century earlier Friedrich Nietzsche attacked reason's claims to be the way to knowledge of the truth. In *The Gay Science* he suggests that what we hold and what we reject does not depend on the judgements of objective reason but on what satisfies our current pattern of life (Nietzsche 1974: 245f.). Reason may even falsify 'the evidence of the senses' to produce grounds which support what subjectively we desire to be the case. However rational it may pretend to be, in the cases of morality and of religion ' "truth" denotes nothing but . . . "imaginings" ' based on misrepresentation and 'misinterpretation' of 'realities which do not exist' (Nietzsche 1990: 46, 65).

A century after Nietzsche thinkers with equal subtlety, sophisticated tools and generally a much less strident tone press home the assault on reason. By rational reflection they identify presuppositions which underlie earlier confidence in the use of reason in order to point out why they should now be regarded as highly questionable, if not obviously mistaken. They thus undermine the confidence in the neutrality, objectivity and competence of reason as the ultimate court of appeal that is typical of 'enlightened' understanding in the modern age. Jean-François Lyotard, for instance, defines the 'postmodernity' characteristic of the current age in terms of, *inter alia*, convictions about 'the obsolescence of the metanarrative apparatus of legitimation' (Lyotard 1984: xxiv; cf. 81). According to Richard Rorty, it is an illusion to hold that it might be possible to establish what is true independently of the conditioning of a particular language-game by reference to criteria that are neutral in respect of any specific context (Rorty 1980: 388). Recognition that there is no 'single set of criteria which everybody in all times and places can accept' means, therefore, that 'one of the less important sideshows of Western civilization – metaphysics – is in the process of closing down' (Rorty 1991: 218).

In the face of such criticisms of the traditional appeal to reason, those who want to make a case for the rational credibility of theological understanding rather than simply confess their faith have two options. One option is to accept the basic validity of the antifoundationalist, postmodernist position and to seek to elucidate the basis of a particular theistic faith in its own terms. Among those exploring versions of this option are Alvin Plantinga and George A. Lindbeck. Plantinga, for instance, considers that what a person considers to be a rational belief is judged by reference to that 'assemblage of beliefs' and their inter-relationships which constitute 'that person's noetic structure'. He then argues that the mature theist does not regard belief in God as self-evident and incorrigible, nor as a tentative hypothesis, nor as a conclusion reached by argument 'from other things he believes: he accepts it as basic, as a part of the foundations of his noetic structure' (Plantinga 1979: 12, 27). As such it is part of that in terms of which the theist understands and acts rather than a product of rational understanding.

While Lindbeck states in *The Nature of Doctrine: Religion and Theology in a Postliberal Age* that the 'true' religion may be identified in principle as that which 'corresponds to ultimate reality', in his opinion the insights of 'postliberal antifoundationalism' make it clear that there are no neutral 'universal principles or structures' by reference to which the credibility of a faith can be established (Lindbeck 1984: 52, 132, 129). Since 'meaning is constituted by the uses of a specific language', it is 'intrasemiotic or intratextual' to a language system (ibid.: 114). Each system provides a comprehensive interpretative scheme for 'constructing reality, expressing experience, and ordering life' (ibid.: 47f.). A religious faith is such a system. People become followers of a particular faith as they learn 'its language, doctrines, liturgies, and modes of action' and develop their skill in using them to make sense of their experiences (ibid.: 39; cf. 131). The credibility of a faith hence arises from 'good performance' in using it as an interpretative scheme (ibid.: 131).

According to such antifoundationalist postmodernism, there is no way of justifying, by reference to ultimate, neutral principles that are independent of a particular system of understanding, the claim that a particular way of understanding is the objectively or absolutely correct (i.e., 'true') way to see things. Those who take up this option and apply it to theological understanding undermine the possibility of natural theology as traditionally understood. While they may claim that they do not deny the rational credibility of theological understanding as a way of interpreting reality, the rationality that they recognize is internal to the system being used. Belief is hence seen as its own warrant. When all the sophisticated defences are reduced to a minimum the basic claim seems to be: 'If you look at things in the way that I do and use my system of interpretation, then you will see that I am justified in seeing them as I do.'

Is there, however, a rationally sustainable alternative to the postmodernist, antifoundationalist understanding of rationality and belief? It is not simply the justifiability of continuing to seek to establish a natural theology that depends upon there being some such option; the possibility of making a rational choice between the different belief-systems found in a pluralistic social context, and of rationally defending the credibility of a particular belief-system may be held to depend upon there being one.

The search for such an option cannot justifiably ignore the various important criticisms that have been made of the arguments traditionally used to establish a natural theology; nor can it expect to be taken seriously if it ignores the relativity of understanding, both as human understanding and as culturally and conceptually conditioned understanding. On the other hand, there may be other ways of establishing a natural theology. The inescapable relativity of a particular way of understanding does not entail that it must be incapable of providing, within the limits imposed by its relativity, more or less objectively 'true' understanding. One possible way forward is by considering the search for a credible natural theology as a search for a comprehensive story of the ultimate character of reality that fits and makes sense of our experience and understanding of it and that bears fruit in further insights into what is and might be.

By 'story' in this context is not meant a fiction but a diachronic description that provides a synchronic insight into the ultimate that is the creative and sustaining ground of being (cf. Pailin 1986). While it may be pointed out that the justification of such a story must inevitably be circular to some extent (since what is apprehended as the components of 'reality' to be made sense of by the story will be seen in the perspective provided by that – or some other – story), it may be maintained in reply that there is a certain stubbornness in things that prevents them being smoothly incorporated into every story that people may desire to tell. Traditional forms of theism have always been aware of this stubbornness in terms of the data posing the so-called 'problem of evil' (a problem that basically arises because of the assumption of a view of God as creator that is unsustainable in a post-Darwinian culture), for this data is material that will not happily fit into the theistic story being considered.

The reasoning that develops and hence shows the credibility of what claims to be the story of reality as a whole is complex (Hodges 1953; Pailin 1971; 1975; Mitchell 1973). It involves reciprocal interactions between evidence and its interpretation, and a recognition that the understanding that is being sought is of the ultimate ground and end of a process of which we are only acquainted with a little part – and do not even know how little that part is, nor where it is located in the process as a whole. Nevertheless, if a coherent and comprehensive story emerges which justifies the claim that reality makes sense in terms of its being fundamentally theistic, that story will form a kind of natural theology that may justifiably claim to deserve serious consideration by theists who accept the canon of reason and who wish to be rationally responsible about their faith. Whether or not such a convincing story will appear in the future, only people who exist then will be able to decide.

If such a story does appear, however, it is likely to indicate the unjustifiability of the long-standing distinction between 'natural' and 'revealed' theology by showing that what have traditionally been regarded as two utterly distinct ways of coming to theological understanding appear on examination to have fundamentally the same logical structure. Traditionally 'revealed' theology has been understood to be based upon propositions that have been disclosed by God, generally with warranting signs (for example, miracles), to certain privileged individuals (for example, to Moses and the prophets – cf. 'thus says the Lord' – and to the apostles of Jesus who witnessed to the incarnate 'Word' – cf. John 1: 14). Assent is to be given to these propositions because of the status and insight of their (alleged) author. This is held to be unquestionable: since God knows what is true and does not tell lies, therefore what God has declared must be accepted as true (and, as was noted earlier in relation to Aquinas, as the touchstone for what people may consider that they have discerned to be true through the use of their reason). In contrast 'natural theology', as was mentioned at the start of this chapter, is considered to consist of truths about the divine that have been perceived through rational reflection on the implications of the intrinsic nature of reason and of what is observed in natural states, historical events and human experiences.

This distinction between supposedly 'revealed' and 'natural' theology collapses, however, once the idea that 'revealed theology' is a matter of reporting and expounding propositional truths disclosed by the divine is recognized to be unsustainable, as is now widely accepted to be the case, and claims to alleged revelatory insights into the divine come to be viewed, as arguably they must be, as the product of the way in which individuals (or groups) imaginatively interpret particular events or experiences as manifesting aspects of the reality and will of the divine (Pailin 1990: 113–39). When what was claimed to have been 'revealed' is so understood, it follows that the claims of so-called 'revealed' theology and those of so-called 'natural' theology have fundamentally the same rational status. They both generalize (and, thereby, seek to justify rationally) insights into the divine, as the ultimate and sacred ground and goal of all, that have been gained from musing on the significance of limited areas of experience in the realms of nature, history and human being. The difference between them is that what is regarded as 'natural' theology seeks to justify its insights by reference to reflection on a wider range of states, events and experiences than is typically the case with 'revealed' theology. In both cases, however, the insights are derived from consideration of a selected band of evidence, whether it be somewhat narrow (as, for example, in the use of the reports of the witnesses to Jesus as the Christ as the normative revelation of God in Christian theology) or more general (as in the use of supposed observations of order and purpose in the processes of reality in teleological arguments characteristic of some forms of natural theology). And, what is generally overlooked by those who seek to preserve the traditional notion of revelation as a basis of faith, belief and theological understanding, insight into the reality of the divine allegedly evoked by such selected states, events and experiences, whether the selection is broad or narrow, is not justified by further consideration of those states, events and experiences but by showing that what is thereby perceived is warrantable as a rationally credible perception of the divine (Pailin 1993). Reflection on the nature of theological understanding thus indicates that its only rationally justifiable form is some form of what has in the past been regarded as natural theology, even though that form, in order to be rationally credible today, may have to use evidence and reach conclusions about the ultimate story of reality in ways that are significantly different from how natural theology has often been understood in the past.

REFERENCES

Alexander, S. (1920) *Space, Time and Deity*, 2 vols, London, Macmillan.
Anselm (1962) *Basic Writings*, trans. S. N. Deane, La Salle, Ill.: Open Court.
Aquinas, T. (1947) *Summa Theologica*, trans. the Fathers of the English Dominican Province, New York: Benziger Brothers.
—— (1975) *Summa Contra Gentiles*, trans. A. C. Pegis *et al.*, Notre Dame and London: University of Notre Dame Press.
Augustine (1873) *Lectures or Tractates on the Gospel according to St. John*, vol. I (Tractates I-XXXVII), trans. J. Gibb, Edinburgh: T. & T. Clark.
—— (1874) *Lectures or Tractates on the Gospel according to St John*, vol. II (Tractates XXXVIII-CXXIV), trans. J. Innes, Edinburgh: T. & T. Clark.
Ayer, A. J. (n.d.) *Language, Truth and Logic*, 2nd edn, New York: Dover.
Baillie, J. (1962) *The Sense of the Presence of God*, London: Oxford University Press.
Barbour, I. (1990) *Religion in an Age of Science*, Gifford Lectures vol. 1, San Francisco: Harper and London: SCM Press.
—— (1993) *Ethics in an Age of Technology*, Gifford Lectures vol. 2, San Francisco: Harper and London: SCM Press.
Barr, J. (1993) *Biblical Faith and Natural Theology: The Gifford Lectures for 1991*, Oxford: Clarendon Press.
Barth, K. (1938) *The Knowledge of God and the Service of God according to the Teaching of the Reformation*, London: Hodder and Stoughton.
Bartholomew, D. J. (1984) *God of Chance*, London: SCM Press.
Bayle, P. (1734) *A General Dictionary, Historical and Critical*, London.
Birch, C. and Cobb, J. B. (1981) *The Liberation of Life: From the Cell to the Community*, Cambridge: Cambridge University Press.
Brunner, E. (1949) *The Christian Doctrine of God: Dogmatics Volume I*, trans. O. Wyon, London: Lutterworth Press.
Brunner, E. and Barth, K. (1946) *Natural Theology*, trans. P. Fraenkel, London: Geoffrey Bles, The Centenary Press.
Bultmann, R. (1969) *Faith and Understanding: Collected Essays*, ed. R. W. Funk, trans. L. Pettibone Smith, London: SCM Press.
Calvin, J. (1953) *Institutes of the Christian Religion*, trans. H. Beveridge, London: James Clarke.
Campbell, C. A. (1957) *On Selfhood and Godhood*, London: George Allen & Unwin.
Clarke, S. (1732) *A Discourse Concerning the Being and Attributes of God, the Obligations of Natural Religion, and the Truth and Certainty of the Christian Revelation*, London.
Clatworthy, J. (1992) 'Editorial', in *Theology in Green*, No. 1, Jan., 3–8.
Cobb, J. B. Jr., (1965) *A Christian Natural Theology*, Philadelphia: Westminster Press.

Collins, A. (1713) *A Discourse of Free-Thinking*, London.

Culverwel, N. (1661) *An Elegant, and Learned Discourse of the Light of Nature: With Several other Treatises*, London.

Davis, C. F. (1989) *The Evidential Force of Religious Experience*, Oxford: Clarendon Press.

Derham, W. (1723) *Physico-Theology: Or, A Demonstration of the Being and Attributes of God from His Works of Creation*, London.

—— (1738) *Astro-Theology: Or, A Demonstration of the Being and Attributes of God from a Survey of the Heavens*, London.

Descartes, R. (1931) *The Philosophical Works of Descartes*, trans. E. S. Haldane and G. R. T. Ross, Cambridge: Cambridge University Press.

Edwards, J. (1692) *An Enquiry into Four Remarkable Texts of the New Testament*, Cambridge.

Ellis, J. (1743) *Some Brief Considerations upon Mr. Locke's Hypothesis*, London.

—— (1747) *The Knowledge of Divine Things from Revelation, Not from Reason or Nature*, London.

—— (1757) *An Enquiry Whence Cometh Wisdom and Understanding to Man?*, London.

Feuerbach, L. (1957) *The Essence of Christianity*, trans. G. Eliot, New York: Harper and Brothers.

Freud, S. (1962) *The Future of an Illusion*, trans. W. D. Robson-Scott, ed. J. Strachey, London: The Hogarth Press.

Gilson, E. (1938) *Reason and Revelation in the Middle Ages*, New York: Scribners.

Harnack, A. (1961) *History of Dogma*, trans. N. Buchanan, New York: Dover.

Hartshorne, C. (1965) *Anselm's Discovery: A Re-Examination of the Ontological Proof for God's Existence*, La Salle, Ill.: Open Court.

—— (1967) *A Natural Theology for Our Time*, La Salle, Ill.: Open Court.

—— (1970) *Creative Synthesis and Philosophic Method*, London: SCM Press.

Hatch, E. (1907) *The Influence of Greek Ideas and Usages upon the Christian Church*, Hibbert Lectures for 1888, ed. A. M. Fairbairn, London: Williams and Norgate.

Hegel, G. W. F. (1892) *The Logic of Hegel, translated from the Encyclopaedia of the Philosophical Sciences*, trans. W. Wallace, Oxford: Clarendon Press.

Hepburn, R. W. (1958) *Christianity and Paradox: Critical Studies in Twentieth-Century Theology*, London: Watts.

Herbert, E., Lord Herbert of Cherbury (1663) *De Religione Gentilium*, Amsterdam: Typis Blaeviorum.

—— (1768) *A Dialogue between a Tutor and his Pupil*, London: W. Bathoe.

—— (1937) *De Veritate*, trans. M. H. Carré, Bristol: University of Bristol.

Hodges, H. A. (1953) *Languages, Standpoints and Attitudes*, London: Oxford University Press.

Hume, D. (1935) *Dialogues Concerning Natural Religion*, ed. N. K. Smith, Oxford: Clarendon Press.

Jaki, S. L. (1986) *Lord Gifford and His Lectures: A Centenary Retrospect*, Edinburgh: Scottish Academic Press.

Kant, I. (1909) *Critique of Practical Reason and Other Works on the Theory of Ethics*, trans. T. K. Abbott, London: Longmans.

—— (1933) *Critique of Pure Reason*, trans. N. K. Smith, London: Macmillan.

Kierkegaard, S. (1936) *Philosophical Fragments or A Fragment of Philosophy*, trans. D. F. Swenson, Princeton: Princeton University Press.

—— (1941) *Concluding Unscientific Postscript*, trans. D. F. Swenson and W. Lowrie, Princeton: Princeton University Press.

Lindbeck, G. A. (1984) *The Nature of Doctrine: Religion and Theology in a Postliberal Age*, London: SPCK.

Locke, J. (1979) *An Essay Concerning Human Understanding*, Oxford: Clarendon Press.

Luther, M. (1848) *The Table Talk or Familiar Discourse*, trans. W. Hazlitt, London: David Bogue.

Lyotard, J.-F. (1984) *The Postmodern Condition: A Report on Knowledge*, trans. G. Bennington and B. Massumi, Minneapolis: University of Minnesota Press.

McFague, S. (1993) *The Body of God: An Ecological Theology*, Minneapolis: Fortress Press.

Macmurray, J. (1957) *The Self as Agent*, London: Faber & Faber.

—— (1961) *Persons in Relation*, London: Faber & Faber.

Macquarrie, J. (1966) *Principles of Christian Theology*, London: SCM Press.

Mascall, E. L. (1943) *He Who Is: A Study in Traditional Theism*, London: Longmans, Green and Co.

Melanchthon, P. (1965) *On Christian Doctrine: Loci Communes 1555*, trans. C. L. Manschrek, New York: Oxford University Press.

Mitchell, B. (1973) *The Justification of Religious Belief*, London: Macmillan.

Newman, J. H. (1870) *An Essay in Aid of a Grammar of Assent*, London: Burns, Oates and Company.

Nietzsche, F. (1974) *The Gay Science*, New York: Vintage Books.

—— (1990) *Twilight of the Idols and The Anti-Christ*, Harmondsworth: Penguin.

Ockham, William of (1957) *Philosophical Writings*, trans., ed. P. Boehner, Edinburgh: Nelson.

—— (1969) *Predestination, God's Foreknowledge, and Future Contingents*, trans. M. M. Adams and N. Kretzmann, New York: Appleton-Century-Crofts.

Ogden, S. M. (1967) *The Reality of God and other Essays*, London: SCM Press.

Pailin, D. A. (1968) 'Some Comments on Hartshorne's Presentation of the Ontological Argument', *Religious Studies*, 4:1, Oct., 103–22.

—— (1971) 'Theistic Verification', in D. Kirkpatrick (ed.) *The Living God*, Nashville: Abingdon Press.

—— (1975) ' "Credo ut intelligam" as the Method of Theology and of its Verification', in *Die Wirkungsgeschichte Anselms von Canterbury*, ed. H. K. Kohlenberger, Analecta Anselmiana, Band IV, 111–29.

—— (1986) 'Narrative, Story, and the Interpretation of Metaphysics', in G. R. Lucas (ed.) *Hegel and Whitehead: Contemporary Perspectives on Systematic Philosophy*, Albany: State University of New York.

—— (1989) *God and the Processes of Reality: Foundations of a Credible Theism*, London and New York: Routledge.

—— (1990) *The Anthropological Character of Theology: Conditioning Theological Understanding*, Cambridge: Cambridge University Press.

—— (1993) 'The Supposedly Historical Basis of Theological Understanding', in S. Coakley and D. A. Pailin, (eds) *The Making and Remaking of Christian Doctrine: Essays in Honour of Maurice Wiles*, Oxford: Clarendon Press.

Paley, W. (1838) *The Works of William Paley*, London: Longman.

Penelhum, T. (1971) *Religion and Rationality: An Introduction to the Philosophy of Religion*, New York: Random House.

Plantinga, A. (1979) 'Is Belief in God Rational?', in C. F. Delaney (ed.) *Rationality and Religious Belief*, Notre Dame and London: University of Notre Dame Press.

Price, H. H. (1969) *Belief*, London: George Allen and Unwin.

Rashdall, H. (1924) *The Theory of Good and Evil*, London: Oxford University Press.

Ray, J. (1722) *The Wisdom of God Manifested in the Works of the Creation*, London.

Rorty, R. (1980) *Philosophy and the Mirror of Nature*, Oxford: Basil Blackwell.

—— (1991) *Objectivity, Relativism, and Truth: Philosophical Papers*, vol. 1, Cambridge: Cambridge University Press.

Russell, B. (1975) *Why I am not a Christian and other Essays*, London: George Allen & Unwin.

Schleiermacher, F. (1928) *The Chrisitan Faith*, ed. H. R. Mackintosh and J. S. Stewart, Edinburgh: T. & T. Clark.

—— (1988) *On Religion: Speeches to its Cultured Despisers*, trans. R. Crouter, Cambridge: Cambridge University Press.

Scotus, J. Duns, (1962) *Philosophical Writings*, trans., ed. A. B. Wolter, Edinburgh: Nelson.

—— (1966) *A Treatise on God as First Principle*, trans., ed. A. B. Wolter, Chicago: Forum Books.

Smith, J. (1660) *Select Discourses*, London.

Sorley, W. R. (1924) *Moral Values and the Idea of God*, Cambridge: Cambridge University Press.

Taylor, A. E. (1932) *The Faith of a Moralist*, London: Macmillan.

—— (1961) *Does God Exist?*, London: Collins.

Taylor, J. (1647) *A Discourse of the Liberty of Prophesying. Shewing the Unreasonableness of Prescribing to Other Men's Faith*, London.

Temple, W. (1934) *Nature, Man and God*, London: Macmillan.

Tennant, F. R. (1956) *Philosophical Theology*, vol. II, 'The World, The Soul and God', Cambridge: Cambridge University Press.

Voltaire (1962) *Philosophical Dictionary*, trans. P. Gay, New York: Harcourt, Brace and World.

Whitehead, A. N. (1978) *Process and Reality: An Essay in Cosmology*, ed. D. R. Griffin and D. W. Sherburne, New York: The Free Press.

Wollaston, W. (1726) *The Religion of Nature Delineated*, London.

FURTHER READING

Abraham, W. J. and Holtzer, S. W. (eds) (1987) *The Rationality of Religious Belief: Essays in Honour of Basil Mitchell*, Oxford: Clarendon Press.

Banner, M. C. (1990) *The Justification of Science and the Rationality of Religious Belief*, Oxford: Clarendon Press.

Blanshard, B. (1974) *Reason and Belief*, London: George Allen.

Ewing, A. C. (1973) *Value and Reality: The Philosophical Case for Theism*, London: George Allen & Unwin and New York: Humanities Press.

Hick, J. (1970) *Arguments for the Existence of God*, London: Macmillan.

Küng, H. (1980) *Does God Exist? An Answer for Today*, trans. E. Quinn, London: Collins.

Pannenberg, W. (1991) *Systematic Theology*, vol. 1, trans. G. W. Bromiley, Edinburgh: T. & T. Clark, ch. 2.

Ross, J. F. (1969) *Philosophical Theology*, Indianapolis and New York: Bobbs-Merrill.

Swinburne, R. (1981) *Faith and Reason*, Oxford: Clarendon Press.

Webb, C. C. J. (1915) *Studies in the History of Natural Theology*, Oxford: Clarendon Press.

Woods, G. F. (1958) *Theological Explanation*, Welwyn: James Nisbet.

See also chapters 13, 17, 18, 20, 21.

20

RELIGIOUS LANGUAGE

Mark Wynn

Religious language embraces a wide range of phenomena. Believers may use the language of religion to make statements (sentences which are true or false), to give expression to feelings, or to bring about some state of affairs in the very act of speaking (as when it is said 'I baptize you . . .'). Or again, believers may speak in religious terms in order to prescribe, to exhort, or to declare their intention of behaving in a certain way. Moreover, the statements of the believer may have to do with for instance putative events in human history, or with ethical norms, or they may offer (what appear to be) descriptions with a metaphysical reference. Clearly, the field of religious language is broad and complex.

For simplicity's sake, we shall concentrate on talk about God and distinguish three kinds of 'problem' which may be posed by such uses of religious language. First of all, there is a question about the relation between the sense of religious expressions and the character of the empirical world. It is clear enough that the sense of a term like 'red' is related to the conditions in which the expression 'x is red' is true. So it is natural to ask whether religious talk is also subject to some such relation, and whether any failure to tie the truth of religious utterances to specific empirical conditions would render them devoid of meaning. This issue we may call 'the problem of anchorage'. Next there is a question about the term 'God'. How does this term succeed, if at all, in identifying its referent, and what sort of reality does it pick out? This issue we might label 'the problem of reference'. Then finally, there is a question about how we ought to understand the terms which we predicate of God. Do these terms bear the same sense when used of God and of creatures? And if not, how are we to keep a grasp of their meaning? We can refer to these issues as 'the problem of predication'.

Following this simple typology, we can pose three questions of a religious sentence such as 'God is good': we can ask about the reference of the term 'God', about the sense of the predicate '. . . is good', and about the relation between the whole sentence and reality. I propose to address these matters by beginning with the problem of anchorage, and will proceed in turn to the problems of predication and reference.

THE POSITIVIST CRITERIA OF MEANING

The first of these problems was posed with particular force by 'logical positivism'. This theory was promulgated in the late 1920s and early 1930s by Moritz Schlick, Rudolf Carnap (1974: 60–81) and other philosophers belonging to 'the Vienna Circle'. The positivists proposed that a sentence is meaningful if and only if it satisfies one or other of two conditions: either the sentence is true by definition (a tautology: in this class they placed the truths of logic and mathematics), or it is meaningful by virtue of the fact that it can be verified (or falsified) by the empirical facts. Now religious claims do not give the appearance of being tautologies. So on the positivist account of linguistic meaning, it seems we must say that the claims of religion make sense only on condition that they are empirically verifiable (or falsifiable), or more exactly on condition that they are verifiable (falsifiable) at least in principle (that is, on condition that there are possible empirical circumstances which would serve to verify or falsify them). Now the positivists ruled that religious claims failed to meet this condition and concluded that the apparent claims of religious believers are in fact meaningless.

In favour of this approach to religious language, we may refer again to the example of 'red' above. It seems that we learn the meaning of such terms by being presented, on the one hand, with objects of which we may truly say 'this is red' (thus verifying the sentence in question) and, on the other, with objects concerning which it would be false to say 'this is red' (here the corresponding sentences are falsified, of course). And this, it may be said, is not just a psychological but a logical truth: if we had been told that 'x is red' was true of every object, or false of every object, then the term 'red' could not (logically could not) have any sense for us. But then the theist seems to be committed to the truth of 'God created the world' or 'God is love' no matter what the situation may be; these claims, it seems, are not advanced as tentative hypotheses, to be revised if the empirical evidence should turn out in a certain way. So should we not say, by analogy with what we have said about the conditions for assigning a sense to the term 'red', that the sentence 'God created the world' is simply devoid of meaning?

To assess this proposal, we need to formulate the positivist's claim more precisely. Perhaps the relevant criterion of factual (as opposed to tautological) meaning can be expressed thus:

1 A sentence is factually meaningful only if it is conclusively *verifiable*.

Or perhaps it is to be expressed as:

2 A sentence is factually meaningful only if it is conclusively *falsifiable*.

But there seem to be clear counterexamples to 1 and 2. For instance, the sentence 'All Australians like the sun' is not conclusively verifiable (even if all Australians have liked the sun so far, it remains possible that some future Australian will not do so); and the sentence 'Some Australians like the sun' is not conclusively falsifiable (even if no Australian has liked the sun so far, it remains possible that some future Australian will do so). Despite their failure to satisfy 1 and 2 respectively, these sentences are surely meaningful. Moreover a hybrid of 1 and 2, claiming that a sentence is factually meaningful only if it is either conclusively verifiable or conclusively falsifiable, seems to work no better. For instance, the sentence 'All Australians are mortal' does not satisfy this further criterion, although it is clearly meaningful.

Recognizing the difficulties with any form of the verification principle which was couched in terms of *conclusive* verification (or falsification), the positivists reformed their account so that it appealed simply to the possibility of confirmation or disconfirmation; that is, they ruled that a sentence was factually meaningful if and only if the empirical evidence could establish with some measure of plausibility its truth or falsity, even if such evidence could not remove all possibility of error. This is the form of the principle advocated in the most celebrated English-language presentation of the positivist case, A. J. Ayer's *Language, Truth and Logic*, which first appeared in 1936. This 'weak' form of the verification principle can admit the meaningfulness of sentences like 'All Australians are mortal'; for the mortality of all Australians is certainly confirmed by the empirical evidence, even if it is not conclusively verified.

But even in this attenuated form, the positivist claim seems open to counterexamples. What about: 'The appearance of fairies is at least sometimes unconfirmable.' Clearly, there is no possibility of confirming this sentence (you cannot confirm that unconfirmable appearances have taken place). But neither can the sentence be disconfirmed (even if you observe the fairies appearing on some occasions, that does not count against the claim that they appear unconfirmably on further occasions). Some may draw the moral that sentences like this are meaningless. But others will disagree; and this disagreement cannot be settled by appeal to the positivists' own criteria of meaning without begging the question of whether these criteria are appropriate (Swinburne 1993: 22–9).

So the different forms of the positivist principle seem in various ways to be vulnerable to counterexamples. It may be that we can offer a general explanation of this fact. In brief, we might suggest that the principle in its various guises postulates too close a relation between knowing the truth conditions of a sentence (the circumstances in which it is true) and knowing the evidence which would serve to establish its truth. Now to know the meaning of a sentence is indeed to know its truth conditions. But knowing the truth conditions of a sentence, it seems, need not involve knowing what evidence would serve to show that the sentence is true (Heimbeck 1969: 46–76). For instance, it is possible to grasp the truth conditions and so the meaning of 'These rocks were laid down five million years ago' without understanding how to provide evidence for this claim. So the positivist proposal that the meaningfulness of a sentence is tied to its checkability fails: even if we cannot specify how a sentence might be confirmed, it may have a meaning, and its meaning may be known to us.

These few remarks suggest that the positivists' criteria of linguistic meaning are too restrictive. So the person who wishes to uphold the truth or falsity of theistic claims, and who thereby presupposes the meaningfulness of these claims, can respond to the positivist challenge by seeking to undermine the verification criterion in something like the fashion outlined above. Another kind of response would seek to show that the meaningfulness of theistic sentences can be maintained without infringing the positivist criteria, or at any rate to show that these sentences can be anchored in empirical experience somehow, even if this means developing a broader conception of the relation between empirical fact and factually significant discourse than the positivists themselves would have allowed. It is certainly worth seeing whether theistic discourse can satisfy (something like) the verification principle. For while the positivists may not have shown that verifiability is a *necessary* condition of sentence meaning, it does seem to constitute a *sufficient* condition. (Think again of the example of 'red'.) So if it can be shown that theistic claims satisfy the verification criterion, that would be one way of removing any doubt about their meaningfulness.

BROADENING THE POSITIVIST CRITERIA

In the tradition of natural theology, many philosophers have argued that the character of the empirical world overall affords good evidence for the belief that God exists. If any of these arguments should prove to work, we would be able to verify the claims of theism not merely in principle but with reference to known empirical facts, so meeting the condition of cognitively significant discourse imposed by the positivists. Any such argument will take the form of first, identifying certain facts and second, arguing that these facts are best understood in theistic terms. So any dispute regarding such an argument may accordingly relate to the former or the latter approach: the sceptic may doubt whether the supposed fact is really a fact, or may allow the fact but question the theist's interpretation of its significance. The positivist complaint against the theist is in effect that disputes between theist and atheist do not (at least do not any longer) turn upon disagreements of the first kind. Both sides agree upon the 'facts', in the sense of agreeing that the world is comprised of this and not that range of empirical phenomena. If that is so, the positivists urge, then surely the claim that there is (or is not) a God is not anchored in the nature of empirical reality, and is therefore meaningless.

To see whether the dispute between theist and atheist can be treated as a factually significant one, even if there is no disagreement as to the empirical facts, we might recall the nature of disputes in other disciplines. For instance, in law there can be agreement on all the facts of the case (whether the defendant turned right at the lights at forty miles per hour, and so on) but disagreement about what label to apply to a certain pattern of behaviour (was the defendant driving 'with due care and attention' or not?). This sort of dispute is not 'factual' in so far as it cannot be settled by empirical enquiry (for the empirical facts are all agreed); but even so we are inclined to say that the dispute is 'factual' in so far as the ruling of the court is not merely an arbitrary affair: arguments on each side need to be weighed, and while the ruling is not simply an empirical judgement, it needs to be sensitive to the empirical facts.

Now if this sort of disagreement is factually significant in the sense just identified, we might ask whether the dispute between believer and unbeliever is not similarly a factually significant dispute, where there is agreement on the empirical facts but disagreement about what name to apply to these facts. Thus we might represent this sort of dispute as a dispute about whether or not the world exhibits an order of the kind that may be labelled a 'mind pattern'. Here again the disagreement is not about individual facts, but about the pattern they present, and about what label it is appropriate to apply in view of the pattern (Wisdom 1953: 149–68). So here is a reason for thinking that it may be possible to anchor theistic sentences in the empirical facts, even if empirical enquiry alone cannot decide whether these sentences are true. This line of argument could be presented as a way of accommodating the positivist criterion of meaning, by showing how theism might after all be open to confirmation by the empirical facts even if it is not itself simply another such fact. At the same time, it amounts to a criticism of the positivist approach, which calls for a broadening of its conception of anchorage.

This sort of argument could be considered as explanatory. But the claim that a person was, for example, driving without due care and attention is more naturally considered not as an explanation of certain events but as a way of characterizing (or labelling) them; and similarly we might suppose that the label 'mind dependent' is to be taken as a description of the data of observation, rather than as an appeal to some further reality which lies behind them. (This interpretation is borne out by Wisdom's closing remarks on the factual significance of Greek mythology, 1953: 166–7.) Other sorts of argument are more clearly explanatory. Thus we may try to anchor the claims of theism by supposing that God is the best explanation of a certain range of empirical phenomena (or perhaps the best explanation of the very existence of finite things). This sort of argument may proceed relatively informally, as in the work of Basil Mitchell (1973: 39–57), or may appeal to a formal calculus of probabilities, as in Richard Swinburne's writings (Swinburne 1991: 64–9). Here again, there need not be any disagreement between the theist and the sceptic about the empirical facts: the disagreement may have to do with what best explains those facts. And this sort of disagreement, like disagreements about naming, seems to be factual. Consider by analogy a scientific debate concerning the need to cite some unobserved entity in order to explain certain observations; on the standard account, this would rate as a factual issue.

These natural theological arguments attempt to establish the truth of theism; and showing the truth of a claim is, of course, one way of demonstrating its meaningfulness. But a further sort of approach is possible, where it is argued that theism is verifiable in principle, and is therefore cognitively significant, even if its truth cannot be established in fact. This is the approach taken by John Hick in his article 'Theology and Verification' (1971: 53–71). Hick argues for the conceivability (not the truth) of the idea that after death I will enter a resurrection world where I will have 'an experience of the reign of the Son in the Kingdom of the Father' (ibid.: 69). Such an experience, he suggests, would serve to establish the claims of Christian theism beyond reasonable doubt. Hick believes that the world is religiously ambiguous, favouring decisively neither the claims of the believer nor those of the sceptic. But, he argues, since theism can (at least in principle) be verified eschatologically in this fashion, it follows that its claims are cognitively significant even so.

It has been objected, for instance by Nielsen (1971: 74–7), that Hick's description of the verifying experience here merely begs the question. It may be said:

> The positivist observes that the language of religion is meaningless in so far as terms like 'God' cannot be grounded in experience; and it is no reply to this objection to say that we could have an experience of being in the Kingdom of God, for the positivist will still want to know how a belief about the Kingdom is to be anchored in experience of familiar kinds.

In Hick's defence, we might try to specify in non-theistic terms (that is, without referring to God) what sort of experience would serve to verify Christian belief. Providing it is confirmation that is required, and not conclusive verification, it seems that certain non-theistic experiences would most reasonably be interpreted in terms of the Christian world-view – experience, for instance, of a figure who answers to the description of Jesus in the Gospels, who works miracles, and so on (Mitchell 1973: 12–14). It seems to me that sense experience could make such an interpretation reasonable independently of any reference to further kinds of experience. But the more difficult issue raised by Nielsen's criticism concerns the possibility of a non-sensory experience of the divine. This is to broach a large epistemological topic; but if we do admit the possibility of such experiences, then the believer could claim that the language of religion is anchored in much the same way as our ordinary perceptual language, with the difference that non-sensory experience is relevant in this further case.

These various ways of tying the claims of theism to the realm of empirical (or at least experienceable) fact seek to preserve the idea that religious claims are factual. In this sense, we may say that in their view religious language is cognitive: such language can be used to make assertions, or (equivalently) to frame sentences with a truth-value. Alternatively, we might seek to keep the connection between the language of religion and empirical claims in a way which confers upon such language a non-cognitive significance. For instance, we may argue as follows. Our willingness to pursue our empirical enquiries without limit rests upon a commitment to the final intelligibility of the world; and the idea that there is such a congruence between reality and our ideals of reason is well expressed by the theistic belief in the existence of a self-explanatory deity who governs the created order in a rationally intelligible manner. In that case, we should say that religious language can be anchored in the realm of empirical fact on account of its role in animating our empirical investigations, even if it does not advance any knowledge claim itself (for we do not know that reality is intelligible in this sense; it is just that we act upon the assumption that it is).

The first *Critique* of Immanuel Kant (1729–1804) is the classical source for the idea that religious language may have such a regulative function (Kant 1933: A619–20, B647–8). But a similar proposal has been advanced by R. M. Hare (1959), who suggests that the principles we apply in distinguishing between fact and illusion cannot themselves be known, but may involve something like a faith in a 'divine order'. This proposal, it seems to me, is an improvement on Hare's earlier but better-known idea that religious beliefs constitute a *blik* (Hare *et al*. 1955: 99–103). According to his earlier account, a *blik* is a perspective on the world which determines the way a person interprets the facts, although it is not itself a factual claim. For instance, suppose that a student believes that his teachers are out to murder him, and suppose that he persists in this belief regardless of all contrary evidence, preferring to explain away such evidence in various ways. Such a belief, or *blik*, is then unfalsifiable, since it determines the way the student understands the evidence, rather than itself resting upon evidence. Hare concludes that the belief therefore lacks the status of an assertion (here siding with the positivists). Nonetheless, he implies, the belief (or 'belief') still has a sense (we know what the student means by his claim). Analogously, Hare suggests, religious discourse may be unfalsifiable, and so non-cognitive, while still having a sense. But this sort of dispute (should we say that the teachers' pattern of behaviour exhibits murderous intent?) is perhaps more satisfactorily treated in the manner which Wisdom outlines in his discussion of the 'logic' of naming; in short, this seems to be a factual dispute.

So there are various ways of meeting the positivist challenge in the sense of showing that there is after all some connection between religious discourse and the world of empirical fact. In sum, religious discourse may provide appropriate labels for certain patterns that we discern in the empirical world; or it may offer a framework in terms of which we can explain the character of our experience (whether now or in some future, possibly eschatological, state); or it may provide a way of articulating a constitutive assumption of empirical enquiry. I have developed these different approaches on the assumption that believers and their interlocutors agree on the nature of 'the facts' with which we need to reckon. But some may argue that religious discourse is grounded in certain special facts which only believers acknowledge. For instance, it may be said that various miraculous events provide a grounding for the language of Christian belief. But this sort of proposal is perhaps less interesting in so far as it depends upon the introduction of factual claims which not all Christians (let alone all those who find the language of Christian belief meaningful) would wish to make.

RELIGIOUS DISCOURSE AND RELIGIOUS PRACTICE

The approaches I have considered so far, whether cognitivist or non-cognitivist, share the idea that the meaning of religious language is grounded in the realm of empirical enquiry (even if that role is the regulative one of guiding such enquiry). But we might prefer to locate the sense of religious claims in relation to their practical rather than their (supposed) theoretical function. Clearly, religious uses of language are interwoven with religious practice, and a person's religious belief seems usually (necessarily, in the view of some) to carry implications for his or her conduct more generally. Perhaps, then, the sense of religious discourse relates to its role in regulating human beings' dealings with one another and with the world in ways which do not relate to our empirical enquiries.

For instance, it may be argued that in expressing a religious belief, a person is subscribing to a certain ideal of conduct, and informing others of his or her intention to conform to that ideal. Of course, this sort of linguistic activity is familiar enough from other, non-religious contexts, and such utterances seem clearly enough to make sense despite the fact that they are not subject to empirical testing (indeed they have no truth-value if the speaker is not describing his or her state of mind but merely expressing an intention). This sort of construal of religious language is apparent in the work of various nineteenth-century authors, for instance Matthew Arnold, but a more recent exponent of the view is Richard Braithwaite (1971: 72–91). Braithwaite postulates a dual role for religious language. First of all, such language serves to express a person's intentions (not just any intention will do: the intention should relate to some general policy of conduct). Second, the language of religious stories serves as a stimulus to moral action: by entertaining (not necessarily asserting) such stories, the believer is inspired to persevere in the moral life.

This approach to the sense of religious language again asks for a broadening of the positivist criteria of linguistic meaning. Here it is suggested that it is not only tautologies and statements which record (or explain or label) empirical data which have a meaning, but also expressions of attitude or intention. (Religious stories can be accommodated straightforwardly within the positivist framework as long as they are comprised of sentences which are verifiable in principle.) The positivists themselves sometimes recognized the possibility of such forms of meaning. For example, Ayer offers an 'emotive' account of moral language, according to which its role is not to describe some putative factual domain, but rather to give expression to feelings, and to encourage others to share these feelings (Ayer 1971: 111). But the positivists did not explore this possibility systematically in relation to religious language. Note that although Braithwaite has departed from positivist theory to the extent of questioning their (official) doctrine of the conditions of meaningful utterance, he has retained an important (perhaps the most important) part of the positivist programme, namely the claim that an utterance is factually meaningful only if it is empirically verifiable. So Braithwaite's theory, like Hare's, is non-cognitivist. In particular, his proposal does not ascribe a factual meaning to religious claims in so far as they function as declarations of intention; and although religious stories may be factually meaningful (if verifiable), Braithwaite is clear that the question of their truth is not important (their religious significance is not diminished if they are treated as fiction).

What are we to make of this account? In its favour, we should note that Braithwaite's theory has no difficulty in explaining the practical import of religious beliefs: if religious belief comes down to the expression of an intention to behave in a certain way, then its role in guiding action is relatively unproblematic. By contrast, it might be said, if we treat religious belief as a more speculative affair, which has to do with upholding various theoretical claims, then its relation to conduct becomes less apparent; and this surely poses a problem for any cognitivist account of religious discourse.

However, few have been persuaded by Braithwaite's theory. D. Z. Phillips urges that his approach is 'reductionist' (Phillips 1976: 139–50). In particular, he suggests, this approach reduces religion to its role as a moral motivator. Braithwaite seems to think that the believer's moral perspective can be specified without recourse to the language of religion, and that the role of religious language is at bottom to help with the implementation of such a perspective, rather than to define it. In place of this view, Phillips argues that religious discourse may serve to constitute a moral vision; that is, it may be that a certain moral perspective cannot be articulated independently of the language of religion. This is one way of developing the thought that Braithwaite's perspective is reductionist. Others will suppose that Braithwaite's reductionism runs deeper: it is not just that he has failed to note the role of religion in defining a moral vision; his construal of religious language is altogether in the practical mode, and so neglects the theoretical, fact-stating dimension of such language. If either of these responses is valid, we should conclude that Braithwaite's theory fails as a descriptive account of religious language; but it may be that some will find the theory attractive as a prescriptive (or revisionary) account of such language. We could read Braithwaite's account as a recommendation concerning the sense that ought to be assigned to religious language by people who have, for instance, an appreciation of the difficulties we may encounter in trying to anchor such language in the domain of empirical fact.

Braithwaite's attempt to supplement the positivist account of the conditions of linguistic meaning reflects his familiarity with the later philosophy of Ludwig Wittgenstein. In his *Tractatus* (which appeared in German in 1921) and in conversation with members of the Vienna Circle in the 1920s, Wittgenstein had enunciated the central principles which the positivists went on to apply with such enthusiasm: the meaning of a statement is given by the method of its verification; the truths of mathematics and logic are tautologies; there are strictly speaking no further possibilities for meaningful discourse. But in his later work Wittgenstein came to question this conception of linguistic meaning, and to suppose that the functions of language are much more various.

This later emphasis upon the plurality of linguistic activities is expressed succinctly in the thought that human discourse is comprised of a multiplicity of 'language-games'. (A language-game comprises a set of linguistic practices appropriate to a given sphere of human life.) By speaking in this connection of 'games', Wittgenstein indicates that these different examples of language use cannot be classified according to some single function that is performed in each case, just as there is no single defining feature of what it is to be a game (Wittgenstein 1968: para. 66). By contrast with the positivist attempt to reduce all (legitimate) linguistic practices to one or other of two basic types, the approach of the later Wittgenstein proceeds in an inductive, piecemeal fashion: instead of deriving in a relatively *a priori* fashion a general account of the conditions of linguistic meaning, we are told to look at the way language in fact works in the many and various language-games that make up human discourse.

This approach relates to the account of justification which Wittgenstein develops in his later philosophy. Any attempt to justify our use of language cannot go on indefinitely, he suggests. In particular, we cannot justify our most basic ways of responding to the world in linguistic and other ways; in other words, we cannot justify what he terms our 'forms of life'. It follows that our language-games also lie beyond the reach of justification, in so far as they help to constitute these forms of life. Within a game, we can make judgements about the appropriateness of a given use of language, by referring to the rules of the game; but the game itself marks a stopping point of explanation. So determining the limits of meaningful discourse is not, as the positivists had supposed, a matter of justifying or criticizing our language use in terms of its conformity to an abstract norm; instead, the task of the philosopher is to describe (rather than to reform or to ground) the contours of our language-games.

A number of philosophers have applied these ideas to the case of religious discourse (a subject about which Wittgenstein himself said relatively little). D. Z. Phillips, for instance, holds that religious and scientific discourse are to be judged according to very different standards of meaning and rationality and therefore constitute different language-games. It follows, Phillips suggests, that there is no more reason to call into question the meaning or rationality of religious language (as a whole) than to call into question the meaning or rationality of science.

More exactly, Phillips proposes for instance that prayer is not concerned with exerting some sort of causal influence upon the progress of events (Phillips 1965: 112–30), and that talk of an afterlife is not to be taken as speculation about some further state of consciousness beyond the grave. Or again, and more fundamentally, he suggests that the reality of God is not that of some superbeing existing beyond this world. Rather, God's reality is to be found within the linguistic and other practices that comprise the believer's form of life. The same sort of point is made concisely by Peter Winch when he remarks that ceasing to pray is better considered as an *aspect* rather than as a *consequence* of ceasing to believe in the reality of God (Winch 1977: 207); in other words, belief in God does not stand independently of practices such as praying to him, and so on, rather as my belief in the reality of my friend Peter stands independently of my practice of addressing requests to him (I could continue to believe that Peter exists without asking him for anything). So expressions like 'asking x of God' and 'asking x of Peter', while they may resemble one another superficially, have very different logical properties (their 'depth grammar' proves to be different). In general, Winch, Phillips and other 'Wittgensteinians' find that religious belief does not stand prior to religious practice (and so does not provide a justification for it); rather, practice is an aspect of belief, so that there are 'internal' (or conceptual) connections between the various dimensions of religious belief (in the reality of God, the efficacy of prayer, the existence of the soul, and so on) and religious practice.

In these various respects, it is clear that Phillips and others of this persuasion postulate a profound difference between the discourse of religion and that of science. Some may prefer to say that while the languages of religion and science are of course very different (God's reality is necessary, the reality of things in the world is contingent, and so on), nonetheless talk about God is still talk about an agent (perhaps of an agent who answers prayer by changing the course of the empirical world, or of an agent whose activity accounts for the enduring existence of the world). The appropriateness of this sort of response will depend partly upon the possibility of mounting an effective natural theology, or providing some other epistemological warrant for metaphysical theism; partly upon the possibility of finding points of connection between our empirical enquiries and the language of religion; and partly upon the possibility of developing a convincing doctrine of analogy, or some other account of how the terms we predicate of a metaphysical God make sense (see below).

My discussion so far has concerned the first of the three 'problems' I distinguished at the outset, what I have termed 'the problem of anchorage'. We have seen the positivists frame this problem in uncompromising terms. And we have seen various responses to the challenge they pose: we might try simply to find individual counterexamples to their criteria of meaning; or more constructively, we might develop another, broader account of the connections between empirical fact and meaningful discourse (in the manner of Wisdom, Mitchell, Swinburne or Hare); or we might try to supplement their typology of the conditions of linguistic meaning by drawing attention to the ways in which religious discourse is related to and helps to constitute our practical commitments (in the manner of Braithwaite or Phillips for instance).

THE PROBLEM OF PREDICATION

The second of the general problems I distinguished above had to do with the sense of the terms we predicate of God. Neo-Wittgensteinians and others who question the metaphysical reference of God-talk will have their own perspective on this issue. (Thus Wittgensteinians will say that the sense of God-talk is evident from the forms of life in which it is embedded.) But if we adopt the approach of metaphysical theism, a rather different set of problems emerges. In brief, the difficulty can be expressed as follows. When we consider the terms which we use of God and of creatures (terms like 'good' and 'wise'), we can suppose first, that these terms have the same sense in divine and creaturely contexts or second, that their senses differ in these two cases. But neither of these approaches seems satisfactory. The former is likely to leave us with an anthropomorphic account of the divine nature. And the latter seems to issue in a kind of agnosticism. For our understanding of our terms derives from the sense which they bear when they are used of creatures; so if terms like 'good' acquire a different sense when they are predicated of God, then we shall not be able to locate their religious sense with any precision.

St Thomas Aquinas (1224/5–74) identifies the same dilemma when he proposes that the relation between the terms we use of God and of creatures cannot be one of univocity (sameness of sense) nor one of equivocity (total difference of sense). Instead, he suggests, we need an intermediate possibility, where the meaning of a term is stretched in the divine case but not stretched so far as to lose all continuity with its original, creaturely sense. This intermediate possibility he terms analogy (Aquinas 1964: 1a 13.5; 61–7). For instance, the term 'healthy' is not used in just the same sense when we speak of 'a healthy complexion' and of 'a healthy man'; but at the same time, it is not used in totally different senses in these two contexts (we are not merely punning when we use the same word in each case). To mark this fact, we may say that the term 'healthy' is used **analogically** of human beings and their complexions.

More generally, in the language of one of **Aquinas's** commentators, Cardinal Cajetan (1469–1534), we may say that there are two kinds of analogy. First, there is 'analogy of attribution' (of which 'healthy' as used above would be an example). In this case a term applies, strictly speaking, to just one of the analogates (in our example the human being) and in a derivative way (or by attribution) to the further analogate by virtue of some relation which it bears to the primary analogate (for instance, the relation of being a symptom, in the case of a healthy complexion, or of being a cause, in the case of a healthy diet). On the other hand we may speak of an 'analogy of proportionality', in cases where a term applies, strictly speaking, to both analogates, but in a different way to each analogate. For instance, we may speak of 'a faithful dog' and 'a faithful spouse', where faithfulness is 'proportional to' the natures of dogs and human beings respectively.

It is natural to ask the question: which of the many terms we predicate of created things may be predicated analogically of God? With reference to the analogy of attribution, we might suggest that any term which can properly be applied in the created order may be used analogically of God also, in so far as he is the cause of all created things. But this approach carries unfortunate implications. It suggests that terms like 'goodness' and 'wisdom' may be used in the fullest sense of creatures (the primary analogate in this case) and only derivatively of God (in so far as he is the cause of the goodness and wisdom of creatures). By contrast, the believer is inclined to say that it is God who is the supreme exemplar of goodness, and that creatures are good only in some secondary sense. More importantly, it suggests that terms like 'round', 'green' and 'hirsute' all apply to God, since they can be truly predicated of God's effects. The analogy of proportionality also poses problems, at any rate if it is treated as a kind of formula for ascribing sense to the terms we use of God. For this approach suggests that in order to give sense to a term like 'good' when it is predicated of God, we need to take account of the fact that God's goodness is in proportion to his nature. And it may be objected as follows: in order to act on this proposal, we must first have some notion of what God's nature is like; but we cannot have such a notion without already understanding what terms like 'good' mean when they are predicated of God; for such terms are basic to our conception of the divine nature; so we are caught in a circle.

To meet these difficulties, the theory of analogy needs development. There are some indications of how to proceed in Aquinas's own account. For example, he suggests that when we ascribe a property to God we should remove from our idea of the property anything which implies imperfection or a creaturely form of existence (the *via remotionis*). The application of this rule will ensure that terms like 'round' are not predicated of God. Aquinas adds that we should suppose that God possesses these 'pure perfections' in a supereminent degree (the *via eminentiae*). This approach gives us some idea of how perfection terms must be stretched when they are applied to the divine nature, although it does not provide a substantive conception of God's perfection.

Some may wonder whether we can dispense with some of these difficulties by adopting a theory of univocity. Following Duns Scotus (d. 1308), it may be suggested that we should draw the boundary between univocal and analogical uses of terms by considering the possibility of various comparisons (Sherry 1976: 439–40). For instance, the comparison 'Your complexion is healthier than I am' sounds logically odd, suggesting that 'healthy' does not have the same sense when used of complexions and human beings. But the comparison 'God is wiser than you are' does not sound so obviously amiss (although Wittgensteinians may detect deep differences of 'logical grammar' here). So there are reasons for thinking that in some central cases we may talk of God and of creatures univocally. Indeed, it may be argued (as Scotus himself suggests) that Aquinas's own doctrine is implicitly univocalist. For instance, Aquinas maintains (1964: 1a 13.3; 57–9) that the *res significata* of terms like goodness is the same in the case of creatures and God (that is, the property signified in the two cases is the same); it is just the *modus significandi* which differs in the two cases (that is, it is just the way in which God possesses the property that differs). But surely, it may be said, if terms like 'wisdom' and so on pick out the same property when used of God and of creatures, then it is best to suppose that these terms are used univocally in the two cases (Swinburne 1993: 80–1).

These arguments suggest, contrary to Aquinas's stated view, that there is indeed a sense in which talk of God and of creatures may be said to be 'univocal'. But this sense is to be distinguished from Aquinas's. For Aquinas's account of univocity (unlike Scotus's) seems to be more than a merely logical doctrine: it also involves a range of metaphysical judgements. In particular, from the way in which Aquinas argues for the impossibility of univocal usage, it is clear that on his understanding the possibility of making certain comparisons is not a sufficient condition of univocity; in addition, it is necessary that the things concerned should not differ too profoundly in their mode of being. For instance, Aquinas argues that we cannot speak univocally of God and creatures because the divine properties are possessed in a simple and undivided way, whereas those of creatures are not. Similarly, his doctrine of analogy involves more than the logical point that certain terms can be used across generic boundaries (terms like goodness and existence). It also involves a metaphysical account of causation, in particular the view that a cause must possess in a higher form whatever perfections it brings about in other things; and it includes the view that as subsistent being itself, God must possess all perfections. In sum, our verdict on the claim that terms may be used of God and creatures univocally, or only analogically, should be sensitive to different connotations of the terms 'analogical' and 'univocal'.

Analogy, univocity and equivocity are all literal modes of discourse. But we also speak of God metaphorically or figuratively, as when we say that 'God is a rock' or that 'God is angry' (assuming the truth of the impassibilist account of the divine nature). Indeed, some have proposed that all human language, including the language we use of God, is metaphorical (Sarot 1992: 141–4). Suppose for instance that I am introduced to the term 'red' in relation to the colour of a certain apple. When I use the term thereafter, it is most unlikely that I will be applying it to things whose colour resembles in all respects the colour of the apple. Instead, in saying that a thing is red, I will be noting that its colour resembles that of the apple in some but not in all respects; so my application of the term in further cases is a creative use of language which extends the term's range of application. But such creativity, it may be said, is characteristic of metaphorical discourse. For instance, if we remark that someone has a 'regal manner', speaking metaphorically, we are using the term 'regal' outside of the context in which its sense was first established, and noting that the deportment of the person resembles that of a king in some but not in all respects.

If we adopt this view of metaphor, it follows uncontroversially that all talk of God is metaphorical, because the terms we use of God we learn first in relation to creatures, and the divine properties are not like those of human beings in all respects. However, if we are using the term 'metaphor' in its everyday sense, then the claim that all human talk is metaphorical is false. And on this same understanding of metaphor, we might argue that the supposition that all talk of God is metaphorical must also be false (Alston 1989: 17–37). (Here the issue concerns positive descriptions of the divine; all parties can agree that negative and relational attributions may be literally true.) Suppose we distinguish between the subject of a metaphor (the thing to which the metaphor is applied) and its exemplar (the thing to which the expression in question literally applies). Using these terms, we may say that a metaphor proposes that a certain exemplar is an appropriate model of the metaphor's subject (ibid.: 22). So a metaphor will be apt or the statement in which it is embedded true on condition that the exemplar is indeed a good model. We might then argue as follows. But in making such judgements of aptness or truth, we must judge that the metaphor's subject is appropriately compared to its exemplar in a given respect. And to make such a judgement, we need to know what the subject is really like in that respect. And this implies an ability to speak of the metaphor's subject in literal terms, at least in principle (that is, on condition that the language contains an appropriate predicate). Similarly, if we wish to say that we can distinguish good from poor theistic metaphors, then we must say that talk of God cannot be irreducibly metaphorical. (Of course, this is not to say that the sense of theistic metaphors can be exhaustively specified in the form of a literal paraphrase.)

Advocates of the 'pan-metaphorical' view would endeavour to escape the force of Alston's argument by questioning the account of metaphor on which it relies. According to Alston's view it does appear that metaphors are true or apt only if they are implicit comparisons and if they impute resemblances between the subject and exemplar which are found to hold. Many would question this account of metaphor as too crude. They would contend that the basic function of a metaphor is to make us think about one thing in terms of another and that this can be fruitful even though there are no literal similarities between exemplar and subject. By metaphorical descriptions of God, we set up associations between divine and mundane realities which help us in thinking about God (for example, by extending upon reflection our negative or relational knowledge of him), without imputing any literal resemblances between creature and creator. In this way the transcendence of God may be preserved (see Searle 1979 and Yob 1992 for the basis of this reply). This debate throws up the question, crucial also in discussions of analogy described above, as to what account of divine transcendence underlies our strategies for interpreting religious language.

Although the claim that all talk of God is metaphorical may be controversial (on some understandings of the nature of metaphor), it seems clear that metaphors do have an important role in the language of religion. In particular, a number of recent philosophical discussions have drawn attention to the importance of models in theology. The relation between metaphor and model is a matter of debate, but models (when they are spelt out linguistically) seem to comprise metaphors themselves and to sponsor the use of further metaphors. For instance in speaking metaphorically of the brain as 'a computer', we use a model to establish a theory; and this model generates further ways of thinking metaphorically about its subject, as when we speak of the 'programming' of the brain. Thus we may distinguish respectively between theory-constitutive metaphors and metaphorically constituted theory terms (Soskice 1985: 101). Analogously we may begin with a model of God as father, or as mother or friend, and use these models to derive further ways of speaking metaphorically of the nature and activity of God.

Soskice elaborates on the parallel between the scientific and theological uses of models, suggesting that the two are more alike than is sometimes supposed. In particular, she suggests that models in religion have an explanatory or cognitive and not merely an affective role. And she suggests that scientific and not merely religious or theological theory is inextricably bound up with the use of models: models constitute the projective capacity of a scientific theory, suggesting new lines of enquiry, as we investigate which of the points of comparison implicit in the model are appropriate and which are not (Soskice 1985: 108–15). These reflections suggest that by noting the referential success of scientific models, we can develop a further argument for the idea that religious language is anchored in our empirical experience even though its ontological claims are not reducible to claims about the data of observation. To substantiate such a case, we would need, of course, to give reasons for rejecting other (e.g. positivist and instrumentalist) interpretations of the status of scientific models.

We have now considered a number of issues relating to the nature of predication in religious uses of language: should our talk of God be understood in metaphorical terms alone, or do some of the things we say of God have a literal significance? If the latter is true, should we suppose that the terms we use of God and of creatures are related analogically, or should we take them to be related univocally (or equivocally)? And does the metaphorical use of language in religion provide a way of anchoring religious claims, by analogy with the ways in which scientific models may be grounded in the empirical data? In these various ways, we may debate the meaning of expressions like '. . . is good' and '. . . is wise' when predicaed of God. But what about the term 'God' itself? How does this term function linguistically?

THE PROBLEM OF REFERENCE

Here we arrive at the third of the problems I distinguished at the outset. The term 'God' seems partly to behave as a proper name. For instance, in response to the question 'Whom do you worship?' I may reply simply: 'God.' But at the same time the term seems to have some sort of descriptive content, and so to differ from proper names like 'Mark' or 'Jane'. Thus in the tradition of Saint Anselm (1033–1109), we may say that God is definitionally that than which nothing greater can be conceived. Thus the term functions syntactically both as a proper name and as a kind of title term. In these respects, the logical role of 'God' is similar to that of a term like 'Caesar', which serves both as the name of a particular individual and also in due course to denote the holder of a particular office (the ruler of the Roman Empire) (Pike 1970: 28–33).

In recent philosophical discussion, two competing theories of the ways in which proper names refer have been canvassed. Following Russell, some philosophers have maintained that proper names are in the normal case implicit definite descriptions (thus 'Aristotle' means 'the man who was a pupil of Plato, taught Alexander, and also . . .'; or more plausibly it means 'the man who did at least a sufficient number of these things: . . .'). The other theory holds that proper names do not have a sense, but apply simply to whatever individual was picked out on the occasion of some initial dubbing (Kripke 1980). (A description may have been used on this occasion to identify the individual, but on this theory the description will not form part of the sense of the term.) The importance of this discussion for religious discourse is apparent if we consider the question: do the different religions refer to the same sacred reality?

If we work with a descriptions account of proper names, then in order to show that 'Yahweh', 'Allah', 'Brahman' and so on all have the same reference, we will need to explain away any incompatible descriptions which are associated with these various names. This suggests that we may find it easier to make a case for common reference across the religions if we adopt the dubbing account of naming. For in this case we need not concern ourselves with differences of description; it may be enough to argue that terms like 'God', 'Allah' and so on serve to denominate (rather than to describe) the source of a particular kind of experience (Soskice 1985: 152–4), an experience which is common to the different religions. Despite offering a simple and attractive solution to the problem of religious diversity, this approach seems unconvincing as it stands. For suppose we were to establish that religious experiences are the product simply of a certain psychological complex; in that case, given the truth of this form of the dubbing theory, we would have to say that the term 'God' referred to this complex. But would it not be more natural to say that in such a case 'God' would not refer to anything? This difficulty may suggest once more that the term 'God' is logically tied to certain descriptions, such as the Anselmian description we noted just now.

CONCLUSION: THE WIDER CONTEXT

In my remarks so far I have treated the problems of anchorage, predication and reference largely in isolation from broader issues in the philosophy of religion. But any developed philosophical perspective on the nature of religion will involve an interlocking set of views on the epistemology of religious belief, the concept of (for instance) God, and various other issues, including the nature of religious language. Views about the nature of language may in some cases play a foundational role in the construction of such a system (as in the case of those philosophers who are sympathetic to the later work of Wittgenstein). But in other cases, views about the language of religion may be 'read off' from a prior understanding of certain conceptual or evidential questions.

For instance, in recent philosophical discussion of religion we can distinguish between those who support the classical concept of God; those like Hartshorne (1969: 152–67) or in a different fashion Ward (1987: 155) who wish to modify this concept by admitting the possibility of change and passibility into the divine nature; those who wish to associate the idea of God with a moral realism of metaphysical dimensions, for instance Sutherland (1984) or, in a neo-Platonic vein, Leslie (1979); those who in the style of Cupitt (1980) prefer to think of God as a moral projection of some sort; those who are persuaded by Hick's (1989: 233–49) postulation of a Real to which we cannot ascribe, with literal truth, any substantial property; those who wish to draw on the insights of feminism to reshape the traditional, 'patriarchal' understanding of divinity; and so on. These different positions, and others besides, tend to be driven by epistemological concerns or by some conception of what follows from the idea of divine perfection, but all carry clear implications for the nature of religious language.

Thus our understanding of whether or not terms implying passibility can be predicated of God in a literal way will depend on whether we follow

Hartshorne or a neo-Thomist such as Davies (1985: 117–71) in our account of the divine nature. Or again, our understanding of the ways in which religious discourse is anchored in experience will vary depending upon whether we follow Sutherland's moral realism (where God does not play a causal role) or Leslie's (where ethical ideals are held to be creatively efficacious). Similarly, the problem of reference will emerge in very different forms and invite very different solutions depending upon whether we adopt Cupitt's account of God as the 'religious requirement' (a representation of the ideal moral state, Cupitt 1980: 85–95) or a metaphysically realist account of the divine nature. So the reader is invited to supplement this discussion of religious language with material drawn from other chapters in this volume, in particular the chapters on natural theology, the concept of God, religion and science, and feminism.

REFERENCES

Alston, W. (1989) 'Irreducible Metaphors in Theology', in W. Alston *Divine Nature and Human Language: Essays in Philosophical Theology*, Ithaca: Cornell University Press, 17–37.

Aquinas, Thomas (1964) *Summa Theologiae*, vol. III, London: Blackfriars.

Ayer, A. J. (1971) *Language, Truth and Logic*, Harmondsworth: Penguin.

Braithwaite, R. (1971) 'An Empiricist's View of the Nature of Religious Belief', in B. Mitchell (ed.) *The Philosophy of Religion*, Oxford: Oxford University Press, 72–91.

Carnap, R. (1974) 'Religious Language is Meaningless', trans. A. Pap, in M. Charlesworth *The Problem of Religious Language*, Englewood Cliffs, NJ: Prentice Hall, 123–31.

Cupitt, D. (1980) *Taking Leave of God*, London: SCM Press.

Davies, B. (1985) *Thinking About God*, London: Chapman.

Hare, R. M. (1959) 'Religion and Morals', in B. Mitchell (ed.) *Faith and Logic*, London: Allen and Unwin, 176–93.

Hare, R. M. *et al.* (1955) 'The University Discussion', in A. Flew and A. MacIntyre (eds) *New Essays in Philosophical Theology*, London: SCM Press, 96–108.

Hartshorne, C. (1969) 'The God of Religion and the God of Philosophy', in *Talk of God*, London: Macmillan, 152–67.

Heimbeck, R. S. (1969) *Theology and Meaning: A Critique of Metatheological Scepticism*, Stanford: Stanford University Press.

Hick, J. (1971) 'Theology and Verification', in B. Mitchell (ed.) *The Philosophy of Religion*, Oxford: Oxford University Press, 53–71.

—— (1989) *An Interpretation of Religion*, London: Macmillan.

Kant, I. (1933) *Critique of Pure Reason*, trans. N. Kemp Smith, London: Macmillan.

Kripke, S. (1980) *Naming and Necessity*, Oxford: Basil Blackwell.

Leslie, J. (1979) *Value and Existence*, Oxford: Basil Blackwell.

Mitchell, B. (1973) *The Justification of Religious Belief*, London: Macmillan.

Nielsen, K. (1971) *Contemporary Critiques of Religion*, London: Macmillan.

Phillips, D. Z. (1968) *The Concept of Prayer*, London: Routledge & Kegan Paul.

—— (1976) *Religion Without Explanation*, Oxford: Basil Blackwell.

Pike, N. (1970) *God and Timelessness*, London: Routledge & Kegan Paul.

Sarot, M. (1992) *God, Possibility and Incorporeality*, Kampen: Kok Pharos.

Searle, J. (1979) 'Metaphor', in A. Ortony (ed.) *Metaphor and Thought*, Cambridge: Cambridge University Press, 92–123.

Sherry, P. (1976) 'Analogy Today', *Philosophy* 51: 431–46.

Soskice, J. (1985) *Metaphor and Religious Language*, Oxford: Clarendon Press.

Sutherland, S. (1984) *God, Jesus and Belief*, Oxford: Basil Blackwell.

Swinburne, R. (1991) *The Existence of God*, revised edn, Oxford: Clarendon Press.

—— (1993) *The Coherence of Theism*, revised edn, Oxford: Clarendon Press.

Ward, K. (1993) *Images of Eternity*, New York: Oneworld.

Winch, P. (1977) 'Meaning and Religious Language', in S. Brown (ed.) *Reason and Religion*, Ithaca: Cornell University Press, 193–221.

Wisdom, J. (1953) 'Gods', in J. Wisdom *Philosophy and Psychoanalysis*, Oxford: Basil Blackwell.

Wittgenstein, L. (1958) *Philosophical Investigations*, trans. G. E. M. Anscombe, Oxford: Basil Blackwell.

—— (1961) *Tractatus Logico-Philosophicus*, trans. D. F. Pears and B. F. McGuinness, London: Routledge & Kegan Paul.

Yob, I. M. (1992) 'Religious Metaphor and Scientific Model: Grounds for Comparison', *Religious Studies*, 28: 475–85.

FURTHER READING

Ayers, R. H. and Blackstone, W. T. (1972) *Religious Language and Religious Knowledge*, Athens: University of Georgetown Press.

Brümmer, V. (1981) *Theology and Philosophical Inquiry*, London: Macmillan.

Charlesworth, M. (1974) *The Problem of Religious Language*, Englewood Cliffs, NJ: Prentice-Hall.

Ferre, F. (1967) *Basic Modern Philosophy of Religion*, London: George Allen & Unwin.

Jeffner, A. (1972) *The Study of Religious Language*, London: SCM Press.

Kenny, A. (1973) *Wittgenstein*, Harmondsworth: Penguin.

McFague, S. (1982) *Metaphorical Theology: Models of God in Religious Language*, Philadelphia: Fortress Press.

Mitchell, B. (ed.) (1959) *Faith and Logic*, London: Allen and Unwin.

Ramsey, I. T. (1957) *Religious Language: An Empirical Placing of Theological Phrases*, London: SCM Press.

Swinburne, R. (1992) *Revelation: From Metaphor to Analogy*, Oxford: Clarendon Press.

See also chapters 17, 19, 24.

21

THEOLOGY AND SCIENTIFIC UNDERSTANDING

Peter Byrne

The relations between theology and the natural sciences are relevant to a range of problems in the philosophical underpinnings of Christian thought. The importance of theology's relation to science arises out of the fundamental ways in which Christianity and natural science are linked with the character and evolution of Western culture. For many centuries Christianity, in the characteristic fashion of religious systems, provided Western culture with its understanding of human nature and of the reality in which this was set. The realms of personal and cosmological meaning were integrated in a Christian-inspired vision of the destiny of humankind in the world. With the growth of natural science since the seventeenth century, Christian theology has faced the challenge of integrating its understanding of human nature and reality with accounts originating in sources in scientific theorizing which are at once autonomous and questioning of many traditional Christian perceptions.

The ways in which theology and natural science may be mutually relevant include the following: through their agreement/disagreement on the facts of the world and its history as they state them; through the explanations they separately offer of such facts; through the metaphysics of reality they affirm or suggest; through the ideals of method and reason in human enquiry they are committed to (see Austin 1976: 6–8). Science discovers and records facts about the world, explains them with hypotheses and theories, and such theories suggest general conclusions about the ultimate character of the cosmos. This entire process of discovery, theorizing and metaphysical inference is underpinned by procedures of justification and proof. Different views may be adopted towards the relations with theology established by the elements and implications of scientific thought (see Barbour 1990: 3ff. for the classification used below). Some thinkers perceive conflict between science and theology. They then assume a choice must be made between scientific and theological understanding. Others contend that the perception of significant inter-relations between science and theology is misguided. In reality the modes of understanding of theological and scientific enquiry are quite independent of one another. This is a decisive way of rejecting the notion of conflict between science and religion. Others contend that science and theology can be integrated into a combined vision of the world. More modest is the claim that there can be fruitful dialogue and consonance between science and theology.

CONFLICT

A great deal of writing on modern science and religion has assumed that with regard to fact, explanation, method or metaphysics there are fundamental conflicts between them. For many decades the historiography of science and religion was dominated by 'the conflict thesis'. This thesis interpreted the history of the rise of modern natural science in Europe as the result of a war between Christianity (representing superstition, authority and prejudice) and science (representing freedom, reason and enlightenment). Superficial support for a conflict thesis is provided by initial reflection on such things as: the Catholic Church's opposition to Copernicanism, the refutation of biblical chronologies by early nineteenth-century geology, and the controversies over evolution and creation. Vivid evidence that some Christians find their theology in conflict with scientific teaching is provided by the bitter hostility of contemporary creationists to neo-Darwinism.

The interpretation of the history of modern science in terms of the conflict thesis has not stood up to test in recent historiography (see Brooke 1991 for a masterly survey and full bibliography). In part this is due to the weakness of the thesis when tested against the details of specific historical events, such as the Victorian reception of Darwinism. The conflict thesis reveals itself under close examination to be an ideologically motivated myth which was read back by late nineteenth-century rationalists and materialists into the history of science. Underlying the conflict thesis is the implausible picture of science and religion as monolithic systems of thought, which may then be thought of as in conflict, in harmony and so on. In fact, such clear cases of mutual interaction between science and religion that we find in history show us that science and religion are not unchanging entities and that it is in the context of the shaping influence of a whole range of intellectual and social concerns that they touch upon one another. This makes the thesis that there has been a conflict between religion and science in the abstract devoid of any clear sense (as contended in Brooke 1991).

Many writers endeavour to argue against the conflict thesis by supporting a counterproposal made famous by Michael Foster (Foster 1934, 1935, 1936). This asserts that the rise of natural science is due to the influence of the Christian doctrine of creation. The fundamental thought here is that only firm belief in a free, yet rational, creator enabled Western thought to develop a commitment to a lawful, contingent universe. Commitment to law and contingency is alleged to be necessary to ground a science that is both mathematical and experimental. There is contemporary apologetic mileage to be gained from the notion that the creation doctrine is at least a necessary condition for the conduct of natural science (see Jaki 1974). As a historical thesis the appeal to creation is meant to answer the question as to why natural science only developed fully (after initial starts in Muslim, Chinese and other cultures) in the Christian cultures of Western Europe. The time lag in Christendom's development of science is then put down to the need to purge the influence of a prioristic Greek conceptions of nature from the Christian world-view. The emergence of modern natural science is traced finally to the triumph of voluntaristic conceptions of creation and God associated with the influence of late-medieval nominalism and reformed thought.

How far this attempt to stand the conflict thesis on its head succeeds is open to question. For example, it asks us to associate the rise of early modern science particularly with intellectual circles influenced by Protestant, biblicist theology. While there have been efforts to link scientific advance with Puritanism, they have provoked endless and somewhat inconclusive debate among historians. Furthermore, these same strands of Christian thought typically taught a strong version of the Fall, which could and did produce denunciations of human reason's ability to operate independently of revelation and also led to downgradings of nature in the drama of human salvation. The 'Christian world-view' is clearly neither homogeneous nor a sufficient condition for the emergence of science – witness the failure of scientific enquiry to emerge in Christian countries dominated by Orthodoxy. Moreover, the scientific enterprise has proved perfectly capable of flourishing in the twentieth century in cultures not influenced by Christianity to any significant degree.

The problem of why modern science, initially characterized by its revolution in astronomy and mechanics, developed out of medieval Christian culture and not out of Islamic and Chinese culture of the same epoch has been exhaustively surveyed in Huff (1993). His answer is much more complex than the thesis passed down by Foster. Huff describes the rise of modern science as due to a fusion of three things in Christian culture of the Middle Ages:

1 A theology which gave great support to human rationality.
2 The impact of the re-discovery of Roman law.
3 The inheritance of Greek science.

The second of these factors allowed the emergence of autonomous, corporate institutions (such as the medieval universities) and gave further impetus to the flourishing of individual conscience and reason. There were no parallels to this in Islam or China, he asserts. Europe of the high and late Middle Ages was thus in a unique position to allow autonomous scientific enterprise, free of the control of religious or traditional dogma, to be born. Thus could a cosmology independent of close ecclesiastical control arise.

Nowadays Christian thinkers who perceive a conflict between their theology and science are likely to be ones who take their Bible 'straight' and cannot stomach neo-Darwinism. Little needs to be said about the folly of associating theology with creationism and 'creation science'. Suffice it to say that, though there are unsolved problems and intellectual difficulties in its application and development (as in all large-scale scientific paradigms – this is what makes them creative), neo-Darwinism is, on grounds of independent testability, fecundity and coherence, a well-confirmed scientific theory. There is no alternative paradigm for the integration of biological knowledge, indeed much biological discovery in the last 150 years is predicated on the truth of evolutionary theory. By contrast, 'creation science' reveals itself to be a mass of *ad hoc* hypotheses, reacting piecemeal to new facts and providing no paradigm for discovery (see Kitcher 1983 and Berra 1990).

Biology teachers might properly balk at the proposition that they should teach their subject on the basis of 2,500–year-old, near-Eastern religious texts. What is at stake here is the autonomy of biological science as an independent discipline of thought. A theological perspective on science has to hold in tension belief in the proper autonomy of human reason in the sciences in relation to various distinct subject matters with the need to integrate the various operations of reason in an overall view of reason as God-given. This need tells against a conflict view of the relation of science to theology that is advanced from a theological perspective.

The dangers in separating modes of reason in science and theology can be illustrated by reference to some of the consequences drawn from the collapse of foundationalism as an ideal of reason. Foundationalism is held to be wrong because it falsely claims that there are independent, universal and self-evident starting points for the operation of reason. Our data in fact are infected with and shaped by the theories and concepts we bring to bear upon them. 'That which a scientist takes as data he does so because of his acceptance of an enormously complicated web of theory' (Wolterstorff 1967: 63). Wolterstorff draws the conclusion that the Christian theologian is as much entitled to take the credal formulae and biblical data of his or her faith as the starting points for, and touchstones of, right reason, as the scientist is his or her theories. Thus he laments the 'radical conformism' of modern theology with respect to science, the implication being that a healthy Christian thought would interpret scientific claims in the light of biblical truth, rather than the other way round. Anti-foundationalism of this kind appears to give the creationists' opposition to the clear testimony of biological and geological science the support of a Procrustean relativism.

The mistake in such reasoning lies in refusing to see that, though observational and experimental data in science are imbued with theory, theories – such as the component parts of neo-Darwinism – are laden with data. There is a range of facts about the natural world and its history which limit how many testable, fruitful and coherent theoretical paradigms can be produced to account for them. The poverty of 'creation science' in this regard is only too well documented. There is a high theological price to be paid for crying against 'radical conformism'. For the anti-foundationalist defender of 'biblical

Christianity' must presume that the operation of human reason that is biological and geological science is deeply deluded. He or she then needs an account of how a God-given reason in a God-given world is led into such fantastic errors. Only a deeply pessimistic and ultimately schizophrenic account of the fallen intellect promises an explanation. Given the success, the reliability and the pervasiveness of the theories and discoveries of modern natural science, any credible theology must accept it as one of the expressions of a providence which cannot be in conflict with itself.

MUTUAL INDEPENDENCE

One important way in which theologies have sought to establish the complete and mutual independence of science and religion is through some version of the distinction between nature and spirit. The foundations of modern efforts to enforce a separation between the concerns of science and theology lie in the thought of such writers as Descartes and Kant. However, it can be argued that the grounds for such a divorce lie deep in early reactions to the complaint that emerging natural science disturbs biblical truth. Galileo contends (in defence of Copernicanism against the literal meaning of famous biblical passages such as Joshua 10:13) that Scripture teaches us how to get to heaven and not how heaven goes. Galileo asserts the principle of accommodation (Galileo 1973: 32), whereby it is understood that the physical truths implied or stated in Scripture are matched to the limitations of its audience's understanding. They may indeed be misleading or false if that understanding is primitive, yet physical falsehood does not disturb the message of personal salvation which is revealed. As Moltmann has noted, such efforts at accommodation were linked with the Reformed stress on the Gospel as a drama of personal salvation, with the result that 'Theology's domain became the soul's assurance of salvation in the inner citadel of the heart' (Moltmann 1985: 35).

It is but a short step to the existentialist and personalist theologies of the nineteenth and twentieth centuries with their stress on a world of human meaning as the locus of theology, while nature is abandoned to the sciences. Existentialist and personalist theologies have mirrored what has happened to religion as a whole in Western culture and to theology in the realm of learning. Anthropologists distinguish between cosmocentric and anthropocentric functions religion may play in society. Many tribal religious systems, they allege, provide their peoples with a cosmology which explains their world. The gods enter into human discourse as the explanation of what happens in the world of nature. In a modern culture this cosmological role is played by the sciences but this still leaves religion to play the further part of speaking of the questions of human and personal meaning which remain after the course of the world's events is explained. Indeed, the very impersonality of the causes of those events established by science threatens to make questions of meaning more urgent and more difficult to answer. However, the question which must be raised is how theology can tackle these problems of meaning if it is completely divorced from questions of a cosmological kind.

The charge against any attempt to divorce theology from science is that answers to questions of human meaning are liable to have at least some implications, however vague, for cosmological thought. If, for example, in the manner of an existentialist, we locate human meaning and theological symbol in the quest for authentic existence, we presuppose the ability of the embodied human person to exhibit free action and a moral and cognitive transcendence. Yet only some accounts of the nature of the world and human evolution will allow these things. At the point of human nature and its place in the cosmos, cosmocentric and anthropocentric concerns will meet. Existentialist and wholly personalist theologies appear to see the problem of the human being's place in nature as calling for so little reflection only because they already assume an answer to it. They assume a radical dualism in which the realms of nature and spirit do not intersect. The former is given over to lifeless mechanism and the latter to a radical, materially ungrounded freedom. Only thus can it become intelligible how such theologies can view the redemption of the individual as being unconnected with the redemption of the universe.

The argument offered implies that theology must have connections, however tenuous, with cosmology. Its thrust is summed up in Moltmann's pithy conclusion: 'If God is not the Creator of the world, he cannot be my Creator either' (Moltmann 1985: 36). That theology has implications for, and must in turn be informed by, the study of the cosmos has somehow to be kept in tension with belief in the proper autonomy of the natural sciences. It is arguable that the Christian doctrine of creation entails the end of a detailed cosmocentric function for religion. Creation banishes the gods from the world, tells us that no part of nature is divine and can imply that the reason in the world is open to discovery by the reason in human persons. Thus the autonomy of the sciences is suggested by one, plausible, theological account of creation. Yet this autonomy cannot be absolute. If the autonomous sciences reach conclusions which are incompatible with the thoughts that God is the creator of the universe they study and that human redemption takes place in this universe, theology must be prepared to offer its own critique of these conclusions. It must feel sure that it has the ground from which that critique can seem relevant and persuasive.

In the light of the above, what appears wrong with 'creation science' is not that it is ready to speak from theological perceptions to limitations in biological thought, but that the ground from which it utters is so naively limited and its critique of biology so stupid and uncomprehending. Its errors should not be taken as proof that science and theology have nothing to do with one another. Theological critique is in order where popularizers of neo-Darwinist socio-biology tell us that human beings are mere machines programmed to act by their selfish genes (Dawkins 1976), or that chance so rules the processes of natural selection that any idea that there can be a purpose to the overall history of life is mistaken (Monod 1974). The first of these ideas would destroy the cognitive and moral transcendence which enables human beings to be capable and worthy of salvation. The second seems plainly incompatible with the notions of creation and providence. Theology must react to such ideas by balancing its belief in the autonomy of scientific reason against its belief in the unity of reason. That is to say, granted that Dawkins and Monod use biological premises to pronounce on areas which are of direct concern to theology and allied disciplines (such as philosophy), theology should hope that scientific or other errors can be found in their conclusions. It is easy enough to show that the demonic portrayal of human life in Dawkins is self-refuting (as are all other reductive philosophies of the human person). They are put forward as opinions for which their authors are responsible and for which they feel reasons can be offered. Yet if they are true, no human selves could stand in that relation to ideas and the very scientific process that fostered them would have been impossible. As to the claim that evolution reveals a world caught between iron necessity and pure chance, the careful study of the nature of chance processes in the light of statistical theory by D. J. Bartholomew (Bartholomew 1984) has shown that randomness in the detailed processes of evolutionary transformation is quite compatible with (and indeed will tend to produce) significant pattern on the larger level of the world's history.

The dual emphasis on the underlying unity but autonomous application of reason produces the need for the kind of dialogue between theology and science so briefly outlined above. Another way of reaching the same conclusion stems from the recognition that it is in the nature of the natural sciences to ask questions about and suggest answers to large-scale questions of human meaning, in addition to their role as searchers after reliable beliefs about the detailed processes of the cosmos. It appears inescapable that enquiries in physical cosmology and biology will provoke thought about the meaning of cosmic, animal and human history. If we see science as a humane enterprise then the fact that its speculations spill over into the realms of ethics, philosophy and theology is not surprising (see Midgley 1985). Seen in this light, it is then no aberration that evolutionary theory has produced what are to all intents and purposes substitute religions. Dialogue between the sciences and those disciplines, such as theology, concerned with human meaning is, all things considered, inevitable.

THE INTEGRATION OF SCIENCE AND THEOLOGY

The plea for a return to theologies of nature offered by Moltmann (1985, see above) has been well heeded by contemporary theology. Attempts to show that the doctrines and methods of Christian theology can be harmonized with, and even illuminate, the doctrines and methods of contemporary science are legion. This effort to integrate theology and science is in part a continuation of the theological critique of the conflict thesis in the historiography of science and in part a reaction to the alleged barrenness of existentialist and neo-orthodox theologies. It goes hand in hand with a rebirth of scientifically informed natural theologies (of which Swinburne (1979) is the best-known example).

The theories of contemporary cosmology, physics and biology seem to offer the theologian ample opportunity to show how Christian belief and the scientific world-view can be integrated. The main themes in this enterprise that can be gleaned from recent writings are the following:

1 Order and contingency.
2 Creation and the finite universe.
3 Temporality and evolution.
4 Life and its conditions.
5 Novelty and emergence.

The composite description of these themes is drawn from: Barbour (1990); Davies (1992); Jaki (1978); Peacocke (1979, 1990); Polkinghorne (1986, 1988); Torrance (1969, 1981, 1985); many more works with similar themes could be cited but my description should not be taken to imply that there are no differences between these authors.

1 Order and contingency

Science requires nature to contain a universal order which is contingent. Order is presupposed and confirmed in the extension of scientific hypotheses to the remotest spaces and times in the investigation of the cosmos. Yet it would be fatal to a science that is ultimately grounded upon experiment and observation if this order were necessary and discoverable *a priori*. But the only guarantee or intelligible explanation of how the universe could be a system of contingent order rests with its creation by a sovereign but rational God. Moreover, its origin in God explains what is otherwise mysterious, namely why this order is such that the human mind can grasp and anticipate it. Here the very existence of science is bound up with the validity of a doctrine of cosmic creation.

2 Creation and the finite universe

Relativity theory and Big Bang cosmology point to a universe which is bounded in space and time. An absolute origin for the universe somewhere between 10 and 20 billion years ago is suggested by the evidence for a cosmic singularity. Such a picture harmonizes with the idea of creation as currently interpreted.

3 Temporality and evolution

Study of both the behaviour of sub-atomic and larger physical systems reveals that the cosmos has an irreducibly temporal direction and reality. Time is real, essential to physical processes and irreversible. The universe is evolving, providing the natural home for a drama of creation which represents the will of a creator in action.

4 Life and its conditions

The evolution of the cosmos has led to sentient and self-conscious life emerging in it. Considerations about the 'fine tuning' of creation suggest that the initial conditions of the cosmos' origin had to be precisely set so as to allow life to emerge. Since these initial conditions are apparently contingent, life is not inevitable or necessary. The purposive character of a divinely ordained creation is here displayed.

5 Novelty and emergence

With the demise of classical physics the universe has emerged as a non-deterministic system. Novelty over the course of time is to be expected as a consequence of the undetermined nature of the basics of physical reality. Moreover, even at the foundations of reality we see that the behaviour of individual components of matter is in part conditioned by their membership of wholes. Physics reveals no less than the ability of matter to take on new properties through the fact of its organization into significant wholes. These facts point to the failure of deterministic reductionism – a programme associated with the ideals of classical, Newtonian science. Biological reality can be seen as displaying the emergence of new levels of reality. Science can allow an account of human personhood which gives it irreducible properties, such as freedom and consciousness, without postulating a duality of substances (physical and mental) in the world. The net effect of the possibility of novelty and emergence is that we no longer have to see the activity of the creator in directing the course of cosmic history and in creating life as involving interventions in a closed system which threaten its order and interconnectedness. Instead, we can see the entire process of cosmic history as open to providential direction. Religion need not be in conflict with science in affirming the reality of matter-transcending rational life and need not posit breaks in the history or constitution of the cosmos.

It has been characteristic of existentialist theologies of this century to regard the cosmology of the biblical world-view as 'mythical' and to glean from Scripture only the portrait of a general, human, existential crisis and the possibility of overcoming it through faith in God and Christ. The contemporary integration of science and theology aims to save essential facets of an outlook to be found (so it is claimed) in the biblical writings and make them serve as the presuppositions and illuminators of modern science. These facets will include: a rational, sovereign creator-God, a dependent but ordered universe, a temporal direction and progress in the universe's history, a universe that is open to direction by its creator, and a human race responsible to God. The theological writers inspired by this vision of integration tend to take sides on philosophical debates about the nature of God. For example they will favour 'realist' as opposed to 'non-realist' accounts of God, seeing such works as Cupitt's *Taking Leave of God* (1980) as the last remnants of a positivist view of science and reality, which forces its exponents into a non-objective God. They will also side with portrayals of God in philosophy which

441

stress his personal character, portrayals which, for example, interpret his eternity as infinite duration rather than timelessness. Such moves are in the service of establishing God as a dynamic providence, involved in cosmic evolution. For reasons which are referred to below, there is a tendency to endorse process theology in consequence.

It is essential for the broad movement of thought described here to contend that scientific and religious explanations of reality can be on a par. Things left partly or wholly unexplained by science can be explained by religious cosmology. Gone is the sharp ideal of scientific explanations functioning through laws, which entails dismissing other spheres of thought as non-explanatory. Instead, the root of explanation may be seen in the notion of pointing to the operative natures of explanatory entities (Schoen 1985: 75), in which case explanations that invoke personal agency can be taken to be irreducible. This leaves open God as a possible source of explanation in cosmology.

The very broad outlines of the theological programme favoured by contemporary integrationists of science and theology are now in place. The main problems and avenues for further exploration associated with this approach can be divided into two groups. First, we must look at those relating to the conception of God contained in it. Second, we must look at the scientific issues relevant to it.

The attempt to present an overall cosmological vision which sets references to the God of theology alongside reference to scientific realities will fail unless the god referred to admits of a certain degree of intelligibility. In particular, such accounts must presume that the relationship between God and the world can be made sufficiently intelligible to enable mention of God to figure as an explanation, however minimal, of facets of the world described by science. Yet it appears there are problems in principle in making this relationship clear enough for these cosmological projects to succeed.

Many of these difficulties stem from the notion of creation. In the first place we have to face the familiar problems created by dualism. The doctrine of creation claims that the world is dependent on God for its existence and character, but that God is not in like manner dependent on the world. A dependence of the world on God of this sort entails that God and the world must be two distinct substances. Efforts to make this further notion intelligible inevitably fall back on a matter/spirit dualism. God as spirit is not one with the universe as matter. But now this very dualism stops the relation of causal action upon the world by God presupposed by creation from being one that carries much, if any, explanatory force. It is open to the stock objections to dualist accounts of the human person, namely that interaction between person (spirit) and body (matter) we find in intentional action, becomes utterly mysterious. A causal link is postulated which of its nature appears incomprehensible.

Added to such worries is the difficulty theologians face in saying what exactly creation consists in. Big Bang cosmology appears to chime in with the idea of creation as an initial act. That cannot be the whole of the story, for, if it were, creation would be divorced from providence and cosmic history. There is a tendency to affirm the necessarily continuous character of creation by opting for the stock formula that what God did in order to create the world *ex nihilo* he must repeat at every instant. God is the world's continuous sustainer and his action is necessary to prevent the universe of contingent things from collapsing into nothingness at each and every moment. Such a line of thought appears to have two major advantages in the present context. It secures the relevance of God to every moment of cosmic history and every detail of scientific cosmology. Yet it does so without disturbing any of those details, since it deals in a relation between events and their divine support which is undetectable because the same for all happenings.

A number of recent writers have endeavoured to show that this modern doctrine of creation is a fundamentally unsatisfactory account of the relation between God and the world of science (see Bartholomew 1984; Byrne 1985; Oakes 1987; Olding 1991). For one thing, creation is normally held to secure divine transcendence, which in turn implies some distinction between the world and God and a measure of independence for the world. But God hardly seems to have secured the production of a distinct, independent creation if it would collapse into nothingness at any and every moment and needs creating *ex nihilo* continually. It may appear in addition as if this halting, limp universe does not consist of enduring, material things if they need sustaining by the divine will in this fashion. They seem more like the collections of ideas that constitute the furniture of the world in Berkeley's philosophy – for it is plausible to suppose that thoughts have reality only so long as the volition of a being with mind sustains them from nothingness. Surely, if God had made real and enduring things, no further explanation would be needed of their habit of continuing in existence. Their eventual demise can easily be explained for they are subject to forces of decay and destruction, but mere continuance in the absence of such forces needs no explanation: this is just what characterizes a substantial, enduring thing.

Whether or not creation *ex nihilo* entails Berkelean idealism, it can be argued more directly to produce a view of the universe which equally destroys any prospect of a realist interpretation of science. The charge is that the current gloss on creation entails occasionalism: the belief that there are no true causes in the world – God is the cause of all, and what we call 'causes' are but occasions for the divine will to bring about every event. If God sustains the world continually and *ex nihilo* at every moment then it appears that things in the world have no power to generate effects. Left to itself no state of the universe would generate any later state. God is then the sole cause of the state of the universe at any one time. Nothing but he, it turns out, has causal power. But, it may be objected, cannot God be thought of as sustaining causal agents (the forces of nature) through every moment and thus allowing them in consequence to produce their effects? The answer is that no sustaining role that is merely cooperative is available to the God who creates *ex nihilo* at every moment. For the effects of natural agents' causal powers and liabilities are included in the list of things that are ready to vanish into nothingness at every instant and which must be preserved at every instant. It is the whole range of nature's 'agents' and effects that must be created *ex nihilo* continually and thus it cannot be that the state of the alleged causal agents in nature is at all instrumental in bringing about any subsequent states of the universe.

At the heart of the accepted view of God's relation to creation is the thought that the initial act of creation, if such there was, and the continued creation that follows it are in perfect symmetry. What God did once to create the world, he repeats at every moment. But the *ex nihilo* part of the doctrine tells us that God's creation was not subject to any necessary conditions for its fulfilment (save any that may be thought to be part of his own nature). He was not in any sense a cooperator with other agents in making the world. He was the absolutely sufficient and necessary condition for the world's existence. If later divine sustaining of the world is symmetrical with this, then it must also be true that it is absolutely sufficient and necessary for every later state of the universe. It follows then that no other agents are even necessary conditions for such states. The perception that things in nature have causal powers, which produce effects and help shape the character of the world, is then just an illusion.

What follows from these points is that we cannot have in one, coherent account of the relation between God and the world the following elements: an initial creation that is *ex nihilo*, a continued creation that is perfectly symmetrical with it, and a universe that contains genuine causes and is describable in realist terms.

Writers seeking to integrate science and religion who have recognized these points, such as Bartholomew (1984), find the most natural response is to deny the symmetry between divine creation and sustaining. What God does to sustain the world is less drastic and radical than what is required to create it. The issues involved in spelling out what God's continuous activity in sustaining and directing the cosmic history might be take us into scientific problems in the contemporary integration of science and religion.

Continued divine direction of cosmic history is ruled out if the universe is a deterministic process whose initial states uniquely fix its future. Contemporary integrationists welcome that interpretation of quantum mechanics which allows us to see a real measure of chance and randomness in cosmic history. Bartholomew's careful study of the mathematics and mechanics of chance processes shows that the argument advanced by Monod and others to the effect that chance in nature is incompatible with purposeful, providential direction is unsound (Bartholomew 1984: 95–102). Chance in individual events in nature is quite compatible with, and will in fact imply, predictability when such events occur as parts of large aggregates. So God could have initially fashioned the world such that it contained both chance and a disposition to develop in one direction rather than another. The presence of chance will apparently allow openings for God to shape the history of nature without the temporary destruction or setting aside of the natural order: producing determinate outcomes out of otherwise random parts of the natural order. The problem is, crudely, how much of the world's history is so influenced and how can we expect to catch God at this activity?

Bartholomew's arguments rule out one kind of answer to these questions. We cannot easily suppose that God directs events at the sub-atomic level, topping up natural indeterminism with divine causality to ensure one future for the world. For if God were to do this, he would have to provide a determinate structure for sub-atomic happenings which gave the appearance (now quite misleading) to our eyes of a process infected by randomness. Bartholomew contends that in principle this is problematic (Bartholomew 1984: 128–31). Moreover, the very insistence on holistic visions of natural processes and events, and on the importance of emergent properties and states within them, favoured by contemporary integrationist accounts gives weight to Bartholomew's conclusion that 'it is very doubtful whether it is coherent to suppose that the world can be controlled from this [the sub-atomic] level' (ibid.: 142). Bartholomew contends that cosmic history seems most amenable to continued divine influence in the area of interaction with human agents and thus in the direction of human history (ibid.: 143). This represents a substantial withdrawal of the exercise of divine power from the world. While it may be advantageous in dealing with the problem of evil, such a withdrawal is suggestive of a return to confining providence and creation (after an initial framing of the world) to human affairs only (for a contrasting account see Ward 1990, especially chapter 7).

That there are these substantial problems in developing accounts of the relation between God and the world which will allow the integrationist programme to proceed explains why pursuit of that programme leads to theological revisionism. We must note the fact that some writers feel that a proper understanding of nature, based in part on natural science, entails abandoning the classical view of God. Visions of God as embodied in the world overcome cosmic dualism. Creation and transcendence are thought of in terms of the way in which a mindful body/embodied mind displays novelty and creativity impossible for mere matter alone (see Jantzen 1984). Process thinkers abandon God's omnipotence in favour of a power for creative persuasion which allows God to influence the world. This influence is most marked in human events, but all happenings have a 'mental pole' which allows God to beckon, not coerce, the future out of the present (cf. Barbour 1990, chapter 8).

Whatever we think of such endeavours to reform the concept of God, we must accept that the drive for a full integration of theology with scientific cosmology will oblige theologians to be ready to entertain metaphysical novelty of this kind. However, the problems in seeing reference to God as an explanation in cosmology might lead us to question whether religious world-views and explanations are as close in meaning and purpose to scientific ones as theological integrationists imply. In addition, it is worth asking whether the nature of scientific conclusions about the origins and fundamental nature of the world makes such efforts at integration worthwhile.

Perhaps the most fundamental reason for posing these questions is the suspicion that contemporary theological integrations of religious and scientific cosmologies are based on an ill-founded and hasty reading of a shifting and complex scientific scene. This is the conclusion argued for at length by W. B. Drees in his impressive study *Beyond the Big Bang* (1990), which contains very extensive reference to scientific literature. I can only summarize his basic case very briefly. It is to the effect that scientific cosmology has not proved, nor has it universally accepted, that the universe has an absolute beginning in time. Rather, though the belief in an origin of the cosmos in an initial expansion is agreed on good grounds, the very first few moments of that primeval expansion remain under debate, largely because current cosmological theories (such as general relativity) break down in application to them. In consequence, contemporary science has explored a variety of quantum cosmologies which would unite relativity theory and quantum mechanics in the hope of providing an understanding of the very earliest moments of the Big Bang. Various competing models and theories result, all still in their infancy. Whilst some support the idea that there was an absolute beginning, some do not. Among those which do not are cosmological models which entertain the thought of our cosmos as the product of a quantum 'bubble' in an underlying substratum (sometimes thought of as a vacuum) that itself is sempiternal. Others, associated with the work of Stephen Hawking, produce models, the consequence of which is that the directionality of time breaks down 'prior' to the stages of the Big Bang retrodicted so far, with the result that the meaningfulness of talking about a first moment is called into question. Moreover, such cosmologies produce closed accounts of time in general which would relegate its apparent directionality to the realm of phenomenological reality only. Some quantum cosmologies also implicitly attack the idea of cosmological evolution (beyond the biological one we have discovered on earth) by suggesting that the world's fundamental structure is mathematically necessary and thus determinate. This in turn throws doubt both on the need to explain the 'fine tuning of the cosmos for life' by design (since pure chance is not the only alternative) and on the idea that the world's order is contingent.

The net result of these reflections is to emphasize a sense of the instability, uncertainty and equivocal character of the input from scientific cosmology to the contemporary integration of science and religion. Theologians in favour of close integration have not been unaware that contemporary science may contain seeds of thought hostile to their preferred ways of integrating science and theology. This has produced in the writings of one of the most vocal theological integrationists, Stanley Jaki, the paradoxical position of someone using theological premises to lick science into shape so that physics and cosmology can then be shown to be part and parcel of the 'Christian world-view'. Here the recognition (essential to a proper dialogue between theology and science) of both the unity of reason in general and the autonomy of reason in the sciences appears to be missing. (See Sharpe 1982 for a full account and critique of Jaki's methods and conclusions.)

Contemporary integrations between science and theology seem open to question when the distinct character of cosmological concepts in religion is brought out and when the shifting and speculative character of scientific cosmology is borne in mind. Theology might set its sights on a lesser task: that of 'consonance' (McMullin 1981: 51) or 'dialogue' (Barbour 1990: 16–23).

CONSONANCE

Consonance, as a middle path between independence and integration, is argued for by Drees (1990), Gilkey (1970) and McMullin (1981). A broadly similar view of the relation of science to theology can be discerned in such works. It denies any irresolvable clash either in claim or method between science and theology. It affirms the necessity for theological symbols to have implications for our understanding of nature as well as humankind, and the possibility of a fruitful dialogue between science and theology. However, it denies that theological notions provide explanations of facts that are continuous with those provided by science, or that Christian thought is committed to the truth of particular, detailed scientific cosmologies. Consonance and integration both demand an intellectual endeavour to keep scientific and religious teaching free of conflict, while yet mutually relevant. But consonance does not require a single cosmology to arise out of the fusion of science and theology, in part because it affirms that theological doctrines and symbols are to a degree different in their function and mode of meaning to those of science. Such differences as exist between the integrationist and the consonance views of the theology/science relation can be brought out by considering what they say about the relation between the methods of science and of theology.

It is characteristic both of conflict and independence accounts of the relationship to assert a sharp opposition between methods of discovery and justification in science and theology. The difference between these accounts lies only in that the former asserts the paradigm status of science's use of reason, condemning all those disciplines that exhibit different modes of thought, while the latter is prepared to allow unconnected, but equally valid, methods in different areas of discourse. Both of these types of view can paradoxically unite in accepting a positivist account of scientific truth and method. This will give a deductivist portrayal of the goals of science, centring these on the ideal of a theory as a series of general statements whose job is to unify and predict observational reports which constitute their independent anchorage and source of meaning. Since doctrinal systems and symbols do not amount to theories related to observations in this way, the road is open to acknowledging the fundamental distinction between modes of meaning and truth in science and theology.

Both consonance and integrationist views wish to deny this positivistic, deductivist ideal for science and thus both can allow for points of contact between methods in theology and science. In this questioning of positivistic deductivism they are at one with the critique found in much recent philosophy of science. In this critique two strands of argument against the earlier models of scientific reason stand out: questioning of the anchorage of science in observation and rejection of the deductivist account of a theory. On the anchorage of theory in experience, harmonizers of science and theology make common ground with epistemologists and philosophers of science who assert that there are no pure observations by reference to which scientific theories may be confirmed or disconfirmed. All observations are to a degree theory-laden. There is no way in which a single component of a theory can be confirmed or disconfirmed in isolation by experience. Hypotheses are not laid against reality singly but in groups, so discrepancy between hypothesis and reality does not tell us which particular hypotheses are false. There is always room for judgement in determining which scientific ideas are well grounded and which not. The deductivist ideal of theory is held to be questionable because it ignores the role of theory in giving us a picture of the generative mechanisms in nature that account for observed phenomena. The aim of science is not simply to unify and predict observation reports, but to provide understanding of the workings of the universe. In this case, models are essential parts of theories. Theories are not merely deductively organized systems of hypotheses but 'statement–picture complexes' (Harré 1970: 101).

Two points arising out of this critique of deductivist/positivist portrayals of science need highlighting. One is that a sharp contrast between scientific beliefs as anchored in experience and theological beliefs as 'metaphysical' becomes hard to sustain. Rather, we have a difference in degree – in the amount of interpretation given to facts of experience and in the freedom belief-systems show in building upon experience in theory construction. The second point worth stressing is that the claimed indispensability of models in scientific theorizing shows that it cannot ultimately present a portrayal of reality free from metaphor. Its reliance on analogical, metaphorical forms of understanding indicates that there must remain a degree of tentativeness and openness in even the most well-confirmed theory. None captures reality 'neat' and in an unrevisable form. All remain products of imaginative understanding and retain the mark of the human imagination upon them. These two points can be used to plead once more the continuity between theological and scientific modes of understanding (see Barbour 1974). Reflection on these ideas leads to the conclusion that it is impossible to sustain the claim in Wiebe's study *The Irony of Theology and the Nature of Religious Thought*

(1991) that academic theology is necessarily destructive of faith and of religion as practised. Wiebe's contention is that religious thinking is 'mytho-poeic' in contrast to philosophical, scientific thinking which is 'critical–rational'. The two cannot mix and the result of trying to do 'scientific', critical theology in universities has been and will be to undermine the pre-critical thought on which the life of religion is based. But if it is the case that scientific thought is essentially tied to the employment of metaphorical modes of understanding, the contrasts on which this general argument rests are neither absolute nor unquestionable.

Integrationists build upon these ideas to present a close continuity between the scientific and the theological enterprises. But they are also compatible with significant differences of degree between science and theology in the reliance on metaphor and in the freedom with which ideas relate to observed reality. Such differences may suggest that something less than the integrationists' ideals may be all that can safely be pursued. For example, in discussing God as creator above I have suggested that appeal to this notion cannot provide a causal explanation of cosmological facts which is on a par with a scientific explanation. The element of mysteriousness at the heart of this notion suggests that it is part of an imaginative picture which explains why the cosmos exists by presenting that fact in the light of an analogy (maker to product) that forever defies precise explication. Causal questions are not thereby answered but searches for other forms of understanding (relating to finding a purpose and value in the cosmos) are given direction. A common experience of the contingency of all things is articulated. The overall imaginative picture must be consonant with science. It should not contradict any well-supported scientific theory about cosmic and human origins and it may imply limits on the range of detailed cosmologies that are compatible with it, but it does not complete the enquiries of science. This could be part of an approach which recognizes the overall force of the notion of the unity of reason as it operates in science and theology, but allows a looser, family-resemblance interpretation of that unity. There is consonance and some overlap in scientific reason and theological reason but also difference of an irreducible kind.

An argument for this irreducible difference, which also provides a way in which science still provides a challenge to theology, can be gleaned from thinking about what tells in favour of a realist interpretation of science. Scientific ideas come and go; so do those of theology. Scientific ideas are also to an extent influenced in their rise and fall by social and historical factors. So are those of theology. Yet we do find across the history of science a steady accumulation of reliable beliefs about every conceivable aspect of the natural world (Harré 1986: 1). This is reflected in the justice with which we can say that an undergraduate physicist in 1992 knows vastly more about the physical universe than Newton. Accumulation suggests realism. It implies that, for all their imperfections and provisional character, a significant proportion of successive scientific theories have reached out, enabled their proponents to refer

449

to realities independent of human cognition and added some truths about those realities to the stock of human knowledge. Such undeniable success also suggests that, within the social-cum-personal-cum-historic factors that have moved scientific belief, there has also been at work a morality concerned with truth and reason (Harré 1986: 6).

Unlike science, but like other disciplines such as philosophy, theology has not shown this accumulation of reliable belief. This implies that either theology fails at the same kind of enterprise science is engaged in, or that it searches after a mode of understanding, which, though it may have continuities with that of science, is nonetheless different. The latter is obviously the preferable conclusion.

So despite the failure of a sharp contrast between scientific method and theological method (as found in positivism), the nature of scientific knowledge does provide a challenge to theology. In the first place that challenge demands an effort to show how theological reflection aims at and sometimes achieves understanding, without that understanding resulting in an increased stock of truths. The most likely account of theological understanding which might yield this result is one that stresses the likeness of theology to modes of practical enquiry and the similarity of the knowledge that it seeks to practical knowledge. The knowledge of God that theology needs is a knowledge of how individuals and communities are to discover meaning, and shape their lives in the light of the creative will of God. Consonance suggests that such knowledge must fit into the picture of the natural world that the best science of the day presents us with, but also that it cannot be offered as on a par with the knowledge provided by science.

The development of natural science in Western, Christian culture has finally yielded the picture (distinctive in the history of religions) of a religion trying to make its way in a thought-world whose cosmology is provided by a largely autonomous system of belief. That is one challenge that theology must face. Furthermore, theology must confront the example science presents of a cognitive community, which, though it has no shining, infallible path to incorrigible belief, preserves a markedly strong morality of inquiry which gets results.

REFERENCES

Austin, W. H. (1976) *The Relevance of Natural Science to Theology*, London: Macmillan.

Barbour, I. G. (1974) *Myths, Models and Paradigms*, London: SCM Press.

—— (1990) *Religion in an Age of Science*, London: SCM Press.

Bartholomew, D. J. (1984) *God of Chance*, London: SCM Press.

Berra, T. M. (1990) *Evolution and the Myth of Creationism*, Stanford: Stanford University Press.

Brooke, J. H. (1991) *Science and Religion: Some Historical Perspectives*, Cambridge: Cambridge University Press.

Byrne, P. A. (1985) 'Berkeley, Scientific Realism and Creation', *Religious Studies*, 20: 453–64.

Cupitt, D. (1980) *Taking Leave of God*, London, SCM Press.
Davies, P. (1992) *The Mind of God*, New York: Simon and Schuster.
Dawkins, R. (1976) *The Selfish Gene*, Oxford: Oxford University Press.
Drees, W. B. (1990) *Beyond the Big Bang*, La Salle, Ill.: Open Court.
Foster, M. B. (1934) 'The Christian Doctrine of Creation and the Rise of Modern Natural Science', *Mind*, 43: 446–68.
—— (1935) *Mind*, 44: 439–66.
—— (1936) *Mind*, 45: 1–27.
Galileo (1973) 'Letter to the Grand Duchess Christina', in D. C. Goodman (ed.) *Science and Religious Belief*, Milton Keynes: Open University Press, 28–49.
Gilkey, L. (1970) *Religion and the Scientific Future*, New York: Harper & Row.
Harré, R. (1970) *The Principles of Scientific Thinking*, London: Macmillan.
—— (1986) *The Varieties of Realism*, Oxford: Basil Blackwell.
Huff, T. E. (1993) *The Rise of Early Modern Science*, Cambridge: Cambridge University Press.
Jaki, S. (1974) *Science and Creation*, Edinburgh: Scottish Academic Press.
—— (1978) *The Road of Science and the Ways of God*, Edinburgh: Scottish Academic Press.
Jantzen, G. (1984) *God's World, God's Body*, London: Darton, Longman and Todd.
Kitcher, P. (1983) *Abusing Science*, Milton Keynes: Open University Press.
McMullin, E. (1981) 'How Should Cosmology Relate to Theology?', in A. R. Peacocke (ed.) *The Sciences and Theology in the Twentieth Century*, London: Stocksfield, 17–57.
Midgley, M. (1985) *Evolution as a Religion*, London: Methuen.
Moltmann, J. (1985) *God in Creation*, London: SCM Press.
Monod, J. (1974) *Chance and Necessity*, London: Fontana.
Oakes, R. (1987) 'Does Traditional Theism Entail Pantheism?', in T. V. Morris (ed.) *The Concept of God*, Oxford: Oxford University Press, 57–71.
Olding, A. (1991) *Modern Biology and Natural Theology*, London: Routledge.
Peacocke, A. (1979) *Creation and the World of Science*, Oxford: Clarendon Press.
—— (1990) *Theology for a Scientific Age*, Oxford: Basil Blackwell.
Polkinghorne, J. (1986) *One World*, London: SPCK.
—— (1988) *Science and Creation*, London: SCPK.
Schoen, E. L. (1985) *Religious Explanations*, Durham, NC: Duke University Press.
Sharpe, K. J. (1982) 'Stanley Jaki's Critique of Physics', *Religious Studies* 18: 55–76.
Swinburne, R. (1979) *The Existence of God*, Oxford: Clarendon Press.
Torrance, T. F. (1969) *Theological Science*, Oxford: Oxford University Press.
—— (1981) *Divine and Contingent Order*, Oxford: Oxford University Press.
—— (1985) *Religion and Scientific Rationality*, Edinburgh: Scottish Academic Press.
Ward, J. S. K. (1990) *Divine Action*, London: Collins.
Wiebe, D. (1991) *The Irony of Theology and the Nature of Religious Thought*, Montreal: McGill-Queen's University Press.
Wolterstorff, N. (1967) *Reason within the Bounds of Religion*, Grand Rapids, Mich.: Eerdmans.

FURTHER READING

Banner, M. C. (1990) *The Justification of Science and the Rationality of Religious Belief*, Oxford: Clarendon Press.
Brümmer, V. (ed.) (1991) *Interpreting the Universe as Creation*, Kampen: Kok Pharos.
Clayton, P. (1989) *Explanation from Physics to Theology*, New Haven: Yale University Press.
Davis, P. (1983) *God and the New Physics*, New York: Simon and Schuster.

Dawkins, R. (1986) *The Blind Watchmaker*, London: Longman.
Heim, K. (1953) *Christian Faith and Natural Science*, London: SCM Press.
Montefiore, H. (1983) *The Probability of God*, London: SCM Press.
Murphy, N. (1990) *Theology in an Age of Scientific Reasoning*, Ithaca: Cornell University Press.
Polanyi, M. (1958) *Personal Knowledge*, London: Routledge.
Russell, C. A. (1985) *Cross-Currents*, Leicester: Inter Varsity Press.
Russell, R. J., Stoeger, W. R. and Coyne, G. G. (eds) (1988) *Physics, Philosophy and Cosmology*, Vatican City State: Vatican Observatory.
Whitehead, A. N. (1925) *Science and the Modern World*, Cambridge: Cambridge University Press.
See also chapters 17, 18, 19, 22.

22

THEOLOGICAL ANTHROPOLOGY

Roger Trigg

The very notion of theological anthropology suggests that ideas of human nature cannot in the last resort be separated from questions about God. Indeed, the problem of who we as humans really are and of our place in the world leads us immediately to the question whether we have been created by a God or not. The issue of theism or atheism is fundamental to any consideration of human nature. It is not a separate problem or an interesting side issue. The nature of human beings is indissolubly caught up with the question of whether they have any role in the purposes of a Creator.

To turn to the ways this matter is now commonly perceived, does human life have a meaning which is given to it from outside? Have we simply evolved as an accidental by-product of blind physical forces at work in an immense and ultimately uncaring universe? Does humanity have a unique place in the scheme of things or are we merely one animal species amongst many? These and similar questions illustrate how understandings based on the development of modern science can easily undercut traditional theological views of the purpose of God in Creation. If human beings are only viewed through the techniques available in the practice of science, it will be inevitable that they are seen as physical objects in a physical universe. Yet the pursuit of science is itself the product of the very human rationality that seems to set us apart from other organisms. We should not only look at scientific theories but note that the very ability to produce them is evidence of a remarkable capacity to reason and recognize truth which goes far beyond any animal characteristic and is certainly not shared by the ordinary physical constituents of the world around us.

Reason, language and consciousness are all aspects of something that seems to give us a unique place in the universe. It is the task of theology to give an explanation of their significance. Its starting point has been the insight that we are all made in the image of God. We are made by God for a purpose, and we reflect, however imperfectly, something of his nature. This immediately sets humans apart from animals, even though it has long been recognized that we also share an 'animal nature' with them. This way of looking at things can encourage the view that there is an inevitable conflict within us between our rationality and our 'instincts', between our 'divine' and 'human' natures. It is easy to make a distinction between an eternal soul which is somehow good, and a perishable body which is the root of evil. This form of dualism has its roots in Plato's understanding of human nature. Apart from the fact that it is unduly dismissive of 'natural' desires, it also ignores the great capacity for evil in rational human choice. Even if a distinction is made between our reason and our passions, our reason can be the source of great evil, just as our passions, or desires, may themselves be good. Christianity, however, has made it abundantly clear, despite occasional aberrations, that it is wrong to think in simplistic terms of the body as evil and the soul as good. The doctrine of the Incarnation has normally been at the heart of any Christian understanding of human nature. God sanctified our physical existence by entering into it in the person of Christ. This is essentially consistent with the view of Judaism, portrayed in the Old Testament, which shows God's care and concern for humans as physical creatures, as well as for their flourishing as responsible moral agents.

It is easy to challenge a Platonic dualism which seems to devalue the material world in favour of some spiritual world. Indeed, many have suggested that the influence of such Greek philosophy on Christian thinking has resulted in the distortion of traditional Hebraic conceptions. Aristotle's vision of formed matter, rather than of separate forms reflected imperfectly by matter, has often met with more favour. An embodied mind has seemed to be more in agreement with Christian teaching than an outright dualism of mind and body. The contrast is sometimes drawn between the Christian teaching on the resurrection of the body and some Greek teaching concerning the immortality of the soul. Certainly one aspect of Christian doctrine that makes it distinct from Greek views of a rational principle lodged in humans is its emphasis on the importance of the whole individual rather than of just some indwelling abstract ability.

IMMORTALITY AND SURVIVAL

Part at least of the meaning traditionally discerned in the phrase 'resurrection of the body' is that you or I survive as recognizably distinct individuals into the Life Everlasting. I am still me, linked by some common thread to the life I have lived on earth. Some views of resurrection have taken this excessively literally, and have then been confronted by such difficulties as what happens when a body has been totally destroyed, or even eaten by someone else. How can it be reconstituted? Even to raise such questions is to fall into error. Whatever resurrection means it surely cannot involve the reconstitution of the original matter of the body in conditions mirroring our previous life. St Thomas Aquinas, following Aristotle, found difficulties in reconciling a view of the person as essentially embodied with the idea of immortality. Some hesitations about the propriety of cremation can be traced back to this kind of difficulty. Yet once it is accepted that, if there is a life after death, we must inevitably be transformed and glorified in ways we cannot here envisage, the idea of resurrection becomes less easy to distinguish from an idea of immortality of the soul. Problems about personal identity may still loom large. We must, however, recognize that our present concept of what it is to be a person is formed in the conditions of this life and by definition cannot apply to circumstances that will be very different. This may mean that much of what we say about any life to come will lapse into unintelligibility. Unless, however, we are verificationists we must recognize that there are limits on our understanding. Not everything that is real may be comprehensible to us here and now. The idea, though, that we are essentially material beings, cannot in the end incorporate a vision of the life to come. The denial of dualism and an assertion of some form of materialism or naturalism must entail that we are dependent for our identity on the continued existence of our bodies in this spatio-temporal world. Once it is accepted, as it must be, that our bodies can be utterly destroyed, it will then seem as if we have no future at all as continuing individuals beyond death.

Does this matter? The answer must be that for Christianity, at least, it always has seemed to. St Paul is often quoted in this context when he claims in 1 Corinthians 15 that if Christ were not raised, our faith is in vain. If Christ was not raised, neither could we be. St Paul says: 'If it is for this life only that Christ has given us hope, we of all people are most to be pitied.' Resurrection lies at the heart of the Christian Gospel, not just as something which once occurred for Christ, but as a hope held out to each and every individual. There is room for discussion in Christian theology about how far Christ's resurrection appearances can serve as a model for human resurrection. As they occurred within this world of space and time, and a life to come will not, they may not be able to serve as a model. The point though is not what form the life to come will take. The assertion that there is one has normally appeared to be a corner-stone of the Christian faith.

The idea of personal survival is seen as giving value and purpose to the life of each individual which can then be set against the backdrop of eternity. Once vision is narrowed to this life, it is suggested that we are all too likely in the end to be afflicted by despair and the feeling that nothing really matters. Indeed, the nihilism that is often explicitly embraced in the modern and 'post-modern' world is often linked to a materialism that restricts its focus to physical events in a physical world. There is in fact a certain instability about such a position in that while nihilism demands the repudiation of all claims to truth, and to insights into the nature of reality, materialism is itself making highly specific claims about what is real. Theological anthropology, on the other hand, often begins with what must be the simple insight that we are each loved by God and should matter to each other because of that. The fatherhood of God seems to entail that we are all related to each other as a family and should care for each other accordingly. Yet if he loves us, the argument goes, could he accept the fact of our inevitable extinction? Without an eternal destiny, people may seem to cease to matter. The promise of life after death, it is held, does not so much distract us from the concerns of this life and from our duty to care for others but gives all that a point and a purpose which otherwise it would not have.

DUALISM AND THE SELF

The theological demand that we do not lose sight of personal resurrection again raises the question of dualism. Is it inevitable that we hold that there is a fundamental distinction in human beings between the mortal and the immortal, the fleshly and the spiritual, the material and the immaterial? Whilst forms of dualism, of the separation of the mind and the body, are consistent with Christianity, are we driven to conclude that theology demands some form of philosophical dualism? As a matter of historical fact it has not, but once materialism is rejected, it may seem as if dualism is the only alternative. This is a matter of vexed philosophical debate, and the onward march of science, with its success in uncovering the functions of parts of the brain, has led many to assume that science will one day be able to explain everything about the human personality. Clearly one risk is that if Christianity is too explicitly dualist, it may seem to be laying itself open to disproof by scientific discovery. Yet whatever the connection between mental events and physical ones, between consciousness and brain processes, it should be clear that Christianity lays stress on the notion of the self, as a responsible and rational agent, able to take moral decisions and be accountable for them. This suggests a continuing subject of experience, which is not reducible to a collection of experiences (or a bundle of perceptions as the eighteenth-century empiricist, David Hume, would have it) nor to an ensemble of brain processes. The idea of a metaphysical self, the continuing subject, appears central to a Christian idea of the individual. If there were no such self, it seems difficult to attribute moral freedom or any form of rationality to a human being. Science cannot make sense of such a notion, and it is not surprising that empiricist philosophy is dismissive of it. How could we ever experience ourselves as the subjects of experience? Hume complained that he could never observe anything but the perception. Yet if the self is purely subjective, it could not convert itself into an object. It could never catch itself discovering itself.

It is also curious to expect physical science to pin the self down, since science is the product of scientists who are themselves rational subjects making judgements about truth. Any attempt to suggest that the self is just a series of events in the brain fails to do justice to the unity of the person, and fails to take account of the fact that science itself depends on a reason which cannot be identified with physical processes. This very process of identification assumes the existence of the rationality and ability to recognize truth which are explicitly explained away by a reductionist strategy.

The idea of a self which cannot be identified with any part of the physical world is ruled out by scientific methodology. Yet it also appears to be presupposed by the same methodology (Trigg 1993). Reasoning towards truth is an ability possessed by subjects and not brains. Modern science, however, tends to refuse to admit that there are limits to its own capabilities. Richard Rorty (1991: 176) refers to the picture of the self 'common to Greek metaphysics, Christian theology, and Enlightenment rationalism'. For him it is the picture 'of an ahistorical natural center, the locus of human dignity, surrounded by an adventitious and inessential periphery'. The picture is, philosophically speaking, an essentialist one, and it is easy to make links between this philosophical conception and religious views of the soul as the continuing essence of what makes each individual what he or she really is. Those who attack such notions do so very often with an explicitly atheist agenda. For Rorty, the self has to be 'de-divinized' (Rorty 1989: 30). Even our moral conscience must be simply traced back to its origins in the contingencies of our upbringing. The self is seen as the human counterpart of God. Indeed, our reason and moral understanding reflect, however imperfectly, his nature, and if the one is to be rejected so is the other. Even radical theologians have been ready to embrace this way of thinking. Don Cupitt (1990: 188) rejects the idea of the 'human subject as a metaphysical subject, a rational soul more or less prior to and independent of history and the body'. Instead he is willing to embrace what he terms 'nihilism' according to which 'everything is under judgement', including, he thinks, whatever standards of judgement we use. We have to recognize that we are continually reinventing ourselves. Who 'we' are is a fiction. As Dan Dennett writes in another context, considering the nature of consciousness (Dennett 1991: 418): 'Our tales are spun, but for the most part we don't spin them: they spin us. Our human consciousness, and our narrative selfhood is their product, not their source.'

The self, consciousness, rationality, moral understanding and free will are all linked in a way that means that an attack on one can easily become an attack on them all. It is not just a question of how we are to be identified with our bodies. The basic question is always who 'we' are. Can I abstract myself from my physical and social surroundings in such a way that I can reason about them and thereby exist as more than their product? Is the very notion of a self a fiction? If the question is posed in this way there is an obvious incoherence. Who are the people making the fictions, or even asking whether they are fictions? If the fiction makes us, it has to be accepted that the concept of a self precedes us and our thinking of ourselves. It is perhaps embedded in the language we use. Yet this only poses the problem as to the origin of that language.

Once the idea of the self is attacked from whatever source, the whole project of metaphysics is at risk. The metaphysical self may be anathema to empiricists in particular, but it is also attacked by anyone who wishes to undermine a metaphysical vision of the world. It is no coincidence that Nietzsche and his followers are as antagonistic to any idea of a self as they are to the concept of God. Not only are both metaphysical, it can be argued that each is the corollary of the other. Don Cupitt correctly sees (1990: 150) that a 'conception of the self as a more-or-less free-standing and self-mastering spiritual subject is by no means a modern aberration'. He accepts that it did not begin with the dualism of Descartes, but was always closely linked to theological tradition. He says:

> For God was seen as a self-founding Creator–Subject who generates both reality and his own knowledge of it, and the human self was regarded as having been made by God in his own image. The self was from the first a little counterpart of God.

It is possible to dispense in the short term with God and to concentrate on the abilities of the self. The Enlightenment tradition, with its own exaltation of human reason, did this. Yet because the self was properly at home in a theological context, it is not surprising that the cult of the rational atheist self was always likely to collapse under the weight of its own internal contradictions. A self granted the absolute freedom of a god but without any external standards by which to be guided may seem magnificently free. In reality, as existentialists discovered, the gift of such absolute freedom carries with it the threat of an ultimate lack of purpose and of meaning. Total creativity can imply that it does not matter what one does, and in turn that nothing matters. An attack on the possibility of a self which is able to rise above the constraints laid on it, can ultimately involve an attack on the possibility of rationality. If we are simply the creatures of our environment, we will be caused to believe certain things, view them in a particular way, and have a particular conceptual scheme. Only if we are able to transcend, however imperfectly, our immediate surroundings, and apprehend, however dimly, what is true, will we be able to reason. Yet it is commonly believed that human beings do not possess this kind of free-floating rationality. Contemporary science of various kinds is often very quick to produce views about human nature which explicitly deny the possibility of genuine reason. As has already been remarked, this is a high-risk strategy for a human activity which seems itself to involve the exercise of reason. Science can, if it is not very careful, find itself removing the conditions of its own possibility.

THE IDEA OF HUMAN NATURE

Nowhere is the danger of science undercutting its own possibility more evident than in the field of the social sciences. Much modern controversy has dwelt on the old question of nature or nurture. Are we the product of our biological inheritance or of our social surroundings? Is heredity or environment the dominant factor in making us what we are? The controversy has political overtones, in that the more it is stressed that human nature is fixed, the less we can, it seems, do anything about it. If it is malleable, and indeed the creation of a particular society, then a change in the conditions of society will inevitably produce a change in the characters of its members. Marxism was always inclined to this view, and it made revolution seem a rational way of changing people for the better. Yet the whole point of such a strategy is that people are created by society and that social structures are the main formative influence on us. If this is so, however, how can Marxists, or social scientists, or whoever, hope to abstract themselves from a particular society, in order to make judgements about how it functions, and about its worth? The very possibility of social science, if it is to be more than the articulation of prejudice, presupposes the ability of individuals to transcend the limitations of whatever society they belong to, and make judgements which claim truth. Any view about the influence of society can over-reach itself in this way. If society is the origin of all our judgements and ways of thinking, then how can even this be articulated from within the society? Social science must aspire to proclaim truth about societies and this is a project that depends on the assumption that we can abstract ourselves, or at least distance ourselves, sufficiently from our immediate culture to make judgements about it. This may be difficult, and may involve us giving up some of our dearest prejudices. If, however, it is impossible because all our thoughts and concepts are deter-mined by our social setting, that must be the death of social science. It is paradoxical that the very practice of social science, which begins to cast doubt on views of ourselves as separate asocial individuals, ultimately depends on the assumption that each of us is a locus of a rationality which can never finally be constrained by its surroundings.

The contradictions implicit in a social science which attacks the idea of rational individuals has not prevented various forms of social determinism from exercising great influence. The question of reflexivity has loomed large for many social scientists. They are aware of the dangers of applying their own theories to their own practices. Nevertheless, many have put forward views which suggest that we are creatures of our culture, and that our social environment is what makes us. This has not just meant an attack on the idea of isolated individuals choosing to cooperate. It has meant a denial of the concept of any human nature constant between different times and places. The issue is crystallized in the words of Hume (1975: 83). He asks:

> Would you know the sentiments, inclinations and course of life of the Greeks and Romans? Study well the temper and actions of the French and English ... Mankind are so much the same, in all times and places, that history informs us of nothing new or strange in this particular.

Is there a common human nature? The more that social conditions are invoked to explain our behaviour, or the concepts embedded in our shared, common language appealed to so as to explain our thought, the more this will be doubted. Societies vary and languages change. Once the differences between them are emphasized to the exclusion of similarities, history becomes crucial. We are then the products of our history, and the problem becomes one of building bridges to other times and places. We can no longer invoke a common humanity as a basis of mutual understanding. To revert to Hume, an ability to understand the Greeks and Romans is put very much in question. Their culture, their economic circumstances, their social background, are so remote from our own that we are likely to understand their thought-forms only after they have been filtered through our own. The question of the translation of their languages becomes especially problematic. Indeed, many would allege that the gap between our own day and Hume's in the eighteenth century is nearly as great as that between now and the first century CE. The revolution in industrial methods and in science has, it is claimed, made a new age, and a new humanity.

The Marxist tradition has been particularly influential in emphasizing the role of society and questioning the idea of a common human nature. With its concentration on the communal nature of human life it has had its own influence in the twentieth century on many theological views and has served as a useful antidote to positions which ignore the crucial fact that humans need society and are culture-producing creatures. We are all embedded in a particular historical background, and an emphasis on the relevance of history and on the potency of social institutions can help to counteract views which see us exclusively as biological organisms or exclusively as isolated, ahistorical individuals. Nevertheless, any theory can over-reach itself by concentrating only on one aspect of human life. Marxists can very often both argue that we are all historically determined, and somehow assume that Marxist theory is itself exempt from being regarded as the product of social conditioning.

In the Anglo-American tradition the later work of Wittgenstein has stressed that all our concepts, and hence our reasoning, are learnt and used in a social setting. Particularly in his argument against the possibility of a private language, Wittgenstein was totally opposed to traditional Cartesian dualism. Instead he emphasized that concepts to be meaningful have to be shared, and misuse publicly corrected. This has the effect of making a shared language the pivot on which all our understanding depends. We are not isolated individuals, each reasoning towards truth in a private vacuum. We are the products of a communal 'form of life', using language according to public rules. We are rooted in what is public and social, and the private and individual is secondary to this. Reason is viewed as a component of our way of life, and cannot be separated from it, or stand in judgement on it. Although Marxists have seized on the priority of the social evidenced in Wittgenstein's stress on the communal nature of language, the idea that we are each members of a tradition, and created by it, is also consistent with facets of conservative thought. Certainly there seems very little motive to change for members of any particular form of life, however it is identified. Deliberate change itself requires the very ability to stand back from a culture which is being denied.

One strong tendency in the thought of those who follow the later work of Wittgenstein is the reluctance to justify attitudes or practices in terms of metaphysics. Our attitudes to each other are, it is suggested, not grounded in a metaphysical picture of what a person is. Rather, we are told (Cockburn 1990: ix) that 'the metaphysics is an expression of the attitude, and the attitude itself has no ground'. Thus, the hunger for metaphysics which motivates much theology is dismissed. Instead, we are told to start with human practices and to avoid the search for rational grounding. Dualism is an example of such an attempt, and it is a characteristic of those echoing the later Wittgenstein that they eschew such grand philosophical doctrines by attempting to take our ordinary social and linguistic practices seriously. Such an approach in effect undercuts the whole idea of a theological anthropology which attempts to ground our thought about human beings in a metaphysics. It does have the virtue of showing that we do not have a simple choice between dualism and materialism. The basic problem with such approaches, however, is that very often it is not just a question of how we do talk and behave, but also whether our traditional ways of regarding each other are rationally justifiable. The repudiation of metaphysics stops us ever facing this crucial question.

All views about human nature, and denials that there is such a thing, have theological import. Theologians are often very quick to adapt them for their own purposes. Theories, however, which stress the priority of the social and which under-value the individual spell danger for Christian theologians. The very fact that they can easily place the responsibility for the ills of humanity solely on society, with little mention of the individual or the fact of an inherited human nature, carries vast implications for ideas of salvation. If what is wrong with us is simply the fault of society, this not only removes any question of personal responsibility and sin. It also suggests that the path to change lies wholly in political, even violent, action in removing structures which are perceived to be the root cause of injustice and evil.

Liberation theology has taken this path, and post-modernist theology in North America is also intent on identifying social causes of oppression and domination. Liberation and emancipation are seen as the routes to salvation, and people are seen as being liberated from concrete political sufferings. Our contemporary experience of injustice becomes the way to an understanding of the Christian message. 'The theme of liberation, so desired by those involved in contemporary struggles for justice, becomes a hermeneutical key to the message's meaning' (Taylor 1990: 179). When liberation of a political kind becomes the key to Christianity, it follows that our understanding of the historical Jesus will also change. Indeed the theologian just quoted sees the heart of Christianity not so much in the man Jesus as in 'historical realms of communal interaction'. He says: 'This approach to the divinity of Christ understands divine presence – ultimate and healing presence, value and

461

meaning – to be operative in a distinctive, interpersonal communal praxis, and in persons as participants in that communal praxis' (ibid.: 173). In other words, Christ is not to be understood as a historical person at all, but merely as the aspiration of a particular community.

The path to this position is clear enough. Once we stress the absolute priority of the social, and the crucial role of social structures in creating individuals, the radical changes of history will make the historical Jesus remote and irrelevant. Without Hume's confident belief in a common human nature, there will be nothing to unite us with the Greeks or Romans. Their life was not ours. There is no point of common reference, and no similarity of understanding of any common world, no shared hopes or fears or anything else. Yet for a faith, like Christianity, based on particular historical events, this is dynamite. If even the practice of history and the possibility of understanding other languages and the thought-forms of other cultures are put in question, the origins of Christianity, and of any other religion, are put beyond our reach. The historical Jesus is made at best irrelevant, and at worst incomprehensible to us. If the most important thing about us is that we are human, we can share that with Jesus. We can identify with him and he can be an example to us. If, though, he is to be dismissed as a product of an alien culture, the speaker of an alien language, and the inhabitant of a world long gone, Christianity, if it is to survive, can only do so by turning its back on the historical Jesus. Instead it will see the Christ as something quite different, something that is the reflection of whatever are the current concerns of our own society. It is questionable whether the result can be Christianity as it has been traditionally understood. Indeed, since we are trapped in our own age, even the traditional understandings of Christianity are going to be beyond our reach.

The Incarnation, in fact, has traditionally been seen as God somehow sanctifying human nature, so that Jesus' nature is somehow meant to be the pattern for all humanity. Yet it can only be of significance to us that the Word was made flesh, if the divine Word is relevant to us today and if the flesh referred to is our flesh too. Christianity, it seems, needs a doctrine of humanity as much as it needs a doctrine of God. Once it is suggested that there is no such thing as humanity or human nature, the idea of Jesus being both human and divine is no longer applicable. This is not just a question of the irrelevance of the thought-forms of one society to our own. The point is that the very category on which the doctrine depends has been undermined. It has always seemed problematic how a particular man could also be God. Now in some quarters, the category of 'man' or 'human' is in doubt. When who we are depends on our social circumstances, it becomes impossible to appeal to a category of being human in a way that can bridge and transcend all particular societies. There is no longer such a thing as the human condition. Human beings as such can no longer be in need of a Saviour. Human needs become localized and made specific to the needs of those in particular societies. There is no possibility of standing outside all societies and talking of human sin, or even of injustice in the abstract, let alone human rights. What we need, it is concluded, must be totally different from what those alien members of far distant cultures once perceived as important and necessary.

In this way sin becomes by definition merely a social category and not one which can be applied to individuals. Responsibility for injustice is laid firmly on social structures. Individuals are seen as mere puppets being directed by social forces of which they may not be fully aware. It is hardly surprising that those who are impelled by this collectivist vision see religion in increasingly political terms. The remedy for evil can only be social. They would deny that changing individuals will do anything to eradicate what is seen as wrong. Yet the relativism implicit in the collectivist emphasis on society is itself corrosive. Not only is human nature denied, but all moral categories have to be viewed as relative to the thought-forms of a particular society. Evil and sin are no longer terms with any cosmic significance. Different societies will see injustice and evil so differently that there is likely to be little connection between what is denounced in different cultures. Without a human nature there can be no natural law nor any fixed moral standards applying to all humans everywhere. Christianity will then inevitably be seen itself to take different shapes in different epochs and places. Even what it is against may vary from time to time. It is, of course, obviously true that Christianity has been expressed in many different social forms over the last two millennia. This fact can itself seem to provide a spur for relativism. Many, however, would still maintain that the basic message of Christianity, addressed to the same human condition, has persisted through that time. Whether there can in fact be such a thing as 'the Christian Gospel' proclaimed unchanged through the ages to meet unchanging human needs remains one of the great controversies of this age. Yet the shifting sands of relativism can provide no firm basis for religion or for theology. There will no longer be any agreement about what is wrong with human beings or what is needed to put it right. Indeed, as we have seen, the idea of 'human' beings is suspect. This in turn means that doctrines of sin and salvation lose their import, unless these are given very particular application to the passing characteristics of one society.

It is not just the person of Christ which is made to seem remote and irrelevant to us. The whole of the Bible, and indeed of any other sacred text in any religion, must be seen as the product of a historical period with which we have little in common. In the case of the New Testament, the denial of any common human nature removes any possibility that the desires and interests of the inhabitants of the Roman Empire in the first century CE will be echoed by our own. In fact the abyss that is thus dug between the two historical periods becomes so great that no amount of hermeneutical understanding will suffice to cross it. It is indeed curious that the discipline of hermeneutics which began with the question of how to understand biblical texts can easily in the end produce the conclusion that all such understanding is strictly impossible. It is always going to reflect our own presuppositions and the prejudices of our culture. Texts can then be read in a myriad ways, with no way being better than any other. That in fact is the post-modernist view.

The collectivist position is mirrored philosophically at the other extreme by a strongly individualist one. Yet just as the collectivist image left no room for individual responsibility, the individualist one can do the same. This time it is not because it fails to recognize individuals, but because it fails to accept that they have any responsibility to each other in a social setting. An emphasis on society and its structure can easily result in human relationships being seen exclusively in terms of power, of domination and oppression. Different impersonal forces meet and clash, and different group interests are pursued. The same emphasis on power, conflict and coercion can occur in a second influential picture of society, which stresses that a society is merely the sum total of its parts. We are each regarded as separate atoms, ultimately unrelated to each other and all ruthlessly pursuing our own interests and desires. Such views often hope that out of this chaos an invisible hand, perhaps God's, will somehow produce a common good. Yet each individual will manipulate and use the other for his or her own ends. Everything is reduced to the calculation of personal interest, and altruism is made to seem deviant. Even morality, if it enters the picture at all, is made merely the object of personal preference. Human beings are regarded simply as the owners of desires. Rationality is seen in a purely instrumentalist fashion as the means to working out the fulfilment of our fixed desires. There is no question of our standing back from what we want and questioning whether we ought to want it. That would presuppose the existence of a self, fully responsible and able to make significant decisions. Once again, as in so many areas of philosophy, the role of reason is downgraded.

The idea of a human community as simply a collection of individuals is nowhere more graphically illustrated than in the engraving at the front of the early editions of Thomas Hobbes's *Leviathan*. There the king sits in his regalia, but on closer inspection his body is seen to be made up of lots of little men, each whole and separate from the rest. The idea is that the state is formed by the voluntary association of selfish individuals banding together for their own protection. This is very different from the picture favoured by St Paul and referred to frequently by him, of the Church as a living organism, identified with Christ or else with Christ as its Head. This idea is that we each belong to each other, as do the various parts of the body to the other parts. Disease in one area affects the whole. It follows that we each have a special responsibility to contribute to the good of the whole. We have an identity apart from the rest, and so this is not collectivism. Yet at the same time we are not isolated egoists but have an obligation to care for the other members of Christ's body. Relationships between people should, it seems, be ones of love and not of power. We each matter, because we are all God's children. We should love because he first loved us. Faced with the alternatives of a collectivism which is also willing to sacrifice the individual for the sake of the mass, and an extreme individualism which seems to exalt the amoral and ruthless pursuit of self-interest, this traditional image of the Church as the body of Christ might seem an attractive one. The relationship of the individual to the community, and in particular to the Church, has, however, been an issue which has caused great divisions. Whether this has occurred because of different visions of our relationship with each other, or just because of competition for power within the Church is another matter. The fact remains that from the authoritarian structures of the Roman Catholic Church to the individualism of a Quaker meeting there is a wide gulf of understanding in how we each relate to a wider community.

SOCIOBIOLOGY

Can biology help to clarify matters concerning human nature? Does our biological nature provide a basis for understanding? Of particular relevance in this area is sociobiology, which was defined by E. O. Wilson, its founder, as the 'the scientific study of the biological basis of all forms of social behaviour in all kinds of organisms, including man' (1978: 222). Based on neo-Darwinian insights about the way genes can be selected and passed on in the course of evolution, it has at times made grandiose claims about the genetic basis of human behaviour. Some are plausible, unless one adopts the extreme thesis that there are no innate tendencies in human beings, and that all our characteristics are the result of environmental influence. Genes encouraging youthful suicide are unlikely to be passed on because those concerned will not live long enough to reproduce. Anything which encourages survival and ensures reproductive success is likely to be under strong genetic influence. For instance, parental care for offspring is likely to be an ingrained tendency in most species.

Sociobiology can offer many insights into the origins of animal behaviour, although it must always be on its guard against supposing that every piece of behaviour must be tailored to the quest for evolutionary advantage. Matters become more controversial when sociobiology turns its attention to the explanation of specifically human behaviour. Human sociobiology can only be an important discipline if it makes the same assumptions about the intimate link between genes and behaviour in the case of humans as it did with birds, animals and even insects. Because the individual is the vehicle of the genes, sociobiology also tends to concentrate on the individual as the source of explanation. In this respect it allies itself with the individualism and egoism of writers like Hobbes. As a result, altruism becomes a major problem. Sociobiology can explain why we care for those who are genetically related to us, and it can explain what it terms 'reciprocal altruism', whereby helpful behaviour to others provokes benefits in return. Genuine altruism, according to which I help others with no hope of any benefit, becomes very problematic to this way of thinking. Anyone who incurs costs without corresponding benefits is going to be at an evolutionary disadvantage compared with those who pursue the interests of themselves or their relatives in a single-minded way.

Wilson even aims to explain religious belief in evolutionary terms. He says that if 'the brain evolved by natural selection, even the capacities to select particular aesthetic judgements and religious beliefs must have arisen by the same mechanistic process' (1978: 2). Religious belief must, therefore, have a biological function which explains its origin and role in human nature. Besides the term 'mechanistic', others such as 'materialist', 'determinist' and reductionist' are also appropriate. When human sociobiology takes this form, it must be the avowed opponent of theology, and in Wilson's eyes it is. His aim is to account for the origin of all religious beliefs by, as he puts it, 'the principle of natural selection acting on the genetically evolving material structure of the brain' (1978: 192).

Sociobiology, at least in some forms, has been the apparent enemy of reason itself. It has looked for explanations in terms of genetic fitness. It starts with the individual, as a basis for its methodology, and accepts no important distinction between humans and animals, however much lip-service it might pay to the relevance of 'mind' or 'culture'. Yet once the importance of human reason and its products is stressed, the scope of human sociobiology is much reduced. It is of course relevant to note that sociobiology is itself the outcome of human reasoning.

Sociobiology has sparked off furious debates about the respective relevance of the social and the natural sciences. Social scientists and sociobiologists argue about which strings really work the human puppet. Christian theology must surely resist this vision of human nature. It must deny that we are merely the vehicles of genes struggling for survival, just as it must refuse to accept that humans are wholly shaped by the society into which they are born. Even accepting that biology and society should not be seen in isolation from each other does not meet the problem. Real though biological and social influences may be, they cannot tell the whole story. The very existence of the human and natural sciences is a sign of the continuing human quest for truth, and an example of the possibilities for human reason as it ranges widely and freely. Whatever the special characteristics of chimpanzees, they cannot possess a science of chimpanzee nature. They do not have the ability to reflect about themselves or their place in the universe. However they may happen to behave, they do not have a conscious morality or anything approaching a religious attitude to life.

The arguments of the materialist and the stringent demands of a strict biological reductionism are themselves evidence of human rationality. Sociobiology claims that religion is mere illusion, but that it is biologically advantageous. E. O. Wilson appears in no doubt of its falsity. Yet in so far as sociobiology tries to undermine religious belief, it is on its own understanding trying to reduce the biological fitness of those it convinces. Why should sociobiologists persist? The simplest explanation is surely that they are using their reason to try to uncover truth. They are attempting to transcend the constraints of biology and society in order to discover what is the case. Since they are still at the stage of sketching a research programme, and are far from having any empirical proof for much of what they claim, their activity is not so very different from that of the theologians they wish to undermine.

The existence of sociobiology as a discipline, like that of science in general, shows that the human mind can rise above the real influences swaying us. Altruism has proved a challenge, because the occurrence of deliberate selfless acts itself bears witness to the ability of humans to rise above the level of animal behaviour. Whatever accounts may be given of clever apes and faithful dogs, there does seem to be a significant divide between humans and non-humans. This is far from being a licence for humans to exploit animals. Indeed we are in a position to know better than to do so. In the end, however, the major dispute between theology and a discipline such as sociobiology must be over this. Whatever truth there may be in neo-Darwinian theories of evolution, we should not confuse questions about the origin of human beings with issues about present human and animal nature. It seems undeniable that we do possess an animal inheritance. Arguments, however, upholding and perhaps exhibiting the possibility of human rationality, point to an important truth. However important animals may be in Creation, and however much we should care for their interests, human beings cannot be classified as merely another animal species. Indeed, the very fact that we can agonize over moral issues about how animals should be treated itself demonstrates a major difference between ourselves and them.

Sociobiology, ethology and allied disciplines apply Darwinian principles to current science. As a piece of scientific methodology, it may be fruitful to see how much human behaviour can be understood by treating it like animal behaviour. Many facets of human nature can be uncovered in this way. For example, there are powerful genetic penalties resulting from incest, and it would be surprising to find this practised with impunity. People who dislike snakes are perhaps less at risk from poisonous varieties than those who like stroking them. The former will survive and the latter are less likely to. Genes discouraging such behaviour are more likely to be passed on. The holders of genes for liking snakes, assuming such a specific desire had been encouraged as a result of genetic mutation, would not be likely to live long enough to transmit their genes to future generations. Examples like this can be multiplied, some perhaps controversial, others less so.

Some of our characteristics, starting with such features as eye colour, are under genetic control. The issue is how many. There are striking continuities between animals and humans. The emphasis in sociobiology on the importance of self-interested behaviour for the survival of an organism does highlight a crucial facet of human nature. We do seem more naturally inclined to pursue our own interests than those of other people. We are more inclined to favour relatives and close family than those who are totally unrelated to us. We are often only willing to help others in the expectation of favours in return. All this is summed up in the sociobiological notions of inclusive fitness and reciprocal altruism.

Opposition to this kind of account can take more than one form. Some will point to society as the major formative influence and deny the relevance of biology to detailed social behaviour. Another possibility, however, is to accept the truth of neo-Darwinian accounts of human nature up to a point, but to insist that they give only a partial picture. The influence and mediation of social factors will be important, but also crucial is the human capacity to reason and to accept moral responsibility. Whereas sociobiology depends for its presentation on a disinterested search for truth, it often seems to be reducing everything to physical factors. It is as if the replication of genes not only provides limits for what is possible for human nature, but also tries to explain everything that humans think. However we describe the situation, humans transcend the capabilities and powers of animals. Aristotle made rationality the mark of the human. Modern thinkers, such as Wittgenstein, also stress the centrality of language, though this is better seen as an instrument of rational thought rather than its master. Thought without language may be possible.

It is often felt that the removal of any distinction, except one of degree, between humans and animals, fails to do justice to the traditional view that we are all made in the image of God. It may also result in a failure to explain the significance of the union of the human and the divine in the Incarnation. It is alleged that there is in human nature a potential to share in something higher than itself, which animals do not possess. The divine *Logos* is then within human reach, and this may suggest that there is a sharp break between what humans and animals are meant to be in the providence of God. Any intellectual discipline which insists on treating humans as merely another animal species challenges this kind of theological understanding of human nature. Whether it is the only possible form of Christian understanding is another matter. Some may fear that too sharp a divide between humans and animals would only serve (and perhaps has served) to encourage the ruthless exploitation by humans of the animal kingdom, which is also, it is pointed out, composed of God's creatures.

The claims of sociobiology and allied disciplines are further complicated by the ambiguity that reference to human nature often exhibits. Not all of such nature is uniformly desirable. A simple example is that there could well be a natural disgust felt by many at the sight of blood. This might be biologically useful, but it is important that people, particularly doctors and nurses, should be willing to overcome it if they are to help others. There is a considerable emphasis in sociobiology, as we have seen, on the selfish aspects of human nature. There are, however, two separate questions. Are they really part of our nature? If so should we, and can we, do anything about it? What is natural may not be good. The traditional opposition between reason and desire may point to an important fact about us. Our basic drives and biological instincts are not always good guides. As we have already seen, not all desires are bad, just as not all human reasoning is good. It is too simple to see human nature as involving a battle between the animal and distinctively human parts of our nature. Animals are not as capable of such deliberate evil and cruelty as humans. Nevertheless our inbuilt tendencies to selfishness need themselves to be restrained. As Bishop Butler pointed out in the eighteenth century, the problem is often that we are endowed not with too much self-love but not enough. It is often not in our own long-term interests to indulge whatever passion may for the moment overwhelm us. The selfish passion can be remarkably imprudent, because short-term interest is preferred to long-term. We must, too, consider other people's interests as well as our own.

RESPONSIBILITY

We have seen how some accounts of humans can locate sin only in the structures of society. It is a strength of a greater emphasis on the role of the individual and of personal responsibility that sin can also be located at the individual level. A determinist must have difficulty in taking sin seriously as there seems little possibility of holding anyone morally responsible for what he or she does. According to such a picture, we are all the products of forces beyond our control, whether social or biological. What then are we to make of the sociobiological emphasis on inherited tendencies to selfishness? One reply might be that this is partly what can still give plausibility to the doctrine of original sin. That has always linked a human disposition to sin and an inbuilt selfishness with our biological inheritance. The doctrine has often been expressed in biological terms as a matter of inherited taint though it has typically implied that humans were once in a sinless state from which they have fallen. Anyone who accepts modern scientific accounts of the transmission of genes might wish to doubt that. The underlying picture remains, though, of an inheritance which presents us with tendencies that are not wholly good. Our agonizing problem is that we are simultaneously in the grip of such desires, and also can stand back from ourselves and see that natural inclinations at times need to be resisted rather than slavishly followed. In fact, even sociobiologists sometimes defend their discipline by maintaining that greater knowledge of our motives may give us the ability to have greater control over ourselves.

Any moral theory has to take account of human nature as its raw material. It has to have a conception of what humans need and what they want. This is yet another example of our ability to stand back from ourselves and reason about ourselves. We seem never wholly the prisoners of our biological nature, even if we may sometimes pretend that we are. In the same way we may not be the prisoners of the culture which has produced us. Biological and social influences, separately and in combination, influence us all the time. They provide constraints and obstacles as well as opportunities. Yet human freedom cannot be totally discounted. Even blaming society or our genes for what we do is an exercise of that freedom. In the end, any theological anthropology has to take seriously the freedom and responsibility which each person possesses.

Our social and physical environment, including our biology, may present us with many disadvantages. Some people have more severe problems to encounter than others. Social status, as well as physical weakness, may provide many obstacles. It is, however, a basic theological insight that, whatever their circumstances, people can never be mere puppets being controlled by someone or something else. How we react to our circumstances is finally a matter for each person, however apparently powerless. It follows that a Christian doctrine of redemption cannot be satisfied with a political programme which aims to correct injustice, let alone with some biological technique which would try to engineer a better set of human genes. We may well wish to improve social conditions, but it can be argued that even the urge to do so will be rooted in the personal responsibility which individuals feel to those who may be worse off. However complicated the relation of individuals to a community may be, it will be individuals who will be able to change society. Society can never change itself. The worth, or otherwise, of an institution, will depend very much on the calibre of its participants. Not even the Church can hope to flourish, if its members are corrupt.

This is why a strong conception of the self as the locus of moral responsibility, as well as of rationality, should be part of any theological understanding of what it is to be human. According to such a position, we each, as individual selves, are accountable to God for the way we live our lives in the circumstances in which we are placed. It has often been recognized that the freedom of the individual cannot be emphasized to the exclusion of all other considerations in a theological context, but has to be seen in the context of the grace, and providence, of God. Too much stress on human freedom and responsibility can appear to detract from the sovereignty of God. This has led some, such as Calvinists, to talk of predestination. We may, it seems, be wrong in thinking that we can rely on our own spiritual resources. That, however, does not mean that we should blame social circumstances as a way of escaping responsibility. Similarly, it is not enough to blame our biological inheritance. Just as we are presented with the consequences of a myriad personal decisions by members of previous generations, so what we make up our minds to do will have consequences for those who are to come. Individuals are not isolated units or atoms. We have a responsibility for others. Any genuinely theological anthropology will hold that we are moral agents with the ability to respond to or reject the will of God. The very term suggests that if God created us, to be truly human must be to live as God intended.

REFERENCES

Cockburn, D. (1990) *Other Human Beings*, London: Macmillan.

Cupitt, D. (1990) *Creation Out of Nothing*, London: SCM Press.

Dennett, D. (1991) *Consciousness Explained*, Boston, Mass.: Little, Brown and Co.

Hume, D. (1975) *Enquiry Concerning Human Understanding*, ed. L. A. Selby-Bigge, 3rd edn, Oxford: Oxford University Press.

Rorty, R. (1989) *Contingency, Irony and Solidarity*, Cambridge: Cambridge University Press.

—— (1991) *Objectivity, Relativism and Truth*, Cambridge: Cambridge University Press.

Taylor, M. K. (1990) *Remembering Esperanza: A Cultural–Practical Theology for North American Praxis*, New York: Orbis Books.

Trigg, R. (1993) *Rationality and Science: Can Science Explain Everything?*, Oxford: Basil Blackwell.

Wilson, E. O. (1978) *On Human Nature*, Cambridge, Mass.: Harvard University Press.

FURTHER READING

Hick, J. (1976) *Death and Eternal Life*, London: Macmillan.

Kitcher, P. (1985) *Vaulting Ambition: Sociobiology and the Quest for Human Nature*, Cambridge, Mass.: MIT Press.

Olding, A. (1991) *Modern Biology and Natural Theology*, London: Routledge.

Pannenberg, W. (1985) *Anthropology in Theological Perspective*, trans. M. J. O'Connell, Edinburgh: T. & T. Clark.

Stevenson, L. (ed.) (1981) *The Study of Human Nature: Readings*, Oxford: Oxford University Press.

Taliaferro, C. (1994) *Consciousness and the Mind of God*, Cambridge: Cambridge University Press.

Trigg, R. (1982) *The Shaping of Man: Philosophical Aspects of Sociobiology*, Oxford: Basil Blackwell.

—— (1983) 'Religion and the Threat of Relativism', *Religious Studies*, 19.

—— (1984) 'Sin and Freedom', *Religious Studies*, 20.

—— (1988) *Ideas of Human Nature*, Oxford: Basil Blackwell.

—— (1988) 'The Metaphysical Self', *Religious Studies*, 24.

Ward, K. (1992) *Defending the Soul*, Oxford: Oneworld.

See also chapters 17, 21, 24.

23

EVIL AND THEOLOGY

Stewart Sutherland

Si Deus justus, unde malum?

(Boethius)

Epicurus' old questions are yet unanswered. Is he willing to prevent evil, but not able? then he is impotent. Is he able, but not willing? then he is malevolent. Is he both able and willing? whence then evil?

(David Hume)

Listen: if all have to suffer so as to buy eternal harmony by their suffering, what have the children to do with it – tell me please? It is entirely incomprehensible why they, too, should have to suffer and why they should have to buy harmony by their sufferings. Why should they, too, be used as dung for someone else's future harmony?

(Dostoevsky)

More than a millennium separates Boethius and Hume, and yet they both identify the same point of pressure to theology applied by the recognition of the presence of evil in the world: that point of pressure lies at the heart of the theological enterprise, viz. The very idea of God. Is God good? Is God powerful? All-powerful? Is God just? Does God know how things are here on earth? Does God care? Dostoevsky, through the towering figure of Ivan Karamazov, gives particular form to these last two questions, and in so doing identifies the mixture of weariness and despair, which characterizes the responses of some in our century to the answers which theologians have given to these questions.

There are two initial points which I wish to make at the outset before embarking on more detailed and systematic discussion. The first is that the problems, for there are many, associated with the presence of evil, pain and suffering in this world, have a very long history indeed. They are not, as is occasionally hinted, a product of the Enlightenment, nor of the particular horrors of this century – Auschwitz and Hiroshima. They are not simply the consequence or product of monotheism, for puzzlement about the lot of human beings is to be found in cultures other than those which are monotheistic – as classical Greek tragedy makes plain. Nonetheless, the character or articulation of the problems does vary from one period to another, and so inevitably does their impact on theology.

My second general point is that amidst all the complexities which we shall find, there is a radical difference between two very different sorts of approach to the issues at stake. On the one hand, there are those who argue, and in that sense at least believe, that there are possible intellectual resolutions of the problems, however difficult it may be to reconcile oneself to the pain and suffering which may be endured by self or others. On the other, there are those for whom no such intellectual resolution is possible. For them, if belief in God remains, theology will have to take a radically different shape from that developed by forms of theology based on philosophical arguments from world to God.

In the context set by these general points, the discussion will cover a variety of different but always related issues. Initially, the focus will be upon those treatments of the problems of evil, pain and suffering which are structured by the attempt to find the most reasonable answers that we can to those deeply puzzling issues. If in the course of the ensuing multi-stranded discussion there is a single underlying question, then it is this: If there is a conflict between theological affirmation and moral perception, which has the priority? As we shall see, most attempts to confront the issues at stake can be seen as being – or at least implying – an answer to this question.

The very idea of theodicy implies an attempt to reconcile human moral perception with the ways of God, for it is quite literally the attempt to justify the ways of God to human beings. The implication is that human moral perceptions of evil, suffering and pain are not to be discounted or set aside, but rather that some further explanation will show how theological affirmation and moral sense can be reconciled without one or the other having to be jettisoned in the interests of consistency. For a believer that is to attach very considerable weight to our moral perceptions.

The problem of evil in its traditional formulations arises just because human moral perceptions are seen to be capable of creating an intellectual difficulty for any religious system that holds that God is omnipotent, omnibenevolent and omniscient. Taken with the statement that God exists, these claims appear to imply or entail that there should be no evil in the world. God, being omnipotent, has the power to remove evil; being omniscient, he has the knowledge of how to remove evil; being omnibenevolent, he will want to remove evil. Yet God, it appears, cannot have the power, knowledge and motive sufficient to guarantee that he will remove evil from the world, if our perception that evil is a monstrous reality is at all reliable.

Theodicies of a speculative kind typically seek to remove the intellectual problem outlined by offering an account of God's power, knowledge and motive which will remove the expectation that they imply God should wish to eliminate evil. They work by endeavouring to discover a morally sufficient reason for God's creation or permission of evil. A good God will try to remove evil so far as he can, but perhaps evils exist as unavoidable parts of a yet greater good, such that not even God can have this good without allowing/bringing about the evils we see around us. A prime example to illustrate this possibility is free will. It may be that the good of creating free creatures can only be brought about by God at the cost of allowing human sin into the world, and it may be that this good is deemed to outweigh sin and its consequences. Theodicy then asks us to contemplate the possibility that all evil is, in a technical sense, 'redeemed'. Given the premise of God's omnipotence, the link between evils and any outweighing good would have to be a strong one: these evils would have to be logically or conceptually unavoidable parts of a greater good. Speculative theodicy then gets to work, filling out the account of evil's nature, its relation to good and the character of divine motives and plans: all with a view to showing how evil might plausibly be part of a divine scheme for the creation of over-arching goodness. Following the example of Hick (1977: 210–11), it is customary to divide Christian-based versions of speculative theodicy into two types: those which see evil as the unavoidable *consequence* of the creation of good ('Augustinian' theodicies) and those which see it as the unavoidable *preparation* for good ('Irenaean').

SPECULATIVE THEODICY

Speculative theodicy is an enterprise with major intellectual ambitions and one that gives many hostages to fortune. It hazards assumptions about the weighing of good and evil, about their conceptual relationships and about the character of divine intentions. Our sample discussions of responses to the problem of evil will show that not all writers wish to go down this path. Many of the complications of speculative theodicy can be avoided if one of the divine attributes is sacrificed at once (see Plato on divine omnipotence below). Moreover some theological writers think the enterprise is radically mistaken. In the last section of this chapter we will look at versions of minimalist and practical theodicies which attempt to avoid the job of speculating about divine purposes and the economy of evil altogether. But first some sample treatments of theodicy in its speculative guise.

In the first example of such discussion which we shall consider, we find Plato simultaneously placing such weight on our moral perceptions and on our belief in the goodness of God, that he is prepared to sacrifice the omnipotence and even uniqueness of God.

> Then the good is not the cause of all things, but of things that are well it is the cause – of things that are ill it is blameless.
> Entirely so, he said.

Neither, then, could God, said I, since he is good, be as the multitude say, the cause of all things, but for mankind he is the cause of few things, but of many things is not the cause. For good things are far fewer with us than evil, and for the good we must assume no other cause than God, but the cause of evil we must look for in other things and not in God.

(Plato 1963: 626)

Plato's view is thus very plain. If it comes to a choice between limiting or denying the goodness of God and the power of God, he would choose to question God's omnipotence. As we see, he spells this out very plainly in the *Republic*, and in the *Timaeus* he elaborates the picture of God as a craftsman who fashions out of pre-existing matter the world in the form in which we experience it.

God desired that all things should be good and nothing bad, so far as this was attainable. Wherefore also finding the whole visible sphere not at rest, but moving in an irregular and disorderly fashion, out of disorder he brought order, considering that this was in every way better than the other.

(Plato 1963: 16)

To put not too fine a point on it, Plato suggests that God did the best that he could ('good . . . so far as this was attainable'). The reasoning has the classical form which Hume used to tease the theologians:

1 God is good.
2 There are elements of the world which we experience which are less than wholly good.
3 God is the creator of this world.
4 God as good cannot be the cause of what is evil.
5 There must therefore be causes which are not dependent on God.
6 God is not therefore an all-powerful or omnipotent creator.

In Hume's terms God is willing to prevent evil, but is not wholly able.

Now whatever the plausibility of Plato's reasoning, there is no doubt that this element of Platonic thought has been present as an undercurrent at least, in the Western philosophical environment in which Christian theology as we know it developed. It resurfaced in various ways, and from time to time almost as a form of Manicheism, at the centre of whose philosophical position is a radical form of dualism which separated matter and spirit, such that even God is thought of as a stranger in this world. This religious movement, encapsulating elements from a variety of religious and philosophical sources, whose founder Mani was born in the second century, attracted the young, sceptical Augustine and was sufficiently vigorous as a proselytizing movement to be selected for specific polemical attention by the mature Augustine. (An interesting illustration of the undirected ebb and flow of ideas is that in his eventual rejection of Manicheism, Augustine drew upon alternative strands of Plato's thought which had for a time much greater positive influence in the development of Christian theology. These were the elements of Plato's thinking which provided the inspiration for the complex of developments grouped under the label neo-Platonism, and I shall return to this in due course.)

The possibility that God might be a God who is not omnipotent has been given a renewed currency in the last century and more by thinkers as radically divergent as John Stuart Mill and those who can be classified as Process Theologians. The one point held in common by Plato, Mill, and the Process thinkers is that some limitation to God's power is to be preferred either to the rejection of the goodness of God, or to the denial of the presence of evil, pain and suffering in the world. For example, Mill binds together the inheritance of Plato and the Manicheans in his own account of *The Utility of Religion* as follows:

> One only form of belief in the supernatural – one only theory respecting the origin and government of the universe – stands wholly clear of both intellectual contradiction and moral obliquity. It is that which, resigning irrevocably the idea of an omnipotent creator, regards Nature and Life not as the expression throughout of the moral character and purpose of the Deity, but as the product of a struggle between contriving goodness and an intractable material, as was believed by Plato, or a Principle of Evil, as was the doctrine of the Manicheans.
>
> (Mill 1874: 116)

The role which this leaves for the believer is then that of 'a fellow-labourer with the Highest, a fellow-combatant in the great strife', hence justifying the claims of a utilitarian for the 'utility of religion'.

David Pailin brings out well how close in certain respects this is to the views of some Process thinkers when, in exposition of the views of some of those who belong to that group, he contrasts their view with that of a more traditional account of salvation, in which God is expected to intervene to prevent suffering:

> It is blasphemy against the divine goodness, furthermore, to try to explain the fates of those who suffer and of those who do not as due to divine choice. Such an 'explanation' transforms the object of unqualified adoration into a monster. So far as handicap, want, disease, and warfare are concerned, theistic believers have to realize that it is their responsibility to find and effectively implement the remedies.
>
> (Pailin 1989: 203–4)

What gives legitimacy to discussing each of these otherwise disparate thinkers together is their refusal to allow the unambiguous assertion of the goodness of God to be displaced from centre stage, even if the price has to be the acceptance of a degree of limitation in the power of God.

My own comparatively bold thesis is that much of the response of Christian theology to the problems of evil and suffering can be read as an attempt to avoid such an evidently heterodox conclusion without compromising belief in the goodness of God. The strand of Plato's thought which I have exposed and compared with a very specific passage in John Stuart Mill's writing implies a form of dualism. By that I refer to the very basic point that if there are limits to God's power, then these limits must be set by what lies outside that power, or what in that sense is 'other' than God. Now, *we* are other than God, but that claim is not thought to compromise the uniqueness of God in Christian theology, for we are creatures, created by God, who are thus expressions of God's power rather than limitations to it imposed upon God.

This brings to light a most important issue for Christian theology, if that theology is to attempt to grapple with the most far-reaching issues thrust upon it by the presence of evil and suffering in this world. If we do not wish to develop a form of dualism in accounting for the presence of evil in the created order, then what account can we give of the relation between God and his creation? Ironically, the source of the most comprehensive theory to be developed in this context is the same Plato as the author of the *Republic* and the *Timaeus* upon whom we drew to formulate the question in the first place. In his extant writings there is no formal reconciliation offered between the Plato who for good educational reasons did not wish to imply that God or the gods were to be held responsible for evil, and the Plato who distinguished between the ideal world of the Forms and the world which we perceive, and who claimed that absolute being or reality belonged only to the world of Forms, of which this world is but a pale and insubstantial imitation. The idealism and monism of Plato the metaphysician was what was preserved in the various legacies which Augustine encountered in neo-Platonism, and which he used to construct a theological and metaphysical system with which to counteract the forms of dualism to be found in the Manicheism of his youth. The presuppositions of the metaphysics upon which Augustine drew are not immediately clear and comprehensible to those of us who are separated by a millennium and a half from then, a period which includes the development of the empirical sciences and their refinement through the Enlightenment. The implications for theology in all this as well as for the theological response to evil and suffering are very great, and they demand elucidation.

A foundation stone of empirical thought and scientific enquiry is that the world in which we live and which we investigate with increasingly sophisticated techniques is the real world; and it is a world of many distinctive and distinctively existing things, be they tables or chairs, planets or galaxies, molecules or microbes. In the end, Plato the metaphysician believed that what was real was not this empirical world, but an ideal world, and that ultimately what was real was unified and unitary in form, rather than plural. Anything which did exist did so only in so far as it was an expression, or instantiation (or in later thinkers an 'emanation') of what existed in ideal form; and it was even the case that what existed in such ideal form did so only as it drew for its reality on the ultimate source of being, the Idea of the Good.

In such a pattern of thought, things encountered in our experience did not exist in themselves independently, but only as expressions of, or emanations of, what did exist absolutely and independently. Things existed only up to a point, or to the degree to which they participated or shared in the being of what existed ultimately or in itself. The implications of this for Christian theology were very great, not least in the account which was given of evil and suffering. If what we experience exists not absolutely but only to a certain degree, then it was important to discover to what degree evil, pain and suffering exist. Augustine's bold answer, adopted thereafter by Aquinas and many others, was that evil came at the very bottom of the order of degrees of reality: indeed, so far down that order that its existence was marked and indeed 'constituted' only by the absence of something else – *privatio boni*, or the absence of good. It was in itself 'no thing'. It had no reality or actual existence to any degree whatsoever. Such a view had a number of significant advantages. On the one hand, since evil did not exist, there could be no question of holding God responsible for it. Thus there was no immediate danger of compromising the goodness of God, or of questioning the omnipotence of God. Nor by implication was there any reason to undermine the foundation stone of this view by opening the door to dualism. By incorporating this, as it now seems to us, 'abstruse' metaphysic, Christian theology had reconciled once again the goodness of God with his omnipotence. Historically, however, there was a price to pay, and as metaphysical presuppositions changed so the whole implicit theodicy came to seem implausible.

The difficulty facing those who would seek to reconcile the goodness of God with the omnipotence of God and at the same time accept the reality of pain, suffering and evil in this world, reasserted itself as the plausibility of the metaphysics of neo-Platonism was questioned and finally rejected. A number of alternative strategies were devised and tested, and I shall consider the most influential of these in the remaining part of the chapter. The first of these combines two related elements, each of which is important. The first element is to assert very firmly that much pain, suffering and evil in this world is the consequence of human action. The second is to stress that the laws under which the natural world is perceived to operate are constant and that if they were not so, then, minimally, human life would be so much the poorer, and, more radically, inconceivable.

THE FREE-WILL DEFENCE

The importance of what has come to be known as the 'free-will' defence should not be underestimated. In the first instance, it correlates closely with our experience and moral intuitions. It is undoubtedly true that we bring much of the suffering of sickness and disease upon ourselves. At a fairly trivial level, the pain, gloom and hangover of what has been known in Scotland as a 'Calvinistic Sunday morning' could well be predicted as the inexorable consequence of a 'Rabelaisian Saturday night'. More significantly, as medical science daily demonstrates, much of the suffering of illness is a consequence of life-styles which contribute in the long run to the malfunctioning of heart, liver and lungs. Equally, the hellish creations of Auschwitz and the Gulag were human in origin.

The theological accompaniment to that perception is to stress that God gave to human beings freedom to act according to their own judgements and priorities. In more fashionable idiom, God empowered human beings to be agents, to bring things to pass. In that case we must accept the good with the bad. Human beings reach great heights in the creation of music, art and literature, in penetrating the secrets of the universe, in devising ways to minimize the pain and suffering of others, and in expressing much more directly and personally love and care. The bad news is that human beings can also deploy the same cleverness and ingenuity in pursuit of rather darker ends. Then again, if we add the unintended consequences of human fallibility, inefficiency and misjudgement, undoubtedly we can attribute to sources other than divine action or intention much of the evil and suffering which are part of the daily human lot.

The theological force of this particular theodicy allows special weight and content to be given to the relationship between creator and creature. In principle, creatures have the freedom to respond or not to respond to the love of God. As the character of love between children and parents changes as children achieve the freedoms and maturity of adulthood, so by analogy, it is suggested, can the love of creatures for creator grow beyond the response of total dependency. Such freedom given by God to human beings creates the possibility but not the inevitability of such a relationship of love between creatures and creator. It also defines human beings as moral agents who have given to them the greatest responsibility of all – the responsibility for what they will become. Such is, according to the related theology, the deliberate choice of a creator God who circumscribes the power of the creator to expand and enhance the possibilities open to the creature. It is interesting to note how far this has moved the framework within which theological reflection takes place from the abstract mysteries of neo-Platonism to the picture of a personal, and one is tempted at times to add 'parochial', God with whom relationships appropriate to such a being are at the centre of the theological web.

In fact, this promise of a quasi-personal relationship with God brought its own difficulty, for, of course, if one presses the analogy between human parents and children too closely, then an urgent question arises. Any loving parent would take steps to prevent a young child being exposed, for example, to the risks of the availability of crack or cocaine. Should not a personal loving God show comparable 'parental' responsibility in comparable situations? Should not God, in giving human beings such freedom, have built in limits to the excesses which that permitted?

One particularly closely examined possibility here centred on the discussion of whether or not creator and creatures could not have had the best of all possible options. Could not an omnipotent and loving God, who wished to express love for creatures through the gift of freedom, have so ordered things that as a matter of fact human beings always choose what is right and good and never what is evil and wrong? In advancing this position, it is pointed out that an omnipotent God can surely create any possible state of affairs. That human beings do always as a matter of fact freely choose the good is a possible state of affairs, therefore a God who is omnipotent could surely have chosen to create that state of affairs rather than the one which is actually the case, viz. that human beings do not always choose the good. John Mackie, the author of this objection, puts the matter thus. If it is logically possible that a human being freely choose the good on some occasions, then it is possible that he or she choose the good on all occasions.

> God was not, then, faced with a choice between making innocent automata and making beings who, in acting freely, would sometimes go wrong: there was open to him the obviously better possibility of making beings who would act freely but always go right. Clearly, his failure to avail himself of this possibility is inconsistent with his being omnipotent and wholly good.
>
> (Mackie 1990: 33)

This enticing counter-theodicy has bewitched a number of philosophers in the second half of this century, but cannot be allowed to have the final word. There is a very important distinction to be drawn between the following two propositions:

1 God so creates human beings (and guarantees) that they always choose the good.
2 God so creates human beings (and guarantees) that they always freely choose the good.

The former is a possible state of affairs, but one in which freedom is left out of the picture. Thus it does not achieve the aim of this particular counter-theodicy. For that, we need the latter. This second proposition, however, contains a contradiction, for it implies that human beings might be both free and yet constrained in their choices, by, so to speak, design. Clearly they cannot be both in the sense required, and what is being required of God is self-contradictory and as such not a legitimate expectation even in the case of a being who is omnipotent.

The reply offered to Mackie clearly shows the theodicist committed to a certain conception of free will, one which sees it as incompatible with causal determination. Mackie is operating with a compatibilist view of free will. The important theological question which this distinction raises is 'how far can a strong doctrine of God as first cause and creator allow for indeterminist freedom?' Theologians who favour a strong doctrine of divine creation and sovereignty will thus find themselves unhappy with the libertarianism at the heart of speculative theodicy and will seek alternative strategies for coping with evil as a result (see Davies 1993: 42–3). Here the argument is, for the moment, stalled.

There are, however, other counter-arguments which have more force. One which cannot easily be set aside is the realization that although human beings can be held responsible for much of the pain and suffering in the world, the Lisbon earthquake of 1755, for example, is clearly, if anything, an act of God rather than man. The effect of the Lisbon earthquake on the sensibilities of eighteenth-century Europe was massive. The self-confidence of an intellectual climate immersed in the universal order of a Newtonian-style nature, and in a belief in progress that was grounded in the application to architecture, society, the mind and the emotions, of a paradigm of order derived from a partly mythical classical world, was almost shattered. Voltaire's *Candide* gave pointed expression to the implausibility of the claim that this is the best of all possible worlds.

However, what this establishes is not the irrelevance of the free-will defence, but its limits. That form of theodicy does explain some of the ills which we encounter in the world, but clearly not all of them. There is, as I suggested earlier, a second related point in the armoury of theodicy which must be brought into play. There are those who would probe further the analogy between God and a human parent, by pointing out that human parents usually attempt to set limits to the impact of the environment upon their children. Thus children may be allowed to swim in shallow quiet waters but not where treacherous currents run. Could not God in some analogous way protect us against the worst excesses of nature?

Those who ask for this must accept that they are asking either for the curtailment of our freedom, or for divine intervention to prevent nature from taking its course. Certainly, it might be argued, an omnipotent loving God could intervene to pluck the drowning fisherman from the raging sea, or to shield the lost child from the tree uprooted by the gale. Surely any human parent given the choice would do so; why not an all-loving omnipotent God? Nonetheless the theologian would be on even more treacherous ground here if his theology allowed the possibility of miracles understood as divine intervention. For if God can and does intervene to cure this illness or to prevent that premature death, why would he not do so in the myriad of other comparable or even more morally pressing cases?

The solution to the problem of non-intervention has therefore two elements. The first is to stress the critical importance of the consistency of the operation of the natural order. The laws we perceive to operate in nature may be very complex, but our belief in their consistency is not negotiable. Our practice as human beings is very clear here. If we come across an anomaly or an exception to an accepted rule of nature, we check our perceptions, or our instruments, we reformulate the law so that what appeared to be an exception now falls within a slightly more complex law. In short, we do everything we can to avoid accepting that there are random events which do not fall under the known laws of nature. Now there are very good reasons for doing this which are too complex to pursue further here, but they have to do with the elusive fact that order in thought and order in nature are not optional extras, which we can take or leave. Order in thought and order in nature are conditions of all that we understand by human life. We cannot conceive of an alternative to this, because the very act of conceiving is an act within established order, not one which is independent of or prior to order.

There is a strong theological corollary to this which has been well appreciated by some theodicists. For them, God is seen not only as the creator of the natural order, but as its guarantor. Thus the constitutive role of order in the natural world and in our perception of it is presented as one of the most unvarying, and for that reason greatest, gifts of God. A God who loves may well at one level share our perception of the suffering caused by the apparently 'blind' operation of the natural order, but may be even more impressed by the even greater calamity of the absence of such order. This has considerable force as an argument, but consistency demands that that force is also sufficient to eliminate miraculous divine interventions from a theology which employs the importance of the inviolability of the laws of nature as part of its theodicy.

With the world thus given some measure of independence from the will of God, the way is open for theodicies like Hick's to go on to build on the free-will defence. He and others do so by in effect arguing that a world with natural evils, evils flowing from the structure of the physical cosmos, is an unavoidable precondition for the possibility of significant free choice. That is to say, a world without natural evil would be one where choices of a morally and spiritually important kind could not be made. Only because human beings are faced with dangers, trials, suffering, want and the like can they use freedom to acquire and exercise moral and spiritual virtues. If they lived in an abundant paradise where no harm could befall them, they could have no significant choices to make. Hick is thus able to display the world as a 'vale of soul-making' (a phrase borrowed from John Keats; see Hick 1977: 259n.). The goal of the process is the perfection of human beings as moral and spiritual agents capable of enjoying a relationship with their maker. Natural evils are the occasion for the making of choices which can lead to the acquisition of traits of character and dispositions which in turn fit us for this relationship. The soul-making theodicist sees an economy in the evils of this world. It is an economy of evolution and progress: present evil is redeemed because it makes possible future good.

Objections to this expansion of the free-will defence into soul-making theodicy are legion. Many centre on the 'efficiency' of the economy of evil it postulates. The process is efficient only to the extent that God has adjusted means to ends in the right way, with the minimal evil allowed or created to produce the outweighing good. Efficiency is an issue when we reflect that many evils do not in fact appear to provide occasions for the significant exercise of free choice – as when the abandoned child of war dies hungry, ill and alone. There is much suffering that is, like this, 'dysteleological'. Moreover, the process seems to break as many souls as it makes. Evil makes *possible* the higher-order good of the choice for moral and spiritual virtue, but it does not *guarantee* it, and, paradoxically, its often overwhelming power crushes the spirits of God's human creatures. The three key attributes of God which create the problem of evil in the first place also seem to entail that any economy of evil in the world should be maximally efficient. This is no muddled, imperfect human scheme we are looking at. Thus we are in danger of seeing our initial problem emerging in a new form.

There are a number of responses that can be made from the standpoint of the expanded free-will defence. Two (relating to the compensations of a life to come and to mystery) are examined below. Another worthy of mention expands on the independence of the world from detailed divine providence already claimed by speculative theodicy. According to this line of reply, the economy of evil and its redeeming good should not be judged by reference to the details of what happens to this or that creature. God's general plan demands that a world be created which obeys its own laws and has its own autonomy and integrity. This entails that much happens in it that is not 'efficient' judged from the standpoint of soul-making. However, it is good overall (and efficient) that the world have this autonomy and thus not be efficient in its detailed operations. One of the odd consequences of this reasoning is that we should not expect to be able to see in the detail of our lives and human history the working out of the providential economy of good and evil. This should make us pause. For now theodicy's promise of insight into the working out of the purposes of omnipotent goodness is apparently not to be wholly fulfilled. Moreover, confidence that God can and will bring a redeeming good from the immensity of evil cannot be supported by the actual progress of things. The God of theodicy, after all, turns out, disappointingly, to be forced to leave the world very much to its own devices. At this point the Christian speculative theodicist will want to leave natural theology behind and to turn to revelation as a source of belief in the final redemption of evil.

In summary, the free will defence, even in its expanded soul-making version, is at best, as well as in reality, a partial theodicy. It reminds us clearly that some very considerable part of human suffering is brought about by human decision and action. Human freedom is the gift of a good and omnipotent God. But freedom is inevitably freedom to do ill as well as freedom to do what is good and right. However, there are some clear theological consequences that follow from such a defence, apart from its limitations. The first is that as the tendency increases – as it certainly does in some theologies – to view God in anthropomorphic terms, on a close analogy with a human parent, then questions do arise about the goodness of God as compared with the admittedly limited perception we have of the goodness of a human being. The only intellectual cure for such a theological and moral malaise is to eschew anthropomorphism, and that carries very severe penalties for most traditional theologies. The second consequence which illustrates this point is that one would have to be much more theologically circumspect in the account which one gives of miracles and divine providence.

RECOMPENSE AND LIMITATIONS

There are two further classic responses of theodicy which should be noted and which are often put forward as supplementary rather than alternative to the free-will defence. They are both well encapsulated in St Paul's haunting expression of human mortality: 'Now we see through a glass darkly, but then we shall see face to face' (1 Cor. 13:12). The two elements are the possibility of recompense and justice in the life to come, and the limitations of human beings in grasping eternal perspectives and strategies, for we can but 'see through a glass darkly', poor temporally bound creatures that we are. They are different faces of the same coin. Each makes play with the contrast between the short-sightedness of those who live life here and now, finite in space and time, and finite in perception, and the perspectives of eternity.

The idea of 'seeing face to face' is both rich and beguiling. Its richness is seen in part by the comfort which the related myths and stories about a life to come provide, via both consolation and hope, to bereft and grieving human beings. In part also it is seen in the many philosophical arguments which have been generated by the possibilities respectively of the immortality of the soul and the resurrection of the body. It is also intellectually beguiling, for it can maintain religious sensitivities about human finitude in the face of the eternity of God, while (and indeed *by*) postponing the possibility of an adequate theodicy until we 'see face to face'.

There are, however, two sorts of difficulty which confront this version of theodicy or its evasion. The first would distract from the main theme of the argument, and I have discussed it elsewhere (Sutherland 1967–8). The issue in question is whether we can speak intelligibly of 'surviving death'. In fact, as I have argued, I think that we can; but that does not solve the problem before us. This brings us to the second sort of difficulty. It is all very well reminding us of our finitude, but this is not a claim that is without moral import. Let us recall the quotation from Dostoevsky which is at the head of this chapter alongside quotations from Boethius and Hume:

> Listen: if all have to suffer so as to buy eternal harmony by their suffering, what have the children to do with it – tell me please? It is entirely incomprehensible why they, too, should have to suffer, and why they should have to buy harmony by their sufferings. Why should they, too, be used as dung for someone else's future harmony?
>
> (Dostoevsky 1968: 250)

This is taken from one of the seminal encounters in *The Brothers Karamazov* in which Alyosha, the novice monk, talks to his elder brother, the atheist Ivan. The argument, as these two brothers get to know each other once again after many years apart, is about what one can 'live by', that is, about one's most fundamental beliefs.

Ivan accepts all the implicit intellectual modesty of realizing that he has only a 'Euclidean' mind not fit to grapple with eternal questions. He accepts, that is to say, that now we 'see through a glass darkly'. He even accepts, at least for the sake of argument, that there might be a God whom we shall see face to face – perhaps even that there is a great cosmic plan at work to bring about, after this vale of suffering, some future harmony and recompense. Even granted all of that, however, there is still a difficulty – the children. In the novel, Dostoevsky gives in graphic detail examples of extreme cases of the abuse of children by adults, which sadly could be replicated very easily from the newspapers of today. The point is no less and no more than the issue raised throughout this chapter: the theodicy, the explanation, the justification of the ways of God to man is being purchased at the cost of dulling the sensibilities of our moral perceptions. If the presence of this suffering, the horrific suffering of young children, is to be justified in the light of some future eternal harmony, would we not in any analogous human plan reject it as flawed, or as a tragic consequence of human fallibility? If we do not follow a comparable line in the case of theodicy, then we are allowing our wish for a consistency in our theology to overcome deeply rooted revulsion at the suffering of small children. Ivan accepts the corollary to this, in what Camus called his 'even if'.

> I don't want harmony. From love for humanity I don't want it. I would rather be left with the unavenged suffering. I would rather remain with my unavenged suffering and unsatisfied indignation, even if I were wrong. Besides too high a price is asked for harmony; it's beyond our means to pay so much to enter on it. And so I hasten to give back my entrance ticket, and if I am a honest man I am bound to give it back as soon as possible. And that I am doing. It's not God that I don't accept, Alyosha, only I most respectfully return Him the ticket.
>
> (Dostoevsky 1968: 251)

And so in one of the most famous utterances in European literature, Ivan Karamazov throws down the gauntlet to theologians inclined towards comprehensive theodicy. It is a challenge recognised by Plato, Augustine, Boethius, Hume, and many others before and since. It is the challenge to ensure that one's theology, if one has one, and the theodicy which is implicit in it, are commensurate with the facts of evil, pain and suffering, and the power of human moral perception (surely one of the greatest gifts any creator could bestow).

OTHER ROUTES

An increasing number of philosophers and theologians find themselves uncomfortable with the ambitions of speculative theodicy. For Ivan's question about the morality of God apparently bringing about or allowing evil for the sake of greater, future good, sounds more forceful to generations brought up with the knowledge of the Holocaust and like tragedies made possible by the powers developed by twentieth-century humanity. One question raised by such events is how far speculative theodicy can see them as tragedies. For on its account they are unavoidable parts of a greater good and therefore redeemed. Thus, the God of theodicy foreseeing them, or at least foreseeing that this kind of thing could arise out of his gift of freedom to creatures living in an autonomous world, thinks they are overall worth allowing or creating. It is difficult to avoid the conclusion that to God, and thus to the theodicist, it is overall good that they should happen, albeit that when taken in isolation from their role in providential economy they are evil.

It can be argued that what is revealed by Dostoyevsky in the light of further reflection is that speculative theodicy demands an alteration of our moral sensibilities – those bound up with our sense of the tragic, unredeemable character of much evil. As James Wetzel puts it, it 'has banked on truncating our sensibilities against the rationalization of evil (Wetzel 1992: 361). We might balk at this endeavour to challenge moral perception and instead seek to abandon the ambitions of the speculative theodicist. Both minimalist and practical theodicists endeavour to do just that.

Minimalist theodicists deny the need for a full-blown theodicy altogether. They opt for a 'defence' against evil instead. (See Plantinga 1977 for the arguments that follow.) This distinction emerges from the precise challenge they see arising out of evil. For minimalists the only weighty intellectual difficulty for theology in evil lies in the possibility that the proposition 'There is evil in the world' is formerly incompatible with the key claims about God's omnipotence, omniscience and omnibenevolence. If this possibility obtained, then Christians would hold beliefs which were logically inconsistent with one another. The minimalist offers a defence designed to show that it is logically possible for the claims about God to be true and for evil to exist. But there is no need to show that it is plausible or likely that the God of theology should create a world with manifold evils in it.

Often this stance goes hand in hand with a rejection of natural theology as an important part of the theological enterprise. Philosophers in the Reformed tradition will draw upon exclusive reliance on revelation by some in that tradition and add to it the fashionable philosophical doctrine that there are no substantive standards of rationality independent of particular belief systems. Then it is open to the minimalist to claim that there are no independent criteria of plausibility or likelihood which enable a speculative intellectual problem about evil and God to be launched and which would, in turn, generate the need for a full-blown theodicy.

If the problem is one of intellectual consistency alone, then there are two ways for minimalist theodicy to deal with it. One is simply to appeal to the intuitively discerned possibility that there could be some way in which God has a morally sufficient reason for allowing evil in the world, for all that we cannot say what this reason might be (Pike 1990: 47). Another route to the same goal is to offer a proof that 'Evil exists' is formally consistent with the claims about God. One way of doing this is to find a proposition which is known to be consistent with those claims and which, if true, would entail that evil exists. In Plantinga the proposition in question is 'Human beings have free will.' And so we have yet another use of the free-will defence, though this time in a different context of argument. It follows that this version of a 'defence' against the charge of inconsistency is open to the challenges from Mackie rehearsed earlier.

Minimalist theodicies exhibit a number of notable features worthy of reflection. In denying that there is any notion of plausibility or likelihood to be applied to theology's assertions of God's goodness and power in the light of evil, they are going to the opposite extreme to the anthropomorphism noted above. We can form no expectations of what purposes for evil a good God is likely to have that are based upon analogies with a good human agent, and so no such expectations can be compared with the reality we find the world to be. Moreover, if we are content with an intuition or proof of mere consistency, then any amount of any type of evil in the world should leave us untroubled about God's goodness and power, so long as it is logically possible that a world of this type is one that God has a morally sufficient reason for creating.

As Wetzel notes (1992: 355–6), such a 'defence' against evil leaves totally unexplained why believers should have been puzzled and challenged by evil in the way they have. And it robs the theologian of the obligation and opportunity to use his or her faith to offer any insight into the character of evil and the purposes it serves. This protective strategy can succeed only at the cost of denying that theology has anything illuminating to offer in this area of human experience and reflection. Wetzel's picture of the limitations of minimalist theodicy must surely apply in equal measure to the practical theodicies of some post-modernist theologians. As represented by Surin in *Theology and the Problem of Evil* (1986), practical theodicy is a whole-hearted attack on any Christian writing about evil which endeavours to offer an apology for it. It is not for this way of approaching the subject to engage in speculations about an economy of good and evil in which the latter might be seen to be redeemed. Surin eschews all such generalizing thought about evil and its purposes. Instead he offers a theodicy whose aim is at least twofold: first, to enable, via the resources of Christian reflection, an authentic appreciation of the reality of suffering; and, second, to suggest means of drawing upon those same resources for responding to and coping with that reality. It is the charge of the practical theodicist that speculative versions of the enterprise, in allegedly apologizing for evil, hinder these two vital tasks.

No theologian would deny the importance of the two tasks Surin sets a proper theology of evil. But the denial of proper interest in the intellectual conundrums arising out of evil's existence in a universe created by a good

God can seem merely like an injunction to change the subject. Does the practical theodicist deny one or more of the attributes of omnipotence, omniscience and omnibenevolence? If he or she does, then of course the intellectual problem may well not arise, but then this denial should be clearly stated and its consequences for belief in God explored. Does he or she instead tacitly make yet another appeal to mystery, supposing that, though we must use the traditional formulations, we understand them so little as to be unable to draw any inferences from them?

The practical theodicist wants us to stop asking what appear to be important questions. We should be wary in general of such aims. We are left (as Wetzel notes, 1992: 363) with another version of theodicy which denies that theology has anything to say about the purposes of evil in the world's design, and which has no insight to offer into the question of how this universe does or might function as a moral order. Existential and spiritual questions have been at the heart of believers' disquiet about evil and suffering, but so have searchings for an overall meaning which illuminates the function of evil in a providential world.

The burden of this chapter is that speculations about evil form an unavoidable part of theology and an unavoidable source of questioning about its presuppositions. It is of the essence of such questioning to make us ask how far our moral sensibilities are challenged by the injunction to respect and worship a God who finds it overall worthwhile to make a world like this.

REFERENCES

Davies, B. (1993) *An Introduction to the Philosophy of Religion*, revised edn, Oxford: Oxford University Press.

Dostoevsky, F. (1968) *The Brothers Karamazov*, trans. C. Garnett, London: Heinemann.

Hick, J. (1977) *Evil and the God of Love*, 2nd edn, London and Basingstoke: Macmillan.

Mackie, J. (1990) 'Evil and Omnipotence', in M. M. Adams and R. M. Adams (eds) *The Problem of Evil*, New York: Oxford University Press, 25–37.

Mill, J. S. (1874) *Three Essays On Religion*, London: Longmans.

Pailin, D. A. (1989) *God and The Processes of Reality*, London: Routledge.

Pike, N. (1990) 'Hume on Evil', in M. M. Adams and R. M. Adams (eds) *The Problem of Evil*, New York: Oxford University Press, 38–52.

Plantinga, A. (1977) *God, Freedom and Evil*, Grand Rapids, Mich.: Eerdmans.

Plato (1963) *Republic*, in E. Hamilton and H. Cairns (eds) *The Collected Dialogues of Plato*, Princeton: Princeton University Press.

—— (1963) *Timaeus*, in E. Hamilton and H. Cairns (eds) *The Collected Dialogues of Plato*, Princeton: Princeton University Press.

Surin, K. (1986) *Theology and the Problem of Evil*, Oxford: Basil Blackwell.

Sutherland, S. R. (1967–8) 'Immortality and Resurrection', *Religious Studies* 3:377–89.

Wetzel, J. (1992) 'Can Theodicy be Avoided?', in M. L. Peterson (ed.) *The Problem of Evil*, Notre Dame, Indiana: Notre Dame Press, 351–65.

FURTHER READING

Camus, A. (1948) *The Plague*, trans. S. Gilbert, New York: Random House.
Farrer, A. M. (1962) *Love Almighty and Ills Unlimited*, London: Collins.
Hume, D. (1947) *Dialogues Concerning Natural Religion*, (ed.) N. Kemp Smith, London: Thomas Nelson.
Pike, N. (ed.) (1964) *God and Evil*, Englewood Cliffs, NJ: Prentice-Hall.
Sutherland, S. R. (1977) *Atheism and the Rejection of God*, Oxford: Basil Blackwell.
—— (1984) *God, Jesus and Belief*, ch. 2, Oxford: Basil Blackwell.
Swinburne, R. (1979) *The Existence of God*, Oxford: Clarendon Press.
See also chapters 17, 22.

24

FEMINISM IN THE PHILOSOPHY OF RELIGION

Grace Jantzen

Although feminist philosophy of religion is in its infancy, it is one of the most dynamic areas of current work in the philosophy of religion. It must be seen within the wider context of feminist theory, and, more generally, within the feminist movement as a whole. The feminist movement is not primarily intellectual: rather, it is seeking to bring about radical changes in patterns of human relationships. Its fundamental premise is that women are discriminated against because of their sex, and that bringing about an end to this discrimination would require major changes in the social, economic, and political world (Delmar 1986: 8). These changes would have to do not only with issues of gender, however, but also with issues of race, class, sexual orientation, differing ability, and many other areas of modern life where groups of people suffer oppression. Feminism is therefore a movement concerned with efforts towards justice.

It is within the movement as a whole that feminist scholarship finds a place. Far from aspiring to an ideal of detached neutrality, feminist scholars seek to develop theories which will be in the service of active efforts for justice, and criticize traditional male-dominated scholarship for its pretence of neutrality which actually serves to perpetuate the social injustices which feminism seeks to overcome. At the same time, feminists recognize that it is essential to give a clear account of what justice involves, in terms of both theory and strategy. At this level, there is much debate and fruitful tension within feminism not only with regard to general theory, both philosophical and political, but also in terms of specific issues, ranging from pornography to genetic engineering. Discussion of these fall beyond the remit of this chapter; but it is important to remember that feminist philosophy of religion is part of the effort of feminist scholars to develop theory in the service of active efforts for justice.

Like feminist philosophy more generally, feminist philosophy of religion therefore both engages in a critical appraisal of traditional approaches in the philosophy of religion, and also seeks to develop creative insight into issues from a feminist perspective. Like the rest of philosophy of religion, feminist philosophy of religion draws heavily on theory developed within mainstream philosophy, especially in epistemology, the philosophy of language, and ethics; unsurprisingly, it also owes a heavy debt to feminist scholars working in these areas, as we shall see more fully below. In addition, feminist philosophy of religion is closely linked with feminist work in theology, biblical studies, and spirituality. Indeed, as will be apparent below, the lines between disciplines are much more fluid in feminist thinking than they have usually been drawn in mainstream thought, not least because the problems which feminists encounter and the solutions that are proposed are often practical, human ones and cannot be neatly confined to single academic disciplines.

FOUR FORMS OF FEMINISM

Within feminist theory generally, four main branches can be distinguished, though there are many interconnections between them: each of them is also represented in feminist approaches to philosophy of religion. Liberal feminism, whose early representatives include Mary Wollstonecraft (1985), John Stuart Mill and Harriet Taylor Mill (1983), has long argued against the inferiority of intellect and morality attributed to women by key figures in the history of philosophy of religion, such as Augustine and Thomas Aquinas. If women are allowed equal education and opportunity, they will show themselves equal to men in every respect: they should therefore be equally eligible as teachers and writers of philosophy and for ordination of Christian ministry. This was the position taken by Mary Daly in her early work (1968), though as we shall see, she moved far beyond it.

It soon became apparent, however, that in their stress on the equal human-ness of women and men, liberal feminists had overlooked the fact that 'human' has been defined and characterized in ways that are normatively male. Furthermore, liberal feminists had largely accepted without question some of the assumptions and the ideals of the Enlightenment, locating our humanity and dignity in our capacity for rationality and autonomy. Radical and socialist feminists began to argue that this location should be scrutinized, not least for its male bias. Why not locate our humanity and dignity in emotion and inter-subjective bonding, for example, at least as much as in rationality and freedom? Hence it was recognized that the oppression of women is much deeper than liberal feminism took it to be; indeed, it is built into the definitions and conceptualizations of what it is to be human. But if that is the case, then it is not surprising that such oppression should also be built into human conceptualizations of God, whose omniscience and omnip-otence are thought to be the religious pattern of human rationality and freedom; consequently, the three subsequent forms of feminism take a much more radical stance religiously than does liberal feminism.

Radical feminism adopts a reversal of the stance of liberal feminism with regard to the Enlightenment values of what is normatively human (Daly 1985b). Rather than accepting the account of a common humanity, radical feminists celebrate women's *difference*, emphasizing emotion, community, and the nurturing characteristics of women, as against male reason, alienation, destruction and warfare. Radical feminists point to the extent to which language, including the language of religion and philosophy, embodies and reinforces sexist attitudes. Instead of merely asserting the right to be admitted as equals with men in areas of study otherwise unaffected by the presence of two genders instead of one, radical feminists seek to change the whole agenda of philosophy, not least in philosophy of religion. If philosophy of religion is based on male conceptualizations, for example, would it not be appropriate to seek new sources of religious knowledge, rooted in women's experience? If God has been conceptualized in terms which valorize spirit, power and knowledge, at the expense of bodies and feelings, in whose interests has it been to argue for and against the existence of such a God? I will discuss these issues more fully below.

The difficulty with radical feminism, as has been pointed out by Beverly Harrison (1985: 6) among others, is that if women are conceptualized as the polar opposites of men, then the logical conclusion for feminist strategy is a separatism which creates for women their own space, not just as an interim measure, but as a final solution. Women are wonderful; men are unredeemable. The result, however, (though I wish to be clear that Daly herself has not followed her argument to its conclusion in this respect) is that women would actually disengage themselves from struggle against concrete injustices, separating themselves from the sordid patriarchal world into a newly woven feminist web. Even if that were desirable, it would at most be possible only for a few affluent and privileged women, and would do little to help those who are most oppressed.

Socialist feminism is a third form of feminism which tries to overcome the problems of both liberal and radical feminist theory. Whereas radical feminism polarizes male and female reason, and calls for women's separateness, socialist feminists take the view that gender, and with it modes of behaviour including reasoning, is socially constructed. Drawing heavily on Marxist theory, socialist feminists like Nancy Hartsock (1985) argue that there are no views from nowhere; that all human knowledge is shaped by the perspective of the knower, and that as knowledge has been constructed in the Western world, those knowers have largely been the dominant males. Contrary to the claims of neutrality and objectivity standardly made by practitioners of science and philosophy, these disciplines actually represent and perpetuate the interests of the oppressor class (Harding 1991: 138–63). Hartsock uses Hegel's master–slave analogy and applies it to gender: just as the slave perforce needed to know things which the master could afford to ignore, so also women, because the conditions of their lives have been immersed in reproductive and nurturing labour, are able to see relationships with men and to account for male structuring of society in a way which men from their more privileged position have not seen. Female experience and perspective thus invert the male-dominant perspective, seeing the dualisms which the latter has constructed, between the mind and the body, God and the world, culture and nature, as life-denying rather than life-enhancing. These dualisms can be understood not as the basis for religion, but rather as male projections of their own alienation from bodiliness and women, who have regularly been identified with the second term of each of the above pairs. Socialist feminists are thus concerned to demonstrate the alienating nature of religion; and their work in the philosophy of religion has not usually been focused on detailed arguments within the discipline but rather a reconsideration of the discipline itself, as serving the interests of the dominant class, just as they hold that religion itself does. There are notable exceptions in the area of ethics, however, where socialist feminists' views have been important in the positive construction of arguments (Harrison 1985; Welch 1990). A central challenge for socialist feminism lies in its use of the Marxist category of class: in what sense can women, in all our diversity, be considered a 'class' for epistemological purposes? Surely the wide variation of women makes the idea of 'a woman's standpoint' problematical, and points to the necessity for a multiplicity of standpoints (Harding 1986: 136–96)?

This insistence on diversity is the common denominator of the fourth form of feminism, post-modernist feminism, some of whose major articulations have come from the French feminist writers Julia Kristeva and Luce Irigaray. They agree with socialist feminists that religion, at least as it has been known in Western societies, is male-defined. The concept of an omnipotent and omniscient deity has been used by men to valorize their own preoccupation with power and knowledge, and the insistence on God as creator serves to deflect attention from the fact that all men are, in fact, born of women and owe their existence and usually their continued nurture to women (Grosz 1989: 152). However, French feminists, especially Irigaray, have urged that abandonment of religious concepts is not the way forward for women. What is needed, instead, is a displacement and diversification of religious concepts, corresponding to women's displacement and diversity. She seeks to explore 'some of the necessary conditions for constructing a *female divine*, God, gods, a heaven, a genre and social position which is feminine, and can represent women's aspirations to an ethical order, as men's God has represented theirs' (ibid.: 162). A discussion of what this means is found below.

These four forms of feminisms, liberal, radical, socialist, and post-modernist, are the major strands of late twentieth-century feminist thought; and it is useful to see the strengths of each as well as the tensions within and between them as we consider issues in the philosophy of religion. However, it should be obvious that feminist writers in the philosophy of religion do not normally consider themselves bound by any one of these four forms, and draw on them as they find them useful to develop their insights. As I have already indicated, feminists usually find the whole project of drawing tightly defined boundaries around or within disciplines a deeply suspect masculinist project, more designed to abet the goals of individual specialism than to foster liberating communal insight.

SOURCES OF RELIGIOUS KNOWLEDGE

Christian theologians have traditionally based the possibility of religious knowledge on three main sources: revelation, tradition, and reason, to which might be added religious experience. Differences between theologians and ecclesiastical divisions have occurred over which of these is to have priority. Philosophers of religion have spent much energy debating the arguments for and against each of these as sources of religious knowledge: the question of proofs or evidence for the existence of God looms large in any standard course or textbook in the philosophy of religion. Feminists, however, have pointed out the deeply gendered and indeed oppressive assumptions within each of these strands: to what sort of God would such methods of argument lead? Biblical scholars have done much to show the patriarchal nature of alleged revelation (Trible 1978; Fiorenza 1983); feminist historians have developed an awareness of the ubiquitous oppression of women in Christian history and theological tradition (Bynum 1987; Miles 1989); and feminist philosophers, especially socialist and post-modernist philosophers, are engaged in deconstruction of patriarchal modes of reasoning, as discussed above (Irigaray 1985). Accordingly, feminist philosophers of religion are on the whole not particularly interested in debating the issues of proof or evidence for the existence of God. To do so would be to accept some of the basic platforms of masculinist thinking in the philosophy of religion which feminists wish to challenge. There have, however, been notable efforts to find in the Bible (Trible 1978) and in tradition (Grey 1993: 38–52) liberating resources for a religious knowledge which will be true to the experience of women.

The feminist movement as a whole is deeply grounded in women's experience: both the experience of oppression, and the experience of possibilities of liberation arising out of a sense of sisterhood or community among women working together for change. Although there has been little systematic analysis of it specific to the philosophy of religion, it can be seen that this dual experience of oppression and liberating sisterhood is also taken by feminists as the primary source of religious knowledge. I have already indicated the way in which the experience of oppression functions as a basis for questioning the standard sources of religious knowledge. The positive experience, also, has been of major significance. For many women connected with the feminist movement, the experience of being heard, affirmed, and valued in women's groups was a novel and life-changing experience, contrasting sharply with the marginalizing and disrespect which they had encountered in other academic, ecclesiastical and domestic settings. So powerful was this experience of solidarity and sisterhood that it has itself been seen as revelatory, not just of new insights, but even of the divine. As Sheila Daveney puts it, 'It has become axiomatic within North American [and British] feminist theological circles that women's experience is both the source for theological reflection and the norm for evaluating the adequacy of any theological framework' (1987: 32). Obviously, what is meant by 'the divine', if this is a primary source of knowledge regarding it, will be very different from what has been meant in traditional Christian theology and Western philosophy of religion, as will be seen more fully below.

How, precisely, should such experience of an 'epiphany of sisterhood' be understood as a source for religious knowledge? No systematic account has yet been undertaken; but several possibilities present themselves. One of these emerges in the works of Elisabeth Schüssler Fiorenza (1984: 43–63) and Rosemary Radford Ruether (1983: 12–46). According to these writers, it is essential to recognize the social character of theological norms, and therefore the fact that whereas current theological systems often present themselves as objective, they are in fact derived from male experience and reflect male interests. The experiences of women who have committed themselves to struggle against all forms of oppression, however, are experiences which are grounded in the liberating presence of God, since God is the cosmic reality on the side of liberation (Fiorenza) as can be seen from the alliance of Jesus with the powerless (Ruether). Hence, while women's experiences are as culturally bound as are those of men, the experiences of God of those who struggle for liberation are more valid than the experiences of those bound to the 'false and alienated' world of patriarchy: here can be seen an application of the socialist feminist standpoint theory epistemology described above.

Such a position can, however, be subjected to several criticisms. In the first place, one can see that whereas the overt appeal is to the primacy of women's experience, there is an obvious appeal, also, to the Bible and tradition as sources for an understanding of God as liberator, or of Jesus on the side of the powerless. At best, therefore, women's experience serves as a principle of selection from these sources; it does not do away with them. While neither Ruether nor Schüssler Fiorenza would deny this, it does considerably qualify their claim that women's experiences are paradigmatically sources of religious knowledge. Furthermore, as Sheila Daveney has pointed out, if human experience and hence human knowledge are grounded in its social and historical context, then this is as true of women's experience as it is of men's. Yet in Ruether and Schüssler Fiorenza there is 'the implicit, sometimes explicit assumption that there is a perspective from which we can perceive the way things really are and that feminist experience provides such a privileged location' (Daveney 1987: 42). Daveney's preferred response is to argue against the possibility of 'one true story', and affirm instead a multiplicity of 'knowledges' based on one's position in specific communities, and an effort of struggling within them for what counts as desirable consequences. While she is prepared to accept the relativism of her position, however, other feminists are less willing to adopt such a stance, since it would then follow that the advocacy by a community of sexism, racism, the extermination of Jews or homosexuals, or the like, could not be named as (unqualified) evil.

Another approach which uses the idea of socially based knowledge and community while trying to avoid relativistic consequences can be found in the work of Sharon Welch (1990: 160–2), who contrasts the traditional idea of the kingdom of God with a new idea of 'beloved community'.

> The kingdom of God implies conquest, control, and final victory over the elements of nature as well as over the structures of injustice. The 'beloved community' names the matrix within which life is celebrated, love is worshipped, and partial victories over injustice lay the groundwork for further acts of criticism and courageous defiance.
>
> (Ibid.: 162)

This love, celebration and resistance to oppression Welch speaks of as the divine; and it is within the context of the 'beloved community' that encounter with the divine is possible. There are, here, echoes of traditional theologies of encounter; but the divine that is encountered is not in any straightforward sense 'a person', let alone the Father God or the (male) Christ of Christian tradition (both of whom are in any case deeply suspect from a feminist perspective). While Welch plays on resonances of Christian vocabulary of the divine, it is not part of her project to claim her theological understanding as Christian, in the way that Ruether and Schüssler Fiorenza wish to do: what she is suggesting is that the experience of the 'beloved community' should be the basis for development of a theology radically different from the oppressive theologies of Christendom. It is to be hoped that in a future book she will develop these tantalizing hints further, and show how this 'beloved community' should be constituted and what would be the basis of the claims that it would make: in particular, why should they be considered *religious?* It would appear that Welch is suggesting not only a new source of religious knowledge, but a new understanding of what religion consists in, or at least an understanding different from that which has characterized much of the theology of Christendom.

Such new sources, and with them a new understanding of religion, are explicitly sought by Luce Irigaray. In conjunction with her project of constructing a new God or gods from women's self-understanding, she utilizes theories drawn from Feuerbach, which see the traditional attributes of God as human projections, and points out that they are gender-specific. *Men* have needed to see themselves in relation to an infinite, bodiless God whose primary attributes are omnipotence and omniscience, because these are the attributes which men, alienated from their bodies and struggling against their finitude, most crave for themselves. Thus God is for men a form of self-completion. Irigaray says:

Man can exist because God helps him to define his genre, to situate himself as a finite being in relation to the infinite ... To set up a genre, a God is needed ... Man did not let himself be determined by another genre: feminine. His only God was to correspond to the human type which we know is not neutral as far as the difference of sex goes.

(Irigaray 1993: 61)

Thus, if women are to accept the project of self-definition, part of that project will include formulating a God or gods of our own, developing an understanding of divinity which will represent 'the possibility of a perfection, an ideal, goal and trajectory of the subject' (Grosz 1989: 160). Such a God or gods can arise only out of women's self-knowledge; yet it is also true that women can only achieve such self-knowledge in relation to God as the ideal of our perfection. Irigaray represents this as reciprocal movement, with women's self-knowledge and knowledge of God nourishing one another.

Only a God in the feminine can look after and hold for us this margin of liberty and power which would allow us to grow more, to affirm ourselves and to come to self-realisation for each of us and in community. This is our other still to be realised, beyond and above life, powers, imagination, creation, our possibility of a present and a future.

(Irigaray cited in Grosz 1989: 162)

There may be echoes here of a Kantian regulative idea, but any notion of a God objectively existing in the heavens has disappeared together with the correspondence theory of truth and the patriarchal understanding of religious knowledge.

THE CONCEPT OF GOD

It is obvious that there is a direct correlation between what are considered to be the privileged sources of religious knowledge and the concept of God or gods that could be derived from them. Feminists like Welch and Irigaray are often reproached with the observation that the divinity they advocate will be purely subjective and relative, a wish-fulfilment on the part of women. Far from denying this, they will respond with astonishment that anyone could think that the patriarchal God of traditional theism is not also such a wish-fulfilment: the God of Western Christendom is so obviously made in the image of dominant males. The concept of God, on which so much energy is spent in the philosophy of religion, is a concept which needs thorough investigation from a feminist perspective, not because of some puzzles about omnipotence or about the coherence of theism or the compatibility of omniscience with human freedom, but because it is a concept which is regularly used in ways that are oppressive of women, which perpetuates economic and racial injustice, and which imperils the earth. In fact, feminists are suspicious that the energy spent in arguing about the finer points of the puzzles surrounding the concept of the God of Christendom is actually a way of colluding with the injustices perpetuated in 'his' name, or at the very least, that making such a debate central to the agenda of the philosophy of religion deflects attention from the weightier issues of how that concept of God is related to practices of injustice.

The obvious starting point is with the representation of God as male. Although it is affirmed that God is without a body and hence without gender, nevertheless God is constantly referred to in male pronouns, and characterized, in line with traditional Christian theology, as Father, Son and Spirit – all of them masculine in the Latin upon which Western theology is deeply reliant. Even feminists who are much more committed to traditional Christianity than are Welch and Irigaray find this masculinization of God problematic. Janet Soskice, in an article entitled 'Can a Feminist Call God "Father"?' asks, 'Can a feminist be at home in a religion where "father" is a central divine title, if not necessarily in current usage, then certainly in the foundational texts and subsequent history to which these have given rise?' (Soskice 1992: 15). Drawing on Ricoeur, Soskice seeks to make a space for feminist understanding of God as Father by analysing its nature and history as a symbol which paradoxically dissolves its own masculinity and 'opens the way for a non-patriarchal religion of hope' (ibid.: 26). Other feminists have shown that there is scope within orthodoxy for extending female metaphors for God (McFague 1982: 145–77), and that there was much greater emphasis upon such female metaphors in medieval thinking, especially among the women visionaries like Julian of Norwich (Jantzen 1987: 115–24), Gertrude of Helfta, and Hadewijch of Antwerp (Bynum 1982: 170–247).

However, most feminists, even those who recognize the possibilities of female imagery, remain deeply dissatisfied with the actual language of theology and the philosophy of religion. Mary Daly stated it with characteristic bluntness: 'if God is male, then the male is God' (1985b: 19). Although sophisticated theological thought has always rejected the maleness of God in any sense stronger than metaphor, the God of the Bible and the God of Christian ideology has been indubitably male, with such few female metaphors as there are in the Scriptures and tradition are very much subordinate to the masculine imagery. Early Christian theologians actually doubted whether women could be made in the image of God, since God was authoritative, as were males, but women were meant to be subservient (Soskice 1992: 19). When such one-sex symbolism is used for God, then 'a woman whose consciousness has been aroused can say that such language makes her aware of herself as a stranger, as an outsider, as an alienated person . . . She cannot belong to this without assenting to her own lobotomy' (Daly 1985b: 20).

Not only is the first person of the Trinity called 'Father', but the second person is called 'Son', his alleged incarnation being Jesus of Nazareth who was unquestionably male. It was Rosemary Ruether who asked 'can a male saviour save women?' (1983: 116). If salvation is understood in terms of some variety of economic transaction, whereby Jesus pays God (or the devil) for the sins of humankind and thereby redeems (buys back) humankind from damnation, then there is no particular reason to suppose that a male Jesus would not do for women as well as men; but such an understanding of atonement is largely discredited among male as well as female theologians. If, on the other hand, Jesus is to be understood not as a ransom but as an exemplar, or as the manifestation of God and the one in union with whom human beings can find fulfilment and true life, then it is much more problematic how a male Jesus could be an exemplar for or the fulfilment of women. The maleness of Jesus is still frequently used, moreover, as an argument against the ordination of women to priestly ministry, since it is said that a woman could not represent him in the celebration of the eucharist. Although there are plenty of arguments against this view (for instance, that it is not the physicality of Jesus but his redemptiveness which the celebrant represents, otherwise priests would have to be not only male but also Jewish), the very fact that such arguments still arise is evidence of the ways in which the maleness of Jesus has been used for misogynist ends, as Daphne Hampson makes clear (1990: 108–12).

However, as Janet Soskice points out, 'what disturbs feminist theologians is not simply that God has been styled as male in the tradition, but that God is styled as male in particular ways and especially has been styled as powerful, dominant, and implacable' (Soskice 1992: 20). Not only does this give a theological perspective which renders God suspect, but because men have seen it as their Christian duty to try to be godly (god-like), the valorization of power has been taken as a licence to cultivate attitudes of domination and power which have had devastating effects on women and on the planet. Sharon Welch points out that 'the idea of an omnipotent and sovereign God . . . assumes that absolute power can be a good' (Welch 1990: 111). Although she recognizes that the doctrine of omnipotence can be articulated in such a way as to deny that such power should ever be assumed by human beings, nevertheless Welch claims that doctrines 'that affirm the absolute power of God . . . also reinforce a human desire for absolute power, a dangerous desire for those who have political and economic power'. This is made all the more dangerous when those claiming such power see themselves as merely fulfilling the will of the omnipotent God: since they abase themselves before 'him', and believe themselves to be carrying out 'his' purposes, they may feel themselves justified in exerting 'total control over others' (ibid.: 112): it is always the case that 'oppressive power gains much of its force through the claim of submission to a greater moral purpose' (ibid.: 114). Welch links such glorification of power, in which the theology of Christendom aids and abets appropriation of power by men in dominant positions, directly with the Third Reich, as well as with the American dream of total control exemplified by the 'star wars' programme. Other writers, notably Dorothee Sölle, seek for these sorts of reasons to offer a different concept of God, a God of vulnerability, whose justice and mercy are of greater importance than power, since a religion based on the adoration of power is much too closely connected with what Sölle calls (with direct reference to the Third Reich) 'the culture of obedience and barbarism' (Sölle 1990a: 86).

Similar arguments as Welch makes in relation to the valorization of power can also be made in relation to omniscience: the God who knows all is the God who is in total control; and those who seek to emulate such a God cannot avoid the interweaving of power and knowledge about which Michel Foucault has written with eloquence (Foucault 1980: 134–45). Thus Anne Hunter has used Foucault's discussion of the panoptic gaze (Foucault 1979: 205) to link the idea of the 'all-seeing male God' with the social control of women by men (Hunter 1992: 7–26); and Joanne Brown and Rebecca Parker have suggested a startling relationship between the Christian doctrine of Jesus' suffering at the behest of his omnipotent Father with a glorification of both power and suffering that can easily result in battering and abuse of women and children by men who claim the right to dominate (Brown and Parker 1989: 1–30).

Many of these ideas still await much more detailed and careful analysis and probing in the philosophy of religion; but it is obvious from this survey that feminist philosophers have a vastly different agenda to that of traditional philosophers of religion, who have not discussed issues of this sort within standard writings on the concept of God. Indeed, it is because of the recognition of the oppressively patriarchal character of Western religion, along with an increased confidence in women's experience as a source of religious knowledge, that there has been an upsurge of a goddess movement, sometimes associated with an effort at revival of pagan rituals or witchcraft, among women. The words of Ntozake Shange at the end of her choreopoem *for colored girls who have considered suicide/when the rainbow is enuf* have found deep resonances in feminist writers:

> i found god in myself
> & i loved her/i loved her fiercely

(Christ 1980: 97–117)

Women seeking to reclaim the dangerous memory of the thousands who were burned as witches in the name of the male deity, and to honour the millions whose voices have been relegated to the margins of history, have developed important connections between the god/ess who is thus found within women's experience and the beliefs and rituals of women of the ancient past (Starhawk 1990: 176). To what extent these connections are historically credible is a moot point; but to many feminists this is not what is important. Carol Christ, is a landmark article entitled 'Why Women Need the Goddess' (Christ 1979: 273–87), discusses the way in which goddess celebration affirms the validity of women, challenges the denigration of women's bodies and bodily processes such as menstruation and childbirth which have been treated as taboo, and positively evaluates women's energy and women's choices and community. It is this reclaiming of women's self-hood and worth, rather than any sort of philosophical claim about the objective existence of such a god/ess, which is the point of god/ess rituals. However, many feminists would argue that their practice of self-affirmation through such rituals differs from male self-affirmation in the more orthodox beliefs and practices of Christendom only by the fact that most women participants are self-conscious about the fact that what is involved in god/ess worship is deliberate projection, while most male worshippers would deny that such projection was taking place. By no means all feminists accept the notion of god/ess as unproblematic. Many reject religion altogether, of course; and many others try somehow to stay within more orthodox Christianity. It is significant, however, that one of the most important recent pieces evaluating the god/ess movement has centred not on issues of historicity or objective truth, but on whether a focus on a god/ess somehow experienced as external, and a preoccupation with archaic rituals and practices, may actually deflect attention from the pressing needs of liberation from the oppressing conditions of life (Lunn 1993: 17–38). Thus once again issues of justice take precedence over strictly intellectual concerns.

CONCEPTS OF PERSONHOOD

One of the first issues to be raised in feminist philosophy of religion and theology in the 'second wave' of the women's movement was put by Valerie Saiving in 1960: is sin the same thing for men as it is for women? As Saiving saw it, the modern theological characterization of human beings as essentially free, and therefore prone to anxiety, pride, and 'the imperialistic drive to close the gap between the individual, separate self and others by reducing those others to the status of mere objects which can then be treated as appendages of the self and manipulated accordingly' (Saiving 1979: 26) is much more accurate of men than of women. Because of social conditioning, women are far less likely to find that their besetting sins are pride and the desire for mastery. Instead, women are more likely to be prone to inappropriate humility, lack of a sense of self-worth, lack of centredness or focus, and consequently triviality and diffuseness. Because theology has 'defined the human condition on the basis of masculine experience' (ibid.: 39), warnings against sins and exhortations to virtue are, if taken seriously by women, likely to actually exacerbate what they are intended to rectify. A woman who already has a poor sense of self-worth, for example, is not helped by sermons on the sin of pride and the need to abase oneself in service to God and neighbour. The same theme is expanded by Mary Daly (1985b: 44–68) and more recently by Daphne Hampson, who also points out the extent to which sin has regularly been construed in modern theology as an individual matter, between a person and God. But as Hampson says, for many feminists sin consists not so much in individual actions but rather in structural sin, the injustices of society. 'Thus sin is the sin of the domination of one class by another, and indeed (and perhaps primarily) the sin of sexism – which has gone unrecognized in male theology' (Hampson 1990: 125).

Hampson points out, furthermore, that if sin is gender-specific, then so, presumably, must be salvation: we have already seen the implications of this for christology. Moreover, the means by which women and men seek to appropriate salvation may be different. Hampson discusses the Protestant tradition as exemplified by Reinhold Niebuhr, who speaks of conversion in terms of the 'breaking of an egotistical self', which is 'crucified with Christ' and thereby finds its pride shattered (Hampson 1990: 127). But if it is the case that women have suffered from too weak (rather than too strong) an ego, then this would be precisely the worst sort of prescription that could be given to women, who need instead to find healing for their brokenness and fragmentation, and strengthening of their inner self. 'If women's ills have been the result of an undervaluation of the self, then their healing must consist in self-actualization' (ibid.).

The lines between philosophy, psychology, and theology are blurred here (and many feminists are in any case scornful of the sharp divisions of disciplines which characterize much male theory); but it is clear that part of what is at issue in the discussion of sin and salvation is a broader question of human personhood and whether it has been correctly described in traditional philosophical and theological thought. As Saiving and Hampson maintain, the concepts of sin and salvation are gender-specific not because of inherent biological differences between men and women, but because of the different socialization which women and men undergo. Other feminists, however, among them Mary Daly, hold that women are *essentially* different from men, differences which are rooted not in nurture or social conditioning but in nature. From this it would follow not only that traditional theological accounts of sin and salvation are unhelpful to women, but that the whole modern characterization of human beings in terms of rationality and autonomy is alienating to women, who must either betray their own femaleness and think of themselves in male terms, or else confront the emptiness of theory in relation to their own condition.

It is somewhat difficult to see, however, how an essentialist account such as Mary Daly's could ever be substantiated. It is not, after all, possible to get back to any pre-socialized state, whether in our own culture or in any other. As long as there are socially instituted differences in gender roles (which there are in every known culture, though, of course, the content of those differences varies) there is no control group against which a socialized group could be measured, nor is there any group whose essential characteristics could be studied uncontaminated by social conditioning. Furthermore, feminists are all too aware of the ways in which theories of biological essentialism have been used to confine women to their reproductive functions, under the rubric that 'anatomy is destiny'. The recognition of the necessity of gendered accounts of sin and salvation, or, in secular terms, vice and virtue, does not entail the unprovable and dangerous doctrine of biological essentialism.

Very significant work has been done by feminists to challenge the ideology of atomic individualism as it has presented itself in modern liberal thought, and to construct alternative models of understanding human personhood and relationship. Thus for example Mary Hunt, in her book *Fierce Tenderness* (1991), uses the model of friendship as the basis for theological as well as anthropological understanding. It is only within our relationships with one another that we find fulfilment as human beings: to suppose that we 'spring like mushrooms out of the ground', as Hobbes once said, is to misunderstand the very nature of humanity. But to relate to one another in 'fierce tenderness' it is necessary that we take responsibility for our mutual relationships, that we seek to be adult in our responses. Mary Hunt sees this as a paradigm also of our relationship with the divine. Rather than being the perpetual 'children' of God, acquiescing in infantilization, women and men need to learn to be adult in relation to the divine, taking responsibility and being accountable within the relationship, and expecting the same thing in return. In a world of violence, the 'sprigs of holiness' of good friendships must be fiercely protected: they are the safe places in which connectedness rather than isolation can be fostered. The erotic elements sometimes present in such friendships have also been taken as a source or paradigm of religious knowledge, notably by Carter Heyward (1989): it is a refreshing change from the suspicion and suppression of the body and sexuality which are a regular part of traditional theological thought. However, voices have been raised in warning against too romantic a notion of the way in which the erotic can be the manifestation or occasion of divine love. For women who have suffered sexual assault or abuse (and while precise estimates vary, it is agreed that that includes a very high proportion of women) it would be much too quick and simple to celebrate sexuality as the channel of divine love and power. Kathleen Sands discusses the significance of the erotic for woman-centred religious thought, and points out that 'to date, the sexual wisdom of feminist theo(a)logy is inhibited by our need to defend Eros, a motive which has taken the place occupied by the defense of God in androcentric theology' (Sands 1992: 8); she stresses, however, that women need to bring to this celebration of Eros much wisdom and healing for the many whose experience of the relation between love and power has been anything but liberating.

Although it is obvious from the disputes about essentialism and about the role of the erotic as a source of connection with the divine that there are considerable differences among feminists regarding the understanding of human personhood, most feminists would agree that the traditional split between mind or soul and body is one of the worst legacies of patriarchy. This split is conceived of as only one of a whole series of dualisms: mind/body, good/bad, light/dark, God/world, male/female, knowledge/ignorance. From the time of Pythagoras, such sets of opposing terms have been a frequent part of religious and philosophical thought, with the left-hand terms usually being thought of as higher in value than the right-hand terms. The various forms of dualism have been shown to be interlinked. For example, I argued in *God's World, God's Body* (Jantzen 1984) that cosmic dualism, the idea that God and the world are utterly different and separate, is a large-scale version of mind–body dualism; and if the latter is philosophically and theologically dubious then so must be the former. At the time, I did not appreciate that both of these dualisms also mirror the male–female dualism: men have from Plato onwards been associated with mind and spirit and transcendence, while women have been linked with the body, reproduction, and the material world. These connections have been clearly demonstrated by several writers, notably Rosemary Ruether (1983: 72–92) and Sallie McFague (1987: 63–9). Whether because of male anxiety deriving from the need of a boy child to separate from his mother to achieve male identity, as Freud and his followers suggest, or whether there is some other cause, male-dominated Western religion and philosophy demonstrate a discomfort with sexuality, the body, and the material world, and have often sought other-worldly alternatives. As Luce Irigaray puts it:

> the patriarchal order is based upon worlds of the beyond: worlds of before birth and especially of the afterlife, other planets to be discovered and exploited for survival, etc. It doesn't appreciate the real value of the world we have and draws up its often bankrupt blueprints on the basis of hypothetical worlds.
>
> (1993: 27)

Feminist philosophy of religion has not only recognized the gendered nature of the various forms of dualism, however, but has also begun to develop more holistic approaches. Some of these have already become apparent in this chapter: the emphasis on justice in the 'beloved community', the recognition of friendship and of sexuality as contexts of divinity, and the emphasis on women's experience, not least bodily experience, as a source of religious knowledge. The most extended feminist treatment to date of the concepts of God, the world, and traditional Christian doctrine from the perspective of the model of the world as God's body and everything within it as radically interconnected is the excellent monograph by Sallie McFague, *The Body of God* (1993). McFague shows how transcendence, both human and divine, needs to be understood not in contrast to embodiment, but *through* embodiment, thus enabling the possibility of a new evaluation of bodiliness and a new perspective on such issues as the ecological crisis. Although much still needs to be done in feminist philosophy of religion in exploration of human personhood and embodiment, and although McFague accepts traditional Christian doctrines to a greater extent than many feminists would find congenial, there is no doubt that she has provided a solid basis for future reflection.

FEMINIST ETHICS

The area of feminist ethics is large and important enough to deserve a chapter to itself; within the context of feminist philosophy of religion, however, a brief account of it must suffice. The impetus to much recent writing in feminist ethics came from the now very famous work of Carol Gilligan, a Harvard psychologist who pointed out that much of the work on the moral development of children by Kohlberg and others was in fact based on studies where all the subjects were male. Gilligan conducted studies which compared the moral responses of groups of boys with groups of girls, matched for age and socio-economic background. Her findings showed that whereas boys tended to emphasize fairness and rule-governed behaviour, girls were more likely to emphasize care for one another, and showed much stronger commitment to finding solutions to problems which would enable them to maintain relationships, rather than insisting on preconceived ideas of justice (Gilligan 1982).

Feminist writers on ethics were quick to use Gilligan's findings to begin a critical analysis of modern ethical systems from Hobbes to Rawls, showing how their ideas of justice are, in fact, ideas which privilege dominant males (Kittay and Meyers 1987; Okin 1989). A constructive effort also developed, in which feminists explored the ideas of care and connectedness as a basis for moral thinking (Noddings 1984; Andolsen et al. 1985; Code et al. 1988). Nevertheless, feminists quickly realized that while ethical theory and moral issues have much to gain from an emphasis on care and connection, it is all too easy to slip back into the notion that women are the ideal carers of society, the ones to whom the 'private' issues of care can be left while the men get on with the more public concerns requiring an emphasis on justice and fairness. Although such a dichotomizing view should certainly not be attributed to Gilligan herself or to feminist ethicists who build on her work, it is clear that feminist ethics requires not only a strong commitment to care and connectedness, but also a robust account of justice, and of the ways in these concepts need to interpret one another (Grey 1991; Jantzen 1992).

The person who has done most to foster rigorous feminist ethics within a framework of Christian philosophy of religion is Beverly Harrison, to whose work a double issue of the *Journal of Feminist Studies in Religion* (1993) has recently been dedicated. Harrison has consistently emphasized the significance of the patriarchal social context within which the formation of the moral character, for both males and females, takes place (Harrison 1985: 54–80; 83–114). Not only the moral character, but all of its specific moral choices too, occur within a social and religious context, and are misunderstood if they are seen as an ahistorical exercise of the autonomous will. Consequently, while Harrison broadly welcomes the work of Gilligan and the formation of an ethic of care, she calls attention back to the patriarchal social determinants of men and women that predispose them to emphasize justice and care respectively. If an ethic of care, by focusing on individual moral decisions, deflects attention from the need to dismantle these oppressive structures, including their religious underpinnings, or if it channels the energy of women away from the struggle for social justice by characterizing that as unfeminine, then more will have been lost than gained by noting the gender differences in (current, white, Western) types of moral decision-making. Harrison speaks of the urgency of ethical revaluation of the complicity of churches and theologies in strategies of oppression, and, far from dampening women's anger at injustice, seeks to mobilize 'the power of anger in the work of love' (Harrison 1985: 3–21).

That 'work of love' demands an effort to change the world, to make it a place for human habitation for women and for men, who learn to live in ways that foster dignity and community. Sharon Welch has explained how well-intentioned liberal efforts to change the world easily end up in 'cultured despair', an abandonment of all effort as useless because no single effort can accomplish everything. Yet as Welch points out, such an attitude is the mirror image of the desire for an unholy omnipotence, an unwillingness to accept risk, to do the next thing. What we need to seek is not for a 'final solution' but for ways that will take the struggle for justice forward (Welch 1990: 103–80). It is this struggle for justice to which the intellectual and imaginative resources of feminist philosophy of religion are dedicated.

REFERENCES

Andolsen, B. H., Gurdorf, C. E. and Pellauer, M. D., (eds) (1985) *Women's Consciousness, Women's Conscience*, Minneapolis: Winston Press.

Brown, J. C. and Parker, R. (1992) 'For God So Loved the World?', in J. Brown and C. Bohn, *Christianity, Patriarchy and Abuse: A Feminist Critique*, New York: Pilgrim Press.

Bynum, C. W. (1982) *Jesus as Mother: Studies in the Spirituality of the High Middle Ages*, Berkeley: University of California Press.

—— (1987) *Holy Feast and Holy Fast: The Religious Significance of Food to Medieval Women*, Berkeley: University of California Press.

Carr, A. E. (1988) *Transforming Grace: Christian Tradition and Women's Experience*, San Francisco: Harper & Row.

Christ, C. P. (1979) 'Why Women Need the Goddess: Phenomenological, Psychological and Political Reflections', in C. P. Christ and J. Plaskow (eds) *Womanspirit Rising: A Feminist Reader in Religion*, San Francisco: Harper & Row.

—— (1980) *Diving Deep and Surfacing: Women Writers on Spiritual Quest*, Boston: Beacon Press.

Code, L., Mullett, S. and Overall, C. (eds) (1988) *Feminist Perspectives: Philosophical Essays on Method and Morals*, Toronto: University of Toronto Press.

Daly, M. (1968) *The Church and the Second Sex*, Boston: Beacon Press. New edition with 'Feminist Postchristian Introduction' and 'New Archaic Afterwords' (1985a).

—— (1985b) *Beyond God the Father: Towards a Philosophy of Women's Liberation*, London: The Women's Press.

Daveney, S. G. (1987) 'The Limits of the Appeal to Women's Experience', in C. W.

Atkinson *et al.* (eds) *Shaping New Vision: Gender and Values in American Culture*, Ann Arbor: NMI Press.

Delmar, R. (1986) 'What is Feminism?', in J. Mitchell and A. Oakley (eds) *What is Feminism?*, Oxford: Basil Blackwell.

Fiorenza, E. S. (1983) *In Memory of Her: A Feminist Theological Reconstruction of Christian Origins*, London: SCM Press.

—— (1984) *Bread not Stone: The Challenge of Feminist Biblical Interpretation*, Boston: Beacon Press.

Foucault, M. (1979) *Discipline and Punish: The Birth of the Prison*, London: Penguin.

—— (1980) *Power/Knowledge: Selected Interviews and Other Writings 1972–1977*, (ed.) C. Gordon, London: Harvester Wheatsheaf.

Gilligan, C. (1982) *In a Different Voice: Psychological Theory and Women's Development*, Cambridge, Mass.: Harvard University Press.

Grey, M. (1991) 'Claiming Power-in-Relation: Exploring the Ethics of Connection', in *Journal of Feminist Studies in Religion*, 7(1): 7–18.

—— (1993) *The Wisdom of Fools*, London: SPCK.

Grosz, E. (1989) *Sexual Subversions: Three French Feminists*, London: Allen & Unwin.

Hampson, D. (1990) *Theology and Feminism*, Oxford: Basil Blackwell.

Harding, S. (1986) *The Science Question in Feminism*, Ithaca: Cornell University Press.

—— (1991) *Whose Science? Whose Knowledge?: Thinking From Women's Lives*, Ithaca: Cornell University Press.

Harrison, B. W. (1985) *Making the Connections: Essays in Feminist Social Ethics*, Boston: Beacon Press.

Hartsock, N. (1985) *Money, Sex and Power: Toward a Feminist Historical Materialism*, Boston: Northeastern University Press.

Heyward, C. (1989) *Touching Our Strength: The Erotic as Power and the Love of God*, San Francisco: Harper & Row.

Hunt, M. (1991) *Fierce Tenderness: A Feminist Theology of Friendship*, New York: Crossroad.

Hunter, A. M. (1992) 'Numbering the Hairs of Our Heads: Male Social Control and the All-Seeing Male God', in *Journal of Feminist Studies in Religion*, 8(2): 7–26.

Irigaray, L. (1985) *This Sex Which Is Not One*, Ithaca: Cornell University Press.

—— (1993) *je, tu, nous: Toward a Culture of Difference*, London: Routledge.

Jantzen, G. M. (1984) *God's World, God's Body*, London: Darton, Longman and Todd.

—— (1987) *Julian of Norwich: Mystic and Theologian*, London: SPCK.

—— (1992) 'Connection or Competition: Personhood and Identity in Feminist Ethics', in *Studies in Christian Ethics*, 5(1).

—— (1993) *Journal of Feminist Studies in Religion*, 9(1, 2).

Keller, C. (1989) 'Feminism and the Ethic of Inseparability' in J. Plaskow and C. P. Christ, *Weaving the Visions: New Patterns in Femininist Spirituality*, San Francisco: Harper & Row, 256–65.

Kittay, E. F. and Meyers, D. T. (eds) (1987) *Women and Moral Theory*, Savage, Md: Rowan and Littlefield.

Lunn, P. (1993) 'Do Women Need the GODDESS?', in *Feminist Theology* 4: 17–38.

McFague, S. (1982) *Metaphorical Theology: Models of God in Religious Language*, London: SCM Press.

—— (1987) *Models of God: Theology for an Ecological, Nuclear Age*, Philadelphia: Fortress.

—— (1993) *The Body of God: An Ecological Theology*, London: SCM Press.

Miles, M. (1989) *Carnal Knowing: Female Nakedness and Religious Meaning in the Christian West*, Boston: Beacon Press.

507

Mill, H. T. and Mill, J. S. (1983) *The Subjection of Women and the Enfranchisement of Women*, London: Virago.

Noddings, N. (1984) *Caring: A Feminine Approach to Ethics and Moral Education*, Berkeley: University of California Press.

Okin, S. M. (1989) *Justice, Gender and the Family*, New York: HarperCollins.

Ruether, R. R. (1983) *Sexism and God-Talk*, London: SCM Press.

Saiving, V. (1979) 'The Human Situation: A Feminine View', in C. P. Christ and J. Plaskow (eds) *Womanspirit Rising: A Feminist Reader in Religion*, San Francisco: Harper & Row.

Sands, K. M. (1992) 'Uses of the Thea(o)logian: Sex and Theodicy in Religious Feminism', in *Journal of Feminist Studies in Religion*, 8(1): 7–34.

Sölle, D. (1990a) *The Window of Vulnerability: A Political Spirituality*, Minneapolis: Fortress Press.

—— (1990b) *Thinking About God: An Introduction to Theology*, London: SCM Press.

Soskice, J. (1985) *Metaphor and Religious Language*, Oxford: Clarendon Press.

—— (1992) 'Can a Feminist Call God "Father"?', in T. Elwes (ed.) *Women's Voices: Essays in Contemporary Feminist Theology*, London: Marshall Pickering.

Starhawk (1990) *Truth or Dare*, San Francisco: Harper & Row.

Trible, P. (1978) *God and the Rhetoric of Sexuality*, Philadelphia: Fortress Press.

Welch, S. D. (1990) *A Feminist Ethic of Risk*, Minneapolis: Fortress Press.

Wollstonecraft, M. (1985) *A Vindication of the Rights of Women*, London: Penguin.

See also chapters 17, 18, 22, 47.

IV

SPIRITUALITY

INTRODUCTION

Leslie Houlden

A vastly greater number of persons concern themselves with what is put under the heading of spirituality and religious experience than with the concepts or content of belief, or indeed with the Bible. Many who would be reluctant to give adherence to formal creeds and churches or even to claim much in the way of religious conviction are ready to testify to experience identified as religious, however hard it is to define or account for. Rivalled only by ethics, this is the area in which religious reflection and activity have their most typical and pervasive expression. That expression ranges from inchoate yet often deeply felt private longings to the most meticulously worded and staged public liturgies. What these have in common is the quest for God or for 'the Other', or else (as it may rather be put) the response to the Other's quest for human creatures. Here we encounter the democratic heart of religion. In this sphere people of the whole gamut of intellectual capacity and of the complete social spectrum are brought to a certain equality. In this area too, deep discernment and foolish credulity may be mixed surprisingly at all levels of mental ability or apparent religious professionalism. From the investigative point of view, this is the prime field for the kind of enquiry that falls within the scope of the anthropology of religion and, in part, of the sociology of religion. The focus of this Part, however, is on religious thought, rather than on religion as a human phenomenon; but in this aspect above all, it would be wrong to lose sight of the inarticulate and even irrational hinterland behind its articulate manifestations.

As some of the following chapters point out, the isolation of spirituality or experience for special treatment, and indeed the very use of spirituality as a special term to describe this aspect of religious life and behaviour, would have mystified Christian thinkers over the greater part of the Church's history. All rational thought about God and the elements of Christian belief were part and parcel of the soul's search for the divine, all bound up with the journey of salvation. For what else could be the purpose of life but the attainment of union with God who had stepped into the human arena in Christ for our rescue? To articulate the faith and to engage in the quest were twin aspects of a single enterprise.

Only with the Enlightenment did it become at all commonly thinkable to reflect on God in a spirit of detachment, scepticism and even disbelief – and (more relevant to our present concern) in the context of a life in which prayer and worship played only a formal part or, eventually, no part at all. The non-practising philosopher of religion or even theologian is a modern phenomenon, who would have seemed to earlier periods as unlikely as a tone-deaf musician or a colour-blind artist. There would have been little sense of the virtues, in the quest for truth (now the motivating goal), of dispassionate and uncommitted enquiry.

Even committed Christian theologians, however, often came to share something of this separating off of Christian thought from the intensity of the quest for God. Symbolically, the home of theology, especially in the Protestant West, came to be the increasingly secular university rather than the monastery. There might (or, increasingly, might not) be a context of worship, but that was not, as in the monastery, the *raison d'être* of the institution, the dominant element in life. The study or library, not the chapel, came to be the place where the action was.

Yet, ironically, it is only in relatively recent times that 'spirituality' has become identified as a distinct object of attention for religious thinkers of various kinds and as an academic discipline – a branch of theology as a whole; quite apart from the widespread popular interest it has come to attract. It is possible to see this development as a natural reaction and even protest against the stunting effects of the prevailing secularism. At the academic level, it is perhaps best looked at as one among a number of examples of the separating out of new objects of study – a much-needed breaking of the traditional mould of the academic agenda. Just as, at the popular level, there can in certain cases be something escapist and distorting, even enfeebling, about the isolation of 'spirituality', with its apparatus of withdrawal from life, from other aspects of Christian thought and activity, so its separation as a discipline of enquiry may have disadvantages. It may, for example, lead to the avoiding of the bracing challenges posed by philosophy of religion, ethics and biblical studies, and may lack something of the rigour of its near neighbour, systematic theology.

All that assumes, of course, that it is impossible to put the clock back – to restore a sense of theology as a unified quest, mustering all resources as appropriate for a single agreed enterprise, to seek that which may now be expressed as the divine mystery. Few people of sensitivity would, after all, deny the ineradicable and enriching character of this 'questing' tendency of the human spirit, whether it be seen as directed inwards, to the depths of the self, or outwards, towards God, however described. Not one unified enterprise surely, however: but perhaps many unified enterprises, with individuals and groups arriving at their own syntheses of theological thought centred on a purpose that transcends the supposed neutrality of the secular and does justice to the totality of human aspiration – that is a way in which spirituality might achieve a stabilizing and focusing role. But, given the present global context of religion as of all else, there is bound to be much diversity, much syncretism, much (in traditional Christian terms) indiscipline and even anarchy. Spirituality as an academic subject will not lack scope for analysing, ordering and assessing a mass of astonishingly diverse phenomena.

The chapters that follow examine Christian spirituality and experience in a number of different ways. They spell out and exemplify matters that have been adumbrated in this introduction. In the first, Philip Sheldrake gives a magisterial overview of the state and character of this aspect of theological enquiry. He draws a strong picture of its width of concern and its potential to give a unifying and practical perspective to theological thought.

The next four chapters are historical. Dealing with some of the major periods of Christian history, they demonstrate the many different styles of language and practice and the different aspirations that have marked Christian life down the centuries. The selected periods are the patristic, where both Eastern and Western Christianity are involved; the medieval West, with its (at least in retrospect) highly integrated world-view; the time of reform, both in the new Protestant sphere and in Catholicism; and the last two centuries, where the wide range of thought, both in the Churches and more under the shadow of the Enlightenment, is amply demonstrated. All these chapters should be read alongside those on the tradition of theology in Part II which they complement and with which, to a degree, they inevitably overlap.

William J. Wainwright's chapter reaches out in the philosophical direction. Moving beyond the narrowly Christian sphere, it discusses the language of religious experience and mysticism, analysing its use and validity.

In some circles in both past and present, spirituality has lived up to the implied rejection, seemingly present in the word itself, of the material context of life in this world. But alongside this world-fleeing tendency and, it may be held, truer to Christianity's foundations in the Incarnation, the thorough involvement of the divine within the world, there is also a persistent tradition of a spirituality that lives in the light of that involvement and seeks to extend it. Here the bond with Christian ethics is at its strongest. The twists and turns of this tradition, down to its modern flowering, notably in liberation theology, are set out by Kenneth Leech.

Finally, Christian spirituality has never been solely concerned with 'what a man does with his solitude'. Again, the essentially corporate and social character of Christian belief from its beginnings, with Christ seen as the inaugurator of a new, or renewed, people, together with the continuous experience of corporate worship, have meant that this side of the divine quest has in practice been dominant, even though it is the more personal side that comes out chiefly in the literary tradition of Christian spirituality. In the final chapter, Gordon Wakefield explores some aspects from Christian history of the liturgical expression of Christian spirituality and experience, in which individuals of many kinds have found common ground and the means of their nourishment.

25

SPIRITUALITY AND THEOLOGY

Philip Sheldrake

'Spirituality' is a word that is commonly used yet difficult to define. Theologians sometimes level the criticism that spirituality as a discipline claims unlimited resources (for example, historical, theological, philosophical, psychological and anthropological) without having its own methodology. In recent years, attempts have been made to provide a coherent definition and methodology from both a theological and historical standpoint (Kinerk 1981; Principe 1983; Schneiders 1986, 1989; Hanson 1990; Sheldrake 1991). As a result, spirituality has emerged as an interdisciplinary subject that is concerned with the specifically 'spiritual' dimension of human existence.

As we shall see, there have been attempts to define 'spirituality' generically by transcending the assumptions of specific religious traditions. However, opinions differ concerning this process. In Christian terms, 'spirituality' relates to how people subjectively appropriate traditional beliefs about God, the human person, creation, and their inter-relationship, and then express these in worship, basic values and life-style. Thus, spirituality is the whole of human life viewed in terms of a conscious relationship with God, in Jesus Christ, through the indwelling of the Spirit and within the community of believers. As an area of study, 'spirituality' examines this dimension of human existence from historical, phenomenological and theological standpoints.

The word 'spirituality' has a relatively short pedigree and was confined, until recently, to Roman Catholic and Anglican circles. What it seeks to describe has changed shape over the centuries, whether subtly or substantially, as understandings of God, Church and human person have evolved in different contexts. Most significantly, in recent decades there has been a paradigm shift in theological method which has had a major effect on how spirituality is understood. Previously, theology was predominantly analytical, logical, deductive in approach, with a stable body of knowledge, rich in tradition and equipped to answer all questions from an *a priori* standpoint. Approaches to the 'spiritual life' were similarly structured and separated from concrete human experience.

Greater reflection on human experience as an authentic *locus theologicus* has facilitated a movement away from static understandings of the Christian life. At the same time that theological thinking has moved towards a more inductive, experiential method, 'spirituality' has become more of a dialectical tension. On the one hand, there is the concreteness of revelation in Jesus Christ and subsequent tradition and, on the other, the appropriation of the Gospel by each person within specific historical and cultural circumstances. Spirituality operates on the frontier between experience and tradition and does not subordinate the former unquestioningly to the latter. Consequently, the realization has emerged that spiritual traditions are embodied initially in people rather than doctrine and begin with experiences rather than abstract ideas (Sudbrack 1975). The problem of defining 'spirituality' in recent years arises in part because it is no longer a single, transcultural phenomenon but is rooted in experiences of God that are framed by the always specific, and therefore contingent, histories of individuals and communities.

HISTORICAL DEVELOPMENTS

History of the term 'Spirituality'

'Spirituality' has become the standard word for the theory and practice of 'life in the Spirit', or of discipleship. However, in its present sense, the word has a relatively short history. *The Catholic Encyclopedia*, published before the First World War, contained no references to 'spirituality' while *The New Catholic Encyclopedia*, published in the 1970s, contained eight articles on different aspects of the subject. Standard reference works such as *The Oxford Dictionary* and *Websters International Dictionary* offer only one definition out of six that corresponds to spirituality as a religious area of study. This, however, supports a dualistic contrast between concern for 'things of the spirit' and material interests.

'Spirituality' derives from the Latin *spiritualitas* which corresponds to the Greek *pneuma*, 'spirit', and its adjective *pneumatikos* as they appear in the Pauline Epistles (for example, 1 Cor. 2:10f. and 12:13). At the risk of simplification, a spiritual–material dichotomy is not implied here because 'spirit' does not contrast with 'matter' or 'physical body' (*sōma*, in Latin *corpus*) but rather with anything that is opposed to the Spirit of God (*sarx*, in Latin *caro*). The 'spiritual' is what expresses the Spirit of God. A spiritual person (1 Cor. 2:14, 15) is simply someone in whom the Spirit of God dwells (Deidun 1988).

In the West, this emphasis predominated until the twelfth century. At this point, the development of philosophical theology, known as scholasticism, led to a sharper distinction between spirit and matter. This was partly because 'spiritual' came to be applied only to intelligent creatures (humankind) as opposed to non-rational creation (everything else). The Pauline moral sense of 'spiritual' gradually gave way to one more radically opposed to corporeality. Although the theoreticians and practitioners of Christian asceticism had always been ambivalent in their attitudes to bodiliness, the intellectual basis for an unhealthy disdain for the body undoubtedly received a further impulse at this point. However, the two senses of 'spiritual' continued to stand side by side in the writings of someone like Thomas Aquinas.

In fact, the theological use of the word declined during the remainder of the Middle Ages and only re-emerged in seventeenth-century France. It sometimes referred simply to affective relationships with God but was often used pejoratively of enthusiastic or quietistic movements. Voltaire used the word in his angry rejection of the over-refined 'salon mysticism' that became popular in upper-class circles. During the seventeenth and eighteenth centuries a variety of words was used for Christian living. 'Devotion' was preferred by Francis de Sales and the Anglican mystic William Law, 'perfection' by John Wesley and the early Methodists and 'piety' among early Evangelicals. The use of the word 'spirituality' declined in reaction to its unorthodox associations and by the nineteenth century was confined to groups outside the mainline Churches.

The word reappeared in France at the beginning of the twentieth century and thence passed into English. It found favour particularly with those theologians and historians who sought a comprehensive term for the Christian life as opposed to those who believed in a radical distinction between ascetical theology (concerning the life of 'ordinary' Christians) and mystical theology (concerning 'extraordinary' people and experiences). The still continuing *Dictionnaire de Spiritualité* (1932 onwards) was highly influential in establishing the respectability of the word. Since the Second Vatican Council, 'spirituality' has established itself across an increasingly ecumenical spectrum (see Principe 1983: 130–5; Sheldrake 1991: 34–6).

'Spirituality' as a subject for reflection

Theology was a unified enterprise from the patristic period of the early Church until the development of the 'new theology' of scholasticism in the West from the twelfth century onwards. Thomas Aquinas divided his *Summa Theologiae* into various component parts which in some senses heralded a slow process of division which would climax in the development of different theological 'disciplines' centuries later. However, patristic theology was not a purely abstract discipline separated from pastoral theory and practice. The unifying feature was the Bible. Thus, theology was a process of interpreting Scripture on different levels with the aim of deepening the Christian life in all its dimensions. This approach encapsulated a synthesis of biblical exegesis, speculative reasoning and mystical contemplation. Doctrinal theology, as well as arising from this biblical base, attempted to provide precise language to incarnate what was essentially a mystical apprehension of God who is revealed in Christ and as the Spirit within every Christian. Early theologians did not write about 'spirituality' or 'mystical theology' as distinct areas of knowledge. Rather the very heart of patristic theology was mystical.

Patristic 'mysticism' is not to be confused with later Western interest in subjective religious experience or in detailed itineraries for the spiritual journey. Rather, it is the life of every baptized Christian who knows God, revealed in Jesus Christ, through belonging to the 'fellowship of the mystery', supported by Scripture and liturgy. In the sixth century this insight fused with neo-Platonic elements in the writings of a theologian, Pseudo-Dionysius, to produce a more explicit 'mystical theology'. Although, to some degree, Pseudo-Dionysius pointed towards the later medieval development of mystical theory he essentially summarized patristic approaches (Bouyer 1981; Rorem 1986).

The Eastern Orthodox, unlike the Western tradition, continued to follow the patristic model of a 'mystical theology' that synthesized ethics, spirituality and doctrine. The classic treatment by Vladimir Lossky defines Orthodox theology as a spirituality that expresses a doctrinal attitude. Theology is inseparable from contemplation and is 'mystical' in that its overall aim is to show forth the divine mystery. True theologians are those who experience the content of their theology. On the other hand, mystical experiences, while personal, are nevertheless the working out in an individual of a faith that is common to all (Lossky 1973).

In the West, the patristic–monastic style of theology drew its inspiration and method from the traditional meditative reading of Scripture, or *lectio divina*. Considerations of what might be called 'spiritual' theology appeared simply as collections of homilies or scriptural commentaries. Apart from this, there were some writings specifically associated with the way to God appropriate to monastic life. Studies of prayer and asceticism, therefore, took for granted a context of separation from everyday life (Leclercq 1978: 1–9, 111–38, 233–86).

In contrast, the new theological method of the schools, with a more 'scientific' approach based on the increased availability of ancient Greek philosophy, led writing on the spiritual life to take new directions. First, there was a slow but inexorable separation of 'spiritual' theory from the rest of theology. Even Thomas Aquinas, the great thirteenth-century Dominican, who tried to maintain the unity between contemplation and theological speculation, knowledge and love, divided his *Summa theologiae* into distinct parts. In doing so he contributed to the classical divisions within theology, for example, between doctrine and ethics. Second, there was a recovery of interest in the mystical theology of Pseudo-Dionysius. These two factors combined in the writings of the Victorine school of theology based on the monastery of St Victor in Paris. The two great writers, Hugh and Richard of St Victor, exercised a major influence on the development of a distinct spiritual theology.

Third, there was a new interest in subjective, particularly affective, mystical

517

experience, and the birth of an associated literature. This had several sources, including a new sensibility born of the 'Renaissance' of the twelfth century. The theme of love, secular and religious, was cultivated to a heightened degree. Also, with qualification, there was an increased awareness of the inner human landscape, if not precisely of the modern concept of the individual 'self'. Affective mysticism and attention to the individual encouraged an interest in spiritual guidance which in turn generated treatises by spiritual directors for those under their guidance. *The Cloud of Unknowing*, the fourteenth-century English mystical text, is a well-known example (Bynum 1982: 82–109).

Finally, the growth of a body of knowledge associated with asceticism, contemplation and mysticism led to the gradual systematization of meditative techniques. While the meditations of, for example, St Anselm in the eleventh century were still associated with unsystematic, prayerful reading of Scripture, the treatises of the fourteenth- and fifteenth-century movement known as the *devotio moderna* discussed methods of prayer and structured them into regular exercises. This tradition of methodical prayer gave rise to a considerable literature over the next few centuries.

In summary, the High Middle Ages in the West were characterized by divisions within theology and the gradual separation of 'spirituality' from theology as a whole. This division went deeper than method or content. It was, at heart, a division between affectivity and conceptual knowledge. Further, within 'spirituality' a concentration on subjectivity and interiority led to its separation from public liturgy and from ethics. By the end of the Middle Ages, the 'spiritual life' had increasingly moved to the margins of theology and culture as a whole. Although late medieval religion was not completely individualistic (the growth of lay confraternities is evidence of the importance of collective experience), there is no doubt that religious practice became more personal and internalized. It also began to demand a new specialized language, distinct from theological discourse as a whole, capable of expressing its separate existence (Dupré and Saliers 1989: xiii–xix; Sheldrake 1991: 40–4).

Although immediately post-Reformation writers such as Teresa of Avila, Ignatius Loyola or Francis de Sales did not yet possess the terminology of 'ascetical' or 'mystical' theology there was a suggestion of distinctive knowledge concerning the 'spiritual life'. It was not, however, until the eighteenth century that the terms 'ascetical theology' (Christian life up to the beginnings of contemplation) and 'mystical theology' (from contemplation to mystical union) came into being.

During the period of the Enlightenment the growth of scientific enquiry as a way to truth and certainty aggravated the split between 'spirituality' and theology. To theologians, spirituality became an object of suspicion. It was unrealistic because it was associated with theologically dubious devotion and was of optional interest because it seemed to relate only to a certain cast of mind. The value of abstract intelligence was overestimated and, consequently, the experiential was to be questioned throughout the analytical journey towards the provable which became the point of intellectual endeavour. The notion that theology was a science united with a sense that science could generate value-free knowledge. This pointed theology towards isolation from context or personal feeling (Louth 1983: chapters 1 and 6).

During the next hundred and fifty years a vocabulary of Christian life and prayer stabilized and a field of study defined as 'spiritual theology' was established. There were, of course, Anglican and Protestant mystical writers who, particularly in seventeenth-century Anglicanism, produced works of spiritual guidance or meditation. However, until the modern era, there was not the same systematic approach as in Roman Catholicism but, rather, some antagonism to it (Leech 1977: chapter 3; Moorman 1983).

Numerous manuals of ascetical and mystical theology appeared in Roman Catholic circles from the nineteenth century until the Second Vatican Council. The overall approach was one of precise categories and definitions. The theology was static and the method deductive despite the experiential subject matter. Divine revelation and rational knowledge were the major sources because universal principles necessarily governed a 'scientific' study of the spiritual life. A. A. Tanquerey and R. Garrigou-Lagrange may be taken as representatives of two contrasting views with regard to whether the spiritual life was fundamentally a unity or not (Tanquerey 1930; Garrigou-Lagrange 1937). Tanquerey believed that there was an essential distinction between ordinary moral life and 'extraordinary' mysticism. In contrast, Garrigou-Lagrange emphasized continuity and that mystical prayer was a goal to which all were called. Immediately prior to Vatican II, writers such as Louis Bouyer moved away from the style of the older manuals. Although now dated, his work espoused a more scriptural, liturgical and even ecumenical approach (Bouyer 1961).

THE DEVELOPMENT OF CONTEMPORARY SPIRITUALITY

From 'Spiritual theology' to 'Spirituality'

In recent decades a major shift has taken place in Western theology. The move has been from a more deductive, transcultural theology towards serious reflection on experience of God in its cultural particularity and pluriformity. In harmony with this shift, and partly provoked by it, understandings of the Christian life have also changed. 'Spiritual theology' has given way to a more dynamic and inclusive concept, 'spirituality'. The result is that the separations noted at the end of the medieval period and reinforced by post-Enlightenment emphases, have begun to break down. First, 'spirituality' is an inclusive term that is not limited to elites such as monastic celibates. 'Spirituality' has broadened beyond attention to a limited range of phenomena, for example mysticism, to include the values and life-styles of all Christians. 'Spirituality' has gained considerable ecumenical acceptance and so studies of spirituality tend to draw upon the riches of a shared Christian heritage rather than to limit themselves to sectarian understandings of 'life in the Spirit'. The term has also found favour in inter-faith dialogue and is no longer limited to Christian experience. More contentiously, 'spirituality' has been used to describe the deepest values of people professing no coherent religious belief system (Schneiders 1986: 253–74; 1989: 687–97; Van Ness 1992: 68–79).

Second, spirituality has become more closely associated with theology and biblical exegesis than it has been over the last few hundred years (Bechtle 1985). A number of major theologians and theological 'schools' once again take experience seriously as a subject for reflection. This has been associated with a renewed theology of grace and of the human person. In some cases, reflection on experience, and the question of the relationship between experience and tradition, have become the heart of theological method. One specific area where there is a fruitful dialogue is the interrelationship between spirituality and moral theology (O'Donohoe 1987). Moral theology has moved away from a concern primarily with the quality of actions to a greater interest in people's dispositions of character. There has been a shift from human actions to the human agent and an increasing awareness of the basic unity between the moral and the spiritual life. A number of writers have suggested that the joint task of contemporary spirituality and moral theology is to explore renewed understandings of 'virtue' (that is, what enables a person to become truly human within a commitment to Christ and aided by the action of grace) and 'character' (or what we should be, rather than do, if we are to become fully human persons).

Third, spirituality is not so much concerned with defining 'perfection' in the abstract as with surveying the complex mystery of human growth in the context of dynamic relationships with God. Equally, spirituality is not limited to interiority but seeks to integrate all aspects of human experience. Clearly this affects its actual definition. The broader the compass, the greater the problem of coherence and the danger of subsuming spirituality into 'religion in general'. Thus, 'the spiritual life is the life of the whole person directed towards God' (Leech 1977: 34). The British theologian Rowan Williams rejects an understanding of spirituality as the science of 'spiritual' and private experience: 'it must now touch every area of human experience, the public and social, the painful, negative, even pathological byways of the mind, the moral and relational world' (Williams 1979: 2). Contemporary theorists accept that definition becomes more complex once we cease to separate the spiritual dimension of human existence from materiality. Whatever the problems, contemporary spirituality as an area of reflection attempts to integrate religious and human values rather than to concentrate exclusively on such matters as stages of prayer.

For some people, the contemporary emphasis on experience as the starting point for spirituality is associated with an attempt to define it in generic terms, that is, 'spirituality as such'. In practice, spiritualities are specific and have particular doctrinal referents. This is what makes it possible to sift the authentic from the unauthentic in spirituality (Principe 1992: 56–60). Every religious tradition has tests for the authenticity of spiritual experience based not only on broadly human considerations but also on the foundational beliefs of the tradition. Generic definitions of spirituality are problematic because spiritualities are always conditioned by context and embody the language of a tradition, its themes and symbols.

The emphasis on experience in contemporary spirituality does not in fact exclude specific reference to tradition. Even if there is some common ground between different faith traditions (e.g. Christianity and Hinduism) regarding the meaning of 'spirituality', that is, the development of our capacity for self-transcendence in relation to the Absolute, nevertheless Christian spirituality is increasingly related to explicitly theological themes. While spirituality, in Christian terms, concerns not some other life but simply human life at depth, our understanding of what this means arises from what Christian revelation and tradition suggest about God, human nature and the relationship between the two. Christian spirituality derives its specific characteristics from a fundamental belief that human beings are capable of entering into relationship with a God who is transcendent yet dwelling in all created reality. Further, this relationship is lived out within a community of believers that is brought into being by commitment to Christ and is sustained by the active presence of the Spirit of God. Put in specific terms, Christian spirituality exists in a framework that is Trinitarian, pneumatological and ecclesial.

Spiritual experience is not 'naked' in the sense of being free from values and assumptions drawn from faith traditions. Nor is it entirely private but exists within systems of religious discourse or behaviour – even if these, in some cases, are implicit rather than expressed in public membership of some faith community. This seems to indicate that members of different faith traditions do not simply *describe* their spiritual experiences differently but actually *have* different experiences in significant ways (Lindbeck 1984: 30–45).

Theologians and religious experience

A number of significant theologians or theological traditions in recent decades have explored the reintegration of spirituality with theology by focusing attention on religious experience. Among these have been the Roman Catholic theologians Bernard Lonergan and Karl Rahner, liberation theology and feminist theology.

The Canadian philosophical theologian, Bernard Lonergan, directed a great deal of his attention to theological method. His 'transcendental method' explored religious experience, and particularly conversion, as the heart of theological enquiry. There is a movement within human consciousness from attention to experience, to understanding what has been experienced, to judgement in the light of understanding, to final choice or decision in terms of what has been understood. In other words, human intentionality moves from desire to knowledge to action in a process that involves personal consciousness being drawn towards the Ultimate, Love, God (Lonergan 1972: 6–20, 101–24, 235–66).

Perhaps more than any other theologian, Karl Rahner has made acceptable the language of 'openness to mystery' and 'self-transcendence', both of which concepts had long been familiar to students of spirituality. The mystery, of course, is God in whom is our origin, within whom we live and towards whom we are drawn in a movement of self-transcendence. Rather than starting with God, Rahner begins his theological enquiry with our shared human experience. There is a kind of knowledge that is acquired by being in existence. This is 'experiential knowledge'. As social beings, this knowledge reaches the level of reflection and communication in us. An aspect of this existence and experience of it is a sense of responsibility and of freedom to choose. To this extent we exist 'beyond' the world and its causes and in this sense transcend it. The questions that arise, therefore, are: where do we come from (if not solely from the world) and where is our transcendence leading us (if the world cannot define our limits)? It is this ultimate questioning (or transcendental experience), confronting us at every turn, that Rahner reflects upon as a starting point for speaking of God (Rahner 1966: 3–22; 1971: 25–46; 1974: 68–114; 1984, passim).

In the case of liberation theology, the method involved is not simply inductive rather than deductive – that is, reflection on human experience in a general sense. It is reflection on the quite specific daily experiences of Christian communities in Latin America, Asia and elsewhere that exist in conditions of massive poverty, human suffering and oppression. It is also reflection on the experience of a people, a collective experience rather than that of isolated individuals. In this tradition, theology and spirituality are essentially intertwined from the start and at all points. There is, therefore, no question of bridging a gap or of bringing two discrete disciplines together. As Gustavo Gutiérrez suggests, 'the kind of reflection that the theology of liberation represents is conscious of the fact that it was, and continues to be, preceded by the spiritual experience of Christians who are committed to the process of liberation' (Gutiérrez 1984: 1). Note, it is a spiritual experience, not merely a socio-political one, that is reflected upon. Equally, it is the case that valid theology is *lived* (orthopraxis) and so the actual following of Jesus Christ in concrete circumstances, not merely reflection on 'discipleship', is an essential theological 'moment' (ibid.: 35–71).

Feminist theology also suggests a profound integration of experience and reflection. 'As the experience of God's salvation in Christ and the response of individuals and groups to that salvation, spirituality can be understood as the source of both theology and morality' (Carr 1990: 202). Again, this is dialectical because theology and morality also work upon spirituality in that they may criticize and transform what is often an unconscious pattern of convictions and behaviour in relation to God. While generalization is hazardous, it seems that much feminist theology seeks to move theological anthropology away from a dual-nature position to a single-nature one (ibid.: 117–33). While there are observable differences between the sexes regarding styles of understanding and relating to self, others and God, these result from the power of historical conditioning (ibid.: 204–6). Thus, it is argued, feminist theology and spirituality are not essentially reflections upon distinctively female ways of relating to God in contrast to male. That is more appropriately termed 'women's spirituality'. By contrast, feminist spirituality has specifically integrated a critique of patriarchal tradition and lives out of this consciousness (ibid.: 206–14).

In such contemporary theological approaches, a disjunction between the God who evokes a feeling response and the God of systematic theology is undermined. Older styles of theology, affected by limited understandings of 'scientific' truth and which set great store on objective, value-free knowledge, as well as on the overwhelming importance of coherent systems, always had problems with spirituality. Personal experience was rejected as having no place in the essentially rational and logical compendium of faith. Today, the frontiers of theology are more likely to seek articulation in a method and process that is experiential.

THE INTERFACE OF SPIRITUALITY AND THEOLOGY

In the contemporary search for renewed connections between spirituality and theology, three areas stand out as follows:

1 Theological criteria for evaluating religious experience.
2 The relevance of hermeneutics to the interpretation of spiritual classics.
3 Different typologies for classifying spiritual traditions.

1 Criteria for evaluating spiritualities

Spirituality as an area of study obviously needs tools both to analyse and to evaluate different traditions, their texts and other modes of self-communication. Given the plurality of contemporary approaches to spirituality, and the apparent novelty of some of them, the question of criteria for assessing what is authentically Christian takes on greater importance. These criteria will be based on central theological principles developed within the faith community. The process will involve addressing questions to spiritualities in order to discern theological dimensions that are often only implicit.

A number of contemporary theologians, both Roman Catholic and Protestant, have responded to the increasing appeal to experience in theology by developing criteria for evaluating religious experience. These criteria are also useful in terms of evaluating different approaches to spirituality. Theologians commonly approach the question on two levels. Prior to an examination of criteria drawn specifically from the Christian tradition, such theologians as Schubert Ogden and David Tracy agree that it is important to show that religious experience meets the basic demands of modern 'secular' knowledge and life. This is in terms of what have been called 'criteria of adequacy'. A further level consists of questions of faithfulness to a specifically Christian understanding of existence, termed 'criteria of appropriateness'. The contemporary work of David Tracy may be taken as a typical example.

The application of criteria of adequacy should not be interpreted as a reduction of Christian theology and spirituality to non-religious norms. What it implies is that neither spirituality nor theology can be innocent of generally accepted developments in human knowledge nor of the ways in which previously over-confident views of human progress have been undermined by recent, painful historical events. To put it simply, we have to take into account the new worlds opened up by cosmology, evolutionary theory, psychology and the social and political sciences. Equally, theology and spirituality can never be the same again after the Holocaust and Hiroshima.

Tracy suggests three broad criteria of adequacy. First, is a particular religious interpretation of experience meaningful? That is, is it adequately rooted in common human experience and related to our lived experience of the self? Put another way, what aspect of ordinary human experience, shared by many or all, is expressed here? And does it relate to reality as commonly understood? Second, is the specifically religious understanding of experience coherent? Any spirituality makes some cognitive claims in that it seeks to reveal meaning. Can these claims be expressed conceptually in a coherent way? Do they also fit with the generally accepted claims of scientific knowledge? Third, does the spiritual tradition throw light on the underlying conditions that make existence possible? Does it have anything to say about our human confidence in life being worthwhile? Does it affirm that 'the good' will have the last word? Does it confirm the underlying conditions for the possibility of existence in the human world? (Tracy 1975: 64–71; see also Ogden 1963: 122, 190–2).

While David Tracy argues the need for criteria of appropriateness (Tracy 1975: 72–9), other theologians such as Dermot Lane and Walter Principe provide useful summaries of what these might be. In general terms, does a spirituality relate us to a God worthy of our complete loving involvement? Does it effect genuine conversion? Does a spirituality offer 'special' or individualistic experience or does it offer a connection to a wider community of experience? This latter criterion seems particularly important in a world where new religious movements sometimes appear to offer experience detached from commitment or open only to special initiates (Lane 1985: 26).

More specifically Christian criteria would be as follows. Is a spirituality consonant with a Trinitarian God who is engaged with the human condition and with a belief in Incarnation and all that this implies? Does it, for example, recognize the priority of God's grace and Jesus' saving work over human effort? Is the view of God adequately personal or is it deist? On the other hand, is it adequately transcendent and 'other' rather than excessively anthropomorphic or pantheistic? Does the spirituality suggest a graced world or a world radically alienated from God? Is there an adequate view of creation as God's outpouring into the cosmos? In general, what theology of grace is implied in a given spirituality? Does a spirituality lead to choice or commitment inspired by the vision and teachings of Jesus Christ? Within the limits of legitimate diversity and of valid emphases, is it sufficiently 'catholic' in the sense of inclusive of the *whole* Gospel rather than selective, exclusive or unbalanced? On the other hand, is it excessively Christocentric by neglecting the role of the Spirit or, indeed, of a transcendent God to whom the teachings of Jesus point? Is the nature of the conversion described and offered related to the dynamics of the death and resurrection of Jesus Christ? Does it not only have an individual dimension but also a social dimension in line with Jesus' teachings about the demands of the kingdom of God? How is the goal of the Christian life viewed? What models of holiness are presented?

What theological anthropology is present in a spirituality? Is the view of human nature excessively materialistic or is it, on the contrary, dualistic with a low theology of the human body and a detached theology of 'the spiritual dimension' of human life? How are human emotions judged? Is sufficient role given to imagination as opposed to an exclusive emphasis on intellect and will? What is the understanding of sin? How is suffering viewed? How is human work viewed? Is there a balanced and healthy evaluation of sexuality?

What understanding of prayer and contemplation is presented? Is its approach to mysticism elitist? Does it view Christian life essentially as one, in a common baptism, or does it tend to perpetuate a hierarchy of life-styles? Is there a balance between contemplation and action?

Does the spirituality, however radical and prophetic, exist in some kind of continuity with the experience of the Christian community across time and place? What is the role of Scripture and tradition? Is it peripheral and accidental or, on the other hand, is the approach fundamentalist? Is the spirituality excessively individualistic or does it relate to communal activity and worship? Does it manifest a balanced approach to authority? Is a spirituality compatible with the hierarchy of truths and values that exists within Christianity? For example, does a spirituality focus on a specific devotion or traditional activity to such an extent that it becomes unbalanced or reduced to antiquarianism?

Finally, does the spirituality have an eschatology and specifically one that encourages an appropriate balance between 'the now' and 'the not yet'? Does a spirituality allow a proper place for the value of human history? What is its understanding of the virtue of hope? (Lane 1985: 27; Principe 1992: 58–60).

When questions of evaluation of theologies and spiritualities are discussed nowadays, the critique offered of traditional approaches by, for example, liberation theology and feminist theory demands a 'hermeneutic of suspicion'. That is to say that questions provoked by contemporary values and understanding will be more critical than hitherto of the theological and social assumptions behind spiritualities. There is a greater awareness of their conditioning and of the need to expose hidden ideologies. Spirituality has, like theology as a whole, tended to marginalize certain groups whether they are women or members of cultures other than the dominant Eurocentric or North Atlantic ones.

Consequently, there may be a number of additional questions that are especially appropriate today. In general, are spiritualities open to the experience of 'the other', whoever that may be? Are they informed by human sciences that open us up to the widest possible spectrum of reality? Are spiritualities aware of the need for indigenization or are they more or less uncritical of their own cultural conditioning and consequent limitations? There may be some more specific questions. Does a given spirituality bear noticeable marks of patriarchy, unrestricted capitalism, racism, colonialism or individualism? Does it emphasize not merely charity but also social justice? Is it oppressive to any group of people and, if so, does this undermine its central values? Does it respect the dignity and rights of the human person? Does it foster maturity or immature dependence?

2 Spiritual classics and hermeneutics

The complexity of historical and textual interpretation in reference to spiritual classics has received increasing attention in recent years. Previously, histories of spirituality tended to present and analyse spiritual traditions in relative isolation from their wider social and historical contexts and paid scant attention to the contingency of their theological assumptions. Classical spiritual texts were treated as though their perspective and language raised no major problems. There was an assumption that the meaning of a text consisted of the literal sense of the words and the intentions of the author.

The adoption of the phrase 'signs of the times' by the documents of the Second Vatican Council in the early 1960s, and the suggestion that Christians must pay proper attention to those signs, were an important indicator of a major theological shift that was taking place more broadly. History was no longer incidental to redemption. Faith was not opposed to history. No separation is possible between religious history and the world which this history unfolds (Ruggieri 1987: 95–104). A consequence for the study of spiritual traditions is that they must be seen as existing within the limitations of history. Their origins and development reflect the circumstances of time and place and the mental horizons of the people involved. For example, the emphasis on radical poverty in the spirituality of the thirteenth-century mendicant movement was both a spiritual and social reaction to the conditions of Church and society at the time. This does not imply that spiritualities, and the texts that arise from them, have no value beyond original contexts. However, in order to appreciate the riches of a spiritual classic we need to take context seriously and to adopt a critical rather than naive approach to their interpretation.

Hermeneutics, the science of interpretation, has long been at the centre of the debate about how Christians are to read the Scriptures. This is because such texts are intimately bound up with Christian identity and experience and are accorded the status of 'revelation'. However, the insights of contemporary hermeneutics have become increasingly important when the interpretation of spiritual texts is addressed. This is because certain texts have been accorded a kind of normative status in some Christian circles, e.g. the Rule of St Benedict in monastic communities or *The Spiritual Exercises* of Ignatius Loyola among many retreat-givers.

While all spiritual texts are historically conditioned, some move beyond the time and place of origin and become significant influences in new contexts. These are what we may call 'classics'. In other words, they continue to disclose something that is compelling, challenging and transformative in terms of what is perceived as central to the Christian experience. Some people have consequently described such texts as 'wisdom documents'. The literary genre of such texts is often related to their continued success. Usually they are pastoral rather than purely technical, stimulate the imagination in different ways and have the capacity to persuade and move the reader to a response that is affective as well as intellectual (see Tracy 1981: ch. 3).

Because we live in a historically conscious age, we are inevitably aware of different perspectives when we read classical texts. If interpretation is not purely for antiquarian purposes, the question arises as to how far to respect a text's conceptual framework, structure and dynamic in relationship to contemporary Christian living. Certain answers would be naive. On the one hand, it is possible to ignore the author's intention and the text's inner structure and to use it, or elements of it, simply as it suits us. On the other hand, it is possible to assume that the author's intention alone is normative, assuming that this can be reconstructed. In the first case we subordinate the horizons of the text to present need and in the latter case we subordinate present horizons to the past. Both approaches assume that to arrive at the relevant 'meaning' of a text is relatively simple. In contrast, a more sophisticated and also more fruitful approach to interpretation would involve a receptive yet critical dialogue with the text. This enables its own wisdom to challenge the contemporary reader and yet accords a proper place to present-day questions.

In the dialogue between the horizons of a text and contemporary questions, the text's historical context is a vital starting point. Spiritual 'classics' usually addressed specific concerns with a specific audience in mind. Modern literary criticism reminds us that even if words in an ancient text initially appear familiar, the assumptions that lie behind the words are different from our own and that, consequently, words change their meaning across time and place in nuanced and even substantial ways. When reading a text it is also important to recall that the moment of its creation and the moment of our reading are not totally disconnected. Between the two moments lie the subsequent history of the text and a tradition of interpretation which affects our own moment of reading.

However, there are limits to the value of historical knowledge in isolation. For example, because texts employ the conventional categories of their age, what we encounter in a text is not direct experience of another time but what a text *claims*. In other words, texts are already *interpretations* of experience rather than merely records of it. Some texts, for example the Long Text of the *Showings* of Julian of Norwich (the fourteenth-century English woman mystic), are explicitly interpretations of experience based on hindsight. However, to acknowledge the interpreted nature of texts does not undermine their value. Indeed, subsequent reflections on experience may be more relevant to those who seek to use a text than the particularity of the original experience alone. For example, the Gospels are creative re-workings of earlier oral and written traditions about Jesus that the Gospel writers allowed to interact with the contexts and needs of their audiences. This creative approach is part of the value of the Gospels for readers in subsequent ages.

There have been developments in hermeneutics in recent years. The conventional approach, inherited from the nineteenth century, had as a basic premise that the values brought to a text by the reader are a problem for a correct interpretation. The new hermeneutics, however, emphasizes that a text has possibilities beyond the original author's conception that may be evoked in a creative way by questions arising from the new religious worlds in which a classic text continually finds itself.

An interpretation of spiritual classics also takes place in the use of texts (for example, *The Spiritual Exercises* of Ignatius Loyola in retreats). For this reason, the example of the performing arts may be helpful in understanding the new hermeneutics. Thus, musicians use a text, the score, which they interpret. A 'good performance' will certainly be true to the score in the sense of accurately reproducing the notes and observing the composer's main instructions. This is because performers cannot do simply anything with Sibelius and still call it his *Seventh Symphony*. However, those of us who have heard 'dead' musical performances will know that a good performance must go beyond mere accuracy. It must also be creative. As with music, so with a classic spiritual text. In this sense, there cannot be a single, true interpretation. Every 'performance' is in some sense a new interpretation (Lash 1986: ch. 3).

Thus, there is a dialogue between a classic text and the reader in which both partners may be challenged. A text may reveal a genuinely new interpretation yet the reader may also be provoked into a new self-understanding. Understanding a text implies not constant *repetition* but constant *reinterpretation* by people who question and listen within their particular historical circumstances (Gadamer 1979). A concrete example would be the way that interpretations of the Rule of St Benedict have, while retaining some common features, produced different monastic life-styles over the centuries.

Finally, as has been mentioned, contemporary approaches to interpretation emphasize a 'hermeneutics of suspicion' as well as one of 'consent'. On the one hand, we 'consent' to a text in that its origins, author's intention and consensus of interpretations over time exert some kind of normative role that prevents the reader from exploiting the text. On the other hand, the questions provoked by contemporary horizons may be critical of aspects of the text and its theological or cultural assumptions. An uncritical reading may simply reinforce hidden prejudices, for example anti-Semitism (John 1988).

3 Typologies and spirituality

There have been a number of attempts to differentiate spiritualities according to 'type' based on theological criteria. To speak of 'types', however, assumes that Christian spirituality is plural. Until the early 1960s it was assumed that all spiritualities were essentially the same. This resulted from the dominance of a systematic and deductive spiritual theology that proceeded from universal principles. It was the collapse of this approach, coupled with a recognition of the relationship of spirituality to historical context that pointed to the plurality of spirituality and made it impossible to reduce the diversity of spiritual experience to universal formulae. It is possible to argue, of course, that a fundamental unity of all spirituality in Christ is prior to any diversity. Christologically, all spiritualities meet and flow together (von Balthasar 1965: 5–13). Yet, Christianity is a religion of incarnation and thus cannot retreat from the particularity of history into some kind of 'timeless truth'. Each generation of Christians, and members of diverse cultures, are challenged to respond to the Gospel within the circumstances of their time and place.

Three typologies of spiritualities in relation to theological emphases merit particular attention. First, there is the classic division between the *via negativa* (or apophatic theology) and the *via positiva* (or cataphatic theology). Second, there have been attempts to distinguish between Protestant and Catholic 'mentalities'. Finally, in recent years, there have been several attempts to classify spiritualities in terms of their eschatologies or their evaluation of history and the world as contexts for spiritual transformation.

Apophatic and cataphatic theologies

The words 'apophatic' (emphasizing silence, passivity and the negation of images of God) and 'cataphatic' (emphasizing images of God, and created reality as a context for God's self-revelation) are often used to describe mutually exclusive spiritual paths and theologies. However, the origins of this distinction in the writings of the pseudonymous sixth-century writer, Pseudo-Dionysius, make a rigid distinction questionable. There, cataphatic and apophatic theologies are essentially complementary. Creation is a self-revelation of God's goodness because it results from an outpouring of divine life. God can be affirmed and named, for example as 'good'. Yet, even the Christian affirmation of God as Trinity ultimately reveals God as unknowable. Paradoxically, through our relationship to God we realize that God is not our possession or an object of knowledge. Consequently, it is through a way of 'denial' that we move towards the deepest knowledge of God. Contemporary usage of the words apophatic and cataphatic simply to describe different forms of prayer is therefore misleading. Any typology must allow for the fact that they are theological concepts related to our ways of apprehending God and as such are mutually complementary (Louth 1989; Sheldrake 1991: 191–8, 211–13).

Protestant and Catholic mentalities

Protestant and Catholic Christianity have developed distinctive forms of religious consciousness, but do these concepts distinguish fundamentally different spiritualities (Sheldrake 1991: 198–205)? One approach to this question contrasts an emphasis on the individual hearer of the Word (Protestant) with an emphasis on membership of a sacramental community (Catholic). The main proponents of this viewpoint are two representatives of the Reformed tradition, Franz Leenhardt and Hieje Faber (Leenhardt 1964; Faber 1988).

The 'Protestant', Abrahamic, type emphasizes dependence solely on God, hearing God's word, repentance, prophecy and an eschatological kingdom. God is transcendent and a figure of authority, is essentially free and continually calls humans to a response. The 'Catholic', Mosaic, type involves a journey of faith within a community and a tradition. God is present and is associated with priesthood, cult and place. The stress is on the glory of God made visible and tangible. The medium of reception is the eye (ritual) more than the ear (proclamation).

Another approach emphasizes different understandings of human communion with God in terms of immediacy (Protestant) and mediation (Catholic). The power of sin and an awareness of separation from God drive one either towards a reliance on human mediation (ritual and priesthood) or towards liberation from sin and guilt by total dependence on God's grace. Both types agree that salvation is by grace and through Christ but the foundations are essentially different. For the Protestant, God forgives sin once and for all and salvation is assured solely by God in a completely free act. Catholic spirituality, by contrast, suggests that God, by grace it is true, actually makes human actions worthy in the divine sight. Room is left for human action even if initiated by and dependent on grace. If Catholic spiritualities speak of the human search for God and of spiritual ascent, Protestant spiritualities speak of God alone seeking and descending to us.

Such attempts to use 'Protestant' and 'Catholic' as absolute types come up against a number of problems. For example, as biblical types, Abrahamic religion allows for ritual and theophany and Mosaic religion emphasizes trust and hope in the promises of God. With regard to immediacy and mediation, it is now better understood that certain strands of pre-Reformation spirituality emphasized the immediacy of communion with God more than mediation and that the Reformers drew a great deal on these in their views on salvation and God's relationship with humankind (for example, Pannenberg 1984: 15–22; Veith 1985: 25). Equally, Protestantism, both in its Lutheran and Reformed strands, in the end encompassed a complex of emphases on grace, free will and human cooperation with God. At the institutional level, 'Protestant' may of course include High Church Lutheranism in Sweden and the fundamentalism of the American 'bible belt', while 'Catholic' encompasses liberation theology and Archbishop Lefebvre.

Eschatologies and spirituality

Finally, there have been attempts to create typologies in terms of attitudes to history and eschatologies. Kinerk asks how spiritualities evaluate the world and human history as contexts for self-transformation (Kinerk 1981). There are four types. The first, classically expressed in mystical spiritualities, says 'no' to the world and history. The second, for example Ignatian spirituality, says 'yes' to both. The third, expressed for example in monasticism, says 'yes' to the world but 'no' to history. The fourth type, for example Francis of Assisi or prophetic movements, says 'no' to the world but 'yes' to history. The four types are not graded but are treated as equally important with equal weaknesses.

A more complex typology, derived from Richard Niebuhr, examines the relationship between Christ and culture from the viewpoint of eschatology and distinguishes a number of possibilities (Wainwright 1986). 'Christ against culture' views the world as hostile to the kingdom of God. Eschatologically, the kingdom is 'not yet' or elsewhere, for history is beyond redemption. Embodiments of this approach include Pentecostalism and primitive monasticism. 'Christ of culture', on the contrary, affirms the world as it is. The eschatology identifies the kingdom with the world or avoids eschatological language altogether by rejecting a human fall from grace. The Reich Church of Nazi Germany would fit this category. Each of these first two types is interpreted as cripplingly deficient. Three further 'types' are more balanced in their attitudes to human culture. 'Christ above culture', while emphasizing a positive view, recognizes the need for purification. The eschatology emphasizes the redemption of all creation. This tends to favour the present effectiveness of Christ's action. Examples cited are Orthodox spirituality and the hymns of Charles Wesley. 'Christ and culture in paradox' is more world-denying. Eschatology is both 'now' and 'not yet'. Spiritualities emphasize struggle and paradox. Contrasting examples are the holy fools of the Celtic and Russian traditions but also Dietrich Bonhoeffer. 'Christ the transformer of culture' views the world positively and suggests that any corruption is a perversion of its essential goodness. The eschatology points to the beginnings of the kingdom in history through various processes of dying to self. Yet there is an urgent impulse towards final completion. Liberation spirituality finds a place in this type alongside Augustine, certain aspects of Methodism, and Ignatian spirituality.

One may argue about the validity of placing specific spiritual traditions in one type rather than another. Equally, the theological assumptions behind any typology need to be exposed. It is dangerous to adopt a single typology as the sole means of differentiating spiritualities. However, the attempts to highlight eschatologies and theologies of history remind us of the necessarily intimate relationship between spiritual experience and theological mentalities.

CONCLUSION

The deeply experiential character of much late twentieth-century theology, from Karl Rahner to liberation and feminist approaches, is a remarkable shift given centuries of *a priori* theological method. Western theology and spirituality are in the process of overcoming an ancient and radical divorce between them. The beginnings of a separation can be traced to the beginnings of 'philosophical theology' around the thirteenth century. This was accelerated and deepened by Enlightenment presuppositions about knowledge. The result has been what T. S. Eliot called a 'dissociation of sensibility' in Western culture that separated thought from feeling, mind from heart, and theology from life. The journey of the mind, the way of knowledge, thought and theory, was contrasted with the journey of the heart, the way of love, prayer and action (Louth 1983: 1–3; Bechtle 1985: 305).

However, the last twenty years have seen a substantial convergence so that theology as a whole has been increasingly able to acknowledge its experiential roots and spirituality has begun to establish itself in the academy as an interdisciplinary subject for study. Theological method and themes necessarily play a large part in the study of Christian spirituality. However, the discipline also increasingly draws upon history, psychology, comparative religion and social anthropology. There are differences of opinion as to whether 'spirituality' is a sub-discipline of theology, whether subordinated, for example, to doctrinal theology or a distinct area entitled 'spiritual theology'. It seems that majority opinion is moving towards an acceptance that 'spirituality' is an autonomous discipline which functions in partnership and mutuality with theology. Thus, theology is an integral part of the study of spirituality because it is essential to the full interpretation of Christian spiritual experience. Yet, spirituality is also integral to theology both because it raises questions which theology must consider and also because, as Karl Rahner pointed out, the empirical realities of spirituality supply data that are necessary for theology and not available from purely doctrinal sources (Schneiders 1989: 689–90).

REFERENCES

Bechtle, R. (1985) 'Convergences in Theology and Spirituality', *The Way* 25, 4, 305–14.

Bouyer, L. (1961) *An Introduction to Spirituality*, New York: Desclee.

—— (1981) 'Mysticism: An Essay on the History of the Word', in R. Woods (ed.) *Understanding Mysticism*, London: Athlone Press.

Bynum, C. W. (1982) *Jesus as Mother: Studies in the Spirituality of the High Middle Ages*, Berkeley: University of California Press.

Carr, A. E. (1990) *Transforming Grace: Christian Tradition and Women's Experience*, San Francisco: Harper.

Deidun, T. (1988) 'Beyond Dualisms: Paul on Sex, Sarx and Soma', *The Way* 28, 3, 195–205.

Dupré, L. and Saliers, D. (eds) (1989) *Christian Spirituality: Post-Reformation and Modern*, London: SCM Press.

Faber, H. (1988) *Above the Treeline: Towards a Contemporary Spirituality*, London: SCM Press.

Gadamer, H. G. (1979) *Truth and Method*, London: Sheed and Ward.

Garrigou-Lagrange, R. (1937) *Christian Perfection and Contemplation*, St Louis: Herder Book Co.

Gutiérrez, G. (1984) *We Drink from Our Own Wells: The Spiritual Journey of a People*, London: SCM Press.

Hanson, B. C. (ed.) (1990) *Modern Christian Spirituality: Methodological and Historical Essays*, Atlanta: Scholars Press.

Kinerk, E. (1981) 'Towards a Method for the Study of Spirituality', *Review for Religious* 40, 1, 3–19.

John, O. (1988) 'The Tradition of the Oppressed as the Main Topic of Theological Hermeneutics', *Concilium* 200, *Truth and its Victims*, 143–55.

Lane, D. (1985) *The Experience of God*, Dublin: Veritas.

Lash, N. (1986) *Theology on the Way to Emmaus*, London: SCM Press.

Leclercq, J. (1978) *The Love of Learning and the Desire for God: A Study of Monastic Culture*, London: SPCK.

Leech, K. (1977) *Soul Friend: A Study of Spirituality*, London: SPCK.

Leenhardt, F. (1964) *Two Biblical Faiths: Protestant and Catholic*, London: Lutterworth Press.

Lindbeck, G. A. (1984) *The Nature of Doctrine: Religion and Theology in a Postliberal Age*, London: SPCK.

Lonergan, B. (1972) *Method in Theology*, London: Darton, Longman and Todd.

Lossky, V. (1973) *The Mystical Tradition of the Eastern Church*, London: James Clark & Co. Ltd.

Louth, A. (1983) *Discerning the Mystery: An Essay on the Nature of Theology*, Oxford: Oxford University Press.

—— (1989) *Denys the Areopagite*, London: SPCK.

Moorman, J. (1983) *The Anglican Spiritual Tradition*, London: Darton, Longman and Todd.

O'Donohue, J. (1987) 'A Return to Virtue', *Church* (Spring), 48–54.

Ogden, S. (1963) *The Reality of God*, New York: Harper & Row.

Pannenberg, W. (1984) *Christian Spirituality and Sacramental Community*, London: SCM Press.

Principe, W. (1983) 'Towards Defining Spirituality', *Sciences Religieuses* 12, 2, 127–41.

—— (1992) 'Pluralism in Christian Spirituality', *The Way* 32, 1, 54–61.

Rahner, K. (1966) *Theological Investigations, 5: Later Writings*, London: Darton, Longman and Todd.

—— (1971) *Theological Investigations, 7: Further Theology of the Spiritual Life*, London: Darton, Longman and Todd.

—— (1974) *Theological Investigations, 11: Confrontations 1*, London: Darton, Longman and Todd.

—— (1984) *The Practice of Faith: A Handbook of Contemporary Spirituality*, (eds) K. Lehmann and A. Raffelt, New York: Crossroad.

Rorem, P. (1986) 'The Uplifting Spirituality of Pseudo-Dionysius', in B. McGinn, J. Meyendorff and J. Leclercq (eds) *Christian Spirituality: Origins to the Twelfth Century*, London: Routledge & Kegan Paul.

Ruggieri, G. (1987) 'Faith and History', in G. Alberigo, J-P. Jossua and J. A. Komanchak (eds) *The Reception of Vatican II*, Washington, DC: Catholic University of America Press.

Schneiders, S. (1986) 'Theology and Spirituality: Strangers, Rivals or Partners?', *Horizons* 13, 2, 253–74.

—— (1989) 'Spirituality in the Academy', *Theological Studies* 50, 676–97.

Sheldrake, P. (1991) *Spirituality and History: Questions of Interpretation and Method*, London: SPCK.

Sudbrack, J. (1975) 'Spirituality', in K. Rahner (ed.) *Encyclopedia of Theology: A Concise Sacramentum Mundi*, London: Burns & Oates.

Tanquerey, A. A. (1930) *The Spiritual Life*, Tournai: Desclee.

Tracy, D. (1975) *Blessed Rage for Order*, New York: The Seabury Press.

—— (1981) *The Analogical Imagination: Christian Theology and the Culture of Pluralism*, London: SCM Press.

Van Ness, P. H. (1992) 'Spirituality and Secularity', *The Way Supplement* 73, 68–79.

Veith, G. E. (1985) *Reformation Spirituality: The Religion of George Herbert*, London: Bucknell University Press.

Viller, M. (ed.) (1932–) *Dictionnaire de spiritualité*.

Von Balthasar, H. U. (1965) 'The Gospel as Norm and Test of all Spirituality in the Church', *Concilium* 9, 1, 5–13.

Wainwright, G. (1986) 'Types of Spirituality', in C. Jones, G. Wainwright and E. Yarnold (eds) *The Study of Spirituality*, London: SPCK.

Williams, R. (1979) *The Wound of Knowledge: Christian Spirituality from the New Testament to St. John of the Cross*, London: Darton, Longman and Todd.

FURTHER READING

Haight, R. (1979) *The Experience and Language of Grace*, New York: Paulist Press.

—— (1985) *An Alternative Vision: An Interpretation of Liberation Theology*, New York: Paulist Press.

Lash, N. (1988) *Easter in Ordinary: Reflections on Human Experience and the Knowledge of God*, London: SCM Press.

Leech, K. (1985) *True God: An Exploration in Spiritual Theology*, London: SPCK.

Megyer, E. (1981) 'Spiritual Theology Today', *The Way* 21, 1, 55–67.

Miles, M. R. (1988) *The Image and Practice of Holiness*, London: SCM Press.

Panikkar, R. (1973) *The Trinity and the Religious Experience of Man*, London: Darton, Longman and Todd.

Ruether, R. R. (1982) *Sexism and God-Talk: Toward a Feminist Theology*, Boston: Beacon Press.

Schneiders, S. (1986) 'Scripture and Spirituality', in B. McGinn, J. Meyendorff and J. Leclercq (eds) *Christian Spirituality: Origins to the Twelfth Century*, London: Routledge & Kegan Paul.

Thompson, W. (1987) *Fire and Light: The Saints and Theology*, New York: Paulist Press.

See also chapters 14, 16, 28, 29, 30, 41.

26

PATRISTIC SPIRITUALITY

Anthony Meredith

Patristic spirituality is the inheritor of two related but distinct traditions, the Hebrew and the Greek. Both of these had offered answers to the all important question, 'How shall I come closer to God?' This means not simply, How shall I find out more about him?, but also (or rather), How can I enter into a relationship with him? Although the two traditions are in many ways sharply distinguished from one another, they are at one on a central point. For the Psalms there can be no climbing the mountain of the Lord without purity of heart (Ps. 24:3) and for Plato there is no way of rising to the contemplation of the absolute Good, without living a good life (cf. above all *Republic* 6, 7). The two indispensible requirements for anyone wishing to approach and experience the divine are in both systems a good life and open mind or eyes. In both traditions God or the absolute is regarded as somehow distinct from the visible world and therefore inaccessible to the eyes of the body.

Faced with such a united front, what were the early Christians to make of it, when faced with the figure of the historical Jesus? How did he 'fit in' to such a scheme, or rather how did it 'fit in' to him? It has already been suggested in the previous chapter that crucial though Jesus was and is to Christianity, he was not ultimate in the sense that God was. Indeed, in the Synoptic Gospels the centre of his preaching is the kingdom of God (Heaven) and the Fatherhood of God. It is only with St John and St Paul that the preacher becomes the one preached, and even there, by and large, he is the one through whom we go to the Father, to whom he reconciled the human race. The vast majority of early Christian writing is concerned with the problem of how the person of Jesus modified or radically challenged received positions about the absolute nature of God. These problems were to some extent 'resolved' in 325 at the first Ecumenical Council of the Church held at Nicaea, modern Isnic in Turkey.

The preoccupation with more strictly theological issues left the Church little space to devote itself to the question of how, given the growing awareness of the true nature of Christ as both human and divine, this 'new' perception should affect the lives of the Christian community in practice. The New Testament itself had given little assistance on this score. It had indeed insisted on the centrality of the sacraments of baptism and the eucharist, and, in the Gospel of Luke especially, presented the example of Jesus praying, but it had little to say about how Christians should set about the task of drawing near to God in religious experience. For example, with one important exception, it had given no advice about how the Christian should pray, apart that is from insisting at times on the need for continual prayer (cf. 1 Thess: 17).

The important exception is the Our Father, of which two variants survive in the New Testament, at Matthew 6 and Luke 11. It was to be the distinctively Christian prayer, available only to those who had been baptized and so incorporated into the body of Christ. A good deal of what the Fathers meant by spirituality can be gathered from the often copious commentaries they wrote on the Lord's Prayer. Before we turn to a closer scrutiny of how some of the early Christian writers understood the path to holiness and the vision of God, it will perhaps help to see what some of them made of the contents of this prayer.

The first extant commentary on the prayer, meant for the instruction of converts to Christian life, comes from the end of the second century and is the work of Tertullian (*c*.160–220). After pointing out the novelty of Christian prayer, he gives a line-by-line comment on the text. The continuous use of this prayer throughout this period and the differing interpretations can be illustrated by seeing what five different Fathers make of the verse, 'Give us this day our daily bread'. In section 6 of *On the Prayer*, Tertullian refers the words to the Word of God, come down from heaven and giving life to the world, and also to the bread of the eucharist. This second sense he connects with the words of Christ at the Last Supper, 'This is my body'. In 231 an Alexandrian writer, Origen (185–254), gives the words a different sense in his treatise *On the Prayer*. In section 27 of that work he applies the words to the Word that feeds us and makes us grow in the Spirit. There is no clear and unambiguous reference in the text to the eucharist. Cyril of Jerusalem, however, towards the end of the fourth century, writes that the 'supersubstantial' bread for which we pray is Holy Bread, an almost certain reference to the eucharist; while another fourth-century writer, Gregory of Nyssa, who composed five homilies on the Lord's Prayer, provides a quite novel meaning to the familiar words. For him, in the fourth homily, the bread is the basic needs of life, as distinct from superfluities. Finally Augustine, in his *Enchiridion* (or 'Handbook'), section 115, of 421 CE, interprets the words to apply to the basic needs of body and soul. There is a refreshing independence about these divergent and on the whole independent understandings of the words of the prayer of prayers, an absence of stereotyping that also marks their approaches to the quest for God, which lies at the root of all spirituality. Further, the various treatments of the Lord's Prayer give us an insight into different approaches to the concerns seen as central to the prayer of Christians.

GOD AND CHRIST

Plato and the Old Testament had been at one in viewing the vision of God as the goal of human life. How does the person of Christ fit into this scheme? As we have seen, the New Testament endorses it, sometimes actually identifying Jesus as God. On the whole, though, he is the way to the Father, the one through whom the knowledge of God is made available to us. He is not 'absolute' himself. The New Testament remains theocentric and the main aim of the early Fathers was to define the special relationship of Jesus to God without endangering the inherited monotheism of the Bible. This means in practice that even after the full deity of Christ had been defined at the Council of Nicaea in 325, the theology and spirituality of the Fathers are primarily interested in the deity of Jesus rather than in his human nature. Jesus worship and Jesus mysticism, centred on the figure of the Gospels, are on the whole rare in the early Church. This fact by itself serves to distinguish the patristic period from the Middle Ages and the Reformation period, where devotion to Christ is central in writers as diverse as Julian of Norwich, Ignatius Loyola and Teresa of Avila.

With a few exceptions, the Fathers preserved the general practice of the New Testament and of the liturgy in making prayers to the Father, through the Son, rather than to the Father and the Son. The Mass did indeed address both the 'Lord have mercy' and 'Lamb of God' to Christ, but these seem to have come into the liturgy at a later date. Outside the liturgy examples of prayers to Christ are rare. The *Sayings of the Desert Fathers*, a fourth-century collection of alphabetically arranged words of the Fathers from the desert of Egypt, do indeed mention prayer to Jesus. And there is the 'Jesus Prayer'. It is not altogether clear at what date this prayer acquired its final form as 'Lord Jesus Christ, have mercy on me a sinner.' Clearly the prayer for mercy has a gospel model in the prayer of the blind men at Matthew 9:28. The invocation of the holy name of Jesus occurs certainly in writings of a fifth-century bishop of Photice, Diadochus. In section 59 of his *Gnostic Chapters*, he recommends frequent remembering of the name of Jesus. This remembrance is to be accompanied by a warmth of feeling, quite unusual among the Fathers, whose general approach to the quest for God is not marked by any great stress on the importance of the emotions.

With the exception of the *Sayings*, which come from a more 'popular milieu' and Diadochus of Photice, the Fathers have little to offer in the shape of 'Jesus Worship' and it is on the whole true to say of them that for them the humanity of Christ is treated as a means through which we can arrive at either the Father or at the divinity shared by Father and Son alike. This reduction of the person of Jesus' role to that of intermediary derives above all from the fact that pretty well all the Fathers begin their theology and their search for God with a highly remote and distanced figure of God. A particularly clear example of this phenomenon is Origen, whose birth in 185 in

Alexandria and subsequent education there under Platonist auspices may help to explain the origin of his idea of God. For him God is a completely spiritual being, bodiless, spaceless, timeless, beyond the reach of our senses and available to us partly through his action in this world and partly through what Origen saw as the 'spiritual senses'. This novel doctrine of his is outlined in his treatise *On First Principles* written in about 230. In answer to the objection that his highly abstract account of God left little or no possibility for any direct apprehension of God, he replied that in addition to the five bodily senses, we also possess senses of the spirit. Basing himself on Proverbs 2:5 in the Greek text, 'You will find a divine sense', he argued that we have spiritual sight (cf. Matt. 5:8), spiritual taste (cf. Ps. 34:8), and so on.

But, if we can know that God exists and something of his nature, and if the knowledge of God is the end of the spiritual life, it may be asked what place the person of Christ plays in all this 'knowing' process. How necessary is Christ and what sort of knowledge can and does he communicate? On the whole it must be admitted that the role of Christ in the Origenistic scheme is essentially supplementary. Christ is in some places spoken of almost as the poor man's Plato, enabling the simple Christians to know something about the divine nature. But even when he is so spoken of, Christ in his person as a historical figure is always a step on the way to God himself. In his great *Commentary* on the Fourth Gospel, Origen treats Christ as a complex figure, made up of several aspects – he calls them *epinoiai* – arranged like steps to a temple. The lowest and least important aspects are those which refer to the temporal life and work of Christ, as propitiation, shepherd and healer. From these lowly foothills the more ambitious ascend by means of self-mastery and mental exercise to the aspects of Christ as justice, wisdom and word. In other words, within the person of Christ we find a union of the historical and salvific aspects of his work and, beyond those, the cosmic and absolute elements. But even these last are not the end of the spiritual quest for Origen. The word and wisdom are essentially directed above to the simple, uncompounded nature of God that lies above all. In another place he makes a distinction between the temporal and eternal gospel, which corresponds exactly to the distinction between the Incarnate and Eternal word of God. The Christian is meant to move upwards, drawn on by the love of heavenly wisdom. The movement of desire is something given to us by God, a love for truth and ultimately for God as the source of all truth, which is part of the very fabric of our created natures. The restless mind can only find satisfaction, and even then not total satisfaction, in the thought and presence of God.

This highly theocentric spirituality clearly has roots in a form of Platonism. In his dialogue the *Symposium*, Plato had also placed us under the impulse of an upward moving eros (love or desire), which finds its rest only in the vision of absolute beauty. The thought of God as beautiful or as beauty appealed to Origen's successors, the Cappadocian Fathers, Gregory of Nazianzus, Basil and Gregory of Nyssa, defenders of the faith of Nicaea in Asia Minor in the last third of the fourth century. For Basil (330–79), underneath the structure of the monastic life, for which he composed a set of rules, there lies the God-given desire to rise upwards to the God who is beauty. In Gregory of Nyssa's early treatise *On Virginity* (370), the absolute beauty of Plato is identified with God.

Undoubtedly the best-known of all such identifications is to be found in a writer who can in no obvious sense be regarded as a follower of Origen, and who on several occasions took pains to distinguish his position from that of Origen, Augustine of Hippo (354–430). In book 10 of his *Confessions* (1991) he addresses God as follows: 'Late have I loved you, beauty so old and so new: late have I loved you.' Augustine was obsessed with the idea of and desire for God. Everything is God-centred. He is the 'one true God', from whom all things derive their being and for whom all things are made as their final end. The tragedy of human life is that we have the power to refuse the essential nature and drive of our beings. Although he is nearer to us than we to ourselves, we can refuse to attend to him and can be far away from him in our minds and hearts. The parable of the Prodigal Son of Luke 15 spoke to Augustine of the perpetual condition of the human heart made for but away from God. 'One does not go far away from you or return to you by any movement through space. The younger son in your gospel did not look for horses or carriages.' The human heart – a word for which Augustine in his *Confessions* shows a marked preference, using it about two hundred times – is a complex reality. It is the centre of the conscious life and of the drive to achieve ultimate satisfaction. And that satisfaction, he tells us at the beginning of the *Confessions*, despite all our attempts to divert the streams of desire, can find rest nowhere else save in God. 'You have made us, O Lord, for yourself and our heart is restless till it rest in You.'

So far the main difference between Augustine and Origen lies in the central object of desire. For Augustine it is the divine Trinity, for Origen it is the simple divine intellectual nature of the Father only. How does Augustine's treatment of the place of Christ in this highly theocentric scheme of things differ from that of Origen? The answer is, hardly at all. Commenting on John 14:6, 'I am the way, the truth and the life', he asks (in his thirteenth tractate on the Gospel) how can the same Christ be both the journey and the destination. His reply is that 'we go through Christ to Christ, through Christ incarnate as man to Christ discarnate as Word'. The principal difference between him and Origen is that for him the Word is fully divine, while for Origen the Word is only secondarily and therefore not fully divine.

Can we travel on the road to God without the help of Christ? On this crucial question Augustine makes an important distinction. We cannot do without the help of the saving work of Christ, the only mediator between God and us. The role of Christ as mediator is supplemented by his office as instructor in humility. Although Augustine seems prepared at times to say that we can know the existence of God and of our eternal home without the help of Christ, we cannot arrive there without him; and again, although one might perhaps know of God by the exercise of the mind, it is only a real possibility for the majority of the human race if they have Christ as instructor. But so strong was Augustine's conviction of the presence of God to himself and indeed to the whole of creation, that the need to go through Christ in order to discover this presence does not seem to have been urgent for him.

Origen and Augustine, without a doubt the two greatest thinkers and writers of the early Church, shared a powerful conviction of the presence and beauty and universal availability of God. It is true that by God Augustine meant the whole Trinity, Origen only the Father as the fount of deity; it is also true that Augustine writes about and to God with a passion which is, by and large, lacking in Origen. But despite these differences their theocentric vision of the world made it hard for them to find a place for the person, above all for the humanity, of Jesus. If the end of life was the entry into a lasting and eternal relationship with God himself, then clearly time and history could not be thought of as anything more than a stage on the way to this goal. This conclusion may disappoint those who expect to see Christ as the centre of Christian spirituality and they may feel inclined to blame the influence of Plato on both Origen and Augustine. This would be unfair, because although it is true that both writers owed an immense debt to Plato and his followers, the idea that Christ is the ultimate object of worship and service is not found in the New Testament either.

LIGHT AND DARKNESS

On several occasions the New Testament 'defines' both the Father and the Son as 'light'. In 1 John 1:5, 'God is light and in him there is no darkness whatever' and in John 8:12 Jesus says, 'I am the light of the world.' The prologue to the Fourth Gospel announces that '[the word] was the true light'. On the other hand, in 1 Timothy 6:16 we read that 'God dwells in unapproachable light.' And at the end of the prologue to the Fourth Gospel we find 'No-one has ever seen God.' Clearly there is a certain amount of unclarity in the minds of the New Testament writers about the availability of God to human nature.

The problem of how much we can know about God lies at the heart of all theology and all spirituality, two activities whose relationship to each other will be discussed in the epilogue to this chapter. Clearly our ability to know God is connected with our understanding of the capacities of the human mind. Is that relationship primarily a matter of the intelligence, or of the feelings, or of the body, or of all three together? The place of the body in patristic spirituality has been the subject of recent study by Peter Brown (1989). There he tries to make the spiritual strivings of the early Church intelligible to people of today, who find the quest for God in the writings of the Fathers difficult to understand and even harder to sympathize with. For Brown, the pursuit of virginity and otherworldliness was not simply a sell-out to a form of Platonism, but an attempt to define oneself against the constrictions of a very demanding secular city. Therefore, virginity as an ideal did not arise from contempt for the body, but from the desire to free it from the constraints of marriage, child-bearing and service to the state. This desire for emancipation, especially on the part of women, had its more positive side, offering an escape from the prevailing social dominance of men. The desire to attend to God needed the exclusion of those elements that got in the way of this vital activity, above all noise, politics and the company of the opposite sex, and perhaps of all human society. The flight from the world was but the other side of the pursuit of God, which led the first monastic heroes to leave their villages and spend their lives in the desert or on the top of pillars, sometimes alone and sometimes in the company of like-minded men or women.

But, even granted the real importance of the body, as shown in Brown's analysis, it is still true that the intellectual aspect remains primary, and this is hardly surprising once it is remembered that from most cultures only evidence from the articulate (and the orthodox) survives. In other words, we are dependent upon the writings of theologians for our picture of the spiritual quest of the early Church. These can be roughly divided into two groups: on the one hand, those who for good reasons have an optimistic view of the human mind and a relatively restricted view of the divine nature, and on the other hand those who have a less exalted picture of the human mind and a much loftier view of God. The former group are often called 'light theologians' because they stress the importance of knowing God, the latter 'darkness theologians' because for them God is ultimately an infinite being, incomprehensible even to the angels. The principal figure in the first class is Origen, and in the latter, Gregory of Nyssa and Denis (or Dionysius) the Areopagite, so called from his supposed identification with St Paul's convert mentioned at Acts 17:34. In reality he was a Christian theologian of the late fifth century, deeply influenced by the late Platonist writer, Proclus (412–85).

Origen's optimism about the possibility of knowing God sprang partly, but only partly, from his consciousness of the need to defend Christianity from two groups within the Church who in his judgement threatened to upset the rational and historically revealed character of the Gospel. The first group against whom he defined his position were the Montanists, the followers of a second-century Christian prophet from Asia Minor, who claimed to have received a new revelation of the faith under the direct inspiration of the Holy Spirit. According to Montanus and his two female followers, Priscilla and Maximilla, the mind when under the influence of the Spirit was totally passive. The moment of divine visitation was also the moment of passive ecstasy. A witness, perhaps hostile, cited by the Church historian Eusebius (1954: 158–62) says that the Montanists prophesied in a state of abnormal ecstasy

542

and frenzy. The movement gave the Church considerable problems. Was such an experience a genuinely divine one? How was it possible to distinguish between the true and the false spirit? Was irrationality a mark of divine presence? Origen's belief in the divine character of human reason, the image of God within us, gave him little natural sympathy for Montanism and he attacked it, though not by name, on several occasions. But before we turn to his own version of the interaction and interrelation of divine and human, something must be said about the second group whom he countered, the Gnostics.

It is perhaps unfair to class all Gnostics together. The finds of Nag Hammadi in 1945 have revealed the extraordinary richness and complexity of the phenomenon, misleadingly called 'Gnosticism'. The word 'Gnostic' comes from the Greek word for knowledge, *gnōsis*, and many Gnostics, though not all, offered their followers a novel entrance into the divine mystery. This mystery usually took the form of a highly complex account of the origin of the world, which was usually regarded as deriving its existence as a result of cosmic sin committed in the upper world, which resulted in the creation of a lower one. Seeing the present order as sin-derived, as a sort of 'cosmic hiccough', they saw the way to God and to salvation as lying in escape from this world order. A negative attitude to this world and to its author is a feature common to most Gnostic systems, as is the promise to redeem the individual from it by secret knowledge. The whole system bore too close a similarity to orthodox Christian systems to be allowed to pass unchallenged. It was not inherently absurd and some of its literature possesses considerable charm. Clement of Alexandria (150–220), not himself a Gnostic, sums up the basic thrust of their teaching as follows: 'Who we were and what we have become, where we were, where we were placed, whither we hasten, from what we are redeemed, what birth is, what rebirth' (Stevenson 1957:75). The seductiveness of Gnosticism can be gauged simply from the number of replies it elicited from the 'orthodox'. A whole stream of writers set about refuting the claims of the Gnostics, including, in the second century, Irenaeus, Clement of Alexandria and Tertullian, and Origen in the third.

In Origen the defence of Christianity, as he conceived it, took the form of an insistence upon the value of reason, freedom and Scripture, above all the Old Testament as a worthy and credible account of the nature of God. Convinced as he himself was that history did not hold the key to the ultimate truth about God and the human soul, he had a difficult path to tread between acceptance of the truth and importance of the historical elements of Christianity, on the one hand, and, on the other, the belief in their non-ultimacy.

In order, therefore, to assert the rationality of religion against the emotional faith of the Montanists and the 'hidden, otherworldly absolute' of the Gnostics, Origen insisted on the availability of God to the rational intelligence. For Origen, God could be known to and by the purified intelligence. He was essentially a 'lightful' being. To the claim of the Montanists that they had been inspired by the Holy Spirit who had taken them outside themselves, Origen replied that it was not the habit of the Spirit of God to act in this outlandish fashion. He moved gently and helped rather than replaced the mind in its activities (1965: 396–8; 1966: 223ff.). When Origen is described as a 'light mystic' what is meant is that he believed that God could be known by the activity of the human mind. He rejected the idea of the utter incomprehensibility of God and also the false notion that in order to be touched by God you have to be 'out of your mind'. But in addition to his distaste for Gnostic incomprehensibility and Montanist ecstasy, Origen was clearly not at home with those passages in the Bible which spoke of the divine darkness. For example, it is remarkable that in those passages in Exodus and the Psalms where God is said to make darkness his dwelling place, Origen either offers no comment at all or takes the text to mean that access to God takes time and effort and is not to be had automatically or for the asking. Commenting on the verse of the prologue to the Fourth Gospel, 'The light shines in the darkness', Origen observes that nothing is absolutely inscrutable; all is available in Christ.

This positive and optimistic attitude to the powers of the mind was not simply a reaction to less hopeful views. It seems to have expressed his own conviction about the nature of the human intelligence and the value of revelation. It was not the only attitude adopted in this period to the value of emotion in religion or to the problem of the availability of God. The fourth century witnessed the flowering of two movements which stand as a contrast and challenge to the Origenistic vision, represented by the so-called *Macarian Homilies* and Gregory of Nyssa. The first of these is far more emotionally charged than Origen and speaks the language of the heart with great and appealing force. The collection of *Homilies*, ascribed to Macarius of Egypt, in reality probably comes not from Egypt but from what is now Iraq. In them, the importance and claims of experience are expressed in a way quite uncharacteristic of Origen. Towards the close of his first homily, Macarius writes:

> If you are not conscious of having experienced any of these things [i.e. the heavenly food of the Spirit], weep, mourn and groan because you have not been made a participator of the eternal and spiritual riches and you have not yet received true life.

Direct experience is made the criterion of being in contact with God. This by itself is enough to distinguish the spirituality of the Macarian homilies from that of the bulk of Eastern spiritual writers, and they represent the more significant of the two movements that contrast with the position of Origen.

There exists within the Eastern tradition a line of thinking about God and our relation to him which is the direct opposite of Origen's 'light' mysticism. Philo the Jew (*c*.20 BCE–*c*.45 CE) from Alexandria exercised a profound influence on the later Christian tradition. Although he almost certainly did not invent the idea of the divine darkness and incomprehensibility, it certainly plays a central role in his thinking. He is the real founder of the so-called apophatic tradition, that is, the tradition that says that God is radically beyond the reach of the human imagination and mind, either because he is so great and infinite that it would be in principle impossible to grasp him, or because the human mind, dwelling in a body and being essentially limited, can never hope to see or fully understand the divine nature. Why did Philo come to this rather startling conclusion? He may have been influenced by contemporary speculation surrounding a citation from Plato's dialogue, the *Timaeus*, which states that 'it is hard to know and difficult to communicate the nature of God'. But Philo goes well beyond this, and in the absence of any evidence of mystical experience on his part we are forced to conclude that he was led to the idea of the divine darkness by reflection on the meaning of certain passages in the Bible (see above) which talk of God's living in darkness. Exodus 20:21 – a key verse for all future discussion, though significantly omitted by Origen in his homilies on Exodus – speaks of God dwelling in thick darkness. This text is used by Philo in his treatise *On the Posterity and Exile of Cain* (5.14) to prove that 'The Existent Being belongs to an unapproachable region where there are no material forms . . . for the Cause of all dwells high above space and time.' The result of this discussion is expressed by Philo as follows: 'We apprehend the real boon of realising that the God of real Being can be apprehended by no one, nor can he be seen by any.' Although God himself is beyond the reach of mind and eye alike, the effects of his action and the power by which he acts in the world can be apprehended by us. Here also we have a foretaste of a similar distinction made by the Cappadocian Fathers in the fourth century.

Philo's personal influence and the way of thinking about God just outlined had a colossal influence on the nascent Church. The apophatic tradition is clear in Clement of Alexandria (*c*.150–220), a converted philosopher from Athens. Unlike Origen he was happy to use the same texts as Philo from the Old Testament which refer to the divine darkness. The modern Russian Orthodox writer, V. Lossky, sees in Clement a genuinely Christian writer, precisely because of his stress on the inaccessibility of the unknown God; and even that awareness is something for which we depend upon the special grace of God.

But it is with Gregory of Nyssa that 'darkness' theology and mysticism move to the centre of the stage. He is rightly regarded as the apostle of apophaticism, a view of God which he roots rather in the divine nature itself than in the limited, sense-bound character of the human mind. He outlines his understanding of the way to God in his *Life of Moses*, most of which is an allegorical account of Moses' pursuit of God, mapped out in three stages. Moses begins in the light of the burning bush and there discovers that God is 'really real'. Then, Exodus 20:21 takes him a step further to the idea of

God as incomprehensible. Finally, Exodus 33:23, where Moses is allowed to see the back of God but not his face, is taken as evidence of the fact that God is infinite. The move from light to darkness serves to underline the difference between Gregory and Origen, for whom God *is* light; but it also serves to distinguish him from Philo, who only got to the second stage of Moses' ascent. The divine infinity is the culmination of Gregory's exploration of the divine nature and occurs in all of his mature writings, whether they are of a dogmatic or spiritual character. Part of Gregory's stress on the infinity of God arises from his awareness that the desire for the divine, which urges the soul to move ever onward in its passionate search for him can be satisfied with nothing limited. God is the 'ever beyond', 'the ever greater', the 'ever more'; in short, he is the infinite, and darkness rather than light is the more appropriate image with which to express this truth. Apart from the language of Scripture, Gregory may well have wished to distance himself from the contemplative tradition of the Greeks, where the accent falls on seeing, and on its intellectual counterpart, knowing. Plato had used the image of the sun to illustrate the nature of the Good; Gregory, perhaps in conscious contrast to this, used the language of darkness, where we cannot see, to suggest the fact that God lies beyond the reach of both bodily and mental seeing. Whatever the precise weight to be attached to the dogmatic and spiritual strands in Gregory's understanding of the divine infinity, his stress on this feature in both types of writing marks a new stage in the history of the idea of God.

The last and in some ways the most influential exponent of the idea of darkness in the patristic period is Denis the Areopagite. The extent of his dependence on Gregory of Nyssa is clear from his work, *The Mystical Theology*. Its first chapter is entitled, 'What is the divine darkness?' and begins with extremely negative language:

> Trinity! Higher than any being, any divinity, any goodness! . . . Lead us beyond unknowing and light, up to the farthest, highest peak of mystic scripture, where the mysteries of God's word lie simple . . . in the brilliant darkness of a hidden silence.

Like Gregory's *Life of Moses* and to some extent indebted to it, Denis bases his account of the progress of the soul and of the divine nature on the same passages in Exodus that had influenced Gregory. The aim of the upward movement for Gregory had been the darkness where God was; for Denis in chapter 2 it is the darkness 'so far above light'. Indeed, Denis is more consistently and resolutely apophatic than his predecessor. Had he received any particular experience which enabled him to speak with such evident assurance about the remoteness of God? We do not know. Like most of his predecessors in the patristic period he is very reticent about himself, in this unlike Plotinus (205–70) the great neo-Platonist mystic philosopher, who did experience ecstasy and vision. It is hard to believe that the strong, convinced and passionate language of Denis springs simply from some abstract theological speculation, especially when it is remembered how close theology and spirituality were for the Fathers. In the absence of any clear evidence, it seems best to conclude that Denis did enjoy some temporary elevation of the spirit, which he calls *ecstasy* and to which he refers on several occasions in his writings. In the opening chapter of *The Mystical Theology* he writes: 'It is by an unrestrained and absolute ecstasy from yourself and from everything that you will be carried up towards the ray of divine darkness beyond being.' The idea of ecstasy here expressed is not that of the Montanists, who had apparently employed the word in order to describe a wholly irrational encounter with the divine Spirit. Far from being irrational, Dionysian ecstasy is the mysterious perfection of our natural powers in the presence and enjoyment of God, who is beyond all being and conception. It is important to make this distinction between rational and irrational ecstasy, in order to avoid the suggestion that once the Montanist challenge was over the Church simply reverted to a Montanist position. Although both Gregory and Denis use the language of divine drunkenness and of ecstasy and darkness to describe their relation to God, they must not be taken to mean by this language a form of irrational religion, but, rather, a form of supra-rational religion.

IMAGE AND LIKENESS

The whole of patristic spirituality could be summed up under the simple rubric: 'we are made in the image of God and are in the process of gradual transformation into his likeness'. This sentence encapsulates the optimistic, realistic and progressive character of much writing on the subject. It is also essentially biblical. Genesis 1:26 had insisted on the image of God in all humanity when it said, in the person of God, 'Let us make man in our image, after our likeness.' This verse expresses the goodness and essentially godlike character of all human beings. However corrupted by original and actual sins this image might have been, none of the Fathers believed that it had been irreparably destroyed, though they did believe that it had been sadly deformed. The process of restoration had been begun by and in Christ, himself seen as 'the image of the invisible God and the first born of all creation' (Col. 1:15). The upward call to holiness given to all is expressed by Christ as 'You must therefore be perfect as your heavenly Father is perfect' (Matt. 5:48).

This positive belief about human nature was in large measure shared by Plato, who in a striking passage describes human beings as having roots in heaven, and in his dialogue the *Theaetetus* (176 B) had expressed the upward call as 'becoming like God as much as possible'. The biblical and Platonist traditions therefore were at one in their assessment of the basic goodness and noble vocation of man.

As with the treatment of the Lord's Prayer, so too with the use of the pair 'image and likeness', the same formula masks a variety of interpretations. On the whole, though, patristic understandings of image are governed by their idea of the divine nature. As God was thought of as a simple, spiritual being, so too must the image of God in us be. This in its turn meant that for the vast majority of the Fathers the divine element, or 'image' element, in each of us is to be sought in the human soul or mind. Though this is true for the majority, there is one notable exception in the shape of the second-century theologian, Irenaeus of Lyons (c.130–200), who insisted, against the world-refusal of some of the Gnostics, on the goodness and godlikeness of the complete human being. Man for him is essentially a mixture of body and soul, material and spiritual, completely made by God with his own hands, the Word and Spirit of God.

This 'holistic' and positive view of human nature, coupled with his tendency to take a mild view of the Fall, has recommended Irenaeus to modern 'creation' theologians, who find the mainstream patristic tradition unsympathetic, either as being too 'spiritual' or as being too 'negative' towards the material order or too preoccupied with sin. On the first point, Irenaeus does form a strong contrast with Origen. For the latter, the image of God of Genesis 1:26 is identified with the 'inner man' of Romans 7:22. He makes it quite clear in his *Dialogue with Heraclides* that it is foolish to find the image in anything less than or other than the unseen, inner spiritual nature all human beings share, of which St Paul speaks both in the passage from Romans just mentioned and also in 2 Cor. 4:16, which distinguishes the inner from the outer man.

Athanasius, bishop of Alexandria from 328 till 373, composed two short treatises, probably at the beginning of his writing career, about 320, which deal with the structure, fall and restoration of the human race. Although differing from Origen in several points, he echoes Origen's belief about the essential character of the image of God in man. It resides, so he tells us in his *Against the Pagans*, in our rational soul. In the companion volume, *On the Incarnation*, the image of God in us is largely concerned with the ability to know God, and there is a close connection between loss of image and loss of the knowledge of God, and by contrast the restoration of the image of God is realized in the knowledge of God given to the human race by and through the Incarnate Word of God. Although Athanasius thought that something tragic happened at the Fall, he never says that the image of God was totally effaced or defaced, but that with the progress of time our ability to grasp spiritual reality was increasingly impaired.

The contrasts and similarities between the Greek Christian vision of the image and that of Augustine in the Latin West are clear. Much of the second part of his work, *On the Trinity*, is devoted to discovering within the structure of the human mind patterns of the divine nature. Basing himself on Genesis 1:26, Augustine argues that because we are in the image of God and because God is Trinity, it should be possible by introspection to find within us something of God's nature, which is there above all reflected. It is true that the interiority of Augustine may well have its roots in the neo-Platonist tradition of Plotinus, especially when both of them insist that the greatest truths are the hidden truths. Even so, Plotinus makes no attempt to prove a trinity within. Augustine found many trinities, or patterns of threeness, within, but probably the most celebrated of them is that of memory, understanding and will, which he explores in book 10 of *On the Trinity*. Now, although Augustine holds this very grand idea of the human soul, he also believes that it is corrupted, *deformis* is the word he uses, deformed. This deformity is a direct result of the choice away from God made by Adam; this choice for self rather than God resulted in a perversion of human nature and a fascination with self and the created universe, which, though not in themselves bad, become so if these objects take God's place within us and become, as it were, a sort of surrogate deity.

It is sometimes said with a good deal of truth that although all the Fathers believed in some form of Fall doctrine, the doctrine in the West, above all in Augustine, is much more sombre than in the East. Irenaeus, Origen, Gregory of Nyssa and Athanasius all believed that something went wrong at the beginning, but not quite as wrong as Augustine thought. Irenaeus does not think we fell quite as far as does Augustine, and even sees the 'Fall' as a step in maturing, like adolescence in human development. All, though, believe that our present condition is imperfect, that we are somehow 'away from God' and must return in order to gain (or regain) the lost paradise, the forsaken likeness of God. This likeness to God, which is to complete us and restore us to God, goes by various names, though the reality remains at root the same. Irenaeus, with reference to Ephesians 1:10 calls it 'recapitulation', Origen calls it 'restoration', Athanasius sometimes calls it 'recreation', but more commonly 'deification'. Gregory of Nazianzus also calls it 'deification', while Gregory of Nyssa follows Origen in referring to 'restoration' or *apokatastasis*, while Augustine's most common expression is 'beatitude', by which he means the perpetual enjoyment of the vision of God.

Beneath this variety of expression there is a basic similarity of idea. We are all made to become as like as possible to God and to see and know him as he is. 'Likeness', therefore, embraces moral and intellectual perfection and satisfaction. It is not something to be had for the asking, without any labour. It assumes the engagement of the whole person in the strenuous demands of the Gospel. Differing symbols appeal to the Fathers as appropriate forms under which to present the image of the spiritual journey. For example, Origen sees this world as a 'school for souls' which will educate us for the vision of God in the world to come. There and in one of his homilies on the book of Numbers he describes how, under the influence of moral discipline and intellectual food, the soul grows, gradually, to its proper size. This idea of the 'growth of the soul' is quite striking and quite un–Platonic. It introduces into the idea of Christian perfection the important idea of *progress*, the absence of which in the ancient world has often been noted. Gregory of Nyssa, both in his *Life of Moses* and elsewhere, uses the image of ascent in order to convey the notion of growing closer to God. In him, however, being a 'darkness mystic', the goal of vision is never reached and the serious Christian is committed to endless progress both in this life and in the future one. Gregory seems to have been influenced in this unusual programme by a verse from the Letter to the Philippians (3:13), which describes the Christian call as ever 'straining forward to what lies ahead'. The word usually used to describe this condition of the created finite spirit before the uncreated and infinite one is *epektasis*, and is derived directly from the verb St Paul uses. Finally, for Augustine the dominant image is that of 'pilgrimage'. The restless human heart longs for peace and can find it nowhere in this world, except in rare moments of ecstasy, and in the next world, 'where we shall see and be at rest'. This longing for eternity will only be fully realized therefore in the life to come. So he begins his autobiography, the *Confessions*, with the celebrated sentence: 'Thou hast made us, O Lord, for thyself and our heart is restless till it rest in thee.'

Even here, therefore, apart from the universally held belief that only God can satisfy the created spirit, and that he will do so with himself only when that spirit has prepared itself for the favour of that presence, there exist many differences. But perhaps the most significant are those between the low esteem in which Augustine holds the soul as it is, and the optimism of the Greek Fathers, and between the changelessness for which Augustine believes we are made and the ever-changing upward mobility of Gregory of Nyssa.

GRACE AND FREEDOM

The New Testament insists that the responsibility for our future rests firmly with us. The parable of the sheep and goats in Matthew 25 makes it quite clear that our free choices, our willingness to help those in need, because they are in the place of Christ for us, are what decide our future with God. We are free to respond positively or negatively to the divine imperative. On the other hand, other passages in the New Testament also make it clear that we can do nothing without the help of God, that is, without grace. St Paul, above all, is the great apostle of the divine grace; but he is not alone. In the Fourth Gospel, we read in 6:44, 'No-one comes to me unless the Father draw him.' Apart from insisting that both are necessary elements in any good action, the New Testament makes no attempt to wrestle with the problem of how to reconcile them.

The early Church offered three basic solutions. Either it stressed the primacy of freedom – as Origen, above all, did – or it did the opposite and asserted the priority of grace and predestination – as many Gnostics and, at a later date, Augustine; or else it resorted to an uneasy middle position, which insisted on the need for both and tried to avoid coming down on either side of the debate – a solution sometimes known as synergism and favoured by Gregory of Nyssa. This case was unlike the previous tensions we have discussed, both in echoing similar debates among Pagans, and in leading to ecclesiastical decisions at councils held in Carthage in North Africa in 418 and at Orange in France in 529. The fact that both were Western assemblies and that both felt the need to assert the primacy of grace over freedom sheds light on the stresses and preoccupations of the West, as distinct from the East, in the patristic period and later. For while the East was trying, in the Second and Third Councils of Constantinople (held in 553 and 680/1 respectively), to define the relation of divine and human in Christ, the West hoped to establish the precise roles of God and man in our response to the call of the Gospel.

Some Gnostics, notably Valentinus, held to the view that our natures and our destinies lie outside our control. We are governed by a providence over which we have no control. From this two conclusions were drawn, not by them but by their critics: first, we are therefore not free in any important sense, we are certainly not 'the captains of our souls' or 'the masters of our fate'; second, the author of our nature may be all-powerful but he is certainly not all-good. It is not altogether clear what led the Gnostics to such an assessment of the world and its author. In defence of their generally pessimistic estimate of the present world order and their consequent urge to escape from it, it may be worth remembering not only that some passages of the New Testament appear to take a similarly jaundiced view of this world, but also that the religious mentality of human beings is very often accompanied by a form of cosmic pessimism. The presence and enjoyment do God must be deferred till this life is over.

Origen, who is himself often accused of having a low esteem of this present order and of the world, stands out as the greatest defender of human freedom and divine goodness against the Gnostics. For him, the goodness of God is a primary article of faith. For its truth he appeals to Mark 10:18, 'No-one is good except God.' Also, underlying his view is that of Plato, who in the *Republic* identifies the supreme principle as The Good. To Plato he also owes the corollary of this. If God is not responsible for evil in the world, then we are. But we are not compelled to do evil; we freely choose to do it. Virtue, vice, good, evil – all exist in this world as a direct result of human choices. Plato had written, at the end of the *Republic*, that virtue is free, that the cause of good and evil lies with the human chooser and that God is not responsible. This strongly libertarian position is echoed by Origen. So convinced was Origen of the need to assert the goodness of God and the freedom of rational beings against the Gnostic, Valentinus, that in his *On First Principles*, the whole world order is attributed to the goodness of God and human free choices (1966: 134). We have all been provided with the inalienable power of free choice, and, according as we choose, so shall be and so is the condition of life in which we are. In other words, for Origen the system of the universe is a gigantic meritocracy in which prizes are awarded in accordance with our just deserts. In a pregnant sentence in his *Against Celsus* (4.3), Origen writes

'Take away free will and you take away virtue' (1965: 186). Finally, in his *Commentary on the Letter to the Romans,* Origen writes that if we were forced by necessity to choose one way or the other, there could be no room for blame of any kind or for virtue. *We* are the choosers. 'The soul, therefore, has the power to decide whether it will choose life with Christ or death with the devil.' Origen's libertarianism is the product of several forces. It is hard to believe that he 'invented' it simply in order to offset the pernicious views of the Gnostics, though that undoubtedly played an important part of his vigorous defence of freedom. More important is his fundamental conviction, for which he could appeal to philosophical and biblical precedent, that good actions done under any form of external compulsion are not good or valuable in any important sense. Freedom is the indispensable condition for excellent and fellowship with God.

Origen's libertarianism was in large measure adopted by the Cappadocian Fathers. Gregory of Nyssa, for example, goes even further than Origen in the importance he assigns to freedom. It is for him the primary expression of and witness to God within us; that in virtue of which we are like him. We may lose some of the features which initially made us like God, but the power to choose for or against him is, paradoxically, that in us which makes us most like him, and of that nothing can deprive us. So Gregory can write, in chapter 5 of his *Address on Religious Instruction,* that 'God would not have deprived us of the most excellent and precious of blessings – I mean the gift of liberty and free will.' In a later chapter of the same work (39) even our rebirth spiritually in Christ depends on our free choice: 'spiritual birth is in the control of the one who is born'. If we are essentially free beings, who make our own souls, does this mean that Gregory left no place for the action of divine grace? Not entirely. In several of his more explicitly ascetic writings, that is, writings which are primarily concerned with what we should do to follow Christ, rather than with what we should believe, he talks of the importance of God's grace. For example, in several passages in a work of Gregory's, *On the Christian Ideal,* he speaks of the goal of the life of the Christian being achieved by the joint action of human effort and the grace of the Spirit. The two forces cooperate to produce that vision of God which the soul craves for. In this treatise the relationship of the two, grace and freedom, is invariably expressed by means of words with the Greek prefix *syn*, with. This is what is meant by calling Gregory a 'synergist': he believes that grace works along with freedom – in other words, it neither precedes nor follows. This can be seen as an attempt to avoid the extremes of libertarianism, or an over-emphasis on human freedom, and predestination, where freedom is secondary and passive. In at least one passage, he departs even further from the position of Origen. In his treatise *On Virginity* (section 12) he writes that 'it is not our work nor does it lie within human power to become like God. This is a work of the divine generosity.' For all his dependence on his master, Gregory is independent-minded enough to acknowledge, in a way quite foreign to Origen, the need for grace in the life of the Christian.

Augustine is sometimes called the 'Doctor of grace' for it was he, above all others, who insisted on the primacy of the divine initiative. There can be no doubt that part of his insistence on this central point derives from his opposition to what he regarded as the un–Christian stance of Pelagius. The latter was by origin a British monk who came to Rome towards the end of the fourth century and did his best to instil a spirit of greater seriousness into the religious life of the capital. He particularly objected to the laxness of morals which he wrongly believed to result from a famous saying of Augustine in book 10 of the *Confessions*, 'Grant what you command and command what you will.' To Pelagius, human effort lay at the very centre of the Christian call to follow Christ. In a letter he wrote to a devout lady, Demetrias, he remarks that 'liberty of choice is our chief glory'. Further, to stress the need of grace was to deprive the action of its human reality. 'Spiritual riches could not exist in you, unless they came from you.' It was not that Pelagius denied the existence of grace; rather, he restricted its importance to what God gives us by way of creation and the sacraments and Scriptures. It was largely, though not entirely, identified with instruction and revelation.

For Augustine, this account of the influence of God upon us was extremely defective. Above all it failed to do justice to two features of Augustine's own consciousness, his own conviction that he had been saved from himself and brought back to God by God's mercy, and his deep acquaintance with the Epistles of St Paul, to which he had given close attention prior to becoming a bishop in 396. How could Pelagius' highly humanitarian ethics do justice to the religious fervour of St Paul's conviction, expressed at Romans 5:5, that 'God's love has been poured into our hearts through the Holy Spirit, which has been given to us'? Ultimately, for Augustine, his opponent's view was moral rather than religious. Instead of springing from the power and love of God and ending in his knowledge and praise, Pelagianism, with its belief in the emancipation of the human race from all constraint, tended to forget that not only do we depend on God for our creation and preservation, but also for the power to will and to carry out God's wishes for the world. 'So it [i.e. the outcome] depends, not on man's will or exertion, but upon God's mercy' (Rom. 9:16).

EPILOGUE

In the foregoing sections I have stressed the diversity of approaches discernible within the patristic period. What has been said by no means exhausts the riches of the spirituality of those early years. Above all they saw the rise of the monastic movement, spearheaded in about 270 in the deserts of Egypt by Antony, and spreading from Egypt to Palestine, Asia Minor and further west to France, culminating in the life and Rule of Benedict in the middle of the sixth century. The whole movement in its divergent forms is a witness not only to the desire for God, which also inspired Origen and Augustine, but to the further conviction that this desire required a 'flight from the world' in order to be realized. Sometimes, as the case with Antony, the flight was solitary, sometimes – and this became the prevalent pattern – it was a flight indeed but not in solitude. Pachomius, who died in 346, founded several communities of immense size who sought God in a common life of prayer and manual labour. Basil of Caesarea's work as bishop and theologian is perhaps surpassed by his work as a writer of *Rules* for his own foundations on the shore of the Black Sea. So popular did the ideal of withdrawal become that writers could speak of the desert as a city.

It is hard to account for the genesis of this powerful movement. It is not easy to see why the monk found it hard to realize the call to perfection and the love of God within the city. Part of the reason must be that the search for God was felt to be increasingly difficult in the presence of the noise and distractions of normal life. Again, with the departure of the age of martyrs at the accession of the Emperor Constantine in 306 and his subsequent victory in 312 at the battle of the Milvian Bridge, it became, in the eyes of many, too easy to be a Christian. The challenge of the Gospel declined when a Christian did not have to endanger his life or property in professing the faith. In other words, monasticism was a response to the challenge of indifferentism. It appealed to the heroic in man and came to be seen as a sort of substitute for 'red martyrdom'. Finally, it was, as Peter Brown has suggested (1989), a way of rejecting the demands of society to be, in effect, a slave of it and to surrender all one's life and powers to its service. This was above all true of women, who were expected to produce children and often to see themselves as mere agents of reproduction in a predominantly male society.

Whatever the precise cause of the rise of monasticism, it shares certain important features with other forms of early spirituality. It and they all believed that the origin and shape of their call were determined in response to some direct prompting from God, mediated by the words of the New Testament. Antony of Egypt heard the words of Christ addressed to the rich young man, 'If you would be perfect, go, sell what you have, give to the poor and come, follow me' (Matt. 19:21), and went and obeyed them. Basil, in his *Rules*, bases his idea of corporate life on passages at the beginning of the Acts of the Apostles, which speak of the importance of the common life. Origen's spiritual conception of the Christian ideal is often linked to 1 Cor. 6:17, 'The one that is united to the Lord is one spirit with him', and Gregory of Nyssa's fondness for Philippians 3:13 has already been mentioned. In other words, whatever we may think about their differences of emphasis and ethos from biblical Christianity, they clearly supposed themselves to be acting under its inspiration and with its clear warrant.

In addition to this external and formal similarity, all the writers acted following a deep-seated desire for the vision and possession of God himself, as the one alone capable of satisfying a profound desire placed by God in the heart of each of us. In the first chapter of *The Vision of God*, Kenneth Kirk (1977) writes that 'the thought of the vision of God as the goal of human life . . . came rapidly to its own'. From Ignatius of Antioch at the beginning of the second century to Denis the Areopagite in the sixth, a desire for God amounting at times to passion is the spring of all their upward movement. For Ignatius in his *Letter to the Romans*, this expresses itself as a passionate desire to 'attain to God'; for Denis it is part of the upward yearning of the finite spirit to be one with the infinite. In both cases the desire is for satisfaction and completion by a God who is quite distinct from themselves. Origen and Gregory of Nyssa found in the Song of Songs a powerful vehicle for articulating the love of the creature for its Creator; and, as we have seen, it was the restlessness of the human heart ever spurred on by God's presence that forms the centre of Augustine's *Confessions*.

Nowadays we are accustomed to make a distinction between what we call theology and spirituality. For us, the theologian is primarily concerned with an abstract, cerebral knowledge about God. It need imply no change in life, no relationship to God forged in the crucible of prayer. Spirituality, on the other hand, is a personal affair, partly of the head, partly of the heart, which presupposes a moral life, perhaps even one which entails a good deal of self-discipline by fasting and lack of sleep. This distinction between theology and spirituality is not particularly new. It can be traced back to the fourteenth century, if not earlier. It was caused by a quite new approach to theology and probably owes a good deal to the spirit of Aristotle, under whose influence theology became more of a science. So wide did the split become between theology and spirituality that a fifteenth-century writer could say that 'mystical theology and scholasticism are no more related than the art of painting and shoe-making'. Nowadays, again, we do not necessarily expect to find that the theologian is particularly moral, or the spiritual man particularly intellectual.

This dichotomy would have been quite unintelligible to the Fathers. For them it was impossible to be a good theologian unless one were living a moral life. In other words, the purity of heart of which the Beatitudes speak was a necessary precondition for the vision and correct understanding of God. So Gregory of Nazianzus (329–89) insists in his *Second Theological Oration* that any attempt to understand God without purity of heart is doomed either to failure or to danger. A deeper understanding of God issues from a serious moral life and accurate thinking about the things of God. The close alliance between knowing *about* God and knowing God may help to explain the difference between patristic and modern approaches to spirituality. It may also help to explain why we find so little reference in the writings of the Fathers to devotion and the place of feeling in prayer. It was not because they had no word for it, or knew nothing about it, but because to know God was simply assumed to mean something much richer than simply a series of abstract truths. It meant the expansion of the heart in the presence of one who was infinitely attractive, and a life lived under the influence of such a conviction.

The distinction we make, and one the Fathers did not make, between knowing God (= spirituality) and knowing about God (= theology) corresponds by and large to a further distinction between their anthropology, or way of understanding human nature, and ours. For them the word 'heart' did not mean simply the organ we feel with as distinct from the mind, as that with which we think. Even the distinction we commonly assume between mind and will only began to take shape with Augustine. For us, on the other hand, the mind, will and feelings are quite distinct. This means that for us thinking about God and willing his will and feeling for him are quite distinct activities, and it would be quite possible to know about God and yet have no sense of relationship to him. It is hard to say precisely when or why this separation took place; but its presence in the post-Reformation Church is quite clear. To put it succinctly and perhaps crudely, it was possible thereafter for the academic theologian to be lacking in devotion and moral seriousness, for theology had become primarily, if not entirely, an affair of the head. Conversely, it was possible for people to be obedient and devout, with little or no understanding of theology. Such a compartmentalization of the self would have been unfamiliar to great saints like Augustine and Gregory of Nyssa, for whom the movement of the self towards God meant one's involvement in that quest for the God who can satisfy head and heart and will.

REFERENCES

Augustine (1953) *Enchiridion*, ed. E. Evans, London: SPCK.
—— (1991) *Confessions*, ed. H. Chadwick, Oxford: Oxford University Press.
Brown, P. (1989) *The Body and Society*, London: Faber.
Eusebius, (1954) *The Ecclesiastical History*, London: SPCK.
Gregory of Nyssa (1954) *Christology of the Later Fathers*, ed. E. R. Hardy, London: SCM Press.
Kirk, K. E. (1977) *The Vision of God*, Cambridge: Clarke.
Origen (1954) *On the Prayer*, ed. E. G. Jay, London.
—— (1965) *Contra Celsum*, ed. H. Chadwick, Cambridge: Cambridge University Press.
—— (1966) *On First Principles*, ed. G. W. Butterworth, New York: Harper & Row.
Stevenson (1957) *A New Eusebius*, London: SPCK.
Tertullian (1953) *On the Prayer*, ed. E. Evans, London: SPCK.

FURTHER READING

Bouyer, L. (1963) *The Spirituality of the New Testament and the Fathers*, London: E. T.
Jones, C. *et al.* (eds) (1986) *The Study of Spirituality*, London: SPCK.
Library of the Great Spiritual Masters, in *Classics of Western Spirituality*, Mahwah, NJ: Paulist Press.
McGinn, B., Meyendorff, J. *et al.* (1986) *Christian Spirituality: Origins to 12th Century*, London: Routledge & Kegan Paul.

Wakefield, G. (ed.) (1983) *A Dictionary of Christian Spirituality*, London: SCM Press.
See also chapters 6, 10, 25, 27, 32.

27

MYSTICISM AND DEVOTION IN THE MIDDLE AGES

Benedicta Ward

Throughout the period that lies between the ancient and modern eras, from the early Church to the Reformation, there was intense exploration of the content of Christian doctrine which arose out of the experience of Christian life and which, in its turn, influenced it. Divisions between private and corporate, theological and devotional, natural and supernatural, secular and sacred, Church and State, were neither conceived nor formulated with modern precision, so that to consider 'devotion' in the Western Church for the period from 500 to 1500 would be to examine virtually the whole of the history of the Church for that period, which is also the history of society seen in its God-ward aspect. Even when limitations have been imposed, it is artificial to separate doctrine from devotion, or mystical prayer from other kinds of devotion, since those who formulated doctrine were also part of the general conversation about God in their times. One particularly important aspect of the devotional world of the Middle Ages is the fact that practically every writer whose texts survive belonged to the monastic or religious orders, so that it is by way of that particular approach to reality that the devotion of others can be studied.

The enormous diversity of the thousand years in question means that some kind of structure must be imposed; in this case, three dominant themes have been chosen under which to group a great spread of material: the first is the concept of the glory of God; the second, the humanity of Christ; and third, the relationship of Christians living in this world to heaven. These correspond roughly to three historical periods, but all can be found in each; it is a question of predominance rather than wholesale development.

THE GLORY OF THE LORD

Medieval devotion to God was based on the Latin Bible, the Sacred Scriptures, heard, read or seen. For a thousand years it formed the imagery through which reality was explored, both as a pantechnicon containing all knowledge and as that to which all learning was to be brought for its elucidation, but above all as a word of God to the soul. It was copied often and gloriously, and studied closely, so that the commentaries upon 'the Sacred Page' (as it was often called) were integral to it. The Old and the New Testaments were read as one single book by one author, God, who spoke to his people both in the time of the Law and in the time of Grace, illuminating the pages of both for the reader by the person of Christ; a comment by Origen (*c.* 183–*c.*254) on the text of Genesis summarizes already the medieval approach to Scripture:

> If anyone wants to hear and understand this according to the literal sense, he should listen to the Jews rather than the Christians. But if he wants to be a Christian and a disciple of Paul, let him hear what is said according to 'the law of the Spirit', and let him consider what is said about Abraham and his wife and sons in an allegorical sense. We are given such allegories, but it is not easy for anyone to discover all their meaning, so we must pray from our hearts that the 'veil might be taken away'. If anyone wants to be converted to the Lord, 'for the Lord is Spirit', let him pray from his heart that the veil of the letter might be taken away and the light of the Spirit come, as it is said, 'we all with open face behold as if in a glass the glory of the Lord and are changed into that image from glory to glory as by the Lord the Spirit'.
>
> (Origen 1976: 61)

This theme of glory communicated through the pages of the Scriptures to the believing heart provided the basis for prayer and devotion; according to Claudius of Turin (died *c.*830): 'Blessed are the eyes that see divine Spirit through the letter's veil' (1844: 617).

The Bible was not read alone; the concept of sacred Scripture was extended in some ways to the commentaries of the Fathers of the Church which were mined by preachers and pastors as well as forming the basis for meditation. This knowledge of the text through symbolic, spiritual commentary affected devotion at every level, usually linking the text with doctrine about Christ or/and interpreting it in relation to the hearer. For instance, in his commentary on Genesis, Bede (673–735) interprets a passage of the Old Testament thus:

> 'Four kings with five . . . took Lot the son of Abraham's brother . . . when Abraham learned that his kinsman Lot had been taken captive . . . he went in pursuit . . . and brought back his kinsman.' (Genesis 14:9, 12, 14, 16.) Here we see Abraham as the mystical figure of Christ who by his passion and death redeemed the world from death in battle against the devil.
>
> (1967: 186)

There is here interest in the text of the Bible as illustrating redemption in Christ, not in the possible meaning of this passage in its original context. Other commentators took this even further, as in Bernard of Clairvaux's (1090–1153) comments on the Song of Songs, which show his primary concern both for Christian doctrine and for its apprehension here and now:

> 'Thy Name is as oil poured forth' (Song of Songs 1:3). Draw near ye nations, your

salvation is at hand; the Name is poured forth, upon which when anyone shall call, he shall be saved. The Name is oil which when poured out feeds the flame and gives light to the soul; as oil nourishes the flesh, so does the Bridegroom's name feed those who meditate upon it; and like oil that eases pain when used as medicine, so does this name when we call upon it. Hidden in this Name of Jesus, o my soul, you have a sovereign remedy against every ill. Keep it in your heart always, ready to hand, so that all your love and desire may be centred upon Him.

(Bernard of Clairvaux 1971: 111)

The medium through which the glory of the Lord and the light of the sacred page were received was for most Christians not so much through reading written words but through hearing them said or sung, most of all through the poem of the liturgy, with the glory of buildings and ritual reflecting for the eyes the wonder of praise. The concentration of attention to what was prayed and seen to be prayed in church formed liturgy so that the church became an antechamber of heaven. Along with eucharistic celebration went the ordered public prayer of the Divine Office where the continual public reading at fixed hours of the day and night of the prayer-book of the Bible, the Psalms, offered a vehicle for the expression of praise and repentance, as their christological sense was drawn out by context and form.

This sense of glory and the wonder of what God has done in Christ was reflected in the gold of the crosses and the richness of other church ornaments; in the beauty of language, of music, stained glass and painting. The buildings contained sacred space in which, as it were, even the stones cried out in praise, though again and again writers and preachers affirmed that external glory was only of value to God if matched by inner conversion. In a sermon for the anniversary of the dedication of the church at Jarrow, Bede added, after commenting on the external glory of church building and ornaments both in the Temple of Solomon and in his own monastery:

The marvellous workmanship that went into the construction of the Lord's earthly house [has delighted] you as you heard about it and so . . . these details spiritually understood [should] arouse our minds to more ardent love of our heavenly dwelling place.

(Bede 1990: 267)

This sense of the immediate presence of the kingdom of God was linked to a view of history which pervaded both speculation and action. Time which had begun with the expulsion of Adam from paradise was with the coming of the new Adam, Christ, in its final phase; this was the sixth and last age of the world, in which glory was constantly breaking through from the majority of Christians already in heaven to those still on earth. The contact of Christians in this world with the saints was no wistful sentimentality but a practical awareness of their united life in Christ: the saints lived in the 'seventh age' of the world which was thought to run concurrently with the sixth or present age from the birth of Christ until the end of the world; both would find their culmination in the eighth and last 'age', the day of the Lord.

It is appropriate to refer briefly here to the tradition of devotion in these centuries in the Eastern parts of the Christendom, that is, in the Greek and Russian Orthodox Churches, since the sense of the presence of the saints and the awareness of glory were there particularly emphasized. As in the medieval West, for the Orthodox East the Divine Liturgy was, and has continued to be, the source of devotion, with its stress on the dimension of mystery and of glory expressed and made personal by the living significance of symbols, gestures and icons, used as doors opening into heaven. As well as continuing this objective dimension of the early Church, Orthodoxy also fostered an intimate sense of prayer as the heart of religion for the individual, by its tradition of personal spiritual direction and also by stress upon the use of the formula 'Lord Jesus Christ, Son of the Living God, have mercy upon me, a sinner' as the focus of personal prayer, both of which traditions can also be found at times in other forms in the medieval West, but which have a continuity in the East which was lost in the different development of Western history.

THE HUMANITY OF JESUS

The sense of living in the antechamber of heaven, with the shadow of judgement as well as the promise of mercy always present, coloured all aspects of medieval devotion, but the eleventh century saw a turning point towards a more personal, interior and humanistic approach. The key figure in this was the theologian–monk, Anselm of Bec, who ended his life as archbishop of Canterbury (1033–1109). He made a break with the long tradition of prayer which flowed mainly through the channels of the Psalms, by creating a new kind of poetic material for the use of those who wanted to pray. His *Prayers and Meditations* arose out of his own prayer, and he sent copies of them to those of his friends who asked for them, together with simple and practical advice about how they were to be used. Naturally his prayers were shaped by his monastic and clerical background and interests, but from the first they were popular with men and woman living a busy Christian life in society, for whom the ideal of prayer was seen in the cloister, an ideal with which they longed to be associated. Anselm's secretary and biographer, Eadmer, wrote of these prayers in his *Life of St Anselm*:

> With what fear, with what hope and love he addressed himself to God and his saints and taught others to do the same. If the reader will only study them reverently, I hope that his heart will be touched and that he will feel the benefit of them and rejoice in them and for them.
>
> (Eadmer 1962: 14)

In Anselm's writings there is no rift between Christian thought and Christian devotion. As well as being a good pastor, a man of prayer and an affectionate friend, Anselm was an outstanding scholar, with one of the keenest minds of all time, and he applied his intellect to the lifelong task of thinking about God. Every part of his fine mental equipment was stretched to its limit, seeking and desiring God; at the end of the *Proslogion* he wrote:

> My God,
> I pray that I may so know you and love you
> that I may rejoice in you
> and if I may not do so fully in this life,
> let me go steadily on
> to the day when I come to that fullness.
>
> (Anselm 1973: 266)

It is clear from this quotation, which comes from his most brilliant philosophical work, in which he first proposed what was later called 'the ontological argument' for the existence of God, that Anselm knew very well that God is not known by the intellect on its own but by the heart and mind together. His own discovery about prayer was what he passed on to others as 'faith seeking understanding'. In his advice about praying, he insisted that the first necessity was to want to pray and to be ready to give up some part at least of concern with oneself in order to be 'free a while for God'. In a quiet place, alone, Anselm offered to the person praying words that he himself had prayed, arising out of but not confined to, the Scriptures, to be used in personal and intimate dialogue with Jesus.

Anselm knew that it is not easy to 'leave one's selfish preoccupations' even for a little while and that to go into a quiet place was only the first step. Indeed, to be absolutely alone was no part of the Christian tradition as Anselm understood it, and so he put into many of his prayers words that give the reader an awareness of the presence of those already in Christ, called saints in a specific sense. In a dialogue with Christ and with the saint, usually a saint from the Bible, like Mary, John the Baptist, Paul or Mary Magdalene, Anselm offered words that were meant to stir the readers out of their lethargy and make them use their emotions and minds as triggers to move the will to seek God, first by awareness of sin and then by an even greater realization of the love and mercy of God. This way of 'compunction', of being pierced by sorrow for sin or joy in redemption, was to lead only to love, which is identified in and with the person of Christ.

These prayers reshaped the devotion of Western Europe: they were at once widely copied and imitated. It is not without interest to compare the imitations with the small number of prayers Anselm himself wrote, and to find that it is only in the latter that the brilliance of imagery, the warmth of emotion, and the beauty of style are so linked to true theology that they can still serve as a path to God. This is most vividly seen in Anselm's third meditation, which is a summary of the theological argument of his treatise on redemption, *Why God Became Man*, set in the form of a heart-felt prayer:

> Lord, my heart is before you; I try, but by myself I can do nothing; do what I cannot. Admit me into the inner room of your love. I ask, I seek, I knock. You

who made me seek, make me receive; you who gave the seeking, give the finding; you who taught the knocking, open to my knock.

(Anselm 1973: 237)

These prayers of Anselm were used not only by monks but also by secular friends. A century later, the Cistercians, and especially Bernard of Clairvaux, made this way of prayer even more popular, but in doing so began its separation from the academic analysis of doctrine. Knowledge by the head began to be set in opposition to the knowledge of the heart, leading eventually to aridity in theology and sentimentality in devotion; as one of his contemporaries, Hugh of St Victor, wrote, 'Love knocks and enters; knowledge stands without.'

The other side of this interiorization of glory was an increasing sympathy with the sufferings of Christ and his mother. Both the mass and the Office increasingly emphasized the links with the passion of Christ provided by the experience of corporate prayer: these were reflected in the increasing number of feasts commemorating the life and person of Christ, of the Virgin Mary, and of the Passion in particular. The Office which, in its daily observance, had been linked with the hours punctuating the Passion story since the third century, now increasingly directed attention to the person of Christ by the addition of the Office of Our Lady and the Office of the Dead. The change can be illustrated by the alteration from the veneration accorded to Christ through the cross of glory in earlier centuries, where he was shown robed and crowned like a king. After the eleventh century in the West, the crucifix became increasingly a depiction of 'the man of sorrows'. It was no longer a matter of presenting 'God in Christ reconciling the world to himself' (2 Cor. 5:19), either by a figure richly apparelled or by the form of a young man with eyes wide open and head erect, mounting the cross 'because he willed it' (John 10:18), but of putting forward a suffering servant whose pains reproached those praying in order to arouse them to compassion and repentance. The change is illustrated by the fact that Francis of Assisi (c.1181–1226) was the first person to receive on his body the stigmata, the wounds of the crucified Christ. The focus of devotion changed, from the receiving of salvation already wrought, to personal involvement with the central action of that salvation.

The passionate emotions aroused by the new devotion to Christ and his mother led to the circulation of relics related to the earthly life of both: the shift of the Virgin Mary which she wore when nursing the child Jesus, the hairs she tore out in her anguish at the foot of the Cross, the nails, spear, crown of thorns, and the blood of the crucifixion joined the better-known pieces of the cross as a focus for devotion and a reminder of the human life and death of Jesus. A negative side of this emotion was the increasing marginalization of the Jews in Western society, as the supposed perpetrators of the death of Christ.

Devotion to the eucharist also underwent a change, from the understanding of the whole sacrament of the body of Christ, linking the believer to the whole Church which was summed up in Anselm's 'Prayer Before Receiving Communion' (1973: 100–1), to a narrow concentration on the matter of the sacrament, the bread and wine as body and blood. Change in theological perspective and formulation was here directly linked to change in devotion, observable, for example, in the use of the consecrated elements as relics in the dedication of churches. The feast of Corpus Christi, introduced and popularized in the thirteenth century, presented a different approach to the mass from that of Maundy Thursday and Easter, focusing on the presence of Christ in the eucharistic elements rather than on the redeeming events that lay at the origins of the rite and formed the identity of the Christian community as 'the body of Christ'.

This shift in devotion produced practical changes in Christian living: where poor and suffering humans had previously been seen as those who by their anguish were nearest to Christ, a privilege they should be allowed to keep, and to whom the rich gave alms not for their alleviation so much as for the good of the donors, now care of the poor, the weak and the suffering began to be seen as service given to fellow Christians as if to the suffering Christ on earth, a duty essential in itself. This change of emphasis showed itself also in attempts to sacramentalize all ways of life in society, and not to see salvation as attained mainly by imitating monasticism. Many of those involved in what was in much of its structure a military society were able to understand their lives as Christian soldiers, not only by agreeing to schemes meant to limit warfare, such as the Peace of God, and the Truce of God, but by pilgrimages to Jerusalem, later called the crusades (a subject to which we shall return). The cult of chivalry was already giving a glamour to the soldier and the romance of the *Quest of the Holy Grail* furthered the sense that it was possible to be a knight of Christ. While a counter-current held to a spiritual sense of warfare (as in Ephesians 6:10ff.) in which the enemy was within, physical death in battle in the crusade was declared to be the equivalent of martyrdom leading straight to heaven by way of actual journeys and vigorous battles.

An unexpected result of the contact of the Western world with Byzantium and Islam in the crusades was the rediscovery in the West of the works of Aristotle, which were appropriated into theology most of all by Thomas Aquinas (1225–74). The revolution in theology and philosophy which this caused had its effect on popular religion, and preaching took on an added dimension due to the training of clerics in the new modes of thought. The importance of defining and presenting doctrine to form Christian life was given further urgency not only by contact with non-Christians such as Jews and Muslims, but by the rise of heresy within the Church in the form of the Cathars, or Albigensians, in the Languedoc area of the south of France, and groups such as the Humiliati in Italy. The dualist creed of the Cathars, with its devaluation of matter and its exaltation of spiritual ideals, attracted a large and organized following, most of all because of the piety and austerity of life of its leaders. It provoked several reactions from the Church. First, the institution of the papal Inquisition was set up to control and examine the teaching of the heretics. Second, the combat against heretical doctrine led to further refinement and restatement of doctrine. Third, the example of holy living shown by the orders of friars, mainly the Franciscans and Dominicans, as well as by the Cistercian monks, with their stress on evangelical and personal poverty and austerity, was given an added urgency by the example of the heretical experiments in such evangelical living. The Gregorian reform of Church life in the eleventh and twelfth centuries had led to an increasing clericalization of Christian life, and at the same time a separation of clergy from laity. And it may well be because of the isolation of theology as a clerical occupation that the most significant changes in the spirituality of the late Middle Ages came about, in spite of the dangers of heresy, among the simple and meek of the earth rather than among the outstanding theologians in the universities.

A GREAT CLOUD OF WITNESSES

This understanding of the glory of the Lord and the nearness of Jesus was joined by a third feature, an urgent sense of the use that could be made of the relationship with the saints, those who were known to be already alive to God in Christ. The theology of intercession was developed in this period especially in the increasing number and scope of prayers for the dead. In the one household of faith, the prayers of the saints were woven into the fabric of daily life at every level, but also increasing responsibility was felt for those who had died but had not yet attained their place in glory. The doctrine of purgatory and the intercession of the saints produced an almost materialistic fervour for the accumulation of merit before God for oneself or one's friends, alive or dead. The offering of indulgences, that is, the use made of the accumulated merits of Christ and the saints for remission of the punishment for sins of those on earth, underlined this attitude, and the building of chantry chapels for prayers for the founders after their death was a result of this very practical and personal approach to religion. This attitude in devotion can be seen most of all in the growing cult of the saints, which can be observed in a number of ways: in accounts of their lives and miracles, in the increasing numbers of pilgrimages which focused on relics of the dead saints, and in the miracles associated with them at shrines.

In the early Church, the liturgical celebration of Christians through the year had revolved around the central mysteries of salvation: incarnation, redemption and the coming of the Holy Spirit, but this had been expanded by the liturgical celebration of the death of those who were seen to be closely conformed to Christ, that is, saints. The first stage in the cult of the saints concerned the people mentioned in the Bible as being closest to Jesus in his earthly life, the Virgin Mary and the apostles. After them came the early martyrs and then those who were held to have shown the charity of Christ in their earthly lives and deaths in every part of Christendom. This accumulation became so extensive that the Fourth Lateran Council of 1215 set up a sifting process for the canonization of saints, which centred on the accounts of their lives and their miracles. Popular curiosity about the saints was not, however, easily controlled. Where accounts of the lives of early saints, including biblical characters, did not exist, they were invented; they provided food for the imagination and so for meditation at all levels of society.

Pre-eminent in the cult of the saints was the Virgin Mary, the mother of Jesus. In Scripture, her place was definite but discreet, always associated with her son; in a sense, hers seemed to be a secret life, not a matter for public speculation. But with the increased interest in the humanity of Jesus in the eleventh century, devotion demanded more. The Protevangelium of James, dating from the second century, had speculated about her parents and named them Joachim and Anna; later centuries were to treat Mary as if she were a contemporary about whom everything could be known and from whom everything could be expected. Since by her flesh she had given human form to God, so all humanity was now seen as included in her flesh. Her growing cult presents a panorama of medieval life and devotion. The prayers of Anselm included three to the Virgin Mary and were replete with carefully wrought theology, as well as with emotion; in them the place of Mary in relation to her son was clearly defined and stirringly presented.

Popular devotion gradually lost sight of the theology in favour of the emotion, to such an extent that Mary was seen as embodying the compassionate love of a saviour and Jesus as administering the severity of a judge, a severity which only his mother could ameliorate. This was not in contradiction to but rather an extension of the increased pity for his sufferings, since the pain Christ endured on the cross was increasingly seen as a condemnation of human sin which had caused it. Miracle stories about the Virgin proliferated with astonishing rapidity, producing a literature numbering thousands of examples and embodying the desire of ordinary people for favour and patronage, to be specially favoured by a powerful and loving one, however sinful and hopeless they might be. It was a devotion for everyman, and it lay at the centre of popular religion for at least five hundred years. The figure of Mary was seen in contemporary terms, as a great lady, a young mother, a desirable girl, who would always be on the side of those who expressed love for her. This devotion could be expressed in prayers such as the Hail Mary, in the saying of the rosary, or in the devotion of the Five Joys of Mary, as well as in the new feasts of the Virgin and the widely used Little Office of the Virgin. An example of the extent of popular confidence in Mary and the power attributed to even the smallest stirring of devotion to her is the story of the thief Ebbo: in the course of a career of crime, he was said to have been devoted to the Virgin and was in the habit of saluting her even on his marauding expeditions. He was caught and hanged, but Mary held him up for two days, and when the executioners tried to fix the rope more tightly she put her hands on his throat and prevented them, until finally he was released.

Interest in later saints included the same kind of curiosity about the details of their lives as was directed towards the Virgin Mary. Increasingly, the question asked about saints was whether these people revealed the love of Christ in terms that could be understood by their contemporaries. Hagiography has always been concerned with the ways in which a saint's life has conformed to that of the basic pattern of Christian sanctity, Christ, but there was growing interest after the eleventh century in what the saints had actually said and done in their earthly lives. This humanistic change produced the lives of Anselm of Canterbury, Aelred of Rievaulx, Hugh of Lincoln and many more, and began a trend which contributed eventually to the modern understanding of biography.

A large part of accounts of the lives of saints concerned miracles which in this period became a major part of the authentication of a saint. A saint's contemporaries could attest the power of divine charity at work during his life, but what mattered even more was that the power and mercy of God should be expressed by miracles, signs of God's work through him, both alive and dead. There was a growing literature of the miraculous, a concentration on shrines and then on handbooks of miracle stories compiled for preachers and for the devout, illustrating themes for meditation.

Frequently, though by no means always, miracles were connected with relics, fragments remaining from the earthly life of the saint, ranging from the whole body to splinters of bone, dust from the tomb, fragments of clothing, or water in which the bones had been washed. Allied to the cult of miracles, then, was the cult of relics which proceeded most clearly of all from a very practical desire for contact with eternity. The bones of the saints, especially the martyrs, were held in great reverence from early times as the remains of places where divinity had been manifested and which would still, since the saint lived on, provide a visible and tangible link with Christ through his holy ones. The sick and those in other kinds of need came or were brought therefore to the tombs of the saints and often allowed to sleep there, to touch the bones, to drink water mixed with dust from the tomb, and to offer prayers in words and by means of gifts. The focusing of devotion on the shrines of the saints was a local and spontaneous phenomenon throughout Europe for the whole of the Middle Ages, and one which was to provide most problems for the theologians of the sixteenth-century Reformation.

Another aspect of the cult of the saints was pilgrimage, which had always been a factor in Christian spirituality but which was, as we have seen, given a new direction by that great feature of the Middle Ages, the crusades, and by an increasing freedom for travel. The Pauline image of Christian life as a quest for another country, a pilgrimage towards man's true home of heaven, took on a very practical and external form. In order to go to 'the Jerusalem which is above', pilgrims went first of all to the actual Jerusalem on earth, especially on the expeditions which were later to be called crusades but which were at first referred to as 'journey' or 'pilgrimage'. The call of Pope Urban XI in 1095 for all Christians to attempt the deliverance of Jerusalem from the hands of the Saracens highlights many of the themes already noted in medieval devotion. The Holy Land to be rescued was the land of the Bible where Adam was created and the glory of God was manifested to men in Christ; it was also the place where Christ would come again in glory. Especially important was Jerusalem, which was seen (as in the Hereford *Mappa Mundi*) as the centre of the world. Since it was the place where the earthly Jesus had lived and suffered, it offered supremely one of those chinks between heaven and earth where contact with heaven was especially available. Pilgrimage there carried the promise of full absolution from sin and gave a chance to the ordinary Christian to become part of the spiritual warfare of Christ and his saints by doing the one thing that was possible for a militarily orientated society, to fight for the release of captives and the protection of poor pilgrims, even when it involved killing and destruction.

Besides Jerusalem, the great places for pilgrimage were Rome and Compostela, where the bones of the apostles Peter, Paul and James afforded other well-tried locations for access to heaven; and among later shrines Canterbury, with its new martyr Thomas Becket (*c.*1118–70), was at times their rival in popularity on an international scale. But there were also local shrines for pilgrimage, some containing fragments of the bones of the early martyrs, others with the bodies of later saints of local repute, which were appealed to for healing and for support in matters of justice, in a fashion which could become a demand for favour rather than a petition for mercy.

It is sometimes said that in the later Middle Ages Church life was at a particularly low ebb, with the complex and materialistic side of popular religion obscuring the realities of belief and theology. Serious-minded people have always criticized formalism and hypocrisy in religion, and this was certainly so in the fourteenth and fifteenth centuries, but such criticism does not necessarily mean that dissent from orthodoxy was widespread. Yet it is true to say that increasingly in the late Middle Ages the most vigorous understanding of Christian life seemed to be found on the fringe of the formal structures of the Church. It is possible to see this as a time of widening gaps, with, on the one hand, a highly efficient and centralized administration in the papacy, international in scope, with a minute and detailed code of law, precise doctrinal formulations and an over-organized clergy, and, on the other, the growth everywhere of independent personal piety, literate and deeply versed in the Scriptures, present in lay life rather than monasticism. Sometimes this vigour took the form of heresy. In England, for instance, this was most usually found in forms of Lollardy, the movement associated with John Wycliffe (*c.*1330–84). Whatever truth there may be in this picture, it can also be said that the late Middle Ages were also a time of great Christian vitality, which issued in robust criticism of hypocrisy but also took the form of mysticism and piety.

The delineation of ways of prayer, thought and feeling had been undertaken since the eleventh century by many theologians from Anselm onwards. But besides the analysers of prayer there were also visionaries and mystics such as Hildegard (1098–1179), the abbess of Bingen in Germany who expressed her insight in images of colour, warmth and beauty, which have recently become known through recordings of some of her music. This breaking through of heaven was beyond intellectual words and concepts, and it seems that it was especially open to those, such as lay-brothers in religious orders and women, who had not had their minds limited by academic systems: as Bernard of Clairvaux wrote in a letter to Hildegard:

> How could I presume to advise or teach you who are favoured with hidden knowledge in whom the influence of Christ's anointing still lives so that you have no need of teaching for you are said to be able to search the secrets of heaven and to discern by the light of the Holy Spirit things that are beyond the knowledge of man.
>
> (Bernard of Clairvaux 1953: 46)

In the following centuries, the life of Christian piety produced more written works analysing and giving instruction about the life of prayer, such as the writings of two German Dominican mystics, Master Eckhart (c.1260–1327) and Johann Tauler, (c.1300–61) and in the Low Countries, Jan van Ruysbroeck (1291–1381), a Canon Regular whose community at Groenendael became prominent in the movement known as the 'Devotio Moderna', which produced a classic of spirituality in *The Imitation of Christ* by Thomas à Kempis (c. 1380–1471). Such writings were associated with the group known as the Brethren of the Common Life, and those who followed this way were concerned primarily with a deep personal piety which concentrated without structures on the inner search of the individual for illumination in prayer. Many of their writings were in German or Dutch rather than Latin and they urged the need for the words of the Scriptures to be made widely available by translation into the vernacular. Manual work had a large place in the lives of those involved in this movement; they were shoe-makers, schoolmasters, lace-makers by trade – town-dwellers of the new lower middle class. They were sometimes called 'Beguines', and an English chronicler reported 9000 in Cologne, following ordinary lives under a private vow of celibacy, while continuing their everyday work.

There was a sombre background to the times, with increasing violence and pain and death. In the various outbreaks of the plague known as the Black Death around 1350, one third of the population of Europe died. A series of wars between England and France, 1337–1453, arising out of the claim of Edward III to the French crown, became a dynastic clash of Plantagenets and Valois, in which, at the battles of Crécy, Poitiers and Agincourt, and the siege of Calais (1356), great numbers died on both sides. Joan of Arc (1433) gave a new and plainly religious focus to the French side of the conflict, with her heavenly guidance and patriotic piety, and was herself a victim of the brutality of these wars. Trade rivalry and the rise of the towns added to the general decay of the countryside and the beginnings of urban overcrowding, with its attendant ills in the new and more dreadful poverty of the unemployed.

During this time of rapid and disturbing change there was also, however, a notable and vigorous growth in devotion. There were in England, for instance, alongside the major secular poets, Langland (1330–86) and Chaucer (1343–1400), five influential writers of literature in the vernacular that was both mystical and popular: Richard Rolle (1300–49); the anonymous author of the *Cloud of Unknowing* (*c*.1345); Walter Hilton (1330–96); Julian of Norwich (1342–*c*.1413); and Margery Kempe (*c*.1373–*c*.1433). All were connected in some way with the increasing numbers of lay-people undertaking a life of devotion in solitude.

Earliest in time was the northern hermit and preacher, Richard Rolle. He was born at Thurgaton in Yorkshire, was educated in Oxford and possibly in France but became impatient with the formality of the schools, which he soon left in order to become a hermit back in Yorkshire. He illustrates the popular unrest with academic learning and the desire for a more personal following of Jesus. Rolle was a prolific writer and preacher, both in Latin and English, and was best known in his own day for treatises such as *The Fire of Love* and *The Emending of Life*. His English religious lyrics have found a permanent place in vernacular literature. He was an exponent of affective mysticism, depending on bodily feelings in prayer, such as heat, sweetness, and song, which he described thus in his *Fire of Love*:

> In the beginning of my conversion I thought that I would be like the little bird that languishes for love of his beloved but is gladdened in his longing when he that it loves comes, and sings with joy and in its song languishes in sweetness and heat. It is said that the nightingale is given to song and melody all night that she may please him to whom she is joined. How much more should I sing with great sweetness to Christ my Jesus that is the spouse of my soul through all this present life that is night in regard to the clearness that is to come, so that I could languish in longing and die of love.
>
> (Rolle 1927: 190).

Devotion to the person of Jesus Christ especially in his passion found a new and delicate expression in Rolle around the 'Name of Jesus', another popular devotion of the times both personally and liturgically, which he expressed in prayers like the following:

> Hail Jesu my creator of sorrowing medicine;
> Hail Jesu my saviour that for me suffered pain;
> Hail Jesu help and succour, my love be aye thine;
> Hail Jesu the blessed flower of thy mother virgin.
>
> (Rolle 1939: 269)

A little later in time and less popular than Rolle, Margery Kempe was in some ways the most typical of her age. She was noted for an emotional understanding of religion very similar to that of Rolle. Born at King's Lynn in Norfolk, she married John Kempe in 1393, and had fourteen children. A severe mental illness followed the birth of her first child during which she had a vision of Christ and thereafter regarded herself as especially bound by devotion. It was not until 1418, when she was 45, that she left home and undertook a life of pilgrimage, accompanied by visions and ecstatic experiences. These were dictated by her (she could not read or write) and form the first autobiography in English, *The Book of Margery Kempe*. It has survived in only one manuscript, which was only recognized as such in 1934. Of immense interest for the history of popular religion, it is of less note for Christian theology and prayer. Margery was an emotional person who wept often and publicly; her 'cryings' were the thing for which she was most famous, as she wrote of herself (in the third person):

> And this creature had great compunction, with plentiful tears and much loud and violent sobbing for her sins and for unkindness towards her creator . . . Her weeping was so plentiful and so continual that many people thought that she could weep and leave off when she wanted and therefore many people said she was a false hypocrite and wept when in company for advantage and profit.
>
> (Kempe 1985: 48)

Margery travelled widely, to Palestine, Assisi, Rome, Compostela, Norway, Aachen and Danzig. She had heard of, and perhaps had had read to her, the works of Hilton and Rolle and she visited Julian of Norwich, to whom she says she spoke about herself:

> She told her about the grace that God had put into her soul, of compunction, contrition, sweetness and devotion, compassion with holy meditation and high contemplation and very many holy speeches and converse that our Lord spoke to her soul and also many wonderful revelations, which she described to the anchoress to find out if there were any deception in them for the anchoress was expert in such things and could give good advice.
>
> (Ibid.: 77)

Margery does not appear to have heard of Julian's work, *The Revelations of Divine Love*; she records Julian as listening with courtesy and recommending obedience, charity and above all patience. There is a great contrast between this emotional, affective, talkative woman, and the wisdom of Julian, Hilton and the *Cloud* Author but, in many ways, Margery reflects the eager and vigorous devotion of the times as truly as do her more restrained contemporaries.

Julian of Norwich also, like Richard Rolle and Margery Kempe, was a mystic outside the institutional boundaries of monasteries and convents. She lived at the end of her life as a solitary in a room built onto the wall of a Norwich church dedicated to St Julian, from which she perhaps took her name. She wrote two works, one a longer version of the other, called *Revelations of Divine Love*. The title itself indicates the direction of her writings. They explore the way in which God loves mankind rather than giving instruction about how prayer and life can be directed to him. She could be regarded as the first theologian to write in English. The continued importance of devout women, whether in their concern for guidance about prayer or as visionaries and mystics, was a striking feature of medieval Church life. Among the most influential were the nuns of Helfta, Catherine of Siena (1347–80), Catherine of Genoa (1447–1510) and Bridget of Sweden (1303–73) – and Julian was to some extent in this tradition. She developed her record of a visionary experience of the cross in a lifetime of thought and commentary on the central mysteries of salvation. Her quiet confidence in the promises of God is a firm counterbalance to the morbid despair that was prominent in her time:

> In this endless love we are led and protected by God, and we shall never be lost; for he wants us to know that the soul is a life, which life of his goodness and grace will last in heaven without end, loving him, thanking him, praising him.
>
> (Julian 1978: 284)

Her use of the image of motherhood in discussing the second person of the Trinity was extended and detailed and took up a tenuous earlier tradition with new insight. Her confidence in God's love was the result of a life of struggle to understand how love and judgement could be held together in God, and her conclusion that 'love was His meaning' and that 'all shall be well' was neither facile nor sentimental, but the product of hard and anguished thought and prayer.

Walter Hilton and Julian of Norwich were the serious and sustained theologians of the group, but Hilton's *The Scale of Perfection* was more definitely a book of instruction than was the work of the other three writers. *The Scale* (scale = ladder here) covers a whole range of teaching about a life of prayer. As with so much spiritual writing, he says it was done at the request of others, in this case an anchoress (= hermit). He wrote to his 'spiritual sister in Jesus Christ' with advice she had asked for about prayer and spiritual life, drawing on his own experience to do so. A firm and clear picture of the life of prayer emerges, carefully arranged, set out with gentleness and tolerance, though with the austere theme of the mystics. In order to reach the vision of peace (which is the literal meaning of the word 'Jerusalem'), one must go through the 'night of murk': 'We may never come to the full knowledge of God till we know first clearly our own soul.' The way to this is as follows:

> You should draw your thought in yourself as much as you can, away from all material things and then . . . if you wish to find Jesus you should suffer the pain of this nothing . . . for right inside this nothing Jesus is hidden in his joy.
>
> (Hilton 1991: 125)

Hilton was reserved about the emotional and affective devotion connected with Margery Kempe and Rolle, and he may have had Rolle specifically in mind when he wrote:

> Hearing of delightful song, feeling a comfortable heat in body, or perceiving light or the sweetness of bodily savor. These are not spiritual feelings ... even when they are best and most true, they are still only outward signs of the inward grace that is felt in the powers of the soul.
>
> (Ibid: 256)

The most brilliant and original of all these writers was the anonymous author of *The Cloud of Unknowing* and other related pieces, some very short, the most important of which is *The Book of Privy Counsel. The Cloud of Unknowing* was a response to a request for help, in this case from a would-be solitary of 24 years of age who asked the author for advice about prayer. The writer was a clear and decisive person, full of wit and acute observation, with no time or patience for sentimentality and hypocrisy. He wrote in a racy English prose style with a single theme, which he explained with wisdom, patience and confidence, offering specific guidance about the way of prayer which is called 'apophatic' (because of its emphasis on the utter transcendence of God and his unknowableness by human faculties – he 'cannot be spoken about'):

> No man may think of God himself. Because he can certainly be loved but not thought. He can be taken and held by love but not by thought ... you are to smite upon that thick cloud of unknowing with the sharp dart of longing love.
>
> (*Cloud* 1982: 130–1)

While presenting a theme of great and mysterious import, he was always briskly alert to the dangers of pride and for those following a life of prayer:

> Labour and toil as much as you can and know how, to acquire for yourself the true knowledge and experience of yourself as the wretch you are ... it is his good pleasure to be known and experienced by a humble soul living in this mortal body.
>
> (Ibid.: 150)

Like Hilton, he warned against reliance upon Rolle's 'heat, sweetness and song', and recommended a way of prayer in which any knowledge through bodily senses was to be purified by darkness:

> If ever you come to this cloud, and live and work in it as I bid you, just as this cloud of unknowing is above you, between you and your God, in the same way you must put beneath you a cloud of forgetting between you and all the creatures that have ever been made.
>
> (Ibid.: 128)

The Cloud author insisted that the way of prayer he described was not to be undertaken lightly but only by those called to it by God, not those qualified by learning or self-confident ability, but those seriously seeking God; the work's present popularity in an equally anti-intellectual age is therefore not surprising.

All these writers were representative of their age, with their freedom within structures, their intense care for the interior life of the individual, their use of the vernacular, and their positive sense of the love of God towards humanity. At a time when the institutions in Church and State seemed to many distant and incomprehensible, delight in the Lord and his works remained alive among such vigorous but basically ordinary people.

In considering the devotion of Western Christians to Christ it should be remembered that there was throughout the Middle Ages a coherent understanding of spiritual reality, an indissoluble link between thought and prayer within a social and historical reality which was not separated from inner devotion and aspiration. It is not the case that theological speculation formed popular practice but rather that the theologians were also men of their time, and addressed themselves to questions which arose out of their situation. They too were involved in what we distinguish as 'popular devotion' and were able to articulate the universal sense of belonging in thought and in prayer to a continuing and living tradition. With regard to this lively tradition of prayer, it is possible to apply some words of the humanist and scholar, John of Salisbury (1115–80):

> We are like dwarfs on the shoulders of giants; by their aid we can gaze further than they did. Clinging to the ancient treatises we rediscover their finer judgements banished from memory by ages past, forgotten by men, and raise them as from death to new life.
>
> (John of Salisbury 1855).

REFERENCES

Anselm (1973) *The Prayers and Meditations of Saint Anselm*, trans. B. Ward, Harmondsworth: Penguin Classics.

Bede (1967) *Libri Quatuor in Principium Genesis*, ed. C. W. Jones, CCSL, CXVIIIA, Turnholt: Brepols.

—— (1990) *Homilies on the Gospels*, Book 2, trans. L. T. Martin and D. Hurst, Kalamazoo, Mich.: Cistercian Publications.

Bernard of Clairvaux (1953) *The Letters of St Bernard of Clairvaux*, trans. B. Scott James, London: Burns Oates.

—— (1971) *On the Song of Songs*, trans. K. Walsh and I. M. Edmonds, Kalamazoo, Mich.: Cistercian Publications.

Claudius of Turin (1844) *In Libros Informationum Litterae et Spiritus super Leviticum Praefatio*, PL, col. 104, Paris.

The *Cloud* Author (1982) *The Cloud of Unknowing*, ed. J. Walsh, London: SPCK.

Eadmer (1962) *The Life of Saint Anselm, Archbishop of Canterbury*, ed. and trans. R. W. Southern, Oxford: Oxford University Press.

Hilton, W. (1991) *The Scale of Perfection*, eds J. P. H. Clark and R. Dorward, New Jersey: Paulist Press.

John of Salisbury (1855) *Opera Omnia*, ed. J. P. Migne, PL, CXCI, col. 900, Paris.

Julian of Norwich (1978) *Julian of Norwich: Showings*, ed. E. Colledge and J. Walsh, London: SPCK.

Kempe, M. (1985) *The Book of Margery Kempe*, ed. B. A. Windeat, Harmondsworth: Penguin Classics.

Origen (1976) *Homilia in Genesim*, ed. and Fr. trans. H. de Lubac and L. Doutreleau, *Sources Chrétiennes* 7, Paris.

Rolle, R. (1927) *Writings Ascribed to Richard Rolle, hermit of Hampole, and materials for his bibliography*, ed. H. E. Allen, New York and London: Macmillan.

—— (1939) *The Life and Lyrics of Richard Rolle*, ed. F. M. Comper, London: J. M. Dent.

FURTHER READING

Brooke, R. and Brooke, C. (1984) *Popular Religion in the Middle Ages: Western Europe 1000–1300*, London: Thames and Hudson.

Dronke, P. (1984) *Women Writers of the Middle Ages*, Cambridge: Cambridge University Press.

Duffy, E. (1992) *The Stripping of the Altars*, New Haven: Yale University Press.

Leclercq, J. (1978) *The Love of Learning and the Desire for God*, London: SPCK.

McGinn, B., Meyendorff, J. and Leclercq J. (1984) *Christian Spirituality: vol. 16, Origins to the Twelfth Century* and *vol. 17, High Middle Ages and Reformation*, New York: Crossroad.

Mursell, G. (1989) *Out of the Deep: Prayer as Protest*, London: Darton, Longman and Todd.

Smalley, B. (1984) *The Study of the Bible in the Middle Ages*, Oxford: Basil Blackwell.

Southern, R. W. (1953) *The Making of the Middle Ages*, London: Hutchinson.

—— (1990) *Anselm: A Portrait in a Landscape*, Cambridge: Cambridge University Press.

Tugwell, S. (1984) *Ways of Imperfection*, London: Darton, Longman and Todd.

Ward, B. (1980) *Miracles and the Medieval Mind*, London: Scolar Press.

Ware, K. (1979) *The Orthodox Way*, London: Mowbrays.

Williams, R. W. (1979) *The Wound of Knowledge*, London: Darton, Longman and Todd.

See also chapters 3, 6, 11, 16, 26, 28, 32.

28

RELIGIOUS EXPERIENCE IN THE ERA OF REFORM

Rowan Williams

Late medieval culture was heavily weighted with symbolism: its world was one in which virtually anything could speak of or point to virtually anything else. But, more specifically, it was a world in which events and objects might be expected to speak of God, in such a way that (in the words of one of the greatest scholars of late medieval thought, Johan Huizinga) 'Nothing is too humble to represent and to glorify the sublime' (Huizinga 1965: 198). Qualities or characteristics in common between things, however apparently trivial, indicated a shared participation in a more profound unity. It is not surprising, then, that the devotional and artistic practice of the late Middle Ages tended to more and more complex levels of elaboration. Writers of the fifteenth century often expressed anxiety that the basic coherence of the Christian liturgical year was being overlaid by the multiplication of new feasts and cults; and, of course, the cult of the saints continued to burgeon, often carrying very significant local and political loyalties or aspirations. Much has recently been made of the importance in the later Middle Ages of the relatively new solemnity of Corpus Christi as a focal point of the year – a celebration of the community's identity and integrity, an occasion for restoring broken or threatened bonds of charity: it would be misleading to say that it overshadowed the historic feasts of Christmas and Easter, which were themselves also elaborated with new liturgical and para-liturgical ceremony at this time, but it is undoubtedly true that the position of Corpus Christi near the summer solstice, at the very end of the cycle of biblical feasts (Christmas, Easter, Pentecost) gave a radically new shape to the calendar. The eucharistic Christ, adored on Corpus Christi, could be clearly seen as the focus of all symbolic action, the point at which the transparency of created reality to God was most authoritatively set forth. The act of God through Jesus Christ, an act continued by Christ's authorized ministers, establishes the identity of two apparently dissimilar things, the eucharistic bread and the flesh of Christ (in the words of a late medieval English poem, the eucharistic host 'is quick [alive] and seems dead'). In celebrating the eucharistic transformation, the people of the late

Middle Ages affirmed their faith in a universe held together by God's creative and redeeming grace, and their trust in the sustaining bonds that held them together as a community within the Body of Christ.

Alongside this were other elements, in some tension with the great synthesis of public liturgy and sign. The beginnings of modern capitalism and mercantilism were already changing and fragmenting social patterns, and challenging the interlocking hierarchical relations of pre-modern community life. The crisis of moral confidence in the papacy and the early fifteenth-century struggles over where supreme authority lay in the Church had intensified popular scepticism about the authority of the clergy. And the spread of various sorts of radical spirituality had introduced an area of religious activity not all that easily contained within the public synthesis. Influential teachers of prayer, from Eckhart and his successors to Dionysius the Carthusian and Nicholas of Cusa, had given new force to the old tradition of insisting that God could only be spoken of by negations, and had aroused anxiety by what seemed to be a position encouraging indifference to the public linguistic and ritual activity of the Church, despite the manifest loyalty of such teachers to Catholic discipline. In a related but rather different context, we find, in the 'new devotion', the *devotio moderna*, the impulse towards a simple life-style, moral earnestness rather than speculative or symbolic imagination, and withdrawal from the public stage. Groups like that from which the *Imitation of Christ* (à Kempis 1952) emerged, reformist religious communities especially in the Low Countries, represented something of a challenge to the prevailing style of Catholic thought and imagining, though not in any overtly revolutionary way.

One final factor to be considered is 'humanism' – the new concern in the late fifteenth century throughout Europe to deploy classical scholarship, above all the possibilities opened up by the diffusion of Greek learning in Western Europe after the capture of Constantinople by the Turks in 1453, in the service of a renewal of the Church. The attempt by Erasmus and his circle to recover a sound Greek text of the New Testament not unnaturally went with a certain discontent with the extravagant elaborations of popular and not so popular religious practice. Earlier medieval reformers, like Bernard or Francis, had worked with an ideal of the 'apostolic life' as lived by the earliest Christians, but the Erasmian movement linked this long-standing and respectable tradition to a far stronger historical sense of how a primitive simplicity had been overlaid. And, like the reformist communities of the Upper Rhineland, Erasmus's circle stressed sincerity and directness in personal and social relations. Much influenced by Stoic literature (Seneca and Cicero in particular), they were aware of the problems created by the gulf between external hierarchy and the 'inner' realities of spirituality and morality. What is the authority of an external power devoid of inner moral probity?

The spirituality of the sixteenth century cannot be easily understood without this background of a growing tension between a sophisticated and resourceful system of public signs and public resolutions of conflict, and a widespread move in quite different areas of social life towards a valuing of inner experience and a consequent scepticism (which appears in varying levels of clarity or explicitness) about the harmonies, and so also the hierarchies, of Catholic society. Much in the medieval synthesis depends on the conviction that there is an authoritative guarantor of the unities and convergences that make the world a coherent communicating whole: unease about authority and unease about the reliability of symbolic systems goes hand in hand. The history of spirituality in the Reformation period is a history of attempts to manage this unease, either by a radical abandonment of the symbolic universe, or by the bringing of interiority into the service of the system itself.

FAITH AGAINST THE WORLD: LUTHER'S DISCOVERY

Luther is hardly a 'humanist'; he has no interest in classical learning as such, let alone classical ethics. But his personal and professional concern with the interpretation of Scripture drives him to a more sustained engagement with what lies behind the surface of the text than can be managed within the framework of conventional scholastic theology, and he shares with the Erasmian circle a problem over reality and appearances. He is also very clearly the heir of the negative mysticism of Eckhart and Tauler: he translated into German the post-Tauler compendium, the *Theologia Germanica*. The stress in Tauler and similar writers on faith as a pilgrimage into a territory without 'means' or methods, into a desert where religious observances guarantee no tangible results, is forcefully reflected in Luther's fierce hostility both to a religious busyness designed to secure divine favour and a 'charismatic' focus on experiences of assurance. In the second decade of the sixteenth century, Luther develops his critique of what he calls a 'theology of glory', a theology that celebrates congruence and harmony, the accessibility or visibility of God in the creation. In the theses Luther advanced at Heidelberg in 1518 (Luther 1962), he gave definitive expression to this critique, insisting that God becomes 'visible' only in situations where there is no congruence, no readable symbolic reference – i.e. above all in the cross of Jesus, where, to the human eye, God is absent. God can only be seen to be God where his utter difference from creation is shown: if he can be confused in any way with the order or process of the world, he is no longer distinctive or free. Thus the beginning of real knowledge of God (and so of real theology) is what Luther very bluntly calls being in hell, experiencing utter dereliction and meaninglessness. From here, and here alone, one can rediscover the experiences of ordinary life as *all* pervaded by grace. If God does not belong with a particular set of positive 'religious' experiences, the kind of experience you may have if you perform religious duties or undergo religious ecstasy, then God is not restricted in his presence in the world. The so-called 'secular' environment becomes a place for God to be found.

Hence Luther's eventual disenchantment with the ideal of monasticism (he ceased to wear the monastic habit in 1524, and married a year later): we encounter God not in a special sort of life, but in performing the ordinary obligations of our human life. There is no way in which we can earn God's favour by doing extraordinary things; so we must do prosaic ones instead. And we do what we do not out of the desire to purchase our eternal well-being, but freely: we imitate the gratuity of God's love by doing what we do not need to – serving and loving each other. All this is set out briefly and powerfully in Luther's treatise on *The Liberty of a Christian*, written in 1520 (Luther 1952); and it expresses with clarity the distinction between reality and appearance, inner and outer, that becomes more and more characteristic of the whole literature of spiritual growth in this period. The goal we aim at is a state in which our outward behaviour perfectly expresses the inner reality – which is union with Jesus Christ through trust in his action on our behalf to redeem us. The process of Christian living, Christian witness, comes *after* the fundamental transition, which is our inner cleaving to God out of the depths of abandonment and helplessness, where God in his humility comes to meet us, without form or comeliness, in that naked sharing of our Godless-ness which is the cross of Jesus. We cannot move from the outside to the inside, from appearance to hidden truth, because this reverses the true order of reality: Christ is not holy because of what he does and suffers externally, he is holy in essence from the beginning. To be identified with Jesus is to share his inner sanctity, a holiness not achieved or purchased, but simply there, purely 'given'. And this is why Luther (notoriously) taught that we could not really theologize about the process of sanctification, why we could not expect outward behaviour to give us any firm indication about inner spiritual states, why we could be called 'righteous and sinners at the same time' (*simul justus et peccator*). We could, of course, rightly and properly work to express our inner union with Christ, and it would be a caricature to suggest that Luther was not profoundly concerned about this; but there is, in his thinking, a kind of timeless quality to our holiness, as there is to the Church's holiness or apostolic integrity.

This was a strategy that enabled Luther to give at least a potentially positive evaluation to styles of life that had been consistently treated as second best in earlier periods – above all, marriage and commercial or civic activity. What distinguishes the Christian is not the particular style or state of life he or she is in, but the inner truth of God's grace and our trustful response. Thus it becomes almost impossible to say in advance that there are states of life or kinds of work incompatible with being a Christian. And here lay the ambiguity of Luther's revolution: the turn to interiority, in this austerely theological and christological context, could easily leave Christian ethics rather stranded, divided by a great gulf from theology and spirituality. The visible forms of Christian social life are supposed to be indistinguishable from those of worldly life at large; and this could lead to the conclusion that Christian faithfulness in external matters was always a matter of loyal and unquestioning belonging to whatever social order happened to prevail. If all external things stand equally under the sign of God's absence and difference, they all stand (or are capable of standing) under the sign of God's approval, by the same token, and no room is left for Christian protest as a legitimate spiritual path. The terror and profundity of Luther himself become part of a passive or pietist ideology for a bourgeois society or worse (the Lutheran heritage was to prove an acute problem in the era of the Third Reich in Germany). In many respects, Luther remains a medieval, the last and most radical of the German mystics of the later Middle Ages, taking to one possible logical conclusion the deep distrust of method and action in spirituality so characteristic of these earlier writers. But the paradoxical effect of his synthesis was to provide something of a theological alibi for certain kinds of modern political structures, centralizing and conformist, and with a supreme authority answerable to no-one – a deeply un-medieval idea.

COVENANT OBEDIENCE: THE REFORMED TRADITION

Luther and Calvin disagreed about christology, among other things; and this disagreement may help to illuminate the differences in emphasis between Lutheran and Reformed concepts and images of the holy life. Calvin (like Knox and some other non-Lutheran thinkers in the Protestant camp) laid a good deal of stress on the way in which Christ's human life 'recapitulates' the human condition, fulfilling at every stage what is required from us by the holiness and justice of God. Christ as man must in every way pay the human debt to God, enacting the obedience that God's covenant demands, even to the point of death and forsakenness. The dereliction of Christ on the cross is as important to Calvin as to Luther, but for significantly different reasons. Christ's faithfulness to God, for Calvin, has to be realized in the most extreme point of the human condition, the point at which God's justice exacts the full punishment for disobedience. Rather, as for Irenaeus, Christ's cross represents the performance of Adam's duty in the very heart of the consequence of Adam's disobedience. Calvin believed that the relation between the divine Word and the human individuality of Jesus was a relation between conceptually distinct agents (even though their action is inseparable in fact), so that the life of God the Word was not exhausted by the identity of Jesus (this is the doctrine of the so-called *extra calvinisticum*); and this allows him to give a creative role to the free human decision of Jesus that is commonly absent in Luther, who made strong claims for the practical identity of Jesus and the divine Word. Thus it would not be possible for Calvin to say, with Luther, that Christ's holiness is simply 'timeless', not achieved through his actions. Certainly Jesus does not become divine as a result of or as a reward for his actions; but this holiness must be (as we might say) constructed in the course of a biography. On this rests much of Calvin's theology of the centrality of the *priestly* humanity of Christ, standing for all human agents and giving them a share in the character of his own active humanity – i.e. making obedience possible for them, not as a way of earning grace, nor (as in Luther) as a way of expressing a given and immutable interior reality, but as the manifestation of the continuity between Christ's glorified humanity and our own in the acts of obedience that are done by Christ in or through us (Torrance 1965).

Calvinism thus does have a doctrine of sanctification, an account of the processes and disciplines by which the Christian life is to be brought to maturity; and this is shown in the typical Reformed concern for the purification of outward things, whether images in churches or inequity in the state. The Reformed polity allows far less to the *de facto* authorities in society than Luther's teaching: the elders of the Church are governors of a people who display in their life together the sovereignty of God's law, and they therefore possess a real independence of the 'magistrate' or 'prince' – though the latter may be called in to enforce the true discipline of the Church in a society where the Church is corrupted or deprived of real power to reform itself.

Calvinism thus produces, not so much a 'spirituality' in the usual sense, but a comprehensive discipline of living, scrupulous about fidelity to the law of Christ the King of the nations. This produced a high degree of sexual rigorism and what we should now see as patriarchalism in family affairs, and an intense sense of the imperative for stewardship of God's gifts in the economic sphere. No less significantly, it led to an intelligent interest in biography, in the ways in which God's direction shaped a life of faith by guidance, providence and answers to prayer. The result of this in second-generation Calvinism – not least in English Puritanism at the end of the sixteenth century – was to lead Christian thinking back towards what Calvin had struggled to lead it *away* from, towards what some Reformed theologians considered (and still consider) the weakness of vulgarized Lutheranism – a concern with the experience of assurance, and introspection devoted to uncovering evidences within as well as without of God's favour.

Calvin's doctrine of predestination had entailed a belief in the necessary victory of God's grace in whomever God might choose to receive it (the 'irresistibility' of grace, in the technical phrase). This was increasingly interpreted as meaning that a falling-off of the sense of security in faith, the sense of the lively favour of God, indicated that grace had never taken root in the soul – and so that the soul had never been chosen by God at all. This curiously subjective account of the workings of grace is alien to the concerns of Calvin himself, but became widely prevalent. Something of it is reflected in the Thirty-Nine Articles of the Church of England (1563), though these take care not to endorse the notion that those predestined for damnation could know this fact for sure. At the crudest level, this might lead to an assumption that material success was an index of divine favour (and its absence a sign of the opposite). Among the more sophisticated and morally sensitive, it led to the emergence of new genres of religious literature – the journal and the religious autobiography (whose only real precedent is Augustine's *Confessions*). In such works, the Puritan consciousness explored its own awareness of its history and its responses to and interpretations of apparently chance circumstances. Living under grace came to mean, for many, striving to make a continuous story of their lives, each occurrence being carefully and systematically related to the purposes of God, mysterious but not completely obscure, so as to exclude the sense of the absolutely contingent, events or thoughts or experiences that failed to carry the meaning rooted in God's will and calling for this particular life. It is not too much of an exaggeration to say that the European novel owes an enormous debt to this kind of literary Calvinism – as becomes very evident in the later seventeenth century.

The theological and pastoral problems that could arise in connection with the doctrine of assurance and its corollary, the final perseverance of the elect in their Godliness, were discussed a good deal in the England of the late sixteenth and early seventeenth century. Richard Hooker, in a very lengthy sermon of 1585 (Sermon I, Hooker 1841; 1989), argued against the usual form of popular Calvinist belief in assurance, on the grounds that faith, like other aspects of Christian righteousness, was always subjectively incomplete; if it were otherwise, we should have no continuing need of Christ. Assurance comes, not through a particular kind of emotional experience, but through the perpetual awareness of one's need and desire for God's favour; and in this sense, assurance is compatible with varying states of worldly success and varying states of subjective conviction or devotion. Some of this looks back (though not in conscious dependence) to an approach more like Luther's. It is echoed unforgettably in the poetry of George Herbert a few decades later. Herbert, undoubtedly Calvinist in the broad outlines of his theology, explores, with a fullness not previously found in English religious verse (and seldom equalled since), the brick wall encountered when the 'inner life' is experienced as stale, useless or meaningless, and God appears absent or even hostile. In such a light, 'assurance' is found only when the poetry itself allows the prior reality of God to emerge, overriding, silencing or rewriting the uninhibited expression of rebellion and suffering. In other words, the poetry works religiously by pursuing the interiority of faith only to dismantle it so as to make room for the interruptions of God.

Mention of Herbert requires us to note two other features in Reformed spiritual writing of the time. Herbert's treatise on the duties of the pastor (Herbert 1941) represents a Protestant adaptation of the new Catholic concern with the spiritual discipline and formation of the secular (non-monastic) clergy. The pastor's duties in relation to his people in terms of prayer and pastoral guidance are spelled out, and there is a careful discussion of the appropriate style and idiom for preaching. The issues raised here relate to a continuing Protestant debate about the use of rhetoric in religious discourse, in sermons and poetry alike. Herbert follows the Erasmian tradition in being suspicious of rhetorical elaboration: the more work is put into techniques of persuasion, the less honour is given to the power of God to touch and move the hearer or reader; thus the appropriate language for the Christian orator is always plain and unadorned.

In seeking a style that is transparent to the (inner) working of God in Christian speech, poetic or homiletic, this concern reflects the humanist preoccupation with honesty and with the critique of misleading appearances. It is of a piece with the Reformed hostility to visual art designed to move or stir religious emotion. Thus any kind of programme designed to elicit particular responses of feeling towards God – the visual and auditory art of the Counter-Reformation or the sophisticated meditational techniques of Catholic writers, from the early Jesuits to Francis de Sales – is unacceptable (Clarke 1993). It is essential to note that this is not a characteristic of what is usually called 'Puritanism' alone: it is not a hostility to skill or beauty or the aesthetic as such, but a coherent theory of how human activity makes itself a vehicle for God's. There is an appropriate 'beauty' for Christian art and utterance, but it is to be judged by how far it draws attention away from the 'real' agent, the divine agent.

Herbert, like earlier Protestant theorists of religious speech such as the humanist Valdes (whom Herbert translated), Sir Philip Sidney and Fulke Greville, is not a political Puritan, an opponent of forms and ceremonies as such in the Church and a critic of the existing order in the name of a primitivist programme of Christian reconstruction; but, although he is a loyal Anglican, he speaks for a view by no means universal in the Reformed Church of England. The sermons of John Donne and Lancelot Andrewes show the high levels of rhetorical skill deployed in preaching, whether to prompt intellectual exercise or emotional intensity or both. The early seventeenth century also saw the beginning of a diffusion of English adaptations of continental (especially French) works of devotion. But there was already a native literature of devotional reflection, going back to the Middle Ages. Some of this survived here and there, and there was a fresh outpouring of comparable material designed for the Reformed faith, books setting out patterns of daily prayer and reading, counsel on matters of behaviour, and forms of preparation and self-examination before receiving Holy Communion (Stranks 1961). It is a literature almost without exception directed at the leisured classes. With the disappearance of the popular devotions of the Middle Ages – pilgrimage, the cultus of the Eucharist and the saints, the rosary, the commemorations of the dead – piety had become largely a matter for the literate in Britain. Only in the eighteenth century did Britain catch up with the Continent in developing (mostly in the Methodist movement) a vehicle of mass piety and theological education by way of popular hymnody.

One further factor should not be ignored. Alongside the evolution of the 'magisterial' Reformation, the styles of thought and piety associated with Luther and Calvin and their immediate followers, there were also far more radical movements, normally emphasizing high requirements of personal purity or holiness, intense communal life, and – a sharp contrast to the generally affirmative attitude of the 'mainstream' Reformation towards civic and social involvement – separation from the compromised life of society around. Some such groups exhibited vivid apocalyptic beliefs, and the most extreme sometimes defended or promoted these with violence. But by the end of the sixteenth century, most had settled down into stable sectarian forms. These were characterized by pacifism, rejection of infant baptism, strong corporate discipline and, often, a stress on simplicity of life-style. In some respects, they represent a style or ethos close to classical monasticism; and in the eyes of the 'mainstream', their emphasis on tangible and disciplined holiness as essential to the Christian life posed exactly the same threat as monasticism had – a weakening of the radicality of grace. The strongest resistance to Calvinist views on predestination often came from sectarian milieux such as these. The modern Baptist churches are the heirs of such of these groups as became more assimilated to a denominational or connectional pattern. But modern Mennonite and Hutterite communities represent a closer approximation to their ancestors in their continuing stress on pacifism and purity of corporate life. They have always exercised an indirect but powerful influence on a good many non-Calvinist Protestant churches, in standing for a sharp, 'separatist' approach to sanctification, by way of a distinctive life-style.

THE CATHOLIC REFORMATION

Catholic reform in the sixteenth century did not begin as a response to the Protestant movements of the age; it is much more accurately seen as a parallel reaction to some of the same problems and stimuli, and it very notably has the same interest in the 'interior' and the individual. Erasmian influence had already spread to southern Europe before Luther's breach with the Catholic hierarchy, and the reforming movements of Spain in particular reflect this independent stimulus. Sixteenth-century Spain unquestionably produced the most important writers on spirituality in our period – the great reformers of the Carmelite nuns and friars, Teresa of Avila (1515–82) and John of the Cross (1542–91), and the founder of the Jesuits, Ignatius Loyola (1491–1556). It also nurtured one of the most independent artistic geniuses of the age in El Greco, whose painting can properly be seen as a rendering in the field of visual art of some of the themes of Spanish Catholic radicalism in the sixteenth century.

The fact that Spain was the nursery of so much religious creativity itself tells us something about the social sources of religious reform. The peninsula had only recently (1492) been reclaimed by Christian armies in its entirety from 'Moorish' (Muslim) occupation and the new society that was developing was aggressively and self-consciously hostile to the presence of 'impure' elements within it – to people of Moorish or Jewish descent, 'New Christians', who were generally regarded as unreliable members of Catholic society. People of Jewish descent in particular were suspected of continuing to practise Jewish rites in secret, and the Spanish Inquisition had originally been set up (in 1480) to deal with this. The result was a society pervaded by concealment and mutual suspicion, as persons of mixed descent sought to establish their credentials. Many town councils, cathedral chapters and religious orders began to enact statutes forbidding entry to people of 'New Christian' background. The secular literature of this time reflects widespread tension over all this, and much of it articulates a plea for sincerity and openness, and for the valuation of people by moral rather than racial standards. In addition to this focal issue, economic vicissitudes had reduced many traditionally aristocratic families to near poverty. From this side also, the potential inconsistency between appearance and truth was an acute problem (Williams 1991).

Several religious orders had begun early in the sixteenth century to reform themselves by returning to the original asceticism of their founders, and this had been part of a wholesale reform movement in the Spanish Church after the 'reconquest'. Part of this movement was an Erasmian interest in the primitive purity of the Christian religion itself, which generated a massive investment of scholarship in biblical research; and this in turn produced in some circles a humanistic ethos, sympathic to Erasmus's stress on inner uprightness and truthfulness, and indifference or contempt towards the ecclesiastical establishment.

The situation was further complicated by the growth of small groups of clergy and laity eager to learn about and practise contemplative prayer. These were much encouraged by some members of the Franciscan order, and became increasingly associated in the popular mind with extreme or outrageous expressions of religious feeling – claims to total unity with God or sinlessness or infallible inspiration – and (predictably) with sexual license. A complicating and novel factor was that women played a leading role as teachers and interpreters of prayer in many of these groups. Such circles were known as *alumbrados*, the 'enlightened'. Their object was to attain total renunciation and submission to God's will, and something like a suspension of normal consciousness and will. More cautious 'reformist' circles preferred to emphasize the disciplines of 'recollection', meditational techniques leading to the simple focusing of the mind on God. Here again, the Franciscans had a crucial role, and the *Third Spiritual Alphabet* of Francisco de Osuna (*c.* 1492–*c.*1540; Osuna 1981), first published in 1527, provided a popular and authoritative guide for many. It is essentially a quite conservative text, drawing on the style and emphases of Augustine and Bernard and other medieval authorities: the soul is to draw closer to God by reflecting on its own nature as spirit; meditation on the person of Christ is a crucial stage on the way, but is finally to be set aside. Along with works by a few other writers of similar background, the *Alphabet* became a favourite text for literate and devout laypeople – like the uncle in whose house the young Teresa first read it.

This widespread interest in 'mental prayer' – i.e. in the progress towards a form of prayer intended to be as perfectly receptive to God as possible, as against prayer that was the performance of verbal or other actions – was far from welcome to anxious authorities. The stress on the hidden working of God within the soul suggested a certain relativizing of the importance of the ordinary activities of Christian life, and of the hierarchy that administered them. As Spain became more and more the flagship of Catholic Europe in the war with 'heresy', concern with doctrinal as well as racial purity intensified; in 1569, the Inquisition prohibited the reading of a large number of books in the vernacular on the life of prayer, including virtually anything that appeared to encourage passivity in prayer for laypeople (women in particular), and some works that favoured frequent communion (also seen as a dangerous recognition of the rights of lay piety). Osuna's *Alphabet* escaped condemnation, but other works of his were named, and the *Alphabet* was not to be reprinted for over sixty years. Throughout the century and beyond, this particular controversy persisted, between those who encouraged all to aspire to a state of pure receptivity or passivity to God in prayer, and those concerned to regulate and control the possibilities open to the laity, and who regarded passivity in prayer as the first step towards the most serious heresy and blasphemy. The dramas of Spain in the sixteenth century were to be rehearsed again within the Jesuit order early in the seventeenth century, when there was a sharp struggle between those who wished the Society to return to a more contemplative vision, and those who sought to reduce the length of time spent in training and spiritual formation so as to make the Society a more practically effective and flexible institution. The result, partly inspired by the remarkable General of the Society, Acquaviva (head of the order from 1581 to 1615), was both a repudiation of activism and a programme designed to 'standardize' the life of prayer as lived in Jesuit houses – a skilful compromise that succeeded in establishing for the centuries ahead a classical form of Jesuit spirituality. And a similar conflict recurred later in the seventeenth century in France with the controversy over 'Quietism', in which the formidable Bishop Bossuet attacked the entire genre of what was now increasingly designated 'mystical' literature.

This is to run ahead; but it helps to set the scene for the struggles and achievements of Teresa of Avila in her day (for works, see Further Reading). As the daughter of a wealthy family of Jewish origin, she inherited one of the most central and persistent social challenges of her society – how to make sense of a social order that granted economic status and respectability to the racially 'impure', but preserved an underlying hostility and contempt that made it impossible for the 'New Christian' ever to belong fully, except at the cost of dishonesty. As a woman, committed to practising and teaching prayer, and even to interpreting the Bible, she was also a highly suspect and vulnerable figure. Part of the impulse of her attempt to reform her order came from deep dissatisfaction with the socially divisive form of religious life common in her convent and most others, where distinctions of class or family secured different levels of privilege and comfort in the common life. And this dissatisfaction was in turn nourished by her own experience as a Christian: she was abidingly conscious that, from the beginning of her monastic life, there had been a complete lack of correlation between the gifts given her by God in prayer, gifts of deep absorption and joy, and the immature or lukewarm level of her actual practice and understanding. Despite early experiences of profound receptivity to God, she had for many years practically given up private prayer; but a moment of visionary insight in the presence of a statue of the suffering Christ recalled her to seriousness, when she realized that she was the object of unconditional divine love, and was 'needed' to give friendship and compassion to Christ in his agony. All this laid the foundation for a consistent and far-reaching grasp of friendship with God as the basis of discipleship, a friendship initiated by the causeless love of God himself, and issuing in the possibility of mutual friendship between Christians. In this way, she learned to repudiate completely any suggestion that worldly 'honour' had any place in the monastic community, and was careful to legislate for small communities, in which each could have direct and equal personal contact with all, and share in the ordinary manual work of the house. Christ's incarnation is the pattern for such a refusal of status and distance: and the honour that matters is being made 'kinsfolk' of Jesus through the Church. Teresa's long discussion of the Lord's Prayer in *The Way of Perfection* takes this as its starting point (Williams 1991: chs. 1 and 3).

Her autobiography, written at the suggestion of her confessors in the early 1560s, is a careful apologia, insisting that she did not seek experiences of passive contemplation: they were given to her, often utterly unexpectedly and disconcertingly. She was thus able to present herself as a loyal Catholic, reluctant to look for extraordinary depths of prayer, yet compelled by God to receive unusual gifts. In this work, which received a good deal of unsympathetic attention from the Inquisition at various points, she elaborates her first theory of how growth in the spiritual life is to be charted – the celebrated image of the four methods of irrigating a garden (by hand, by a water wheel, by irrigation ditches and by rainfall). The significant progression is from a state where everything appears to turn on human effort to one where the agency of God is all-important. This is not a *method* for spiritual growth, but a structure for interpreting its evolution; Teresa nowhere commends a specific method, and her whole approach depends, in one sense, on the impossibility and unreliability of methods. The autobiography makes extravagant claims about the higher reaches of prayer, where union with God – she alleges – is manifested in preternatural experiences of total absorption and ecstasy. When she wrote her masterpiece, *The Interior Castle*, in 1577, she had rethought this issue, and was able to produce a new synthesis of great power and comprehensiveness. Here the dominant image is of the soul or self as a many-roomed castle: growth is progression towards the centre of the castle, which is where God already lives. We pass through seven different sorts of 'mansions' (*moradas*, stages on the journey) in this process: as in the *Life*, the progression is from activity to passivity and also from uncertainty to assurance, the assurance represented by the imagery of betrothal and marriage. Only from the final level can we look back and see how at a particular point a 'pledge' occurs between God and the soul of such a kind that there can be no final rupture. Very significantly, she now denies that final union is identical with experiences of rapture and suspension of ordinary consciousness: the ultimate state is one in which contemplative activity has become habitual to the soul, so that we can go about our normal business while God is consistently and harmoniously at work within us.

There is much of incidental interest in the *Castle*: Teresa discusses how to distinguish between different kinds of visions and 'locutions' (words or statements heard by the inner intelligence), how to cope with the periods of agonizing unsettlement caused by the sporadic visitation of preternatural effects in mind or body (including levitation), and, most significantly, the role of the incarnate Christ in prayer and meditation. In sharp and deliberate contrast to Osuna and the tradition he speaks for, Teresa, always profoundly incarnationalist, denies that there is ever a stage at which we can properly stop thinking about or at least fixing our regard upon the humanity of Jesus.

In this respect, she appears at first a little at odds with her close friend and follower, John of the Cross (for works, see Further Reading); yet closer examination suggests that the difference is not after all so marked. Certainly John's influence on the *Castle* in general is considerable, and it is usually agreed that Teresa's more cautious approach here to exceptional and dramatic spiritual experiences is the result of the continuous contact with John's teaching that she had experienced for some years, when he was confessor to her and her community in Avila. John is a very different writer in all sorts of ways. His background is in the ranks of the impoverished gentry; he grew up in something like real destitution, having to support a widowed mother by manual labour. But, as a Carmelite friar and candidate for the priesthood, he acquired a thorough education in scholastic theology, and his prose writings are technical and painstaking in a way Teresa's never are. He was also a poet of extraordinary skill and power, turning the idioms of lyrical and erotic Spanish verse to his own purposes (Thompson 1977). While the parallels between sacred and secular eros had been often exploited before (by Bernard of Clairvaux, Richard Rolle and numerous lyricists of the fourteenth and fifteenth centuries), John gives new and radical emphasis to the sense of erotic loss. The loving self is essentially a homeless and disoriented self, desperately seeking to recapture an intimacy and presence that has apparently vanished for ever. John even recasts, in his *Romances*, the entire story of creation and incarnation in terms of an erotic history, the finding and winning of a partner for the Son of God. The incarnation is the point when the Son and the bride embrace each other; it is also, however, a moment when humanity and divinity exchange some of their properties, God assuming the sorrow of the human condition and humanity receiving the eternal joy of the Godhead. The union of the incarnation depends on a reciprocal dispossession, God abandoning what is proper to him and humanity abandoning the self-obsession that keeps it from God. Christ alone can be the agent of both acts of renunciation.

Thus, although John follows earlier writers in suggesting that there comes a point where actual meditation on the human life of Jesus can be a distraction, there is no point at which this humanity does not underpin and make sense of the Christian's spiritual journey. In the most systematic and orderly of his prose works, *The Ascent of Mount Carmel/Dark Night of the Soul*, John gives a very important place to the idea that Christ is the paradigm for spiritual renunciation. Just as he is on the cross 'reduced to nothing', deprived of everything, including spiritual consolation, unable to do anything in particular, so we must confront the calling to a total emptying out of what we think of as action, understanding and joy – since it is on the cross that Jesus most decisively acts to bring God into the world, and completes the task his Father has given him. The *Ascent/Night* describes in painstaking detail how all the ordinary capacities of human consciousness and subjectivity have to let go of their usual objects and gratifications, both material and spiritual. Faced with the *nada*, the 'nothing', that then emerges, they can begin to discover God as the proper object of all the self's activity, and so advance towards perfect union with God, a state in which all we are and do is shaped by the obscure presence of God in us – not as an object for the mind, but as an agency given free rein in our inner life. The whole process is summed up neatly by John when he says that the three 'faculties' of the soul as defined by Augustine and the tradition flowing from him, the capacities of memory, intelligence and will, must be completely transformed into the three 'theological virtues' named by Paul as hope, faith and love. And for this to happen, they must first of all enter into darkness – the 'night of sense', in which all gratification of the outer, material perceptions and aspirations disappears, and the 'night of spirit', in which we leave behind even what we think of as the proper and due rewards of prayer and piety. Both 'nights' have an active and a passive dimension – what we do and what God does. The ultimate purification is the passive night of the spirit, which John famously describes as the most intense loss and suffering imaginable, a state where all landmarks disappear and we are thrown back on naked faith with no definable content. In this deepest darkness, the movement towards the dawn begins; not that it is succeeded simply by 'positive' instead of 'negative' experiences; but the self becomes aware of 'touches of union' in the depths of its being. In the imagery of *The Living Flame of Love*, one of his most mature, though diffuse, works – the fire of the Spirit begins to transform the whole self as it consumes all that resists or holds back God the Holy Trinity. And in this condition, the world around ceases to be just a sign of God's absence, tantalizingly pointing away from itself: we rediscover our environment as charged with the love that is transfiguringly at work within us, an insight spelled out especially in the last sections of John's commentary on his *Spiritual Canticle*: the contemplation of God leads to 'contemplative' knowledge of creation.

All John's prose works are in fact commentaries on his poems; but, for all the complexity of the commentaries, it would be a mistake to think, as it has become rather fashionable to do, that the poems are everything and the commentaries a kind of misunderstanding by John of his own genius. The prose has its own beauty, its own distinctive energy, often carried along by free and imaginative allusion to Scripture; and it is where we see most clearly how the scheme of our pilgrimage into hope, faith and love is anchored in a trinitarian and incarnational context. But the lyrical intensity and delight of the poetry is, of course, essential to disabuse us of the caricature that John is simply rejecting the created order without qualification. Perhaps his most central message is that only by learning detachment from our affective responses to things, learning, that is, not to regard 'satisfying' responses as an end in themselves, are we set free to encounter reality as it is, both creation's reality and God's. Certainly he is as austere as could be in encouraging us not to seek or cling to happiness and comfort in our prayer, and in suspecting 'religious experiences' as a goal. But this is to allow us to be open to that receiving of God (and God's creation) that we could never predict or imagine, the utterly surprising meeting of the desires too deep in us to be at first visible.

The parallels with the agenda of Luther and Calvin are clear (it is striking that all the writers so far discussed are driven to put the dereliction of Christ on the cross near the heart of their discussions). All look for a refinement of suspicion in our apprehension of ourselves and our world, for a turn inwards to seek the truth; all, however, insist also on suspicion of certain kinds of interiority (superficial emotion, good intentions, the sense of security or rightness). What we find in the work of Ignatius Loyola, founder of the Jesuits, is above all a set of guidelines for constructively training such suspicion and acquiring an instinctive discernment. Ignatius's *Spiritual Exercises* (begun in 1522, but not published until 1548; Loyola 1991) represent the central element in the formation of members of the new community, the Society of Jesus, which spread so rapidly and influentially in sixteenth-century Europe and beyond (Teresa was greatly helped by Jesuit guides in her struggles to discern God's will for the reform of her own order). The *Exercises* are a month-long programme of daily reflection, centred almost exclusively on the Bible, the Gospels in particular, aiming at uncovering what one most deeply wants, so as to enable the choice of a new and more faithful state of life. The technique is startlingly novel, requiring careful and sustained examination of conscience over a set period, the disciplined use of the imagination in bringing before the eyes and 'inner' sense the circumstances of the Gospel history, and a programme for techniques of intensifying appropriate affective responses to the nature and action of God. Although it is a short work, it is very hard to summarize, being nothing if not practical. It should be noted, though, that, despite all the formal and highly organized provisions of the *Exercises*, the goal is the same as that of Teresa or John – proper receptivity to God. And both the *Exercises* and Ignatius's other works, autobiographical and reflective, make it clear that the life and experience envisaged is one marked by many traditional signs of spiritual advance – spontaneous and uncontrollable weeping, for example, sensitivity to the diverse sorts of impulses or 'motions' in the soul, and the development of skills to discern those that come from God from those coming from the devil or our own self-love, the learning of rhythmical forms of prayer that involve the body's 'attention' as well as the mind's – all things that we can find in the classical spiritual writings of the Christian East a thousand years before. In the century or so following Ignatius's death, there were those who used his and other methods of imaginative reflection on the Gospels in a wooden and legalistic way, not allowing the transition to be made to contemplative receptivity (Teresa and John complain of insensitive directors and confessors, and the Anglo–Welsh Benedictine Augustine Baker (1575–1641) is scathing about the psychological effects of forcing this sort of meditation on those ready for other paths). But this is very far from Ignatius's own intent, and more recent thinking about the *Exercises* has conspicuously rediscovered their original flexibility and dynamism.

CONCLUSION

It has been said with truth that the sixteenth century saw a sea change in Christian spirituality. On all sides, the movement is towards the responsibility of the individual to shape his or her journey to God according to charts and programmes of spiritual advance far more detailed than ever before, and far more attuned to the analysis of subjective states – though, as we have seen, the greatest writers in this area point us to the subjective only to place it too under the shadow of suspicion. It is not hard to see why issues about prayer came to be of political importance, given the claims made for the freedom and authenticity of the inner life: for both Catholicism and Protestantism, the issue of religious control was to become more and more complex as the old corporate forms of devotion broke down or changed drastically. Very broadly speaking, the Catholic resolution was to place the new concern with interiority at the service of a rigorous training of the will: for the Carmelite saints and their followers, the disciplining of the will to be faithful in experiences of darkness and inward suffering, for the Jesuits, the formation of a habit of disinterested obedience to the imperatives of the Church's mission. Protestantism had more, and more various, difficulties: while some Protestants drifted further towards a new style of biblical literalism as a way of resolving problems over authority, others moved in the direction of rationalist universalism – the reliance on truths available to the introspection of every reasonable human subject, without the intervention of any external authority. The problematic results of that are familiar enough to anyone with an eye to our current cultural situation. But it can certainly be said that, in one way or another, the spirituality of the Reformation era helped to fix, for good and ill, the shape of the modern psychological subject, which, in its suspicion and restlessness and awareness of unsatisfiable desire, has, in the words of a recent French study of this period, 'kept the form and not the content' of the spiritual journey mapped out in the sixteenth and early seventeenth centuries (de Certeau, 1993: 293).

REFERENCES

Clarke, E. (1993) ' "Divinitie and Poesie Met": The Origin and Strategies of Sacred Rhetoric in George Herbert's Poetry', unpublished D. Phil. thesis.

de Certeau, M. (1992) *The Mystic Fable*, vol. 1: *The Sixteenth and Seventeenth Centuries*, Chicago: University of Chicago Press.

Herbert, G. (1941) *The Works of George Herbert*, ed. F. E. Hutchinson, Oxford: Clarendon Press.

Hooker, R. (1841) 'A Learned and Comfortable Sermon of the Certainty and Perpetuity of Faith in the Elect', in J. Keble (ed.) *The Works of Mr Richard Hooker*, vol. 3, Oxford.

—— (1989) *The Folger Library Edition of the Works of Richard Hooker*, vol. 5, eds L. Yeandle and E. Grislis, Cambridge, Mass. and London: Harvard University Press.

Huizinga, J. (1965) *The Waning of the Middle Ages*, London: Penguin.

à Kempis, T. (1952) *The Imitation of Christ*, trans. L. Sherley Price, London: Penguin.

Loyola, I. (1991) *Spiritual Exercises and Selected Works*, ed. G. E. Ganss, Mahwah, NJ: Paulist Press.

Luther, M. (1952) *Reformation Writings of Martin Luther*, vol. 1, ed., trans. B. L. Woolf, London: SCM Press.

—— (1962) *Early Theological Works*, ed., trans. J. Atkinson, London.

Osuna, F. de (1981) *The Third Spiritual Alphabet*, trans. M. Giles, New York and London.

Stranks, C. J. (1961) *Anglican Devotion*, London: SPCK.

Thompson, C. (1977) *The Poet and the Mystic: A Study of the 'Cantico Espiritual' of San Juan de la Cruz*, Oxford: Oxford University Press.

Torrance, T. F. (1965) 'Justification: Its Radical Nature and Place in Reformed Doctrine and Life', in *Theology in Reconstruction*, London, 150–68.

Williams, R. (1991) *Teresa of Avila*, London: Geoffrey Chapman.

FURTHER READING

Bossy, J. (1985) *Christianity and the West, 1400–1700*, Oxford: Oxford Paperbacks.

de Guibert, J. (ed.) (1964) *The Jesuits: Their Spiritual Doctrine and Practice*, Chicago: Institute of Jesuit Sources.

Dicken, E. W. T. (1963) *The Crucible of Love: A Study of the Mysticism of St Teresa of Jesus and St John of the Cross*, London: Darton, Longman and Todd.

Dickens, A. G. (1968) *The Counter Reformation*, London: Thames and Hudson.

Duffy, E. (1992) *The Stripping of the Altars: Traditional Religion in England 1400–1580*, New Haven and London: Yale University Press.

John of the Cross (1934–5) *Complete Works*, trans. E. A. Peers (3 vols), London: Sheed and Ward.

—— (1979) *Collected Works*, trans. K. Kavanaugh and O. Rodriguez, Washington, DC: ICS Publications.

Leith, J. H. (1989) *John Calvin's Doctrine of the Christian Life*, Atlanta: John Knox Press.

McGrath, A. E. (1992) *Roots that Refresh: A Celebration of Reformation Spirituality*, London: Hodder & Stoughton.

Rahner, H. (1968a) *Ignatius the Theologian*, New York.

—— (1968b) *The Spirituality of St Ignatius Loyola: An Account of Its Historical Development*, Chicago: Loyola University Press.

Raitt, J. (ed.) (1987) *Christian Spirituality II: High Middle Ages and Reformation*, London: Routledge.

Richard, L. J. (1974) *The Spirituality of John Calvin*, Atlanta.

Rupp, G. (1953) *The Righteousness of God*, London: Hodder & Stoughton.

Stachniewski, J. (1991) *The Persecutory Imagination: English Puritanism and the Literature of Religious Despair*, Oxford: Clarendon Press.

Teresa of Jesus (1946) *Complete Works*, trans. E. A. Peers (3 vols), London: Sheed and Ward.

—— (1976–85) *Collected Works*, trans. K. Kavanaugh and O. Rodriguez (3 vols), Washington, DC: ICS Publications.

von Löwenich, W. (1976) *Luther's Theology of the Cross*, Belfast.

von Rohr, J. (1986) *The Covenant of Grace in Puritan Thought*, Atlanta.

Wallace, R. S. (1959) *Calvin's Doctrine of the Christian Life*, Edinburgh and London/ Grand Rapids.

See also chapters 12, 27, 32.

29

THEOLOGY AND SPIRITUALITY IN THE NINETEENTH AND TWENTIETH CENTURIES

Terry Tastard

Early in the nineteenth century there was a hopeful mood in Western Europe. The spread of industrialization and scientific advance had created a new confidence in human ability. The defeat of French expansionism and the apparent concert of European powers at Vienna in 1814 led to new hopes for international co-operation. The spectre of war created by religious or political fanaticism was diminishing. The power of human understanding seemed to be fulfilling the hopes expressed for it by Immanuel Kant, who in 1784 had described Enlightenment as 'man's release from his self-incurred tutelage. Tutelage is man's inability to make use of his understanding without direction from another ... *Sapere audere!* [Dare to know] – that is the motto of enlightenment' (Kant 1959: 85). Yet in the early nineteenth century a darker mood was also discernible. The industrial revolution seemed to be pursuing its course with the cunning of a logic that ignored the consequences. Among the poor, especially in the teeming cities, the price was plain to see. There was also a growing feeling that industrial progress had meant ugliness and alienation from nature.

Religion was discovering that its traditional pillars of reason and revelation no longer commanded the respect once afforded them. To take reason first: the confidence of theology had been shaken by Kant's argument against supernatural knowledge. Kant's critique had weakened the traditional *apologias* for divine existence. To Kant they typified the illusory nature of appeal to transcendence, by starting in the world of space and time only to end in a realm beyond all knowledge and experience. Kant argued that the true role of religion was to be the practical adjunct of moral life. Doctrines were of little significance in his account of reality. The traditional reliance on revelation was also under attack. Sceptics were questioning claims that the Bible described miraculous events and fulfilled prophecies. The atavism of some Old Testament passages was also felt to belie claims of divine inspiration, as were occasional discordances between different passages. Just as the spirit of the age was seeking a broader understanding of the human subject, so theology was drawn to look afresh at human experience. It was felt that the encroachment of secularization could be turned back once feeling, rather than reason, was seen as the road to God: Nicholas Lash comments, 'The place at which religion takes its stand, and builds its redoubt, is the inmost recesses of feeling or "pure experience" ' (Lash 1988: 44).

THE INWARD TURN: FRIEDRICH SCHLEIERMACHER

Friedrich Schleiermacher (1768–1834) provided a ground-breaking account of why theology should take experience more seriously. Religion, according to Schleiermacher, is a universal tendency evolving from the innate awareness of the human mind. In *On Religion: Speeches to its Cultured Despisers* (1799) he calls this capacity a 'sense and taste for the infinite' from which flows all religious faith. Later in *The Christian Faith* (1821–2) he refines this to 'the feeling of unconditional dependence'. Schleiermacher constructs everything upon his principle that religion grows from 'the consciousness of being absolutely dependent, or, which is the same thing, of being in relation with God' (Schleiermacher 1968: 12). There is, in each of us, a subjectivity which is more than our responsiveness to the world around us. Our self-consciousness 'is itself precisely a consciousness of absolute dependence' because we become aware that 'the whole of our spontaneous activity comes from a source outside of us' (ibid.: 16). This provenance which is within yet beyond the human is what makes possible both our receptivity and our activity. God, says Schleiermacher, is this mysterious 'Whence' on which we depend.

Precisely what Schleiermacher meant by absolute dependence is notoriously uncertain. But he seems to be pointing to each person's unique inner stream of awareness, proceeding from depths beyond scrutiny and yet enabling each one to take a stance towards the world. Feeling, then, is not to be understood as a form of emotion but rather as an immediate self-consciousness, what Robert Williams calls 'a global consciousness of self in correlation with the world' (Williams 1978: 23). This absolute dependence is what carries human freedom. Indeed, each person's sense of self, of identity, would not be possible without it. In Schleiermacher's system, God is apprehended and identified through this feeling, which amounts to 'a co-existence of God in the self-consciousness' (ibid.: 126). Absolute dependence, he adds, has been expressed in many ways in different cultures, but is most purely expressed in monotheism. Descriptions of divine attributes and modes of actions, and metaphysical statements generally, are seen as developing out of the feeling of absolute dependence (ibid.: 125–6). The ability to grow in awareness of this inner presence is the essence of religious practice. Salvation lies in cultivating this consciousness, in which we respond to the infinite inner presence with a corresponding love, and are drawn towards the infinitely good and the infinitely true. Jesus of Nazareth is regarded by Schleiermacher as the supreme example of such God-consciousness. Showing how we can be in touch with God within, Jesus redeems us by empowering us. But concepts such as atonement, resurrection and ascension add nothing to our awareness of God and become redundant (ibid.: 417–19). Schleiermacher also argued that religion enabled a deeper union of the human spirit with the divine ground of being, thus protecting science, art, and morality from scepticism and decay (Redeker 1973: 111).

With Schleiermacher the centre of gravity in Protestant theology shifted. It was no longer taken for granted that Scripture or tradition would be the starting point. Theology had a new approach more in keeping with the intellectual currents of a critical and scientific age. Richard Brandt comments that most Protestant theologians in the succeeding generation followed Schleiermacher in his insistence on the autonomy of religious experience. The foundations of faith were now to be found in the dynamics of human nature itself (Brandt 1971: 307). To be human was to have the source of piety within oneself in a direct and immediate relationship created by God, who revealed himself through it. In this respect Schleiermacher was clearly influenced by Pietism: he was mostly educated by Moravian Brethren, who stressed the importance of a vividly experienced communion with the Saviour (Redeker 1973: 10). Among other influences was Spinoza, to whom Schleiermacher is indebted for his view of God as the pervasive loving presence through whom the universe is maintained in being and finds a unity. God, however, does not interfere in the closed system of nature.

Schleiermacher's achievement is immense, yet has some serious weaknesses. Perhaps the most serious is the privacy of the experience on which he bases his religious system. Doctrines and the community of faith are traced back to the religious experience of the individual. Although he argues that the Church takes shape through inter-action and co-operation (Schleiermacher 1968: 532), there is very little room in his system for a sharing of the ideas which express human experience and shape it further. Schleiermacher's theology reinforced the tendency of Protestant theology to make the inward dimension of faith the most important one, at the expense of its relational dimension. It is also instructive to reflect on Schleiermacher's defence against the charge of pantheism: 'It is quite inconceivable how one could attribute pantheism to me, for I fully separate the feeling of absolute dependence from any relation with the world' (quoted in Redeker 1973: 115). This tendency to introversion is increased by the deterministic way in which Schleiermacher views the God–world relationship. Although he insists that God is not responsible for discrete events, nor involved in time (Schleiermacher 1968: sects. 50–2), it is difficult to escape the impression that he associates causality in nature too closely with the will of God. Prayer, for example, is to be limited to resignation or thankfulness, or better still, should simply move beyond these to a deeper trust in God (ibid.: 669). Finally, despite some spirited defenders (e.g. Redeker 1973: 131–2), Dilthey's criticism is correct: Schleiermacher shapes his picture of Christ to fit his theology of experience. He sees no sense in vicarious suffering, and his theology of the cross is skimpy and unsatisfactory (cf. Moltmann 1991: 214–15).

In sum, Schleiermacher gives grounds for treating human experience with new seriousness. The sense of self is seen as containing an inherent dynamism which points back to God. In this account there is much to encourage respect for the uniqueness and responsibility of human nature. On the other hand, its privacy means that there is little room for either salvation or sin as a shared experience in the life of believers. Nor is it easy to construct from him an account of how communities and societies can shape and be shaped through religious discourse. This neglect of evil, and the relative downgrading of the need for human solidarity, were true also of much subsequent liberal Protestant theology. The turn to experience often concealed within it a confident belief in progress.

THE INFLUENCE OF ROMANTICISM

In the nineteenth century Romanticism profoundly influenced the role of religion in society, particularly through broadening people's understanding of what counted as religious experience. The Romantic movement reminds us that spirituality is not confined within the limits of formal religion.

Romanticism was fed by an astonishingly diverse band of writers from whom flowed a torrent of poetry, novels, philosophy, theology and cultural criticism: people like Blake, Wordsworth, Shelley, Rousseau, Goethe, Schelling, Pushkin, Coleridge, Emerson and Thoreau. Romanticism emerged towards the end of the eighteenth century and was most influential around 1840, after which it slowly declined. It was a reaction against both the rationalistic spirit of the Enlightenment and the dispiriting dreariness of industrialization. Romantics sought a new world in which the values of the heart would lead humankind forward and individualism would be prized. They stressed original genius, artistic creativity, and emotional depths (Furst 1979: 26–8). The Enlightenment had esteemed the power of human rationality to comprehend and exploit the laws of science hidden within nature. By contrast, the Romantics sought a more harmonious way of life which would draw on the purity, dynamism and spontaneity of nature. Many Romantics believed that a life force flowed through the world and could be gasped intuitively. They therefore plunged into nature, to deepen their communion with the source of life within themselves and all beings. In a letter Coleridge describes his reaction to the beauties of nature:

My mind feels as if it ached to behold and know something great – something one & indivisible – and it is only in the faith of this that rocks or waterfalls, mountains or caverns give me the sense of sublimity or majesty! – But in this faith all things counterfeit infinity.

(Quoted in Watson 1970: 115).

Given the vast and sometimes contradictory nature of the Romantic movement, this brief account will focus on manifestations of Romanticism through Wordsworth and Emerson.

William Wordsworth

In Britain, William Wordsworth (1770–1850) was a leading figure of the Romantic movement and effectively popularized many of its ideas. Many Victorians found in his poetry 'a peculiar emotional and religious power' (Prickett 1976: 89). Wordsworth typifies Romantic fascination with the mystical unity running through nature. In 'Tintern Abbey' he writes that looking on nature

> I have felt
> A presence that disturbs me with the joy
> Of elevated thoughts; a sense sublime
> Of something far more deeply interfused,
> Whose dwelling is the light of setting suns,
> And the round ocean and the living air,
> And the blue sky, and in the mind of man;
> A motion and a spirit, that impels
> All thinking things, all objects of all thought
> And rolls through all things.

In this poem Wordsworth also refers to nature as 'The guide, the guardian of my heart'. God is mentioned only indirectly, as 'a presence'. In his odyssey of faith Wordsworth moved from radicalism to nature mysticism and on to more conventional Christianity. Reardon suggests that Wordsworth's poetry appealed to Victorians by offering a non-theistic spirituality which consoled doubters for the loss of traditional convictions (Reardon 1971: 361–3). Prickett sees the autobiographical element of the poems playing an analogous role. Wordsworth, in bringing spiritual crises into his nature poetry, 'enabled his readers to feel in "the language of nature" an emotional unity and sense of wholeness in face of the ambiguities and doubts of an increasingly fragmented and complex intellectual climate' (Prickett 1976: 89).

Wordsworth's nature poetry appeals to the revelatory and revivifying power of nature, experienced through feeling. But this raises the question, inescapable in the Romantics, of whose feeling is being articulated. In the preface to the *Lyrical Ballads* (1801) Wordsworth declares that his principal aim is 'to make the incidents of common life interesting by tracing in them . . . the primary laws of our nature'. With this in mind he will draw from 'low and rustic life', with its plainer and more powerful language and its closeness to 'elementary feelings' (Wordsworth 1989: 155). Yet he could also write of 'the lower orders accumulating in pestilential masses of ignorant population' (Quoted in Byatt 1989: 125). Wordsworth was acutely aware of people's suffering through causes as diverse as agrarian pauperization and child labour in factories, and could depict these movingly (e.g. 'Michael', 'The Excursion'). But he saw such abuses in an existential light, illuminating a greater sadness that was part of the human condition. Moreover, as the years passed his Romantic fascination with the medieval evolved into a nostalgia which esteemed feudal-style benevolence and respect, in which all classes would be linked in one organic whole (Byatt 1989: 128, 155–6). This was in an England where the human experience was often of desperate poverty and pell-mell urbanization.

Against this background Wordsworth's nature mysticism, like that of much Romanticism, seems like a *fuga mundi*. While the poetry was about feeling, to many readers it must have been a safe category of feeling, in an age where poverty and uncertainty were all around. Certainly, Wordsworth and others like him made possible the expression of a broader religious sensibility which would otherwise have remained silent. The Romantics believed that each person could find, through communing with nature, a source of power and direction in which the physical and the spiritual could be reconciled (Taylor 1989: 370–3). But this expressive individualism, while it enlarged the understanding of religious experience, drifted away from the community of the suffering and the oppressed, and indeed was one further step in the developing Western understanding of seeing religious experience as essentially an individual affair.

Ralph Waldo Emerson

Romanticism's ascription of a revelatory power to nature inevitably raised questions about historical revelation in Christianity. Some of the German Romantics, such as Schelling, were effectively pantheists, influenced by their reading of Spinoza. Among those carried towards a generic pantheism was Ralph Waldo Emerson (1803–82). Emerson was formed by New England Unitarianism, imbibing from it a strong sense of integrity and a selective attitude towards historical doctrine. Sydney Ahlstrom considers that the role Emerson took on himself was that of the poet as seer and prophet – the one who speaks of the life he sees surging within the universe (Ahlstrom 1985: 38). This was certainly a typical trait of the Romantics – Schelling had believed that the artist was the one in whom the unconscious life of the universe comes to conscious expression. In *Nature* (1836) Emerson argued that the natural world was an incarnation of the divine spirit, expressing itself in the manifold life of nature and culminating in humankind. Human openness to divine influence meant that the divide between subject and object was reconciled, for in human perceptions of the world, God – the underlying unity of the world – was the perceiver also. In *Nature* Emerson writes:

In the woods, we return to reason and faith . . . Standing on the bare ground, – my heart bathed by the blithe air, and uplifted into infinite space, – all mean egotism vanishes. I become a transparent eye-ball. I am nothing. I see all. The currents of the Universal Being circulate through me; I am part or particle of God.
(Emerson 1981: 11).

In 'The Oversoul' he expanded his account to argue that 'Oversoul' was the uniting and vivifying factor underlying all the expressions of nature. '[W]ithin man is the soul of the whole . . . the act of seeing and the thing seen, the seer and the spectacle, the subject and the object, are one.' Human beings see the world in discrete parts, 'but the whole, of which these are the shining parts, is the soul' (ibid.: 210–11).

Emerson considered that Christianity had taken a wrong turn into dogma: 'They will have Christ for a Lord but not for a brother. Christ preaches the greatness of man, but we hear only the greatness of Christ' (quoted in Ahlstrom 1985: 50). Emerson believed in liberating human potential by harmonizing it with the operations of the universe, which could be seen, in the long run, to reward generous-spiritedness and to nullify selfishness (Emerson 1981: 74). This not only required him to present an optimistic picture of the world, in which evil had no real existence but was simply the absence of good. It also required him to be a determinist. In his essay 'Fate' he wrote (ibid.: 373): 'Let us build altars to the Beautiful Necessity, which secures that all is made of one piece; that plaintiff and defendant, friend and enemy, animal and plant, food and eater are of one kind' – that is, being subsumed into a steadily evolving higher unity. Despite attempts to systematize Emerson (e.g. Gelpi 1991) much of what he wrote was intended to be spoken and to evoke a mood rather than to conduct a suasive argument. Catherine Albanese points out that sometimes he writes as if the material world is sacramental, sometimes he writes as if it is a trap and an illusion, to be transcended if we are to see true reality. The first approach will emphasize harmony with nature, the second will emphasize mastery over nature; she accuses Emerson of resolving this tension with deft rhetoric (Albanese 1991: 81–5).

Emerson, in fact, had arrived at religion without theology. In this respect the Transcendentalists are a development of the Romantic stress on the heroic individual and the power of feeling. Religious experience is no longer that which grounds individuals linked in communities. Rather, religious experience is a personal communion with nature. Religion becomes the individual experience of transcendence felt by the self-reliant person, rather like those favoured by William James (see below). In this respect Emerson and his followers represent a further turn in the privatization of religious experience. Sometimes it is said that this inward turn diminished interest in American social institutions and debates in the crucial years before the Civil War. Yet Ann Rose argues that while the Transcendentalists turned aside from politics, they sought social reform through their immediate influence as individuals, as families and in co-operative experiments. Among women in particular effective networks were established (Rose 1981: 225, 174–84). We may note, too, that the pioneer American conservationist John Muir drew heavily on Emerson to create a kind of ideology for his work (Albanese 1991: 93–105). On the other hand, Robert Bellah and his fellow writers say that American society today is characterized by an individualism so extreme as to weaken social cohesion. They point the finger at Emerson as one of those whose influence has created the impression that the interests of the individual and those of society are opposed to one another (Bellah 1986: 55) They say, 'the dead end of radical individualism' has been 'inherited from Wordsworth, Emerson and other romantics'. The resulting language of radical individual autonomy has reduced people to 'arbitrary centers of volition' (ibid.: 81). This, of course, is not an exclusively American problem: Alasdair MacIntyre (1985) stimulated considerable debate with his suggestion that ethical discourse generally has become vitiated by sundering the individual from community and tradition.

The legacy of Romanticism

Whether these analyses are correct is open to debate. They do, however, indicate ongoing unease about the contemporary individualistic depiction of human nature. The concern about the role of the will is particularly significant, and points back to the role of Romanticism in creating present-day images. Romanticism sought to transcend polarities by an appeal to the power of feeling, which was intended to integrate subject and object, conscious mind and unconscious mind, human beings and nature. With this development religious experience was effectively deinstitutionalized. Spirituality now became for many an aspect of the pursuit of beauty or the appreciation of nature. Richard Tarnas comments that '[A]rt itself – music, literature, drama, painting – now took on a virtually religious status for the Romantic sensibility . . . for many modern intellectuals disillusioned with orthodox religion, art became the chief spiritual outlet and medium' (Tarnas 1993: 373). With its more subtle sensibilities, Romanticism broadened the category of religious experience. Paradoxically it also foreshortened the horizons of religious experience. Religion was increasingly how individuals expressed their identity and found individual fulfilment, rather than a shared understanding in communal or social life (cf. Taylor 1992: ch. 21). Such individuals were attuned to nature, and thus in theory in harmony with it. And yet, the Romantic stereotype was the person of genius, of originality, of courage, in whom the unconscious creativity of nature burst into conscious understanding and action. This led easily to an esteem of strength of will in developing human gifts and visions, and to a view of human beings as separate from and even dominating nature. Romanticism did not transcend polarities in the way that it had first hoped.

One stream of Romantic influence carried on through the churches and sought a new mystagogy. The clear windows and interlocking proportions of eighteenth-century churches, with their delight in rationality, gave way to neo-gothic architecture. Sacredness and mystery were evoked by decoration, interplay of light and shade and the separation of sacred space by means of altars and sanctuaries. The sacraments, like nature as a whole, were seen as imbued with mystery and divine self-disclosure. They could only yield their secrets to those with respect for the mystery. There was a stress on Church and ministry as divinely willed. Prayer and worship focused anew on the mystery of the incarnation. A second stream rolled away from the churches into a gnostic nature religion. A divine presence is seen in nature, and salvation is to be found in recovery of harmony with nature and thus with the ground of being. Some spirituality associated with ecology is the heir of this stream today. A third stream of Romantic influence helped create the nascent discipline of psychology, by drawing attention to the inexhaustible and complex depths of human nature.

EXPERIENCE WITHOUT DOCTRINE: WILLIAM JAMES

One of the characteristics of Western culture in the twentieth century has been the influence of psychology. There is now widespread acceptance that each person has unconscious depths which, if explored and analysed, will yield valuable insights about the person concerned and perhaps about human nature itself. Among the first to apply psychology to religion was William James (1842–1910). His conclusions helped shape – and limit – the interpretation of religious experience. James's influence in religious studies has been ongoing, helped by his Gifford Lectures with their evergreen title, *The Varieties of Religious Experience*. His assertion that religious experience can be valued for itself, with doctrine being set aside, fits neatly within the mind-set of much late twentieth-century thinking about religion.

In *The Varieties of Religious Experience* William James says that he is bent on 'rehabilitating the element of feeling in religion and subordinating its intellectual part' (James 1971: 478). Like Schleiermacher he is influenced by Romanticism's stress on the primacy of feeling. William James not only emphasizes feeling over intellect, but also stresses individual accounts of religious experience. He rejects experience filtered through tradition or formulated within a community: 'When a religion has become an orthodoxy, its day of inwardness is over; the spring is dry; the faithful live at second hand exclusively' (ibid.: 330). Hence he avows that 'feeling is the deeper source of religion . . . philosophic and theological formulas are secondary products, like translations of a text into another tongue' (ibid.: 414–15). He tries to select vibrant stories of 'great-souled persons wrestling with the crises of their fate'. James defines religion as *'the feelings, acts and experiences of individual men in their solitude, so far as they apprehend themselves to stand in relation to whatever they may consider the divine'* (ibid.: 50; italics in original). He gives a key role to subliminal mind with its storehouse of: 'obscurely motivated passions, impulses, likes, dislikes, and prejudices. Our intuitions, hypotheses, fancies, superstitions, persuasions, convictions, and in general all our non-rational operations come from it . . . In it arise whatever mystical experiences we may have' (ibid.: 462). Profound religious experiences take place when this surd of memory boils up into the immediate consciousness. In conversion experiences, for instance, a person in a divided and unhappy state surrenders to an incursion from the subconscious. The person finds unity and new energy in recentring his or her life around religious ideas which were previously peripheral (ibid.: 200–2).

In his analysis of mysticism, James assigns four keynotes to mystical experiences.

1 They are ineffable, having a quality which cannot really be conveyed but needs to be experienced for itself.
2 They are noetic, yielding 'insight into depths of truth unplumbed by the discursive intellect'.
3 They are transient.
4 They are experiences of passivity, in which the mystic feels 'grasped and held by a superior power' (ibid.: 367–8).

These keynotes help to ensure that mysticism fits into his account of religious experience as drama, the inrush of powerful insights and images from a subliminal mind which has been storing and sifting material. The self feels open to a wider consciousness through which saving experiences come. As a source of new life, this other mental 'world' is undoubtedly real, for it works profound changes in people; and, says James, 'that which produces effects within another reality must be termed a reality itself'. As supreme reality it can be termed God (ibid.: 491). This wider consciousness and source of power depend, however, on the rich world of the subliminal consciousness. James does say that if there is a power beyond the human, then it may get access only through the subconscious (ibid.: 243; cf. 493). He has a panpsychic view of God, holding that there is 'a continuum of cosmic consciousness, against which our individuality builds but accidental fences' (quoted in Brennan 1961: 59). Lash hardly caricatures when he says that James sees God as a kind of cosmic consciousness occasionally 'leaking into' individual human minds (Lash 1988: 80).

James was influenced by Charles Peirce's pragmatism. In James's terms, truth is to be found in what concepts do, rather than in any objective truth they might have in and of themselves. 'There can be no difference . . . in abstract truth that doesn't express itself in a difference in concrete fact, and in conduct consequent upon that fact' (James 1921: 49–50). An idea's meaning is found in the conduct it produces: '[T]hat conduct is for us its sole significance' (James 1971: 425, 427). If a truth-claim has no consequences in conduct, it is to be dismissed. James accordingly sweeps aside divine attributes like necessary existence, infinity, and personality. Since they can make no difference in conduct, it makes no sense to say whether they be true or false. God's moral attributes, on the other hand, provide challenging standards, and inspire fear, hope and expectation, and are thus useful. He concludes that 'The uses of religion, its uses to the individual who has it, and the uses of the individual himself to the world, are the best arguments that truth is in it' (James 1971: 439). This elision from meaning to use makes James's approach seem so contemporary nearly a hundred years later. We live in times when, say, a Chicagoan can decide to try Zen Buddhism, while a Londoner selects Native American spirituality. The conceptual frameworks of religions do not matter, and there is no real consideration as to how belief interacts with practice in the life of a community. What counts is whether concepts yield valuable effects. A devotee can seek the experience without carrying the luggage of doctrine.

This approach raises the question of whether the subject in such instances would experience anything beyond the self. James portrays religious experience as a moment of privileged immediacy of perception, occurring to an individual whose insights spin out of the contents of his or her mind. At best, society could be said to be implicitly present, presumably having contributed some of the subliminal memories. This interpretation of experience, however, yields a picture of human personhood centred on itself with all the problems of the lonely Cartesian ego. Hans-Georg Gadamer reminds us that advances in understanding require us to mediate between different horizons: between, for example, received tradition and reason, past and present, self and community. Understanding evolves out of this process in which horizons of interpretation are enlarged and eventually fused (Gadamer 1975: 269–74). To appeal to objective procedures, while denying any power to tradition, is to be particularly dominated by unseen prejudices (ibid.: 324). James offers us basically one horizon, that of the individual seeker; he seems to believe that his scientific approach obviates questions of religion's cultural settings.

This same problem arises in another of James's works, his essay 'The Will to Believe' in the eponymous book (1897) in which he draws on Pascal's wager. James argues that questions of faith are choices which are living, forced and momentous. That is, each option attracts, choosing is unavoidable, and the outcome is of great significance. There is no clear evidence for choosing either way. But scepticism runs the risk of losing a possible gain, whereas to choose to believe might reap a rich benefit. This, says James, justifies taking a step which might otherwise seem unjustified. James's argument is more than wish-fulfilment. He is keen to underline how convictions are often influenced through our 'passional nature' by factors such as fear, hope, prejudice, passion and imitation (James 1897: 9). Given this reality, we have the right to choose, as an act of will, the most insistent tendency within us (ibid.: 10–11). But, as Gerald Myers points out, religious believers appeal to something beyond themselves, to 'historical episodes, sacred writings, and authoritative institutions'. James's will to believe 'assumes a total absence of objective evidence, with only internal feelings to go by' (Myers 1986: 454).

In *The Varieties of Religious Experience* James does, of course, appeal to evidence, but underlying it is the same reliance on feeling and the same absence of any wider community of faith. If we shift our focus away from James's sample of individuals with dramatic stories, then our interpretation of religious experience changes too. Grace Jantzen has compared James's analysis of mysticism with what we know of the mystics Bernard of Clairvaux and Julian of Norwich. She notes that James, while occasionally making concessions to a broader concept of religious experience, in fact concentrates on its more dramatic manifestations. By contrast, Bernard and Julian portray union with God as gradual transformation, the patient discipline of seeking to bring heart and mind into harmony with God's love. Special experiences are at best a help on the way to this, may even be a hindrance, and are never to be sought for themselves (Jantzen 1989: 313). By highlighting subjective elements and sidelining the objective content of religion, James misuses mysticism.

Nor is James's pragmatic approach without its problems. Pragmatism implies, as he himself said, that 'an idea is "true" so long as to believe it is profitable to our lives' (James 1921: 75). Now, James is not necessarily reducing ethics to self-interest, although Bertrand Russell and others have accused him of this (Russell 1910; reprinted in Olin 1992). To take an example: in a discipline like history, people may value ideas simply for their usefulness. Yet these ideas may have objective truth-value, both stimulating and verifying further research, even though as individual items they may be changeable and rejected when no longer useful. In other words, utility and truth are not exclusive of each other, but interrelated in a complex way (Phillips 1992: 243–4). However, it is difficult to escape the conclusion that a spirituality along the lines of Jamesian pragmatism would turn in on itself. It would fit handily the needs of the more powerful, and say nothing to the poor and vulnerable, for there would be no transcendent standard by which action could be judged. Russell observed that James radiates a genial North American optimism, in which 'successful men of action . . . expect the world to be malleable to their wishes, and . . . find their expectation justified by success' (Russell 1910: 122–3). James frees religious experience from the straitjacket of being examined only in its own terms. The price paid, however, is a further twist to privatization of such experience, and the danger that his emphasis on effects, and effectiveness, could degenerate into the dangerous adage that the end justifies the means.

EXISTENTIALISM AND POSTMODERNISM

The speculative philosophy of Hegel left a deep mark on early nineteenth-century thinking. Hegel argued that the apparent chaos of history manifested spirit coming to self-consciousness in society and its institutions. No development is ever truly mistaken, wasteful or destructive, for everything is subsumed into higher forms. Everything is rational, and is constantly evolving. Søren Kierkegaard (1813–55) was one of the strongest opponents of this Hegelian revisionism. He lashed the complacent Christianity which he felt was the result. In particular, he objected to religion being blandly undemanding, with faith being presented as the reasonable response to a Christianity that fitted neatly into everything known. Kierkegaard aimed to show that what mattered was the divine irruption into the world, cutting across conventional reason by appearing in Jesus as human being and God. Christ being eternally present, faith could now be seen as the challenge to accept the truth of his incarnation. This was a spirituality of disjuncture. To believe meant launching forth in faith, continually re-making one's life in a decision for Christ which could not be shown to be reasonable. Truth was found in the way an individual came to awareness in the encounter with God. Initially (e.g. in *Either-Or*) Kierkegaard contrasted the loneliness of ethical fidelity with the pleasure of aesthetic pursuits. Later he went further, to argue (e.g. in *Fear and Trembling*) that nothing supersedes the encounter with God, not even ethics. He cites Abraham's preparedness to sacrifice Isaac as demonstrating the validity of the 'teleological suspension of the ethical': goodness is found in faithfulness to God's prompting rather than in any system of laws. With no suasive proof to carry faith forward, faith, in such uncertainty, will imply anguish, which for Kierkegaard is a sign of authenticity.

Kierkegaard feared that a mixture of forces was creating a mass human identity, eroding the basic sense of awareness and individual responsibility which was so central to being human. State religion, Hegelian theology turning evil into part of human progress, even the rise of democracy – these and other forces he saw as encouraging a mass mentality in which no-one would have the courage to stand out. Kierkegaard thus anticipated the sense of unease about collectivism which has been a feature of the last century. Part of the attraction of faith in Christ was that it jolted people out of drifting along with the herd. Faith was an act of will, not an act of understanding. Herbert Wolf says that Kierkegaard opposed 'anything that attempts to deny or replace the decision-character of faith. To establish a historical basis for faith . . . is to substitute knowledge for faith, security for risk' (Wolf 1965: 62). Kierkegaard fitted well into the traditional Reformation emphasis on justification by faith alone, and scholars as diverse as Barth and Bultmann drew on Kierkegaard in shaping their own thought. His picture of the believer *contra mundum* encouraged a faith which refused to compromise with popular culture. But Kierkegaard leaves the believer a lonely figure, scarcely linked to others in the community of faith. Faith itself is an act of resistance. There is little to learn from the surrounding world (indeed, there is little to learn from the history of Christianity). Kierkegaard had stressed the infinite distance between human beings and God, a distance bridged only by the incarnation on one side and by radical faith on the other. Kierkegaard's suspicion about human nature discourages any spirituality in which believers reach God by weaving links between their experiences in life in general and their faith beliefs. There is no room for the Holy Spirit as the God of relationships, bringing together the Church and wider society (cf. Wolf 1965: 57).

Kierkegaard was to be hailed retrospectively as one of the inspirations of existentialism. Another proto-existentialist was Friedrich Nietzsche (1844–1900). Nietzsche's jaundiced eye surveyed the confident, expanding world of capitalist entrepreneurialism and detected an underlying anxiety. The very fact of human self-reliance meant that any sense of an overarching ethic or point of reference had collapsed, and could never be pieced together again. There were no longer any universal truths and hence, said Nietzsche, God was dead. Human beings had only themselves to rely upon, which was just as well, since systems of ideas were the creation of weak people to shackle the strong. With no universal laws to be observed, the only limits to individual wills were other wills. What was needed was strong leaders whose will to power could sweep aside all timidity and obscurantism and seize every opportunity. He attacked Christianity for its deification of weakness and its depreciation of the passions. The joint influence of Kierkegaard and Nietzsche can be seen in Martin Heidegger (1889–1976), who argued that Western philosophy's treatment of metaphysics tended to obscure the reality of being. Ideas of absolute truth closed off discussions about alternative ways of viewing reality. In particular, the twentieth-century technological culture was creating a myth of scientific reason as the master of all things. This confidence in self-mastery obscured the essential understanding of being as something unpredictable, contingent, and manifold. Those influenced by Heidegger came to see the alliance of capitalist technology and consumerism as producing an omnivorous culture of uniformity.

The baton of suspicion is now handed on to postmodernism, with its desire to dethrone absolutes of meaning. One consequence of this, in spirituality, has been a new interest in the recovery of voices and traditions that have been squashed by the dominant culture of reason and technology. Probably the main influences in postmodernism have been Jacques Derrida (b. 1930) and Michel Foucault (1926–84). Derrida helped popularize the idea of deconstruction, a term he takes from Heidegger. Deconstructive postmodernism steps outside the traditional framework of philosophical rationality to question metaphysical categories, for these implicitly assume a grounding in some ontological certainty. Derrida holds that there is no such grounding, for 'there is nothing outside the text'. Any discourse can be shown to contain variant readings which contradict or subvert any attempt at a fundamental meaning, such as that intended by the author or surrounding culture. Moreover, we cannot apprehend an essential 'meaning' because the very fluidity of language itself sets up endless deferrals, in which we pursue meaning through one field of social constructs after another. What can be sought outside the text is that which was denied in its composition. Universalizing systems of thought have operated by suppressing whatever is opposite to themselves. They constitute themselves by this act of exclusion, which means that they carry the trace of that which they deny. According to Derrida the tendency in Western philosophy towards such totalizing discourses is another expression of the obsession with power and domination underlying so much of Western culture. The deconstructive postmodernist approach strives, rather, for an openness to that excess of being which is beyond all categorization or expression and which disrupts attempts at such. Truth is that which dissolves every attempt at a metanarrative.

Michel Foucault takes a thoroughly Nietzschean line to argue that normative ideas such as justice, sanity and sexuality have been plastic, changing radically within different periods of history and different communities. Not only are there no absolutes, but the very norms we have taken for granted have been contingent expressions of the power relations within society. People have developed their identities within understandings of normality which seemed immutable but which were in fact spun out from the controlling forces within society. Freedom demands the recovery of alternative vision, the truth which eludes us unless we go beyond the margins of convention to seek a different construction of reality (e.g. Foucault 1988: 154–6).

Foucault and his followers have a particular cutting edge to their critique: their insistence that in contemporary society relations of power and control have been internalized. No longer are the dominant values imposed from above. The influence of the Enlightenment means that the values of instrumental rationality permeate people's thinking, in such a way that they freely co-operate in creating a disciplinarian society. Crucial here is the idea of surveillance, which Foucault treats extensively in *Discipline and Punish* (1979) and which he sees as characterizing modernity. Along with the Enlightenment view that all people are equal there grew the acceptance of supervision within society. It was felt that the basic truths of society were so clear, distinct and persuasive that their value should be seen by all. There is an expectation that the resulting codes will be observed, an expectation helped by the background awareness we have of being monitored and recorded by bureaucracy with its files and computers. The culture of modernity is thus one of spontaneous compliance. Initially, Foucault's answer was to call for the recovery of 'subjugated knowledges', judged to be useless, dangerous or deluded by the prevailing culture (Foucault 1980: 82). He later refined this to a call for 'free speech', in terms of which subjugated knowledge is not so much an alternative worldview; rather it is that which challenges and subverts the paradigms of understanding prescribed by modernity. Such knowledge, and the experience of groups which has yielded it, are intended to resist the normative view and stimulate action against domination and exploitation.

From Kierkegaard to Foucault, there has been a strong element of cultural criticism in nineteenth- and twentieth-century philosophy and theology – a hermeneutic of suspicion, in fact. Integrity is seen as resistance to a world of conformity and of misleading sophistries. Truth is seen as cutting across conventional understandings. In deconstructive postmodernism the very idea of truth is problematical, but it is that which upsets expectations, which cannot be accommodated within the known forms. (The irony here is that the turn to the subject, which accelerated with the Enlightenment, has now turned against the Enlightenment concept of reason as that can be shown to apply universally.)

This sketchy overview has been necessary to indicate some of the intellectual antecedents of a significant influence on contemporary spirituality. In the twentieth century the deinstitutionalization of spirituality has proceeded apace. Many groups on the fringe of organized religion or outside it now seek to recover their own subjugated knowledge as part of the quest for human growth and liberation. Rowan Williams points out that although all human beings are liable to be drawn into the fantasy lives of others, cultural power reaches in to shape the self-perception of the powerless (Williams 1988: 140). This is what many today set out to resist. Spirituality, with its integration of under-standing and practice, is seen as central to this process. Examples include gay and lesbian groups, feminists interested in recovering the lost wisdom of women through the ages, neo-pagan circles, African Americans seeking the memory of slave religion, and followers of creation-centred spirituality.

A hallmark of postmodernist criticism is 'commitment to indeterminacy, openness and multiplicity' and to continual decentring which refuses to anchor itself in any normative world-view (Connor 1989: 18–19). Postmodernists share common ground with many feminists in offering a critique of universal accounts of reality. An example might be Francine Cardman, who sees an emerging spirituality of compassion characterized by critique of domination in all its forms, and by respect for difference and acceptance of a multiplicity of viewpoints:

> Reorienting oneself to pluralism is a spiritual as well as an epistemological and practical process. It requires a radical decentring on the part of the privileged whose reality has occupied the centre, whatever its defining terms (e.g., economic, geopolitical, sexual, even christological).
>
> (Cardman 1992: 8)

Part of this transformation will involve rejection of values that were previously central to Christian spirituality, such as self-sacrifice, obedience, submission and suffering, with an accompanying 'dismantling or replacement' of associated theological concepts such as 'predominant understandings of sin and redemp-tion, atonement and Jesus' relation to the Father' (ibid.: 10).

Some aspects of this process are notable developments. For example, the search for appropriate spirituality usually takes place in a group. The subject does not regard his or her growth as a private matter; the personal is not reduced to the individualistic. It is seen that holiness involves challenging the unholy within society. There is a shift, too, in that the spiritual is not a realm of special experiences, but a dimension of experience as a whole. Spirituality is, in part, that which informs and illuminates ordinary life. Yet we may feel that this broadening of spirituality has come at a price. To follow postmodernism is to accept that every delineation of truth is partial and susceptible to corruption by power. Mary Grey uses Foucault's idea of subjugated knowledge to construct a feminist account of redemption. But she insists that 'the claims of liberating faith spring from fidelity to the vision of "shalom", or Divine righteousness, which stand their ground despite the quicksands of political systems which may surround them' (Grey 1989: 10). A nuanced assault on deconstructive postmodernism comes from Charlene Spretnak (1991), who is strongly committed to respect for difference and relatedness. She argues that wisdom spirituality, through its grounding in the cosmological processes, can help to nourish wonder and hence to appreciate difference, subjectivity and communion. In this way it subverts exploitation and domination (Spretnak 1991: see ch. 6, esp. 220–3).

A spirituality of radical decentring impresses by its empowerment of the dispossessed and by its preparedness to embrace vulnerability. Also, its acceptance of the limitations to knowledge is close to that respect for mystery which is part of Christian tradition. Yet many will hesitate to accept the accompanying argument that any idea of transcendent truth is oppressive. The vision of God which evokes free assent is one which can unify and reconcile people in a divided world. It can make possible a sharing of values, and a creative exploration of new possibilities through these. Moreover, deconstructive postmodernism seems at times actually to celebrate how global capitalism dismembers cultures with their explanations of reality (Spretnak 1991: 127). There is surely a danger that there is nothing left with which to criticize this commercial engine (cf. Connor 1989: 234). Every recovery of truth is contingent, which would mean there was no real concept of liberating truth against which corrupt systems could be tested (cf. Taylor 1986: 70). At the very least, however, postmodernism's discontents make us aware of how often ideas of doctrinal purity have been associated with violence and exclusion. If in future spirituality is to speak from a vision of the whole in a way that attracts, it will have to speak in the language of service, kenotic prophecy, and respect for mystery.

ROMAN CATHOLICISM

There is some justification in considering Catholic experience separately. For most of the period under discussion the Roman Catholic Church kept its distance from other Christians. The Catholic Church also in many ways resisted the spirit of the age. In his encyclical *Quanta Cura* (1864) and its attached Syllabus of Errors Pius IX condemned those who said that the Catholic Church should come to terms with modernity. Then as the twentieth century opened, Pius X acted vigorously to extirpate liberalism in biblical and doctrinal studies, in a drive against modernism. Some modernists – like the Hegelians so detested by Kierkegaard – explained the elements of Christian faith as symbols of the human spiritual quest rather than as aspects of revelation. Yet the modernists were small in number and the Catholic response to them excessive. Aidan Nichols says that 'much of the anti-Modernist response went to an extreme'. One result was the freezing of discussion within the Catholic Church of those questions the modernists had been asking (Nichols 1991: 241, 332–4).

One of these questions was how religious experience related to Christian doctrine. This in turn meant re-examining how grace was understood, how God acted in persons who retained their freedom and responsibility. Aquinas had depicted grace as a divine gift working within human nature to deepen a person's responsiveness to God. Over time this divine gift would become 'habitual grace', enabling the subject to grow in faith, hope and love. These virtues in turn modified the intellect and the will so that the person could live in co-operation with God's will and works. Divine activity within human nature was therefore seen as helping the person to transcend human limitations and be drawn into union with God. Such language was abhorred by the Reformers, especially those in the Lutheran tradition, for it seemed to imply a religion of works. Two aspects of the Catholic defence against the Reformers were particularly formative of post-Reformation Catholic spirituality. The Council of Trent (1545–63) said that no-one could be absolutely certain whether or not they were in a state of grace or saved. Yet Trent also said that mortal sin would drive the grace of justification out of a person's life. Trent, together with the earlier influence of scholasticism, shifted Catholicism towards a narrower account of grace. It was now more difficult to see how grace related to the whole of life as a possible field of divine activity. Grace was presented in what Roger Haight calls 'the abstract, technical and static language of being' (Haight 1979: 73). In consequence, Catholic spiritual theology tended to think of grace as something lost and gained in an almost mechanistic way, through sin and confession. Grace seemed less a dynamism at work within human nature, more a precarious possession. Frequent confession became a feature of Catholic spirituality, utilizing the language of the penitent returning to a state of grace. It gave a seriousness to penitence in the Catholic Church that was perhaps equalled only in Protestant revivalism. However, it could also create the impression that sin was limited to a few areas which were gone through almost by rote. Looking back with the hindsight of the late twentieth century it is striking how sacramental confession for much of the time tended to limit the area of life under review, and how little it encouraged reflection on the wider experience of life, with its joys, sorrows, tensions, hopes and dreams. The consequences in Catholic spirituality were profound. Grace was widely seen as something added on to life rather than discovered or experienced within it (ibid.: 72–3, 113–14).

A similar dynamic can be discerned in eucharistic theology. The eucharist has long been understood by Catholics as a sacrificial action in which the bread and wine, through consecration, become the body and blood of Christ. The concept of transubstantiation had been accepted by the Lateran Council in 1215. Aquinas had later explained it by using the Aristotelian concepts of substance and accidents: the bread and wine retained their discernible characteristics (accidents) but in the essence of their being (substance) were transformed by God to become the body and blood of Christ. Trent reaffirmed this teaching. Easily criticized as mechanistic by detractors, the Thomistic account was actually more subtle than was often realized, drawing on an underlying concept of God as source and sustainer of the entire created order. The difficulty was that the presence of Christ could easily be perceived as a static one, so localized within the eucharistic elements as to exclude other senses of Christ's presence. Antony Archer describes the Tridentine rite as ostensibly floating free of any particular time or culture. He adds: 'Any creativity or varying contributions on the part of the people were excluded.' In effect the primary concern of Catholic worship was to establish a different, sacred world into which people entered (Archer 1986: 98–9). Moreover, the worshipper was cast in a passive role. David Power considers that

> [T]he popularization of the Tridentine teaching ... concentrated attention almost exclusively on the consecrated and reserved species and did not place the eucharistic presence of Christ in the context of celebration and eucharistic action. As a result it encouraged adoration and devotion but not communion and active participation in the ritual memorial.
>
> (Power 1992: 587)

Despite these weaknesses, in the life of the Catholic Church the Tridentine Mass was a rite of great numinousness. For many it yielded an intense experience of the presence of Christ.

By the mid-twentieth century, however, Catholic theologians themselves were increasingly aware that the theology underlying much Catholic spiritual practice needed renewal. The most important influence was Karl Rahner (1904–84). Rahner insisted (e.g. Rahner 1974: 18) that sacramentality as a whole was only made possible by God's constant initiative towards the world. Sacraments drew their living power from a revelation of the divine presence in our midst. Christ, as the supreme revelation of God, was the primal sacrament. But it was the Church that continued to be the sign by which Christ was known in the world, so if Christ was the primal sacrament, the Church was the fundamental sacrament. Rahner's reworking of the Catholic tradition was influential at the Second Vatican Council (1962–5) when the Catholic Church set out on a path of renewal. The sense that the Church itself was sacramental brought a growing awareness of its importance as a sign. A key Vatican II document about the nature of the Church, *Lumen Gentium* (Abbott 1966), describes the Church as being 'in the nature of sacrament – a sign and instrument, that is, of communion with God and of unity among all men' (para 1). This fitted in neatly with the developing Catholic social awareness, and the desire for the Church to be prophetic. It also allowed a good deal of Catholic self-criticism.

A second major shift in understanding was a new appreciation of spirituality as running through the whole of life. The previous understanding of grace had tended to localize spiritual life within certain observances. But Rahner's influential anthropology portrays each person as always in relationship with the mystery of God, whether this is realized by him or her or not. Rahner draws attention to the many forms of self-transcendence, such as creativity and conscience, and to how every answer to a question is never final but enables a fresh assessment and new questioning (Rahner 1978: 32). Human beings carry within them a call to truth. Truth is not 'a proposition which is equally valid in all its possible applications'. Rather, says Rahner, truth is an omnipresent and all-encompassing horizon in each person's life, impinging upon his or her awareness in many ways:

> And this is that truth which supports all other particular truths and is not itself supported by any. It is that which is uniquely self-authenticating (in itself) and, precisely in virtue of this fact, that which is to us the incomprehensible mystery.
> (Rahner 1971: 233)

This is, in other words, the luminous divine presence within. Rahner's approach chooses to go via God as absolute mystery rather than God as absolute being, which may leave a weakness in how he ultimately links these two divine aspects. Critics have also argued that his approach effectively undermines Christianity's claim to a unique revelation (cf. DiNoia 1989: 190–200). But his influence and that of his fellow-thinkers enabled a profound shift within Catholicism. Spirituality, including sacramental practice, was now less likely to be seen as the creation of a divine–human relationship where none had previously existed. Rather, it meant becoming aware of God who was always there, the subject now appropriating and celebrating this presence. Together with other developments, such as the women's movement, this trend encouraged a declericalization of spirituality within Catholic tradition, and a freeing of talents within the community of faith.

The same opening up can be partly attributed to the work of Edward Schillebeeckx (b. 1914). Schillebeeckx, drawing on personalism, stressed the element of sacramental encounter with God. Christ, who was once encountered through his bodily presence, now made himself known through the sacraments, which were 'a personal act of the Lord in earthly visibility and open availability' (Schillebeeckx 1963: 44). Just as the Church met Christ through the sacraments, so the world met Christ through the Church, which was a sacramental sign of Christ's living activity reaching out to the world (ibid.: 48–54). At this time, scriptural studies suggested that the sacraments, instead of being seen in abstract terms of grace, should be seen as part of salvation history inseparable from Christ's death and resurrection. Patristic studies suggested that sacraments were not isolated acts of individuals but communal events. Liturgical studies stressed participation and celebration of the sacraments rather than administration and reception (Martos 1983: ch. 4). Scholars such as Yves Congar, M.-D. Chenu and Odo Casel were among those at work here. They enabled a huge shift in Catholic sacramental emphasis, from the laity as done unto to doers themselves. Even Catholics who have a strong sense of priestly ministry as pastoral would hesitate today to use the language of Ronald Knox, who wrote that just as God intended the human race 'to look after the dumb beasts . . . so he would have priests to look after the faithful, to fold them and guide them and feed them in the ways of the supernatural life' (Knox 1959: 18). The foreword to the new *Roman Missal* (a normative document of Vatican II) states (para 5) that 'the celebration of the Eucharist is an act of the whole Church . . . The celebrating people are in fact the People of God . . . who continually grow in holiness by active, conscious and fruitful participation in the eucharistic mystery.' The phrase here, the People of God, recurs throughout the documents of Vatican II and inspired Catholic renewal thereafter. The adoption of this as one of the key images highlighted how all the members of the community of faith constituted the Church, not just the hierarchy. As Richard McCormick notes, 'This has immediate implications for the elaboration and development of moral doctrine, for consultative processes and for the free flow of ideas in the church' (McCormick 1991: 65).

It is worth noting briefly the change wrought in eucharistic spirituality. A symbol of this is the devotion in the eighteenth and nineteenth centuries to Jesus, the 'prisoner in the tabernacle' (i.e. in the reserved sacrament). Devotion to the eucharistic presence of Christ is still a potent form of prayer in the Catholic Church. But such prayer is now balanced within a larger, dynamic understanding of Christ present in the community and in the Scriptures. This also provides the context for understanding transubstantiation. David Power suggests that we go beyond anthropological or phenomenological categories if we talk of substantial change in the eucharistic elements:

> They can be better appreciated for what they say of Christ's presence if the starting point is the resurrection and the Spirit that assures the presence of the risen Lord in the church. After the memorial thanksgiving over them, the bread and wine are indeed no mere material substances. They belong in the world of communion with the risen Lord and thus assume a new reality whereby he is present in the midst of his faithful.

> (Power 1992: 608)

This draws out the eschatological aspect of the eucharist and its challenge that those who celebrate the presence of Christ should themselves be a transforming presence in the world.

Catholic spirituality at the close of the twentieth century is quite different from its earlier decades, when on the one hand, there were books of devotion, some of them quite saccharine, and on the other, manuals about the spiritual life for seminaries and novitiates. Even before Vatican II the tide was changing. Pierre Teilhard de Chardin (1881–1955) captured the imagination of many with his picture of the universe as full of divine life, in which Christ energized and drew all things towards himself as the omega point of evolution (cf. Corbishley 1971; King 1980). His respect for the material order was profound: 'Nothing here below is profane for those who know how to see' (Teilhard de Chardin 1960: 38). Some aspects of de Chardin anticipated the Gaia hypothesis in which the earth is seen as a single interacting biosystem (cf. Lovelock 1989). He continues to influence those in the New Age movement who seek a spirituality which speaks to ecological concerns (Woods 1993), but his influence within the churches has faded. More staying power has been shown by Thomas Merton (1916–68). Less systematic than de Chardin, he combines the mystical tradition of Christianity (and towards the end of his life, of other religions) with a sharp-eyed critique of the pretensions of Western culture. A more analytical critique was offered by liberation theologians, many of them Catholic and seeking to speak from the experience of suffering and oppressed people.

This section has focused on priestly writers, but this could give a false impression of Catholic spirituality today, in which women and men from many walks of life reflect on their experience in the light of their faith. This raises, though, the question of the extent to which Catholic spirituality now exists as a discrete entity. Unlike their forebears, Catholic authors no longer assume that they are writing for the ghetto: most want to address persons of goodwill interested in spiritual aspects of the human condition. Some, like Merton, bring together the insights of tradition and the questions of modernity. Others make little attempt to mediate between received truths and present-day concerns, seeking a fresh and untrammelled look at the latter. In this respect the Catholic Church reflects the same situation as much of the wider Christian community.

CONCLUDING QUESTIONS

For some two centuries the trend in spirituality has been towards an immanent view of God. Schleiermacher linked God with the human sense of absolute dependence; the Romantics sought God in nature; psychological approaches (e.g. James) used the analysis of human emotions to give meaning to the concept of God; postmodernism has led some to reject claims of absolute truth and to seek God in the pluriformity of insights suppressed by master discourses; even some recent Catholic spirituality has proceeded from human experience to divine mystery. Much of the initial impetus in this trend came from the Kantian critique of ideas of transcendence, but history played its part too. Jürgen Moltmann draws attention to how trust in human power to plan and achieve has shifted people away from living according to tradition, or in terms of the laws of the cosmos revealed in natural law (Moltmann

1988: 3–4). Today, the immanentist trend of spirituality is often linked with a sense of empowerment, fuelled in part by a desire for justice.

This trend poses awkward questions for both institutional Christianity and for those who believe that God is found within and nowhere else. It questions the Churches, because spirituality today proceeds increasingly from a situation in which people learn from their own experience. They trust themselves, and believe that they can speak from their own lives.

The evidence of this is seen in the declericalization of spiritual direction, in the emphasis on faith as world-transforming, in the shift of authority from institution to individual. Can the Churches find ways of incorporating this, of learning 'from below'? If not, then the renewal of spiritual life will flow more and more in non-institutional channels, outside formal Christianity.

There are questions, too, for those who endorse a strongly immanentist spirituality. Voices such as Alasdair MacIntyre (1985), Robert Bellah (1986) and Charles Taylor (1989) have drawn attention to a problematical self-orientation. They highlight such issues as the separation of right conduct from shared values, and the drive for self-expressive fulfilment which seems to override any communal or social interests. Some contemporary spirituality does indeed suggest that people can seek salvation, or healing, or growth, in isolation from the needs of others. In this trend there is little by which spirituality can be assessed – my way is my way, your way is your way. Is there any way of being open to God as transcendent, a living standard of love and holiness by which human searching can both assess itself and be inspired at the same time? If not, the danger is that spirituality becomes simply another consumer option. Ecological concerns also suggest that reports of the death of natural law may be premature. Empowerment needs to respect the mystery of God revealed through the cosmos in all its diversity, intricacy and interdependence. Enlightenment brought human self-mastery of a kind, but also a new vulnerability. Today, spirituality can learn from both.

REFERENCES

Abbott, W. M. (1966) *Lumen Gentium*, in *The Documents of Vatican II*, London: Geoffrey Chapman.

Ahlstrom, S. E. (1985) 'Ralph Waldo Emerson and the American Transcendentalists', in Ninian Smart *et al.* (eds) *Nineteenth Century Religious Thought in the West*, vol. 2, 29–68, Cambridge: Cambridge University Press.

Albanese, C. L. (1991) *Nature Religion in America: From the Algonkian Indians to the New Age*, Chicago: University of Chicago Press.

Archer, A. (1986) *The Two Catholic Churches: A Study in Oppression*, London: SCM Press.

Bellah, R. (1986) *et al.*, *Habits of the Heart: Individualism and Commitment in American Life*, New York: Harper & Row (Perennial Library).

Brandt, R. (1971) *The Philosophy of Schleiermacher: The Development of His Theory of Scientific and Religious Knowledge*, Westport, Conn.: Greenwood Press.

Brennan, P. (1961) *The Ethics of William James*, New York: Bookman Associates.

Byatt, A. S. (1989) *Unruly Times: Wordsworth and Coleridge in their Time*, London: The Hogarth Press.

Cardman, F. (1992) 'Liberating Compassion: Spirituality for a New Mellennium', *The Way* 32(1): 5–12.

Connor, S. (1989) *Postmodernist Culture: An Introduction to Theories of the Contemporary*, Oxford: Basil Blackwell.

Corbishley, T. (1971) *The Spirituality of Teilhard de Chardin*, London: Collins.

DiNoia, J. A. (1989) 'Karl Rahner', in David Ford (ed.) *The Modern Theologians: An Introduction to Christian Theology in the 20th Century*, 183–204, Oxford: Basil Blackwell.

Emerson. R. W. (1981) *The Portable Emerson*, ed. C. Bode, London: Penguin (revd edn).

Foucault, M. (1980) *Power/Knowledge: Selected Interviews and Other Writings*, ed. C. Gordon, New York: Pantheon Books.

—— (1988) *Politics, Philosophy, Culture: Interviews and Other Writings 1977–1984*, ed. L. D. Kritzman, New York: Routledge.

Furst, L. (1979) *Romanticism in Perspective: A Comparative Study of the Romantic Movements in England, France and Germany* (2nd edn), London: Macmillan.

Gadamer, H.-G. (1975) *Truth and Method* (2nd edn), London: Sheed & Ward.

Gelpi, D. L. (1991) *The Religious Quest of Ralph Waldo Emerson*, New York: University Press of America.

Grey, M. (1989) *Redeeming the Dream: Feminism, Redemption and Christian Tradition*, London: SPCK.

Haight, R. (1979) *The Experience and Language of Grace*, Dublin: Gill and Macmillan.

James, W. (1897) *The Will to Believe and Other Essays in Popular Philosophy*, New York and London: Longmans.

—— (1921) *Pragmatism: A New Name for Old Ways of Thinking*, London: Longmans.

—— (1971) *The Varieties of Religious Experience: A Study in Human Nature*, London: Collins.

Jantzen, G. M. (1989) 'Mysticism and Experience', *Religious Studies* 25: 295–315.

Kant, I. (1959) *Foundation of the Metaphysics of Morals and What is Enlightenment?*, Indianapolis: Bobbs-Merrill.

King, U. (1980) *Towards a New Mysticism: Teilhard de Chardin and Eastern Religions*, London: Collins.

Knox, R. (1959) *The Priestly Life: A Retreat*, London: Sheed & Ward.

Lash, N. (1988) *Easter in Ordinary: Reflections on Human Experience and the Knowledge of God*, London: SCM Press.

Lovelock, J. (1989) *The Ages of Gaia: A Biography of Our Living Earth*, Oxford: Oxford University Press.

McCormick, R. A. (1991) 'Changing My Mind about the Changeable Church', in J. Wall and D. Heim (eds) *How My Mind Has Changed*, 63–74, Grand Rapids, Mich.: Eerdmans.

MacIntyre, A. (1985) *After Virtue: A Study in Moral Theory* (2nd edn), London: Duckworth.

Martos, J. (1983) *The Catholic Sacraments*, Wilmington, Del.: Michael Glazier.

Moltmann, J. (1988) *Theology Today*, London: SCM Press.

—— (1991) *The Crucified God: The Cross of Christ as the Foundation and Criticism of Christian Theology*, San Francisco: HarperCollins.

Myers, G. E. (1986) *William James: His Life and Thought*, New Haven and London: Yale University Press.

Nichols, A. (1991) *The Shape of Catholic Theology: An Introduction to its Sources, Principles and History*, Edinburgh: T. & T. Clark.

Olin, D. (ed.) (1992) *William James: Pragmatism in Focus*, London and New York, Routledge.

Phillips, D. C. (1992) 'Was William James Telling the Truth After All?', in D. Olin (ed.) *William James: Pragmatism in Focus*, London and New York: Routledge, 229–47.

Power, D. (1992) 'Eucharist', in F. S. Fiorenza and J. P. Galvin (eds). *Systematic Theology: Roman Catholic Perspectives*, 583–612, Dublin: Gill and Macmillan.

Prickett, S. (1976) *Romanticism and Religion: The Tradition of Coleridge and Wordsworth in the Victorian Church*, London: Longman.

Rahner, K. (1971) *Theological Investigations*, vol. 7, London: Darton, Longman and Todd.

—— (1974) *The Church and the Sacraments*, London: Burns and Oates.

—— (1978) *The Foundations of Christian Faith: Introduction to the Idea of Christianity*, London: Darton, Longman and Todd.

Reardon, B. (1971) *From Coleridge to Gore: A Century of Religious Thought in Britain*, London: Longman.

Redeker, M. (1973) *Schleiermacher: Life and Thought*, Philadelphia: Fortress Press.

Rose, A. C. (1981) *Transcendentalism as a Social Movement 1830–1850*, New Haven: Yale University Press.

Russell, B. (1910) *Philosophical Essays*, London: Longmans.

Schillebeeckx, E. (1963) *Christ the Sacrament of the Encounter with God*, London: Sheed & Ward.

Schleiermacher, F. (1968) *The Christian Faith*, eds H. R. Mackintosh and J. S. Stewart, Edinburgh: T. & T. Clark.

Sheldrake, P. (1991) *Spirituality and History: Questions of Interpretation and Method*, London: SPCK.

Spretnak, C. (1991) *States of Grace: The Recovery of Meaning in the Postmodern Age*, San Francisco: HarperCollins.

Tarnas, R. (1993) *The Passion of the Western Mind*, New York: Ballantine Books.

Taylor, C. (1986) 'Foucault on Freedom and Truth', in D. Hoy (ed.) *Foucault: A Critical Reader*, Oxford: Basil Blackwell, 69–102.

—— (1989) *Sources of the Self: The Making of the Modern Identity*, Cambridge: Cambridge University Press.

Teilhard de Chardin, P. T. (1960) *Le Milieu Divin*, London: Collins.

Watson, J. R. (1970) *Picturesque Landscape and English Romantic Poetry*, London: Hutchinson.

Williams, R. (1978) *Schleiermacher the Theologian: The Construction of the Doctrine of God*, Philadelphia: Fortress Press.

Williams, Rowan (1988) ' "Nobody Knows who I am Till the Judgement Morning" ', in D. D. Honoré (ed.) *Trevor Huddleston: Essays on His Life and Work*, Oxford: Oxford University Press.

Wolf, H. C. (1965) *Kierkegaard and Bultmann: The Quest of the Historical Jesus*, Minneapolis: Augsburg Publishing.

Woods, R. (1993) 'What is New Age Spirituality?', *The Way* 33: 175–88.

Wordsworth, W. (1989) *Selected Poetry and Prose*, ed. P. Hobsbaum, London: Routledge.

FURTHER READING

Brown, D. (1987) *Continental Philosophy and Modern Theology*, Oxford: Basil Blackwell.

Dupré, L. and Saliers, D. E. (eds) (1990) *Christian Spirituality* vol. 3: *Post-Reformation and Modern*, London: SCM Press.

Fox, M. (ed.) (1981) *Western Spirituality: Historical Roots, Ecumenical Routes*, Santa Fe, NM: Bear & Co.

Lane, B. C. (1988) *Landscapes of the Sacred: Geography and Narrative in American Spirituality*, New York/Mahwah, NJ: Paulist Press.

Miles, M. R. (1988) *The Image and Practice of Holiness: A Critique of the Classic Manuals of Devotion*, London: SCM Press.

Murdoch, I. (1992) *Metaphysics as a Guide to Morals*, London: Penguin.

Passmore, J. (1970) *The Perfectibility of Man*, London: Duckworth.

Steiner, G. (1989) *Real Presences*, London: Faber.

Taylor, C. (1991) *The Ethics of Authenticity*, Cambridge, Mass.: Harvard University Press.

Welch, C. (1988, new edn) *Protestant Thought in the Nineteenth Century*, vol. 1, *1799–1870*, New Haven: Yale University Press.

Woods, R. (ed.) (1981) *Understanding Mysticism*, London: Athlone Press.

See also chapters 13, 14, 25, 30, 31, 41, 44, 45, 46.

30

RELIGIOUS EXPERIENCE AND LANGUAGE

William J. Wainwright

Modern philosophers have focused almost exclusively on two aspects of the spiritual life – spiritual states and their epistemic status. What is the reason for this? A remark made by William James in 1902 suggests an answer. 'Feeling is the deeper source of religion . . . philosophic and theological formulas are secondary products, like translations of a text into another tongue.' While 'conceptions and constructions are . . . a necessary part of our religion', 'these intellectual operations . . . presuppose immediate experiences as their subject-matter. They are interpretative and inductive operations, operations after the fact, consequent upon religious feeling, not coordinate with it, not independent of what it ascertains' (James 1902: 423–4). This kind of emphasis on religious experience is new. Traditional Christianity explored the nature of the spiritual life in detail. It also believed that (some) spiritual states involve perceptions. But the epistemic status of mystical states was not an issue, and there was little interest in other spiritual traditions. Nor were religious experiences appealed to to justify religious belief.

The modern belief that *sui generis* religious feelings are the primary source of religious beliefs and concepts has several sources. One is an eighteenth- and nineteenth-century emphasis upon 'heart religion' and Romanticism's valorization of feeling. There are historical connections, for example, between James and Edwards who, with other leaders of the Great Awakening, insisted that 'true religion consists, in great measure, in vigorous and lively actings of the inclination and will of the soul, or the fervent exercises of the heart' (Edwards 1959: 99). Friedrich Schleiermacher and Jacob Friedrich Fries were both educated by Moravians. James's attitudes towards Romanticism are ambivalent but the affinities are real. Another source is the Enlightenment's preoccupation with natural religion – the belief in a 'religious *a priori*' which is part of human nature and underlies the diversity of religious belief and practice. Deism identified the religious *a priori* with reason's ability to establish basic religious and moral truths. The Romantics identified it with feeling or intuition. In either case, the religious *a priori* could be used to explain and evaluate the historical religions. A third source was the widespread conviction that Kant had demonstrated the bankruptcy of natural theology and that, therefore, religious belief lacked justification or could only be justified by appealing to the exigencies of practical life or feeling.

Modern philosophers, then, have frequently held that religion can be adequately explained by religious feeling. Many have also thought that religious feelings are its only justification. So their interest in the varieties of religious experience, and in its cognitive validity (or lack of it) is not surprising. Nor is it surprising that much of their attention has been devoted to visions, raptures, and other ecstatic experiences with a pronounced perception-like quality. For these would justify religious beliefs and practices if they were veridical.

TYPOLOGIES OF RELIGIOUS EXPERIENCE

One of the most important early typologies of religious experience is Rudolf Otto's. Otto identifies the religious *a priori* with numinous feeling. Numinous feeling is woven of five strands. The relation between them is indicated by the following diagram:

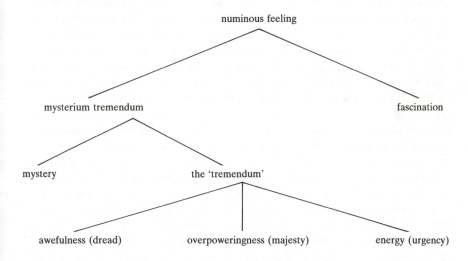

The experience involves 'blank wonder, an astonishment that strikes us dumb, an amazement absolute' (Otto 1958: 26). Its apparent object is wholly other, a mystery that is in principle opaque to understanding. Religious dread is distinct from ordinary fear. It is more like a fear of ghosts or a dread of haunted places, feelings which make our flesh creep and our blood run cold. One experiences a sense of 'impotence and general nothingness as against overpowering might', of being 'dust and ashes as against majesty' (ibid.: 21).

621

The experience's apparent object seems overwhelmingly alive and urgent, a quality indicated by terms suggesting 'vitality, passion, . . . will, force, . . . activity, impetus' (ibid.: 23). But the mysterium tremendum is only an aspect of the numinous. It is also fascinating, compelling, alluring, enchanting – a value so great and splendid that all other values seem insignificant in comparison.

As religious experience develops, numinous experience is 'schematized' by rational concepts to yield the 'complex concept of the Holy'. Mystical experience, on the other hand, is a form of numinous experience which 'shows a preponderance of its non-rational elements' (Otto 1958: 85n). *Mysticism East and West* (1957) distinguishes two types – the 'mysticism of introspection' and the 'mysticism of unifying vision'. In the first, the mystic withdraws from outward things and turns inward, sinking deep into the self in an attempt to find the holy power or depth or ground which he or she believes lies at the centre or summit of his or her soul. This holy power may be identified with the mystic's true self or with the world-ground. The second sort of mystic turns outward. The mysticism of unifying vision has three stages. In the first, the mystic perceives nature's unity. Natural phenomena are identified with each other and the mystic. They become 'transparent, luminous, visionary', and time stands still (Otto 1957: 46). The object of experience in the first stage is nature but a nature transfigured, timeless, and mysteriously one. The object in the second stage is not only nature but a power behind it which supports it and manifests itself through it ('the one behind the many'). In the third stage, nature drops away and the mystic experiences the 'one apart from the many' – Samkara's Brahman without attributes or Eckhart's "silent void of the Godhead" into which difference or multiplicity never entered' (ibid.: 52).

Numinous and mystical experiences, however, seem phenomenologically distinct. The former tend to be I–thou experiences in which the subject is confronted by a transcendent 'will' or 'emotional temper' which thrusts itself into his or her own. The latter are unitive experiences in which the sense of distance or otherness is largely overcome, and they are often described in impersonal or transpersonal terms (see Smart 1960). Why did Otto fail to see this? There are similarities between the experiences. The objects of both experiences 'fascinate' the beholder. The mystical object, too, is incomprehensible and therefore a mystery. Furthermore, the mystic experiences a loss of self and is hence 'nothing' before the One. But the similarities seem insufficient to justify assimilating them. Philip Almond suggests that Otto's principal reason for doing so is his commitment to Fries's metaphysics which postulates a religious *a priori* underlying empirical religious phenomena. Otto identifies Fries's *Ahnung* with numinous feeling. This commitment prevents him from appreciating the 'phenomenological disparities' between the two experiences (Almond 1982: 107–17).

The most influential typology that has appeared in recent decades is Walter

Stace's. Mystical consciousness is characterized by a 'sense of objectivity or reality', a 'feeling of blessedness, joy, happiness, satisfaction, etc.', and a sense 'that what is apprehended is holy, or sacred, or divine'. It is also characterized by parodoxicality, and alleged ineffability. The mystic offers descriptions of his experience which are contradictory if taken literally, and claims that it cannot adequately be put into words (Stace 1960: 79). Mystical consciousness assumes two forms. The extrovertive mystic perceives all things as one. Ordinary objects appear to be identical with each other and/or rooted in some unity which lies behind them. The world is also experienced as alive or conscious, or as rooted in life and consciousness. It is a 'living presence'. The mind of the introvertive mystic, on the other hand, is empty of ordinary contents. Awareness of the phenomenal world vanishes and space and time are no longer experienced. Ordinary mental activity is suspended and the mystic's soul is stripped of abstract concepts and sensuous images. Having purified his or her consciousness, the introvertive mystic becomes aware of a One with which he or she experiences union or identity. (Stace's introvertive mysticism appears to be identical with what others have called 'pure consciousness' – a state in which the mystic is conscious but conscious of nothing.)

While Stace's typology has been widely influential, it oversimplifies and thereby distorts the richness and variety of spiritual experience. Two examples will make this clear. Buddhists cultivate an experience in which spatio–temporal reality is perceived as 'empty' – a conceptually unstructured flow of 'dharmas' (momentary physical or psychological events or states that resist further analysis). The object of the Buddhist's experience is not some permanent substance or force underlying things. It is the process of becoming itself – but viewed without attachment and without attempting to conceptualize it. This is not a form of introvertive mystical consciousness, for the 'object' of the mystic's experience is the phenomenal world. But neither is the experience extrovertive in Stace's sense. Viewing things as a conceptually unstructured flow, and without attachment, appears to be phenomenologically distinct from perceiving their identity or seeing them as rooted in some larger life or unity. (For similar reasons, Otto's typology cannot handle this experience.)

The major difficulty with Stace's account, however, is its failure to mention love. This is extraordinary in view of the central role played by love in the accounts of both Eastern and Western theistic mystics. R. C. Zaehner hardly overstates the case when he concludes that Stace's 'failure to mention love can only be due to an obvious anti-Christian [or anti-theistic] bias reinforced by a massive ignorance of the whole tradition of love-mysticism within Hinduism itself' (Zaehner 1957: 200). The experiences that interest Stace are primarily knowledge experiences. Theistic mystical experiences, on the other hand, are primarily love experiences, and love experiences and knowledge experiences are phenomenologically distinct (see Dhavamony 1971).

Zaehner attempts to rectify this mistake. Nature mysticism (cosmic consciousness) and monistic (or soul) mysticism are distinguished from theistic mysticism. The first two are roughly identical with Stace's extrovertive and introvertive mysticism. But theistic mysticism cannot be accommodated within Stace's categories. It does involve introversion. The theistic mystic's mind empties itself of precepts, images, and all but a few of the most general and abstract concepts (such as 'being', 'presence', or 'love'). But unlike monistic experiences, theistic experiences have an object or content which is distinct from the self. This object, however, is not identical with a part of the space–time world or with the space–time world as a whole. The experience's character or tone is indicated by the fact that these mystics employ erotic imagery to describe the felt quality of their relation to its object. Bernard, Teresa of Avila, and John of the Cross furnish obvious examples.

Zaehner is also guilty of oversimplification. The uniqueness of Buddhist experience is ignored (Zaehner identifies it with cosmic consciousness), and theistic mysticism itself is more variegated than he recognizes. Zaehner focuses on introvertive modes of consciousness which are experienced as states of mutual love, noetic experiences in which the mystic not only loves but has an 'experimental perception' of the beloved's love for the mystic. But other theistic and quasi-theistic experiences seem different. For example, there is an introvertive state in which theistic mystics direct their will and affections towards God without experiencing his presence. In another, God is not experimentally perceived but his presence is inferred from the soul's sense of well-being, its advances in virtue, sensations of 'sweetness', and feelings of love (see Martin 1959: 123–4). Orthodox mystics cultivate experiences in which the soul is invaded and permeated with a light which is identified with the divine energies. The experience is achieved by introversion but involves purified senses as well as a purified intellect (although the blind can have it). Other introvertive theistic experiences appear to have a great deal of conceptual content and to be primarily knowledge rather than love experiences. Teresa's intellectual vision of the Trinity is an example. Finally, the relation between theistic mystical experiences and monistic experiences may be closer than Zaehner is prepared to admit. There are introvertive experiences which culminate in a loss of self but seem distinct from pure consciousness. Plotinus and possibly Tauler provide examples. Both are metaphysical dualists, and both construe the object of their quest as transpersonal (though not impersonal like Nirvana). Both regard *eros* (the soul's love of God) as a necessary means to union and neither clearly speaks of experiencing God's love of the soul. (Although Tauler's language is ambiguous, and he does suggest that God's life is a life of love.) These states differ from Zaehner's theistic mystical experiences because they are not experiences of mutual love. But the fact that love is their prelude, and that they are more aptly described as experiences of an object with no subject than as experiences of a subject with no object, suggest that they are also distinct from pure consciousness. Again, Nelson Pike has convincingly argued that experiences of mutual love sometimes culminate in experiences of identity ('union without distinction'). This state 'is not a distinct kind of mystical experience. It is, rather, the climax moment . . . of two distinct mystical states, namely, Full Union and Rapture (or ecstasy).' It is 'an interval in a more comprehensive experience which . . . occurs very rarely and then only for an instant.' The mystic temporarily loses the sense of God as 'not me' and in doing so loses his or her sense of self (Pike 1992: 38, 40). Pike thinks that 'union without distinction' is Stace's introvertive mysticism. This is doubtful. The moment in question is experienced as the temporary culmination or climax of an experience of intense mutual love. Its phenomenological ancestry is distinctive and seems to colour the experience itself. Thus Ruysbroeck characterizes the unity from which one cannot distinguish oneself as 'an eternal fire of love' and describes union as being 'burnt up in love' (Ruysbroeck 1951: 186).

The problematic character of these typologies raises important methodological questions. The typologist has to rely on texts and personal interviews. How is one to distinguish description from interpretation? And if one cannot, how is one to determine the phenomenological features of the experiences being investigated? Ninian Smart points out that Zaehner thinks that Buddhists, Yogins, and Advaitins are all monistic mystics. Nevertheless, they interpret their experiences differently. The Buddhist claims that 'there are no eternal selves, but only impermanent' empirical egos which 'go out like a flame' when they pass into Nirvana (Smart 1965: 83). Yoga thinks that a plurality of eternal selves exist. Each can free his or her own eternal self from its entanglement in nature and thus achieve liberation (*moksa*). Advaita maintains that there is only one eternal self (the *Atman*) which is identical with the ground of being (the *Brahman*). Liberation consists in recognizing one's identity with the *Atman–Brahman*.

If Zaehner is correct, it is a mistake to argue from the differences between these interpretations to differences in the experiences which are being interpreted. Is it any less of a mistake to argue (as Zaehner does) that since theistic and monistic mystics offer different accounts of their experiences, their experiences differ? The question is critical because differences between theistic and Advaitin accounts seem no greater than those between Advaitin and Buddhist accounts. We are not hopelessly at sea. It seems reasonable to privilege first-person accounts, to be more suspicious of descriptions which employ doctrinal concepts than of those which do not, to pay attention to analogies with more familiar experiences (if mystical experience A is more like ordinary experience x than ordinary experience y and if mystical experience B is more like ordinary experience y than ordinary experience x, then A and B are probably distinct), and so on. But the criteria are loose and agreement on their correct application is unlikely.

In the face of these difficulties, a number of scholars have recently suggested that cross-cultural typologies of religious experience are impossible. The most influential spokesman for this view is Steven Katz. Katz believes there are no 'pure' or 'unmediated' experiences. All experience is shaped by the attitudes, expectations, beliefs, and intentions we bring to it. Since these vary from one religious tradition to another, mystical experience too varies. There are as many types of mystical experience as there are traditions. A cross-cultural typology of mystical experience is therefore impossible. Katz's thesis, then, is that a mystic's experience is largely constructed by the concepts, beliefs, attitudes, etc., which the mystic brings to it. Since the mystics' traditions are significantly different, so too are their experiences.

How credible is this? Two questions should be distinguished: 'Is a cross-cultural typology possible' and 'Are mystical experiences largely constructed?' These questions are independent. Even if mystical consciousness is constructed, experiences from different traditions may be significantly similar. Katz points out that there are not only great differences between the experiences of (e.g.) Christian and Buddhist mystics, there are also significant differences between the theistic mysticism of the Bhagavad-Gita, Ramanuja, Teresa, Isaac Luria, and al-Hallaj, and between the monism of Samkara, Spinoza, and Eckhart. This is true but inconclusive. Things significantly different in some respects can be significantly similar in others, and the similarities may justify classifying them as things of the same kind. Although rabbits, bass, grasshoppers, whales, and butterflies are very different, the animal kingdom can be usefully divided into relatively few kinds (mammals, fish, insects, etc.). Similarly here. Whatever their differences, the religious experiences of Christians and Vaisnavas are more like each other than either are like the experiences of Yogins, Advaitins, and Jains, and the experiences of the latter resemble each other more than they resemble either Christian or Vaisnava experiences or Buddhist experiences. Even if religious experiences are constructed, significant cross-cultural typologies are still possible.

But are mystical experiences largely constructed? There are reasons for thinking that at least some of them are not. For one thing, it is difficult to see how the experience of pure consciousness could be constructed. As Anthony Perovich points out, constructivism can be understood in two ways. On one interpretation, the mind is presented with a conceptually unstructured manifold or continuum which it then unifies or divides by imposing concepts. Unification results in a 'synthesized manifold'. Division 'introduce[s] difference, multiplicity, and form rather than [does] away with them' (Perovich 1990: 242). In either case, the constructed experience involves multiplicity. In the experience of pure consciousness, on the other hand, distinctions disappear.

On the second interpretation, constructivism denies that there is a mystical 'given' which is then structured by consciousness: the mind does not impose form on something immediately presented to it but produces its objects *de novo*. This form of constructivism fares no better than the first, however, since pure consciousness has no objects.

Constructivism is also disconfirmed by some Buddhist experiences. The experience of emptiness is not obtained by imposing concepts on the flow of sensations but by deconditioning. Meditation involves a progressive decon-struction of ordinary perception and thinking (including Buddhist thinking) until a stage is reached in which the mind no longer imposes its categories on what is immediately presented to it.

Nor is it clear that mystical or numinous experiences which have objects are primarily structured by the religious, rather than non-religious, concepts which the mystic brings to them. The fact that Christian mystics typically use Christian concepts to describe their experiences is not important if there are non-theological descriptions which they would find acceptable. (For example, 'I had a non-sensory experience in which I seemed to merge with an overwhelming, loving, reality.') It should also be noted that the general and abstract concepts which sometimes inform theistic mystical consciousness ('being', 'reality', 'presence', 'love', etc.) are part of our ordinary conceptual equipment. (Specifically Christian experiences like Teresa's intellectual vision of the Trinity are comparatively rare in Christian mysticism.) It is not clear, then, than these experiences are primarily structured by peculiarly religious concepts. If they are not, it is not obvious that they are artifacts of the mystic's religious tradition.

Constructivism also has difficulty accounting for novelty. As Robert Forman points out, 'it is not unusual to hear of an untrained or uninitiated neophyte who has a mystical experience without any deep preconditioning' (Forman 1990: 20). Richard Bucke and Alfred Tennyson are familiar examples. The course of an adept's experience is also sometimes unexpected.

> St. Teresa was at first quite astonished by her apprehension of God's presence in all things, and in the presence of the Trinity in her soul, since she had not previously known that such experiences were possible . . . St. John of the Cross likewise encountered some difficulty in trying to fit certain comtemplative states into the categories of the scholastic theology of the day, [and said] that pious souls often tend to resist new and deeper mystical communications because they do not understand and had not anticipated them.
>
> (Payne 1990: 149)

Although the uninitiated neophyte's experiences could be the product of religious beliefs and concepts the neophyte had unthinkingly absorbed from his or her environment, and the adept's unanticipated experiences could be determined by the religious beliefs, intentions, and attitudes he or she holds, 'the theory starts to sound *ad hoc*' (Forman 1990: 20).

Of course if all human experience is constructed, then so is mystical experience. But why think that it is? Few contemporary philosophers believe that the thesis can 'be established a priori. Consequently, it must be an empirical claim' (Perovich 1990: 245). Why accept it in the face of apparent counter-examples like pure consciousness? That ordinary human experience is constructed does not entail that experiences which the soul obtains when ordinary mental activities are suspended also are.

Nor is it clear that religious experiences which have objects are artifacts of their traditions. The empirical evidence for this thesis consists in correlations between the sorts of experience the mystic has and distinctive features of his or her tradition. Buddhists do not have intellectual visions of the Trinity or Christ's presence, and Christians do not have visions of celestial Buddhas or experience the emptiness of things. These correlations, however, prove little. They are consistent with the claim that the beliefs, attitudes, intentions, and expectations which constitute (e.g.) theistic traditions produce theistic experiences. They are equally consistent with the claim that the latter determines the former. The second and more radical form of constructivism places all the explanatory weight on the interpretative systems which the subject brings to his or her experience. But what accounts, then, for the interpretative systems themselves? It may be more illuminating to suppose that religion grows out of real or apparent divine disclosures than to suppose that these disclosures are produced by religion (its beliefs, practices, institutions, and so on) for the latter leaves religion inadequately accounted for. None of the alternative explanations (priestcraft, wish-fulfilment, or their more sophisticated variants) seem as plausible as the hypothesis that among religion's principal causes are experiences which, while sometimes conceptually structured, are not specifically Christian, or Buddhist, or Muslim although they may be implicitly theistic, pantheistic, or monistic in the sense that they are more naturally interpreted in one of these ways than another. The typologies of Otto, Stace, and Zaehner are oversimplified but the enterprise they were engaged in has an explanatory power which radical constructivism lacks.

In a series of recent articles, Grace Jantzen has argued that modern philosophical discussions of mysticism are skewed by their obsession with visions, trances, raptures and other extraordinary experiences, and by their emphasis on these experience's veridicality (or lack of it). While experiences of this kind do occur in the life of mystics, they should not be abstracted from their context. Religious experience in the broad sense ('a lifetime of "being towards God"') is the heart of a life of prayer. 'Religious experience in the narrow sense of visions and ecstasies' is not (Jantzen 1989: 301–2). Jantzen's caution is useful. The experiences we have been discussing can only be fully understood in the context of the spiritual life to which they belong, and their value is a function of the help they provide in achieving the goal of the spiritual path which the contemplative is pursuing. Our estimation of the degree of cross-cultural similarity between different mystical traditions will also be affected by whether we focus on religious experience in the narrow or broad sense. If we focus on the first, we find much similarity. The experience of pure consciousness, for example, appears to occur in a number of traditions and so does the experience which some Christian mystics call 'marriage'. If we focus on the mystic's identification of his or her experience's object, on his or her aims and methods, or on other features of the spiritual paths in which these experiences are embedded, the differences are more striking. For example, Yoga identifies the object with the mystic's *purusa* – one of a plurality of pure selves. According to Advaita Vedanta, the object of mystical experience is the *Atman–Brahman* – the unique ground of both world and self. Yoga's aim is isolation. The adept attempts to free his or her *purusa* from its entanglement in nature (*prakriti*) so that it may exist in splendid solitude. Advaita aims at the intuitive and existential appropriation of the fact that one is the *Atman–Brahman*. Patanjali's yoga (which involves special postures, breathing exercises, the withdrawal of the senses from sense objects, concentration upon an object of meditation, etc.) provides the means to isolation. The Advaitin believes he or she can achieve his or her aim by *jnana*-yoga – a study of, and meditation upon, scripture. Thus while the experiences of isolation and identity are arguably the same (viz. pure consciousness), the objects, aims, and methods of the two spiritual paths are significantly different. Again, there are striking similarities between Christian and Vaisnava theology, experiences (in the narrow sense), and values. But the centrality of the Incarnation in some Christian mysticism (e.g., that of Father Berulle) is uniquely Christian and it is tendentious to argue that it is not essential.

Whether these considerations vitiate modern philosophy's approach to mystical phenomena, however, is more doubtful. In the first place, the extraordinary experiences that interest Otto, Stace, and Zaehner are more significant features of the spiritual path than Jantzen's remarks suggest, for they are typically regarded as anticipations or foretastes of its goal. Thus, the experience of cessation (which may be pure consciousness but is more likely the temporary extinction of consciousness) is sometimes regarded as 'nirvana in life'. Again, spiritual marriage is an anticipation of the eternal participation in God's own life which the saints enjoy in heaven – a divine life in which God is known and loved as he knows and loves himself. Furthermore, ordinary religious experience is parasitic on the experience of the saints, prophets, and teachers who are the tradition's exemplars and principal authors. Visions, ecstasies, and other 'transcendent experiences' are important features of these figures' lives. If they are delusive, the value of the lives is called in question. Finally, if apparent cognitions of the divine really are one of religion's root causes, then it is natural to focus on the extraordinary experiences in which the noetic or perception-like quality is particularly striking. The interest in cross-cultural typologies which focus on experiences in the narrow sense, and a concern with these experiences' validity, is not just misguided.

THE EPISTEMIC STATUS OF RELIGIOUS EXPERIENCE

Attention to spiritual experience's epistemic status has taken two forms. Some have attempted to explain the mechanism of spiritual perception, i.e., to show how it works, its place in the human psyche. Others have offered reasons for believing that these perceptions are (or are not) veridical.

The most interesting examples of the first approach are Rudolf Otto's

Philosophy of Religion and *The Idea of the Holy*, and discussions among Roman Catholic theologians and philosophers in the first half of the century.

Following the neo-Kantianism of J. F. Fries, Otto argued that we possess an immediate knowledge of Reality (the noumenal world) which expresses itself in 'feelings of truth'. These intuitions are brought to consciousness as Ideas.

When the categories of theoretical reason (cause, substance, relation, etc.) are 'schematized' by space and time, they apply to appearances. But when they are schematized by 'the principle of completeness' (which expresses reason's 'perception and knowledge' that real existence is necessary, one, and complete), they apply to Reality. A category which has been schematized by this principle is an Idea of theoretical reason. These Ideas are essentially negative. Reality is thought by negating the limitations imposed by space and time. Practical reason also has its 'feeling of truth'. Although it cannot be completely conceptualized, it is the source of the Idea of Reality as a 'reign of purpose'.

Kant thought that the Ideas of reason were empty because no concrete intuition corresponds to them. Fries and Otto disagree, arguing that the Real is directly given in feelings or concrete intuitions (*Ahnung*). These feelings are aesthetic judgements in Kant's sense. They can be communicated and are inter-subjectively valid since they are expressions of reason's essential structure. Although they cannot be 'expressed in terms of a concept' and hence are not knowledge in the strict (i.e., conceptual) sense, they are genuine cognitions or 'perceptions' (Otto 1931: 93) Examples are feelings of beauty and of the sublime in which the Transcendent is obscurely grasped, and religious intimations and intuitions such as our dissatisfaction with the temporal or sense of absolute dependence. In *The Idea of the Holy*, feelings of the beautiful and sublime are more sharply distinguished from religious intuitions (they are mere analogies of the latter), and religious intuitions are identified with numinous feelings.

Three positions emerged in debates between Roman Catholic philosophers and theologians in the first half of the century. According to the first, God's presence is merely inferred from effects he creates in the soul. According to the second, the mystic immediately perceives God but does so through these effects. According to the third, God is perceived directly; there is no intervening medium.

While the best-known exponent of the first position is R. M. Garrigou-Lagrange, it was most carefully developed by Henry Browne and August Saudreau. Faith believes something because God has said it. It thus typically has two objects – God and the proposition he proposes for belief. Browne thought that mystical 'vision' is a form of faith in which the soul is directed only towards faith's primary object (God). Saudreau, however, believed that the objects of the mystic's intellect are 'the truths known by faith: the greatness, perfections, amiability, incomprehensibility of God' (Saudreau 1924: 57).

There is no direct perception of God. Mystics misleadingly speak of immediate perception because God's presence is spontaneously inferred from the effects he produces in their souls ('feelings of love', 'progress in virtue', 'sweetness', and so on), and because they sometimes enjoy an infused and irresistible conviction (not perception) that God is present. (There is an interesting similarity to sceptics like James Leuba and Wayne Proudfoot who also think that mystical 'perception' is an inference from interior feelings, unusual physiological states, and so on, to a supernatural cause but believe that the inference is fallacious.)

This theory was widely rejected because (as Albert Farges said) it did not adequately account for the fact that the mystic's knowledge is ' "experimental" ... concrete, intuitive, and without reasoning, analogous to that of the senses' (Farges 1926: 612). Why then did Saudreau and others adopt it? In part because they wanted their theory to account for mystical states like aridity in which God is felt to be absent as well as states in which he is experienced as present and, in part, because they tended to focus on the 'prayer of simple regard' or 'loving attention'. In this prayer, the mind is empty except for a 'naked [and loving] intent stretching unto God, not clothed in any special thought of God' (McCann 1964: 105). But God is not immediately experienced.

The most fully developed defences of the second position are Jacques Maritain's and Albert Farges's. An *objectum quo* is a 'mental object' such as a concept or image or sense impression that provides the 'means by which we know'. The *objectum quod* is 'the object which is known' (Maritain 1959: 120–1). *Objectum quo*s are not objects of knowledge from which we infer the existence or presence of their non-mental counterparts; they are mediums through which the object of knowledge is immediately grasped 'in the sense that no *quod* mediates it' (ibid.: 394). Contemplation includes a knowledge of God 'as present, in which the soul undergoes an action exercised upon it by that object and perceives in virtue of this very passion' (ibid.: 263). Maritain (but not Farges) thinks that the consciously experienced effects of infused charity are the medium (*objectum quo*) through which God's essence (the *objectum quod*) is experimentally (although obscurely) grasped.

Why must mystical perception be indirect? First, it is only in the beatific vision that 'the Divine Selfhood will be grasped just as it is', 'without the mediation of any creature or concept' (Maritain 1959: 249). Second, Farges (but not Maritain) points out that mystical knowledge is obscure. Contemplatives more often speak of touching or tasting God than of seeing him. In the third place, human (as distinguished from angelic) intellects can only grasp things through concepts, impressions, and other media. Indeed, the soul can only grasp itself through its operations. Fourth, Maritain and Farges both think that 'A (experimentally) perceives X' entails 'A is aware of X's presence through effects which X produces in (the soul of) A'.

But why should the medium of spiritual perception be identified with the experienced effects of infused charity? For two closely related reasons. First, mystical knowledge is (as John of the Cross says) a 'light which is the union of love', a 'wisdom of love', a 'loving awareness of God' (Maritain 1959: 338–43). Union is attained through love and is a form of love. Second, the mind has emptied itself of everything but its loving awareness of God. If mystical awareness has a medium, it must therefore be love, for love is the only thing other than this awareness which has not been 'buried beneath the cloud of forgetting'.

It seems reasonable to identify the experienced effects of infused charity with mystical knowledge's *objectum quo* if mystical perception involves a medium. But the arguments for the latter are inconclusive. First, some orthodox divines have believed that the beatific vision can be (briefly) enjoyed in this life. Augustine and Aquinas thought that Moses and Paul had done so. In any case, that the mystic cannot directly apprehend God's essence does not entail that he or she cannot directly apprehend God's being, or presence, or attributes. (Unless God is simple. If he is, apprehending God's being or attributes involves apprehending his essence although one need not recognize that one is doing so.) Second, touching and tasting are as direct as sight. Furthermore, direct experiences can be obscure. Our experience of some of our inner states or moods is an example. Obscurity is often a function of inadequate conceptual resources and not of indirect perception. In the third place, some mystical experience appears to be direct and unmediated. (Monistic experiences and Pike's 'union without distinction' are examples.) To assume that they cannot be so because all human experience is mediated begs the question. Fourth, there are forms of 'experimental perception' in which the subject is not aware of the perceived object through effects that the object produces in him or her. Our awareness of sense data and our own mental states are examples.

Maritain's and Farges's arguments are therefore inconclusive. Nor is it clear that their theory best fits the mystical texts. The fact that authors of very different theories (such as Saudreau) appeal to the same passages suggests that they are at best ambiguous.

If theories like Saudreau's fail to respect mysticism's experimental character, and if views like Maritain's are inadequately supported, one should seriously entertain the third possibility – that in some mystical states, God's substance, or presence, or attributes are perceived directly. Although not as frequently espoused, this position was sometimes held. For example, Ambrose Gardeil thought that the mystic's awareness of God, like the soul's experience of itself, is direct and not dependent on such things as 'sense impressions, phantasmata, intelligible species, concepts', and so on (Butler 1966: 1).

The question of mystical perception's mechanism and the question of its validity are related but distinct. The authors we have discussed assume that spiritual cognition is in order and ask how it is possible. Just as Kant's first two critiques showed how scientific and moral knowledge are possible, Otto's neo-Kantian theory shows how knowledge of the Real is possible. Saudreau's and Maritain's theories show how experimental knowledge of God can occur in a theistic universe. These theories implicitly refute the charge that mystical knowledge cannot be veridical because spiritual cognition is not possible.

But even if spiritual perceptions are possible, they might not occur; apparent perceptions can be delusive. Other authors have addressed this issue directly.

Walter Stace offers three arguments for mysticism's epistemic reliability. First, the experience is not subjective. Objective experiences (e.g., my visual experience of the pen I am using) exhibit 'internal' and 'external' order. The object of experience conforms to empirical law. Subjective experiences are disorderly. If I dream that the water in a kettle freezes when heated, my experience exhibits internal disorder since what I experience conflicts with empirical laws. The experience of a mirage exhibits internal order but 'a breach of natural law occurs' in the object's 'external relations . . . with the other areas of experience which immediately surround it . . .' (Stace 1960: 142). (For example, no water is perceived when we arrive at the place where we thought we saw it.) Mystical experiences have no object and hence cannot be orderly or disorderly. They cannot, then, be objective. But neither can they be subjective. Second, the mystic is convinced that his or her experience is not 'shut up entirely inside his [or her] own consciousness' for he or she experiences himself or herself as 'becoming one with or becoming dissolved in an infinite and universal self' (ibid.: 145, 147). This conviction can be supported by argument. Stace identifies selves with streams of consciousness and argues that they are distinguished from each other by differences in their empirical content. The pure self which the mystic experiences is devoid of content. Since the One is an undifferentiated unity, it too is devoid of content. So nothing distinguishes (pure) selves from each other or the One. They are therefore identical. In experiencing his or her (pure) self the mystic consequently experiences all other (pure) selves and the One. His or her experience is thus 'transpersonal'. In the third place, weight should also be given to the mystic's sense of objectivity or reality. 'The self-transcendence of the experience is itself experienced, not thought' (ibid.: 153).

Stace's defence of mysticism's epistemic reliability is open to criticism. First, his first two arguments assume that all (pure) mystical experience is monistic and therefore devoid of content. We have seen that this is doubtful. Second, the first argument only shows that mystical experience is not subjective in Stace's sense. It does not show that it is not subjective in other senses. Stace's conclusion is compatible with the possibility that mystical experience is more like pain or depression (which also lack objects) then sense perception, memory, rational intuition, and other paradigmatic cognitive experiences. It is also compatible with the possibility that the experiences are delusive in the sense that they systematically mislead us. Finally, selves and the One are identical if they are not distinguished by differences in their properties. That there are no differences in empirical content does not entail that there are no differences in properties. And, on the face of it, (pure) selves have different attributes. For example, self A has the essential property of being identical with A, self B has the essential property of being identical with B, and so on. Selves (streams of consciousness) are also contingently connected with different bodies, and occupy different segments of the space–time continuum.

Stace's arguments are therefore inconclusive. Furthermore, according to his view, the ontological status of the One is paradoxical. Mystics describe it as full and empty, with and without qualities, active and inactive, existent and non-existent. Stace assumes that the contradictions are genuine. If they are, and logic is applicable, the One is logically impossible and therefore unreal. Stace concludes that logic does not apply. Logic is a tool for handling 'a multiplicity of separate items' and is therefore 'applicable to all those experiences, realms, or worlds where there is a plurality of existences. But [it is] not applicable to the undifferentiated unity of the mystic' (Stace 1960: 270–1).

Yet even if we were to grant that logic only holds in possible worlds with two or more members, it would not follow that it does not apply to the One or to experiences of undifferentiated unity. For the mystic does not inhabit a world with one member; he or she experiences the underlying reality in a possible world (namely our own) which contains a multiplicity of separate items. Stace believes that monism (which holds that nothing is real but the undifferentiated One) is false. Hence logic should apply to the experience and its object.

Stace recognizes that some mystical paradoxes seem to be about a 'plurality of existences'. Examples are 'The world is both identical with God [the One] and distinct from him', and 'The many – "blades of grass, wood, and stone" – are one.' Stace responds to these counterexamples by arguing that the difficulty they create and its solution have meaning only from the standpoint of logic and multiplicity. Fully enlightened mystics see no distinction between the One and the many, the realm of logic and the realm of non-logic. They do not inhabit the realm of everyday experience and so the problem does not arise for them. But this is a non sequitur. The problem may not arise for the mystic but it does arise for us. That the mystic does not see a problem does not imply that there is not one or that it is not serious.

Richard Swinburne argues that the 'principle of credulity' ('if it seems [epistemically] to a subject that X is present, then probably X is present') is a basic principle of rationality (Swinburne 1979: 254). Without it, we would not be able to justify our reliance on memory, sense perception, and rational intuition. If the principle is sound, the presumption is initially in favour of how things seem to us although the presumption can be overridden. If one can show that the subject was not in a position to perceive X if X were present, or that X was not present, or was present but was not a cause of the subject's apparent perception of X, then the claim to have perceived X should be withdrawn.

Since the principle of credulity applies to all experiences, it applies to religious experiences. Hence, if it appears to someone that God is present, probably God is present. Can the presumption created by apparent perceptions of God be overridden? Swinburne thinks not. 'Most religious experiences are had by men who normally make reliable perceptual claims' (Swinburne 1979: 265), and are not had in circumstances which are known to be correlated with unreliable perceptual claims. Again, if God exists, he is present everywhere and is a cause of everything. Hence, barring a disproof of God, there is no reason to think that God is not present and causing the experience. The presumption therefore stands.

Swinburne's position appears to imply that all apparent perceptions of God which normal people have are probably veridical. Thus if Smith is normal and it seems to Smith that God is commanding him to destroy the godless, then probably God is. For God is present everywhere and therefore to Smith, and God is a cause of everything including Smith's apparent perception. Swinburne must therefore show that Smith is deranged or otherwise not in a position veridically to perceive God. It is doubtful whether this can be done in most cases of this kind. What is needed, rather, is a way of showing that God is not causing Smith's experience in the right way. For it is not enough that X causally contributes to the experience of X; it must causally contribute to it in the way objects contribute to veridical experiences of those objects. (The presence of a table might cause a researcher to stimulate the brain of a blindfolded subject so that he has an apparent perception of the table. The apparent perception is not veridical even though the presence of the table causally contributes to it.) How is the distinction between appropriate and inappropriate causal chains to be drawn? Swinburne does not discuss the issue but the problem seems analogous to that of distinguishing between special acts of God and his general providential activity.

Swinburne focuses on perceptual experiences. William Alston focuses on perceptual practices. A doxastic (belief-forming) practice is basic if it provides our primary access to its subject matter. For example, memory is basic because it provides our primary access to the past. Sense perception is basic because it provides our primary access to physical objects. The reliability of basic practices cannot be established without circularity. Sense-perceptual practices, for instance, cannot be justified by appealing to scientific theories since these theories are acceptable only if the observational data on which they are based are correct. Nor can we appeal to the fact that perception enables us successfully to find our way about in our environment because our belief that it does so is based on perception.

But if a basic doxastic practice like sense perception or memory cannot be justified without circularity, why should we trust it? First, the practice is internally consistent. (Its outputs are, on the whole, mutually compatible.)

Second, its outputs are also consistent with the outputs of other well-established doxastic practices. Third, the practice is socially established. Finally, it is self-supporting in the sense that its outputs support its claim to reliability. Sense perceptual practice, for example, displays the features it would have if it were reliable. Our senses seem to put us in contact with a public world of spatio-temporal objects that interact in law-like ways. Suppose that perceptual experience was reliable and therefore was effectively controlled by objects of this sort. We could use these experiences to make accurate predictions about the course of future experience. (The behaviour of the objects is law-like.) Perceptual claims would be intersubjectively testable. (The objects are public and their behaviour is regular.) And people would conceptualize their experience in roughly the same way. (For their experiences are controlled by the same sorts of objects.)

The practice of forming beliefs about God on the basis of a sense of empowerment, guidance, or forgiveness, classical mystical experiences, and other apparent perceptions of God ('Christian mystical practice') displays these features. First, as a basic practice it provides our primary access to its subject matter (God). As such, its reliability cannot be established without circularity. Attempts to do so will appeal to beliefs about God which ultimately rest on the practice itself. Second, Christian mystical practice is internally consistent and, in the third place, consistent with the outputs of other well-established practices. (Philosophical and scientific objections to Christian beliefs can be met.) In the fourth place, the practice is socially established. Finally, it displays the features it would have if it were reliable. If the practice was reliable, it would provide access to a God who is good but 'too "wholly other" for us to be able to grasp any regularities in His behavior', or to be able adequately to grasp what he is like (Alston 1983: 129). We would therefore expect to find that we could not predict God's behaviour with much accuracy. Nor would the practice's outputs be intersubjectively testable in the way that ordinary perceptual claims are. (Intersubjective testability depends on publicity and regularity.) Because our grasp of God is partial and inadequate, people would also conceptualize him differently. Furthermore, if the practice were to promise certain ethical and spiritual fruits to those who engage in it, they would experience them.

Christian mystical practice, therefore, is epistemically on a par with sense-perceptual practice. It is thus arbitrary to countenance one while rejecting the other. If it is reasonable to engage in a socially established doxastic practice in the absence of good reasons for thinking it unreliable, it is also reasonable to engage in Christian mystical practice.

The most serious objections to Swinburne and Alston are that the relevant experiences are produced by causal mechanisms (e.g., psychosis or wish-fulfilment) that are known to be unreliable, and that religious experiences are used to justify inconsistent claims.

For the first line of attack to be effective, the critic must not only show that the unreliable mechanism is capable of producing the experiences and beliefs in question, he must also show that it actually does so. This has not been successfully done.

The second objection is more formidable. Swinburne admits that (e.g.) Buddhists and Christians back apparently inconsistent claims by appealing to religious experience but suggests that Buddhists could describe their experiences in 'less committed ways' (e.g., as an experience of the divine). 'Religious experiences in non-Christian traditions are experiences apparently of beings' similar to God, or of states of affairs which are compatible with his existence (Swinburne 1979: 267). There is therefore no real conflict. Whether this response respects the integrity of (e.g.) Buddhist beliefs and experiences, however, is doubtful. Alston concedes that Christian and (e.g.) Buddhist mystical practices may conflict, and that a genuine inconsistency should diminish the Christian's confidence in his practice's reliability. But he argues that it is nonetheless rational for the Christian to continue to form beliefs about God in the way he does because his practice is socially established, self-supporting, and has not been shown to be unreliable. One may agree that it is pragmatically rational for the Christian to continue to do so. Whether it is *epistemically* rational may depend on the existence of independent (of religious experience) metaphysical and empirical evidence for Christian theism. Swinburne's and Alston's arguments are most persuasive when regarded as part of a cumulative-case argument for the Christian world-view.

MYSTICISM AND LANGUAGE

William James thought that ineffability was a defining characteristic of mysticism; 'the subject of' a mystical state 'immediately says that it defies expression, that no adequate report of its contents can be given in words' (James 1902: 371).

James seems to have believed that the mystic's difficulty is akin to that which we encounter when we try to express other unusual or deeply emotional experiences. Others have thought that it is a consequence of the nature of the experience's object. However it is to be explained, though, mystics do seem to experience 'some [special] difficulty about verbalization' (Stace 1960: 79).

Ineffability can be interpreted in at least four ways:

1 Nothing can be truly said of the experience and/or its object.
2 No true literal assertions can be made about them.
3 All true literal assertions about the experience or its object are negations or descriptions of their extrinsic features. We can say something about the experience's causes and effects, for example, or describe its object as the ground of the world or as the object of universal desire. But we cannot

give a positive, true, and literal description of the experience's and/or object's internal characteristics.

4 The most adequate language is paradoxical in the sense that it violates laws of logic.

The first two claims should not be taken seriously. For one thing, they are self-stultifying. If one says that nothing can be truly (or literally and truly) said of mystical experience or its object, one means to say something literally true about them. If the experience or object are ineffable in the first or second sense, one cannot truly (or literally and truly) say that they are. The claims are also false. Mystics successfully describe their experiences, and some of the things they say about them are literally true. (That they have a positive affective tone, for example, or that they are empty of conceptual content.) Some of their descriptions of their experience's object may also be literally true. (That it is a-spatial, for instance, or a-temporal.)

The fourth claim is also dubious. There are two ways of interpreting it. The first is Stace's. True literal descriptions of the experience or its object violate logic. The second is that our best attempts to express the mystical datum violate rules of logic (and so are not literally true). We saw that Stace's claim is false. The second cannot be summarily dismissed. Paul Henle has demonstrated that some (true) thoughts cannot be expressed in some languages. (He shows, for example, that there are algebraic schemes in which attempts to express $a+b=b+a$ or $b-a \neq a-b$ result in empty tautologies or contradictions.) It is thus possible that some truths (e.g., those the mystic is trying to express) cannot be expressed in any known symbolic language without violating rules of logic. Whether this possibility is realized, however, is doubtful. Peter Moore suggests that we should distinguish between autobiographical accounts of mystical experience (those of Teresa, for example, or Suso), 'impersonal accounts' which describe mystical experience in general and abstract terms (for example, the works of John of the Cross, or the anonymous *Cloud of Unknowing*), and theological and speculative accounts of the experience's apparent object (for example, Plotinus' *Enneads*, Eckhart's speculative theology, or Samkara's reflections on the *Atman–Brahman*). As Moore points out, genuine paradox most often occurs in speculative accounts of the experience's object and only rarely in autobiographical and impersonal accounts of the experience itself.

The third claim should be taken seriously. Stace is correct in thinking that the special difficulty in describing mystical experience lies in its object. It is significant that a long and respectable tradition maintains that the intrinsic features of this object can only be described negatively and symbolically.

For example, the Pseudo-Dionysius claimed that the only 'intelligible [conceptual] names' of God are names of forms such as The Good, or Life, or Wisdom. These names express God's relation to the world. Thus 'The Good' expresses his boundless outflowing. God can also be described symbolically by applying the names of creatures since every created being is a (potential) theophany or manifestation of him. The truth is most closely approximated, however, by negating the content of intelligible names and symbols, 'advancing through the negation and transcendence of all things . . . towards that which is beyond all things' (Rolt 1957: 152). So God can be truly (albeit inadequately) described although we must ultimately cease to 'see or know [that] we may learn to know that which is beyond all perception and understanding' (ibid.: 194).

Rudolf Otto's position is similar. The object of numinous feelings can be characterized in two ways. We can 'schematize' the 'numen' by such rational concepts as unity, necessity, and completeness. But these should be understood negatively. Necessity, for example, negates contingency and dependence. We can also employ 'ideograms'. Ideograms denote properties which elicit feeling responses analogous to those evoked in numinous encounters. The numen, for example, evokes religious dread. Since this is analogous to fear, we can indicate the property of the numen which evokes dread by using a term ('wrath') which refers to a property that typically arouses fear.

Symbol theories are sometimes criticized on the grounds that metaphorical assertions are only intelligible to those already possessing a non-metaphorical understanding of the metaphor's subject. Hence, the mystic's metaphors cannot help the non-mystic. But this objection is not compelling. The theories in question identify the subject of predication by negative and extrinsic predicates. These are understood literally. One can also understand a metaphor if one is directly acquainted with its terms. For example, I understand 'The sound of a trumpet is like scarlet' because I know what scarlet looks like and what trumpets sound like. Mystics believe that they are directly acquainted with the objects they describe. But they also typically assume that there is sufficient continuity between their own experience and that of non-mystics to make their descriptions at least partially intelligible to the latter.

General discussions of ineffability are helpful but inconclusive. A careful examination of individual mystics is needed to determine the senses in which they do and do not claim that their experiences are ineffable. Steven Payne, for example, has examined relevant passages in John of the Cross.

Although John says that 'the delicateness of delight in this contact is inexpressible', and speaks of being reluctant to describe this state because he fears he will not do it justice or will mislead his readers, this is the 'familiar "ineffability" associated with any profound emotion'. The main source of difficulty is the absence of 'sensible and intelligible species' (i.e., sense impressions and the concepts abstracted from them). John accepts the scholastic view that human knowledge proceeds by abstracting from sensible species. He also appears to think that 'an X is strictly and properly described only by . . . a "name" associated with a sensory "form" or intelligible species of X'. Sensory images and concepts are excluded in the mystical state, and God's essence cannot be grasped through sensory forms and concepts abstracted from them. Neither the mystical state nor its object, then, can be 'strictly and properly described'. It does not follow that we can say nothing about them. Although the mystic's knowledge of God is 'obscure' and 'general' (since it is 'unmodified by the boundaries of form, species, and image') John explicitly states that it can be described 'in certain general terms' and expressed in 'figures and similes'. Proper weight must also be given to his success in conveying the nature of his experience (Payne 1990: 29–30, 100–2). An examination of John of the Cross provides little support for the first, second, and fourth ineffability theses.

REFERENCES

Almond, P. (1982) *Mystical Experience and Religious Doctrine*, Berlin: Mouton.

Alston, W. P. (1983) 'Christian Experience and Christian Belief ', in A. Plantinga and N. Wolterstorff (eds) *Faith and Rationality*, Notre Dame: University of Notre Dame Press.

—— (1991) *Perceiving God*, Ithaca and London: Cornell University Press.

Browne, H. (1925) *Darkness or Light: An Essay in the Theory of Divine Contemplation*, St Louis and London: Herder.

Butler, E. C. (1966) *Western Mysticism*, New York: Harper & Row.

Dhavamony, M. (1971) *Love of God According to Saiva Siddhanta*, Oxford: Clarendon Press.

Edwards, J. (1959) *Religious Affections*, New Haven: Yale University Press.

Farges, A. (1925) *Mystical Phenomena*, New York: Benziger Bros.

Forman, R. K. C. (1990) 'Introduction: Mysticism, Contructivism, and Forgetting', in R. K. C. Forman (ed.) *The Problem of Pure Consciousness*, New York and Oxford: Oxford University Press.

Garrigou-Lagrange, R. M. (1944) *Christian Perfection and Contemplation according to St. Thomas Aquinas and St. John of the Cross*, St Louis and London: Herder.

Henle, P. (1949) 'Mysticism and Semantics', *Philosophy and Phenomenological Research* IX: 416–22.

James, W. (1902) *The Varieties of Religious Experience*, New York: Modern Library.

Jantzen, G. M. (1989) 'Mysticism and Experience' *Religious Studies* 25: 295–315.

Katz, S. T. (1978) 'Language, Epistemology, and Mysticism', in S. T. Katz (ed.) *Mysticism and Philosophical Analysis*, London: Sheldon Press.

Leuba, J. H. (1925) *The Psychology of Religious Mysticism*, London: K. Paul, Trench, Trubner.

McCann, H. J. (ed.) (1964) *The Cloud of Unknowing together with The Epistle of Privy Counsel*, London: Burnes & Oates.

Maritain, J. (1959) *Distinguish to Unite, or the Degrees of Knowledge*, New York: Scribners.

Martin, H. (1959) *On Loving God and Selections From Sermons by St. Bernard of Clairvaux*, London: SCM Press.

Moore, P. (1978) 'Mystical Experience, Mystical Doctrine, Mystical Technique', in S. T. Katz (ed.) *Mysticism and Philosophical Analysis*, London: Sheldon Press.

Otto, R. (1931) *The Philosophy of Religion Based on Kant and Fries*, London: Williams and Norgate.

—— (1957) *Mysticism East and West*, New York: Meridian Books.

—— (1958) *The Idea of the Holy*, New York: Oxford University Press.

Payne, S. (1990) *John of the Cross and the Cognitive Value of Mysticism*, Dordrecht: Kluwer Academic Publishers.

Perovich, A. N. Jr. (1990) 'Does the Philosophy of Mysticism Rest on a Mistake?' in R. K. C. Forman (ed.) *The Problem of Pure Consciousness*, New York and Oxford: Oxford University Press.

Pike, N. (1992) *Mystic Union: An Essay in the Phenomenology of Mysticism*, Ithaca and London: Cornell University Press.

Proudfoot, W. (1985) *Religious Experience*, Berkeley and Los Angeles: University of California Press.

Rolt, C. E. (ed. and trans.) (1957) *Dionysius the Areopagite on the Divine Names and the Mystical Theology*, New York: Macmillan; London: SPCK.

Ruysbroeck, J. van (1951) *The Adornment of the Spiritual Marriage, The Sparkling Stone, and The Book of Supreme Truth*, London: John M. Watkins.

Saudreau, A. (1924) *The Mystical State, Its Nature and Phases*, London: Burns, Oates, and Washbourne.

Smart, N. (1960) *A Dialogue of Religions*, London: SCM Press.

—— (1965) 'Interpretation and Mystical Experience', *Religious Studies* 1: 75–87.

Stace, W. T. (1960) *Mysticism and Philosophy*, Philadelphia and New York: J. B. Lippincott.

Swinburne, R. (1979) *The Existence of God*, ch. 13, Oxford: Clarendon Press.

Zaehner, R. C. (1957) *Mysticism: Sacred and Profane*, Oxford: Clarendon Press.

—— (1970) *Concordant Discord*, Oxford: Clarendon Press.

FURTHER READING

Broad, C. D. (1953) 'Arguments For the Existence of God', in C. D. Broad *Religion Philosophy and Psychical Research: Selected Essays*, London: Routledge & Kegan Paul.

Davis, C. F. (1989) *The Evidential Force of Religious Experience*, Oxford: Clarendon Press.

Gale, R. (1991) *On the Nature and Existence of God*, ch. 8, Cambridge: Cambridge University Press.

Gilson, E. (1940) *The Mystical Theology of St. Bernard*, New York: Sheed & Ward.

Gutting, G. (1982) *Religious Belief and Religious Skepticism*, ch. 5, Notre Dame: University of Notre Dame Press.

Martin, C. B. (1959) ' "Seeing" God', in *Religious Belief*, Ithaca: Cornell University Press.

Mavrodes, G. I. (1970) 'The Experience of God', in *Belief in God: A Study in the Epistemology of Religion*, New York: Random House.

Poulain, A. (1950) *The Graces of Interior Prayer*, St Louis: Herder.

Wainwright, W. J. (1981) *Mysticism: A Study of its Nature, Cognitive Value and Moral Implications*, Brighton: Harvester.

Yandell, K. E. (1992) *The Epistemology of Religious Experience*, Cambridge: Cambridge University Press.

See also chapters 17, 20, 25, 29, 30, 42.

31

SPIRITUALITY AND LIBERATION

Kenneth Leech

Christian theology, spirituality and social commitment are rooted in a belief in the importance, significance and sanctifying potential of matter. This belief is expressed formally in the doctrines of creation, incarnation and resurrection, and is manifested visibly in the materiality of the Church's sacramental celebrations, and in Christian action in the world. In contrast to the Platonist tradition, which lacked any real historical concern and saw the world in static terms, Christian theology is rooted in the historical and material realities of the flesh of Christ and of the community which grew out of his life, death and resurrection. Yet, although the opposition of soul and body, which we find in such writers as Plato, is alien to the orthodox Christian incarnational tradition with its emphasis on the central place of the body and of matter in the work of salvation and sanctification, it can hardly be denied that such dualistic ideas have influenced the Christian movement, Eastern and Western, at many levels, not least in its attitudes to sexuality and politics. A fear of flesh and politics has haunted the Christian tradition from its early days.

In the West, from Tertullian and Irenaeus in the early Church to Julian of Norwich in the fourteenth century, the life of the spirit was seen as originating in the material and physical. The flesh, claimed Tertullian, was the pivot of salvation. Irenaeus laid particular emphasis on the reality of Christ's flesh and on the offering of material things in the eucharist, while Julian claimed that both our substance and our 'sensuality' are in God and together constitute 'our soul'. In the East, the mystical theology of Orthodoxy and its iconography have laid great stress on the transfiguring of the material world and of human personality. The Eastern theologian Gregory Palamas (1296–1359) was one among many to stress the importance of the passions in spiritual life, and the need to transfigure the passions, not to transcend them. Other mystics of the Orthodox East, such as John of Damascus in the eighth century, stressed the need to deal with holy things in a bodily manner. As the leading figure in the opposition to the iconoclasts, John insisted that, while he did not worship matter, he did worship the Creator of matter, who, for his sake, 'became material', dwelt in matter, and through matter brought about his salvation. 'I will not cease from reverencing matter', he insisted, 'for it was through matter that my salvation came to pass.'

A Christian spiritual vision as expressed in such statements is thus a materialistic vision. It is a vision which is deeply and unashamedly materialistic, which values the creation, which rejoices in the physical, in the flesh, in human sexuality, and which is rooted in the principle that matter is the vehicle of spirit, not its enemy. When William Temple said that Christianity was the most materialistic of all religions, he stood within a long tradition of incarnational and sacramental materialism. It not only saw bread and wine as symbols of the transformation of all human resources; it saw the material world as the primal sacrament from which all others derived. Orthodox Christian theology refuses to tolerate a division between matter and spirit, or any disparaging of matter or the physical. To despise and undervalue the creation is to despise its Creator. Catholic Christianity stands or falls on this sacramental principle: and this must involve a break with those movements of Christian thought which see the spiritual as the antithesis of the material, and concern for social and economic justice as a hindrance to true spirituality. Such dualism is deeply alien to a sacramental materialism.

In spite of such witnesses, the influence of dualism and even of Gnosticism, with its view that matter and spirit are opposed, has been considerable. For the Gnostic, both sex and the *polis* (i.e. socio-political life) were sources of contamination. True spirituality consisted in an ascent from the realm of the carnal and worldly to that of the supernatural. One consequence of this kind of dualism has been a tendency, evident throughout Christian history, to associate 'spirituality' with passivity, and 'Christian discipleship' with social action and struggle, movements of change and reform, perhaps revolutionary political activity. It is widely assumed that a 'spiritual' emphasis is associated with the realm of the inward, and a lack of concern for the transformation of society; and that 'social concern' goes hand in hand with a lack of interest in the deeper realms of the spirit. So spirituality comes to be associated with dependence, activism with the assertion of autonomy. Some writers have approached the study of Christian spirituality itself by way of the theory of bimodal consciousness in which the features of the receptive mode (such as surrender, intuition, symbol) are contrasted with those of the active (such as logic, control, analysis.)

Yet the polarization of passive prayer and active discipleship in the world represents a fundamental mistake which has damaged the history of spirituality, and from which there has, in the last thirty years or so, been a growing process of recovery. Prayer is not passive, nor is action intrinsically hostile to reflection. Much early Christian writing on prayer stressed its active and dynamic features: Augustine saw prayer as the 'affectionate reaching out of the mind for God' while Gregory of Nyssa characterized the spiritual life as one of *epektasis*, straining forward. Prayer was closely linked with work, particularly with manual work, as in the Rule of St Benedict.

The importance of a balance between action and contemplation was expressed clearly by Augustine whose *City of God* was so important in shaping both the spirituality and the political thought of the early Middle Ages.

> No one ought to be so leisured as to take no thought in that leisure for the interest of his neighbour, nor so active as to feel no need for the contemplation of God . . . It is love of truth that looks for sanctified leisure, while it is the compulsion of love that undertakes righteous engagement in affairs.
>
> (Augustine 1972: 880).

While Augustine certainly encouraged the division between the earthly city (ultimately the city of Cain and of the Devil) and the city of God, his work helped to create a world in which men and women could live together in community. According to Augustine, the city of God was both a pilgrim living by faith amongst the wicked, and a presence within the 'the stability of the eternal resting place for which it now waits in patience' (*City of God* 1). The design of medieval cities, made from stone and glass, in which God's people could live in peace, was the result of the theology of such thinkers as Augustine and Isidore of Seville (Sennett 1991).

From Augustine's time to the present, it has been widely recognized that movements of social transformation, if they are to survive and flourish, need a reflective, critical dimension, and a certain inner spiritual discipline of patience, stability and persistence. On the other hand, one strain in Christian thinking, from an early period, saw activity as particularly associated with the Devil. One amusing example of this approach is the Vulgate translation of the passage about the Devil from Psalm 90(91):6, used in the Office of Compline: *negotium perambulans in tenebris* – literally, the business that prowls around in the shadows!

In spite of such aberrations, the Catholic culture of the Middle Ages was rooted in a sense of the integration of activity and contemplation, and of individuals and community. The emergence of what was to become known as 'Christendom', while it was open to severe criticism, did seek to embody the unity of spirit and matter within a unified social order. The history of the medieval Church was marked by a complex dialectic of social upheaval and intense personal devotion with the eucharistic liturgy at the very heart of the culture (Rubin 1991). The monastic tradition, while at times it encouraged a view of the 'religious' life (i.e. in monastic and other similar communities) as spiritually superior to that of men and women in 'the world', was an attempt to embody Gospel values within a social framework of common life and activity rooted in prayer and worship. As such, it formed a microcosm of medieval culture as a whole. Within this essentially sacral context the idea of a fundamental cleavage between spirit and matter was inconceivable.

It was the awareness of this unity which led the Anglican social theorist Maurice Reckitt to write:

> If you had told any typical Christian thinker in any century from the twelfth to the sixteenth that religion had nothing to do with economics, and that bishops must not intrude in these matters upon the deliberations of laymen – propositions which to many of the correspondents to our newspapers appear to be axiomatic – he would either have trembled for your faith or feared for your reason. He would have regarded you, in short, as either a heretic or a lunatic.
>
> (Reckitt 1935: 12)

It was the disintegration of this culture which reinforced and developed some of the emerging fissures between the dimensions of Christian prayer and Christian life in society. Recent historical work has suggested that the ending of medieval Catholic culture had serious effects on the sense of Christian community, on the understanding of the transcendence of God, and on the experience of the holy (Duffy 1992; Somerville 1992).

SPIRITUAL DECLINE

However, the history of Christian spirituality prior to the collapse of the medieval synthesis was itself marked by a shift towards individualism and pseudo-interiority. In the West, while the fourteenth century saw both a flowering of mysticism and a rebirth of the radical Christian tradition of social protest, there was a marked tendency towards an individualistic and passive approach from the twelfth century onwards. We can already see the beginnings of the split between spirituality and action in the devotional life of the fourteenth and fifteenth centuries. The Flemish mystic Ruysbroeck speaks harshly of what he terms 'false vacancy':

> It is a sitting still, without either outward or inward acts, in vacancy, in order that rest may be found, and may remain untroubled. But a rest which is practised in this way is unlawful: for it brings with it in men a blindness and ignorance and a sinking down into themselves without activity. Such a rest is nought else than an idleness into which the man has fallen and in which he forgets himself and God and all things in all that has to do with activity. The rest is wholly contrary to the supernatural rest which one possesses in God.
>
> (Ruysbroeck 1951: 155)

Rarely has a mystic spoken so strongly against the false subjectivism of interior passivity when cut off from communion with God and humankind.

As a wedge came to be driven between heart and head, affections and intellect, there was a further decline into subjective pietism in the fifteenth century. This was evident in the Free Brethren of the Netherlands, in the Waldensians and Huttites, in some of the German mystics, the *devotio moderna*, and many devotional writers. It reached its peak in the *Imitatio Christi* of Thomas à Kempis (1380–1471), which, while it reflected the deepest experience of the sacramental piety of the later Middle Ages, was 'individualistic through and through' (Ramsey 1956: 168). In à Kempis's thought, concern for the needs of the body constituted a burden on the inner self. The passions, the emotions and desires, even the body itself, were enemy forces, hindrances to the attainment of salvation. His focus is on the wretchedness of life and on the need for withdrawal from the world and from humankind in order to attain union with God. This book has been tremendously influential throughout the Christian West and was more popular than the Bible among Roman Catholics before the Second Vatican Council. Along with individualism there was an increasing stress at this time on passivity and reliance on the action of God in the soul. Thus John Tauler (1300–61) compares such spiritual reliance to the state of sleep: 'Joseph', he reminds his readers, 'was asleep when the angel called him.' The Beghards, condemned by the Pope in 1312, held that meditation on Christ's humanity was a descent from the pure spirituality of contemplation. In addition, in much devotional writing, the activity of God comes to be located in 'the soul' which is seen in ahistorical terms and as somehow separate from the totality of the human person in community. This dualistic and private focus has made its impact on many of the manuals of devotion down to the present day (Miles 1988).

IGNATIUS AND THE CARMELITES

On the surface, it would seem that both the individualism and the passivity are perpetuated in the great Catholic writers of the sixteenth century. Certainly there is little here which directly confronts the social dimensions of grace. However, there has been in recent years a growing recognition of the strength and value of these spiritual guides, and a reappraisal of their work within the contemporary context. There are a number of reasons for this. One is that in these writers there is both an insistence on the integration of prayer and ordinary life, and a stress on the confrontation with illusion. Ignatius Loyola stressed discernment and the need to find and serve God in the midst of the activities of life, while John of the Cross and Teresa of Avila placed the mystical path firmly within the context of ordinary life. Teresa insisted that the foundation of Christian discipleship could not consist only of contemplation, but must also include the practice of the virtues. Without such practice, she says, we will remain dwarfs.

Another factor in the renewed attention on these writers is the realization that the teaching of John of the Cross, focused on the symbol of the dark night of the soul, has much to teach modern men and women who are struggling with newer forms of darkness and alienation. John sees this central experience of darkness as a necessary part of the way of illumination. For illumination means the running out of language and the need to move beyond the limits of one's ordinary conceptual apparatus. There is a need to look into the darkness of God, and to enter into both that mystery and the recognition of our own vulnerability, failure, and contradiction. Far from being a passive and purely 'spiritual' experience, this encounter with darkness is one of extreme turbulence and passionate intensity. One contemporary Carmelite has emphasized the dynamic and active dimensions of the dark night:

> In the Dark Night the passion flames forth unchecked by any barrier because it is perfectly pure – and purity is essentially freedom from limits. That is why mystics, men and women who plow through the tremendous upheavals and torrential storms of the Dark Nights, are the most passionate of all people, exploring as they do the terrible uncharted regions of human evolution.
>
> (McNamara 1977: 11)

Recent thinkers have emphasized both the need to reinterpret Ignatian spirituality in the light of social and political factors, and the need to read the dark night in terms of corporate and intellectual experience. So we find such language as 'corporate dark night', 'the dark night of our institutions', and so on.

It was in the seventeenth century that the problem of 'quietism' became a matter of discipline in the Roman communion, and there were condemnations of Miguel de Molinos (1687), Madame Guyon (1695), and some of the claims of Fénelon (1699). The issue was about exaggerated forms of supernaturalism. Yet, as the authentic tradition went into decay, many of these forms were to become accepted and promoted at the level of personal devotion.

BEYOND THE REFORMATION

In spite of the Reformers' concern to recover something of the purity of the apostolic Church, their spirituality failed to restore the catholicity and solidarity which was so central to its life and practice. The tendency towards a spirituality which was not wholly Christian and which neglected the material base of spiritual life, as expressed in the doctrines of creation and incarnation and in the sacraments, was continued and strengthened within many parts of Protestantism. Some followers of Calvin laid so much stress on sin and fallenness that any concern with human society was lost (though Calvin himself emphasized the need to contemplate the divine image within the human person). The early Calvinist concern for political reconstruction decayed as many of those within the Reformed Churches came to abandon any hope for this world and its institutions. Lutheranism moved steadily towards an individualism in which *sola fide* came to mean that the concern for justice in the world was of no importance. The role of 'two kingdoms' theology in preparing the way for Nazism remains a matter of controversy, but it is beyond dispute that Lutheranism was seriously deficient in its social theology. It was the Anabaptists who stressed the social demands of the Gospel, with their insistence on discipleship, community and sharing of goods, their view of the Church as a counter-sign to the world, and their Johannine understanding of salvation as a communion in the divine life. In line with the theology of the Orthodox, the Anabaptists believed in the divinization of humanity through Christ (Beachy 1963: 17). Their spirituality was social, hopeful and focused on the power of grace.

It is often assumed that in later Protestant spirituality there has been a polarization between the personal piety of the evangelicals with their stress on the 'quiet time' and on the relationship of the soul with the Saviour, and that of the liberals and followers of the 'social gospel' with their emphasis on commitment and action in the world. Like other polarizations, this is also misleading. There were links between spirituality and social action in Jonathan Edwards (1705–58) and the Quaker John Woolman (1720–72), as well as in some aspects of the Wesleyan revival. There was a strong concern for social justice among many of the revivalists, such as Finney, while many proponents of the 'social gospel', both in liberal Protestantism and, particularly, in Anglicanism, laid great emphasis on prayer and worship. There has in recent years been a recovery of many of the neglected elements of the theology of the Reformation. Nevertheless, it is true that from the nineteenth century until recently, the history of most forms of Protestantism has been marked by a retreat into interior pietism.

So in recent years many Christians have come to believe that the only way out of the present crisis of the Church in the West is by the transcendence of the conceptual limitations of Reformation theology, especially of its individualism. But they see that this cannot be accomplished by a return to medievalism or to the Catholicism of the European Counter-Reformation. The only hope for a Christian response to the contradictions and dilemmas of the contemporary world lies in a renewed spirituality which can respond to the spiritual hunger, the nihilism and despair, the need for community, and the quest for transcendence of modern men and women. Many people today speak of the need for a 'new reformation'.

In repudiating the corruption of the medieval Church, the reformers and radical innovators of the sixteenth and seventeenth centuries abandoned much of the earlier corporate understanding. It has been a task of twentieth-century Christians, influenced by biblical, liturgical and ecumenical movements of renewal, to recover something of this corporate sense. The rediscovery of the Bible has led to a richer understanding of the social character of the work of God in redemption, and of our need to respond to this activity as a liberated people.

THE LIBERATING WORD: THE REDISCOVERY OF THE BIBLE

The 1960s initiated a period of self-criticism and renewal in many areas of Christian life and thought, leading to shifts in Christian consciousness of a very profound kind. One key area was the recovery of biblical wholeness. In these years new translations of the Bible became popular, and, for the first time for centuries, readings from the Old Testament became an established feature of the eucharistic liturgy. These, and other factors, were important in bringing about a renewal of biblical study, not least among oppressed and marginalized communities in the Third World. The birth of liberation theology at the end of the 1960s was closely connected with the reading of the Bible as a collective enterprise within a context of worship and reflection on concrete experience. This rediscovery of the Bible as a resource for people in struggle has been a major element in nourishing a spirituality of resistance and liberation in many parts of the world. While the rhetoric of liberation has been associated particularly with Latin America, the movement which has developed there since about 1968 has many parallels, some of them going back to an earlier age.

The biblical revival has undermined many established positions and raised the level of awareness of Christians in relation to the world. We can speak of a new biblical consciousness during these years. Attention to the biblical narrative led to a realization of the unity of worship, common life and struggle for justice which was bound to call into question the simplistic individualism of earlier approaches both to biblical study and to spirituality. William String-fellow, a powerful influence on the growing Christian radicalism in the United States in these years, expressed it in this way:

> The biblical topic is politics. The Bible is about the politics of fallen creation and the politics of redemption; the politics of the nations, institutions, ideologies and causes of this world and the politics of the Kingdom of God; the politics of Babylon and the politics of Jerusalem; the politics of the Antichrist and the politics of Jesus Christ; the politics of the demonic powers and principalities and the politics of the timely judgment of God as sovereign; the politics of death and the politics of life; apocalyptic politics and eschatological politics.
>
> (Stringfellow 1973: 14–15)

In another study, Stringfellow turned his attention to biblical spirituality:

> There is no biblical spirituality to be found in a vacuum cut off from the remainder of humanity within the totality of creation. Indeed biblical spirituality is significantly about the restoration or renewal of these relationships throughout the realm of created life ... From a biblical perspective ... the assertion of some species of so-called spirituality which is privatised and nonpolitical or antipolitical is simply nonsense.
>
> (Stringfellow 1984: 20, 21)

The new attention to the Bible has led to a recovery of the central biblical concern with holiness and justice. The holy God has been rediscovered as the God of justice. Justice and salvation are interlocked (Isa. 45:21–4; 46: 12–13, etc.) To do justice is to know the Lord (Jer. 22:15–16). Communion with God, according to the prophets, is incompatible with injustice and oppression. Those who sell the righteous for silver and the poor for a pair of sandals, and who trample the poor into the dust, are the objects of prophetic condemnation (Amos 2:6ff.), as are those who decree unjust laws and embody oppression in legislation (Isa. 10:1). Many Christians have read these words with a new urgency and have tried to relate them to their contemporary context. They have sought to live within a biblical world-view.

Again, the realization that it is impossible to sever Jesus from his Jewish roots has led to a new emphasis on the centrality of the Kingdom of God and of the proclamation of Jubilee (in Judaism, a time of periodic social renewal) in Jesus' teaching, and therefore to a move away from the personal and inward interpretations which had affected much earlier biblical study (see Luke 4:18f.). Books such as John Howard Yoder's *The Politics of Jesus* (1972) have had a profound effect, particularly among the newer breed of evangelicals, while Norman Perrin's work on the Kingdom of God (Perrin 1963) affected other sections of the Church. So the nature of the Gospel itself has come under scrutiny, for much conventional preaching, including evangelical preaching, has not been a proclamation of the Kingdom of God with any kind of social dimension.

Closer attention to the biblical record has also led to a stronger sense of the *koinōnia hagiōn*, the common life of the holy, and indeed of the holiness of the common. In early Christian thought, nothing was common or unclean (Acts 10:14–15). Here the revival of interest in the *koinōnia* of the apostolic Church ran in parallel with the liturgical movement and the renewal of eucharistic sensibility which was also occurring during the 1960s. After centuries of decay and distortion, Christians of many traditions came to discover their character as a community bound together by the apostolic doctrine, common life, the breaking of the bread, and prayer (Acts 2:42). Twentieth-century Christians, after centuries of Constantinian ideology, came to see themselves as being very close to the life of the early Christian community.

One of the most striking features of early Christian spirituality is its social and corporate perspective. Rarely if ever do the New Testament writers concern themselves with personal spirituality or with the fate of the soul in isolation from that of the community, the *sōma Christou* (body of Christ), which is so central to the theology of Paul (1 Cor. 12; Rom. 12). Here it is difficult to over-emphasize the influence of John Robinson's small work *The Body* (1961) in which he showed the centrality of this idea to Paul's theological outlook. The entire concentration of Paul's writing is on the body, the community, the social movement towards fullness of life in Christ within a new creation. The phrase *en Christō*, in Christ, is used 164 times in Paul's writings. To be *en Christō* is to be part of a redeemed community, a new order of being. Christians are one body in Christ (Rom. 12:5; 1 Cor. 10:17; 12:12). This Christian community is constituted and manifested in the life of the eucharistic assembly, the gathering of disciples who meet to break bread and drink wine together, but, more importantly, to share life in its fullness beyond the assembly.

So a reading of the New Testament has led to a reorientation of the very foundations of spirituality. Spirituality is not a private relationship with God in isolation: it is to know Christ and the power of his resurrection (Phil. 3:

10) within a community which shares his life. Holiness is social. We die together and we live together (Rom. 14:8). We are to be transfigured (2 Cor. 3:17; Rom. 12:2) by our incorporation into a new creation. Later work by such writers as Gottwald, Brueggemann, and Wink (Gottwald 1979, 1983; Brueggemann 1978, 1985, 1991; Wink 1984, 1986, 1992) has led to a deeper engagement with such areas as the theme of liberation in the history of Israel, the prophetic imagination and prophetic witness, and the place of the contemporary struggle with principalities and powers.

It is clear that, while it is not the only influence, the rediscovery of the Bible has been an important factor in the renewal of spirituality in its social and political aspects. Many people have come to realize that 'when the Bible speaks of God, it is almost always in political language' (Cox 1969: 21).

OUT OF PESSIMISM AND APATHY

The 1950s in Britain had been a period of pessimism and retreat in much Christian thinking. The older 'social gospel' had given way, with the advent of the welfare state, to an inward-looking Church, concerned with reunion schemes and other ecclesiastical issues, and to a more individualized approach to the Gospel. The preaching of the Gospel itself had gone awry, commented Michael Ramsey in 1955 (Ramsey 1955), while a writer in the previous year referred to 'a crisis of Christian thought' marked by a flight from the idea of the Kingdom of God as an earthly reality, the denial that human society can be redeemed, and the acknowledgement only of an interior kingdom within the individual consciousness (Evans 1954: 25–9). Among evangelicals, the older social consciousness associated with such figures as C. G. Finney (1792–1875) and the movement of Christian perfection which grew up around Oberlin College, for many years 'a laboratory of both spirituality and radical social action' (Smith 1981: 125), had deteriorated into the more individualized pietism of Billy Graham who led his first British crusade in 1954.

The return of Trevor Huddleston from South Africa in 1956 alerted British Anglicans to the existence of a tradition within their own Church which combined orthodoxy of faith with passionate resistance to injustice. The South African Church struggle was marked by a combination of traditional faith and radical commitment. John Davies, writing many years later, was even reluctant to use the word 'radical', insisting on the traditional character of the resistance movement.

> There has been nothing radical or intellectually daring about this. The South African situation has required Catholicism to be thoroughly conservative and oppose the novel nonsense of upstart racism with a traditional orthodoxy which insists that there must be a visible fellowship of believers and that Christian love must be acted out in visible terms.
>
> (Davies 1983: 188)

The return of Huddleston marked a turning point in the history of radical

Christianity in Britain. Significantly it had been Huddleston's order, the Community of the Resurrection, which had done much to prepare the ground for the renewal of liturgy which was to transform the consciousness of the Church in the 1960s.

THE LITURGY AND THE RENEWAL OF CHRISTIAN COMMUNITY

The liturgical movement, which has restored the centrality of corporate worship, especially eucharistic worship, to the life of the Church, has also given to Christian spirituality and life a more earthy and material focus. At the heart of the renewal of the liturgy was an emphasis on the Church as the body of Christ and as an integral element in the proclamation of the Gospel. The origins of liturgical renewal go back to the nineteenth century, to such figures as Dom Prosper Guéranger, the Abbot of Solesmes, though the work of the Anglican socialists of the Percy Dearmer school in building up an early 'Parish Communion' movement in the first half of the twentieth century has recently been stressed (Gray 1986). But it was the 1930s and 1940s which saw a more widespread development of the concern to restore the liturgy to the people, and to create a more dynamic and active framework for the celebration of Christian worship. Pioneers included Odo Casel in Maria Laach, Pius Parsch in Vienna, and Virgil Michel in the United States, while Pope Pius XII's encyclical *Mediator Dei* (1947) placed the seal of official endorsement on the movement.

Within Anglicanism, Michael Ramsey's study *The Gospel and the Catholic Church*, published in 1936 (Ramsey 1956), was of fundamental importance in shaping a theological tradition which took seriously both the Bible and the liturgical renewal, and it did so in an ecumenical way. It undermined the theological liberalism of the time, with its impatience with doctrine and its division between Gospel and Church, and it prepared the theological path for later developments in the world Church. But its major significance was as a statement of the roots of spirituality in the very nature of the eucharistic and Gospel-living community.

It was many years after Ramsey's formative work that the movement made significant headway in both the Anglican and Roman Churches. Again the 1960s was a crucial decade, although there had been pioneering work by the movement 'Parish and People' prior to this. John Robinson's book *On Being the Church in the World* (1964) was significant in that it sought to relate liturgy to the concern for justice in the world. Robinson restated the belief that 'Christianity stands or falls by the sacramental principle that matter and spirit are not separate or antithetical' (Robinson 1964: 34). In its work of celebrating the liturgical action, the Christian community manifested its character as the body of Christ in the world, and this doctrine of the body of Christ was 'the specifically Christian clue to the renewal of society'. The eucharist was the pattern of all Christian action, the germ of all society redeemed in Christ (ibid.: 70–1).

The recovery of the centrality of the eucharist has brought about a profound revolution in most Christian traditions as the Church has come to see itself as a liturgical community. It has been argued that this growing 'eucharistic sensibility' has been the most important event in the recent renewal of spirituality (Pannenberg 1986: 31, 43), and has led to a spirituality which is more materialistic and more socially aware. The image of the officiant or preacher addressing a passive congregation has given way to the sense of 'being the Church', and of a dynamic and shared liturgical action in which there is movement and increased participation.

Robinson's other writing during the 1960s was important in helping many people to see the connections between prayer and engagement with human realities. It was Robinson (in *Honest to God*, 1963) who introduced the prison reflections of Dietrich Bonhoeffer to a wider public. Bonhoeffer stressed that whoever evades the world does not find God, and that any attempt to escape the world leads in the end to sinful surrender to the world. Yet, although Bonhoeffer's name was to become linked with the phrase 'religionless Christianity', he was a man of deep prayerfulness and ascetic discipline, strongly committed to liturgical prayer and the use of the Psalms. He wrote of the importance of the *disciplina arcani* (in effect, a reticence and shunning of worldly prominence) of the Christian community, and suggested that for the foreseeable future all Christian practice would be restricted to the two activities of prayer and righteous action. It was out of these two activities that all Christian thought, speech and organizing would be born (Bonhoeffer 1972: 300).

Although the early work of Robinson and others tended to stress prayer as occurring in the midst of relationships, there was a growing need for deeper interiority and for spiritual resources which this emphasis could not satisfy. So as the 1960s moved on, there was a revival of interest in contemplative prayer and mysticism.

CONTEMPLATION AND RESISTANCE

A key figure in the spiritual renewal of these years was the Trappist monk, Thomas Merton, who died in 1968. Merton was a transitional figure, bridging various worlds: the world of the nuclear arsenals and that of the counter-culture, the world of Tridentine Catholicism and that of the new liberating vision of Vatican 2, the world of Western Christianity and that of the Asian mystical traditions, the world of middle America and that of the emerging Christian radicalism. Merton died as that explosive and seminal year, 1968, drew to its close. His death occurred as liberation theology, the mystical wing of the counter-culture, the charismatic renewal, and the beginnings of modern feminism were emerging. His own journey was a microcosm of the spiritual currents of the age, reflecting the strivings and struggles, the dilemmas and upheavals of an entire generation.

During the 1960s Merton wrote over twenty books, over half of them on social and political issues. The years from 1963 to 1968, when he was most prolific, were the years of his matured political consciousness. Behind the nuclear build-up, the war in Vietnam, and the racial rebellions in Detroit, Los Angeles and other cities, he saw a threat to the very nature of humanity. He believed that the integrity and freedom of the human person were under attack, and the defence of human integrity was central to his spirituality. In articulating his thoughts, he found that he was engaging with the minds of people far removed from him, and he became a prophetic guide and interpreter to many of those involved in the social and political struggles of the period. In the reflections of this solitary monk, many of those who were searching for a more human and more engaged spirituality found a solidarity in struggle, a sensitivity to the alienation and confusion of men and women in the modern world, and a clear analysis of, and commentary on, the violence and racism in Western culture.

Merton's message for activists was simple and direct. He believed that solitude was essential to any true experience of communion, and that activists needed the discipline of silence and contemplative prayer. He saw that they could easily succumb to a form of violence, expressed in hyper-activism and overwork, as they became carried away by too many demands and projects. Their frenzy neutralized their work for peace, for it destroyed its fruitfulness and killed the root of inner wisdom within them. For many Christian activists of these years, Merton was a source of inspiration and spiritual strength. He played a crucial role in the integration of contemplation and resistance.

Merton's vision was pluralist, ever open to new insights, open to the wisdom of the East, particularly of the Zen tradition, and of the insights of other faith traditions. He saw the main role of the monk in the modern world to be that of listening profoundly to the neglected voices of the world (Merton 1973a: 35). The monk, in his view, was a marginal figure, a person outside all establishments, one who withdrew to the margins in order to deepen fundamental human experience (Merton 1973b: 305). The monk's central task was one of continual scrutiny, watchfulness and interrogation. But, most of all, he was concerned to confront and unmask illusion and falsehood within religious and irreligious life, and it is here that Merton was a source of illumination, critical support and inspiration for so many.

For some years there had been a growing movement of Christian resistance to the evils of modern war, racism and injustice. It was inevitable that this movement would seek to discover spiritual roots and a theological basis for its activity. The year 1973 seems to have been a turning point. In January of that year a conference took place in Huddersfield on the theme 'Seeds of Liberation'. It was concerned with the spiritual roots of political struggle, and it brought together some of the key figures in the new radical spiritual quest – Daniel Berrigan, Colin Winter, and Jim Forest, among others. One commentator wrote: 'A new term has entered the vocabulary of politically radical Christians in Britain – spirituality' (Kee 1973: 3). The task which these young Christians saw was not a cerebral critique of theology and politics so much as a flesh and blood discovery of spiritual roots.

It was the coming together in these years of Christian faith and the experience of structural injustice, particularly of modern war and racism, which led many Christians to see the need to work out their quest for holiness within the arena of political struggle. But at the practical and experiential level, many of the activists of the 1960s were moving to a deeper appreciation of the place of contemplative spirituality within the active life of discipleship, a development which was seen clearly in the career of the American theologian Harvey Cox. Many were realizing that terms such as 'activist' and 'spiritual', which in the 1960s were rarely found together in the same sentence, in fact belonged together. If people were to avoid exhaustion and 'burnout', a concern for one's inner resources was essential (Woodard 1983). Some drew on older traditions, such as that associated with the Catholic anarchist, Dorothy Day, whose Catholic Worker movement had set up houses of hospitality in the run-down urban areas of America since the 1930s. The Catholic Worker was a pioneering movement both in the creation of a Catholic radicalism and in the integration of liturgy and justice (Piehl 1982). By the 1970s its witness was having a powerful effect among young evangelicals.

As awareness of the nuclear, racial and ecological crises deepened, many Christians came to value the material world and human dignity with a renewed seriousness, and sought to nurture a spirituality which would support such concern. Out of these turbulent years came black theology, feminist theology, a new evangelical radicalism, and liberation theology, each of them movements which sought to grapple with concrete forms of oppression in the light of the Christian tradition.

BLACK THEOLOGY AND THE STRUGGLE AGAINST RACISM

The black theology movement grew from a sense of solidarity in oppression, rooted in skin colour and aligned with slavery, poverty and inequality. Black people were the first community to create a vocabulary to counter the oppression of those defined by something other than class. Later concepts such as 'sisterhood' and 'gay power' helped to define movements of those whose experience of oppression was rooted in gender and sexual orientation. But it was the black struggle which provided the impetus for the later movements.

In the movement for civil rights in the USA, the black Church became the main sphere for the creation of survival strategies, and the context within which visions of liberation were nourished and expressed. More widely, the Church became a bulwark against the meaninglessness and desolation of the ghetto, and black Christian discourse became the principal language of subversive dissent and visionary energy. The black Church was, and in many places remains, a source of corporate and personal identity, a source for the definition of meaning and of humanity, while to this day, all over the United States, the prophetic black Church is a major source of social and political leadership.

In recent years the experience of black Christians, particularly in the United States, has found expression in the black theology of writers such as James Cone, Gayraud Wilmore, Cornel West and Katie Cannon (Cone 1970, 1972, 1975; Wilmore 1972; West 1982, 1988, 1993a, 1993b; Cannon 1988). Black theology is an effort to relate the experience of blackness to the tradition of Christian theology. From its beginnings it has been seen as a black theology of liberation. According to Cone and all writers in the tradition of black theology, if a theology is indifferent to liberation it is not Christian theology. There can be no theology without the experience of an oppressed community. Along with theological reflection has come a dynamic black spirituality, strongly biblical and prophetic, and rooted in the life of local communities. Black theologians are highly critical of those black churches which have moved towards conformity and away from a critical prophetic stance.

In Britain, the struggle against racism has brought together black and white Christians from a range of traditions. At the same time, as most white Christians have avoided committed social involvement, so there has been a resurgence of black pietism, and some have withdrawn into an otherworldly stance. The black-led churches have developed a spirituality which draws on classical Pentecostal sources (with their origins in the southern plantocracy and white revivalist missions) as well as on the prophetic tradition of the American black Church and on the experience of racism within the British urban context. Often these tendencies coexist in an uneasy tension, and what the future will bring is unclear. It may be that more radical groups within the black churches will form alliances across denominational divides, and that the conservatives will withdraw into the growing fundamentalist scene. It is likely too that alliances will be built between radical black groups, Christian and non-Christian. For many black and white Christians, the experience of racism has been a source of spiritual renewal and spiritual empowerment, a crucial point in the present-day conflict with the principalities and powers.

FEMINIST THEOLOGY AND SPIRITUALITY

Feminist theology is not a homogeneous entity: like theology as a whole, it comes in a variety of forms, some of them extremely conservative and conformist. I exclude from this account those forms of theology which call themselves feminist but which in fact merely offer a 'feminine dimension' to dominant theological assumptions, or which seek to modify language without questioning relations of power and domination. Modern feminism began as a critique of patriarchy and male domination within Western capitalism, and its theological forms have developed important critiques of Christian spirituality at a number of levels.

First, feminists have attacked the separation of two hemispheres of the brain – rationality (seen as male) and intuition (seen as female), with all the ideological baggage which goes with this separation. While some feminist theorists have tended towards a form of female essentialism, offering female ways of knowing and acting as being essentially different from, and perhaps superior to, male ways, the general thrust of feminist theory has been against this approach. Writers such as Lynne Segal have been critical of the apocalyptic feminism in which a 'Manichean struggle' occurs and where the female is represented exclusively in such symbols as motherhood, nurturing, and 'nature' (Segal 1987: ix). Feminism is to be sharply distinguished from the 'cult of the feminine' which exalts 'femininity' in a 'pedestalist' way.

Again, while some types of feminist spirituality have led to an increased privatization and have moved towards a sentimental nature mysticism of 'womanspirit', there has also been a great deal of emphasis on the need to combat sexism at the heart of Christian culture. This kind of feminist theology is thus a form of liberation theology which seeks to unmask illusion and ideology. In its liturgical expression, such feminism shows a strong emphasis on the demands of justice and the need for liberation (Morley 1988, 1992).

A third feature of feminist spirituality is its insistence on the concrete origins of reflection and of prayer. It begins with experience within history, often with such specific and painful experiences as rape, violence and abortion. There is a stress on the body in relationship. The critique of atomized individualism is central to feminist spirituality and ethics (Fox-Genovese 1991) and this emphasis is clear in the cooperative style of feminist scholarship itself.

Fourth, feminism is critical of male understandings of sin as self-assertion which tend to lead women to positions of dependence and self-negation. It seeks to reclaim neglected emotions such as anger and pride within a framework of love. Fifth, feminist theology rejects the mistrust of sexuality and the view of women as the source of sexual temptation, which have often been the main representations of sex in Christian tradition. Devotional manuals only seem to notice sex as a distraction. Recognizing the 'threadbare inadequacy of the Christian tradition on these issues' (Miles 1988: 159–60), feminist writers see sexuality as that which deepens and shapes personal beings in their most intense interaction with the world. So they reject the tradition deriving from Augustine for whom sex was 'an abiding unhealed fissure in the soul' (Brown 1989: 418). In Augustine's work there is no integration: sex is a punishment, not a foretaste. Feminist theology thus challenges Christians on their attitude to sex and the body. Sexual justice is recognized as 'the most trivialised, feared and postponed dimension of social justice in western society and possibly in the world' (Heyward 1989: 4).

657

Finally, in its approach to political struggle, feminism demands 'much more exacting inner standards' (Rowbotham *et al.* 1979: 42) than is common in most political movements. The personal becomes political, and friendship is seen as a major element in both spirituality and political struggle (Raymond 1986). It is not surprising that much of the recent writing on spiritual direction has come from a feminist perspective (Fischer 1989).

THE NEW EVANGELICAL RADICALISM

One of the most striking features of the early 1970s was the emergence of a new evangelical radicalism in both the United States and Britain, as well as in many Third World countries. The beginnings of a more socially aware current within the evangelical world can be seen in the founding of the American journal *The Other Side* in 1965, and in the Wheaton Declaration of 1966 which criticized 'unscriptural isolation from the world'. Similar assertions of the need to hold together the *kērygma* (the message) and the *diakonia* (service), evangelism and social action, were made at gatherings at Lausanne (1966) and at Keele (1967), while the Chicago Declaration of 1973 prepared the way for more militant 'radical discipleship' groups to appear (Sider 1974). These groups were rediscovering a lost evangelical heritage, the heritage of Finney and the Oberlin College movement and other early radicals of the Holiness movement (Dayton 1976: 15–25). David Moberg's 'great reversal', by which the earlier radical social tradition among evangelicals gave way to individualism and otherworldliness, was itself reversed, and a new phase began (Moberg 1972).

One of the most articulate exponents of the new type of evangelical radical spirituality is Jim Wallis, leader of the Sojourners Community in Washington DC. Wallis has argued, in numerous books and articles, that the Church needs once again to become alien, pilgrim, and prophet, a counter-cultural community of outsiders, living out its discipleship in a deepening disentanglement from the values of the dominant order. In his view, modern Christians must choose between established religion and biblical faith. Establishment Christianity has lost its adversary relationship with the world. As both the 'new left' and religious liberalism declined, he predicted in 1976, the strongest and most sustained thrust towards social justice was likely to come from people of Christ-centred, biblical faith. So he called for a 'new biblical radicalism' (Wallis 1976: 11). Wallis and his followers deplore the division into those who see the Gospel as primarily spiritual and those who see it as primarily political. His study *The Call to Conversion* (1982) is an attack on such divisions and on the individualism of evangelical preaching. He argues that the Gospel has been moulded to suit a narcissistic culture. Conversion has come to mean self-realization, the uncovering of human potential. Christ comes into our hearts to help us do better, to improve our lives rather than to transform them. Such narcissistic conversion is far removed from the biblical message of the Kingdom of God. Thus, he argues, the integrity and central core of the Gospel have been lost. 'The disastrous result is "saved" individuals who comfortably fit into the old order while the new order goes unannounced' (ibid.: 34).

Since 1973 the *Sojourners* magazine (originally called *The Post-American*) has been a unique forum where those who have been influenced by the charismatic renewal have come together with those affected by the new social consciousness. In addition, what began as a rigidly evangelical journal has, over the years, come to incorporate insights from the Catholic contemplative tradition of Merton and Henri Nouwen, and the Catholic radical tradition of Dorothy Day and the Berrigans. Contributors to its pages reflect the presence throughout the USA of churches and communities which seek to hold together the contemplative and active dimensions of ministry such as the Church of the Saviour in Washington DC and the Church of the Messiah in Detroit. The movement is ecumenical, liturgical, and biblical, defying earlier categories of definition.

Two thinkers who have influenced Wallis and Sojourners are Stanley Hauerwas and John Howard Yoder. Yoder is a Mennonite while Hauerwas is deeply affected by Mennonite theology. Both argue that Christian spirituality is about the formation of a new community, characterized by non-violence and by a distinctive life-style. According to Hauerwas, the task of Christians is not to transform the world but to be the Church (Hauerwas and Willimon 1989: 38). The Church is to be a community of contrast, offering a political alternative to the politics of the secular order (Hauerwas 1981). Like Wallis, these writers emphasize the character of the Christian community as a confessing Church, marked by worship of God and faithful discipleship.

A SPIRITUALITY OF LIBERATION

For much of its history the Church has seen liberation in entirely inward, personal or futuristic terms, and has denied, or devoted little attention to, its relevance to social, economic and political structures, to the freedom of minorities, to the attack on racial oppression, or to the future of the planet itself. There has been particular resistance to the idea that liberation involves dealing with the specific and concrete demands of groups of oppressed people. However, in recent years, a spirituality of liberation has arisen out of a concrete identification with oppressed people and a commitment to end oppression. It is a practical, corporate and revolutionary kind of spirituality, rooted in the experience of oppressed communities and groups. Though associated particularly with Latin America, it exists wherever there is oppression and a spiritually conscious opposition to it.

The spirituality of liberation arose from the liberation theology of Latin America (although one of the first books on liberation theology was by the North American theologian Rosemary Ruether (Ruether 1972)). This is a theology which starts from the experience of oppression, a theology which shares the life of very poor people, and exists in an atmosphere of great physical danger. It seeks to unite contemplation and political struggle and has been marked since its early years by its concern for the deepening of spiritual life. Indeed rarely can there have been a theological movement which is so clearly and so deeply rooted in spiritual experience.

In his first book Gustavo Gutiérrez, the father of the movement, referred to a 'serious crisis' about prayer, and he suggested that this crisis could lead to a purification of the life of the spirit. The recovery of the contemplative life was central. He claimed that there was a 'a great need for a spirituality of liberation' (Gutiérrez 1972: 208). Such a spirituality would be concerned with following Jesus. Later Gutiérrez spoke of 'the spiritual journey of a people' (Gutiérrez 1984) and the stress on the spiritual journey as a collective enter-prise has been continued in his subsequent writing (Gutiérrez 1990). He insists that any authentic theology must be a spiritual theology, and his works are steeped in a mystical theology which unites prayer and action in a way which few contemporary Christian writers can match. In a study in 1984 he pointed out that there had been a marked growth in spirituality over the years among Christians within the liberation tradition: 'a growing maturity in their solidarity with the commitment to liberation has . . . brought with it a new emphasis on prayer as a fundamental dimension of Christian life' (Gutiérrez 1984: 22).

Since Gutiérrez's call, many writers have devoted attention to this theme. The Chilean pastor Segundo Galilea has been one who has constantly focused on the need for a rich devotional life. Galilea is steeped in the Spanish mystics, and his work consists of small but profound devotional studies on the nature of contemporary discipleship and prayerfulness. Galilea in 1973 wrote of a 'crisis of spirituality' associated with the split between contem-plation and politics. He believed that liberation was fundamentally a problem of spirituality, and that there was a need for a meeting of mystics and militants (Galilea 1973). Christian mysticism is a mysticism of commitment, and it is in commitment that contemplation and action come together.

In Britain, a more secularized society than Latin America, the articulation of oppression has taken less typically Christian forms. Yet the question of what a spirituality of liberation means for Britain remains vital. To answer it we need to look at the experience of oppressed groups here. Two communities which have experienced both oppression (a widespread culture of bias resulting in structural contempt) and discrimination (a specific series of acts having adverse social results) are those people suffering from HIV and AIDS, and those who are the victims of racism. There can be no spirituality of liberation unless these people's voices are heard. So the process of listening to neglected voices is central. At the time of writing, single mothers are the target of considerable hostility. Their voices must be heard also. Only from such careful listening can a genuine spirituality emerge.

The experience of HIV and AIDS is worthy of study for it has brought out the best and the worst in Christian people. At its worst, it has brought to the surface an appalling mass of hatred, prejudice, bigotry and loathing. Positively, the Christian community has found itself both wounded and healed by the AIDS crisis. AIDS has been a painful and healing process for Christians as they have been forced to face unresolved issues in sexuality as well as the terrible reality of disintegration and death. It has also brought tremendous renewal and liberation as Christians have found resources of life and love in the depths of this terrible scourge. These movements and upheavals have brought Christian spirituality into a place of turbulence and upheaval, a new kind of dark night of faith, in which much has been weighed in the balances, much as been tested and purified.

THE PROSPECTS FOR A RADICAL SPIRITUALITY

For many people today the quest for spirituality must take place outside the framework of institutional Christianity. Since the counter-culture of the late 1960s, there has been a marked shift away from the 'mainstream' churches into a variety of new religious movements (including new churches) while for many the spiritual landscape is increasingly idiosyncratic and syncretistic. The women's movement, therapy groups, new age, movements for peace and ecological renewal, are among many areas within which people are trying to shape a new spiritual consciousness in which the polarities of individual and social, active and passive, are transcended.

A spirituality of human liberation cannot be built by lonely militants in isolation from the common people. It is a movement which can only be built on solidarity and comradeship. It calls for the creation of what Alasdair MacIntyre has called networks of small groups of friends, local forms of community within which the virtues and the vision of a human future can be sustained. MacIntyre even invokes a new St benedict as a symbol of the future (MacIntyre 1981: 244–5). Yet, as Sebastian Moore has said: 'Unlike the birth of contemplative prayer in the medieval monastery, its birth today will be political, and generate a holy rage against the suicidal policies of our time' (Moore 1986: 53). So a spirituality of liberation must be characterized by solidarity. For the work of liberation is corporate work, not private enterprise. Those involved in this work are called into comradeship and communion. They will need a common spirituality to nurture and strengthen them. A central feature of such a spirituality will be the creation and strengthening of these networks of friends and pilgrims in truth and love, networks of people who guide and help one another.

A spirituality of human liberation is bound to take seriously the fact that, while there is no possibility of a return to a medieval-type sacral unity, there is today a desperate need for a sense of community and common life, and for a sense of the holy. Much of our current distress is related to the breakdown of these realities: its resolution will involve their renewal. A spirituality of liberation therefore must be marked by discontent and yearning, sanctified unease combined with joyful longing. It is this seed which contains the hope of the future.

REFERENCES

Augustine (1972) *Concerning the City of God* (ed.) H. Bettenson, Harmondsworth: Penguin.

Beachy, A. J. (1963) 'The grace of God in Christ as understood by the major Anabaptist writers', *Mennonite Quarterly Review* 37(1): 5–33, 52.

Bonhoeffer, D. (1972) *Letters and Papers from Prison*, New York: Macmillan.

Brown, P. (1989) *The Body and Society*, London: Faber.

Brueggemann, W. (1978) *The Prophetic Imagination*, Philadelphia: Fortress Press.

——— (1985) 'The prophet as a destabilising presence', in E. E. Shelp and R. H. Sunderland (eds) *The Pastor as Prophet*, New York: Pilgrim Press.

——— (1991) *Interpretation and Obedience*, Minneapolis: Fortress Press.

Cannon, K. G. (1988) *Black Womanist Ethics*, Atlanta: Scholars Press.

Cone, J. H. (1969) *Black Theology and Black Power*, New York: Seabury Press.

——— (1970) *A Black Theology of Liberation*, Philadelphia: Lippincott.

——— (1972) *The Spirituals and the Blues*, New York: Seabury Press.

——— (1975) *God of the Oppressed*, New York: Seabury Press.

Cox, H. (1969) *God's Revolution and Man's Responsibility*, London: SCM Press.

Davies, J. (1983) 'The Catholic movement for export', in K. Leech and R. Williams (eds) *Essays Catholic and Radical*, London: Bowerdean Press, 181–92.

Dayton, D. W. (1976) *Discovering an Evangelical Heritage*, New York: Harper & Row.

Duffy, E. (1992) *The Stripping of the Altars: Traditional Religion in England 1400–1580*, New Haven: Yale University Press.

Evans, S. G. (ed.) (1954) *The Return to Reality*, London: Zeno Press.

Fischer, K. (1989) *Women at the Well*, London: SPCK.

Fox-Genovese, E. (1991) *Feminism Without Illusions: A Critique of Individualism*, Chapel Hill: University of North Carolina Press.

Galilea, S. (1973) 'Spiritual awakening and movements of liberation in Latin America', *Concilium* 9(9): 131.

Gottwald, N. (1979) *The Tribes of Yahweh: A Sociology of the Religion of Liberated Israel 1250–1350 BCE*, Maryknoll: Orbis.

——— (1983) *The Bible and Liberation*, Maryknoll: Orbis.

Gray, D. (1986) *Earth and Altar: The Evolution of the Parish Communion in the Church of England*, London: Alcuin Club Collections, no. 68.

Gutiérrez, G. (1972) *A Theology of Liberation*, Maryknoll: Orbis.

——— (1984) *We Drink From Our Own Wells: The Spiritual Journey of a People*, Maryknoll: Orbis.

——— (1990) 'Expanding the view', in M. H. Ellis and O. Maduro (eds.) *Expanding the View*, Maryknoll: Orbis.

Hauerwas, S. (1981) *A Community of Character: Towards a Constructive Christian Ethic*, Notre Dame: University of Notre Dame.

Hauerwas, S. and Willimon, W. H. (1989) *Resident Aliens: Life in the Christian Colony*, Nashville: Abingdon Press.

Heyward, C. (1989) *Touching Our Strength: The Erotic as Power and the Love of God*, San Francisco, Harper & Row.

Kee, A. (1973) *Seeds of Liberation: Spiritual Dimensions to Political Struggle*, London: SCM Press.
MacIntyre, A. (1981) *After Virtue*, Notre Dame: University of Notre Dame Press.
McNamara, W. (1977) *Mystical Passion*, New York: Paulist Press.
Merton, T. (1973a) *Contemplative Prayer*, New York: Doubleday.
—— (1973b) *The Asian Journal of Thomas Merton*, New York: New Directions.
Miles, M. R. (1988) *The Image and Practice of Holiness*, London: SCM Press.
Moberg, D. O. (1972) *The Great Reversal: Evangelism versus Social Concern*, London: Scripture Union.
Moore, S. (1986) *Let This Mind be In You*, San Francisco: Harper & Row.
Morley, J. (1988) *All Desires Known*, London: Movement for the Ordination of Women.
—— (1992) *Bread of Tomorrow*, London: SPCK and Christian Aid.
Pannenberg, Wolfhart (1983) *Christian Spirituality*, Philadelphia: Westminster Press.
Perrin, Norman (1963) *The Kingdom of God in the Teaching of Jesus*, Chicago: University of Chicago Press.
Piehl, M. (1982) *Breaking Bread: The Catholic Worker and the Beginnings of Catholic Radicalism in America*, Philadelphia: Temple University Press.
Ramsey, A. M. (1955) 'Faith and Society', *Church Quarterly Review*, CLIV, 360–6.
—— (1956) *The Gospel and the Catholic Church*, London: Longmans Green and Co.
Raymond, J. G. (1986) *A Passion for Friends: Towards a Philosophy of Female Affection*, London: Women's Press.
Reckitt, M. B. (1935) *Religion and Social Purpose*, London: SPCK.
Robinson, J. A. T. (1961) *The Body*, London: SCM Press.
—— (1963) *Honest to God*, London: SCM Press.
—— (1964) *On Being the Church in the World*, London: SCM Press.
Rowbotham, S., Segal, L. and Wainwright, H. (1979) *Beyond the Fragments: Feminism and the Making of Socialism*, London: Merlin Press.
Rubin, M. (1991) *Corpous Christi: the Eucharist in Late Medieval Culture*, Cambridge: Cambridge University Press.
Ruether, R. (1972) *Liberation Theology*, New York: Paulist Press.
Ruysbroeck, John of (1951) *The Adornment of the Spiritual Marriage, The Sparkling Stone, The Book of Supreme Truth*, trans. C. A. Wynschenk Dom, London: Watkins.
Segal, L. (1987) *Is the Future Female?: Troubled Thoughts on Contemporary Feminism*, London: Virago Press.
Sennett, R. (1991) *The Conscience of the Eye: The Design and Social Life of Cities*, London: Faber.
Sider, R. J. (ed.) (1974) *The Chicago Declaration*, Carol Stream, Ill.: Creation House.
Smith, T. L. (1981) 'Holiness and radicalism in 19th Century America', in T. Runyon (ed.) *Sanctification and Liberation*, Nashville: Abingdon Press, 116–41.
Sommerville, C. J. (1992) *The Secularisation of Early Modern England*, Oxford: Oxford University Press.
Stringfellow, W. (1973) *An Ethic for Christians and Other Aliens in a Strange Land*, Waco, Texas: Word Books.
—— (1984) *The Politics of Spirituality*, Philadelphia: Westminster Press.
Wallis, J. (1976) *Agenda for Biblical People*, San Francisco: Harper & Row.
—— (1982) *The Call to Conversion*, Tring: Lion Books.
West, C. (1982) *Prophesy Deliverance!: An Afro-American Revolutionary Christianity*, Philadelphia: Westminster Press.
—— (1988) *Prophetic Fragments*, Grand Rapids, Mich.: Eerdmans.
—— (1993a) *Prophetic Thought in Postmodern Times*, Monroe, Maine: Common Courage Press.
—— (1993b) *Prophetic Reflections*, Monroe, Maine: Common Courage Press.

Wilmore, G. (1972) *Black Religion and Black Radicalism*, New York: Doubleday.
Wink, W. (1984) *Naming the Powers*, Philadelphia: Fortress Press.
—— (1986) *Unmasking the Powers*, Philadelphia: Fortress Press.
—— (1992) *Engaging the Powers*, Minneapolis: Fortress Press.
Woodard, J. (1983) 'How can activists stay spiritually sane?', *The Witness*, March, 4–5.
Yoder, J. H. (1972) *The Politics of Jesus*, Grand Rapids, Mich.: Eerdmans.

FURTHER READING

Berdyaev, N. (1935) *Freedom and the Spirit*, London: Geoffrey Bles.
Elliott, C. (1985) *Praying the Kingdom: Towards a Political Spirituality*, London: Darton, Longman and Todd.
Kovel, J. (1991) *History and Spirit: An Inquiry into the Philosophy of Liberation*, Boston: Beacon Press.
Leech, K. (1981) *The Social God*, London: Sheldon Press.
—— (1984) 'The social dimensions of Christian spirituality', *The Way*, 24(3): 167–74.
—— (1990) *Care and Conflict: Leaves from a Pastoral Notebook*, London: Darton, Longman and Todd.
—— (1992) *The Eye of the Storm: Spiritual Resources for the Pursuit of Justice*, London: Darton, Longman and Todd; San Francisco: Harper.
—— (1994) *Soul Friend: Spiritual Direction in the Contemporary World*, revised edition, London: Darton, Longman and Todd.
Ramsey, A. M. (1965) *Sacred and Secular: A Study in the Otherworldly and This-Worldly Aspects of Christianity*, London: Longmans.
Soelle D. (1977) *Revolutionary Patience*, Maryknoll: Orbis.
Tinder, G. (1991) *The Political Meaning of Christianity: The Prophetic Stance*, San Francisco: Harper.
See also chapters 26, 27, 28, 29, 32.

32

SPIRITUALITY AND LITURGY

Gordon S. Wakefield

There are some definitions from which one would deduce that Liturgy and Spirituality are one and the same. Regin Prenter has said that 'Liturgy is service, and every human service, whatever its content, consists in serving God. Thus our whole life may be called a service to God i.e. a liturgy.' He goes on to maintain that liturgy 'is a most comprehensive term consisting of the whole of Christian life' (Prenter 1977: 139, 140). This is implied in the favoured dismissals at the end of some new rites, which, after a blessing, send the people, out, as in the Methodist Sunday Service of 1975, 'to live and work to God's praise and glory', and in an essay of the English Joint Liturgical Group on 'The Liturgy after the Liturgy', 'Christian worship and Christian living constitute a single liturgy' (Hunter 1988: 140). It is almost identical with Alexander Schmemann's preference for speaking of 'the Christian life' rather than 'spirituality', a term which, he says, has become

> Ambiguous and confusing . . . For many people it means some mysterious and self-contained activity, a secret which can be broken into by the study of some 'spiritual techniques' . . . (T)he very essence of Christian spirituality is that it concerns and embraces the whole life. The new life which St Paul defines as 'living in the spirit and walking in the spirit' (Gal. 5:25) is not another life and not a substitute; it is the same life given to us by God, but renewed, transformed and transfigured by the Holy Spirit.
>
> (Schmemann 1976: 107)

We may applaud both Prenter and Schmemann, but liturgy for our purpose is restricted to communal worship, prescribed and ordered, embodied, if not in set and authorized forms, in procedures and customs which include certain invariable elements such as praise, penitence, intercession and the reading and exposition of Scripture. As its historic Christian norm, it involves and centres on fidelity to what was believed to be Christ's command in the Upper Room on his betrayal night, to take bread and wine and eat and drink in remembrance of him.

In the New Testament, worship is a spiritual activity, inspired by the Holy

Spirit, though in danger of being invaded by an enthusiasm, a spirit-possession which could deny Christ. For the early Christians, the sacrifice they offered was of themselves, their whole lives (Rom. 12:1). It was also the sacrifice of praise, 'the tribute of lips which acknowledge [God's] name', but offered 'through Jesus' and his self-offering, inclusive and made once for all (Heb. 13:15). The temple was no material edifice but the Christians themselves indwelt by the Holy Spirit (1 Cor. 3:9b-17).

While this gave to the worship of Christians a great freedom from rites and ceremonies, they inherited certain liturgical forms, the Psalms and synagogue prayers. At first, according to the Acts of the Apostles, their leaders attended the prayers in the temple at Jerusalem. They believed that the Lord himself had given them a prayer, which in some manuscripts is concluded with a liturgical form – 'for thine is the kingdom, the power and the glory' – (Luke 11:2f.; Matt. 6:9ff., Rom. 8:15) and they devised liturgical forms and hymns of their own (Phil. 2:5-11; Eph. 5:14; 1 Tim. 3:16). And the eating of bread and drinking of wine, believed to have been instituted by Christ himself, had, it would seem, originally a sevenfold shape, taking, giving thanks, breaking and distributing the bread, taking, giving thanks, distributing the wine.

LITURGY: SPIRITUALITY CONTAINED

There always have been dangers in spirituality, as we have seen: a tendency to mistake some experience or phenomenon for a manifestation of the Holy Spirit, or to seek a spiritual religion in some sense free of 'rough, crude history' and the particularities of the first-century 'Christ-event'. Josef Jungmann wrote in a brief study of the Eucharistic Prayer, that 'the remembrance of the facts of redemption is essential and fundamental for Christianity. This is what distinguishes Christianity from all natural religions, by they pantheistic, polytheistic or monotheistic' (Jungmann 1956: 3).

Liturgy may correct and restrain the excesses and aberrations of spirituality. And this was necessary in the first decades of the Church. We learn from Paul of the institution of the Eucharist as he deals with the recalcitrant, charismatic Corinthians (1 Cor. 11:23–5). He is concerned to deter not only enthusiastic blasphemy, without quenching the Spirit, but also the making of the Christian table fellowship an orgy, which *inter alia* divided rich from poor. 'Let everything be done decently and in order' (1 Cor. 14:40). The heart of the Christian meal is the *anamnesis*, the proclamation of the Lord's death, as the Church awaits his coming. This must not be obscured or profaned either by spiritual exuberance, gastronomic excess or social divisiveness in the Christian community.

Centuries later, John Henry Newman, in his Anglican days, preached on 'Religious Worship, the Remedy for Excitements'. He is not concerned with religious excitements alone. The mind agitated by secular ambitions and anxieties may be steadied by the opportunity to be in church for Divine Service which lasts, uninterrupted, for a certain length of time, sufficient, he thinks, to compose the mind and save the person from restlessly hurrying to and fro. There is no doubt, though, that Newman is thinking chiefly of evangelicals, the rapture of the newly-converted, who often find opportunity for its expression in the free, less inhibited worship of sects, rather than in the staid and sober rituals of the mainstream Church. He wishes that his own Church would act more according to its professed principles, have 'more frequent Services of praise and prayer, more truly Catholic plans for serving God and man'. But liturgy does bring people to prayer and he appeals to those who need comfort and the presence of Christ in the heart, or who, filled with the energies of the Spirit would do 'the highest and most glorious things for the whole world':

> Come to our Services: come to our Litanies: throw yourself out of your own selfish heart: pour yourself out upon the thought of sin and sinners .. upon the contemplation of God's Throne, of Jesus the Mediator between God and man, and of that glorious Church to which the dispensation is committed. Aspire to be what Christ would make you, His friend: having power with Him and prevailing. Other men will not pray for themselves. You may pray for them and for the general Church: and while you pray, you will find enough in the defects of your praying to remind you of your own nothingness, and to keep you from pride while you aim at perfection.
>
> (Newman 1875: 348–9)

This is an anti-Methodist sermon, troubled by revivalism and the vulgarity of the corybantic. It is doubtful if the lower middle-class converts of the Wesleys and their successors, pitmen redeemed from drunkenness, or condemned felons, brought to Christ in the cell or at the gallows, could have found their spiritual milieu in the Anglicanism of Newman's day, which he himself came to reject in favour of the Roman Mass,

> so piercing, so thrilling, so overcoming. . . . There are little children there, and old men, and simple labourers and students in seminaries . . . there are innocent maidens and there are penitents; but out of these many minds rises one eucharistic hymn, and the great Action is the measure and scope of it.
>
> (Graef 1965: 106)

He would, presumably not without some wishful thinking with regard to so mixed a congregation, have seen this as the supreme containment of excess, where fears are calmed and devotion soars. But it must not be forgotten that early Methodism, though noisy, raucous and some would think over-excited, was saved both in England and the Caribbean from degenerating into hysteria by the Wesley hymns and *The Book of Common Prayer*. The former would be thought by the Tractarians, who feared that Keble's *The Christian Year* might be too Methodist for comfort, to be the very hallmark of enthusiasm. In fact, the hymns channelled enthusiasm into systematic biblical theology and the faith of the historic creeds. There has also been a tradition of using the Methodist hymnbooks not only in the assemblies and congregations, but in private prayer. Many of the Wesley hymns, little known outside Methodism, are especially suited for this, expressing as they do an intimate personal relation with God and a burning desire for holiness or perfect love. These would have formed a bond with Newman and the Oxford Movement had there not been the repellent danger of 'perfectionism', the doctrine of 'the second blessing', the perilous idea that a believer might become instantaneously perfect in this life.

LITURGICAL SPIRITUALITY

Authorized common prayer

There are and have been those whose whole Christian life and prayer are, in a phrase of Neville Ward's, the extension of the Liturgy into their seven weekly attempts at living (Ward 1967: 17). Liturgy is fixed and authoritative. It was so in the beginning in those rudimentary forms we mentioned above, which co-existed with a great deal that was immediate, spontaneous and extempore. The earliest Eucharistic prayers were probably composed by each individual bishop. It was before long necessary to have set forms in each centre of primitive Christianity to guard against heresy and ensure catholicity and the essential elements. Ever since, liturgy has carried the imprimatur of the Church which devised it, whether it be a rite of Jerusalem, or Antioch, Alexandria or Byzantium, the Roman Missal or the *Book of Common Prayer*. It rests ultimately on the 'givenness' of the Gospel, mediated by scholarship and the meeting of appointed minds, not on individual experience or personal preference. Its aim is to unite diversities of temperament, age and Christian understanding, to make possible 'common prayer', which embraces not only the Church throughout the world but the Church throughout the ages and, as C. H. Dodd said, 'reconstitutes the crisis of our redemption'. When the formularies of the liturgy are used in private prayer, it means that religion is being seen not as 'what the individual does with his solitariness', but as a means of deliverance from the loneliness of the spiritual conflict.

This is universally true, though as the historic event of Jesus Christ moved out into the Roman world and its cultures, it was interpreted in terms very different from those of its origins and influenced by the bewildering variety of religions with which it came into contact even though they were its rivals and largely to be opposed. The need for Christian worship to go underground through danger of persecution at some times and places, and the constraints of a way of life in conflict with social mores resulted in the Church seeming anti-social. Were Christians not 'atheists' (rejecters of the gods) in their abstention from public religious activities? Pliny, the Governor of Bithynia, writing to the Emperor Trajan around 112, was puzzled because their worship and their meals together seemed to be harmless, yet he felt constrained to punish them. Later, Justin Martyr gave an account of Christian worship to defend it from charges both of sedition and of indecency (Bettenson 1943: 3–6; Jasper and Cuming 1980: 17–21). But Christianity did acquire some of the features of a mystery religion, its faith expressed in clandestine and exclusive rites, which by the fourth century, when Christianity was officially recognized, had reached an awesomeness that was 'spine-chilling' (Yarnold 1972). The encounter of Christianity and other cultures has influenced liturgy and spirituality from the beginning, not least as the Church broke out of Europe, to India, Latin America and Africa.

> The notion of absolute and general fixity in the whole range of liturgical phenomena even in the period of the Counter Reformation is valid only in terms of official curial policy. For the living Church, whether in Europe or elsewhere, it is more fable than fact.
>
> (Kavannagh 1990: 96)

Nevertheless, liturgy has been a great preservative of continuity and identity. Though forms and appurtenances and interpretations have come to differ astronomically over the centuries – the Latin High Mass seems a long way from the Upper Room, or from a Congregationalist Lord's Supper – and controversies have raged unto death, certain elements have never been lost. There is always some link with the Institution narrative.

The Orthodox Churches

The Liturgy (i.e. the eucharist) is the centre of the spirituality of the Eastern Orthodox Churches. There is a story of the 1920s of a young Englishman who after a visit to Mount Athos was accompanied on a hill walk to Salonika by one of the elderly monks. Overnight they stayed at country inns where they had to share a bedroom. Neither morning nor night was the monk seen to pray or engage in any devotions. In the end the young man's curiosity could not be restrained and he made bold to ask the monk why he had omitted so essential a duty. The old man seemed surprised. He pointed out that he was a member of a community which offered regular daily prayer in the Liturgy and offices. When he was in the monastery he participated to the full; when he was not, the prayer went on just the same (Hankey 1937: 147).

That is an extreme case. The Orthodox Liturgy presupposes a correlation between personal devotions and corporate worship in the community. The former are both the preparation and the sequel to the latter, but, as Georges Florovsky wrote (the italics are his),

> *Prayer is intrinsically subordinate to sacraments.* It is possible only on the basis of our sacramental incorporation into the body of Christ, through Holy Baptism. Accordingly, the ultimate 'encounter' is realized also in a *sacramental* way, in the mystery of the Holy Eucharist. All 'private devotions' must be directed towards this sacramental goal.
>
> (Mother Mary and Ware 1969: 34).

669

The eucharist is the ultimate mystery and is itself the most perfect and intimate union, more than the sum of individual experience and sense of the presence of God. It comprehends the whole Church, both on earth and in heaven. The Liturgy is the weekly entrance of the Church into the Kingdom, to eat and drink with Christ at his table.

> Secretly, unseen by the world, 'the doors being shut', the Church, that 'little flock' – to whom it was the Father's good pleasure to give the Kingdom (Luke 12:32) – fulfils in the eucharist her ascension into the light and joy and triumph of the kingdom.
>
> (Schmemann 1987: 43).

This is eschatological rather than mystical in the Western sense, the communal anticipation of the consummation of all things, God's final triumph in Christ, the new heaven and the new earth, rather than the union of the individual with God.

No Orthodox theologian would describe the Christian assembly, young and old, gathered together on a Sunday morning, as 'partners in learning' or regard worship as a 'learning experience'. Contrasting Eastern with Western worship, Aidan Kavannagh has said that it 'tends to be less cerebral and more open to movement, sense experience, contemplation and individual initiative'. The East is 'iconic'; the West 'pictorial'. 'Pictures are about meaning. Icons are about being' (Kavannagh 1984: 4). The Christ of Orthodox spirituality is not predominantly the Christ of Gethesemane and Golgotha, as in the West, so much as of the Transfiguration: and as we reflect his Divine radiance, 'we are changed from glory to glory' (2 Cor. 3:18).

Some Western types

Michael Ramsey, Archbishop of Canterbury from 1961–74, was an undergraduate when he came to find in Anglo-Catholic worship

> the sense of mystery and awe, and of another world at once far and near . . . a sense that we were vividly in the presence of the passion of Jesus and also vividly near to heaven, to which the passion mysteriously belonged, so as to be brought from the past to the present.

He came to value communion after careful preparation at 8.00 a.m. and then High Mass at which (in that period) no-one but the priest took the sacrament. This set his mind free for pondering and adoring (Chadwick 1990: 375). He expressed reservations about the Parish Communion movement which had swept Anglicanism by the time he was a bishop in the 1950s. He thought that people merely 'tripped along' to their communion, spiritually unready. He might have had sympathy with the old Scottish Presbyterian custom of Communion Sundays, which took place but once or twice a year. Ramsey would have wanted communion more frequently than that, daily indeed (a practice virtually unknown in Eastern Orthodox liturgical practice).

T. S. Eliot was also converted to Anglo-Catholicism, in his case because it provided a liturgical spirituality of confession, Mass and communion in which the profoundest scepticism was combined with the deepest faith. One was not signing a statement of faith, clothed in the ambiguities beneath the apparent clarities of language, but was caught up in a rite – Eliot compared it to a drama – in which one was not always asking for 'meaning' and 'the series of acts themselves may be the only justification for those who perform them'. He received communion with rapt devotion (Ackroyd 1984: 163).

There have been those who have found the source of their private prayers in the liturgy. Lancelot Andrewes's private prayers are a mosaic of passages from Scripture, the Fathers and ancient liturgies (Brightman 1903). He prayed with his pen in his hand and did not like to use his own words. He thought extempore prayers, in the heat of the moment, might be unworthy of God's majesty and 'he wanted a historic formula to pray with; one tested by the Church and by time'. And this was also because 'he felt his own private prayers, however inadequate, to be part of something far bigger, a little living voice inside a multitude of voices praising' (Chadwick 1986).

The modern Liturgical Movement in the West has insisted on the communal nature of liturgical worship and that we should 'Pray the Mass' rather than 'Pray at the Mass'. We are to participate at each moment, gathered around the table, near to the priest or minister, aware of one another as well as of the bread and wine. The Church is the celebrant, not the individual ordained to preside. The emphasis has changed from the act and moment of consecration as the priest recites the words of institution over bread and cup, to the whole Eucharistic prayer, if not the whole rite, as being 'a holy action from beginning to end' (Kilpatrick 1983: 83). This results in a very different eucharistic spirituality, participatory rather than contemplative, with less opportunity to 'ponder and adore'. It is less numinous, the Divine not 'up there and out there', but in the worshipping people of God, their reconciliation in Christ enacted at the revival of the ancient greeting of the Peace, rather than in the consecrated elements and the sacramental presence in them. It certainly attempts to bring liturgy to life and unites the Church around the altar with the Church in the world of human relations and political and social action.

Some of this was anticipated at the Reformation. The Reformers insisted on the congregation receiving communion and in both kinds (i.e. not bread alone, as for the past three centuries at least), while Cranmer does not speak of a prayer of consecration (i.e. drawing attention to the bread and wine themselves) in either of his Prayer Books (1549 and 1552). The term was applied to the third part of the anaphora of the *Book of Common Prayer* in 1662 at the instance of Caroline high churchmen. This was in reaction to what Protestants have regarded as the departure of the Roman Catholic Church of the high Middle Ages from biblical truth. The supreme moment of the Mass had become the elevation of the Host (i.e. the consecrated bread).

To see that rather than to communicate was the means of grace and salvation. Before summoned to kneel and adore, the congregation might be lost in their own private devotions, perhaps from an appropriate manual – the origin of pews may lie in the desire to concentrate on these – or telling their rosary beads (or even discussing business in the nave). Eamon Duffy has disputed the conventional wisdom that medieval Western Christians were largely non-participants in a largely clerical liturgy as untenable over-simplification. The Mass permeated society, its themes were assimilated by the laity in a variety of ways, and if the Sunday Parish Mass was indeed celebrated at a high altar, distant from the people, the low Masses on weekdays, and often on Sundays simultaneously with the main service, were at side or nave altars where the action could be accessible to the worshippers. What is more,

> each Mass was framed within a series of ritual moments, at which the ministers, often carrying sacred objects, such as the Host itself at Easter, or on ordinary Sundays, Gospel texts, the paxbread, or sacramentals like holy water or holy bread, passed out of the sanctuary into the body of the church.
>
> (Duffy 1992: 112)

Mass books for instruction offered moralized or allegorized meditations on the stages of the rite, some working out its correspondences with the events of the Passion, in the belief that, as one tract put it, 'the processe of the masse representyd the very processe of the Passyon off Cryst'. The Sunday Mass was surrounded with light and colour and music, which made the Reformers' liturgies seem over-solemn, verbose and stark in comparison. This was mitigated for Protestants by the vernacular and, eventually in England, by congregational singing (Whale 1936: 161ff.). Scripture read at length was new and exciting, its teaching seen as centring on justification by faith, 'a most wholesome doctrine and very full of comfort'.

The seventeenth-century Anglican understanding, turned into hymns in the next century by the Wesleys, is dominated by *anamnesis*, remembrance, which by faith makes worshippers the contemporaries of Calvary. The once-for-all Sacrifice is re-presented in the eucharist. These ideas are in fact anticipated in Theodore of Mopsuestia (*c*.350–428) and are congenial to twentieth-century Catholic theologians such as Casel and de la Taille (Casel 1962; Yarnold 1972: 219). We may find also a hint of Jeremias's exegesis of Christ's command: 'Do this that God may remember me', with its eschatological implications – that God will bring in the kingdom (Jeremias 1966: 237ff.). Anglican liturgical spirituality has often held that the belief that bread and wine become the body and blood of Christ is a mystery about which we should be agnostic rather than devising scholastic theories (Hooker 1907: II: 328–31), while holding that in the sacrament Christ himself is given to his Church on earth in his real presence (Rattenbury 1948).

672

The Office

The Office, with its basis in the Psalms and the Bible, has for many centuries been a bridge between liturgy and spirituality. It is a liturgy of time, of daily prayer at set hours. In the early third century, Hippolytus commended seven daily hours for prayer to Christians at home or at work – on rising and before any work; at the third hour when Christ was nailed to the cross; at the sixth hour when there was darkness at noon as Christ suffered on the cross; at the ninth hour of the piercing when Christ slept in death; on going to bed; about midnight (though this will mean rising for a while from bed and possibly retiring for the purpose to a separate room, if one's partner is not among the faithful) for then, it is believed, all creation is for a moment still and in Christ's parable the bridegroom came; and at cockcrow (Cuming 1976: 29–31). Origen (c.233) taught that to pray without ceasing was to combine action with prayer. 'Virtuous deeds and commandments fulfilled [are] included as acts of prayer.' This is why the whole life of the saint is one great unbroken prayer. 'That which is commonly called prayer' should take place not less than three times a day as with Daniel. Origen also stresses, with scriptural reference, the importance of prayer during the night, as does Chrysostom in Byzantium at the beginning of the fifth century (Oulton and Chadwick 1954: 261–2).

After the end of persecution, when Christian assemblies became legal and public

> the morning and evening times of prayer began to emerge as pre-eminent and to be celebrated daily as public services everywhere, while as a general rule the other pre-Nicene hours remained as purely individual observances, increasingly becoming the activity of the especially devout and ascetic alone.
>
> (Bradshaw 1981: 72)

Work prevented most people from keeping all the hours of prayer congregationally. Services morning and evening, with praise and thanksgiving dominant and with an element of penitence, since those soiled by the world's transactions needed God's forgiveness, were held 'daily at the place which the bishop appoints for them' (Cuming 1976: 28–9). Because of its link with the authority of bishops, modern scholars have called this twice daily form 'the Cathedral office' (Baumstark 1958: 111). The Office was also, however, the backbone of monastic prayer. Monasticism had pre-Christian antecedents, for instance in Judaism, and, it has been argued, was 'always simply there in the life of the Church', in the sense that there are signs from the start that some Christians felt called to a stricter observance of daily prayer. Origen, in the third century, envied Mary sitting at the Saviour's feet (Luke 10:38–42) and John who 'departed into the desert where the air was purer, the sky more open and God more intimately nigh'. But the overwhelming influence of monasticism began in the fourth century. It was an expression of the eschatological character of Christianity

as an almost unconscious and instinctive reaction against the secularisation of the
Church – not only in the sense of a reduction of her moral ideal or pathos of
sanctity, but also of her entrance into the 'service of the world' – of the Empire,
civic society and natural values

which, after the downfall of paganism, were waiting to receive from Christianity a religious gloss and authorization (Schmemann 1966: 102).

It began as a lay movement and was never primarily liturgical in its
creativity. Most often it has accepted the currently authorized principles of
liturgy, even though some orders have had their own rites. The eucharist has
always been central and obligatory, but what has been of most significance for
Christian worship is monastic devotion to prayer and psalmody expressed in
the daily offices – at eight hours of the day and night as described already
in Hippolytus (c.217) and then taken up in the rules of St Basil in the East
and St Benedict in the West. It was a quest for perfection attained through
unceasing prayer, understood, as with Origen, as including work. Accompanying prayer was the chanting of Psalms. Augustine once said that 'A love of
psalmody gave birth to monasticism.' The Psalter was no longer used as a
hymnbook as with the Jews and earlier Christians, with Psalms for suitable
occasions being chosen out of it, but sung in 'course', that is simply in the
order of the Psalter itself. The Rule of St Benedict divides the 150 Psalms
among the Offices, so that they are all recited each week.

Not all the consequences of monasticism have been beneficial to Christian
spirituality: sometimes it has appeared as an elite, even an affluent elite, apart
from and superior to the life expected of ordinary Christians. Today, when
vocations have diminished (after some nineteenth-century revival and its recovery in the Church of England), it is seen very much in relation to the Church
as a whole. The exploration, practice and teaching of the life of prayer are
for the good of all. Monasteries provide both powerhouses of prayer and
havens of quiet in a frenetic world, and the common life is sustained by
liturgy and office, free in certain ways from some of the dangers that beset
other Christians. Monastic life seeks to represent what Christian community
should be, while the other orders, with a base in community life under vows,
venture into the violent and most depressed places of the earth with the love
of Christ. But in its patristic and medieval heyday, there was a tendency that
instead of life being prayer, as for Origen, and his Alexandrian predecessor,
Clement, prayer replaced life. Liturgy was privatized. The eucharist became
an ascetic act for the spiritual succour of the individual in his or her pilgrimage
to perfection rather than the 'making real' of the Church in the eschatological
feast of the kingdom (Schmemann 1966). Monasticism became the ideal to
which life in the world should approximate. The fuller monastic office took
over from the 'cathedral office', becoming the norm for the parish clergy. A
particular form of spirituality, valuable for those called to it, came to provide
a model for the ordered and disciplined prayer of those whose needs it did
not altogether serve. Thus, in medieval Europe, monasteries were, somewhat

paradoxically, both oases of gospel life within a society operating on lower standards and ideals to which clergy and devout lay people aspired.

The Breviary, which has undergone slow evolution since the thirteenth century, was intended as the prayer book for those using the monastic pattern in ordinary life (Jones *et al.* 1978: 378f.). It has been imitated outside Roman Catholicism. When Charles I's Queen, Henrietta Maria, brought over from France her Roman Catholic ladies-in-waiting to the Court, a wave of conversions to Rome followed, together with an interest in Catholic devotional forms. John Cosin, then a Prebend of Durham, compiled in 1627 a Liturgy of the Hours for members of the English Church, together with the penitential psalms, litanies, collects and prayers for various occasions (Stanwood 1967). Viciously attacked by Puritans in the years that followed, it never attained popularity. *The Book of Common Prayer* was already established as the flagship of the Church of England, with its two daily offices, of which Evening Prayer, with its fusion of the Breviary services of Vespers and Compline, is considered one of its masterpieces.

The Office retains its use amid all changes in the Churches and the world. Twentieth-century Free Churchmen have commended it as a help in dry seasons and an anchorage in the wider Church. Nathaniel Micklem, the Congregationalist, devised morning and evening offices, which used his own tradition of hymnody as well as devotions from the centuries (Micklem 1941). The British Joint Liturgical Group produced proposals resulting from a lengthy discussion of the Office, the first edition introduced by a Baptist, Stephen Winward (Jasper 1968). These ecumenical efforts have not caused general satisfaction. There is a feeling that Protestants use the Office for edification, whereas for some Catholics it is not at all didactic, or emotional, but an impersonal offering to the glory of God apart altogether from feeling and experience, or else an act of identification with the Church (Thornton 1957).

Paul Bradshaw wrote in 1981 that

> we need to discover and create a truly 'cathedral' office, not necessarily by reconstructing what was done at Jerusalem or Antioch or wherever in the fourth century, but by using insights provided by historical study in order to establish the essentials of our pattern of daily prayer and spirituality and then express these in forms appropriate to our own age.
>
> (Bradshaw 1981: 153f.)

The Psalms

In spite of the near absence of Morning Prayer in the Sunday worship of present-day Anglican and Methodist Churches and diminished congregations at Anglican Evensong, there is among many devout Christians an increased appreciation of the Psalms. Jesus himself quoted them according to the tradition of the Gospels and used them to interpret his own mission. The evangelists read them as illuminating his life story. Psalm 22 underlies the Marcan and Johannine narratives of the Passion. They express what George Herbert, in the seventeenth century, called the 'bitter-sweet' of Christian experience:

> I will complain yet praise;
> I will bewail, approve;
> And all my soure-swet days
> I will lament, and love.

Some feel that the Psalter is incongruous for Christians, as did John Burnaby in a fine essay on 'Christian Prayer'. The Psalter owed its place in the Church's liturgy 'primarily to the ease with which it lent itself to interpretation by the early Church as prophetic of Christ'.

It has established its hold by the supreme beauty and truth of many of the Hebrew hymns and prayers which it contains. But the type of *Klagelied*, of complaint or expostulation, to which not less than a quarter of the psalms belong, is animated by a temper which even the most reckless allegorizing can scarcely baptize into Christianity.

(Burnaby 1962: 235–6)

The imprecatory verses, bringing down curses on the writer's enemies, are a particularly acute problem. They have been bracketed in the 1928 Prayer Book and elsewhere. John Wesley considered them 'highly improper for the mouths of a Christian congregation'; and Bishop Gore, earlier this century, said that no amount of singing the Gloria at the end could make them Christian. To allegorize – in Psalm 137 for instance, with 'Babylon's children' as our sins and Christ as the rock against which they should be dashed – seems an evasion and an escape from historical reality. What must never be forgotten is that the Psalmists are often calling on God to establish divine justice, and many of the Psalms are the cries of the poor, the oppressed and the needy. They cannot easily condone the violence done to them and to others. Modern users have seen them as all too relevant to our times: those who perpetrated the Holocaust cannot simply be excused, or their iniquities condoned by easy talk of forgiving love. The Psalmists do not propose to take vengeance into their own hands but rather demand God's action. And yet in these prayers for justice there is all too obviously human sin, that which is incompatible both with the teaching of Jesus and with God's atoning action in him.

HOUSEHOLD RELIGION

The Reformed tradition regarded every household as a religious community, a conviction which Anglicans shared (de Waal 1983: 145–6). 'A Christian family', says Baxter, echoing many others, 'is a church . . . a society of Christians combined for the better worshipping and serving God' (Baxter 1830: IV,

75), and Puritans quoted Augustine: 'what the preacher is in the pulpit, the same the householder is in the house' (Bayly 1669: 158n.). Though like George Herbert they were aware of religious advantages in the single life (Martz 1986: 200), marriage was certainly no inferior spiritual state. In this they had been anticipated by Wycliffites and other reforming Catholics (Tripp 1991: 77n.). As much as Catholics and Orthodox they believed that all prayer, wherever offered, alone, in family, or in public worship, was one. The praying individual or group was primarily a member of the Body of Christ. In this tradition, prayer should be twice daily and corresponded to the temple sacrifices under the old covenant. It was the continuous burnt offering of Leviticus 6:13, a passage applied to Christian devotion in Matthew Henry's commentary and echoed in Charles Wesley's hymn:

> O Thou who camest from above
> The pure celestial fire to impart
> Kindle a flame of sacred love
> On the mean altar of my heart.

It was the incense which ascended to God (Ps. 141:2; Rev. 8:3, 4).

Domestic spiritually was holistic in that it encompassed 'not only worship but instruction, governance, discipline, and the exercise of charity and justice'. Fasting was practised regularly. Household religion was inclusive of women. Many treatises regard women as deputy household priests able to take over should the male default (Tripp 1991: 77–82). Children were integral members of the people of God. Their instruction began almost at birth and precocity in religion was not unusual, even though it might be difficult to distinguish 'playing church' from a real devotion. Servants were taught to read the Bible and were always included with the children in daily prayers. The Christian week more than the Christian year was the focus of devotion and all was an extension of worship in church on the Lord's Day, so that this spirituality was often liturgical in form, using prayer books of various kinds. The Lord's Day itself was 'the schoolday, the faire day, the market day, the feeding day of the soul', the day of sublimest recreation when the sheep heard Christ's voice and found pasture (Wakefield 1957: 59–63). This tradition was strong in nineteenth-century evangelical spirituality, but it often became didactic and moralistic. The sacrificial and mystagogical elements were lost in evangelical pedagogy and the young frequently became embarrassed by the desire to capture their souls through family prayers. As the family itself gradually declined, so there departed with it the religion of which the aim was to be 'true to the kindred points of heaven and home'.

NON-LITURGICAL SPIRITUALITY

Liturgical spiritually was anathema to some elements in Protestant Christianity. The nineteenth-century Danish philosopher, Søren Kierkegaard, wrote:

'what Pascal says about Christianity is entirely true, the truest words ever spoken about Christianity, that it is a society of men who, with the help of a few sacraments, exempt themselves from the duty of loving God' (Plekon 1992: 221). George Fox, founder of Quakerism, and Pascal's contemporary, used sacramental language, but did not believe that there was any warrant in Scripture, where the word Sacrament is not found, for the ordinances of the Church: Jesus' saying at the Last Supper, 'This is my body', is metaphorical, like 'I am the true vine' – a not infrequent Puritan contention. The phrase 'as oft as you take it' does not mean 'you must take it always'. His protest is against the observance of an outward, formal act, which may make no apparent difference to living.

> For after yee have eaten in remembrance of his death then yee must come into his death & die with him if yee will live with him as ye Apostles did: & yt is a neerer & a further state to be in ye fellowshippe with him in his death, then to take bread and wine in rembrans of his death.

There is here both the desire for immediacy of communion with Christ and ethical concern (Nuttall 1947: 100–1).

The Society of Friends, as the Quakers came to be called, do not worship with a liturgy but by silent waiting upon God. This is seen, not as a prelude to mystic union, but rather to the guidance of the Spirit who will give them the words to speak. Quaker devotional writing has been powerful. Examples include John Woolman's *Journal* from eighteenth-century America and the work of Rendel Harris (1852–1941), the textual scholar. In one of his many spiritual writings, *Union with God*, he imagines himself being asked, 'Why don't you say that religion means being baptised, taking the Lord's Supper, saying the Ten Commandments and reading your Bible? Well, because this is not the way the New Testament sees it' (Harris 1913: 32). The writings of Thomas R. Kelly (1893–1941) still bring refreshment and relief from 'the vagaries of ritualism' or 'the dull institutionalism' of much Christianity as they expound in language of great beauty the eternal truths of the inner life and the peace that passes understanding. Even so, there has in recent years been a two-way traffic between Quakers and Roman Catholicism, finding common ground in the contemplative rather than the liturgical tradition of prayer.

Some seventeenth-century extremists were totally against 'stinted forms' and opposed congregational singing of psalms or hymns or the use of prayers (even the Lord's Prayer) composed in advance as being a denial of the Holy Spirit, whose inspiration must be an immediate and present reality. John Bunyan was not one of the most radical sectarians, but liturgy provokes his most sarcastic invective. He sneers at those who have:

> both the Manner and Matter of their Prayers at their finger-ends; setting such a Prayer for such a day, and that twenty years before it comes. One for Christmass, another for Easter and six dayes after that. They have also bounded how many

syllables must be said in every one of them at their public Exercises. For each Saint's day also, they have them ready for the generations yet unborn to say. They can tell you also when you shall kneel, when you should stand, when you should abide in your seats, when you should go up into the Chancel, and what you should do when you come there. All which the Apostles came short of, as not being able to compose so profound a matter.

(Greaves 1976: 247–8).

Bunyan believes that liturgy is the enemy of spirituality. 'Spirit' is the operative word. He fears that religious duties and obligations may be fulfilled in a 'legal spirit', so that faith becomes a business transaction (a covenant of works) rather than a personal relationship of grace, so that the 'spirit' in the sense of the inward disposition, the Holy Spirit taking possession of the whole being, is of no concern provided the rules are kept and the bargain honoured. He was too well aware of quarrels over liturgy, not least the bitter controversies among his own people over Baptism. It must not be forgotten that the English liturgy in Bunyan's day and for long afterwards was an instrument of political oppression. It represented a Church by law established so that those who could not conform to its use were victims of social and political discrimination. It represented a governing hierarchy, and though it helped to maintain the good order of the State, it denied what many believed was the rightful freedom of Christians, as well as in their view being dubiously faithful to Christ and to Scripture.

Spirituality may be the great critic of imposed and authorized forms of worship, yet it influences liturgy; so that it may be said that today's liturgy is yesterday's spirituality. For good or ill, and for many kinds of social, cultural and intellectual reasons, ways of praying develop which, in due course and often subtly, come to affect the form or, more commonly, the actual practice of liturgy. Only perhaps in modern Western mainstream Churches has liturgy become responsive to changes of mood and outlook. Readiness to change liturgy in this way is a recent and significant development.

Liturgy has also, however, had the great virtue of being a preservative of truths of the Christian faith which may lie buried within it until their hour has come. The Tractarians of early nineteenth-century Anglicanism believed that there was a Catholicism in the Prayer Book communion rite which had been obscured by the bias in church life and practice towards Protestantism, but which a Catholic emphasis on reverence and ceremonial could recover. Their successors, the Anglo-Catholics, were not content with that rite and incorporated into it prayers from other (chiefly Roman Catholic) sources, to make up for its deficiencies. Liturgy cannot remain intact if it does not express the spirituality of those who use it.

TENDENCIES TO LITURGICAL IMBALANCE

The expression of spirituality in liturgy may lead to imbalance within the actual practice of liturgy itself; even if spirituality does not actually move away from liturgy, as Aidan Kavannagh fears is a danger today, when charismatic and evangelical experience does not feel the need to find expression in liturgy or feels restricted by it (Kavannagh 1983: 20).

Candlemas

Throughout history, particular features of liturgy have gained disproportionate prominence because of their popular appeal. Some of these have been minor. For example: there is no mention of candles in the Gospel narrative of the Presentation of Christ in the Temple (Luke 2:22ff.), but by the high Middle Ages the feast on February 2nd, 'celebrated as of lesser solemnity only than the supreme feasts such as Christmas, Easter and Pentecost, but of equal status to Trinity Sunday, Corpus Christi and All Saints' had become Candlemas (Duffy 1992: 15–22). The story itself is of a tenderness and beauty to inspire devotion. It depicts Mary and Joseph, and infant Jesus who is being offered to God; together with the aged pair, Simeon and Anna, who represent the vigilant faithful of Israel. And it includes Simeon's song, hailing the child as 'a light to lighten the Gentiles' (the reason why candles were introduced), and his words to Mary prophetic of her sufferings. There is plenty here to arouse the imagination, yet the candles were seized on and became 'sacramentals' – conveyors for many of numinous, indeed magical, power, featuring in stories of miraculous healing.

Marian devotion

Mary, the Mother of Jesus, is central to the story of the Presentation and became increasingly prominent in both personal prayer and liturgical worship in both Eastern and Western Christianity. Devotion to her had its germ as early as the second century and her story was elaborated during the patristic period. She was believed herself to have been miraculously conceived by aged parents and her perpetual virginity became an article of faith for the Roman tradition from Jerome onwards. The fourth-century title *Theotokos* (Mother of God) was, in original intent, primarily Christological, affirming the unity of the human and divine natures in Christ, but it undoubtedly stimulated veneration of Mary – eventually in a distorted manner. The term's emphasis on Christ's divinity reflected a tendency to underplay his full human reality and, in due course, by the early Middle Ages, to dwell on his awesome role as mankind's future judge. In this scenario Mary was the human, feminine figure to whom the guilty might turn for intercession with her Son. Contemporaneously there was, it is true, a new devotion to the sacred humanity of

Jesus, notably in Bernard of Clairvaux and Francis of Assisi (and not found to the same extent in the Eastern church); but Marian devotion became – and has remained – immensely important in spirituality and liturgy; witness the popularity of the Hail Mary, the use of the Rosary, the singing of the 'Salve Regina' which celebrates Mary's part in redemption and sees her as the mediatrix of its victory and blessings. The Second Vatican Council took a momentous decision, in terms of the theology signalled thereby, when it included discussion of Mary in the document on the Church and not in a separate document all to herself. It also avoided the medieval title 'Mother of the Church'.

There is a modern re-thinking of the place of Mary which has led perhaps to a correction of former imbalance. Feminists have seen in devotion to her a perverse testimony to the male clerical oppression of women, who are simply to be submissive and obedient 'handmaidens' in a Church dominated by men. She has been adored, but only once she is placed on a 'safe' pedestal of virginity, and made innocuous in liturgy – quite remote from the potentially threatening women of real life. But in Latin America, people are now coming to see in her a prophetess of liberation who sang the Magnificat, who listened attentively to God's word and was open to his will, however revolutionary it might be.

The Ministry of the Word

Of another order is the tendency of the Word to dominate Protestant worship. Liturgy is a union of Word and Sacrament, but it has often been held that Christianity was born in preaching. With the tradition of the Hebrew prophets in the background, Jesus proclaimed the kingdom of God and the first apostles went preaching into the world, outwards from Jerusalem. The Fathers preached, as did the priests and friars of the Middle Ages, but there can be no doubt that the Reformation re-emphasized its necessity, and to some extent substituted the pulpit for the confessional (McAdoo 1949: 12). Moralists, like Bishop Butler, taught through sermons, the Evangelicals (like the later Anglo-Catholics) preached to convert individuals. In Great Britain, from the last half of the nineteenth century until at least 1914, the great Free Church preachers drew such crowds that they had to build larger chapels (Munson 1991: 112–14). Eloquence 'seemed to make heaven near and the invisible clearly seen', wrote J. C. Carlile. Preaching certainly overshadowed the Sacrament in Nonconformist Churches, and the primary purpose of going to church was to hear a preacher. And if the preacher had sufficient gifts and graces, they rarely came empty away, and sometimes they would emerge changed people. It is rarely so now, though Evangelicals have managed to retain the tradition of substantial preaching while also giving a greater place than in earlier days to the sacrament of Communion.

CONCLUSION

There is throughout history a two-way traffic between spirituality and liturgy and sometimes a tension between them. Both need the control of theology, though both also breathe religious life into theology. This may seem a disputable statement and uncongenial to an age where anti-intellectualism is in vogue and there is in the churches great suspicion of theologians, if not downright hostility. As Aidan Kavannagh declared, what happened at the burning bush was a revelation not a seminar (Kavannagh 1984: 92). However, the revelation resulted in a lengthy theological colloquy out of which action came and indeed the whole subsequent history of the children of Israel! Both Kavannagh and the late Richard Hanson have pointed out that

> the great majority of the theologians of the fourth century were bishops. Not one of them was a professional theologian. The early church did not know of the phenomenon of a professional theologian. Most of them might have agreed with Kierkegaard, that to be a Professor of Theology was to crucify Christ. They all had pastoral responsibility.
>
> (Hanson 1989: 149)

This is a necessary reminder and warning. Theology should not be divorced from any part of human activity, whether it be politics or prayer, because it is the quest for truth in the belief that everything is related to God, whether human relations or what we identify as 'religious' experience.

Yet the value of theology lies in the fact that it is religious emotion recollected in tranquillity, in Butler's 'cool hour'. It does not worship reason for it knows its fallibility; nor does it despise or fail to use it. Spirituality and liturgy need the control of theology, with its knowledge of the Christian tradition, which it will accept with realism while trying to read the signs of our times.

Paul Tillich says in one of his sermons that, like the liturgist and the spiritual man or woman, the theologian is one who is 'grasped, within the Church, by the Divine Spirit' (Tillich 1949: 120) whose mission, according to John 16:13, is to guide the disciples of Jesus into all truth. So, the theologian will be 'the loving nurse' of both liturgy and spirituality making sure that the experiential does not supplant the given, yet aware (in T. S. Eliot's words) that Christianity is always adapting itself into something that can be believed and practised.

REFERENCES

Ackroyd, P. (1984) *T. S. Eliot*, London: Hamish Hamilton.

Baumstark, A. (1958) *Comparative Liturgy*, Maryland: The Newman Press.

Baxter, R. (1830) *Works IV*, ed. W. Orme, London.

Bayly, L. (1669) *The Practice of Piety*, London

Bettenson, H. (1943) *Documents of the Christian Church*, Oxford: Oxford University Press.

Bradshaw, P. F. (1981) *Daily Prayer in the Early Church*, London: Alcuin Club, SPCK.

Brightman, F. E. (ed.) (1903) *The Preces Privatae of Lancelot Andrewes*, London: Methuen.

Burnaby, J. (1962), 'Christian Prayer', in A. R. Vidler (ed.) *Soundings*, Cambridge: Cambridge University Press.

Casel, O. (1962) *The Mystery of Christian Worship and Other Writings*, Maryland: The Newman Press.

Chadwick, O. (1986) *Lancelot Andrewes*, Barry Lecture, Southwell Minster.

—— (1990) *Michael Ramsey*, Oxford: Clarendon Press.

Cuming, G. J. (1976) *Hippolytus: A Text for Students*, Nottingham: Grove Booklets.

de Waal, E. (1983) 'Family Spirituality', in G. S. Wakefield (ed.) *A Dictionary of Christian Spirituality*, London: SCM Press.

Duffy, E. (1992) *The Stripping of the Altars: Traditional Religion In England 1400–1580*, New Haven and London: Yale University Press.

Graef, H. (1965) *God and Myself: The Spirituality of J. H. Newman*, London: Peter Davies.

Greaves, R. L. (ed.) (1976) *John Bunyan, Miscellaneous Works II*, Oxford: Clarendon Press.

Hankey, C. P. (1937) in A. G. Hebert *The Parish Communion*, London: SPCK.

Hanson, R. (1989) 'The achievement of orthodoxy in the fourth century AD', in R. Williams (ed.) *The Making of Orthodoxy*, Cambridge: Cambridge University Press.

Harris, R. (1905) *Union with God*, London: Hodder and Stoughton.

Hooker, R. (1907) *The Laws of Ecclesiastical Polity V*, Oxford: Clarendon Press.

Hunter, V. L. (1988) 'The Liturgy after the Liturgy', in D. Gray (ed.) *The Word in Season*, Norwich: The Canterbury Press.

Jasper, R. C. D. (ed.) (1968) *The Daily Office*, London: SPCK and Epworth Press.

Jasper, R. C. D. and Cuming, G. J. (1980) *Prayers of the Eucharist: Early and Reformed*, London: Collins.

Jeremias, J. (1966) *The Eucharistic Words of Jesus*, London: SCM Press.

Jones, C. P. M., Wainwright, G. and Yarnold, E. J. (eds) (1978) *The Study of Liturgy*, London: SPCK.

Jungmann, J. (1956) *The Eucharistic Prayer*, Wheathampstead: Anthony Clarke.

Kavannagh, A. (1983) 'Liturgy and Ecclesial Consciousness: A Dialectic of Change', Societas Liturgica IX Congressus Internationalis Vindobonae MCMLXXXIII Talks.

—— (1984) *On Liturgical Theology*, New York: Pueblos.

—— (1990) 'Liturgical Inculturation: Looking to the Future', *Studia Liturgica*, 20, 1, 95–106.

Kilpatrick, G. D. (1983) *The Eucharist in Bible and Liturgy*, Cambridge: Cambridge University Press.

McAdoo, H. R. (1949) *The Structure of Caroline Moral Theology*, London: Longman.

Martz, L. L. (ed.) (1986) *George Herbert and Henry Vaughan*, Oxford: Oxford University Press.

Mother Mary and Ware, K. (eds) (1969) *The Festal Menaion*, London: Faber and Faber.

Micklem, N. (1941) *Prayers and Praises*, Oxford: Oxford University Press.

Munson, J. (1991) *The Nonconformists: In Search of a Lost Culture*, London: SPCK.

Newman, J. H. (1875) *Parochial and Plain Sermons III*, London: Rivingtons.

Nuttall, G. F. (1947) *The Holy Spirit in Puritan Faith and Experience*, Oxford: Basil Blackwell.

Outlon, J. E. L. and Chadwick H. (eds) (1954) *Alexandrian Christianity, Library of Christian Classics*, London: SCM Press.

Plekon, M. (1992) 'Kierkegaard and the Eucharist', *Studia Liturgica*, 22: 214–36.

Prenter, R. (1977) 'Liturgy and Theology', in *Theologie und Gottesdienst: Gesammelte Aufsätze*, 139–51.

Rattenbury, J. E. (1948) *The Eucharistic Hymns of John and Charles Wesley*, London: Epworth Press.

Schmemann, A. (1966) *Introduction to Liturgical Theology*, London: Faith Press.

—— (1976) *Of Water and the Spirit*, London: SPCK.

—— (1987) *The Eucharist*, New York: St Vladimir's Seminary Press.

Stanwood, P. (ed.) (1967) *John Cosin: A Collection of Private Devotions*, Oxford: Clarendon Press.

Thornton, M. (1957) *Pastoral Theology: A Reorientation*, London: SPCK.

Tillich, P. (1949) *The Shaking of the Foundations*, London: SCM Press.

Tripp, D. K. (1991) 'Daily Prayer in the Reformed Tradition: An Initial Survey', *Studia Liturgica*, 21: 176–207.

Wakefield, G. S. (1957) *Puritan Devotion*, London: Epworth Press.

Ward, J. N. (1967) *The Use of Praying*, London: Epworth Press.

Whale, J. S. (1936) *Calvin*, in N. Micklem (ed.) *Christian Worship*, Oxford: Oxford University Press, 154–71.

Yarnold, E. (1972) *The Awe-Inspiring Rites of Initiation*, Slough: St Paul's Publications.

FURTHER READING

Allchin, A. M. and Hodges, H. A. (1968) *A Rapture of Praise*, London: SPCK.

Austin, G. (ed.) (1991) *Fountain of Life*, Washingon, DC: The Pastoral Press.

Bonhoeffer, D. (1982) *The Psalms*, Oxford: Sisters of the Love of God.

Bouyer, L. (1956) *Liturgy and Life*, London: Sheed and Ward.

Bradshaw, P. F. (1992) *The Search for the Origins of Christian Worship*, London: SPCK.

Brooks, P. (ed.) (1975) *Christian Spirituality*, London: SCM Pres.

Cabasilas, N. (1960) *A Commentary on the Divine Liturgy*, London: SPCK.

Childs, B. S. (1989) 'The Struggle for God's Righteousness in the Psalter, in T. A. Hart and D. P. Thimell (eds) *Christ in Our Place*, Exeter: The Paternoster Press.

Cuming, G. J. (1982) *A History of Anglican Worship*, London: The Macmillan Press Ltd.

Davies, J. G. (ed.) (1986) *A New Dictionary of Liturgy and Worship*, London: SCM Press.

Duquoc, C. and Florestan, C. (eds) (1990/3) 'Asking and Thanking', *Concilium*, London: SCM Press.

Morris, C. (1972) *The Discovery of the Individual*, London: SPCK.

Power, D. N. (1990) *Worship, Culture and Theology*, Washington, DC: The Pastoral Press.

Wakefield, G. (1992) *Bunyan the Christian*, London: HarperCollins.

White, J. F. (ed.) (1992) *Documents of Christian Worship*, Edinburgh: T. & T. Clark.

See also chapter 27, 28, 29, 31.

V

PRACTICAL THEOLOGY

INTRODUCTION

Peter Byrne

The notion that theology should have practical applications in social and personal life is integral to thinking about its status as a discipline of intelligence. Is it a mode of enquiry that leads to genuine insight or not? If it has nothing interesting to say about the practical dilemmas facing human beings, the answer can only be 'no'. All the chapters in this Part are committed to the conclusion that theology does offer insight into human affairs and seek to show what that insight might amount to in a number of areas of the ethical life. However, there are major problems in working out what that insight might be.

These chapters collectively, and James Gustafson's broad survey of the field of Christian ethics in particular, point to the unavailability in the contemporary world of simple models of the application of theology to ethics. They show that we cannot expect theology to offer a set of dogmatic claims about human life, or a set of biblical precepts, and then deduce moral conclusions from these. Dogmatic construction in our age is too aware of its own relativity and of the diversity among dogmatic theologies to provide that kind of basis for ethics. Biblically based ethics, be it drawn from teachings of the Bible or the exemplary portrait of Jesus, is likewise too aware of relativity and diversity in the understanding of Scripture to function in that geometric fashion.

This is to suggest that the theology *from* which moral insight may be drawn is no longer of the kind that could lead to a straightforward deduction of morals from dogma. Moreover, we must reflect that there is a new diversity in the ethical life *to* which theological insight is to be applied. This diversity arises in part out of the fact that theological moralists, even those in Western Europe and North America, no longer speak to a predominantly Christian culture. This latter fact suggests a crucial dilemma for the contemporary application of theology which is raised both in Gustafson's chapter and in John Morgan's on medical ethics. To the extent that substantive theological principles and models are used to guide moral reflection, that reflection runs the risk of simply being ignored as irrelevant to society at large. To the extent that theological ethics speaks to a wider culture in a moral language it comprehends, then it risks having no specific Christian theological content at all. Secular thinkers will see this dilemma as the basis for a rebuttal of the very possibility of theological ethics. The rebuttal can proceed further by noting that it is an apparent definitional truth about moral thought that its conclusions and modes of reasoning should be publicly accessible. Publicity and universality are what distinguish morality from a private code and moral reasons from mere personal hunches. Therefore, there could not be a distinctive ethics which was the result of the application of theology to practical life, since the price of its being distinctively theological would be that it was no longer ethics but rather the code of a closed group.

There is a theoretical response to be made to this secularist rebuttal of the possibility of the practical application of theology, but its possibility still leaves much work to be done in individual areas of the ethical life. The fact that modern culture is no longer Christian does entail that theological ethics must face with renewed determination the problem of how it can be ethics and theological. It must surely see itself as a contribution to a conversation whose goal is the moral advancement of humankind. To engage in that conversation with profit is to recognize theology's obligation to speak from itself but with a universal voice. All partners in this conversation – that is, all traditions, all reflective human beings – must likewise speak from themselves but with a universal voice. There is no prior, neutral language of ethical insight into which the traditions and viewpoints that engage in the conversation must first translate their contributions; so to think is one of the errors of contemporary, secular liberalism. The conversation will be enriched to the extent that those participating respect their own distinctive voices but use them to promote universal conclusions. In other words, the dilemma of particularity and universality in practical theology is to be solved by being true to particularity in the starting point of ethical reflection, but to seek universality in its endpoint.

One way in which Christian ethical teaching can maintain its relevance for a non-Christian culture is through seeing itself as a contribution to a natural law understanding of moral reality. This is in essence how Barrie Paskins treats traditional Christian perspectives on violence and warfare. It is his contention that the just war doctrine of moral theology remains relevant as a source of necessary moral restraints upon the conduct of warfare. It is not his concern to interrogate the theological sources in order to discern whether an authentic Christian concern should embrace a total pacifism. Rather, he judges the viability of moral teaching on warfare by reference to whether it makes sense of political realities. In the light of these, a just war ethic based in natural law remains valid, he concludes.

Edward Norman's chapter on the nature of the state is also concerned with the relations between Christian ethics and the political. Using the terms of this Introduction, we may say that one of his chief concerns is that the conversation between practical theology and contemporary, non-Christian culture has become too one-sided. That is to say, it is characterized by too ready an acceptance by theology of the final validity of contemporary political liberalism and its affirmations of the possibility and importance of the pursuit of human well-being through political advance. He characteristically affirms the existence of what he sees as an older wisdom which places limits on the final importance and success of reforming politics.

If Norman's chapter displays an attempt to free practical theology from too great an accommodation with secular modes of thought, Jack Dominian's attempt to set forth an ethic of pastoral counselling exhibits a readiness to re-shape theological attitudes by drawing upon insights from outside. His theme is the manner in which theological attitudes towards sin and the sinner need development in the light of Freudian and post-Freudian depth psychology. The result of his reflections is not the abandonment of theological models in the understanding of personal growth, but rather a re-examination of them in the light of insights from psychology. The ethic of counselling offered is still theologically driven, but the theology has altered in dialogue with external sources.

Dominian's chapter illustrates the shift in contemporary Christian ethics away from thinking that theology supplies ethics with a set of rules for conduct. This modest shift towards a more antinomian, personalist ethics is further illustrated in Helen Oppenheimer's general discussion of personal ethics. The person- and relational-centred paradigms for the ethical life she explores are, of course, partly in vogue because of developments, social and moral, in society as a whole. Like Dominian, she shows how such acceptance of external influences leads, not to an abandonment of theological resources in ethics, but to their revaluation. She also clearly demonstrates, through her critique of extreme libertarian emphases on autonomy as the be-all and end-all of ethics, that those resources have the power to correct and modify its partner in dialogue.

John Mahoney's discussion of the ethics of wealth exhibits a clear concern to relate the most pressing of contemporary concerns about wealth and social justice to theological fundamentals, in particular the Old Testament's prophetic tradition and the central Christian beliefs in creation, sin, incarnation and completion. He finds in these sources a complementary message which licenses both an injunction to individuals to use their God-given creativity to make wealth and an injunction to regard that wealth as having a social purpose and function.

The final two chapters in this Part illustrate the development of theological resources to cope with newly emerging problems. Medicine and medical ethics are not new. But the emergence of scientifically based health care in the twentieth century has brought a range of problems with it which cannot easily be catered for in the traditional humanist and theological codes that governed pre-modern medicine. John Morgan's chapter brings out the diversity of response to this range of problems evident within modern theology. In this way he reminds us of the diversity within the modern theological discussion of ethics and takes us back to James Gustafson's initial survey. Despite this diversity, Morgan's chapter brings out the way in which contemporary theological ethics has distinctive and worthwhile things to contribute to the contemporary debate about the purposes and parameters of medical science.

Christian theology evidently contains a doctrine of creation but the notion that this creation faces an ecological crisis which requires a review of human responsibility towards the animate and inanimate world is a feature of the present age. Stephen Clark's discussion of environmental ethics takes on board the standard criticism of the Christian doctrine of the creation as the part-cause of the humanly created ecological crisis. He nonetheless argues that Christian theology has resources to offer a better perspective on humanity and nature than the variety of 'pagan' responses he identifies in contemporary ecological thinking.

Careful study of the chapters in this Part will reinforce the point made in the beginning of this Introduction: the notion of 'applying' theology to practical life to produce a Christian ethics is too simple as it stands. Application involves construction and development. Contemporary theology bears upon practice and conduct via a process of dialogue. Dialogue is multifaceted. Theology is in dialogue with the practical problems themselves. Old problems acquire new aspects and entirely new problems arise. Hence existing theological models and doctrines must be looked at afresh in the light of new practical realities. Theology is in dialogue with other sources of insight into ethical life – at the cost of making itself irrelevant or turning itself into a private code for a sect. In the course of the dialogue that is ethics, theology finds its own modes of understanding under investigation. Hence, application leads to re-examination, construction and development in the ways illustrated by the chapters in this Part. The general problem for theology in this process, abstractly stated, is how to retain its identity and distinctiveness. These chapters collectively illustrate how that problem can be overcome.

33

THE IDEA OF CHRISTIAN ETHICS

James M. Gustafson

Long before Christian ethics became an academic and ecclesiastical discipline there were writings that prescribed or commended particular moral actions for Christians; the sorts of outlooks, dispositions and ends they ought to have; the justifying reasons for them; and the powers that made proper forms of life and action possible, or restrained them. The Bible does not provide the Church with an abstract coherent theory of Christian ethics, and thus within it are the seeds of various ideas that developed in the tradition in relation to different cultural contexts, to practical social and moral issues that emerged, and to varying theological emphases that were articulated.

In the Bible there are moral/legal codes of conduct, e.g. the Holiness code in Leviticus, proscriptions of certain actions in Pauline writings, and general commands such as the commandment to love. There are passages which take the form of exhortation and admonition more than precise prescriptions; these are found in the parenetic passages in the Pauline letters, in exemplary parables in Luke and other Gospels, and the description of actions which are mimetic of the life and death of Jesus. Thus there is biblical precedent for normative Christian ethics to be developed in the form of rules, of counsels, of ideals, and of exemplary narratives. In Pauline writings, e.g. 1 Corinthians 7 and 10–11, one finds discursive passages which in effect state various points that Christians ought to consider in determining their proper conduct without a decisive closure.

Passages which are both descriptive of the life of Christians and their community, and exhortative of what they ought to be are common in New Testament writings. There is no theory of virtue, such as Aristotle's and Aquinas's, but there are qualities of life that are presumed to be present as fruits of faith, or are expected to be present if trust and faithfulness are present in the community. Certain qualities, as in Galatians 5, love, joy, peace, patience, kindness, goodness, fidelity, gentleness and self-control, are described as gifts of the Spirit. Other qualities and actions are described as belonging to 'lower nature' and thus condemned: fornication, impurity, indecency, idolatry, quarrels, a contentious temper, envy, fits of rage, selfish ambitions, dissensions, party intrigues and jealousies. The Sermon on the Mount has been widely interpreted to indicate conditions which are blessed by God. Thus, certain conditions of human persons should display the proper being of faithful people, and presumably will issue in appropriate actions.

The possibilities of these commendable qualities are credited ultimately to the work of the Spirit, to thankful response for the work of Christ (1 John 4), to faith, or to proper obedience. But there are realistic interpretations of the constraints that inhibit the realization of these qualities, the powers of sin that continue to plague members of the community, e.g. as in Romans 7. The anthropology of the New Testament is the basis for interpretation of the being and acts of human beings, including Christians.

The prescriptions, proscriptions and admonitions, and the praiseworthy and blameworthy dispositions and actions are all given justifying reasons which are based in doctrines, or beliefs, about God, about Christ and the Spirit, and about the human condition. Christian ethics, unlike 'secular' ethics, are always set in a theological context, and in a context of the life and experience of those who believe. Even those passages which are adduced as support for natural law, e.g. Romans 1 and 2, function religiously as well as morally; they show a basis for a natural morality but make the point that this leaves all persons without excuse.

Thus the idea of Christian ethics is set within the larger framework of the ends and purposes of God, particularly God revealed in Christ, and the ends and purposes of human life which are never reducible simply to the moral but always are, in some sense, related to the creative, ordering, or redeeming work of God. In the Christian context, morality is never an end in itself. It is related to what God has done (as in the Covenant or in the work of Christ) as an 'indicative' that grounds the 'imperatives' or the possibilities of fruitful and faithful lives and actions; or it is related to the purposes of God who is the creator and ultimate orderer of all things and whose ends, e.g. God's kingdom, are to be realized either in present time or in the ultimate future, or to God's authoritative law or commands.

The singular and determinative event for interpreting the Divine for Christians is Jesus Christ, and thus, in one way or another, for ethics to be Christian they must be grounded in some interpretation of his person and/or work. This particular historical feature also distinguishes ideas of Christian ethics from ideas of ethics based solely on presumably natural or purely rational principles. Even in the New Testament the person and work of Christ have various significances for ethics; he is a teacher with authority because of who he is, his life is a pattern to be followed, his death and resurrection are the conditions of the freedom of Christians to be lived out in acts of love; the coming of God's kingdom which he proclaimed, and of which his life is at least a sign, assures hope; he reveals the graciousness of God so that all actions are responsive to the Divine goodness; and the power of the Spirit enables a transformation of the lives of those who have faith and even of all of creation.

Given the 'excess of meaning' which the Bible provides for the Christian community, there are grounds for developing a variety of ideas of Christian ethics in the tradition, including our own time. Different strands of the biblical sources become related in different ways to historical conditions, moral and social problems, patterns of philosophical thinking, and human experiences. When the community confronts new events, experiences and knowledge, either as threats or as resources, the idea of Christian ethics takes particular shapes. And different historic traditions, Orthodox, Roman Catholic, Anglican, Lutheran, Calvinist and Anabaptist, tend to authorize particular emphases in their ideas of Christian ethics.

Comprehensive accounts of Christian ethics, it follows from all of the above, have at least a rough coherence between doctrines of God as creator, redeemer and sustainer, emphases in christology, doctrines of human life, views of history and nature, the kinds of life that Christians are enabled and required to live, and even the appropriate or prescribed ways in which persons and groups ought to make moral choices. For example, churches stemming from the Radical Reformation appear to have a distinctive emphasis in their ethics, an emphasis on an ethics of faithful discipleship to Jesus, which includes readiness to bear the cross as well as conform to his earthly deeds and teachings as described in the Gospels. But this emphasis is improperly understood if it is not set in the context of that community's shared beliefs with other communities in the justifying and sanctifying work of Christ, of its understanding of sin and 'the world', and of the kind of ecclesiology that is normative for Christians.

It is not possible in this chapter to develop fully all the points of reference that are adduced in various ideas of Christian ethics. (For a different approach to organizing these ideas, see Gustafson (1986 and 1978: 139–43)). For interpretations of various christological to ethical themes, see H. R. Neibuhr (1951) and Gustafson (1968).

'ACTION GUIDES' AND CHRISTIAN ETHICS

One aspect of the idea of Christian ethics is how Christians do, or ought to, make choices which determine their actions. Two moments in this can be distinguished. What are the standards, values, ends, ideals, rules, or principles that ought to govern their actions? And, what processes of choice do, or ought, they to use? Casuistic applications of principles and rules, means/end calculations, intuitive insight, etc., are some of the alternatives.

The first moment points to the controverted issue of whether there are distinctive, specific or singular, unique standards that are obligatory for Christians, or whether the positive morality of Christians is in its content the same as for all other persons. Uniqueness is obviously the strongest claim; to establish it requires comparative historical studies. There can be distinctive emphases in positive Christian morality which are not unique, and there can be specific moral obligations or expectations for Christians which are not sufficient to determine their conduct in all areas of life. From such a position procedures of application of the distinctive emphases to general issues have to be developed. Claims that there is no distinctive positive Christian morality require philosophical and/or theological justification. These issues are very much a part of current discussion in Christian communities. (For positions taken in recent Roman Catholic and Protestant moral theology, see Curran and McCormick (1980 and 1991).) For the sake of verbal economy, 'distinctiveness' is used to cover all claims for a positive Christian morality.

Historically there have been strong claims for distinctive Christian morality. Some biblical bases have been alluded to above. The command to love not only one's neighbour as oneself, but also one's enemies; the exhortation to live so that conduct is mimetic of the life and death of Jesus and as literal adherence as possible to the 'hard sayings' of Jesus are examples. Dietrich Bonhoeffer's *The Cost of Discipleship* (1959), with its theme of suffering as the mark of Christian life, is probably the most powerful statement of this in our century. Part of the historical legacy has been the distinction between counsels of perfection that are not obligatory for all Christians but are for those with special vocations, and the standards of moral conduct applicable to all persons. Actions beyond normal standards are supererogatory. Countering this distinction have been the claims of some radical Reformation authors that Christians ought not to bear arms, not hold offices in the secular state, and ought to hold property in common, as well as Calvin's dictum that there is no supererogation in the Christian life. And certainly, in our time both within and outside the churches, Christian ethics is understood popularly to require behaviour according to historically distinctive standards; this is seen in the senses of guilt or inadequacy that many conscientious Christians feel in having to 'compromise' in their actions, and in the charges of moral hypocrisy that others often make against Christians.

For many students of Christian ethics, Ernst Troeltsch's differentiation of the ideal-type of the Church and its ethics from that of the sect and its ethics is used. The christology of the Church type is Christ as the universal Redeemer which recognizes that actions in 'the world' can be Christian even though they 'compromise' the stringent ideals and requirements of literal discipleship to Jesus. That of the sect type requires adherence to the pattern of life that the New Testament portrays Jesus as having led and taught since faithfulness to him is the fundamental mark of Christian ethics (Troeltsch 1949: 1: 321ff.).

Two contemporary American authors are the most visible proponents of distinctive positive Christian morality, John Howard Yoder and Stanley M. Hauerwas. Both establish their positions relative to their interpretations of the dominant forms of Christian ethics in both Protestantism and Catholicism.

Yoder, in *The Politics of Jesus*, cites what he believes to be six errors in the ways 'mainstream' Christian ethics has interpreted Jesus and his teachings: as an interim ethic, as a Franciscan and Tolstoyan simple rural figure, as living in a world over which Jesus and his followers have no control, as an ahistorical message by definition, as a radical monotheist, and as the unique one whose life was given for the atonement of human sins. As a result of these kinds of interpretation it is claimed that Jesus had no intention 'to provide any precise guidance in the field of ethics'. Thus for the content of decision-making other sources have to be used (Yoder 1972: 15–19). For Yoder, however, the lordship of Christ is the centre which must guide value choices 'or even to reject those values which contradict Jesus' (Yoder 1984: 11).

Yoder's position is authorized, as implied above, by the acceptance of 'biblical realism' which is not to be confused with literal inspiration types of fundamentalism. His supporting argument is necessarily exegetical, and is theologically backed by the conviction that God has been revealed in Jesus in the Scriptures. Among the moral outcomes of this view is not just the establishment of an exemplary community but also a passive but resistant response to evils in the world. How choices should be made in the light of these convictions is through a 'hermeneutics of peoplehood' in the disciplined Christian community, a process of corporate discernment (Yoder 1984: 15–45).

Hauerwas wrote that 'we Christians are not called on to be "moral" but faithful to the true story about God' who is perfectly faithful. The story is that humans are creatures under the lordship of God who wants nothing more than our faithful service; by this service we become not 'moral' but like God, 'holy'. Ethics is made Christian by the content of our conviction; 'it helps to understand the implications of the story for the kingdom' (Hauerwas 1983: 67–9). Becoming Christian cannot be reduced to being human in some universal sense for Hauerwas; there is a specificity to Christian conduct determined by the Christian story whose truth is made personal by participation in the community. In one development of this position Hauerwas's polemic is against Roman Catholic moral theologians, Timothy O'Connell, Josef Fuchs, Richard McCormick, Gerard Hughes and others for whom the content of morality is 'the human', and not distinctively Christian (see below). For Hauerwas, the biblical revelation is the authorization of his view.

There are different ways in which authors who claim a distinctiveness for Christian ethics relate that to various choices about life in the world, personal and social. Love, for example, has often been claimed to be the distinctive feature of Christian ethics, and *agapē* has been differentiated from other forms of love, e.g. *eros*, or *philia* (e.g. Nygren 1953; Barth 1958: 727–51; Tillich 1963: 135–40; Toner 1968; Outka 1972; Singer 1984: 268–311). Precisely what *agapē* means as an ethical term or reality is subject to a variety of interpretations. Gene Outka, in his cogent ethical analysis of *agapē* stresses 'equal regard', i.e. 'regard is for every person qua human existent, to be distinguished from those special traits . . . which distinguish particular personalities' (Outka

1972: 9). This focus requires critical assessment of other emphases, e.g. self-sacrifice, and the relation of *agapē* to self-love and to justice, its application to human relations in which special traits of persons are important, e.g. friendship and its application by subsidiary rules. Central to the discussion is the possibility of *agapē* being universally applicable. (Outka's is the most philosophically sophisticated examination of love as the distinctive theme of Christian ethics in the literature.)

Applications of love as the distinctively Christian theme in ethics vary according to how *agapē* is defined and the procedures adopted by various authors. Paul Ramsey (1950: 100) held a stringent view of *agapē* as 'inverted self-love' which has to be applied through justice when the needs of two or more neighbours conflict. In later writing he continues to adhere to love and faithfulness as the mark of Christian ethics and 'in-principles' it so it supports just war theory and is applicable to many procedures of medical experimentation and therapy. Reinhold Neibuhr's view of love as self-sacrificial is applied in a dialectic between *agapē*, mutuality and justice (Niebuhr 1943: 68–90). His procedure always maintained a critical tension between these terms so that, e.g., justice without the judgement of *agapē* tends to become less than justice, and *agapē* without justice remains an inapplicable ideal for politics, economics and international relations. Interestingly, Ramsey's procedures relieve the tension that Niebuhr's create; Niebuhr always leaves one with a sense of remorse, if not guilt, for not fulfilling love.

Critics of *agapē* as self-sacrifice adduce biblical, experiential, and philosophical evidences in their favour. Mutuality is seen to be a theme in the New Testament; Daniel Day Williams, for example, claims that love there 'is affirmed, not as a new ethical principle, but as the spirit of a new relationship of man and God' (Williams 1968: 41, see 41–51). Feminist theologians find the emphasis on self-sacrifice to be a denial of the proper self-love of which women have been deprived and argue that Christian love builds mutuality and community rather than demanding radical self-denial (Andolsen 1981). Process theology provides the philosophical basis for mutuality as characteristic of reality, ontological as well as interpersonal, for Williams and other authors.

Others move from love to particular problems through the development of middle axioms which define, in a sense, general goals and boundaries of appropriate policies and actions without precisely determining them. James Nash, for example, begins with love as the distinctive Christian ethical principle (and motive) and states six axioms to be followed in the politics of environmental issues, e.g. that the economics–ecology dilemma must always be resolved, and that the interests of future generations must be protected (Nash 1991: 192–221).

The issues involved in maintaining distinctive features of Christian ethics while engaging in 'public choices' with people of other religions traditions and with philosophers and others who eschew religious bases for morality receive heightened attention as Western nations become more pluralistic in their cultures and as Christian communities in dominantly non-Christian cultures seek to work with others to resolve social and political issues. (For an analysis of this issue in the ethics of Barth, Brunner, and Bonhoeffer, see Lovin, 1984). To put the issue in terms used by Josef Fuchs, what is the relation between the *Christianum* and the *humanum* in ethics (Fuchs 1983: 53–67)? For Yoder, Hauerwas and some others the Christian provides a prophetic critical stance towards the culture and society Christianity finds itself in as well as direction as to how the Christian community and its members ought to conduct their activities. For Ramsey, Niebuhr and many others not cited, the Christian ethic, whether by way of distinctive values, principles, or ideals, has to be applied procedurally to broader issues while retaining its particular identity. The other alternative is to claim that there is no distinctive positive Christian ethics, and that the *humanum* provides the content.

The contemporary forms of this general position have antecedents in the tradition. While Thomas Aquinas's treatise on natural law must be placed in its theological context of all things returning to God, it lays the ground for a rational basis for ethics in which all humans participate. The 'New Law' is not a different positive morality, but the work of the Spirit. Luther's ethics under the law are based upon rational determination of the forms of conduct that are appropriate to social roles and responsibilities which the Turk as well as the Christian can grasp. Richard Hooker laid a foundation for much subsequent Anglican ethics by developing reason and natural law as a basis for morality in distinction from the biblicistic 'Puritans' of his time. And many contemporary Protestants who wish to stress a distinctiveness to Christian ethics would agree with Gilbert Meilaender that 'although the Christian way of life is itself a particular one sustained within particular communities, it has within it more universal elements' (Meilaender 1991: 20).

Recent discussion within Roman Catholicism has been particularly vigorous. Bernard Häring is the most prominent author who stresses the biblical images and bases for Christian ethics, while also absorbing natural law. In *Free and Faithful in Christ* (1978), as in his earlier *The Law of Christ* (1961), he combines New Testament theological themes with ethics in a way that has wide appeal for many Roman Catholics. The theology accents love, liberty and fidelity, and issues in guidelines and norms that are both binding and liberating. These norms 'depend thoroughly on faith and thus are distinctively Christian' (Häring 1978: 1: 22–3). He distinguishes his position from that of Franz Böckle (1980), and by implication arguments similar to Böckle's, whose norms 'do not yield much in favor of a distinctively Christian ethics' (ibid.: 1: 23).

Strong arguments against distinctive positive Christian ethics have been developed by distinguished Jesuit and other Roman Catholic moral theologians. Josef Fuchs, the Jesuit writer, concludes that the norms of Christian morality are valid 'to the extent to which they proclaim truth', that is, 'are universally human and therefore also Christian – hence not distinctively Christian' (Fuchs 1983: 53). The categorical content of Christian morality is the *humanum*, a universal value and quality of human beings. Bruno Schüller comes to similar conclusions. Biblical ethics in his view is primarily exhortation, and he acknowledges that Christian faith and biblical ethics can be the 'genesis' of the morality of Christians. But the 'truth-value' of moral norms and insights is not dependent on their genesis. '[E]ven for the Christian the knowledge of the requirements of morality is, with logical priority, the object of his reason and not his faith' (Schüller 1986: 41; see also Schüller 1991). The English Jesuit, Gerard Hughes, argues that the use of biblical material as the ultimate authority for ethics leads to exegetical, hermeneutical and theological difficulties and concludes sharply 'that an independent morality is an essential tool in interpreting Christian tradition, since it enables us to distinguish the voice of God from the human voices' that speak in the tradition. One will only discover what God is saying in the Christian tradition 'by patient methods of moral philosophy which enabled us to hear him in the first place' (Hughes 1978: 24–5; cf. Kant 1960). These positions, interestingly, support the autonomy of ethics, a position argued for by many secular moral philosophers. (See also Curran and McCormick, and others in Curran and McCormick (1980 and 1991).) For all these authors it is reason and, in some sense, natural law that are the bases of ethics; for ethics to be ethics it must be universal and not historically particular. The distinctiveness of Christians' and the Church's moral activity is located elsewhere – in motivation, intentionality, interiority (see below).

Roman Catholic authors cite Protestant authors who come to virtually the same position on the non-distinctiveness of Christian morality, e.g., Rudolf Bultmann. Knud Løgstrup, a Danish Protestant theologian, was influenced by Bultmann and Friedrich Gogarten in the development of his ethics. His descriptive promises do not rest on traditional natural law, but on a phenomenology of moral experience; trust and distrust are its fundamental aspects. There is an 'unspoken demand' in relationships that calls for obedient action. After the development of such themes, Løgstrup has a chapter, 'The Impossibility of "Christian" Ethics'. In the proclamation of Jesus, God's demand to serve the other person's welfare is central; every word and deed should care for the other person. Decisions about what acts meet the silent demand are made by Christians 'on exactly the same bases as those upon which anyone else decides'. The Christian message is about the truth of our existence, and if one attempts to define specific Christian arguments about marriage, the purpose of punishment, etc., Christianity has become an ideology. The Christian 'must use reason, insight, and human considerations to clarify' action, and must appeal to the same sources in the other person (Løgstrup 1971: 111–21).

Other Protestants, who also appeal to the human, stress the transformation of people through faith and grace as necessary to grasp the universal. Paul

Lehmann arrived at 'the human' or 'humanization' as the purpose of morality via a biblical theology, rather than by reason alone. God's activity in the world is 'to relate men to each other in and through the enterprise of the new humanity', that is through enabling human maturity (Lehmann 1963: 131). This occurs in the context of particular events under ever-changing conditions. But formed by life in the community of faith, Christians can have theonomous consciences. 'The theonomous conscience is . . . immediately sensitive to the freedom of God to do in the always changing human situation what [God's] humanizing aims and purposes require' (ibid.: 358). The norm is the divine activity; conscience is the means to perceive what that is.

Knowledge of 'the human' is arrived at very differently by Fuchs, Schüller and other Roman Catholics and by Løgstrup and Lehmann, but what is truly human is universally so. This literature also never takes much account of the diverse interpretations of the human, the right and the good, that moral philosophers, psychologists and other scientists, and creative writers offer. To suggest that 'the human' is the norm for Christian ethics only moves the controversy to another sphere. It resolves nothing in and of itself.

The second moment, how Christians make their choices, or ought to make them, has been alluded to in some of the above. H. Richard Niebuhr's typology of humans as makers, as citizens or law abiders, and as answerers or responders, while stated as appropriate to all moral life, is applied to the life of Christians (Niebuhr 1963). 'Maker' suggests ideals, or ends which activity realizes, or approximates, or compromises in particular situations. K. E. Kirk, in his classic study of *The Vision of God* as the telos of the Christian life, wrote that 'the principal duty of the Christian moralist is to stimulate the spirit of worship in those to whom he addresses himself, rather than set before them codes of behavior' (Kirk 1931: x). For some others the end is the kingdom of God which is to be 'built' on earth, or which is delineated as a kingdom of love with practical approximations in cooperative, just social policies, e.g. Walter Rauschenbusch. In such a view historical social reforms are the means to begin to realize the kingdom. For others love is the ideal; means/ends thinking is the procedure for fulfilling Christian duties or opportunities.

'Citizen' suggests rules to be obeyed or applied, or commands to be heard and obeyed. When love becomes primarily a rule term, the strategy to apply it properly is to develop principles or middle axioms which are generated by it. Similarly, the precepts of natural law have to be applied as precisely as possible to courses of action. For many Christian fundamentalists the Bible provides rules of conduct which are to be obeyed, though they are selective as to which have current or continuing authority. Reason functions in the application of principles or rules; it can issue in stringent rigorism, as it has in ascetic Christianity and some contemporary Protestant and Catholic materials, or in more probabilistic ways (see Jonsen and Toulmin 1988).

Obedience to the commands of God continues to be defended as the most fitting approach to Christian morality. Karl Barth's ethics, with its stress on the particularity of divine commands in changing and specific occasions is the most widely known twentieth-century programme of this sort. One is to hear the divine command; to make choices on the basis of traditional practical reasoning is to usurp the prerogative of God. But Barth permits a 'practical' casuistry informed by Scripture (since the gracious God's commands are recorded there and God will not command anything contrary to his grace) and reflection on the occasion of action (Barth 1961). More recently, Richard Mouw has developed a 'comprehensive' divine command theory in which virtue ethics, agapism, 'a divinely implanted sense of justice', and an ethics of 'external law' become diverse strategies for moral surrender to the divine will (Mouw 1990: 2). Many Protestants have objected to the 'citizen' or law-abider view of ethics because it becomes heteronomous and legalistic, and can lead to works-righteousness, e.g. among others Paul Tillich.

For the 'responder' type as developed by both H. Richard Niebuhr and Paul Lehmann the first question is not what humans ought to do, but 'what is God doing?' As seen above, for Lehmann, that is humanizing work perceived by the theonomous conscience; for Niebuhr it involves a complex process of interpretation of events in solidarity with the community to establish what actions are fitting.

These, and other procedures, all require that the specific sphere (Barth's term) or context in which human action occurs has to be interpreted. The debate of 'context vs. principles' that flourished for some years was, in fact, contention over which of the terms was to be dominant. The 'contextualism' of Joseph Fletcher (1966) and J. A. T. Robinson (1963) was an example of one extreme; neo-Thomist manuals of moral theology and Paul Ramsey's reaction to Fletcher, Robinson and Lehmann are examples of the other extreme.

MORAL AGENTS AND CHRISTIAN ETHICS

A second aspect of the idea of Christian ethics is the construal of moral agents and activity, personal and collective, in the light of Christian beliefs and experiences. Moral philosophers provide different interpretations of the nature of moral agency; some stress rationality and the capacity of reason to determine volitions, some stress basic drives or orientations of persons, e.g. towards pleasure of happiness; some stress the power of traditions and the communities that embody them to shape and form persons. Moral philosophers have to account for human failure; it is wrong reason, or weakness of will, or improper socialization. They also have views on how to correct moral failures. The formal structure of moral anthropologies is shared by all, or most, moral theorists. The moral anthropologies of Christian writers set these issues in a particular theological and religious context. Moral failure, for example, has historically been defined as disobedience to the will of God;

it is a form of sin, and sin is a theological and religious term as well as a moral term. Its antidote is not only better practical reasoning, but the effects of religious faith and openness to the redemptive powers of the Spirit, for example. Confining attention to the significance of sin and grace does not permit a description of all relevant features of Christian moral anthropology, but does provide a way to indicate the importance of choices made by theologians.

Christian ethical ideas are affected by the extent of corruption theologians claim to be the effect of the Fall, whether that is interpreted historically or mythically. Generally the Orthodox, Roman Catholic, and Anglican traditions have had more confidence in the continuation of powers of the image of God in the human than classic Reformation theologies and their descendants. Appeals to the use of reason to give knowledge of the universally human content of morality in both historic and contemporary moral theologians assume less corruption than many Protestants accept. If rational capacities are corrupted by sin, our knowledge of the right and the good is distorted. Classically, and throughout the tradition, one locus of the moral fault is in the 'will', the power to determine one's conduct according to the good and right that can be known. Thus St Paul, in Romans, claims that we have natural knowledge of what we ought to be and do, and therefore are without excuse in not doing it. The good we would, we do not; the problem is in the weakness or corruption of the will. Radical conversion of the person is required; participation in Christ and the presence of the power of the Spirit are correctives which enable people to have commendable dispositions and to act in morally proper ways.

For the purposes of this chapter, four loci of sin will be distinguished as follows (they are not necessarily mutually exclusive):

1 Disorientation of the ends of natural desires.
2 Unfaith or misplaced trust.
3 Disobedience.
4 Historical social structures.

Each affects the locus of accountability, and the remedy is to some extent determined by it.

1 Disorientation of the ends of natural desires

Disorientation of natural loves or desires is interpreted by Anders Nygren (1953) and others as continuing the influence of the *eros* interpretation of love, and the neo-Platonic influences on theology and ethics. Classic statements of it can be found in the theology and ethics of Augustine and in the basic framework of Thomistic theology. Humans are by their created natures oriented towards their good, and the human community by its nature is oriented towards its common good. The fault lies in the improper ends towards which our desires are directed, and in the disproportion of the intensity of our love, i.e. in excessive or deficient love for proper objects. The trajectory of not only our eternal well-being but also our personal and historic well-being is diverted from those proper ends by sin. Thus, as Augustine says, when our love is curved in upon ourselves, our actions and orderings of life are corrupted.

In Aquinas's anthropology more precise distinctions of aspects of the human are made according to categories adapted from Aristotle; we are vegetative, sensible, and rational beings. If our inclination and actions were rightly ordered by our rational apprehension of the proper ends of the human we would also be rightly ordered as agents. The theoretical correlative of this is confidence that there is an objective moral order of nature that is human, social and also cosmic, an order of Being. The ultimate end of life is union with, vision of, or friendship with God. A properly ordered moral life keeps us oriented towards this end; our particular sinful acts keep us from this end.

The corrective of sin comes through the redemption of humans in Christ; it is only in Christ that the grace which empowers and directs human life towards its proper temporal and eternal ends is possible. Humans can cooperate with this grace; they can participate in the divine love, *caritas*, which is the mother and root and form of all the moral virtues. The structure of the moral anthropology makes it possible to grow, or develop, in the moral life; infused theological virtues, in a sense, penetrate, order and direct us towards our proper ends.

Thus, the remedy for sin as disorientation is the power of divine grace, known in Christ and through the Church, to direct life towards God as its true end, and thus reorder our desires and the action we choose towards proper moral ends. The fundamental theology of the Eastern Orthodox tradition provides one example of this. As in all traditional Christian theology, the chief end of the human is not properly morality, but salvation, in this case participation in the divinization (*theosis*) of all of life: human, social and cosmic. *Theosis* is the central concept which integrates the Trinitarian and mystical theology of the Orthodox tradition with the true end of humans and all creation, and with the efficacious remedial processes of human experience in the liturgical and communal life of the Church. The triune God is the good, and the goodness of the world is formed by the divine presence in the world as Spirit, as divine energies. Dumitru Staniloae writes that Spirit 'is experienced as a kind of fluid spiritual atmosphere which rises within us and raises us up towards God in ever greater understanding and love' (Staniloae 1980: 25; also Harakas 1983). Love is not so much a moral principle as it is 'a total disposition toward life' (Guroian 1987: 43); it is the mother of every good. It develops and enhances the capacity for self-determination in people so that they can act more in accordance with *theosis*. In a sense somewhat similar to classic Roman Catholic ethics, the divine love becomes the mother and root of all moral virtues, empowering them and directing them through choices that are in accord with the divine will and powers.

2 Unfaith or misplaced trust

Evidence for the idea of sin as unfaith or misplaced trust can be found in the Bible and throughout the history of theology. The idea was accented in the Reformation, in part due to the rejection of moral anthropologies which tempted people to claim righteousness before God as a result of their moral growth. A classic formulation of this is found in Luther's 'Large catechism' (Tappert 1959: 365):

> [T]he trust and faith of the heart alone make both God and an idol. If your faith and trust are right, then your God is the true God. . . . That to which your heart clings and entrusts itself is . . . really your God.

The root term in the moral anthropology is no longer love or desire, but trust; sin, rather than being disorientation of desire, is trust in the wrong objects.

With various alterations this idea has been present in the work of recent Protestant theologians. Against the background of his philosophical theology, Paul Tillich could write that the Protestant principle 'is the guardian against the attempts of the finite and conditioned to usurp the place of the unconditional in thinking and acting' (Tillich 1948: 163). It functions as a prophetic stance against the absolutization in personal and social life of all that is less than 'God'. Reinhold Niebuhr's interpretation of anxiety as the precondition of sin leads to the idea of sin as overcoming that anxiety by undue trust in all that is less than God; this issues in a distortion of valuations by individuals and by collectives (Niebuhr 1943: 1: 178–240). H. Richard Niebuhr interprets faith as a reality in all human experience; it names the objects of our confidence and our loyalty, our trust and our faithfulness (H. R. Niebuhr 1960: 16–23). His monotheism points to the One beyond the Many which relativizes all the many loyalties and calls humanity to a universal object of confidence and loyalty. In different ways for all three of these thinkers the Christ event gives knowledge which makes God ultimately trustworthy; e.g., in H. Richard Niebuhr it is only through Christ that we have assurance that God is the Redeemer, that we can know God as friend rather than enemy (H. R. Niebuhr 1963: 174–8).

As with other interpretations of sin, a theologian's account of the person and work of Christ is crucial to the ethical outcomes that are claimed. In Reinhold Niebuhr, the stress is on the freedom to restrain the evil in the world in somewhat pragmatic ways, though grace is also a new empowerment. As with Luther, strong powers of sin continue, and thus excessive confidence in human moral achievements can lead to pride and to actions with morally bad outcomes. But the coming of the kingdom, known through Christ, points to an assurance of the fulfilment of the right and good 'beyond tragedy' which necessarily accompanies life in history. Trutz Rendtorff, after quoting Romans 12: 1–2, states that 'the Christian life is by its nature a life lived through faith. It is living out of freedom.' The exposition of the significance of this Pauline theme is a description of how human beings, in this defined way, structure relationships and act through 'their personal and social, historical and political individuality in their relationship to God' (Rendtorff 1986: 1: 151 and 152).

The language of sin as unfaith, misplaced faith, or idolatry has its antidote in proper faith, in God revealed as Redeemer, in one sense or another. Whereas the language of love or desire as the primary term in moral anthropology lends itself to 'growth in grace', and thus to a more virtue-centred ethics, the relationship of trust is a more personalistic analogy, stressing freedom more radically, and tends to limit the possibilities of an ethics of virtue such as one finds, for example, in Aquinas. Sometimes these matters have been stated so as to show a fundamental difference between Roman Catholic (and by implication Orthodox) ethics and Protestant ethics. Thus, Barth wrote, 'between the Roman Catholic view and our own stands a difference in the concept of God, of man, of the sin of man, and grace which comes of him' (Barth 1981: 30). The analogy of Bring in contrast to the analogy of faith lends itself to an anthropology of desires and loves, of sin as disorder in relationship to the order of being, and to grace as infusion and penetration of the characteristics of humans.

3 Disobedience

The idea of sin as disobedience is also deeply rooted in biblical materials and in various ways throughout the history of Christian ethical thought, and has been related to sin as both misplaced desires and misplaced trust. Deontological patterns of ethics have coexisted historically with teleological patterns, and been integrated into them. The corollaries of obedience are law and commands. In Augustine and throughout the tradition one finds statements that sin is disobedience to the law of God, or to the commands of God. The idea of the law of God takes different forms.

In classic theological natural law theories, the moral law of God is part of the structure of humans, of their relations to each other, and the relations of all things which are ordained to serve the common good. Practical inferences of 'secondary' laws or rules can be derived from the descriptive premise that we incline towards the good and shun the evil. In a teleological structure, nonconformity to principles and rules is a diversion from an orientation to the true temporal and eternal good of humans; conformity keeps us in the right trajectory.

Thus, sinful acts can be delineated, numbered, graded with reference to their severity, in a way that assumes a somewhat legalistic structure of Christian ethics (Mahoney 1987: 2–36). The penitential disciplines in Roman Catholic life developed the norms of precise conduct to which the stated types of action are to conform. Indeed, Christian ethics in this strand of history, present most vividly in the neo-Thomist manuals of moral theology, becomes strategies to avoid sin, and disciplines required to compensate for sinful acts. Acts of disobedience to moral laws and rules are impediments to being rightly oriented towards our true temporal and eternal ends.

This pattern has been defended in relation to the biblical authority of Christian ethics. For some the revealed moral laws in the Bible are positive statements of the natural law. Calvin, for example, agreed with the received Catholic tradition on this. While no theory of natural law can be found in the Bible, Romans 1 and 2, the doctrine of the *imago dei*, and the christology that sees all things created in and through Christ have been argued to be a basis for it (Fuchs 1965).

For some authors whose view of Christian ethics must be grounded solely in the Bible, the revealed law of God is that which is to be obeyed. Historically a distinction has been drawn between the revealed ceremonial laws, which are abrogated by Christ, and the revealed moral law, which continues to have authority. Revealed moral law has had different degrees of authority for ethics that adheres to it.

In biblical literalism, laws are presumably applicable to current circumstances, though there is always selection of what is most important.

> The Christian ethic is a specially revealed morality.... It gains its reality in and through supernatural disclosure.... Its fountainhead is the will of God. It is received in the Divine confrontation of man by commandments, statutes and laws, and face-to-face in the incarnation.
>
> (Henry 1957: 193)

One possible practical application of revealed law is through casuistic processes, for which there is ample precedent in the Covenant Code in Exodus and the Holiness Code in Leviticus. Another is more immediate application to particular conditions deemed sinful, e.g. homosexuality. In this pattern the laws and commands of God are right because God commands them; God does not command all of them simply because they are right. Sin is disobedience to these commands and laws.

Not all Christian ethical systems that are presumably based solely on the Bible take this more legalistic form. Karl Barth, for example, argues that the moral laws in the Bible are summaries of individual commands of God. The theological support for this view is the freedom of the gracious God to command what is proper in particular contexts. Sin is disobedience to the particular commands of God given to particular people; the biblical commands and laws, including the teachings of Jesus, are not likely to differ from a present command of God, and thus the obedient person will presume that their direction is morally correct, but he or she will not apply them casuistically because this is to usurp the divine prerogatives, i.e., to make the person the determiner of the right and the good rather than God the commander. Thus the deeper sin is this usurpation; Barth can even suggest that human ethics is sin precisely because of this (Barth 1957: 631–61). The antidote is faith in the gracious God revealed in Christ, in the Gospel; its effect is to endorse the reality of the good, which is God, in obedient actions to God's commands.

4 Historical social structures

In recent years a new emphasis has been put on sinful social structures, or structural sin. This comes from the recognition that there are evil institutional and cultural patterns of economic and political injustice and oppression, of racism and sexism, which have determinative power, with dehumanizing outcomes for people and communities. They serve the interests of specific groups to the exclusion of the dignity and the fundamental human needs of others.

Perhaps the root sin in this view is injustice, which takes a variety of forms: failure to respect the dignity and full basic humanity of all people regardless of their specific racial, gender or other characteristics; exploitation of others for personal or corporate gains; violation of the rights of others by using subtle as well as overt tactics; victimization which results from this and often is interpreted so that the victims are responsible for their plight; unfair exclusions from access to social and economic power which are the conditions for people and communities to determine their own destinies; wanton destruction of the natural environment for economic gains which has deleterious outcomes not only for the environment but also for the long-term well-being of humans and other life forms.

Theologies of political and economic liberation, feminist theologies, black theologies, *dalit* theology in India and its counterparts in other parts of Asia and elsewhere all are fuelled by the fundamental perception that concentrations of power, backed by ideologies or cultural custom, demean people who under these conditions are not responsible for their conditions of poverty and discrimination. The tools for the exposure of the structural sins are social, political, economic, and psychological analyses developed from the perspective of their victims. Christian social ethics' first task, in this general perspective, is one of prophetic indictment not only of current realities all over the world but also of those aspects of the Christian tradition which have explicitly or implicitly sanctioned them. For example, natural law ethics has tended to justify existing orders of society as expressions of the natural moral order; harmony between people and parts of the social order has been its tacit norm and conflict has been judged aberrant. Conflict models of society, based upon the striving for forms of justice, is the alternative. Patriarchalism is held up as a heritage of the biblical and Christian traditions which have legitimated male dominance, and still dominate life in churches as well as society in spite of appeals, made by Pope John Paul II and others, for respect for fundamental human dignity.

The practical antidote to sinful structures is radical social reform, and even in some cases violent revolution. The redeeming and salvific purposes of God are not only, or even primarily, directed towards the eternal well-being of individuals, but must penetrate the ways in which economy, politics, and social relations are structured and conducted in present historical circumstances. The kingdom of God is not just a future reality, but must be actualized more and more in history. Its symbol is the basis for radical relativization of all current social arrangements, as in the theology of Jürgen Moltmann as well as Roman Catholic and other theologians.

Accountability for sinful social structures is more diffuse than views of sin which are focused on individual people, their acts and the consequences of them. These structures are the effects of many choices and processes over long periods of history, and of institutionalized centres of power within which accountability is also diffuse. Systems, and not just individuals, are at fault. Rarely, if ever, in the traditional ideas of Christian ethics has such analysis appeared. Indeed, this view of sin might well be the major innovation of moral theology in our time.

Some personal acts of traditional sins are conditioned by the powers of domination which are not under the control of individuals. For example, divorce, considered sinful by much of Christian tradition, is set in the context of the repressive effects of certain traditions of marriage and of the wider social factors which make commitments to lifetime marriage more tenuous. Thus divorce does not have the same blameworthiness that was attributed to it historically. The sins and crimes that are committed in conditions of racial segregation and poverty are interpreted in the light of those conditions, and thus a moral indictment of society becomes prominent. Violence, traditionally justified by just war theory in relations between states, can now be justified as a last resort within political communities and societies. Human actions in pursuit of justice, motivated by the sense of injustice, and in Christian contexts seen to be a violation of dignity of the human and the justice of God, are the means of redemption.

'SPIRITUALITY' AND CHRISTIAN ETHICS

Several ways in which the person and work of Christ have effects upon the idea of Christian ethics have been noted in parts of this chapter: Christ as pattern, as teacher, earlier as redeemer whose work brings inner freedom, as mediator of grace that heals and restores nature, as empowering a theonomous conscience, as the source of specific new interiority and motivation. Other examples are now noted to call attention to the wide range of claims that may be made.

K. E. Kirk's classic study argues that 'Christianity came into the world with a double purpose, to offer men the vision of God, and to call them to pursuit of that vision' (Kirk 1931: 1). The fundamental problem of ethics is 'What is humanity's true end?' As he demonstrates, there are many interpretations of how the vision is to be pursued. But various elements are usually included: transition from darkness to light, or from incompletion to completion, or from illusion to truth; joy and conformity to the divine will, and perhaps most importantly 'the sense that personal contact or intercourse with God is of the essence of that towards which the good life is directed' (ibid.: 466). Here we have a profoundly mystical element, as in Eastern Orthodoxy and other forms of Christianity, stressed as an essential part of the moral life.

The idea of vision has more recently taken a moral epistemological direction. Hauerwas and others, in part influenced by Iris Murdoch, have stressed that Christian faith provides a way of viewing life in the world which calls attention to aspects of its goods and evils and gives guidance to the ends and means to be pursued. Timothy Sedgwick develops 'sacramental ethics' that gives 'a vision of the Christian life which signifies the meaning of the paschal in relations and conflicts of daily life, and thereby enables such a life' (Sedgwick 1987: 24).

Worship, liturgy, and spirituality are united to moral life in these recoveries of an ancient tradition. A contemporary interpretation of Orthodox ethics states it well: there is a unity, continuity, and commensurability of *lex orandi*, *lex credendi*, and *lex bene operandi* when 'the human being is, above all else, a worshipping creature whose very act of worship . . . is to establish or deepen belief and to do good'. There is a 'process, once worship is present, of each mode of activity informing, influencing, and strengthening the other' (Guroian 1987: 52).

Moral theology influenced by the work of Karl Rahner, e.g. that of Josef Fuchs, emphasizes that 'Christian existence, and especially its vitality, is a work not only in actors of reflective consciousness but also in those non-thematically and non-reflectively conscious acts which animate and penetrate conscious moral behavior' (Fuchs 1983: 27). The conduct of human ethics for Christians is 'open and related to Christian existence', to the reality of 'the person of Christ, the Spirit at work in us, the Christian community, the hierarchical Church, the sacraments, Christian anthropology' (ibid.: 63). The different 'interiority' of agents is effective in both conscious and unreflective moral activity.

Somewhat different is the interpretation of Christian ethics that is grounded in the resurrection of Christ, and develops the consequences of this both for the world in which we live and in persons as moral agents. Oliver O'Donovan's complex 'Outline for Evangelical Ethics' is based on the following, among other claims: 'Christian ethics depends upon the resurrection of Jesus Christ from the dead' (O'Donovan 1986: 13). The outcome of the resurrection is a vindication, redemption, and transformation of the objective moral order (ibid.: 56), thus Christian ethics has an objective ground. The incarnation reveals the moral order, and Christ's resurrection 'publically and cosmically' vindicates it. Its 'subjective reality' is the powerful work of the Spirit, of God at work within us, which restores our access to reality, and evokes our free response to it (ibid.: 112 and 102). The emphasis of O'Donovan on the significance of the resurrection, one notes, is very different from that of Jürgen Moltmann, for whom it is the ground of confidence that humans are not in bondage to unchanging forms and orders of life (Moltmann 1971: 102–26). Whereas other authors focus on the crucifixion of Jesus as the central event for Christian moral life, O'Donovan focuses on the resurrection.

The ways in which the person and work of Christ have been taken to affect the idea of Christian ethics have not been exhausted. The fact that those noted, and others besides, all find precedent in the New Testament points again to the 'surplus of meaning' in the Bible, and to the fact that different emphases occur in relation to particular traditions, philosophical interests, and events.

ESCHATOLOGY AND ECCLESIOLOGY AND CHRISTIAN ETHICS

In comprehensive interpretations of the idea of Christian ethics several aspects of Christian doctrine are related to each other as well as to the ethical system which coheres with them. This has been stated and implied above. Attention is here called to some features which have not been isolated for development.

The import of eschatological views has only been noted. Whether the kingdom of God is primarily a future reality that assures the ultimate triumph of good over evil, as e.g., in Reinhold Niebuhr, or is more a present reality that is to be realized in the ordering of life, as e.g. in American social gospel teaching, makes a difference in the ethics which cohere with each view. Whether the final fulfilment of all things is primarily developed in terms of history, or whether it is the consummation of nature as well makes a difference in what sources of moral norms are appropriate, e.g., the realization of social justice in historical liberation, or nature as a source of moral ends and principles (see Schuurman 1991). The kingdom can be the basis for a radical prophetic critique of all existing structures of life, and an assurance of the possibility of radical historic change without providing much particular guidance to human activity, or it can provide a vision of peace, justice and the integrity of creation (as in current vogue) which becomes the basis both for care and for ends and principles in the conduct of life relative to the natural as well as the social world. Clearly, how writers delineate views of eschatology affects their interpretations of history and society, as well as their interpretations of the final ends of individual humans. These, in turn, affect but do not determine the loci of concentration of moral issues, the sources of moral norms, and the ways in which Christian ethics is ultimately justified theologically.

Ecclesiological issues have also only been noted. Ideas about the Church in more systematic treatments of Christian ethics are correlated with other doctrines. This can be shown by suggesting, more than he himself does, the ecclesiological corollaries of H. Richard Niebuhr's familiar typology of Christ and culture (1951). The idea of 'Christ against culture' tends to issue in a strong stress on the Church as a community clearly differentiated from the world, on the requirements of explicit faith and belief for membership in it, on internal discipline of its members, on either a model of an exemplary community with an alternate culture and/or one of a prophetic community which both judges the world and acts against its moral and social evils. The idea of the 'Christ of culture' tends to issue in a somewhat complacent view of the Church, often the bourgeois Church in Western societies, in which the culture is viewed as strongly Christianized, and thus the tensions between it and Christ are lessened. 'Christ above culture', as Niebuhr delineates the type, is seen in classic Roman Catholicism which could defend existing social institutions but be basically concerned with the supernatural ends of individuals. 'Christ and culture in paradox' suggests a Church which is primarily concerned with the preaching of the Gospel for salvation together with assurance that the political and social orders are realms of God's law or ordering activity. 'Christ transforming culture' tends to be seen in ecclesiologies which, while distinguishing between Christ and culture, see the Church as engaged in the transformation of institutions and culture through the activity of its members.

CONCLUSION: THE CONTINUING ISSUES

Some of the continuing issues for Christian ethics have formed the structure of the body of this chapter, and alternative positions have been described. (For my own position on these and others, see Gustafson (1975, 1981 and 1984).) To conclude this survey and analysis controverted issues will be isolated and stated more abstractly. Any comprehensive and coherent development of Christian ethics requires choices about these issues: various positions are briefly stated.

The relations between theology and ethics

1 Theology is clearly prior to ethics in determining the content and structure of ethics. The procedures for authorizing the ethics might be quite strict deductive logic based on metaphysical theology or on themes of biblical theology. Or the theology might be used to provide vindicating beliefs which set the basic direction of Christian ethics and the parameters within which it develops, i.e. not relying on strict deductions.

2 A coherent correlation between theology and ethics can be developed without claiming strict priority of authority for one or the other. This position opens the possibility of particular inconsistencies when the general coherence

has failed; either the theology will get preference over the ethics, or vice versa.

3 The ethical is clearly prior to the theological. What are judged to be necessary theological or metaphysical assumptions to defend the ethical position become the theology in some cases. In others, more common in recent literature, various theological principles and themes are adduced, or simply borrowed, to show a plausible theological justification for the ethical.

The authority and role of the Bible

1 The Bible is understood by some to be the revelation of propositional truths about God, and to be a revealed morality, though selection is made of which 'propositions' are more valid and which moral prescriptions are absolute.

2 A more common position among Protestants is that ethics must be grounded, informed and directed by biblical exegesis. Judgements have to be made about which theological and ethical themes of the Bible are critical in determining both the form and the dominant content of motifs of the ethics.

3 Examples of different themes are law and Gospel; liberation; eschatological ethics of hope; orders of creation; love as the central reality of God and thus of Christian ethics; transformation of moral agents through grace; *theosis* – the gracious transformation of the cosmos; faith and participation in the sacraments; ethics of the imitation of Christ or discipleship; and the kingdom of God as an ideal moral social order; humans as deeply corrupted sinners, etc.

4 Differences with reference to form are the interpretation of God in terms of active agent in events, and thus ethics as a response to God's prior action; God as law-giver and commander which can lead to more casuistic ethics or ethics of divine commands; and God as the ordering power of the right relations of all things to each other as they move to their *telos*, issuing as the ethics of natural law.

5 The Bible can be understood as the sole source of sacred doctrine, as the divine revelation about salvation, while ethics has a somewhat independent grounding available to all humankind, as in classic Roman Catholicism.

6 The Bible places particular obligations on Christians following from their faith, e.g. to live a life of self-denying service, which are not incumbent on all people, in addition to obligations they share with all others.

7 The Bible is an informing and corroborative authority for ethics without being decisive for particular moral actions.

711

The adaptation and use of non-biblical, non-theological materials

This heading refers to philosophical, scientific and social scientific, literary, experiential, and other resources that play ancillary or decisive roles in the formulation of Christian ethics. The scope of this heading is vast; only suggestions of what materials are used and how they are used are listed.

1 A moral theory, Kantian, Aristotelian, neo–Platonic, utilitarian, pragmatic, or other, provides the morphology of a position in Christian ethics.

2 A social theory, Marxist, hierarchical, consensual, feminist, or other, is used to analyse circumstances being addressed, and as one basis for the desirable outcomes of intentional moral activity.

3 Epistemological theories are used to analyse critically other positions and to provide backing for a position espoused, e.g. the current debate between 'anti-foundationalism' and 'foundationalism'.

4 Interpretations of the nature and activity of humans are adapted in forms of moral anthropology, e.g. historically, the free-will controversy; more recently, various positions from psychology, cultural anthropology, biology, and other sciences.

5 Issues that emerge in the society and culture give direction to the practical and theoretical issues addressed by Christian ethics, e.g. in recent times, sexism, racism, classism, emancipatory vs. oppressive forms of expression in literary and other cultural and social activities, etc. A focus of the agenda is shaped by issues emerging from technology and science as well, e.g. the ecological crisis turns authors towards the descriptive and analytical materials that depict that problem and affect the selection of theological and ethical themes.

6 Quite untheoretical observations are made about various human experiences, and about the nature of historical events which are adduced as evidences or as illustrations of Christian ethical positions.

The reconstruction of Christian ethics in the light of recent movements

1 For example, some innovations of the past decades have not had lasting influence, e.g. radical situation ethics, theologies of secularity and of the laity. Others have become so widely accepted that they are conventional wisdom, particularly theologies and ethics of liberation. At the time of writing, feminist Christian ethics are being developed in various parts of the world, but no dominating account has emerged.

2 The interaction between historic non-Christian and new religious movements with Christian theology has been the focus of more attention than the relations of the ethics and ways of life of these movements to Christian ethics. Comparative religious ethics is likely to develop more rapidly than it has in

the past decades during which it was formed as a sub-discipline in religious studies.

3 The persisting issue, discussed more fully above, will remain how Christian ethics will maintain a historic identity while at the same time communicating and supporting or criticizing not only secular ethical theories but also public policy and moral issues of modern society. These junctures can be addressed from two directions:

(a) efforts to resolve the general and theoretical issues of the relations of historically particular ethics to some universal form of ethics, or

(b) focus on specific areas of moral activity and social policy to find such consensus as is possible, when supporting views from different background beliefs, including Christian ones, are adduced.

This 'conclusion' does not exhaust the continuing issues for the idea of Christian ethics; it is suggestive enough for readers to extend it, and to make its implications more precise. One conclusion can be made with certainty: there will continue to be various patterns of Christian ethics with various emphases on different forms, themes, contents, and problems. The surplus of meaning in the Bible, the continuing effect of different historic traditions, and the emergence of new and different contexts for writing have this effect. What will be interesting to watch is this: whether coalitions of Christian ethics around particular themes and issues, e.g. liberation, feminism, spirituality, and ecology which already cross boundaries of historic traditions will lead to radical reformulations of ideas and thus to an alteration of historical alliances and identities, and perhaps to formulate novel issues of Christian ethical theory. Feminist Christian ethics, so far mostly addressed to particular social and moral issues, and public affairs is likely to become innovative in radical ways.

REFERENCES

Andolson, B. H. (1981) 'Agape in Feminist Ethics', *Journal of Religious Ethics*: 9: 69–83.

Barth, K. (1957) *Church Dogmatics*, II/2, Edinburgh: T. & T. Clark.

—— (1958) *Church Dogmatics*, IV/2, Edinburgh: T. & T. Clark.

—— (1961) *Church Dogmatics*, III/4, Edinburgh: T. & T. Clark.

—— (1981) *Ethics*, New York: The Seabury Press.

Böckle, F. (1980) *Fundamental Moral Theology*, New York: Pueblo Publishing Company.

Bonhoeffer, D. (1959) *The Cost of Discipleship*, London: SCM Press.

Childress, J. F. and Macquarrie, J. (1986) *The Westminster Dictionary of Christian Ethics*, Philadelphia: The Westminster Press/SCM Press.

Curran, C. E. and McCormick, R. A. (eds) (1980) *Readings in Moral Theology*, vol. 7, *Natural Law and Theology*, New York: Paulist Press.

—— (1991) *The Distinctiveness of Christian Ethics*, vol. 2, *Natural Law and Theology*, New York: Paulist Press.

Fletcher, J. (1966) *Situation Ethics*, Philadelphia: The Westminster Press.

Fuchs, J. (1965) *Natural Law*, New York: Sheed and Ward.

—— (1983) *Personal Responsibility and Christian Morality*, Washington: Georgetown University Press.

Guroian, V. (1987) *Incarnate Love*, Notre Dame: University of Notre Dame Press.

Gustafson, J. M. (1968) *Christ and the Moral Life*, New York: Harper & Row.

—— (1975) *Can Ethics be Christian?*, Chicago: University of Chicago Press.

—— (1978) *Protestant and Roman Catholic Ethics*, Chicago: University of Chicago Press.

—— (1981, 1984) *Ethics from a Theocentric Perspective*, 2 vols, Chicago: University of Chicago Press.

—— (1986) 'Christian Ethics', in J. F. Childress and J. Macquarrie (eds) *The Westminster Dictionary of Christian Ethics*, Philadelphia: The Westminster Press/SCM Press, 87–90.

Harakas, S. (1983) *Toward Transfigured Life*, Minneapolis: Light and Life Publishing Company.

Häring, B. (1961) *The Law of Christ*, vol. 1, Westminster: The Newman Press.

—— (1978) *Free and Faithful in Christ*, vol. 1, New York: Seabury Press.

Hauerwas, S. (1983) *The Peaceable Kingdom*, Notre Dame: University of Notre Dame Press.

Henry, C. H. F. (1957) *Christian Personal Ethics*, Grand Rapids, Mich.: Eerdmans.

Hughes, G. (1978) *Authority in Morals*, London: Heythrop Monographs.

Jonsen, A. and Toulmin, S. (1988) *The Abuse of Casuistry*, Berkeley: University of California Press.

Kant, I. (1960) *Religion Within the Limits of Reason Alone*, New York: Harper Torch Books.

Kirk, K. E. (1931) *The Vision of God*, London: Longmans, Green and Company.

Lehmann, P. (1963) *Ethics in a Christian Context*, New York: Harper & Row.

Løgstrup, K. (1971) *The Ethical Demand*, Philadelphia: Fortress Press.

Lovin, R. (1984) *Christian Faith and Public Choices*, Philadelphia: Fortress Press.

Mahoney, J. (1987) *The Making of Moral Theology*, Oxford: Clarendon Press.

Meilaender, G. C. (1991) *Faith and Faithfulness*, Notre Dame: University of Notre Dame Press.

Moltmann, J. (1971) *Hope and Planning*, New York: Harper & Row.

Mouw, R. C. (1990) *The God Who Commands*, Notre Dame: University of Notre Dame Press.

Nash, J. A. (1991) *Loving Nature*, Nashville: Abingdon Press.

Niebuhr, H. R. (1951) *Christ and Culture*, New York: Harper and Brothers.

—— (1961) *Radical Monotheism and Western Culture*, New York: Harper and Brothers.

—— (1963) *The Responsible Self*, New York: Harper & Row.

Niebuhr, R. (1943) *The Nature and Destiny of Man*, 2 vols, New York: Charles Scribner's Sons.

Nygren, A. (1953) *Agape and Eros*, London: SPCK.

O'Donovan, O. (1986) *Resurrection and Moral Order*, Leicester: Intervarsity Press.

Outka, G. (1972) *Agape*, New Haven: Yale University Press.

Ramsey, P. (1950) *Basic Christian Ethics*, New York: Charles Scribner's Sons.

Rendtorff, T. (1986) *Ethics*, 2 vols, Philadelphia: Fortress Press.

Robinson, J. A. T. (1963) *Honest to God*, Philadelphia: Westminster Press.

Schüller, B. (1986) *Wholly Human*, Washington: Georgetown University Press.

—— (1991) 'A Contribution to the Theological Discussion of Natural Law', in C. E. Curran and R. A. McCormick (eds) *The Distinctiveness of Christian Ethics*, vol. 2, *Natural Law and Theology*, New York: Paulist Press, 92–3.

Schuurman, D. (1991) *Creation, Eschaton, and Ethics*, New York: Peter Lang.

714

Sedgwick, T. (1987) *Sacramental Ethics*, Philadelphia: Fortress Press.
Singer, I. (1984) *The Nature of Love*, vol. 1, Chicago: University of Chicago Press.
Staniloae, D. (1980) *Theology and the Church*, Crestwood: St Vladimir's Seminary Press.
Tappert, T. G. (ed.) (1959) *The Book of Concord*, Philadelphia: Muhlenbery Press.
Tillich, P. (1948) *The Protestant Era*, Chicago: University of Chicago Press.
—— (1963) *Systematic Theology*, vol. 3, Chicago: University of Chicago Press.
Toner, J. (1968) *The Experience of Love*, Washington: Corpus Books.
Troeltsch, E. (1949) *The Social Teachings of the Christian Churches*, 2 vols, Glencoe: The Free Press.
Williams, D. D. (1968) *The Spirit and the Forms of Love*, New York: Harper & Row.
Yoder, J. H. (1972) *The Politics of Jesus*, Grand Rapids, Mich.: Eerdmans.
—— (1984) *The Priestly Kingdom*, Notre Dame: University of Notre Dame Press.

FURTHER READING

Cone, J. H. (1970) *A Black Theology of Liberation*, Maryknoll: Orbis Books.
Farley, M. (1986) *Personal Commitments*, San Francisco: Harper & Row.
Harrison, B. (1985) *Feminist Christian Ethics*, Boston: Beacon Press.
Hauerwas, S. (1975) *Character and the Christian Life*, San Antonio: Trinity University Press.
Jones, G. (1990) *Transformed Judgment*, Notre Dame: University of Notre Dame Press.
Long, E. L. Jr. (1967) *A Survey of Christian Ethics*, New York: Oxford University Press.
—— (1982) *A Survey of Recent Christian Ethics*, New York: Oxford University Press.
Miguez Bonino, J. (1983) *Toward a Christian Political Ethics*, Philadelphia: Fortress Press.
Rauschenbusch, W. (1917) *A Theology for the Social Gospel*, New York: Abingdon Press.
Ruether, R. R. (1992) *Gaia & God*, San Francisco: Harper & Row.
Thielicke, H. (1966 and 1969) *Theological Ethics*, 2 vols, Philadelphia: Fortress Press.
Welch, S. (1990) *A Feminist Ethic of Risk*, Minneapolis: Fortress Press.
See also chapters 24, 34, 36, 39, 47.

34

VIOLENCE, WARFARE AND PEACE

Barrie Paskins

This chapter is concerned with war and a variety of closely related phenomena including nuclear deterrence and proliferation, rebellion, military intervention, terrorism, the arms trade and conscientious objection to military service. The first section examines a number of theories about war; the second section considers their relation to contemporary problems.

CHRISTIAN AND NON-CHRISTIAN THEORIES OF WAR

Broadly speaking, there are four main types of theory about war: just war, holy war, pacifism and realism. Of these, a just war tradition has been the mainstream of Christian moral theology since Augustine. The early Church was in some sense pacifist. It is, however, unclear to what extent this derived from a principled objection to war as such. The early Church was a persecuted minority largely preoccupied with its own concerns, from which the wars of its hostile host the Roman Empire may well have seemed a dangerous distraction. Furthermore, the Empire's requirement that its soldiers worship the Emperor must have seemed blasphemous, so that attempts in the twentieth century to represent modern pacifism as simply a return to the purity of the early Church are widely considered to be anachronistic.

The Empire's conversion to Christianity confronted Christian intellectuals with cruel dilemmas concerning the use of force, which Augustine summarized in the question 'May the Christian without sin wage war?' Three features of this question invite comment.

1 '*May* one wage war?' poses the issue as one of what is *permitted*, not what is *required*, and it is an important feature of the just war tradition that it continues to speak in terms of permission to wage war, *not* in terms of a duty to do so.

2 May *the Christian* wage war? For Augustine and his medieval successors, the non-Christian was so radically immured in sin (short of conversion) that

it can hardly have seemed worth asking whether the pagan or Jew or (later) the Muslim might wage war 'without sin'. In the modern world, some theologians are less sure that things are so clear cut, so we have to ask whether Augustine's question is best understood as applying not only to Christians but to adherents of all the world's religio-ethical traditions. As we will see in a moment, the way in which the Christian just war tradition has developed lends itself to a universalist interpretation.

3 May one wage war without *sin*? It is striking that the question is framed in theological terms. It is not 'May one wage war without *injustice*?' Many theologians will be confident that the distinction is in one sense without practical significance: if God is perfectly good and all-powerful, it may well be that he never lays upon us demands of a sort which would require us to be unjust; so in practice it amounts to the same thing whether we ask if one may wage war without sin or without injustice. But there are two important complications. First, some theologians consider human reason to be radically corrupt and this may result in a stark contrast between what revelation is thought to show to be sinful and what radically flawed human reason considers to be (humanly) unjust. Further, one might hold as revelation the belief that government is appointed by God for the punishment of sin and as such is to be obeyed without question, regardless of what human reason might judge to be unjust. A second complication is that some ethical traditions, such as Buddhism, do not have the concept of *sin*, while others, such as secular humanism, know nothing of any cosmic grounding for ethics. If the just war tradition is concerned with sin, then its hold within these traditions is problematic. For example, the modern secular humanist may wonder whether the tradition is binding upon her or him. Thus, the formulation of Augustine's question in terms of sin makes explicit the issue of whether the just war tradition is susceptible of universalist interpretation.

In Augustine and his successors, an answer developed to the question 'May the Christian without sin wage war?' which it is convenient to call 'the classic just war doctrine'. According to this doctrine, war can be just only if a number of conditions are met. Failure to meet any one of the conditions is enough to show that the war is unjust and participation in it sinful. To be just, a war must be for a just cause. War must be the last resort and there must be legitimate authority for it. There must be no direct attacks on noncombatants. There must be a reasonable prospect of success and the war's ultimate aim must be peace. The good which it is reasonable to expect from the war must outweigh the evil which will certainly be involved. If all these conditions are met, the war may be permissible though, as we have already noticed, the tradition does not purport to say when war is a duty.

According to the classic doctrine, these principles are part of natural law. They are discoverable by any rational human being, regardless of creed, and are therefore binding on Christian and non-Christian alike. In this way the classic doctrine certainly claims to be universalist, but under what conditions is the claim plausible given its authors' understandable non-engagement with the issues which are internal to non-Christian perceptions of war? This question has been discussed much less fully than it deserves and this chapter permits only a brief treatment. Generally speaking, we should perhaps distinguish between two possible types of attitude to the relation between reason and the moral problem of war. One type of attitude is grounded in the assumption that each human life is sacred; the other type of attitude lacks this assumption. Thus, the sanctity of human life which is assumed not only in Christianity but also in Judaism, Islam, Buddhism, etc., is not assumed in Social Darwinism. For anyone who assumes the sanctity of human life, war is problematic in a special way since it seems certain to involve deliberate destruction of the sacred. Buddhist and Muslim will therefore confront essentially the same problem as the Christian in thinking about war. The Social Darwinist, for whom individual human life is in principle expendable, will on the other hand not have the same problem about war, since, in Social Darwinism, reason is an instrument of the survival of the social units into which the human species is supposedly divided.

In any tradition which holds each individual human life to be sacred, the problem of war can be transformed or overcome by the radical denial of reason's competence, which is familiar from Christian history as the assertion that reason is so radically corrupt that immediate revelation is the only valid source of guidance. By the same token, any tradition such as Islam or Buddhism is likely to contain varieties according to which revelation completes and does not supersede reason, and in every such tradition it is reasonable to believe that there will be scope for very much the same line of thought which has produced the classic just war doctrine in Christian history.

This argument does not imply that Islam, Buddhism, etc., will necessarily have already developed a body of thought as articulate as the classic just war doctrine or that there will necessarily be agreement on all points. The suggestion is that the classic doctrine is a product of at least four necessary conditions, and the absence of any of these would be ample explanation if a substantive just war doctrine were lacking in a given tradition. The assumption that each human life is sacred and the belief that revelation completes and does not supersede reason are two factors. A third is that penetrating attention of the sort which theists call theological is brought to bear on the issue of war, and a fourth is that this is done by persons whose concerns are closely aligned with concerns of state. These third and fourth conditions were possibly not met in Christian history before the time of Augustine. In each tradition it will be historical contingencies rather than theological essentials that determine whether something akin to the predicament of Augustine and his successors has yet been confronted.

The just war tradition's status in a world of many faiths and of none is a question of intense practical importance, as a single example may serve to illustrate. When the Cold War ended, there was considerable casting-around in 'the West' for a 'new' enemy to take the place of the defeated Soviet Union and a prime candidate was 'fundamentalist Islam'. This shadowy entity was held to be devoted to the violent overthrow of the West and its presentation tended to dehumanize and demonize important developments throughout the Muslim world. There was thus much work to be done not least in dialogue between Christian, Muslim and Jewish theologians to articulate the varieties of attitude towards war in each of the three faiths. If, as suggested above, the classic just war doctrine has essentially the same status in each of the three faiths, then it provides an appropriate focus for such mutual exploration despite the fact that it developed in Christian history.

Just war and holy war

In many times and places, people of many traditions have believed particular wars to be directly ordained by God or the gods. In many but not all cases, the enemy are thought to be divinely marked out for destruction. To kill them is to do the Lord's will so there can be no question of mercy. The just war tradition's concerns for limitation and restraint are bound to be rejected as impious and the result is almost certain to be savage from the viewpoint of anyone who does not share the holy warrior's beliefs. Such ferocity is frequent in Christian history and has often found sanction in the biblical account of Israel's conquest of the promised land. Indeed, it is convenient to call this type 'biblical holy war', though it is not confined to the religions of the Bible nor should the label be taken to imply that a correct biblical understanding requires one to be a holy warrior! Some historians of the classic just war tradition (notably J. T. Johnson) have argued persuasively that there is a recurrent tendency for just war ideas to be sucked into the rhetoric of the holy warrior's certainty that destruction of the enemy is pleasing to the Lord. According to this view, the greater elaborateness of the just war idea in later writers, such as Vitoria and Suarez in the sixteenth century, is in part a response to this tendency, an attempt to re-assert the tradition's essential concern for limitation and restraint when this has been eroded by the drift towards holy war.

The type of holy war which finds ready biblical support needs to be distinguished from another which appears to be more characteristic of a society or caste of warriors. This second type may or may not regard particular wars as commanded by God or the gods. It is marked by the belief in a god-given code of military practice and the code is often of such a kind as to make the violation of certain prohibitions and restraints inherently 'sinful' by direct divine command. Let us call this 'militaristic holy war', since what lies behind it is the sanctification of certain particular military practices and the forbidding of others.

How are the two varieties of holy war related to the just war tradition?

The belief that particular wars are ordained by God and are against enemies divinely marked out for destruction rules out the emphasis upon the primacy of reason which typifies the classic just war doctrine. The just warrior is made aware of limitations upon what he may do by reason and it is natural for him to regard war as a regrettable necessity. For the biblical holy warrior, on the other hand, there is precious little scope for the exercise of reason. The humanizing effects of the realizations both that particular wars are accounted just and unjust by the operations of fallible reason and that even a just war is at best a sad necessity are excluded on principle for the biblical holy warrior. If the just warrior loses sight of them, this will be through a deficient understanding of his moral position. The just war idea tends inherently towards moderation; the biblical holy war towards destruction without limit.

In practice, holy war of the biblical type tends to allow the end to justify any means because the aim is supposed to be directly god-given and the divinely sanctioned destruction of the enemy removes all basis for restriction of the means of war. Holy war of the militaristic type readily tends in two contrary directions: towards the irrational prohibition of certain means (as perhaps when the crossbow was regarded as an illicit weapon of war to which chivalry objected for its plebeian character); and towards the irrational determination of ends, as when considerations of honour or face are allowed to become absolutes. In contrast to both of these, the classic just war doctrine purports to embody the rational understanding that war is a regrettable means to certain ends, where both ends and means are subject to inherently rational limits.

Just war and pacifism

There are many varieties of pacifism (Yoder's *Nevertheless* (1971) distinguishes thirty-four types!) of which three are especially important. First, so-called 'pacificism' is not pacifism in the strict sense but the belief that war has become intolerable or irrational. Much of the pacificism which followed the First World War collapsed during the 1930s as it became clear that the world was faced with an evil so radical that even the horrors of modern war could arguably be justified as the only viable collective response. There are times when the pacificist's insistence on the evils of war is a much-needed corrective to any temptation to make light of war, but pacificism of this first kind cannot contribute deep insights into the moral realities of war precisely because it rests exclusively on a contingent judgement of the proportion between the evils of a particular kind of war and the estimate of the good at which the war might be aimed.

'Just war pacifism' is a second type that is not pacifism strictly speaking. It is the belief that in practice there are no just wars because in reality every actual war is bound to violate the principles which are required for a war to be just. Such 'pacifism' is a species of just war thinking and differs from other types not in the principles which it deploys but in the prudential judgements to which it comes.

An important kind of strict pacifism is the pacifism of *witness*. Some adherents of the Quaker peace testimony are a good illustration of this. They reject all participation in war in order to witness to certain values which cannot find direct expression in war. They tend not to claim that such a witness is possible for the State. Theirs is an individual witness, upholding peaceful values in a world of war, and many will gladly make themselves useful, for example as medical orderlies ministering equally to casualties on both sides of the conflict. It is a revealing characteristic of what their witness consists in that these very same individuals will sometimes be involved in quiet diplomacy between conflicting third parties when their own country is not at war.

What disagreement is there between the just warrior and the pacifist of witness? The pacifist is likely to emphasize that just war thinking is liable to degenerate into holy war, as discussed above, and is likely to insist on a very strict application of the just war principles, as does the 'just war pacifist'. The just warrior cannot accuse the braver of pacifists of individual cowardice but is likely to emphasize that individual witness is no basis for State action. The just warrior also tends to ask the pacifist about an especially difficult kind of case: suppose that A is being attacked by B and that you are the only third party near enough to A. If you can protect A only by force, do you stand idly by, witnessing to supposedly higher values, or do you intervene? If you fail to intervene, the meaning of your witness becomes obscure; if you intervene, where is your pacifism? Let us call this 'the intervention dilemma'. The thoughtful pacifist tends to concede two points in response to the intervention dilemma: first, that there are hard problems in life to which there are no easy answers, and this may be one of them; second, that the just warrior's tendency to identify with the State represents the taking of a different point of view from the pacifist's avowedly individual stance, and no more irresponsible for that. The State does have its proper tasks. It needs loyal servants and the just warrior may be one of them.

One further point might be made which tends to clarify the divergence between just warrior and pacifist. The difference in their points of view may have much more substance to it than can be apparent in the one's readiness to engage in just war and the other's refusal to do so. The pacifist of witness whose life is devoted to quiet unofficial diplomacy is not performing an office of state but may nevertheless be engaged in activity which is vital to the optimal functioning of society. It is becoming increasingly recognized that the inevitably rigid and somewhat stereotyped functioning of formal international relations can benefit greatly from the complementary flexibility of non-governmental organizations which are enabled by their unofficial status to do what governments cannot. There are, for example, important things which Amnesty International can say and do that are practically out of the question for government. Similarly, if the pacifist is one who works quietly and unofficially between embattled communities then she or he may well be performing as necessary a social function as the just warrior though at a greater distance from the State.

Just war and realism

All the approaches to war that we have discussed so far lean heavily upon moral judgements. The more convincing forms of 'realism' tend to mistrust this central reliance on moral judgement and to strive instead for a more 'dispassionate, objective' attitude to 'the phenomenon of war'. Self-styled realists tend to be a mixture of two ideal types which are in theory starkly contrasted. One type might be called 'the reductionist'; the other type is the pragmatist. One of the ways in which realists differ from one another is that reductionism and pragmatism can be mixed together in a variety of ways.

According to the reductionist, political and/or military realities can be reduced to a small number of fundamental forces or factors, notably self-interest and/or power. The fine words of politicians are a mask and the reductionist is not deceived, even if the politician succumbs to self-deception. When the politician talks the language of just or holy war what is really happening is an assertion of power or self-interest. However coherent and morally attractive the just war tradition may seem, it is ultimately unrealistic. The war to evict Iraq from Kuwait may have been called just but the reality was that the US acted to protect its interests and power in the Middle East. The fine words were empty rhetoric, as can be seen by examining how Washington has acted in other situations where just war requirements have not coincided neatly with the realities of power or interest. This is the view of the reductionist.

According to the pragmatist, there is only one valid simple, generalized response to political questions, and this is that issues are rarely clear cut. Issues become political often because they are an awkward mix of categories: power, interest and justice all scrambled together in a way that only a political decision can unravel; and the unravelling can at best be a partial satisfaction of any of the demands that make the question an urgent one. If moral demand A can be met it can only be at the expense of moral demand B, and seeing to A will also involve furthering interest C at the expense of interest D and advancing the power of E at the expense of F's power.

Clearly, the reductionist and the pragmatist disagree in theory. The reductionist holds that the phenomena are basically simple – 'It's all power really' – whereas the pragmatist insists on irreducible complexity – 'Who knows what may come to the fore in the next controversy?' We must therefore ask why these apparently contradictory approaches tend to combine in practice. An example may suffice to clarify the issue. Consider the dilemma of a morally concerned foreign secretary in a modern democracy. Her or his own experience may well conform to the pragmatic pattern of irreducible complexity, but there is bound to be a problem of how to explain this to public opinion, which is notoriously unreceptive to the detail of foreign affairs. Furthermore, what broad guidelines are one to employ in analysing the flood of new problems and new opportunities constantly impinging on the foreign office? As regards public opinion, it may well be that what most needs emphasis is the all-pervasive importance of the international balance of power. When public opinion is swept by a gust of moral enthusiasm, the grinding demands of long-term intervention may need to be faced. When public opinion is disaffected and inclined to dismiss foreign problems as the product of domestic interest groups (such as the military–industrial complex), then the inescapable involvement of one's country in the world balance of power may need to be stressed. In innumerable such ways, the most appropriate simplifying map of the world may be a reductionist one. Being human, a politician who speaks reductionism for such reasons may easily forget the tensions between reductionist and pragmatic forms of realism and be drawn into the over-simplifications of simple-minded reductionism, especially if there is a strong tendency in this direction within the political milieu.

How, then, does realism relate to the classic just war doctrine? The pragmatist's most searching question to the classic doctrine concerns its understanding of the relation between principle and prudence. Just warriors are usually well aware that just war principles do not apply themselves but have to be brought to bear upon the disorder of everyday reality by a quality of mind and character which is traditionally called both judgement and prudence. This comprises both the intellectual penetration to grasp complex realities and the moral strength to resist such temptations as sentimentality, arbitrary harshness and impatience. Whether the just war doctrine delivers any judgements that are absolute (e.g. that noncombatants are never to be subjected to direct attack is a controversial question within the just war tradition. But however that may be, the doctrine's tendency is undoubtedly towards the imposition of prohibitions and restraints on the resort to and conduct of war. A pragmatist cannot but ask whether this restrictiveness is too rigid and narrow. The pragmatist believes that decision-makers are constantly assailed by a large number of incompatible demands which cannot be reduced to any simple formula. The start simplicities of the classic just war doctrine are bound to strike the pragmatist as one of the many factors to be taken into account, rather than as the authoritative framework for decision-making.

This pragmatic questioning of the basic simplicity of just war doctrine becomes the more sceptical to the extent that a realist mixes pragmatism with reductionism. Many pragmatic realists believe that most of the inputs into different decisions about war are considerations of self-interest and/or power, and that a good deal is known about how it is necessary to behave in order to flourish in a power-political world. Many a realist is therefore in the interesting position of sharing many of the concerns of the just warrior while believing that the classic doctrine is over-simple. A more accommodating attitude to such imperatives as the need to preserve the balance is the beginning of wisdom; or so the realist tends to believe.

How is the just warrior to respond? In our discussion of the pacifist, we saw reason to think that the most responsible of pacifists may be those who take an informal role in peace-making in international society. The State, we thought, could not be so straightforward in its support for peace. The just warrior, it seemed, might fairly claim to be shouldering the heavy responsibilities of State. Now we hear the realist saying that in actuality decision-makers have to be pragmatic and respectful of such sordid requirements as the balance of power to a greater extent than the classic just war doctrine can allow. There is no easy resolution of this painful tension in our public life. Perhaps the most that one can say is as follows. Politics is the clash of a great many somewhat indefinite ideas. Some of these ideas, such as racial purity, are pernicious and must be combated in all their forms, but a great many are more ambiguous. Words such as 'justice', 'freedom' and 'the national interest' admit of many interpretations and most of those who engage in politics have core allegiances which are their sticking points, their resigning-matters. Different politicians have different core allegiances but it would be an ignoble and fruitless politician who was so radically pragmatic that she or he had no sticking points whatever. Those for whom the classic just war principles sum up certain basic allegiances have a peculiarly intelligible and challenging set of sticking points, as we may see by reminding ourselves that their basic demand is that the coercive apparatus of the State be organized and operated in such a way as to avoid violating the will of God ('May the Christian without sin wage war?'). Whatever we think of more 'flexible' attitudes, we can hardly doubt the grandeur and rigour of the just warrior's position.

Furthermore, we must remember that there are no sticking points in realism as such: pragmatism says be flexible and reductionism directs attention to considerations of power and/or interest. Anyone who was a *pure* realist would be on a slippery slope to the readiness to do anything whatever in the service of interest and/or power. Few would doubt that these are false gods and our discussion of holy war provides ample material for informed speculation about what actually tends to happen on the slippery slope to the service of mere interest and/or power. What tends to happen is that some such thing as the national interest (alias 'survival') becomes identified with the will of God; opponents are marked out as enemies of God, and war without limit against them appears to be sanctioned. The more moderate realist is faced with a danger that is the reverse of that which the pragmatist attributes to the just warrior: if the classic just war doctrine is too rigid, greater flexibility brings with it the risk of a slippery slope towards the readiness to permit anything in war.

CONTEMPORARY PROBLEMS

We have examined the inter-relationships of four types of theory about war: just war, holy war, pacifism and realism. Let us now consider their relation to contemporary problems. A sketch of the modern period must serve to define the context. The modern period of military affairs is usually regarded as beginning in the eighteenth century, an era of limited wars between dynasts whose aims were confined to family aggrandizement and whose military commitments were proportionately moderate. It was a time in which the classic just war doctrine was despised. Every belligerent would call its cause just and war would be conducted on the basis of power politics. With the French Revolution the stakes of war increased enormously, for whole peoples came upon the stage of history for the first time and the age-old tendency towards holy war of the biblical type began to develop a modern variety, that of nationalism in arms. War remained an instrument of politics, a legitimate instrument of foreign policy, but the content and passion of war were changed. During the nineteenth century another far-reaching change in the nature of war was brought about by industrialization, which soon permitted the deployment of armies far larger than any that even Napoleon had been able to wield. The changed character of warfare began to be apparent in the American Civil War but it was only between 1914 and 1918 that the new issues became etched into popular and elite consciousness.

The individual sufferings and the destruction of empires effected by the First World War convinced many that war was no longer a legitimate instrument of foreign policy. Something had to be done to outlaw war, so it was felt widely but with insufficient universality. The League of Nations was created as a framework for the prohibition of all but defensive war. It failed to contain the resentments and ambitions of defeated Germany and victorious Japan; it failed to involve the mighty US in preserving the balance of power; it left out the self-preoccupied USSR.

The Second World War completed the tendency of industrialization to forge an intimate link between science and war. For the first time a group of the world's greatest scientists worked in deep secrecy on a military project and invented nuclear weapons. Military thinkers at once began to wrestle with the wholly new idea that peace might be located not in prohibitions and restraints or international organizations but in terror. Fission bombs were soon followed by fusion bombs of virtually unlimited destructive power and the means were devised to 'deliver' these, with ever greater accuracy, to any point on the earth's surface. Nuclear weapons seemed to promise or threaten that their possessors need no longer fight wars but could instead deter them.

By 1945 thinking was already well advanced for an organization to replace and improve upon the failed League of Nations. US President Roosevelt wanted the new United Nations to be based on the organized cooperation of the great powers, but Roosevelt died and was replaced by his Vice-President

Truman, a vociferous anti-Communist with little knowledge of foreign affairs. For reasons which remain the subject of intense historical disagreement, the great powers were soon at odds. There was 'Cold War' between the 'capitalist' US and 'communist' USSR and their respective allies and puppet-states. Furthermore, the US was firmly opposed to the British and French ambition to re-establish their empires (though not inclined to free Latin America from US domination). In theory, the five Permanent Members of the UN Security Council were a powerful oligarchy of the great powers; in practice, their bitter hostility reduced the UN to a marginal role until the end of the Cold War. When the Soviet Union collapsed, its place among the Permanent Members was taken by Russia. It was increasingly argued that Japan and re-unified Germany should be Permanent Members, and the claims of India to be a 'third world' Permanent Member were vociferously argued (and as vehemently opposed by India's enemies such as Pakistan).

During the Cold War, moral debate focused above all on nuclear deterrence. A standard just war argument against nuclear deterrence was as follows. A major nuclear war would certainly be both indiscriminate and disproportionate, therefore contrary to the just war principles. Deterrence requires both the capability to wage such a war and also the political will to do so. There must be political will at two levels. Those manning the deterrent must have the steady determination to fire nuclear weapons if ordered to do so and at the political level there must be the readiness to stand up to testing by crisis, as Kennedy did in the Cuba missiles crisis of 1962. Either the firm political intention to use nuclear weapons must already exist, and there is no question but that nuclear deterrence is the conditional intention to wage disproportionate and indiscriminate nuclear war, or the decision on whether to use nuclear weapons is being deferred to the worst possible moment for rational decision-making, namely, the depth of an international crisis, in which case the deterrent posture stands condemned as irresponsibly irrational. It might be imprudent to abandon one's nuclear weapons unilaterally, but nuclear deterrence cannot be accepted as a durable centre-piece of security policy. If it can be accepted at all then the tolerance is only in the interim, while deterrence is used to make possible the abolition of nuclear weapons.

A number of ingenious alternative assessments more favourable to deterrence were proposed during the Cold War debate about the bomb, and will probably return to prominence if and when the great powers' continued reliance on nuclear weapons returns to the centre of political controversy. But more pressing in the aftermath of the Cold War were issues concerning nuclear proliferation. Few were confident that nuclear weapons could safely be allowed to spread in an unregulated way. In so far as deterrence was thought to have contributed to preventing war among the great powers in the Cold War period, it was argued that mutual deterrence kept the peace, and especially each side's possession of an invulnerable second-strike capability, that is, the capacity to count on being able to inflict massive damage on an opponent even if the opponent attacked first. Unregulated proliferation of nuclear weapons has no inbuilt guarantee that pairs of enemies will acquire invulnerable second-strike capabilities at the same time. An unbalanced spread of nuclear weapons might bring dangerous incentives to strike one's opponent pre-emptively. Also, many believe that some states are more unstable and irresponsible than were the great powers during the Cold War, though this is an argument which fits ill with the contention that nuclear deterrence forces states to exercise restraint and moderation whatever their ideology and organizational defects.

If nuclear weapons cannot be allowed to spread freely, then it is a natural thought that primary responsibility for their control should lie with the Permanent Members of the Security Council who happen also to be the only self-confessed possessors of nuclear weapons. Hypocrisy apart, it might be argued that the Permanent Members alone have the power to offer security guarantees backed by deterrence to states on the brink of acquiring de-stabilizing nuclear weapons as well as the power to intervene to prevent de-stabilizing proliferation. Could it be legitimate to argue in this way? Many a realist would consider such an argument utopian: states seek their own interests and the Permanent Members would intervene and offer security guarantees only in so far as these served their own interests. We could be sure, for example, that the US would treat Israel differently from Arab and other Muslim states.

Other realists are less certain. For them, the hazards of uncoordinated nuclear proliferation seem so great as to have the power to press all of the Permanent Members into perceiving a common problem requiring a common response. To emphasize hypocrisy, such realists will argue, is to misunderstand what is possible and constructive: though states will not act contrary to what they believe to be in their own interests, it is nevertheless possible for them sometimes to think in terms of enlightened common self-interest.

The theme of hypocrisy and enlightened self-interest also made itself felt in moral debate about response to Iraq's invasion of Kuwait. The ethical debate about nuclear weapons and the introspection prompted by US intervention in Vietnam combined to make it seem that the relatively simple pattern of just war response to flagrant aggression would not be repeated in the sophisticated post-war world, so that the application of just war principles would be unavoidably problematic. It is therefore striking that the war to evict Iraq from Kuwait conformed closely to the requirements of the classic just war doctrine. Iraq's naked and unprovoked aggression against Kuwait was the clearest possible just cause for war. In the months before the decisive coalition attack on Iraq a great many kinds of remedy short of conventional war were tried without success. Sanctions were imposed. Start UN resolutions were issued. Inter-state diplomacy and visits by distinguished private citizens brought no lessening of Iraq's determination to keep Kuwait. The UN Secretary-General visited Baghdad only to be humiliated there. The traditional principle that war must be the last resort was clearly meaningful and clearly satisfied. The requirement for legitimate authority also proved to have a special significance. The US and its closest allies, notably the UK, sought the widest possible agreement to the terms on which Iraq was to be evicted from Kuwait. Realists will say that they had their own power-political reasons for doing so (oil, Israel, US prestige) but it remains notable that the war was halted when its UN-endorsed objectives had been achieved: coalition forces did not drive to Baghdad, and Saddam Hussein was suffered to remain in office, a torment to his people and an irritant to the great powers. Considerable efforts were made to avoid direct attacks on noncombatants. Some said that sanctions had not been given sufficient time, but this is an ambiguous claim: sanctions *as a warning* had ample time to work; sanctions *as a blockade or siege* were not given time to work, but it is unclear whether this is contrary to just war principles, for a blockade to impose the UN's will upon Saddam Hussein was likely to have required catastrophic suffering among the Iraqi population before the ruling elite began to experience the kinds of suffering which might conceivably have made them submit.

Most of those who question whether the Gulf War was justified assume that the traditional principles were more or less satisfied but doubt whether the US and its allies were in any serious sense committed to justice. The objection needs to be formulated with more care than is often shown. It will not do to call into doubt the purity of the coalition's motives, for many moral principles are addressed to the will rather than the heart and can be satisfied by being obeyed, whether the agent's motives for obeying are pure or mixed. Perhaps the strongest form of the objection is to argue that the coalition's aims merely happened on this occasion to coincide with the demands of justice. If on other occasions, when the just war principles seemed less expedient, they were not obeyed but dismissed as an irrelevance by the very people invoking them on this occasion, then it would be to the point to argue that these principles were not really guiding the will of the coalition.

This issue is in another guise the question of whether the UN oligarchy can legitimately intervene to prevent nuclear weapons proliferation by a judicious mix of security guarantees and coercion. In both cases, the classic just war doctrine's concern with what is justified on a particular occasion, such as Iraq's invasion of Kuwait, is felt to be insufficient because we want to know what national policies or international institutions will ensure regular compliance with justice, if not justice for its own sake. In the classic tradition there is little guidance on such issues. The ruler is enjoined to consult a council of the wise and we have already noted the tradition's basic assumption that reason can be and should play the leading part in determining policy. On the other hand, the medieval just war writers have little to offer on the role of public opinion in decisions of war and peace. They assume that ordinary people are uninformed about such matters and entitled to entrust the decisions entirely to their rulers. If conscience forbids an action then conscience, even erring conscience, must be obeyed, but the medieval writers allow very little scope for conscience to be disturbed by matters of war and peace.

Whether we are nowadays in any better position to improve the rationality of our rulers' decision-making is debatable, but the inter-actions between ruling elites, other opinion-formers and public opinion are so influential that their impact on the classic just war doctrine may be one of the most important areas in which the doctrine needs to be elaborated. Much detailed work remains to be done, but a worthwhile outline of some of the principal issues is perhaps already discernible. According to the classic just war doctrine, a war can be just only if it is backed by legitimate authority. This principle is directed against arbitrary warfare. It is often said that the principle is satisfied if war is authorized by a sovereign state, but opinions about the war to evict Iraq from Kuwait suggest that state authorization is not enough. What more might be demanded in the spirit of the classic just war doctrine? What could make the authorization of war less arbitrary, more rational?

One very interesting possibility can be illustrated by the office of UN Secretary-General. Because the Secretary-General's principal loyalty can be to the UN system as a whole rather than to any one or group of the UN members, it is possible to imagine the Secretary-General being empowered to pronounce with special authority on which wars are legitimate. For example, he or she might be equipped and constitutionally authorized to draw attention to problem cases, first by resort to the Permanent Members and then, if appropriate action is not forthcoming, by resort to the General Assembly. A realist will point out that the Secretary-General's office has no power of its own apart from the will of the UN's members, but this does not in itself settle whether the office might be given an autonomy which might be likened to that of an investigating magistrate, to draw attention to victims who are being neglected and to wars which lack legitimacy. War is so much a struggle for hearts and minds that a reform of this kind within the formal structure of international relations could go some way to making the conduct of war less arbitrary, and the observance of just war principles less opportunist.

The war against Iraq did not show the UN's international institutions as having this degree of authority. The US, UK, and their allies were eager to develop the widest possible coalition of states and to secure formal UN authorization if possible. Nevertheless, they expressly reserved the right to act in collective self-defence (Article 51 of the UN Charter) and their being able to fall back on the right to act as they judged to be necessary undoubtedly helped to concentrate minds within the UN. It is hard to imagine the great powers relinquishing a final right of autonomous action, but it may be conceivable that the pressure for this right to be exercised only for the common good might be increased by strengthening the Secretary-General (whose humiliation in Baghdad was perhaps the clearest sign that all means short of war had been tried without success).

In addition to changes of the UN structure, the development of international public opinion could conceivably improve the rationality of decisions about peace and war, though arguments about this are far from conclusive. In a democracy, it is open to individuals to develop a concern about foreign affairs and to take a well-informed interest in the justice of their own and other governments' policies. Furthermore, many agree with J. S. Mill's argument that if all opinions can be freely debated then the truth will emerge. These considerations suggest that democracies can play an especially constructive part in making war conform to justice. On the other hand, many are pessimistic about modern media, which seem to them to propagate exploitative images rather than to provoke rational debate. Furthermore, the nineteenth-century liberals' belief that democracy would end war because the people who suffer by war would be reluctant to engage in it has proved a two-edged sword: though popular reluctance to suffer inhibits reckless warfare, it also promotes appeasement and the irresponsible neglect of victims of aggression, confining a democracy to self-righteous, unrestrained wars of self-defence against aggressors who should have been confronted earlier on behalf of the weak.

Although democracy is no panacea, it does seem fair to say that concerned citizens of democratic countries can play an informal part in making decision-making about war less arbitrary. Through a host of organizations such as Amnesty International and the national Red Cross and Red Crescent societies, as well as through the quiet diplomacy mentioned above in our discussion of pacifism, there is scope for informal work to press the exercise of State power in the direction of justice. The widespread feeling of helplessness to influence affairs is thus in part a failure to realize what is actually being done, in part an unreasonable perfectionism.

Rebellion

Attitudes to armed rebellion in Christianity and other religions have varied in ways that are closely connected with the distinctions that we have drawn between pacifism, holy war, realism and just war. The pacifist will no more take arms against the State than on behalf of one State against another. A person or group filled with the type of enthusiasm that motivates holy war of the biblical type will take arms against a godless State without compunction. A kind of mirror image of such zeal is that absolute submission to the State which mistrusts human reason and pictures the government of the day as being directly appointed by God for the punishment of sin: whatever evils it may bring upon its subjects, it cannot be the target of rebellion since the divine will is for it to be obeyed in reverence to God, who will punish his sinful ministers in his own good time. Unlike the pacifist, the just warrior does not shrink in principle from the use of armed forces. Unlike the absolutely submissive holy warrior, the just warrior has sufficient trust in reason to think it possible to recognize when rebellion is necessary. And unlike the holy warrior who fights against the State of which he or she is a subject as a target appointed by God for destruction, the just warrior is subject to the same rational reservations, the same prohibitions and restraints, in rebellion as in war. Let us discuss these before examining the relation between the classic just war doctrine and realism in their applications to rebellion.

To be just, a war must be authorized by legitimate authority. The authorities in question are the State and the UN if the war is between States, but what of rebellion? A special case might be a rebellion sanctioned by the UN, and one might suggest (though many would deny) that the Palestine Liberation Organization (PLO) received sanction for its rebellion against Israel from the UN when its leader Yasser Arafat was permitted to address the General Assembly. Against this particular argument it could be replied that the General Assembly has no authority to authorize rebellions whereas the Security Council might have. But the general thought remains that one special kind of authorization of rebellion might be that international organization which has authority over states.

This can, however, only be a special case because rebellions are not initiated by the UN, it is scarcely imaginable that they should come to be so, and many *prima facie* legitimate rebellions are most unlikely to be endorsed by the UN, dominated as its workings are by the diplomacy of governments. The usual case of armed rebellion is that in which groups of people resort to force without the legitimizing authority of an established government.

What insights has the tradition to offer such people? First, a formative influence in the tradition has been its opposition to private war, e.g. one of baron against another. Private parties should take their quarrels to a higher court rather than use force. From this we should presumably infer that rebellion can be just only if there is no court available which can deliver a credible adjudication of the rebels' quarrel with their government.

Second, the tradition recognizes an inherent and inalienable right of individual self-defence without identifying this with war. If an individual or a family are attacked they are permitted to defend themselves as best they can against the oncoming aggressor. This individual self-defence differs from war in several fundamentals: self-defence in an emergency does not as such involve training or organization to fight, nor the creation of fighting forces, nor the construction of a military command structure, nor the subordination of the military to political control. An armed rebellion, on the other hand, is bound to involve all of these collectivizing complications, so the demand that war be authorized goes much wider than individual self-defence. It includes the demand that a certain kind of collective entity be authorized, a political entity with military means at its disposal. In short, a rebel is not a purely private person but a participant in a collective entity whose existence needs to be justified.

Where, then, might such justification be sought? It may be that no comprehensive generalizations are either possible or necessary, for rebellions are not like states. The continued existence of states is a normal and proper part of fallen human life, and the proper task of each state is to cope with innumerably various challenges and opportunities. Rebellions, on the other hand, arise in response to specific grievances and ought to cease (occasionally perhaps by the transformation of the rebel movement into a state) with the resolution of the quarrel. Because rebellions are *ad hoc*, we should not expect to be able to generalize about them as readily as about states. Our best procedure may therefore be to consider a selection of particular cases.

1 The PLO, like the ANC in South Africa, has the striking feature that it was a legitimate peaceful organization which developed a military wing only under extreme provocation (i.e. as the just war tradition's 'last resort'). Furthermore, it had popular support before turning to arms and continued to do so, though the role of conscription in its military activity raises issues which we will examine later. This is an example of one kind of assurance that the individual can find that 'joining the rebellion' will not be a merely private war, for participation in this case may be participation in the last resort activity of a legitimate organization with a just cause.

2 When Pétain's government surrendered to Nazi Germany, De Gaulle summoned Frenchmen to resist in the name of a government-in-exile. This 'government' was created *ex nihilo* and could not draw legitimacy from an earlier non-military existence. Nor could it derive legitimacy from the majority of French citizens, who gave tacit consent to Pétain's regime. It could, on the other hand, point out that it had recognition (however unenthusiastic) from the countries which were at war with Germany, whose occupation of part of France could hardly be said to be legitimized by the consent of the French people and whose detested domination was the principal reason for such widespread consent to Pétain's regime. It was also able to demonstrate a capacity for State-like behaviour which was unnerving in its competence. De Gaulle's ability to speak as a statesman and to organize like a ruler make it impossible to think of his as a merely private war. Here perhaps is a second type of organization which can count as a legitimate rebel movement so long as it can meet the usual just war criteria of just cause, last resort, etc.

3 The Provisional IRA is a rebel movement which is in conflict with both Ireland and the UK. As the 'military wing' of the political party Sinn Fein it runs a well-trained, well-equipped and tightly organized fighting force. Its cause, to create a unified, socialist Ireland, commands meagre support at democratic elections in both Ireland and the UK. One of its objectives is to create 'no-go' areas from which the UK army is excluded and in which it can begin to exercise the functions of government, e.g. by punishing drug traffickers with knee-capping. Can it be regarded as a legitimate rebel movement? One reason to doubt that it can is the lack of popular consent that it is able to command in Ireland. There appear to be many who give willing

shelter to IRA fighters, but this is from a romantic kindness to young men in trouble with unpopular forces rather than from consent to the political aims of Sinn Fein. The contrast with De Gaulle's Free French is stark and crucial. De Gaulle in exile was able to speak as a credible political authority. The sympathy shown to IRA fighters is to a large extent at quite a different level. Many cultures show a deep fascination with the romantic young rebel. It is one thing to harbour him as an individual, quite another to consent to the political aims of the organization that lies behind him. In a democracy, an organization such as Sinn Fein has little hope of establishing that the resort to arms is a last resort because it can (as it does) operate as a political party.

4 In 1965, Che Guevara left his influential post in the Cuban revolutionary government to attempt to bring about revolution in Bolivia. The failure of his attempt can give us deeper insight into what can count as a legitimate rebel movement. Che did not seek, as Mao had done in China, to gain the understanding and consent of the oppressed peasantry. Instead, he sought to gain ascendancy by guerrilla warfare, hoping that his military organization would then become the organizing focus of revolution. Lacking popular support, his guerrillas were a relatively easy target for government forces and he was wounded, captured and killed in 1967. Strategists emphasize the *de facto* weaknesses imposed on his guerrillas by a strategy that failed to draw strength from the overwhelming mass of the people. But what did Che's isolation mean for the legitimacy of his movement? A generalization suggests itself which, if correct, has far-reaching implications. It is this. The meaning of any social idea becomes determinate through the thoughts, feelings and actions of the individuals in whose life it finds expression. For example, the meaning of 'democracy' cannot be spelled out entirely in a dictionary, for any abstract meaning which one can write down is incomplete without the minute practicalities and emotional colour that the word receives in the life of a democracy. When Mao strove to gain the understanding and consent of the Chinese peasantry he inevitably suffered his revolutionary terminology to be influenced by the people. However harsh and unequal his domineering attitude, the peasants played their part in defining what the revolutionary words meant as the struggle unfolded. To the extent that they were not deceived, manipulated and bamboozled, the peasants were making *their* revolution. Che, on the other hand, in trying to short-circuit the painful process of mobilizing the masses, was inevitably entrusting the practical definition of his revolutionary ideas to a narrow, military elite. It was *their* revolution, not the people's, and therein lay not only its power-political weakness but also its lack of legitimacy.

We can fruitfully compare this with our earlier examples. The PLO and ANC developed their ideas in close contact with the people for whom they claim to speak, and De Gaulle was at pains to find a style which any Frenchman could recognize as quintessentially French. In each of these cases, and perhaps to a greater extent than in Mao's, the rebel movement was actively shaped by those for whom it claimed to speak. In the IRA's case, the movement's politics is so separate from the romantic kindness attracted by its young fighters than Sinn Fein cannot credibly claim to speak for any but a small minority in the two democracies of Ireland and the UK. Thus in all of these cases, the shaping hand of those for whom the rebels claim to speak, or its absence, can be regarded as an important factor in deciding whether the movement is legitimate, and thus whether the rebellion can meet the just war requirement of legitimate authority.

This reading of the connection between consent and legitimate authority needs to be distinguished from two other things. First, it is distinct from a widespread conservative interpretation of the classic just war doctrine. Second, it does not commit one to the dangerously anarchic idea of the self-determination of peoples.

Many conservatives seek to contrast traditional rebellions and modern revolutions. They say that traditional rebellions had limited political aims and were sometimes justified, whereas modern revolutions give violent expression to the utopian idea of radically transforming the totality of human life – an aim so unrealistic that it can never be legitimate and in practice always degenerates into cynically power-political usurpation. This contrast relies on emphasizing the perfectibilist elements in such modern traditions as Marxism (while also downplaying the radicalism of some earlier rebels). It sets dogmatic limits to what might turn out in practice to be a legitimate political aspiration because it fails to consider what, say, Marxist ideas may come to mean in practice. It directs attention only to the abstract, dictionary definition and ignores the transformation that words can undergo in the creation of a revolutionary movement. By drawing the line in terms of political consent, we can avoid this dogmatism.

The self-determination of peoples idea is, at its most extreme, that any group which considers itself to be a people is so and as such entitled to be a nation-state if such is what the group's members desire. Our emphasis on consent differs from this dangerous recipe for the infinite multiplication of states in two vital ways. First, it is concerned only with rebel movements, not with states. Second, a legitimate rebellion must meet numerous conditions including a just cause and the just conduct of hostilities.

We have examined four types of theory about war and have concentrated on connections between just war, pacifism and realism. The differences between the just warrior and the pacifist have proved to be less stark than many would expect, and it has emerged that much remains to be done in the cause of peace and justice about which adherents of these two theories can agree and cooperate both with one another and with the more pragmatic, less doctrinaire types of realist. Our guiding thread has been the thought that revelation completes and does not supersede reason, so that reason in the service of God's will or the Buddhists' universal compassion can allow us to identify principles of justice within which to confine such apparently irrational outpourings of violence as war and armed rebellion. If the argument is sound then these same principles will illuminate all other topics in the field of military affairs. Let us conclude by noticing three topics which are thus illuminated.

Terrorism

Terrorism is a much-used word which in practice is apt to be discredited by the cliché that one person's terrorist is another's freedom-fighter. The classic just war doctrine allows much greater precision. It directs us to ask whether the case is one of rebellion, and whether the rebellion is just or unjust. If the cause is unjust (e.g. the IRA's anti-democratic activities) then there are no legitimate targets. If the cause is just and there is legitimate authority and last resort, it still remains to ask whether noncombatant immunity is respected. In such ways, the classic doctrine brings precision to an issue which is often treated with wearisome emotionalism. A special case is that of 'state-sponsored terrorism', on which the classic doctrine's implication is clear. If the State is overtly supporting the rebellion then it is party to it, a belligerent, and the question to ask is whether the war is just. If the State's involvement is covert, so that the State is seeking to disown responsibility for its involvement, then an issue arises which is well worth connecting with the sale and transfer of arms, as follows.

The arms trade

The supply and transfer of weapons is widely felt to be reprehensible, but arguments to this effect are often weak. It is said that scarce resources are wasted on weapons, but this is to forget that the arms trade is driven by demand rather than supply. It is insecure States and weak rebels who seek to buy weapons and it is not obvious how to put a price on the 'security' that they seek. From a just war perspective, however, certain crisp observations suggest themselves. First, the tradition's concern for legitimacy works against covert actions such as State-sponsored terrorism and secret arms deals. If the State's actions are honourable, why should they be secret? There is rarely a good answer. Second, whoever puts a lethal weapon into the hand of another, especially the hand of one with such a dubious record as that of many a state or rebel movement, should surely beware of becoming an accessory to murder. Third, there are simple guidelines which could easily impose tight and rational restrictions on any one state's arm supply policy. One could, for example, supply arms only when these are authorized by the opposition as well as the government of the purchasing country. One could supply arms only where one is also prepared to offer security guarantees, thus making explicit one's moral commitment. In such ways, State conduct could be shifted towards conforming with the letter and spirit of the classic just war doctrine.

Conscientious objection to military service

Conscientious objection to military service is a perennial issue which brings into sharp focus many of the issues of individual responsibility that we have been discussing. During the Vietnam war, US courts granted exemption from the draft to pacifists but not to objectors who based their arguments on just war principles. Similarly, UK exemption from conscription was (and if conscription returned would almost certainly again be) confined to pacifists. The reason is clear. The just war objector is taking a selective attitude which claims the right to second-guess government policy. The State's sensitivity on this matter is clear enough, but if the just war principles are as powerful and authoritative as has been argued in this chapter then there is strong reason to think that a well-informed just war objector has an especially strong claim to be heard and heeded. The claim is strong whether the objection is at the point of conscription or within the military or within a military scientific research establishment.

In the early 1990s outrages committed during the military–political disintegration of the former Yugoslavia prompted the UN to institute a war crimes tribunal for the first time since the Nuremberg and Tokyo trials after the Second World War. Such a tribunal raises numerous issues of which perhaps the most fundamental concerns individual responsibility. The UN appears to be reiterating that individuals and states are morally and legally accountable for their actions in war and rebellion. To impose this doctrine on warring factions in the former Yugoslavia is one thing; to incorporate it into our own public life by according due respect to conscience that is informed by the just war principles is another and in some ways a more searching task. In this as in so many ways there is much to be done and much guidance to be derived from the universally valid Christian just war tradition.

FURTHER READING

Donelan, M. (1990) *Elements of International Political Theory*, Oxford: Clarendon Press.

Ferguson, J. (1974) *The Politics of Love: The New Testament and Non-Violent Revolution*, Cambridge: James Clarke.

Goodwin, G. (ed.) (1982) *Ethics and Nuclear Deterrence*, London: Croom Helm.

Howard, M. E. (1978) *War and the Liberal Conscience*, London: Temple Smith.

Johnson, J. T. (1984) *Can modern war be just?*, New Haven: Yale University Press.

Midgley, E. B. F. (1975) *The Natural Law Tradition and the Theory of International Relations*, London: Elek.

Niebuhr, R. (1940) *Christianity and Power Politics*, New York: Scribner.

O'Brien, W. V. (1981) *The Conduct of Just and Limited War*, New York: Praeger.

Tusa, A. and Tusa, J. (1983) *The Nuremberg Trial*, London: Macmillan.

Vincent, J. (1974) *Nonintervention and International Order*, Princeton, NJ: Princeton University Press.

Walzer, M. (1992) *Just and Unjust Wars*, 2nd edn, Harmondsworth: Penguin.

White, N. D. (1990) *The United Nations and the Maintenance of International Peace and Security*, Manchester: Melland Schill.

Yoder, J. Y. (1971) *Nevertheless: The Varieties of Religious Pacifism*, Scottdale, Pa: Herald.

See also chapters 33, 37.

35

ETHICS AND THE PERSONAL LIFE

Helen Oppenheimer

TERMS OF REFERENCE

Discussion of 'personal ethics' must begin with demarcation. All ethics are personal ethics: only persons can live morally well or ill. What manageable topic is to be considered here? What is to be left out? 'Personal ethics' as a distinct subject is about people's private lives: not necessarily hidden, nor even beyond the reach of the law; but excluding their public roles, their citizenship, their trades, their professional services to their fellow human beings, their large- or small-scale politics. Such exclusion, to allow concentration elsewhere, is practical; but even so, feminists disapprove. As Susan Dowell put it:

> Feminism challenges the whole concept of 'personal morality' as a separate category of ethics. 'The personal is political', we say. Our sexuality is not a separate or neutral part of our existence; it embodies our whole being.
>
> Dowell 1990: 38

Whether she is saying that no ethics can leave out sexual ethics, or that sexual ethics can leave nothing out, she has a point; but a point which if taken too much to heart would make it practically impossible to discuss anything but feminism.

Of course, in principle, ethics must be a whole without boundaries: taking 'personal ethics' as a distinct subject is like projecting one area of a globe on a flat map. The Equator or the Poles will be distorted: and Alaska will be distant from Siberia. Map-making for particular areas is still a valuable enterprise, offering opportunities of overcoming common distortions rather than fostering them. The petty parochialism of confining 'personal life' to domestic life is a distortion; personal life is more than kitchen sinks. The hasty oversimplification of reducing the 'personal' to the 'erotic' is a grave distortion; personal life is more than sex. One main task for a personal ethic is to set the sexuality of human persons in context.

The late twentieth century is a strenuous time, full of danger and hope.

738

One of its best hopes is a renewed appreciation of our embodied natures. The tendency of high-minded people to try to keep 'the soul' separate from the body is being replaced by a good emphasis on the wholeness of the human being. There are practical explanations for this change. Medicine, hygiene, and reliable contraception make the body less of an enemy, easier to appreciate (Oppenheimer 1988: 33–4). There are possibilities today of a more generous and lively understanding of human embodiment. If the upshot turns out to be traditional, encouraging faithful monogamous unions, it can be based on promise rather than on threat.

Tradition: help or hindrance?

For an incarnational religion, Christianity has had remarkable difficulty in coming to terms with embodiment. Christian theologians have found it harder than the children of Israel to comprehend how physical and spiritual are united in one creature. Angels or animals have seemed more comprehensible than people.

Human sexuality has been approved, sometimes grudgingly, as a divine arrangement for populating the world. The union of a man and a woman has seemed a matter of duty and obedience; and delight, devotion and even companionship have looked like optional and unofficial extras. Meanwhile, realists have understood that men want pleasure as well as parenthood: so marriage has been conceded the secondary role of providing harmlessly for male waywardness. When women claim the same rights to pleasure as men, longer-term human happiness still goes by default. The reduction of sexual relationship to pleasure constrained by duty is hard enough on men: it is even harder on women.

Christian men and woman may now wish to repudiate these attitudes; but for Christians to abandon tradition is to cut off the branch on which they need to sit. Theology which claims to be Christian can move forward only in some kind of continuity with the past. Something must be done with the world-denying, rigorist and patriarchal tendencies in the Bible and in Christian history.

There is no need to be mesmerized by the choice 'accept asceticism, rigorism, and patriarchy or reject Christianity itself'. These ways of thinking, now so unfashionable, are not the whole story of Christian ethics. In this incarnational religion, asceticism has never had its head. Mercy has tempered and even overcome rigorism. Against patriarchy, there has always been some notion that women and men alike are beloved children of God. The story is too complex to be monochrome. From the days of the earliest Churches there have been successes and failures. Christians have been partly responsive, partly deaf to divine inspiration. There is scope for different versions of the complex story. It is not always apparent what counts as success or failure; as obedience, sin or muddle; as insight or prejudice; nor whether new ideas are rooted in faith or rebellion.

People who are confident that twentieth-century knowledge makes nonsense of older beliefs should try to inform themselves more thoroughly what it was like to be alive in earlier times, what seemed obvious, what hopes and fears explain brutality or timidity. In a world without reliable contraception, is it surprising that sexual pleasure was feared, and that women's vulnerability seemed all-important? (Oppenheimer 1990: 31; 1991a: 370.) Maybe celibacy is comprehensible if not congenial (Brown 1989). Maybe patriarchy is excusable though not justifiable. Unless Christians can achieve some appreciation of older attitudes, how can they accept the testimony of earlier Christians about the Gospel itself?

On the other hand, people who are confident about the whole tradition might remember that a tree is known by its fruits. Does the history of the actual sufferings of women indicate that God's will has been rightly understood? If we no longer think it part of the natural order for husbands to be entrusted with total control over their wives and families, and if we believe this control has often been abused, is it so evident that Christian faith requires men to be entrusted with total control over Christian ministry?

The conviction is growing today that women are oppressed. The straightforward charge of ubiquitous cruelty is too simple to stick. Millions of women down the centuries have been happy, fulfilled and indeed appreciated. What has been systematically wrong has not been plain unkindness so much as compulsory specialization. Men know that there is more to life than sexuality: for men. They have many possibilities of achieving goodness, success, happiness, fulfilment and of finding satisfying compensation for their failures. They are people first and lovers, husbands, fathers as part of their larger life stories.

Women find it harder to estimate themselves simply as people, assorted human beings: neither denying nor emphasizing their gender. However much loved and respected, they have had to be women first, married or single, attractive or unattractive. Most of their roles have been gender roles. They are faithful wives, comfortable mothers, pretty girls, fair ladies, virtuous matrons or pure virgins. When the gender roles fail, for whatever reason, there are fewer promising alternatives. Among the voices urging women quietly to accept their allotted place, the voices of Christian theologians have not been silent.

In entering into or coming to terms with their tradition, Christians must now let that tradition be confronted with the challenge of feminism. If that challenge is given priority it limits the terms of reference and confines the argument in an adversarial straitjacket. Discussion is reduced to consideration of what gender means, as if gender were all. Feminists and anti-feminists meet in unconstructive attack and defensive replies, while the not-quite-feminists can hardly gain a hearing. But to ignore the challenge is no longer a live option.

Men, women and people

Children of God come in two kinds, men and women; and through most of history, for reasons bad and good, women's lives have had a narrower scope than men's. Feminists believe it is high time for women to enter the full heritage of humanity, but there are better and worse ways of this happening. In reaction against ancient stereotyping, the first instinct of people who want to liberate women may be to deny that gender matters and try to make men and women interchangeable. Though a man cannot bear a child, and a woman cannot lift a heavy weight, maybe with creches and machinery these differences can be minimized. Women must be strong-minded and men gentle, and remaining prejudices must be legislated away. Sadly or triumphantly, people find that gender still matters: that 'unisex' is not practical; and indeed that neither men nor women much want it to be practical. So traditionalists try to refurbish 'complementarity', while feminists begin to emphasize, not deny, that women are different from men. Their basic premise has changed from 'Women can do what men can do' to 'What men have done is treat women badly.'

It is a strength and a perplexity of the Christian Churches today to have become belatedly aware of long-standing forms of oppression. 'In Christ', said St Paul, 'There is neither Jew nor Greek, there is neither slave nor free, there is neither male nor female' (Gal. 3:28). For people who believe themselves to be children of a loving Father, it should go without saying that humanity matters more than race, class, gender . . .

When it comes to gender, the very premise of the Christian argument is part of the problem. Once consciousness is raised, the Fatherhood of God is part of 'patriarchy'. 'The brotherhood of man' from being inspiring has become objectionable. Knowledge of good and evil is an uncomfortable acquisition. The clash of principles cannot readily allow a moratorium and this war is a civil war. Women have fathers and brothers, and even if they reject husbands they may still have sons. Sisterhood cannot be enough any more than brotherhood is. In a civil war the victory of either side is a defeat for both. There is reason to fear that a victory of either anti-feminism or feminism would be a defeat for humanity. What women need cannot be independence from men; nor a legalistic notional 'equality' which remains vulnerable to the facts of biology. They need, of course, attention to specific grievances; but there remains the problem of the pervasive asymmetry which is summed up by saying that it is difficult for women to enter the heritage of humanity. When a man says, 'We are men', he usually means, 'We are human beings; we have something in common', not 'We are male.' When a woman says, 'We are women', she usually means, 'We are female: we are different'; and 'different' probably implies 'superior' or 'inferior'. Unlike a man, she cannot take her gender for granted. The quest for inclusive language can even be a hindrance. What are women to do, for instance, with Wordsworth's mourning over Venice?:

741

Men are we and must grieve when even the Shade
Of that which once was great is passed away.

Complacency supposes that there is no problem, that 'men' includes women; but substituting 'people' or 'human beings' is not always easy or even possible. The overdue raising of consciousness has had the unhappy side-effect of reinforcing the notion that femaleness is the problem. Woman have achieved the doubtful freedom to repudiate disapprovingly those areas of our common past where it has become clear that women are not included.

It is too late to establish a genuinely inclusive language of 'mankind' in which women too could say naturally 'We are men', not *viri* but *homines*; but perhaps it is not too late for women to avoid the temptation to exclude men in their turn. The language of humanity is less neat and elegant that the language of 'man', but men and women need to learn to speak it and think it: not in a 'unisex' way, but indeed in a *humanist* way, which will recognize gender among the vital and valuable ways in which human beings differ from one another (Oppenheimer 1990: ch. 11).

PERSONALISM

Problem or solution?

At this point it seems obvious to some, and question-begging to others, that we must develop a true personalism before the question becomes too polarized. 'Personalism' has various connotations and its commendation needs care. If one believes that personalism properly understood is profoundly congruous with the Christian faith, one should be the more careful not just to assume its obviousness, still less to treat it as almost synonymous with Christianity. For some traditionalists, personalism is almost synonymous with secularism. They are suspicious of Christian personalist enthusiasm for human flourishing as important in God's sight: they see it rather as a dangerous rival to creaturely obedience.

Personalists are apt to be liberal-minded people who mean well and dislike extremes. They are therefore easily made to feel guilty. It is a familiar experience for moderate liberals to find good ideas logically applied not bringing increased human happiness after all, but 'opening the floodgates' and endangering comfortable certainties. So will the personalist affirmation that fulfilment matters in God's eyes turn out to be another case of a noble-sounding principle which does not stand the test of practical experience?

Traditionalists oddly converge with feminists in distrust of personalism. Feminists notice a personalist tendency to assume that persons are men. They suspect that this friendly-sounding view will turn out to be another way of ignoring women and setting up the superiority of the male. Meanwhile traditionalists suspect that emphasis on 'personal relationships' will flatten out the God-given distinction between male and female. Their fear is that personalism amounts to an individualist and unisex permissiveness which treats human beings as interchangeable units.

In deciding whether personalism is breakthrough or false emphasis, much depends upon what questions are being asked. Personalism at its best is a promising way of understanding the nature of human beings. When it is advocated as a theory about sexual ethics it is more controversial and less convincing. There is substance in the criticism that it offers a limited understanding of human life. It is also fair to suggest that this is a limited version of personalism. The distinction is worth spelling out, lest criticism of the limited version should be deemed to refute a personalist understanding of people.

In recent discussion of sexual ethics, a three-way contrast has developed. On the one hand is the traditional view that sexual behaviour has laws laid down by God. On the other hand is the libertarian view that sexual behaviour has no laws of its own and is governed only by ordinary right and wrong, so that 'anything goes' but cruelty and exploitation. Between these, 'personalism' has been identified as the view that 'what matters in sexual behaviour is the quality of personal relationship that it serves to express and confirm' (*Homosexual relationships* 1979: para. 137).

Such mediating personalism comes under criticism, for all its attractiveness, as a temptation. It is said that in the USA it has 'a good chance of becoming the going christian ethic of sex'; and that 'among "liberal" clergy, the personalist position has already carried the day' (Turner 1985: 37). Not everyone sees this as a breakthrough. Even liberal-minded thinkers are arguing against this fashionable personalism in sexual ethics as inadequate and even dangerous. There is weighty criticism here which deserves attention: especially the accusation that 'the person exists more and more as an atomistic individual whose gender is swallowed up in the transsexual world of "personhood" ' (ibid. 47–9).

Personalists should protest that such narrowing of the meaning of 'personalism' also deserves attention. Personalism ought to mean a concern with human flourishing which has nothing to do with self-centred individualism, but rather with integrity and fidelity; and with the kind of love which can both take and give and not always know which of these is which. Personalism applied to sexual ethics can reject 'unisex' and the idolatry of 'relationships' and agree with the affirmation that 'We are not free to make of sex just what we will' (*Homosexual relationships* 1979: para. 148).

Personalism as ghost-buster

When personalism is claimed as a breakthrough it has more to offer than short-term concern with the sexual fulfilment of individuals. The clue is the imputation of atomism. A main point, even *the* main point, that personalists want to make is the *denial* of atomism. Something has gone wrong, at least with the vocabulary.

Personalism considered as the most promising way of understanding what human beings are should be contrasted, not with traditional or radical sexual morality, but with rationlist dualism. Philosophers since Descartes had let themselves get into the habit of looking on people as 'selves', lone intellectual beings, who each had to think *his* own way out of solipsism if *he* were to have any grounds for believing that the physical world was real or that there were any other people, 'other minds', in it. Wittgenstein broke the grip of this theory of knowledge. Gilbert Ryle in *The Concept of Mind* (1949) let in a wind of change to blow away the bad habits of solipsism. 'The ghost in the machine' could retire from active service and the wholeness of the person could come into its own.

Pesonalism offers the rediscovery of a proper emphasis on embodiment; on minding as well as knowing; and on persons in relation to one another not solipsistically divided. Instead of lone thinkers trying to discover whether there are any other minds, we are human beings learning from each other about the world and how to live in it. 'I participate, therefore I am' can replace 'I think, therefore I am' (Taylor 1963: 49–50; Oppenheimer 1973: 118–24, 131–9; 1988: 30–60; Pobee 1979: 49). Knowledge based on lonely theorizing has nothing but lonely theorizing to build on, so that awareness of other people remains puzzling. Unless relatedness is built into the foundations of our identity it will hardly fit into the superstructure. Solipsism given an inch takes an ell: we need a less abstract comprehension of what persons are. Since more women have found a voice it seems less of a philosophical solecism to notice the interdependence of human beings from their babyhood.

From relatedness to relationship

Christian personalists propose to banish not only solipsism but *legalism*. They take the personalist theory of knowledge, in which relatedness is more fundamental than separateness, and build on it an ethic, in which people matter to one another rather than merely bargaining with one another. Self-conscious rectitude must abdicate in favour of *generosity*.

Moral philosophers have emphasized the autonomous 'moral subject' who is primarily characterized as owing duties and bearing rights (Oppenheimer 1974: 82–4; 1991b: 9–12). Personalists can afford to demote this character. Like the lone thinker, he is an abstraction (Byrne 1991: 101). For personalism, tautologically, persons are primary, and persons are people. It is people, not 'subject–selves', who are real: people who have wants and needs and especially needs for companionship.

The ethic of rights and duties has nothing but rights and duties to build on, so that supererogation remains puzzling. Unless generosity can somehow be built into the foundations of ethics it will hardly fit into the superstructure.

744

Legalism given an inch takes an ell: but personalism can decline to put on the legalistic straitjacket. The supremacy of obligation is eclipsed by magnanimity.

Human beings who have recently discovered human rights are afraid of finding themselves on the wrong side here; but the good can be the enemy of the best. Rights are necessary and rights can be deadly. Fixation on rights bedevils moral problems such as divorce and abortion (Oppenheimer 1990: ch. 6; 1992), not to speak of theological problems such as atonement and divine judgement. Personalists are allowed to notice that in order to flourish people require more than their rights: more indeed than they can *fairly* demand. They need to enable one another to transcend rights: in other words, to love and be loved.

This ethic may be mistrusted, from left or right, as 'individualist' or as 'liberal'; and indeed it is both. As individualist, its enemy is totalitarianism, not community (Oppenheimer 1991c: 3). As liberal, it opposes rigorism, not order. If it emphasizes human happiness more strongly than obedience, the happiness it commends is not the immediate satisfaction of a separate and selfish 'self' but the long-term flourishing of real people who are aware of belonging to each other. The concept of relatedness, which belongs to theory of knowledge, cannot remain morally neutral but needs to be expanded into a concept of relationship, which belongs to ethics; and even to develop into a concept of enabling grace, which belongs to theology.

Does the smooth transition from persons, via other people, to relationships which enable human flourishing really allow and encourage the further, Christian, transition from human grace to the grace of God? This kind of personalism is indeed miles away from atomism; but is it therefore close to the Christian Gospel? Is personalism suspiciously humanist? If the answer is to be, 'humanist' yes, 'suspiciously' no, something will have to be done to relate personalism to the Christian tradition (Oppenheimer 1983, 1988, 1989a).

Can personalism be Christian?

Christian moralists have been much influenced, indeed too much, by Anders Nygren's magisterial and profound book *Agape and Eros*. True Christian love is supposed to be 'unmotivated'. Modelled on the love of God, *agapē* must not expect its beloved to be lovable or deserving. This orthodoxy would make the personalist emphasis on the value and the flourishing of human beings too selfish to be part of Christianity. Nygren said many fine and important things about *agapē*; but in so far as he belittled *eros*, the love that wants, neglected *philia*, the love that appreciates, and cast doubt upon whether human beings could be said to love God, it is as well that a reaction has set in (Oppenheimer 1973: 184–7; 1983: 104–10; 1986: 153). It is time to bring the hope of fulfilment back into human and divine love.

The LORD GOD of Israel from all eternity wanted like a GOD. He wanted the Communication of His Divine essence, and Persons to enjoy it. He wanted Worlds, He wanted Spectators, He wanted Joys, He wanted Treasures. He wanted, yet he wanted not, for he had them.

(Traherne 1958 I: para. 41)

Fulfilment rightly understood is not selfishly individualistic, because what fulfils people is loving and being loved. So *agapē* can make room for *eros*: *eros*, of course, not just in its limited sense of erotic love, but as desire in its widest and deepest meaning. People are not lone atoms but need one another to be themselves. Their relatedness is not extra but fundamental. There is nothing unworthy about needing and wanting, when what people need and want is the company and attention of one another.

The selfish/unselfish dichotomy is too simple. Liking is supposed to be selfish, benevolence unselfish: yet most people would rather be naturally liked than made the object of disinterested philanthropy or even 'respect for persons'. There is more hope in liking more people than in 'loving' people one dislikes (Oppenheimer 1983: 124–31).

Nygren treated the emphasis on friendship in the Fourth Gospel with a certain anxiety, as a decline from *agapē*; but Christian personalism need not be so nervous. To make friends is to find out each other's value, to enjoy each other's company and to want each other's fulfilment. Finite as we are, we are limited in our friendships. Nobody but God can appreciate the endless variety of human beings; the attention span of each of us is tiny and our days are short; but friendship is not intrinsically exclusive. Friendship is not an excuse for turning one's back upon most of the world, but can be a model for the way any human being might be appreciated. Rather than a rival to *agapē*, the appreciative love which is *philia* is like a pattern sum ready worked out, a picture of possibilities (Oppenheimer 1973: 188–92, 1983: 118–21, 132–9).

If people may be valued, they should be valued in their individual distinctiveness. Instead of being afraid of the notion of partiality, personalists could almost define *agapē* as partiality extended to infinity, on the pattern of the infinite love of God who ascribes special and unlimited value to each human being, not generalized but particular for every one. As Milton said,

Then long eternity shall greet our bliss
With an individual kiss.

BIBLICAL BASIS

Creation stories

Traditional theological views need to be shown to make contemporary sense. Novel theological views need to be related to characteristic Christian affirmations. Christian personalism claims to be almost platitudinously traditional: in ascribing such importance to people, it treats them as God's children. If this sounds novel, is that an indictment of Christians? Or is the very assumption that fulfilment is truly Christian itself an accommodation to the spirit of the age? Personalism generally seems to have more work to do to please traditionalists than liberals.

One way to relate personalism to traditional Christianity is by giving it a biblical though not a fundamentalist base. The early chapters of Genesis are not a history of our origins, but can be taken more timelessly as an inspired interpretation of what human creatures are. There is moral theology packed up here in mythical form. The insistence that men and women are made 'in the image of God' makes a firm foundation for a personal ethic. The concept of the 'one flesh' union of husband and wife has been a basis for Christian sexual morality at its most positive. If excuse is needed for taking this ancient myth-making seriously, the belief that Christ himself took it seriously is firmly embedded in the Gospels (Mark 10: 6–9; Matt. 19: 4–6).

It is worth making the effort to extricate the stories in the first two chapters of Genesis, not only from the debate about human origins which goes back to Darwin, but also from the more recent debate about sexism. Feminists are now looking at these chapters, and the prejudices they have collected, with new eyes. Has an imbalance or even corruption distorted the interpretation by fallen human beings of their fallen condition? (Trible 1978; Clines 1990: 25–48; Dennis 1991: 1–23). Since the stories have been understood for so long as upholding the superiority of men, the change of perspective required cannot be achieved in a moment. The debate goes on, with some overstatement on both sides.

Meanwhile these myths have more to offer than a controversial sexual ethic. If twentieth-century Christians put aside the notions that Genesis is essentially anti-evolutionary, anti-feminist and outdated, they can find in these ancient stories a holism and even an implicit humanism appropriate for an incarnational faith. From the biblical accounts of creation can be drawn a theological analysis of human beings: their double nature, embodied and spiritual, akin to the dust of the earth and the breath of God; their need for each other and capacity for union; their fertility as blessed by God (Oppenheimer 1989a: 89–90; 1990: 9).

Double nature

The emphasis on embodiment presents the physical as vehicle for the spiritual. The picture language about dust and breath need not be dualist or sexist, but properly materialist. The physical and more than physical character of human beings can be interpreted in terms of *word* and *sacrament* (Oppenheimer 1973: 26–32; 1988: 48–66; 1989a: 114–15; 1990: 63–4).

Words need body. Matter, far from being insignificant, is our means of communication. Communication is more fundamentally human even than sexuality. Bodies are the means by which people keep in touch, literally and metaphorically, with one another and the outer world. Dualism is unsatisfactory because it detaches spirit from body. All human relationships, from mere acquaintance to close friendship, including of course erotic relationships, depend upon hearing, sight, or touch. In this 'materialism' the Christian concept of incarnation finds a foothold: in due time, the Word of God was made flesh and dwelt among us, communicating with us humanly.

Sacraments need body. Matter, far from being unworthy, conveys spiritual reality. Some Christians elaborating upon this idea ignore its simplest meaning. They appreciate the erotic as holy, yet meanwhile overlook an even more obvious aspect of our humanity: physical creatures live by nourishment. Contemporary Christians rightly point out that the story of the Fall does not ascribe the origin of sin to sexuality. They may not notice that the sin of eating forbidden fruit is likewise a matter of embodiment. More seriously, they miss a literal truth in the myth of creation: the fruitfulness of the earth has to do with the nourishment of creatures.

Feeding one another is a fundamentally human activity. People till the ground, or it is tilled for them. They nurture their children. They provide food, or prepare it, for themselves and for each other. Not trivially, they offer refreshment to their guests. They mark out their ordinary lives by mealtimes. In our physical need for nourishment we are animals; in the meanings we give to food and drink and the rituals we build upon these meanings we find a large part of our humanity. Food and drink for human beings are means of grace as well as means of sustenance.

No interpretation of what human creatures are which omits this physical aspect can claim continuity with biblical tradition. More 'spiritual' believers patronize ancient sacrificial systems as materialistic; but people who have taken bodies as seriously as 'souls', making offerings from their first fruits and their herds, eating and drinking with their God as well as with each other, have laid the foundations of an understanding of *communion* as beginning in embodiment but not ending there.

Needing each other

The creation stories emphasize not only embodiment but relationship: at least an affirmation of the human need for one another's company, which the animals cannot assuage. Genesis 2 ends with the union of Adam and Eve (Trible 1978: 102–4). Love, not just duty, can find a foothold here. This triumphant conclusion has been under-emphasized in Christian art: many minds have been formed by Michelangelo, who moves straight from Eve's creation to the Fall. But the emphasis from Genesis taken up by Christ is not sinfulness nor even fertility, but the one-flesh union of a man and a woman (Mark 10: 6–8); Matt. 19: 4–5).

Of course there is a sexual ethic here. Its positive character is plain, though not always well heeded by moralists: what God has made is 'very good'. But besides this general affirmation the creation myths offer a specific understanding of human sexuality, as expressed from the beginning in the pairbond. We can call the first human beings Adam and Eve if we wish. What we need to say about them, if we believe there is inspiration in the Book of Genesis (Clines 1990: 47–8), is that men and women found from the first that they belonged to each other. The story of creation culminates in human marriage as 'one flesh' union (Gen.1: 23–4).

To found sexual ethics upon 'the mutual society, help and comfort, that the one ought to have of the other' (*Book of Common Prayer*) is neither unbiblical nor unrealistic. There is good hope of regaining this emphasis today. 'When Vatican II defined marriage as a community of love it effectively endorsed the view ... that love was not something to be forced in among the so-called secondary purposes of marriage' (O'Callaghan 1970: 104).

Fertility

Traditionalists may be unhappy with the personalist emphasis on relationships, and prefer to emphasize the command, 'Be fruitful and multiply' (Gen. 1: 28). Some have seen sexual love as justified only by procreation. Up to a point, they can call biology to witness. The human pairbond has evolved for continuing our species, as the context in which children are most safely born and nurtured. Believers may affirm that the raising of children within marriage is in accord with 'natural law', and that for people to marry and have children is in a clear sense a 'norm': provided that these concepts are used in gratitude not in exclusiveness, and that questions are not prejudged about the legitimacy and indeed the value of other ways of life (Oppenheimer 1990: 13–14, 48).

The human 'one-flesh' union has far transcended its biological function and Christians believe such transcendence to be according to the purpose of God (ibid.: 86–7). 'Be fruitful and multiply' is encouragement more than command. God's blessing on procreation belongs with the announcement that human beings are made in God's image and likeness: they are fit to be granted a share in God's creativeness.

Relationships and community

The image of God in human beings is both creative and relational. God says, 'Let us make man in our image.' Christian Trinitarian hindsight has relished that 'Let us'. Without naive over-emphasis, one can appreciate Sherwin Bailey's judicious summary: 'Man in the image of God is essentially a "being-in-relation", and human existence is essentially "existence-in-community"' (Bailey 1959: 267). Since Bailey's great book was published, these ideas of 'relation' and 'community' have been much bandied about. They have lost much of their vitality and have become triggers of approval or disapproval, mechanical aids to slogan-thinking. They are no less needed but require care to make them work with any precision.

It is worthwhile to keep struggling with the idea of 'persons-in-relation'. Though the meaning of 'relationship' is elusive, sliding from geometry to sociology, its slipperiness can be put to use, with caution, to illuminate what persons are by making connections between fact and value (Oppenheimer 1973: 143–4; 1983: 71–3). Likewise it is worthwhile to keep struggling with the idea of 'community'. The trouble is that 'community' has to be a 'Good Thing' and so becomes a too convenient substitute for argument or even a hasty plunge into politics. An appeal to 'community', without precise context, can be used to knock 'individualism' on the head as the characteristic 'Bad Thing' of our times, without specifying what is being meant by 'individual' or what kind of community, 'we' or 'they', is to be given such priority of esteem (Oppenheimer 1991c: 3).

The affirmation that human beings find their true existence in community need not imply that any collective, nation, neighbourhood, family or even Church, has priority over individual people; nor that 'joiners' are better than 'non-joiners'; nor indeed that hermits who abandon human company to seek the vision of God are selfish. What it means is simpler and more basic: that human beings are social creatures, that 'it is not good', nor even possible, for them 'to be alone'. They need each other and depend upon each other, even for their very identity (Oppenheimer 1973: 136). The kind of individualist who neglects, rejects or tramples upon other people is going against the grain of creation. 'Hell is other people' is perversely wrong: hell is solipsism, the isolation of the ingrowing self.

PROVING TOO MUCH

The two shall become one

Various oversimplifications and overstatements hinder the sorting out of what needs to be said about Christian personal ethics. The trouble with creation stories as a theological foundation is not that they are 'unscientific', provided that they are not taken as proofs but as elucidations; nor that they are sexist, if they are given a chance not to be; but that, in using them as a resource, it is tempting to try to make them say everything that needs to be said all at once.

1 Personalists are not exempt from this tendency to prove too much. The temptation is to spoil a good case by trying to go too fast. It is not special pleading for Christian personalists to emphasize the 'one-flesh union' and to offer an interpretation which aspires to be both liberal and traditional. But there is a short cut which substitutes a part for a whole, letting an excellent doctrine of marriage do duty for an ethic of persons-in-relation.

Personalism can happily fit the two creation stories together. According to

Genesis 1, humanity is created, in the image of God, as male and female: which suggests that human beings are fundamentally relational. In Genesis 2: 18 this is spelt out: 'It is not good that the man should be alone.' Adam welcomes Eve with the words, 'This at last is bone of my bone and flesh of my flesh.' So the honourable estate of matrimony (*Book of Common Prayer*) goes back to the beginnings of humanity; and is revalidated in the teaching of Christ. 'Therefore a man leaves father and mother and cleaves to his wife, and they become one flesh' (Gen. 1: 23–4; Mark 10: 7–8. But if marriage is supposed to be the sole point of creation the argument has over-reached itself.

Where liberals make relationships all-important and traditionalists make offspring all-important, this version of personalism makes marriage all-important. What has it to say to people who are not spouses? The ethics of marriage must not take over the whole of ethics. The marriage union is an excellent example of what human relatedness can mean: not the only example, though maybe a paradigm case.

Christian personalism at its best is about human beings made in God's image. It needs spelling out ethically and metaphysically. Such spelling out will sooner or later need the difficult but rewarding idea of 'unity-in-plurality'. The three-in-oneness of God, the Pauline and Johannine notion of abiding in Christ and in one another, the experience of enabling grace whether divine or human, are all instances of a concept which may be called personal immanence: in which, strangely but compellingly, unity turns out to enhance, not swallow up, individuality. Marriage is the most conspicuous and familiar example of unity-in-plurality in human life; and as such it is an available analogy for the theological concept of immanence (Oppenheimer 1971; 1973: 165–80). We can avoid the invalid syllogism: the image of God is relational; marriage is relational; therefore the image of God is matrimonial. The Trinity is not a marriage; but the union of husband and wife in human marriage can be used as one valid illustration of what it might mean to say that the concept of personal immanence makes sense.

2 Traditionalists, having so frequently given priority to celibacy, may feel secure from any risk of making marriage too important. What they have over-stressed has been 'Christian marriage'. They have allowed the human pair-bond, as blessed by the Creator, to disappear into a would-be loftier notion of a kind of union founded by Christ, reserved for Christians. Such possessive-ness offers a *doctrine of Christian marriage* which impoverishes the *Christian doctrine of marriage* by cutting it off from 'the beginning of creation'. The teaching of Christ illuminates the meaning of marriage as it already existed in God's purpose for human beings. The wedding at Cana was not a Christian sacrament (Oppenheimer 1971: para. 24; 1990: 8–9, 57, 59, 75–6).

The definition of marriage in English law, the voluntary union for life of a man and a woman, is practically a paraphrase of the words of Genesis quoted by Christ (Mark 10: 6–8). Christians can build on this, taking seriously the idea of faithfulness implicit in it. Marriage is a man and a woman consenting to belong to each other for life, whatever religious or secular ceremony they find suitable for blessing, or simply for making public, their commitment. What Christians may still think wrong with 'fornication' is lack of commitment, not lack of ceremony. Christian affirmation of monogamy can encourage life-enhancing hopes: that sexual union expresses fidelity and nourishes it; and that fidelity deserves the time it needs to become deep-rooted.

3 While traditionalists suggest that valid sexual ethics must be Christian, liberals suggest that valid personal ethics must be sexual. Their characteristic overstatement has been to assimilate 'relationship' with 'erotic relationship'. Any relationship which is evidently not erotic is deemed to be minor, or undeveloped, or frustrated, or dishonest. Friendship is inadequately distinguished from romantic love and becomes hard to place. Human dealings with one another are placed along one scale, ranging from casual to intimate according to their degree of physical commitment; so that sexuality is allowed to colonize human life and human love. How, for instance, can we say that this husband and wife are friends if 'friend' has no distinct meaning from 'lover'? The very attempt to build up the significance of personal relationships seems to make them at the same time oddly one-dimensional.

There is not only overstatement but confusion in this. The double character of human beings as both embodied and spiritual, dust and breath, is not the same doubleness of their sexuality, male or female. A human being is embodied *and* spiritual; a human being is man *or* woman. Human embodiment is sexual not asexual, but gender differentiation is not the whole significance of embodiment. The myth of the union of Adam and Eve expresses a truth, even a fundamental truth, but not the whole truth about human relationships in their variety.

Well-intended tyrannies

Exaggerations react against each other, making overstatement hard to eliminate. The liberal oversimplification which assimilates relationships, permissively, is reacting against a traditional oversimplification which distinguishes relationships, prohibitively. Liberals make the pair important at the expense of the bond, indignant at the tyranny of making the bond important at the expense of the pair.

Traditionalists reasonably deny that the rigorism they commend ignores human happiness. They can quote Wordsworth: 'the weight of too much liberty'. Human beings may be happiest living their lives within a firm framework. To want to be good and to have to work out for oneself all the way what goodness means is a kind of freedom which looks much like nightmare. What is fair? What is loyal? What is prudent? How far can we go? What can I expect? Should I leave him? Situation ethics is like Alice's croquet with flamingoes for mallets.

Whereas liberal optimism expects faithfulness to operate in a vacuum, traditionalist logic ties up faithfulness in formality. Firm moral frameworks become unyielding legal frameworks. When Christians relish the idea of the law of Christ and forget how dangerously antinomian the ethics of the kingdom must have looked, there is shrinkage and distortion. The breaking of Christian marriage vows, unlike monastic vows, is made into a metaphysical impossibility rather than a tragic fact. Can this divorcee marry again, not because her sin has been forgiven, but because she was baptized after she was first married? Are these young people 'living in sin', not because they refuse to commit themselves, but because they do not see the paraphernalia of getting married as relevant to their circumstances? The idea that what counts is the ring on one's finger is a taunt of Faust's Mephistopheles, not a command of Christ. With good intentions traditionalism has given support to various kinds of legalistic over-emphasis.

A high view of marriage can slip into cruelty: not only to sinners penitent and less penitent, but to people who through no particular fault of their own do not fit into the natural categories which make for an uneventful moral life. Sexual ethics becomes tyrannical when blessings, especially heterosexual marriage and the procreation of children, come to look like conditions for acceptability. When the norm of family life is taken for granted, single people, childless people and people whose marriages are in trouble have to bear the loneliness and indignity of being odd ones out, as well as the sadness of missing ordinary human happiness. 'Norm' ought to be a useful neutral word establishing a good firm base from which constructive variations would be possible and unhappy variations would be manageable. It can become a device for damning nonconformity by definition.

Lack of imagination can look like disapproval. Actual disapproval, hiding behind attempts to 'hate the sin but love the sinner', shows itself as reprobation. Would-be tolerance can fall into such well-meaning insensitivities as the expectation that celibacy will surely be the Christian solution to other people's problems. Though the recommendation of celibacy to divorced people is less in fashion than it used to be, Christian moralists have by no means given up the idea that such renunciation must be expected of homosexual people. So it comes to look like a positive suggestion, still in the name of tolerance, that same-sex lovers should be exhorted, not to faithfulness, but to secrecy. It is not surprising when they angrily repudiate the norm in whose name this advice is given, and reject the notion that homosexuality constitutes a 'problem' at all (Oppenheimer 1990: 105).

These matters are not now being neglected in the Christian Churches. A good deal of work is going on, some of it dogged by prejudices, harsh or sentimental, much of it inconclusive: but much of it determined to look loyally and constructively at the meaning of the Christian Gospel. Theologians and pastors are taking into account the experience of individuals and the real needs of our times. Commissions meet and wrestle and report, congregations consider, and although nothing happens immediately as a result attitudes begin to change and progress is made.

WORK IN PROGRESS

Pros and cons

The thorniest recurrent problems are how to avoid the perennial optional/compulsory dichotomy; and how to be generously flexible about exceptions without letting exceptions swallow up valuable norms. Permissiveness is the obverse of rigorism, part of the same trap. Christians need to appreciate, not smugly but gratefully, what really is life-enhancing, and not allow what they know to be good to be reduced to optional extras or unrealistic ideals. To let fidelity go by default in discouragement or cynicism could be to sin against the Holy Ghost. Understanding is hampered by backlashes on both sides which are not even attempting tolerance. There is a traditional backlash against liberalism which makes no effort to understand discontent, and unimaginatively 'upholds standards'. This reaction fuels a radical backlash which actively sets about denying ancient blessings and destroying ancient standards.

Sometimes it is supposed that everything is different today, for good or ill; sometimes that morality at least is unchangeable. The feeling that we are living in frightening times, in too big a universe with alien powers in charge, is not new: nor the conviction of successive generations of elders that 'young people today have no standards'. There never was a golden age. Goodness is always in jeopardy, and nagging could never be the answer: nor the kind of self-fulfilling defeatism which brandishes alarming statistics (Oppenheimer 1990: 1–4).

There was no golden age: but there is a revolution, mostly medical, with real ethical consequences. Right and wrong abide but terms of reference change. Effective safeguards against disastrous pregnancy really have altered the demands of prudence. It is understandable that the notion of a 'human right' to sexual experience has gained ground. The menace of AIDS has not abolished that notion, though it has polarized attitudes. For some, the old idea of natural law has acquired increased authority; for others, the idea of safe casual sex has been positively advertised by the recommendation of sensible precautions. Those who believe that the demands of faithfulness are as valid as ever have the responsibility, indeed the opportunity, to explain faithfulness anew in its fresh context.

Panic, resentment and aggressiveness are unconstructive. What Christians need in sexual ethics, as everywhere, is objective information; courage looking steadily at ascertained facts; faith remembering God's presence; and imaginative goodwill, transcending tolerance, entering into other people's situations. Some of the troubles which cluster around sexual ethics arise from attempts to enforce love rather than enable it (Oppenheimer 1986: 160–2). Legislation cannot work unless legislators understand the limitations of law; but there is plenty of scope for providing frameworks for flourishing: legal, social and educational. Timing needs attention. For example, when vows are broken and reconciliation is impossible there can be conciliation; like the terminal care a hospice provides when cure is impossible. A marriage, like a human being, can make a 'good end'. If we would rather it made a good start, the foundations are best laid long before. Children learn about relationships from babyhood: that is when encouragement can begin for their development into men and women who will be able to love one another (Oppenheimer 1990: 109). The Christian personalist contribution is emphasis on human happiness: not instant satisfaction of the most vocal but the long-term flourishing of all concerned according to the purpose of their Creator.

Little ones

Who are those concerned? It is strange how, in many of the arguments about sexual ethics, the children have been the least considered. Liberals, concentrating on relationships between adults and the excellence of sexuality, have over-ridden the interests of children: a serious indictment against followers of Christ. The strong argument, which many people have found out the hard way, against the hope that a more relaxed family law will make unhappy people happier is the miserable effect which unstable relationships really do have upon children of all ages. When loving parents, stuck in their own troubles, are unable, not unwilling, to give their children the security everyone knows they need, and when pastors and legislators are preoccupied with helping the course of true love to run smooth, who is to speak for the whole family? The belated appreciation of this priority is an encouraging factor in recent discussion (English Law Commission 1993; Burgoyne et al. 1987). As the children of more and more broken homes grow up and begin to shape their own lives, complex ethical ramifications are developing: instability and lack of good role models no doubt, and many teeth set on edge; but also, much truly moral determination to learn from the mistakes and hypocrisies of previous generations. What will happen to marriage in this combination of pressure and promise is not predetermined for good or for ill.

It might be expected that renewed emphasis on children would vindicate traditionalists, who surely, with their emphasis on procreation, could be expected to get family life right; but sometimes they have seemed to pay more attention to unborn and even unconceived children than to actual families. While theologians have stressed the duty of married couples to have children, the duty to cherish existing children, within and outside wedlock, has become a characteristic emphasis of secular writers (e.g. Fletcher 1973; Burgoyne et al. 1987).

It is not too late for Christian moralists to be constructive and convincing about family life. They can affirm that the one-flesh union of a man and a woman is characterized, but not defined, by fertility (Oppenheimer 1990: 89). In other words, human love in the image of divine love is not self-enclosed but creative. Procreation is by no means the only kind of creation, but it is an ordinary and excellent example of it. In the purpose of God, new people originate in love, are nourished in love, and grow up to love and be loved. At whatever stage love is lacking or inadequate, the Christian faith is that God's purpose is not eventually defeated; but the cost may be heavy in the short, middle and even long run.

Fidelity

What human relationships need, all human relationships not just marital ones, is faithfulness. If this seems vague outside the context of marriage, there is a promising way of making it more specific: encouragement of ordinary and not so ordinary truthfulness to one another. If people stopped using big and little deceptions as an appropriate oil for the wheels of relationship, they and their spouses, children, friends, acquaintances, colleagues, could live in a less uncertain and inhospitable world. The ethics of personal life, sooner or later, is about integrity and its application to people's variegated callings (Bok 1978; Oppenheimer 1990: 22–4).

Marriage has a particular faithfulness: 'forsaking all others, keep thee only unto her – keep thee only unto him – so long as ye both shall live'. This lifelong requirement evidently goes beyond the evolutionary imperative to provide security for offspring. Childless people, whether heterosexual or homosexual, may claim exemption: at the price of missing one of the most life-enhancing forms of fulfilment available to human beings. For vows to fail means tragedy, because the loss of a great good is a great loss. To belong to one another for life is to have time and space to tend and reap a harvest of trust, with the live hope of bringing to fruition happiness, vitality, generosity, effectiveness and wisdom. Taking each other for granted is faith, not exploitation. What spouses promise is not to make a strange unnatural sacrifice of their freedom. On the contrary, they promise one another a firm base from which to meet the rest of the world. All manner of fidelities can be built upon the fidelity of marriage (ibid.: ch. 3)

Again, it is important not to prove too much. Marriage is not the only form of faithfulness upon which human beings can build their lives. Celibacy, when it is positive vocation not negative renunciation, is precisely a form of fidelity. The claims of faithfulness upon human beings are wider than either marriage or celibacy: as wide as the claims of generosity and on the same basis, that human beings are so made that faithfulness and generosity are the raw material of their flourishing and fulfilment.

REFERENCES

Bailey, D. S. (1959) *The Man–Woman Relation in Christian Thought*, London: Longman.

Bok, S. (1978) *Lying, Moral Choice in Public and Private Life*, New York: Pantheon Books.

Book of Common Prayer (1662) 'The solemnization of matrimony'.

Brown, P. (1989) *The Body and Society*, London: Faber & Faber.

Burgoyne, J., Ormrod, R. and Richards, M. (1987) *Divorce Matters*, Harmondsworth: Penguin.

Byrne, P. (1992) *The Philosophical and Theological Foundations of Ethics*, Basingstoke and London: Macmillan.

Clines, D. A. J. (1990) *What Does Eve Do to Help?*, Sheffield: Sheffield Academic Press.

Dennis, T. (1991) *Lo and Behold: The Power of Old Testament Story-Telling*, London: SPCK.

Dowell, S. (1990) *The Two Shall Be Made One*, London: Collins.

English Law Commission (1993) *Looking to the Future: Mediation and the Ground for Divorce*, London: HM Stationery Office.

Fletcher, R. (1973) *The Family and Marriage in Britain*, Harmondsworth: Penguin.

Homosexual Relationships: A Contribution to Discussion (1979), A report published for the Church of England Board for Social Responsibility, London: CIO Publishing.

Marriage and the Doctrine of the Church of England: Study Extracts from the Reports of Two Recent Marriage Commissions, (1985), House of Bishops Marriage Education Panel, Cambridge: Cambridge University Press.

Nygren, A. (1969) *Agape and Eros*, New York: Harper.

O'Callaghan, D. (1970) 'Marriage as Sacrament', in *Concilium* 5: 6.

Oppenheimer, H. (1971) 'Marriage as illustrating some Christian doctrines', in *Marriage, Divorce and the Church* (The Root Report), London: SPCK.

—— (1973) *Incarnation and Immanence*, London: Hodder & Stoughton.

—— (1974) *The Character of Christian Morality* (2nd edn), Leighton Buzzard: Faith Press.

—— (1983) *The Hope of Happiness: A Sketch for a Christian Humanism*, London: SCM Press.

—— (1986) 'Divorce' 'Desire' and 'Marriage', in *A New Dictionary of Christian Ethics*, ed. J. Childress and J. Macquarrie, London: SCM and Westminster Press.

—— (1988) *Looking Before and After: The Archbishop of Canterbury's Lent Book*, London: Collins.

—— (1989a) 'Two shall become one', in P. Turner (ed.) *Men and Women: Sexual Ethics in Turbulent Times*, Cambridge, Mass.: Cowley Publications.

—— (1989b) 'Handling Life', in G. R. Dunstan and E. A. Shinebourne (eds) *Doctors' Decisions: Ethical Conflicts in Medical Practice*, Oxford: Oxford University Press.

—— (1990) *Marriage* ('Ethics: Our choices' series), London: Mowbray.

—— (1991a) 'Ethics, sexual', in *Dictionary of the Ecumenical Movement*, Geneva: WCC Publications.

—— (1991b) 'Ourselves, our Souls and Bodies', in *Studies in Christian Ethics* 4: 1–21.

—— (1991c) 'Belonging and the Individual', in *Trust* 5: 2–4 London: SCM Press.

—— (1992) 'Abortion', in *Studies in Christian Ethics*, 5: 46–60.

—— (1995) 'Marriage' and 'Partnering', in P. A. B. Clarke and A. Linzey (eds) *Dictionary of Ethics, Theology and Society*, London: Routledge.

Pobee, J. S. (1979) *Toward an African Theology*, Nashville: Abingdon.

Rogerson, J. (1991) *Genesis 1–11*, Sheffield: JSOT Press.

Ryle, G. (1949) *The Concept of Mind*, London: Hutchinson.

Taylor, J. V. (1963) *The Primal Vision*, London: SCM Press.
Traherne, T. (1958) *Centuries: Poems and Thanksgivings*, Oxford: Oxford University Press.
Trible, P. (1978) *God and the Rhetoric of Sexuality*, Philadelphia: Fortress Press.
Turner, P. (1985) *Sex, Money and Power*, Cambridge, Mass.: Cowley Publications.
See also chapter 38.

36

THEOLOGY, WEALTH AND SOCIAL JUSTICE

Jack Mahoney

Both historically and in the present a variety of Christian attitudes can be identified towards wealth, influenced to a significant extent either by explicit teaching about it in the Bible or by reflecting on wealth in the light of various basic Christian beliefs. Thus, the powerful words of Jesus on the spiritual dangers of money and wealth (Mark 10:23–7) have imprinted themselves so deeply on the Christian community through the centuries that those who are well off, or even comfortably off, often feel uneasy and troubled in conscience. Moreover, the whole subsequent Christian tradition of suspicion towards wealth, with its stress on the evils of materialism, consumerism and worldliness, has provided scant comfort, far less encouragement, to those whose job in life is to create wealth and make money, whether for themselves and their dependants, or for others, or for the society in which they live. Added to that, the plight of the increasing millions of poor people living often in otherwise affluent countries as well as in the less developed areas of the globe raises very serious ethical and theological misgivings about the economic structures of modern society which can result in such striking disparities of wealth among human beings.

BIBLICAL THEOLOGIES OF WEALTH

The question needs to be considered, however, whether the sum total of the Christian evaluation of wealth is that it constitutes a major source of temptation and is nothing more than an occasion of sin for individuals, or whether the New Testament's silence on wealth as a social issue, for whatever reason, can be supplemented for believers who live more consciously in the long haul of history than did the early Christian community, and who have come to adopt a wider view of their place in human society.

It is notable, for instance, that if we look elsewhere in the Bible as it reflects the historical development of Israelite society, we find a variety of insights on how wealth and riches were regarded among God's people. In the period of the nomadic small cattle-breeders whom we know as the patriarchs, personal wealth was considered a gift from God and a sign of his favour and blessing, a view which was to recur in Christian history in the Calvinist incentive which considered earthly success as a sure sign of divine election. At the same time, however, such God-given wealth was also regarded as something to be shared with others, notably within the family and the tribe, but also by extending hospitality to the visitor and the stranger.

It was this idea of the social purpose and function of wealth which came into prominence as Israelite society settled into an urban way of life, and social stratifications increased, with a growing gap between wealthy and powerful employers and owners on the one hand, and a vulnerable workforce and the poor on the other. This was the period of the great prophets of Israel, with their dramatic social preaching against the exploitation of the poor and powerless whose only refuge and recourse was to be found in God, as contrasted with the wealthy and powerful, who were castigated for their self-sufficiency and their single-minded pursuit of interest, profit and property at the expense of others and without regard either for God or for God's poor.

Thus a triple message emerges from the Hebrew Bible on the right approach to wealth: a theology of gratitude to God for his bounteous generosity to his favoured ones; a social theology on the need for a just distribution of wealth in society to meet the needs of all without exception; and a spiritual theology on the dangers for the wealthy of becoming so immersed in making or enjoying their wealth that they lose all proportion and forget their radical need to centre their whole life on God. It was this last spiritual theology of the risks to the individual's soul arising from the possession and accumulation of wealth which figured prominently in the teaching of Jesus, while the New Testament has scarcely anything to say on the more positive idea of wealth as a divine gift, or on the more social theology of the role of wealth creation in society (though compare James 5). It is true, of course, that part of the messianic salvation to come involves remedying the distress of the poor, but there is no indication of how this will come about. It is also true that the early Christian community seems to have made some attempts to redistribute wealth among its members, notably by the great collection for the poor of Jerusalem (cf. 1 Cor. 16:1–3). But such actions were either short-lived or seen in terms of almsgiving and philanthropy rather than as recognizing a social role for the creation of wealth, or as identifying, or identifying with, any particular economic theory.

One way, then, to aim at identifying and developing a full Christian attitude towards wealth, as indeed towards other aspects of life, involves incorporating other insights into the subject which are to be found in the Old Testament, whether explicitly or implicitly. It is only in this century, for instance, that the predominantly negative and cautionary approach of the New Testament to human sexuality has been dramatically corrected and enriched by the Christian Church's realization of the full significance of the creation story narrated in the opening chapters of the Bible. For according to that God created the sexes, male and female, not only to increase the race, and not just as sources of temptation for each other, but also to complete and fulfil each other as human individuals. Likewise, it is only very recently in this century through a deeper insight into the biblical account of creation that Christians have come, rather late in the day, and with very little help from the New Testament, to a new sense of respect for God's world into which we are created, with corresponding responsibilities in the ways in which we treat our environment and the earth's resources.

It is salutary to note how in these important aspects of life a fresh appropriation of the Judaeo–Christian doctrine of creation has enriched Christian reflection and brought a deeper understanding to human living. For in similar fashion an approach to wealth and riches by way of the theology of creation can help us to appreciate that, for all their risks and temptations, they have a positive purpose in the continuing work of creating human society. Developing the earth's resources to produce goods and services to satisfy the needs and aspirations of the increasing millions of its inhabitants not only adds value in economic terms. It enhances the human value and quality of living, by expanding human freedom and culture, and by providing a social environment in which human dignity too can develop and prosper. Hence, while the insights of Jesus on the spiritual risks attendant on the pursuit or possession of wealth remain of abiding and piercing moral significance, they cannot be the complete Christian account of wealth. They must be situated within a deepened social context and an expanded awareness of the positive calling of Christians to develop God's world for the well-being of all his human creatures.

CHRISTIAN DOCTRINES AND WEALTH CREATION

A properly developed theology of wealth, however, does not just depend on returning to earlier and hitherto neglected or forgotten passages of the Bible in order to supplement what teaching we have in the sayings of Jesus and the early Church. It becomes a matter of developing and appreciating a fuller theology and doctrine of creation, and of noting how considering or reconsidering this doctrine can throw light on various aspects of contemporary living, including how Christians should relate to exploiting the potential of the earth's and humanity's resources to meet and satisfy the economic and other needs of God's human creatures.

Christians, however, subscribe to other major doctrines alongside that of creation, and it is interesting to note how the influence of such other doctrines can powerfully affect the ways in which Christians, whether as individuals or as groups in society, can look on the activity of creating wealth. Indeed, Christian attitudes towards wealth and riches provide an interesting illustration of how major Christian beliefs may in general be considered to have ethical implications and to seek expression in Christian behaviour. For what may be considered the central beliefs of Christianity – creation, sin, incarnation and fulfilment – can have, and have had, significant impact on how Christians regard wealth and riches.

Thus, concentrating on the idea of God's bringing his creative enterprise to completion at the end of history can give rise to two contrasting basic attitudes towards the present life. One is to view it as of little significance by comparison with the life to come which God will bring about in due time, and consequently to consider it wrong to become immersed in the affairs of this passing world and ignore one's true future in the world to come. This emphasis can be seen most clearly in traditions and attitudes of quietism and sectarianism, which regard with suspicion, or at least with moral reserve, all secular or worldly activities, including the accumulation and possession of wealth, engaging in business and the whole enterprise of wealth creation, particularly so far as Christians are concerned.

Concentrating on the Christian doctrine of completion can, however, also take the form of viewing that divine work as already in process, and as a result Christians can consider it a duty for human beings to cooperate with God by working to create conditions in society which enable all people to live even now lives worthy of their destiny. This application of the Christian belief in completion can be found in various social reform movements, liberation theology, and other critiques modelled on the denunciations of their society by the Hebrew social prophets. Its attitude is not one of hostility towards wealth or riches as such, so much as one of radical opposition to what are considered unjust economic and social structures which enable some sectors and individuals within society to profit at the expense of others. It is the achieving of this social purpose of wealth which has become so dominant today in Christian preaching, in the face of the glaring economic disparities which exist, and may be increasing, not only among individuals within the same society, but also between countries and the different regions of the globe.

Both these ways of interpreting the Christian belief in a divine completion, the quiescent and the impatient, have this in common, that they regard the present condition of society as falling short of what it will be, or of what it could be. In order to explain the present unsatisfactory state of human existence they rely on another of the four major Christian beliefs identified above, that of human sin and sinfulness, which many Christians also view as the outstanding characteristic of society. There is no sharper ethical divide among Christians, both in history and in the present, than in the prominence which they attach to the presence and influence of sin in all areas of life, including those connected with riches or wealth; that is, in the degree to which they view all human behaviour as subject to, and expressive of, a profound predisposition to moral wrongdoing, whether this is understood in terms of disobedience to the commands of God or of inflicting harm on one's fellow human creatures. As was noted above, it is the alluring potential of

762

wealth and riches to entrap individuals and cause them to succumb to greed, pride and self-sufficiency to their spiritual destruction which figures prominently in the teaching of Jesus on wealth. Yet it also has to be asked, as was done at the beginning of this chapter, whether such a negative attitude exhausts a Christian evaluation of riches and wealth. In fact, behind such influential New Testament perceptions may lie not only a foreshortened view of human history with its lack of concern for the future of society as such, but also a stress on human sinfulness which requires to be balanced by giving due significance to other Christian beliefs, including belief in the incarnation and the actual achievement of Jesus.

For in its strongest form an emphasis on sin would lead to despair of humanity, were it not for the Christian belief in the incarnation; that is, in God's gracious mercy in bringing forgiveness and hope to human beings in the life and passage through death to new life of Jesus Christ. As with the Christian belief in divine completion, however, this belief in the incarnation can give rise to two contrasting attitudes to life in the present state of society, and towards wealth and riches as one manifestation of such living. For many Christians what is central to a concentration on this belief in the incarnation is not just the fact that Christ has saved humanity from its sins, but also the fact that humanity still stands in recurring need of being forgiven for its inherent self-centredness, its proud trust in its own resources, and its continual proneness to succumb to the allurements of worldly goods and worldly success. As a consequence, in the view of such Christians, who are largely representative of the Protestant tradition, human reason and motivation cannot be a trustworthy guide to human moral behaviour, since they remain infected by sin and are inherently suspect. The sole reliable source of proper human behaviour is to be found only in biblical revelation and above all in the teaching and example of Christ. This interpretation of the incarnation as not dispelling the prevalence of sin or the propensity to sin and as therefore requiring powerful dependence on the moral teaching of Jesus can obviously result in stressing the negative nature of such dominical teaching and at the same time in confirming a Christian suspicion of the malign seductions of much in modern life, including riches and wealth, together with any social activities which are connected with them.

By contrast, other Christians take a more positive and optimistic view of the effects of sin in the lives of individuals and society. They do not consider the presence and effects of human sinfulness as so pervasive and destructive as we have been considering, and thus are enabled to emphasize confidence in the continuing creational goodness of humanity and of the world. They are more disposed to trust the reliability of human motivation and of human moral reasoning as developed, for instance, in the tradition of a natural moral law, to which all humans, and not just Christians, have access. They also stress the constructive and honourable nature of many occupations in society, rather than concentrating on their occupational ethical hazards. In particular,

763

they view the creation and use of wealth and riches as in principle a positive cooperating by humans with God in the ongoing creative work of developing the earth's and humanity's resources for the common benefit of all.

Such a less destructive view of the effects of sin on the human constitution then sees the work of the incarnation as continuity and confirmation rather more than as rehabilitation, and it finds its positive appreciation of the basic creational trustworthiness of human intelligence and enterprise enhanced by belief in the incarnation as not just a remedying of sin but a reaffirmation and enhancement of the goodness and potential of creation by the divine identification with it. This strong perception of the effects of incarnation is shared also by those who believe that, even granted a more cataclysmic effect of sin on humanity, the saving and healing work of God in Christ is even now capable of having some positive, and even widespread, influence for good on the attitudes and behaviour of all human beings, including even those who may be unaware of it. In this more typically Catholic approach, what belief in the incarnation adds to the doctrine of creation, apart from any remedial consequences it might have, is an enhancement of the radical goodness of creation by the Creator's deigning to identify with it in such a way that 'the Word became flesh' (John 1:14).

If Christianity, then, can be summarized as centrally concerned with beliefs about creation, sin, incarnation and completion, and with the ethical implications of living out those beliefs, this helps us realize that historically, as well as in the present, the placing of particular emphasis on one or other of these beliefs by individual Christians or groups of Christians shapes their attitude to human behaviour in all walks of life, including the possession and creation of wealth. There thus exists a variety of Christian attitudes towards wealth depending on whether Christians give particular weight to one or other of the basic beliefs outlined above. Yet, to have a complete Christian view of wealth, alongside the spiritual aspect of its risks for individuals, which is the main message of the New Testament, and alongside the social aspect of its proper distribution, which is the main thrust of social prophecy both in the history of Israel and in the present, there is a need also to put in place its creational aspect: the increasingly complex ways in which wealth is produced and possessed in society and in which further value is added to the creation with which God continues to gift his human creatures. Without that third creational element a spirituality of wealth runs a Manichaean risk of treating it as evil and as no more than a material source of temptation without regard for its positive purposes. And without a creational theology of wealth the social view of wealth distribution incurs a utopian danger of disregarding the necessary conditions for creating the wealth to be distributed. Perhaps the continual challenge for Christians is to give due weight to all their basic beliefs, in what can be termed a form of dynamic equilibrium. When this balanced tension is applied to the human activity of possessing and creating wealth, Christianity can then address to those who possess wealth words of encouragement and approval on the one hand, for what they are capable of doing and to some degree actually are doing with their wealth, and also words of criticism and impatience on the other, for what they may not be doing or not yet doing sufficiently with it. This can perhaps be summed up from the Christian viewpoint in acknowledging a continuing moral tension between the God-given goal of humans cooperating to develop the earth's resources for their common well-being, and the historical reality of a human inclination to pursue individual interests at the expense of others and thus frustrate the ultimate purpose of God's work of creation.

INDIVIDUAL RESPONSIBILITIES FOR WEALTH

These various theological considerations on wealth have evident ethical application in the way in which individuals use their personal resources. If the teaching of Jesus warns of the dangers which wealth can bring individuals, the complete picture of a Christian attitude to wealth here identified can also give a more positive orientation to the responsibilities of ownership, and to the creative use of one's personal income and resources. Thus, one form which this can take is in recognizing the social purpose of taxation, both direct and indirect, when this is resorted to by society in the service of redistributing wealth for the benefit of its more needy and less fortunate members. So much so that honesty and accuracy in paying one's taxes, and a disinclination to be involved in any form of tax avoidance, not to mention tax evasion, can be seen as one yardstick by which individuals may assess their sense of moral responsibility in using and administering their wealth. Similarly, willingness to embrace the Christian tradition of giving alms according to one's means in order to relieve the distress of the poor can be seen as a further expression of responsibility in one's stewardship of one's possessions. Early Christian tradition tended to view wealth beyond one's needs as belonging by moral right to the poor of God. That criterion can continue to be of value today as enabling one to recognize that almsgiving must be a matter of giving relative to one's particular means and other responsibilities, and yet it can also be a reminder of the importance of incorporating into one's life the evangelical values of simplicity and frugality in the use of material possessions which have found consecrated and wholehearted expression in the monastic and mendicant movements and lifestyles in the Christian Church.

Individual responsibility for wealth can also find expression in the positive ways in which it is used in consumer choices in the market. One such expression, as noted above, can lie in decisions not to make certain purchases of goods or services as superfluities or luxuries which are unwarranted in the light of the needs of one's fellow human beings. Actual purchases, however, can also express responsibility in the choices made of goods and services. Most obvious, and most fashionable today, are purchases made in the light of environmental and ecological criteria. Other purchasing decisions may take a more dramatic form and constitute in their refusal varying degrees of economic pressure and even boycott in pursuit of various social or political aims. Yet others may signify social approval of the good or service on offer, and the using of one's economic purchasing power as a market vote in support of it.

Such consumer ethics, as a creative and responsible use of one's wealth, is probably at its most enduring and influential when the purchase takes the form of shares in various companies, in what is becoming increasingly recognized as the ethical investment movement. The most obvious manifestation of this expression of responsibility for one's wealth is when one declines to invest it in companies of whose products or whose behaviour one ethically disapproves, whether the products take the form of tobacco, armaments or luxury goods, or the company's behaviour includes mistreating its workers or its suppliers or unethical marketing or advertising behaviour. In such cases the refusal to invest betokens both an unwillingness to support and be party to the activities which one considers wrong, and also a moral repugnance to increasing one's wealth as a result of investing or colluding in such activities.

More public impact of one's economic power is to be seen, not when one declines to invest, but when one actively divests from a company of which one may have come to disapprove, and does so with the maximum of publicity with the intention of using one's economic power to attempt to deter the company from behaving as it does. A more activist way of exercising one's economic power to an ethically responsible end consists in acquiring or keeping shares in such a company in order to be in a position to influence its policy or behaviour from time to time, by making one's views known to its management either as an individual or in concert with other shareholders. Finally, probably the most constructive responsible use can be made of one's wealth as a shareholder when it is deliberately directed to supporting companies of whose behaviour one positively approves as providing goods or services which are of genuine value to society. Such creative use of wealth can even extend to undertaking a policy of ethical venture capital, perhaps aimed at financing measures to alleviate global poverty, and with inevitable risks, not now to one's soul, but to one's resources, but with possible potential results in human betterment which will more than justify incurring such risks.

One modern method of exercising individual responsibility for one's wealth, then, consists in using one's economic power in the market as an investor and part-owner in order to influence companies and corporations in their conduct, and to do so not just with the aim of discouraging and deterring bad business policies and practices but, more importantly, with the intention of encouraging and supporting good enterprises and practices. To such considerations it is sometimes objected that the number of small private investors in the market is tiny, and their influence negligible, by comparison with the large institutional investors, the pension funds, insurance companies, banks and investment trusts. While there is obvious truth in this observation, nevertheless to the extent that private share-ownership is on the increase in society, partly stimulated by the privatization of utilities, more individuals are coming to have a possible influence on the conduct of companies. Moreover, the large institutional investors are often themselves subject to being influenced in their business decisions affecting other companies by those individual pensioners, policy holders, etc., whose interests – and presumably wishes – they represent.

SOCIAL JUSTICE

A full theological appreciation of wealth, however, must see it as a shared human asset and not just as a matter of individual possessions and how they are to be used responsibly. The steady Christian tradition, stemming from the theology of creation, views the world's resources as brought into existence to meet and satisfy the needs of all God's human creatures. Hence a consideration of the responsibilities which wealth brings cannot ignore the economic structures of capitalism and the market economy which are now most common in modern society, and which have proved most effective as contrasted with socialist models and the command economies which until recently characterized Eastern Europe and the USSR.

The importance of shared human well-being as the ultimate goal of wealth is highlighted for Christians by one insight which all their beliefs have in common: the fact and the challenge of human solidarity. God's enterprise of creation, salvation and completion is viewed as one which encompasses humanity as a whole. The divine moral commandment to be found in Judaism and singled out by Jesus, to love one's neighbour, places no conditions on who among one's fellows is to qualify as neighbour – unless it be those particularly who are most in need (cf. Luke 10:25–37). Christianity as a whole thus finds itself at odds with any view of society which depends on or leads to any form of elitism, adversarialism or alienation, whether of ethnic origin, sex, class, or geographical location or wealth.

It is thus incumbent on Christianity to scrutinize and where necessary to de-absolutize all worldly structures, whether of a political, social, or economic nature, against this criterion of a shared human destiny for all the earth's present and future inhabitants. One consequence which follows from this is the duty incumbent on society to ensure that various economic instruments are not regarded ideologically as ends in themselves, and to contrive that whatever economic success they produce is not gained for some of its members to the ultimate social detriment of their fellows.

For all their evident economic success in history, particularly as compared with alternative systems, capitalism and the market economy arouse misgivings for many Christians which can be summed up as their relying for their success on human self-interest and on competition. Such reliance appears tantamount to accepting, on the one hand, individual acquisitiveness and greed as the engine of wealth creation, and, on the other, a zero–sum game, which inevitably creates losers as well as winners, sometimes with dire economic consequences for the loser and his or her dependants and for whole countries, and frequently also with resulting loss in self-esteem or in the perception of one's social worth. It is not clear, however, that the arguments adduced against competitiveness among humans, namely that it creates losers and that by accepting inequalities it undermines human dignity, are as compelling as some would maintain. For human equality takes a variety of forms. Within a religious context it is a commonly held belief that all human creatures without exception are equal in the sight of God, and are thus as his creatures entitled to equal respect and treatment simply as human beings, a belief which provides the religious basis for the popular and increasingly important idea of universal human rights. Another expression or form of equality concerns not just equality of treatment but equality of access to various resources within society, and equality of opportunity to engage in social activities, whether as individuals, or as groups within society, or as nations on the international scene. Here there appears little scope for disagreement and much to be done to promote such fairness of access and of opportunities, by creating and building upon various forms of human cooperation in society, rather than relying simply on impersonal factors of supply and demand.

Where, however, matters may become more problematic is in a third form of equality advocated by some in society on almost ideological grounds, namely, equality of outcome or of results. For this seeks to eliminate or to prevent disparities in the achievements of individuals on the ground that this diminishes the worth of those who turn out to be less successful. But there is a difficulty in arguing for such a view of equality of outcome as essential to maintaining respect for individuals. For the argument itself presupposes that human worth is dependent on achievements or on merits, rather than being an inherent quality which belongs as a matter of human right to all individuals, regardless of their performance in any human or social arena.

However, what the stress on equality, including equality of outcome, does serve to highlight is that in society no-one should suffer unduly from economic failure or from the lack of material resources or welfare as a result of the workings of a free market. And that safeguarding against such consequences is a social duty which falls upon all in society, including businesses, as a matter of distributive justice and taxation policy. It does not necessarily invalidate the principle of the market economy, although it clearly sets some limits to its wider consequences in society. For the free market is simply at best an economic instrument which may be given its place in society, provided that place is limited, and provided that the economic values of efficiency and profitability are not considered to be the be-all and end-all of social living. The ethically important point is to ensure that lack of success in the creation of wealth does not lead to human impoverishment and diminishment; to accept that capitalism is a good servant, but a bad master; that it has its rightful place in modern society, but that that place needs to be carefully identified and continually monitored, and its economic consequences to be remedied by positive social measures at national, continental and international levels. Concern for the victims of competition, whether as individuals in the labour market or as less developed nations in the global market, requires society to create structures, from individual and family welfare provision to World Bank programmes, which will satisfy the claims of social justice and, while respecting the inherent dignity of individual persons and peoples, will contribute in some degree to distributing the wealth created within a society by business. Hence also the requirement on society to monitor and regulate the conduct of business in its enterprise of wealth-creation, and to encourage business to fulfil its primary ethical purpose of providing a service of value to society and of making its profit in the process.

This reference to profit recalls the other major misgiving with which many Christians regard the entire enterprise of business, that it is motivated by self-interest and acquisitiveness, which appear scarcely honourable reasons for engaging in the creation or possessing of wealth. There is no doubt that many abuses of the power of business are the result of greed, whether on a petty individual or on a colossal international scale. Nevertheless, there can be a legitimate and even desirable place for a measure of self-concern and self-interest in one's conduct. It seems an unduly ascetical approach, even bordering on the Jansenist, which would require individuals to be entirely other-regarding in their behaviour.

A healthy spiritual theology takes into account the proper flourishing of the human self uniquely created by God, while it does not concentrate exclusively on cultivating one's own spiritual well-being. The entire enterprise of Christian medical ethics has as one of its pillars the duty of individuals to safeguard and protect the life and health with which God has endowed them, while not necessarily making physical well-being their top priority in life. Likewise, there seems to be no Christian reason why of all the spheres of human existence and activity one's material well-being should be matter for disapproval or suspicion. That having been said, however, and a legitimate place accorded to a certain measure of concern for self in all one's activities, there remains here also, as in the spiritual and the health-care areas of life, the possibility of concentrating exclusively on one's own material or financial interests, frequently involving in business the pursuit of a competitive advantage over others. What this possibility of excessive concern for the profit motive perhaps exemplifies is the perennial tension to be found between regard for the self and regard for others in society and the need to seek continually to balance the two.

For the Christian belief in the solidarity of humanity in its creation and destiny which we have earlier considered does not absorb in anonymous collectivism the value, worth and interests of individuals, any more than its belief in the dignity and vocation unique to each human being fragments society into solitary adversarial individualism. Indeed, contemporary Christianity proposes two ways in which the relationship between the individual and society can be more positively expressed and advanced, with consequences for social conduct, including the conduct of business. One is to take up and develop the biblical idea of covenant as a model for all truly human relationships and for the mutual respect and regard which should characterize them. The divine bonding initiated by God with Adam, Noah, Abraham and the people of Israel and, as Christians believe, renewed with humanity in the person of Jesus Christ, goes far beyond contractual rights and responsibilities, to inculcate a view of human existence in the world as a gift to be received from God in gratitude, to be held in mutual promise and trust, and to be administered and developed in stewardship.

In this approach the Christian Church can be viewed as the community of the new covenant, called to exercise towards and among its own members the covenant qualities identified above, but also called to epitomize for society the promise and even now the possibility of forming a truly human community characterized by such qualities. Historically, it must be confessed, the absorption with wealth and riches from which the Church has suffered at various periods, and the abuses of power to which this gave rise, have been frequently more a scandal than an inspiration to society. Yet the Christian belief in the Church as at least capable of providing a living instance and exemplar of covenant relationships can indicate how relationships between men and women throughout society as part of the universal creative, incarnational and fulfilling work of God can also be viewed as ideally covenantal. As such they do not constitute an arena for convenience, self-interest and destructive rivalry, but rather provide a partnership of solidarity and mutuality based on a shared pledge and commitment to a common purpose, within which place can still be found for self-interest and individual enterprise and success.

Freely entering into, or willingly acknowledging, such a covenant with one's fellows is the supreme exercise of individual choice and of moral responsibility; whereas disrupting or repudiating a covenantal relationship is an act of irresponsibility and self-seeking more than it is the genuine expression of individual freedom. The consequence of such an approach to business relationships in society is to invest them with a quality and a texture much richer than the requirements of purely contractual or legal compliance, and to introduce into the consideration of business decisions human and relational factors of which the terminology of stakeholders can be only a pale expression.

The other Christian approach in recent times to identifying and promoting a positive relationship between the community and the individual is to explore the nature of human personhood as offering a bridge between the two. In this view, Western philosophical theories and popular traditions which have stressed the radical distinction between human individuals have usefully done so in order to vindicate and enhance the identity, autonomy and the social, political and economic independence of all human beings. In so doing, however, they have worked in a vacuum which takes no account of the inherently social disposition of humanity, and of the possibility of relationships which express not just human dependence or independence, but the richer quality of human interdependence.

This human characteristic of individuals interacting in community is what the concept of person attempts to express, as, for instance, when it views life in community not just as providing individuals with the occasion to claim various human rights, but also regards living responsibly in community as providing a balancing context for moderating the claim and exercise of such rights. It acknowledges the importance of community support and structures for the development and flourishing of individuals, while at the same time it recognizes the worth and significance of individuals in contributing to the maintenance and prospering of their fellows and of the community which they share. The implication of such an understanding of the human person for ethical behaviour in all human activities, including business, is to view not only collectivism but also individualism as depriving both individuals and communities of the respective strengths which they contribute to, and derive from, each other. In particular it includes the challenge to the necessarily collective nature of much modern business activity to recognize and encourage, rather than suppress, the contributions which individuals can uniquely and valuably make, including their moral insights, when all are engaged in a shared communal enterprise.

MODERN BUSINESS ETHICS

If society as a whole has responsibilities for the ultimate well-being of all its members in terms of the distribution of wealth and of access to the earth's resources and the value which can be added to them, when one focuses on the theological and ethical considerations which apply to the actual creation of wealth in society, then attention inevitably turns to the business sector as that part of society which is most involved in this process. For the shape and the conditions of contemporary business have developed in such a way that the challenge of moral values is being addressed now not just to individuals as they go about their business, but to business companies and corporations, and, indeed, to the whole activity and role of business in modern society.

The development of large public corporations, with the important distinction between the ownership and the management of such enterprises, resulted in increasing power on the part of such companies and their managers over the lives of many millions of people, whether as customers and consumers, employees and labour forces, marketing areas at national, overseas and increasingly multinational levels, suppliers at home or overseas, including the Third World, and whole communities and countries with their local and national governments. One way of summing up the agenda of modern business ethics is to see it as the study and analysis of the power possessed by business throughout society, and of the ways in which businesses acquire and exercise their power, whether for good or for ill.

771

In fact, one of the major incentives for the development since the 1960s of a new approach to business ethics was the incidence of a massive and continuing misuse of business power in various parts of the globe, exemplified in bribery and corruption scandals; systematic racial and sexual discrimination; dangers to workers, consumers and the public at large; disregard for environmental and ecological considerations; and a growing awareness of the plight of undeveloped nations in the southern hemisphere, including the growing burden of international debt and many of the conditions attached to financial grants and aid. In all these circumstances it is not surprising that society began to formulate new ethical and social expectations of business, which can be summed up in requiring business to respect the legitimate interests of those other sectors of society who came to be identified as its 'stakeholders', that is, all those constituencies which had a stake in how business operated, including its owners, managers and workforce and their dependents, its customers or clients, its suppliers, cooperators and competitors, and the local and national communities of people in which it found itself and operated, and of which business was considered to be an integral part.

In such ways the social agenda for business changed and diversified, and with the growing awareness of the power of business and the consequent responsibilities of the growing managerial class in society, the focus of ethical concern turned to the behaviour not of business men and women but of businesses themselves, in terms of their corporate, and not just individual, responsibility, and of their broad social, and not just financial, accountability.

One way in which ethical attention can be focused on the power of business is by considering the different human relationships which are to be encountered in business activities, and to identify and explore the ethical implications of those relationships as they find expression within four areas of activity which are common to all business organisations:

1 The inner workings of the company itself.
2 Its relationships with customers and clients.
3 Relationships with other companies, whether as collaborators, suppliers or competitors.
4 The company's relations with society as a whole.

It is thus possible from an ethical point of view to identify the desirable qualities which should characterize human relationships in general and then to apply those qualities as appropriate in each of the business areas identified and consider how their presence or absence makes for good or bad business in ethical terms.

Thus, within the company's interior organization and activity and the structures and relationships which desirably should govern the inner workings of a company, attitudes which can be identified include the recognizing and respecting of the human personal dignity of all involved in the enterprise, and the implications which this has for such issues and questions as employment and dismissal, wages and working conditions, discrimination in employment and promotion, mutual confidentiality and mutual loyalty. It is also within this circle of relationships internal to the company that attention can be focused on its shareholders, not only in regard to the general business activities of the managers who are their agents, as already noted above, but also in regard to possible acquisitions and mergers and their effect on workforces, dependants and local communities. In this inner circle of the business organization's activities much concern is rightly directed today at the whole area of corporate governance and the ways in which managers ought to render an account of their stewardship to owners, as well as the ways in which owners discharge their own responsibilities, not all of which can simply be delegated to others. If one of the reasons for the economic success of modern business has been the distinction between ownership and professional management, it appears that one of the manifestations of new-found ethical sensitivity in business is the recognition that such a distinction must not constitute an ethics gap or perpetuate the mistaken idea that owners have no ethical responsibilities for the behaviour of their agents.

The process of wealth creation relies critically on sales of goods and services, and so particular ethical concern needs to be directed at a company's relationships with its customers as exemplifying, above all, concern for the dignity and autonomy of individuals, as well as their capacity for cooperating with others to their mutual advantage. Particular issues which thus fall to be considered here include questions of product safety, reliability and durability; the ethics of certain marketing and advertising techniques, especially when directed at impressionable or vulnerable groups or societies; and the ongoing debate about whether advertising exists to satisfy actual needs or is designed to create new needs, and to what extent this latter is humanly desirable. In this area considerable concern is directed today at the marketing and sale of credit, whether to individuals or to less developed nations, and at the moral, and not just the legal, responsibilities of both debtors and creditors, whether the latter are the High Street banks or the World Bank and the International Monetary Fund.

Business relations with suppliers raise questions of respect for those who are in a subordinate position in a relationship of inequality or dependency, with particular concern centred on speedy payments to vulnerable suppliers, and on pricing and other conditions imposed on Third World producers. Competition, too, calls for mutual respect and raises ethical issues relating to contracts, bribing for business to secure unfair advantage, and monopolistic and price-fixing arrangements, as well as the seeking of unfair selective government protection.

Finally, the ethics of business power exercised for good or ill can consider the ways in which companies relate to the various communities on which they depend and which they claim to serve. Here inevitable attention is paid today to the physical environment, but there should be no less concern for the social and political environments and the ways in which corporations relate to local communities, as well as to local and national governments and legislation. How a corporation practises what has been called 'good citizenship' in terms of public philanthropy has become a fashionable question in some countries today, but how far that should extend beyond the immediate and long-term business interests of the company, and in particular whether such business philanthropy is an acceptable alternative to social justice on the part of government, are questions which require careful elucidation. Likewise, consideration needs to be given to the desired cooperation between a local community and a particular company or industry involved in opening, or closing, plants within that community, including the immediate and knock-on costs and the likely effects on the economic and social ecosystems within a particular community.

A THEOLOGY OF BUSINESS

When one thus considers the myriad possibilities for the exercise of power in modern business and wealth creation and the ethical responsibilities which are entailed, then perhaps one will return with fresh appreciation to the spiritual warnings of Jesus. For all its positive creational and social justification, participation in the enterprise of wealth-creation does need to be balanced by other, spiritual, considerations. It *is* a risky occupation spiritually, as are many other worthwhile human activities. Perhaps today the increasingly global scale of business, the speed and urgency – and the secrecy – with which it is often conducted, and the sheer power which modern business offers individuals, managers and corporations, all make it an occupation which should carry its own particular spiritual health warning. Nevertheless, the modern creation of wealth also involves social, and over-riding, responsibilities which justify its pursuit in the interests of the common good. Within this line of reflection, the business of creating wealth and contributing to economic growth in and for society is then seen to be a positive and constructive social occupation for men and women, as well as an honourable calling for Christians.

Aiming to work for a fair access for all humankind to the goods of God's creation and for a standard and quality of living and working in society which respects their dignity as God's human creatures gives the men and women who are engaged in business not only an honourable programme, but also a formidable portfolio of responsibilities. So much so that the idea of business as an honourable 'calling', and of the Christian in business as responding to a divine 'vocation' of service to society, is one which many today find inspiring and encouraging.

The appeal to a vocation, or literally, the unique 'calling' which individuals receive personally from God took the form in medieval times of some individuals feeling called by God out of secular society to embrace a separate and distinct monastic or clerical way of life, in a way which expressed, and confirmed, the view that secular occupations, including trade, were morally unsuited to those wishing to live a fully Christian life. Since the sixteenth century, however, the Christian idea of vocation, as part of the Protestant Reformation, has become less elitist and has been interpreted more as a divine calling to all individuals to worship God from within the particular way of life in the world in which they find themselves, or in which they consider God has providentially placed them. The consequence of this belief in a 'worldly' vocation was twofold. One was to act as a corrective by recognizing the intrinsic dignity of many social occupations as providing a context in which individuals could devote themselves to God by pursuing their calling with diligence and simplicity, an attitude which came to be termed the 'Protestant work ethic', and which may have contributed to the development of capitalism.

The other consequence of the belief in each one's personal vocation within, rather than out of, society was to enable one's ordinary social activities to be invested with the religious motive and ideal of serving others, as the practical working out of the command to love one's neighbour and to follow the example of Christ who spent his earthly life in service of his fellows.

In one of the most famous biblical passages referring to wealth Jesus is recorded as warning that one cannot serve both God and money (Matt. 6: 24). But there is a third possibility: to serve society, one's fellow men and women. If the acquiring and use of wealth in society, whether by individuals or nations or businesses, can be seen as just that, adding human value to life by creating employment, by contributing to society in the payment of personal and corporate taxes, and by the provision of goods and services of value to others, then those engaged in such mundane activities are also by that fact serving their Creator in their calling, and also cooperating with God in his continuing good work of human creation in a world whose resources he destined for the common enrichment of all.

FURTHER READING

Curran, C. E. and McCormick, R. A. (eds) (1986) *Official Catholic Social Teaching: Readings in Moral Theology*, No. 5, New York: Paulist Press.

Davies, J. (ed.) (1993) *God and the Marketplace: Essays on the Morality of Wealth Creation*, London: Institute of Economic Affairs Health and Welfare Unit.

De George, R. T. (1995) *Business Ethics*, New York: Macmillan.

Gonzalez, J. L. (1990) *Faith and Wealth: A History of Early Christian Ideas on the Origins, Significance and Use of Money*, San Francisco: Harper & Row.

Griffiths, B. (1982) *Morality and the Market-Place*, London: Hodder & Stoughton.

Harries, R. (1992) *Is There a Gospel for the Rich?*, London: Mowbray.

Heelas, P. and Morris, P. (eds) (1992) *The Values of the Enterprise Culture: The Moral Debate*, London: Routledge.

Minus, P. M. (ed.) (1993) *The Ethics of Business in a Global Economy*, Amsterdam: Kluwer.

Preston, R. H. (1991) *Religion and the Ambiguities of Capitalism*, London: SCM Press.

University of Edinburgh Centre for Theology and Public Issues (1992) *Capital: A Moral Instrument?*, Edinburgh: Saint Andrews Press.
Vallely, P. (1990) *Bad Samaritans: First World Ethics and Third World Debt*, London: Hodder & Stoughton.
Wogaman, J. P. (1986) *Economics and Ethics: A Christian Enquiry*, Philadelphia: Fortress Press.

See also chapters 33, 37.

37

POWER AND THE STATE

Edward Norman

CHURCH AND STATE

There has been much discussion in the last couple of decades about the notion of 'doing' theology: in the area of Christian political thinking this idea can be given a particularly apposite meaning. For although there has been quite a lot of recent writing about the State and public policy from a Christian viewpoint – and especially much occasional writing in the press – it has all been rather episodic and, compared with the systematic offerings of the past, fragmentary. As this doubtless corresponds to the divided condition of values within society, and within Christian society, it is unavoidable and even desirable. But it does mean that in a brief critical survey of opinions, like the present one, it is impossible to separate the contributions made by academic theologians from the attitudes and policy preferences of the church leadership. This is not because the church leaders are especially notable for theological insights, but because politics is a practical matter, and 'doing' theology has an immediate application in this sphere of human activity. Even in the Catholic Church, with a tradition of achieving balance between capitalist and socialist systems of ideas – expressed within the teaching of papal encyclical letters – there has been little that can really be called systematic political philosophy in the years following the Second Vatican Council.

From the immediate perspective of Western liberal society it must seem as if contemporary Christianity seeks to distance itself from political power. Church and State are in most countries constitutionally separated, and in those in which a link persists, as in England or Sweden, there is little real sense in which they have any functional relationships; politicians act without special reference to the traditional guardians of religious truth and morality, and the clergy, for their part, are anxious to show themselves as critics of public policy rather than, as their predecessors so often were, agents of it. The moral agenda in these societies is set by an extremely articulate secular intelligentsia, and by the charitable and relief agencies whose purpose, as informers of the public mind about the condition of society and the imbalances of the international order, echoes that of the established Churches of the past. The Churches have, in effect, privatized themselves. Their appeal, now, is to the individual conscience, with exhortations to scrutinize public policy from the outside, and to instruct their own members, and any of the public who will listen, about 'moral' dimensions of political and social 'issues'. They tend to be as instinctively hostile to the moral claims of the State as were the Protestant Dissenters in Victorian Britain, to whom the State often appeared as no other than the institutional monopoly of the landed classes. In its place the Dissenters sought a moral capitalism – the sovereignty of private judgement in spiritual discernment, freedom of religious choice, a private enterprise in worship. For Christians today, however, it is the very capitalism sustained by the State which is liable to arouse suspicion. To the public at large, indeed, and to the press, it often seems as if the Churches have become the mouthpiece of progressive political ideas, so insistently have their leaders pressed 'prophetic' criticism of the ideals of 'the enterprise society'. The Victorian Dissenters managed to combine their *laissez faire* in religion with an insistence that government should enforce Christian personal morality with the use of State power; there was to be no private enterprise when it came to sexual behaviour or to what are now called 'family values'. This paradox is exactly reversed in modern Christianity. The Christian leaders of today are anxious to reserve matters of personal morality to the area of private determination, yet to demand that the State involve itself with a high level of central economic and social planning. During the *Aufklärung* of the 1960s the church leadership went over, in virtually all its departments, to an acceptance of liberal attitudes (and some would say to humanist values) in sexual and personal moral questions. The State, they are now in effect contending, is no fit body to legislate in a manner which would seem to favour one life-style code rather than another, since views about private morality have proved to be controversial. At the same time, however, they are saying that the State is suited to determine and to enforce collective morality in the economic and social spheres. For in those spheres, as the church leadership sees it, the State's recent desire to limit its capacity to intervene, and to allow the forces of the market to operate, has prompted the emergence of an uncaring social order and randomized social ethics. Christian assemblies and Christian thinkers have become, in contrast, thorough collectivists. That was the burden, for example, of the Church of England's 1985 report *Faith in the City: A call for action by Church and Nation*. It was a call for increased State involvement, and increased public expenditure, in urban planning. Such a clear Christian endorsement of moral action by government is indeed an embracing of the power of the State, and every Western country has in recent years seen comparable declarations by Christian writers and bodies in support of State action for welfare reasons. How did they ever originally come to see themselves as critics of State power? It has been, after all, the very idea of Church institutional involvement with political power, and not merely particular distasteful types of government or governing ideologies, which Western Christians have rejected. Despite the widespread rhetoric about the impossibility of separating religion from politics the fact is that when church leaders identify an area in which Christianity should get involved they always make it clear that they do so on moral grounds and not political grounds. The Western Churches of today are actually notable for a very low level of political involvement.

HUMAN RIGHTS AND NATURAL LAW

In the old 'Christendom' model of Church and State relations organized society was seen as a unity divided into spiritualities and temporalities by function. The two areas of responsibility, for the souls and for the bodies of men and women, were regarded as equally Christian and as interdependent. The great strength of the arrangement was that it recognized that social organization unavoidably embodies ideological preferences, and it simply imposed Christian beliefs and practices rather than countenance the supremacy of others. The world in which this state of affairs flourished could offer no other models: everywhere government experienced single ideological propositions, and the apparatus of the State protected the consequential social values. Modern liberal society, in contrast, seeks to contrive a balance between enforced sacral values and the reservation of areas of life in which individuals can be protected in the enjoyment of their own moral preferences. The latter are now conventionally rendered in the vocabulary of Human Rights. The necessary accompaniment of a liberal polity is a diminution of the power of the State in the reserved areas – religious belief, or sexual morality, for example. As these are precisely the kinds of areas in which the individual citizen's most deeply held convictions reside, the liberal State becomes a kind of balancing mechanism intended to prevent mutual intrusions by citizens themselves into the freedoms of society in general. The whole trend of thought and action in the Western world has been towards individual liberty in this sense, and it is only comparatively recently, under the guise of 'family values', that attempts have been made to return to the older practices of the confessional state, of the 'Christendom' variety, in which the details of individual moral choice are restricted by State action. Churchmen of the political Right, and Evangelicals, have readily lent themselves to this renewed understanding of the function of government. In the United States the 'Moral Majority', who were particularly influential politically in the early years of the 1980s, showed a good deal of sensitivity about the problem of seeking law enforcement of Christian values whilst at the same time respecting the separation of Church and State. But they have not managed to resolve the clear incompatibility. What their various campaigns have disclosed is the wide gap between their supporters and the prevailing Christian leadership, most of whom, as elsewhere in the Western world, have embraced liberal ideals. The leadership has been especially insistent on the right of individuals to choose their own moral values. It is commonplace to hear church leaders denounce as an evil the existence of legal discrimination against individuals on the basis of their religious or moral beliefs – an attitude which corresponds closely to the moral sense of the contemporary secular intelligentsia. The area of medical and biological ethics, it is true, has raised some difficult questions for the Christian leadership (as for liberal opinion in general), for here the intervention of the State, in determining the limits of research, and so forth, is plainly necessary.

At times Christian leaders seem unaware of how greatly their opinions contrast with those of Christian society in the last two millennia. Yet is is in order to separate themselves decisively from the 'Christendom' model, from the use of the power of the State to enforce Christian beliefs, that Western Christians have come to reassess their public role and to see themselves as external critics of the political management. They eschew privilege, and in recognition of a society of plural values they opt for freedom to propagate their religious truths alongside the practitioners of other and rival systems. Many theologians writing today assume the inherent virtue of moral pluralism in society, and they are probably right to do so – in the sense that after a couple of thousand years there is no agreement among reflective people about the moral basis of life on earth. There sometimes appears, it is true, to be a measure of agreement; the agenda of Human Rights seems at first sight to offer a tariff of shared moral beliefs about some basic human claims, but when scrutinized closely, these turn out to be labels whose meaning is so wide that when they are attached to concrete historical situations the area of agreement diminishes to nothing.

The acceptance or the rejection of liberal attitudes towards the organization of society is one of the major causes of division among Christians today, though it is often confused, by external observers, with the simultaneous acceptance or rejection of liberal methods of intellectual enquiry as applied to theological scholarship. The calculations here are not exact, and a scholar open to all kinds of intellectual liberalism may also sustain a very structured view about social organization. There is a widespread feeling, however, that the days are past when the Church should look to the power of the State to give religious beliefs institutional expression. It is the arrival of political democracy which has reinforced this conviction. Democratic choice by mass electorates is a new experiment in human history – scarcely a century old anywhere – and it echoes the distribution of popular education. Nothing in Christian thinking or teaching during the preceding centuries suggests that Christianity would be particularly friendly to democratic practice, and in the nineteenth century, in fact, Christian opinion was broadly hostile to the political forces which were beginning to advance democratic theory. That is in itself, of course, no reason why Christians should not be able to identify democracy as a Christian expression. Christian faith is a dialectic with the world, and its passage through time shows many instances where new insights can set old adversaries into a more favourable context. It is surprising, however, that the Christian churches of the Protestant tradition, have (often as a necessary consequence of their separation from a relationship with the State) contrived internal systems of government which are indebted to the democratic devices of modern secular society – for there can be no sense in which religious truth can be decided on a majority principle. God is not known to be God by the counting of heads. When it comes to the conduct of public life, modern Christians show an extraordinary unanimity about the virtue of political democracy, however. So closely have they identified themselves with its practices, in fact, and so exactly have they matched it with applied Christian teaching, that many have felt themselves able to justify the use of force (as in guerrilla warfare against political regimes of the Right) to secure the attainment of democratic systems of government. The point is this: since religious values cannot actually be authenticated by popular choice, the achievement of democracy necessarily implies a separation of religion from some areas of political power. Religious values are among those which are reserved from the competence of the State, and are seen to be in the realm of individual choice. But then a difficulty arises. What are the moral values of the State to be if there is no institutional religious tradition to which it may refer, and if there is no agreed philosophical alternative, as there is not in Western societies at present? What is the State to say when people ask why they should obey the law? All law implies a prior moral sanction, and if the Churches do not supply the moral basis then ideological rivals may. This unresolved problem lies at the heart of contemporary liberal society. In practice one of the ideological rivals of Christianity – secular humanism – is, on a day-to-day basis, filling in the need, but in a very incoherent fashion, and without any great public consciousness that that is what is happening. Materialist views of humanity are always at their most successful when they are presented as commonplace responses to the needs of human welfare.

There are still those who believe that the old concept of Natural Law is a possible solution. It is certainly true that the prevalent Human Rights ideology is merely a modern checklist of individual liberties which once would have been expressed in Natural Law language, and that the Western Church, following medieval Aristotelianism, has a tradition of associating Christian moral teaching with Natural Law formulations. Positive good may be achieved if the State uses its power to enforce propositions which are agreed to be true because they correspond to truths that are universally written in men's hearts, and so are common to Christian and non-Christian alike. Alas for this simplicity, Natural Law formulations have strongly fictional qualities, since what is in men's hearts does not appear to be precise enough to provide the contents of real rights in civil society. Society is in practice divided ideologically, and the 'Laws' are either too general to have agreed individual applications or they are too controversial to be 'Natural'. The failure in the 1970s of the Warsaw Pact and the NATO alliance to agree what the Natural Law freedoms enshrined in the Helsinki Accords actually meant illustrated the difficulty – the Communists interpreted Human Rights as collective ones, and the Western Liberals saw them as individual liberties. Among Catholic theologians, nevertheless, there has been a distinguished continuing tradition of writing on modern political problems in terms of Natural Law theory, particularly in relation to issues of defence policy, warfare, and the moral questions of social justice. The shift of emphasis to Human Rights rhetoric, and away from more classical formulations of Natural Law, is, indeed, one of a number of indicators that contemporary Christian understanding of political processes is becoming increasingly secularized.

It is now usual for Christian leaders and thinkers to categorize the Church as being like a moral agency, operating alongside others within the boundaries of a society of plural values. Where once Christianity had taught that the State (as in a passage of Romans 13) is a divine institution, it is now seen as a secular device, responsive to the public will. The State, in fact, needs to be perpetually scrutinized to ensure that its behaviour corresponds to the supposed injunctions of natural rights, and that it does not interfere with the liberties of individuals. The State has lost its organic character – which is now considered potentially totalitarian – and has come to be viewed atomistically. So far from being God's instrument for curbing the viciousness of mankind, it is now commonly thought of by Christians as a provider of welfare. Acceptance of the legitimacy of diverse interpretations of basic values, of the plural society, implies that the State, which is their institutional representative, is no longer properly able to have a relationship with religious bodies. There are in some societies, as it happens, all kinds of anomalous relationships between government and religious institutions: even the constitutional separation of Church and State in the American Constitution has not eradicated the persistence of links between the law and religious opinion in a number of areas of both federal and state experience. These sorts of survival, however, are not regarded by Christian observers as of any ideological significance, though they often are by the public generally, who still arrange them into symbols or components of a 'Christian' country or society. The twentieth century has seen an overall shift in Western democracies towards a redefinition, by Christian leaders, of the relationship of institutional religion to government. The churches are now much more usually regarded as external critics of the morality of state action than they are as spiritual or moral adjuncts of it. The last remnants of the old 'Christendom' model were probably the so-called 'National Security' regimes of Latin America in the 1970s, in countries like Chile, Argentina and Brazil, when Church and State stood together to preserve what was perceived to be Christian civilization from the assault of Communism. Europe had witnessed comparable essays in the 1930s. In practice this soft of organized Christian support for 'stable' values has meant an alliance with the political Right.

CHURCHES AND THE LEFT

It is often contended, by unsympathetic commentators, that the leading thinkers and officers of the Western Churches are actually committed in some
sense to the political Left. The impression derives from their sympathy for
Third World radical movements, from the undoubtedly socialist preferences
of the World Council of Churches in the 1970s and 1980s, from the apparent
preoccupation of Christian bodies with welfare issues which bring them into
conflict with conservative political forces, and from the association of the
Christian message of peace with actual peace movements under the ultimate
direction of radical political influences. In fact Western theologians and church
leaders have in recent decades demonstrated, not ideological commitment, but
a suprising measure of ideological innocence. The 'Christian–Marxist Dialogue' of the 1960s and 1970s was perhaps the last occasion on which Christian
thinkers seriously addressed the philosophical issues of historical materialism
in a way which attracted professional intellectual attention. Individual writers,
and a number of academic groups, explored the common ground between
Christian and Marxist beliefs. The traditional hostility between a Christian
insistence on the transcendence of humanity and Marxist teachings about the
determinism of historical materialism seemed, at the time, frayed at the edges
by the intellectual and political upheaval of the 1960s. Radical theologians
were questioning received Christian ideas about the nature of human understanding, and Marxists, in a revolt against Stalinist Communism, had rediscovered Marx's own early writings, and with them the evident possibility of
a more flexible attitude towards the phenomenon of religion. In the event
the dialogue, conducted in many parts of the world, proved sterile, and the
contending parties eventually disengaged. Marxism subsequently collapsed, at
the end of the 1980s, as the vehicle of the moral seriousness of both the
Western and Eastern intelligentsia, and Christianity, for its part, emerged little
altered by its exchanges with its ideological rival. The persistence of Christianity had little to do with the demise of the Marxist regimes, which was due
to economic mismanagement, ordinary interior corruption, and intellectual
adhesion to the Westernized (and secularized) doctrine of Human Rights. In
a few places, as in the German Democratic Republic, the churches took part
in the initial upheaval, but this was solely because they were the only available
institutions free of State control who could offer a platform for dissent.

It is not difficult to see why the churches were so modestly affected by
the 'Christian–Marxist' exchanges. Leading Christian thinkers, and academic
institutions, have shown themselves more concerned with the ethics of social
welfare than they have with the philosophical questions which lie at the basis
of political organization. There are few distinctly Christian contributions today
to political debate or political theory. For many Christians the matter scarcely
seems important since it is already settled: democracy is the Christian form
of government. After two thousand years, Christian involvement with classical

political thinking – with determining the philosophical references by which the bases of political society may be located – seems to have run into the ground. There is much heat generated among Western Christians over merely party differences, and these are often mistaken for really serious ideological divergence. But they are not. Most Christians (and certainly all those who look for acceptance by the Christian leadership) adopt a version of bourgeois liberalism and quarrel about its detailed applications, contending that the moral dispositions or policy programmes of this or that party are more 'Christian' than those of another. The test of political virtue is no longer reference to transcendent values of some sort or other, but is simply one of 'caring'. Social compassion is sovereign.

ENDORSING DEMOCRACY

The extent of Christian endorsement of democracy cannot be understated. Yet there have been few coherent and considered theoretical explanations offered by contemporary Christian thinkers which display the religious basis of what, after all, has for most of the history of civilization been regarded as the worst form of government. Many Christian apologists are content with accepting secular justifications, depicting democratic practice, therefore, as having to do with just social order and with human claims to equal participation in material rewards. It is in this sense that Christian support for democracy has centred on the notion of equality, even though the relationship between egalitarianism and political expertise remains unclear. There have been a few distinguished analyses: R. H. Tawney's *Equality* (1931), for example. A direct translation from an inclination to regard all men and women as equal before God to the sovereignty of a majority is a very large and dramatic movement, however. The English tradition of Christian Socialism, in the understanding of great nineteenth-century thinkers like F. D. Maurice, was originally extremely insistent that mutual esteem between classes, and social fairness, were quite separable from political democracy – which was to be postponed until the whole of society has been raised to a high level of educational accomplishment. To put it rather bluntly – the people were only to be admitted to political decision-making when they had been conditioned into accepting the rules of the game. That, in renditions of varying degrees of disguise and sophistication, is how democracy in liberal society still operates. Only those political forces are politically acceptable which recognize the essential moral purposes that the democratic political classes who operate the existing system are prepared to tolerate. In a society of rather low ideological division, as much of the Western world has become in recent decades, this restriction of meaning will not seem confining, and many, including many Christians, are quite prepared to go along with the legal exclusion of those ideological groups who resort to force, or whose views on issues (race relations, for example) which are at variance with the consensus, seem to threaten the political status quo. All this is to point out that political democracy as it operates in bourgeois society – in a society whose political terms of reference are laid out by the educated classes and their clients – is actually the form of politics which Christian apologists have come to endorse when they speak about the essentially 'Christian' nature of democratic practice. Democracy, under this interpretation, is really only acceptable so long as false consciousness guarantees a quiescent mass backing for the ideals of the liberal intelligentsia. As the intelligentsia is internally divided into parties over largely superficial differences of emphasis within the liberal set of ideals, there is a deceptive appearance of authentic political choice.

That truth, wise counsel, virtue, ultimate values, or religious knowledge, cannot be derived from the resolutions of majorities, or rest for their acceptance by the individual on mass electorates, does not in itself invalidate democratic practice – provided democracy is understood as a kind of last-resort political mechanism. After two and a half millennia of political thinking the most reflective minds are unable to agree among themselves about the philosophical basis most appropriate to the organization of life on earth; nor does the historical record provide any indicators as to which of the many so far tried political arrangements is most conducive to the cultivation of human virtue, or even, if that is a desired good, of human happiness. Democracy can thus be justified on the grounds that the counting of heads is the safest way of arranging public life since it is arguably the least likely to issue in the imposition of ideological tyranny. That is only true, however, if very large areas are removed from the competence of the State and reserved for the citizens. Hence, Western liberal democracy. All the effective twentieth-century political tyrannies have rested on mass assent, sometimes directly through the ballot box: democracy does not, in itself, provide a safeguard against the exclusivity of ideas whose presentation is within the idealism or the greed of mankind. But contemporary Christian endorsements of democracy do not envisage democratic practice as a low-level mechanism. They regard it, on the contrary, as among the finer fruits of Christian thinking – thereby also ignoring the fact that the roots of democratic theory, like the roots of contemporary liberalism, are not (though historically linked to some Christian ideas, because the culture in which they were first conceived was a Christian one) by nature distinctly Christian. Christian theologians and leaders today tend to refer to democracy as if it was an unambiguous structural expression of the love of neighbour spoken of by Christ. That is to confuse ordinary benevolence with political wisdom. It corresponds to a strong current in modern Christianity which would place human welfare above ideology, which sees the material needs of humanity as more pressing than the ultimate purposes for which life on earth is intended (unless it is intended for its mere survival, as some materialists argue), and which envisages democracy as the most virtuous form of government because it corresponds to what people think they are entitled to receive.

Since existing governments are rarely capable of travelling ahead of public expectations, and since the moral judgements of the educated classes are these days highly attuned to a whole series of issues to which virtually no government could provide satisfactory solutions, and since a heightened preoccupation with public issues has become a kind of surrogate religion, it is clear that the level of criticism now aimed at governments is very high. Christian leaders like to see themselves as independent evaluators, observing and criticizing the morality of government actions from the standpoint of the Gospel. In reality, however, their moral and political sense is very closely related to that of the secular intelligentsia, whose agenda on public issues they largely share. Where Christian moralists are divided among themselves this invariably parallels a division of view within educated opinion in general. That is the reality of the 'prophetic' voice which the leadership of Christian opinion offers. Behind the endorsement of liberal ideals, and the thoroughly proper inclination to regard the existence of a society of plural values (of which they constitute a unit) as a positive gain in the development of human society – in the sense that it recognizes the legitimate diversity of philosophical and moral positions – Christian acceptance of democracy has a further consequence. For individual lives, in a highly organized society, are in some measure moulded by public institutions, and especially by public education. Through frank if necessary acceptance that those institutions may be determined on a majority principle, the leaders of Christian opinion are potentially handing the culture in which the future of society will be shaped to ideological opponents. This may already be seen to be in existence in Western countries. Here the classrooms of schools conducted through public agencies freely teach children views about humanity itself which are plainly materialist: which depict men and women as creatures of circumstance, their lives decisively influenced by environmental, cultural, social, and economic conditioning, to the exclusion of transcendence. Hence, again, the necessity that Christian endorsement of democracy be allied to a limited view of the competence of the State. In practice, as already noticed, this does actually operate within contemporary Christianity when issues of personal life-styles are involved. But when it comes to social and economic arrangements a very different priority exists.

CHRISTIANS AND THE POWER OF THE STATE

Something has now been said about the relative rejection of State power within modern Christianity, and about the consequent limitation of the competence of the State. There must next be an examination of a quite contrary direction within Christian thinking – an acceptance of the expansive morality in some areas of State power. It has already been contended that the State's lack of a coherent ideological base, its dependence on the democratic majority principle, its presidency over a society of plural values (reinforced in some particulars by ethnic as well as cultural diversity), ensure that the modern State must reduce its control of the purveyance and enforcement of values. Christians often disagree among themselves, as does society in general, about the extent to which this resignation may be effected. When it comes to economic and social direction, however, there is an extensive area of consensus within Christian thinking: the leaders of contemporary Christianity are thorough collectivists. They look to the power of the State for the provision of welfare, and to the regulatory machinery of the State for the creation of what are regarded as goals of economic and social justice. Just beneath the leadership level there are, of course, many Christians who are sceptical of State direction in these areas, who see individual liberty as eroded by State intervention in society and the economy, and who believe that market forces are also simply more effective at achieving the desired end of enhanced material well-being. But there can be little doubt that within the most influential Christian thinking the prevailing disposition, throughout the Western world, sustains a high level of collectivism, and for moral reasons. Although Christian thinkers have no agreed coherent doctrine of the State, and in practice endorse democracy without really setting it within an intellectual framework, their insistence on the moral office of the State in using its power to achieve a more 'just society' receives hardly any internal criticism.

In many Western countries, and perhaps especially in North America and Britain, the endorsement of collectivism has in recent years drawn the leadership of the churches into political conflict with conservative political interests. Yet on neither side, that of the Church or that of the State, have the philosophical differences really been exposed – or even thought through. As a result the differences have remained on the surface of public life. Christian thinkers, for their part, have tended to argue for advanced collectivism on the simple ground of the morality of welfare. The priority, very often, has not been a transcendent view of humanity and its need for instruction into the truths of religion, but human material need. Only the State, they insist, has the capacity, through taxation, to accumulate the necessary resources for welfare benefits, and only the State has the legislative sanction to enforce social justice and overcome individual and vested interests. There is nothing peculiarly religious in this series of attitudes; public commentators, secular writers, and the intelligentsia generally are also characterized by the paradox of a simultaneous option for individual choice over personal moral values and for State enforcement of economic and social morality. There is a widespread supposition that collectivist solutions in certain areas of public life are self-evidently required. In supporting collectivism Christian thinkers are, however, giving their assent to very extensive State power. So the State which is too internally divided by moral pluralism or cultural values to be allowed to prescribe life-styles and ultimate beliefs for its citizens is also the State which is capable of identifying and enforcing very precise and detailed moral norms over economic and social life. Christian thinkers have not done much to resolve this contradiction in their attitudes, nor have they actually shown themselves especially aware of its existence.

As the centre of Christianity moves more and more decisively to the Southern hemisphere, to the countries of the developing world, it is important to notice that there, too, Christian leaders are increasingly advocates of State power for reasons of social justice. In some areas there has been an alliance of nationalism and socialism: socialism, too, not of the latter-day Western variety, shot through with ideological heresies and critical of Communist state *Apparat*, but socialism in a vigorously collectivist sense. With the demise of the Marxist governments in Europe at the end of the 1980s and, in a domino sequence, in other parts of the world, socialist collectivism has been modified as the goal in some countries. Yet socialism was not the only reason for the appeal of State power among the developing nations – the need for central planning to defeat colonialist influences, for a coherent national response to Western agencies seeking to have economic or welfare relations with the emergent countries, for a mechanism for preventing or else for securing the dominance of one ethnic group against others, and for a symbol of nationhood – all these have tended to the aggrandizement of the State. Christian thinkers and writers have often been among the first (since often the first educated) to propagate these features of Third World nationalism, and to associate them with Christian values. They have envisaged social justice as attainable by State power.

The history of apartheid in South Africa illustrates the point. Although South Africa is, by most tests, scarcely a Third World country, the relationship of its non-white population to government shows many features which are characteristic of the developing world, and the preoccupation of Western Christian opinion with the apartheid question, since the 1950s, provided some clearly defined Christian arguments and attitudes. The creation of apartheid, especially over educational issues, emphasized its inherent collectivism as much as its racism. In opposition to the apartheid system the leaders of black opinion also, over the decades, gradually came to assume the need for extensive State powers (in a future black state) to create a unitary society. This actually involved a good deal of internal conflict, particularly between the rigorous Marxism of the African National Congress and the decentralizing liberalism of the more rural and less well-organized groups. Christians were to be found in all of the various organizations, including the Marxist ones, yet Christian criticism of apartheid, both inside and outside South Africa, increasingly emphasized State power as the necessary way to create a just society. The radical Black Consciousness movement of the 1970s (which was in some measure influenced by black American writers like James Cone) was unusual among the articulate critics of apartheid precisely because of its scepticism of State action and its flirtation with anarchism. Hence its unpopularity – not exposed to the public, especially the Western liberal public – with the hard-line Marxists of the ANC. The history of Christian involvement with the anti-apartheid movement in South Africa is the history of Christian endorsement of State power. Only the State power of a country run by blacks will achieve justice. The arguments used by the Christians involved have been intellectually unsophisticated: it has not seemed necessary, in view of the plainly unjust nature of apartheid society, to set the assumptions being made about State power within a tradition or interpretive framework of political theory or political philosophy. The issue of racial equality, furthermore, has been lumped together with political democracy as if they were necessarily inseparable. The history of the world, however, shows that most societies have not enjoyed democratic systems, and their moral basis, or the legitimacy of their laws, has not in consequence been invalidated.

LIBERATION THEOLOGY

There has been one important area of modern Christian concern with the political process which *has* been discussed in terms of basic political theory. The school of liberation theology (for it is systematic enough and universal enough to be regarded as a school) has allied theological categories with Marxist intellectual methods in a way which has achieved a good deal of prestigious support. The most seminal of its writings have come from the Peruvian *pensador* Gustavo Gutiérrez, and especially from his work of 1971, *A Theology of Liberation: History, Politics and Salvation.* Here, and in the outpourings of the radical political criticism of which it was the first fruit, liberal Christians have thought to discover the authentic voice of the Third World. Gutiérrez in fact combines pretty standard Marxist social analysis with primitive biblical exegesis and a theological understanding virtually unacquainted with most development in contemporary theological scholarship. It is his voice, identified as that of the world's powerless, which attracts the admiration of liberal Christians in the West. He was invited to give the keynote address at the start of the Anglican Lambeth Conference in 1988, and what he said on that occasion was greeted by the assembled bishops with enormous enthusiasm. Few of these bishops, surely, can actually have agreed with the succession of Marxist precepts which Gutiérrez offered on that occasion. Of all contemporary theological writing on political issues, however, liberation theology has been the most widely respected and the most widely read. Its origins lie in the radical political ferment of Europe and North America in the 1960s, whose idealism and intellectual dispositions were rapidly developed by Catholic priests in Latin America. These men were often themselves teachers in universities and colleges, or exercised their ministries among the bourgeoisie of Latin American cities. They were already acquainted, that is to say, with the well-established Marxist intellectual tradition of the Latin American intelligentsia. This existing tradition had been assembled in hostility to the Catholic Church, and was a crucial dimension of the secularism of Latin American liberalism. Liberation theology was always intended, therefore, to be something of a paradox: the priests who adopted the political theories of their ideological opponents; the members of the professional class who sided with the poor; the teachers of peace who nevertheless exhorted their flocks to revolution.

Christian love of neighbour has always inspired a continuing spiritual tradition of concern for the world's poor, in an attempt to follow the poverty of Christ himself, who had nowhere to lay his head. What was new in liberation theology was the concept of 'solidarity' with the poor – and a mass poor, who were now identified as 'the oppressed'. For poverty came now to be seen as the fruit of exploitation; the poverty of the Third World was recognized as the consequence of exploitation by the developed world, and the poverty of the peasants and the working classes was diagnosed as the result of internal capitalist exploitation. Here was a ready-made class analysis of social reality, and it was a single step to a realization that existing academic theology, which seemed inattentive to such matters, was the theology of the status quo. The Church had the duty, according to liberation theologians, of prophetic unmasking – to end the myth of a possible 'Christian' society within prevailing social structures, and to recognize that society in fact represented a conflict of social classes, just as the international order depicted the capitalist exploitation of the world's poor by the transnational corporations of the developed countries. What was needed, according to the liberation theologians, was for theology to become specific. Its agenda must be set by historical circumstance; in this case the conflict of classes. Ordinary people, the exploited themselves, must be, as the Brazilian Marxist Paulo Freire put it, 'conscienti-zed'. They must be re-educated, that is to say, into a sense of their own social reality, removed from the false consciousness of social palliation and Catholic charitable relief, and made aware of their own humanity. Then they would grasp history: the apocalyptic tone is central to the appeal of Marxist analysis. The content of theology should be set, not by the prevailing learning of the academics and the ecclesiastics, but by the praxis of social reality. Thereafter the revolution was to be a real one, not just a shift of attitudes or the permeation of Christian good intentions. The poor were to seize their own destiny and create a socialist society; reformism was merely a disguise for the continuation of exploitation. Basic changes were needed in the consciousness of men and women themselves, so that they could become free, as Gutiérrez expressed it, from all that impeded self-fulfilment. There are echoes here of the radical intelligentsia's rediscovery, made in the 1960s, of Marx's own early critique of 'alienation', and of Mao Zedong's concept of a permanent revolu-tion of culture. Gutiérrez sought a 'new man' purged of the psychology of repression, re-fashioned in each generation to be critically emancipated from the thrall of bourgeois values. This vision, common enough in the secular redemption breathlessly held out by the 1960s intellectuals, was now given a theological basis by the liberation theologians and made the foundation of a reappraisal of State power. For however much the newly emancipated, after the purification of the revolutionary experience, may find themselves able to dispense with the familiar structures of the bourgeois State, they would need a strong and centralized State power during the transition to social justice. At first sight the liberation theologians appear to embrace the scepticism about State power characteristic of the 1960's intellectuals; looked at from a closer perspective, however, it is plain that the need for perpetual renewal of the revolutionary experience, as the case of Marxism in China was to indicate, would always involve strong and effective centralized direction. In Latin American terms, that meant the retention of the enduring Hispanic tradition of a central power. It is diverting to wonder how aware of all this the bishops who applauded Gutiérrez at the Lambeth Conference really were.

There are all kinds of variations and subtleties of emphasis within liberation theology. It is also true that the school has produced some writings of theoretical sophistication, at least as far as internal applications of Marxist methodology are concerned. As its influence spread to other areas of the developing world, and especially to Southern Africa, in the mid-1970s, the social analysis of liberation theology acquired considerable enrichment. In the Republic of South Africa, particularly, the conflict of classes was re-read as a conflict of races, with the result that an existing inclination by liberals to ignore the fact that the anti-apartheid movement was penetrated with Marxist political elements was reinforced. In all other areas of the developing world, however, the agents of liberation theology have encountered tough resistance from traditional Christianity, sometimes in alliance with the ruling classes, and sometimes simply because the social diagnosis of liberation theology, with its emphasis on revolution and State power, has seemed religiously inappropriate and too secular. It has been within the liberal leadership of the Christianity of the Western world that liberation theology has enjoyed its most sustained following.

Behind liberation theology lies the assumption that when 'the Christian' policy for society has been identified it is legitimate to use political force to bring it into actual existence. There is much commentary in the writings of liberation theologians about employing political violence as an instrument of Christian love – to liberate oppressors from their own oppression. Using the power of the State to give institutional reality to Christian ideals, however, is in direct contrast to the methods envisaged within contemporary Western liberalism, and therefore condemned, at least in relation to their own circumstances, by most Western Christian leaders. Liberation theology, under the banner of Marxism, is in effect a resuscitation of the old 'Christendom' model: the ethical State is conceived as a unitary one. In Western liberalism divergencies of ethical thought and practice are recognized, if selectively, and it is not thought proper that the State should be entrusted with the enforcement of a single ethical norm if it is seen to be in conflict with the ethical ideals of other sections within the prevailing pluralism of values. The idea that the Christian community and civil society are co-extensive has long been abandoned in the face of acknowledged diversity. Historically, the notion of a single Christian society was first questioned because it was in clear conflict with divergencies of views among Christians themselves; later it was considered inappropriate that Christianity itself should receive the sanction of the State as against other systems of belief. Church leaders are themselves reluctant to resort to the power of the State for the protection or endorsement of their religious teaching. Where they do in fact call for State action – most commonly in social and economic issues – they do so beneath the umbrella of a consensus of the educated: the morality of a particular policy is thus in accord with an identifiable area of secular opinion. Reforms are sought not because they are in themselves embodiments of religious teaching, but because they are conducive to human welfare. The Church's necessary concern with the social policy is both a cause of its own internal secularization and also an indication of the extent to which it associates its teaching with the moral goals that are general in society. As the possibility of making the Christian community and civil society co-extensive recedes, the Church progressively recognizes itself, once again, as a gathered society. It sees its mission as that of a community within a community, a leavening agent, a witness to the society of those called by Christ to 'engage the world' (to use an expression common among contemporary theologians). The insoluble problem of public policy remains: some group, some system of belief, has to undertake government, and government, even at a very reduced level of activity, still moulds the public culture within which law receives its sanction and citizens are nurtured in virtue. Christians may decline to use the power of the State to implement their beliefs, but others, ideological rivals, will not hesitate to do so, though the moral incoherence of modern political society may for a time disguise the fact. Collectivism is, in effect, the old 'Christendom' model in a secularized form. Its supporting system of ideas is an ill-defined humanism which tends, often with no clear intention of doing so, to cultivate a materialist view of human life.

CONCLUSION

Attitudes of modern Christian leaders to the power of the State have thus demonstrated considerable ambiguity. They no longer regard the State as providing a suitable structure for the cultivation or propagation of religious ideas. Governments, therefore, should have, in their view, no concern with religious doctrine, and it is the duty of the churches to see that their own adherents are the agents who will seek to establish the kingdom of Christ on earth. Yet the Christian leaders simultaneously hold that the power of the State should be used for the enforcement of moral goals – but selectively. The State should be concerned with the economic and social order, with securing and guaranteeing certain sorts of basic human rights, and with issues (like those now raised by medical technology) in which inventiveness appears to advance ahead of agreed moral understanding. Yet in areas of personal morality, modern Christian leaders tend to follow liberal opinion in seeking areas reserved to individual judgement. It does not need to be said that all the definitions employed to determine the extent of these various issues are controversial. The modern Church does not look to the State for the establishment of transcendent values, but for securing the conditions of human welfare in the material world.

REFERENCES

Gutiérrez, G. (1971) *A Theology of Liberation*, London: SCM Press.
Faith in the City: The Report of the Archbishop of Canterbury's Commission on Urban Priority Areas (1985), London: Church Publishing House.

FURTHER READING

Boff, L. (1987) *Jesus Christ Liberator: A Critical Christology for Our Time*, London: SPCK.
Bonino, J. M. (1983) *Towards a Christian Political Ethics*, London: SCM Press.
Gibellini, R. (1987) *The Liberation Theology Debate*, London: SCM Press.
Kee, A. (1974) *A Reader in Political Theology*, London: SCM Press.
Metz, J. B. (1981) *The Emergent Church*, London: SCM Press.
Moyser, G. (ed.) (1985) *Church and Politics Today*, Edinburgh: T. & T. Clark.
Norman, E. (1984) 'The Imperialism of Political Religion', in *Liberation Theology*, ed. R. Nash, Michigan: Mott Media Press.
—— (1990) 'Do British parties need philosophies?', in *Christianity and Conservatism*, ed. M. Alison and D. Edwards, London: Hodder and Stoughton.
Pope Paul VI (1967) *Popularum Progressio*, London: Catholic Truth Society.
Ratzinger, J. (1988) *Church Ecumenism and Politics*, New York: St Paul Publications, Slough & Crossroad Publishing.
Scarfe, A. and Sookhdeo, P. (1982) *Christianity and Marxism*, Exeter: Paternoster Press.
Turner, D. (1983) *Marxism and Christianity*, Oxford: Basil Blackwell.
Wilson, B. (1982) *Religion in Sociological Perspective*, Oxford: Oxford University Press.
Wren, B. A. (1977) *Education for Justice*, London: SCM Press.
See also chapters 33, 34, 36, 37.

38

THE PASTORAL EXPERIENCE

Jack Dominian

The object of the Christian life is to know, love and serve God. In fact Jesus made it clear that the heart of faith is love.

> But when the Pharisees heard that He had silenced the Sadducees they got together and, to disconcert him, one of them put a question, 'Master, which is the greatest commandment of the Law?' Jesus said 'You must love the Lord your God with all your heart with all your soul and with all your mind. This is the greatest and the first commandment. The second resembles it: You must love your neighbour as yourself. On these two commandments hang the whole Law and the Prophets also.'
>
> (Matt. 22:34–40)

Clearly, love is at the centre of the relationship between God and man, and between human beings themselves. This love involves the heart which means affect, the mind which contains reason, and the soul which is the sphere of spiritual discernment. But men and women are not dualistic entities, they are not matter and spirit, they operate as whole beings. In this operation their awareness of what is right and wrong, their freedom to choose between the two and their capacity to assent to their decisions have been traditionally the elements making up responsibility for their actions.

What is right and wrong has been discerned from revelation through the inspired word of the Bible. Here there are two traditions that have held sway. The Roman Catholic one which claims that the teaching Church interprets the word of God, and the Protestant one which encourages a more direct dialogue between the Bible and the individual believer. For both, however, revelation is a primary source of teaching of divine truth.

Revelation is supplemented by reference to tradition and natural law. Thus revelation, tradition and natural law form a core of truth to which the Christian tries to adhere. This adherence is achieved by a combination of discernment by the soul and the individual's rationality. In this respect freedom plays a vital part in the choice and consent of an individual action.

Traditional psychology emphasized that human action was ultimately focused on the will which chose from a spectrum of right and wrong and finally gave assent to a decision. In this perspective, which belonged to all the Churches but was emphasized particularly by the Roman Catholic Church, sin consisted of an action which was wrong, for which the individual had full freedom and exercised full consent. Sin thus constituted the free decision of the whole personality against the will of God. Sin was divided into serious or mortal, and minor or venial.

Having committed a sin, the Catholic Christian went to Confession which is the Sacrament of Penance. In Confession the minister acts in the name of the Church as the forgiving presence of Christ.

> In the evening of that same day, the first day of the week, the doors were closed in the room where the disciples were, for fear of the Jews. Jesus came and stood among them. He said to them 'Peace be with you', and showed them his hands and his side. The disciples were filled with joy when they saw the Lord, and he said to them again 'Peace be with you. As the Father sent me, so I am sending you.' After saying this he breathed on them and said 'Receive the Holy Spirit for those whose sins you forgive they are forgiven, for those whose sins you retain they are retained.'
>
> (John 20:19–23)

Initially in the early Church, confession was carried out publicly and allowed (though with some variety) once in a lifetime. Eventually it became private and could be repeated, and, indeed, in recent centuries frequent Confession was considered a good Christian practice. Those who went to Confession disclosed their sins, sought absolution and made an act of contrition. Until the mid-seventies this form of Confession was very common, in particular in the Roman Catholic tradition. In pastoral practice it presented a number of problems. The absolution received often became mechanical; the penitent repeated the same sins between one weekly confession and the next. There was no basic transformation of the personality. Confession became superficial and, although large numbers attended, it became a routine without much meaning.

In the 1970s private confession became less common, and currently very few people go to Confession in the Roman Catholic Church, despite repeated attempts to re-activate the Sacrament. The demise of Confession is a complex phenomenon. It is associated with a drop in all Church activities, including liturgical attendance. But at a deeper level there is an awareness that traditional Confession did not involve the whole personality and that psychological factors play a much greater role in human responsibility and freedom in action. Whilst Confession continues with diminished frequency there is a much greater awareness of the impact of dynamic psychology on the human personality and on what we understand by sin.

Millions of Roman Catholics and Christians of other denominations grew up with this understanding of sin which presupposed clear knowledge, free consent and, for mortal sin, grave matter; and the manuals of the past spent a great deal of time interpreting what constituted clear knowledge, free consent and grave matter. This language has virtually disappeared today; in fact, over the last thirty years, there has been a shift from this rational psychology to the present model which will be considered in this chapter.

PASTORAL COUNSELLING

The way has become open to move to what has come to be called pastoral counselling. By pastoral counselling is meant the understanding of human behaviour in terms of the psychodynamic model instituted by Freud (1910, 1915–16, 1916–17), and Jung (1933) in a setting where there is a dialogue between dynamic and spiritual factors. The rest of this chapter will spell out what this involves.

Psychodynamic factors

The prevailing psychology of the first half of the present century was concentrated on will and reason. The essence of this psychology made the will the determining factor which controlled behaviour, aided and abetted by reason. Thus, rationality was the basis for examining human responsibility. What was asked in moral manuals was, first how far the individual knew and understood what he or she was doing was wrong and, second, how far they had the ability to give full consent. But Sigmund Freud (1923–5) revolutionized this sin-centred model of interpreting human behaviour. He emphasized that the human personality was constructed on a three-layer system. In the unconscious part were to be found the instincts and wishes, such as sexuality and aggression, that fuel the drives of human beings. These drives are controlled by the conscious part of men and women, the ego, and also are controlled by a censor which is unconscious called the superego. Shortly we shall look at a more detailed plan of human development than this crude outline. The point to be made here is that, within the structure of the mind, one of its central features is that of conflict or ambivalence. The clear-cut analysis of human behaviour of the previous psychology is now replaced by uncertainty, conflict and ambivalence in which we hold two contradictory feelings at the same time.

The word 'feeling' introduces another aspect of psychodynamic theory. Behaviour is controlled as much by feelings as by rationality, and these feelings play a vital part in the direction that behaviour takes. For a previous generation feelings were ignored as being of subsidiary importance. Today they are recognized as playing a prominent role in behaviour.

The inner world of the mind in which conflict and affect play a part is subject to trauma. The child goes through a sequence of phases which leaves a permanent impact on its personality. Two features emerge from the world of childhood. The first, as already stated, shapes adult behaviour, and the second, which is just as important, is that the personality develops ways of coping with both trauma and conflict by forming psychological defences which are unconscious. These defences play a vital role in our personality. We use mechanisms such as suppression (the conscious suppression of facts), repression (the unconscious repression of knowledge), denial mechanisms (the denial of facts and responsibility), projection (pushing unconsciously onto somebody else our own feelings from one situation to another), and so on. The point about these psychological defences is that they influence our behaviour by suppressing the anxiety which the original trauma, conflict or ambivalence causes.

The advent of psychodynamic theory allows us a whole new view of human behaviour in which awareness, freedom and motivation take on a new meaning. In particular, the freedom to act in a particular way is influenced by the way our childhood has been shaped, and the traumas received then. The tendencies of some people to behave in a certain way, such as persistent promiscuity or aggressiveness, which previously have been interpreted as stubborn, sinful features, take on a new understanding when we see the background of such people as one deprived of love. The promiscuous behaviour is a desperate seeking of affection and the anger is a repeated response to rejection. Before the behaviour can be modified it has first to be understood. Understanding, of course, is not enough. It has to be followed by a movement towards maturity.

For psychodynamic theory the goal of development is maturity which involves autonomy, control and fulfilment of essential needs. Maturity has now become a goal for Christian spirituality as well. What has emerged from psychodynamic theory is a pastoral care which is influenced by the essentials of listening, empathy and a non-judgemental approach.

Listening, empathy and non-judgemental approach

The pastoral care which will be outlined as part of pastoral counselling is a derivative of psychoanalysis. This is not the place to describe psychoanalysis, but to emphasize three of its key features. Until the advent of psycho-analysis doctors and ministers heard a problem, proceeded to make a diagnosis or a moral judgement, and then laid out the solution in terms of medical or spiritual cure. Freud changed all that. Instead of doing the talking himself, he allowed the patient to talk uninterruptedly, and he listened. Attentive listening has become the order of the day when we are communicating with people who have problems, whether they are psychological or spiritual.

This listening requires special qualities. We must be in touch with the feeling world of those we listen to. We need to be in touch with their moods. Are they hurt, angry, joyful, perplexed, anxious or depressed? This has come to be known as empathetic listening. In other words, we need to be in touch not only with their reasoning but with their feelings, their defences and their understanding of their situation. In addition to empathetic listening we have to be non-judgemental. This is one of the most difficult aspects of pastoral care that takes its references from pastoral counselling. Traditionally, the Christian moralist listened and then judged according to the rules. In this pastoral care we do not judge. The fact is that the person concerned already feels guilty enough and does not need any further admonition. So that the triad of listening, listening empathetically and non-judgementally have become the principles of pastoral care. Most people can practice these. There is no need of detailed theoretical knowledge or learned practice to put into operation these simple principles. This is the first stage of pastoral care, it is an approach in which those concerned are listened to, their feelings are heeded, and they are not judged.

The next step is to proceed to pastoral counselling. Now the pastor needs to be acquainted with a schema of human development so that a better understanding is achieved of the two concepts of maturity: autonomy and the fulfilment of emotional needs. It is no good talking about spiritual goals until human needs have been met. A great deal of the attraction of counselling is the realization of psychological needs, and the pastor who wants to influence the person in front of him with spiritual values must graft these on to human integrity.

There may appear to be a certain tension in this situation. Psychodynamic psychology aims at a maturity which realizes autonomy and realization of needs. Christianity seeks to fulfil the commandment of Jesus to be as perfect as our heavenly Father which implies the donation of self, love of others and sacrifice on their behalf. At first sight the two goals appear incompatible. However, this is a superficial judgement. It is only when we are whole people, that is when we are capable of realizing our potential, that we can empathize with the needs of others and not reject them when they make demands on us, and have the fullness of being to donate ourselves to others. In other words, psychological maturity is a prerequisite of the Christian life. Put another way, we can only really love God and others when we love ourselves. Loving ourselves requires that we recognize our physical, intellectual and emotional needs. Most of us can recognize our physical and intellectual needs because of the advances that Western society has made in these fields. It is our emotional needs, or phases of development, that we have problems with, so what follow are two theoretical models of personal development which emphasize the emotional side of ourselves.

The model based on E. Erikson, with additions of J. Bowlby and M. Klein

This model describes some of the most important human needs we know, and anyone who enters the world of pastoral counselling must at least be aware of them. In this model we follow the child in its various stages of development and delineate its basic needs as it proceeds to adulthood. Erikson writes of acquiring 'a sense of' and these acquisitions are a permanent feature of our adult life.

As the British psychoanalyst, John Bowlby (1969) has taught the first and principal human experience, going right back to birth, is to form an attachment first with our mother and then our father, then subsequently with key figures in our life. This attachment is an affective bond which we form through vision. We become familiar first with the face of our mother, and then the rest of her body. Second, we form an attachment through sound as we become familiar with the sound of mother's voice. Third, we form a bond through touch, in holding and being held. Emotional attachment becomes the cornerstone of our human relationships. It is the way we link up with other people. There is a world of difference between secure and anxious attachment. In the former we feel sure of the love of the other person, in the latter we are unsure of their love or commitment and we live with the fear that we are going to lose them and of being abandoned.

Human attachment is vital to the fabric of our personality. It is the way we feel we belong and others belong to us. Anxious attachment, when we feel insecure with those close to us, can be the result of genetic factors, but it is also due to our parenting, e.g. being insecure through abandonment, being passed from one person to another, or our mother threatening to go away or to kill herself. Such insecure childhoods make us grow into insecure people, fearful of being let down by God and mankind. We are afraid that people who love us will leave us, that they will go away and not return. Insecurity makes it difficult to trust others and to disclose ourselves. We may fall prey to the first person who loves us, to whom we disclose ourselves. If we are fortunate, they can cope with our insecurity; if not, they let us down. So the first year of life teaches us to acquire the ability to form attachments which are repeated in our friendships and our marriage.

Erikson (1968) writes of our acquiring in the same first year a sense of trust or else a sense of mistrust. In the first year of life the child's sense of being safe depends on mother and increasingly on father as they quietly meet its needs in a continuous, reliable and predictable fashion. The infant begins to recognize in a dim way that what it requires will be fulfilled, be it food, cuddling, change of nappy, or sleep. The mother has the capacity to make its world trustworthy. When the environment is not reliable and the home is unstable, the child develops a sense of basic mistrust. This basic mistrust can continue in childhood and adulthood where we continue to fail to trust people. It is out of this basic mistrust that we become paranoid, that is, we expect people to hurt and attack us. Our world is insecure. We expect to be let down.

Erikson (1968) links the various stages of development with certain virtues. When the infant's capacity to trust is greater than its fear of mistrust then it acquires the capacity to hope. It is interesting to tie the acquisition of this human virtue with that of St Paul's triad of faith, hope and love. Long before our time, St Paul realized that hope is a fundamental human feature in spiritual life. We now see the link between psychology and spirituality in that the latter has an infrastructure which is psychological.

The infant's basis of hope lies in the fact that its aspirations, masteries, achievements will overcome its failures, frustrations, losses, and in this way it will achieve its fervent wishes. A trustworthy childhood is background of that quiet confidence that inspires men and women to attempt apparently impossible tasks, and must have been a basic acquisition of Jesus in his belief that the kingdom of God had arrived with him.

In the second and third years of life the child acquires the capacity to feed itself, control its defecation and urination, dress itself, walk and speak. It is an enormous range of achievement. When things go wrong in one or more of these areas shame and doubt are experienced; and so Erikson (1968) describes these years as the time for acquiring a sense of autonomy, or else a sense of shame and doubt. The virtue that Erikson establishes in this period is that of the will. The will is the unbroken determination to exercise free choice as well as self-restraint, in spite of the unavoidable experience of shame and doubt in infancy.

Returning to John Bowlby (1969–80) and Melanie Klein (1965), there is another vital experience that takes place during these two years. A child can leave the mother's side, go to another room and play alone with its toys. Nothing unusual about that, but it is in fact a feat of considerable achievement. It is now realized that the toddler takes inside it the memory of mother and holds on to her in her physical absence. This awareness of her presence in her absence is brought about by the psychological process of internalization. Making people part of ourselves in their physical absence plays a vital part in our everyday life. We leave home every day and we leave behind our loved ones. Their only way of keeping in touch with us is to preserve us in their memory during the day until we return home.

When people die we mourn them and after a while we internalize them, that is, take them inside us and make them part of ourselves. Internalization plays a vital part in the way we acquire a sense of God. God is not a reality we can see and touch. Unlike our parents we do not have a physical image of God, we cannot see or touch him. So how do we develop an understanding of God? As children, particularly at this early stage, we are told stories about Jesus and God, and we picture God in our imagination. This image of God we gradually internalize. We build up a picture of God inside us which is supplemented by the Jesus of the Scriptures. So internalization plays a vital role in the formation of our faith. A third feature of these years of autonomy is the advent of forgiveness and reparation. During this period the child wants to do things in its own way, and the mother in her own way. Inevitably there is going to be a clash, a shout and even a smack. For a moment the world of the child collapses. Its heaven of intimate relationship is interrupted. Within a very short time the mother forgives and there is a reconciliation. This sequence of events, conflict, forgiveness and reparation, becomes a standard sequence of human behaviour and ties in with the forgiveness which we receive from God and practise with each other.

The capacity to seek forgiveness depends on feeling loveable enough to merit it. There are men and women who are steeped in self-rejection and who cannot find anything good about themselves which can permit them to seek forgiveness. They feel thoroughly bad and unloveable. We can see that this phase of autonomy, the second and third years of life, is packed with crucial psychological experience which remains important for the rest of life.

After trust and autonomy, according to Erikson (1968), the child proceeds to a stage of initiative. The youngster is a person, but must discover what kind of person he or she is. Children are helped to appreciate themselves by their ability to run, climb and explore their surroundings. The use of language becomes more extensive and precise. It should be noted that trust is now linked with language. Trust in the first few years was primarily physical, being held, feeling secure, but from now on trust will extend to the veracity of the spoken word. The child needs to be told the truth and comes to rely on the accuracy of verbal statements.

Thus, the key characteristic of this stage is the child's growing capacity to initiate actions, thoughts and fantasies. Erikson relates this phase to a sense of guilt when things go wrong. The child has the ability to plan from now onwards, and the virtue which is developed is that of purpose. Purpose is the courage to envisage and pursue valued goals uninhibited by the defeat of infantile fantasies, by guilt and by the fear of punishment.

At the same time as the young person realizes that he or she is a person, a sense of being lovable is acquired. This is an important development in which the child feels unconditionally loved. All that has preceded in the way of attachment, trust, autonomy makes it realize that it is unconditionally loveable. This will be compared shortly with a sense of achievement at school in which it will feel loved and appreciated for what it achieves.

This is a crucial distinction: men and women feel loved first unconditionally and then for what they have achieved. There are men and women who have never felt loved unconditionally, and their sense of achievement comes only from their creativity, from what they achieve. These people find it difficult to believe that God loves them. They can only appreciate acceptance in terms of what they deserve. They are not aware of unconditional love.

Here are two important theological issues. The first has been the argument between the Roman Catholic tradition and the Protestant one about meriting and not meriting God's love; about earning God's approval through good works and being graced unconditionally. The roots of this debate have psycho-logical overtones. Do we feel unconditionally loved or do we have to work hard for our approval? The psychological experience sets the scene for our spiritual feelings.

Second, it can easily be seen from the psychological development described so far that we depend utterly on our parents for their love so that we may feel loved. We can love thus because we were first loved ourselves. This is echoed in the first Epistle of St John: 'We are to love, then, Because he loved us first' (1 John 4:19). We can thus see the sequence of events. God first loved the world and taught us what love is through our parents. In so far as this love experience from our parents is flawed, so we become wounded people. At the heart of pastoral care and pastoral counselling is the reversal of this wounding. This is where psychology and spirituality meet in our capacity to be loving people.

We now continue with Erikson's (1968) schema. With basic trust in the first year the personality becomes 'I am what I am given'. In the second and third years the stage of autonomy, the identity, is entered on 'I am what I will'. At the third stage, when the child is four or five, its identity becomes 'I am what I can manage to be'. Now we reach the school years the child acquires a sense of industry or else a sense of inferiority. The industry comes from progressive achievement in scholastic work, and the sense of inferiority from any unsatisfactory results. A successful resolution of the tension between industry and inferiority leads to the development of a new virtue, that of competence. Competence is the free exercise of dexterity and intelligence in the completion of tasks, unimpaired by infantile inferiority. So school offers a second opportunity to acquire self-esteem. It is the self-esteem which flows from achievement and it compares with the self-esteem acquired at home through the first five years of unconditional loving.

During the school years at about age twelve or thereabouts the child enters puberty. It acquires secondary sexual characteristics typical of its sex, and it moves away sexually from its parents. There is an important psychospiritual step to be achieved from now on. The young man or young woman will be driven by adult sexual drive towards someone, usually, but not always, of the opposite sex. This sexual drive is physical and is directed towards the body; but the encounter is between people and this is where the love acquired in the first dozen years of life becomes important. The person who attracts us sexually has to be the target both of our physical sexual drive and of our personal love, all of which involve care and concern. Here lies one of the most common problems of morality. The problem is the dislocation between the sexual drive and love. Sex with a prostitute epitomizes this issue. In this instance there is a union between bodies but not persons. Both psychological and spiritual integrity require that there should be union of the physical and the loving, and when the two are not united there is a lack of integrity. There are many difficulties in achieving the perfect blend between the sexual drive and love. Those who have not been loved want sex alone, indeed, they cannot cope with the combination of sex and affection. They do not know how to handle the two together. Alternatively, when love is missing, sex is mistaken for love, and here we find people who are promiscuous who believe that the more sex they have, the greater is their experience of love. So sexual problems are tied in with the psychological upbringing of the person and morality is entwined with the psychodynamic evolution of the individual.

Moving on, Erikson (1968) now describes the stage of adolescence which spans puberty and covers the years between twelve and twenty-two. This phase is called acquiring a sense of identity versus role confusion. The adolescent has to retain a sense of sameness and continuity in the middle of much change.

The changes are in sexuality, in status (from child to adult) and in the move from study to work. In all these areas there may be confusion. With regard to sexuality, time is needed to acknowledge one's vibrant physicality, and to learn to direct it towards another person. Sexual attraction will shift from person to person. A generation ago this attraction and relationship was achieved without sexual intercourse. Today sexual intercourse has become part and parcel of these transient relationships. The issue revolves around answering the question 'What is sex for?' Is it for pleasure or is it a seal of a permanent relationship? Young people are confused and want their sexuality to mean several things, ranging from a pledge of fidelity to a casual exchange of sexual excitement. Clearly pastoral counselling has to distinguish sexual disturbance from the normal spectrum of uncertainty which adolescents face nowadays. Within the concept of what has been described, sexuality has the meaning of being a seal to a personal commitment, and the spiritual assessment has to gauge how far the person is ready for personal commitment.

Nevertheless we have acquired a great deal of knowledge in the last thirty years about stable relationships of marriage, and one of the things we have learned is that marriages that start before the age of twenty are likely to be unstable and more prone to divorce. So it is important not to drive young people into early marriages in order to satisfy commitments. There may be a lot to be said for cohabitation as an intermediary between promiscuity and marriage. Whatever is chosen, we want to avoid promiscuity at any cost. Finally, there is work to be negotiated. Work of course, depends on the employment situation of a particular country or locality. Even when there is employment, young people experience a strange transformation. At school they were at the top of their development and position depending on their abilities. At work they have to start at the bottom of the ladder. It requires a certain degree of confidence to move from one position to the other. For some young people the transition is negotiated by further advanced study at college or university. There are two or three further years to attain maturity before the adolescent, now nearly an adult, is plunged into work.

Most adolescents negotiate the transition from childhood to adulthood without difficulty. But there are young people who do not, and the pastor is likely to be faced with them. The more common manifestations are excessive rebellion, outrageous dressing, refusing to come to church on Sunday, being rude, staying in bed at all hours of the day, going out at night and coming back in the early hours of the morning. There are also some serious problems.

Adolescents can attempt suicide, drink excessively, take hard drugs, become promiscuous or phobic, and refuse to get out of the home or whilst in it remain aggressive. Adolescents need careful handling. They will not be patronized or censured. As stated above, their confidence needs to be gained. They need an adult as a friend. This friend needs to understand the turbulence of their inner world. They are anxious, isolated, lack self-esteem, are eager to establish their independence and yet frightened to be on their own. The counsellor has to establish trust, not to be authoritarian, and yet to be firm. As always, one has to listen to what the adolescent is saying about his or her inner world, and to discern what degree of confidence has been achieved. The pastor has to reassure and receive the anger and the apparent unreasonableness of the world. Little by little the young person begins to trust himself or herself, to establish rapport with older people, to find friends among their peers and to try out the things he or she is afraid of. Counselling the adolescent can be a very satisfying experience and it is a common need in our society which imposes such complex expectations on adolescents.

With the arrival of adulthood, men and women enter into the stage of their life where they make a commitment, usually to a person of the opposite sex, to live together in a permanent relationship which we call marriage. There are two points to be noted about this stage of development. The first has already been referred to in the tension between psychological and spiritual maturity. Is the object of psychological development the emergence of an autonomous adult who merely satisfies his or her needs? The answer is clearly not. Beyond autonomous adulthood is the person who has committed himself or herself to another person, to love and to cherish.

The same applies to Christian spirituality. The pinnacle of Christian spirituality is to love God and your neighbour. The emphasis is on loving God, that is to say, making one's potential available to him, offering oneself to him. At the same time we have to be mature enough to be the recipients of God's call to us. In order to be open to this call we have to be whole people, that is, to negotiate all the phases of our development, and not be stuck or paralysed at any one stage. If we are fixed at a particular level of development all our energy is taken up with negotiating that phase long after it should have passed.

If we have problems with trust, then we shall have problems in trusting that there is a God who exists and loves us. Trust is intimately linked with faith. Faith is also linked with the balance between dependence and autonomy. If we are afraid to grow up, we will look at God as a figure of authority, not as a source of love, on whom we are dependent for our survival. If the church is an authoritarian church, then obeying rules and regulations becomes a substitute for loving. The link between the development of our various phases and loving God is intimate.

The same applies to loving our neighbours. We need to trust people to get close to them. If we do not trust them, we keep ourselves at a distance, and we do not let them come close to us. When we let people come near us, do we respect them or do we manipulate them to serve our needs? Do we use them as parental figures or do we try to dominate them because we are afraid that otherwise they will control us? Is there mutual respect? The capacity to love our neighbours depends on our ability to get close to them, trust them, make ourselves available and donate as much of ourselves as we receive back. All this requires mature psychological development, making the link with spirituality essential.

To come back to Erikson (1968), he describes this stage as one of acquiring a sense of intimacy versus a sense of isolation. When one looks at what Erikson calls genital love he has in mind the following criteria. There should be mutuality of orgasm with a loved partner of the other sex, with whom one is able and willing to share a mutual trust, and with whom one is able and willing to regulate the cycles of work, procreation and recreation, so as to secure for the offspring all the stages of a satisfactory development.

Erikson calls the next stage, which is clearly to be attained within marriage or a permanent relationship, the achievement of a sense of generativity versus a sense of stagnation. Merely wanting children is not enough. Parents need to extend themselves, to give themselves to the future. This is what Erikson calls generativity, whose chief mark is care.

On marriage

At this point I will interrupt Erikson's account of emotional progress to the final stage and give a brief summary of my own concept of marriage as passionate and compassionate love. Childhood is a time when parents are giving life and love to their children, but this is part and parcel of giving love to each other in their marriage. The world sees marriage as a relationship of love, and theology sees marriage as a community of love and life. For the overwhelming majority of men and women, probably nearly 80–90 per cent, they will experience their God in the love they have for each other in their married life. It is true that some of these marriages will be marred by divorce and adultery, but even then the couple will often re-emerge and try a second time. The point that is being made here is that in marriage the psychological and the spiritual meet in the experience of love, so it is important to understand what we mean by love in contemporary marriage.

The first stage of love is falling in love. This is the stage when a young couple idealize each other. They feel that each other's bodies, minds and spirits are the most wonderful entities on earth. They celebrate and find good in each other. They rejoice in each other's presence. They want to be together as much as possible. They forgive and forget readily. There is good evidence, both from research and from actual experience, that the phase of being in love subsides after a year or two. The intensity of mutual excitement recedes, and imperceptibly they move to the next phase of loving each other. Whilst everyone recognizes the falling in love stage, there is no consensus as to what this next phase of loving consists of. Loving continues for fifty years or more, and it has to be a deep experience to hold the couple together.

I have suggested that there are three aspects of loving which are at the source of maintaining love in marriage. These are sustaining, healing and growth. By sustaining I mean the moment-to-moment maintenance of an effective relationship. This is carried out on the basis of carrying out five patterns of behaviour.

The first is availability, both physical and emotional. By physical availability is meant sufficient closeness between the couple to maintain an optimum degree of togetherness. This is expressed in time together at home and outside. The working patterns of couples make availability a difficult task, but a minimum of proximity is essential to express love. There has to be a balance between closeness and distance which each couple has to decide for itself. Here the couple have to become aware of each other's inner world. They have to appreciate their mutual feelings and respond accurately to each other. The second parameter is communication. Contemporary marriage relies heavily on communication to reach the other's inner world. Women are very much better at communication, so much so that men label women's communication as 'nagging'. The third factor is demonstration of affection. Once again women complain that men do not show that they appreciate them. Men can be pretty demonstrative at the beginning of the relationship, but they tend to take their wives for granted thereafter. The fourth factor is affirmation. There is evidence that one of the differences between stable and unstable marriages is the degree of approval bestowed by spouses on each other. Finally there is the resolution of conflict. Arguments and fights are normal within marriage. The important thing is not to win battles, but to learn from the hurt that has been caused what is destructive to the relationship and to avoid it next time. When couples are relating with this degree of intimacy they discover not only the strengths of each other but also their weaknesses.

We have seen how people emerge from childhood with a variety of traumas. When it comes to intimate relationships they may have anxious attachments, being afraid of losing their partner, or they may feel insecure, with various degrees of feeling unloveable and unwanted. In the past it was usual to respond to these wounds by indicting people and passing moral judgements. We called them lazy, selfish, self-centred, obstinate and difficult. We told them to pull themselves together. Nowadays we appreciate that more often than not these men and women are wounded people emotionally and need a healing response rather than chastisement. The healing response consists in offering them security for their insecurity, acceptance for their rejection, love for their feelings of being unloveable. In this way, healing takes place as men and women receive from each other a second chance to experience love. Thus marriage becomes the single most important healing experience in society.

Finally there is growth and maturation. A couple may stay together for fifty years or more. During that time they either grow together or they become alienated. They have to learn to adapt to each other physically. With the passage of time the ravages of physical change take their toll. Love has to remain constant and spouses have to respond to each other's physical changes positively. Intellectually there is a shift from intelligence to wisdom. The partners are the most attentive listeners to each other's word. They can help to clarify each other's ideas, develop them and facilitate further growth. Emotionally they can appreciate each other's strengths and weaknesses and respond accordingly. They can learn to avoid hurting each other by critical remarks and reinforce each other by encouragement. They can act as facilitators to each other's development by encouraging new ideas and supporting new ventures.

All this loving is reinforced by sexual love. Sexual intercourse becomes a language of loving. When couples make love they are communicating with each other. What do they say? At least five things. First of all they tell each other they recognize, want and appreciate each other as the most important person in the world. In this way they affirm each other's personhood. Second, when they make love they fulfil each other sexually. The man makes the woman feel most completely feminine, and the woman makes the man feel most completely masculine. Thus they affirm each other's sexual identity. Third, as we have seen, couples argue and fight. They usually forgive and forget quickly, but sometimes the pain is too much. A few days elapse and then the couple make love, and in this way become reconciled. So sexual intercourse becomes a language of reconciliation. Fourth, we all long for meaning in our lives, and the knowledge that someone wants us at regular intervals fills us with hope and meaning. So in this way sexual intercourse becomes an act of hope. Finally, sexual intercourse is a way of expressing thanks to each other for the other's presence yesterday, today and hopefully tomorrow. It is a major expression of gratitude for each other's presence.

If at the heart of the Christian religion is to be found love, then marital love becomes one of the most powerful means of discovering God. The term 'Domestic Church' has been coined for the spirituality of marriage. Within the confines of marital life the daily events of getting up, washing, communicating with each other, going out to work, taking the children to school, looking after the home, returning from work, having a meal, talking to each other, going to bed, making love, become the liturgy of the Domestic Church. Couples will find God in and through each other and their children. That is why pastoral care must make marriage a priority. The parish must become a centre where married life is put on the map. This can be done by adequate preparation for marriage, by support for it after the wedding, by an appropriate liturgy to remind people that their married life and the word of God match and by support for the separated and divorced. The overwhelming majority of men and women will marry, some more than once. There is a small minority of homosexual and single people; they too need love in their lives.

807

Homosexual men and women may be orientated sexually towards a person of the same sex, but in all other aspects their needs are the same as heterosexual people. In other words, they too need to form a dyadic relationship in which sustaining, healing and growth are achieved. The objective of homosexual men and women is the same as that of their heterosexual counterparts, which is to form a stable, permanent and exclusive relationship in which they can nurture each other. Within this relationship, they have to exercise their conscience, whether to express their love sexually or not. The evidence is accumulating in favour of this expression, but we need further understanding of what the scriptural condemnations are saying before there can be universal agreement on sexual expression for homosexuals. As far as single people are concerned, it must be remembered that there are several categories of single people, those in their thirties and forties who have delayed marriage or whose lives have not given the opportunity for marriage, those who remain single for vocational reasons, those who are separated and divorced and those who have lost their partner through death. Psychology shows clearly that we all need intimacy, the presence of which safeguards against physical and psychological ill health. The single person needs intimacy too and has to achieve this through good friendships. Friendship permits closeness, self-disclosure, interaction and commitment, all of which are necessary for human integrity. The Christian community has to foster the needs of homosexual and single people as well as of the married, despite the appearance of homosexual expression as a sexual counter-culture where the flight from stability and intimacy is celebrated.

The final phase according to Erikson (1968): ego integrity versus despair

Life proceeds inexorably towards death. How we face death is an enormous physiological and spiritual challenge. For Erikson the climax of the life cycle is reached when the foundations of infantile trust have made possible their adult counterpart which is integrity.

Adults in whom ego integrity has fully developed realize that their individual lives are but one life cycle in the flow of history. They are convinced that what had to be came to be and was satisfying. Those who have integrated the previous phases can face the ultimate of death without the fear of oblivion. There is a psychological infrastructure which accepts life as meaningful and that one has played a part in the history of mankind. One has been significant by being of value and by having meaning. Against this experience there is a sense of despair which is the feeling of protest of a person who is not yet satisfied with a life that perhaps has never been satisfactory. If, on the other hand, wisdom has been achieved, there is a confirmation of an awareness that new ideas, new meanings, new persons have been personally created. These new creations are immortality. It is this acceptance of self which forms the infrastructure of old age and allows us to face death with a confidence that it will not shatter our reality. That self-acceptance was most complete in Jesus Christ who had a life of complete acceptance and love of self to the point that his certainty of being was rewarded with the resurrection. The resurrection is the meeting point between psychological and spiritual integrity. It is the bridge, the transformation of the human into the divine. Jesus accepted himself so completely that death could not dent the integrity of his life. There was such fullness of being that it survived the disintegration of biology. In approaching death we can see that a supernatural belief in after-life is not enough to see us through. Our belief must be based on a psychological integrity which has negotiated the various phases of life with the conviction that their meaning has been lived to the full.

We are a mixture of the psychological, the social and the spiritual; and the spiritual must be based on nature which has been fulfilled. The new approach of living the spiritual on the foundations of the social and the psychological is the basis of pastoral care.

The spiritual

So far this chapter has stressed that spiritual integrity must be grafted on to psychological intactness, and it has developed the Erikson model of the various phases of development. But these phases of development give us a humanistic foundation only. We have now to examine briefly the spiritual foundations. According to modern philosophies, our human capacity for spirituality is our ability for self-transcendence. Self-transcendence consists of our ability to go beyond ourselves in truthful knowledge, having loving relationships, and making free commitments.

Religious spirituality refers to the actualization of human self-transcendence, i.e. the capacity for loving, relating and committing ourselves to whatever is acknowledged to be the ultimate or the Holy. The ultimate in the Judaeo-Christian tradition is God. Religious spirituality is related to religious experience, be it Roman Catholic, Protestant, Hindu, Muslim, Jewish, or whatever. We can now see the essence of pastoral care which is a delicate interaction between the human and the spiritual. Traditionally spirituality was invoked without reference to the underlying psychological basis. Humanistic thinking is insufficient without any ultimate spiritual meaning. This is the crisis of our contemporary society. Its high level of psychological and biological understanding appears to make the spiritual redundant. But the physical and psychological do not offer ultimate values and the human personality is always searching for them. Psychology helps religion by correcting its tendency to promote dependency and authoritarianism, and its suspicion of legitimate pleasure. Religion can be helpful when it criticizes psychology's tendency to reduce the human personality to needs and satisfactions. At the heart of being human is relationship. There are three basic relationships in life, relationship to self, to God and to others. Let us look at what pastoral care can offer to these three basic relationships.

Relationship to self

Traditional Christian spirituality emphasized self-denial and stressed one's sinfulness. In this way Christianity has relied a great deal on guilt; guilt for wanting to fulfil one's needs and have satisfaction; guilt for breaking the rules and regulations; guilt for being aggressive; in brief, guilt for being bad. There is a tendency, particularly in the Reformed tradition, to luxuriate in badness and being a sinner. These are the conditions in which we receive God's love, forgiveness and compassion. But contemporary men and women are rebelling at this notion of self. Psychology in particular has made us aware how often we are victims of our childhood circumstances, and are not basically bad. We are much more aware of our wounds than our badness. We are more conscious of our incompleteness than our guilt. But we do not have to apologize for the desire to feel good in relation to ourselves. The Christian model of integrity is Jesus. Jesus based his whole life on his capacity to love his Father and others. In order to do this he had to accept himself wholeheartedly. In order to love others he had to feel good, accept himself, feel loveable. In order to donate himself to others he had to feel that what he offered was good. Jesus had the supreme confidence that he was loveable and that his Father loved him. In this way he basked in his self-acceptance and that is what we have to strive for.

In practice what we have to face in relation to human beings is that Christianity tells them simultaneously that they are sinners and that God loves them. This is a contradiction. They feel that in order to be loved they have to be bad. But this is contrary to their childhood experience which is that they felt loveable because their parents accepted them unconditionally. Pastoral care needs to shift its emphasis from self-rejection to self-acceptance. The pastor has really to help people to feel good about themselves.

Love of self has had a bad press in Christianity. It is a chapter that has been opened again by psychology. The psychology I have described here implies that self-love is experienced by accepting the various capacities which arise in us as we develop. Our parents are the first people to confirm our value, but when this confirmation goes wrong we have a second chance through the intervention of minister, spouse or friend to accept us unconditionally. Part of this acceptance takes place in the dialogue between ourselves and others. When we receive them unconditionally, listen to them non-judgementally, and accept them lovingly, we are already on the way to help them to accept themselves. This self-acceptance is a rejoicing of their gifts, an acceptance of limitations and the feeling of being loveable. Such self-acceptance gives rise to peace, consolation, joy and these are the fruits of being at one with oneself.

A stable and loving childhood lays the foundations of this self-acceptance, and therefore a spirituality of feeling accepted by God depends on us accepting ourselves. This is not an acceptance on the basis of being bad but of being good. Of course, we are flawed human beings, wounded, incomplete. All these concepts are really included in the Christian term of being sinners. But God does not love us for being these things. God does not rejoice in our limitations. He rejoices in our wholeness, in our completeness. The whole strategy of pastoral care is to help people to accept themselves in a balanced way, conscious of their strengths and weaknesses, but, beyond all, to feel loveable whatever their resources. Another way that people present themselves is feeling empty. This is an emptiness which seeks to be filled up with power, money, sex, drugs, alcohol, arrogance, inflated sense of significance. Traditional spirituality has offered the grace of the sacraments and, in particular, the bread and wine of the Eucharist as the body and blood of Christ to nourish us.

As with the love of God, the receptivity of persons depends on their underlying state. Emptiness is a feeling that one has no resources, is lacking the essential ingredients of power, energy and the ability to take the initiative. Such men and women fill their emptiness with a sense of nothingness. Their emptiness is not humility. Humility is an expression of the ability to feel full but not to boast about it. Emptiness is also not poverty of the spirit. When our Lord talks about the blessedness of the poor in spirit he refers to an openness to receive God's presence, to be filled by the Spirit. This filling of the Spirit presupposes a human capacity to receive. The empty person is someone who is like a bucket with holes. All that is poured into the bucket is lost. It is like the seed that the sower set out to sow which fell on poor soil. Once again in these circumstances trying to fill someone with the sense of God depends on an underlying human structure which has the readiness to receive and to conserve what it receives. Pastoral care aims at restoring to people their sense of significance and in this way giving them a readiness to receive the fullness of God.

Between them, feeling unloveable and feeling empty are the two most common psychological conditions that the pastor or the counsellor meet. They need to be handled with care so that God's presence is grafted onto a functioning human recipient.

Relationship to God

The acquisition of a sense of God has been described already. Very early in life those in a Christian setting are informed about Jesus and God through stories and pictures from the Gospels. We internalize these, that is, we acquire a sense of God in the absence of physical, visual and sound stimulation. We cannot see or touch God, but we can have a sense of God which is real and personal. It is this sense of God that spirituality tries to build up over a whole lifetime through prayer, following the words of God and the sacraments. Faith is the active acceptance of the reality we call God.

This faith can be attacked by cultural factors. We live at a time when the mystery of creation is threatened by a scientific approach which claims to have made God unnecessary. This is, however, pseudo-scientific. At the heart of creation is to be found a mystery. However good the explanation of science, what is unfolded in creation is a phenomenon of untold complexity, beauty and wonder. Evolution may explain how we came about, but no scientific explanation can offer an answer to the 'why' of life. Why did life start and what is its purpose? These are spiritual questions and require faith to answer them, or even to consider them in depth. Nearer the psychological dimension men and women wonder how a loving God can permit suffering and pain in this world, particularly when it is personal. There are no easy answers to these dilemmas. The pain and suffering of the individual are a constant challenge to grow and mature, and for society as a whole there is a demand for a response of care and compassion. Psychology is more pertinent when the experience of a parent, be it a father or mother, is unloving, rejecting or hostile, which makes it difficult to identify with a loving father or with Mary, the mother of God.

Perhaps the most significant contribution that psychology has made to our relationship with God is that related to authority and dependence. In the course of our childhood, we emerge from a relationship with our parents in which we see them initially as figures of authority on whom we are dependent. The possibility of dependence remains a marked feature of our whole life. We can become dependent emotionally on our spouse, friends, relatives, the priest or the boss. Dependence means that we rely on authority for guidance, taking decisions, running our lives, doing our own thing. Dependence makes us remain perpetually childlike, living by kind permission of others. Dependence on God has been a subtle issue. In one sense we are all dependent on God. The relationship between God and man has been clearly portrayed in the Gospel of John. There, Jesus' dependence on the Father is shown in more than one passage: 'I tell you most solemnly, the Son can do nothing by himself; he can only do what he sees the Father doing: and whatever the Father does the Son does too' (John 5:19).

In another sense we have been created by God to be redeemed by Jesus Christ and to have a relationship of equality, in and through him, with the Father. God wants us to realize our potential and not to grovel. The grovelling sinner is an image which the world has rejected and it is totally inappropriate as a relationship with God.

Religion in the past has reinforced emotional dependence on God. In churches where there is an authoritarian structure the people of God have been placed at the bottom of the pyramid and these churches are finding it difficult to mobilize the initiative and talent of the People of God. In the Roman Catholic Church, the priest as 'Father' was the authority which had to be obeyed. Millions of Christians grew up with the notion of God as a figure of authority who had to be obeyed, who knows our innermost secrets and from whose wrath we cannot escape. This is a God of judgement, awe and punishment. There is no doubt that man offends against God and that God is a figure of authority who understands and forgives. 'Yes if you forgive others their failings, your heavenly Father will forgive you yours' (Matt. 6:14). But the important thing is not to sustain a child/parent relationship with God. It is not surprising that after 100 years of psychology such a picture has been dismissed by modern men and women. Instead, we are one with Jesus, the adult and the mature son of God and our relationship with the Father aims to realize this adult relationship with God the Father. 'You will understand that I am in my Father and you in me and I in you' (John 14:20). In pastoral care we have to help people release themselves from the infantile dependence on God, we have to cease to project on God our own images, reflecting our dependence and personal experiences of childhood.

Relationship with others

Our relationship with God is mediated through a vertical experience of prayers and openness to the mystery, and through our interpersonal relationships of love. Mention has been made of the tension between the psychological goal of autonomy, the realization of needs, and the spiritual goal of loving our neighbour, which puts our neighbour before ourselves. The resolution of this conflict lies in developing our resources in terms of autonomy, self-acceptance and realization of our potential in order to donate ourselves fully to others. So long as we are in relationships with others, their care is our concern, and the way we fulfil this obligation depends on the resources we have. The more completely fulfilled we are, the greater will be our ability to make ourselves available to others. What we have to offer to others is our bodies, minds and hearts and, in the section on marriage, I indicated how we can love our partner but in fact the same applies to any person with whom we have an intimate relationship.

Being in a loving relationship with others always runs the risk that our anger will damage it. Anger is a stumbling block in Christian circles. We do not know what to do with our anger. The Gospels do not refrain from depicting Jesus as frequently angry. He was angry with Peter and the other apostles, he was angry in the temple, and he was angry with the Pharisees.

There are two types of anger. The first is legitimate when we use anger to protect ourselves from any form of violence in our life. Anger in these circumstances is self-defence. We can be angry and defend ourselves, when our lives are threatened, when our loved ones are attacked, when truth is violated, when injustice is perpetrated. In all these situations anger is creative. There is also destructive anger when we go beyond registering a protest, when we want to destroy another person. That is not legitimate.

Whether it is anger, or mistrust, or fear, we do indeed interrupt our relationship with others. We are temporarily alienated from each other. When our relationships are interrupted we have to restore them by forgiveness. Forgiveness is a gratuitous offer to lift the justified resentment, anger, which we feel when we have been hurt. Forgiveness is an important Christian virtue which is central to human and God–mankind relationships. Without forgiveness human relationships would come to a full stop.

The dynamic psychology which has been the background to this chapter goes beyond forgiveness. When someone close to us habitually hurts us, then we have to try to understand what is wrong with him or her. The problem is usually psychological. They may be expecting us to register their existence, they may be afraid and not carry out our wishes. They may be insecure or feel unloved, wanting our attention. Whatever it is, we have to make a diagnosis of what is wrong and respond both by forgiveness and by an attempt to offer the sort of response that is needed to overcome the problem.

The pastor as a healer traditionally listened to a moral dilemma and passed judgement and helped the person to come to terms with whatever was needed to be done. In this chapter the pastor responds to the person by listening empathetically and non–judgementally. He is not there to pass judgement on the person. That does not mean that he has to avoid being objective about the psychological and moral integrity of the situation. Being non–judgemental does not mean fudging the truth. It means helping people to reach the truth and to take responsibility for their actions. If they take responsibility for their actions, they are in charge of their own lives. Helping them to take charge of their own lives means that they do not become dependent on the pastor for decision–making. Initially they are dependent for emotional support, and this needs to be given in a way that their self-esteem grows. The pastor has to be affirming of people so that slowly their potential is realized. The greater their self-esteem, the greater is their capacity to accept their limitations without feeling completely defeated.

In the course of listening to people the pastor has to be familiar with two key concepts, namely, transference and defences. Each one of us tends to hide from the truth by using defences. People reciting their stories have to be helped to understand when they are avoiding the truth through denial, projection, rationalization, exaggeration, etc. In this way reality can be faced. People can be helped to look at their feelings and to take measure of the things that generate anxiety. When the anxiety is experienced the pastor can be reassuring and allow people to overcome their fears and move nearer to authenticity and integrity.

The second experience for the pastor is to understand transference. This is to say, the pastor must distinguish between the feelings of the client who sees him as a parental figure, a figure from the past, and as he is in reality. This can help the client to understand the possibility of experiencing people as they are and not as they are expected to be. The combination of understanding, transference and defences allows the pastor to shift the man or woman being counselled towards reality and also to take charge of his or her own life. Slowly the person moves from dependence to independence, rejection to acceptance, lack of confidence to more certainty, insecurity to security, all of which build self-esteem and help to make the person feel loveable. In this way we feel accepted by our neighbour and God.

CONCLUSION

In this chapter I have traced a pastoral approach in which spirituality is experienced as an interaction between the psychological and the spiritual, which is the expression of an ultimate reality called God, experienced through the foundations of our humanity. The traditional belief that grace builds on nature is now seen in a new light.

The psychological growth of each one of us shapes our vulnerability in terms of our awareness of what is right and wrong, our freedom to choose between the two and to give our assent. Psychological maturity is the background to our spiritual development and our spirituality in turn shapes our personality. We have now realized that psychology and spirituality go hand in hand and the fruit of this insight is expressed in pastoral counselling.

REFERENCES

Bowlby, J. (1969) *Attachment and Loss*, vol. 1, London: Hogarth Press.
—— (1970) *Attachment and Loss*, vol. 2, London: Hogarth Press.
—— (1980) *Attachment and Loss*, vol. 3, London: Hogarth Press.
Erikson, E. H. (1968) *Identity: Youth and Crisis*, London: Faber & Faber.
Freud, S. (1910) *Five Lectures on Psychoanalysis*, vol. XI, *The Standard Edition of the Complete Psychological Works of Sigmund Freud*, London: Hogarth Press.
—— (1915–16) *Introductory Lectures on Psychoanalysis*, Parts I and II, vol. XV, *The Standard Edition of the Complete Psychological Works of Sigmund Freud*, London: Hogarth Press.
—— (1916–17) *Introductory Lectures on Psychoanalysis*, Parts III and IV, vol. XVI, *The Standard Edition of the Complete Psychological Works of Sigmund Freud*, London: Hogarth Press.
—— (1923–5) *The Ego and the Id*, vol. XIX, *The Standard Edition of the Complete Psychological Works of Sigmund Freud*, London: Hogarth Press.
Jung, C. G. (1933) *Modern Man in Search of a Soul*, London: Routledge & Kegan Paul.
Klein, M. (1965) *Contributions to Psychoanalysis*, London: Hogarth Press.

FURTHER READING

Bowlby, J. (1988) *A Secure Base*, London: Routledge.
Capps, D. E., Parsons, R. D. and Wicks, R. J. (eds) (1985) *Clinical Handbook of Pastoral Counselling*, Mahwah, NJ: Paulist Press.
Coleman, P. (1980) *Christian Attitudes to Homosexuality*, London: SPCK.

Dominian, J. (1991) *Passionate and Compassionate Love: A Vision for Christian Marriage*, London: Darton, Longman and Todd.
Erikson, E. H. (1965) *Childhood and Society*, Harmondsworth: Penguin.
May, R. (1953) *Man's Search for Himself*, London: Souvenir Press.
Monte, C. (1987) *Beneath the Mask*, New York: Holt, Reinhart, and Winston.
Nelson, J. B. (1978) *Embodiment*, Minneapolis: Augsburg.
Pruyser, P. (1974) *Between Belief and Unbelief*, London: Sheldon Press.
See also chapter 35.

39

THEOLOGY, MEDICINE AND HEALTH

John Morgan

In this chapter we shall examine what resources are available in the Christian tradition for a theological approach to the concepts of health and disease and then proceed to see how these are developed by some theologians. The principal theological themes discerned are the doctrine of creation and the limits of the power of human beings exercised in self-transcendence as part of both original creation and redemption. The application of these themes in dealing with some particular problems in bioethics is also discussed.

THE BIBLE AND CREATION AS RESOURCES

Religion, as distinct from theology, has an intimate historical relationship with healing and medicine. Many of the earliest religious functionaries in human civilization were involved in healing ministrations as part of their religious activities as priest-physicians. The religious element is also represented in the identification of religious offences as causal factors in illness, for example in various Babylonian stories, and in the story of the suffering Job. Healing takes place when various infractions against the deity and the community are made up for by some act of reparation. The priest-physician healed the body by healing the spiritual ill that caused the disease. However, an empirical basis for medical practice also existed in both Mesopotamia and Egypt. The Code of Hammurabi gave professional status to the physician and controlled his activities (Harrison 1962: 331).

In the Old Testament, healing miracles were part of the powers that the prophets were able to exercise, as in the cure of Naaman the leper by Elisha. The priests of ancient Israel did not, however, function as physicians as did the priests in other cultures during the period. The relationship between the work of the earlier prophets, in proclaiming God's will for the people of Israel, and the carrying out of healing works, underscores an implicit theological view within Judaism that sickness and death are part of a disrupted original order. The order has been disrupted because of human misuse of divinely conferred freedom that allows the entry of the marks of human finitude into creation: these include illness and disease which become part of the human condition. The healing work of the prophets on this view is the assertion of God's power in the midst of a disrupted order (Amundsen and Ferngren 1982: 61–7).

Health and physical strength are regarded in the Old Testament as a great blessing, as is length of days and material prosperity. A concern with hygiene is manifest in the Mosaic Code and obviously here the priests had some concern with health (Jakobovits 1986: 115–16). Healing in the Old Testament is a matter of a right relationship with God. Physicians in something like the modern understanding are honoured in the inter-testamental period especially in the writings of Ben Sira in Ecclesiasticus which has obvious Hellenistic influences (Ecclesiasticus 38:1–15).

In the New Testament, the healing work of Jesus – as God's supreme agent – is at once a display of divine compassion and an inbreaking of the kingdom of God in which the sick are healed (i.e. made whole) as foretold in Isaiah. The word *shalem*, meaning healthy, is related to the understanding of wholeness, and is an aspect of *shalom* – peace. Jesus showed a concern for the sick in body and mind and did not support the view that disease is sent as a punishment by God upon a particular individual: rather, it is part of the operation of evil in the world. It was as an aspect of his mission in opposing evil and showing the work of God in the world that Jesus engaged in healing works. See, for example, the healing of the man born blind in John 9 where Jesus dismissed the idea of prenatal sin or the transmission of parental sin. However, these works generally required the operation of faith – either stated or implicit – for him to be able to heal. It is significant that the New Testament word *sōzō* means both to save and to heal in the sense of freeing from disease. Luke, 'the beloved physician', is the traditional author of Luke–Acts and is the missionary companion of St Paul. In the apostolic period and that of the early Church, healing is carried out in the name of Jesus, frequently accompanied by anointing and prayer.

The creation story of Genesis, that human life is given by a creative God, and that human beings are made in the image of God, provides the basis for the view within both Judaism and Christianity that human life is sacred. From this basic insight various theological and moral implications are drawn. In this development Judaism moves into an absolutist normative view regarding the value of physical life as infinite and thus the preservation of life as an absolute good in itself (Jakobovits 1975: 45–98 and 1986: 120). This is not generally held in Christian ethics. Christianity sees life as a value, but this is in relation to other values of human existence, all of which stem from God's act of creation and his desire that humans should achieve the ends he desires for humanity. These values are discernible by human reason as it interprets revelation in the light of faith. An understanding of a God-given creation in which God has participated through the self-giving of Christ in incarnation and crucifixion, and of the body as the temple of the Holy Spirit, are the principal theological warrants for basic health care within the Christian tradition. At the same time there are powerful constraints against making an idol of the body and, with it, having an over-exalted view of physical existence without reference to the other values of human existence.

Within the different contemporary strands of Christian theology we can see similar themes being played out as between Judaism and Christianity in relation to the sanctity of life: not so much in regard to the preservation of life, although that is a theme, but in relation to what we may describe as 'human self-manipulation'. Those theologies that are directly informed by the biblical sources and attempt to extract a deontological morality for human life from Scripture will tend to take something close to an absolutist position regarding the value of physical human life, i.e. that the human being from conception to death is inviolable. This is apparent in relation not only to such bioethical questions as euthanasia, but extends also to abortion, human embryo experimentation and decisions regarding termination of treatment. Those theologians who are influenced especially by the writings of Karl Barth will tend to follow this approach. Included in this category are such theological moralists as Paul Ramsey and Oliver O'Donovan. The theme of covenant is also especially prominent in the writings of Paul Ramsey. However, those Christian theologians who work within a theological tradition that is informed by a high regard for human reason as able to assist in discerning the divine end for humanity by use of the natural law may also take an absolutist position in this area. This was a feature of much Roman Catholic moral theology in the period prior to the Second Vatican Council. It is represented in the writings of such contemporary ethicists as Germain Grisez, William E. May and John Finnis.

The theological approach which assumes a more personalist perspective stresses the requirement for human beings to use divinely given freedom in a responsible manner and allows for the development of power over themselves, while remaining faithful to the insights derived from both an understanding of creation and human reason as divinely given. This view does not desert the understanding that God is the author of creation, but allows for a legitimate exercise of human power within creation as something that is in accord with divine purpose. Such an approach also sees that ethical reasoning may be developed out of insights drawn from Scripture and interpreted both by natural law and a developing view of the human person, as well as being informed by tradition. Versions of this approach are represented in the writings within the Roman Catholic tradition of moral theologians such as Bernard Häring, Richard McCormick, Joseph Fuchs, Jack Mahoney and Charles Curran, as well as amongst some Anglicans, for example, Ian Ramsey, Gordon Dunstan and John Fletcher, and also amongst such Protestant writers as James Gustafson, Roger Shinn, Paul Lehmann and Kenneth Vaux.

The foregoing is not meant to be an exhaustive list. Other theological moralists working in the field of medical ethics, while having a high regard for a doctrine of creation and the place of reason, have taken a line of thought that is more conditioned by revelation and the place of covenant within the life of the Christian community. Here we may consider, respectively, such writers as Stanley Hauerwas and William F. May (a former pupil of Paul Ramsey), both of whom defy any easy categorization.

THEOLOGY, BIOETHICS AND PUBLIC DEBATE

While the theologians mentioned above are all entitled to the label 'Christian', the different theological presuppositions frequently result in ethical positions that are at considerable variance with each other when applied to various moral problems in the biomedical area. Two important questions arise for those who approach bioethics from a theological perspective. These questions may be asked in this way: 'What, if any, is the relevance to public debate of a theologically based or influenced ethic, when approaching particular ethical problems in health care or medicine? To whom, and for whom, do theological moralists write?' The danger is that the theologically based medical moralist will fall into either of two traps. The first is that of particularism. This implies that the theological approach taken will be of a kind that only those who share the particular orientation of the theologian will either comprehend it, or find that it in any way engages their interest. It will have little impact on the wider society. However, there are those who would defend this approach on the basis that the ethics of the Christian community, or whatever part of it is represented by a particular writer, is the ethical stance of that group and that any work carried out within the tradition is part of the process of self-definition. This may lead those outside any religious group whatsoever to deny that traditions of theological ethics may make any constructive contribution to bioethics and health care. However, the individual theologian and group may even feel affirmed by the rejection of their viewpoint.

The opposite theological approach, which involves a conscious attempt to speak simultaneously to both a faith group and the wider society, may end up with a position which has no distinctive stance which in any way marks it off from a secular-based bioethics. Those theologians who work within this tradition would probably assert that this is a legitimate development of their initial theological viewpoint and methodology. An argument in favour of this position would claim that, from a theological perspective, the doctrines of creation and revelation, and their interpretation by the application of reason, point to the building up of the distinctively human in accordance with a developed understanding of natural law. It is claimed that it is consistent with such a viewpoint that there should be a seeking after dialogue and commonality of purpose among people of different faiths and no faith. Another variant to this approach is to seek a kind of equivalence or 'enrichment' by way of the use of theological terms like 'Image of God'. This, it is claimed, leads, for example, to a fuller understanding of the idea of person, while a concept such as beneficence in secular moral philosophy may be seen as only a lesser version of Christian neighbour-love.

If we are to assert that theology has something distinctive to offer in the area of bioethics it is necessary that it should be accessible and that its proponents should be prepared to be clear in what they believe they have to offer. It has been said that theology, in fact, 'rarely yields precise and concrete directives for bioethical decision making, or commends insight and actions that are inaccessible to non religious persons' because of both concepts and language (Gustafson 1975; Cahill 1990: 11). It is in the realm of practicality that theology may enter – perhaps unconsciously at first – into a dialogue. Ideally this takes the form of a dialogue between partners informed at the empirical level who are concerned about the nature of a common practical moral obligation. It is possibly also at this level – the level of public ethical discourse – or dialogue – that theology, of whatever kind, may make its most visible contribution (Cahill 1990: 11). The theologian may appear both as representative of a particular tradition and as citizen, often playing a role as member of a consultative group where he or she will contribute, both as a theologically educated person and as one with a faith commitment, engaging in open dialogue with those of other viewpoints and those who lack any faith commitment. In this situation, the theologian will bring into the dialogue such concerns as the well-being of creation, God's providence, human responsibility and human finitude and sinfulness. This is in addition to such broad ethical themes as love, forgiveness, mercy, concern for the specially vulnerable and a respect for individual persons which may be shared with nontheologically informed bioethicists.

Distinctive theological stances may influence which of the themes looms largest in the background to the contribution which a particular theologian makes, but it is of course nuanced by reference to the context, including the degree to which, if any, of the theological assumptions are shared by the larger group. It will be the task of the theologian both to listen and to explain, as well as to argue. Such an approach might not be particularly amenable to those who see themselves as working solely within the traditions of their own religious community and interpreting biomedicine to its members for their edification. Those theologians who engage in public discourse must be clear about their goals in so doing, but, as noted earlier, there are theological approaches that seek to use language and insights that can be shared by those outside the religious community without abandoning their self-understanding as Christian theologians faithful to a tradition. Yet at the same time there is usually an element in their work of a sense of the Other, the transcendent and immanent God, who originates and sustains creation. For a theological moralist to engage only in universal moral discourse without a sense of the Other – to accept fully the assumptions of secular humanistic bioethics – will be to employ a variety of moral Esperanto that diminishes the perspective that theology has to offer (Stout 1988: 163–88).

BASIC THEMES IN THEOLOGICALLY INFORMED BIOETHICS

One of the most significant themes in theology is the relationship between faith in a transcendent and loving God and the existence of suffering in the world – the problem of theodicy. In examining the relationship between theology, health and medicine we face head-on the practical problem of dealing with suffering, especially that part of it attributable to physical pain. Likewise death itself, so frequently seen by both society and medicine as the ultimate defeat, takes on a new understanding when seen within the context of Christian faith. Both suffering and death, viewed in the light of the death and resurrection of Christ, may be seen as necessary parts of the human condition, not capable of a fully rational explanation, yet understandable as part of the business of living in a fallen creation which is nevertheless one which God seeks to redeem. Thus every healing and pain-relieving encounter is a demonstration of both God-given grace and the application of the powers we are able to exercise over ourselves, employed rationally to good ends.

Suffering, seen in the light of Christ's redemptive suffering, may lose some of its particular psychic pain and allow the opportunity for a new approach to both God and others (Vaux 1978: 110–11). This does not of course mean that we should not where possible avoid pain, but neither should we flee from it by way of euthanasia. While death itself is something not to be actively sought according to the Christian approach, neither is it to be staved off at all costs. Acceptance of the human condition as involving the possibility of suffering and death allows us the more to discover meaning in our lives and those of others. For those working as professionals in the work of medicine and medical science, it means that our power is given by God and that, if faith informs the exercise of medical knowledge and skills then, as Christians, the response must be one of service and self-giving, no matter what the context. At the same time a recognition of creatureliness and human sinfulness prevents technological hubris from asserting that we are truly as God, although he shares creative power with us.

Concern over the degree of freedom which humans should properly exercise in the use of the creative powers which God has called human beings to share has caused some theological moralists to question the exercise of responsibility in the biomedical area. Those theological moralists who feel more constrained by the givenness of the created order, including some who perhaps hold a less than optimistic view of human nature, are likely to be suspicious of overconfidence in the exercise of the sharing of God's creative powers. An understanding of the limits of human creatureliness thus acts as a restraint on any over-optimism. On the other hand, the theological view that ascribes a high value to human reason exercised within the limits of humility, will allow for a questioning of proposals and will examine them in terms of means/ends, their possibility for life enhancement, and whether or not any disvalue is present.

While humans are part of creation as God's people, there is a sense in which we are able to transcend creation. Yet all theologians would agree that this must not be done in such a way as to deny the ultimate ownership of who and what we are as children of God, valuable in his sight and to each other. This approach is particularly important when we approach such topics as reproductive technologies, gene therapy, and the probing of our own internal structures through the human genome project. These are all areas in which the potential for both achievement and abuse is great, and the procedures and projects must be kept under constant questioning both from within the medical and scientific communities and by those outside. The Lutheran theologian Helmut Thielecke has expressed this succinctly, contrasting our human ability to advance technologically with our not being able to accept suffering as a part of the basic human condition, a development he ascribes to secularization:

> This dogma of man's ability to do anything and everything constitutes the Promethean variant of our time. It is a new excess of misunderstood human autonomy. It is not that man can do so much which is godless. Man can do these things under God, if he does so as administering the talent entrusted to him. But to believe in man who thinks he can do these things by his own power – this leads to excess and hubris. There is one thing that this man who can do everything cannot do. He is no longer capable of accepting suffering. He can no longer accept, because he no longer knows the One who gives and sends all things.
>
> (Thielecke 1964: 267)

Understandings of what it means to be healthy derive insights from both creation and redemption. The Hebrew notion of human beings as *nephesh*, i.e. that human beings are a unity of body, mind and spirit, not spirits inhabiting a body as in dualistic understandings of human nature, common in much Christian theology, calls us to think of wholeness. The view of human nature as being a psychosomatic unity is further supported by the Christian understanding of resurrection. The resurrection of the body, either as historical fact or metaphor, adds another dimension to medicine which requires us to consider illness or a medical condition as something which affects the whole person, not merely an isolated part of the body, or the body as distinct from the real self. The understanding of health as total wellness – as wholeness – is also underlined by it.

Bodily health may be viewed as one aspect of the search for an integration of personal and social life. Paul Tillich notes that health is considered in the Bible as an individual possession deriving from social or cosmic health. Biblical usage makes no distinction between the psychic and the somatic and does not make something like 'health' in the modern definition the *summum bonum* of human life (Tillich 1946: 348–84). Health and religion cannot be separated in his view; there is no religion that is a mere optional decision in life. Man is 'multi-dimensional unity'. A view of health in contemporary terms involves a multi-dimensional view of health, disease and healing so that each dimension is present in the other: mechanical, chemical, biological, psychological and spiritual are united. The *sōtēr* – the saviour/healer – makes healthy and whole and Jesus is the one healer showing the unity of the religious and the medical (Tillich 1961: 162–4).

The image of the Church as the body of Christ is of assistance here, speaking against fragmentation and individualism. This has important ramifications also for attitudes to individualism in health care ethics that relate to the organization and delivery of health care. The understanding of neighbour-love, the New Testament teaching of *agapē*, displayed in the selfless giving of Jesus on the Cross, serves to underline this and to provide both a warrant and an incentive for theological concern in this area. Likewise, this is drawn on in discussions of the allocation of scarce resources. Justice, powerfully underlined in both Old and New Testaments is the accompaniment of *agapē* and often in tension with it. In discussion of the distribution of scarce health care resources a theological approach will not make an easy and immediate distinction between those selected for treatment and those deemed to be not suitable or simply unselected. It will certainly not make an immediate decision on the basis of social utility, but will seek a solution which combines care for the individual with the interests of the whole society.

THEOLOGICAL PERSPECTIVES ON SELECTED PROBLEMS IN MEDICAL ETHICS

We shall now examine theological approaches to some of the more common ethical dilemmas or quandaries which are presented in medical ethics. There is a tendency to adopt a problem-based approach in medical ethics. While this is certainly not eschewed in theologically informed medical ethics, there is an inclination towards a more holistic approach which allows the application of a general underlying principle – i.e. of God as creator, sustainer and redeemer. Much of traditional theologically based medical ethics is casuistical in form, precisely because, originally, particular questions were put to moral theologians which required answers which in turn related to a total understanding of creation as a unified whole and a developed scheme of salvation. Even Protestant medical ethics turns its attention to particular problems in medicine rather than encouraging reliance on private consciences drawing on generalized insights and making individual decisions.

It is also perhaps only by looking at the detailed applications of more generalized theological positions that we shall explore adequately the differences between approaches consistent with Christian belief and those which reject it, as well as seeing the differences in theological understandings thrown into relief. The particular areas which we shall examine are those concerning assisted reproduction, the care of malformed neo-nates, euthanasia, human experimentation, and doctor–patient relations.

Theology and self-creation: assisted reproduction.

The use of medical technology to assist men and women to have families, where previously they would have had to remain childless, by such means as *in vitro* fertilization or its later developments, or by the use of artificial insemination by donor or husband, is an area in which there are obvious conflicts between different theological viewpoints. These in turn reflect different understandings of the relationship between God and humanity and of the application of the powers given to human beings to order their own lives.

The English Evangelical moralist Oliver O'Donovan sees the intrusion of human technique into this area as leading to the transformation of human procreation into a technical operation, as well as causing concerns about the essential characteristics of human existence (O'Donovan 1984: vii). In particular, he is concerned with what it is appropriate for human beings to do. When he also examines the question of human embryo experimentation, as an aspect of the experimental transcendence involved in the use of new reproductive technologies, he rejects it as not displaying respect for persons. It is, in his view, a rejection of the resurrection fellowship into which God has called us in Christ, which means that all human beings, regardless of their manifest status or the ambiguity or uncertainty of their humanity, are to be treated with brotherly love (ibid.: 49–66). No human being therefore should become the creature of another, which is the risk inherent in separating the unitive and procreative aspects of human reproduction and creating human zygotes for observation, therapy or experiment.

The views of the American Protestant moralist Paul Ramsey on this point are similar. He is concerned that human beings should not become artifacts, products of their own technological ingenuity and attempting to manipulate themselves without reference to the purpose for which they were created – namely the attainment of the love of Christ. Ramsey believes that love and procreation cannot be in any way separated and this belief too is related to eschatology or teleology. We have to examine and question the means whereby we attain ends which seem in themselves good – this is part of Ramsey's rejection of any form of consequentialism arising out of his all-embracing understanding of covenant fidelity. Love, procreation and physical union must go together. 'Any person or society or age, expecting ultimate success where ultimate success is not to be reached, is peculiarly apt to devise extreme and morally illegitimate means for getting there . . . [M]en have another end than the receding future contains' (Ramsey 1970: 31). Ramsey is also concerned about the changes which may take place in human preferences as the result of focusing on the ends sought. For him the important thing is to accept the bounds of our created status. We must not seek to have limitless dominion over ourselves. The relationship between God and humanity is one of creation and covenant and so too should it be in human procreation:

God created nothing apart from his love; and without the divine love was not anything made that was made. Neither should there be among men and women love set out of the context of responsibility for procreation, any begetting apart from the sphere of love.

(Ramsey 1970a: 38)

On this basis Ramsey rejects not only adultery, but the use of gamete and egg donations, artificial insemination and surrogacy. There is neither a right to have a child nor a necessity to do so. When, however, a life has been begotten there is a responsibility not to exploit it.

Some of the basis of this tradition is spelt out by Karl Barth in his *Church Dogmatics* where he writes that:

The one God, who is of course the lord of life and death, the Giver of this life and that which is to come, will in all circumstances and in every conceivable modification demand respect for life. He will never give to man liberty to take another view of life, whether his own or that of others. Indifference, wantonness, arbitrariness or anything else opposed to respect cannot even be considered as a commanded or even permitted attitude. They are frontiers which are necessarily set by God, and cannot be claimed as emancipations of man.

(Barth 1961: 343)

The important term here is 'respect for life'. Barth does not favour any kind of absolutist 'reverence for life' even though human beings are endowed with a God-given dignity in their possession of it.

When we turn to other writers more inclined to a natural law position who follow the post-Vatican II approach to moral theology, we can see a distinctly different approach to the notion of humanity and the power of humans over themselves. Both Karl Rahner and Joseph Fuchs in their reflections on human self-manipulation are prepared to allow for a greater degree of freedom and responsibility by those working in the biomedical field. Rahner laid the basis for a more open approach to the understanding of human self-development in terms of man being free in relation to God and able to align himself towards his own ultimate goal of self-determination. Yet Rahner's view is not one of unbounded optimism. Christianity warns self-manipulating man that in his movement towards God, who is his end and his goal, he must pass through the zero hour of death (Rahner 1972: 205–24). As Curran comments also, 'A proper human anthropology must recognize both our freedom and our limits' (Curran 1982: 157).

Fuchs has developed some of Rahner's work by pointing to contrasting concepts of human nature. He contrasts first the idea of the givenness of humanity, of human life as a gift, against the possibility – perhaps the commission – of human self-realization, and second, the call for humanity to be a responsible partner with God as opposed to being irresponsible. Faith provides the final horizon for humanity while at the same time it assumes the role of a light in that it guides reason. Faith does not replace reason but shows us that a full concept of the human involves seeing human beings in nature as believers, as well as rational creatures (Fuchs 1984: 91–8).

Some of the practical difficulties in this area include the question of whether or not it is ever possible to engage in study of and experimentation upon the early human embryo *in vitro*. This means that the question of when human life begins – significant also in the abortion debate – must be canvassed. Gordon Dunstan, an Anglican theologian, and thus heir to a methodology which has always made use both of natural law and of scriptural insight, has sought to hold together three dimensions: the understanding of God as source and giver of life, the idea of humanity as made in God's image, and the preciousness of both created and redeemed humanity. At the same time he has sought a point at which we may licitly, from a moral perspective, engage in study and experimentation on the human embryo which may offer great therapeutic benefits to humanity. Dunstan has sought to ground his approach to this in both embryology and theology, finding in the use of Karl Rahner's thought by Bernard Häring (Häring 1972: 75ff.) an understanding of a 'threshold at which experiment must cease, a step which must not be crossed. For beyond it lies the life of a man, the image and glory of God: and this is holy ground' (Dunstan 1974: 71). In a later work, writing on the more sensational possibilities of the new reproductive technologies, Dunstan has written of the requirement of the moralist to address his mind to the moral claims as they occur in the empirical features of the study. He is not to be concerned with fanciful cases or practices presented to him (Dunstan 1984: 7). There is thus no fundamental difference regarding the respect which is to be accorded to human life between Dunstan, Ramsey and Barth. The question is still partly when life as human life begins.

A similar approach to this problem is taken by the British Jesuit writer Jack Mahoney. He argues, in the light of the insights of both Rahner and Teilhard de Chardin, that 'it is possible . . . to maintain that human personhood cannot be ascribed to it [i.e. the embryo] in its earliest stages of development, but that the intrinsic promise which it does contain even then cannot be discounted or simply disregarded' (Mahoney 1984: 86). While he does not seem to advocate embryo-experimentation directly, it seems that Mahoney is prepared to countenance it as being 'in the interests of human life as such', where it is carried out in a way that is directly relevant to clinical problems and 'contributory to human biological life and to the well being of such individuals as do develop' (ibid.: 98). Earlier in the same work Mahoney has demonstrated that for him, *in vitro* fertilization may be warmly welcomed by Christians as a means of filling the void of childlessness within many families, and so of achieving one of the major purposes of marriage.

The question of when human life begins, as opposed to when biological life – seen as cellular activity – comes into existence, has allowed some theologians then to draw a line at which point human embryonic life takes on the inviolable characteristics of personhood. The original work of Häring and Dunstan in this area has thus been built on by Mahoney and Ford using empirical biological data, so as to allow the beginnings of human individuality to date from the appearance of the primitive streak in the zygote fourteen days from conception. This is said to be the point at which 'a living human body is actually formed with the active potential to develop further without change in ontological identity' (Ford 1988: 181). Such an understanding would permit, prior to this stage, a range of experimentation designed to help humanity and thus be a legitimate exercise in self-manipulation, not an abuse of the power over self given by God at creation.

Since children are commonly viewed as a blessing upon human relationships it seems hard to dismiss as 'unchristian' that which can bring this about where previously it seemed impossible. Nevertheless, in our exercise of human power over nature the theological dimension causes us to question what we may do with ourselves in the exercise of the freedom with which we have been endowed. Whether we choose to follow some all-embracing ethic regarding the value of life as part of divine creation and with it a covenantally required approach of fidelity, or to act upon a basis of reasoned freedom in the light of God's disclosure, there seems little doubt that in all theologically inspired approaches the gift element of creation looms large. Similarly, research carried out on early embryos, designed to help us to understand childlessness, or to eliminate genetically transmitted diseases, either for the particular embryo, or for humanity in general, is treated by some theologians as an imperative while for others it is to be viewed with caution, or even ruled out.

Any answer given to the problems presented by this aspect of human self-manipulation must be based not only upon respect for life, but also upon the theological understanding of the normatively human which will be influenced by a view of the morality of the possibilities, theologically considered. For Joseph Fletcher in his earlier manifestations as a Christian writer there were few constraints. Others have seen a boundedness, defined either initially at creation or by a covenant of faithfulness which sets definite limits. Again, others have seen a more open, but yet limited, sphere in which we may use freedom and developing knowledge for self-improvement, while we explore the limits and respond in moral seriousness to the new possibilities that emerge under new circumstances (Gustafson 1974: 270–1).

The care of malformed neonates

Particular ethical problems arise in the care of those children who are born with congenital malformations. Modern medicine is able to keep alive many children who in earlier decades would have probably died at or shortly after birth. Many of these children now survive with what some commentators refer to as 'impaired quality of life'. The range of medical problems under this healing also includes very low birth weight infants who require intensive treatment in order to survive. Many of these are children born before term, or are the children of parents who have medical conditions that have not been diagnosed. The use of pre-natal diagnosis by means of amniocentesis raises the question of abortion in order to prevent the foetus coming to term, although now in some cases, foetal diagnosis may be followed by foetal surgery *in utero*. In the cases of children suffering from spina bifida, hydrocephalus and mongolism who have actually been born, there are many instances where a decision has been made not to treat and to allow death to occur. Such non-treatment regimes have frequently been challenged by theologically informed moralists. In deciding how to act medically in such cases, it is often argued that a form of substituted judgement is exercised, i.e. that if these infants were able to make a choice then they would choose for their life to come to an end rather than endure a painful, and in some cases, short-lived future. Theological considerations may offer a perspective which allows a case to be made for active intervention or non-intervention, but not for the infanticide argued by such secular moralists as Singer and Kuhse (Singer and Kuhse 1985).

James Gustafson has pointed to the obligation within Christianity to be 'as much for others as we are for ourselves' when it comes to making a decision in this area where on some occasions parental rights must be balanced against the right of a child to develop, even at a cost to the parents. On this basis he concludes, in a well-known analysis, that a particular child afflicted with Down's Syndrome and suffering from duodenal atresia should have been operated upon and not just kept 'comfortable' and allowed to starve to death at the behest of the parents. He bases this upon 'the intrinsic worth of the child as a human being, which is regardless of any person's intelligence or capacities for productivity, or potential consequences of the sort that burden others' (Gustafson 1973: 535).

Paul Ramsey argued, in his Beecher Lectures at Yale in 1969, that often we should recognize when people are dying and resolve to 'keep them company', rather than seek to intervene dramatically with all the medical technology at our disposal. However, in a later work, he dismissed the distinction between ordinary and extraordinary means in the area and criticized the American Jesuit Richard McCormick who, on the basis of proportionalism, had argued for a quality of life view as a basis for ceasing to treat when treatment merely preserved a life either of excruciating pain, or without potential for other values of human life such as relating to others. In relating this to the case of grossly malformed infants Ramsey rejected McCormick's view of 'potentiality for other values', asking rather what fidelity to another human life requires of an agent. For Ramsey:

> patients are to be loved and cared for no matter who they are and no matter what their potential for higher values is, and certainly not on account of their responsiveness. Who they are in Christian ethical perspective, is our neighbour ... I merely supposed that Christian love and its derivative, a strong sense of medical care, could reach their own limits of usefulness, in their inability to convey the care or attention needed.

(Ramsey 1978: 227)

McCormick had seen biological life as a relative rather than an absolute value and concluded that for some infants their potential for life had been reached at birth. McCormick was adamant that life as such is

> a basic good but not an absolute one. It is basic because it is the necessary source and condition of every human activity and of all society. It is not absolute because there are higher goods for which life can be sacrificed.
>
> (McCormick 1989: 202)

For McCormick the relationship of love is higher than life, because only through love of neighbour can we adequately express our love of God. If, then, the basic conditions for relations with neighbours are lacking, and life can only be maintained in such a way that the interpersonal goods for which life is given are overwhelmed by the maintenance of physical life, then it is permissible to allow life to end by forgoing treatment.

McCormick certainly would not advocate such an approach in all cases of malformed neonates. The basis of the method he employs is a modern variant of natural law reasoning and of the traditional distinction between ordinary and extraordinary means, adding to it the notion of 'burdensome treatment', defined as treatment which offers no sustained benefit in proportion to the means employed. In his view we are under no obligation to employ such treatment (McCormick 1974: 174).

A very different approach is represented in the writings of Stanley Hauerwas who would object to a policy which in any way suggested that we should simply seek to eradicate suffering. Rather we must concentrate on the building up of communities which bear with those who are afflicted. Such communities will be those who have confidence in the Lordship of Yahweh as the truth of our existence and, in particular, of our community. So a society will be created that is capable of engendering persons of virtue and trust, who see the neighbour as essential for their own life (Hauerwas 1981: 86).

In dealing with the problem of suffering, as part of his discussion of the retarded, Hauerwas distinguishes between suffering that happens to persons and that over which they have some control. He claims that attitudes towards the retarded often disguise the unwillingness of people to have amongst them those who are different and who will in some way remind them of their own need. By extension this sort of approach could be said to apply to those cases of severely handicapped infants who would have some length of days if medical intervention took place, but in regard to whom decisions not to intervene are justified on the ground that they would suffer, if they lived. The question for Christians becomes one of what they think of God and what is the community they seek to build in order that they can welcome the other in the person of the retarded or handicapped (Hauerwas 1986: 179).

The task of theology in this area does not simply relate to the care of the defective newborn. As Hauerwas reminds us, it forces us to attend to basic questions about Christian identity in the face of suffering. With regard to who shall decide about intervention or non-intervention, it also causes us to consider the place and meaning of parenthood. Finally, a theological consideration of this area makes us ask deeper questions about our loyalty both as parents and as people of God (Smith 1987: 515).

Euthanasia – death, dying and withdrawal of treatment

One of the earliest works in the field of modern bioethics was Joseph Fletcher's book, *Morals and Medicine*, first published in 1954. This work, like his situation ethics, is an application of act utilitarianism as a form of casuistry based on the notion of the most loving act. Fletcher made out a case for voluntary euthanasia on the basis of a right to die, saying that the issue here was not the choice between life or death, but rather, what kind of death? In line with his later work on medical ethics, emphasizing the capacity of human beings to plan their own lives and to take control over themselves, he asserted that 'we are not as persons of moral stature to be ruled by ruthless and unreasoning physiology, but rather by reason and self-control'. He claimed that those who faced issues of euthanasia with a religious faith would not submit to 'the materialistic and animistic doctrine that God's will is revealed by what nature does, and that life, *qua* life, is absolutely sacred and untouchable' (Fletcher 1954: 208–9). Fletcher also looked forward to what he regarded as the exercise of mercy, so that science would not merely seek to keep people alive in the midst of pain and suffering.

There have been few other theologians who have followed Fletcher in his position. Christians have, however, always argued that not everything which can be done for a patient should be done, and that there is no need for extraordinary treatment or that which is out of all proportion to the benefits gained. This is very much the position which was developed within natural law-based ethics, well prior to the Second Vatican Council. Discussions of euthanasia cannot, however, be easily separated from discussion of death itself. As we noted, Christian theology offers a distinct perspective on suffering, dying and death because of the death of Jesus. Bernard Häring expressed it thus: 'Christ suffered physically but he went beyond bodily pain to assume the profound suffering of dismay and anguish in the hour of death. He thus overcame death felt as something meaningless and redeemed it through unbounded trust and forgiveness' (Häring 1972: 123). Initially the Christian approach to death must be seen not as solving a problem but as facing it as part of the problem of suffering.

William F. May has warned against the idolizing of either death or life – the positions of the pro-euthanasia movement and the pro-life movement respectively. Both revere a creaturely good, not the Creator (in this he echoes Karl Barth). The danger is in putting the argument simply in terms of life versus quality of life, since this ends by not truly considering patients themselves and what is happening to their fundamental identity in the midst of suffering. So far as the practice of medicine is concerned, it raises questions regarding paternalism and autonomy, perhaps needlessly pitting the physician and the tradition of medicine against the patient. As he sees it, the problem with the euthanasia movement is that it 'engineers death rather than facing dying'. However, May also warns Christian believers against two over-emphases which may develop from theology. The first is derived from a romanticized view of Christ's suffering and death which leads to too active an embrace of these elements in human experience. The other is an over-triumphalist emphasis on the resurrection, which can lead to not taking death seriously at all (May 1983: 69–73).

Because he takes both human community and the body seriously, so too May regards death in relation to both society and the individual. However, against either giving way to the overwhelming possibilities of death or attempting to ignore it, May poses the existence of the sovereign God who does not rule an abstract kingdom but who did, in Christ, truly suffer and die. The consequences of this solidarity with the suffering and dying are that a human response to disease and death which is defined wholly by a desperate resistance is forbidden (May 1991: 205).

Paul Ramsey has written movingly of our duties towards the dying and, while he was no advocate of an easy letting go, he allows for differences between patients by asking whether there are any qualifications of our duty always to care for the dying. He bases his answer on a medical indications policy and concludes that a point may come when we may cease to do something which was once called for and begin to do what is now called for by what he describes as 'always only caring for the dying'. Yet we must keep covenant, according to Ramsey, and this involves not giving way to what might be thought of as small acts of mercy which may weaken our resolve within medicine to save life where possible. Because of his conviction that life is given by God as a good, there cannot, for Ramsey, be any absolute right for a patient to refuse treatment, nor any situation where human beings pronounce that a life is not worth living. There are times to let go, but these are indicated by the medical condition of the patient, not chosen by others. It is the point at which the incurable becomes the dying and we then treat the patient in an appropriate way (Ramsey 1978: 187–9).

With regard to any attempts to frame a regulated euthanasia policy, the understanding that human life is possessed of sanctity is one of the strongest influences which Christian ethical insights have upon contemporary society. There are differences of emphasis between theologians as to how this is to be expressed in quandary situations, but even while there are differences, there is no endorsement of a euthanasia policy for society. The difficulty which hard cases always pose in this area was well recognized in an Anglican report which nonetheless concluded:

The good and simple principle that innocent human life is sacred has influenced profoundly our conviction that the old and the dying should be cared for and consoled, no matter what their condition. It has been accepted by the law and the profession of medicine. For our society to recognize any departure from it, involving consequences that we cannot predict and may not desire, would require clear, cogent and conclusive justification. For ourselves we do not think that such exists.

(Amulree 1975: 24)

Some situations where withdrawal of treatment is concerned pose particular problems for the theologically based medical moralist: in particular, the withdrawal of nutrition and hydration from patients in a persistent vegetative state. The giving of food and water is highly symbolic since it is basic to human dignity. Hence the deliberate deprivation of them seems to go against basic Christian principles, not only towards those in desperate circumstances, but against the very basis of physical life. Richard McCormick has, however, argued that such patients may be seen as instances where the use of medical technology makes the difference between a dying and non-dying patient. The moral question is whether we should use the technology for feeding and hydration or not. We must make a value judgement in such cases, based on whether or not any return to normal health and ultimate independence from the technology is possible.

The most important factor is a weighing of the benefits – what benefits will the patient receive from the treatment? McCormick does not believe that life in a persistent vegetative state is a benefit or a value to the one in such a state. Consistent with his views on care of the grossly malformed infant, McCormick considers the question in relation to the kind of life enjoyed or endured by such a patient. At the point at which such treatment is introduced, the patient in persistent vegetative state has ceased to be an embodied person and become a mere body only. For McCormick the crux of the argument here lies in what he believes is the Christian position: a refusal to absolutize either life or death. It is, therefore, morally licit to remove feeding tubes from those in persistent vegetative state. Medical technology can help or hurt us, individually and societally, according to McCormick, and in relation to artificial nutrition and hydration the personal and social evidence suggests the latter. The theological perspective of McCormick, both in his view of death and his questioning of the use of technology on the basis of likely benefits, allows for a cessation of treatment (McCormick 1989: 385).

Human experimentation

The use of human beings as experimental subjects raises acutely a number of points regarding our attitude towards the value of persons. Ever since the enormities of the Nazi medical experiments, Western society has been aware of the possibilities for holding a narrowly utilitarian view of humanity where medical experiments are carried out in non-therapeutic circumstances, i.e. with no direct benefit to the patient being envisaged. The various Codes and

Declarations by which biomedical research is guided, from the Nuremberg code to the Declaration of Helsinki and its various modifications, have as their primary concern the protection of the human subject as part of the general concept of respect for persons. Along with this goes a concern for the scientific value of any proposed research. In order to be truly valid from an ethical standpoint, there must be a discernible prospective benefit to scientific knowledge which justifies the use of human subject research. The latter must be undertaken only when animal research has already been undertaken and where risks are minimal.

While it may seem, on the surface, that any research on humans which is not directly for their benefit cannot be justified, the doctrine of free and informed consent can act as a release from this presumption and satisfy notions of human rights as well as doing service to the Christian concern for the integrity of the individual person and his or her capacity for free choice. When we consider the motives for offering to be a research subject, the theological virtue of charity is of assistance. The donative element in human relationships, characterized by disinterested concern for one's fellow humans, may provide a justification for volunteering to be a research subject, as it may for organ donation. Indeed, theological reflection in this area may well lead to the conclusion that if medical experimentation holds no risk for us, and a piece of research seems to hold great hope for humanity while having minimal risk, then we are obliged to offer ourselves. On the other hand a purely secular approach would possibly regard this either as purely supererogatory or a case of 'tit for tat'. There can be no unwitting or unwilling research since from the Christian perspective this absence of freedom diminishes the personhood of the subject. Mahoney points out that

> the opportunity for generous or heroic personal collaboration in seeking further alleviations of man's ills can not only enhance the person but, for the believer, give expression to that love of neighbour in effective terms which sums up so much of the Judaeo-Christian ethic.

(Mahoney 1984: 105–6)

One particularly vexed area in medical experimentation is that involving research on special subject groups: prisoners, the institutionalized, and children. A notable exchange occurred between Paul Ramsey and Richard McCormick on the issue of experiments involving children. Ramsey's concern regarding the possibility of exploiting the vulnerable was so great that in the case of institutionalized children he believed that any non-therapeutic experimentation should be outlawed. Christian love means protecting research subjects from exploitation: the possibility of consent makes experimentation in the case of competent adults a human enterprise, but 'no child or adult incompetent can choose to become a participating member of medical undertakings, and no-one else on earth should decide to subject these people to investigations having no relation to their own treatment' (Ramsey 1970b: 14).

No doubt Ramsey was powerfully influenced in his thinking on this point by the hepatitis experiments which occurred at the Willowbrook School in New York State, where retarded children were deliberately inoculated with live hepatitis, following their parents' consent, so that the disease could be studied (ibid.: 47–55).

For Richard McCormick there are some situations – rare though they may be – where non-therapeutic experimentation is permissible on children. These are where the parents have given proxy consent and there is no discernible risk. It is permissible morally to expose a child to some slight risk for the good of others, but the situation ought also to be one that involves no undue discomfort or inconvenience. The justification which McCormick offers is that the child has the same duties as any other human being and that there are things we ought to do for the human community – bearing our share so that all may prosper. If it can be argued that it is an aspect of social justice that we ought to do such things as taking part in experiments, then a presumption of consent is reasonable, even where children are involved, and proxy consent therefore becomes legitimate.

The differences between Ramsey and McCormick on this point partly illustrate the difference between Protestant and Catholic approaches. Ramsey sticks with his overarching principle of no experimentation without consent and, while he argues by using a form of casuistry, he will not allow any exception or other supervening principle to intrude. On the other hand, McCormick is prepared to consider an exception to the principle involved while still maintaining it, and only allowing the exception where there are other equally strong Christian moral insights which command attention and which have a moral claim as forming a part of the Christian life. This is part of what is involved in his notion of proportionate reason. McCormick's methodology is informed by reason, almost as much as by faith. This approach does not necessarily begin by being informed by revelation, but rather sees ethics as an autonomous exercise. The employment of a form of consequentialism (in the shape of proportionate reason) by McCormick has been the subject of criticism from within his own communion, as well as by Paul Ramsey (McCormick and Ramsey 1978; Finnis 1983 and 1991).

The use of proportionalism – as a form of teleologism or consequentialism – by Roman Catholic moral theologians has also been criticized by Pope John Paul II in his encyclical *Veritatis Splendor* as possibly justifying some acts deemed to be intrinsically evil, which, according to the encyclical, can never be transformed either by circumstances or intentions into good or defensible choices (John Paul II 1993: 111–28).

The doctor–patient relationship

As we have noted, the physician is honoured in the Judaeo-Christian tradition. The physician in the modern Christian tradition is called to the service of humanity by the exercise of his or her knowledge and skills. Their possession gives an authority to the physician, but the danger is always that a degree of paternalism may enter the relationship on this account because of an over-exercise of beneficence. It may be shown in such acts as not fully imparting to patients the nature of their condition or not enlisting their co-operation in their treatment.

The most insightful discussion of the physician from a contemporary theological perspective is that of William F. May who sees medicine as a covenanted profession (May 1975 and 1983: 106–45). The professional is, he says, marked off by the claims of his profession and is indebted to the community which has educated him and confers power upon him. Rather than see the profession as one which is regulated by a code, or even by contract, both of which may lead to minimalism, May sees the physician as guided by the notion of covenant in which there is a response to patient needs. In this relationship there is a move beyond any simple form of gratuitous philanthropy to a respect of the patient as a part of the community which has nourished the physician. Thus the physician approaches his or her patient as someone with whom he or she has more than a contract. Rather, the patient is someone with whom there is a bond, and towards whom the physician must act as both teacher and debtor. In this there must be no hint of being a benefactor on the part of the physician, instead the role must be seen in the light of the transcendent, 'of gift answering to gift' (May 1975: 36).

Oliver O'Donovan has pointed to the danger inherent for the doctor–patient relationship in the combination of the technologization of medicine and the over-exercise of compassion. It leads, he believes, to the view that there must always be a specific cure because of a specific cause. This develops from a consumeristic view of patient care in a society where freedom is largely conceived in a passive way. In this context, the patient has freedom not to suffer, and thus: 'The old conception of medicine as a collaborative enterprise, in which doctor and patient each have freedom and responsibilities, can no longer be sustained' (O'Donovan 1984: 10). This is, in his view, essentially a misreading of compassion which presupposes that there is always an effective answer to the question, 'What is to be done?', and results in the situation that inevitably more technology is required. The mutual responsibility between doctor and patient can be recovered, according to O'Donovan, by a consideration of 'their equality as co-operating human agents, in ways that only the Christian confession can open to us', by which he means, 'faith in the transcendent ground of human brotherhood' (ibid.: 13).

In the relationship between physician and patient there is a clear role for the theologian. Bernard Häring expressed it from within the Roman Catholic tradition in terms of being a 'mediator between the *magisterium* and medical field workers' (Häring 1972: 36). Revelation gives general contours while the Church has always sought an understanding of the nature of man and his journey which is made more definitive in the light of revelation. The physician becomes involved, according to Häring, in the 'effort to distinguish what is permanent from what constitutes only changing aspects of our knowledge and values'. The theologian interprets the teaching of the Church in the light of the historical context, in conjunction with physicians. The physician will always be responsible before God for his personal judgement and his conscience. At the same time, the physician must respect the conscience of his patient and, with it, the responsibility of the patient for his or her own health. A full and frank disclosure of any proposed methods of treatment should lead to an informed decision by the patient and the physician must abide by this, even if he does not believe in it. An example would be the refusal of a blood transfusion by a fully conscious adult patient. At the same time the patient must accept the right of the doctor's conscience not to give a treatment or intervene in a way that goes against his own moral conviction.

Häring, like May, also sees the relationship of doctor and patient in terms of a covenant which goes beyond the impersonal basis of many other relationships. It should be characterized by such personal attitudes as fidelity, reverence, respect, truthfulness and mutual trust. Its concern is summed up by the title of Paul Ramsey's work, *The Patient As Person* (1970b). Yet Häring does not see the doctor as violating the covenant if he or she goes against the particular wishes of a patient, where the patient may not be responsible and is acting selfishly in not considering his or her essential relationships and responsibilities to fellow citizens (Häring 1972: 199–200). The social dimension thus qualifies autonomy, and so too it would seem does a theological perspective; but the corollary is not to resort to a variety of medical paternalism. Dunstan has expressed strong reservations about the unqualified exercise of patient autonomy as being likely to erode the true professional nature of the doctor–patient exchange. In this he represents a more empirical approach in which the decision must be made by the practitioner, not the moralist (Dunstan 1983: 21–2; Dunstan 1989).

CONCLUSIONS

The direct bearing of theology on medicine cannot be accurately charted. Proclaiming the autonomy of the two and then seeing what points of contact exist is one possibility. What we have attempted to explore in this chapter are the possible points of contact – the direct and independent bearings that each has on the other. As we observed, there have been close contacts between religion and medicine throughout history and the bringing of healing, of wholeness, into human life is part of the mission of Jesus as being the restoration of humanity to a full relationship with the divine source of all life. Salvation and healing are linked in the notion of therapy as restoration.

The distinctive insights of Christian theology into medicine concern the authorship and stewardship of life. Together with those factors there is also the question of the right use of freedom in relation to ourselves. 'Religion qualifies morality' is the way it was aptly expressed by one Christian moralist (Gustafson). Another has spoken specifically of the 'corrective vision' which theology brings to the practice of medicine (May), while yet another (McCormick) has seen it as not having a direct originating influence, but rather a 'compenetration' of protective, dispositive and directive dimensions.

Christian ethicists will often take very different positions from each other when they approach particular problems within bioethics. However, as fashions in secular-based ethics change, and we move from one set of specific solutions to particular problems to yet another set of problems, finding neat or comprehensive solutions becomes impossible to discover. The human dispositions and virtues of which Christian faith and the Christian story speak so strongly, may therefore have greater cogency in our attempts to come to grips with understanding health and how we may begin to solve particular problems in bioethics, rather than enabling us to codify ready-made answers to every problem.

Faith must always tend to speak to faith and sometimes people of faith can only use the language of faith, even when in dialogue with those of no faith. However, it is the case that to try to lay out on every occasion what is the exact difference between a Christian and a secular perspective is to misrepresent the nature of Christian faith (Cobb 1985: 306). For most of the time the story by which Christians live remains in the background as having made them the people that they are. For that reason there can be no glib answers to the questions posed by Alasdair McIntyre about the difference it makes to be a Jew, Christian or Muslim, rather than a secular moral thinker, or how this may lead to a critique of secular culture and, finally, how what has been said on the first two may relate to the specific problems of modern medicine (McIntyre 1979: 435–55).

In his reflections on belief, medicine and suffering, Stanley Hauerwas claims that most people want an explanation, in particular, of the illness or death of children. It is 'as if we have a positive need to know that such an illness or death does not render our existence and God's existence absurd' (Hauerwas 1990: x). This 'primitive need' for an explanation he sees as impeding the care which medicine can offer. What we require instead, in his view, is a community capable of absorbing our grief – people who worship God and seek to be more faithful. In this we need to be sustained by the faith carried in our faith narrative, because

> we have no theodicy that can soften the pain of our death and the death of our children, but we believe that we share a common story which makes it possible for us to be with one another especially as we die.
>
> (Ibid.: 148)

On the other hand, secular humanism – in the Enlightenment sense – has not provided or justified a canonical moral content for the moral life, apart from a general justification, by a general secular humanism, for a moral cohesion, universal in scope and able to withstand the onslaughts of nihilism. Despite the attempt by moralists such as Engelhardt to frame such secular bioethics, he believes (not unlike the French sociologist Durkheim) the problem remains, that pure reason or secular humanism 'Cannot [e]nsure, or perhaps even motivate moral deportment in general or a just health care policy in particular. The service is intellectual.' Engelhardt is forced to ground both a general secular morality and secular health care in 'the possible bond of mutual respect among persons, the only beings who pose moral questions and attempt to answer them' (Engelhardt 1991: 140).

The ethical insights provided by aspects of the Christian understandings of creation and self-transcendence also allow for the possibility of dialogue among moral strangers, i.e. those who have different religious beliefs or none at all, and provide for believers the emotive and motivational factors which are prior to action. Lisa Sowle Cahill, in addressing the relation of Roman Catholic medical ethics to this problem, sees their 'natural law' language as a commitment to the business of consensus: 'to find a degree to which the language of each partner can resonate with the experience of other as overlapping moral perceptions are clarified, refined, and redefined toward some consensus' (Cahill 1989: 101).

On the other hand, Kenneth Vaux writes that our prevalent medical ethic is a pragmatic one in which

> all good consists in sheer human will power and control. We look scientifically and technically at cells, tissues and organs with a view to fixing or replacing the parts which malfunction. . . . the western scientific world view and technology have displaced traditional belief and values.

So, 'we are left in a bewildering situation because our deeper traditional convictions conflict with the values inherent in current technological capacities' (Vaux 1989: ix–xi).

Vaux proposes, by way of an alternative to the moral bewilderment engendered by modern science and its applications, a comprehensive and inclusive ethic for medicine because 'it is evident that humans are by nature *Homo religiosus*, but there is also a universal substance to theological truth'. There are, he believes, universal convictions which could be affirmed by all faiths which involve God, the moral imperative, humanity as made in the image of God, and the fact of human malevolence and apathy. Ethics culminates for him on an eschatological plane – as they do for most Christian believers – in a situation in which hope (*elpis*) and fear (*phobos*) are in conflict, and a sense of what we might be as humans can emerge and triumph over despair, both in individual decisions and in final outcomes, 'the denouement of nature and history' (ibid.: 192–3).

Theological ethics will rarely give hard and precise answers to medico-moral dilemmas, but rather, a direction will be indicated and enough will be given to enable us to probe beneath the surface of any answers that come too easily, whether they deny or invoke the divine in relation to human life in its dimensions of birth, life, death, tragedy and happiness and the decisions surrounding them. In this, there is no reason for the Christian theologian to be shy regarding his or her religious belief when discussing health and disease as part of the human situation, and when analysing the problems posed by particular aspects of them and the practice of medicine in contemporary society, whether it be what constitutes good health, the distribution of resources or the more obvious hard cases of medical ethics, including developments in medical research and their utilization. In the words of Bishop Ian Ramsey, the spiritual person, who is saved and made whole,

> under the inspiration of the haunting vision of the gospel, can pioneer whatever changes come to [m]an or society as scientific exploration takes us further into unknown and exciting terrain. He goes forward in faith, confident that under the inspiration of his vision there can be a creative outcome to the travail in which we endeavour to match medico-scientific development with the needs and possibilities of human life and society.

> (I. T. Ramsey 1971: 130–1).

REFERENCES

Amulree, Lord (Chairman) (1975) *On Dying Well: An Anglican Contribution to the Debate on Euthanasia*, Westminster: Church Information Office.

Amundsen, D. W. and Ferngren, G. B. (1982) 'Medicine and Religion in Pre-Christian Antiquity', in M. E. Marty and K. L. Vaux (eds) *Health, Medicine and the Faith Traditions*, Philadelphia: Fortress Press, 53–92.

Barth, K. (1961) *Church Dogmatics*, vol. III, *The Doctrine of Creation*, Parts one and four, (eds) G. W. Bromiley and T. F. Torrance, Edinburgh: T. & T. Clark.

Cahill, L. S. (1989) ' "Theological" Medical Morality? A Response to Joseph Fuchs', in E. M. Pellegrino, J. P. Langan and J. C. Harvey (eds) *Catholic Perspectives in Medical Morals*, Dordrecht/Boston/London: Kluwer Academic Publishers, 93–102.

—— (1990) 'Can Theology Have a Role in "Public" Bioethical Discourse?', in D. Callahan and C. S. Campbell (eds) *Theology, Religious Traditions, and Bioethics*, 10–14, supplement to *Hastings Center Report*, 20 (4), July/August.

Cobb, J. B. (1985) 'Does Theology Make a Contribution to Bioethics?', in E. Shelp (ed.) *Theology and Bioethics*, Dordrecht: Reidel Publishing, 303–7.

Curran, C. E. (1982) *Moral Theology: A Continuing Journey*, Notre Dame: University Of Notre Dame Press.

Dunstan, G. R. (1974) *The Artifice of Ethics*, London: SCM Press.

—— (1984) Introduction to *Human Procreation: Ethical Aspects of the New Techniques*, Report of a Working Party, Council for Science and Society, Oxford: Oxford University Press.

—— (1989) 'The Doctor as Responsible Moral Agent', in Dunstan, G. R. and Shinebourne, E. A. (eds) *Doctors' Decisions: Ethical Conflicts in Medical Practice*, Oxford: Oxford University Press, 1–9.

Dunstan, G. R. and Seller M. J. (1983) (eds) *Consent in Medicine*, London: King Edward's Hospital Fund.

Engelhardt, H. T. Jr. (1991) *Bioethics and Secular Humanism*, London: SCM Press.

Finnis, J. (1983) *Fundamentals of Ethics*, Washington, DC: Georgetown University Press.
—— (1991) *Moral Absolutes*, Washington, DC: The Catholic University of America Press.
Fletcher, J. (1954) *Morals and Medicine*, Boston: Beacon Press.
Ford, N. (1988) *When Did I Begin?*, Cambridge: Cambridge University Press.
Fuchs, J. (1983) *Personal Responsibility and Christian Morality*, Washington, DC: Georgetown University Press.
—— (1984) *Christian Ethics in the Secular Arena*, Washington, DC: Georgetown University Press.
Gustafson, J. M. (1973) 'Mongolism, Parental Desire and the Right to Life', *Perspectives in Biology and Medicine*, 16 (Summer), 529–57.
—— (1974) 'Basic Issues in the Bioethical Fields', in *Theology and Christian Ethics*, Philadelphia: United Church Press.
—— (1975) *The Contributions of Theology to Medical Ethics*, Milwaukee: Marquette University Press.
Häring, B. (1972) *Medical Ethics*, Slough: St Paul Publications.
—— (1981) *Free and Faithful in Christ*, vol. 3, *Light to the World, Salt for the Earth*, Slough: St Paul Publications.
Harrison, R. K. (1962) 'Medicine', in G. A. Buttrick (ed.) *The Interpreter's Dictionary of the Bible*, Nashville: Abingdon Press, 331–4.
Hauerwas, S. (1981) *A Community of Character*, Notre Dame, Indiana: University Of Notre Dame Press.
—— (1986) *Suffering Presence*, Notre Dame, Indiana: University Of Notre Dame Press.
—— (1990) *Naming the Silences*, Grand Rapids, Mich.: Eerdmans.
Jakobovits, I. (1975) *Jewish Medical Ethics*, New York: Bloch Publishing Company.
—— (1986) 'The Jewish Contribution to Medical Ethics', in P. Byrne (ed.) *Rights and Wrongs in Medicine*, London: King Edward's Hospital Fund, 115–26.
John Paul II, Pope (1993) *Veritatis Splendor: Encyclical Letter of John Paul II, On Certain Fundamental Questions of the Church's Moral Teaching*, Homebush, Sydney: St Pauls.
McCormick, R. (1974) 'To Save or Let Die: The Dilemma of Modern Medicine', in *Journal of the American Medical Association*, 229(2), 8 July, 172–6.
—— (1989) *The Critical Calling: Reflections on Moral Dilemmas Since Vatican II*, Washington, DC: Georgetown University Press.
McCormick, R. with Ramsey, P. (eds) (1978) *Doing Evil To Achieve Good: Moral Choice in Conflict Situations*, Chicago: Loyola University Press.
MacIntyre, A. (1979) 'Theology, Ethics and the Ethics of Medicine and Health Care: Comments on Papers by Novak, Mouw, Roach, Cahill and Hartt', *The Journal of Philosophy and Medicine*, 4(4), December, 435–43.
Mahoney, J. (1984) *Bioethics and Belief*, London: Sheed and Ward.
May, W. F. (1975) 'Code, Covenant, Contract or Philanthropy', *Hastings Center Report*, 5(6), December, 29–38.
—— (1983) *The Physician's Covenant: Images of the Healer in Medical Ethics*, Philadelphia: Westminster Press.
—— (1991) *The Patient's Ordeal*, Bloomington: Indiana University Press.
O'Donovan, O. (1984) *Begotten Or Made*, Oxford: Clarendon Press.
Rahner, K. (1972) *Theological Investigations*, vol. IX, *Writings of 1965–71*, London: Darton, Longman and Todd.
Ramsey, I. T. (1971) 'Human Personality', in I. T. Ramsey and R. Porter (eds) *Personality and Science*, London: Churchill Livingstone, 125–32.

Ramsey, P. (1970a) *Fabricated Man*, New Haven: Yale University Press.
—— (1970b) *The Patient As Person*, New Haven: Yale University Press.
—— (1978) *Ethics at the Edges of Life*, New Haven: Yale University Press.
Singer, P. and Kuhse, H. (1985) *Should the Baby Live?*, Oxford: Oxford University Press.
Smith, D. H. (1985) 'On Religious Traditions and the Treatment of Infants', in S. E. Lammers and A. Verhey (eds) *On Moral Medicine: Theological Perspectives in Medical Ethics*, Grand Rapids, Mich.: Eerdmans, 511–16.
Stout, J. (1988) *Ethics After Babel: The Language of Morals and Their Discontents*, Boston: Beacon Press.
Thielecke, H. (1964) *Theological Ethics*, vol. 3, *The Ethics of Sex*, Grand Rapids, Mich.: Eerdmans.
Tillich, P. (1946) 'The Relation of Religion and Health: Historical Considerations and Theoretical Questions', *Review of Religion*, X(4), May, 348–84.
—— (1961) 'The Meaning of Health', reprinted in S. E. Lammers and A. Verhey (eds) *On Moral Medicine: Theological Perspectives in Medical Ethics*, Grand Rapids, Mich.: Eerdmans, 161–4.
Vaux, K. (1978) *This Mortal Coil: The Meaning of Health and Disease*, San Francisco: Harper & Row.
—— (1989) *Birth Ethics: Religious and Cultural Values in the Genesis of Life*, New York: Crossroads Publishing Company.
See also chapter 33.

40

ENVIRONMENTAL ETHICS

Stephen Clark

Nature no longer seems inexhaustible, at the very moment when most modern thinkers have been persuaded that Nature is all we have to hope for. The latter crisis is not my concern, except to remark that the case against 'super-naturalism' has yet to be made. It is not that we have reason to believe that there is nothing beyond Nature, but that 'we' have decided to ignore the possibility. The former crisis seems certain.

> For generations, we have assumed that the efforts of mankind would leave the fundamental equilibrium of the world's systems and atmosphere stable. But it is possible that with all these enormous changes [population, agricultural, use of fossil fuels] concentrated into such a short period of time, we have unwittingly begun a massive experiment with the system of this planet itself.

The words were Margaret Thatcher's, on 27 September 1988 (Pearce *et al.* 1989: 27). Responses to the crisis have ranged, in terms first suggested by the Norwegian philosopher Arne Naess, from the 'shallow' to the 'deep'. 'Shallow' environmentalists identify the damage to human interests done by too careless a treatment of natural resources; 'deep' ones advocate a radical revision of our purposes in the world, urging that the integrity of the whole terrestrial ecosystem is the one proper concern of all enlightened folk (Naess 1983). Those for whom such deep environmentalism, or ecologism, amounts to a revived paganism tend to blame 'Judaeo-Christian Thought' (itself an uncomfortable amalgam of rather different traditions) for elevating human nature above that of the whole. Objections to dichotomies of this kind, 'dualism', tend to go along with a more or less verbal admiration for 'matter'. Whereas our predecessors divided 'mind' and 'matter, 'spirit' and 'flesh, 'humanity' and 'nature' (and even 'man' and 'woman'), we should instead impute to matter itself the value once divorced from it. There is also a strand of environmentalist thought that objects to objectivity: where science gives ontological priority to objects stripped of all evaluative or symbolic properties, 'new age' thinkers – borrowing from the pragmatist tradition – concern themselves with the richly perceived environment, suffused with just such symbolism. Finally, there is an element in popular moral culture that elevates the 'natural' above the conventionally moral.

This melange of doctrine amounts to the beginnings of a distinct religion, naturism, not all of whose prophets are acceptable to any humane or liberal intelligence, but which might still have something to offer. It is important for theologians and others to identify the wrong turns that religious feeling and commendable environmentalist concern may take, and to formulate a proper piety towards the earth and our fellow-inhabitants. The historian Arnold Toynbee, conversing with Daisatsu Ikeda in the early 1970s, spoke as follows.

> A right religion is one that teaches respect for the dignity and sanctity of all nature. The wrong religion is one that licenses the indulgence of human greed at the expense of non-human nature. I conclude that the religion we need to embrace now is pantheism, as exemplified in Shinto, and that the religion we now need to discard is Judaic monotheism and the post-Christian non-theistic faith in scientific progress, which has inherited from Christianity the belief that mankind is morally entitled to exploit the rest of the universe for the indulgence of human greed.
>
> (Toynbee and Ikeda 1976: 324)

I share Toynbee's belief that a crisis is upon us, but wish to argue that pantheism, or what I have called 'naturism', in all its forms is exactly what we do not need, and that Christian faith, along with the other great religions of the Book, does already teach respect for the dignity and sanctity of God's creation. The attitudes he criticizes are actually unChristian, and unJewish. We must not be panicked into abandoning either reason or true religion.

SHALLOW AND DEEP ENVIRONMENTALISM

Even the shallowest of environmentalists would agree that we have duties to more than our present convenience. People who do not care what happens to our children and grand-children are recognizably rogues.

> As we feel it wicked and inhuman for men to declare that they care not if when they themselves are dead, the universal conflagration ensues, it is undoubtedly true that we are bound to study the interest of posterity also for its own sake.
>
> (Cicero De Finibus 3.64)

We should not live in ways that would make our descendants' lives enormously difficult, should not use up or destroy what they will need. As Thomas Jefferson insisted, in line with the common law of England, we have no claim upon the land itself, but only on its lawful fruits (see White 1978: 223): we do not inherit the land from our ancestors, but rather hold it in trust for our descendants. Nothing, said Locke, was given to man to spoil or destroy (Locke 1963: 332). It does not follow that we should never use up non-renewable resources on the plea that this would leave no such resources for our descendants to use: if they may use them, so may we. But ordinary counsels of prudence (which include concern for those of our kind that come after us) suggest that we should not use things up without good reason, and without any effort to locate alternative resources. 'To plant a tree, to cultivate a field, to beget children; meritorious acts, according to the religion of Zoroaster' (Hume 1962: 180).

The burning of fossil fuels is, of its nature, an energy source that must, eventually, eliminate itself. The transformation of metals first into implements and then into metallic dust, rust and volatile gases, may also, sometime, have an inevitable end. It may not be at all easy to say when all available fossil fuels, all available metallic ores, will have been transformed into unusable residues. Retrieval techniques improve, and sources that once were not worth exploiting will become valuable resources when other wells run dry. Even residues may have a use, once the price and the techniques are right. It follows that prophecies of an imminent end to 'the earth's capital resources' are likely to be proved false. Certainly the prophecies made twenty or thirty years ago have not been vindicated by the markets. Earlier generations imagined that a worked-out mine might gradually renew itself, that ores and jewels grew like living things. Moderns, more accurately, reckon that such things are 'non-renewable', and appropriate the image of a worked-out mine to intimate our future. But that future may be so distant that geological processes, working even on our poisonous residues, will actually create some new resources for our remote descendants. Even before the ages have created such new fossil fuels, we will have found an economic profit from recycling waste. 'Non-renewable resources' are not so easily defined as some environmentalists have held, and human ingenuity not so limited (see Simon 1981). But we can agree that, in the near future, there are resources that are less likely to be renewed, or are more easily eliminated, than are others. Paradoxically, it is not the inanimate products of geological ages that are most vulnerable, but the animate. In one sense, trees are renewable resources in a way that coal is not. There is a finite, and fixed, amount of coal in the earth's crust, even though we do not know what it is; the amount of biomass embodied in the world's trees is also finite, but indefinitely renewable (at least until the sun's light fails). But whereas there is no known case of an inanimate kind's being finally extinguished, there are many actually extinguished species, of plant and animal alike. A species, while its members live, can be renewed; once they are gone, it is extinct for ever. It would seem to follow that anyone concerned to maintain a livable world for his or her descendants should take more care not to extinguish biological kinds than geological. The chance that we will ever 'use up' all the zinc, iron, aluminium is very small, especially if we take account of new techniques for retrieving such elements from 'wastes'. We may use up all readily available fossil fuels, but no-one can quite say when, or what alternatives will then be economic. We already have 'used up' all the dodos, passenger pigeons and no-one knows how many other denizens of degraded habitats, and continue to use up literally irreplaceable species by direct assault and, more effectively, by destroying their homes.

The question is, of course, why we should care. Shallow environmentalists, concerning themselves with the needs of future individuals, especially of our species, can point out that the irreplaceability of species is a function of their chemical complexity. Substances are produced by living beings that could not be produced in any less complex, less synergetic way. It took a supernova to produce such elements as iron or carbon, on which our life depends, but the process is well understood. It took four billion years of evolutionary change to produce normal features of our (and our habitat's) biochemical makeup. We cannot retrace the steps that led to them, and only very rarely synthesize the thing from elementary parts. Some substances will, probably, be found in every living thing; many will be produced in only one kind of plant or animal. How many of those special substances are likely to be important to us we do not know – that many of them will be important to us we can, by precedent, be convinced of. Everything in the modern pharmacopeia, as much as in the medieval herbalist's, is taken from nature's workshop. Damaging that biochemical factory would be far worse than trashing a multi-million pound laboratory without even finding out what is on its shelves. Nor can we always console ourselves by thinking that the loss of one species can be easily contained: the nature of the living world is such that everything changes when one thing changes. Each kind is part of other kinds' environment, and the causal chains that bind the world together are too complex for us to model accurately beforehand.

Does it follow that we should do nothing? Or perhaps withdraw to careful enclaves, isolated from the rest of nature, so as to allow that great magician to go on churning out new drugs and opportunities? Obviously not, if only because establishing such enclaves, perhaps at the earth's Trojan points, is beyond our power. Even if it were not, the argument would be inconclusive. If the value of the natural world is that it is a marvellously productive biochemical factory from which we can profit, we should take care not to damage it. But we can be confident that, despite local and occasional disasters, it is also very resilient, and works by responding to new challenges. It is easy to fall into the belief, easily confirmed by anecdote and personal memory, that 'nature' in the developed world is gradually growing less complex. There are fewer wild flowers, fewer butterflies. We glimpse the prospect of a domesticated world, with only a few tamed species occupying pre-determined spaces. But though evolution may be relatively slow in its macroscopic effects, it has not halted. Species adapt (or do not) to new situations, and do so most quickly at the bacterial or viral level. There is no evidence that the total biomass has declined, nor even that there is less variety within the living world than once there was. We may, as many have said, be living through a period of species-extinctions unknown since the last great dying, when the dinosaurs went down. But if we do not know what marvellous chemicals exist already (and might seek to preserve them), we equally do not know what marvellous chemicals are coming into being (and might seek to permit them). The assumption that extinctions reduce chemical variety is, so far, unproved.

This is not to say that nothing follows from the observation that biochemical variety is good. Bureaucratic efforts to diminish the variety of edible fruits and vegetables are not merely irritating to those who like the forbidden fruits. They are themselves the product of a profoundly mistaken notion of good health: trying to keep things within a narrow range of possibilities makes sense only if the enforcers seriously believe that real kinds should be preserved against mutation, that we cannot trust the unexpected, unplanned results of myriad interactions. Conservationists and bureaucrats may sometimes be the very same people, seriously concerned to prevent change, and to preserve the values that they have noticed. The notion of 'equilibrium' cited by some (not all) environmentalists may be no more than bureaucratic fantasy. The impulse to keep things clean and tidy, to resist 'pollution', may issue in environmental activism, or in bureaucratic conformism (see Douglas and Isherwood 1979). What causes the undoubted differences?

The needs that even 'shallow' environmentalists detect are not themselves entirely 'material'. Material needs are always liable to 'use up' material, gradually degrading it to a point where nothing else, at the moment, can be done with it. Non-material needs are only really satisfied if the thing is not used up. There is a real difference between eating the apple and enjoying it.

> It may be that vice, depravity and crime are nearly always, or even perhaps always, in their essence, attempts to eat beauty, to eat what we should only look at. . . . If [Eve] caused humanity to be lost by eating the fruit, the opposite attitude, looking at the fruit without eating it, should be what is required to save it.
>
> (Weil 1959: 121)

Someone who wishes only to make use of a landscape, plant or animal is missing its main use, which is simply to be appreciated as it is. Even shallow environmentalists recognize that it is the perceived beauty of the world of nature (a beauty that is often very far from cosy) that demands our care. We wish to preserve the world in beauty for our offspring, and not just to leave them with appropriate materials for their life together. If we could guarantee their survival by providing trace elements and drugs from our own factories, we would be bound to wonder what they were surviving for. Would their lives be worth living without any trace of beauty? Maybe they could create it by themselves, but what could their standard of beauty be, if not the world of nature that has created us? Do we imagine that we would make their lives worth living by drugging them into 'happiness', causing them to delight in what gives us no pleasure at all? Why should we bother with the delights of aliens? If we mind about our distant offspring it is as creatures with whom we can identify: amongst our goals must be to preserve the world in beauty, in what we can see as beauty, for their benefit. The question is, what counts as beauty?

These shallower varieties of environmentalism do no more than draw attention to the inescapable and sometimes irreparable effects our actions have on human and sentient life. The most anthropocentric of such moralists are ready in principle to remake the world for the sole benefit of humankind, but can be brought to agree that we are in no position thus to replace Nature with a human technosphere, and that amongst the benefits that most human beings seek is the sight of natural beauty. It is occasionally suggested that this is a recent development, the product of romantic disaffection. Burnet, writing in his *Sacred Theory* in 1691, suggests that earth and moon alike 'are both . . . the image or picture of a great Ruine, and have the true aspect of a World lying in its rubbish' (Burnet 1965: 91): a few years later even ruins and rubbish dumps were regarded with respect. The Beautiful and the Sublime are different, it is said: Beauty lies in the world of human, humane order, and the Sublime in the wild woods and mountains that owe us no obedience. It may be true that there are fashions in aesthetic judgement: it is far less clear that what romantics call 'sublime' is not what earlier and later generations have simply called 'beauty'. The greatest of late antique philosophers, Plotinus, did not equate the beautiful with the tame and orderly, but with the forms of life, no one of which was sufficient to represent Beauty Itself.

Less anthropocentric, 'deeper' moralists also acknowledge the moral claims of other sentient beings whom we presently kill, torment and dispossess. Sustaining the world in beauty for our offspring is an activity that blends imperceptibly with another duty: of care towards those creatures who now share the land with us. The Torah ruled long since that we should not take everything as if it were ours alone, but leave resources for the wild things of the world, who also seek their food from God (see Lev. 26:6f.). We hold the land in trust for our descendants, maybe: but we also hold it in company with God's other creatures. From this it follows that it is not enough to plant such trees as our descendants may find useful: we must also weigh up the interests of other animals who also need trees (and their sustaining habitat). Our medieval predecessors at least debated whether wild things should be evicted from a piece of land to make room for a monastery or farm or city (and sometimes decided in the wild things' favour). St Kevin, it is said (Waddell 1934: 136), refused an angel's offer of a splendid monastery, with the plea that he did not wish the wild things of the mountain to be dispossessed on his account. We have of late taken humanism so much for granted that pleas for the non-human have had to be couched in carefully 'un-sentimental' terms. Just so the case against killing all adult males in Mytilene had to be put to the Athenian Assembly purely in terms of the perceived advantages of mercy to the Athenians. Less determinedly egoistic a people might more openly have acknowledged that it was the harm to Mytilenians that made such slaughter wrong, not merely to Athens' reputation (see Thucydides *History of the Peloponnesian War* 3.42ff.). It is one thing to regulate the killing of whales so as to leave our children whales to kill; another to slow the killing so as to leave them whales to enjoy; yet another to stop it just because of the harm it does to whales.

Some moralists, having absorbed the insight that pain is an evil whoever or whatever it is that suffers it, have imagined that a sort of 'scientific calculation' of total utility can be made. There are more or less sophisticated versions of this thesis, of which the best is perhaps the kind of cost-benefit analysis or 'Comprehensive Weighing' proposed by the majority of the St Cross working group (Attfield and Dell: 1989). I devote no space to describing this, however. All such would-be 'scientific' analyses seem to me to rely on specious formulae and figures plucked out of the air. We cannot describe the total utility of any action or political programme, and all the really interesting moral problems are answered by other methods, even by those who appeal to such utilitarian calculation. Who bears the cost? Who benefits? What is the common measure of such transactions? Should any be enforceable? Are all things 'negotiable' (even when no actual negotiation can occur)? Is there really nothing, as the majority report asserts (ibid.: 37) that is 'literally priceless'? We should certainly not surrender to the thesis that everything has its price, for moral insight rests on realizing that some things cannot be sold. Nor should we denigrate the real concerns of the poor by characterizing them as so much superstition (since an identical retort can be made to any moralist, even the most egotistical). Yet these are the effects of cost-benefit analysis in the hands of rulers secretly contemptuous of those they control. If such calculation has any distinguishable meaning it is bound to excuse judicial murder, gang-rape and the transformation of the wilderness into Disneyland. If it does not produce those answers (as of course it does not, in the hands of the St Cross group) it is only because the moralists have chosen to outlaw them for quite unutilitarian reasons. All this is familiar enough in other regions of rational morality, and there seems no reason to explore the environmental results any further.

The deeper sort of environmentalist reckons even the rhetoric of animal liberation egoistic: as long as we select one class of living thing, whether it be the human or the sentient, as the object of our moral concern, we are guilty of too great discriminations. On this account trees, rivers, forests, ecosystems do not need to be sentient to be morally considerable. We ought not to think only of what harm we cause to humans or to animals but what damage we do to the integrity of the ecosystems within which we live. The last man alive, in a world bereft of any 'higher' sentient life-form, would still be in the wrong if he were to destroy the last living forests, or irrevocably poison all the seas. Even if no alien intelligence ever saw this monument to human folly it would be, objectively, an evil. In making such a claim deep environmentalists abandon two premises of much modern thought: first, that individual sentient beings are more morally significant than insentient systems; second, that all value is subjective value, resting in the perceived pleasure or discomfort of those sentient beings. It can be argued that they are wise to do so, that the two premises are actually incompatible. If all value is subjective value, it cannot be true that sentient beings are objectively more valuable than insentient ones. If (on the contrary) they are, then not all value is merely subjective. But it is equally difficult to understand what sort of value such objective value could be: theists may identify it with God's approval of each stage of creation; non-theists must postulate absolute moral laws independent of anyone's recognition.

Disagreement about the metaphysics of morals is conjoined with a disagreement about other metaphysical issues: are 'individuals' (chiefly the middle-sized individuals of our ordinary lives) more real than the systems of which they are inescapably a part? Although Enlightenment thinkers are now regularly blamed for abstracting individuals from their social and physical context, they actually tended to insist that the only true substance (that is, the only self-subsisting individual) was God: we, and other ordinary individuals, were only modes of that one substance. According to Descartes, whom modern environmentalists regularly blame for rampant individualism,

> though each of us is a person distinct from others whose interests are accordingly in some way different from those of the rest of the world, we must still think that none of us could subsist alone and each one of us is really one of the many parts of the universe, and more particularly a part of the earth, the State, the society, the family to which we belong by our domicile, our oath of allegiance and our birth.
>
> (Descartes 1970: 172 (15 September 1645))

Descartes actually attacked both individualism and solipsism: so far from elevating his own will and reason, or that of each rational individual, above the truth, his whole effort was to bring to our attention something not ourselves that merited our worship. A true Cartesian recognizes himself or herself as a dependent, confronted and contained by a world not of his or her making (see Clark 1992), the one true substance.

This monism has recently received psychological (though not logical) support from the 'Gaia hypothesis' of James Lovelock (1979, 1985). Although Lovelock himself is environmentally fairly 'deep' it is not entirely clear that the hypothesis has the moral effect that some have suggested. According to the hypothesis, living things have always been altering their environment to suit themselves. The bacterial population of the Earth, in particular, ensures that temperature and chemical condition stay within a narrow range whatever outside forces do. Other living things reinforce these bacterial pressures, or create further opportunities for the bacterial population (the sole population of the earth for most of its history). Ecomystics and very deep environmentalists prefer to think of Gaia as a single, thinking or quasi-thinking being, the Goddess, who will sustain herself in beauty even if it means devising some new plague to strike us down. Some, turning full circle to become just like the shallower sort of moralist, imagine that Gaia has devised us human and would-be space-travelling beings to scatter her seed around the universe. A few have joined forces with, as it were, 'drylanders', the very people who most pollute the globe. Maybe Gaia – for her future profit – requires us to promote the greenhouse effect, or scatter mutagens to increase the rate of evolutionary change. These moralizing uses of scientific hypothesis were not the point of Lovelock's first speculations, but clearly fit into a late twentieth-century religiosity. This is often expressed as a re-affirmation of an immanent, nurturing divinity, the Goddess rather than the God. But the Goddess may easily be depicted as one that delights in the blood of her enemies (see Heine 1988: 46), and threatens immediate judgement on the cancerous growth of human industrial intelligence (unless she intends the 'cancer' too).

Recognizing the terrestrial ecosystem as something like a living organism may indeed excite the kind of love that we need to feel. We need, perhaps, to wonder at its beauty, and treasure pictures of the whole Earth seen from space (the greatest single justification of the whole space programme). Feeling that love, we may be a little more inclined to leave large tracts of the whole earth alone. We may also, seeing how complex are the inter-relations of the living systems that go to make up Gaia, be sensitive to the thought that what we do here–now may have unpredictable effects elsewhere. Gaia, despite the rhetoric of an earlier decade, is not 'Spaceship Earth'; we have blueprints of machines, and can make good guesses about the effect of what we do to them – though the arrival of complex computer systems has already shown us that we cannot altogether predict what programs will do when they are executed on particular hardware, in conjunction with existing systems. That is why cautious businessmen and administrators do not really want to be the first to use a program: who knows what bugs it holds? We have no blueprint at all of Gaia, and should be still more cautious. But even if we wish Gaia well, and love 'her' as she is, her unpredictability, and strength, may not, in the end, be what environmentalists will wish to hear. The trouble is that, on the evidence, almost nothing we could do would seriously damage 'Gaia': not even a nuclear winter. That, after all, is the evidence that there is such a living system: it has survived enormous cataclysms in the past, and the bacterial population, largely unaffected, has maintained the climate until other larger organisms fill up the world again. Acting so as to preserve the 'integrity' of the whole can be given some content when we consider little systems (forests or wetlands, rivers and savannas), but what state of Gaia is better or worse – for Gaia – than any other? Lovelock himself suggests that, judged by the amount of biomass, Gaia was 'healthiest' during the Ice Ages (Lovelock 1985: 135ff.). A nuclear winter, on those terms, would be quite good for her! But actually the assumption that health is measured by amount of biomass seems as arbitrary as any other.

Loving the whole world – or rather that fragment of the whole that we identify as the living earth – is an important element of any proper piety. The problem is that in the absence of a clear account of how the earth should be, of what actually counts as 'Gaia's health', it does not seem that we can give much content to any duty of benevolence – over and above our duty not to steal, torment or slaughter those we can hurt. If we could really destroy Gaia then of course we shouldn't, but even a planet-wrecker of the kind conceived by science fiction writers (namely a large asteroid, crashing down to earth) would probably not finish Gaia for good. Our duties of non-maleficence, for the moment, merely require us not to destroy creatures of our own rank, and not to make their habitats too harsh for them to adapt. This may be a wider duty than merely to be kind to animals, but it need not involve a radical restructuring of our morality.

MINDS, MATTER AND INDIVIDUALS

Environmentalists tend to agree with fashionable thinkers in philosophy and the biological sciences in denouncing dualism.

> Because Descartes, or Augustine, or Plato, divided body and mind, and identified the real self with the mind, we are culturally afflicted with a disdain for the physical environment. What we think is real, and what we feel and handle is unreal or insignificant. To avoid this moral disaster we must realise that our mental capacities are those of a physical organism, that we are deeply, unavoidably and rightly involved with the physical universe, and that right-living does not require us to divorce ourselves from matter but to enjoy it.

According to Matthew Fox, a Catholic figure roughly silenced by the Vatican, 'Creation spiritually takes opposite positions on just about all of Descartes' principles' (Fox 1991: 102). Actually Fox misrepresents those principles, in ways that go beyond my present concerns. Descartes insisted, as I have already observed, that we were dependent beings, and that we were 'in our bodies' not as angels (or ghosts) in a machine, but as living persons. 'If an angel were in a human body he would not have sensations as we do, but would simply perceive the motions which are caused by external objects and in this way would differ from a real man' (Descartes 1970: 128 (January 1642)). Even (or especially) Augustine denounced then-fashionable disdain for the physical as heresy. And even Plato 'looked away' from the physical only in the sense that he saw the One in the Many, and pursued Beauty rather than being obsessed with particular passing beauties. If Beauty were only what we have so far seen as beautiful, such worship would be the kind of conservation beloved of bureaucrats: that nothing be allowed to change. It is because Platonism does not equate Beauty with particular beauties that we can be reassured: change need not be an evil, because Beauty is realized in indefinitely (infinitely?) many ways.

> All things counter, original, spare, strange;
> Whatever is fickle, freckled (who knows how?)
> With swift, slow; sweet, sour; adazzle, dim;
> He fathers-forth whose beauty is past change:
> Praise him.
>
> (Hopkins 1970: 70)

If Western dualism, and a rejection of material values, are the root of our ecological crisis it is at least strange that other, supposedly less dualist cultures have done no better, and that it is in the West that the greatest exploration of the physical universe has yet taken place. It has in the past been argued that we are more, not less, concerned with matters physical.

Whatever the truth of historical claims about the origins of our crisis, it can be argued that metaphysical dualism is false, and that an ethical dualism, even if not as pernicious or as influential as some have said, should also be dismissed. The metaphysical claim is that we need not postulate a different sort of thing than the merely physical to explain consciousness or qualitative experience. Material things can think, and so we need no 'minds' to be added to the physical to explain how we can think. It may be agreed at once that Cartesian dualism, which denies that even chimpanzees have minds, is deeply unconvincing (though many biologists and psychologists still act as if it were true). But there are more difficulties than are fashionably admitted about materialistic monism: either we do not understand matter correctly when we characterize it in terms drawn from the ordinarily physical sciences, or we should (incoherently) abandon all talk of conscious experience as mere superstition, or we must admit the existence of sheerly inexplicable conjunctions in the world (for there can be no physical reason why things should be qualitatively conscious). Calling this latter 'emergence', as if the term explained anything, is to rely on magic (see Nagel 1979; Clark 1984: 121ff.). That a world made up entirely of objects should ever contain subjects remains as absurd as Descartes, and William James, believed it. The point is not that we do not (yet) understand the mechanism involved in transforming 'matter' into 'mind', but that such transformations make no sense at all.

> The problem is admirably expressed by Joseph Glanvill, a fervent Cartesian, in his *Vanity of Dogmatizing*, in the course of an enumeration of the limitations of human knowledge. 'How the purer Spirit', he writes, 'is united to this Clod, is a knot too hard for fallen Humanity to unty. How should a thought be united to a marble statue, or a sun-beam to a lump of clay! The freezing of the words in the air in northern climes is as conceivable, as this strange union ... And to hang weights on the wings of the winde seems far more intelligible'.
>
> (Willey 1934: 84, quoting Glanvill 1661: 20)

The problem is not, as some suppose, that Descartes arbitrarily invents a mind distinct from matter. The point is that science rests on the construction (the hypothesis) of a world where wishes are not horses, where things are not the case merely because we say they are. To admit that they sometimes are is to admit that 'an empty wish should remove Mountains', as Glanvill puts it. To deny that they ever are seems to leave no room for efficacious volition. Deep environmentalists who reject dualism should also reject materialism, or be left with no reason at all to worry about the life or continued being of matter.

Ethical dualism may be more easily dismissed: that is the notion that what should be important to us is not the fulfilment of our more physical urges, but the intellectual or spiritual passage from the world of sense to that of intellect or spirit (these need not be the same). Animals, trees and ecosystems should not matter much to us (we shall outlive them all, or now surpass them by contemplating eternal truth), and neither should the concerns (if any) that we once shared with them. Those who care for non-human animals have regularly been denounced for caring for the things such animals themselves do care for (food and sex and sleep). Because human beings should care for other things they should not trouble themselves with those who care for merely material matters. Paradoxically this has then been made the excuse for using animals, trees, ecosystems just to satisfy the material wants we had been told we should not care about. Almost as paradoxically the environmentalists who denounce ethical dualism actually, like moralists of old, wish us to turn our eyes away from immediate and physical satisfactions so as to delight in the ongoing life of the non-human universe. It would seem as easy to conclude instead to physical hedonism and make use of matter for our pleasure's sake. If we should instead acknowledge that what we had dismissed as merely material is as valuable as any dreams of heaven then perhaps we must, perforce, practise an ascetic discipline as dualist as any in our past. Present enjoyment must be deferred to allow the world to be in beauty. The more we are involved in it as material beings on a par with alligators or coral insects the more we shall employ it for our present use; if we are to avoid that trap we have to distance ourselves, and not be merely 'animal'.

Should this involve us in a move from 'individualism'? And can we afford this move? As long as we do not fully realize that we are parts of 'nature', we may imagine that our interests are at odds with 'hers'. Once we realize that we depend on 'nature' in everything, we shall have to respect 'her', while at the same instant standing a little aside from all that nature makes us. 'If men spit upon the ground they spit upon themselves. Man did not weave the web of life, he is merely a strand of it. Whatever he does to the web he does to himself' – as Chief Seattle of Washington State did not say in 1854 (for the speech recalled as his was written 'by one Ted Parry as a film script for a movie called "Home" produced by the Southern Baptist Convention in 1971–2' (Callicott 1989: 204)). Alligators make the swamps of Florida, and depend on them, but do not – we presume – know that they do. The wise know that there is no escape from nature, that we are not independent agents, free to discard our past. In fact, the wise are individual in understanding that they have never been strict individuals. The thought is not a new one: it is indeed exactly what the Stoics said, who sought to honour 'God and Nature' by seeing themselves as strands within that larger whole, their actions as determined as the ocean waves. Their problem, frequently observed, was that their system left no room for moral freedom: wrong-doing was only action that led, in general, to a personal disaster, but no-one could rationally be blamed for it, nor any other action wished for. If we are not individual agents, but only parts of a world we must respect, we can take no more offence at 'environmental degradation by human agency' than at thunderstorms, or alligators.

It is still more alarming to notice that in rejecting dualism and individualism we are in danger of losing sight of everything that matters to environmentalists. Consider another respected theologian, Teilhard de Chardin, who is popularly supposed to have praised the material world, and identified with its travails. In fact, his interests were entirely anthropocentric, and he spared few tears for any 'lesser tribes' that might hold back 'progress'. 'What attitude should the advancing sector of humanity adopt towards static and decidedly unprogressive ethnic groups?' (Teilhard, writing in 1937; Speaight 1967: 234). At the same time his praise of Matter leaves no room for the discriminations necessary to an environmentalist ethic. Matter as such will survive any cataclysm, any degradation that we can conceive, even more securely than Gaia. The desolation that lay before Mordor, 'a land defiled, diseased beyond all healing – unless the Great Sea should enter it and wash it with oblivion' (Tolkien 1966: II, 251), is just as material as Lothlorien. If matter were all that mattered we could have no problem. The problem lies in the forms that matter is constrained or coaxed to take, the way that matter becomes *this* material thing or *that*. A merely reductive materialism, insisting that 'in reality there are only atoms and the void' (as Democritus declared; Kirk *et al.* 1983: 410), can make no room for such notions as 'extinction' or 'pollution'. Nothing real can ever be extinguished, or polluted. Such notions only make sense if there are real kinds, real standards of good health, and these in turn seem to require the real existence of minds to discriminate them.

If there are no minds distinct (even in thought) from matter, then the existence of sentient individuals is called in question. All material bodies have fuzzy edges, and all kinds are fuzzy too. Our usual language incorporates a deeply held conviction that there are indeed real individuals (which is, real indivisibles), and real kinds, but we should not rely on this 'usual language' to 'cut the world at its joints'. In the absence of real minds, can there be real individuals or real kinds? One stretch of land is Bosnia, and another Croatia, by changing political fiat: nothing in the land itself dictates what conventional nation it is. Similarly a human neonate is part of its mother, its father, its family or is itself alone by changing moral and legal practice. The words that issue from this mouth or that may once have been thought the speech of this real mind or that: in the absence of minds, they are the product of a larger situation, a biological complex. 'My' words do not belong to 'me', because there is no single thing really identified by 'me'; this body, whose sounds or key-strokes they are, is an artificially abstracted segment of a larger four-dimensional reality.

In that case, if there are any morally significant entities at all, there is no need to think they are only entities 'with minds'. Any functional segment of the physical universe, whether it be a single body or a clan, or hive, or ecosystem, has as strong a claim to be an important element of the whole. So the shallower sort of environmentalist, who attends only to the needs of 'minded' or sentient entities, gives way to the deeper kind, devoted to the continuing being of any functional segment. Not only people, not only higher animals, but also rocks and river-valleys, wetlands, herds and species, are indistinguishably part of the whole earth. Care for such ongoing wholes, within the larger whole, is actually compatible with what shallower moralists will consider a regrettably callous attitude to individual mortality – because there are no important individuals, whether or not there are real 'mental properties' distinct, in thought, from more 'material' ones.

There is, of course, a certain paradox in this approach. It is only if there are minds, and moral consciousness, that it makes sense to require us to exercise any moral concern for anything at all, even trees and river-valleys. If there are no individual minds to mind *about*, there are equally no individual minds to mind. Monistic environmentalism is in danger from the 'Lazy Argument' which was deployed against Stoics: whatever it is thought we do is really part of the ongoing being of the whole of wholes, and asking any segment of the whole to reconsider its alloted status is insane. The very claim that Enlightenment dualism is a cancerous growth, a deeply felt delusion, only makes sense to those infected by it. Environmentalism itself would be part of the same strange disease. It seems easier to propose that there are real individuals, with varying capacities to consider themselves apart from any physical whole of which they are, in a sense, a part. Only such individuals can be expected to care what they do. They must therefore conceive themselves to be such individuals, and therefore not just material segments of a whole whose behaviour is all of a piece. In other words, we are both bodies (extended fragments of an infinitely discriminable whole) and spirits (moral and meta-physical dependents on a wider truth) – as Descartes said.

OBJECTIVITY AND THE RULES OF REASON

The oddities of 'new age' religiosity about the environment can be set in context by considering again the step that made the Enlightenment, and modern science. Science began in the seventeenth century with a piece of self-denial: the determination not to moralize the world. Instead of describing things in terms from (or at least associated with) human purposive action, scientifically minded thinkers decided to describe them as 'objectively' as possible. Final causes, substantial forms, conscious feeling were not to be offered as real explanations of what was going on. Instead, the world was to be described by measuring such changes as could be assessed without the help of sympathy or moral judgement. The idea of the world that has been constructed over the last few centuries is a triumph of the human imagination – but it is one, of course, that has no place at all for its creator. A world that is to be described solely in terms that do not depend upon the presence of human consciousness, moral judgement or immediate feeling plainly cannot explain, or even allow for, those features of our actual, living world. Having divested the world of any features that imply the existence of particular feelings, or the propriety of particular actions, we are naively astonished to discover that we cannot, from the facts we have admitted, demonstrate the existence of such feelings or the propriety (even the existence) of such actions. Still more naively we conclude that because we cannot prove (for example) that chimpanzees have feelings or that it matters if they do, we are therefore entitled to believe that they do not, or else it does not (thereby drawing conclusions of the kind that we have said we cannot)!

Objectivism of this kind may seem deeply flawed. If the dead, mechanical world is revealed, or created, by objective reason, so much the worse for reason. Better trust to feelings, and especially those feelings of identification, participation that the Enlightenment renounced. On those terms 'there is no inorganic nature, there is no dead, mechanical earth; the Great Mother has been won back to life'. The words are those of Ernst Krieck, a Nazi ideologue writing in 1936, and cited by Pois (1986: 117). For the problem is that the one 'environmentalist' party to win power in this century was the Nazi party, and its rhetoric was sufficiently like that of modern 'Greens' to alarm older Germans who remember it (see Bramwell 1985; Spretnak and Capra 1985).

Making sense of Nazi ideology is probably a lost cause: those who have abandoned the good of intellect (including any commitment to the laws of non-contradiction and excluded middle) cannot sensibly be expected to make sense. Heidegger apparently believed that National Socialism would cure humanity of technologism, the belief that things were only implements for the use of people: he was compelled to admit that National Socialism was itself a symptom, not a cure, and that it ended in making implements, or worse, of people. The Nazis acted out a dream of technocratic control while speaking as if they respected 'nature'. Death camps and factory farming were alike, founded on a careful attempt to evacuate all worshipful meaning from the creatures they oppressed. It is perhaps a mark of moral myopia that Heidegger's comment on the identity of camp and farm is usually now cited as evidence that Heidegger was a moral monster. If his intention was to mitigate the Nazis' offence I could have no quarrel with those who cite the remark against him. If it was instead a belated recognition that the Nazis evacuated the world of meaning in much the way that factory farmers, or some experimentalists, must do, and that they were therefore guilty of exactly the same disorder as the technological or humanist civilization they, and Heidegger, denounced, he might be forgiven it.

Those who think that the world (apart from their own intentions) is to be conceived 'objectively', enshrining neither intentions nor 'objective values', are preparing it for any use they please. If the tree is to be cut down – or at any rate, cut down without apology – it must be evacuated of its attendant dryads, or any sentimentally inspired fantasms. If the dog is to be cut open without anaesthetic, poisoned, burned or drowned 'for the sake of science', it must be conceived as 'an animal preparation', 'matter in that state known as living', not as 'faithful hound' or 'affectionate mammal' or Pythagoras' friend. If Jews or Gypsies are to be eliminated, as enemies of the true, organic folk, they must be made to seem like waste, like bacterial infections, and their elimination be a painful duty. The closer we come to creatures who seem to be of our kind, the more difficult will this necessary 'objectification' be, and the more likely will it be that some of those assigned to the task will come to enjoy inflicting what looks like distress even as they deny that any real distress is caused. But sadism is almost a humane vice, a recognition of pain that might involve a distorted mutuality: sadists actually want their victims to be sentient, valued organisms. 'Objectivizers' only want results, and no more think it sensible to torture their victims (when there is no actual gain) than to flounder in the manure they're sweeping out of sight.

What I have described are fake objectivists, precisely because they are not objective about their own intentions, and unthinkingly equate the 'objectively valueless' with what has no value: the merely actual with the dispensable or the disgusting. The strength, the moral strength, of Enlightenment objectivism rested on the realization that merely conventional values could be transcended. 'When Adam delved and Eve span, who was then the gentleman?' Instead of seeing things (fellow humans, animals, trees, rivers) through a haze of mis-placed sentiments, irrelevant memories and outdated symbolism, we should be guided by what was 'really' there. A human being stripped of merely subjective associations could be met face-to-face; an animal (say, a wolf) that was not treated as a symbol of rapacious evil might turn out to be friendly, and even if dangerous was not worth hating. A land that was not intrinsically French or English, 'mine' or 'yours' could be bargained around, and not be bled over. Fake objectivism forgets to be objective about our actual intentions, and merely denies that anything we deal with has intentions, or values, of its own, to interfere with. Under the pretence of objectivity such fakes actually subjectivize the world: everything is matter for their purposes because they deny that there are purposes at all. Making things merely material is not just denying that they have objective value, but asserting that they have disvalue.

One answer to such fake objectivism is to insist that there is a better way of being truthful. Objectivists insist that the right way to uncover truth is to discard all empathy, projection, participation in the life or being of objects. It is sometimes a necessary asceticism so to do, since we are all too ready to attribute qualities to others that are only what we would wish them to have. An amorous adolescent who wants to get to know someone might be well advised to discard his erotic fantasies, and try to think in some more disin-terested way. It certainly does not follow that he ought to think of people as so much stuff – and any attempt to do so will issue in the fake objectivism that I have described before. Instead of understanding the girl he fancies as she is he will see her only as an erotic object, while pretending to himself that he is seeing her 'objectively'. It would (obviously) be better to rely upon an educated sensibility that uncovers a truthful response in others by being open to such responses. Instead of pretending that we only understand the world when we see it without affect (and therefore as available for the crudest of our own desires), it would be better to think that we understand it best when we see it companionably. Truth is what is revealed to us as something we should acknowledge: recognition is a moral consent.

Companionable or convivial understanding is sometimes associated with 'feminine' modes of cognition. 'Masculine' understanding, it is said, is simultaneously abstract and objectifying. Men (biologically or culturally) are trained to ignore their own immediate emotional responses to a situation, to think of it in the way that any disinterested observer might manage, as an example of some very general, abstract principle. What matters to a 'masculine' intelligence is high-principled consistency, and (equivalently) an object purged of any merely subjective, accidental, historical qualities. Knowledge is understood as abstract or expert knowledge, best expressed as a system of interlocking propositions, such that one who knows can 'justify' his knowledge by detailing exactly why things must be as they are believed to be. One anecdote makes the point: in the 1984 Grange Inquiry into a number of infant deaths at a hospital in Toronto,

> when lawyers, who were mostly men, questioned doctors, the questions were phrased in terms of what they knew. When nurses were on the stand, the question was, 'Based on your experience . . .'. Experience in our society is considered second-class compared to knowledge. Nurses should not know.
>
> (Code 1988: 64)

We ought not to believe anything without the right kind of justification, and all trains of justification should, ideally, begin from self-evident principles which are either logical axioms or reports of immediate, unprejudiced sensory experience. The twin projects of empiricism and rationalism (taking sensory reports or logical axioms as foundational) are in some disarray, not least because the epistemological axiom just stated is pragmatically self-refuting (it being neither logical axiom or sensory report nor deducible from anything else that is), but 'masculinist' epistemology is still the preferred option amongst educators. The great alternative, the 'feminine' mode, is to reject foundationalist, abstract, systematic epistemology, in favour of more personal modes. Experience, craft-knowledge, educated sensibility are all, in fact, crucial even in self-consciously scientific disciplines. Our knowledge of each other's life and meaning is always of this kind. We cannot *know* without putting ourselves 'at risk' (or what seems risk) in a personal encounter. We cannot know without accepting our dependent status, as inheritors of a tradition and as faced by truths we should acknowledge.

'Feminine' or 'tacit' knowledge may be especially relevant in environmentalism, for two reasons. The first has to do with the issues already addressed:

whereas the abstract, objectifying form of knowledge tends to identify its object as outside value, or even (speciously) without value, more personalized modes of knowing cannot make this error. We know someone or something best when we can comfortably live with them. This mode of knowing does not aspire to leaving things as they are, as if we could *know* only what is not affected by our knowing. Knowing is an ongoing project, a dance of mutual accommodation, not a pretended separation of subject and object which is magically transcended through the subject's power. That model of knowledge is grotesque. It is absurd to postulate a world of 'pure matter', having no necessary qualities or values and then express surprise that qualities and values cannot be explained in terms referring only to that 'pure matter'. It is just as absurd to postulate a subject divorced from any object and then pretend that the subject could still have an accurate picture of the object. Matter that does not have any mental aspect cannot explain mind; subjects that are not united with their objects cannot know that what they have is knowledge. Real knowledge must arise from union, as minds arise from a world that never was 'pure matter'. It follows that the model of the earth and its inhabitants that is abstracted from our personal response to the organic world is an idol. 'The Great Mother has been won back to life.'

The second feature of this methodology is a distrust of the demand for proof. What cannot be 'proved', by more abstract canons, should not be believed: from which it follows, in practice, that what cannot be proved is disbelieved, even though its contradictory is also unprovable. If we cannot 'prove' that unanaesthetized dogs 'feel pain' we are entitled to assume that they do not even though this is just as far from proven. Clearly we cannot prove that they feel pain if 'proof' requires us to deduce that they must feel pain from logical axioms, mathematical theorems, physical laws and sensory reports, all of which have been carefully phrased to avoid any reference to the 'unknown' inner life of dogs or anything else. But 'proof' is suspect for another reason. It may sometimes be right to demand certain kinds of 'proof'. What is admissible in a court of law often does depend on our experience of errors: eye-witnesses, and expert witnesses, have been mistaken, especially when they have let their moral fury or prejudice dictate what they report. But some rules of evidence may – all too obviously – favour one side or other. If rape cannot be 'proved' without an independent witness, few rapists will be convicted. If the cause of infant leukaemia near a nuclear installation, or of one particular incident, cannot be 'proved' to be the radiation around the site, unless all other explanations are ruled out, then no-one will win compensation for what – commonsensically – must be an injury. To 'prove' is to compel particular people to act upon a certain theory, and the engines of proof, of such compulsion, are in the hands of (largely male) authority). As long as the Soviet authorities held all the cards it was impossible to 'prove' what damage they were doing: nothing at all could count as 'proof' that they were lying scoundrels. Even the most ardent radical can agree (and should) that the West is not so wicked, nor so damaging, as that seventy-five-year experiment. But even if that regime was worse than anything the West has done it is difficult not to suspect that there can be no true proofs until political and economic power is more equal. 'Proving', till then, is always an exercise of power, and the harder it is made to 'prove' a thesis, the less such changes will occur. A genuinely rationalist methodology would place as severe a standard on theories approved in the present as on radical ones: someone who has failed to 'prove' his or her point might reasonably ask whether the established theory can be proven. At present far less rigorous tests are imposed on what 'the great and the good' affirm, even though we have ample experience of error in what such authorities have said.

Environmentalists of this kind put more trust in the reports of those immediately involved with the living world than in the predictions of abstract theoreticians. The testimony and fears of indigenous peoples, the empathetic understanding of (some) women, artists, and craftspeople, the suspicions of those who are likeliest to suffer the effects of novel engineering projects – all are given more weight than they would be by more conventional standards. It is not enough to reply to environmentalist fears by saying that our present meteorological and evolutionary models are as yet too crude to prove any particular prediction (and we are therefore entitled to believe, without proof, what suits the prosperous to have us all believe). It is not enough to explain those fears away by suggesting that they are projections of personal or social inadequacies (of which the spokesmen for the prosperous are free). It is certainly not enough to say that our present health and prosperity, greater by far than that of any generation until now, must 'prove' that we are doing something right (and should go on). We should be at least as suspicious of those who defend the uses of power as we are of those who attack them. We should be at least as suspicious of those who demand 'proof' while making it impossible to provide such proof, as we are of those who demand that the sentence should precede the trial. What counts in knowledge, as it counts in any responsible politics, is to build towards a genuinely convivial culture, which does not outlaw anyone's experience of life. There is a role for system, and for objectivity: neither can long survive, or be worth having, outside the personal, unsystematized, and value-laden Knowing that is – not our foundation, but – our home.

NATURE AND CONVENTION

But what is home? That what is 'natural' is good, and the conventional (or merely conventional) is bad is an ancient theme, since first we noticed that customs differed. What better guide in uncertainty than what Nature or the gods have made us all to do, or made all the 'unfallen creatures' do? What happens or happened naturally is what was 'meant' to happen, till human beings decided that they could do better. What we do not condemn 'animals' for doing we should not condemn in 'human beings'; what we condemn in human beings we refuse to see in nature (concern for the bubble reputation, for example). Mainstream moral philosophers regularly insist that 'natural' does not necessary mean 'good': it is possible to think (since many do) that morality and the law exist to deny or transform nature. What happens naturally need not, as a matter of logic, be good. But by the same token, what is natural can be taken as the criterion of right conduct, and many moralists do. There would certainly be something very odd in denying all value to nature: as Plotinus pointed out to the Gnostics who despised the physical universe, 'if God is not in Nature, He is not in you' (*Enneads* 2.9.16). In common parlance the natural is opposed to the conventional, the artificial, the spurious or deceitful. Returning to nature, or being guided by nature, is a goal with many attractive features. What happens naturally does not depend on us, and avoids all moral disputes. The conventional is the disputable, and dependent on our strength to support it. It is also suspect, in that our natural selves may not be well adapted to the artificial world, of approved conduct or artificial chemicals. We find 'civilization' terribly restrictive, and its produce possibly harmful. Would it not be better to return home?

Only a few moralists have ever really acted out the return to nature, seeking to live as naked primates. Only a few, because – paradoxically – we are very ill-adapted to life 'in nature', without clothes, cookery or social customs. Custom is our second nature, and a refusal to be ruled by it is as unnatural as any. But less extreme renunciations have been practised: the Tupi-Guarani Indians, it seems, rejected the kind of state-authority that blossomed amongst the Incas, or the Aztecs, preferring to live as equals among the trees (see Clastres 1977). Individual Cynics, or Hindu *sannyasin*, sought to do without encumbrances, as did Christian monks – always to be mocked by those who could not conceive that any 'normal', 'natural' human being could renounce the delights of ownership. Both those who renounced and those who mocked, in other words, employed a rhetoric that rested on the value of what came naturally.

In an environmentalist context the worship of nature and the natural decrees that we 'respect the integrity of living systems', that we do not seek to invent new ways of being nor lay claim to more than we need here–now. The immediate paradox is that those who seek to live 'naturally' must often, in any developed society, take more trouble about what they eat and drink than those content to go along with second nature, custom. Running wholefood cooperatives, living low on the food-chain, not wearing synthetics (woven from the world's non-renewable resources) all take time and energy: they are, in a sense, unnatural because they do not follow the line of least resistance, and because they hold back from what advantages we could acquire. Life feeds on life, the retort must come: living things all seek to maintain themselves and gain an advantage, usually by following the easier, straighter track. Behaving naturally might, after all, be what those labelled 'anti-environmentalists' are

862

doing. Being rational, of course, most of us can defer the satisfaction of desire so as to achieve it, but thrift is a virtue only if we wish, in the end, to spend. Those who really live at least a little 'closer to nature' than do city-dwellers are rarely thrifty: instead they rely on what they can easily take from their surroundings, without wishing to save up for any rainy day (see Sahlins 1972).

The prayer that Christians teach their children asks God to give us enough bread for today, and Christ is reported to have told his disciples not to prepare for any tomorrow, but to trust in God (see Luke 12:22ff.). It is understandable that we rarely take this literally. Those who expected a swift Second Coming, and decided not to plant their crops or lay in stores were speedily rebuked: 'who will not work let him not eat' (2 Thess. 3:10). It is up to us to do our duty in the world while it is light, and not to count on rescue. The notorious remark by James Watt, sometime secretary for the environment in Reagan's administration, that there was no need to husband earth's resources since the Lord would soon return, was yet more absurd. What he thereby advocated was not renunciation of material gain, but open season on the living earth. If we should accumulate no treasures here on earth this is hardly a good reason to cut down the forests for the sake of present gain. Such gains are transitory, and we can hardly think that God delights in the destruction. 'What are your endless sacrifices to me? says Yahweh. I am sick of holocausts of rams and the fat of calves. The blood of bulls and of goats revolts me': the Lord's rebuke through the prophets to those who imagined that he wished us to destroy God's creatures (Isa. 1:11ff.).

A 'return to nature' that really involved what Sahlins has called the 'Zen solution' to the problem of scarcity (namely, to limit our desires) is not without its merits. It is certainly very easy to mock the spurious desires engendered by commercial society, and prefer Plato's 'city of pigs' to the luxuriating, fevered state that needed a philosophical elite to order it. But very few of us will willingly 'return to nature' in that sense. Most of those who try will really only abandon one set of luxuries, for which they happen not to care, while contentedly equating their own hobbies with the 'simple life'. Merely limiting our desires, in any case, is likely enough to make the problem worse. There are no universally acknowledged truths of economics, nor any science of economic prediction. But it seems likely enough that the Zen solution is only really available to hunter-gatherers, content to live as one species amongst many. Ever since we adopted agricultural and industrial techniques we have had to keep the economy moving: if we do not buy each other's goods, we will have none to sell. If we have none to sell we will have no surplus wealth with which to clean up after ourselves – and it is merely romantic to suppose that early industry or agriculture is non-invasive, non-polluting, and environmentally friendly. The earliest civilizations of the Middle East are deserts now.

Why should we suppose otherwise? Why are we so prone to imagine that Time Past contains the answer, that we can 'return' to a form of life 'at one with its environment' by merely abandoning an arbitrary few of our recent acquisitions? The date of that lost world may vary: the most conventionally conservative identify it with an Edwardian summer, or early Victorian idyll; more radical reformers look back before the Civil War, the Revolt from Rome, the Norman Conquest or the Christian Era. Every time we realize the flaws of our preferred period (and why it led to us) we look still further back – very much as idealistic communists transferred their affections from one failed revolution to another as they found out what each was like. The safest bet, no doubt, is to conceive of a pre-historical utopia, a lost aeon. Radical environmentalism, deep ecologism, naturism is a religious form that has not yet had its John Evangelist or Muhammad, let alone their scholastic successors. There is, that is, no paradigmatic vision of how things are and should be, no sacred text, no creed, no clerisy and no agreed-upon utopian age. Many different streams are flowing together, but without any certainty that they will one day be a river, riding to the sea. Some 'ecofeminists' have proclaimed themselves as witches (e.g. Starhawk 1990), and drawn on romantic theories of the Goddess allegedly once worshipped by those 'close to nature'. Similarly romantic fantasies encourage people to believe that Native Americans, Australian Aboriginals, Celts or what you will retain a real devotion to our earthly Mother. Those who say so rarely notice how condescending they are being, how influenced by very familiar stories about defeated peoples. Invading peoples always assimilate their victims to the world of nature, and some of those victims profess to believe them: in the British Isles both Welsh and Scottish Highlanders have suffered from the theory that they are 'naturals'. Claiming that this is true is actually as insulting as the similar claim that 'women' are close to nature. Both claims amount to accepting the dichotomies created by imperial culture so as to exclude the losers.

But a rational, objective criticism of these historical fantasies is not enough. Whether we seek to conserve wetlands and the whooping crane, or Ely cathedral and its surrounding buildings, what matters is the vast sweep of our imagined past and the pledges it offers the future. Our concern is not only with the 'actual', present beings and the profit or pleasure they afford us, or even what they afford themselves, but with their meaning, and the fantasies we build around them and ourselves. It is no answer to say that things were never as easy, as utopian, as we loosely suggest, and that the relics or reminders of past fantasy are not worth preserving. Images of the past, even if literally false, are promises for the future. That the great cathedrals are not really proofs of 'Merry England' (any more than the pyramids are proof of 'merry Egypt') does not show that, properly understood, they are not promises of such a future. There has really been no time at all when people lived 'in harmony' with each other and the world, but the phantom memory that once, sometime, they did still has the force of prophecy.

An eighteenth-century English Whig landowner, who had put his treasure into the founding of a family, would plant avenues which even his grandchildren would not live to see with the eye of the flesh in the glory of the timber's full-grown stature. A twentieth-century Ministry of Agriculture planted soft wood to replace the hard wood that it felled; and in this greediness for quick returns, it was advertising its disbelief in its own immortality.

(Toynbee 1954: 518)

It is true that there was no world in harmony, just as it is true that 'ancient lineages' are mostly spurious or shameful. But if we are ever to live in anything approaching harmony we had better try to 'remember' how. The best way of ensuring that things last is to pretend that they already have. The myth of Gaia, and of a primordial bargain with the world, may be what we most need to help bring about a future, unknown peace. In ordinary political theory the 'social contract' that some philosophers imagined had been made back in the very beginning has helped to guide our peoples towards a bargain that, in fact, no-one made before. The actual beginnings of civil society lie in brigandage and (sometimes) piety: the idea that every subject willingly keeps the peace is a pious hope. So also is the idea that we might live at peace with all our fellow travellers in 'the odyssey of evolution' (Leopold 1968: 109).

CONCLUSION

Environmentalists will often say – with support from those like Watt – that Christians claim domination, in God's name, over all the earth, and thereby license any amount of destruction. Nature, it is said, is a 'great Ruine' whose elements should be re-used in building the celestial city. Value lay in the controlling power, the covenant we had with God: God gave the land to us, on the bare condition that we served him, and all the creatures of the world are in our hands. That doctrine, of an absolute dominion over creatures who do not embody any value in themselves, has given us environmental degradation. The trees and animals that the fake objectivist was to empty of all value, save as material, had already been prepared for use by Christian missionaries who warned against idols, demons, animal exemplars. In the Middle Ages, of course, this message was not wholly heard: it was agreed that the material universe embodied images of the divine, that many things were so because they ought to be, that the 'natural' was indeed God-given. Many of the slogans now in use amongst environmentalists (as not to use a bulldozer on one's mother) are drawn from medieval rhetoric (see Merchant 1982: 29ff.). It was those who emphasized God's freedom to create whatever he pleased who denied that nature contained anything of value, and bizarrely licensed us to do as we pleased in turn. 'Natural theology', that sought to identify God's purposes from a study of the world of nature, demanded that we respect that script. If nothing could be learnt from it (since God's decision was arbitrary) then we need not respect it. All that mattered was the covenant, the convention, made with God, and the content of that agreement was just to obey commands that we could only learn about from books, and from the Church. So began the long decline into irreligion and disobedience.

There is just enough truth in this account to be uncomfortable. There is certainly no difficulty in finding arguments within the Fathers for an indifference to natural creatures that might reasonably be blamed for some of our insouciance in injuring them. Can God be supposed to care for oxen, Paul enquired? Did Jesus not reveal the unimportance of pigs by using them as a home for devils, Augustine asked? There could be no covenant with non-rational creatures, said Aquinas (after the Stoics). Whatever happens, human purposes must have precedence, and nothing is outlawed merely as being destructive of non-human purposes. More recent religious rhetoric (James Watt excepted) has preferred to emphasize that any 'dominion' granted us must be that of a steward, that we have a duty to care for God's garden and our fellow-creatures. 'Stewardship' is what counts, not tyranny. No doubt this is an improvement. But we should surely notice that 'stewards' and 'guardians' are what brigands always claim to be when they have seen reason to settle down amongst their victims. Every invading tribe in history has claimed, in the end, to be the people's friends. The people are not usually asked to say whether they wanted such protectors. Possibly they might prefer to be left alone – and so might the world of nature. The image of stewardship may help us to 'conserve' resources, just as brigands might be well advised – in their own interests – not to destroy their prey but cultivate them. Such brigands readily convince themselves that their victims could not manage without their guiding hand. But the claim is not too plausible, especially when 'stewardship' appears to license most of the same behaviour that tyranny once did, as long as we do it with a friendly smile.

The historical or sociological claim that Celts and the rest are 'closer to nature' or 'kinder to nature' than their conquerors is dubious, and condescending. But it may be that the experience of defeat is one from which we sometimes learn. 'Stewardship' is the fantasy of the kindlier sort of despot, convinced of his superior power and learning. The brutal truth is that the world can get on well enough without us, and that the best we can do for it is usually to leave well enough alone. We are not God's gardeners, and those who have had to scrape a living among the ruins are perhaps in a better position to realize their, our, abject dependency. This is no new religion. In the book of Job 'Yahweh describes himself as the wisdom that makes for the survival of the wild ass, the hamster, the eagle, the ostrich, of all living nature, and the wisdom that uproots mountains and annihilates angels' (Kallen 1969). The vision of things before which Job at last bowed his head, and repented in dust and ashes, was a cosmic democracy, in which each creature gets its turn, and is allowed its own integrity. So far from dictating that we human beings should think all nature at our disposal, the Bible constantly insists that humankind is not alone, not privileged above all others, not like God. When Babylon the great has fallen at last,

> there no Arab shall pitch his tent, nor shepherds fold their flocks. There marmots shall have their lairs and porcupines shall overrun her houses; there desert owls shall dwell and there he-goats shall gambol; jackals shall occupy her mansions, and wolves her gorgeous palaces.
>
> (Isa. 13:20f.)

> The whole earth has rest and is at peace; it breaks into cries of joy. The pines themselves and the cedars of Lebanon exult over you: since you have been laid low, they say, no man comes up to fell us.
>
> (Isa. 14:7f.)

'Woe to those who add house to house and join field to field until everywhere belongs to them and they are the sole inhabitants of the land' (Isa. 5:8). If we do not spare the land, we shall be driven from it, and 'the land shall enjoy its sabbaths to the full' (Lev. 26:34). That judgement, in Hosea's mouth, becomes in turn a prophecy of hope: stripped and driven out into the wilderness Israel will turn again to God and he 'will make a treaty on her behalf with the wild animals, with the birds of heaven and the creeping things of the earth; [he] will break bow, sword and battle in the country, and make her sleep secure' (Hos. 2:20).

REFERENCES

Attfield, R. and Dell, K. (1989) (eds) *Values, Conflict and the Environment* Oxford: Ian Ramsey Centre.

Bramwell, A. (1985) *Blood and Soil: Richard Walter Darré and Hitler's Green Party*, Abbots Brook: Kensal Press.

Burnet, T. (1965) *The Sacred Theory of the Earth*, intr. B. Willey, Fontwell: Centaur Press.

Callicott, J. B. (1989) *In Defense of the Land Ethic*, Albany: State University of New York Press.

Clark, S. R. L. (1984) *From Athens to Jerusalem*, Oxford: Clarendon Press.

—— (1992) 'Descartes' debt to Augustine', in M. McGhee (ed.) *Philosophy, Religion and the Spiritual Life*, Cambridge: Cambridge University Press, 73–88.

Clastres, P. (1977) *Society against the State*, trans. R. Hurley, New York: Urizen Books.

Code, L. (1988) 'Credibility: a double standard', in L. Code, S. Mullett and C. Overall (eds) *Feminist Perspectives: Philosophical Essays on Method and Morals*, Toronto: University of Toronto Press, 64–88.

Descartes, R. (1970) *Philosophical Letters*, ed. A. J. P. Kenny, Oxford: Clarendon Press.

Douglas, M. and Isherwood, C. (1979) *The World of Goods: Towards an Anthropology of Consumption*, London: Lane.

Fox, M. (1991) *Creation Spirituality*, San Franscisco: Harper.

Glanvill, J. (1661) *The Vanity of Dogmatizing*.

Heine, S. (1988) *Christianity and the Goddessses*, trans. J. Bowker, London: SCM Press.

Hopkins, G. M. (1970) 'Pied Beauty', in W. H. Gardner and N. H. Mackenzie (eds) *Poems of Gerard Manley Hopkins* (4th edn), London: Oxford University Press, 69–70.

Hume, D. (1962) *Enquiries* (2nd edn), ed. L. A. Selby-Bigge, Oxford: Clarendon Press.

Kallen, H (1969) 'The Book of Job', in N. N. Glatzer (ed.) *The Dimensions of Job*, New York. Schocken Books, 17ff.

Kirk, G., Raven, J. E. and Schofield, M. (eds) (1983) *The Presocratic Philosophers*, Cambridge: Cambridge University Press.

Leopold, A. (1968) *A Sand County Almanac*, New York: Oxford University Press.

Locke, J. (1963) *Two Treatises of Government*, ed. P. Laslett, New York: Cambridge University Press.

Lovelock, J. (1979) *Gaia: A New Look at the Earth*, New York: Oxford University Press.

—— (1985) *The Ages of Gaia*, Oxford: Oxford University Press.

Merchant, C. (1982) *The Death of Nature*, London: Wildwood House.

Naess, A. (1983) 'The Shallow and the Deep, Long Range Ecology Movement', *Inquiry* 16: 95–100.

Nagel, T. (1979) *Mortal Questions*, Cambridge: Cambridge University Press.

Pearce, D., Markandya, A. and Barbier, E. B. (1989) *Blueprint for a Green Economy*, London: Earthscan Publications.

Pois, R. (1986) *National Socialism and the Religion of Nature*, New York: St Martin's Press.

Sahlins, M. (1972) *Stone Age Economics*, London: Tavistock.

Simon, J. L. (1981) *The Ultimate Resource*, Oxford: Robertson & Co.

Speaight, R. (1967) *Teilhard de Chardin: A Biography*, London: Collins.

Spretnak, C. and Capra, F. (1985) *Green Politics*, London: Paladin.

Starhawk (1990) *Dreaming the Dark*, London: Unwin Hyman.

Tolkien, J. R. R. (1966) *The Lord of the Rings* (2nd edn), London: Allen & Unwin.

Toynbee, A, (1954) *A Study of History*, vol. VII, *Universal States, Universal Churches*, London: Oxford University Press.

Toynbee, A. and Ikeda, D. (1976) *Choose Life*, London: Oxford University Press.

Waddell, H. (1934) *Beasts and Saints*, London: Constable.

Weil, S. (1959) *Waiting for God*, trans. E. Crawford, London: Collins.

White, M. (1978) *The Philosophy of the American Revolution*, New York: Oxford University Press.

Willey, B. (1934) *The Seventeenth Century Background*, London: Chatto and Windus.

FURTHER READING

Attfield, R. (1983) *The Ethics of Environmental Concern*, Oxford: Basil Blackwell.

Berry, W. (1990) *What Are People For?*, London: Rider Books.

Clark, S. R. L. (1989) *Civil Peace and Sacred Order*, Oxford: Clarendon Press.

—— (1994) *How to Think About the Earth*, London: Mowbrays.

Cobb, J. B. (1972) *Is It too late?: A Theology of Ecology*, Beverley Hills: Bruce.

Elliot, R. (ed.) (1995) *Environmental Ethics*, Oxford: Clarendon Press.

Kohak, E. (1984) *The Embers and the Stars*, Chicago: University of Chicago Press.

McDaniel, J. B. (1989) *Of God and Pelicans*, Louisville: Westminster/John Knox Press.

McKibben, D. (1990) *The End of Nature*, Harmondsworth: Penguin.

Passmore, J. (1974) *Man's Responsibility for Nature*, London: Duckworth.

Primavesi, A. (1991) *From Apocalypse to Genesis*, Tunbridge Wells: Burns & Oates.

Rolston, H. (1986) *Philosophy Gone Wild*, Buffalo: Prometheus Books.

Seed, J., Fleming, P., Macy, J. and Naess, A. (1988) *Thinking like a Mountain: Towards a Council of All Beings*, London: Heretic Books.

See also chapters 24, 33, 47.

VI

CHRISTIAN THEOLOGY: SCENE AND PROSPECT

INTRODUCTION

Leslie Houlden

What, in the light of the present scene, is the future for Christian theology? Or, more sceptically, can there seriously be a future for Christian theology? As the following chapters illustrate, there are quite different ways of responding to this question. Broadly, there are intra-mural answers and extra-mural answers.

And there are also rather practical, workmanlike answers. The latter will take it for granted that, like it or not, justifiably or not, Christian thinkers, as indeed thinkers of other faiths, are going to continue being active for the foreseeable future. Then, what are they likely to interest themselves in? In a global perspective, given the overwhelming problems of famine, the North–South divide, and political instability randomly erupting into barbarism, liberation theology and its associated movements, especially some forms of black theology, and also styles of Christian thought heavily adapted to local cultures that are far removed from its old, long-lasting matrix of the West, are the most likely candidates for attention. Other close relatives of liberationism, feminist theology in particular, are products of the West itself and find their most fertile ground in that half-hospitable, half-resistant setting.

The matter of the intra- and extra-mural perspectives is more intriguing and of more far-reaching intellectual significance. What distinction is in mind here? For the intra-muralists, it is a matter of taking one's stance within the tradition as a relatively self-contained entity, of course affected by external currents of thought and culture, but thoroughly identifiable and more or less coherent in its own right, and then discerning possible lines of growth. What intellectual clarifications are desirable, perhaps already in process of emerging? Those who adopt this perspective necessarily consider present and future in the light of the past and a good deal of history features in their contributions (see especially chapters 43 and 44). They are dealing with an organic whole where continuities figure prominently.

The extra-mural observers are on the whole less assured and more sceptical. They might well be, for their task is daunting. For one thing, they have chosen to view Christian thought in one form or another of universal perspective: how does Christian theology now appear once one opts to step outside its own circle and look at it from another standpoint, one that is of necessity more detached? After all, to take one way forward along this route, Christianity has planted itself in almost every country of the world, and, while it may be most at home in the West, it has, both factually and in its missionary stance, as it were 'taken on' every form of thought under the sun. Moreover, the full recognition of its minority status in humanity at large, as one element among many and as itself irretrievably diverse and fragmented, is relatively new, and demands quite new responses.

These responses are of two kinds. It is possible to come to the conclusion, explicitly or implicitly, that Christian theology has no sensible or viable future. It will continue, of course, just as Christianity will continue, no doubt in all kinds of new varieties and manifestations. Within its own shrinking confines, the vigour of Christian theology may be undiminished and create for the insiders a great feeling of strength; but, at least as far as every measurable intellectual criterion is concerned (peer-esteem, number and prestige of academic posts, notice in the general educated world), it will cut less and less ice, and its talk will turn into more and more of a private discourse. In some respects and in some places, it has already almost reached rock bottom; though in the context of modern academic fragmentation (oddly coinciding with a growth of inter-disciplinary endeavours) it shares many features with other disciplines. But unlike the others, it has the character of a survivor, concerning itself with issues which, however much their shape may have been updated, belong essentially to and had their heyday in times long past. There can even be a sense of poignancy in so far as that past is so rich and includes towering achievements of mind and spirit. The hinge of the Enlightenment, coming up for comment so often in this volume, really did make all the difference, and there is no mileage to be gained in trying to exorcize it as a devilish intruder. Indeed, much in Christian theology itself would point to a duty to come to terms with the given cuckoo in the nest, to make something good out of even the most threatening new presence.

But it is certainly not surprising if some extra-muralists exhibit an anxious pessimism for Christian theology. And they are not cheered by what they see as the complacency and a-priorism of the intra-muralists, for all their fertility of mind and success in achieving their own agendas.

There are, however, other kinds of extra-mural response. If Christian theology, as traditionally conceived, has reached something of a terminus, that need not be the end of theology itself. We live in the global village, and maybe there are brighter prospects if we bring all the world faiths within our sights, discover common ground and, to our mutual enrichment, seek to unify the religious quest of the human race in its diverse profundity. This more positive response is plainly virtuous and has important devotees, who are attracted to it academically as well as for religious and public-spirited reasons.

Not unnaturally, membership of an increasingly worldwide academic 'club' prompts sympathetic scholars to foster a universal fellowship of faiths too. But, in the face of the staggering traditionalism and perhaps increasing self-assertion of the vast majority of the adherents of the great faiths (including Christianity itself), the proposal has something of the well-meaning but hopeless common sense of the Esperanto movement in the area of language; however socially desirable its efforts, especially in some multi-cultural Western societies, once more the Enlightenment broods gloomily over the scene.

Intellectual Christianity having come through that ordeal (or process of stimulation and purification, according to taste), it is divided formidably from the other world faiths that have not undergone the same experience or anything approaching it. That day may be dawning, but not much more so far, and its prospect is not wholly reassuring. In the meantime, common ground is found at the level of conceptual tendencies, sometimes over-generalized or abstracted perceptions of what a religion is said to stand for (as if religions were monoliths), and of course out of a common concern for the religious dimension of human life.

This is not the only extra-muralist response of a positive kind. It is possible still to hope to formulate a purged and credible way of Christian thinking that has digested the lessons stemming from the Enlightenment and since – and has not despaired. For getting a hearing, it can count on those who, while dissatisfied with traditional Christianity and with those in the theological world who fail to come to terms with what seem compelling criticisms, sailing on regardless, are still equally dissatisfied with the secularist alternatives, whether intellectual or social, whose capacity to impoverish seem inexhaustible. These ideological orphans need not (though they may) be wistful for a past that they recognize to be irrecoverable; they may be conscious rather of the dimension of what can be called 'unfinishedness' in human life and aspiration. It is certainly necessary, to do justice to this constituency, to pitch it more widely than the merely ethical: they are concerned for more than the degeneration of society, which they may see as symptom or effect rather than as the heart of the matter.

The beliefs that may be acknowledged in relation to this style of transcendence will vary greatly, from types of demythologized orthodoxy, long on the scene, through the exploration of non-conceptual, narrative styles of theological statement and sensibility, endeavouring to raise their stock in Christian esteem, to attempts to build up valid responses to the mystery in things and the aesthetic and moral demands upon us, in essence, some form of renewed natural theology. It is impossible to tell whether such attempts to frame various versions of 'atheist Christianity' or belief in a 'non-realist God' will have any drawing power or indeed any survival power, religiously or theologically; even though their proponents often claim that they represent what many (including their outspoken opponents) actually believe – if the test of belief is what makes a difference to the way you think and act. The world which extra-muralists of this ilk look out on is, obviously, much more secular, generally more Western, than that of the 'world faiths' response. In one sense, it is a less exclusively religious world: these are not people who are chiefly focused on the religious inheritance of humanity but rather on the human predicament as they encounter it. In another sense, it is more Christian, for however far-reaching its denial of traditional Christian beliefs, it stems from a profound sense of the religious dimension in all things, whose roots lie in the old Christian convictions of creation and incarnation – the divine pervasiveness (however you define 'divine'), 'the dearest freshness deep down things'.

Readers of the following chapters (and the later chapters in Part 2, on the Tradition, also bear on our subject) will not find it hard to allocate them to the different tendencies and reactions that have been discussed and may like to indulge in the game of identification. Some are clear cut, others replicate within themselves aspects of the debates and conflicts that are to be found on the present scene. This is, after all, not the end of a story, only one more moment in a very long process. It is a process in which it has proved far easier for new ideas to appear than for old ones ever quite to be laid to rest. As now, so often in the past, Christian thought has seemed to contemporaries to be in crisis, even on the verge of dissolution and extinction. To those coming after, whether they look back with gratitude or regret, the episode in question has looked rather less catastrophic – and certainly not as constituting an end under which a line had finally to be drawn. Things have a way of falling into place. At the time, it is rarely possible, and often rash, to foresee how things will go. The intra-muralists have caution on their side and a certain kind of realism when it comes to looking towards a future for Christian theology. They can also point to its formidable sticking-power, protected in the past (but in the future?) not just by inherent conservatism of a kind that modern circumstances of communication and information render outmoded but by strong institutions like the papacy and episcopate, often the temporal power, and even great authoritative books of theological synthesis. The extra-muralists, with their broader horizons, have a more hazardous task, but they too may trust in the inexhaustible well-spring in the Christian spirit. We can be virtually certain that the outcome will surprise us.

41

THE CHARACTER AND POSSIBILITY OF CHRISTIAN THEOLOGY TODAY

John Kent

CHRISTIAN IDENTITY

Is there still, in the last years of the twentieth century, a sustainable, as distinct from a recognizable, Christian identity? The major churches, in answering this question affirmatively, appeal to the authority of their sacred Scriptures, historic creeds and confessions; as churches, they present themselves as authoritative, and even as supernaturally guided, interpreters of what has been handed down from the primitive Church in text and tradition. They base their ecumenical policies on the assumption that despite existing differences in doctrine, worship, and ethics they share a common identity which could be expressed in a common theology and structure. This does not mean that their attitude to doctrine is entirely static; they accept, in theory at any rate, the possibility of theological change, but the theories of development which they prefer do not justify either radical rejection of traditional doctrine or more than minor doctrinal adjustment to changing historical conditions. Nor do these churches officially admit that within their ranks – in what might be called the existential, as distinct from the institutional, Church – reinterpretation of some traditional doctrines, for example that of eternal punishment, has gone so far as to be tantamount to a repudiation of what earlier Christians generally believed. For the churches as institutions the identity of Christianity, supernaturally revealed and guaranteed, has not changed, whatever the appearances. The final authority of Scripture and tradition remains unimpaired, however diverse interpretation may become: although there are many cases in which Scripture and tradition settle nothing, nothing can be settled apart from them. The strength of this position explains the anxiety of innovating Christian individuals or groups to claim religious and theological continuity with the past: in the sixteenth century Protestants argued that they, and not Roman Catholics, were faithful to the traditions of the primitive church, while in the nineteenth century what was decisive for John Henry Newman in his shift from Anglicanism to Roman Catholicism was his belief in the closer identity of Roman Catholicism with the patristic Church. In the 1990s, Anglican opponents of the ordination of women attacked the proposal as a departure from Scripture and tradition so radical as to make it impossible to guarantee the future identity of Christianity.

In these examples one sees an anxiety to establish identity in the most detailed terms possible. Christianity was to be objectified as a specific visible institution, the Church, which offers through the unbroken succession of apostles and bishops from the time when Jesus lived the only divinely provided means of salvation from divine judgement; for this reason the Church is justified in seeking to impose on any surrounding culture a 'Christian' world-outlook, ethical system and liturgy. The problem of protecting this underlying identity, a problem shared by all the main branches of Christianity, is not a new one. This traditional solution has been described (against an eighteenth-century background) by the American scholar, Hans Frei, in *The Eclipse of Biblical Narrative* in these terms.

> there was only one seemingly watertight device for protecting the theological indispensability of historical revelation against deistic insinuations of a natural, nonpositive, saving knowledge of God. This was a root and branch affirmation of the specific historical event of original, inherited, and naturally unexpungeable guilt, the fatal moral, metaphysical, and noetic flaw which could be wiped out only by a similarly factual saving occurrence (the Work of Christ).
>
> (Frei 1974: 61–2)

Starting from this basis in the notion of the Fall there was constructed what Frei calls a simple, over-arching narrative, broadly based on the Bible, which ran from the Creation to the Final Judgement. Frei's use of the word 'narrative' seems inaccurate, however, to the extent that this theological scheme was for long regarded as fixed in historical time by the recent birth, death, resurrection and ascension of Jesus, as well as by the historically 'factual' human fall. As far as the first seventeen hundred years of Christianity were concerned, this theological account of the universe and of humanity's place in it was therefore much more than myth (or 'narrative' in Frei's sense): God had intervened once and for all in Herod's Palestine and in doing so had guaranteed the truth of the Christian explanation of past as well as future human experience.

General cultural confidence in the absoluteness of Christian theology gradually declined as the political West expanded into the non-Christian world. One can see an earlier version of this process in the magnificent thirteenth-century Norman cathedral at Monreale in Sicily, where Frei's narrative is pictured in vivid clarity in the mosaics which cover the walls. But although the walls of Monreale seem to declare that the identity of Christianity is absolutely secure, it is worth remembering that the Norman rulers of early medieval Sicily were fascinated by the Arab society which they had conquered; they had no policy of forcible conversion to Christianity. This did not mean that they had a problem with the identity of Christianity, but that, living and fighting on the southern frontier of the Christian West, they also encountered at first hand the identity of Islam.

We cannot discuss the encounter here: it is enough to say that from the end of the medieval period the validity of Christian theology has always been under pressure from outside as well as inside the institutional Churches. The decline of the intellectual hegemony of the Christian world-view in the West became more obvious after 1945 because the collapse of the old colonial empires transformed the context of Christianity in all the traditional centres of Christian missionary expansion. At the same time the population of Europe became much more mixed in religious terms, a process which is likely to continue. In a post-missionary situation the Churches had to decide whether to acknowledge the possibility of individual salvation (however defined) through religions other than Christianity. To grant the idea of parity in the matter of salvation would have shattered the mainstream Churches' traditional sense of Christian identity, and so one finds the Second Vatican Council, for example, in its declaration on *The Relation of the Church to Nonchristian Religions* (Flannery 1975) saying cautiously that the Catholic Church rejected nothing that was 'true and holy' in other religions. Nevertheless, *Nostra Aetate* said, the Catholic Church was bound to proclaim Christ, in whom God reconciled all things to himself, and in whom 'men find the fulness of their religious life' (Flannery 1975: 739).

The presence of the world 'fulness' implied the use of an inclusivist theological system which sought to reconcile other religions to Christianity in an all-embracing religious unity whose centre would be the Christian Trinity. The Anglican theologian, Brooke Westcott, was already exploring this possibility in the late nineteenth century, and, more recently, Raimundo Panikkar has offered a Roman Catholic version of the same approach. There was no official question of parity between religions, only of respect: for example, in the post-conciliar *Guidelines on Religious Relations with the Jews* (1974) Rome stated that 'lest the witness of Catholics to Jesus Christ give offence to Jews, they must take care to live and spread their Christian faith while maintaining the strictest respect for religious liberty' (Flannery 1975: 744). The propriety of seeking to convert Jews to Christianity was not questioned.

For Protestantism there was no similar voice of central authority, even after the formation of the World Council of Churches in 1948, but the main Protestant Churches would not have gone further than the Vatican. The Churches could not easily accept a Christian identity which had now to be shared on something like equal terms with that of other religions. Individual Protestant theologians, like Karl Barth in the late 1930s, still advocated the absolute truth of Christianity to the exclusion of the non-Christian religions, on the ground that the human knowledge of God depended entirely on God's revelation of himself in Jesus Christ. After the Second World War, however, as the intercultural situation began to change rapidly, the intellectual drive to historicize (i.e. see in their original context) the basic documents of

Christianity, a drive which had developed gradually since the later seventeenth century, reasserted itself strongly. It is significant that at this time Roman Catholic scholars, under the influence of Hubert Jedin, historicized the Tridentine theological system, which for generations had seemed almost as absolute as Scripture. Protestant theologians like Wilfred Cantwell Smith and Ninian Smart, taking a much wider view, argued that religious systems are not divinely revealed, but are a product of the human imagination in a specific historical context; one should not, therefore, assert that any one system is the only true one. From this historicizing point of view the establishment of Christian identity does not depend on an absolute ecclesiastical authority supernaturally empowered to define the Creed and discipline the faithful. Christian theologies would be better thought of as possible sets of symbols concerned with the meaning of existence: their authority depends on their intellectual and existential persuasiveness. In such a context the visible Churches remain more or less authoritative guides to the past identities of Christianity: its future identity has become an open question. One of the driving forces behind this position is historical relativism, to which we now turn.

HISTORICISM AND HISTORICAL RELATIVISM

By the early nineteenth century the link between historical writing and philosophy had been loosened. Increasingly, historians parted company from the theologians and philosophers who had previously set the framework of their thinking for them. 'What man is, only his history tells', said Wilhelm Dilthey (1833–1911), and he meant that Christianity, together with all other religions, was a product of human history, not a supernatural power introduced into human history from outside. What had happened in the past had left traces ('documents' of written and other kinds) from which the historian, working (as R. G. Collingwood suggested) like an ideal detective, could produce an imaginative but critical approximation to truth. It even seemed possible that the historian might be able to go beyond the documented presentation of 'what had actually happened' in a limited series of events such as, for example, the Glencoe Massacre, and that one might be able to work out from the facts generalizations which would have the status of laws of history.

By the end of the nineteenth century there was a strong tendency to assume that the historical process must be explicable in terms of development or progress, and that a thorough analysis of the facts was bound to show the overall direction of events, a position which implied an analogy between historical science and physical science. Nevertheless, there was no necessary connection between nineteenth-century historicism and theories of progress: professional historians were above all concerned with the improvement of historical method. Karl Popper, in his book, *The Poverty of Historicism*, argued that historicism aspired to predict the course of human history by scientific or other rational methods, but this view exaggerated one side of historicism, especially that of the materialist utopianism of the Marxist tradition, which itself grew out of the very different Hegelian vision of human history as the temporal theatre of a supernatural process. Popper rejected both the Hegelian and the Marxist positions, and with them 'the possibility of a theoretical history, that is to say, of a historical social science that would correspond to theoretical physics' (Popper 1963: 6).

Most professional historians, however, were less concerned with theoretical sociology than with how one used documents in order to visualize and reproduce specific events in the past. At this level historical method gradually influenced the traditional conservatism of biblical scholarship in its approach to the New Testament text. The professional historian, for example, took for granted his freedom to reject, in certain circumstances, what his authorities (the documents) said. The New Testament scholar, on the other hand, has usually been committed to theological assumptions which had priority over what the professional historian has regarded as historical enquiry. This has meant that, apart from a brief period at the beginning of the twentieth century (when, for example, Ernst Troeltsch (1865–1923) wrote *The Absoluteness of Christianity and the History of Religions* in 1901, in order to question the absoluteness of Christianity), Christianity has been described and analysed in its own terms, as though other religions, their history, religious texts and ethical attitudes existed in an outside, religiously irrelevant, world. One of the results has been a distortion of the history of the Jews, both before and after the first century CE, to suit Christian assumptions, and a reliance on a version of Judaism as a religion to which Christianity is automatically taken to have been superior. Another traditional tendency has been to approach the Gospels through the Epistles, so that interpretations of the material about Jesus have often been dominated by theological interpretations of the meaning of Paul.

Given the assumptions of the professional historian, however, one is obliged, as the Finnish New Testament scholar, Heikki Räisänen says, to face the fact that

> the actual pluralism of the religious traditions forces a scholar concerned with truth-questions to a certain kind of reductionism which will affect the model of Christianity which emerges: he is bound to reduce the often absolute claims found in his sources to a more relative size, if for no other reason than that he has to relate them to claims found in other sources (unless he is content with simply reproducing the rival claims). Taking one's sources seriously cannot possibly mean that the scholar must give everything the same significance as the sources themselves do. For instance, it is impossible to accept simultaneously on an objective level both the claims made by the New Testament writers about Jesus and the claims made in the Qu'ran about the revelations received by Muhammad.
>
> (Räisänen 1990: 135–6)

In effect, Troeltsch was making the same point in 1901, when he wrote that

> it is impossible for historical thought to believe the Christian miracles but deny the

879

nonChristian. Again, however frequently one may discern something supernatural in the ethical power of the inner life, no means exist by which to construe the Christian's elevation above sensuality as supernatural while interpreting that of Plato or Epictetus as natural.

(Troeltsch 1972: 48)

The argument also applies to religious experiences: 'the religious experiences of mankind neutralise themselves, as it were, on the level of interpretation; no single experience can be provided with such emphasis as the person in question claims' (Räisänen 1990: 199). One may isolate Christianity from the rest of history and then define it as the absolute norm, but the result is implausible. There has been a growing awareness of the extent to which both religions and ethical systems are culturally conditioned. As Dilthey said, the new historical consciousness revealed the relativity of every metaphysical and religious doctrine.

What became clear was that the historian, however rich his documentation might be, could not demonstrate the absolute truth of a particular interpretation of history but was left with his own subjective version of events, which others might or might not find plausible. The classic criticism of the 'objectivity' which historicism pursued can be found in Friedrich Nietzsche (1844–1900), who described it as 'a condition in the historian which permits him to observe an event in all its motivations and consequences so purely that it has no effect at all on his own subjectivity'. The analogy (he said) was with the aesthetic detachment with which a painter was supposed to react to a landscape: 'it is a superstition, however, that the picture which these things evoke in a [painter] is a true reproduction of the empirical nature of the things themselves'. The outcome of artistic creation

may be an artistically true painting but cannot be an historically true one . . . To think of history objectively in this fashion . . . is to think of all things in relation to all others and to weave the isolated event into the whole, always with the presupposition that if a unity of plan does not already reside in things it must be implanted in them. Thus man spins his web over the past and subdues it, thus he gives expression to his artistic drive – but not his drive toward truth or justice. Objectivity and justice have nothing whatever to do with one another.

And he quoted from the Austrian dramatist, Franz Grillparzer: 'What is history but the way in which the spirit of man apprehends events impenetrable to him?' (Nietzsche 1983: 91–2).

Nevertheless, the cult of objectivity died hard, and a distinguished mid-twentieth-century Christian historian like Herbert Butterfield still thought it possible that one could divest oneself of one's own moral, political and religious assumptions, and interpret the past for its own sake in its own terms. There is a sense in which the historian can, by an effort of the imagination, transcend his own cultural situation and comprehend other perspectives; one must not, as Karl Popper has said, transform something which is difficult into something which is altogether impossible. In the case of the New Testament, however, this does not in itself dispose of the challenge of historical relativism. One can, for example, describe a typical Greek temple, with its external sacrificial platform and its inner, symbolic cella. One can suggest a relationship between the killing of animals *outside* and the presence of the god/goddess *inside* the temple, and one can introduce an intellectual discussion of sin and sacrifice. One can make similar suggestions in the case of the sacrifices at Jerusalem, where Herod's temple was essentially similar in design (as E. P. Sanders does, for example, in *Judaism, Practice and Belief 63BCE-66CE*, 1992, especially pp. 103–18). One can in some ways relate the societies in which this was (or seems to have been for the majority of people) normal behaviour, to modern Judaeo-Christian society, in which there is, strictly speaking, no such behaviour, though the Judaism of the Diaspora seems to have abandoned physical sacrifice (which involved the shedding of blood) more thoroughly than was the case in some varieties of Christian eucharistic theology. It is much less convincing to say that we 'comprehend' these pre-Christian and indeed ancient Christian religious perspectives.

Great edifices have been reared on the basis of Hans-Georg Gadamer's proposal, in *Truth and Method* (1960), of the possibility of a 'fusion of horizons', a process in which the 'horizon' of the contemporary reader, which includes the prejudices and preconceptions carried from his/her presence in a tradition, is to be transformed by the 'horizon' of the pre-modern text which is being read. There remains, it can be said nevertheless, a gap which one cannot cross between the late twentieth-century self and the ancient societies which expressed themselves religiously through the temple sacrifice. One of the principal aims of the modern historical tradition was to recreate past events in the living experience of the present, but one cannot recreate the temple sacrifice, either in Greece, or in Jerusalem, or in Aztec Mexico. One can play it out as drama, as sophisticated fiction, but one cannot re-enact it. Playing it out is certainly an act of the imagination, but it remains an act of a twentieth-century imagination, and this is the core of the historical relativist's perception. One can seek to study, in the manner of the school of modern French historians who took their name from the periodical, *Annales*, the 'mentalité' of the Jews who lived at the time of Jesus, but how far is it possible to understand in what sense Jesus and those who knew him while he was alive accepted or rejected the Temple sacrifices? And to what extent is what we are studying here the mentality of popular religion, which is usually thought of as having a certain coherence, and to what extent is it the mentality of a small elite, for whom the existence of many alternative sets of ideas would have allowed freedom for individual choice, thus weakening the force of any attempt at generalization? Despite much confident writing, there is no way in which we can speak with certainty about what went on in the mind of Jesus himself. The widely differing images of Jesus which scholarship has produced even since 1945 tell their own story. The use of the historical method has seemed at times to cut Christian symbolism off from any historical root, leaving a series of pictures – the Fall, the birth of Jesus, his miracles, death, resurrection and ascension – like so many poetic images, which can be used to support statements about God, men and women in history, but which draw little strength from history themselves.

Nevertheless, some recent scholars seem unworried by the problem of Christianity's historical roots. Robert Morgan, for example, in *Biblical Interpretation* (1988), said that

> Christian theology is reflection on a faith in God which centres on the incarnate, crucified, and risen Lord Jesus. This faith is nourished by the Gospel story and stories. Such a faith does not need the historical reality of Jesus to be laid bare or fully disclosed. But it does need to know that it is based on historical reality, and that it has nothing to fear from historical research.
>
> (Morgan with Barton 1988: 121)

The two parts of this statement, 'the Gospel story and stories' and 'the historical reality of Jesus', are not very convincingly attached together. When he turns later to the question of Jesus' eschatological teaching, moreover, Morgan says that

> a degree of agnosticism is appropriate among historians. Jesus' understanding of God and the future was probably more elusive than that of his questioners or his followers, and even the latter can only be fragmentarily known. The argument back to Jesus from Paul's eschatology (itself not wholly clear), through the first followers, who have left no records and were perhaps slow to understand, and so to Jesus' grasp of what can never be adequately expressed, is highly precarious.
>
> (Ibid.: 244)

It is surely the theologians, rather than the historians, who need 'a degree of agnosticism' here. Morgan's argument draws its force from the assumption of an external, ahistorical perspective from which the 'history' of the New Testament can be seen in a desirable light.

For the historical relativist, who prefers the historical to the theological method of reading the text, the content of the New Testament is one example of the way in which cultural systems produce their own particular religious accounts of human existence. At the historical level, both the biblical stories in the form in which we have received them and the 'mentalité' of the Jewish society in New Testament Palestine, either before or after the life of Jesus himself, are not easy to decipher, and there is the further problem that in the late twentieth century our reading and interpretation of the New Testament are moulded partly by theological systems inherited from periods (and 'mentalities') much later than that of the New Testament itself, those of the Reformation and of Counter-Reformation Catholicism, for example, and partly by a world-view transformed by scientific knowledge. As Maurice Wiles wrote with the doctrine of the Incarnation in mind:

> the rise of the modern historical consciousness has, in some degree or another, made historical relativists of us all . . . I mean that when we think and speak most carefully, we recognize the need to assess all statements, especially statements of

fundamental belief, in relation to the particular cultural situation of the time . . . This makes it extremely difficult for us (I am tempted to say impossible, but that would be to prejudge the issue) to ascribe absolute authority to any particular occasion or to any particular set of experiences within the world.

(Wiles 1974: 45)

More strongly still, a critical theologian like Van Harvey (1967) was prepared to argue that

we cannot see the world as the first [Christian] century saw it. We can, it is true, imaginatively understand how they could have believed what they believed, but these beliefs are no longer practically possible for us . . . We have a new consciousness, and although we can transcend it from time to time in an act of historical imagination, we judge what we understand in the light of our own present knowledge and interpret it in the terms of our own existing 'world'.

(Van Harvey 1967: 114)

It follows from this that, instead of defining Christianity as though it possessed a knowable supernatural identity essentially independent of the culture within which it was formed, historical relativists, and the theologians influenced by them, treat it as a historical phenomenon. Such a definition does not make a modern Christian identity impossible: one still has, in the late twentieth century, a recognizable religion in a variety of more or less justifiable forms, with a particular past in the course of which change, from the religiously uncommitted historian's point of view, legitimately took place. Neither identity nor the question of truth disappear in a flood of subjectivism. What is lost is the plausibility of asserting that there is a specific historical basis for identifying Christianity as the one true religion over against others; and the plausibility of arguing that if, for example, a male priesthood had ascertainable historical roots in the first five centuries of the Christian era then there can never be female priests in any later period. Nor is there anything necessarily sacred about the historical forms which Christian institutions have taken, either in theology or in organization, as though the true Christian identity were ineluctably bound up with a certain form of thought or Church. It follows that when one looks at the Church-in-history, and tries to write ecclesiastical history, one has to remember that one is, in the broadest sense, making it up, for the narrative differs radically according to whether one chooses an official Roman Catholic, a feminist, an independent Protestant, or some less committed interpretation. Karl Barth's attempt, for example, to cut free from historical contingency in the name of a Church founded on a divine revelatory intervention in Jesus Christ fails disastrously if one considers that Barth was not really defending 'revelation', truth against liberal heresy, but defending a particular, post-Reformation interpretation of the Bible which slanted the text in the way that the sixteenth-century mainline Protestants preferred. As Dennis Nineham put it: 'Barth demands that a modern Christian should work with categories which belong to fifth-century and sixteenth-century cultures and have no natural link with the rest of his Weltanschauung – are indeed irresolubly paradoxical within it' (Nineham 1977: 158).

There is no simple intellectual way, therefore, of privileging the New Testament text and its interpretations, so that they remain untouched by the relativism inherent in our post-modern situation. An authoritarian social system can will ecclesiastical absolutes into existence and equip them with legal power, but such a policy never lasts. There is no certainty that the human past has conformed to any significant, knowable underlying structure other than that which scientific research is gradually clarifying. The fresh theological emphasis placed in some quarters on an ahistorical final judgement which will somehow make good the moral ambiguities of history, shows an awareness of this.

FEMINISM AND CHRISTIAN THEOLOGY

There is yet another aspect of modern cultural change which may influence the historian and which throws considerable doubt on the stability of the traditional identity of Christian theology. This is the possibility that radical changes in some aspects of human consciousness may have taken place since the time of Jesus. The philosopher, Leon Pompa, for example, has pointed out that such a change may place the historian in considerable disagreement with the assumptions and conclusions of his predecessors.

> Dependent on the nature of the change, it may . . . involve the more or less complete abandonment of a certain kind of account as being based upon presuppositions which are now held to be false or partial or unacceptable in some other way. Examples of this might be . . . the growth of feminist history which is currently occurring under the influence of changing beliefs about the nature of women and their place in society.

He said that although feminist history originally began as though it were simply a matter of attending to previously overlooked aspects of the past,

> it is now developing into a new genre as it is coming to be realised that what is required is a new framework within which to write histories in which women are viewed not under traditional categories but in quite different relations to almost the whole range of activities, interests and attitudes to be found in social life.
>
> (Pompa 1990: 221)

This is not a matter of asserting that 'human nature' has changed, but of arguing that our perception of what is indicated by human nature has altered greatly.

From this root stem feminist history and feminist theology, which have combined to cut deeply into the assumption that we have an acceptable Christian interpretation of history, which is what both traditional theologians and ecclesiastical historians have for the most part assumed that they possessed. It is no longer just a question whether there is 'a great cultural gap which separates Jesus and his contemporaries from all things "modern" ', as Professor Nineham wrote in *The Myth of God Incarnate* (1977a: 192). There is also the question how far the historian's attempt to understand Palestinian culture in the time of Jesus has been distorted by assumptions which a feminist historian and theologian like Elisabeth Schüssler Fiorenza would reject as part of the dominant patriarchal culture of the West. The historicist tradition (and this was also true of biblical scholars) had been predominantly male. Fiorenza applied the hermeneutic of suspicion to historicism (she had no love for von Ranke) and claimed to have demonstrated the existence of a persistent Christian tradition of androcentric scholarship which had ignored or suppressed the role of women in the early Church, treating them as a naturally subordinate part of a male culture. This had involved the distortion of a primary, egalitarian 'Jesus Movement', in which women were often the leaders, into hierarchic Christian churches which had absorbed a Graeco-Roman ethos and had integrated an Aristotelian patriarchy into their life and theology – although, Fiorenza commented, 'there is not one story or statement transmitted in which Jesus demands the cultural and patriarchal adaptation and submission of women' (Fiorenza 1983: 247). It is interesting to note that Fiorenza's feminist picture of the early Church resembles in some ways what has been a recurrent radical image of the ecclesia in Christian history. Despite the constant pressure of the social and ecclesiastical hierarchy, there has been intermittent conflict between hierarchical and egalitarian versions of the Christian community. In the present century the hierarchical (and episcopal) ideal has been in the ascendant in the main Christian Churches, and it is not untrue to say that the dissenting tradition has been given a minor role in most historical work.

Nevertheless, however much Fiorenza's reconstruction and reinterpretation of the history of the early Church may be open to criticism on evidential grounds, it offers a substantial challenge to accepted ideas about the identity of primitive Christianity. Feminist history as ruthless as this threatens to complete the process of cutting off Christian theology, radical as well as orthodox, from its historical links with Roman Palestine, by adding to the older relativist's picture of the cultural otherness of the Ancient World, and our sense of the general fallibility of modern historical perspectives, the revelation of a one-sidedness in the canonical text of the New Testament which reflects a failure in its own perception of men and women in society; this in turn weakens the religious authority of the image of God which has traditionally been established on the basis of the text. As Dorothee Sölle, the most distinguished German feminist theologian of the post-war generation, has written:

> I am concerned with more than the 'feminine characteristics' [in God] which enlightened men are prepared to recognise today. Such talk disturbs me because it is as if God might be in himself and above all male, and as if the Feminine which had remained hidden 'in him' must now be worked out as an additional trait.

According to this way of thinking, the feminine exists in God as the child is recognisably in the man. But it is not enough to want to discover the hitherto unrecognised feminine in the familiarly masculine God: the feminist critique has not gone far enough yet within the work of such deconstruction . . . Our inward difficulty does not lie in the more or less false images of God which have been transmitted to us; and we cannot overcome the spiritual alienation in which we live by setting up statues of the goddess, images of matriarchy, in the emptied temples. We are not lacking in images but in definable experience of God. We are trapped in a strait-jacket of male authoritarian language, incapable of giving a name to what is experienced, the secret of life which we call God.

(King 1992: 42)

If, from the feminist point of view, the available Christian theological language turns out to reflect a secular patriarchal culture, then women's religious experience lacks definable expression, and one has to take great care to avoid being drawn back into using images which conceal what has taken place.

Another feminist theologian, Dr Daphne Hampson, whom some would label post-Christian, has argued on essentially historical grounds that Christian theology has no intellectual space in which to evolve out of the errors of the past: for her, Christianity is trapped in its origins, bound to a perceived revelation of God, through a particular man, in a particular place, at a particular time; as a religion it depends on its claim to have been given a specific historical revelation and it cannot abandon its historical origins and give a fresh account of itself by discovering feminine characteristics in God. For Hampson, therefore, the historical issue is paramount: Christianity is immoral, because historically patriarchal and sinful, because of the damage which it has done to women historically. One cannot make a theological escape from the historical problem by asserting that the truth of the Christian theological system has to be found at the level of myth, because this only means using the myth to justify patriarchal society. Feminism raises the question whether the Christian myth is either moral or true, and here Hampson goes further than other leading feminist theologians, Dorothee Sölle, Rosemary Ruether and Mary Grey, for example, and argues that the central Christian theme of sacrifice, salvation through suffering, might appeal to the male warrior but not to the woman who has freed herself from male role-models.

Feminist theology has been treated with caution by other scholars, and there is force in the comment by Ann Loades that non-feminist theologians should make a serious attempt to appreciate feminist theology of a constructive kind, 'unless, of course, they are content to maintain unchanged a tradition some elements of which are deeply offensive to those women who want to remain within mainstream Christianity' (Ford 1989: 249–50). In this context it is interesting that a leading New Testament scholar, Robert Morgan, allows that Fiorenza, for example, makes a good historical case for separating Jesus himself from the patriarchal ethos, and continues:

since the New Testament records aim to interpret Jesus theologically, such a claim

886

to the historical truth about him has to be taken seriously. It would be very bad theology to allow a purely historical interpretation of Jesus to replace the evangelists' theological interpretations, but within a christian theological frame of reference new historical insights can find a valuable role.

He concludes, however, that 'especially in Old Testament scholarship, Jewish and Christian feminist interests are best articulated through a literary criticism which explores the feminine imagery which is present in the tradition but insufficiently appreciated' (Morgan with Barton 1988: 158–9). This is an example of the position criticized by Sölle as limiting feminist theology to the discovery of 'feminine characteristics in God'. For Morgan, the theologian has to work from the faith, which has already been largely organized into a doctrinal system, of a believing community. Fiorenza's use of the historical approach to the New Testament as a way of generating a new theological understanding of Christianity, is interpreted as a reversion to a historicist method which reduces the Bible to source-material for the history of religion, and which does not sustain and structure the faith of the contemporary religious community (Morgan with Barton 1988: 199). This is tantamount to saying that only in the most extraordinary circumstances would the faith in its organized forms yield to the pressure of the critical historian of religion. Morgan seems to share the position of the American 'post-liberals' – Hans Frei, George Lindbeck, and Stanley Hauerwas – for whom the clear articulation of the believing community's apprehension of its own theological tradition is the nearest that it can come to establishing authority. A large edifice has indeed been built on the basis of Hans Gadamer's *Truth and Method* (1960). None of these theologians envisages the possibility that there may be a large 'community' of believing women whose outlook is not very different from that of Fiorenza, Ruether and Sölle, for example, and who share the hermeneutic of suspicion.

Here the orthodox defence against historicism is to leave the historian as little theological room as possible: in academic terms, he must write from within the community or be classed as a student of the history of religion. Morgan made this attitude clear when he wrote that 'disinterested historical research is quite likely to lead away from contemporary religious use of the Bible' (Morgan with Barton 1988: 184). The historical method has not produced agreed results but a tangle of competing hypotheses: therefore the 'community' must cut the tangle by turning to its own theological interpretations of the biblical text with the aim of criticizing religious faith from within in order to purify it, not destroy it (ibid.: 197). This has the added advantage that it is what the Churches already see themselves as doing. The theory assumes the existence in the community of both a self-authenticating faith and also of an inherited systematic theology of largely unquestionable value. This explains why, in *The Nature of Doctrine* (1984), George Lindbeck defended a regulative approach in which the job of the systematic theologian is to describe the rules of the religious language accepted in the community (in his case Lutheran): any significant shift of theological definition would require the assent of faith.

James Mackey, however, a more radical theologian, tries to liberate an existential community from the absoluteness of the institution (in his case what he calls 'the straitjacket' of Roman Catholic ecclesiastical law) by arguing, in *Modern Theology: A Sense of Direction* (1987), that the primary Christian community is the eucharistic community. 'The eucharistic criterion has priority because formal teaching is subservient to the drama in which divinity is encountered and to the story told in the drama, both of which formal teaching must simply seek to explain' (Mackey 1987: 152). At first sight, the appeal to the experience of eucharistic faith solves the historical question, but Mackey's radicalism also depends on the claim that

> there seems to be no gainsaying Schillebeeckx's conclusions that in the beginning it was the local community that celebrated, or, as modern jargon would have it, concelebrated, the eucharist. Nobody had to be specially ordained to celebrate the Supper or preside at it. No special 'sacred power' was conferred on anyone for the purpose. There were no priests in this new religion. Its founder was not a priest.

> (Ibid.: 142)

Schillebeeckx's position will not surprise anyone familiar with liberal Protestant scholarship, but his are far from uncontested views (not least in the Vatican) and Mackey's use of them suggests once again that serious arguments about Christian origins, and therefore about the kind of Christian community which should exist at the present time, cannot be settled properly either by appealing to Gadamer's 'fusion of horizons', as Mackey does, or by restricting the conversation to 'the contemporary religious use of the Bible' in the light of faith and theological traditions, in the style of the post-liberals. Another specific instance of the way in which historical judgements may affect theological opinions may be found in the controversy about secularization.

SECULARIZATION

Strictly speaking, secularization is a word used to describe the historical changes, starting in the sixteenth century and accelerating in the late eighteenth, through which the Christian Churches in the West have been gradually stripped of most of the economic, social and political influence which they once had. Much of the social work which they did in the past is now carried out by the so-called caring professions, whose members have no necessary connection with the Churches. Empirical evidence also exists of the Churches' loss of religious influence over individuals: there is, for example, a twentieth-century decline in Western church attendance, in the number of the clergy, both Catholic and Protestant, in the number of live births followed by baptism, and in the general acceptance of ecclesiastical law where sexuality is concerned.

Sociologists of religion have studied such data intensively in search of a

888

general theory, and have postulated a secularizing process, associated with the growth of a scientific, industrial, urban mass culture; they have sometimes suggested that this process would finally bring about the disappearance of religion. One should distinguish, however, between religious behaviour in general, which seems to be surviving such pressures, though often in privatized forms, and the weakening of specific religious institutions like the main Christian Churches. As far as Christianity is concerned, there has undoubtedly been an increase in the number of people in the modern West who consciously assimilate and analyse their everyday experience without reference to Christian theological ideas. The American sociologist, Peter Berger, called this attitude 'subjective secularisation' (Berger 1969: 113). 'Subjective secularisation' is always likely to be incomplete, because the consciousness which has become empty of specific Christian beliefs about the transcendent may still harbour religious ideas and impulses, but the detachment from traditional Christian ideas makes the survival of a Church, a community created by a common theology, as well as the theology itself, difficult.

> Any religion loses influence when the social–psychological roots by which it is anchored in the everyday life of its adherents – a unanimous though implicit assent to belief and the assumed community so achieved – are disrupted ... religious belief denied these underpinnings becomes subjective, and its truth value becomes relative.
>
> (Christiano 1987: 124)

At the same time, Christianity still seems plausible to some social groups, those, for example, which see religion as a way of maintaining the family rather than the ecclesia. Subjective secularization actually leads to 'subjective' religious beliefs, that is, in the choice of beliefs the balance of authority shifts away from the religious community to the individual. This works against the significant survival of systematic theologies.

No-one really disputes that Christianity, especially as an intellectual system of theology intended by the Churches to influence society politically and ethically, as well as religiously, has moved from the centre to a point closer to the margin of Western culture. The problem is why this happened, and how far, at the level of theology itself, the truth-value of doctrine has been permanently relativized. Is the long-term secularizing drift a social phenomenon, which might be reversed by subsequent social changes, or is secularization itself, as far as Christian doctrine is concerned, in part the result of intellectual movements which are now irreversible?

Immediately after the Second World War Karl Löwith, in *Meaning and History* (1949), offered a theological interpretation of secularization which rejected the value of the direction in which Western culture had developed since the late Middle Ages. He identified 'progress' as the key concept of the 'modern'. This was the belief, especially powerful from the eighteenth century, that a new, successful human beginning was possible, based on the rejection of older, including Christian, authority and assumptions, and on the use of the inherent problem-solving capacities of human beings. Löwith asserted that this idea of progress was no more than a groundless appropriation of the hope expressed in Christian eschatology. Without the Christian faith and tradition which alone could guarantee and legitimize its promises, 'progress' remained a 'secularized eschatology', an empty version of the Christian belief that the tragedy and contradictions of history could be overcome. Such a belief in progress was asking for the End without the means, because the human mastery of history was impossible outside 'the community of faith'. From Löwith's point of view, therefore, modernism, by which he meant broadly the general movement of scientific humanism, was an aggression (though it did not always understand itself as such) against theology, from which it had derived anything of any value in its understanding of history. Essentially, however, modern culture had done violence to the facts of the human situation, was illegitimate, as he put it, and was bound to fail. From the Christian point of view, the time for a new start was in the present, but it would require repentance and submission to ecclesiastical and theological authority.

This was by no means a new approach. Catholicism had never officially reconciled itself either to the Protestant Reformation or to the eighteenth-century Enlightenment. The Russian Orthodox theologian in exile, Nicholas Berdyaev, had written in 1936:

> the Christian idea rests on the hope of an end to historical tragedy and contradiction valid for all human generations, and of resurrection in eternal life for all who have ever lived. But the nineteenth-century conception of progress admits to the messianic consummation only that unborn generation of the elect to which all preceding generations have made their sacrifice.
>
> (Berdyaev 1936: 190)

Orthodox Protestantism was no less hostile: secularization was the product of the sin of pride.

Löwith's position, which strongly influenced the sociology of religion, was vigorously contested by Hans Blumenberg in *Die Legitimität der Neuzeit* in 1966 (translated, from the second edition, by R. M. Wallace as *The Legitimacy of the Modern Age*, 1983). Blumenberg gave a different account of modern European cultural history. He said that so far from secularization resulting from sinful (or sometimes 'tragic') human self-assertion, what had happened since the fifteenth century had been in reaction to a perceived failure of Christian theology, above all in the case of the doctrine of providence. It was the failure of the theological system to balance the actuality of a cruel, 'fallen' world with convincing assurances about the providential power of an interventionist God – to offer, that is, a plausible theodicy, in the sense of a vindication of God in having created a world in which evil exists – which made a shift in attitudes inevitable sooner or later. The failure was decisive, because without a compelling description of the way in which God governed nature, humanity and history, the idea of God was bound to become increasingly irrelevant to human existence. As traditional religion lost its plausibility, secularized interpretations of life became more plausible: modernism justified itself, either by solving problems which a transcendence-based Christian theology could not solve, or by accepting the insolubility of problems which theology claimed to have solved. Blumenberg's position was based on the practical success of scientific humanism; secularization, understood above all as the rejection of the restrictions which traditional Christian theology had placed on human reason and, consequentially, human behaviour, was the legitimate, necessary concomitant of greater understanding of the possibilities and limits of life.

Where Blumenberg stressed the positive value of secularization, Berger (1969) emphasized the cumulative impact of events on the internal plausibility of the Christian doctrine of providence. The religious wars of the sixteenth and seventeenth centuries may well have been the decisive turning point, but Berger also noted the effect of the Lisbon earthquake (1755) on educated opinion, the implication in Darwinism that conflict was inherent in the development of life and the worldwide cruelty of the twentieth century. For a long time orthodox theologians stuck to the view that humanity was endowed with some degree of freedom and must therefore blame itself, not its creator, who had at least offered a way of redemption in Christ, so that divine justice was not impaired. Some modern theologians have modified the doctrine by saying that God's action is on the personal life of the individual; process theologians, though not restricting divine action to the human order, suggest that God acts persuasively, not coercively; others again, Jürgen Moltmann for example, look forward eschatologically to a new creation in which the righteousness of God will make itself clear. When one speaks of secularization, however, one is pointing, for example, to the evidence that by the end of the twentieth century Providence was no longer widely expected to preserve the planet from human self-destructiveness. Here the truth-question returns insistently: either one is praying to an interventionist God or one is not, and if one no longer expects God to intervene, either within or beyond the human order, then one has moved a long way from traditional Christianity, and from most forms of religion as such. Theology hovers between the sometimes hopeful, sometimes defiant reiteration of past absolutes and individual adventures into territories where absolutes belong to the past.

ACADEMIC THEOLOGY AND THEOLOGY IN THE CHURCH

All this inevitably created a gap between 'theology in the University' and 'theology in the Church'. As higher education expanded in Britain and other countries after 1945, it was often held that no university was complete without a theology department as a witness to Christianity as the country's civil religion, and there was vague and hopeful talk about theology still being 'the queen of the sciences'. In the 1990s it remained official Conservative education policy in Britain that state schools should promote and preserve the country's Christian heritage and values. At first the new British theology departments, which depended almost entirely on public, not ecclesiastical, money, followed the pre-war pattern, taking for granted the unique truth of Christian theology and emphasizing biblical studies, Christian history and theology down to 451 CE, together with an apologetic line in the philosophy of religion. These courses had originally been framed when university departments and faculties were closely related to theological seminaries. It was assumed that staff and students, virtually all male, shared a common Christian faith, and many of the students intended to enter the priesthood. Yet the courses contained little or nothing about what had happened to the Christian Churches since 1789.

In view of all the changes which we have been discussing here it should be obvious that such a situation could not last. The move towards more pluralistic departments of 'Theology and Religious Studies' developed swiftly after about 1960. One important internal factor was the worldwide drop in the number of students for the professional ministries, whether Catholic or Protestant; in order to survive convincingly university departments everywhere had to recruit other students, women as well as men, and this required a broader curriculum, much less concerned with supplementing the work of theological seminaries. In Britain, what took place was hardly revolutionary: only one department, set up at the new university of Lancaster in 1967, was actually called a Department of Religious Studies. This was headed by an Anglican philosopher of religion, Ninian Smart, a powerful advocate of the study of world religions, who later became Professor of Religious Studies at the University of California, Santa Barbara. Other British departments cautiously changed their title to 'Theology and Religious Studies'.

'Religious Studies' often meant not much more than the introduction of courses on modern Christian theology and history, the sociology of religion, and some varieties of Buddhism. There are still comparatively few posts for the teaching of non-Christian religions: the Old Testament is frequently taught from a Christian point of view as though it were primarily a Christian text; and Judaism is rarely treated as a religion in its own right with a tragic modern history.

The gradual emergence of 'the study of religion' did not produce much ecclesiastical comment. What excited hostility by the 1970s, as might have been expected from the general political direction of the decade, was the pluralistic and radical tendencies of the Christian theology which some, though by no means all, university scholars were publishing, not only in America and Britain, but also in European Catholicism. In Britain, the symbolic books were *God and the Universe of Faiths* (1973) by John Hick, and the symposium, *The Myth of God Incarnate* (1977). The problem was not so acute in the USA, where the old unofficial 'Protestant establishment' crumbled to pieces in the 1960s, but in Britain many in the Churches though that university departments of religion, whatever they called themselves, should, like state schools, teach and believe in 'traditional Christianity', as though there were no problem about either the intellectual or the social status of Christian systematic theology in the late twentieth century. Much as the National Trust preserved 'the English Country House' so the Department of Theology should preserve 'traditional Christianity': other religions might be studied, as had sometimes been the case in previous generations, as fields of missionary analysis. This view is not unrepresented within universities, where some academics still think of their departments as part of the ecclesia. There is still a strong and conscientious desire to maintain the uniqueness and absolute-ness of Christianity, whatever may be done about other world religions, and these 'other' religions are still often taught by Christian scholars. However, what individual Churches tolerate or discipline in the name of faith in their own institutions is a matter for them and for the teachers whom they employ. There is ample evidence, for example, of recent papal interference in the freedom of Catholic universities, especially in the United States; in Europe, the case of Hans Küng is a notorious example. In public university depart-ments for the study of religion, including Christianity, however, departments which depend on public money and which should serve society as a whole and not the Christian Church in isolation, the pluralism of theological study and the freedom of teaching, research and publication should be axiomatic.

REFERENCES

Berdyaev, N. (1936) *The Meaning of History*, London: Geoffrey Bles.
Berger, P. (1969) *The Social Reality of Religion*, Harmondsworth: Penguin.
Christiano, K. J. (1987) *Religious Diversity and Social Change: American Cities 1890–1906*, Cambridge: Cambridge University Press.
Fiorenza, E. S. (1983) *In Memory of Her: A Feminist Reconstruction of Christian Origins*, London: SCM Press.
Flannery, A. (1975) *Vatical Council II: The Conciliar and Post Conciliar Documents*, Clonskeagh, Ireland: Dominican Publications.
Ford, D. F. (ed.) (1989) *The Modern Theologians* 2 vols, Oxford: Basil Blackwell.
Frei, H. (1974) *The Eclipse of Biblical Narrative*, London: Yale University Press.
Gadamer, H.-G. (1960) *Truth and Method*, London: Sheed and Ward.
Hick, J. (1973) *God and the Universe of Faiths*, London: Macmillan.
—— (ed.) (1977) *The Myth of God Incarnate*, London: SCM Press.
King, U. (ed.) (1992) *Liberating Women: New Theological Directions*, Bristol: Bristol University Theology Department.
Lindbeck, G. (1984) *The Nature of Doctrine*, London: SPCK.
Loades, A. (1989) 'Feminist Theology', in D. Ford (ed.) *The Modern Theologians*, Oxford: Basil Blackwell.
Löwith, K. (1949) *Meaning and History*, Chicago: University of Chicago Press.
Mackey, J. (1987) *Modern Theology: A Sense of Direction*, Oxford: Oxford University Press.
Morgan, R. with Barton, J. (1988) *Biblical Interpretation*, Oxford: Oxford University Press.
Nietzsche, F. (1983) *Untimely Meditations*, trans. R. J. Hollingdale, Cambridge: Cambridge University Press.

Nineham, D. (1977a) 'Epilogue', in J. Hick (ed.) *The Myth of God Incarnate*, London: SCM Press.
—— (1977b) *Explorations in Theology 1*, London: SCM Press.
Pompa, L. (1990) *Human Nature and Historical Knowledge: Hume, Hegel and Vico*, Cambridge: Cambridge University Press.
Popper, K. R. (1963) *The Poverty of Historicism*, London: Routledge and Kegan Paul.
Räisänen, H. (1990) *Beyond New Testament Theology*, London: SCM Press.
Sanders, E. P. (1992) *Judaism, Practice and Belief 63BCE–66CE*, London: SCM Press.
Sölle, D. (1991) 'Liberating our God-Talk', in U. King (ed.) *Liberating Women: New Theological Directions*, Bristol: Bristol University Theology Department.
Troeltsch, E. (1972) *The Absoluteness of Christianity and the History of Religions*, London: SCM Press.
Van Harvey, A. (1967) *The Historian and the Believer*, London: SCM Press.
Wiles, M. (1974) *The Remaking of Christian Doctrine*, London: SCM Press.

FURTHER READING

Hamnett, I. (ed.) (1990) *Religious Pluralism and Unbelief*, London: Routledge and Kegan Paul.
Hampson, D. (1990) *Theology and Feminism*, Oxford: Basil Blackwell.
Hauerwas, S. (1991) *A Community of Character*, Notre Dame: University of Notre Dame Press.
Hick, J. (1989) *An Interpretation of Religion: Human Responses to the Transcendent*, London: Macmillan.
Kaufman, G. D. (1981) *The Theological Imagination*, Philadelphia: Westminster Press.
Küng, H. (1987) *Christianity and World Religions: Paths of Dialogue with Islam, Hinduism and Buddhism*, London: SCM Press.
Ruether, R. R. (1983) *Sexism and God-Talk: Towards a Feminist Theology*, London: SCM Press.
Surin, K. (1989) *The Turnings of Darkness and Light: Essays in Philosophical and Systematic Theology*, Cambridge: Cambridge University Press.
Swinburne, R. (1991) *From Metaphor to Analogy*, Oxford: Clarendon Press.
Tracy, D. (1982) *The Analogical Imagination: Christian Theology and the Culture of Pluralism*, London: SCM Press.
Ward, K. (1991) *A Vision to Pursue: Beyond the Crisis in Christianity*, London: SCM Press.
See also chapters 4, 7, 9, 13, 14, 24, 25, 48.

42

MAKING SENSE OF GOD

Theodore Jennings

How are we to 'make sense' of talk about God? The question as thus formulated supposes that, in some way, this talk is not self-evident. But of course in many contexts 'God' is self-evident, in that many users of the discourse in which this or a cognate term occurs find the term unproblematic. Those who move within a religious discourse as 'fish in water' find nothing especially odd about using this term in accordance with the conventions of the culture or sub-culture within which they live and speak.

The possibility of the theme that we are to discuss requires that we be distanced, or distance ourselves, from the discourse and the discursive culture within which the talk about, and to, and on behalf of, the divine is self-evident. Historically such a move occurred in a variety of ways. In the ancient world, for example, it sometimes occurred by way of a confrontation with alternative discourses in which, it seemed, the term, name or category of the divine had a noticeably different character. In such a case it was necessary to clarify in what way one's own discourse either was 'superior' to that of others (more truthful or what have you), or to discover ways of adapting one's own discourse in order to incorporate the apparent advantages of alternative discourses, especially those of more powerful or prestigious cultures. For a militant religious movement, one that seeks to attract adherents from a wide variety of sub-cultures, this may involve the co-option of elements from competing discourses together with a strategy of disqualification of other elements as superstitious, idolatrous and so on. All of these strategies may be found in the work of early Christian theologians.

In modern Europe this set of issues was largely replaced in academic theology by another, namely, the question of whether talk about the divine or God is meaningful as such; that is, with the question of atheism. This challenge has taken a number of forms. In some cases the issue is formulated as to whether talk of a 'supreme being' is compatible with the onward march of the scientific world-view or with the forms of rationality that have proved themselves to be effective in the scientific liberation of humanity from poverty, disease, superstition, ignorance and authoritarianism. In other cases we have to do with 'protest atheism' that unmasks the ways in which religious language generally and god-language in particular have functioned to legitimate the production of neuroses (Freud), of systems of economic oppression (Marx), or have entailed the resignation of humanity to its victimization by an absolute divinity or tyrannical fate (Camus).

Whether in ancient or modern times, what is at stake then are the strategies for rendering sensible or intelligible what has been called into question. Generally we make sense of something by first locating it within a meaningful or useful discursive context. Naturally, this will work in so far as the discourse within which we situate talk about God makes sense to a larger public. However, any such strategy will be successful only for those for whom that discourse itself appears meaningful. Thus, in the world of Christianity's early centuries, those ways of making sense of God that appropriated the world-view of the Hellenistic cultural elite, to the extent to which they were successful, made sense for the elite. But not for those whose world-view was markedly different, as, for example, the popular classes not schooled in the conceptuality of that cultural elite.

Where the task of making sense of God in the discourse of the cultural elite comes to be specialized and separated from the religious discourse of the 'faithful', the impression grows of a disjunction between the religion of the philosophers (theologians) and that of the faithful. In fact these languages are quite distinct. The ways in which talk of God makes sense in each are quite different. But both technical theological discourse and popular religious language are the product of the attempt to make sense of God for distinct populations with distinctive discursive traditions.

Of course, this picture is greatly over-simplified since in the religious world of Hellenistic culture there were in fact a great many different discourses available, for example, to the popular classes. Thus when Christianity sought to make itself understood, it had to make sense in the thought worlds of public cult, mystery religion, myth and legend as well as the political and legal and commercial discourses available to wide sectors of the public. At the same time the cultural elites also had available a variety of discourses: neo-Platonism, Gnosticism, stoicism and so on. Each of these discourses is employed in early Christian attempts to make sense of its own distinctive view of God. And the view of God undergoes adaptation to these perspectives and world-views.

The situation is quite similar when it comes to the modern period. The challenges posed to the meaningfulness of talk about God by the Enlightenment and its aftermath provoke a variety of responses that correspond to the multiplicity of discourses and world-views that 'make sense' to people in the modern era. Academic theology seeks to adapt its talk of God to the discursive worlds of European cultural elites while popular theology and religion seek to 'make sense' in terms that are familiar or plausible to the groups within which they seek adherents. Thus contemporary theology is characterized by a multiplicity of ways of seeking to make sense of God.

How are we to make sense of the diversity of ways of attempting to make sense of God? Even if we restrict ourselves to what may be termed 'academic theology', we are still confronted with a great variety. However, much academic theology can be characterized as having in view the question of whether talk about God does in fact make sense at all; that is, with the question of atheism. This way of setting the issue places our reflections within the problematic of the Enlightenment. However, it is also the case that a number of reflections upon God in academic theology do not take this problematic as a starting point, that is, do not contend with the possibility of atheism but with the older questions of idolatry and superstition. Thus many contemporary theologians seem to take for granted that god-talk is meaningful but seek to contest false gods. This is true of liberation theologians and feminist theologians. To be sure, these work within a cultural sphere affected by the Enlightenment, but they proceed from the use made of god-talk to ask whether this use is justifiable in relation, for example, to basic principles of prophetic and biblical discourse.

The task of this chapter then must be to make sense of the variety of ways in which theologians in the contemporary period seek to make sense of God. In this chapter we will begin where many of our readers begin, with the question of theism and atheism inherited from the Enlightenment. Then we will attempt to clarify the range of proposals that emerge following the collapse of theism. The provenance of this *Encyclopedia* dictates that greater emphasis is to be placed on the post-Enlightenment problematic and its permutations than would be justified either by the practice of ordinary Christians within this cultural sphere or by the importance of this problematic for those operating on the margins of this sphere. While Euro-American academic culture can no longer claim for itself the self-evident pre-eminence and even hegemony of earlier eras, it nevertheless has a legitimate role to play as one of the partners in the discussion about God. However, it is also crucial to give an account of those proposals that are less concerned with the issue of the possibility of meaningful god-talk than with the question of the truthfulness or appropriateness of alternative ways of speaking of the divine. These proposals have in common that they usually emerge from the 'margins' of European Enlightenment culture, whether in the 'Third World' or from 'liberationist' perspectives within the cultural sphere of the Enlightenment. These proposals are contributing to the fundamental reshaping of academic theology as they offer a voice to previously silenced or marginalized groups of Christians.

In a final section of the chapter we will attempt to identify some of the characteristics shared by these diverse proposals for making sense of God, thereby offering a kind of map of the altered landscape of theology as this is now emerging.

THE RISE AND FALL OF THEISM

The classical framework

We have already indicated the way in which early Christianity sought to make itself understood within a variety of philosophic and religious discourses and practices of the Hellenistic world. One feature which many of these discursive traditions, especially among the cultural elites, had in common was a critical attitude towards religious practices regarded as superstitious or magical. Christianity with its inheritance from Jewish monotheism found a positive point of contact with Hellenistic views that sought to reduce the plurality of divine beings and forces to a single divine principle.

To this was joined, however, the sense that the world of experience was chaotic, hostile, inimical to human well-being. Christianity could associate itself with this view to the extent that its God was understood to be not the immanent principle of the world but transcendent to the world. The soteriological hopes of Hellenistic religions for escape from the world could then be linked to the one God conceived of as radically distinct from the world. In order for this to work, however, it was necessary to speak of the divine not only as transcendent to the world but also as not subject to change or mutability, in short, as absolute. Thus the perspective that came to characterize official Christian theology was a view of God as eternal, immutable, without passion and completely independent of the world (absolute).

Now this understanding of the divine being stands in tension with the idea that the divine 'becomes flesh', which derives from the ascription of divinity to Christ. Not surprisingly then, the question of the divinity/humanity of Christ and the attendant issues of the characteristic features of divine being become the preoccupation of Christian theology in this period. The 'result' of this discussion is the trinitarian structure of Christian thought about God. This trinitarian structure serves as a way of taking into account both the absolute transcendence of God and the soteriological focus upon christology.

This formulation of the distinctive Christian way of making sense of God became standard for 'the Christian tradition' (although allowance must be made for variations like European Arianism and Eastern Monophysitism and Nestorianism that continued alongside 'Catholic' and 'Orthodox' Christianity for several centuries). Yet this trinitarian formulation is unstable. It does not succeed in clarifying the specific features of the third person of the Trinity (Holy Spirit) or in clarifying fully the relation between the first person of the Trinity and divinity as such (Lampe 1977).

As a consequence of the last of these issues it becomes possible, especially in the West, to separate the discussion of the oneness of God (and the divine nature and attributes) from the discussion of the triune God. This is precisely what happens in the theology of Aquinas, under pressure from the Islamic and Jewish theological appropriations of Aristotle. Aquinas's attempt to 'make sense of God' within this Islamicized (and thus anti-trinitarian) Aristotelian discourse produces a bifurcation between trinitarian thought as specialized and isolated dogma and the doctrine of the divine as such.

Emergence of theism

The religious strife that engulfed Europe in the century following the Reformation served to undermine the credibility of specifically Christian discourse concerning God. This discourse, with its characteristic trinitarian form, also seemed incapable of translation into the increasingly prestigious discourse of the 'scientific world-view'. However, the development by Thomas Aquinas and his successors of a philosophical discourse concerning God that was viewed as not incompatible with specifically Christian discourse offered a way to make sense of God without recourse to the issues of confessional dispute. Thus was born the specific form of modern theism.

In addition to being severed from specifically Christian discourse (with its talk, for example, of sin and salvation, of christology and pneumatology), theistic discourse was characterized by its view of the divine as the supreme being whose relation to the world was that of causation. In this way the inheritance from Aristotle by way of Aquinas was preserved. Considerable variation, however, was to be found, ranging from views that attributed every event to specific divine causation (Zwingli) to those views that supposed that the divine direct causation was restricted to the moment of creation of the world (deism). But the plausibility of causation as the model of divine activity was increased by the way in which this idea predominated in the language of the emerging sciences. To this model of causation, however, was added that of entire beneficence and wisdom derived from the Christian view of God as supremely concerned for human welfare.

Despite the apparent advantages of theism, it also encountered grave difficulties precisely at the point where it seemed most promising – in the view of the divine as the principle of causation. For this cast the problem of theodicy in an especially acute form. If 'the Supreme Being' was omnipotent causation, then the existence of evil, and especially 'natural evil', appeared to become inexplicable. Of course it was logically possible to resolve the difficulty by way of supposing the divine to be morally neutral or even arbitrary, but this would so completely sever talk of God from its basis in the religious traditions of Christianity as to render it senseless.

This was impossible for another reason as well. Theism also took on the moral imperative and social character of the divine as articulated in dominant strands of the Judeo-Christian tradition. The goodness or beneficence of God was related positively to social and personal morality. To deny the absolute goodness of the divine would leave the personal and social world without a moral anchor or basis. Yet it was precisely by alleging that the idea of God served to found or secure personal and social morality that talk of God was rendered plausible in the emerging middle-class culture of Europe.

God as the supreme being whose beneficence served to anchor morality and whose omnipotent causality served to tie the idea to the emerging scientific world-view: this is what may be termed the modern form of theism as a way of 'making sense of God'.

THE PROBLEMATIC IN THE SPHERE OF THE ENLIGHTENMENT

Revisions of theism

While modern theism continues to have its defenders, academic theology has concerned itself increasingly with either the revision of, or the development of alternatives to, that way of making sense of God. We will attend first to those proposals that may be regarded as revising rather than abandoning the main tenents of classical theism.

1 Process theology

Perhaps the most influential revision of theism in the twentieth century has been the development of process philosophy by Alfred North Whitehead (1929) and Charles Hartshorne (1964), and its appropriation as process theology by John Cobb (1965), Schubert Ogden (1966) and others. Instead of speaking of God as absolute, which had been the self-evident presupposition of theology since the Hellenistic period, this view maintains that God can be understood as a being or actual entity in mutual relation with all others. This being is not characterized by absolute but by relative power, as supremely influential in relation to all other entities but also as always limited as well by the autonomy or integrity of all other entities.

This revision of theism, based upon a new cosmology that took into account relativity theory in physics, served to open the way for a correlation between the idea of God and the scientific world-view, a correlation that had been in dispute since Hume and Kant. Moreover, process thought appears to be able to provide a solution to the difficulties of theodicy. The divine benevolence could be maintained in ways that prior forms of doctrine of God made problematic or where those forms had had to compromise in order to emphasize the divine omnipotence. Further, like modern theism as described in the last section, it is able to prescind from the specifically confessional forms of Christian discourse concerning God and so to become a potential vehicle for interreligious dialogue.

Despite the fact that this way of understanding God is able to make sense of God in terms of the presuppositions of modern natural sciences and to give a cogent account of reality in terms of its view of God, process theology has been limited in its influence to segments of the liberal Church and academy. This may be partly due to a general lack of interest in or concern about issues of cosmology generally or to the greater prominence of questions of social and psychological meaningfulness in late modern culture. It may also be due to the apparent distance between the language and problems of speculative metaphysics and the kinds of language regularly employed by believers, even those few who are conversant with issues of the natural sciences. The sense that questions concerning the natural sciences are best left to specialists and are too arcane for the laity may account for the lack of interest in the contributions of process thought to the revitalization of theism.

Nevertheless, some of its features, like the limitation of divine power by the freedom of other beings and the idea of mutual relatedness between God and the world and the concern to develop a positive relation between God and time, have had wide influence even where the specific structure of Whiteheadian speculative philosophy has not. These elements are not restricted to the sphere of process theology properly so–called but have characterized other views in the late modern period as well.

Among the most influential of the views that are sometimes compared to and interact with process theology is the vision of cosmogenesis advanced by Teilhard de Chardin (1959). Taking evolutionary models of biology rather than relativity models of physics as its starting point, this view suggests that the whole development of earth and life and human history may be understood as aiming at the 'omega point' which corresponds to the vision of the divine. While process thought has enjoyed wider influence in Protestant theology, Teilhard's views have been more influential in Catholic circles, despite the considerable reserve shown to his vision by the magisterium.

2 Renunciation of cosmological horizon

Although process philosophy and theology show that it is at least possible for talk about God to make sense within the horizon of cosmology and the natural sciences, it is the case that much modern talk of God has surrendered this cosmological horizon. This is already prefigured in Kant's displacement of the divine from science and metaphysics to the area of ethics and morality. Kant's view was that God could not be understood to be a presupposition of our knowledge of the world but was instead a presupposition of humanity's moral sense. This view of course meant surrendering the problematic sphere of the natural world and thus the advantages (connection to science) and the disadvantages (theodicy) that had accrued to theism from this association. But it meant that it was possible to make sense of God on the basis of moral order. Given the surrender of the sphere of the sciences to specialists and the concentration upon social and personal life of the emerging middle-class culture, this move made eminent sense to many theologians.

Once the way had been opened in the direction of making sense of God apart from the world, a number of connected options appeared. Among these we may count the development by Schleiermacher of an analysis of the sense of absolute dependence constitutive (as he thought) of human being and correlative to the emphasis upon faith as trust that had developed in pietism. This emphasis upon the individual relation to the divine is taken up also in the transcendentalism of Emerson and the Unitarians in the United States. Others, like Rudolf Otto, made sense of God by identifying a special sphere for the apprehension of the divine as the holy. Still others have continued Kant's project of making sense of God by way of an appeal to the moral life. In the late nineteenth century this was understood increasingly in social terms by such thinkers as Ritschl and Harnack in Europe and by proponents of the Social Gospel in America.

These revisions of theism have in common that they surrender the horizon of cosmology and the natural sciences and instead make sense of God in terms of personal experience. Some of these thematize the specific domain of ethics while others opt for an aesthetic or even a specifically religious domain as the sphere in terms of which talk of the divine may be rendered intelligible. Thus the discussion of the experience which grounds talk of God has produced a number of proposals among which we may include the rumours of transcendence suggested by Berger (1970) and Gilkey (1969) and the identification of the experience of limit proposed by Kaufman or of basic trust by Ogden (1966).

3 Pannenberg

Of contemporary theologians, Wolfhart Pannenberg (1991) remains most committed to the attempt to make renewed sense of 'god' as a principle of explanation on the order of the Thomistic and classical theistic perspective. In Pannenberg's case this explanatory principle is connected to the problematic of self-and-world as opposed to those views that see God as correlative of the self alone as in Kierkegaard, Rahner (1978) and Schleiermacher.

Pannenberg has gradually distanced himself from the attempt to ground talk of God in an *a priori* structure of human experience and has increasingly appropriated the Barthian view of the centrality of biblical revelation. However, more clearly than Barth, he has oriented the meaningfulness of this way of speaking of God to its capacity to make sense of our world and history. Thus 'god' is still viewed as an explanatory principle for world historical experience. However, as Pannenberg insists, this claim can only receive full verification with the consummation of history. The Christian claim is that the divine goal has been actualized in advance in Jesus of Nazareth, his mission and ministry. The truth of this claim, while it may be made sense of in advance (by attempts to clarify worldly and historical existence on its basis), can only be truly compelling at the end of history.

4 Discourse analysis

One of the challenges that beset the defenders of theism in the middle and latter part of this century, in addition to the challenge of atheism and of the theodicy question, has been the question of the meaningfulness of talk of God at all, regardless of whether God were conceived of as the supreme being or as being itself. This challenge, mounted most forcefully by A. J. Ayer (1936) and his successors, initially maintained that to be meaningful a proposition must be either tautological (as in mathematics) or empirically verifiable. The debate that ensued has been most useful, not only for clarifying the character of talk about God, but also for clarifying a great many features of language and thus of human experience and consciousness generally. One effect of this discussion has been to correlate talk of God more closely with general human experience. The 'empirical' turn which this has fostered in theology has served to connect talk of the divine to ordinary human experience, with a gain in credibility as a result (Gilkey, Jennings).

The other response has been to investigate more carefully the character of language generally as this bears upon religious discourse and specifically on the question of God. This has served to open up new areas of research into the character of biblical language and the discovery that there are a great many different ways for talk of God to function, many of which had been overlooked by theism and its defenders. The motto of Wittgenstein (1953) 'the meaning of a word is its use', as well as the suggestion that forms of discourse have their own rules (and that there are many more possibilities of rule-regulated discourse than the two suggested by early positivism), serve to open the way for far greater sophistication in the analysis of the meaning of assertions about or concerning the divine.

Post-theistic options

In addition to these modifications of theism, there are a number of proposals which seem to move beyond theism's preoccupation with the character of a divine being and which are therefore understandable as post-theistic in character.

1 Being itself

A somewhat more drastic revision of theism than those already mentioned surrenders the idea that God is to be conceived of as the supreme being or even as a 'being' at all, and instead proposes that it is better to make sense of God as the being of beings, as the source or ground of beings but not as one of these beings. This view, derivative from older German Romanticism and from the newer existential ontology of Heidegger, identifies the divine with what in process terms was called 'creativity'. According to this view, God is like a kind of vital force or the source or fount of being.

The most influential versions of this perspective are those articulated by Paul Tillich (1951, 1957, 1963) and John Macquarrie (1966, 1967). According to Tillich's view the 'God beyond God' is the ground of the possibility of any being's existence. According to Macquarrie's view this is to be understood as the power of being that 'lets being be'. In both cases there is a sense of connectedness to this source in the feeling of dependence reminiscent of Schleiermacher. But the view of the divine in Tillich and Macquarrie has a stronger connection to the whole of reality (rather than simply human historical experience), owing to its relation to an explicit general ontology. These views have also been useful for the development of feminist and other alternatives to theism (see below).

2 Trinitarian

Deserving of special mention is the recuperation and transformation of a trinitarian form for the doctrine of God. The process of recuperation begins with Karl Barth, especially in the *Church Dogmatics* (1932). This reverses the trend towards the relegation of the doctrine of the Trinity to an appendix as in Schleiermacher. This reformulation of the doctrine of the Trinity as the foundation for any understanding of the doctrine of God and indeed for Christian doctrine as a whole, begins with a critique of the Enlightenment problematic of God and the attempts of modern theology to respond to this problematic.

The renovation of trinitarian perspectives in European theology is carried further by Jüngel (1983) and Moltmann (1974) who shift the emphasis from the analysis of the event of revelation characteristic of Barth to an analysis of the meaning of the cross. For Moltmann this means that the distance between God (as Father) and the abandoned Christ (as Son) opens up a space in God bridged by the Spirit which makes God not an observer of, but a participant in, the suffering of humanity. For Jüngel the concentration on the cross means as well that the divine is to be understood as fully engaged in the temporality and perishability of worldly experience. For both, trinitarian categories provide the framework for the rethinking of the identity of God as relational and temporal.

The essentially social character of the trinitarian view of three persons is developed by Leonardo Boff (1988). Thus the equality and communion of three persons is understood to represent the goal of history as the establishment of a society of mutual love, a community of all beings integrated into the communitarian form of the doctrine of God. In consequence, trinitarian thought is connected positively to the protest against unjust social structures of domination and division and is made also to represent the utopian aspiration for just community which animates the struggle of and for the poor in all societies. By being thus connected to the protest, struggle and aspiration of the masses of people, talk of God is rendered more plausible for those who take up or sympathize with this struggle.

More recently, feminist theologians have adopted the trinitarian perspective as an illustration of non-hierarchical relations within God and thus as generative of non-hierarchical relations generally. Thus revisions of trinitarian discourse proposed by Lacugna (1991) and Johnson (1992) have emphasized the connection between talk of God and the aspiration for mutual relatedness and generative communion that connect powerfully with previously discredited or ignored aspects of the experience and insight of women.

This turn to a recuperation and revision of trinitarian discourse on the part of theologians of such diverse types may be regarded as one of the most striking features of late twentieth-century theology.

3 Radical

In apparent conflict with the recuperation of trinitarian discourse are more radical strands of theological reflection which have their point of departure not in the Barth of the *Church Dogmatics* but in the earlier Barthian emphasis on the extreme dialectical juxtaposition of the divine and the worldly. Already, for the early Barth, this meant a profound break with theism. By insisting on the otherness of the divine, dialectical theology essentially breaks the causal link between God and the world. Thus the divine is not regarded as the principle of explanation of what is, whether metaphysically or psychologically or socially. This stands over against the attempt of Pannenberg to rehabilitate the use of God to account for the possibility of the self–world relation. The severing of this chain, especially in the earlier Barth (1933), identifies the divine with the interruption of the world, penetrating the world 'slantwise' from above. Thus reflection upon God is freed from the attempt to account for the way things are.

This break was carried further by the suggestion that the divine occurs in the word-event which is located entirely within ordinary language between persons (Ebeling 1973). Others have suggested that the divine should be understood as the occurrence of genuine meeting between persons. Dorothee Sölle (1990) has carried this radical position into the reformulation of a range of doctrines. In common among the more radical proposals is the denial of the usefulness of the notion of a supreme being and even of the idea of being itself. The rejection of metaphysics and the critique of theism's complicity in the horrors of our century make for the development of a 'Christian atheism' which understands the divine not as a being or as being itself but as the occurrence of that which truly humanizes.

Deserving of special mention among the anti-theistic proposals of radical theologians is the movement in North American theology of 'death of god theology'. While quite diverse perspectives were originally lumped indiscriminately together under this heading, it is apparent that the most fruitful of these perspectives has proved to be that of Thomas J. J. Altizer (1993). Here the view is maintained that the divine as a separate absolute and transcendent reality has abolished itself in order to become fully and completely flesh in history. The event in which this occurs is the incarnation. Thus the view of the divine is largely determined by a christological concentration reminiscent of Hegel (1910) and Barth. Unlike Barth, however, Altizer supposes that the Church is characterized by the refusal of the divine kenosis. Thus the reality of the divine is not to be encountered there but in the movements of late modern culture which reject theism and conventional Christianity. Moreover, the denial of theism which this view entails has also provided Altizer with the possibility of an appropriation of Eastern modes of thought, thus grounding in a new way the possibility of inter-religious dialogue.

An alternative radical proposal is made by Gordon Kaufman (1993) who suggests that God should be understood as an 'x', orientation to which serves a humanizing function for persons and for history. The key to this 'x' he finds in the 'serendipitous creativity' that may be discerned in the world historical process which produces life and humanity and the emergence of humanistic values. In order to give this serendipitous creativity greater purchase on the imagination, he proposes that the task of making sense of God is both critical and constructive. It is critical in that it undermines all attempts to know what cannot be known; it is constructive in that the idea or concept of God is recognized as a human construction which fosters human development. Feminist theologians like Sallie McFague (1993) have found this perspective congenial for developing new ways of imaging or constructing models of God. Like the other proposals that may be regarded as radical, this constructivist view renounces not only theism but also its revisions, in favour of a concentration upon aspects of this-worldly experience that fund discourse concerning the divine.

VOICES FROM THE MARGIN

As the discipline of theology has become a global or planetary project, the self-evident character of the Enlightenment project has eroded. To be sure, this problematic still characterizes much Euro-American theology. But the task of making sense of God is no longer the exclusive preserve of Euro-American consciousness. Indeed, even within this sphere alternative agendas are at work.

While some contemporary attempts to make sense of God offer a modified or attenuated theism (process, being, Pannenberg) others are characterized by a renewed exploration of the religious imagination generally and of biblical images particularly. Thus images and metaphors for God have proliferated. This approach is driven by the following:

1 Attention to the religious language of marginalized minorities and majorities in liberationist theologies.
2 The search for alternatives to patriarchal images.
3 Engagement with the rich resources of other religious and cultural traditions.

Standing behind these (negatively) is a suspicion of the hegemony of Hellenistic and Enlightenment forms of the doctrine of God and (positively) an appreciation of poetic–imagistic discourse as a fully legitimate equal to rationalistic discourse.

In this section we will attend to characteristic proposals that bracket the Enlightenment problematic. These are feminist, African-American, Latin American, and 'Third World' indigenizing proposals for making sense of God.

Feminist

At an early stage feminist theology appropriates the view that god-language is constructed of diverse metaphors. It then seeks to bring to the surface alternative metaphors for the divine that correspond to the experience of women. This entails the appropriation of feminine metaphors for the divine and a reflection on the significance of such metaphors for an understanding of the divine as matrix of creativity and so on. These attempts make use of process views of creativity and Heideggerian and Tillichian views of the self-giving of being itself.

This metaphorical turn to symbolism, funded in part by Suzanne Langer's understanding of symbolics (1942), also turns to a wider field for the discovery of such metaphors including those of mother goddess and Wicca (Daly 1973). The development of an alternative symbolics encounters the ways in which traditional symbolics have served to legitimate patriarchal and hierarchical structures and consciousness. Thus, instead of simply supplying an alternative symbolics, feminist theology begins to challenge the appropriateness of patriarchal symbolics and to demonstrate the greater adequacy of the feminist symbolics. Thus not only are there female images for the divine but these are also to be preferred to masculinist images that are appropriated from the patriarchally structured dominant culture. The test of adequacy is some combination of greater correspondence to the heart of biblical religion as liberated from the accretions of patriarchal presuppositions, and greater adequacy to the experience of women.

In any case what is at stake is the attempt to make greater sense of the idea of God. This 'making sense' may be understood at the level of widening the range of liturgical semantics or at the level of an alternative metaphor for God (McFague 1993) or of combating the patriarchy (Ruether 1983, 1992). Some argue that Christianity is entirely circumscribed within patriarchy and so call for an alternative religious symbolics (Daly 1973) or seek instead the liberation of Christianity from patriarchal assumptions (Ruether 1983, 1992).

More recently there has been a recognition of the way in which feminist theological reflection has been bound by the cultural assumptions of the Euro-American middle class. This recognition propels attention to alternative cultural expressions. The consequence is greater sensitivity to the ethnic or racial as well as the class limitations of conceptuality (Thistlethwaite 1989) and it produces a growing body of womanist and mujerista religio-theological literature.

Black theology

In North America there has been a growing body of literature which seeks to render talk of God answerable to the struggle for the dignity of African-Americans. This has meant taking the imagery of popular religious traditions with more seriousness than has been customary in academic theology in order to relate theological reflection concretely to the struggle and the insight of the people. This move has also meant that the idea of God has been transformed. The transformation may be regarded not as an abandonment of theism (as in the 'radical' proposals discussed above) but as its reformulation. That reformulation entails that God not be understood as outside history and its struggles nor as essentially neutral with respect to concrete historical struggles but as affected by the suffering of racism and as committed to the struggle against racism. Here the Enlightenment problematic, in so far as it concerns theodicy, is addressed but it is also transcended, in that the principal issue is not the defence of the existence of God or the plausibility of the idea of God, but rather the struggle against the idolatrous features of theism in both its popular and its academic representations. That 'God is black' (Cone 1975) means that God is not the supreme being who legitimates existing structures or a bystander to history but the one who provokes struggles for justice and human dignity.

Latin American liberation theology

A similar move is made by Latin American liberation theology. Here again the divine is understood to be engaged in history on the side of the poor and oppressed majorities and against the structures of domination and exploitation. As in black theology (but unlike much feminist theology) the Latin American liberation theologians have found a re-reading of biblical materials especially fruitful for discovering new ways to make sense of God in their own situation. Both social analysis and biblical hermeneutics converge upon the notion that God is to be conceived as principally the 'God of the poor' (Araya 1987) who is leading history towards the reign of justice (Miranda 1974). In this way the concerns of 'protest atheism' are addressed, although the questions of the post-Enlightenment era concerning the existence of the divine are bypassed or are rendered moot. Instead, a wager that it makes sense to side with the divine activity as thus conceived is invited.

Indigenization

In a variety of contexts theologians are finding it appropriate to make sense of God in terms of indigenous non-Christian religious traditions. While elements of this may be discerned in North American discussions of black theology and in attempts to honour Native American spirituality, the urgency of these proposals is most keenly felt in certain sectors of African theology (Mbiti 1970; Oduyoye 1986) and especially in Asian theology.

At first this move of indigenization was governed by the attempt to find cognates for Western concepts of the divine. But increasingly this has meant a positive appropriation of insights specific to other religious traditions. In the early stages of academic theology's dialogue with other religious traditions, there was a concentration on the views of the religious and intellectual elites of India and Japan, of Hinduism and Buddhism. But the emergence of Asian theologians has resulted in attempts to take far more seriously than ever before the expressions of popular religious traditions of Hinduism, Buddhism and Confucianism (Song 1982) as well as shamanistic traditions.

While some of the proposals that have emerged develop liberationist themes similar to those of black and Latin American theology (for example the development of 'minjung' theology in Korea), the main characteristic of these proposals seems to be their attempt to re-symbolize the divine immanence to the world of nature and history through the use of indigenous traditions. Unlike Latin American theology but like feminist theology, this means not so much a re-interpretation of biblical imagery as a turn to alternative, indigenous images, symbols, and representations of the divine. Typically the 'Christ event' serves a regulative function in the selection and interpretation of these images, but the images themselves are derived from extra-Christian sources.

The emerging view of God is one which refuses to separate God from nature and history, or to restrict the data to biblical or Western conceptuality. God is increasingly perceived as immanent to the world, as the victim of its suffering and the source of its transformation. Thus the divine is not separated from time, from perishing, from suffering, or from relationship.

COMMON THREADS

What are we to make of the considerable diversity of ways of making sense of God that characterizes the contemporary scene? Are there some common threads which, while not universal, seem to unite a variety of proposals across the lines that we have adopted for this taxonomy?

The most striking feature of the contemporary scene is precisely this multiplicity. Academic theology can no longer concern itself exclusively with the issues that 'make sense' to the traditional intellectual elites of modern European culture. Instead, a multiplicity of constituencies and a corresponding multiplicity of discourses clamour for attention. The absence of a single or even a dominant discourse is often represented as the very heart of the 'post-modern' situation. The absence of a 'meta-narrative' (Lyotard 1984) in terms of which intellectual proposals make sense means the appearance of a diversity of views, each making sense within the context that provokes or receives it. The opening to previously silenced voices and ignored experiences and discourses produces an enrichment in theological discourse and a recognition that even with respect to making sense of God no single proposal can hope to escape the limitations of its discursive context, its cultural assumptions. Does this mean the reign of chaos, of unbridled relativism? At first it may seem so. But closer attention to the contemporary situation suggests the emergence of a number of common threads. It is this that produces the impression of a fundamental sea change in the attempt to make sense of God. In this concluding section I will attempt to identify some of these commonalities.

The treasure of language

One thread common to many proposals is a fresh attention to the rich resources of language. In some cases what is at stake here is attention to the variety of ways in which terms function within particular 'grammars'. This has proved useful in British, American and Scandinavian theology, often with an indebtedness to Wittgenstein.

Other theological proposals have exploited the richness of metaphor and symbol. In black and Latin American liberation theology, this has usually meant a turn to biblical metaphor and narrative to supply the richness apparently lacking in analytical traditions. In feminist and Asian theologies it has meant the freedom to select images and metaphors from other religious and cultural traditions. This is the case with indigenizing trends in African and Native American theologies as well.

The exploration of the richness of language for making sense of God is accompanied by fundamental transformations in the way in which divinity is conceived.

From absolute to related

Christian, as well as Jewish and Muslim, theology inherited from the Greek and Hellenistic world the view that the divine must be conceived of as fundamentally distinct from the world of change and time. The absoluteness of the divine thus meant that the divine must be understood as without essential or internal relatedness to the world and its vicissitudes. This view of God which had dominated theology for millennia has, in this century, been superseded by a growing consensus that the divine is to be understood as related to the world (and thus as subject to change) and therefore as not only eternal but also temporal. While there is considerable diversity in the ways in which this fundamental change in the form of the understanding of the divine is appropriated, scarcely any contemporary proposal is immune to the effects of this radical reorientation in the conception of the divine.

The idea of the relatedness of the divine to the world of change and suffering has at least two roots. The first is the greater role now given to the 'religious imagination'; that is, to the symbols and narratives by which the divine is represented in the myths and symbols of the religious traditions themselves. These materials regularly suppose that the divine is engaged in the events of human life and history. The greater attention to this symbolic discourse has resulted in the development of a philosophical discourse more amenable to the acceptance of mutability in the divine, whether we think of Hegel or Whitehead.

In addition to the greater prestige accorded the symbolic and narrative discourse of religion, the willingness to conceive of the divine as related rather than absolute owes much to the realization that the theodicy problem is otherwise insoluble. The absoluteness of the divine as this came to be formulated in theism made the suffering of humanity irreconcilable with the goodness and power of the divine. Accordingly, the view of the divine as the 'fellow sufferer' (Whitehead 1929), or the exposition of 'the pain of God' (Kitamori 1965) or the 'humanity of God' (Barth 1961), have grown from isolated suggestions into a significant consensus in a relatively few years.

In European theology this has generally been accompanied by an emphasis on the cross as the decisive point of disclosure of the truth about the relation of the divine to the world as suffering. Thus both Moltmann and Jüngel may be understood as proposing a theopaschite view of the divine (that is, that the divine suffers the suffering of Christ and therefore of humanity). This is, as well, the impetus for the 'death of God' theology of Thomas J. J. Altizer in North America. Jewish theology has been led in a similar direction through an attempt to grapple with the Holocaust (Rubenstein 1966). All of these views have Hegel (and, to a certain extent, Nietzsche) in their background and some rely upon a Lutheran view of the *communicatio idiomatum* (the interchange of characteristics between Christ's divinity and humanity).

The relatedness of the divine to the world, and especially to human suffering, has also made possible and even necessary a much greater attention to the possibilities of the trinitarian form of the doctrine of God among Christian theologians. The Trinity offers a way of showing how relatedness is not something simply external to the divine reality but is something internal to the divine life as well. While Barth and Rahner had earlier argued for a view of the Trinity as determinative for the specifically Christian view of revelation, the newer theological proposals (like those of Moltmann, Jüngel, Pannenberg) argue for the possibility of understanding the divine as essentially a relational field (Pannenberg) that incorporates humanity and humanity's suffering (Moltmann) into the divine reality. This emphasis on the internal and external relatedness of the divine has also been taken up in feminist theological proposals (Lacugna 1991; Johnson 1992) and in liberationist modes of thought (Boff 1988) as suggestive of the goal of the divine history. Indeed, even proposals as apparently 'agnostic' as that of Gordon Kaufmann take seriously the trinitarian structure of the divine.

This transformation of the structure of the concept of the divine has also transformed the way in which the 'divine attributes' are conceived. Thus the immutability of the divine has become the faithfulness of the divine, the omnipotence of God has become the invincible patience of the divine, the eternity of the divine has become everlastingness, and so on.

In short, it is difficult to exaggerate the fundamental sea change that has overcome the way of making sense of God. Orthodox, liberal and radical proposals for making sense of God share a common frame of reference in which the absoluteness of the divine has been radically modified by or exchanged for the relatedness of the divine.

Temporality

Inseparably connected to the relatedness of divine being is the positive understanding of the temporality of divine being. The radical distinction between time and eternity has served as the presupposition for the development of the idea of God for many centuries. It simply seemed inconceivable that the divine should be immersed in or subject to the vicissitudes of temporality, especially since time is the domain of suffering and perishing. Although this disjunction was expressed with renewed vigour by Kierkegaard and Barth, it was decisively altered by the application of a dialectical 'coincidence of opposites' by which the eternal coincided with, without being dissolved into, temporality. This move made possible a positive reappropriation of the images of historical engagement characteristic of biblical narrative.

In the later twentieth century, a number of ways of positively relating the divine to temporality have emerged. Within the sphere of European Protestant theology there has been a tendency to identify the divine with the occurrence of the event character of time. In the case of Ebeling this has meant a focus on the notion of a word-event in which the divine 'happens' in the speaking of words that open up a new future. This 'eventful' character of the divine can be radicalized as the occurrence of true relationality (Sölle), or as the encounter with truth (Scharlemann 1981), or as the rupture in the structures of language/experience (Jennings 1985).

Where, following Hegel, the temporality of the divine is seen most clearly in the event of the incarnation/crucifixion, the divine is seen as incorporating into itself the perishability that comes with temporality (Jüngel, Altizer,

Moltmann). In process thought and other currents of liberal and neo-liberal theology, the divine is viewed as the ever-changing yet essentially self-identical companion of history.

Of perhaps even greater importance is the tendency to locate the divine not in the past as the source of what is, not in the present as the event of encounter, but in the future as the goal or aim of the world-historical process. This view was enunciated with visionary power by Teilhard de Chardin in relation to the evolutionary process as a whole. On this view the divine was to be conceived as the aim or end, the 'omega point' which lured the evolutionary and historical process towards completion. The more recent proposal of Gordon Kaufman, while more tentative in character, similarly identifies the divine with the serendipitous creativity of the universe that aims at the humanization of the planet. Operating with considerably greater attention to biblical resources, Pannenberg has plausibly rendered the divine as the telos of history. That the divine is to be identified with the consummation of history rather than as the source of being is a view that resonates quite strongly as well with various currents of liberation theology.

What all these proposals have in common is the modification (through dialectical methods) or the abandonment of the absolute distinction between the divine and temporality. Thus a genuinely new situation opens up for the theological task of making sense of God. The 'historical' sense of modernity (and 'post-modernity') is incorporated fully into the idea of the divine.

From legitimation to critique and transformation

In addition to the attention to the resources of language and its symbolic resources as a source for alternative ways of making sense of God, and in addition to the apparent abandonment of the notion of the divine as self-contained (unrelated) and as eternal (non-temporal), we should also note an emerging consensus concerning the function of the concept of God. In general, this change may be represented as the shift from understanding the divine as identified with, and legitimative of, the structures of nature, history and society to the view of the divine as a critical principle in relation to these same structures.

Already in the first half of the twentieth century, with the collapse in the legitimacy of the structures of the European social world, dialectical theology emphasized that the divine was to be understood as the 'crisis' of all such structures. From this point of view, traditional theism had become bankrupt by having invested its plausibility in the social structures of the late nineteenth century. But these structures were regarded as having exposed themselves as simply the legitimation of the narrow interests of nation states. This critique could be allied with the critique of capitalism (Barth and Tillich) and served as the basis for an opposition to the pretensions of National Socialism in Germany (Barth; Bonhoeffer 1971).

In North American theology the critique of latent idolatry animated the proposals of the Niebuhrs and the reception of Tillich's 'Protestant principle'. Common to these views was the initial supposition that the divine should be conceived of as absolute transcendence, standing over against all attempts at the appropriation of the divine to legitimate worldly social structures and institutions.

However, when the absolute transcendence of the divine was reconceived in terms of relativity and temporality, the critical function of the idea of God was not given up. For example the 'naturalistic' proposal of Gordon Kaufman, that identifies God with the serendipitous creativity and mystery of the world-historical process, continues to identify idolatry as the chief enemy of a proper conception of the divine. Similarly the radical non-theism of Dorothee Sölle has understood the divine to stand over against the structures of domination and division.

A variety of ways in which the divine is understood to be a critical and transformative principle rather than a principle of legitimation of given structures has been put forward. The conception of the divine as event rather than structure serves to undermine pretensions of god-talk to legitimate social and cosmic structures. Similarly, the relationality of the divine in feminist discourse has served to oppose non-mutual or hierarchical (and patriarchical) structures of social reality. The conception of the divine as 'located' in the future similarly serves to criticize structures received from the past. Thus the divine is not the legitimating origin of these structures but the eschatological principle of their transformation. The 'utopian' function of talk of God in liberationist perspectives serves to bring into question the self-evidence of systems of oppression. Even where greater attention is paid to the natural and cosmic sphere as the locus for making sense of the divine, there is a marked tendency to focus not upon perduring regularities as the indication of the divine but upon transformative and creative moments (as in Teilhard de Chardin or Moltmann).

What is common to this great variety of proposals is a relinquishing of the legitimating function of talk of the divine common to ancient myth and traditional metaphysics, in favour of understanding the divine as the principle of critique and transformation. It is this factor, especially in relation to the openness to a greater variety of images for the divine, that makes possible a far greater openness to inter-religious dialogue than has been true of Christian theology in the past. This dialogue opens up the prospect of a mutual transformation of religious traditions and of the theological conceptualities in terms of which these traditions come to be expressed.

In summary then, the great variety of ways of making sense of God in the contemporary world does not mean a sheer multiplicity without common features. The multiplicity of options, together with the attempt to contend with this multiplicity, are one of the common features of the contemporary problematic of God. But beyond this we have noted other common features which together mark our epoch as decisively different from earlier periods of theology. The attention to the treasures of language, including the resources of other religious discourses, breaks down the barriers between academic theology and popular religions and among religious traditions. The transformations in the structure of the concept of the divine that give greater place to relationality and temporality mark a radical departure from the received category of the divine. And the alteration in the function of talk of God from legitimation (origin, structure etc.) to critique and transformation means that ways of making sense of God are now characterized by a fundamentally different orientation than that of traditional theism.

REFERENCES

Altizer, T. J. J. (1993) *The Genesis of God*, Louisville: Westminster.

Araya, V. (1987) *God of the Poor*, trans. R. R. Barr, New York: Orbis.

Ayer, A. J. (1936) *Language, Truth and Logic*, London; Gollancz.

Barth, K. (1932) *Church Dogmatics*, Edinburgh: T. & T. Clark.

—— (1933) *The Epistle to the Romans*, trans. E. E. C. Hoskyns, London: Oxford University Press.

—— (1961) *The Humanity of God*, London: Collins.

Berger, P. (1970) *A Rumour of Angels*, Harmondsworth: Penguin.

Boff, L. (1988) *Trinity and Society*, trans. P. Burns, New York: Orbis.

Bonhoeffer, D. (1971) *Letters and Papers From Prison*, London: SCM Press.

Cobb, J. B., Jr. (1965) *A Christian Natural Theology*, Philadelphia: Westminster.

Cone, J. H. (1975) *God of the Oppressed*, New York: Seabury.

Daly, M. (1973) *Beyond God the Father*, Boston: Beacon.

Ebeling, G. (1973) *Introduction to a Theological Theory of Language*, Philadelphia: Fortress.

Gilkey, L. (1969) *Naming the Whirlwind: The Renewal of God-Language*, New York: Bobbs-Merrill.

Hartshorne, C. (1964) *Man's Vision of God*, Hamden, Ct: Archon.

Hegel, G. W. F. (1910) *The Phenomenology of Mind*, trans. J. B. Baillie, London: Macmillan.

Jennings, T. W., Jr. (1985) *Beyond Theism: A Grammar of God-Language*, New York: Oxford University Press.

Johnson, E. (1992) *She Who Is: The Mystery of God in Feminist Theological Discourse*, New York: Crossroad.

Jüngel, E. (1983) *God as the Mystery of the World: On the Foundation of the Theology of the Crucified One in the Dispute between Theism and Atheism*, trans. D. L. Gruder, Grand Rapids, Mich.: Eerdmans.

Kaufman, G. D. (1993) *In Face of Mystery: A Constructive Theology*, Cambridge, Mass.: Harvard University Press.

Kitamori, K. (1965) *Theology of the Pain of God*, Richmond: John Knox.

Lacugna, C. M. (1991) *God for Us: The Trinity and Christian Life*, San Francisco: Harper.

Lampe, G. W. H. (1977) *God as Spirit*, Oxford: Clarendon Press.

Langer, S. (1942) *Philosophy in a New Key*, Cambridge, Mass.: Harvard University Press.

Lyotard, J.-F. (1984) *The Post-Modern Condition: A Report on Knowledge*, trans. G. Bennington and B. Massumi, Minneapolis: University of Minnesota Press.

McFague, S. (1993) *The Body of God: An Ecological Theology*, Minneapolis: Fortress.

Macquarrie, J. (1966) *Principles of Christian Theology*, London: SCM Press.

—— (1967) *God-Talk: An Examination of the Language and Logic of Theology*, London: SCM Press.

Mbiti, J. S. (1970) *Concepts of God in Africa*, London: SPCK.

Miranda, J. P. (1974) *Marx and the Bible: A Critique of the Philosophy of Oppression*, trans. J. Eagleson, New York: Orbis.

Moltmann, J. (1974) *The Crucified God*, trans. R. A. Wilson and J. Bowden, London: SCM Press.

Muñoz, R. (1990) *The God of Christians*, trans. P. Burns, New York: Orbis.

Oduyoye, M. A. (1986) *Hearing and Knowing*, New York: Orbis.

Ogden, S. (1966) *The Reality of God*, New York: Harper & Row.

Otto, R. (1950) *The Idea of the Holy*, London: Oxford University Press.

Pannenberg, W. (1973) *The Idea of God and Human Freedom*, trans. R. A. Wilson, Philadelphia: Westminster.

—— (1991) *Systematic Theology*, vol. I, trans. G. Bromiley, Grand Rapids, Mich.: Eerdmans.

Rahner, K. (1978) *Foundations of Christian Faith*, New York: Seabury.

Rubenstein, R. L. (1966) *After Auschwitz*, New York: Bobbs-Merrill.

Ruether, R. R. (1983) *Sexism and God-Talk: Toward a Feminist Theology*, Boston: Beacon.

—— (1992) *Gaia and God: An Ecofeminist Theology of Earth Healing*, San Francisco: Harper.

Scharlemann, R. P. (1981) *The Being of God: Theology and the Experience of Truth*, New York: Seabury.

Sölle, D. (1990) *Thinking About God*, London: SCM Press.

Song, C. S. (1982) *The Compassionate God*, New York: Orbis.

Teilhard de Chardin, P. (1959) *The Phenomenon of Man*, London: Collins.

Thistlethwaite, S. (1989) *Sex, Race and God: Christian Feminism in Black and White*, New York: Crossroad.

Tillich, P. (1951, 1957, 1963) *Systematic Theology*, 3 vols, Welwyn: Nisbet.

Whitehead, A. N. (1929) *Process and Reality: An Essay in Cosmology*, New York: Macmillan.

Wittgenstein, L. (1953) *Philosophical Investigations*, 3rd edition, Oxford: Basil Blackwell.

See also chapters, 14, 17, 20, 24, 41, 43, 44.

THE FIGURE OF JESUS CHRIST IN CONTEMPORARY CHRISTIANITY

John Macquarrie

'What is bothering me incessantly is the question . . . who Christ really is for us today' (Bonhoeffer 1971: 279). The question was asked by Dietrich Bonhoeffer in a letter from the prison where he was held, just about a year before his execution. He was writing in Nazi Germany, in a country which had turned away from its long Christian tradition to embrace a neo–pagan ideology. The Nazi ideology has now been left behind, but Bonhoeffer's question remains, for to a large extent virtually all the countries of Europe have become secularized and Christianity has for long been a declining influence.

Perhaps there was a time in Europe when most Christians believed that they knew the answer to the question 'who Christ really is'. They believed that the New Testament contains a veridical account of his words and deeds. They believed that he had performed miracles, had died for the salvation of the world, had risen from the dead and would some day return to the earth in power. They believed the teachings of the early councils of the Church that Jesus Christ is 'of the same being' as God the Father, and that he has two complete natures, one human and one divine. But the whole structure of Christian theology was shaken to its foundations about the eighteenth century by the intellectual revolution which we call the Enlightenment. That revolution affected every area of human knowledge and belief, and not least the Church's belief in Jesus Christ. Questions were being raised about the reliability of our information concerning events of the distant past, about the possibility of miracles or, more generally, of divine interventions in the world, about the authority of venerable documents which had up till then been considered beyond criticism, or indeed about any authority which is unsupported by rational validation. Obviously major difficulties were being raised for the Christian faith as it had been traditionally presented.

Our present questions had their origin in the Enlightenment and in the controversies which followed. In the words of Hans Küng, 'The christological debate that has persisted since the dawn of the modern age has not yet been resolved' (Küng 1987: 19). The difficulties that appeared so forcibly in the eighteenth century are, for the most part, still there and in some cases have even been aggravated. On the other hand, the tremendous efforts at restatement and reconstruction in which Christian theologians engaged throughout the nineteenth century yielded many new insights and new possibilities of interpretation and cannot be easily dismissed.

This chapter considers the situation as it is in the second half of the twentieth century, let us say roughly from the time when Bonhoeffer wrote the letter quoted above (1944) to the present day. There has certainly been no lack of effort in the search for an answer to Bonhoeffer's question, and it would seem to be vital for the future of Christianity that a satisfactory answer should be found. On the other hand, it needs hardly to be said that no single answer or set of answers has emerged. Even among Christian theologians, there seems to be a pluralism just as bewildering as the wider pluralism which we see among the many religions and ideologies when we look beyond Christianity to the world scene at the end of the twentieth century. Yet even in New Testament times there was a plurality of emerging christologies, and we may find that now as then some trends stand out and point the way to future interpretations of the figure of Jesus Christ. Also we shall find that in spite of two hundred years of criticism the classical formulations of belief in Christ still have their champions, including some of the foremost theologians of our time.

NEO-ORTHODOXY

In the middle of the century traditional Christian theology was not only surviving but, in the form known as 'neo-orthodoxy', was surprisingly the dominant school of Protestant theology. By the closing decade of the century, its influence had certainly faded, but it still has many representatives. The man chiefly responsible for this revival of the theological tradition was Karl Barth (1886–1968), a Swiss theologian who had grown up under the influences of liberal Protestantism but had then rebelled against his teachers. Rightly or wrongly, he blamed the nineteenth-century Protestant theologians for having diluted and humanized the teaching of the New Testament to the extent where it had become little more than an endorsement of the prevailing European culture. Barth believed that the gradual blunting of the Christian proclamation had been a significant factor in bringing on the crisis which culminated in the Great War of 1914–18. At the end of that war, Barth published his famous commentary *Romans*, which served as the manifesto for a radical change of direction in Protestant theology. He quoted Kierkegaard: 'Remove from the Christian religion, as [liberal theology] has done, its ability to shock, and Christianity is altogether destroyed' (Barth 1933: 98). The new theology was to return to the message of the Bible, to the eschatological theme of crisis or judgement.

When he came to express his mature thought in his great *Church Dogmatics*, written over three decades from the 1930s to the 1960s, Barth adopted a calmer tone, but the general direction of his teaching was opposed to that which had prevailed in the previous century. Whereas the theologians of that century had usually begun their thinking about Christ from the human Jesus or the Jesus of history, Barth goes back beyond history to the doctrine of the Trinity and to Christ as a divine person of the Trinity. His christology is founded on a doctrine of election, an 'event' which took place before the creation of the world, if one may so speak. 'In the beginning of all the works and ways of God' (Barth 1956: 2/2, 50) Jesus Christ was elected, and with him the whole human race, to be the partners of God. This teaching seems to give to the human race a dignity which was not accorded to it in Barth's early work, where he still held with Kierkegaard the view that between God and man there is an 'infinite qualitative difference'. Now, forty years on, he can speak of a 'humanity in God' and even says that 'theology would be better called theanthropology' (Barth 1967: 9). But we must ask whether the transposing of so much of the action to a beginning before history does not render the whole historical element in Christianity superfluous, and whether it does not also call into serious question the true humanity of Jesus Christ.

Barth does of course seek to maintain the doctrine of the two natures in Jesus Christ, and at the heart of his christology is a dialectical balancing of descent and ascent, the way of the Son of God into the far country (i.e. this world), and the exaltation of the human Jesus as he returns to the Father. In his exposition of these themes, Barth makes extensive use of the Christ-hymn from Philippians 2:6–11. One might think that he is going to follow the kenotic ('self-emptying', Phil. 2:7) path beloved of so many earlier theologians, but not so. God does not need to shed his divinity in order to humble himself. 'God is always God, even in his humiliation. The divine Being does not suffer any change, any diminution, any transformation into something else, let alone any cessation' (Barth 1957: 4/1, 79). Barth had a much clearer grasp of the dialectical being of God than had the kenoticists. Yet we have to note that there are grave questions about the genuine humanity of Christ in Barth's thought.

Among the many associates of Barth in his efforts towards a theological renascence, special mention may be made of another Swiss scholar, Emil Brunner (1889–1966). In an early monograph on Jesus Christ, he clearly expressed his polemical intentions towards nineteenth-century theology: 'The present exposition . . . is deliberately and uncompromisingly opposed to the modern conception of the [christological] dogma, introduced by Ritschl and Harnack' (Brunner 1934: 249). At that stage of his thinking, Brunner had, like the early Barth, heavily emphasized divine transcendence and likewise the divine nature of Christ. One critic has gone so far as to declare that Brunner's early christology was 'unquestionably docetic' (McGrath 1986: 101).

In his *Dogmatics* of 1949, Brunner sought to correct the earlier bias. Quoting Luther, he writes, 'We must begin at the bottom, and afterwards rise to the heights' (Brunner 1949: 2/322). By this time Brunner had become deeply influenced by the personalist or 'I-thou' Philosophy of Buber and Ebner, and he believed that his adoption of this philosophy would prove to be his major contribution to theology. It is in the meeting of person with person that revelation takes place. Brunner writes: 'Jesus Christ is more than all words about him. The Word of God, the decisive self-communication of God, is a person, a human being, the man in whom God himself meets us' (ibid.: 2/15). One consequence of this teaching has been to move the idea of revelation away from the medium of words to the broader medium of personal encounter, and this is a point that has been widely accepted among contemporary theologians, both Protestant and Catholic.

EXISTENTIALIST INTERPRETATIONS OF CHRIST

Rudolf Bultmann (1884–1976) had been at the beginning of his career an ally of Barth, but he later came to follow a very different course. Bultmann was primarily a New Testament scholar and soon gained the reputation of taking a very negative attitude towards the historical trustworthiness of the Gospel records. In many ways, his thought was close to that of D. F. Strauss. Just as Strauss had pointed to the gap between the first-century mentality which believed in supernatural interventions in human affairs and the modern mentality which believes that the causation of events in the world is due to other innerworldly events, so Bultmann held that one cannot accept modern science and the applications which we make of it and at the same time believe in miracles and other supernaturally caused events as these are related in the New Testament. Like Strauss, Bultmann did not hesitate to use of the word 'myth' for those parts of the New Testament which introduce supernatural agency, and he also applied it generally to the whole framework of the narrative which claimed that God had sent his Son to die for the sins of the world and had then raised him from the dead and exalted him to eternal life.

But Bultmann's problems about the trustworthiness of the New Testament went far beyond the general application of a ban on the supernatural. In particular, he took up (though he did not originate) the method of form-criticism. According to the form-critics, the Gospel narratives can be analysed into distinct paragraphs – this is very obvious as we read these narratives – and the paragraphs can then be classified according to their form. As early as 1921, Bultmann had carried out a detailed examination of the synoptic Gospels along these lines. His finding was that the paragraphs had originally circulated as independent units of teaching in the primitive Church and then they had been (to use the comparison that was often applied to the process) strung together like beads on a string. Although, as Bultmann did not deny, many of the sayings and deeds of Jesus have probably been preserved, we are in uncertainty about the order in which they occurred and are therefore unable to reconstruct the life, career and development of Jesus, except in very broad and inexact lines. So although we can derive from the New Testament some idea of *The History of the Synoptic Tradition* (the title of Bultmann's book), we are unable to reach the history of Jesus. But Bultmann does not believe that we read the New Testament for historical information. We read it in the hope of finding answers to questions raised by our own existence. This is the point at which Bultmann's thought makes contact with existentialist philosophy, especially the analysis of human existence offered by the early philosophy of Martin Heidegger. Bultmann's 'demythologizing' is the attempt to translate the mythological and even the historical elements in the New Testament into a language which interprets human existence.

So when Bultmann was asked how he could still have faith in Christ when so little is said to be known about him, he could give several answers. One, which might make some appeal to a Lutheran, was that since historical research is a work, and faith cannot be built on works, it is a mistake to try to base faith on historical assertions. Again, if we read the New Testament to learn about our own human existence and the way that leads from an inauthentic to an authentic existence, we need not be too much concerned with the historical or literal accuracy of the stories, provided we appropriate their saving message. Finally, however, this seems to mean that we need not be too much concerned about the person of Jesus Christ himself. Bultmann believed that the personal history and character of Jesus had been absorbed into his historical significance, so that we need only know the 'that' (*dass*) of Jesus, the fact that he lived and gave the message, not the 'what' (*was*), the content or character of his life. His significance seems to be exhausted in his being the bearer of the message.

Bultmann was strongly opposed to any 'objectifying' of the belief in Christ. Here we find echoes that go back to Ritschl, Melanchthon and the early Luther. To confess that Christ is God is not, according to Bultmann, to make a statement about his nature but to acknowledge his significance for one's own existence. This is perhaps the key instance of Bultmann's systematic demythologizing or existential interpretation of the New Testament. But surely a critical question arises at this point. Can a rational being give a wholehearted existential commitment to Jesus Christ or accept the proclamation that he is the way to an authentic human existence without some assurance about who or what Jesus was? Though many theologians of the present day have attempted to get away from objective questions of history and likewise of metaphysics, can faith and theology really be insulated from such questions? Would Bultmann himself have spent all the energy and ingenuity that he did in wrestling with the questions of Christian origins if he had really believed that only the 'that' and not the 'what' of Jesus has any existential significance?

Paul Tillich (1886–1965) may be included among those who viewed the figure of Jesus Christ from an existentialist point of view, for although he drew on other parts of the philosophical tradition, he expressed a special debt to existentialism. So although we find in him remnants of German idealism

(Schelling), of the mystical tradition (Boehme), and of depth psychology (Jung), his starting point, like Bultmann's, is the questioning that arises out of human existence. But Tillich differs from Bultmann in two important points. For the questions, he looks to the contemporary culture in general, rather than to the individual; and in seeking answers to the questions in the Christian revelation, he is concerned not just with human existence or human society, but with general ontology.

Does this mean that Tillich offers a more adequate interpretation of Christ than does Bultmann? In some ways, perhaps he does. In theory at least, he maintained that 'Jesus Christ is both a historical fact and a subject of believing reception' (Tillich 1953–64: 2/98). He insisted on this for the good reason that if one leaves out the historic factuality of Christ, one has left out what appears to be an essential part of Christian faith, namely, the assertion 'that essential Godmanhood has appeared within existence and subjected itself to the conditions of existence without being conquered by them' (ibid.: 2/98). It would seem that quite a weight of historical material is covered by Tillich's expressions, but in fact he has very little to say about it, and is far more interested in what may be called the symbolic or universal significance of Jesus Christ. Indeed, among twentieth-century theologians, Tillich must be counted among those who set least value on historical information. On the other hand, by concentrating attention on the symbolic significance of Jesus, Tillich was able to give a far more affirmative account of the religious quest of mankind than Barth had done, and was able to commend an affirmative attitude among Christians towards people of other faiths.

SECULAR CHRISTIANITY

By relating Christian teaching to the existential and cultural questions that arise in contemporary society, both Bultmann and Tillich were setting up a dialogue between Christianity and the secular world. But it was another German theologian, also one who had formerly been an ally of Barth, who advocated an affirmative attitude towards the phenomenon of secularization, claiming even that secularization is an implicate of the Christian revelation.

This was Friedrich Gogarten (1887–1967). Like Bultmann, he wanted to address the 'modern' man or woman, and he embraced Bultmann's demythologizing as a step towards doing this. But whereas it has been objected that Bultmann was too vague in what he understood by the 'modern' mentality, Gogarten is more careful in trying to analyse the changes which the Enlightenment brought to the European mind. One of his main points was that in the modern period history has taken the place of metaphysics as our frame of reference. According to Gogarten, this means that the world has become man's own world, in the sense that he has now to shape the world rather than to adapt himself to its pre-established order. Thus, for Gogarten, secularization is historicization, the bringing of everything into the historical reality, the *saeculum*.

This understanding of history is quite different from the nineteenth-century quest for the historical Jesus. It is a question of reading the history of Jesus in such a way that it illuminates our own history and enables us to lay hold on its possibilities. Gogarten can declare that the word of Jesus is the word of God, and it is obvious that his position is very close to Bultmann's. But in a book entitled *Christ the Crisis* (1970) Gogarten explores more fully than Bultmann had done the grounds for equating the word of Jesus with the word of God. Perhaps this involves him, whether he likes it or not, in metaphysics and objective history. At any rate, Gogarten claims that Jesus was the first member of the human race to break with the confusion between God and the world, and therefore to take full responsibility for the world. The biblical authority cited for this is Paul's teaching that the Christian has come of age (like the man of the Enlightenment!). Jesus brought the old world to an end with its oppressive powers and inaugurated the kingdom of God in which human beings are free to become co-workers with God (Gal. 4:1–9). So Jesus appears here as the pioneer of modern secularity. But an obvious problem for this view is that modern secularity seems to get along very well without either Jesus or Christianity. As Gogarten ruefully acknowledges, 'The difference between modern historical thought and Jesus' understanding of history is that virtually nothing remains of responsibility before God' (Gogarten 1970: 157).

The idea of a secular Christianity spread to the United States and, in a lesser degree, to England. Harvey Cox (1929–) took up Gogarten's point that Jesus had freed human beings for a new responsibility towards the world and claimed that the rise of Western science and technology could be attributed to the influence of Christianity in 'disenchanting' or 'desacralizing' the world, so making it open to investigation. In his very widely read book, *The Secular City* (1965), Cox argued that secularization is so far from being the enemy of Christianity that it may be considered an implicate of the Gospel. However, it was just about that time that people were beginning to perceive the ambiguities of technology, and it seemed that the total desacralization of nature might be a serious danger.

A different form of secular Christianity was proposed in Paul van Buren's *The Secular Meaning of the Gospel* (1963). The author of this book was a student of Barth and was also versed in analytic philosophy. Though he later modified his position, his secular interpretation of Christianity was meant to reduce it to history and ethics, so that his teaching could have a secure place within the limits of knowledge laid down by the positivist philosophy of the day. The best-known British writer on these topics was Ronald Gregor Smith (1913–68), especially in a book called simply *Secular Christianity* (1966). He was very critical of the American secularizers, both for their naive optimism and for their equally naive reductionism. His own view was close to Gogarten's

– that secularization is primarily historicization, but that this does not eliminate God, who is the transcendent reality which we meet within history, especially the history that has its centre in Jesus Christ.

CHRIST AS AN ESCHATOLOGICAL FIGURE

By the 1960s, it became obvious that new ideas were stirring in theology. The great theologians who had dominated Protestant thinking for decades – Barth, Brunner, Bultmann, Gogarten, Tillich – were dying off or becoming inactive. The leadership passed to younger theologians, and among them an interest in eschatology became apparent. It is true that since the beginning of the twentieth century, theologians had been aware that in the New Testament an expectation of the end of the present age played an important part, more important than the nineteenth-century liberals had allowed. But Johannes Weiss and Albert Schweitzer, the two scholars who had done most to show the importance of eschatology for the New Testament, had been somewhat embarrassed by their own discovery that such a mythological idea played such a key role in the thought of primitive Christianity, and even of Jesus himself. Both Barth and Bultmann talked much about eschatology, but they both played down the futuristic aspects of the idea. Now some younger German theologians were bringing back eschatology and emphasizing its futuristic character. Instead of seeing it as a mistaken idea of the first Christians, they were claiming that it belongs to the essence of the Christian proclamation.

A leader in this new phase of German theology is Jürgen Moltmann (1926–). His first major writing was his *Theology of Hope* (1964), subtitled 'On the Ground and the Implications of a Christian Eschatology'. He was writing in conscious opposition to Bultmann, and denied that eschatology is merely a mythological trapping of first-century belief. Instead, Moltmann claims, eschatology in its full futuristic sense is at the very heart of Christianity. The theologians of the previous generation had made revelation central to their enterprise, but Moltmann believes that the central place belongs to promise. The whole Bible has a future reference and God is to be understood not so much as a present reality but rather as the power of the future or the power of resurrection. Moltmann can even speak of the present world as 'godless', but this is not to be understood in an atheistic sense, but in the sense that God is 'not yet' – a phrase that comes from the neo-Marxist philosopher Ernst Bloch. This philosopher visualized not only the human race but the whole universe as imbued with a striving towards the future – a quasi-mystical idea which brought him into conflict with orthodox Marxists.

For Moltmann, therefore, the notion of resurrection is central, and by this he understands both the resurrection of Jesus Christ and the ultimate resurrection or renewal of the whole creation. So in opposition to all demythologizers, Moltmann declares: 'Christianity stands or falls with the reality of the raising of Jesus from the dead by God' (Moltmann 1964: 165). The resurrection of Jesus he takes to be the promise or guarantee of the future resurrection.

We may wonder whether Moltmann is not relapsing into a kind of remythologizing. He never succeeds in making clear just what he understands by resurrection. It is not myth, but it is not empirical fact either. On the other hand, we should note that the future resurrection is not conceived as only supernatural or otherworldly, but it is linked firmly by Moltmann with social and political action for the renewal of human society. He is, among contemporary theologians, one of those most involved in the social applications of Christianity. We should note also that in later writings Moltmann sets alongside the resurrection the cross and the tragic elements in Christianity. This is the case especially in his notable book, *The Crucified God* (1974). Here it is Christ in his suffering who is placed at the centre, and Moltmann argues persuasively for a form of panentheism in which the relation between Jesus Christ and the Father is so conceived that the Father too suffers at the cross.

Another German theologian who has taken up the eschatological theme is Wolfhart Pannenberg (1928–). Like Moltmann, he is critical of Bultmann and, more generally, of what he calls 'positivist' history. In particular, he believes that the theologian must have a conception of history that allows room for resurrection and other eschatological ideas. In his words:

> One must be clear about the fact that when one discusses the truth of the apocalyptic expectation of a future judgement and a resurrection of the dead, one is dealing directly with the basis of the Christian faith. Why the man Jesus can be the ultimate revelation of God, why in him and only in him God is supposed to have appeared, remains incomprehensible apart from the horizon of the apocalyptic expectation.
>
> (Pannenberg 1964: 82–3)

The fact that Pannenberg lays this great stress on resurrection should not mislead us into supposing that he is making an appeal to the supernatural. On the contrary, he adopts a rationalist (but not 'positivist') attitude to history, and believes that 'resurrection' is the most reasonable 'explanation' of the traditions concerning the end of Jesus' career and the rise of Christianity. Unlike Bultmann, Pannenberg does not think that the story of the empty tomb is merely a legend, but an independent tradition supportive of the appearance stories. So he can accept the resurrection as an event of history. Yet at the same time he insists very strongly on the full humanity of Christ. We must begin from the full acceptance of this humanity, and it is not breached even by the event of resurrection. Nevertheless, one must not be too hasty in attributing to Christ something 'more' than humanity. 'All christological considerations tend toward the idea of the incarnation; it can, however, only constitute the conclusion of christology. If it is put instead at the beginning, all christological concepts . . . are given a mythological tone' (ibid.: 279).

Can we arrive at a clearer idea of Pannenberg's concept of history, which allows for resurrection though it is not, he claims, mythological? He advances two considerations in support of his view. One arises from the existentialist analysis of the human being. The human existent is constantly projecting itself into the future and this projecting goes beyond death. 'It is inherent in man to hope beyond death' (Pannenberg 1970a: 44). This may indicate that for the human individual something like an expectation of life beyond death belongs to his or her existential constitution. But Pannenberg has a more ambitious and more comprehensive argument. Dissatisfied with the positivist view of history as a series of episodes, he seeks to revive the idea of a philosophy of history, a unitary view of the historical process. It is God who gives unity to history and reveals himself in history. This is possible only if history moves towards an end. Such a view, Pannenberg claims, does not imply any supernaturalism. 'Proper theological research into history must absorb the truth of the humanistic tendency toward an immanent understanding of events. It may not supplant detailed historical investigation by supernaturalistic hypotheses' (ibid.: 79).

LIBERATION CHRISTOLOGY

We have noted how Christ has been interpreted in the frame of secular theology by Gogarten, and how political implications have been drawn from eschatology by Moltmann. This is part of the contemporary desire to recapture the full humanity of Christ, and we now come to a further manifestation of the trend in liberation christology. This has flourished mainly in Latin America, though one might also include similar movements in other parts of the world.

Perhaps the most important contribution of the liberationists towards the interpretation of the figure of Jesus Christ is a book of Jon Sobrino (1938–), known in its English translation as *Christology at the Crossroads* (1978). Sobrino makes the very reasonable point that 'there is no reason why christological titles should be the exclusive prerogative of one particular culture, even that of the New Testament writers' (Sobrino 1978: 379). His own suggestion is that at the present day people in Latin America would be much more responsive to the title 'liberator'. This of course was the title used for Simon Bolivar and other leaders in the revolt of the Spanish American colonies against the mother country in the early nineteenth century. The use of this title would, of course, associate Jesus Christ with the political sphere, but we should remember that the same could be said of the title 'messiah' in the first century. Though Sobrino tends to exalt 'praxis' over theory, he is not cutting Jesus Christ down to the size of a politician. In some ways his christology is quite traditional, and he affirms clearly that 'it is through Jesus that we learn what liberation really is and how it is to be achieved' (ibid.: 379).

There is, however, a danger in this type of theology that difficult intellectual questions are passed over in the concern for 'praxis'. Sobrino severely criticizes both Harnack and Pannenberg for their absorption in historical scholarship.

926

He blames them for being 'explicative' rather than 'transformational' theologians. But since he appeals himself to the historical Jesus, he can hardly evade the kind of problems with which Harnack and Pannenberg have wrestled.

Leonardo Boff (1938–) has also written a full-scale work on christology, *Jesus Christ Liberator* (1972), subtitled 'A Critical Christology for our Time'. He lists his priorities, and they are similar to Sobrino's – praxis over theory, social over individual, human over institutional, and so on. But Boff too is quite traditional in most matters. Although he insists that salvation must affect economic, social and political structures, he acknowledges that this is less than the salvation which Jesus envisaged, though it is part of it. There is again an appeal to the historical Jesus, but again there is the problem of the limitation of our historical knowledge and the difficulty of moving from what we do know of the first-century Jesus to the socio-political problems of the twentieth century. Is it really the case that 'the historical Jesus puts us in direct contact with his liberative programme and the practices with which he implements it'? (Boff 1972: 279).

SOME BRITISH AND AMERICAN CHRISTOLOGIES

In our discussion so far of the figure of Jesus Christ in contemporary Christianity, very little has been said about the contributions of theologians in the English-speaking world. It is true that the leadership in theology has belonged to thinkers from the European continent, especially Germany, but solid work has been done both in Britain and the United States and although much of this has been stimulated by and dependent upon European influences, the English-speaking theologians have brought clarification and criticism to bear on the continental works and, not least, have curbed some of the excesses.

An outstanding example of this work of sifting, refining and constructing is the classic treatise of the Scottish theologian, Donald Baillie (1887–1954), *God Was in Christ*. The book was first published in 1947, and opens with a survey of the scene as it was then. Baillie noted two apparently contradictory tendencies. One he called the 'end of docetism', for there seemed to be a new determination among theologians to take the humanity of Jesus Christ with full seriousness and to combat that largely unconscious docetism (i.e. that he merely *seemed* human) which is deeply entrenched in popular Christianity and even in much theology. The other tendency was a new historical scepticism, which had come about partly as a result of the criticism of the nineteenth-century quest for the historical Jesus, partly as a result of the sceptical researches of Bultmann. In general, Baillie welcomed the first of these tendencies, but believed the second needed modification. The mere fact that Jesus had existed and had been crucified or even had been resurrected could hardly have any significance for us unless we knew something of who and what he was.

Baillie acknowledged that the idea of a God–man is the 'supreme paradox', but he was not content just to leave it at that. He believed that light can be thrown on this paradox from the Christian experience of the operation of grace in human lives. From Paul onward, Christians have done things, yet they have said that it was not really they who did them, but God working in and through them. Yet, according to Baillie, it is exactly at such times that human beings are most truly themselves. Here we have the essence of his christology. Jesus Christ is the man fully surrendered to God, the man in whom grace reigns supreme, yet he is for that very reason truly man. Baillie tells us the idea comes from Augustine, but the use which he made of it seems quite original.

In his book Baillie includes a full discussion of the atoning work of Christ, and here we see how he corrected some of the excesses of continental theologians. He returns to the point that we cannot ignore questions about the Jesus of history, for the meaning of the cross cannot be understood apart from what we know about the one who died on the cross. This seems to be directed against Bultmann. He makes the further point, directed against Barth, that atonement cannot be purely an objective happening, for it is 'a spiritual process in the realm of personal relationships' (Baillie 1947: 200).

In the United States especially, there has developed a type of theology which seems to be genuinely Anglo-Saxon, in the sense that it derives much of its conceptual structure from English-speaking philosophers rather than German-speaking. This is 'process theology' and it is deeply indebted to the philosophy of Alfred North Whitehead and also to his American disciple, Charles Hartshorne.

How the figure of Jesus Christ appears in process theology is perhaps best seen in the work of Norman Pittenger, who about a decade after the appearance of Baillie's book published a full-length study of christology entitled *The Word Incarnate* (1959). He later updated this with a sequel, *Christology Reconsidered* (1970).

The process theologian, as the name implies, sees events in terms of continuous development, rather than as sudden jumps or irruptions from outside the process. So Pittenger is determined to consider even incarnation in this way. This obviously demands that Jesus Christ should be understood as in solidarity with the whole human race, and Pittenger frequently insists that the difference between Jesus Christ and other human beings is one of degree, not of kind. He believes too that Jesus Christ is not an anomaly in the universe but 'the unique focus for a universal presence and operation' (Pittenger 1959: 192). He connects this view with the traditional Christian teaching about the divine Logos. We may note here that Pittenger is anxious to show that his teaching is continuous with the Catholic tradition, especially as it was expressed in the patristic age. He believes he preserves the 'intention' of that teaching, though he is not tied to its words. And he asserts that 'if the intention which determined the classical formulations . . . be denied, Christianity is certainly destroyed' (ibid.: 85).

Another American theologian, generally counted as belonging to the process school, though, as we shall see, with a somewhat different approach, is Schubert Ogden (1928–). Ogden's early work was dominated above all by his enthusiastic (though not uncritical) acceptance of Bultmann's existential interpretation and demythologizing. But he saw that Bultmann's views could easily be transformed into a subjectivist or non-realist version of Christianity because they lacked any metaphysical underpinning. So he advocated the bringing together of existentialism and process philosophy as a basis on which to construct a theology that would treat adequately not just human existence but divine existence as well. 'We would suggest', he writes, 'that an adequate solution to our theological problem waits on an attempt to think through in an integral way the respective contributions of these two movements in contemporary philosophy' (Ogden 1962: 177).

In the next phase of his thinking, Ogden emerged as perhaps the most effective critic of the 'death of God' school of theology, at that time active in the United States. Ogden was now drawing heavily on the 'neo-classical' theism of Whitehead and Hartshorne. However, when he returned specifically to the figure of Jesus Christ in his book *The Point of Christology* (1982), Ogden also reverted to existentialism, and declared: 'The point of christology is an existential point. Its assertion about who Jesus is, is even more an assertion about who we are' (Ogden 1982: 42). Perhaps the welding together of existentialism and process philosophy had proved to be unfeasible.

The British theologian and bishop, John Robinson (1919–83), was attracted to process theology and was a great admirer of Norman Pittenger, but he never fully embraced the process point of view, and based himself primarily on New Testament studies, rather than on any particular philosophy. He shot to fame with his book *Honest to God* (1963) which was not only a critique of the somewhat deistic image of God cherished among many church people, but equally a critique of the docetism which characterized the way in which they thought of Jesus Christ. In popular belief, Jesus was regarded as a figure from some realm 'out there', he had pre-existed in heaven, he had sojourned briefly on earth and then he had returned to his supernatural abode. Robinson tended to caricature popular belief, but there was substance in his complaints and if the idea of Jesus as the God–man seems incredible to many people in the twentieth century, the responsibility for this state of affairs must in the main be ascribed to inadequate teaching on the part of the Church.

Robinson's major contribution to christology, *The Human Face of God* (1973), was a determined effort to dispel the obscuring clouds of docetism and to present Jesus Christ as a genuinely human person, something which was clearly affirmed by the Chalcedonian fathers in the fifth century and is essential if Jesus is to have any significance for the human race. But although Robinson was critical of supernaturalism and of the way in which ideas like the 'pre-existence' of Jesus and his 'sinlessness' had been understood, he remained committed to the central Christian belief in incarnation. This belief is not dependent on pre-existence and related ideas.

I believe 'that the word can just as truly and just as biblically (in fact, more truly and more biblically) be applied to another way of understanding it. This is: that one who was totally and utterly a man – and had never been anything other than a man or more than a man – so completely embodied what was from the beginning the meaning and purpose of God's self-expression (whether conceived in terms of his Spirit, his Wisdom, his Word, or the intimately personal relation of Sonship) that it could be said and had to be said of that man, 'He was God's man' or 'God was in Christ' or even that he was 'God for us'.

(Robinson 1973: 179)

So it was not surprising that when a collection of essays by some English theologians, *The Myth of God Incarnate*, was published in 1977, it was sharply criticized by Robinson who considered it unduly reductionist.

SOME CONTEMPORARY ROMAN CATHOLIC CHRISTOLOGIES

This chapter has up to this point been almost totally confined to Protestant and Anglican theologians. The reason is that until recently Roman Catholic studies of Christ were for the most part reiterations of the classical christology of Chalcedon, and throughout the nineteenth and early twentieth centuries, Catholic theology held itself aloof from the 'liberal' tendencies manifesting themselves in Protestantism. As Karl Rahner has observed, textbooks of Catholic dogma published in 1950 were scarcely distinguishable from the textbooks of 1750, in spite of all the revolutionary changes that had taken place in the world of ideas in the two hundred years between them. But since the middle 1960s, that is to say, since the Second Vatican Council, new developments have appeared. During these years, it is also the case that the leadership in Christian theology has passed from Protestant to Roman Catholic thinkers. The traditional doctrines have not been abandoned, but fresh language and fresh emphases have brought a new intelligibility, and this has happened not least in the interpretation of the figure of Jesus Christ.

Karl Rahner (1904–84) himself affords a good illustration of the new spirit animating Catholic reflection on the person of Christ. One of the strengths of his theology is that it rests upon a carefully elaborated anthropology (i.e. belief about the human being), and this attention which he pays to the constitution of the human being results in a corresponding importance attaching to the humanity of Christ, so that we see in Rahner the same tendency observed in many other theologians, namely, a desire to recapture the humanity of Christ, so often obscured in the past.

Rahner's anthropology is contained mainly in two books of philosophical theology. One is *Spirit in the World* (1957) and in this book, the concept of spirit is taken as the clue to what it means to be human, and spirit is understood as the outreach towards the infinite. The human being is a finite creature who is nevertheless conscious of moving towards an infinite horizon. A further book, *Hearers of the Word* (1969), claims that the human being has an openness for revelation. The argument is that we are aware of ourselves

930

as embarked on a limitless process of transcendence towards a spiritual infinite, and to be in this situation is to have the expectation of some revealing word from that infinite.

The foregoing sketch of Rahner's anthropology already suggests its significance for his christology. Rahner succinctly expresses the relation thus: christology is transcendent anthropology, anthropology is deficient christology (Rahner 1961: 164). His remarks on the relations between anthropology and christology are reminiscent of Schleiermacher (1768–1834), though not of course directly derived from him. Rahner reminds us too that a christology which begins from Christ's humanity has a precedent in the New Testament and should not be allowed to fade from view because of more sophisticated christologies based on the eternal Word or Logos (from John's Gospel on). He asks:

> Is the christology of the Acts of the Apostles, which begins from below, with the human experience of Jesus, merely primitive? Or has it something special to say to us which classical christology does not say with the same clarity?

The more strictly incarnational idea of the coming of God into the creation is discussed by Rahner in connection with the idea of evolution (Rahner 1978: 178–203). Some of his views are similar to those of Teilhard de Chardin, discussed below. Rahner believes that God has, in the evolutionary process, been progressively communicating himself in and to the creation. Jesus Christ is the climax of this process of communication, so that he has for Rahner a cosmic significance, again an idea with a New Testament pedigree, in Ephesians.

The wide variety to be found in post-Vatican II Catholic theology is obvious if we set alongside the christology of Rahner that of the Belgian Dominican, Edward Schillebeeckx (1914–). He too begins from the humanity of Jesus Christ, but not from a philosophical understanding of what humanity is and might become, rather from an attempt (in spite of everything!) to reconstruct the historical Jesus. In two massive volumes, the first called *Jesus* (1979) and the second *Christ* (1980), he searches through the New Testament material, and in particular tries to bring to light the earliest impressions of Jesus. This involves him in a difficult and precarious attempt to isolate the earliest strata of tradition in the New Testament. He attaches special importance to the hypothetical document known as Q (*Quelle*), alleged to lie behind Matthew and Luke, though it must be noted that New Testament experts are divided about the merits of Schillebeeckx's findings. Jesus, he claims, is best described as a prophet, proclaiming the kingdom, giving evidence of its advent in healings and exorcisms, and communicating its spirit in teaching and in table fellowship with both disciples and social outcasts. Already these hearers were undergoing in themselves something like a salvific experience through their fellowship with Jesus, so that even before the climactic events of crucifixion and resurrection, if we accept Schillebeeckx's reconstruction, Jesus through his teaching and ministry was liberating his hearers from constricting ideas of God and of human community, and giving them a fuller vision of what human life can become.

But even if we admit this, it is hard to admit Schillebeeckx's claim that the idea of 'prophet' had all the weight that he ascribed to it and that the early perception of Jesus as prophet was already on the way to the classical christology. Schillebeeckx does respond to the need to ask who and what was the person crucified and resurrected, but he does not adequately treat crucifixion and resurrection themselves.

The Jesuit Pierre Teilhard de Chardin (1881–1955) belonged to an earlier generation than that of Rahner and Schillebeeckx, but since he was not permitted to publish his work during his lifetime, it was only in the period of Vatican II and after that it became generally known. His most important book, *The Phenonenon of Man* (1959), appeared in the year of his death, and many other writings in the decade which followed.

In his youth, Teilhard had become interested in the biological sciences and had been influenced by the philosophy of Henri Bergson, who had attacked the materialism of the nineteenth century and had argued for a creative principle at work in evolution. Teilhard came to see evolution as a vast ordered process moving towards a goal. Some scientists criticized him for taking too simplistic a view of evolution by ignoring its apparently groping and tentative character, while some theologians questioned whether the immanent creative principle of evolution as described by Teilhard could be rightly called 'God'. Our concern is however not so much with the general merits or demerits of Teilhard's philosophy as with his view of Jesus Christ. He sees Jesus Christ as the reflection back into the present of the future goal towards which evolution is moving. This is called by him the 'omega-point', which appears to mean all things gathered up in God, an idea which has its roots in the New Testament, especially Ephesians. This is the understanding of Christ as a cosmic figure, indeed the goal of the cosmic process. In Teilhard's own words, 'The exclusive task of the world is the physical incorporation of the faithful in the Christ who is of God' (Teilhard de Chardin 1964: 318). It would be hard to imagine a more exalted christology than this. At the same time, Teilhard is far from any docetic or gnostic attitude. On the contrary, he has a quite astonishing reverence for the material and the potentialities of the material, without parallel since the days of John of Damascus (eighth century) and the controversies over icons. When one has in mind the astounding potentialities of matter–energy, then Teilhard's vision of the whole universe as the body of Christ, that is, of the Logos which is the principle of its order and unity, does not seem quite so sweepingly imperialistic as it might at first sight. But his theories stand in need of rigorous sifting and revision, due to the fact that, as he was unable to publish in his lifetime, he did not get the scholarly criticism that would normally have been due to him.

932

THE PRESENT SITUATION

The foregoing survey of christological thinking in the second half of the twentieth century reinforces the comment of Küng quoted near the beginning of the chapter: 'The christological debate that has persisted since the dawn of the modern age has not yet been resolved.' We are in a time of pluralism, when long-established ways of understanding the figure of Jesus Christ seem to have become worn out, and no one new statement has taken their place. Yet amid the pluralism we can discern some trends which keep recurring. Now that the change of direction signalled by neo-orthodoxy no longer exercises the powerful influence that it had a generation or so ago, ideas which first appeared in the immediate post-Enlightenment period and throughout the nineteenth century are appearing again. When his influence was at its strongest, Karl Barth remarked that it had become apparent that Ritschlianism had been only an episode. Today, a few decades further on, it looks as if Barthianism too was only an episode. Yet one would have to say that even if some of the ideas of the pre-Barthian period are returning, they have been chastened by the discussions which were provoked by the theological renascence under Barth. We shall briefly consider some of the current trends.

The historical question

In the nineteenth century, writers about Jesus Christ were much concerned about reconstructing his history, disentangled from the theological and mythological ideas that had grown up around him. This 'quest of the historical Jesus', which aimed at showing his genuine humanity, was severely criticized by Albert Schweitzer and others (Schweitzer 1954). Many of the theologians discussed in this chapter were therefore very sceptical about the need or even the possibility of getting reliable information about the Jesus of history – this would be true of Bultmann, Gogarten, Barth, Tillich, though in different ways. But we have seen that as early as 1947 Baillie was calling for a new and more affirmative attitude to the historical questions. Soon after, Ernst Käsemann and other disciples of Bultmann launched a 'new quest' of the historical Jesus. This 'new quest', like the contemporaneous 'new hermeneutic', never really came to much and the historical question is one that still needs investigation – and still receives it, from both Christian and Jewish scholars and others. Among contemporary writers, Pannenberg and Schillebeeckx take history very seriously as a medium of revelation, but they are aware of the dangers of slipping back into the old quest.

The humanity of Jesus Christ

The traditional christology attributed to Jesus Christ both a human nature and a divine nature. In post-Enlightenment thought, for instance in

933

Schleiermacher, a strong emphasis was laid on his human nature, which had hitherto been obscured by the excessive stress on his divinity. During the period of neo-orthodoxy, the true humanity of Christ was again in danger of being obscured. But since the 1960s, the stress has again been on the humanity, and the humanity has usually been the starting point for christological reflection, as may be seen in Rahner, Schillebeeckx, Pannenberg, Robinson and others. These recent thinkers have made use of contemporary philosophical anthropologies which have claimed that there is no fixed human 'nature' and that the human person is a being in process of transcendence.

The divinity of Jesus Christ

If formerly the stress on the divinity of Christ obscured his humanity, the new interest in his humanity now threatens to obscure his divinity. The idea of 'incarnation' has been subjected to criticism (Hick 1977), though it has also had restatements. It is difficult to see how Christianity could survive without its divine claim for Christ, which is deeply entrenched in theology and liturgy. The trend today is not to think of divinity as an additional 'nature' somehow added to Christ's humanity or of his humanity as a 'nature' assumed by his divinity, but rather that a transcendent humanity fully images God, to the extent that is possible under the conditions of finitude.

Saviour-figures

A question which is not new but is receiving new prominence is that of the relation of Jesus Christ to other 'saviour-figures' such as Confucius, Muhammad, Krishna, Buddha *et al.* Is Christ the only or even the ultimate revelation of God or do some parts of the human race find salvation through one of these other figures? Or, more speculatively, if, as we may think nowadays, there may be many intelligent or spiritual races of creatures in distant parts of the universe, do they too have their saviours, their messengers from God or even their incarnations of God? The New Testament itself gives no completely unambiguous answer to such questions, and even so central a theologian as St Thomas Aquinas speculated on the possibility of a plurality of incarnations. This is a problem that will have to engage the christology of the future, and although numerous articles and books are already being written on the subject, there are many difficult questions to be settled. For instance, is there a plurality of rationalities, of moralities, of spiritualities? Or is there one universal Logos who is manifested (though perhaps in varying degrees of clarity) in the many saviour-figures? It seems that there are still unfinished tasks for christology.

REFERENCES

Baillie, D. (1947) *God Was in Christ*, London: Faber & Faber.
Barth, K. (1933) *Romans*, Oxford: Oxford University Press.
—— (1956) *Church Dogmatics 2/2*, Edinburgh: T. & T. Clark.
—— (1957) *Church Dogmatics 4/1*, Edinburgh: T. & T. Clark.
—— (1967) *The Humanity of God*, London: Collins.
Boff, L. (1972) *Jesus Christ Liberator*, London: SCM Press.
Bonhoeffer, D. (1971) *Letters and Papers from Prison*, London: SCM Press.
Brunner, E. (1934) *The Mediator*, London: Lutterworth Press.
—— (1949) *Dogmatics*, Philadelphia: Westminster Press, 3 vols.
Bultmann, R. (1963) *The History of the Synoptic Tradition*, trans. J. Marsh, Oxford: Basil Blackwell.
Cox, H. (1965) *The Secular City*, New York: Macmillan.
Gogarten, F. (1955) *Demythologizing and History*, London: SCM Press.
—— (1970) *Christ the Crisis*, London: SCM Press.
Hick, J. (ed.) (1977) *The Myth of God Incarnate*, London: SCM Press.
Küng, H. (1987) *The Incarnation of God*, Edinburgh: T. & T. Clark.
McGrath, A. (1986) *The Making of Modern German Christology*, Oxford: Basil Blackwell.
Macquarrie, J. (1990) *Jesus Christ in Modern Thought*, London: SCM Press.
Moltmann, J. (1964) *Theology of Hope*, London: SCM Press.
—— (1974) *The Crucified God*, London: SCM Press.
—— (1990) *The Way of Jesus Christ*, London: SCM Press.
Ogden, S. (1962) *Christ Without Myth*, New York: Harper & Row.
—— (1966) *The Reality of God*, New York: Harper & Row.
—— (1982) *The Point of Christology*, London: SCM Press.
Pannenberg, W. (1964) *Jesus: God and Man*, London: SCM Press.
—— (1970a) *What Is Man?*, Philadelphia: Fortress Press.
—— (1970b) *Basic Questions in Theology 1*, London: SCM Press.
Pittenger, N. (1959) *The Word Incarnate*, New York: Harper & Row.
—— (1970) *Christology Reconsidered*, New York: Harper & Row.
Rahner, K. (1957) *Spirit in the World*, London: Sheed and Ward.
—— (1961) *Theological Investigations 1*, London: Darton, Longman and Todd.
—— (1969) *Hearers of the Word*, New York: Herder & Herder.
—— (1978) *Foundations of Christian Faith*, London: Darton, Longman and Todd.
Robinson, J. A. T. (1963) *Honest to God*, London: SCM Press.
—— (1973) *The Human Face of God*, London: SCM Press.
Schillebeeckx, E. (1979) *Jesus*, London: Collins.
—— (1980) *Christ*, London: SCM Press.
Schweitzer, A. (1954) *The Quest of the Historical Jesus*, London: A. & C. Black.
Smith, R. G. (1966) *Secular Christianity*, London: Collins.
Sobrino, J. (1978) *Christology at the Crossroads*, London: SCM Press.
Strauss, D. F. (1972) *The Life of Jesus*, Philadelphia: Fortress.
Teilhard de Chardin, P. (1959) *The Phenomenon of Man*, London: Collins.
—— (1964) *The Future of Man*, New York: Harper & Row.
Tillich, P. (1953–64) *Systematic Theology*, Chicago: University of Chicago Press.
Van Buren, P. (1963) *The Secular Meaning of the Gospel*, New York: Macmillan.

FURTHER READING

Bultmann, R. (1958) *Jesus Christ and Mythology*, New York: Scribner.
Cullman, O. (1959) *Christology of the New Testament*, London: SCM Press.
Dunn, J. (1980) *Christology in the Making*, London: SCM Press.
Fuller, R. H. (1965) *The Foundations of New Testament Christology*, New York: Scribner.
Knox, J. (1962) *The Church and the Reality of Christ*, New York: Harper & Row.
—— (1967) *The Humanity and the Divinity of Christ*, Cambridge: Cambridge University Press.
Küng, H. (1987) *The Incarnation of God*, Edinburgh: T. & T. Clark.
McIntyre, J. (1966) *The Shape of Christology*, London: SCM Press.
Meyendorff, J. (1969) *Christ in Eastern Christian Thought*, Washington: Corpus Books.
Sanders, E. P. (1985) *Jesus and Judaism*, London: SCM Press.
Vermes, G. (1973) *Jesus the Jew*, London: Collins.
See also chapters 9, 10, 14, 15, 26, 44, 45, 46.

44

THE TRINITY IN MODERN THEOLOGY

Colin Gunton

Three main phases can be distinguished in modern discussion of the doctrine of the Trinity in the West. In early modernity, its fate tended to be bound up with that of christology, so that early modern criticism of the dogma of the divinity of Christ, classically that of Socinus (d. 1604), naturally called the doctrine into question. Aspects of that anti-trinitarian teaching, sharpened by the Enlightenment, are repeated without much variation by F. D. E. Schleiermacher (1768–1834), who is in that respect representative of one strain of nineteenth-century Protestantism. However, in the constructive dimensions of his theology Schleiermacher took the discussion into a second phase, as did some of his contemporaries. W. G. F. Hegel (1770–1831) developed a speculative theology of the Trinity in the process of developing his wide-ranging philosophy. In England, the doctrine of the Trinity in a more traditional form became increasingly important in the thought of Samuel Taylor Coleridge (1772–1834), as he engaged with problems of religion, morality and society against the background of the philosophy of the Enlightenment.

The third phase comes in the twentieth century, and takes its direction particularly from the dogmatic work of the Swiss Reformed theologian Karl Barth (1886–1968) which began in the late 1920s. The increasingly ecumenical spirit of the era has meant that there is much cross-fertilization between traditions which previously tended to go relatively independent ways. Major contributions to trinitarian thought have been made by Roman Catholic and Eastern Orthodox writers, and recent decades have witnessed a wide range of publications from many places in the theological spectrum, so that it is even possible to say that the subject has become fashionable.

It must be recognized that to speak of phases of development in this way is highly schematic. In all periods there have been competent theologians, Catholic and Protestant alike, who have continued to work with traditional trinitarian categories while being aware of the reasons that have led others to question, modify or reject traditional orthodoxy. The history of theology is more complex than that recorded in even the most comprehensive histories of doctrine. Inevitably, however, in a chapter of this kind it will be work that has been most prominent that will be in the forefront, as well as that which at present appears to offer the most likely and interesting possibilities for future development.

THE HISTORICAL AND CONCEPTUAL BACKGROUND

The early modern reaction against trinitarian theology can be understood only in the light of the problematic history of earlier theology. In referring to some early discussions, I shall hope not to duplicate material from earlier chapters, but to call upon such material only as is necessary to place modern developments in their context. In this respect, the relevance to modern thought of patristic treatments of the doctrine of the Trinity is that there originated conceptual possibilities which are only now being exploited, but whose development led by long and complex paths, particularly but by no means solely in the West, to a widespread modern belief in the practical irrelevance of the doctrine. The aim of this chapter will therefore be first to outline the chief conceptual advances, second to trace their fate, particularly in recent centuries, and third to give some account of recent and potential developments.

There are two chief conceptual developments to which reference is to be made. First is the teaching, associated with the decision of the Council of Nicaea (325 CE) and its outcome, that God the Son is 'one in being' (*homoousion*) with God the Father. Trinitarianly, this functions to express the equality of divinity of God the Father and God the Son. In its historical context it served to deny the Arian teaching that the Son is in some way less fully divine than is God the Father. While the precise meaning of the *homoousion* in its historical context is the subject of much debate (Stead 1977), the kind of function that the concept performs can be described quite simply. It is to establish a new ontological principle: that there can be in God a sharing in being which does not serve to subvert his unity. According to the Greek ontology which forms its background, to be is either to be universal or to be individual: that is, being is defined either by virtue of participation in universal form or by virtue of material separation from other beings. By insisting that God is Son as well as Father, the Nicene theologians introduced a note of relationality into the being of God. God's being is defined as a being in relation. 'To say that the Son belongs to God's substance implies that substance possesses almost by definition a relational character' (Zizioulas 1985: 84).

It was a commonplace of some nineteenth-century scholarship, often repeated in recent writing, that teaching of this kind encased the Christian Gospel in some kind of alien metaphysic. In this respect, as with what follows, the reverse is the case. Concepts whose origin was in Greek thought were developed in a way unacceptable to mainstream Greek philosophy in order to secure against distortion a theology whose basis lay in historical and particular divine action. Thus a relational trinitarian ontology is in sharp contrast and conflict with the doctrines of extreme divine transcendence propagated by Plotinus and other neo-Platonist philosophies.

The second conceptual innovation came with the further development of trinitarian thought by the Cappadocian theologians later in the fourth century. Largely as a result of their concern with the third person of the Trinity, the Holy Spirit, they further advanced the intellectual revolution, enriching the concept of relationality with one of communion. According to this, God is understood as one whose being is not absolutely simple – as neo-Platonism taught and as the mainstream Western tradition was to continue to teach – but is a being in communion. God is 'a sort of continuous and indivisible community'. The innovatory character of this ontological teaching was recognized by its authors, who themselves claimed that in it they had developed 'a new and paradoxical conception of united separation and separated unity' (Basil of Caesarea, cited by Wiles and Santer 1975: 34, 35). (For the character and implications of this development, see Zizioulas 1985.)

Once again, the development denies the assumptions of contemporary philosophy about the relation of matter and form, particular and universal. To be sure, the exponents of this theology were sometimes rather ambiguous about its expression, and appear to make appeal to the Platonic assumptions that their theology implicitly undermines. Nowhere is this more the case than in Basil of Caesarea's much cited comparison between human and divine individuality and essence in his letter on the difference between *ousia* and *hypostasis* (Basil 1989: 137–8). It has led to widespread suspicion either that by comparing Father, Son, and Spirit to Andrew, John and James he is effectively understanding the being of God in terms of Platonic forms, or (on the opposite side) that he is implying that there are three Gods, as instances of a prior universal. In point of fact, as a careful reading of the letter will reveal, he is chiefly interested in showing how the three persons of the Godhead are distinctively what they are in relation to each other in the being of the one God.

The intellectual achievement of the Cappadocians will be appreciated if account is taken of the fact that the drawing of a distinction between *ousia* and *hypostasis* achieves what Coleridge called desynonymization. This is the process whereby the capacity of language is enhanced by enabling two words which once were synonymous to achieve distinct meanings. In this case, the first term, 'being', continued to be used for the being of God as one, while the latter comes to express his threeness, what the Latin tradition had already begun to call the persons. In a doctrine of God as communion, according to which the three persons by their inter-relationship make up or constitute the being of God, there is no final competition between unity and trinity, because a revised understanding of what it is to be allows it to be realized that God's unity, far from being endangered by his threeness, in point of fact consists in the relational threeness of the particular persons. It is here that the perennial question of the coherence of trinitarian theology is answered, for in a relational conception such as this, unity and plurality are understood as complementaries, rather than having to be in some way reconciled.

More positively, it can be suggested that the fruitfulness of the development should be judged in terms of its capacity to generate understanding, and the ecclesiological, anthropological, social and political implications will be developed later in this chapter. But there is a case for arguing that the implications were drawn out adequately in neither the Eastern nor the Western traditions, both of whose theologies have been impoverished as a result. In an important article, Dorothea Wendebourg has argued that in the East the development of the conception of the energies of God crowded out crucial dimensions of the doctrine, and so led to what must be called the 'Defeat of Trinitarian Theology' (Wendebourg 1982). In effect, it may be glossed, the energies crowded out the persons of the Son and the Spirit as the mediators of divine action in and towards the world, so that the implications of the relational ontology became submerged.

Despite this, the Trinity has remained the focus of Eastern Orthodox liturgy and life in a way that has not been the case in the West (British Council of Churches 1989: 6), where among the results of the failure to allow trinitarian categories to permeate life and thought has been, as we shall see, a reaction against traditional and institutional Christianity in the modern era. The root of the alienation has been traced by some authors to aspects of the theology of Augustine of Hippo (354–430), who is alleged to have weakened the impact of both of the Cappadocian intellectual developments traced above. First, in his fusion of neo–Platonic and Christian categories he reintroduced a strong dualism of the sensible and the intelligible, the material and the ideal, and so neutralized the notion of relational being made possible by the *homoousion*. This had a major impact in a number of areas. First, it undermined the priority of the person, about the definition of which Augustine is vague, admitting that he cannot see the point of the Cappadocian *hypostasis* and claiming to use the concept of the person only 'in order not to remain silent' (Augustine 1963: 5.10). Second, correspondingly, it stressed the unitary being of God at the expense of the plurality, and effectively generated a modalism in which the real being of God underlies rather than consists in the three Persons (Harnack 1898: 131). The importance of this as a cause of modern 'protest atheism' will become apparent below. Third, characteristically of Platonism, it tended to a disparagement of the material dimensions of human being, and has in recent times led to the charge that Augustine shares responsibility for the misogynist strain in Western Church history. The dogmatic effects of the development were that the doctrine of creation was reduced to the margins of theology (Nebelsick 1992: 17) and that the incarnation tended to be reduced to a timeless point, so that the importance of the human and historical Jesus was minimized (Ritschl 1967).

The second complaint against Augustine is that he effectively obliterated the Cappadocian claim that God is 'a sort of continuous and indivisible community' and so blunted its ontological cutting edge. By seeking his analogies for the being of God in the individual human mind – what is sometimes known as the 'psychological analogy' – Augustine effectively aborted the social, ecclesiastical and practical, as distinct from the chiefly devotional, impact of the doctrine. Again, the root of the dogmatic aspects of the development, which many modern writers are anxiously working to undo, is a cutting off of the 'inner' and eternal Trinity from the economic and revealed. It is as if much that is of interest to writers about the Trinity in later Augustinian theology could be said almost without reference to the divine economy of creation and salvation made real in the Son and the Spirit. Conversely, the doctrine ceases to be constitutive of the Christian understanding of God. Thus it is that in the eleventh century Anselm's major treatise on the existence and nature of God contains one brief incantatory passage which does no more than repeat Augustinian themes (Anselm 1956: 88), while in the fourteenth century William of Ockham completes a process of effective movement towards unitarianism by his understanding of God as unitary and arbitrary will.

The long-term effects of Augustine's failure to understand and develop the conceptual possibilities of trinitarianism – though it must be emphasized that this judgement would be resisted by some modern scholars – have been noted in a number of twentieth-century writings. These can be summarized under a number of headings as follows:

1 Theological
2 Ecclesiastical
3 Cultural
4 Political.

1 Theological

Karl Rahner has pointed out that the divorce of immanent from economic Trinity has led to a corresponding breach in Catholic dogmatics between treatises 'on the one God' and 'on the triune God' (Rahner 1970: 10–21). The result is that the doctrine of the Trinity has appeared to be irrelevant, because everything worth saying about God has already been said by the time it is reached. Another way of putting the same problem would be to say that a divorce has been engendered between the being of God and his act: between who God is and what he does historically. The absolute simplicity and immutability of the God of the metaphysical theism that in effect took the place of the Trinity appear to militate against a conception of divine involvement in the world in incarnation and inspiration.

2 Ecclesiastical

The Church, it is sometimes contended, has rarely been understood as a communion in the image of the Trinity, and so has succumbed far too readily to inappropriate political and military models of her being (British Council of Churches 1989: 27f.). The consequent repressiveness has in its turn, it is argued, encouraged the millenarian and sectarian splintering which so mark the Christian era and which are fed by a perception of the difference between church practice and biblical models (Gunton 1991: 64).

3 Cultural

Michael Buckley (1987) has argued that modern atheism is a direct result of the tendency, from medieval to early modern times, to defend Christianity in merely monotheistic, non-trinitarian terms. Similarly, it has been argued that the highly monist and voluntarist God of late medieval nominalism generated by way of an intellectual reflex the denial of God that marks modernity (Blumenberg 1983).

4 Political

It is widely argued that the practical monism – sometimes misleadingly called 'monotheism' – of Western Christian concepts of God has helped to father the association of God with repression.

While in all these cases one must beware of simplistic tracings of cause and effect, and certainly of attributing them all to Augustine, the cumulative case is very strong that modern alienation from Christianity would not have taken the form that it did if trinitarian possibilities had been more adequately developed. (For continuing defences of an Augustinian position, see Hill 1982 and Mascall 1986.) Certainly, during the Enlightenment it was argued that human liberation involved freedom from the shackles of dogma, tradition and the institutional Church. How could it happen, however, that a faith centred on one who went to the cross rather than call on military assistance, a faith, moreover, which taught a gospel of liberation and which first took institutional shape as a persecuted minority, should come to be seen as the seat of obscurantism and repression? When we come to an account of recent developments, we shall see that modern exponents of trinitarian theology often explicitly argue that certain of these inherited problems at least appear differently if viewed through the focus of features of trinitarian theology that were previously obscured or suppressed. We now move to the modern era, and begin in the nineteenth century, when the anti-trinitarian developments alluded to above had fully worked themselves out.

THE NINETEENTH CENTURY

Schleiermacher and the modern crisis of religion

Schleiermacher represents a qualified form of modern anti-trinitarianism. In early modern times, the doctrine of the Trinity met the fate of most of the particular dogmatic claims of Christianity. For a number of reasons, among them the revulsion against dogma fed by the wars of religion and the confidence of the Age of Reason that there was one rational religion of which all particular religions were more or less inadequate versions, a Christianity mediated by Church, tradition and dogma was rejected by leading secular thinkers of the time. The doctrine of the Trinity, along with the doctrine of the divinity of Christ, often served as a model of the irrelevant and intellectually absurd. Just as it is easy to argue, according to a certain simplistic view of things and of language, that 'man' and 'God' are contradictory predicates, so it appears absurd that a being should be both one and three.

Schleiermacher's brilliance was shown in his conceding only some of the claims of the critics. To the view that particular religions were but deficient versions of the one simple religion, he responded in Romantic fashion with a hymn to the virtues of historicity, variety and particularity. Yet his defence of Christianity's particularity was based upon not its dogmatic particularity but its distinctiveness as a mode of communal experience or religion. With this, he combined an acceptance of Kant's dogma that things, and *a fortiori* God, could not be known as they were. Rejecting the view that the being of God in himself can be known, and therefore virtually all forms of the doctrine of the Trinity that the tradition offered, Schleiermacher began what is now a long modern tradition of arguing that God can be known only through the filter of experience, which is of such a kind that nothing not so reached may be predicated of him. Because it is in no way the implication of immediate experience, the teaching that God is triune in himself is consigned to the dustbin of history.

Despite this, however, a form of trinitarianism does survive. The structure of Schleiermacher's dogmatics is trinitarian after a fashion, because he believes that there is a threefold way in which experience of the Christian God takes shape. Although it is sometimes disparagingly said that the Trinity appears in Schleiermacher only as an appendix to his thought, it is rather the case that he describes his treatment as the conclusion. In an organically and systematically constructed work such as his *The Christian Faith*, the conclusion is, as he says, the coping-stone of the intellectual arch, and therefore the theology of the Trinity can be said to be of some importance. His reasons are that the being of God in Christ is essential to his conception of redemption, while without 'a union also in the common Spirit of the Church, the Church could not ... be the Bearer and Perpetuator of the redemption through Christ' (Schleiermacher 1928: 738). It is noteworthy that

Schleiermacher admits that his teaching is consistent with Sabellianism, that it to say that the three persons are but modes of the divine being, with the implication that the finally real God is concealed somewhere beneath or beyond his historical manifestations. Here, the seeds of modalism in the earlier Western tradition have under the impact of Kantian agnosticism developed into full flower.

It is important to keep Schleiermacher in mind when appraising the works of more recent theologians, for two features of his work frequently recur: an experiential approach to the doctrine, and a tendency to share his suspicion of anything claiming to be knowledge of God's eternal truine being (the 'immanent' Trinity). This is particularly pervasive in the writings of those Roman Catholics who have become in recent times suspicious of their tradition's tendency to dogmatic confidence about the inner being of the deity. A striking, perhaps rather extreme, example of a neo-Kantian and experiential account of the Trinity is to be found in Mackey (1983), who is sceptical about the consistency of the orthodox doctrine and highly agnostic about the possibilities the doctrine offers for the knowledge of God.

Hegel and the crisis of Western culture

Hegel's concern was rather different, because he did not share Schleiermacher's concern with religion as experience, of which he was contemptuous, but rather attempted to obviate the kind of alienating dualism between God and the world that has its roots in Plato and is mediated to the West by Augustine. The aim of Hegel's thought is integration, and at a number of levels. Conscious that, since the break-up of the medieval Christian synthesis, Western culture was in danger of fragmentation through loss of a unifying vision, he sought integration in a new theory of the Trinity. But he was also conscious of the deficiencies of traditional Christian theology and devotion, which he held to open up a breach between God and the worshipper (the 'unhappy consciousness') rather than to reconcile them. Thus his programme was both philosophical, in a wide sense, and theological: to renew at once the culture of the West and Christian theological integrity.

All aspects of culture and society were brought within the purview of a system whose central concept was *Geist*, or rational spirit, a clear allusion to the third person of the Christian Trinity. But Hegel's Trinity is not so much an order of eternal being-in-relation as a triadic process or movement in which the reality of Spirit is realized through and in the processes of human thought and culture. The basis of the process or dialectic is an absolute indeterminacy rather like that of Plotinus' One. But instead of giving rise to other forms of being by a timeless process of emanation, this One negates itself by giving rise to otherness or determinateness in process of time. The final moment takes place as Spirit realizes itself through a 'sublation', or resolution through elevation to a higher level, of the apparently contradictory moments of indeterminacy and determinacy.

In more traditional terms we may say that for Hegel the dialectic represented by the Father as indeterminate origin and the Son as historical centre are completed in the movement of Spirit. At the centre, as in the orthodox Trinity, is christology, because for Hegel that represents the reconciliation, in human history, of the apparently contradictory moments of the infinite and the finite. Crudely put, christology represents the claim that the 'other', transcendent, God of traditional theism dies in order that his final being as Spirit should be manifested and realized. But this is not identical with the later claim, associated with Friedrich Nietzsche, of the death of God as an achievement of human culture. As Jüngel has argued (1983: 55–7, 63–100), it should be seen in the light of Luther's radical association of God with the death of Jesus on the cross. Hegel's concern is to maintain the elements of historical particularity in Christian theology, while elevating them to a higher level as a universal philosophical teaching about human destiny. It is the trinitarian shape of God's christological self-revelation that is the reason for Hegel's description of Christianity as the absolute or revealed religion.

There is much dispute about Hegel's contemporary significance for Christian theology. One view, which has recently been defended by Andrew Shanks (1991), is that Hegel's transmutation of the transcendent, authoritarian, deity of the tradition into historical terms is of major constructive value. More moderate Hegelians, like Wolfhart Pannenberg, while welcoming the note of immanence, hold that Hegelian categories require control by a stronger assertion of historical particularity. A more hostile view would be that the outcome of Hegelian immanence is likely to be a form of pantheism, that identification of God and the world which it is one of the points of the doctrine of the Trinity to obviate, and that its rationalizing of the historical Gospel is inevitably Gnostic in is implications. Without doubt, Hegel's form of the Trinity is strongly modalist, with Father, Son and Spirit succeeding each other through the process of historical dialectic. It is certainly a whole world away from the conception of the eternally tri-personal deity of the tradition, some of the virtues of which engaged the attention of our third representative nineteenth-century thinker.

Coleridge and the Enlightenment's erosion of values

Coleridge is a characteristically English theologian, very much the moralist. That is not to say that he was insular, as many English theologians later in the century were to become in face of German 'rationalism and unbelief'. He read widely in German, and was deeply influenced by Kant, by German biblical criticism and by the dispute about pantheism that took place with the rise of the Romantic movement, with which he, like Schleiermacher and Hegel, was associated. The key to his development of a trinitarian theology which was distinctively different from theirs was his growing alarm about the moral implications both of the philosophy of mechanism and of the Romantic pantheism that succeeded it.

While he never succumbed entirely to those movements which shaped his early theology, Coleridge's intellectual pilgrimage can be understood as a movement from the rationalist unitarianism of the late Enlightenment, through the pantheism of Romanticism, to a form of orthodox trinitarian belief (McFarland 1969). The outcome of his thought was that all monistic forms of belief, whether mechanistic or organic, Deist or Romantic, tended towards the suppression of human moral freedom. Against all monism he asserted the rich plurality-in-unity of the Trinity. While the underlying basis of his trinitarianism was biblical, his defence of the doctrine was rational, in the broad sense of an articulation of its relation to the context in which human life was lived. In his quest for ideas, which should be understood as those indispensible notions which fuel the dynamic of the human mind in response to truth (Coleridge 1853b: 407), he came to hold that the doctrine of the Trinity was, as the 'idea of ideas', the basis for all thought (Coleridge 1976: 12–22).

This should not be understood abstractly. For Coleridge, as one of those minds who sought, like Hegel, to integrate all the dimensions of human being, thought was always a broad quest for an understanding of the human relation to the world. Its focuses were alike moral, social, epistemological and cosmological. But the outcome of his trinitarianism was very different from Hegel's, because he believed that human freedom is realized not in the immanent self-realization of God within human culture but in the difference-in-relation that a doctrine of the immanent Trinity allows. His concern was for a doctrine of God rich enough to allow space for an adequate conception of the relation between God and the world (Coleridge 1853a). His doctrine of the Trinity is therefore far more traditional than those of his two contemporaries, in that it focuses an understanding of the being of God in himself in distinction from God in relation to the world. Much of the point of his thought is that freedom requires that ontological otherness of God from the world as a result of which the creature is established in its own proper being in relation to its creator.

THE TWENTIETH CENTURY

As in the nineteenth century, the development of trinitarian theology in the twentieth is associated with a number of leading figures, notably Karl Barth and Karl Rahner. But in view of the wide range of interests that have come to emerge, the discussion will here be classified by topic rather than by theologian.

Towards a renewal of the Christian doctrine of God

Both Barth and Rahner focus their retrieval of the doctrine on the inadequacies of their inheritance. As is well known, Barth's early fame derived from an apparently root and branch rejection of the theology of the nineteenth century, and indeed his movement towards a trinitarian framework for theology does represent part of his reassertion of classical Reformation theological forms. It is not often noticed amid all the discussion of justification, predestination and the 'Protestant work ethic' that one of the ways in which Calvin differed from his medieval predecessors was in the constitutive role that trinitarian categories played in his theology. Despite its qualified appropriation of Calvin, however, Barth's trinitarianism should also be understood in terms of its characteristically modern orientation to epistemology.

He faced two main problems which were in fact the same problem from different perspectives. The first was the Kantian interdiction on all knowledge of a transcendent God gained from the world; the second, the consequent tendency of Protestant thought since Kant, Schleiermacher and Hegel to identify the divine in or as immanent or this-worldly phenomena. Early in his career, Barth had rejected the latter as an improper identification of the Gospel with human history, activity or culture. The former he faced (or evaded, according to the judgement of many critics) with an epistemological *tour de force*, according to which the doctrine of God's self-revelation provides a modern way into a doctrine of God. If God does make himself known within the contours of worldly being, then he can so do, and the Kantian denial of this is shown to be simply *a priori* and dogmatic (Barth 1975: 316). The key to Barth's proposal, however, is not simply an appeal to revelation, but to the fact that revelation takes a particular rational form. Revelation demonstrates the lordship of God because through it God himself enables us to know him as Father, Son, and Holy Spirit. In Jüngel's words, the doctrine of the Trinity is theology's interpretation of God's self-interpretation (Jüngel 1976: 15).

In all this, Barth was developing far more than a polemic against the stranglehold that Enlightenment epistemology had taken on modern theology. He was also engaging in a critique of the way in which large parts of the Christian tradition had come into thrall to distorted conceptions of God. He himself pointed out that only Bonaventure and Peter Lombard among all his predecessors had placed the Trinity at the head of their systems of dogmatics. This was symptomatic for him of the fact that theology had in the past come to the Trinity only after crucial decisions about the being of God had been made on other grounds. T. F. Torrance has argued that against this tendency Barth's theology represents an attempt to integrate the being and act of God more satisfactorily than had been done in the past (Torrance 1962). While traditional natural theology establishes the being of God and then tries, unsuccessfully for the most part, to integrate with it God's historical acts in

947

the economies of creation and salvation, Barth's programme is to integrate being and act, somewhat after the manner of the Cappadocian Fathers, by deriving the former from the latter. In Robert Jenson's words, 'God is what he does among us. All the complicated subtleties of Barth's developed doctrine of the Trinity say this one thing at all the different places where it might be forgotten' (Jenson 1969: 113). This point has been influentially developed by Eberhard Jüngel in one of the best studies of Barth's trinitarian theology, *The Doctrine of the Trinity* (Jüngel 1976).

It is here that the interests of Barth and Rahner in trinitarian theology coincide, though there are crucial differences in the way the doctrine takes shape in their thought. As we have seen above, Rahner's complaint is against the manner in which Catholic dogmatics introduces a breach between its treatments of the one God and the triune God. In response, Rahner develops a twofold strategy. First, he effects an integration of the realms of nature and grace by attempting to demonstrate the universal trinitarian shape of human experience. Second, he follows Barth in moving from the economic to the immanent Trinity, but even more radically identifies the economic and immanent. Barth's strategy was to link the economic activity of God – his triune action in revelation – logically with the doctrine of what God is in himself, eternally. Because God's revelation is genuinely revelation of himself it follows that he is in eternity what he reveals himself to be in time. Barth certainly does not take the step of saying that there is no more to God than his historical action. The immense stress he places on the freedom of God in revelation rules that out absolutely. Rather, the historical revelation has its basis, so to speak, in the inner and eternal Trinity to which it bears witness.

Rahner is less cautious in his identification of historical and eternal trinities. '*The "economic" Trinity is the "immanent" Trinity and the "immanent" Trinity is the "economic" Trinity*' (Rahner 1970: 22; italics are the author's). There has been much debate about the nature of the identification, which is certainly not intended to be absolute but to exclude all speculation about the being of God apart from the economy. There is, however, in Rahner a tendency to reduce the being of God to his historical manifestations. This gives clear echoes of Hegel's programme, though it appears to be mediated to Rahner through later German neo-Kantianism. A strongly Hegelian and immanentist note is also apparent in the work of Jürgen Moltmann, the main consideration of whom will appear below.

A feature shared by Rahner and his Protestant counterparts is a suspicion of speculation about the inner and eternal being of God. This is particularly apparent in the American Lutheran, Robert W. Jenson, whose chief criticism of Barth, about whose trinitarian theology he has written extensively (Jenson 1963, 1969), is that he does not take far enough the criticism of 'religion' that is for him one of the main functions of trinitarian theology. According to Jenson, religion is the innate human drive to escape our being in time for a timeless realm beyond, and with its eternalizing drive Western Christianity has capitulated to the anti-gospel of timelessness. In contrast, the Gospel, which speaks of God's radical involvement in our time, is encapsulated in the doctrine of the Trinity. There is therefore no spatially conceived transcendence of God and the world, for that leads back to the timeless. Rather, God's transcendence is to be conceived temporally, as one of futurity, expressed by the priority of the doctrine of the Holy Spirit as the goal of the trinitarian history.

The refusal of speculation about the inner being of God sits well with Kantian agnosticism about the world in itself and with the associated modern impatience with metaphysics. But the trinitarian price to pay is modalism. As Kant well knew, the human mind is irremediably metaphysical in its drive, so that what is driven out of one door creeps back by another. All of the theologians reviewed in this section make strenuous efforts to avoid modalism, and, indeed, they are all best understood as seeking ways out of modalism by returning again to the economy as the historical and real presence of God. The question to those in particular who would radicalize the Barthian method is whether modalism can be avoided without a robust conceptualization of the inner being of God to provide ontological support for the claim that the economy is a divine one. Without this, the impression is unavoidable that the historical manifestation is but the mask for something unknown lying beyond it.

Ecumenical concerns

The doctrine of the Trinity has served both as the unifying confession of universal Christendom – which it remains – and as the focus of its first major schism, that between the Churches of East and West which resulted in part from the West's unilateral addition to the creed of the clause 'and from the Son'. The split became entrenched probably in the eleventh century, when the Popes ceased to be commemorated in Constantinople. What, other than ecclesiastical politics, hangs on whether or not the Spirit is confessed to proceed 'from the Father' or 'from the Father and the Son'? For the East much indeed, and Lossky (1957) sees the *Filioque* as the root of all the weaknesses of Western theology.

Two focuses can be identified. First, it is argued that a tendency to modalism is established if two principles of origination for the Spirit – the Father and the Son – are posited, because the human mind will inevitably seek for a principle of being underlying the two, who will thus effectively be reduced to being surface appearances of an underlying *impersonal* deity. Although there are differences between Eastern accounts of this matter, Zizioulas (1985: 88–9) is probably representative in holding against this that the principle of deity must be *a person*, that is, the Father. Second, the effective subordination of the Spirit to the Son means that the work of the Spirit is marginalized, so that he tends to become little more than the one who applies the benefits of the Son to the believer. The impoverished state of pneumatology in Western theology, in contrast to the immense energy expended on christological dispute, is often cited as evidence for this claim. Much intellectual energy is now being devoted to a solution of this problem. (See, for example, Smail 1988; British Council of Churches 1989: 12–13, 30–4.) It is significant that there is now serious consideration among Western Churches as to whether this offending expression should be omitted from their creeds.

Of equal, if not greater, importance in ecumenical conversations is a measure of convergence on the relevance of trinitarian considerations in the worship of the Church. One of the driving forces of the early development of the doctrine of the Trinity was the trinitarian shape of Christian worship, beginning as it does in a number of New Testament expressions, perhaps most clearly in the so-called 'great commission' recorded in Matthew 28:19, to baptize 'in the name of the Father and of the Son and of the Holy Spirit'. Both baptism and the Lord's Supper presuppose a high doctrine of Christ and the Spirit, which was in turn used by early theologians as an argument for their co-equal deity with the Father. Drawing on recent arguments that Christian worship has been impoverished through neglect of its trinitarian framework (see Torrance 1975 for an account, utilizing both Catholic and Protestant scholarship), the recent report of the British Council of Churches' Study Commission opened with an affirmation that the primary relation of the Church to God is to be found in worship, 'in which we are brought to God the Father through his Son and in his Spirit' (British Council of Churches 1989: 3). It is, moreover, possible to build on such a basis as this to argue that trinitarian worship founds a conception of Christian theology as the articulation of the implications of faith in the God who is worshipped. Building on an article by Edmund Schlink (1967), the Methodist theologian Geoffrey Wainwright recently published a systematic theology whose framework is the worship of the triune God (Wainwright 1980).

The Trinity and protest atheism

In his call for the reintegration of economic and immanent Trinity, Karl Rahner used the term 'monotheism' in a pejorative sense, to allude to the problematic and unitary deity of much of the Western theological tradition. Much is now made of the link between this deity, conceived largely in terms of power, and the objection taken to Christian belief on the grounds that its God is demonic (as in Dostoevsky's much cited parable of the Grand Inquisitor) and encourages authoritarian or repressive forms of political order. It is argued that much of what is called 'protest atheism' is directed against such a God, and correlatively, that the doctrine of the divine tri-unity acts as a corrective to this unitary deity. There are two focuses of attention, the christocentric and the social. First, concentrating attention on God's suffering involvement in the world on the cross, in particular reference to the Holocaust,

Moltmann (1974) uses trinitarian categories as the basis of a theodicy, while Jüngel (1983) shows how non-trinitarian conceptions of the deity have been associated with the subversion of human freedom. Second, drawing on the link that can be drawn between a triune God and pluralist and open forms of social order, Moltmann (1981) develops work pioneered by Erik Peterson in the context of Nazi totalitarianism (Peterson 1935) for the doctrine's political relevance. While the originators of this approach, which has some links with Barth's strongly christocentric theology, were chiefly Protestant, a parallel approach is to be seen in Catholic writers, among whom is Walter Kasper (1984).

Within their limits, the points made by these and other theologians are valid, but two warnings need to be borne in mind. The first is that they sometimes presuppose a very naive view of the relation of theology and social practice, against which it is easily countered, after the projectionism of Feuerbach and Marx, that trinitarian theology projects a 'plural' rather than a unitary God simply because the preferences of the age are for a more democratic form of government. The second is that they encourage an instrumentalist conception of doctrine, recommending that which appears to promise the most appropriate results. That is not to say that no implications should be drawn from doctrine to practice; indeed, it could be argued that a theology which remained merely theoretical would scarcely qualify as Christian. Rather, caution is necessary about the way in which links are made and implications drawn. The next section will offer a test case.

The Trinity and the concept of community

Much recent trinitarian theology has called attention to the way in which the doctrine of the Trinity can provide the basis for a theology of community and, more generally, a relational conception of the person (Zizioulas 1985; Gunton 1991; Schwoebel and Gunton 1992). The common theme of much writing in this area is the inadequacy alike of the individualism and collectivism associated with the apparently monist tendencies of Western theology, and especially Augustine's. It must be stressed, however, that this does not involve naive playing of the Cappadocian tradition against the Western, for, as we have seen, there is a case for arguing that the East also ran into the sands. Rather, attempts are being made to realize in modern conditions the conceptual possibilities of trinitarian theology for social and political thought. Nor are they derived only from Cappadocian sources, for there are in Western theologians anticipations of the points being made. In the fourth century, Hilary of Poitiers argued for the importance of the distinct persons in God, so that the error should not be made of supposing that God is solitary (Hilary, *De Trinitate* 3.24.3f), while Richard of St Victor in the twelfth century argued for the necessity of three persons if God is truly to be conceived as love. 'Shared love is properly said to exist when a third person

951

is loved by two persons harmoniously and in community' (Richard of St Victor, *De Trinitate*, 3.19).

The doctrine of the Trinity is particularly illuminating in discussions of the relation between, and the arguments for and against, collectivist and individualist social orders. Indeed, it might well be pointed out that, in the light of trinitarian considerations, the choice is a false one (British Council of Churches 1989: 21f.). However, it must be remembered that, for example in radical feminist arguments, such considerations sometimes provide the basis for a rejection of the Trinity. According to them, the concept of the Fatherhood of God and the apparent masculinity of the Son are the source, not solution, of all the problems of modern society. The matter is a complicated one, but at the centre of the debate are the questions of whether the doctrine of God as Father is definitive of Christian belief; of whether it inevitably implies masculinity and a 'patriarchal' social order; and, on the other side, of whether the concept of a feminine deity inevitably generates the very pantheism which leads to the slavery to that unitary and non-relational deity which Coleridge saw to be the enemy of all human freedom (Kimel 1992). For something of a moderating position, which rejects 'patriarchalism' while recognizing the complexity of the predication of Fatherhood of God, see Lacugna (1991). There can be little doubt that questions such as these will exercise theologians for some time.

Other recent developments

On the face of the matter, the doctrine of the Trinity is an 'exclusivist' doctrine that militates against an appropriate stance towards non-Christian religions. However, some theologians are now arguing that the opposite is the case, and that it opens a middle way between aggressive christological assertiveness and a vacuous pluralism that is unable to encompass the real differences between faiths. Gavin D'Costa and others have made the points that a trinitarian approach is a way of avoiding a false polarization between, on the one hand, 'christocentric' and 'theocentric' approaches to the theology of religions, and, on the other, 'exclusivist' and 'inclusivist' theories. It is for its reconciliation of elements of particularity and plurality that the doctrine is particularly valued, either because pneumatology allows the particularity of Christ to be related to the universal activity of God in history (D'Costa 1990: 19), or because 'a Christian theology of religions based on the particularity of the self-disclosure of the Trinitarian God seems to be better able to preserve the independence and distinctive particularity of the partners in dialogue' (Schwoebel 1990: 43). And the point can be taken further. The theological fruitfulness of a trinitarian approach in opening up questions which are restricted by a too strongly christological approach is argued as a general point by Geoffrey Wainwright in his introduction to a volume designed to celebrate the centenary of the publication of *Lux Mundi* (Wainwright 1989: xxiii).

Another area where exploration is beginning is the doctrine of creation. The medieval tendency to treat creation in largely philosophical terms, and therefore as the act of unitary deity, came to a head in the highly voluntaristic theology of William of Ockham, according to whom it was rather seen as the arbitrary work of a deity largely conceived in terms of will. This is now being argued to be at the root both of the modern rejection of God in the name of the human will and of the consequent assertion of the human will to power that underlies the ecological problem. The possibilities for a return to a more relational view of the matter, adumbrated as they are in Coleridge's trinitarianism, are shown in the contention that the doctrine of the Trinity enables it to be said both that God is truly related to that which he has made, and that the relation is a free one (Gunton 1991: 142–61). The opportunities for exploration of this area, which has implications for cosmology, aesthetics and ethics, are immense.

Nonetheless, there is little doubt that at the centre of all trinitarian thought is the question of personal being. In what sense is God personal, and in what sense are we, those creatures created in 'the image and likeness of God'? How are we to understand the relation between divine and human persons, and how in its light are we to bear ourselves to each other and the world in which we are set? It is persons whose being is violated by our wars, market arrangements and social organization, and whose integrity is at stake in the way that the created world is being treated. On the one hand we have the massive totalitarianisms which so disfigure our modern world, and which are inseparable from the modernity of which we sometimes boast; and on the other, those forces of modernization whose outcome appears to be the increasing homogenization of people and societies into identical consumers of identical goods. Everywhere either the many are subordinated to the one, or the oneness and interconnectedness of things are lost in the ('postmodern') fragmentation of experience (Gunton 1993).

It is at this place above all that conceptualities developed by the great trinitarian theologians of both East and West are set to engage with the horrors and alienations of modernity, for they affirm two things above all. The first is that at the heart of things is the personal being of the God who is himself persons in eternal and inseparable communion, and whose being is a celebration of the centrality of the particular person in free and loving relation to other particular persons. It is the incorporation in the deepest structure of reality of both relation and otherness that is at the centre of the doctrine's irreplaceable contribution to human culture. To be a person, to be made in the image of God, is to take what one is both from being created in and redeemed into the image of the God whose being is personal communion. This means in turn that being a created and redeemed person is to be constituted in one's unique personal being not only by God but also in relation to others. We are only uniquely what we each are in relation to others, so that to be human, too, is to be a being-in-relation.

So many of our social and political theories and realities deny this polarity. In the light of the triune revelation, they are revealed to stem from precisely the same refusal of being-in-relation, and so to demand a choice that is a coincidence of opposites. This means that the second great contribution of the doctrine is to show us that there is no final choice to be made between the one and the many, between Parmenides and Heraclitus, because the many need not be reduced to the one, nor the one to the many. As God is one only as three persons in relation, so the world is what it is only as a universe of interrelated particularities. Here we find the basis for the development of Coleridge's concern to understand reality as the creation of a personal God whose world, for all its fallenness and need for redemption, is a place in which to learn and exercise the personal virtues of love and freedom, or rather love as the exercise of freedom in being freely for and from the other.

CONCLUSION: A CAUTIONARY NOTE

There has, then, been a widespread revival of trinitarian theology in the twentieth century. The pioneering work of Barth, Rahner and Lossky has been succeeded by a plethora of enterprises the quality of whose output has yet to be assessed. What is being discovered is that the doctrine is not, as has sometimes been supposed, simply a dogma to be affirmed or denied, but a resource for the life of the Christian community and for thought not only about God but about all aspects of human life in society and in the world. The capacity for the generation of new insights is being explored in many places. Indeed, so fashionable has the pursuit become, that the impression is sometimes given that here we have a cure-all, the solution to all problems. It is here that the dangers lie, and they are twofold.

First, if the doctrine is turned into a general principle for thought, it becomes an abstract philosophy, as a second-rate Hegelianism became in the generations after Hegel a kind of magic key to open all locks. Second, if the being of God is too much identified with all or part of the economy of creation and redemption, for example with the 'suffering God' on the cross, there is a similar danger that a merely superficial appeal to divine involvement in the world will result. The recurring problem of modalism – sometimes hidden under appeals to the merely 'doxological' character of trinitarian affirmation – can hide an evasion of the most promising and most difficult of all aspects of trinitarian thought, ontology. If our understanding of human life and the world is not grounded in some account of who the God is to whom we make appeal, then an implicit appeal will be made to other and often hidden ideological factors, and the very process of distortion, about whose development in the history of theology there is something like an emerging consensus, will simply be repeated in a modern form.

The twin dangers are of claiming to know too much or too little. The recovery of trinitarianism will do much to recover parts of a treasure that has remained buried for centuries. Yet it must also be remembered that the doctrine is not a general principle so much as a way of identifying without exhaustively plumbing the depths of the being of God. It thus offers a way of responding theologically to revelation: to the way in which God is truly believed to have made himself known in Christ and the Spirit. That being not only remains in one sense unknown, but is made known primarily in the life of one who died on a cross. There thus remains an offence to the human intellect which cannot be removed by appeal to the number of problems that are supposedly solved in its light.

As has already been illustrated, the list of topics whose development has been encouraged by appeal to the doctrine are as much the locus of further questions as of solutions. And there are others which have not been mentioned. One problem which must to be faced is the relation of the doctrine to biblical studies. Despite Claude Welch's judgement some years ago that 'the doctrine of the Trinity is ... the objective expression, the "crystallization" of the gospel itself' (Welch 1953: 238), caution is necessitated by what sometimes appears almost a consensus against the doctrine among professional biblical critics (though see W. A. Wainwright 1969). Despite this, there is some reason to believe that with the recent questioning of some of the assumptions underlying the historical–critical method, the possibilities are growing for the renewal of genuine dialogue between the disciplines, and that the doctrine of the Trinity is at their heart (Watson 1994), as it is at the heart of everything else.

REFERENCES

Anselm of Canterbury (1956) *An Address (Proslogion)*, trans. E. R. Fairweather, in *The Library of Christian Classics*, vol. X, *A Scholastic Miscellany: Anselm to Ockham*, London: SCM Press: 69–93.

Augustine of Hippo (1963) *Saint Augustine: The Trinity*, trans. S. McKenna, Washington, DC: Catholic University of America Press.

Barth, Karl (1975) *Church Dogmatics*, vol. 1/1, trans. G. W. Bromiley, Edinburgh: T. & T. Clark.

Basil of Caesarea (1989) 'Letter XXXVIII', in *The Treatise de Spiritu Sancto, the Nine Homilies and the Letters*, trans. B. Jackson, in P. Schaff and H. Wace (eds) *A Select Library of Nicene and Post-Nicene Fathers of the Christian Church*, second series, vol. VIII, Edinburgh: T. & T. Clark, 137–41.

Blumenberg, H. (1983) *The Legitimacy of the Modern Age*, trans. R. M. Wallace, Cambridge, Mass. and London: MIT Press.

British Council of Churches (1989) *The Forgotten Trinity. 1. The Report of the BCC Study Commission on Trinitarian Doctrine Today*, London: British Council of Churches.

Buckley, M. (1987) *At the Origins of Modern Atheism*, New Haven and London: Yale University Press.

Coleridge, S. T. (1853a) 'On the Prometheus of Aeschylus', in W. G. T. Shedd (ed.)

The Complete Works of Samuel Taylor Coleridge, vol. 4, New York: Harper and Brothers, 344–65.

—— (1853b) 'Notes on Waterland's Vindication of Christ's Divinity', in W. G. T. Shedd (ed.) *The Complete Works of Samuel Taylor Coleridge*, vol. 5, New York: Harper and Brothers, 404–16.

—— (1976) *On the Constitution of the Church and State*, in J. Colmer (ed.) *The Collected Works of Samuel Taylor Coleridge*, vol. 10, London: Routledge & Kegan Paul.

D'Costa, G. (1990) 'Christ, the Trinity and Religious Plurality', in G. D'Costa (ed.) *Christian Uniqueness Reconsidered: The Myth of a Pluralistic Theology of Religions*, New York: Orbis Books, 16–29.

Gunton, C. E. (1991) *The Promise of Trinitarian Theology*, Edinburgh: T. & T. Clark.

—— (1993) *The One, the Three and the Many. God, Creation and the Culture of Modernity*, Cambridge: Cambridge University Press.

Harnack, A. (1898) *History of Dogma*, vol. 4, trans. E. B. Speirs and J. Millar, London: Williams and Norgate.

Hill, W. J. (1982) *The Three-Personed God: The Trinity as the Mystery of Salvation*, Washington, DC: Catholic University of America Press.

Jenson, R. W. (1963) *Alpha and Omega: A Study in the Theology of Karl Barth*, New York: Nelson.

—— (1969) *God After God: The God of the Past and the God of the Future, Seen in the Work of Karl Barth*, Indianapolis and New York: Bobbs Merrill.

—— (1982) *The Triune Identity: God According to the Gospel*, Philadelphia: Fortress Press.

Jüngel, E. (1976) *The Doctrine of the Trinity: God's Being is in Becoming*, trans. H. Harris, Edinburgh: Scottish Academic Press.

—— (1983) *God As the Mystery of the World: On the Foundation of the Theology of the Crucified One in the Dispute between Theism and Atheism*, trans. D. L. Guder, Edinburgh: T. & T. Clark.

Kasper, W. (1984) *The God of Jesus Christ*, trans. M. J. O'Donnell, London: SCM Press.

Kimel, A. (ed.) (1992) *Speaking the Christian God: The Holy Trinity and the Challenge of Feminism*, Leominster: Gracewing.

Lacugna, C. M. (1991) *God For Us: The Trinity and Christian Life*, New York: Harper Collins.

Lampe, G. W. H. (1977) *God as Spirit: The Bampton Lectures 1976*, London: SCM Press.

Lossky, V. (1957) *The Mystical Theology of the Eastern Church*, London: James Clark.

McFarland, T. (1969) *Coleridge and the Pantheist Tradition*, Oxford: Clarendon Press.

Mackey, J. (1983) *The Christian Experience of God as Trinity*, London: SCM Press.

Mascall, E. L. (1986) *The Triune God: An Ecumenical Study*, Worthing: Churchman Publishing.

Moltmann, J. (1974) *The Crucified God: The Cross of Christ as the Foundation and Criticism of Christian Theology*, trans. R. A. Wilson and J. Bowden, London: SCM Press.

—— (1981) *The Trinity and the Kingdom of God*, trans. M. Kohl, London: SCM Press.

Nebelsick, H. (1992) *The Renaissance, the Reformation and the Rise of Modern Science*, Edinburgh: T. & T. Clark.

Peterson, E. (1935) *Der Monotheismus als politisches Problem: Ein Beitrag für Geschichte der politischen Theologie in Imperium Romanum*, Leipzig: J. Hegner.

Rahner, K. (1970) *The Trinity*, trans. J. Donceel, London: Burns and Oates.

Ritschl, D. (1967) *Memory and Hope: An Enquiry Concerning the Presence of Christ*, London: Collier-Macmillan.

Schleiermacher, F. D. E. (1928) *The Christian Faith*, trans. H. R. Mackintosh and J. S. Stewart, Edinburgh: T. & T. Clark.

Schlink, E. (1967) 'The Structure of Dogmatic Statements as an Ecumenical Problem', in *The Coming Christ and the Coming Church*, Edinburgh: Oliver and Boyd, 16–84.

Schwoebel, C. (1990) 'Particularity, Universality and the Religions: Towards a Christian Theology of Religions', in G. D'Costa (ed.) *Christian Uniqueness Reconsidered: The Myth of a Pluralistic Theology of Religions*, New York: Orbis Books, 30–46.

Schwoebel, C. and Gunton, C. (eds) (1992) *Persons, Divine and Human: King's College Essays in Theological Anthropology*, Edinburgh: T. & T. Clark.

Shanks, A. (1991) *Hegel's Political Theory*, Cambridge: Cambridge University Press.

Smail, T. A. (1988) 'The Holy Trinity and the Resurrection of Jesus', in A. Walker (ed.) *Different Gospels*, London: Hodder & Stoughton, 63–78.

Stead, G. C. (1977) *Divine Substance*, Oxford: Clarendon Press.

Torrance, T. F. (1962) *Karl Barth: An Introduction to his Early Theology, 1910–1931*, London: SCM Press.

—— (1975) 'The Mind of Christ in Worship: The Problem of Apollinarianism in the Liturgy', in *Theology in Reconciliation: Essays towards Evangelical and Catholic Unity in East and West*, London: Geoffrey Chapman, 139–214.

Wainwright, G. (1980) *Doxology: The Praise of God in Worship, Doctrine and Life. A Systematic Theology*, London: Epworth Press.

—— (ed.) (1989) *Keeping the Faith: Essays to Mark the Centenary of* Lux Mundi, London: SPCK.

Wainwright, W. A. (1969) *The Trinity in the New Testament*, London: SPCK.

Watson, F. B. (1994) *Text, Church and World. Biblical Interpretation in Theological Perspective*, Edinburgh: T. & T. Clark.

Welch, C. (1953) *The Trinity in Contemporary Theology*, London: SCM Press.

Wendebourg, D. (1982) 'From the Cappadocian Fathers to Gregory Palamas: The Defeat of Trinitarian Theology', *Studia Patristica* 17: 194–8.

Wiles, M. and Santer, M. (eds) (1975) *Documents in Early Christian Thought*, Cambridge: Cambridge University Press.

Zizioulas, J. D. (1985) *Being as Communion: Studies in Personhood and the Church*, London: Darton, Longman and Todd.

—— (1992) 'On Being a Person: Towards an Ontology on Personhood', in C. Schwoebel and C. Gunton (eds) *Persons, Divine and Human*, Edinburgh: T. & T. Clark, 33–46.

FURTHER READING

Brown, D. (1985) *The Divine Trinity*, London: Duckworth.

Kaiser, C. B. (1982) *The Doctrine of God: An Historical Survey*, London: Marshall, Morgan and Scott.

Thompson, J. *Modern Trinitarian Perspectives*, Oxford: Oxford University Press.

See also chapters 10, 12, 14, 17, 25, 26, 42, 46.

45

THEOLOGY IN THE NARRATIVE MODE

Brian Horne

THE UNIVERSALITY OF NARRATIVE

In 1966 the French philosopher and critic, Roland Barthes, began his influential essay 'Introduction to the Structural Analysis of Narrative' with the observation that 'narrative is present in every age, in every place, in every society . . . narrative is international, transhistorical, transcultural: it is simply there, like life itself' (Barthes 1977: 79). In the Prologue to his study of the origins and function of myth Joseph Campbell, the American anthropologist, made a similar observation: 'Man, apparently, cannot maintain himself in the universe without belief in some arrangement of the general inheritance of myth' (Campbell 1960: 4). His investigations into societies both ancient and modern, Eastern and Western, have demonstrated that we do not know of a human culture that has sustained itself without myths, and that the myths have taken the form of narrative. For Campbell narrative is not 'simply there, like life', but the means by which a society is shaped and maintained.

What the science of anthropology has tried to demonstrate about social and communal existence, the science of psychology has tried to demonstrate about individual, personal existence. Carl Gustav Jung, for instance, dealt extensively with the power and purpose of mythical formations in the structure of the human psyche; and in one of his last essays he wrote of the significance of myth in words which echo those of Joseph Campbell:

> The need for mythic statements is satisfied when we frame a view of the world which adequately explains the meaning of human existence in the cosmos, a view which springs from our psychic wholeness, from the co-operation between conscious and unconscious. Meaninglessness inhibits fullness of life and is therefore equivalent to illness.
>
> (Jung 1978: 372)

Without the ordering of reality into mythical structures the self disintegrates. A representative of a quite different school of psychology, Bruno Bettelheim, provided, in his book *The Uses of Enchantment*, a detailed analysis of the purpose and function of fairy stories, in the context of his work with mentally disturbed children.

> As an educator and therapist of severely disturbed children, my main task was to restore meaning to their lives. This work made it obvious to me that if children were reared so that life was meaningful to them, they would not need special help ... Just because his life is so bewildering to him, the child needs even more to be given the chance to understand himself in this complex world with which he must learn to cope. To be able to do so, the child must be helped to made some coherent sense out of the turmoil of his feelings ... The child find this kind of meaning through fairy-tales.
>
> (Bettelheim 1976: 5)

We may not agree with Bettelheim in his analysis of particular fairy tales or the concept of the order which the stories impose upon the confused mass of experiences which is characteristic of early human life, but we must note that he is at one with Campbell and Jung in believing that an essential means of discovering meaning and of giving shape to a life is to be found in the encounter with a narrative form. I am aware of the distinction Bettelheim draws between fairy tale and myth in *The Uses of Enchantment* and his unwillingness to put myth to the same use as fairy tales in his treatment of disturbed children; but he does not deny the narrative character of myth, and he is in complete agreement about the necessity and inescapability of narrative as a dominant mode of human experience and understanding.

From our earliest years we are caught in, held in, and, in some sense, even constructed by a web of stories, so that it is impossible to envisage a life without stories. The belief in this basic narrative quality to life has become, in our own day, a fundamental principle of both psychoanalysis and most forms of psychiatry. The recovery of a person's past by the discovery of suppressed or forgotten incidents and feelings begins the movement towards personal integrity; and the way both to self-understanding and to healing is the way of a narrative. A person will remain in a condition of psychic disturbance until the disconnected events of an individual's history have been ordered into a coherent pattern which, then, offers resolution. But, of course, the process cannot end there: the individual cannot achieve integrity merely by locating himself or herself within the confines of his or her own story. One cannot live only in one's own myths. Because the individual is also related to a community it is necessary that successful relations are made with other members of the community; and the group has its own story by which it comes to some knowledge of itself. So there must be a meshing of the private and the public spheres: the story of the individual must be woven into the story of the world he or she inhabits, and vice versa. The two narratives may sometimes contradict one another and produce tension and frustration: they may co-inhere to produce peace and harmony.

In ancient societies and oral cultures places of honour were reserved for those who possessed the gift of story-telling, and the gift itself often interpreted as a mark of divine favour. In each generation the story-teller preserved, perpetuated and conveyed the tales by which the tribe lived. Without them the community was in danger of degenerating into separate and antagonistic entities (see Eliade 1963). In modern societies, more fissiparous in character, the function of the story-teller has become disseminated through numerous agencies, some more obvious than others. The work of the fiction writer is still a tangible link to the story-telling of ancient civilizations. When a storm of controversy blew around the head of James Joyce on the publication of his novel *Ulysses* in 1922, T. S. Eliot defended the book on the grounds that Joyce, by correlating his fictional account of a day in the life of a man in modern Dublin with the Homeric saga of Odysseus, had found a way of 'giving a shape and a significance to the immense panorama of futility and anarchy which is contemporary history' (Eliot 1923: 482). The seashore and the streets, the river and the houses, the laughter and the quarrels, the loves and jealousies of modern Dublin are contained within the framework of the story of Odysseus' wanderings and return to Penelope. In turn the Homeric world is absorbed into contemporary Ireland. The modern and the ancient, fiction and saga interpenetrate and inform one another.

In the fourth decade of the nineteenth century a storm of even greater ferocity had been raised by the publication of a book in which the author, D. F. Strauss, dared to introduce the word 'myth' as a description of the Christian faith in his *Das Leben Jesu* (1836) (Strauss 1972). Dismissing the belief that the supernatural events described in the New Testament could actually have occurred, Strauss depicted the writers of the Gospels as creative myth-makers and the subsequent development of Christian dogma and tradition as a type of mythology engendered by the Christian community for the purpose of laying hold upon the experience of a spiritual reality. The book was to have a profound influence upon German Protestant theology: it suggested that a serious consideration of the concept of myth in relation to Christian thought and practice might not only be possible but even necessary. In the twentieth century Rudolf Bultmann's exegetical work on the New Testament texts furthered this approach and opened the way for a systematic programme of 'demythologizing' Christianity (Bultmann 1960). The narrative theologians of our own day have developed the notion of myth still further but stand in an ambivalent relation to Bultmann and the demythologizers. While acknowledging a debt to the scholars of a previous generation who had emphasized the mythical dimension in the texts of the Christian faith, they have strongly argued against a process of demythologizing which would attempt to re-read the texts in such a way that the narrative element is resolved into abstract moral, spiritual or philosophical precepts.

Joseph Campbell returned to consider the ways in which myth functioned in the final volume of *The Masks of God*. He identified four elements in the process:

The most vital, most critical function of a mythology, then, is to foster the centering and unfolding of the individual in integrity, in accord with d) himself (the microcosm), c) his culture (the mesocosm), b), the universe (the macrocosm) and a) that awesome ultimate mystery which is both beyond and within himself and in all things.

(Campbell 1982: 6).

We shall see, when we come to look more closely at the work of modern theologians of the narrative mode, how their perception of the way in which religious narratives work resembles or differs from Campbell's analysis.

NARRATIVE FORM

An extensive discussion of narrative is contained in Wesley Kort's book, *Story, Text and Scripture*. After noting the apparent ubiquity of narrative in all societies at all stages of their development he reinforces what we have already seen implicit in the work of Campbell, Jung and Eliade: 'the study of a culture's narratives is an enquiry that quickly becomes a study of culture, even of humanity itself' (Kort 1988: 8). (A similar point is made, more provocatively, by Roland Barthes in the closing sentences of 'Structural Analysis of Narratives'.) Kort presses this further in his examination of the relation between narrative form and language itself by suggesting that 'rather than arising from language, narrative is either co-existent with the origination of language, or in some way or other, even the originator of language' (ibid.: 22). This is a controversial theory. While one may agree that narrative might be regarded as a primary rather than a secondary form of discourse, one may be justifiably sceptical about claiming for it the status of 'the originator of language'. The origins of human utterance are still a widely debated issue among philosophers and anthropologists and nothing has been proved conclusively. Nevertheless, we can still maintain with some certainty that there is 'no point so deep in the life of a culture that is free from narrative form' (ibid.: 12), even if we remain agnostic about whether there is or is not any form of speech 'prior to narrative upon which narratives depend' (ibid.).

The story-teller of ancient societies may have almost disappeared from most cultures but in Western culture there has been an astonishing proliferation of stories in the last two hundred years. Frank Kermode has drawn attention to the growth and development of the novel in Western literature in *The Sense of an Ending*. 'It happens that in our phase of civility, the novel is the central form of literary art' (Kermode 1967: 28). It cannot be accidental that narrative theology, as a recognizable mode of discourse, should have arisen at a time and in a culture which invented and has been nourished by the novel.

But before moving on to explore the various kinds of narrative, it will be useful to give some attention to the character of narrative as such: to try to answer the simple question: what is a narrative? Here there is some confusion and a variety of definitions. For some scholars, like C. S. Lewis and Don

961

Cupitt, the terms 'story' and 'narrative' seem almost interchangeable. For others, like Roland Barthes, Robert Scholes and Robert Kellogg, they can be distinguished: 'story' becomes synonymous with 'plot' and forms only one part of a narrative discourse. It might be recognized, too, that not all of the writers are consistent in their own usage and, sometimes, create ambiguities by using the same words in different senses or different words to refer to the same thing. A notable feature of the debate is that it has been conducted by scholars not only in conversation with each other but in dialogue with Aristotle.

It is, perhaps, inevitable that Aristotle should figure so prominently, for it was he who, in his discussion of tragedy in the *Poetics*, drew attention to the significance of narrative, and was the first to attempt a systematic (if brief) analysis of it as a mode of discourse. His definition of tragedy as 'the imitation of an action' led him to emphasize plot at the expense of character. 'The imitation of the action is the fable [story]: for by fable I now mean the contexture of incidents or the plot' (Aristotle 1955: 15). Character is derived from action. (This reverses the usual Western European perception that it is character or personality that causes things to happen.) His words are of particular interest for the bearing they have on the relationship between narrative and time. An action, by definition, moves through time, and a narrative must mirror and convey the sense of the passing of time. There are some art forms which seem to want to escape from the time sequence: a lyric poem which, paradoxically, takes time to read, may be attempting the capturing of a single moment of ecstasy or agony deliberately isolated from 'before' or 'after', though it might be argued that the true understanding of the frozen moment may depend upon the supposition of a 'before' and an 'after'; and, as I said, the contemplation of the emotion embodied in the poem takes place in a time sequence. Aristotle, by focusing on action rather than character (tragedy is the imitation of an action) emphasized the narrative quality of our experience. We live in a sequence, experiencing existence as a pattern of before and after. Actions have beginnings and ends. When we see the connection between an event of the past and an occurrence in the present; when we predict an outcome of an action in the present, we have created a plot. In a timeless world there would be no action and no stories, there would only be character. And without story there would be no narrative.

In *What is a Story?* Don Cupitt cites Parmenides as the first person to have attempted the creation of a 'metaphysics of the Absolute': proposing 'an ideal of knowledge that is anti-narrative, timeless and divorced from action' (Cupitt 1991: 4). But as Cupitt points out (and as I remarked in the case of the lyric poem) the attempt is fraught with paradox for despite having given the impression of 'having conjured up something absolute and eternal' Parmenides 'has done so in a text which like every other text is a succession of relativities'. This poses the problem of the relation of text to time in its most acute form. It is obviously absurd to say that all texts are narrative, but it is not absurd to say that the apprehension of texts is unavoidably narrative in so far as the reading of them takes time and the action of reading is an action which becomes part of the reader's own narrative. We, as readers, are already placing each text in a sequence of events that constitute our history and promote our self-understanding.

However, the elevation of plot to the dominant position in a narrative structure has been questioned by some scholars, though it must be admitted that the experience of telling stories to young children would suggest that it is precisely plot – 'what happened then?' – which engages their attention at the most basic level. Character, as Bruno Bettelheim has pointed out, is of relatively little interest to children. Nonetheless, as one grows older one becomes aware of other ingredients in a narrative, and in one of the most important of recent books on the subject of narrative, Robert Scholes and Robert Kellogg have argued both for the greater significance of character and the complicating factor of 'point of view'. Wesley Kort developing their arguments suggests four necessary, interdependent elements in the constitution of a narrative: 'subjects (character) involved in processes (plot) under certain limits and conditions (atmosphere) and in relation to a teller (tone)' (Kort 1988: 14–15). It might be argued that the equal interplay of all these elements may assume different roles. 'Any one of the four is sufficiently complex and effective in force and meaning to dominate a particular narrative and to deform the other three towards itself' (ibid.: 17).

An example of such 'deformation' is provided by Erich Auerbach in a book to which many of the writers on narrative refer and which has assumed the status of a classic text on literary theory: *Mimesis* (published originally in German in 1946). In a famous passage in the opening chapter the author tried to demonstrate the difference between the narrative technique of Homer and that of biblical writers. (The specific narratives under scrutiny are those of the return of Odysseus and the account of the sacrifice of Isaac.) Homer, in the Odyssey, he contends, 'knows no background. What he narrates is for the time being the only present, and fills both the stage and the reader's mind completely' (Auerbach 1957: 2–3). He is discussing the incident of the discovery of Odysseus' scar: the narrative here abruptly breaks away from the story of the hero's return to recount a much earlier incident in his life. This sudden diversion comes as a surprise to modern readers accustomed to a different manner of story-telling. But, writes Auerbach, 'any such subjectivistic perspective, creating a foreground and a background . . . is entirely foreign to the Homeric style; the Homeric style knows only a foreground, only a uniformly illuminated, uniformly objective present' (ibid.: 5). This, if Auerbach is correct, would be an example of 'deformation' by the dominance of 'atmosphere'. There are characters (Odysseus and Euryclea) and a plot (the return of the warrior to his house and wife in disguise) and a story-teller, but all are subsumed under the presentation of atmosphere. The story of Abraham and Isaac in the book of Genesis is quite different: here 'background' predominates. The aim is not 'to bewitch the senses, and if nevertheless they produce lively sensory effects, it is only because the moral, religious and psychological phenomena which are their sole concern are made concrete in this sensible matter of life' (ibid.: 11). In this instance, it would seem, 'tone' is all-important; what Scholes and Kellogg might call 'point of view'. 'Doctrine and promise are incarnate in them and inseparable from them; for that very reason they are fraught with "background" and mysterious, containing a second, concealed meaning' (ibid.: 12). There is here, too, a stronger emphasis on 'character': the reader is invited to consider the nature of the God who makes the demand and the psychological state of the one who finds himself caught in the dilemma of having to choose between love for his son and obedience to the Almighty. Whether Auerbach was correct in his interpretation of these narratives, in particular that of the book of Genesis, is a question to which I shall be returning.

It must be remembered, as we are considering the nature of narrative, that Aristotle was voicing his opinions about the relation of plot to character in a specific context: the analysis of tragedy. He was not addressing the question of narrative as a genre; and there is no way of knowing if the rules he applied to tragic narrative would have been applied generally to all narrative. Even if one finds, as I do, Kort's analysis instructive, one might still ask: is there a yet more basic structure; a simple pattern to all variations in the narrative mode? Some scholars (Scholes and Kellogg and Kermode) seem to suggest that there is: a pattern of tension passing into resolution. All fairy stories appear to be based upon this pattern, however horrible the resolution may sometimes be. It is certainly a structure which Aristotle maintained was a necessary pattern of tragic narrative – which is one of the reasons why he thought tragic poetry superior to epic poetry. He was dismissive of plots that were 'episodic', i.e. stories in which events 'follow one another without any probable or necessary connection' (Aristotle 1955: 21). And he divided plots into two kinds: simple and complicated. He called an action simple 'when its catastrophe is produced without either resolution or discovery; complicated when with one or both' (ibid.: 22). The stories of Judaism, Christianity and, possibly, also Islam can be seen to be of both kinds. What is basic, however, is the idea of denouement: a movement of one state of being to another. Aristotle's vision is, of course, bounded by the tragic horizon of Greek civilization, and the change of the state of being is invariably catastrophic. This is not the vision of the Judeo-Christian religions; the stories cannot be catastrophic (tragic) because of the promise of God to his creation. In a discussion of fairy stories by J. R. R. Tolkien this point is taken up and developed. He introduces the word 'eucatastrophe' to describe the movement from one state of being to another in the Jewish and Christian view of the world.

The eucatastrophe tale is the true form of the fairy-tale and its highest function. The

964

consolation of fairy-stories, the joy of the happy ending . . . is not essentially 'escapist', nor 'fugitive' . . . It does not deny the existence of dyscatastrophe, of sorrow and failure . . . it denies (in the face of much evidence if you will) universal final defeat and in so far is *evangelium*.

(Tolkien 1966: 81)

While all plots depend upon tension and resolution, it must be admitted that not all of those verbal constructs which we call narrative articulate this pattern at the surface level. But I would argue that for a plot to be a plot there can be nothing which is totally redundant or sheerly arbitrary: an event which is unconnected to any other event, or a series of events which is radically discontinuous destroys narrative structure. Whether we are given catastrophe or eucatastrophe as the resolution is immaterial; unless one believes that catastrophe is not a resolution at all – but that belief could not arise out of one's understanding of narrative. We might not deny the name of narrative to a story which had no resolution, but our recognition of the absence of resolution would seem to indicate our expectation of there being one. We expect stories to have an ending; and the notion of a permanently unfinished study is incompatible with Jewish and Christian theology which is profoundly eschatological and, therefore, narrative in character.

THEOLOGY AND NARRATIVE

I have already referred to the fact that the term 'narrative theology' is of comparatively recent origin and that the recognition of it as a distinct mode of discourse dates back no more than a quarter of a century. It began to emerge with the publication, mainly in the United States of America, of a number of books and articles in the 1970s asking similar questions and finding similar answers. A number of things contributed to the appearance of these writings. First, biblical scholarship was beginning to open itself up to influences from literary criticism and literary theory. Interest was shifting away from textual and historical questions to considerations which were more obviously literary and philosophical in character: authorial intention, scriptural rhetoric, mythography, the concept of the canon, the methodology of hermeneutics. A dissatisfaction with source criticism and form criticism led to the introduction of an important concept like inter-textuality: the theory that texts are interdependent (especially so in the case of the Bible) and not only echo one another but 'absorb and transform' one another (Kristeva 1980: 66). An impetus was also provided by the various forms of structuralism which drew attention to the possibility of discerning similar basic structures in apparently different genres of writing. At the same time social anthropologists and philosophers also began to take an interest in biblical material. It was inevitable that the concept of narrative would rise to the surface and demand close examination.

In 1966 Roland Barthes published his seminal essay on the structural analysis of narrative. This was followed in 1971 by his essay 'The Struggle with the Angel', a structural reading of the text of Genesis 32. In 1967 Frank Kermode published *The Sense of an Ending*, his investigation of 'fictional modes' in which he argued that the specifically religious category of apocalypse had to form part of our understanding of the mode.

> I have used the theologians and their treatment of apocalypse as a model of what we might expect to find not only in more literary treatments of the same radical fiction, but in the literary treatment of radical fictions in general.
>
> (Kermode 1967: 28)

Fifteen years later there appeared Northrop Frye's *The Great Code*, an attempt to 'read' and present the Bible, in all its diversity of forms, as an interlocking textual system, a structural unity with an overarching purpose: a self-referential text, plotted in metaphor and myth as a vast narrative. And the work of Paul Ricoeur, philosophical, theological, literary, too diffuse and difficult to be summarized, has constantly provoked and informed the minds of those who have been concerned with the process of hermeneutics. In particular his focus on the relationship between narrative and time (which will be discussed later) has stimulated debate on the narrative mode for theology. This emphasis on narrative as a constitutive element of human experience, and consequently of religious experience, has affected all branches of theology. It has been instrumental in altering and shaping thinking not only in the expected areas of biblical interpretation and homiletics but also in the fields of doctrine, liturgy and ethics.

One of the most influential books to have been published in these years, and one to which many later scholars refer, was Hans Frei's *The Eclipse of Biblical Narrative: A Study of Eighteenth and Nineteenth Century Hermeneutics* (1974). This was a historical investigation which presented a theological thesis: an attempt to show that up until the seventeenth century, Christians of all traditions were accustomed to reading the Bible narratively, as one coherent story. This habit of reading and interpreting was lost or abandoned in the period of the Enlightenment when the attitude to the understanding of texts began to take a different course. Positivism, Empiricism and Idealism in their different ways combined to make the realm of experience primary. Reading became atomistic and biblical texts came to be evaluated by their approximation to and congruity with some essential, already known absolute Truth. Consequently, the narratives of the Faith, principally the Bible, became the illustration of the Truth and could be, in some way, separable from it. In contrast, Frei argued for the re-discovery of truth mediated by, and inseparable from, the text; and central to this thesis is his notion of 'realistic narrative'. 'Meaning', he wrote, 'is not illustrated (as though it were an intellectuality presubsisting or preconceived archetype or ideal essence, but constituted through the mutual, specific determination of agents, speech, social context, and circumstances that form the indispensable narrative web)' (Frei 1974: 280). Life is narrative in texture and the text is, primarily, narrative in structure: the two are correlate. In his insistence on 'the location of meaning in narrative of the realistic sort in the text, the narrative structure or sequence itself', he seems to contradict Erich Auerbach's reading of the biblical writings who, as we saw, argued that the stories were 'fraught with "background" and mysterious, containing a second, concealed meaning'. But Auerbach is aware of the possible extrapolation of his reading into just such a theory of the separability of narrative and doctrine conceptually expressed, and guards against it by adopting a position similar to that of Frei when he notes that biblical stories 'are in constant danger of losing their own reality, as very soon happened when interpretation reached such proportions that the real vanished' (Auerbach 1957: 12). (However, unlike Frei, he does not blame the positivism of the Enlightenment for the dissolution of the text.)

One might wish to disagree with Frei in his exposition of the history of biblical interpretation and also about the way in which meaning and narrative are correlate, but one cannot ignore his significance in the field of narrative theology. He did not go so far as to imply that the narrative mode was the basic and primary mode of human discourse, as some later scholars were to do, but he thrust the mode forward in such a way that it could never again be omitted from any serious study of biblical texts. As a result, it can no longer be maintained that the Bible is primarily a collection of doctrinal propositions or a set of ethical precepts accompanied by illustrative tales. The question of the nature of biblical authority inevitably arises. Narrative theology questions the assertion that authority lies in the way of the Bible enunciates timeless truths in propositional form. Moral principles, dogmatic formulations may be understood, but cannot be appropriated apart from the narrative that gives rise to them: they do not possess authority until the reader is caught up into the world that the narrative proposes.

And so we can begin to frame a description of theology in the narrative mode. A clue to its nature has been supplied already by Erich Auerbach when he wrote:

> far from seeking, like Homer, merely to make us forget our own reality for a few hours, it [the biblical narrative] seeks to overcome our reality: we are to fit our own life into its world, feel ourselves to be elements in its structure of universal history.
> (Ibid.: 12)

It is a matter of reading ourselves in the light of the text: interlacing the narrative of our own lives with the narrative of the book. It would be the conviction of most theologians doing theology in this mode that 'our basic convictions about the nature and meaning of our lives find their ground and their intelligibility in some sort of overarching paradigmatic story' (Goldberg 1983: 381). If it is true that we are, inescapably, creatures who experience the world narratively then what is said there by Michael Goldberg becomes more than probable. The narrative of God becomes the paradigmatic story for the narrative, not only of the whole human race, but of every human being. In the words of George Stroup, 'revelation occurs when the Christian narrative collides with personal identity and the latter is reconstructed by means of the former' (Stroup 1984: 124). This mode of theology, as we shall see, has far-reaching implications for both the concept of revelation and the perception of the way in which human beings respond to and lay hold upon the saving truths of revelation.

In contrast to both Hinduism and Buddhism (both of which are replete with stories), Judaism, Christianity and Islam are fundamentally narrative in nature. The stories of Hinduism and Buddhism are not connected into a continuous narrative sequence, but are discrete entities illustrating different facets of an absolute Truth. Furthermore, time and history are illusory concepts, and life is cyclical until it manages to break free of the moving prison of time. The Judaeo-Christian tradition is one which moves in and through time forming a salvation history and a history of salvation. Time, as an integral part of the structure of the material universe, has, like matter, to be redeemed. The process of redemption is inescapably narrative. There is an end and a purpose – a denouement. It could even be said that it is the end that causes and explains the process; and the anticipation of the end that makes the process endurable. It is easy to see how neatly the basic pattern of plot which was discussed earlier – tension finding resolution – coincides with the narratives of these religions. Promise and fulfilment are the dominant motif. At the heart of Judaism is the story of the Exodus: a story of a people moving out of slavery into freedom. At the heart of Christianity is the story of Jesus Christ: a story of death and resurrection. By the constant repetition of these stories, liturgically and privately, both the community and the individual achieve their own resolution of tension. Their stories collide with those of the past; a revelation can occur and the process of 'reconstruction' can begin. The narrative theologian, then, is one who proposes that the narratives of a religion do not exist primarily for the purpose of the extraction of transcendent truths that can be expressed in more precise and more abstract terms, nor for the purpose of producing a coherent code of conduct, nor for the purpose of providing stimulus to ecstatic experiences. Some, indeed, have suggested that the process of elucidation into dogmatic formulation and ethical precept is itself a questionable procedure; others have merely been concerned to indicate the discomforting gap that seems to separate the narratives themselves from the philosophical speculations and moral maxims that come later. It is stressed, for example, that the Christian Church should see itself not so much as a community of individuals who share the same beliefs and live by the same moral code, but as a community that is held together by a common narrative and gathers regularly to tell itself stories.

It may have been only in recent years that a theology focusing on narrative has been articulated and named but, in practice, some such process has been vital to both Jewish and Christian communities for as long as the religions have been in existence. The record of a people, believing that they have been chosen by God, moving through history towards a goal, will inevitably have, as its predominant literary form, narrative. 'When Israel went out from Egypt: and the house of Jacob from a people of strange language' (Ps. 114). The early scholars of the Christian Church developed a refined and sophisticated variation of the narrative mode: typology. These interpreters of Scripture and history saw the events and persons described in the Hebrew Bible as 'types' of those which were to come in the Christian era. The story of the miraculous passage of the Israelites through the Red Sea, for example, became a 'type' of the Sacrament of Baptism: darkness into light, death into life. The sacrifice of Isaac became a 'type' of the sacrifice of Christ. It is important to recognize that in this way of reading the Bible and history they 'did not empty the Old Testament or post-biblical personages and events of their own reality, and therefore they constitute a powerful means for imaginatively incorporating all being into a Christ-centred world' (Lindbeck 1984: 117). They were, in effect, narrative theologians after their own manner; and every time one reads oneself into and out of a story one is engaging in an activity that is similar to that of the formal typologist of earlier centuries.

Modern examples of the way in which the narratives of the Hebrew and Christian Bibles have been used can be seen in the various forms of liberation theology. The emphasis upon 'praxis' and the 'bias towards the poor' turn these theologians away from the philosophical speculation of much Western European theology and also from much of the code of social and moral conduct which, to many of them, seems to have arisen in and been caused by a historical context unrelated to their own. The narratives of Scripture and the tradition are liberating in the sense that in their imaginative 'open-endedness' they seem to offer a more relevant basis for reconstructing the lives of the dispossessed in Latin America or Africa. The Bible is frequently read as a vast story of liberation. The collision of the stories of liberation in both the Old and New Testaments with the stories of those who suffer from oppression and poverty produces the hope of the possibility of change. For some, the narrative of God's action in delivering the Israelites from slavery in Egypt has become paradigmatic. In contrast to the way in which much of the traditional Christian preaching and teaching has 'spiritualized' and 'internalized' historical events, these stories are used as models for the achievement of liberation at the concrete political and social level.

Ironically, it is also the story of the Exodus that, until recently, has been the paradigmatic narrative of the Afrikaaner people of South Africa. They have read their own history in and out of the history of the Jews: a chosen race singled out for a peculiar destiny. Their departure in the early nineteenth century from the Cape Colony, their escape from British domination, their wandering into the hinterland of South Africa, their violent encounter with and eventual defeat of native peoples were all sustained by the narratives of the Old Testament. Their preachers and teachers were, no less than the early

Christian fathers or the Latin American advocates of liberation, doing theology in the narrative mode.

By introducing the example of nineteenth- and early twentieth-century Afrikaaner theology I have indicated one of the problems of narrative theology: the ease with which a story can be appropriated and the power which the form itself exerts upon the imagination. Once the story is read as one's own story it is difficult to escape the cycle of mutual reinforcement. The sheer power of narrative entrenches theological, social and political positions, and the only way of overcoming such positions is not by rational argument but by the discovery of another more powerful and convincing story. Just the opposite problem arises when a person or a group of people find that there is no narrative in a given tradition which is capable of speaking to their own condition. Then the power of narrative is felt as positively alienating and oppressive, and is blamed for creating conditions of alienation and opposition in everyday life. This is the view that has been expressed by some feminist theologians in relation to Judaism and Christianity. They have complained that women are without stories which express their own experience and therefore have been made invisible and have lacked authentic ways of understanding themselves. It is not clear whether women should consciously invent new stories for themselves or if the old stories, from the Bible and the tradition, should be re-fashioned from the feminist point of view. Different theologians have given different answers to this question.

I shall conclude this section by suggesting that narrative theologians have raised a serious question about the relation of faith and the imagination in the life of believers. If one believes that 'our basic convictions about the nature and meaning of our lives find their ground and their intelligibility in some sort of overarching paradigmatic story' (Goldberg 1983: 381) and that narrative is the primary mode of our being, is not faith displaced by imagination? If we are to read ourselves into and out of narratives we cannot do so by acts of faith, only by the activity of the imagination. If revelation is not propositional we cannot 'assent to a proposition' in any way that will be more than trivial. If grace and truth are inseparable from the narrative form by which they are conveyed, faith can only arise when the imagination has grasped the implications of the encounter with the story, and justification by faith will be preceded by the reconstruction of the self by use of the imagination. I know of no narrative theologian who has dealt with this question but it seems to have far-reaching implications for the way in which we understand our response to God to be structured.

NARRATIVE THEOLOGY CRITICIZED

George Stroup has wondered about the propriety of the term 'narrative theology' suggesting that the satisfactoriness of the term is dependent upon idiosyncratic definitions of the two words which comprise it. It is clear that the actual process of reflection and interpretation involves the use of linguistic techniques which are not, in themselves, narrative (Stroup 1984). The Chalcedonian Definition or the dogma of *creatio ex nihilo* are, in their specific formulations, propositional, not stories; though they may arise out of stories. It is equally clear that the tale of David and Bathsheba or the conversion of St Paul are not dogma, though both are redolent of religious 'attitude', and theological interpretations of the stories are contained within the texts themselves. It cannot have escaped anyone's notice that, unlike fairy stories and most myths, there is almost nothing in the Bible that remains at the level of sheer story. (Here we are reminded of the distinction between the Homeric style and the biblical style that was central to Erich Auerbach's thesis about the representation of reality.) The most usual biblical form is the theological interpretation which accompanies the story as a commentary: theology and narrative sit side by side explaining one another. Surprisingly few stories come 'unvarnished', and even then they are embedded in a larger interpretative context. It is for this reason that one has to approach claims that what is understood in the narrative is inseparable from the narrative itself with some caution. If any form of propositional theology is rejected, meaning becomes unavailable apart from the actual words in which it is contained. Commentary becomes not only superfluous but impossible. There can only be story telling; and the interpretation of stories (and of the Christian 'myth'), which has traditionally been the task (and description) of theology, must be seen as a process of linguistic falsification.

Anthony Harvey addressed some of the problems that arise out of this position in his essay 'Christian Propositions and Christian Stories' (Harvey 1981). He recognized the fact that 'the primary source for all knowledge about Jesus is . . . not a doctrinal thesis, but is essentially narrative' and that a more appropriate way of expressing 'Jesus' relationship with God and God's relationship with men' might be a way 'which is more characteristic of the Bible: that of story-telling' (ibid.: 5). However, unlike Northrop Frye, he has difficulty with viewing the Bible as one long story, and in detecting the presence of a number of stories, he argued that 'the story cannot be identical with Scripture'. How, then, do we establish criteria for distinguishing the value of stories and judging between them? The stories themselves are not self-authenticating. To avoid tautology the process must involve extrapolation from the stories. This does not necessarily throw us into the arms of those who claim that we have some *a priori* knowledge of absolute truth by which all value is discerned and judgements made, but it does suppose that, even though the story may be indispensable and prior in experience, truths may be perceived in separation from the story and used to form criteria by which to judge between stories. Not all knowledge is narrative and not all narratives are truth-bearing. As I have already indicated, many women find the narratives of Jewish and Christian traditions to be false narratives. On what grounds is this judgement made? On the ground of other narratives? But the complaint of feminist critics is that there are no other narratives in the Christian repertoire and that this lack is the cause of alienation. If there is no alternative female narrative by which to judge the dominant male narrative the judgement must be made on grounds that are initially non-narrative.

If one of the strengths of narrative theology has been its demonstration of the inadequacy of the account of revelation known as 'propositional', one of its weaknesses has been that in drawing attention to narrative as a basic mode of both revelation and experience, it has sometimes seduced scholars into proposing that narrative is a mode which subsumes all others into itself (Schneider in McConnell 1986). So, for example, Don Cupitt has exuberantly pronounced that it is only story which 'structures time and the world, and keeps darkness and death at bay . . . Narrative, and only narrative, conquers darkness and the void' (Cupitt 1991: 80). It is against the background of such exaggerations that we should read Hans Frei's subtle protest against a certain kind of theology which would construct a theory of 'a general and inalienable human quality called "narrative" or "narrativity" within which to interpret the Gospels'. The fact that the Gospels are narrative cannot provide 'foundational warrant for the possibility of their existential and ontological meaningfulness' (McConnell 1986: 73). A far more complex process, he argues, is at work which involves the concept of a community, its shared rituals, language and sign-systems, how it comes into being and how it decides which texts should be read. Simply to utter 'narrativity' is not to provide an adequate explanation of a complex organism. It might be only the use of texts that properly determines their narrative sense.

Criticism of a different but related sort comes from writers, philosophers and critics who deny the proposition that narrative can or should be regarded as a primary mode of human self-awareness and self-expression. This criticism has taken various forms. In the writings of the philosophers of deconstruction, such as Jacques Derrida and Michel Foucault, a radical assault is made upon the belief that a narrative enables the discovery of meaning. Instead, it is argued, the relation between a text and the world (or the individual person) must be seen as highly problematic and no text can offer a single indissoluble meaning. Meaning is, in a sense, never there, but is always being deferred by the nature of language itself: the absence of what is said, which cannot be defined, is as important as what, apparently, is present. On this premise the kind of theological discourse which is symbolic and metaphoric is less illusory than that which purports to provide concrete information – often in a narrative mode: history and doctrine. More recently still the work of Jean-François Lyotard has tried to argue that the world in which we now live has become inimical to interpretation by a single narrative. In *The Postmodern Condition* he offers a description of the modern era as a world in which all the great stories have been emptied of their power to persuade and direct. 'I define "post-modern" as incredulity towards the meta-narrative' (Lyotard 1986: xxiv). Not only are the meta-narratives of religion discarded, so are those of the agnostic Enlightenment: reason and the scientific paradigm. All have become incredible, in their place there is generated a countless number of language-games which do not have any reference beyond themselves. Some of these systems may have narrative features from time to time, but they are fundamentally unstable and undergo transformations as circumstances demand. Contrary to the claims of narrative theologians there can be no over-arching 'world-story' any longer; no-one is able to fit his or her own life into a single paradigmatic model.

It is difficult to see how the complete abandonment of a narrative mode of articulation could co-inhere with belief in the God of either Judaism or Christianity. It would represent a radical challenge to all notions of time and revelation. Only the ecstatic and the mystic sever the connection with time and history to claim a unique 'timeless' revelation. Jewish and Christian faith happens to be tied both to the concept of the community and to the concept of fact. Acts of faith are personal but related to a community; and rooted in the history of the community as well as the self. Moreover both community and individual acknowledge the unfinished quality of life and are expectant of fulfilment in the future. Caught between memory and hope, life becomes inescapably narrative. It is only if one removes God from the world that the religious person can escape the necessity of narrative in theology; it is only if one removes oneself from time (as in ecstasy) that one can discard a narrative mode for faith. There may be much more ecstasy in religion than we suppose, much more room for lyric poetry in theology than we allow; but so long as there is belief in a revelation in history and an appropriation of that revelation in and through time, a narrative mode will be inevitable.

REFERENCES

Aristotle (1955) *Poetics and Rhetoric*, trans. T. A. Moxon, London: J. M. Dent.
Auerbach, E. (1957) *Mimesis*, trans. W. Trask, New York: Princeton University Press.
Barthes, R. (1977) 'Introduction to the Structural Analysis of Narrative', in *Image, Music, Text*, trans. S. Heath, London: Collins.
Bettelheim, B. (1976) *The Uses of Enchantment*, London: Penguin.
Bultmann, R. (1960) *Jesus Christ and Mythology*, London: SCM Press.
Campbell, J. (1960) *The Masks of God: Primitive Mythology*, London: Secker and Warburg.
—— (1982) *The Masks of God: Creative Mythology*, London: Penguin.
Cupitt, D. (1991) *What Is A Story?*, London: SCM Press.
Derrida, J. (1978) *Writing and Difference*, trans. A. Bass, Chicago: Chicago University Press.
Eliade, M. (1963) *Myth and Reality*, New York: Harper & Row.
Eliot, T. S. (1923) 'Ulysses, Order, and Myth', in *Dial*, LXXV.5: 480–3.
Frei, H. (1974) *The Eclipse of Biblical Narrative*, New Haven: Yale University Press.
—— (1986) 'The Literal Reading of Biblical Narrative in the Christian Tradition', in F. McConnell (ed.) *The Bible and the Narrative Tradition*, New York: Oxford University Press.
Frye, N. (1982) *The Great Code*, London: Routledge and Kegan Paul.

Goldberg, M. (1983) Expository review in *Interpretation*, vol. XXXVII, no. 37: 389–91.

Harvey, A. E. (1981) 'Christian Propositions and Christian Stories', in A. E. Harvey (ed.) *God Incarnate: Story and Belief*, London: SPCK.

Jung, C. G. (1978) *Memories, Dreams, Reflections*, London: Collins.

Kermode, F. (1967) *The Sense of an Ending: Studies in the Theory of Fiction*, New York: Oxford University Press.

Kort, W. A. (1988) *Story, Text and Scripture: Literary Interests in Biblical Narrative*, London: Pennsylvania State University Press.

Kristeva, J. (1980) 'Word, Dialogue, and Novel', in L. S. Roudiez (ed.) *Desire in Language: A Semiotic Approach to Literature and Art*, New York: Columbia University Press.

Lewis, C. S. (1966) 'On Stories', in C. S. Lewis (ed.) *Essays Presented to Charles Williams*, Oxford: Oxford University Press.

Lindbeck, G. A. (1984) *Religion and Theology in a Postliberal Age*, London: SPCK.

Lyotard, J.-F. (1986) *The Postmodern Condition*, trans. G. Bennington and B. Massumi, Manchester: Manchester University Press.

McConnell, F. (ed.) (1986) *The Bible and the Narrative Tradition*, New York: Oxford University Press.

Scholes, R. and Kellogg, R. (1960) *The Nature of Narrative*, New York: Oxford University Press.

Strauss, D. F. (1972) *The Life of Jesus*, Philadelphia: Fortress.

Stroup, G. (1984) *The Promise of Narrative Theology*, London: SCM Press.

Tolkien, J. R. R. (1966) 'On Fairy-Stories', in C. S. Lewis (ed.) *Essays Presented to Charles Williams*, Oxford: Oxford University Press.

FURTHER READING

Alter, R. (1981) *The Art of Biblical Narrative*, London: Allen and Unwin.

Cone, J. H. (1975) *God of the Oppressed*, New York: Seabury Press.

Fackre, G. (1978) *The Christian Story: A Narrative Interpretation of Basic Christian Doctrine*, Grand Rapids, Mich.: Eerdmans.

Ford, D. E. (ed.) (1989) *The Modern Theologians: An Introduction to Christian Theology in the Twentieth Century*, vol. II, Oxford: Basil Blackwell.

Funk, R. W. (1988) *The Poetics of Biblical Narrative*, California: Polebridge Press.

Hampson, D. (1990) *Theology and Feminism*, Oxford: Basil Blackwell.

Hauerwas, S. (1983) 'Casuistry as a Narrative Art', in *Interpretation*, vol. XXXVII, no. 37: 377–88.

Hauerwas, S. with Bondi, R. and Burrell, D. (1977) *Truthfulness and Tragedy*, Notre Dame: Notre Dame University Press.

Kermode, F. (1979) *The Genesis of Secrecy: On the Interpretation of Narrative*, Cambridge, Mass: Harvard University Press.

Nelson, P. (1987) *Narrative and Morality: A Theological Inquiry*, University Park and London: Pennsylvania State University Press.

Palmer, H. (1986) 'Stories', in *Modern Theology*, vol. 2, no. 2: 107–25.

Ricoeur, P. (1984 and 1985) *Narrative and Time*, vols I and II, trans. McLaughlin and Pellawer, Chicago: Chicago University Press.

Root, M. (1986) 'The Narrative Structure of Soteriology', in *Modern Theology*, 2(2): 145–58.

Tribble, P. (1984) *Texts of Terror: Literary Feminist Readings of Biblical Narrative*, Philadelphia: Fortress Press.

Wilder, A. N. (1983) 'Story and Story-World', in *Interpretation*, vol. XXXVII, no. 37: 353–64.
Wright, T. R. (1958) *Theology and Literature*, Oxford: Basil Blackwell.
See also chapters 3, 8, 9, 16, 25, 27, 28, 29, 32.

46

THEOLOGY IN THE DOGMATIC MODE

Paul Avis

A WORKING DEFINITION

Theology 'in the dogmatic mode' represents the crowning achievement of the whole theological enterprise. While the alternative expression 'Systematic Theology' brings out the feat of conceptual organization involved in dogmatics, it does not convey the overriding intention that is intrinsic to dogmatics, namely to offer an authoritative and normative statement of Christian truth. To what extent the authority and normative status of dogmatics can be preserved in our relativistic and pluralistic age is a fundamental question that we shall need to consider.

Dogmatics may be provisionally defined as the presentation of the substance of Christian belief in a coherent, credible and critical form. This is the aim that has motivated the articulation of Christian theology from the beginning. Let us now try to unpack this definition.

The substance of Christian belief

The substance of Christian belief is drawn from various authoritative sources: Holy Scripture, especially the New Testament; the ecumenical creeds, especially the Niceno-Constantinopolitan Creed familiar to worshippers from the eucharistic liturgy; the confessional statements of the various Christian traditions and denominations, especially those of the Reformation period such as the Lutheran Augsburg Confession, the Anglican Thirty-nine Articles and the Roman Catholic decrees of the Council of Trent (though Trent has conciliar and universal authority for Roman Catholics, as do the First and Second Vatican Councils); the writings of major theologians within these traditions, such as Aquinas for Roman Catholics, the Greek Fathers for Orthodox, Luther for Lutherans, Calvin for Reformed and John Wesley for Methodists. But what of Anglican theology?

It is comparatively rare for Anglicans to invoke the authority of their major theologians from the classical period of Anglican theology – Jewel and Hooker, Bramhall and Stillingfleet, Hammond and Thorndike – but then, Anglicans are notoriously diffident about theologizing in the dogmatic mode. As William Temple put it in his chairman's introduction to the Church of England's Doctrine Commission report *Doctrine in the Church of England* (1938): 'There are systems of Catholic Theology and of Protestant Theology . . . But there is not, and the majority of us do not desire that there should be, a system of distinctively Anglican Theology.' The Anglican Churches draw on Catholic and Reformation traditions, Temple continued, 'but they have exhibited a rich variety in methods both of approach and of interpretation' (ibid.: 25). This statement should not be received uncritically. It implies the questionable assumption that Roman Catholic or Protestant systematic theologies cannot be ecumenical in their sources and vision and that other traditions do not permit any real latitude of interpretation. An Anglican systematic theology would indeed be 'distinctively Anglican' in some degree, for good or ill – perhaps in reflecting an eclectic catchment of sources and a self-conscious liberty of interpretation.

Liturgy, hymnody and the writings of mystics and poets may also be drawn upon to illustrate the substance of Christian belief. Those dogmatics that, in the tradition of Schleiermacher and Troeltsch, see the task of dogmatics as to interpret the religious consciousness of the present age, tend to privilege these sources.

Dogmatics intends to be comprehensive in its scope – to embrace the full orbit of Christian belief: the doctrine of the trinitarian God – Father, Son and Holy Spirit; creation and theological anthropology; biblical salvation-history, revelation, the Incarnation and atonement (soteriology); the Church with its worship, sacraments and ministry (ecclesiology); the Christian life; and the last things (eschatology).

The abundant and diverse sources of dogmatics, combined with its aspiration to comprehensiveness of coverage, demand some organizing and unifying principle. This requirement raises the question of the essence of Christianity (see below) and is also a function of the coherence of dogmatic theology – to which we now turn.

The coherence of Christian belief

The coherence of Christian belief that dogmatic theology seeks to attain is twofold: it aims to be coherent within itself and coherent with relevant established non-theological knowledge. It is one of the merits of Macquarrie's approach to dogmatics in his *Principles of Christian Theology* that he strikes this note in the opening paragraph:

> Christian theology seeks to think the Church's faith as a coherent whole. It aims not only at showing the internal coherence of the Christian faith, that is to say, how the several doctrines constitute a unity, but also at exhibiting the coherence of this

faith with the many other beliefs and attitudes to which we are committed in the modern world. Only if these tasks are accomplished can the faith be held intelligently and be integrated with the whole range of human life.

(Macquarrie 1977: *v*)

First, dogmatics attempts to present a rounded statement of doctrine in which every part is included and is related to every other part, at least implicitly. Dogmatic theology must be self-consistent and must hold together. This raises the question of the systematic nature of dogmatics. Dogmatics can never be intentionally unsystematic without renouncing the criterion of coherence. An incoherent presentation of Christian doctrine would not obtain a hearing from serious students of theology. On the other hand, however, system cannot become an end in itself. When the form is dominant over the content we tend to speak of scholastic or text-book theology.

Troeltsch argued that a 'dogmatic system' should take the form of 'a consistent, coherent exposition of Protestant Christian beliefs, with reference to all other human knowledge, in such a way as to serve as the centre of a normative, comprehensive worldview'. The requirement of system is rooted, Troeltsch aptly remarked, in 'the systematic nature of human thought, which strives to connect, organise, and unify its diverse contents, never resting until it has achieved a relatively unified perspective' (Troeltsch 1991a: 11).

Pannenberg has insisted that the systematic nature of dogmatics is given in the undivided attention that it devotes to God and thus to all things in God:

As Christian doctrine is systematically presented by the relating of all individual themes to the reality of God, i.e., as systematic theology, the truth of Christian doctrine also becomes a theme. For all the statements of Christian doctrine have their truth in God. They stand or fall with his reality . . . A systematic presentation of the world, humanity, and history as they are grounded, reconciled and consummated in God is thus dealing with God's own reality. In such a presentation the existence of God is at stake, and with it the truth of Christian teaching.

(Pannenberg 1991: 59f.)

How do the great expositions of Christian theology rate on the coherence scale? The criterion of coherence is strong in Aquinas and the *Summa Theologiae* represents the summit of comprehensiveness and coherence; yet Aquinas is saved from becoming a slave of system and from arid scholasticism by the urbane manner in which he weighs various texts of Scripture and authorities as weighty as Aristotle and Augustine, before calmly offering his own judgement (Aquinas 1964). Though Calvin may be identified in the popular mind with the tyranny of system, the *Institutes* are equally urbane on the whole, notwithstanding the outbursts of abusive polemic, and Calvin does not quibble about details (Calvin 1975). Luther's writings were not intended as systematic treatises: they are occasional and therefore polemical pieces, written under enormous psychological and political pressure. Luther is not a model of coherence and his corpus, though it provides important raw materials for dogmatics, could not be dignified with the description 'systematic theology' (Luther

978

1955). Hooker's *Of the Laws of Ecclesiastical Polity* has the limited aim indicated in the title but is nevertheless beautifully systematic, the dignity of the style matching the elevation of the argument (Hooker 1954).

Post-Reformation scholastic theology, Roman Catholic and Protestant alike, was marked by rigorous systematizing. The Enlightenment, with its faith in critical analytical reason, continued to privilege coherence. But Romanticism tended to regard system as speculative and arid. Hamann declared that 'system is itself a hindrance to truth'. Thus Schleiermacher, who bridges the Enlightenment and Romanticism, combining the critical rigour of the one with the profound imaginative insight of the other, has an advanced and sophisticated understanding of system – one that seeks to follow the inherent logic of faith as experienced in the Christian community, rather than imposing one on the phenomenon of Christianity from outside.

In modern dogmatics – Barth, Tillich and Pannenberg – coherence is strong. Like Schleiermacher, Barth asserts that the structure of his dogmatics merely follows, in humble, patient, and faithful obedience, the intrinsic order of the Christian faith – not, as with Schleiermacher, the logic of religious experience, which Barth viewed with grave suspicion, but that of divine revelation, which Barth understood in a highly realist sense, as an empirical reality that could be 'read'. Critics of Barth, notably Pannenberg himself, treat Barth's claim here as a colossal illusion and regard his delineation of the logic of revelation as highly subjective, if not perverse. Pannenberg's own programme of systematics is at present incomplete but so far exhibits the steady march of argument towards a predictable goal. It is Tillich, however, who must take the prize for the conceptual clarity, architectonic symmetry and presentational accessibility of his systematic theology – though some critics have denounced him as one of the most conceptually befuddled of modern theologians whose clarity of argument is superficial and spurious.

The climate of post-modernism today is hostile to system. Those prophets of post-modernism, Kierkegaard and Nietzsche, echoed the Romantics in denouncing the drive to system in philosophy and theology. For Nietzsche the will to a system morally speaking, is a subtle corruption, a disease of the character and evinces a lack of integrity (Nietzsche 1968: 25). We shall shortly see this prejudice against system picked up in the suspicion of the concept of totality.

Karl Rahner (1904–84) reacted against the cut-and-dried text-book dogmatics of the Roman Catholic seminaries and never attempted a systematic theology himself. His voluminous writings comprise prolegomena to dogmatics and belong to the genre of fundamental theology. They bristle with warnings of the impossibility of creating a comprehensive system of thought under the present conditions of the expansion of knowledge and increasing specialization (Rahner 1965–). This brings us to the second aspect of the coherence of dogmatics.

Dogmatics aims at coherence with all relevant assured knowledge about human existence and the world that is provided by non-theological disciplines. This demand entails the elaboration of an explicit or implicit world-view, an overall framework or perspective on reality. For A. Ritschl, Tillich and Pannenberg, the construction of a Christian world-view is imperative, but Barth and Bultmann regard it as a betrayal of the specific theological task which is to respond in obedience to the Word of God within the community of faith. However, this restriction did not make Barth and Bultmann any less subject to secular intellectual influences. The relation of dogmatic theology to secular thought may often be unreflective, but in modern theology it has become an object of conscious methodological reflection. Let us take some examples of the interaction of theology with non-Christian ideas.

The Fathers were influenced by a Platonic or neo-Platonic philosophy and built assumptions derived from the ancient cosmology, anthropology and political theory into their thought. Aquinas attempted a synthesis between traditional theology and the philosophy of Aristotle, thereby effecting a theological revolution that was viewed with grave suspicion at the time. The Reformers still worked with a pre-Copernican cosmology, though they accepted some late medieval developments in political theory. Schleiermacher and Ritschl – though they professed to exclude all metaphysical considerations from their theology – were patently influenced by speculative thought, notably by Kant's veto on our finite knowledge of absolute reality.

Tillich's systematics is overtly hospitable to both archaic notions from philosophical idealism (Schelling) and to modern insights from Marx and Freud. Barth protested that he had no philosophical loyalties and that his theology was derived solely from the Word of God, but students of Barth have had a field day discovering an assortment of philosophical and literary influences, together with epistemological assumptions derived from a superannuated positivistic philosophy of science that emphasizes the givenness of the data and plays down the interpretative element in perception (Barth 1956–).

In Pannenberg, dialogue with non-theological disciplines, especially the physical and social sciences and metaphysics, is elevated to a principle of theological method. Though this has involved Pannenberg in working through several volumes of inter-disciplinary prolegomena (notably Pannenberg 1976, 1985), it has not, as some might have predicted, prevented him from producing his own systematic theology, which is now well under way and is turning out to be rather conservative. In adopting this strategy Pannenberg has done theology the service of making an object of explicit, critical reflection what has too frequently remained an implicit, uncritical assumption, though it must be said that it is difficult to see how all the interdisciplinary labours have made any difference to the heart of his – and all – dogmatics, the doctrine of God (Pannenberg 1991).

Credibility of theology

The criterion of credibility has always been implicit in the enterprise of theology. The first attempts to demonstrate the rationality of Christian belief were made by the second-century Apologists, such as Justin Martyr (*c.* 100–165 CE) who matched Christian affirmations about God and Christ with philosophical insights about *logos* and *sophia*. As R. M. Grant has written:

> Apologetic literature emerges from minority groups who are trying to come to terms with the larger culture within which they live ... They address their contemporaries with persuasion, looking for links between the outside world and their own group and thus modifying the development of both. An apologist who finds the link in philosophy or cultural life will lay emphasis on aspects of philosophy or culture that favour his own group's attitudes or ideals and, at the same time, will emphasise a philosophical or cultural analysis or structuring of his group's views.
>
> (Grant 1988: 9)

The medieval schoolmen hoped to commend their systems over against the rival constructions of alternative theological traditions – Dominicans such as Aquinas were in competition with Franciscans such as Bonaventure. Any credibility gap remained internal to Christian theology. At the Reformation, Protestant and Roman Catholic theologians defended their credibility against each other and against the more radical thinkers who were the precursors of the modern pluralistic culture. Since the Enlightenment, most theologians have been acutely aware that they must commend their theology to a sceptical and secular age, i.e., one that has witnessed the collapse of the public operational relevance of Christian belief systems.

Thus Schleiermacher's dogmatics built on the apologetic intention expressed in his earlier *Speeches to the Cultured Despisers of Religion* (Schleiermacher 1928, 1958). Tillich developed his celebrated method of correlation which aimed to connect our existential questions with the divinely revealed answers. Tillich insisted that all theology must be cast in the 'answering' mode which takes the human quest for the object of our ultimate concern seriously, for no-one can receive an answer to a question that they have not asked (Tillich 1953–68).

Together with Tillich, it is Rahner who has developed the strongest case, methodologically speaking, for dogmatic theology to attend to its credibility throughout. Rahner advocated the integration of apologetics and dogmatics. Apologetics should no longer be regarded, in Roman Catholic theology bearing the *Nihil obstat* and *Imprimatur*, as a prolegomenon to Christian doctrine, which would establish the credentials of Christian revelation, and of the Church's teaching office (Magisterium) as an aspect of this, and could then be discarded. The apologetic intent should inform the project of dogmatic theology from first to last. Dogmatics should therefore be conducted in dialogue with the concerns and insights of contemporary culture, both arts and sciences. Fundamental theology would no longer be restricted to apologetic preliminaries, but would become the critical self-reflection of theology, attending to its aims and methods, as well as its credibility (Rahner 1965–, 1978).

Rahner's strategic reinterpretation of fundamental theology has been developed by his erstwhile student and colleague J. B. Metz who has, however, redirected the criteria of theology's credibility towards social, political and historical sources. Metz has developed a political fundamental theology centred on the themes of memory, narrative and solidarity, and in this Metz has been profoundly influenced by the Frankfurt school of ideological criticism with its galaxy of thinkers that includes Horkheimer, Adorno and Marcuse (Metz 1980).

In contemporary theology, Pannenberg too has powerfully reasserted the criterion of credibility by defining systematic theology as the task of defining the truth claims of Christianity. Like Rahner, Pannenberg attempts to overcome the division between apologetics, which defends the truth of Christian doctrine, and dogmatics, which merely expounds the content. On the contrary, Pannenberg insists, dogmatics may not assume the truth of the doctrines it handles: these must be scrutinized and defended in the process of exposition. Systematics explores religious traditions and their explanatory relevance to the world by means of doctrines which have the status of hypotheses. These hypotheses may be affirmed, modified or abandoned in the process. Christians should not fear the risk involved in this exercise, but 'should have such confidence in the truth of their faith that they can let its divine truth shine forth from the content without any need for preceding guarantees' (Pannenberg 1991: 52).

However, not all Christian theologians would accept the criterion of credibility for dogmatics. Barth held that there was no point of contact, of *rapprochement* between revelation and natural human insight. One could neither justify revelation nor prepare for its reception. Theology was the exegesis of the Word of God which was self-authenticating and carried its credentials within itself. Barth insisted that the apologetic function and the dogmatic function of the theologian were incompatible. He was implacably hostile to all attempts to commend Christian beliefs, to make them seem relevant and reasonable. This led Barth to oppose equally vehemently the Thomist synthesis grounded in the 'analogy of being' (*analogia entis*) between the creator God and human creatures, Schleiermacher's attempt to base specifically Christian religious feeling on an *a priori* sense of absolute dependence, Brunner's acceptance of natural theology focused on a point of contact between revelation and natural reason, Bultmann's translation of Gospel imperatives into terms borrowed from existentialist philosophy, and Tillich's method of correlation.

In taking this stance, Barth was influenced by the writings of Kierkegaard who had defined apologetics as the attempt to make Christianity plausible. Kierkegaard insisted that 'every defence of Christianity which understands what it would accomplish must behave exactly conversely, maintaining with might and main by qualitative dialectic that Christianity is implausible'

(Kierkegaard 1955: 59f.). In his early work (notably Barth 1933) Barth certainly put this advice into practice!

A critical theology

The critical criterion of systematic theology has a threefold reference. First, dogmatics is critical of its sources in Scripture and tradition. It patently cannot draw on all the sources of Scripture or tradition because they are so diverse and even contradictory. Dogmatics is therefore unashamedly eclectic. Luther, for example, was highly selective in his use of Scripture and tradition. He found the true message of Scripture in St Paul and the doctrine of justification by faith. He had no use for the Epistles of James or Jude and was doubtful about the book of Revelation. In tradition, Luther harked back to Augustine, dismissing the medieval synthesis of the Bible, Augustine and Aristotle.

But perhaps the most rigorously selective of current theological options is feminist theology, for which the whole corpus of Scripture and tradition is tainted with patriarchy and its concomitant devaluation and oppression of women. Feminist hermeneutics looks for the neglected and marginalized voices and roles of women in the Bible and in Church history. It attempts to exploit the chinks in the armour of historical patriarchy (Fiorenza 1983; Ruether 1983).

Second, dogmatics is also overtly critical of its rivals. It is compelled to establish its credentials over against alternative systematic theologies. Therefore it is bound to proceed polemically, demolishing those of its predecessors and contemporaries which appear to be in competition with it. However, this is no excuse for brusqueness or dismissiveness – and least of all for deliberately distorting and misrepresenting other positions. Augustine's writings against the Manichees, the Donatists and the Pelagians are thoroughly polemical, while the *Confessions*, the treatise on the Trinity, and the *City of God*, for example, are more reflective. Luther's writings, being almost entirely occasional and called forth by a succession of challenges, are among the most polemical of all theological *œuvres*.

Barth, though he purports humbly to expound the Word of God in Scripture, developed his distinctive theology in polemical dialogue with the shade of Schleiermacher (Barth 1982). And his *Protestant Theology in the Nineteenth Century* is a prolonged encounter with a succession of theologians who are brought out simply to be demolished (Barth 1972). Of all his predecessors, Barth reserves his greatest hostility for A. Ritschl, whom he scorns and denigrates (Schleiermacher he at least treats with respect). But it is not difficult to show how much Barth has in common with Ritschl: suspicion of religious experience, hostility to metaphysics and a central focus on the biblical word. Young scholars have of course always cut their teeth on their teachers and mentors, but caricature and distortion are out of place at any age!

Finally, dogmatics must learn to be self-critical. This is the hardest form of criticism of all. Here Barth is a model for us, for he himself abandoned unfinished his *Christian Dogmatics* (1927) as soon as he came to see that dogmatics could not be undertaken in detachment from the Christian community, the Church. It was not a freelance or freewheeling enterprise but (to borrow a phrase of Rahner's) demanded to be conducted 'in the bosom of the Church'. Barth took up the task afresh with the significantly entitled *Church Dogmatics* (1932–67). Towards the end of his life, Barth acknowledged that his early theology, with its radical stress on the otherness of God who intervenes in revelation and redemption vertically from above, was one-sided. It needed to be complemented (Barth did not actually retract anything) by an affirmation of what Barth called, in a celebrated lecture, *The Humanity of God* (Barth 1967). Augustine took one step further than Barth in self-criticism, writing his *Retractions* at the end of his life in which he repented of his theological errors.

Turning to contemporary theology, the question may be asked of feminist theology, whether it is still so engrossed in exposing the flagrant abuses entailed in patriarchy, that it has not yet begun to turn its formidable critical powers upon itself, to curb its own excesses and distortions.

A CONCISE MODEL OF SYSTEMATIC THEOLOGY

The contemporary context

Dogmatics is not produced for their own amusement by theologians sitting in proverbial armchairs. It takes its rise from specific urgent questions generated by the contemporary context of religious faith. Systematic theologians are usually practising Christians, often ordained. The questions that generate dogmatic work frequently emerge from the pastoral, liturgical, catechetical, social and evangelistic work of the Church. Theology is a highly existential activity and demands our highest efforts.

For example, theological reflection on the relation between God and the world may be spurred by the problem of innocent suffering and apparently meaningless tragedy in human life and history. To what extent is God the Creator ultimately responsible for what happens in the world? How does it help that humans have been created responsible and free? How involved must God be in the world process to be present to bring strength and succour? Can we even say that God suffers in or with the sufferings of God's creatures? Again, theological work in christology does not take the form of academics in ivory towers pondering the obscure formulae of early councils. It is much more likely to be energized by the problems of making sense of the uniqueness of Jesus Christ in a world increasingly conscious that there are many non-Christian religious traditions which appear to find their well-being (to put it no stronger) in God. The question of the uniqueness of Jesus Christ as saviour is also raised by feminist theology which asks whether modern women, seeking their own identity, value and personhood, can identify with Jesus, the male saviour and the founder, in some sense, of an institution which has consistently oppressed women.

A distinctive method

'Method' is literally 'following a way', a procedure for attaining an end in view. Method conveys us from a starting point that is known, to a destination that is hidden from us. Every discipline has a method or methods and engages in critical reflection on it. The philosophy of science reflects critically on the practice and methods of the physical and social sciences. Modern theology is methodologically self-conscious. Systematic theology has tended to discuss method interminably and so postpone the daunting challenge of actually reconstructing Christian doctrine. J. Stout has aptly accused theologians of being 'reduced to seemingly endless methodological foreplay' (Stout 1981: 148). Reflection on method belongs to fundamental theology which is an integral part – but certainly not the whole – of dogmatics.

It has rightly been claimed that 'systematic theology does not have a special method of its own' (Schwöbel 1992: 22). As the crown of the theological enterprise, it draws on the methods of various theological disciplines: exegetical, historical, philosophical, sociological and psychological. The exegetical and historical work serves the criterion of adequacy: is our dogmatics faithful to the givenness of the tradition (without merely parotting past formulations)? Philosophical method serves the criterion of coherence: are our concepts as clear as they can be and consistent with one another? Sociological and psychological methods serve the criterion of relevance: how does our theology relate to contemporary insights into the nature of human being and society?

The crucial issue in theological method, however, concerns the respective authority of the sources of dogmatics (Scripture, tradition, the present teaching authority of the Church, non-theological input, even the insights of other faiths) and the criteria for interpreting them (for example, the degree of recognition given to such genres as myth and symbol). While Scripture gives us the raw material of dogmatics, it does not contain in explicit form several central Christian doctrines such as those of the Trinity and christology. These have been worked out by theologians and synods subsequently, by rational reflection on Scripture and tradition. Three stages in the process of doctrinal formulation may be discerned.

First, there is *normative* doctrine, consisting of the decrees of Church councils expressed in the creeds. These are regarded as definitive and as belonging to the trust deeds, as it were, of the Church. They are intended to exclude gross errors and to set parameters for interpretation, but certainly not to put an end to theological exploration. They exert restraint on theologians operating 'in the bosom of the Church' (as Rahner puts it), especially those who are ordained and hold, say, a bishop's licence, but naturally they cannot inhibit theologians who do not accept such a fundamental loyalty.

Second, there is *formative* doctrine which belongs to the formative period of a church's history when its identity was decisively defined – for Protestant churches, the sixteenth century – and is embodied in confessions and liturgies. Such sources are likely to be regarded as witnesses to Christian truth, but not as definitive statements of doctrine.

Third, there is *adaptive* doctrine which emerges as theologians or church bodies grapple with the questions and challenges that are generated by interaction with the cultural environment. In adaptive doctrine, we draw on normative and formative resources of the Christian theological heritage, together with the information and insight that can be gleaned from any relevant source. However no church claims the authority to make new doctrines and the theories of systematicians are likely to resemble either ancient orthodoxy or ancient heresy. Even when apparently radical positions are put forward – as in Christian feminist theology – which are subversive of tradition, precedents can usually be found.

Thus feminist theologians appeal to divine immanence rather than divine transcendence, to *sophia* (wisdom) rather than *logos* (word), to reconciled polarities over against dualistic dichotomies, and here it may be suggested that they are recovering early Christian insights that soon lost ground in the Western Church. The challenge to ordain women to the priesthood in churches with the traditional threefold ministry finds a mandate and paradigm in the controversial admission of the Gentiles to full Christian privileges in the early Church. So adaptive doctrine is simply a method of applying the theological heritage to fresh issues.

These sources and stages of doctrinal formulation are all problematic today and call for sophistication in theological method. As far as the sources are concerned, the Scriptures are problematic because biblical scholarship is bringing out ever more conclusively the complex and diverse character of the biblical literature. We do not seem to have a concept of biblical inspiration or authority commensurate with the highly contingent and profoundly human character of the texts. A similar process of comparative and critical study has exposed the contingent character of ecclesiastical tradition and the dubious methods often employed in carrying a particular doctrinal decision in the Church's synods. In particular, it has become difficult to see the hand of a directing providence in the unfolding of an oppressively patriarchal tradition.

The stages of doctrinal formulation are equally problematic. First, *normative* doctrine, located in patristic creeds, liturgies and writings, incorporates an outmoded world-view and philosophical concepts that are no longer part of our mental furniture. Hence normative doctrine seems remote and arcane to most Christians – including theologians. The better one understands these notions in their original setting, the more alien they become, for some though by no means all theologians (T. F. Torrance believes that to return to classical

Christian concepts, for example in the thought of Athanasius, is a precondition for the renewal of modern theology).

Formative doctrine, embodied in the classical confessions, is also historically specific – recognizably the product of a particular time, place and culture – and only by a great effort of historical imagination can we put ourselves in the shoes of the sixteenth-century Reformers, for example. Moreover, formative doctrine is patently polemical, directed against the 'errors' of other Christian churches, with ensuing distortions (as we see in the Thirty-nine Articles).

Adaptive doctrine too is problematic, for it is tightly constrained by the proliferating pluralism of the contemporary Church – a pluralism that is rife both within and between the churches. While church bodies such as synods can utter merely bland platitudes because anything sharper would not enjoy consensus support, individual theologians can still speak with a prophetic voice. But the voice of an individual theologian is not yet doctrine – for that it has to be corporately received and promulgated with some authority.

Method is not decided arbitrarily or *a priori*. It is worked out as we grapple with theological problems and should never become absolutized. It is commended by its fruitfulness in practice. Macquarrie writes: 'If it leads to a coherent and intelligible presentation of what is recognisably the content of the revelation as that has been held in the community of faith, then a theological method vindicates itself' (Macquarrie 1977: 34). Method should never be elaborated apart from attention to content nor content apart from reflection on method; the two should proceed dialectically.

Back to the sources

Systematic theologians are driven by the pressure of topical questions back to the authoritative sources of Christian theology in Scripture and tradition. They will not achieve anything by simply citing isolated texts taken out of context or by appealing to the fiction of a monolithic tradition. Biblical and traditional statements are not conclusive in dogmatics. They constitute evidence that is treated with respect, weighed and evaluated by setting it alongside other evidence. The method of Thomas Aquinas in the *Summa Theologiae*, where he ranges biblical texts, the teaching of Aristotle, quotations from the Fathers and the opinions of other schoolmen, on both sides of the argument, before exercising his own judgement, simply makes explicit (in an admittedly crude manner) the procedure that is implicit in all systematic theology worth its salt. Systematic theologies tend to try to commend themselves as mere expositions of Scripture – Calvin's *Institutes of the Christian Religion* (1559) and Barth's dogmatics are prime examples – but while the text of Scripture is given a pre-eminent place, its interpretation is governed by other considerations, to which we now turn.

Our Creative Contribution

What input do we, as theologians, amateur or professional, bring to this task? We bring our own reason – with all that that involves of experience, imagination, creative insight, moral discernment and aesthetic appreciation. First, we use our reason, to identify the sources, allocating them to various literary genres (Gospel, epistle, poetry, vision, etc.), for this will affect our interpretation, and going on to discern within these genres the constituent semantic types (metaphor, symbol, myth, for example), for this discernment will similarly profoundly affect our interpretation.

Second, we use reason to criticize the sources, not accepting them at face value but testing them by standards of religious insight and ethical acceptability. Christian feminist theology is perhaps the most critical of all contemporary forms of theological interpretation: its leading exponents (Ruether and Fiorenza) adopt a particularly mordant form of the hermeneutic of suspicion. Post-Christian feminist theology (Daly and Hampson) is so critical of Christian sources that it finds them actually beyond redemption and virtually unusable.

Third, we employ our reason to appropriate 'secular' information and insight from non-theological disciplines which can shed light upon the nature of the world, history and humankind. History among the human sciences, sociology and psychology among the social sciences, cosmology and biology among the natural sciences, metaphysics and linguistic and conceptual analysis among the philosophical disciplines will all be called upon here by the accomplished theologian. Latin American political theology is an outstanding example of a theology that has drawn on secular disciplines (in this case sociology and political thought, particularly that of Karl Marx) to shape its presuppositions.

In a word, the theologian adopts a proactive, creative role throughout the whole process of theological construction. There is no theological 'technique' that bypasses the personal dimenson. Theology is preeminently a form of what M. Polanyi called personal knowledge.

The discipline of the given

There is one further dimension in this model of systematic theology, which may be called the discipline of the given or, as theologians such as Barth and Torrance would put it, conformity to the object of our enquiry. As theologians we work with a concept – tacit or explicit – of what is central to Christian belief, and in practice we seek to allow this to shape our theology, bestowing structure, symmetry and momentum on our discourse. We do not spin the web of Christian doctrine out of our own fancies and preferences; we aim to conform our thinking to the central message of Christianity. This once again introduces the issue of the essence of Christianity. This concept has become peculiarly attractive to theologians in the post-Enlightenment period as we have become increasingly conscious of the diversity of theological options and their cultural relativity.

In *The Christian Faith* Schleiermacher defined the essence as that everything in dogmatics is related to the redemption accomplished by Jesus of Nazareth (Schleiermacher 1928: 52ff.). This was a dynamic definition, grounding the essence in Christian experience of redemption. W. Adams Brown in *The Essence of Christianity* (Brown 1903) proposed 'Christ's transforming influence', thus strengthening the dynamic character of the essence. A. Sabatier, in his posthumous *The Religions of Authority and the Religion of the Spirit*, located the essence in 'the spirit of Christ in our consciousness' – 'a state of soul' (Sabatier 1904: 362, 365). S. W. Sykes, in his early discussions of this topic, followed this Protestant tradition in offering 'the character or spirit of Christ' (Sykes 1971: 121ff.) as the essence.

In this sequence of discussions we see a steady shift away from the particularity of Jesus of Nazareth towards the universality of the Christ. This reflects the perennial problem of faith and history: to what extent can the salvific assurances of faith be founded on the shifting sands of historical research? But it also suits Christian feminist theologians who are uncomfortable with a Christianity that stresses the particularity of the male Jesus of Nazareth. However, it seems inevitable that in a historical religion such as Christianity, respect will always have to be paid to the particularity of its origins.

Tillich, in his *Systematic Theology*, defined the essence (or 'the material norm of systematic theology') as 'the New Being in Jesus as the Christ as our ultimate concern' (Tillich 1953–68, I: 56). This may perhaps commend itself to feminist theologians since, while not neglecting the historical manifestation (the New Being had to appear in a historical person, according to Tillich) it focuses on the existential relevance and ontological import of the essence. Needless to say, feminist theologians would not find much to commend in Harnack's famous formula (Harnack 1904) that the essence of Christianity consists of the Fatherhood of God and the brotherhood of man!

It is ironic that, while the essence project commended itself to modern Protestant theologians as a way of maintaining coherence in the face of chronic diversity, that diversity is now recognized at the heart of the essence concept. It was E. Troeltsch who insisted that 'the essence of Christianity can be understood only as the new interpretations and new adaptations, corresponding to each new situation, produced by Christianity's historical power' and that 'the essence of Christianity differs in every epoch, resulting from the totality of the influences in each age'. The essence, for Troeltsch, cannot therefore be located in an unchanging doctrinal formula, but only in that very power of adaptation, reinterpretation and reconstruction that synthesizes the historical legacy of Christianity with the contemporary world-view (Troeltsch 1991b: 97).

In *The Identity of Christianity* Sykes has taken this line of argument one step further in dubbing the essence or identity of Christianity 'an essentially contested concept' (Sykes 1984: 251 ff.). This is almost to locate the essence in the phenomenon of argument over what Christianity is all about. It seems unlikely that this melancholy conclusion will put an end to the essence quest which will become increasingly urgent as dialogue with other world faiths is increasingly taken to the heart of systematics. And as feminist theology moves from a predominantly critical mode into a constructive mode, it may well want to attempt its own definition of the essence.

All responsible theology accepts the discipline of the given. This has tended to have a christological focus but also to presuppose a particular interpretation or framework of the relation of God and the world. Our view of the person of Christ becomes a paradigm of our understanding of God's relation to the world. Thus a highly supernaturalistic Christ – Virgin born, omniscient, walking on water, raising the dead, stage-managing his passion, rising and ascending bodily – reflects a dualistic and interventionist concept of God and the world. On the other hand, a profoundly human Christ – wrestling with temptation, doubting, genuinely suffering, resurrected in the spirit rather than the flesh – reflects an immanental concept of God, present in and working through the world process and our fundamental human aspirations. As long as Christian theology engages with christology it will – tacitly or explicitly – grapple with the problem of the essence of Christianity.

What sort of conclusions?

The solutions that systematic theologians arrive at are unlikely to commend themselves to sceptical observers as 'answers' in any normal sense of the word. The problems of theology are insoluble and its dilemmas perennial. The theologians of today are still working on the questions that perplexed their forefathers in the fourth, the thirteenth, the eighteenth, or the nineteenth century. Their solutions are strategies for coping with the tensions inherent in any theology that talks about the conjunction of the world and God, the human and the divine, freedom and sovereignty, unity and plurality, uniqueness and universality. The far-from-final product of systematic theology is likely to be little more than a serviceable model that can contain our questions and address our needs. But it will be a model that is intellectually satisfying and that will not disgrace us when set in the midst of the dominant paradigms of our contemporary world-view. It is this ever-renewed pursuit of theological coherence that renders dogmatics an ongoing enterprise.

The dilemma inherent in the concept of dogmatics is that it attempts to be authoritative – it is an exegesis of the given – yet it is infinitely varied. Systematic theologies speak to their age and its concerns. They are not valid for all time. The conclusions of dogmatics are merely provisional. Any authority that a dogmatics may acquire will consist in the recognition that, to some significant extent, it has succeeded in doing justice both to the heritage of

Christian theology and to the challenge of its own age. There will always be a need for the work of systematic theologians and the churches should take care that they encourage vocations to this form of ministry.

A BRIEF APOLOGIA FOR 'DOGMATICS'

The terms dogma and dogmatic are now pejorative and are repellent to the modern liberal outlook. They savour of blind commitment, intolerance and fundamentalism. They seem utterly unsuitable to describe the crown of all theological endeavour. Hence some alternative expressions have been favoured – less redolent of closure and finality. 'Teaching of faith' (*Glaubenslehre*) was employed by Schleiermacher and Troeltsch; 'Systematic Theology' by Tillich and Pannenberg. However, there is a meaning contained in the term dogmatics that should not be lost sight of.

The Greek *dogma* meant either a personal opinion or an authoritative decree. In the first sense, it came to be used of the tenets of various philosophical schools and could be applied to the true philosophy of Christ. In the second sense it is used in the New Testament of the decisions of the council of Jerusalem in Acts 16:4 which were intended to be binding on the Gentile churches. After the adoption of Christianity by Constantine, when conciliar decisions received state legal sanctions, the unquestionable, authoritative aspect of Christian dogma became dominant. In the history of the Church, dogmas have been those fundamental teachings, enshrined in the creeds and enforced by law, that could not be questioned with impunity.

But what becomes of dogma in a democratic, pluralist and secular society, when state protection for Christian beliefs is withdrawn and there are no penalties for questioning the truth of Christian doctrines? Does it follow that the givenness and authority of doctrines must evaporate and that one opinion is as good as another?

The doctrines that we are free to criticize, to accept or reject, have been mediated to us from a source outside ourselves. To them we owe our theological formation, our theological vocabulary and the inventory of metaphors, symbols and myths with which we operate theologically. They are not ours to dispose of as we will. We are dependent on them and our critique is, so to speak, parasitic on the enduring substance of Christian theological tradition. If we could rival the great artificers of Christian doctrine, and match them in learning, insight and zeal, we might have a better right to disregard what they have handed down to us. Dogmatics, as a term for the coherent presentation of Christian beliefs, reminds us of the givenness of the Christian mystery and of our limited role as its latter-day explorers and exponents.

THE POST-MODERN WATERSHED

In our present cultural situation there are peculiar difficulties attendant on the task of systematic theology. The pluralism and fragmentation of 'truth' in our post-modern age has tempted some to take refuge in the givenness of the Christian story presented in Scripture. Their theology is intra-textual and confines itself to the biblical world. It does not attempt a continual traffic across the boundary between Scripture and the modern world. However, narrative theology of this kind offers no escape from pluralism and fragmentation, for these are precisely characteristics of Scripture itself. In so far as it serves as a form of escapism, purely narrative theology must be judged to be on a par with fundamentalism. In fact, far from invalidating the theological enterprise, the conditions of post-modernity point to an exciting, though daunting, opportunity. However, it should be borne in mind that theologizing in the situation of post-modernity (which is inevitable) is not the same as developing a theology that adopts or invites the label 'post-modernist' (which is an elective stance).

The inter-faith context

Traditionally, dogmatics has been conducted in dialogue with competing theological positions, Protestant versus Roman Catholic, Lutheran versus Reformed. Where it has engaged with hostile non-Christian thought, that has tended to take the form of alternative world-views (for example Augustine's battle with Manichaeism and Aquinas's dialectical engagement with Arabic neo-Aristotelian philosophy). These opponents have been succeeded in modern times by Marxist materialism, Freudian reductionism or the form of linguistic philosophy identified with the Logical Positivism of the early A. J. Ayer.

Only recently, as theodicy (the problem of reconciling the innocent or disproportionate suffering in the world with the existence of an almighty and all-just Creator) has assumed a higher priority in the aftermath of the Holocaust (Shoah), has dogmatics taken Judaism as a serious dialogue partner. Certainly dogmatics has not looked to non-Christian religious traditions as one of its sources of insight. However, it has now been challenged to do precisely that in a programmatic article by G. D'Costa which posits the end of systematic theology as we know it (D'Costa 1992). He argues that the Hindu and Buddhist (as well as the Jewish) world-views should be allowed to shape specifically Christian dogmatic assertions.

This thesis is not entirely novel, though it remains radical. E. Troeltsch argued that the dogmatic exposition of the distinctive character of Christianity should be conducted in relation to 'the stream of the universal development of the history of religions' and that the first task of dogmatics was, therefore, to establish, on the basis of a philosophy of the comparative history of religions, 'the fundamental and universal supremacy of Christianity'. Our warmly appreciative engagement with these religions, Troeltsch suggests, confirms our intuitive sense of the superiority of Christianity (Troeltsch 1991b: 90–5). Troeltsch's conception of the Christian theological appropriation of other religious traditions remains, then, ultimately imperialistic, but the principle of inter-faith fertilization of Christian systematic theology is present. Similarly, Pannenberg's method of employing received doctrines as hypotheses for the critical exploration of religious traditions is hospitable to input from other religious traditions and he postulates that the systematic theology of the future will engage in 'a systematic comparison between the competing conceptions of the world religions' (Pannenberg 1991: xiii).

This programme suggests several reflections:

1 D'Costa is right to propose that a knowledge of world religions should be part of every theological education and that departments of theology must, therefore, incorporate religious studies if they are truly to remain departments of theology (D'Costa 1992: 332).

2 This programme is already going on to some extent: the doctrine of the Trinity is an area where illumination from Hinduism has been brought to bear (cf. Whaling 1986: 145ff.).

3 The burden of research and range of knowledge for any but the most exceptional theologians will become impossible and team work with an inter-disciplinary complexion – already desirable – will become essential.

4 We should be aware that doctrinal concepts are not necessarily commensurable between religions. For example, not every religion has a concept of salvation in the Christian sense; the idea of incarnation is anathema to others; there are opposing assessments of the value of the material world. Inter-faith theological dialogue will not achieve a synthesis that transcends particular religions (D'Costa has not suggested that it will). The exercise will remain one of Christian theologians borrowing selectively from traditions that have some apparent affinity with Christianity in order to enrich and criticize their own material.

The cognitive status of doctrine

Traditional theology cannot be accused of neglecting the transcendence, mystery and ineffability of God. But alongside those affirmations, it placed the fundamental assumption that, thanks to propositional revelation, its statements nevertheless described the ultimate reality of God – not literally, of course, but analogically. Some recent linguistic philosophy and critical theology have questioned the ability of the concept of analogy, as found classically in Aquinas, to bear the weight of this claim (cf. Pannenberg 1991: 337–47).

G. Lindbeck (1984) has distinguished three interpretations of the nature of doctrine, which he rejects, and added a fourth of his own. The first is the traditional or orthodox cognitive view which takes doctrines to be informative and reliable statements about objective realities – naively true. The second is the experiential–expressive view which understands doctrine as the articulation of religious experience, Schleiermacher and Sabatier being its great exponents. The third is an attempt to combine the grounding in experience of the second with the objective reference of the first. Lindbeck cites Rahner and Lonergan – presumably for their notions of veridical insight arising out of the impact of experience, a sort of symbolic realism; but this third view remains elusive and shadowy in Lindbeck's account and he subsumes it under the first and second. Fourth, Lindbeck argues that the sociology of knowledge and the Wittgensteinian concept of language games rule out any direct or indirect reference to objectivity and render doctrines cultural–linguistic constructs (Lindbeck's own view) which have a merely regulative role within their own culture. Their criteria of validity are purely intra-textual.

Lindbeck's emphasis on the reality and finality of the text as given buys into the current fascination with narrative. A narrative is a linguistic and semantic world that does not necessarily make any cognitive claim on reality. But because it is structured as story, we may see our identity quest, either as individuals or a community, reflected in it and so find our faith enhanced. Narrative theology is a way of breaking out of the crudest subjectivity of faith – because the text is external to us – without getting involved in metaphysics. Non-realist theologies stop there, but narrative remains a component in realist theologies too, though it is not required to take all the strain.

Of all intra-textual, expository dogmatics Moltmann's is the most powerful. He dwells within the world of the text, illuminating and applying it by rhetorical heightening rather than by interdisciplinary engagement like Pannenberg. For example, when discussing the virginal conception of Jesus (Moltmann 1990: 78 ff.), he does not apply either a biological or a sociological critique – he asks neither about chromosomes nor about patriarchy – but asserts that the texts in the infancy narratives are *intended* to be taken symbolically.

How should we assess Lindbeck's proposal? His emphasis on the social function of doctrine is a welcome antidote to ideological naiveté and his protest against theological literalism is well taken. But he goes too far in discounting the cognitive status of theological statements. Doctrines exist because they have been believed to be true. The fact that we now see that doctrines also serve human interests and are culturally relative does not invalidate their cognitive status. Doctrines may be cognitive without necessarily being wholly veridical, just as scientific theories enable us to interpret the physical world and to harness its resources even though these theories also are distorted by human interests. Some scientific theories are eventually found to be false, others are heavily modified, but it would not do to say that they had simply a cultural–linguistic function, serving group identity or social cohesion. In all human disciplines concerned with the boundaries of knowledge we see through a glass darkly. Lindbeck seems to need a concept of critical or symbolic realism that does not equate contingent human knowledge with ultimate truth.

The texture of theological discourse

It is the symbolic and mythic nature of religious language that has led Lindbeck and others to question its cognitive status. The presence of myth and symbol in both first-order religious utterances (prayers, hymns and narratives) and second-order theological discourse is undeniable. Symbolic language is a refinement of the ultimately metaphorical nature of all meaningful utterance. Myth weaves numinous symbols into narrative sequence. Wherever we speak of the origin or destiny of the world or of a people, whenever we attempt to describe the great transformations of our being, or divine intervention in the world, we resort to myth. Myth is not confined to Genesis 1–11 or the book of Revelation: it impinges on christology, especially the Incarnation ('He came down from heaven and was made man'), the virginal conception, the resurrection, the ascension and the second coming (in fact all eschatology that is not wholly 'realized', i.e. reinterpreted existentially and in terms of personal or ecclesial spirituality, is mythic). What does the category 'myth' entail?

In modernity, under the influence of scientistic positivism, the prevalent conception of myth has been reductionist: myth is primitive philosophy, just as legend is primitive history. The ideal has been that significant truths should be expressed in a clear and precise form free from myth. Of course, the truths that can be expressed in such a way are extremely limited: metaphysical assertions can only be expressed in symbolic and mythic form. Bultmann's demythologizing programme is a case in point: while Bultmann acknowledged that myth contains a serious religious meaning, he insisted that the scope of that meaning was purely subjective. It could only refer to an inner disposition, not to any transcendent reality (Bartsch 1954; Bultmann 1960).

The challenge to theology in the post-modern situation is now to go beyond Bultmann and develop a realist concept of myth which allows that myths are cognitive and intend to say something about ultimate reality which can then be critically appropriated. A concept of mythic realism would enable us to interpret the myths of the Bible and Christian doctrine, not in a reductionist sense but in a way that left room for the impact of divine revelation in some sense. That would not involve baptizing all myths as equally true, valid or appropriate, but would retain the transcendent reference of myth. Thus, for example, the mythic components in the doctrine of the Incarnation could be acknowledged while the essential affirmations that this doctrine intends to make would be respected – namely the identity of God with Jesus in his mission, suffering, death and resurrection.

Can we attain a total perspective?

Pannenberg has given a timely reminder to a theology that is in danger of losing its nerve, that in postulating God as the reality that determines all reality, theology is committed to venturing assertions about the totality of all that is (Pannenberg 1976). Traditional theology had no qualms about this: the medieval *Summa* intended to reduce the entire scope of created and uncreated reality to concise definitions. The Hegelian system similarly embraced all of history in its metaphysical scheme. Theologies of history have inveterately tended to identify the world of thought and the world of actuality, the rational and the real. They have often been devised to legitimate the current regime and the status of the Church's hierarchy within it. Their total perspective has been employed to justify the suppression of dissent and to absolutize prevailing power structures. The Aryan ideology of the Nazis was a perverted theology of history. Total perspectives on reality are particularly exposed to the temptations of ideology as political power accrues to conceptual value.

For the twentieth century, inevitably, the concept of totality has particularly grim overtones of intellectual tyranny and totalitarianism. The thinkers of the Frankfurt School, Horkheimer and Adorno, indicted – precisely on these grounds – all totalistic thinking as detrimental to freedom (Jay 1984). For Adorno, truth was to be found only in the margins and crevices of life within the 'administered society' of the modern world. Post-modern thought has taken this further in its insistence that there can be no picture of the whole, no all-embracing story: all we have is fragments. 'Let us wage war on totality' is the battlecry of post-modernists (Lyotard 1984: 82).

While theology in the dogmatic mode could not be content with fragments, it should certainly learn a becoming humility. A comprehensive theological system seems unattainable. However, it is difficult to see how theology could continue without some implicit concept of totality. As Rahner has insisted, the word 'God' performs this role in theism. It confronts us with the question of the totality of reality and the wholeness of our own existence. 'God' stands for the ultimate unity and meaning of everything. And Rahner claims that only 'God' does this (Rahner 1978: 48). But while some notion of totality is indispensable, it need not be approached head on and in an undifferentiated way.

Theology must be willing to approach the object of its enquiry obliquely, homing in from more than one direction at once. The theological tradition can be seen to have often done this. It spoke of God's involvement in the world in a twofold manner: in the mode of nature and in the mode of grace. It construed the source of the knowledge of God in a dual mode: that of revelation and that of reason. It affirmed the relation of the Creator to the creation by employing the complementary images of transcendence and immanence. In this way, theology avoided a totalizing concept of God which

996

could so easily have become an idol. It left room for manoeuvre in the realm of the sacred and affirmed the reality and integrity of the natural, created sphere. This tradition of dialectical theism (cf. Macquarrie 1984) avoids the extremes of identifying God and the natural process and the dualism that fails to relate them. A theology such as that of Tillich, which is structured by antinomy and paradox, respects this profound instinct of orthodoxy in a way that the one-sided theology of Barth does not.

A notion of polarity has thus been implicit in the Christian theological tradition. In the post-modern context, this is ripe for further development – possibly in the light of aspects of the philosophy of science such as Bohr's principle of complementarity or Northrop's 'epistemic correlation'. A sophisticated notion of polarity could preserve theology from the excesses of intellectual hubris and enable it to present an appropriately chastened image in a world that is deeply suspicious of all totalizing pretensions.

THE CHALLENGE OF DOGMATICS

Troeltsch regarded the construction of a dogmatics as the specific ultimate theological problem (cf. Troeltsch 1991b: 91). Ultimate presumably because it presupposes extensive groundwork in biblical, historical and philosophical studies, as well as the development of an appropriate theological method – but why 'problem'? Writing a dogmatics is unquestionably problematic if we follow Troeltsch's definition of dogmatics as 'the exposition of a normative Christian worldview' (ibid.). Having already touched on the issue of the systematic nature of dogmatics, let us focus on the epithet 'normative'. Dogmatics sets out to produce a normative account of the content of the Christian faith. This is certainly implicit in the definition of dogmatics as coherent, credible and critical. Dogmatics purports to expound, not just a particular personal standpoint, but the true faith. How can this ambitious claim be justified? What is the source of our authority in dogmatics? Is it not ludicrous to speak of a normative dogmatics in an age of burgeoning religious pluralism and rampant theological individualism?

If a work of systematic theology receives the *Imprimatur* of ecclesiastical authority and is issued with its blessing, that will commend it to some. That form of conferred authority has recently been abandoned by the Roman Catholic Church, though it still maintains a list of authorized teachers of theology. But if, as in Protestant dogmatics, that route is not available, there are two further options.

First, the normative status of the dogmatics may be derived from its faithfulness to some controlling focus, the central reality or essence of the Christian faith. Although this determining principle will not be invented by the dogmatician, but will be drawn out of the mainstream tradition of Christianity, the quest for the essence of Christianity remains a controverted area where debate continues. Moreover, we see in the work of Schleiermacher,

Ritschl and Troeltsch that it requires extensive and sophisticated prolegomena which, as it were, set the theological scene, in the interaction of God and the world and in the phenomenon of religiosity, for the appearance of the essence or principle of Christianity.

Alternatively, a dogmatics may seek, less ambitiously, to express a tacit consensus of scholarly conclusions concerning the fundamental truths of Christianity, limiting its assertions to what carries broad agreement, refraining from idiosyncratic interpretations, and curbing the apparently innate tendency of dogmatics to superfluous polemics (as in Barth) and inflated rhetoric (as in Moltmann). Such a dogmatics will be ecumenical by definition, for it is now meaningless as well as retrograde to speak of a consensus that does not transcend particular Christian traditions. But it will remain, in Troeltsch's words, 'a normative Christian religious system' – one of a plurality of interpretations of Christianity, normative as a valid presentation of phenomenon that exceeds our human grasp, but not ultimate, not by any means the last word. Such a dogmatics will inevitably have a personal slant: its distinctive vision will reflect the narrative component of one theologian's journey of faith.

A fine example of such a modest, serviceable dogmatics is Jan Milič Lochman's *The Faith We Confess: An Ecumenical Dogmatics* (1985). It articulates a modern ecumenical consensus on fundamental Christian beliefs, as enshrined in the Apostles' Creed. The personal dimension is provided by the author's biography as a mediating theologian whose background stems from the Czech Reformation, and who has worked in Christian–Marxist dialogue. If the title 'dogmatics' seems a little pretentious for a work that is compact, clear and distilled, that may be because Karl Barth's massive achievement has created the impression that a dogmatics has to run to a dozen solid volumes of small print. But Barth's monumental work would be counterproductive if it inhibited more modest efforts that were not necessarily works of genius. The challenge of dogmatics is both to the production of exhaustive explorations of the theme, that are the work of a lifetime and influence the future direction of systematic theology, and to the creation of useful compendia that, because they are well meditated in their content and hardly radical in their assertions, nourish reflective Christians in the faith, assist enquirers, and stimulate the clergy to deepen the theological content of their sermons!

REFERENCES

Aquinas, T. (1964) *Summa Theologiae*, 60 vols, Cambridge: Blackfriars.

Barth, K. (1933) *The Epistle to the Romans*, trans. E. Hoskyns, Oxford: Oxford University Press.

—— (1956–) *Church Dogmatics*, 12 vols, ed. T. F. Torrance and G. W. Bromiley, Edinburgh: T. & T. Clark.

—— (1967) *The Humanity of God*, London: Collins.

—— (1972) *Protestant Theology in the Nineteenth Century*, London: SCM Press.

—— (1982) *The Theology of Schleiermacher*, ed. D. Ritschl, Edinburgh: T. & T. Clark.

Bartsch, H. W. (ed.) (1954) *Kerygma and Myth*, London: SPCK.
Brown, W. A. (1903) *The Essence of Christianity*, Edinburgh: T. & T. Clark.
Bultmann, R. (1960) *Jesus Christ and Mythology*, London: SCM Press.
Calvin, J. (1975) *Institutes of the Christian Religion*, 2 vols, trans. F. Battles, *Library of Christian Classics*, London: SCM Press.
Daly, M. (1986) *Beyond God the Father*, London: The Women's Press.
D'Costa, G. (1992) 'The End of Systematic Theology', *Theology* 95: 324–34.
Fiorenza, E. S. (1983) *In Memory of Her: A Feminist Reconstruction of Christian Origins*, London: SCM Press.
Grant, R. M. (1988) *Greek Apologists of the Second Century*, London: SCM Press.
Hampson, D. (1990) *Theology and Feminism*, Oxford: Basil Blackwell.
Harnack, A. von (1904) *What is Christianity?* (3rd edn), London: Williams and Norgate.
Hooker, R. (1954) *Of the Laws of Ecclesiastical Polity*, 2 vols, London: J. M. Dent.
Jay, M. (1984) *Marxism and Totality*, Berkeley: University of California Press.
Kierkegaard, S. K. (1955) *On Authority and Revelation*, trans. W. Lowrie, Princeton, NJ: Princeton University Press.
Lindbeck, G. (1984) *The Nature of Doctrine*, London: SPCK.
Lochman, J. M. (1985) *The Faith We Confess: An Ecumenical Dogmatics*, Edinburgh: T. & T. Clark.
Luther, M. (1955–) *Luther's Works*, 56 vols, ed. J. Pelikan and H. T. Lehmann, Philadelphia: Concordia/Fortress Press.
Lyotard, J.-F. (1984) *The Post-Modern Condition: A Report on Knowledge*, Manchester: Manchester University Press.
Macquarrie, J. (1977) *Principles of Christian Theology*, rev. edn, London: SCM Press.
—— (1984) *In Search of Deity*, London: SCM Press.
Metz, J. B. (1980) *Faith in History and Society: Toward a Practical Fundamental Theology*, trans. D. Smith, London: Burns & Oates.
Moltmann, J. (1990) *The Way of Jesus Christ*, trans. M. Kohl, London: SCM Press.
Nietzsche, F. (1968) *Twilight of the Idols*, trans. R. J. Hollingdale, Harmondsworth: Penguin.
Pannenberg, W. (1976) *Theology and the Philosophy of Science*, London: Darton, Longman and Todd.
—— (1985) *Anthropology in Theological Perspective*, trans. M. J. O'Connell, Edinburgh: T. & T. Clark.
—— (1991) *Systematic Theology*, vol. 1, trans. G. W. Bromiley, Edinburgh: T. & T. Clark.
Polanyi, M. (1958) *Personal Knowledge*, London: RKP.
Rahner, K. (1965–) *Theological Investigations*, 23 vols, London: Darton, Longman and Todd.
—— (1978) *Foundations of Christian Faith*, London: Darton, Longman and Todd.
Ruether, R. R. (1983) *Sexism and God-Talk*, London: SCM Press.
Sabatier, A. (1904) *The Religions of Authority and the Religion of the Spirit*, London: Williams and Norgate.
Schleiermacher, F. (1928) *The Christian Faith*, ed. H. R. Mackintosh and J. S. Stewart, Edinburgh: T. & T. Clark.
—— (1958) *On Religion: Speeches to its Cultured Despisers*, trans. J. Oman, New York: Harper & Row.
Schwöbel, C. (1992) *God, Action and Revelation*, Kampen: Kok Pharos.
Stout, G. (1981) *The Flight from Authority*, Notre Dame: University of Notre Dame Press.
Sykes, S. W. (1971) *Christian Theology Today*, London: Mowbray.
—— (1984) *The Identity of Christianity*, London: SPCK.

Temple, W. (1938) in *Doctrine in the Church of England: The Report of the Commission on Christian Doctrine appointed by the Archbishops of Canterbury and York in 1922*, London: SPCK.

Tillich, P. (1953–68) *Systematic Theology*, 3 vols, Welwyn: Nisbet.

Troeltsch, E. (1991a) *The Christian Faith*, trans. G. E. Paul, Minneapolis: Fortress Press.

—— (1991b) 'The Dogmatics of the History-of-Religions School', *Religion in History*, trans. J. L. Adams and W. F. Bense, Edinburgh: T. & T. Clark.

Whaling, F. (1986) *Christian Theology and World Religions*, Basingstoke: Marshall Pickering.

FURTHER READING

Avis, P. (1986) *The Methods of Modern Theology*, Basingstoke: Marshall Pickering.

—— (ed.) (1988) *The Threshold of Theology*, Basingstoke: Marshall Pickering.

—— (1995) *Christianity in the Fires of Criticism*, London: Darton, Longman and Todd.

See also chapters 10, 14, 15, 17, 20, 25, 41, 42, 43, 44.

47

THEOLOGY AS PRAXIS

Dan Cohn-Sherbok

The term 'praxis' is derived from the Greek, meaning practice. Recently it has become a central notion in contemporary Christian thought. In Latin America, as well as in other countries in the Third World, a new Christian theological development drawing on German Christian theologies of hope expressed by such writers as Jürgen Moltmann has been taking place over the last few decades. Liberation theology, as it is frequently called, has captured the imagination of Roman Catholics and Protestants alike. Combining theory with practice, this movement attempts to use the insights of Marxist social criticism to forge a new vision of the Christian message. Most importantly for Jewish–Christian encounter, liberation theologians have gone back to their Jewish roots in the Hebrew Scriptures. Suddenly Jewish and Christian writers find themselves using the same vocabulary and motifs, and this bond paves the way for a shared examination of common religious ideals.

For these Christian theologians, the biblical account portrays the Israelites as an oppressed people. Suffering torment, their complaints led to new burdens rather then to relief (Exod. 1:8–14). But the Israelites were not alone: God heard the groaning of the people and remembered the covenant (Exod. 2:23–5). Moreover, God declared that the people would be liberated from their bondage. Moses was delegated to lead the people out of Egypt, and after many trials, this was accomplished (Exod. 3:7–10). This story of hope has inspired the oppressed in Third World countries, particularly in Latin America. It is of solace to hear that God does not remain aloof from situations of human history, that God acted against Pharaoh, and that Israel's liberation was not simply from individual sin and guilt. Israel's freedom means liberation from oppressive political and economic structures. It is clear that God has a real concern with life on earth.

This transformation of Christian theology to a policy of social praxis has not been without its critics. According to a number of Christian writers, the prime aim of the Church is individual salvation; the concern for social justice is therefore of secondary importance. Christ's work is his activity within the

Church, they argue, not in the world. Thus the life of the Church is more important than any social programme. Liberation theology is also dismissed as a passing fad. In the view of these critics, liberationists are guilty of putting too much hope in politics and even of glorifying violence. Another attack levelled at liberation theology is that it reduces the Gospel to ethics, politics, or Marxism.

Despite such objections, Christian liberation theology – with its emphasis on praxis – continues to be a vibrant force in the Third World and elsewhere. For many Christians, this new movement has provided a radically important framework for understanding God's action on behalf of the poor: as a result of this reorientation of the faith, liberationists insist that Christians must take an active role in eradicating exploitation, discrimination and oppression. For these writers, Christians must become a saving remnant in the modern world: like Abraham they should hope against hope in labouring to build a just and humane world, thereby becoming an Abrahamic minority attentive to the cry of oppression.

HISTORY AND PRAXIS

The Bible is a record of divine intervention in human history. What was required of Israel was obedient participation in the fulfilment of God's plan of emancipation. The faith of Israel was portrayed as synonymous with acting in consonance with God's will. For liberation theologians the biblical witness leads to a historical orientation of the Christian faith. Praxis, rather than theological conceptualization, serves as the foundation of Christian commitment and obedience.

> Over against a theology of the word or of abstract principles, Latin America now posits a theology of lived faith, of committed action. Here a complete shift has taken place, and faith is understood as orthopraxis rather than as orthodoxy.
>
> (Pérez-Esclarín 1978: 109)

For liberation theologians authentic theology must start from actions committed to the cause of liberation. In this service theology is a praxis of liberation. Within this context Míguez Bonino stresses that Christianity must concern itself with modern society.

> We are not concerned with establishing through deduction the consequences of conceptual truths but with analyzing a historical praxis which claims to be Christian. This critical analysis includes a number of operations which are totally unknown to classical theology. Historical praxis overflows beyond the area of the subjective and private.
>
> (Míguez Bonino 1975: 93)

Theology is here conceived as a critical reflection on praxis. In this context charity has been given a central place in the Christian life; it is understood as the motivating force, the giving of oneself to others. In this light Gutiérrez remarks, 'the understanding of the faith appears as the understanding not of the simple affirmation – almost memorization – of truths, but of a commitment, an overall attitude, a particular posture toward life' (Gutiérrez 1973, 7). The theoretical basis to the identification of orthopraxis with orthodoxy is complex. It rests in large measure upon the key idea that any interpretation of Christianity is inevitably practical/social/ethical in its main thrust. So the only question becomes which political message is the best basis for a contemporary version of the Christian proclamation. Behind the elevation of orthopraxis lies, among other things: a version of the pragmatist theory of truth (the notion that what is true is what works); and a belief in the situated nature of all thought, including theological, so that it must invariably reflect the relativities of the human situation and speak to these. These ideas are deepened and strengthened by acceptance of the Marxist idea of theory as essentially critique. This is well set out by Charles Davis thus:

> Marx rejected the concept of theory as immune from practice and its variations. He refused the claim of theoretical thought to be a presuppositionless, contemplative recognition of a stable object. Theory and practice are interdependent and theoretical activity . . . is a product of the changing reality of society. This new understanding of the relation of theory and practice implied the abolition of philosophy as traditionally understood and its sublation or transformation into critique, namely into critical thought as the conscious component of social practice.
>
> (Davis 1980: 3–4)

As Davis notes, these ideas are given pithy expression in Marx's *Theses on Feuerbach*:

> II. The question of whether objective truth can be attributed to human thinking is not a question of theory but is a practical question. Man must prove the truth, i.e. the reality and power, the this-sideness of his thinking in practice. The dispute over the reality or non-reality of thinking that is isolated from practice is a purely scholastic question.
> XI The philosophers have only interpreted the world, in various ways; the point is to change it.
>
> (Marx 1977: 57–8)

The logic behind the liberationists' identification of orthodoxy with orthopraxis reveals that, even before it offers its analysis of social ills and their cure, liberation theology is indebted to some of the fundamental ideas of Marxism. It is such ideas that entail a radical transformation of Christian doctrine in the hands of liberation theology.

Similarly, Christian spirituality has undergone a major transformation. In the early centuries of the Church, contemplative life was characterized by withdrawal from the world. Today, however, liberation theologians emphasize that religion must engage actively in modern life.

> The revitalisation of the religious life is come by way of our option for the poor classes on our continent. It is there that the following of Christ will find its embodiment in real history. If a people is capable of overcoming exploitation and

building a fraternal society, in that very process it will be creating new forms of consecration to Christ and fidelity to our baptism.

(Cussianovich 1979: 164)

Christian action thus conceived must extend beyond the boundaries of the Church. Instead of using revelation and tradition as starting points – as in the past – Christian reflection must begin with facts and questions derived from history and the world. As Gutiérrez notes, it is precisely this openness to the totality of human history that allows theology to fulfil its critical function vis-à-vis narrowly ecclesiastical praxis (Gutiérrez 1973: 12). Theology linked to praxis fulfils a prophetic function in so far as it interprets historical events in the light of God's purpose for humankind. The aim of such a theology is to make the Christian commitment clear and meaningful. Only in this fashion can the theologian engage in historical reality.

> He will be engaged where nations, social classes, people struggle to free themselves from domination and oppression by other nations, classes and people. In the last analysis, the true interpretation of the meaning revealed by theology is achieved only in historical praxis.
>
> (Ibid.: 13)

Liberation theologians insist that theology and action are inextricably linked. In the past many theologians believed that timeless truths could be applied to a finished universe. In contrast to this traditional view, both the world and human comprehension are viewed as incomplete; each requires refinement and development. Gutiérrez said that 'knowledge is not the conformity of the mind to the given, but an immersion in the process of transformation and construction of a new world' (in Brown 1978: 71). This process involves a constant interaction of practice and theory. For the Christian, praxis is a means by which the new world of the kingdom of God can be formed. It is transforming action in tension with theory. Praxis therefore grows out of and responds to historical circumstance. Further, it is subversive engagement: 'Since it is praxis commited to the poor and to the transformation of the world, undertaken from "the view below", we can describe it, in the precise technical meaning of the word, as subversive action' (ibid.: 72).

Thus theology is a critical reflection on historical activity. Unlike traditional theology, which was concerned with eternal realities, liberation theology is oriented to action. Truth is not defined *a priori*, independent of its historical verification; the theology of liberation insists on a historical basis. Faith can only be historically true when it becomes true, when it is effective in the liberation of humankind. In this way the truth dimension of faith is directly linked to its ethical and political dimension (Assmann 1975: 81).

Such a historically rooted view of theology has serious implications for understanding the meaning of Jesus' ministry. A theology of the cross must be stripped of alienating mystifications. Instead of seeing Jesus as the sacrificial offering and reconciler, the theology of liberation aims to give back to the man Jesus his full integrity as a human being and to give his death its real historical and political meaning. From this vantage point, liberationists argue, it is possible to unravel the true meaning behind the symbolism of the passion narrative (ibid.: 86).

THEOLOGY AND MARXISM

In rendering an account of historical reality, liberation theologians have appealed to the social sciences to provide a basis for their view of society. In the past Christians utilized various philosophical systems to elaborate their views of God and humanity; for this reason liberationists feel fully justified in appropriating certain features of Marxist thought. Marxism, they believe, is a valid instrument of social analysis. By using the Marxist framework, liberation theologians find themselves better able to understand the world.

The interpretive context reveals that society is in a state of conflict in which major forces are polarized, unable to work together: the oppressors and the oppressed. Those who are exploited are not in control of their destiny; they are economically, politically, and culturally dependent on others. Class struggle is thus a fact of life; to deny its reality is to side with the oppressors.

> When the Church rejects the class struggle, it is objectively operating as a part of the prevailing system. By denying the existence of social division, this system seeks to perpetuate this division on which are based the privileges of its beneficiaries.
>
> (Gutiérrez 1993: 275)

In such situations, one must inevitably take sides. Not to do so is in fact a decision to side with those in power; neutrality is impossible. In the past, Christians tended to interpret evil in individualistic terms. Liberation theologians, however, insist that a society must itself change if evil is to be eliminated. For this reason, social and political action are central to the Church's message. The Church cannot rest content with being a holy enclave in a corrupt society.

A Marxist perspective provides a basis for understanding the nature of class conflict. For liberation theologians the struggle against oppression is seen as necessary and critical. The outcome of this conflict is not a new oppression, but the removal of oppression and the elimination of evil. Míguez Bonino explains:

> Class struggle is not seen as a permanent fate of human existence and history but as an evil, triggered by the oppressive character of the present economic (social and political) system; an evil that we must try to overcome by the elimination of this system.
>
> (Míguez Bonino 1975: 107)

The quest for a more human understanding of work is linked to class struggle. According to Marxism, workers in capitalist society are estranged from their work; labour is simply a purchased commodity. The response of many

Christian liberation theologians is to protest against this dehumanized conception of human toil. What is needed instead is for labourers to realize themselves in their work. This can only be done, liberationists insist, by changing the structure of production, by replacing capitalism with socialism.

> Socialism, which is characterized by social appropriation of the means of production, paves the way for a new economy which makes possible autonomous development at a more accelerated pace and which overcomes the division of society into antagonistic classes. But socialism is not just a new economy. It should also generate new values which will pave the way for a society that evinces more fellowship and brotherhood. In this society the worker will shoulder his proper role with new dignity.
>
> (Eagleson 1975: 3)

Such a structure, liberationists believe, will provide a basis for recovering the real meaning of work and re-establish a proper relationship between labourers and the products they create.

According to some liberation theologians, such a transformation of society can only take place through violent revolution. The theory of revolution is based on an analysis of the structures of injustice and oppression. Inevitably those who possess wealth and power will resist change. 'So we are presented', Ellacuría writes, 'with the necessity of exerting force against the unjust will of those who hold power in the oppressive structural setup which crucifies the weak' (Ellacuría 1976: 209).

Violence is therefore legitimate if it is used to redeem the enslaved. In this context the struggle against violence should not be regarded as violence against humankind. Such an understanding is well illustrated in the life of Camilo Torres, the Colombian priest who died as a guerrilla fighter. He believed that taking part in the revolutionary struggle was a Christian and priestly act. Love could, he felt, only be sustained through revolution, and he therefore established a political faction. Eventually he joined the guerrillas and was killed in a military encounter.

Camilo Torres represents an extreme position within liberation theology; nevertheless, liberationists agree that social and political action is necessary in the face of exploitation, oppression, and injustice. In attempting to liberate humankind from servitude, liberation theologians have been guided by the vision of a utopian society. Their quest involves the creation of a new social consciousness and political structure. To accomplish this objective, faith and action must go hand in hand.

> Faith and political action will not enter into a correct and fruitful relationship except through the effort to create a new type of person in a different society ... Political liberation appears as a path toward the utopia of a freer, more human man, the protagonist of his own history.
>
> (Gutiérrez 1973: 236)

Such a conception of utopia proclaims that human unity is possible through the abolition of human exploitation. In the view of liberation theologians,

God calls us to the task of humanizing social and economic structures. Belief in God places humankind at the heart of the historical struggle for justice and freedom proclaimed by both the prophets of the Old Testament and Jesus in the Gospels.

The belief in a utopian vision of the future to be created through human action is far removed from traditional Christian eschatology. As we have seen, the hope of the kingdom has often worked against social and political activity; liberation theologians aim to change the world, and their writings are intended to galvanize others into action. In transforming Christian thought, these Christian writers look to their Jewish heritage for models of divine activity. In the Exodus narrative in particular they find the essential elements of a theology in which divine will and human response were bound together. Thus, as we saw, the Jewish Scriptures serve as the starting point for a theology of liberation in which

> God's action takes place in history and as history. It inextricably involves human action and, conversely, there is no human action reported outside the relation with God's purpose and world . . . Yahweh's sovereignty does not appear in history as an abstract act or an interpretation but as announcement and commandment, as an announcement which convokes, as promise and judgment demanding and inviting a response.
>
> (Míguez Bonino 1975: 134)

JUDAISM AND MORAL ACTION

Here then we can see the Jewish background to this emphasis on the significance of history in liberation theology, and it is instructive to examine the ways in which Judaism is, in terms of its tradition, particularly hospitable to praxis-centred faith. For Jews, as for Christian liberationists, history matters. The Jewish hope for the future lies in God's sovereign rule on earth. From ancient times the synagogue liturgy concluded with a prayer in which this hope was expressed:

> May we speedily behold the glory of Thy might,
> when Thou wilt remove the abominations from the earth,
> and the idols will be utterly cut off;
> when the world will be perfected under the kingdom of the Almighty,
> and all the children of flesh will call upon Thy name;
> when Thou wilt turn unto Thyself all the wicked of the earth.

This is the goal of the history of the world in which God's chosen people have a central role. In this context the people of Israel have a sense of a historical mission to be a light to the nations. Judaism did not separate religion from life; instead, Jews were called to action, to turn humankind away from violence, wickedness, and falsehood. It was not the hope of bliss in a future life but the establishment of the kingdom of justice and peace that was central to the Jewish faith. Moral praxis was at the heart of the religious tradition.

The people of Israel as a light to the nations reflected the moral nature of God; each Jew was to be like the creator, mirroring the divine qualities revealed to Moses: 'The Lord, the Lord, a God merciful and gracious, slow to anger, and abounding in steadfast love and faithfulness, keeping steadfast love for thousands, forgiving iniquity and transgression and sin' (Exod. 34:6–7).

Emphasis on the moral life was reflected in the prophetic condemnation of cultic practices that were not accompanied by ethical concern. The primacy of morality was also reflected in the prophetic warning that righteous action was the determining factor in the destiny of the Jewish nation. Moral transgressions referred to in such contexts concerned exploitation, oppression, and the perversion of justice. These sins had the potential to bring about the downfall of the nation. Similar emphases are to be found elsewhere in Scripture and throughout the tradition of rabbinic teaching from post-biblical times onwards. This shared vision can serve as a bridge between the Jewish and Christian traditions. Liberation theology's sharing of traditional Jewish ideals should make it possible for both faiths to work together for the first time in areas of social concern. Liberation theologians have paved the way for such a common endeavour by explaining how ethical values rooted in the Bible can be put into practice.

SOCIALISM

Liberation theologians have emphasized the importance of building a more socialist order. Recognizing the existence of class conflict, they advocate the abolition of its causes. In particular, they seek to restructure the socioeconomic foundations of society. What is needed, they believe, is a more egalitarian structure. According to the body of liberationist priests who gathered together in Santiago (Chile) in April 1972, unbridled capitalism is responsible for numerous ills (Eagleson 1975: 3): marginal living and alienation, excessive inequality between different social classes, the continuing and increasing frustration of people's expectations; the unjust exercise of repressive power by dominant parties and rulers; tensions resulting from the dependence of countries on other centres of economic power, growing imbalance and perversion of international trade; the flight of economic and human resources; the evasion of taxes by various countries; rising indebtedness; international monopolies and the imperialism of money (ibid.: 100).

To escape from these evils, liberation theologians contend that a major transformation must take place. The Christian must press for the adoption of socialist principles and policies. Such a programme would ideally result in a more equal distribution of goods and services. Facilities such as schools, hospitals, housing, subsidies for the ill and elderly, and employment opportunities would be available for all. By incorporating such values into the fabric of society, liberationists assert that it would no longer be possible for the few to maximize profit for themselves alone; instead the material benefits of labour would be spread throughout the community. Many Jews today would welcome such reforms.

THE POOR

At the heart of the desire to transform society is an identification with the poor. Liberation theologians stress that in the past Christians interpreted Jesus' words of blessing on the poor (Matt. 5:3; Luke 6:20) as meaning that one should accept poverty because injustice will be compensated for in the hereafter. Such an interpretation gives material poverty a positive value: it is understood as austerity and indifference to the things of this world. According to liberation theology this is a mistake. Poverty is not to be idealized; it must be seen for what it is – an evil to be abolished. Further, the existence of poverty is not an accident, but the result of greed.

> It is intolerable because it contradicts the very purpose of God's mighty act of deliverance – to rescue his people from the slavery of Egypt. It robs man of his humanity as a steward and transformer of the world and it therefore contradicts the mandate of creation . . . It breaks human solidarity and consequently it destroys friendship among men and with God.
>
> (Míguez Bonino 1975: 112)

For liberation theologians the starting point of theological reflection is the fact of the poor, not abstract metaphysical theories; the view 'from below' is essential. Liberation theology claims that God is to be found in the situation of the poor, just as in Scripture God is the saviour of the enslaved. What is required then is solidarity as a protest against poverty. Gutiérrez explains that solidarity is a 'way of identifying oneself with the interests of the oppressed classes and challenging the exploitation that victimized them' (Gutiérrez 1975: 14). Poverty is to be fought against and destroyed; God's salvation is achieved in the process of liberation. The problems and struggles of the poor are our own. The vocation of every person is to opt for human love and compassion. 'Solidarity with the poor implies a commitment to turn human love into a collective experience from which there is no turning back' (Cussianovich 1979: 139). As God's suffering servant through the ages, the Jewish people should find this message of solidarity with the poor of paramount significance, and the Hebrew Scriptures contain both legal provisions for the relief of the needy and the strictures of prophets against oppression by the wealthy.

THE THIRD WORLD

In pleading the case of the poor, liberation theologians – who are predominantly Latin American – have focused on the plight of the oppressed in the Third World. The underdevelopment of the poor countries, they point out, is the consequence of the development of other countries. 'The dynamics of the capitalist economy lead to the establishment of a center and a periphery, simultaneously generating progress and growing wealth for the few and social imbalances, political tensions, and poverty for the many' (Gutiérrez 1973: 84). The countries of Latin America were born into this context: they emerged, from the last century on, as dependent societies in consequence of economic exploitation. Such unequal structures dominate and determine the character of the particular cultures of these countries, and they necessitate a defence of the status quo. Even modernization and the introduction of a greater rationality into the economies of these societies are dictated by the vested interests of the dominant groups. Imperialism and colonization are thus hallmarks of the past and present economic climate. From a cultural point of view as well, the imbalance between 'developed' and 'underdeveloped' countries is acute – the underdeveloped areas are always far away from the cultural level of the industrialized centres.

The perception of the fact of this dependence and its consequences has made it possible to formulate a policy of reform. According to liberation theology, human freedom cannot be brought about by a developmentalist approach that maintains elitism. Instead, liberationists grapple with the existing relationship based on injustice in a global frame. By analysing the mechanisms that are being used to keep the poor of the world under domination, liberation theologians assert that authentic development can only take place if the domination of the great capitalistic countries is eliminated. A transformation is needed to radically change the conditions in which the poor live. In this process, human beings assume conscious responsibility for their own destiny. Gutiérrez explains:

> This understanding provides a dynamic context and broadens the horizons of the desired social changes. In this perspective the unfolding of all of man's dimensions is demanded – a man who makes himself throughout his life and throughout history. The gradual conquest of true freedom leads to the creation of a new man and a qualitatively different society.
>
> (Gutiérrez 1973: 36–7)

FIRST WORLD CONCERNS

Preoccupation with the Third World does not preclude concern for the oppressed in First World countries. Liberation theologians stress that grave inequalities between the rich and the poor also exist in the First World. Despite the higher general standard of living in these countries, many suffer substandard living conditions, poor health, concern about jobs, and constant worry about money.

> The epidemic rates of alcoholism and other forms of drug abuse, of rape, wife-beating, child abuse, and other forms of violence, of psychosomatic diseases like

certain kinds of ulcers and heart disease, suggest the depths of anguish and alienation which many experience in our society.

(Cormie 1981b: 29)

Liberation theology points out two segments in the labour market: primary sector jobs with high wages, good working conditions, employment stability and job security, and secondary sector jobs with low wages, poor working conditions, harsh and arbitrary discipline, and little opportunity for advancement (ibid.: 33). Consumerism is a dominant ideology that contributes to inequality. The most important questions deal with lowering taxes and getting the best prices for goods.

This attempt to focus our interests and life priorities on hairspray, cat food, and traveling to the Virgin Islands represents an assault on the One in whose image I am created. It is an assault on human dignity. Consumerism means that my eyes are offended, my ears are obstructed, and my hands are robbed of their creativity.

(Sölle 1981b: 9)

Exploitation in the First World is thus different from exploitation in Third World countries. Inhabitants of the First World nations have become enmeshed in a cultural system that frequently perceives value in quantitative economic terms; the emphasis is on having rather than being. Such hedonistic tendencies – generated by fiercely competitive economic interests – divide the affluent from the poor.

Nowhere is this more apparent than in the black community. In the United States, Cormie explains, slavery did not disappear with the disintegration of the plantation economy. After the Civil War most blacks were relegated to work as sharecroppers. Even after the expansion of northern industries, most blacks were channelled into the least desirable jobs and forced to live in dilapidated areas of the cities. Only a minority of blacks have gained access to the privileges and status promised by the American dream (Cormie 1981b: 33).

THE INNER CITY

In connection with First World poverty, liberation theology has focused on life in the inner city. Here the distinction between the powerful and the powerless is most clearly evident. In the cities – as opposed to the suburbs – are to be found the unemployed, families unable to cope, single parents, people with only part-time jobs, individuals on welfare, drop-outs, and recent immigrants. These are

the people in the area of your town you don't go to, the place you pass through to get to a city or suburb, the place you keep your children away from, the place you pray for, thanking God you do not belong there.

(Vincent 1982: 17)

In such areas inhabitants are divorced from the powerful forces that shape

1011

their lives: the inner city is the place of failure and hopelessness. The graphic social divide between the rich and the poor is an everyday reality for those who live in large metropolitan centres. All too often the poverty of the inner city is the converse side of middle-class suburban life. The situation of the poor is an integral part of the elaborate hierarchy of wealth and esteem. The existence of rich suburbs is linked to the existence of ghettos and marginal sectors.

A new consciousness is needed to remedy this situation, an awareness of the calamities of inner-city deprivation. First World theologians influenced by liberation theology contend that the proper Christian response is to engage in urban mission. By ministering to those at the bottom of society, Christians can affirm through their efforts that God is concerned with the plight of those facing adversity. Such activity constitutes an acted parable of the kingdom, bringing into focus the meaning of the Gospel. Such a parable declares that the Christian cause is served best not by those in places of power and influence but by those in situations of vulnerability and powerlessness. According to liberationists, Christ is incarnate in the inner city. In his own life he belonged to the lower end of the society of his day; in today's world he is also to be found among the lowly. Urban mission thus aims to discover Jesus' message in the economic and cultural impoverishment of city life; from this vantage point, the Christian can strive to ameliorate the conditions of the downtrodden. From the standpoint of its tradition, Judaism shares these aspirations.

THE UNEMPLOYED

As liberation theologians have noted, the unemployed are generally found in the destitute parts of the inner city. Unemployment is a growing problem. Liberationists have therefore directed attention to this deprived group. Gutiérrez, for example, stresses that the Church has an obligation to those who are without work: they should be a focus of pastoral and theological activity. Christians must labour on behalf of the 'underemployed and unemployed, who are dismissed because of the harsh exigencies of economic crises, and often because of development-models that subject workers and their families to cold economic calculations' (Gutiérrez 1983: 134). Such individuals face particular difficulties in coping with their misfortunes. The unemployed do not know what to do with their time, and as a consequence, they are unfulfilled in essential areas: in the basic human needs – for human relationships, for financial income, for social status and identity, and for satisfaction and fulfilment.

Recently Christian writers have made a number of suggestions about the kinds of activities that could be undertaken: ways must be sought for creating new work opportunities; labour not traditionally regarded as paid work (such as housework) must be accepted as valid and necessary; new manufacturing enterprises that stimulate the job market should be encouraged; apprentice-ships for the young should be reintroduced; jobs need to be spread out through job sharing and part-time work; education must be seen as a preparation for life; voluntary activity should be stimulated and seen as a legitimate means of helping those in need (Handy 1983: 24–5).

FEMINISM

Liberation theology has also been concerned about the plight of women. Feminist theologians have attempted to delineate the biblical traditions encap-sulating the liberating experiences and visions of the people of Israel so as to help free women from oppressive sexist structures, institutions, and internal-ized values. In the view of these writers, women have been and continue to be socialized into subservient roles: either they are forced into domestic labour or they hold low-paying jobs. Only a few women manage to occupy jobs in traditionally male professions.

> Work segregation is still the fundamental pattern of society. Women's work uni-versally is regarded as of low status and prestige, poorly paid, with little security, generally of a rote and menial character. The sexist structuring of society means the elimination of women from those activities that allow for and express enhance-ment and development of the self, its artistic, intellectual and leadership capacities.
> (Ruether 1983: 178)

Throughout society, these theologians maintain, the full humanity of women is distorted, diminished, and denied.

To encourage the restoration of women's self-respect, liberationists focus on a number of biblical themes: God's defence and vindication of the oppressed; the criticism of the dominant systems of power; the vision of a new age in which iniquity will be overcome; God's intended reign of peace. Feminist theology applies the message of the prophets to the situation of women; the critique of hierarchy thus becomes a critique of patriarchy. For these writers, images of God must include feminine roles and experiences, and language about God must be transformed. For Christians, they believe, it is necessary to move beyond a typology of Christ and the Church that represents the dominant male and submissive female role. In church structures women must be given full opportunities to participate at every level, including the ministry. In the civil sphere women must be granted full equality before the law – a stance that calls for the repeal of all discriminatory legislation. There must be equal pay for equal work and full access to all professions. Many liberationists also insist on women's right to reproduction, self-defence, sex education, birth control, and abortion as well as protection against sexual harassment, wife-beating, rape, and pornography.

Similarly, in the Jewish community awareness of discrimination against women has been growing. Over the last two decades a significant number of Jewish feminists have attempted to restructure the position of women in traditional Judaism. In the past, Jewish women were not directly involved with most Jewish religious activity. Today, however, Jewish women are trying to find ways to participate fully in their faith. In their attempt to reconcile Judaism and feminism these women are rediscovering various aspects of Jewish life: some study the place of women in Jewish history; others examine religious texts for clues to women's influence on Jewish life; still others redefine and feminize certain features of the Jewish tradition.

THE ENVIRONMENT

Not only do liberation theologians advocate a programme of liberation for all humankind, they also draw attention to human responsibility for the environment: ecological liberation is an important element in their policy of emancipation. Since the scientific revolution, nature has been gradually secularized; no corner of the natural world has been untouched by human domination. Yet in this expansion of material productivity, the earth has been exploited to such a degree that pollution, famine, and poverty threaten humanity's very existence. Liberationists assert that human beings must accept responsibility for the environment.

> The privilege of intelligence ... is not a privilege to alienate and dominate the world without concern for the welfare of all other forms of life. On the contrary, it is the responsibility to become the caretaker and cultivator of the welfare of the whole ecological community upon which our existence depends ... Although we need to remake the earth in a way that converts our minds to nature's logic of ecological harmony, this will necessarily be a new synthesis, a new creation in which human nature and nonhuman nature become friends in the creating of a livable and sustainable cosmos.
>
> (Ruether 1983: 87–8, 91–2)

Reform in this area calls for a different attitude towards the natural world; human beings must accept balance in nature as an essential characteristic of the earth's ecosystem. Human intervention inevitably upsets the natural balance; thus steps must continually be taken to restore equilibrium to the earth. In particular, environmentalists point out that care must be taken about the use of pesticides. Habitats previously available to many living creatures have been destroyed; for agricultural purposes, we should attempt to maintain diversity within nature and this requires a careful monitoring of the use of chemical substances.

CONCLUSION

The aim of this chapter has been to reveal the nature of the challenge liberation theology presents to traditional theology. This challenge can be seen at two levels. First, liberationist thought seeks to reverse the social and ethical conservatism of much past Christian teaching. It does so through its identification with what it sees as the voice of the poor and the oppressed and through using socialist, Marxist analyses of the circumstances that constitute and lead to injustice in the world. These analyses are not self-evidently true. The last decades of this century have seen both the revival of classical, liberal economic and political thought and the collapse of socialist economic and political systems in so many parts of the world. Here, then, liberation theology promises to be the occasion and focus of deep debate within moral and social theology. Many of the issues relevant to this debate can be seen in the chapters on the State and on wealth in Part 5 of this *Encyclopedia*.

At a second and more fundamental level, liberation thought challenges the separation between dogmatics on the one hand, and ethical–political thought, on the other, customary in previous Christian thinking, as it challenges the philosophical foundations traditionally seen as underlying the structure of doctrine. As shown above, the identification of orthodoxy with orthopraxis involves liberation theology in a prior borrowing from Marxism. The gauntlet thrown down to traditional dogmatics consists in the demand that it give some account of the nature of truth and reference in theology which will enable these to transcend in a new and practical way the relativities of changing human social circumstances and the practical imperatives that arise out of them. Debate on these matters of high theory has already been joined and promises to lead to re-examination of the very fundamentals of theology. Moreover they show discussion of the methods and aims of theology to be linked to the most basic questions about the nature and function of the human intellect (see Meynell 1981: 67–8).

REFERENCES

Assmann, H. (1975) *Practical Theology of Liberation*, Tunbridge Wells: Search Press.

Bowker, J. (1973) *Jesus and the Pharisees*, Cambridge: Cambridge University Press.

Brown, R. M. (1978) *Theology in a New Key: Responding to Liberation Themes*, Philadelphia: Westminster Press.

Cormie, L. (1981a) 'The Challenge of Liberation Theology', in D. L. Richesin and B. Mahan (eds) *The Challenge of Liberation Theology*, New York: Orbis Books.

—— (1981b) 'Liberation and Salvation', in D. L. Richesin and B. Mahan (eds) *The Challenge of Liberation Theology*, New York: Orbis Books.

Cussianovich, A. (1979) *Religious Life and the Poor: Liberation Theology Perspectives*, trans. J. Drury, Dublin: Gill and Macmillan.

Davis, C. (1980) *Theology and Political Society*, Cambridge: Cambridge University Press.

Eagleson, J. (ed.) (1975) *Christians and Socialism*, New York: Orbis Books.

Ellacuría, I. (1976) *Freedom Made Flesh*, trans. J. Drury, New York: Orbis Books.

Ellis, M. (1987) *Toward a Jewish Theology of Liberation*, New York: Orbis Books.

Gutiérrez, G. (1973) *A Theology of Liberation*, trans. C. Inda and J. Eagleson, New York: Orbis Books.

—— (1975) 'Liberation Praxis and Christian Faith', in R. Gibellini (ed.) (1980) *Frontiers of Theology in Latin America*, London: SCM Press.

—— (1983) *The Power of the Poor in History*, trans. R. Barr, London: SCM Press.

Handy, C. (1983) 'The Future of Work', *Christian* 8: 24–5.

Marx, K. (1977) *Selected Writings*, ed. D. McLellan, Oxford: Oxford University Press.

Meynell, H. (1981) *Frend, Marx and Morals*, London: Macmillan.

Míguez Bonino, J. (1975) *Doing Theology in a Revolutionary Situation*, Philadelphia: Fortress Press.

Pérez-Esclarín, A. (1978) *Atheism and Liberation*, trans. J. Drury, New York: Orbis Books.

Ruether, R. R. (1983) *Sexism and God-Talk*, Boston: Beacon Press.

Sölle, D. (1981a) *Choosing Life*, London: SCM Press.

—— (1981b) 'Liberation in a Consumerist Society', in D. L. Richesin and B. Mahan (eds) *The Challenge of Liberation Theology*, New York: Orbis Books.

—— (1981c) 'Thou Shalt Have No Jeans Before Me', in D. L. Richesin and B. Mahan (eds) *The Challenge of Liberation Theology*, New York: Orbis Books.

Vincent, J. J. (1982) *Into the City*, London: Epworth Press.

FURTHER READING

Boff, L. (1975) *Jesus Christ Liberator*, New York: Orbis Books.

Cohn-Sherbok, D. (1992) *Exodus: An Agenda for Jewish Christian Dialogue*, London: Bellew.

Dussel, E. (1976) *History and the Theology of Liberation*, New York: Orbis Books.

Ferm, D. W. (1986) *Third World Liberation Theologies: A Reader*, New York: Orbis Books.

Miranda, J. (1974) *Marx and the Bible*, New York: Orbis Books.

See also chapters 34, 36, 37, 38, 39, 40, 41, 48.

48

THEOLOGY AND THE FUTURE OF THE CHURCH

Walter Hollenweger

THEOLOGY IN TODAY'S CHURCH

We theologians, who write books like this one, often learn Greek, Latin and Hebrew. We are drilled in all the methods of critical exegesis and critical thinking. In form-criticism we learn to distinguish between myth and history, between parable and allegory, between the literary structure of the Gospels and a biography of Jesus. We learn in redaction-criticism that biblical texts are the theological product of authors who are responsible to and sometimes in conflict with a narrative community. Yet in our churches almost nothing of this is made fruitful for the people of God. Whilst we are trained in the details of critical theology, our church members still discuss whether or not Adam and Eve, Noah and Methuselah, were historical persons. They still discuss whether or not God could have created the universe in seven days. They still read the Gospels as straightforward biographies and are strengthened in this by our confessions of faith, our liturgies and hymns. And, worst of all, this is considered to be Christian faith. That is why non-believers think that to be a Christian means to give up one's critical faculties.

The reader who considers the above to be an over-statement may remember the storm which the statements of David Jenkins as Bishop of Durham created some years ago. Yet what he said was nothing but what an educated theologian would be expected to know. He or she would fail the examinations if not conversant with this type of argument. That his statements created such an upheaval – in non-Christian circles and amongst the clergy, not to speak of ordinary Christians – proves just how little of our scholarship has been conveyed to our churches or the general public. We have not learned to communicate important and indispensible insights in such a way that they become edifying and devotional, a life-sustaining and critical tool, in the best sense of the word. These insights may appear here and there in sermons or in religious television programmes and thus produce irritation, but critical theology seems irrelevant to the Church of our time. This can be seen by the fact that it almost never appears in our prayers, in our liturgies, in our hymns or in our confessions of faith.

This situation is made more difficult by the rise of house-groups (Thurman 1982; Walker 1989), the charismatic movement (McDonnell 1980; Burgess *et al.* 1988), and other religious revivals in the Church. Since most Christians ask the question: 'What does the biblical text say to me today?', the fundamental questions of theological research are overlooked. These are: 'What did the biblical authors, Church fathers and reformers mean?' or perhaps more precisely: 'What did the narrative community in which the texts emerged mean?' This is followed by the second question: 'What is their significance for us, for the ecumenical community of the Church?' In order to answer these questions some basic knowledge of the social, cultural and religious context of these texts is necessary, not to speak of competence in biblical languages and, in the case of the sixteenth-century reformers, Latin, German and French. But these insights are considered an unnecessary luxury even by priests, and sometimes also as dangerous by the majority of the people of God. It is a false understanding of the Reformation to think that everybody can understand and interpret biblical and other ecclesiastical traditions without the slightest knowledge of their cultural and historical setting.

The reason for this is that academic theology has not been successful in making its insights available to the ordinary Christian and in many cases not even to the average parish priest. 'The theologians may do their research in their ivory towers,' it is said, 'we rely on practical religious experience.' But this 'practical approach' is very unpractical. When one is faced with questions of war and peace, Aids and homosexuality, the ministry of women in the Church, the consequences of Christian discipleship for trade and commerce, the dialogical relationship to non-Christian religions (and these involve important value judgements for the Christian), there is no yardstick, no hermeneutical tool available to deal with these questions. Instead of a solid debate we are faced with a heap of prejudices. 'For all its homage to the authority of Scripture, conservative Christianity continues to mix and confuse the regional, parochial interests of the American middle class with the promises, claims, and demands of Christian faith' (Stroup 1981: 23). The Church has lost its anchor in the Bible. 'Very little that the pastor learned about how to read and interpret Scripture is passed on to the laity' (ibid.: 28). Even more, when certain religious experiences like healing (Hollenweger 1989a) or Spirit baptism (Lederle 1988), like confirmation or re-baptism, occur in part of the Christian community, there are no criteria for dealing with this bewildering religious and ethical pluralism. So uniformity is either enforced through the power structures of the Church hierarchy, through certain specially gifted charismatic leaders, or else each has his or her own theology and morality. Thus the Church is fragmented into bits and pieces, each part (and sometimes each person) putting forward its favourite interpretation and backing it up with the authority of its own experiences and with some quotations from the tradition of the Church. As far as I can see, there is hardly any link between Christian religion as it is lived, both in traditional churches and in more radical revival movements, and theological research (for an exception see Hollenweger 1992).

To take the latter first, of what use is a stated doctrine of inspiration of Scripture in the conservative camp if this inspiration only applies to the original autographs?

> Since no autograph is known to have survived, it would appear that the conservatives have not only an impregnable position – one cannot prove an error in something one does not possess – but also a highly dubious one. Of what use is an inerrant Scripture which is unavailable?

Thus writes Paul J. Achtemeier (1980: 52), himself certainly not a liberal theologian.

But the critical, more liberal camp is also in trouble. That is why Walter Wink declared historical–critical exegesis to be bankrupt. 'If anonymous scribes, not Moses, wrote the Pentateuch, and Jesus never spoke the Sermon on the Mount as we have it, who is to be believed? – the scholars, of course!' (Wink 1973: 35), and that even if they disagree on important points. Augstein, the polemical editor of the widely read German magazine *Der Spiegel*, put this more bluntly:

> What right has a Christian church to base her teachings on a Jesus who never lived, on doctrines which he never taught, on an authority which he never transmitted, and on a claim of him being the son of God which he never made and which he would have regarded as impossible?
>
> (Augstein 1972: 7)

Even if some of these statements are discounted as journalistic exaggerations, one must agree with Walter Wink when he writes that our way of reading the Bible and using biblical and ecclesiastical precedent must 'be examined for its implicit theological bias and blindness' (Wink 1973: 45). But because we discard this, our historical–critical exegesis is bankrupt. Wink uses 'bankrupt' in the exact sense of the term. 'A business which goes bankrupt is not valueless, nor incapable of producing useful products . . . The one thing wrong – and the only thing – is that it is no longer able to accomplish its avowed purpose for existence: to make money' (ibid.: 45). The reason for this is that methods and goals (e.g. 'objectivity') as practised in our theological departments are incommensurate with the intention of the texts. ' "Objective neutrality" thus requires a sacrifice of the very questions the Bible seeks to answer . . . Objectivism is not simply in error, however. It is a false consciousness' (ibid.: 3, 6).

> It pretends detachment when in fact the scholar is attached to an institution with a high stake in the socialization of students and in the preservation of society and when he himself has a high stake in the advancement in that institution by publication of his researches. It pretends to be unbiased when in fact the methodology

carries with it a heavy rationalistic weight which by inner necessity tends toward the reduction of irrational, subjective or emotional data to insignificance or invisibility. It pretends to search for 'assured results', 'objective knowledge', when in fact the method presumes radical epistemological doubt, which by definition devours each new spawn of 'assured results' as a guppy swallows her children. It pretends to suspend evaluations, which is simply impossible, since research proceeds on the basis of questions asked and a ranked priority in their asking. But such judgements presuppose a system of values and an ontology of meanings which not only give weight to the questions but make it possible to ask them at all. Even the choice of syntax and vocabulary is a political act that defines and circumscribes the way 'facts' are to be experienced – indeed, in a sense even creates the facts that can be studied.

The political, theological and cultural bias of language has already been revealed by the editor of the *Theological Dictionary of the New Testament* (Friedrich 1976: in particular, 650ff.). Emil Brunner (1943) has also unsuccessfully pointed to the weakness of 'objective knowledge'. What is, is unknown to us. We only know what reacts with us or with our instruments of observation. If that is true in physics, how much more in theology and biblical studies? Therefore a true scholar will not pretend to be 'neutral'. On the contrary, he or she will declare his or her interests in the subject so as to give the reader or listener the opportunity to understand from which point of view he or she argues. This applies also to this chapter. My interest is a theology which fulfils its function in the body of Christ, a theology which emerges together with the people of God and in which theologians have a clear-cut function but not the last word.

But nowadays theology has 'become cut off from the community for whose life its results might be significant' (Wink 1973: 10). This division of labour (here the producers of theology, the theologians, there the consumers of theology, the lay people) has produced a 'series of grave mistakes' (*Fehlleistungen*) in biblical research, about which Stuhlmacher complains (Stuhlmacher 1979: 28). The scholarly theologian cannot do theology without being in dialogue with the church community for whom he does his research. This separation is responsible for the exclusion from academic research of certain questions because they are not answerable with our methods (as we shall see later). Another approach would be to change the methods and the questions. Once upon a time biblical criticism and critical theology were revolutionary. But 'here, as in other revolutions, those who were fit to overthrow were not fit to govern' (Wink 1973: 12).

PROPOSALS TO SOLVE THE PROBLEM

So, what is on offer to resolve this dilemma? A number or more or less viable proposals have been made as follows:

1 Teaching the lay people.
2 Escape into personal experience.

3 The psychological approach.
4 The structuralist approach.
5 Ecumenical theology.

1 Teaching the lay people

The first and most common proposal is to teach the lay people and to introduce further education for the clergy. That is a laudable aspiration but so far it has been ineffective.

2 Escape into personal experience

The easiest way out, which is in fact an escape, is to make an advantage of a disadvantage and to make one's own understanding or misunderstanding the touchstone for testing the Church. This is a very common approach amongst theologians and lay people. It is said: 'That's what I experienced. Full stop.'

3 The psychological approach

However, there are more sophisticated ways of justifying one's own theology, e.g. in the several psychological approaches to the Bible. Here the texts are no longer simply 'there', over against one, but a tool to understand the archetypes in one's own life. The best-known author on this is the Catholic Drewermann. Less controversial are the French psychoanalyst Françoise Dolto and the German theologian Yorick Spiegel, plus a host of self-styled bibliodramatical and psychodramatical experts who sell their skills for hard cash. All of them have of course a limited value because they help people in their self-understanding but not in the understanding of the tradition of the Church.

4 The structuralist approach

The most sophisticated experts in this vein are the structuralists. They start with linguistic observations in non-theological disciplines. 'Descartes, who wanted to found a theory of physics, separated man from society. Sartre, who wanted to found an anthropology, separated his society from other societies' (Lévi-Strauss (1962), quoted by Schiwy 1969: 14). We could continue by saying: XY, who wanted to write a critical theology, separated his interpretation from the grassroots of and, in fact, the majority of the people of God. Gerhard Ebeling puts this more politely:

> The danger of a highly developed but sterile academic technique cannot be underestimated in particular in New Testament studies. This corresponds to the danger of resignation in so far as one no longer expects anything either from the New Testament or from its scholarly interpretation.
>
> (Ebeling 1975: 23)

1021

Indeed a sorry state after a couple of centuries of critical New Testament studies.

The scholarly interpretation of the Bible is inaccessible in its present form. As 'language is itself a model of the world' (Schiwy 1969: 27), this means that the groups who speak different and not mutually understandable languages, live in different worlds, often without knowing it. They talk to each other, but their language dominates the talk so far that the language forgets to serve its purpose; this language ceases to be a living language (ibid.: 43). One could not describe better the lack of communication between the different churches, between lay Christians and theological scholars, and between Christians and non-Christians.

Schiwy calls this an 'ideological determinism'. Man does not speak. He is spoken. He does not think. He is thought (ibid.: 51). 'Ça parle ... Ce n'est pas seulement l'homme qui parle mais ... dans l'homme et par l'homme ça parle' (Lacan 1966: 688). Claude Lévi-Strauss, Jacques Lacan, Michel Foucault and others propagate a modern kind of nominalism. The 'I' is destroyed (think only of modern literature), now that we discover the 'there is'. There is a 'one'. In a certain sense we return to the standpoint of the seventeenth century, but with the following difference: man is not replacing God, but man is replaced by an anonymous thinking, a knowing without a subject, a theorizing without an identity. Humanism pretends to solve questions for which it is not competent, e.g. the relationship of man to the world, the problem of reality, of happiness – all these obsessions in no way deserve to become theoretical problems. We face the end of all these verbose attempts which, for example, try to reconcile Marx with Teilhard de Chardin. Humanism has condemned intellectual work to sterility. Therefore our task is to liberate ourselves from humanism. In this sense, according to Foucault, our work is political, in so far as it declares the end of all this trafficking under the banner of humanism, in East and West (Schiwy 1969: 17).

The 'there is', 'the one', is in language. This 'positivism not of the facts but of the signs' of course contradicts not only humanism but also all brands of Marxism and Christian theology. The structuralist can integrate all these thought-systems into his system and by seeing in them a language of the 'there is' he devalues them. He does not ask: What was the meaning of Hegel, Wesley, Paul or Jesus? He asks rather: What is the 'there is' which appears here?

Applied to theology that means the parables of Jesus should not be interpreted in the situation in which Jesus spoke them, nor in the situation in which they have been handed down and re-interpreted by the early Church. The theological symbols should not be interpreted against their cultural and religious background. They are in themselves a statement. This then is the exact opposite of historical–critical exegesis. This method is important for the structuralist because, in his opinion, language transcends the power of the thought and the interpretation of the author. It does not really matter whether or not Paul, or Jesus, Cranmer or Luther has seen the full implications of his words. Language makes it possible for an author 'to say more than he knows'. No doubt this last statement is true, but is it permissible to dispense with all attempts at finding out what our 'fore-thinkers' really meant?

Claude Lévi-Strauss describes the same situation much more pessimistically.

> All models of a world-view, from the old myth to the modern 'myths' of science [and of economics, see Collier 1990] have led man astray, in so far as man has not come to the insight that there is no objective truth for man other than that of absolute meaninglessness. The 'relative truth' then of all human world-views consists in that they are all more or less successful attempts to veil the horror of meaningless existence.
>
> ('Tropiques tristes' in Schiwy 1969: 25)

The result of this combination of acumen and precise observation of language and cultures in all continents is simply this – 'There is' no meaning in this world, only attempts at camouflaging this meaninglessness. The instruments for this camouflaging are not only religion, Christian and others, but also – and this is new – the myths of science.

In the end 'there is no route to conscience (passage à la conscience) but only an emergence of the word (passage à la parole)' (Lacan 1956: 206). In more popular forms this produces all kinds of psychological and bibliodramatic interpretations of biblical texts and religious symbols. The symbol cannot defend itself against this imperialism. The only criterion is whether or not it makes me vibrate. Neither the authority of the Church, nor the statements of theologians, nor what others say, is of any relevance. What I experience, what I find in the word, in the symbol, determines its meaning for me. Transcendence becomes simply a 'trip into transcendence'. God is a symbol for something like integration and religion makes me feel better. On an institutional level the question of truth is replaced by the question of success, as the electronic church shows in a most revealing way (on this see *Pneuma* 13/1, 1991, and Hollenweger 1993).

This development contradicts the prophets of secularism. We are now not facing an age of secularism but a bewildering pluralism of religious experiences and ideas. To hold on to a true atheism, man would have to have a very deep and committed faith in atheism. This obviously is not the case. Therefore religion has become the business of our time. The more expensive, the more exotic, the better. The very people who couldn't care less about their parish around the corner will travel to a Philippino ghost-healer, to an Indian guru, to a self-styled shaman, to an expensive psychodramatic or spiritualist conference anywhere in the world. After owning clothes and food in abundance, the Western man and woman is looking for new tastes, new sounds and, above all, new feelings. The one who can offer new feelings, new self-awareness experiences, does the business. Religion has become a consumer good like anything else. The only criterion for the customers is whether they think it works. After the commercialization of sex, we now experience a commercialization of religion. A number of pentecostal theologians have discovered the dangers in this kind of religious salesmanship, in this theology of success (*Pneuma* 1991), but too many of their colleagues, some with a decent academic education, on the impulse of charismatic renewal still ride on this wave (Hollenweger 1993).

The Church tries very hard to argue against this trivialization and commercialization of religion but without success. The appeal to Church authorities, to theology, even to common sense and decency has no currency any more. Having been told for centuries that the only thing that ultimately matters is individual religious experience, people will no longer accept guidance from external authorities. Their only teacher is their heart.

5 Ecumenical theology

In spite of brave attempts, ecumenical theology is in a similar crisis. Why should somebody who has thrown off the tutelage of the Roman Catholic Church, of his or her parish priest, or of so-called biblical theology, now accept the authority of the World Council of Churches and its statements? Certainly not if they conflict with his or her economic and personal interests. So, what is the way ahead?

THE WAY AHEAD

How do we produce a body-of-Christ-theology, a theology which is not only understood by the people but a theology in whose production the people of God participate and which they can recognize as their own? The people of God are not just consumers of theology, they are also – in a different way from academic theologians – producers of theology. Theology cannot just declare the principle of dialogue to be fundamental, it must also produce a method by which the production of theology is experienced in a dialogical process. Theology cannot just declare theology 'to be a function of the church', as Karl Barth maintained; it must show how the Church participates in the production of theology. A number of observations may be helpful for this purpose.

The pluriform biblical texts

The biblical texts show us a most helpful and creative pluralistic approach to religion and ethics without giving up the decisiveness of God's revelation in the man Jesus of Nazareth. This position has come to be recognized by many, including evangelical theologians (e.g. Dunn 1977). The central argumentation for this approach is clear, but how far inculturation into different cultures and situations can go, is controversial: the differences, e.g. between Johannine christology and the christology of the various other Gospels, between the eschatology of Revelation and the eschatology of the Gospel of John, are quite substantial. If historical–critical exegesis has shown us one thing, then it is this wide diversity. If the New Testament presents us with a number of christologies, liturgies, theologies, ethics, how much more do we have to say farewell nowadays to a streamlined universal theology, when Christianity has taken root in many more cultures and languages. A universal theology, seen as a set of sentences to be believed, is a fiction, *de facto* even in the Roman Catholic Church. Since theology always expresses itself in language and since languages belong to different world-views and ontologies, theology is culturally defined. More than ever we need an intercultural theology, that is, a theology which is aware of its cultural conditions and seeks bridges between these different cultures (Hollenweger 1979, 1982). Even evangelicals, despite conservatist inclinations, may admit this very clearly (Kraft 1979). This is all the more important at a time when the centre of gravity of the Christian Church is moving away from the West to the South, as is demonstrated in David Barrett's *World Christian Encyclopedia* (1972). Black theology (Gerloff 1992) and Third World theology (Hollenweger 1987a) are emerging. Taking them seriously could open up new avenues to those sections of our populations which do not communicate through definitions but through descriptions, not in concepts but in banquets, not in theses but in dances, not in systems but in symbols. That a critical theology in these categories is possible is evidenced already in Christian origins by Jesus and the apostles, and in a minor way also by the Centre for Black and White Christian Partnership in Birmingham (Mazibuko 1987; Gerloff 1992). Jesus and the apostles belonged to a narrative community of the Middle East and not to a European scholarly community. This did not hinder them from producing highly critical theological texts and impulses. On what grounds do we dismiss their theological methodology? The only reason I can think of is that we are not experts in oral and narrative theology. But another consequence of the ministry of Jesus and his apostles could also be that we train ourselves to become bilingual, i.e. conceptual and narrative. That narrative oral theology is not scholarly is a belief for which there is no evidence. In both forms, narrative and conceptual, there are competent and incompetent scholars.

Grassroots

Kurt Marti, a Swiss poet and theologian, complains that

> nowadays theology does not any longer emerge from the grassroots. It is unrelated to the processes of thinking and living of the ordinary Christians. Here too we have a division of labour, separation of experts and lay people, of producers and consumers, of theory and praxis, of theology and experience.
>
> (Marti 1976: 95–6)

What is the alternative? How can 'a word emerge' not only in the 'there is' of the structuralists or in Lacan's psychoanalytical sessions (see above p.1022) but also in the ordinary people of the Church of Jesus Christ? How can they together with the specialists and experts find a language, a word, which does not veil the horror of meaningless existence but becomes a vehicle by which they remind each other in the contexts of this world of the Good News, of the death-overcoming life of Jesus for this world? This grassroots theology is emerging not at the universities but in bible studies around the world (Weber 1981). There is nothing more important than this theological task. Neither Hans-Ruedi Weber from the World Council of Churches, nor his colleagues and friends who use similar methods, nor myself after twenty years of bible studies in small circles and in big meetings at the German Kirchentag (up to 10,000 participants in one Bible study session), want a return to a naive study of the Bible. What is called for is a Bible study which does not gloss over the ethical, theological and liturgical differences in the Bible and thus encourages participants to become self-reliant, to think for themselves and not to be afraid of differing from the others, but – and this we still have to learn – not to take theological conformity as the basis of the unity of the Church.

> It encourages participants to endure patiently but attentively the differences between the participants and between participants and text. It encourages them even to endure conflict and if necessary to become intolerant over against those who do not want to or are not able to exercise tolerance.
>
> (Stollberg 1978: 225)

Some may call this simply bourgeois liberalism. It may, however, be the case that bourgeois liberalism is not only part of God's fallen but also of God's good creation.

One of the methods for such Bible studies is what may be called narrative exegesis. This is to be distinguished from what is described as bibliodrama: in bibliodrama, the question is: What does the text say to me? What do I feel? etc. This is a legitimate way of dealing with the Bible but it is unusable for theological debate, because it interprets the reader and not the text. Narrative exegesis asks the question: What did the author want to say? It introduces people into the critical dimension of biblical texts. (As an example take Hollenweger 1989b.)

Taking another approach, this has also been demonstrated by Juan Luis Segundo and other Third World theologians. The title of Segundo's five-volume dogmatics, *A Theology for Artisans of a New Humanity* (1974), already shows his intention. Segundo worked out his theology with a group of people involved in the struggles in Montevideo. It is a theology that has been written together with groups of people at the grassroots of society in the turbulence of a Latin American city. This theology was perceived as revolutionary by the authorities. Whenever people begin to think – be it 'only' on a critical interpretation of their religious sources – the powers that be realize the revolutionary potential, which is why Segundo has been harassed several times.

Those, however, who expect a handbook on revolution in Segundo's books will be disappointed. He is of the opinion that solid theological thinking with and at the grassroots is more revolutionary than 'action' and fiery, but vague, convictions. This was also Karl Barth's opinion during the German Church struggle in the period of Hitler's Reich. Segundo wants to be a biblical theologian, and his liberation of theology does not mean the liberation of theology from its biblical roots but much more a liberation of the biblical message from the interpretation of a mono-cultural imperialism, such as is prevalent in our universities under the disguise of 'scholarship'.

Similar topics are treated in other Third World theological approaches, e.g. in the work of Frank Chikane, a South African pentecostal pastor and general secretary of the South African Council of Churches, or in James H. Cone's works, in this case with the poetry and the wit of a black author. 'After Mannheim, Stark and Berger, whatever may be their differences among themselves or our differences with them, the assumption that theological thinking is objective or universal is ridiculous' (Cone 1975: 45). The interesting thing in Cone's approach is that this statement is verified in exact and yet humorous analyses of European theologies. He does not pretend that black theology is universal. Black theology, just as any other theology, is co-determined by the interests of its authors (that is why the title of one of his works is *God of the Oppressed*). This is inevitable. All theology is culturally, economically, socially and biographically pre-determined. To deny this would be to deny the incarnation! Therefore one expects a scholarly theologian, in so far as he is a scholar, first to try to discover his own interests and not to deny them, and to take cognizance of those theological reflections which reflect cultural media other than his own, in particular the majority cultures of the Christian Church world-wide which is miles apart from the theologian's university culture. A selective concentration on our own university culture is an example of what some call 'sectarian theology', and for Cone it is the essence of racism. Cone has set a good example by taking cognizance of 'stories', of 'theologies and exegetical approaches' other than his own. For him that means studying white American and European theologies. Is it too much to ask from us that we too take a step in the direction of theologies from other cultures, i.e. from the oral majority cultures in our own countries and world-wide?

Syncretism and oral theology

However, if theology is articulated in culturally conditioned forms and if cultural conditioning is recognized, then the central question can no longer be avoided – how do we express the catholicity of the Church? One thing is sure, the present ecumenical and catholic documents do not express the catholicity of the Church. At best they express the catholicity of those experts who have learned to express themselves in Western conceptual categories. Although the World Council of Churches is the major ecumenical fellowship of Protestant, Eastern Orthodox and Anglican Churches, it recognizes that at least half of all non-Orthodox and non-Roman Catholic Churches in the Third World do not belong to this formal ecumenical community (Vanelderen 1991) and that percentage is growing continuously. What does that mean for an organization which considers itself to be the spokesperson for the Third World? How can it speak for the Third World if that Third World does not recognize itself in the WCC's language? It seems as if whoever wants to be heard on the international platform has to use the language of the English parliamentary system which the WCC has inherited because of the dominant role of the British churches during its years of formation. Globally speaking, it is a small minority language!

What is the alternative? A way forward was shown by important worship events during the Full Assemblies of all the member churches of the WCC (with many Catholic, Evangelical and Pentecostal observers) in Vancouver (1983) and Canberra (1991) (van der Bent 1991). The statement by the Korean theologian Chung Hyun Kyung on the Korean pre-Christian culture's significance for Christian theology have been understood (and partly rejected) because they were presented in an oral and visual way (Abraham 1991; King 1991). I am astonished that Western Churches, which are knee-deep in syncretism (in Leonardo Boff's words, 'The Christian church is a syncretism par excellence'), and which probably owe more to their Celtic and Germanic ancestors and to Greek and Roman culture than to the Bible (think of our burial rites, some of our buildings, our liturgies, our liturgical vestments, our church music), could be shocked by a Korean woman who tries to take her own pre-Christian heritage as seriously as we take our pre-Christian tradition.

Not only must the Church be syncretistic, it must produce different syncretisms in different cultures. The touchstones for a theologically responsible syncretism – over against a theologically irresponsible syncretism – are first, the willingness to learn from the biblical authors the methodology of such a theologically responsible syncretism. When Paul, for example in 1 Corinthians 13, composes a collage of contemporary popular religious statements (see the critical commentaries) and manages even to avoid the name of Christ, he shows us how such syncretism works. His process of composition, and not the resulting collage, is the touchstone. To understand him, we enter his workshop and with patient observation learn from him and other biblical authors (the evangelists, the Old Testament writers) how they managed to introduce into their witness a Canaanite temple as the central holy place of Judaism (the idol of the Canaanite temple being replaced by the Ark of the Covenant); how Matthew could tell the story of the Magi from the East who found the way to the cradle using their pagan astrology; how Paul could use the *Haustafeln*, the commonly accepted ethical rules for households of his time (e.g. Col. 3:18–4:2). We learn to see this syncretism at work by reading and re-reading these passages against their religious and cultural background: in many cases, relevant pre-Judaistic or pre-Christian texts are available to us. We learn to handle it as one learns to play the violin, by learning from a master player. Our master players are the biblical authors, not with regard to their resulting collage but with regard to their workmanship.

The second criterion for a theologically responsible syncretism is a willingness to enter into dialogue with Christians from other syncretistic backgrounds. The common language is not so much the language of theology as the language of celebration, singing and praying. By joining others in their liturgy, or perhaps even by creating common liturgies, we may discover our common heritage and our unity, and our theologies may become comparable. That much of our theology is perhaps not 'celebratable' just shows that it has imprisoned itself in the cultural ghetto of academia. That medicine, psychology, economics and other disciplines have the same problem – they too are no longer understandable by those who finance their activities – does not make the matter easier. It is certainly no excuse for theology. In using the term 'celebratable', I do not have in mind an uncritical theology, but a critical theology which reaches those for whom it is intended. Otherwise it is a waste of resources. Certainly that which is indispensable in Christian tradition, critical reflection and exegesis, must become part and parcel of our hymns, liturgies and proclamation. Examples for such a policy are the black churches in the United States (Cone) and the Centre for Black and White Christian Partnership at the University of Birmingham (Hollenweger 1987b).

All this suggests to me that theology in the Church of the future will no longer be just a science but – following the example of the Christian past – also an art. Not for nothing are many of our departments of theology in the faculty of arts!

A missionary theology in a missionary Church

Theology in the Church of the future will have to be a missionary theology in a missionary Church. 'Missionary' does not mean propaganda, nor does it involve the intention of changing others into 'my' image. It means – as in the New Testament – a theology and a Church which are in dialogue with Christians from other traditions, with unbelievers, and with people from other religions. All missionary incidents in the New Testament are of a dialogical nature. In all instances the evangelist/theologian learnt something about the Gospel from his non-Christian partners. The key example for this is the encounter between Peter and Cornelius (Acts 10). Peter learnt from the Roman officer of occupation that forms of Christianity different from his own were both possible and in fact the will of God, i.e. a Christianity without sabbath, circumcision, temple, sacrifices and food taboos. Of course, Peter got into trouble with his colleagues in Jerusalem when he took this new insight seriously. That will happen to us. It seems clear to me that the Church of the future needs a theology which encourages the people of God to enter into these dialogical encounters not just for missionary purposes but much more in order to learn something about the Gospel from non-believers or those who believe in other ways from oneself (Hollenweger 1976).

The attraction of Jesus and the rejection of our christologies

This is particularly important in christology. Jesus of Nazareth has become in our time the most important religious symbol, and that for all religious and even for non-believers. No other religious figure has the same radiance. Think only of Gandhi. Ghandi would not have been Ghandi had he not read and studied the Sermon on the Mount. Muslims have a very high opinion of Jesus of Nazareth and are prepared to give him (not Muhammad) the final word at the Last Judgement. Atheists have discovered the importance of Jesus, e.g. in what I consider the best book on Jesus written in recent years, namely Milan Machovec's *A Marxist Looks at Jesus* (1976). Machovec, a Czech philosopher (who was sent into the wilderness after the Prague spring), an expert on both Catholic and Protestant New Testament exegesis, asks himself in the manner of materialist exegesis – who has written what, and what for, in the New Testament? In applying materialist exegesis strictly and to the very end, he also comes to the limits of this type of exegesis. He does not fall into the temptation of believing that such an exegesis can always give an answer to the question: Why were these authors writing and believing what they wrote and believed? Laying bare the interests, circumstances and determining material factors does not necessarily reveal the reasons for such action and thought.

This is beautifully demonstrated in his extraordinary chapter on Easter which has the simple title 'Christ'. Over a hundred pages of careful exegesis lead to the conclusion:

> At first – and second – sight it is somewhat remarkable that the 'cause' of Jesus did not come to an end with his tragic death on the cross and that his disciples did not simply scatter and vanish without trace like the supporters of all the many other rebels, prophets, preachers of doom, reformists, insurgents and revolutionaries who have fallen victim to the state's concern for law and order . . . How was it that a prophet whose predictions had not been fulfilled should be at the origin of the greatest of world religions?
>
> (Machovec 1976: 164)

How could Peter convince the handful of frightened and confused disciples that that for which Jesus lived and died had not died with the death of Jesus?

Machovec answers this question – in a strictly historical–critical way, as Adolf von Harnack (1958) had already done (Kümmel 1973: 357) – by referring to the Easter belief of the first disciples. If one asks further for the reasons for the emergence of such a belief, Machoveč discusses the well-known atheistic 'explanations' but finds them all wanting, superficial and historically unconvincing. He does not try to 'explain' the Easter belief against the background of the disciples' socio-economic context or their psychological development. On the contrary, one gets the impression from reading Machoveč that the interests of the disciples are in conflict with the belief in the resurrection and its consequences. As an honest atheist, Machoveč leaves open the question, 'Why did the disciples believe?' In the final analysis this is the question of God, of his intervention in life and death. If there is a God, says Machoveč, he could 'explain' the resurrection. Because the hypothesis of God is inaccessible for him, he must leave the question open.

Jesus of Nazareth is a central figure in universal culture. How else could a non-believer write a musical like 'Jesus Christ Superstar' and make a fortune? The explanation of such phenomena is clear: the Jesus-story is extra-ordinary, and this in spite of what we have done in theology to castrate it and in spite of horrors committed in the name of Christ, such as those inflicted on the Latin American Indians, on Africans and on the black slaves in the Caribbean and the United States.

Implications for christologies

The fact that Jesus is central to most cultures does not make these people Christians. They reserve the right to arrive at christologies other than those of Christian theology (Muslim, Jewish, atheistic, Hindu, etc.). And that fills us Christian theologians with a mixture of irritation and gratitude. We are suffering the same experience as the English in relation to their language. After having invented the English language, the English now discover that the majority of English speakers are not English. And these English speakers change and sometimes mutilate the language (think of the Americans). The English cannot defend themselves because they are now a minority in the English-speaking community. That too fills them with a mixture of irritation and gratitude. Gratitude that the whole world speaks English and irritation that 'good' English has become a minority language. This is also the reaction of Christian theologians and Christians. They are thankful for the fact that no-one can ignore Jesus and they are irritated because others interpret Jesus very differently, in effect produce their own christologies. This situation creates a theological task of the highest importance and at least as important as the interpretation of the classical christological controversies.

CONCLUSIONS

So the way ahead is a body-of-Christ theology thoroughly corporate and collaborative; a theology which is not only understood by the people of God but a theology in whose production both they and the non-Christian followers of Jesus participate. They are not just consumers of theology, they are – in a different way from academic theologians – producers of theology. Theology cannot just declare the principle of dialogue to be fundamental, it must produce a method by which the production of theology is experienced as a dialogical process. The Church of the future must learn to produce its liturgies, hymns and prayers not only in the context of its own traditions, not only in debate with its theological specialists, but also together with the people of God, the Christian and non-Christian followers of Jesus. It is obvious that such an understanding of theology and the Church would be much nearer to the early Church's process of theologizing.

The future Church would also be a missionary Church and, finally, it would become a Church which out of faithfulness to its tradition would become relevant in its specific cultural context. This applies not only to theology but also to theological education, to forms of worship and to the sacraments. The last point is particularly tricky. The sacraments, and the eucharist in particular, have become celebrations for the insiders – contrary to our Master, who celebrated the last Passover with people with little theological understanding and a very broken loyalty. I agree with one of my Roman Catholic colleagues who said to me: If Jesus could celebrate the first eucharist with his disciples who were a very mixed bag and certainly on a theological and political level less than that of a harmonious and streamlined company, then I cannot think of anybody in my city with whom I could not celebrate the eucharist, if he or she wished it. That, in ecumerical negotiations, the eucharist has become the seal on some future theological, ideological or even political uniformity, is one of the tragedies of modern Church life. In New Testament times, on the contrary, the eucharist was offered to those who were prepared to celebrate their loyalty to Christ (not to the Church). That implies an understanding of the Church which is not the Church because of the theological or ethical quality of her members but because of the real presence of Christ in their midst.

Since the process just described is not yet realized, it is not possible to foretell exactly the shape of this Church. But it is possible to say that this Church would be both faithful to her tradition and a place where the relevant questions of the past and the present would meet.

As a scholarly article needs a definition of the Church, such a definition is now offered: the Church is that narrative community which celebrates the real presence of her Lord. She is helped in this celebration by specialists in her traditions, by hosts who bring the differing parties together (the bishops, the priests), by forms of liturgy which are the result of syncretisms of the past and which are now adapted to new, culturally relevant and theologically responsible syncretisms. The catholicity of this Church is articulated by mutual recognition, by common celebrations and by common political and social service. The mission of the Church is indispensible as that process in which Christians and non-Christians discover together the relevance of the Gospel.

Critical theology helps the Church not to absolutize her own insights but to discover them as elements in an ongoing process. The responsibility of Church authorities is to make sure that this process is not blocked either by tradition or by the specialists, by the insiders or by the outsiders. This is obviously an unstable balance since the Church does not exist because of its firm structures but because of God's promise.

In case there is a tendency to dismiss these theses as theoretical and therefore irrelevant, one should consider that a number of scholars have tested these insights in the Third World, at the German Kirchentag, in the World Council of Churches (Weber) and in other contexts (Hollenweger, Vogt). With non-Christian dancers and musicians, with folk music groups and choirs, with professional and lay actors (many of them not church-goers), liturgies, eucharists, biblical and religious musicals (e.g. a requiem on Bonhoeffer) have been produced. From these non-church-going people important insights on the Gospel, the liturgy and prayer have appeared. There were more 'sinners' (if this word be allowed for non-church-goers and non-Christians!) taking part in these events than in all the so-called evangelistic campaigns taken together. The reception which biblical texts received from choreographers and producers, from singers and musicians, was on many occasions most remarkable. These people realize, first and foremost, the quality of biblical texts, when they are not used as proof-texts for our ideology but as texts of our common humanity. Whether these people become Christians or not is not our responsibility but the responsibility of the Spirit of God. Perhaps it is not even desirable that they become members of a church. The churches might destroy their emerging faith. On the other hand the churches might repent of their ghetto existence and welcome those who try to become Christians in a new and different way. Thus they will discover aspects of the Gospel which they have so far ignored. Since dialogue is not the opposite of mission but the biblical praxis of mission, a church must be by definition a missionary church and therefore a changing church, a church which changes in the light of her coming Lord.

REFERENCES

Abraham, K. C. (1991) 'Syncretism is not the Issue. A Response to Professor Chung Hyun Kyung', in *International Review of Mission* 80:319–20, July/Oct., 339–46.

Achtemeier, P. J. (1980) *The Inspiration of Scripture: Problems and Proposals*, Philadelphia: The Westminster Press.

Augstein, R. (1972) *Jesus Menschensohn*.

Barrett, D. B. (1972) *World Christian Encyclopedia*, Oxford: Oxford University Press.

Burgess, S. M. *et al.* (eds) (1988) *Dictionary of Pentecostal and Charismatic Movements*, Grand Rapids, Mich.: Zondervan.

Brunner, E. (1943, 1963) *Truth as Encounter*, London.

Chikane, F. (1988) *No Life of My Own*, Braamfontein, South Africa: Skotaville Publishers.

Collier, J. (1990) *The Culture of Economism: An Exploration of Barriers to Faith as Praxis*, New York: Peter Lang.

Cone, J. H. (1975) *God of the Oppressed*, New York: Seabury.

Dunn, J. (1977) *Unity and Diversity in the New Testament: An Inquiry into the Character of Earliest Christianity*, London: SCM Press.

Friedrich, G. (1976) 'Pre-History of the Theological Dictionary of the NT', *Theological Dictionary of the New Testament*, vol. X, Grand Rapids, Mich.: Eerdmans, 613–61, in particular 646, 650ff.

Gerloff, R. I. H. (1992) *A Pleas for British Black Theologies: The Black Church Movement in Britain in its Transatlantic Cultural and Theological Interaction*, 2 vols, New York: Peter Lang.

Hollenweger, W. J. (1976) *Evangelism Today: Good News or Bone of Contention?*, Belfast: Christian Journals Ltd.

—— (1979, 1980) *Erfahrungen der Leibhaftigkeit: Interkulturelle Theologie 1*, Munich: Chr. Kaiser.

—— (1982, 1992) *Umgang mit Mythen: Interkulturelle Theologie 2*, Munich: Chr. Kaiser.

—— (1987a) 'Towards an Intercultural History of Christianity', *International Review of Mission* 76/304, Oct., 526–56.

—— (1987b) 'Interaction between Black and White in Theological Education', *Theology* 90/737, Sept., 341–50.

—— (1988) *Geist und Materie: Interkulturelle Theologie 3*, Munich: Chr. Kaiser.

—— (1989a) 'Healing Through Prayer: Superstition or Forgotten Christian Tradition', *Theology* 92/747, May, 166–74.

—— (1989b) 'Music in the Service of Reconciliation', *Theology* 92/746, July, 276–86.

—— (1992) 'The Critical Roots of Pentecostalism', *Journal for Pentecostal Theology* (University of Sheffield) 1.

—— (1993) 'Verheißung und Verhängnis der Pfingstbewegung', *Evangelische Theologie*.

King, T. M. (1991) 'Theological Controversy in Canberra: A Reflection', *International Review of Mission* 80/319–20, July/Oct., 355–60.

Kraft, C. (1979) *Christianity in Culture: A Study in Dynamic Biblical and Cross-Cultural Perspective*, New York: Orbis Books.

—— and Wisley, T. N. (eds) (1979) *Readings in Dynamic Indigeneity*, Pasadena, Calif.: William Carey Library.

Kümmel, W. (1973) *The New Testament: The History of the Investigation of its Problems*, London: SCM Press.

Kyung, C. H. (1991) 'Come, Holy Spirit – Renew the Whole Creation', in M. Kinnamon (ed.) *Signs of the Spirit*, Official Report Seventh Assembly of the WWC at Canberra 1991, Grand Rapids, Mich.: Eerdmans, 37–47.

Lacan, J. (1956) *La Psychoanalyse*, vol. I, Paris: Seuil.

—— (1966) *Ecrits*, vol. I, Paris: Seuil.

Lederle, H. I. (1988) *Treasures Old and New: Interpretations of 'Spirit-Baptism' in the Charismatic Renewal Movement*, Peabody, Mass.: Hendrickson.

Lévi-Strauss, C. (1956) *Tropiques tristes*, Paris: Plon.

—— (1962) *La Pensée sauvage*, Paris: Plon.

McDonnell, K. (1980) *Presence, Power, Praise: Documents on the Charismatic Renewal*, 3 vols, Collegeville, Minn.: The Liturgical Press.

Machoveč, M. (1976) *A Marxist Looks at Jesus*, London: Darton, Longman and Todd.

Marti, K. (1976) *Grenzverkehr*, Neukirchen-Vluyn: Neukirchener Verlag.

Mazibuko, B. (1987) *Education in Mission – Mission in Education: A Critical Comparative Study of Selected Approaches*, New York: Peter Lang.

Schiwy, G. (1969) *Strukturalismus und Christentum: Eine Herausforderung*, Freiburg/Basel/Vienna.

Segundo, J. L. (1974) *A Theology for Artisans of a New Humanity*, 5 vols, Maryknoll: Orbis.

Spiegel, Y. (ed.) (1972) *Psychoanalytische Interpretationen biblischer Texte*, Munich: Chr. Kaiser.

—— (ed.) (1978) *Doppeldeutlich: Tiefendimensionen biblischer Texte*, Munich: Chr. Kaiser.

Stollberg, D. (1978) 'Tiefenpsychologische oder historisch–kritische Exegese? Indentität und der Tod des Ich (Gal. 2.19–20)', in Y. Spiegel (ed.) *Doppeldeutlich: Tiefendimensionen biblischer Texte*, Munich: Chr. Kaiser, 213–26.

Stroup, G. W. (1981) *The Promise of Narrative Theology. Recovering the Gospel in the Church*, Atlanta: John Knox Press.

Stuhlmacher, P. (1979) *Vom Verstehen des Neuen Testaments: Eine Hermeneutik*, NTD suppl. vol. 6, Göttingen: Vandenhoeck & Ruprecht.

Thurman, J. (1982) *New Wineskins: A Study of the House Church Movement*, New York: Peter Lang.

Van der Bent, A. (1991) 'WCC, Assemblies', in *Dictionary of the Ecumenical Movement*, Grand Rapids, Mich.: Eerdmans, 1090–6.

Vanelderen, M. (1991) 'WCC, Membership of', in *Dictionary of the Ecumenical Movement*, Grand Rapids, Mich.: Eerdmans, 1098–100.

Via, D. O. (1967) *The Parables*, Philadelphia: Fortress Press.

Vogt, T. (1985) *Bibelarbeit*, Stuttgart: W. Kohlhammer.

Von Harnack, A. (1958) *The Rise of Christian Theology and of Church Dogma*, New York: Russel & Russel.

Walker, A. (1989) *Restoring the Kingdom: The Radical Christianity of the House Church Movement*, London: Hodder & Stoughton.

Weber, R. (1981) *Experiments with Bible Study*, Geneva: WCC.

Wink, W. (1973) *The Bible in Human Transformation: Toward a Paradigm for Biblical Study*, Philadelphia: Fortress Press.

See also chapters 41, 42, 43, 44, 45, 46, 47.

INDEX

a posteriori arguments, natural theology 396, 397
a priori arguments
  Enlightenment 620–1
  natural theology 390–1, 396, 397
  spirituality 514, 532
Abelard, Peter 62, 213, 214
abortion 745, 819, 827, 828–9
Abraham 8, 343, 963–4
absoluteness, Christianity 876–8, 880–4
absolution 795
Acacian Schism 207
academic theology 891–3
accidents, substance distinction 612
Achtemeier, Paul J. 1019
Acquaviva 586
'Action Guides' 693–700
activity, contemplation relationship 644, 645, 654, 660
Acts of the Apostles 93–4
  see also Luke, St
ad fontes 236, 238
Adam, sinfulness 61–2
adaptive doctrine 986, 987
adequacy, criteria of 524
adolescence, emotional development 802–4
adoptionism 124
Adorno 996
adultery 805, 826
Advaitins 625, 626, 628–9
advertising, ethics 773
aestheticism 70, 327–8, 331
African National Congress (ANC) 732, 733, 788
African theology, indigenization 909
Afrikaaners, Exodus significance 969–70
agada see haggada
agape 695–6, 745–6, 824
'Age of Faith' 206
Ahlstrom, Sydney 599–600
Ahnung 630

AIDS 660–1, 754
Alan of Lille, Isaiah 63
Albanese, Catherine 600–1
Albigensian Crusade 218
Albigensians *see* Cathars
Albright, W. F. 78–9, 148, 150
Alexander III, Pope 220
Alexander, Samuel 399
Alexandria, Egypt 344
alienation
  feminism 492
  gender 502
  projection 496
allegorical interpretation
  Augustine of Hippo 52
  ceremonial aspects of law 48
  New Testament 103, 106
  Origen 105–6
  parables 119
  Philo of Alexandria 33
Almond, Philip 622
almsgiving 760, 765
Alston, William P. 380, 635–7
altarpieces 323
Altizer, J. J. 906, 911
altruism
  human nature 464
  sociobiology 465–6, 467
alumbrados 585
Ambrose of Milan, creation 61
Amnesty International 722, 730
amniocentesis 828–9
Amos, prophet paradox 55–6
Anabaptists 240, 242–3, 647–8
anagogical interpretation 52
analogy
  doctrine 364, 423
  religious language 419, 424–5
analytic philosophy, theological role 338–9
anamnesis 666, 672
anaphora 198, 202

anatomy, reproduction 502
ANC *see* African National Congress
anchorage 413, 417, 419, 424, 428, 448
Andrew of St Victor 48
Andrewes, Lancelot 583, 671
Aner, Karl 265
Angelico, Fra 325
angels 181, 852
Anglican Church *see* Church of England
Anglo-Catholicism
    communion 670–1
    liturgy 679
animals
    duty towards 848, 851–2
    extinction 845–6
    human nature 453–4
    importance to God 866
    sacrifice 863, 881
    sociobiology 465, 467
anointing 42
'anonymous Christianity' 300–1
Anselm, St
    concept of God 346–7
    concept of reason 369
    Cur deus homo 328–9
    meditations 518, 561
    natural theology 390
    prophecy 56
    Proslogian 562
    religious language 429, 430
    Satan 62
    Trinity doctrine 941
    Why God Became Man 262–3
anthropocentrism 437, 438
anthropology
    concept of reason 376
    friendship 503
    myth 958
    scientific understanding 437
    spirituality 511, 525
    theological 453–71, 919, 930–1
anthropomorphism
    concept of God 348, 365
    free-will defence 483
    minimalist theodicy 487
    spirituality 525
anti-foundationalism 405, 406, 436
anti-Semitism 114, 118, 303–5
anti-trinitarianism 943–4
Antichrist 54, 55
antinomianism 753

Antiochenes, biblical interpretation 107, 110
antonomasia 53
Antony of Egypt, monasticism 553, 554
apartheid, South Africa 788–9
aphorisms 11
apocalyptic literature
    Daniel 19–20
    eschatology 39
    inspirational 131
    narrative 966
    Revelation of John 88–9
apocrypha 29
apodeictic form, law 10
apologetics
    concept of reason 376, 377
    dogmatics 981–2
    post-foundationalist 379–83
apophatic theology
    Dionysius 346
    Gregory of Nyssa 545
    Philo the Jew 545
    prayer 573
    rationalism 352
    spirituality 529–30
apostles
    poverty 215, 221
    status among laity 214–15
Apostolic Fathers 97, 104
apostolic life 105, 214–15, 216–18, 577
appropriateness, criteria of 524
Aquila, Greek Bible translation 30
Aquinas, St Thomas
    see also Thomism
    Aristotelian teachings 337, 564
    Beauty 330
    Catholic Reformation 248–9
    Christ and culture 317
    Commentary on the Sentences 249
    concept of God 347–9, 357
    concept of reason 369, 372, 373, 375
    dogmatics 219, 978
    ethics 701–2, 704
    feminism 491
    grace 611
    immortality 454–5
    infinity 351
    intellectualism 235
    the Law 57–8
    literalism 108
    natural law 697
    natural theology 391–2

non-rational creatures 866
plurality of incarnations 934
poverty of Christ 221
realism 234
religious language 424–5, 426
scholasticism 213, 232
speculative theodicy 478
Summa contra Gentiles 222–3
Summa Theologica 222–3, 247, 248–9, 516, 517, 987
systematic theology 980
theism 899
transubstantiation 612
Trinity 898–9
Arabic, Koran 149–50
Arafat, Yasser 731
Aramaic
Hebrew Bible translation 30–1
post-Exile usage 151
archaeology, Old Testament historicity 78
Archer, Antony 612
architecture
early Christian 322
Gothic 317, 324
Arianism 195, 938
Aristotelianism
assimilation into Christian thought 213
Calvinism 246–7
humanism 237
natural law 781
scholasticism 232, 236
Aristotle
concept of God 337, 347, 349
conditional futurity 56
crusades 564
ethics 702
human nature 454
natural philosophy 373
Poetics 962
reason 367
substance and accidents 612
theology as science 555
tragedy 962, 964
arms
bearing of 694
trade 735–6
Arnold, Matthew 315, 316, 420
Arnold, Thomas 75, 78
art
Church guidelines 323–4
definition 321
early images of Christ 322

Old and New Testaments link 59–61
religious experience 324–6
theological significance 328–32
artificial insemination 825, 826
artists, role 326–8
ascension, redundant concept 596
asceticism
bodiliness 516
meditation 518, 519
monasticism 517
personal ethics 739
Spanish reconquest 585
Asian theology 897, 909
associators 203–4
assurance, doctrine of 582
astronomy 397, 435
Athanasius of Alexandria
divine Christ 195
Fall 549
Holy Spirit 199
image of God 548
sin 61–2
atheism
Christian 873, 905
design argument 374
faith in 1023
human nature 453
importance of Jesus 1030–1
monotheism 942
protest 896, 950–1
validity of religious language 895, 897
Athenagoras, triune God 189
Atman-Brahman 625, 628–9
atonement
Hegelian interpretation 354
purpose 73
redundant concept 596
atonement theology 302
Auerbach, Erich 963, 967
Aufklärung 251–71
Augsberg Confession 72, 976
Augstein, R. 1019
Augustine of Hippo, St
absolute power 234
animals 866
anti-Pelagianism 232
beauty 540–1
biblical style 52
Christ and culture 318
concept of God 345–6
concept of reason 369
Confessions 330, 540

creation 54, 61
De Trinitate 203
dualism 852
ethics 701–2
feminism 491
God, image of 548–50
grace 57, 553
Holy Spirit 197
humanity of Christ 928
just war 716–17
Law and grace 57
Lord's Prayer 537
Manicheism 475, 477, 478
music 330
natural theology 390
Old/New Testaments relationship 50
original sin 62
pagan philosophy 337
pilgrimage 550
polemical writings 983
prayer 643–4
Psalms 62
Retractions 984
sexuality 657
sin 704
spirituality 556
Trinity 203, 940–2, 944, 951
Augustinian Canons 215
authority
  see also canon
  epistles 86–7
  Gospels 88
  Hebrew Bible 28
  Mishnah 36
  New Testament 97–8, 110
  Old Testament 47–8
  post-modern dogmatics 997–8
  rabbis 35–6
  Revelation of John 89
  Scripture 4–5, 155, 156
  spirituality 525
Authorized Version *see* King James
  Authorized Version
autobiography, religious 582
autonomy
  ethics 505
  feminism 491
  gender 502
  reason 436, 439
Averroes, concept of God 347
Avicenna, concept of God 347
awefulness, numinous feeling 621

Ayer, A. J. 405, 415, 421, 903

babies *see* abortion; children; embryos;
  procreation
Bailey, Sherwin 749
Baillie, Donald 927–8
Baillie, John 364, 399, 400
Baker, Augustine 591
Balthasar, Hans Urs von 301, 330
baptism
  adult 242, 243
  New Testament 537
  Trinity 197, 198, 950
  typology 969
Baptist Church 584
Bar Kokhba 36, 173
Barbour, Ian 399, 401, 440
Barmen Declaration 278
Barrett, David 1025
Barth, Karl
  biblical interpretation 883, 902
  biblical laws 705–6
  Christ and culture 317
  Christian Dogmatics 984
  Christocentricism 951
  Church Dogmatics 282, 826, 904, 918–19,
    984
  Church and theology 1024
  concept of God 359, 360–1
  dialectical theology 354
  doctrine of God 947–8
  Enlightenment criticism 264–6
  eschatology 924
  ethics 700
  Holy Spirit 200
  inviolability of human life 819, 826
  language 278
  natural theology 389–90
  neo-orthodoxy 918–20
  non-Christian religions 877
  *Protestant Theology in the Nineteenth
    Century* 265, 983
  radical theology 905
  religious images 330
  Romans 918
  sin 704
  systematic theology 979, 980, 982
  temporality of God 912
  The Humanity of God 265
  theology and philosophy 282
  Trinity 904, 937
Barthes, Roland 958, 961, 965–6

Bartholomew, David 401, 444–5
Basic Belief Apologetic 380–3
Basil I, Emperor 209
Basil of Caesarea, St
  see also Rule of St Basil
  creation 61
  individuality 939
  monasticism 554
  Trinity 200
Basil of Nyssa, God as beauty 539–40
Basle, Council of 225
Baxter, R., domestic church 676–7
Bayle, P., sceptical fideism 377
Beatific Vision 221–2
Beauty
  art 330
  God 539–40
  nature 847–8
  Plato 852
  Puritanism 583
Beccaria 252
Becket, St Thomas à 212
Bede 50, 53, 559–60
Beghards, Christ's humanity 646
Beguines 569
behaviour
  feminism 492
  sociobiology 465
Bellah, Robert 601, 616
Ben Sira 12, 17, 19, 818
Benecke, Gerhard 264–5
Benedict XII, Pope 221–2
Benedictines 215, 324
Berdyaev, Nicholas 890
Berger, Peter 889, 891, 902
Berkeley, George 443
Bernard of Clairvaux
  artistic austerity 324
  Christ as illuminator 50
  Cistercian order 216
  commentaries 559–60
  letter to Hildegard 569
  mysticism 605, 624
  papal law 212
  prayer 563
Berrigan, Daniel 655, 659
Bettelheim, Bruno 958–9, 963
Beza, Theodore 242, 246, 247
Bible 1–159
  see also canon; Hebrew Bible; New
    Testament; Old Testament;
    Septuagint

Aramaic versions 31
artistic and literary features 331–2
authority of 393
'Book of Books' 146
book order 3, 143–5, 157
Calvinist teaching 350
codes of conduct 691–2, 699, 705
commentaries 108, 559
concept of God 342–3
contemporary relevance 1018
creation stories 746–50, 760–1, 767
criticism 102, 259
early church 104
ethics 687, 697–8, 711, 746–50, 866–7
exegesis eighteenth century 257–9
formation 28–9, 143–6
four senses 107–8
glory of God 559
health 823
historicism 887
holy book 3–6, 142–59
Holy Spirit 198–9
holy war 719
homosexuality 808
importance 3–4, 108
inviolability of human life 819
language 152, 200–2
liturgical component 681
Medieval devotion 558–61
metaphor 153
narrative 876, 966–7, 971
neo-orthodoxy 918
patristic theology 516
pluralism 1024–5
post-modernity 992
prayer 562
prophetic nature 73
psychological approach 1021
Reformers 108–9
scepticism 594–5
scrolls 143
sin 703
sola scriptura 242–3, 244
study 1026
systematic theology 983, 987
theocentrism 168–9
theological method 985
tradition 3, 108–9, 165, 875
translation 238
triune God 188–93
twentieth century rediscovery 648–50
uniqueness 157–8

Virgin Mary 566
Vulgate 231, 238–9
wealth 759–61, 775
women's place in 285
word of God 168–9
biblical interpretation
see also exegesis
contemporary 1017–20
critical/traditional contrast 110
doctrinal 102
epistles 87
figurative 51–4
Hebrew Bible 32–8
historical 52, 103–10
iconographic 60
medieval 5, 107–8
morality 15, 52, 62
New Testament 89–91, 102–21, 122–5
Old Testament 44
rationalist 67–9
Reformation 108–10
romantic 67–9
theological 124
Third World 126–7
traditional 102–21, 122–5
typology 969
biblical scholarship
dogmatic method 986
hermeneutics 966–7
historicism 879–80, 886–7
humanism 238–9
laity 1018
narrative theology 965–7
structuralism 965–7
biblical theology 67, 74, 79
bibliodrama 1021, 1026
Biel, Gabriel 233, 235–6
Big Bang 440, 443, 446
binitarian formulae 115
bioethics 780, 817–42, 820–4
biography
Calvinism 581
religious autobiography 582
saints 567
biology
see also sociobiology
scientific understanding 436, 438, 439
bishops
investitures 211–12
marriage 214
Black Consciousness 788
Black Death 569

black theology
concept of God 357
critical theology 1025
future of 871
imagery 908
origins 284–6
spirituality 655–6
structural sin 706
universal theology 1027
Blake, William 156–7, 327
blik, definition 419
Blumenberg, Hans 890–1
Böckle, Franz, ethics 697
Bodin, Jean 55
body
dualism 504
embodiment 747–8
feminism 492, 498, 504
modern attitude 739
patristic spirituality 541–2
personhood 503
taboos 500
virginity 542
Body of Christ
Christian community 564, 650, 652–3
era of reform 576–7
family 677
feast of Corpus Christi 564
Boethius, Anicius Manlius Severinus 472, 484, 485
Boff, Clodovis 127, 137
Boff, Leonardo 904, 927
Bohr, complementarity 997
Bonaventure, St 235, 947
Bonhoeffer, Dietrich
Christology 286, 917–18
The Cost of Discipleship 694
eschatology 531–2
19th century 273
secularization 276–7
spirituality 653
Boniface, St, mission to Germany 208
Boniface VIII, Pope 224
Bonino, Míguez 1002, 1005, 1007
Book of Common Prayer 667, 671, 675
Book of the Covenant 9, 10, 15, 22
'Book of the Twelve' 17
Bossuet, Bishop 586
Bouyer, Louis 519
Bowlby, John 799, 800
Boyle Lectures 396–7
Brahman 625

Braithwaite, Richard 355, 420, 421–2
Brandt, Richard 596
Brethren of the Common Life 569
Breviary 675
Bridget of Sweden, St 226
Bridgewater Treatises 398
British Council of Churches 942, 950, 952
Brown, Joanne 500
Brown, Peter 541–2, 554
Brown, W. Adams 989
Browne, Henry 630
Brümmer, Vincent 364
Brunner, Emil 278, 389, 919–20, 982, 1020
Buber, Martin 325, 400, 920
Bucer, Martin 245–6
Buckley, Michael, atheism 942
Buddhism
    indigenization 909
    inter-faith dialogue 992
    religious experience 623–7, 636–7
    sanctity of human life 718
    sin 717
    statistics 291
    stories 968
    universal compassion 734–5
Buffon, *Natural History* 258
Bullinger, Heinrich 242
Bultmann, Rudolf
    demythologizing 277
    eschatology 924
    ethics 698
    exegesis 123–4
    existentialism 281, 920–2
    Heidegger's influence 360
    myth 995
    natural theology 397
    New Testament texts 960
Bunyan, John, liturgy 678–9
Buren, Paul van 277
Burnaby, John, Psalms 676
Burnet, T., *Sacred Theory* 848
business
    covenant 770
    ethics 771–4
    'good citizenship' 774
    greed 767–8, 769
    stakeholders 772–3
    theology of 774–5
Butler, Bishop Joseph 257, 261–3, 376, 469
Butterfield, Herbert, objectivity 880
Byrne, Peter 337–41, 433–52

Byzantine Church *see* Eastern Orthodox
    Church; Greek Orthodox Church
Byzantine Emperors
    see also Eastern Empire
    authority over church 207
    inconoclasm 208
    protection of popes 208
    remarriage dispute 209

Cahill, Lisa Sowle 839
Caird, G. B. 151
Cajetan, Cardinal 425
calendar, feasts 576
Calvin, John
    Christology 580
    concept of God 350
    doctrine of the Church 245–6
    ethics 694
    idolatry 318
    Institutes of the Christian Religion 244,
        246, 978, 987
    natural theology 393
    New Testament commentaries 108–9
    predestination 470
    Reformation 239–40
    Reply to Sadoleto 246
    voluntarism 235
Calvinism
    Aristotelianism 246–7
    Christ and culture 318
    distinction from Lutheranism 247
    exclusivism 296
    grace 581–2
    predestination 247
    Reformation 240, 241–2
    sanctification 581
    sin 647, 705
    Trinity 947
    wealth 760
Cambridge Platonists, natural theology 395
Campbell, Charles Arthur 399
Campbell, Joseph 958–9, 960–1
Camus, Albert 485
Candlemas 680
candles 680
Cannon, George 154
Cannon, Katie 656
canon
    Christian Bible 143–4
    Hebrew Bible 14–20, 143–4
    Jewish scriptures 28–9
    New Testament 85–6, 97–8, 100, 105

Canon Law 213
canonization, saints 566
Canons of Windesheim 215
canticles 322
Cantwell Smith, Wilfred 383
capitalism
  Cold War 725–6
  era of reform 577
  labour 1005–6
  liberation theology 1008
  morality 778
  social justice 767–9
  spirituality 526
  Third World 1010
  work ethic 775
Cappadocia, Turkey 344
Cappadocian Fathers
  freedom 552
  God as beauty 539
  knowledge of God 545
  Trinity 939–41, 951–2
Capreolus, Johannes 248
Cardman, Francine 609
care, ethic of 505–6
caritas 702
Carmelites 646–7
Carnap, Rudolf 355, 414
Carolingian dynasty 208
Carroll, R. P. 139, 144
Cartesians 850, 853
Casel, Odo 652, 672
Cassian, John 52
casuistic law 8
cataphatic theology 346, 529–30
catastrophe, narrative 964–5
Cathars 215, 218, 564–5
Catherine of Siena 226
Catholic Reformation 240, 243, 584–91
Catholic Worker movement 655
Catholicism see Anglo-Catholicism; Roman
  Catholic Church
causality
  concept of God 353, 394
  scientific understanding 442, 443–4, 449
causation
  modern theism 899–900
  radical post-theism 905
  religious language 426
cave paintings 321
celibacy
  Brethren of the Common Life 569
  clerics 114, 213–14

contraception 740
divorce 753
fidelity 756
homosexuality 753, 808
traditionalists 751
Celsus 189
Centre for Black and White Christian
  Partnership 1025, 1029
Chalcedonian Definition 971
chance, scientific understanding 444–5
charismatic movement 680, 1018
charity, praxis 1002
Charlemagne, Emperor 208, 228
chauvinism, epistemic 380
Chicago Declaration 658
Chikane, Frank 1027
childbirth, taboos 500
children
  see also procreation
  assisted reproduction 825–8
  divorce 755–6
  emotional development 798–805
  environmentalism 844, 847–8
  experimentation on 834–5
  foetal surgery 829
  malformed neonates 828–31
  marriage 749
  right to have 826
  stories 963
  suffering of 838
  unconditional parental love 801–2
China, missionaries 218
chivalry, cult of 564
choice, human nature 454
Christ see Jesus Christ
Christ, Carol 500
'Christendom' model, Church and state
  777–9, 782, 791–2
Christian atheism 905
Christian Socialism 784
'Christian-Marxist Dialogue' 783
Christianismus renascens 238
Christianity
  absoluteness 876–8, 880–4
  distinguishing feature 666
  essence of 989–90, 997–8
  historical praxis 1002–5
  identity 875–8, 883
  inter-faith dialogue 872, 873, 877, 992–3
  Islam relationship 142–3, 149–50,
    306–8, 877
  Judaism

relationship 99–100, 104, 168, 173, 181, 303–6
  split 44–5, 180–1
repression 942
statistics 291
Christiano, K. J. 889
Christmas, Middle Ages 576
Christocentrism
  pluralist view 293–4
  spirituality 525
  Trinity 952
Christology 917–36
  anti-Judaism 303, 305
  art 322
  British/American 927–30
  Calvin 580
  current views 933–4
  early church 124
  exegesis 43–4
  Hegel 945
  inclusivism 299, 300
  inculturation 1024–5
  interfaith dialogue 308
  liberation 926–7
  neo-orthodoxy 918–20
  non-Christian 1030–1
  Old Testament 44
  Paul 177
  pluralism 918, 933
  Roman Catholic 930–3
  theocentricism 294
  traditional interpretation 115–16
Chronicles 9, 18–19, 22
Chub, Thomas 256, 259
Chung Hyun Kyung 287, 1028
Church
  see also Church of England; Eastern Orthodox; Roman Catholic Church
  academic theology relationship 891–3
  Calvinism 581
  centrality of 170–1
  change in meaning 231
  Christian identity 875–8
  class struggle 1005
  commercialization 1024
  communion in image of Trinity 942
  conservatism 1018–19
  critical theology 1017–18
  democracy 780–1
  departure from Jesus' teachings 170, 171
  divine kenosis 906
  doctrine of 245–6

  established 679
  future of 1032
  historical relativism 883
  liturgical community 653
  Middle Ages 558
  missionary theology 1029–30
  narrative 968
  pacifism 716
  patriarchy 885
  politics 777–9, 783–4
  salvation 876
  secularization 888–91
  socialism 783–4
  State 207, 777–9
  syncretism 1027–8
  trinitarian worship 950
  wealth and riches 770
Church of England
  see also Anglo-Catholicism
  Doctrine in the Church of England 977
  establisment 247–8
  ethics 697
  Faith in the City: A call for action by church and Nation 778
  Lambeth Conference 1988 789, 791
  liturgy 652, 672
  ordination of women 876
  Reformation 248
  theology 976–7
  Thirty-Nine Articles 59, 255–6, 581, 976, 987
Church of the Messiah, Detroit 659
Church of the Saviour, Washington DC 659
Cicero 577
circumcision 48, 49, 104
Cistercians
  anti-heretical preaching 215–16
  art 324
  prayer 563
citizen, ethics 699–700, 774
civil religion
  Hanoverian 255–6
  Rousseau 268
civil rights, black theology 284
civil servants, celibacy 213–14
Clarke, Samuel 373, 396
class
  feminism 493
  Marxism 358
class struggle 1005, 1008
Claudius of Turin 559

Clement of Alexandria
  apophatic tradition 545
  figurative interpretation 51, 52
  Gnostics 543
  Gospel of John 111
  prayer 674
Clement of Rome 104
clergy
  see also priesthood
  authority 577
  celibacy 213–14
  communal life 214
  dissolution of marriage 220
  education 1021
  Protestantism 582
clericalization, Gregorian reform 565
Clifford, W. K. 379
Clines, D. J. A. 129–30
Cloud of Unknowing 518, 573
Cluny, order of 210
Cobb, John 900
Code of Hammurabi 9, 817
codes of conduct
  Bible 691–2, 699
  Code of Hammurabi 817
  Covenant Code 705
  Holiness Code 705
codex 143–4
cognition
  doctrinal statements 993–5
  post-modernism 995
  scientific understanding 450
cohabitation 803
Cold War 719, 726–7
Coleridge, Samuel Taylor
  creation 953
  desynonymization 939
  natural beauty 597–8
  non-relational deity 952
  religious truth 275
  Scriptures 261
  Trinity 937, 945–6
collectivism
  Church and state 787–8, 792
  human nature 463–4, 465
  social order 951–2
  unease 606
Collins, Anthony 253–4, 256, 259
colonialism 292, 526
commentary
  Gloss 107
  Lord's Prayer 537

medieval 559
  Mishnah 37–8
commercialization 1023–4
communal worship 665–76
communion see Eucharist
communism 725–6, 782
community
  Augustinian canons 215
  Christian 650, 652–3, 659
  clergy 214
  ethics 506
  eucharistic 888
  feminism 492, 494, 496, 504
  liberation spirituality 661–2
  relationships 749–50
  Second Vatican Council 614
  taboos 500
  theological dialogue 1017–20
  Trinity 939, 951–2
competition
  ethical 773
  market economy 767–9
complementarity 997
completion, doctrine of 762
Compostela, pilgrimage 568
computer systems 851
Concertatio 220
conscientious objectors 736
conditional futurity 56
Cone, James H. 284, 656, 788, 1027
confession 216, 611, 795
confessional orthodoxy 72–4
conflict, scientific understanding 433,
    434–7, 447
Confucianism, indigenization 909
Congress on World Mission 297–8
consciousness
  see also cosmic consciousness; pure
    consciousness; self-consciousness
  human nature 453
conscription 736
consecration 671
conservationism, environmental ethics 847,
    852, 864
conservative theology 125, 278
Consolamentum 215, 218
consonance, scientific understanding 434,
    447–50
Constance, Council of 225
Constantine, Emperor 554
Constantinople, Council of 187
constructivism, religious experience 626–8

consubstantiation 245
consumerism
  ethics 765–6
  liberation theology 1011
  religion 1023
contemplation
  activity relationship 644, 645, 654, 660
  mystical knowledge 631
  spirituality 517, 525
contextual theology 125, 127–8, 284–5,
  286–9, 700
contingency, scientific understanding
  434–5, 440, 443
contraception 739, 740, 754
conversion experiences 502, 525, 603,
  658–9
conversionism, culture 318
Copernicanism 434
Copleston, Frederick 401
corporeality, spirituality 516
Corpus Christi 576
Cosin, John 675
cosmic consciousness 623–4
cosmocentrism 437, 438
cosmogenesis 901
cosmological argument
  concept of reason 373, 376
  natural theology 394, 400–1
cosmology
  process theology 900–1
  scientific understanding 438–40, 442–3,
    445–7, 449
Cotoni, Marie-Hélène 260
Cottret, Bernard 254, 259
Council of Basle 225
Council of Constance 225
Council of Constantinople 187
Council of Florence 225
Council of Lyons 219
Council of Nicaea 144, 187, 537, 538, 938
Council of Trent
  authority 976
  Catholic Reformation 240, 243
  grace 611
  Scripture 231
  transubstantiation 612
counselling, pastoral 796–815
Counter Reformation see Catholic
  Reformation
covenant
  dual 304–5
  human relationships 770

inviolability of human life 819–20
  medical profession 836, 837
  New Testament 110–11
  obedience 580
  Old Testament 78
Covenant Code 705
Cox, Harvey 276–7, 655, 923
creation
  Augustine doctrine of 345
  bioethics 819–20
  embodiment 747–8
  environment 761
  erotic history 588–9
  evolution 931
  Hexaemeron studies 61
  human life as sacred 818
  patristic spirituality 548
  Pelagianism 553
  personalism 746–7, 750–1
  prophetic interpretation 54
  purpose 73, 74
  relationships 748–9
  scientific understanding 434–6, 438,
    440–5, 449, 812
  sexuality 760–1
  spirituality 530
  Trinity 940, 948, 953
  wealth 761, 767
creativity, nature of God 904, 907
credulity, Principle 634–5
Creed 170, 187, 188, 210, 976, 985–6
cremation 455
critical theology
  black theology 1025
  contemporary Church 1017–20, 1033
  Third World theology 1025
cross
  meaning of 904
  spirituality 579, 580, 587, 589, 590
  suffering of God 911
crucifix
  glory 563
  image of Christ 182, 323
  man of sorrows 563
crucifixion
  moral life 709
  temporality of divine 912
crusades
  Albigensian 218
  Christian soldiers 564
  cult of saints 568
  first 210

fourth 218
culture
  biblical 146–8
  Christ 316–21, 710
  definition 314–15
  feminism 492
  gender 502
  human nature 459–60
  medieval Catholic 645
  narrative 961
  popular 328
  power 500
  responsibility 470
  scientific understanding 433, 435
  spirituality 531–2
  theology 314–34
Culverwel, Nathanael 395
Cunaeus, Petrus 66
Cupitt, Don
  human nature 457, 458
  narrative 961–2, 972
  religious language 430, 431
  scientific understanding 441
  subjectivism 276, 281
Curran, C. E. 826
Cynics 862
Cyril of Alexandria 200
Cyril of Jerusalem 537

dalit theology 706
Daly, Mary 491, 492, 498, 502, 907–8
damnation, concept of God 346
Damrosch, D. 148
Danei, Paul 255
Daniel 20, 29, 40–1, 54
Dante Alighieri 327
'dark night of the soul' 589, 646–7
darkness, patristic spirituality 541–7,
  549–50
Darwin, Charles 398
Darwinism 76, 434, 467, 891
Daveney, Sheila 495–6
David 8, 17, 18, 42
Davies, B. 430
Davies, John 651
Davies, M. 128
Davies, P. 440
Davis, Charles 1003
Dawkins, R. 438–9
Day, Dorothy 655, 659
D'Costa, Gavin 283, 952, 992–34
de Gaulle, General Charles 732

de Maistre, eighteenth century radicalism
  252
de Wette, W. M. L. 69–72, 77
deacons, marriage 214
dead, prayers for 112
Dead Sea Scrolls 16–17, 32–3, 173
death
  acceptance 808–9
  duties towards dying 829, 832
  euthanasia 831–3
  life after 926
  mourning 800
  resurrection 132, 134, 822
  right to die 831
death of God theology 905–6, 911
decalogue 10, 58
decentring 609–10
decision-making, moral 506
Declaration of Helsinki 834
declericalization 613, 616
deconstruction
  biblical criticism 128
  culture 318
  feminism 494
  narrative theology 972
  natural theology 405
  post-modernism 607–9
deductivism, consonance 447, 448
deinstitutionalization 601, 609
Deism
  biblical criticism 259
  concept of God 350–1, 353
  concept of reason 374, 375–6
  divine causation 899
  France 264
  John Locke 253–6
  natural religion 261–2, 266
  rationalism 249
  religious *a priori* 620
  religious experience 256–7
Delitzsch, Franz 74, 78
Demetrias 553
Demiurge, Platonic teaching 344
democracy
  Christian endorsement 784–6
  definition 733
  just war 730
  Protestantism 781
  separation of Church and state 780
  Trinity 951
demythologization 277, 921, 922, 924, 960
Denis the Areopagite 542, 546–7, 555

Dennett, Dan 457
denouement, Judaeo–Christian theology 964, 968
dependence, on God 595, 812
Derham, William 396–7
Derrida, Jacques 607–8, 972
Descartes, René
  concept of reason 252, 370–3
  deism 351
  dualism 458, 852–3, 856
  epistemology 379
  individualism 850
  natural theology 394–5
  scientific understanding 437
  solipsism 744, 850
design
  concept of reason 373–4, 376
  natural theology 398, 401
desires, sin 701–3
determinism
  human nature 340–1, 459
  responsibility 469
  sociobiology 466
Deutero-Isaiah 14
Deuteronomistic History 9, 15, 18–19, 22
Deuteronomists 78
Deuteronomy 10, 28
devil *see* Satan
devotio moderna 518, 577
devotion
  see also spirituality
  Christian living 516
  Church of England 583
  Mary 680–1
  Middle Ages 558–75, 576–7, 583
dharmas 623
d'Herbelot, Barthélemy 306–7
Diadochus, Bishop of Photice 538
diakonia 658
dialectic
  Hegelian 354
  Marxist 358
Diatessaron 111
Didache 49
Diderot, Denis 256, 264
Diet of Worms 241
Dilthey, Wilhelm 878, 880
DiNoia, J. 298, 302
Dionysius the Areopagite *see* Denis the Areopagite
Dionysius the Carthusian 346, 577
dipolarity, concept of God 363, 402

discipleship
  ethics 693, 711
  friendship 587
discourse, religious 420–4
discrimination, sexual 490
disease, attitude towards 817–18
disobedience, sin 704–6
Dissenters, State 778
divine command theory 700
divine inspiration
  biblical theology 67
  historical–critical exegesis 125
  New Testament 109–10
  Old Testament 47–8
divine intervention 876
Divine Liturgy, Orthodox Church 561
Divine Office, Middle Ages 560
divorce
  celibacy 753
  children 755–6
  conciliation 755
  human rights 745
  psychology 805, 808
  sinful 707
docetism 927, 929
doctors 817–18, 835–7
  see also medicine
doctrine
  adaptive 986, 987
  Church of England 976–7
  cognitive status 993–5
  coherence 977–9
  contemporary reinterpretation 875
  development 219
  ethics 693
  formative 986, 987
  Middle Ages 558, 563–4
  New Testament sources 109, 111–13
  normative 985–7, 997
  systematic theology 976–98
  wealth 761–5
dogmatics 976–1000
  see also systematic theology
  apologetics 981, 991
  authority 990–1
  biblical interpretation 67, 72
  coherence of 977–80
  contemporary 984–5
  definition 976, 991
  discipline of the given 988–90
  eclecticism 983
  ecumenical concensus 998

inter-faith dialogue 992–3
narrative theology 968, 971
total perspective 996
Dolto, Françoise 1021
domestic church 676–7, 807
domination
    feminism 499
    justice 505
    male 500
    sin 501–2
Dominic, St 216
Dominicans 215, 216, 217, 221
Donatists, Tyconius 52
Donne, John 583
Dostoevsky, F., evil 472, 484–5, 486
Dowell, Susan 738
doxastic duties 368, 379
Dragonnades 264
drama, liturgical 59, 62
dread, numinous feeling 621
Drees, W. B. 446, 447
dual covenant 304–5
dualism
    Cartesian 850, 853
    Cathars 564–5
    embodiment 747–8
    Enlightenment 856
    environmentalism 843, 852–6
    ethical 853–4
    evil 476–7
    feminist theology 492, 523
    God and the World 944
    health 823
    human nature 454, 460, 461
    Manicheism 475–6
    materialism and spirituality 643
    metaphysical 853
    patriarchy 503–4
    physical 853
    rationalism 744
    scientific understanding 438, 442, 445
    self 456–8
Duffy, Eamon 672
Dunn, James 124, 1024
Dunstan, Gordon 827

Eadmer, *Life of St Anselm* 561
early church
    Christology 124
    diversity 92
    New Testament focus 96–8
    Scripture 104

worship 665–6
writings 90
Earth
    body of God 504
    Gaia hypothesis 850–2
Easter 576, 1030–1
Eastern Empire
    see also Byzantine Emperors
    Church and state 207
    relation to West 207–11
Eastern Orthodox Church
    devotion 561
    doctrinal development 222–3
    ethics 708
    Filioque 949
    iconoclasm 207, 208, 331
    iconography 323, 330–1, 642
    marriage of priests 214
    mystical theology 517
    prayer 669–70
    Theosis 702
    tradition role 3
    Trinity 940
Ebbo, devotion to Mary 566–7
Ebeling, Gerhard 905, 912, 1021
Ebner, I-Thou philosophy 920
Ecclesiastes 16, 40, 69
Ecclesiasticus 12, 19
ecclesiocentricism 293
ecclesiology, ethics 709–10
Eckhart, Johannes 217, 360, 569, 577, 578
ecofeminism 864
ecology
    see also environmentalism
    feminism 504
    Old Testament 81–2
    spirituality 615
economics, feminism 497, 499
economy 194–6, 201–2, 941, 948–9
ecstasy 542, 544, 547
ecumenical theology 287–8, 1024
ecumenism
    Apostle's Creed 998
    liturgy 675
Edict of Milan 322
education
    clergy 1021
    laity 224, 1021
    Old Testament 75
    priests 223–4
    Religious Studies 891–3
Edwards, J. 620

Edwards, Jonathan 648
egalitarianism 66
Egocentric Predicament 371
egotism, sin 502
Egyptian influences, Old Testament stories 151
Eichrodt, Walther 78
election doctrine 919
Elijah 181
Eliot, T. S. 532, 671, 960
Elisha 817
Elizabethan Settlement 248
Ellacuría, I. 1006
Ellis, John 397
emanation, concept of God 344
emancipation, monasticism 542
embodiment
    body 738–9
    creation 747–8
    gender 752
    materialism 747–8
    nourishment 748
    transcendence 504
embryos
    experimentation 819, 825, 827
    life 827–8
emergence, scientific understanding 441
Emerson, Ralph Waldo 599–601
empathic listening 797–8, 814
empiricism
    concept of God 351
    design argument 374
    dominant role 341
    dualism 456
    sense-perception 371
    theological role 338–9
Empiricus, Sextus 370, 377
employment, sexism 1013
End see eschatology
Engelhardt, H. T. Jr. 839
English Civil War 255
Enlightenment 251–71
    anti-Trinitarian teaching 937
    atheism 897
    belief in Jesus Christ 917–18
    biblical reading 158
    Christ and culture 316
    doctrine of God 900, 904, 907, 911
    dualism 850, 856
    empiricism 341
    erosion of values 945–6
    eternal truths 123

feminism 491, 492
    hermeneutics 966, 967
    human understanding 594, 597
    influence 608
    legacy of 273, 872–3
    liberation 942
    modern mentality 922
    narrative 972–3
    natural religion 620
    New Testament interpretation 102
    objectivism 858
    Old Testament interpretation 64–5
    progress 263–4
    rationalism 457, 458
    Roman Catholic Church 890
    scepticism 512
    science 856
    spirituality 512, 518–19, 532
    systematic theology 979
    theism revisions 900–6
    theodicy 472, 477
    theological credibility 981
Enoch 181
enthusiasm, eighteenth century 256–7
environmental ethics 843–68
environmentalism
    conservationism 847
    consumer ethics 765–6
    creation stories 761
    dualism 852–6
    liberation theology 1014
    love 696
    Nazis 857
    return to nature 864
    stewardship 866
epektasis 550
Ephesians, Epistle 98
episcopal appointments 209, 211, 212
epistemology
    chauvinism 380
    concept of reason 379
    Enlightenment 947
    feminism 491, 492, 495
    foundationalism 371, 372, 373
epistles
    see also Paul, St
    context 117
    Ephesians 98
    Hebrews 97
    New Testament genre 86–8
    pastoral 98
    Philemon 86

rhetorical analysis 119
  Timothy 98
  Titus 98
equality, economic 768
equivocity 426
Erasmus, Desiderius
  Catholic Reformation 584
  core doctrine 255
  Greek New Testament 238–9, 577
  rhetoric 582–3
  sceptical fideism 377
  Spanish Catholic reform 585
Erikson, E. 798–805, 808–9
Ernst, C. 147
eros 503, 539–40, 701–2, 745–6
eroticism, personhood 503
eschatology
  contemporary views 924–6
  cosmic 131–5
  ethics 709–10
  Eucharist 614, 670, 674
  Hebrew Bible 39–41
  Jesus' teaching 882
  liberation theology 1007
  narrative 965
  neo-orthodoxy 918
  New Testament writers 49
  secularization 890, 891
  spirituality 525, 531–2
Esler, Philip 130
esoteric believers 293
essence, Christianity 989–90, 997–8
essentialism 502–3, 503
eternal existence, Plato 61
eternity 912
ethics 687–715
  see also morality
  Bible 687, 711
  bioethics 780, 819
  business 771–4
  Christian distinctiveness 693–8
  consumers 765–6
  dualism 853–4
  environmental 843–68
  feminism 491, 492, 505–6
  medical 769, 780, 817–42
  moral agents 700–7
  personal 738–58
  resurrection 708–9
  sacramental 708
  scientific understanding 439
  shareholders 766–7, 773

spirituality 707–9
  universally human 697–8
  war 716–37
ethology 467
eucatastrophe, narrative 964–5
Eucharist
  central position 652–3
  community 888
  consubstantiation 245
  creed 187, 189
  future theology of 1032
  Holy Spirit 198
  medieval devotion 563–4
  Middle Ages 576, 583
  New Testament 537
  presence of Christ 245
  Roman Catholicism 612, 614
  spirituality 665–72
  transsignification 245
  Trinity 939
Eugenius IV, Pope 225
Eunomius, Trinity 200–2
Eusebius 54, 144, 147, 542
euthanasia 819, 822, 831–3
Evangelicals
  piety 516
  preaching 681
  radicalism 658–9
evangelism
  exclusivism 297
  state morality 779
evidential philosophy 339–40, 380
evil
  human nature 454, 463
  illness 818
  omnipotent God 899
  oppression 1005
  Plotinus' teaching 343–6
  poverty 1009
  problem of 338, 472–89
  scientific understanding 445
  society 1005, 1008
  theodicy 890
  theological responses 340
evolution
  creation 931
  omega point 932
  reality of God 398
  scientific understanding 434, 436, 440
  sociobiology 466
  Teilhard de Chardin 932
exclusivism

analysis of 296–9
pluralist view of 292–4
Trinity doctrine 952
exegesis
  see also biblical interpretation
  Alexandrian 5, 105–7
  Antiochene 107
  Christology 43–4
  eighteenth century 257–9
  Greek 147
  historical–critical 69–70, 73, 122–30,
    1022
  Jewish 102
  Jungian approach 126
  Latin 52
  liberation 118
  materialist 1030
  medieval 5, 107–8
  Old Testament 43–4, 47–9
  pre-modern 103–5
  presuppositions 118–19
  theology contrast 107, 123–4, 128
Exile, Hebrew Bible formation 7–27
existentialism
  concept of God 359–61
  meaning of Christ 920–2
  post-modernism 605–7
  scientific understanding 437, 438, 440,
    441
  theodicy 488
  Wordsworth 599
Exodus
  authoritative nature 28
  narrative 8, 968–70
  Third World countries 1001
  utopian vision 1007
exoteric believers 293
experience see conversion experiences;
    religious experience
experience-reinterpretation model 135–9
experiential knowledge 522
experimental perception 632
extra calvinisticum 580
extrovertive mysticism 622, 623
Ezekiel 13, 28–9, 62
Ezra, prophetic era 16, 20

Faber, Hieje 530
fairy stories 958–9, 964–5
faith
  challenge 606
  critical theology 1017

eucharistic 888
formation 636
Gospel accuracy 921
historical Jesus 882
imagination 970
Jahwists 78
New Testament interpretation 109
political action 1006
praxis 1002–3
pre-Descartes interpretations 367–70
propositions 630
relationship to God 811–12
sin 703–4
statements of 86
trust 804
Faith and Order Movement 288
Fall
  see also original sin
  corruption 701
  eighteenth century attitudes 253, 263
  embodiment 748
  Hexaemeron studies 61–2
  historical event 876
  image of God 548–9
  narrative 876
  New Testament inclusion 112
  nineteenth century attitudes 72, 73
  patristic spirituality 548, 549
  rationalization 68
  scientific understanding 435
  sexism 747
false vacancy 645
falsification principle 414–16
family
  see also children; marriage; parents
  domestic church 676–7
  Jesus' teachings on 175
'family values' 779
Farges, Albert 631–2
Farmer, H. H. 364
fascination, numinous feeling 621
fasting, domestic church 677
Father
  see also God; Son; Trinity
  feminist theology 952
  impersonal deity 949
  meaning 201
  Old Testament 201–2
  relationship to Son 168, 938
Fathers of the Church
  see also patristic theology
  commentaries 559

feasts, Middle Ages 576
Feathers Tavern Petition 256
feelings
  feminism 491, 492
  numinous 621–2
  religious 620
  Romanticism 595, 598–9, 601
fellowship, divine/human 73
feminism
  creation 747
  ecofeminism 864
  history 884–8
  Judaism 1013–14
  language 491, 492, 498, 741–2
  liberation theology 1013–14
  personal ethics 738
  personalism 742
  radical 491–2
  socialist 491, 492–3, 494, 495
  tradition 739–40
  witches 864
feminist theology
  biblical interpretation 79–81, 127
  Christ, uniqueness 984–5, 989
  concept of God 357
  culture 315
  ethics 713
  feminine aspects of God 885–6, 887
  future 871
  history 284–6, 884–8
  metaphors 498, 907–8
  method 986
  models of God 906
  narrative 970, 971–2
  natural theology 404
  patriarchy 983
  philosophy 490–508
  pluralism 296
  post-modernism 341
  relatedness of the divine 912, 914
  religious language 430
  self-criticism 984
  self-sacrifice 696
  source criticism 983, 988
  spirituality 521, 522–3, 526, 609–10, 656–8
  structural sin 706
  symbolism 907–8
  Trinity 905, 952
Fénelon, François de Salignac de la Mothe 647
fertility, personal ethics 749

Feuerbach, Ludwig Andreas 403, 496
fiction see fairy stories; myth; narrative
fideism 367, 373, 377–8
fidelity, relationships 752–3, 756
figurative interpretation 51–4, 102, 148
Filioque 210, 949
Finney, C. G. 648, 651, 658
Finnis, John 819
Fiorenza, Elisabeth Schüssler 285, 495, 885, 887
First Crusade 210
First World, liberation theology 1010–11
Five Joys of Mary 566
Flannery, A. 877
Fletcher, Joseph 700, 828, 831
Flood, early sources 150
Florence, Council of 225
Florovsky, Georges 669
foetal surgery 829
food
  grace 748
  taboos 38–9
Foreman, Robert 627
Forest, Jim 655
forgiveness
  emotional development 800–1
relationships 814
form criticism 25, 117, 122
formative doctrine 986, 987
Former Prophets 9, 16, 145
Forms, Platonic teaching 344
Foster, Michael 434, 435
Foucault, Michel 500, 608, 972, 1022
foundationalism
  concept of reason 370–3
  decline of 368, 379–84
  epistemology 371, 373–6
  modern theology 331
  pluralism 295
  scientific understanding 436
Fourth Crusade 218
Fourth Lateran Council 216, 566
Fowler, R. M. 129
Fox, George 678
Fox, Matthew 852
Francis of Assisi, St 216, 218, 563
Franciscans 216, 217, 221, 585
Francisco de Osuna 585–6
Frankfurt School 285, 996
Free Brethren 645
free will
  compatibilism 480

Old Testament history 73–4
  patristic spirituality 550–3
  secularization 891
  theodicy 478–84, 487
freedom
  creation doctrine 345–6
  feminism 497
  human 942, 946, 951–3
  individual 779
Frei, Hans 280–3, 876, 966, 966–7, 972
Freire, Paulo 790
French Revolution 252, 725
Freud, Sigmund 403, 504, 796, 797
friars 216–18
Friedrich, G. 1020
friendship
  agape 744–5
  discipleship 587
  feminism 504
  personal ethics 752
  personhood 503
  single people 808
Fries, Jacob Friedrich 70, 620, 630
Frye, Northrop 966
Fuchs, Josef 697–8, 708, 826
functionalism, concept of God 357–8
fundamentalism
  apologetics 981–2
  biblical codes of conduct 699
  orthodoxy 278, 280
'fusion of horizons' 881, 888

Gabler, J. P. 67–9
Gadamer, Hans-Georg 604, 881, 887
Gaia hypothesis 615, 850–2, 865
Gale, Richard 364
Galilea, Segundo 660
Galileo 370, 372, 437
gamete donation 826
Gardeil, Père 632
Garrigou-Lagrange, R. M. 519, 630
Geist 944
gemara 37
gender
  embodiment 752
  feminism 492
  God 498
  importance 741
  language 741–2
  roles 740
  sin 501–2
generosity, personalism 744

genes
  gene therapy 823
  genetic engineering 490
  human genome project 823
  responsibility 469, 470
  scientific understanding 438
  sociobiology 465, 467–8
Genesis
  authoritative nature 28
  creation 54
  historical narrative 8
  older texts 150–1, 155
Geneva, Reformation 240, 241–2
genre
  epics 150
  Hebrew literature 7–27
  holy book 142
  New Testament 88–9, 111
geology, scientific understanding 434
German Confessing Church 278
Gertrude of Helfta 498
Ghandi, Mohandas K. (Mahatma) 1030
Gifford, Adam 399
Gifford Lectures 399, 401
Gilkey, L. 447, 902–903
Gilligan, Carol 505
Gilson, Etienne 392
Glanvill, Joseph 853
global theology 283
Glory of God 558–61
Gloss 107
Gnostics
  art 329–30
  biblical interpretation 104–5, 106
  creation 61
  Gospel composition 111
  grace 550–1
  nature 862
  Romantic influence 602
  spirituality 543–4, 643
  Trinity 945
God
  see also Father; Holy Spirit; Kingdom of
    God; Son; Trinity; Word of God
  absolute nature 536, 898, 900, 910–11
  absolute power 234
  all-loving 293, 294–5, 298
  arguments for existence of 391, 394–5,
    398, 400, 562
  attributes of 392, 399
  authoritarian figure 812–13
  Beauty 330, 539–40

being of beings 903–4
black theology 908
causation 899–900
communion with 77–8, 939
concept of 339, 340, 342–66, 497–501
cosmic conciousness 603
death of 905–6, 911, 945
dependence on 595, 812–13
divine-human relationship 13, 73–4,
    611, 613, 811–13, 953
doctrine of 295, 300, 947
dualism 504, 944
encounter 606
eschatology 132–3
ethics and morality 65, 700, 704, 901
feminist theology 492, 885–6, 887, 952,
    1013
Glory of 558–61
Hebrew world-view 79
historical acts 9, 10, 78–9
human welfare 899
image of 547–50
impersonal deity 949
indigenization 909
innate knowledge of 254
internalization 800, 811
knowledge of 539, 542, 548, 578, 943
language 424–30
liberal view 75
liberation theology 79–80
love 80, 202–3, 745–6, 801, 804, 810–11,
    951–2
Lutheran theology 578–80
male representation 496–7, 498
natural theology 388–412
non-realist 873
omega point 615, 901, 913, 932
omnipotent 899
Other 511
parent analogy 480–1, 483
patristic spirituality 538–41
post-modernist meaning of 996–7
poverty 908–9, 1009
providence 890–1
quest for 511, 512, 541–2
reason 369–71, 373–8, 380–4
redeemer 703–4
relationality 900–1, 910–11, 917, 938–9,
    990
religious experience 630–2, 634–5, 636
repression 942, 950
Roman Catholicism 611–15

scientific understanding 441–3, 895, 900
self 902
as spirit 275–6, 277–8
suffering 822, 911
temporality 901, 912–13
terminology 413
theism 895–915
transcendence of 71, 180, 898, 914
Trinity 187–203, 937–56
wealth 760
Yahweh 79
Goddess 500–1, 850–1, 864, 907
Godmanhood 920–2, 929
gods
    Egyptian 153–4
    Greek 71
Goethe, Johann Wolfgang von 256, 327
Gogarten, Friedrich 698, 922–4, 923
Goldberg, Michael 967
Gospel of John
    accuracy 176
    divinity of Christ 94, 180–1, 812
    doctrine 111
    Incarnation 124
    prologue 96–7
    Synoptic Gospels 117
    theological nature 92
    Word of God 169, 192
Gospel of Luke 93–4, 104, 111
Gospel of Mark 93, 111, 117, 135
Gospel of Matthew 93, 98, 111, 117, 129
Gospel of Thomas 97, 104
Gospels
    accuracy 175
    diversity 92–4
    earlier texts 123
    form-criticism of 920–1
    genre 88, 111
    historical accuracy 920
    imaginative reflection 590–1
    interpretation 117, 122, 528, 658–9, 879,
        920–2
    interrelationship 129
    missionary theology 1029–30
    moral teaching 98
    myth 960
    narrative 972
    pagan philosophy debate 337–8
    secularization 277
    synoptic 175–6, 920–1
    Trinity 949
Gottwald, N. K. 79, 127

government, appointed by God 717
grace
  doctrine debate 114
  exclusivism 298–9
  history 77
  inclusivism 299–301
  irresistibility 581–2
  Luther 109
  Old Testament Law 57–9
  patristic spirituality 550–3
  Reformation 244
  Roman Catholicism 611
  unconditional 801
Graham, Billy 651
Gratian, *Decretum* 212–13
Great Awakening 620
Great Schism 206, 225–6
Great War *see* World War I
Grebel, Conrad 242
El Greco 584
greed
  business 769
  market economy 767–8
  poverty 1009
Greek
  Hebrew Bible translation 30
  New Testament language 151–2
  use in Palestine 173
Greek Bible *see* Septuagint
Greek Orthodox Church
  conflicts with Pope 208–10
  devotion 561
  reunification with West 219, 225
  separation from West 206
Greek philosophy
  concept of God 343–6
  human nature 454
greenhouse effect, Gaia 851
Gregory I, Pope *see* Gregory the Great
Gregory VII, Pope 210
Gregory X, Pope 219
Gregory the Great, St
  exegesis 107
  Ezekiel 62
  figurative interpretation 52
  Job 62
  mission to England 208
  Old/New Testaments relationship 50
  prophecy 55–6
  visual art 330
Gregory of Nazianzus
  Fall 549

Father and Son 202
  God as beauty 539
  Holy Spirit 198–9
  theology and morality 555
Gregory of Nyssa
  biblical language 200–2
  darkness 542, 544–7
  economy 195
  Fall 549–50
  free will 552
  God as beauty 539–40
  Holy Spirit 199
  Lord's Prayer 537
  progress 549–50
  spirituality 554, 556, 643–4
Gregory of Rimini 233, 235–6
Gregory of Tours 54
Grey, Mary 610, 886
Griffin, David 361
Grillparzer, Franz 880
Grisez, Germain 819
Grosseteste, Robert 213
Guéranger, Dom Prosper 652
guerrilla warfare 733, 1006
Guevara, Che 733
Guibert of Nogent 52, 53
guilt
  emotional development 801
  traditionalism 810
Gulf War 722, 727–8
Gunkel, Hermann 76
Günther, Anton 74
Gustafson, James 687, 829
Gutiérrez, Gustavo 789–91
  faith 1002–4, 1006
  poverty 1009–10
  spirituality 522, 660
  unemployment 1012
Guyon, Madame 647

Hadewijch of Antwerp 498
haggada 34, 37, 102
hagiography 567
Haight, Roger 611
Hail Mary 566
halakha 34, 36, 37, 102
Hampson, Daphne 499, 501–2, 886
Hampson, N. 258
Hanson, P. 131–2, 136
Hanson, Richard 682
Hare, R. M. 419, 421
Häring, Bernard

biblical bases for ethics 697
doctor-patient relationship 836–7
embryo experimentation 827
Free and Faithful in Christ 697
Law of Christ 697
suffering and death 831
Harnack, Adolf von
dogma 404
essence of Christianity 989
historical Jesus 274, 926–7
moral life 902
Harris, Rendel 678
Harrison, Beverly 492, 505
Hartshorne, Charles
natural theology 401, 402
process theology 361, 900
religious language 430
Hartsock, Nancy 492
Harvey, Anthony 971
Hatch, Edwin 404
hatred, Scripture theme 132
Hauerwas, Stanley M.
Christ and culture 316
Christian community 659
ethics 694, 695, 697
good and evil 708
suffering 830–1, 838
Hawking, Stephen 446
Haydn, Franz Joseph 316
healing
fragmentation 502
history 817–18
personhood 503
salvation 837
health, medical ethics 817–42
heaven, Hebrew Bible 41
Hebraica veritas 48
Hebrew Bible
see also Bible; Old Testament
apocrypha 29
authorship 8
context 21
eschatology 39–41
formation 4, 7–27, 28–9
interpretation 3, 32–8, 147–8
liberation theology 1001
poverty and wealth 1009
religious focus 45
secular texts 2224
translation 30–2
Hebrew Christians 305
Hebrew language 48, 68, 151, 155

Hebrew nation 69, 70, 77, 79, 342–3
see also Israel; Judaism
Hebrews, epistle 97
Hegel, Georg Wilhelm Friedrich
concept of God 354, 355, 357
death of God 911
feminism 492
history 71, 76, 605–6, 879
Marxism 357–8
natural theology 404
reason 274
theological construction 337
Trinity 937, 944–5
Heidegger, Martin
creativity 907
existentialism 359–60, 607, 921
God as being of beings 903–4
National Socialism 857
philosophical theology 281
Heilgesichte 73
Hell
concept of God 350, 352
solipsism 750
Hellenistic culture
Judaism 30, 32
Palestine 173
world-view 896, 910
Heloise 214
Helsinki Accords 782
Helsinki, Declaration of 834
Henle, Paul 638
Henry II of England 212
Henry VIII of England 247
Heracleon 105
Herbert of Cherbury, Baron Edward 350, 394
Herbert, George 582–3, 676
Herder, Johann Gottfried 67–9, 155
heresy
biblical study 105
iconoclasm 208
inquisition 217
Middle Ages 564–5, 568–9
passive prayer 586
philosophical debate 368
Spanish Catholic reform 586
hermeneutics
feminist theology 983, 988
narrative 966–7
spirituality 526–9
hermeneutics of suspicion 80, 286, 526, 529, 609

Herodotus 148
hesed 79
Hesychast spirituality 222
Hexaemeron 61
Hexapla 51
Heyward, Carter 503
Hibbert Lectures 404
Hick, John
  ambiguity 382–3, 418
  evil 474
  exclusivism criticism 298
  free-will defence 482
  global theology 283
  God and the Universe of Faiths 276, 892
  Incarnation 138
  interfaith dialogue 308
  The Myth of God Incarnate 276, 892
  reality 357
  religious language 430
  theocentricism 293–5
Hilary of Poitiers 195–7, 951–2
Hildegard, visions 569
Hilton, Walter 572, 572–3
Hinduism
  all-loving God 294
  indigenization 909
  inter-faith dialogue 992–3
  love-mysticism 623
  statistics 291
  stories 968
Hippolytus, prayer 673, 674
historical relativism 878–84
historical-critical method, New Testament
  103, 117, 122–30
historicism 778–84, 878–84, 880–1, 922–4
historicity
  Jesus Christ 95, 100
  New Testament events 122–3
  Old Testament events 73, 77–9, 127
Histories, Christian Old Testament 145
historiography, Israel 8–9
history
  divine goal 902
  eighteenth century attitudes 257–9
  feminism 884–8
  Gospel inaccuracy 920–1
  historical method 879
  Jesus of history 274–5
  Judaism 1007
  Luke and Acts 93–4
  narrative theology 973

New Testament interpretation 103–10,
  116–17, 120
  Old Testament *vs* academic 77–9
  philosophy 878
  praxis 1002–5
  prophetic interpretation 54–7
  religions 70, 71–2, 76
  scientific understanding 439
  spirituality 526, 532
  temporality 913
HIV sufferers, discrimination 660–1
Hobbes, Thomas
  ethics 505
  human nature 464, 465
  personhood 503
Hofmann, Johannes Christian Konrad von
  73–4, 78
holiness
  books 142–6
  spirituality 525
Holiness Code 10, 15, 691, 705
Holiness movement 257, 268, 658
holism
  feminism 504
  patristic spirituality 548
Hollenweger, W. J. 1019
Holocaust 304, 911, 950–1
holocaust literature 324–5
Holy Bread 537
holy days, apostles 214
Holy Grail 564
Holy Land, Medieval pilgrimages 568
Holy Spirit
  bridge between Father and Son 904
  Cappadocian theology 939
  feminine image 287
  love 202–3, 702–3
  manifestation 666
  nature of 197–200, 898
  patristic spirituality 542, 544
  prayer 678–9
  priority 949
  Scripture 109–10, 198–9
  subordinate to Son 949
holy war 716, 719–20, 730
Homer, *Odyssey* 963
homoousion 938, 940
homosexuality 705, 753, 807–8
Hooker, Richard
  assurance doctrine 582
  core doctrine 255
  ethics 697

Of the Laws of Ecclesiastical Polity 979
Hopkins, Gerard Manley 326
Hosea 13
Houlden, Leslie 135
house-groups 1018
household religion 676–7
Huddleston, Trevor 651–2
Huff, T. E. 435
Hugh of St Cher 56
Hugh of St Victor
  Bible unity 50
  biblical teaching 107–8
  devotion 563
  irony 53
  literal sense 52
  spirituality 517
Hughes, Gerard, ethics 698
Huizinga, Johann, symbolism 576
human experimentation 833–5
human genome project 823
human nature
  anthropology 453
  idea of 458–65
  sociobiology 468
  theories of 340–1
human rights
  business 768
  Marxism 783
  natural law 779–82
  personalism 745
human self-manipulation 819
humanism
  anonymous thinking 1022
  gender 742
  Medieval 577, 578
  moral cohesion 838
  personalism 745
  Renaissance 236–9
  scientific, secularization 890, 891
  sin 717
  state morality 781
humanity
  Old Testament 71
  solidarity 767, 769–70
Hume, David
  concept of God 351
  concept of reason 376
  dualism 456
  human nature 459–60, 462
  natural theology 397
  sceptical fideism 377–8
  theodicy 472, 475, 484, 485

Hume, John
  An Enquiry Concerning Human
    Understanding 257
  Dialogues Concerning Natural Religion
    255, 257, 258, 261–3
  history 258
  intolerence 252
  miracles 257
  The Natural History of Religion 259
Humiliati 216
Hunt, Mary 503
Hunter, Anne 500
Hus, Jas 227
Hussein, Saddam 728
Hussitism 227
Huttites 584, 645
hygiene, Mosaic code 818
hymnody 667–8, 675
hymns, Psalms 12
hypostasis 939–40, 940

I-thou philosophy 920
iconoclasm 207, 208, 331
iconography 59–61, 323, 330–1, 642, 670
Idea, reason 630
idealism
  concept of God 353–5
  natural theology 400
  nineteenth 274, 275
ideological criticism 129–30, 132–4
idolatry
  Calvinism 318
  critique of 897, 913–14
  exclusivism 297, 298
Ignatius of Antioch 104, 194, 555
Ikeda, Daisatsu 844
illness
  evil 818
  religious offences 817
imagery
  apocalyptic literature 88–9
  Black 908
  feminine 498, 887, 907
  indigenous 909
  patristic spirituality 547–50
imagination
  contemplation 590–1
  relationship to faith 970
Immaculate Conception 244
immanence
  economy 948
  personal 751

transcendence 325–6
Trinity 944, 946
immortality, human nature 341, 454–6
imperialism 292, 296
impurity, ritual 38–9
in vitro fertilization 825, 827
incarnation
  Aquinas 349
  central theological position 642
  debate 138
  divine as flesh 906
  divine/human fellowship 73
  dualism 454
  erotic history 588–9
  evolution 931
  faith and reason 370
  Gospel of John 124
  Greek tradition 343, 344–5
  Hegelian interpretation 354
  historical relativism 882–3
  human nature 462
  humanity of Christ 929–30
  interpretation 138
  mysticism 629
  myth 995
  non-Christian view 993
  plurality 934
  revelation of God 105
  spirituality 513, 525, 645–6, 648
  temporality of divine 912
  wealth 763–4
  worship focus 602
inclusivism 292, 294, 299–302, 877, 952
inculturation
  Christology 1024–5
  inter-religious dialogue 303
  Islam 306
  Third World theology 287
independence, science and theology 447
indigenization
  God 909
  inter-faith dialogue 303
  Islam 306
  Judaism 305
  language 910
individualism
  absolute dependence 595–7
  America 601
  community 750
  Descartes 850
  dualism 854–5
  feminism 494

gender 503
health care ethics 824
human nature 464–5
personalism 743, 745
pietism 645–6
social order 951–2
sociobiology 465
spirituality 525, 526, 648
wealth 769–70
inductive reason 368
indulgences 219, 225–6, 240, 565
ineffability 343, 637–40
infanticide, malformed neonates 829
infinity, concept of God 351
injustice
  feminism 497–8
  sin 717
  Third World 1010
inner city, liberation theology 1011–12
Innocent III, Pope 216, 218, 219
Innocent IV, Pope 219
Inquisition 217, 565, 585
instruction literature 11
integration, science and theology 441–2,
    444–7, 449
intellectualism 235
inter-faith dialogue 126–7, 137–8, 291–313
inter-subjective bonding, feminism 491
inter-testamental period 5
intercession, theology of 565
interiority
  Lutheranism 579
  Middle Ages 577–9, 582
  Spanish Catholic reform 585
internalization 800, 811
international debt 772
International Monetary Fund 773
introvertive mysticism 622, 623
intuition 630
investitures, bishops 211–12
investment, ethical 766–7
IRA *see* Provisional IRA
Irenaeus, St
  economy 194
  eschatology 49
  Fall 549
  Gnostics 543, 548
  Gospel plurality 111
  Hebrew Scripture incorporation 147
  matter and spirituality 642
  monarchianism criticism 190
  New Testament canon 144

traditional interpretation 105
Irigaray, Luce 493, 496, 497, 504
Isaac 8, 179, 963–4
Isaiah
  Alan of Lille 63
  authoritative nature 28–9
  content 13–14, 17
  resurrection 40
Isidore of Seville 50, 53, 644
Islam
  all-loving God 294
  associators 203
  Christianity relationship 142–3, 149–50,
    168, 306–8, 877
  concept of God 347
  fundamentalist 719
  Jesus 1030
  Koran as holy book 149–50
  narrative 968
  sanctity of human life 718
  statistics 291
  war 719
Israel
  see also Hebrew nation; Judaism
  attitudes to wealth 759–60
  chosen people 1007–8
  Exile 7–27
  historiography 8–9
  law 9–10
  national literature 7–8, 20–1
  oppression 1001
  women 1013

Jacob 8
Jacobins 252, 267
Jahwist, theology 78
Jains 626
Jaki, Stanley 440, 447
James, epistle 97
James, William
  dualism 853
  experience 600, 602–5
  mystical ineffability 637
  natural theology 399
  religious feeling 620
  theism 378–9
Jantzen, Grace M. 341, 490–508, 605, 628,
  629
Jedin, Hubert 878
Jefferson, Thomas 844
Jenkins, David 1017
Jennings, T. W. Jr. 903, 912

Jenson, Robert W., Trinity 948
Jeremiah 13–14, 28–9
Jeremias, J. 672
Jerome 48, 50
Jerusalem
  medieval importance 568
  vision of peace 572
Jesuits 249, 584, 586
  see also Society of Jesus
Jesus Christ 168–86
  see also Christology; crucifixion; Son;
    Trinity
  anger 813
  atheist view 1030–1
  birth 182
  Calvinistic theology 580
  centrality of 168–72, 989
  concept of God 343
  critical theology 1025
  cultural relationship 316–21, 710
  death of 174
  divine goal 902
  divinity of
    current thought 917–36, 934
    Trinity 115–16, 188–9, 898, 937
    worship 180–1
  early Christian beliefs 92–5
  eschatological teaching 132–3, 882,
    924–5
  ethics 692–3, 695, 708–9, 711
  existentialist interpretation 920–2
  feminism 495, 498–9
  God-consciousness 596
  healer 818, 824
  historical
    contemporary view 183–4, 933
    context of Gospels 95–6, 172–5,
      881–2, 920–1, 931–2
    critical method 117–18
    early church 181–3
    indirect writings 95, 100
    objectivity 274–5
  humanity of
    current thought 933–4
    Deism 254–5
    doctrine of election 919
    human nature 462–3
    liberation theology 1004–5
    medieval devotion 561–5
    paradox 927–8
    Roman Catholicism 930–2
    systematic theology 990

identity 917–18
imagery
  contemporary 917–36
  early 322
  eighteenth century 255, 259–61, 267
  nineteenth century 274
  twentieth century 881–2
incarnation 588–9
Judaism 94, 304
judge 566
kingdom of God teaching 175–7
Koran 306
as legislator 254–5
liberation theology 286, 461–2
liberator 926–7
Lutheran theology 578–9
man of sorrows 563
marriage 748, 751
Marxist view 1030–1
mediator 540–1
medieval devotion 561–5
Messiahship 43–4, 115
Muslim view 1030
narrative 971
neo–orthodoxy 918–20
new Adam 61, 560
New Being 989
New Testament depiction 6, 87, 93–6, 124
Old Testament fulfilment 47, 49, 65, 70, 89, 104
omega point 615
Orthodox emphasis 670
patristic spirituality 538–41
Paul's view 99
poverty 221, 1009
prayer to 168, 180, 538–41
pre-existence 169, 929
prophecy 174–5, 179, 931–2
Redeemer 694
relationship to God 536, 812, 904
religious symbol 1030–1
resurrection of 124, 175, 177–80
revelation 109
Roman Catholicism 930–3
Ruler of universe 322
sacrifice 179–80, 881
saints' lives 567
secular interpretation of 922–4
self-acceptance 809, 810
Son of God 176
Son of man 176

structuralist interpretation 1022
suffering 500, 822, 911
supernaturalistic 990
systematic theology 989
theological meaning 100
two natures 115
uniqueness 984–5
wealth 759, 760–1, 762–3, 775
Wisdom 169, 190–1
women 885
Word of God 169, 191–2, 920, 923
Jesus Christ Superstar 1031
Joachim of Fiore 55, 221
Joan of Arc 570
Job
  environmentalism 866
  experiential exploration 69
  Gregory the Great 62
  life after death 40
  wisdom 11, 16
John, St 536
  see also Gospel of John; Revelation of John
John XXII, Pope 220, 221
John XXIII, Pope 164
John Chrysostom, St 107, 673
John of the Cross, St
  The Ascent of Mount Carmel/Dark Night of the Soul 589
  categorization of experience 627
  Catholic Reformation 584
  culture 323
  darkness 646–7
  imagery 624
  ineffability 639–40
  The Living Flame of Love 589
  Spiritual Canticle 590
  spirituality 588–9
  'wisdom of love' 631–2
John of Damascus, St 203–4, 642–3
John of Freiburg 223
John of Naples 220
John of Salisbury 574
John Paul II, Pope 707, 835
Johnson, E. 905
Joint Liturgical Group 675
Joseph II, Emperor 264
Josephus 16, 29, 32, 48, 66
Joshua 8, 15, 28–9
Joyce, James, *Ulysses* 960
Jubilee law 66, 82, 650
Judaeus, Hermmanus 52

Judah, history 18
Judah the Prince, Rabbi 36–7
Judaism
   see also Hebrew nation; Israel
   academic theology 892
   all-loving God 294
   biblical interpretation 137–8
   Christianity
      relationship 99–100, 104, 168, 181,
         303–6
      split 44–5, 180–1, 188
   Christ's divinity 180–1, 188
   concept of God 347
   cultural expression 320
   Dead Sea Scrolls 173
   death of God theology 911
   discrimination against women 1013
   evolution 72
   feminism 1013–14
   foundation documents 21
   God's care 454
   heavenly mediators 180–1
   Hellenization 30, 32
   history 879, 1007
   images 322
   inter-faith dialogue 992
   Jesus' relationship 94
   liberation theology 1001, 1007
   messianic Jews 305
   moral action 1007–8
   narrative 968–70
   Old Testament 169–70
   post-Exile development 28
   poverty 1009
   rabbinical communities 33–4, 35–6
   revelatory status 298–9
   rituals 38–9
   Roman Catholic Church 877
   sanctity of human life 718, 818–19
   Shema 188, 195–6
   sickness and death 817–18
   Spanish radicalism 584–5
   statistics 291
   suffering 179, 1009
   temple sacrifice 881
   war 719
Judgement, purgatory doctrine 112
Judgement Day, concept of God 343
Judges 8, 28–9
Julian of Norwich
   devotion to Jesus 538
   female metaphor 498

matter and spirituality 642
   mysticism 571–2, 605
   Revelation of Divine Love 183, 571–2
   Showing 528
Jung, Carl Gustav 796, 958–9
Jüngel, Eberhard
   death of God 945
   divine suffering 911
   Trinity 904, 947, 948, 950–1
Jungmann, Joseph 666
just war 716–19
   arms trade 735–6
   conscientious objectors 736
   Gulf War 727–8
   holy war 719–20
   nuclear deterrence 726
   pacifism 720–2
   realism 722–4
   rebellion 730–5
   terrorism 735
justice
   agape 696, 824
   ethics 505–6
   God 499–500
   paganism 501
   social 767–71, 788–9
justification, doctrine of
   by faith 57, 109, 606, 611, 672
   language-games 422
   Martin Luther 241, 244
   Old Testament events 65
   scholasticism 235–6
Justin Martyr 189, 669, 981
Justinian, conquest of Italy 208

Kafka, Franz 327
Kähler, Martin 274–5
Kant, Immanuel
   aesthetic symbols 329
   concept of God 351–2, 353–4, 357
   concept of reason 372, 373, 376
   deism 351
   feminism 497
   God and science 901
   human reason 273
   intolerance 252
   language 419
   modalism 949
   moral conviction 267
   natural theology 397–8, 399, 400, 404,
      621

Religion within the Limits of Reason Alone
254
religious experience 257, 269
salvation 253
scientific understanding 437
spiritual perception 630
theological construction 337
transcendence 594
Trinity 944
Karlstadt, Andreas Bodenstein von 241
Käsemann, Ernst 124
Katz, Steven T. 625–6
Kaufman, Gordon D. 138, 281, 902, 906,
913
Kavannagh, Aidan 669, 670, 680, 682
Keats, John 482
Kehl, Medard 132–3, 136
Kellogg, Robert 963–4
Kelly, J. N. D. 197
Kelly, Thomas R. 678
Kempe, Margery 570, 571–2
kenosis 906
kenoticism 919
Kermode, Frank 961
kerygma 78, 658
Ketuvim 29
Kevin, St 848
Kierkegaard, Søren
apologetics 982–3
Christ and culture 327
collectivism 606–7
concept of God 359
concept of reason 377, 384
liturgy 677–8
natural theology 403–4
neo-orthodoxy 918
relationship of God and man 919
subjectivity 275, 276
temporality of God 912
King James Authorized Version 149, 152
Kingdom of Christ 178
Kingdom of God
centrality 650
Christs' teaching 175–6
ethics 699, 709
immediate presence 560
meaning 137
praxis 1004
Kings 8, 18–19, 28–9
Kirchentag 1033
Kirk, K. E. 554–5, 699, 707–8
Klein, Melanie 800

Knitter, Paul 295–6
knowledge
dualism 503
feminism 492, 493
God 500
mystical 632–3
objectivity 859–60
sources of 494–7
Knox, Ronald 614
Kohlberg, – 505
koinōnia hagiōn 650
Koran 142, 149–50, 203–4, 306–7
Kort, Wesley 961, 963, 966
kosher rules 38
Krieck, Ernst 857
Kristeva, Julia 493
Küng, Hans 301, 893, 917
Kydones, Demetrios 222–3

Lacan, Jacques, nominalism 1022
Lacugna, C. M. 905
laity
apostles' status 214–15
biblical interpretation 1018
church role 614
education 224, 1021
piety 224–5
theology 1017–18
Thomism 223–4
Lambeth Conference 1988 789, 791
Lane, Dermot 524
Langer, Suzanne 907
language 413–32
Bible 149–52, 152, 157, 903
concept of God 357–8
desynonymization 939
empiricism 338
feminism 491, 492, 498, 741–2
gender 741–2
God 424–5, 498
human nature 453
Koran 149–50
male 498, 741–2
mysticism 637–40
narrative 420–1, 961
partriarchialism 886
preaching 582–3
prophecy 56–7
resources of 910
secularization 277–8
shared 460
sociobiology 468

spirituality 522, 526–7
structuralism 1022–3
symbolic 995
syncretism 1028–9
trust 801
language-games, definition 422
Lash, Nicholas 595, 603
Last Judgement 258
Last Supper, Lord's Prayer 537
Lateran Council, Fourth 216, 566, 612
Latin America
  biblical study 649
  liberation theology 908–9
  Mary's role 681
  spirituality 659–60
Latin Empire 218
Latin Vulgate *see* Vulgate Bible
Latitudinarianism 249, 254
Latter Prophets 145
Law *see* Pentateuch; Torah
Law, William 516
law genre
  canonization 15–16, 18
  context 22–3
  development 9–10
laws
  Israelites 81
  Jubilee 66, 82
  rabbinic Judaism 36
  Roman 435
  sexual behaviour 743
laymen, control of church appointments
  211
League of Nations 725
lectio divina 102
Leenhardt, Franz 530
Leeuwen, A. T. 276–7
legalism 744–5
legends 8
Lehmann, Paul 699–700
Leibnitz, Gottfried Wilhelm von 351, 361,
  373
Leo IV, Emperor 207, 209
Leo IX, Pope 210
Leslie, J. 430
Lessing, G. E.
  Christianity and religion 266–8
  The Education of the Human Race 266
  image of Jesus 259
  Reimarus 260
  religious intolerance 252
letters *see* epistles

Leuba, James, mystical perception 631
Lévi-Strauss, Claude 1022, 1023
Leviticus 28
Lewis, C. S. 961–2
liberal feminism 491
Liberal Protestantism 274
liberal theology 279
liberalism
  backlash against 754
  children 755–6
  Church leadership 778, 779–80
  human rights 782
  marriage 751, 752–3
  personalism 742, 745, 752
liberation
  feminism 495
  paganism 501
liberation theology
  biblical interpretation 79–80, 127–8,
    134, 137, 969–70
  black theology 655–6
  Christology 926–7
  completion doctrine 762
  concept of God 357, 358, 360
  consumerism 1011
  culture 315
  definition 279, 284–6
  divine temporality 913
  emergence 654–5
  environment 1014
  future of 871
  human nature 461
  inner city 1011–12
  Jewish tradition 1007–8
  Latin America 908–9
  making sense of God 907
  Marxism 1001–3, 1005–7, 1015
  oppression 659–61
  pluralism 293, 295–6
  poor 1009
  power and the state 789–92
  praxis 1001–4
  relatedness of the divine 912
  socialism 1006, 1008–9
  sociology 1008
  spirituality 521, 522, 649–51
  Third World 1009–10
  unemployment 1012–13
  violence 1006
  women 1013–14
life
  embryos 827–8

quality of 828–9
respect for 826
sanctity of 718, 818–19, 832–3
life after death, Hebrew Bible 39–41
light, patristic spirituality 541–7
likeness, patristic spirituality 547–50
Lindars, Barnabas 108
Lindbeck, George 301, 405–6, 887–8,
   993–5
Lindsey, Hal 131
literacy, laity 224–5
literalism 52, 107, 108
literary criticism 91, 125, 128–9
literary genre
   New Testament 86–9
   Scriptures 52–3
literature
   biblical influence 146–7
   Calvinism 582
   devotional 583
   Hebrew 7–27
   holocaust 324–5
   instruction 11
   medieval universities 329
   sentence 11
litigation, Church 212–13
Little Office of the Virgin 566
Liturgical Movement 652–3, 671
liturgy
   see also prayer; worship
   communal worship 665–76
   domestic church 677
   drama 59, 62
   meaning 665
   Middle Ages 560–1, 565
   patristic spirituality 538
   Psalms 12, 24
   ritualism 677–9
   set forms 668
   tradition 3
   Word/Sacrament balance 681
Liturgy of the Hours 675
Loades, Ann 886
Lochman, Jan Milic 998
Locke, John
   concept of reason 371, 374–5, 376
   core doctrine 255
   enthusiasm 256
   evidentialism 380
   natural religion 253–6, 395–6
   *The Reasonableness of Christianity as
     delivered in the Scriptures* 254, 257

resources 844
tolerance 255
logic, mystical experience 634
logical positivism 355–6, 405, 414–16
Logos
   see also Word of God
   Forms 345
   process theology 928
   Roman Catholicism 931–2
   Trinity 191–2, 344
   universal 934
Logstrup, Knud, ethics 698
Lollardy 227, 568
Lombard, Peter 213, 233, 947
Lombards, threat to Rome 208
Lonergan, Bernard 521–2
Lord's Prayer 537, 547, 666
Lord's Supper, Christ and the Spirit 950
Lossky, Vladimir 517, 545, 949
Lotze, Hermann 76
Louis XIV, Protestants 264
love
   agape 695–6
   caritas 702
   divine-human relationship 794
   for Earth 851
   eros 503, 539–40, 701–2, 745–6
   faith and hope 799–800
   God of 810–11
   Holy Spirit 702–3
   human experimentation 834
   marriage 749, 805–8
   mysticism 623–5, 632
   non-treatment of patients 830
   personalism 745–6
   procreation 825–6
   revolution 1006
   self 798, 810
   sexual 802–3, 807
   Trinity 202–3
   unconditional 801–2
Lovelock, James 850–1
Löwith, Karl 889–90
Lowman, Moses 66–7
Lowth, Robert 156
Loyola, St Ignatius
   devotion to Christ 538
   prayer and activity 646–7
   Spanish Catholic Reformation 584
   The Spiritual Exercises 527, 528, 590–1
   spirituality 518
Luke, St

see also Gospel of Luke
Jew/Gentile relationship 130
Lumen Gentium 612
les Lumières 251
Luther, Martin
  see also Enlightenment
  biblical interpretation 108–9
  biblical translation 157
  Christ and culture 317–18
  communicatio idiomatum 911
  consubstantiation 245
  death of God 945
  Disputatio contra scholasticam theologiam
    235–6
  dogmatics 978–9
  ethics 697
  faith 921
  justification doctrine 235–6, 241, 244
  Large catechism 703
  the Law 58
  The Liberty of a Christian 579
  natural theology 393
  Reformation 239–40, 241, 245
  sacraments 245
  sceptical fideism 377
  scholasticism 236
  Scripture 983
  simul justus et peccator 579
  Theologia Germanica 578
  'theology of glory' 578
Lutheranism
  Augsburg Confession 976
  distinction from Calvinism 247
  doctrine 248
  exclusivism 296
  individualism 647
  interiority 579
  Reformation 240–241
  spirituality 531
Lux Mundi school 275
LXX *see* Septuagint
Lyons, Council of 219
Lyotard, Jean-François 405, 972–3

Macarius of Egypt, *Macarian Homilies* 544
Maccabees 29, 41
McCormick, Richard 614, 829–30, 833,
  834–5
McFague, Sallie 504, 906
Machoveč, Milan 1030–1
MacIntyre, Alasdair 601, 616, 661, 838
Mackey, James 888, 944

Mackie, John 364, 480, 487
McMullin, E. 447
Macmurray, John 399
Macquarrie, John
  God as being of beings 904
  method 987
  natural theology 389
  phenomenology 281
  Principles of Christian Theology 977–8
magisterial Reformation 241, 243
Magisterium, apologetics 981
Mahoney, Jack 827
Maimonides, concept of God 347
Malbon, E., narrative criticism 128
Malcolm, Norman 401
Manicheism 475–6
Mao Zedong, Chairman 733–4, 790
Mappa Mundi 568
Marcion
  Gospel of Luke 104, 111
  Hebrew Scripture 14, 89, 298
  New Testament canon 144
Mariology 112
Maritain, Jacques 631–3
Mark
  see also Gospel of Mark
  character 128
market economy 767–9
marketing, ethics 773
marriage
  academics 213–14
  adolescents 803
  adultery 805
  annulment 240
  biblical basis 747, 748–9
  Cathars 218
  children 749, 755–6
  conciliation 755
  creation stories 748–9, 750–1
  dissolution of 220
  divorce 707, 805, 808
  doctrinal basis 114
  domestic church 676–7
  fidelity 752–3, 756
  generativity 805
  Greek Christianity 209
  in vitro fertilization 827
  male control 740
  one flesh union 747, 748
  personalism 751–2
  priests 214
  psychology 805–8

repressive traditions 707
role 739
sacrament 239
spirituality 807
unconsumated 220
Marti, Kurt 1025
Martin IV, Pope 219
martyrdom, Judaism 41
Marxism
African National Congress 788
Christian dialogue 783
feminism 492–3
functionalist analysis of 357–8
historicism 879
human nature 459, 460
liberation theology 790–1, 1001–3,
1005–7, 1015
natural theology 404
revolution 734
Mary, Virgin
cult of 566
devotion 680–1
emotional response 182–3
feasts 563
saviour 566
Mascall, Eric Lionel 401
mashiah 42
Mass
see also Eucharist
congregational participation 671–2
patristic spirituality 538
Tridentine 612
master-slave analogy, feminism 492
materialism
collectivism 792
dualism 456
embodiment 747–8
environmentalism 853, 855–6
human nature 455, 461
Jean Meslier 259–60
Marxism 783
sociobiology 466
spirituality relationship 643
mathematics, chance 444
matter
dualism 442
Manicheism 475–6
Matthew see Gospel of Matthew
Maurice, Frederick Denison 75, 78, 784
Maxmilla 542
May, William F. 819, 820, 831–2, 836
mechanics 351, 435, 444

medicine
covenanted profession 836, 837
doctor-patient relationship 835–7
ethics 769, 780, 817–42
natural 846
non-treatment 829
persistent vegetative state 833
Medieval Schools 107
meditation
Buddhist 626–7
Loyola's Spiritual Exercises 591
Spanish Catholic reform 585
megaliths 321
Meilaender, Gilbert, ethics 697
Mekhilta 34
Melanchthon, Philip 236, 245, 393
memoria 210
memorialism 245
men
control over women 740
gender roles 740
knowledge 859–60
objectivism 859
pleasure 739
mendicant movement 526
Mennonites 584
menstruation, taboos 500
mentalités, New Testament Palestine
882–3
mercy, God 499–500
merkavah 41
Merton, Thomas 615, 653–4, 659
Meslier, Jean 259–60
Mesopotamia 9–10, 151
Messiahship 41–4, 115, 176
messianic Jews 305
metalēpsis 53
metaphor 53
doctrine development 991
feminist 498, 907
mystical experience 639
New Testament 119
post-modernism 995
religious language 427–8
richness of 910
scientific understanding 448–9
Ugaritic texts 150–1
metaphysics
concept of reason 372
human nature 461
natural theology 405
theological role 338–9, 340

Methodism 516, 667
Metz, J. B. 982
Michael Cerularius, Patriarch 210
Michael VII, Emperor 210
Michael VIII Palaeologus, Emperor 219
Michaelis, Johann David 259, 260
Michel, Virgil 652
Michelangelo 327, 748
Micklem, Nathaniel 675
Middle Ages
    Christendom 206–29
    Church and State 207
    devotion 576–7
    Eastern and Western churches 207–8
    meaning 232
    mysticism 558–75
Midrash Rabba 34
Milan, Edict of 322
Milbank, John 302–3
military service 736
Mill, Harriet Taylor 491
Mill, John Stuart 476, 491, 730
millenarianism 133
Milton, John 63, 746
mind
    dualism 503, 504
    feminism 492
miracles
    Butler, Bishop J. 262
    Deism 253, 257
    Enlightenment 917
    healing 817
    Rousseau 267–8
    saints 566–7
    science 282, 920
Mishnah 23, 36–8
mission
    China 218
    colonial imperialism 296
    Congress on World Mission 297–8
    Jewish people 305
    Letter of James 97
    other religions 872, 877
    pluralism 294
    urban 1012
missionary theology 1029–30
Mitchell, Basil 417
Moberg, David 658
modalism 944–5, 949, 954
models, theological use 428
modernism
    Catholic attitude 610–11

Old Testament interpretation 5, 64–84
Mohammed 306–7
moksa 625
Molinos, Miguel de, supernaturalism 647
Moltmann, Jürgen
    The Crucified God 925
    divine suffering 911–12
    dogmatics 994
    eschatology 924–5
    immanence 615–16, 948
    Kingdom of God 707
    nature 439
    resurrection 709
    scientific understanding 436, 438
    secularization 891
    suffering 950–1
    theological position 279
    theology of hope 924, 1001
    Trinity 904
    truth 358
monads 351, 361
monarchianism 190, 194–5
monasticism
    Luther 578–9
    Middle Ages 209–10
    patristic spirituality 553–4
    prayer 207–8, 673–5
    purpose 644, 654
    reform 586–7
    spirituality 517
monism
    denial of God 942
    moral freedom 946
monistic mysticism 623–6, 632, 633–4
Monod, J. 444–5
monotheism
    centrality of Jesus 170
    demonic God 950
    modern atheism 942
Montaigne, Michel de 252, 377
Montanism 542–4, 547
Montesquieu, Charles Louis de Secondat
    258–9
Moore, Peter 638
Moore, Sebastian 661
Moors, Spanish radicalism 584
moral agents, ethics 700–7
'Moral Majority' 779
morality
    see also ethics
    creation 746–8
    dualism 456

feminism 505
goodness of God 899–900
Gospels 98
moral failure 700–1
Old Testament 65, 75
social 787
speculative theodicy 485–6
state responsiblity 778, 779–80
theology 687–8, 746–8
welfare 787
Morgan, Robert 882, 886–7
Mosaic code, hygiene 818
Mosala, Itumeleng 287
Moses
apophatic tradition 545–6
as heavenly mediator 181
liberation theology 1001
morality 1008
Pentateuch 15
Torah authorship 28
Mount Athos 210
mourning, internalization 800
Mouw, Richard 700
Mozart 316, 323
Muir, John 601
Murdoch, Iris 708
music
Calvin 318
Church 322
Martin Luther 317–18
medieval universities 329
relation to religion 316
Muslims see Islam
Myers, Gerald 604–5
mysterium tremendum 621–2
mystery, numinous feeling 621
mysticism
Eastern Orthodoxy 642
English 570–4
epistemic status 629–37
experience 517–18, 625, 626, 629, 636–7
introvertive and extrovertive 622–4
language 637–40
Lutheran 578–80
middle ages 558–75
paradoxes 638
patristic period 516–18, 519
prayer 288
typology 621–9
William James' analysis 603, 605
'womanspirit' 657
myth

Christianity 960
eschatological Christ figure 924–6
existentialist interpretation 920–2
feminist theology 886
post-modernism 995
psychology 958–9
truth of 1023

Naess, Arne 843
narrative 958–75
biblical scholarship 965–7
canonization 15
concept 146
definition 961–2
deformation 963–4
development 8–9
exegesis 1019, 1022, 1026
Fall 876
false 971–2
form of 961–5
hermeneutics 966–7
language 961
nature of doctrine 994
old/new texts interaction 18–19
paradigmatic 967, 969–70, 973
post-modernity 992
psychology 958–9, 960–1
religious language 420–1
social context 21–2
structuralism 965–7
theology 965–73
typology 969
universality 958–61
narrative criticism, New Testament 118, 128
Nash, James 696
nationalism 725
natural law
AIDS 754
Aquinas 617
Bible 692, 705
bioethics 820
divine truth 794
ethics 698
euthanasia 831
human rights 779–82
infanticide 830
inviolability of human life 819
just war 717–18
marriage 749
medical ethics 839
morality 688, 763

structural sin 706
theological construction 337
natural religion 374, 620
natural sciences 76–7
natural theology 388–412
  concept of reason 374, 376, 383–4
  Kant 621
  wisdom 11
nature
  see also ecology; environmentalism
  beauty 847–8
  convention 861–5
  dependence on 854
  divine presence 602, 615
  mysticism 623–4
  nurture debate 458, 502
  return to 861–5
  Romantic writing 597–600
  secularization 1014
naturism 843–4
Nazis
  Christian anti-Judaism 304
  environmentalism 857
  German Christianity 278–9
  human experimentation 833
  Lutheran heritage 580
  neo–paganism 917
  objectification 857–8
  theology of history 996
  totalitarianism 951
Nebi'im 29
neighbour, definition 767
neo–Darwinism 435–6, 438, 465, 467, 468
neo-Kantianism, economic Trinity 948
neo-orthodoxy 278, 289, 918–20
Neo-Platonism 548–9, 939–40
nephesh 823
Neuheitserlebnis 147
New Age movement 615
New Testament
  see also biblical interpretation; exegesis
  ahistorical approach 128–9
  authority 105, 110
  baptism 950
  canon 85–6, 97–8, 100
  character 5, 85–101
  Christology 931–2
  concept of God 343
  contemporary reading 89–91, 98
  context 90, 117, 122–3
  contradictions 124–5, 134
  doctrinal omissions 112–13

dogma 991
Erasmus 577
eschatology 131–5, 924
excluded writings 95
existentialist interpretation 920–2
feminist theology 885, 886–7
freedom of choice 550–3
Gnostics 104–5, 106
Greek 238
healing 818
historical–critical exegesis 122–30
historicism 257–9, 879–80, 917, 931–2
influence 120
interpretation 102–25, 882
Jesus as saviour 95
medieval view 559
myth 920
narrative criticism 118
neo–orthodoxy 918–20
Old Testament relationship 47, 49–63,
    65, 70, 105, 115
polemics 113–14
prayer 537, 538
pre-Enlightenment view 917
as Scripture 105
textual criticism 116–17
theocentricism 538
translation 114
unifying factors 95–8, 124
virtue 691–2
wealth 760–1
witness 109
Newman, John Henry
  Christ and culture 317
  conversion to Catholicism 875–6
  inwardness of faith 275
  literature 329, 330
  liturgy 666–8
  natural theology 404
Newton, Isaac
  concept of God 350–1
  concept of reason 373
  scientific understanding 449
Nicaea, Council of 144, 187, 343, 537, 538,
    938
Nicene Creed
  authority 976
  'Filioque' issue 210
  Jesus 170
  Son of God 195
  Trinity 188
Nicholas I, Pope 208–9

Nicholas of Cusa 577
Nichols, Aidan 611
Niebuhr, H. Richard
    Christ and culture 315, 316, 320, 710
    eschatology 531
    morality 699–700
    sin 703
Niebuhr, Reinhold
    agape 696
    kingdom of God 709
    Protestant tradition 502
    sin 703
Nielsen, K. 418
Nietzsche, Friedrich
    death of God 911, 945
    dualism 458
    existentialism 607
    God as repressor 359
    historicism 880
    natural theology 405
    systematic theology 979
nihilism, human nature 455
Nikolaos Mystikos, Patriarch 209
Nineham, Dennis 883–4, 885
Nirvana 357
nominalism
    concept of God 223, 349
    contemporary 1022
    denial of God 942
    science 435
    universal human nature 234
non-cognitivism, religious language 419, 421
non-realism 355–8, 380, 441
normative doctrine 985–7, 997
nourishment, embodiment 748
Nouwen, Henri 659
nuclear weapons 725, 726–7
Numbers 28
numinous feeling 353, 621–2, 630
Nuremburg code 834
nurture
    feminism 492
    nature debate 458, 502
Nygren, Anders 701–2, 745

Oakeshott, Michael 252
obedience, covenant 580
Oberlin College movement 651, 658
objectification 857–8
objectivity
    environmentalism 856–61

experience 633
    feminism 495
    historians 880
    theology 1019–20
objectum quo 631–2
oblates 215
O'Brien, C. C. 153
occasionalism 443
O'Donovan, Oliver 708–9, 819, 825, 836
Office 673–5
Office of the Dead 563
Office of Our Lady 563
Ogden, Schubert 302, 524, 900, 902, 929
Old Testament
    see also Hebrew Bible
    accuracy 73, 75
    chosen people 75
    Christian adoption 47–63, 89
    concept of God 342–3
    divine inspiration 47–8
    early influences 150–1, 153–6
    ecological concerns 81–2
    eucharistic liturgy readings 648
    feminist theology 80–1, 887
    God as Father 201–2
    healing 817–18
    Judaism/Christianity link 4
    liberation theology 79–80
    literature 82
    Matthew's use 93
    medieval view 559
    modernism 5, 64–84
    New Testament relationship 49–63, 65, 70, 115
    order of books 3, 143–5, 157
    political reading 65–7
    pre-existent Christ 169
    religious studies 892
    Septuagint as source 30
    sequence 143–5
    sociological study 76–7
    theocentricism 538
    typology 969
    wealth 759–60
Oman, John 364
omega point 615, 901, 913, 932
omnibenevolence, theodicy 473, 486, 488
omnipotence
    ethics 506
    evil 473, 474–6, 479–80, 899
    feminism 491, 493, 497, 499
    projection 496

theodicy 486, 488
omniscience
  evil 473
  feminism 491, 493, 497, 500
  projection 496
  theodicy 486, 488
ontological argument
  concept of God 562
  concept of reason 373, 376
  natural theology 390–1, 400, 401–2
ontology 903, 938–41, 954
oppression
  ethics 506
  evil 1005
  feminism 491–2, 494, 496–7
  First World 1010–11
  Israel 1001–2
  liberation 659–61
  psalms 676
  women 740
optimism, eighteenth century
  'improvement' 262–3
oral theology 1027–9
oral tradition
  authority 104
  Gospels 88
  Hebrew narrative 22
order, scientific understanding 440
ordination of women 499, 876, 883, 986
Orientalism 306–7
Origen of Alexandria
  Christ as God 196
  economy 195
  eschatology 49
  figurative interpretation 51
  free will 551–3
  Gnostics 543–5
  God as spiritual being 538–9
  image of God 548–9
  light 542, 546
  Lord's Prayer 537
  marginalization of history 182
  New Testament exegesis 105–6
  prayer 673, 674
  Scripture 559
  spirituality 554
  theocentricism 541
  triune God 189–90
  Wisdom 191
  Word of God 192
original sin
  see also Fall

New Testament basis 112
  responsibility 469
  salvation 268
  sexuality 748
  will 62
origins of religion 153–4
Orosius, creation 54
orthodox theology 278–9, 280, 289, 1002–3
Orthodoxy, Eastern see Eastern Orthodox
  Church
orthopraxis 522, 1002–3
Otto II, Emperor 210
Otto III, Emperor 210
Otto, Rudolf
  concept of God 353
  divine as holy 902
  mystical experience 639
  natural theology 400
  religious experience typology 621–2, 629
  spiritual perception 629–30, 632
ousia 939
Outka, Gene, agape 695–6
overpoweringness, numinous feeling 621
Oxford Movement 317, 668

Pachomius, monasticism 554
pacifism
  early Church 716
  just war 720–2
  rebellion 730
  sixteenth century sects 584
pagan philosophy 337–8, 344
paganism 500–1, 843, 917
Pailin, David 340, 388–412, 476
Paine, T. 154, 156
Palamas, Gregory 222, 642
Palestine
  context to Jesus' life 172–3
  Jewish 'mentalité' 881–2
  primitive Christianity 885
Palestine Liberation Organization (PLO)
  731, 732, 733–4
Paley, William 373, 398
pan-metaphorical view, religious language
  427–8
Panikkar, Raimundo 877
Pannenberg, Wolfhart
  divine as telos of history 913
  eschatology 925–6
  God as reality 996
  historical scholarship 926–7
  immanence 945

systematic theology 978, 979, 980, 982, 993
theism 902–3
theological position 279
theology and philosophy 281–2
Trinity 196
panoptic gaze 500
pantheism
concept of God 351, 360
dipolar concept of God 402
environmentalism 844
feminine deity 952
German Romantics 599
immanence 945
Romanticism 945–6
Schleiermacher's teaching 353
Spinoza's teaching 351
spirituality 525
papacy
annulment of marriages 240
arbiter of interpretation 108
Byzantine Emperor 208, 209
control of episcopal appointments 212
decline 225–6
election 211
government 212–13
inerrancy 219
interference in universities 893
justice 212–13
political influence 207
Papias 104
parables 119, 1022
paradise see heaven
paradox
Amos 55–6
dual nature of Christ 116
mystical experience 623, 638
ontology of the One 634
science and Greek mysticism 146
parental sin 818
parents, childhood development 799–803
Paris University 217
Parish Communion movement 670
Parker, Rebecca 500
Parmenides 962
Parsch, Pius 652
Pärt, Arvo 325
participation, liturgy 671
Pascal, Blaise 374, 377, 678
Pascal's Wager 378–9
Passion, feasts 563
Passionist Order 255

passions, human nature 454
Passover, lamb of 179
pastoral care 794–816
Pastoral Epistles 98
pastoral psychology 125
Pater, Walter 316–17
paternalism, medicine 832, 836, 837
Patriarch of Constantinople 207
patriarchs 8, 759–60
patriarchy
Calvinism 581
Christianity 886
concept of God 357
dualism 503, 504
early Church 885
ethics 505–6
Fatherhood of God 741
feminist theology 657, 952
modern criticism 118
Old Testament 80
revelation 494
spirituality 526
structural sin 706
symbolics 907
tradition 739–40
patristic theology
doctrinal formulation 986
mystical theology 513, 516–17
spirituality 536–57
Paul, St
animals 866
body of Christ 650
Christ as God 196
Christocentricism 536
codes of conduct 691
conversion 971
emphasis on Jesus 177
epistles 58, 86–8, 157
equality 741
Eucharist 666
faith hope and love 799–800
free-will defence 484
Gospel interpretation 879
grace 553
human nature 464
immortality 455
the Law 104, 125, 130
New Testament influence 98–9
Son of God 197
spirituality 548, 550
syncretism 1028
will and morality 701

wisdom 169
Payne, Steven 639–40
Peace of Westphalia 249
Peacocke, A. 440
Peirce, Charles, pragmatism 603
Pelagianism 57, 244, 553
penance 239, 795
Penelhum, Terence 339–40, 367–87, 389
penitence 611
Pentateuch
   see also Torah
   Bible component 144–5
   Christian subjection 48–9
   development 15
   final editing 15, 28–9
   grace relationship 57–9
   historical narrative 8–9
   religious motivation 22
Pentecost 198, 576
Pepin, protection of Rome 208
perception
   experience 634–7
   mystical 630–3
   practice 635–7
perfection
   concept of God 346–7, 348
   Methodism 516, 668
permissiveness 743, 754–5
Perovich, Anthony 626, 627
Perrin, Norman 136, 650
persecution, Roman Empire 668–9
persistent vegetative state 833
person, relational concept 951
personal ethics 738–58
personalism
   bioethics 819
   concept of 364–5
   creation stories 747, 750–1
   fertility 749
   I-thou philosophy 920
   marriage 751–2
   personal ethics 742–6
   scientific understanding 437, 438
personality, development 796–7
personhood 501–4, 770–1
perspective
   ecology 504
   feminism 492–3
pesher 32
pessimism, cosmic 551
Pétain, Henri Philippe 732
Peter of Celle 50, 51

Peter the Chanter 53
Peter Lombard 213, 233, 947
Peterson, Erik 951
Pharisees 158, 173
phenomenology 281, 622–3
philanthropy 760, 765, 774
Philemon, epistle 86
philia 745–6
Philip IV of France 225
Phillips, D. Z.
   concept of God 355, 380
   religious language 421, 423
   theology and philosophy 282–3
Philo of Alexandria
   allegorical method 33, 51, 147–8
   darkness 544–5, 546
   messianic ideas 43
   Old Testament authority 47
   Psalms 17
philosophical theology 515–16, 532
philosophy
   biblical theology 67
   feminist 490–508
   Hegelian 71, 76
   historicism 878
   Kantian 70
   linguistic 405
   medieval 337, 339, 346–9, 390–2
   natural, concept of reason 373
   pagan 337–8, 344
   Schelling 73
   speculative 74
   theology as branch of 280–3
Photius 208–9
physics 447
pietism
   black 656
   medieval 645–6
   Protestantism 647–8
   relation of individual to divine 596, 902
piety, spirituality 516
Pike, Nelson 624–5
pilgrimage 210–11, 550, 564, 567–8
Pittenger, Norman 928–9
Pius IX, Pope 610
Pius X, Pope 611
Pius XII, Pope 652
Plantinga, A. 381, 383, 405–6, 487
plants, extinction 845–6
Plath, Sylvia 327
Plato
   Beauty 852

concept of God 344–5, 349
dualism 454, 504
eternal existence 61
God and the world 944
good and evil 551
goodness of man 547
knowledge of God 545
medieval philosophy 346, 347
pagan philosophy 337, 368–9
patristic spirituality 536
sensory world 344
supreme principle 551
theocentric spirituality 538, 539–41
theodicy 474–5, 477, 485
Platonism
art 329–30
effect on early Christianity 182
humanism 237
realism 234
Trinity doctrine 939–40
pleasure, sexuality 739, 803
plenior sensus 118
Pliny 189, 668–9
PLO see Palestine Liberation Organization
plot, narrative 962–5
Plotinus
beauty 848
concept of God 344
divine transcendence 939
ecstacy 546
image of God 548–9
mystical experiences 624
nature 862
One 944
Plumb, J. H. 148
pluralism
adaptive doctrine 987
analysis of 292–6
biblical texts 1024–5
Christology 918, 933
interfaith issues 291–2
morality 696–7, 780, 787
Religious Studies 892
spirituality 609
structuralism 1023
plurality-in-unity 946
pneumatology, schism 949–50
Poetical Books, Old Testament 145
poetry
see also Psalms
Christ and culture 316
Hebrew Bible 12–13

John of the Cross 590
Medieval inner life 582–3
origins 24
Romantic 598–9
Polanyi, M. 988
polarity, post-modern dogmatics 997
polemics
ecumenical concensus 998
Les Ruines 153–5
New Testament 113–14
systematic theology 983
political theology 65–7, 284
politics
biblical topic 649
Christian attitude 642
Church involvement 777–9, 783–4
feminism 499
human nature 458–9
just war 724
Polkinghorne, J. 440
polytheism, Trinity doctrine 189
Pompa, Leon 884
pope see papacy
Popper, Karl 878–80
pornography 490
positivism
broad criteria 416–20
concept of God 355–6
criteria of meaning 414–16
scientific understanding 441, 447, 448
post-liberalism
feminist theology 887
natural theology 405, 406
post-modernism
concept of God 357
existentialism 607–10
feminism 341, 493–4
human nature 455, 461
liberation theology 79–82
natural theology 405
Old Testament interpretation 64
practical theodicy 487
sense of God 910–15
systematic theology 979, 992–7
trinitarianism 953
post-mortem revelation 298
poverty
Christ and the Apostles 215, 221
First World 1010–11
inner city 1011–12
liberation theology 790, 908–9, 1002–4, 1009, 1011–13

mendicant movement 526
Old Testament message 80
paradigmatic narrative 969
praxis 1003–4
structural sin 706–7
theology of wealth 759
Third World 1009–10
Trinity 904–5
wealth distribution 760
power
adoration of 500
feminism 492, 493, 499
personhood 503
Power, David 612, 614
praeparatio evangelica, inclusivism 299
pragmatism
concept of God 352, 360
William James 603–5
praxis 1001–15
prayer
see also liturgy
active 643–4
Anselm of Bec 561–2
apophatic 573
for the dead 112, 565
domestic church 677
Eastern orthodoxy 669
Enlightenment 512
extempore 671
feminist theology 657
Hesychast spirituality 222
Jesus Christ 168, 180, 537, 538–41
language 423
methodical 518
Middle Ages 560. 569, 572
modern spirituality 288, 653
monasticism 517, 674
New Testament 537, 538
Office 673–5
Orthodox Church 561
passivity 586
patristic spirituality 537
precomposed 678–9
Psalms 12
receptivity 586
Reformed patterns of 583
saints 565
structure of day 207–8
thankfulness 596–7
typology 530
prayer books, laity 224
pre-existence, Christ 169, 929

preaching
apostles 215
friars 216
liturgy balance 681
predestination
Beza 246, 247
Calvin 581
conditional futurity 56
patristic spirituality 550–2
responsibility 470
predication, problem of 413, 424–9
prejudice, natural theology 404
Premonstratensians 215
Prenter, Regin 665
Presbyterian Church 241–2
Presentation of Christ 680
Price, Henry Habberley 399
priesthood
see also clergy
academic theology 892, 1018
authoritarian figures 812–13
contemporary Roman Catholicism 614
education 223–4
healers 817
historical roots 883
marriage 214
ordination of women 499, 876, 883, 986
Priestly Code 23
Priestly school 78
Principe, Walter 524
Priscilla 542
privatization
feminist spirituality 657
liturgy 674
religious experience 596, 599, 600, 605
process theology
concept of God 361–4, 402–3, 900–1
evil 476
Jesus Christ 928–9
temporality 912–13
Proclus, darkness 542
procreation
see also children
assisted 825–8
love 825–6
marriage 805
pair bond 749
Prodigal Son, patristic spirituality 540
profit motive 769
progress, secularization 890
projection
feminism 492, 496–7

paganism 501
prolēpsis 53
promiscuity 797, 802–3, 804
proof, objectivity 860–1
prophecy
    apocalyptic 131
    black-led churches 656
    canonization 17–18, 19–20
    conditional futurity 56
    development 13–14
    fulfilment in Jesus 47, 49, 65, 73
    interpretation 52, 54–7
    messianic 107
    Montanism 542, 543–4
    praxis 1004
    social context 25
    verb tense 56
Prophets
    authoritative texts 28–9
    authorship 13–14
    healing miracles 817–18
    schools 13–14
    Scriptural Books 145
    theology 78
proportionalism, infanticide 829, 835
protest atheism 908
    Trinity 950–1
Protestantism
    concept of God 353
    culture 319
    democracy 781
    Dissenters 778
    divine temporality 912
    eighteenth century orthodoxy 255
    ethics 693, 697, 700, 711
    French prophets 256–7
    immanence 947
    incarnation 763
    Liberal 274
    medical ethics 824
    medieval rhetoric 583
    myth 960
    neo-orthodoxy 918–20
    nineteenth century 265
    parity between religions 877
    post-Reformation 246–9
    primitive church 875
    Pyrrhonic scepticism 377
    rebellion 66–7
    Reformation 239–43, 244–6
    religious images 323, 330
    revelation 794

secularization 890
sin 502, 703
spirituality 530–1, 578–84, 647
tradition role 3
unconditional grace 801
vocation 775
Word dominance 681
work ethic 775
Proudfoot, Wayne 631
Proverbs 11, 23
providence, doctrine of 439, 890–1
Provisional IRA 732–3, 734
Psalms
    canonization 16–17
    culture 322
    early church use 666
    experiential exploration 69
    familiarity 62
    history 12–13
    liturgical use 675–6
    Office use 674
    patristic spirituality 536
    usage 17, 24
Psalms of Asaph 13
Psalms of Ascents 13
Psalter *see* Psalms
pseudepigrapha 29
Pseudo–Dionysius 517, 529–30, 638
Pseudo-Jonathan 31
Pseudo-Philo 32
pseudonymity, epistles 117
psychoanalysis 797–8
psychodynamic model 796–7
psychology
    counselling 796–8
    development 798–809
    marriage 805–8
    myth 958–9, 960–1
    pastoral 125
    religious experience 602
    right and wrong 794–5
    spirituality 809–10
public opinion, war 728–9, 730
pure consciousness 623–4, 626–9
pure reason 368
purgatory, doctrine of
    development of 219
    judgement 112
    materialistic fervour 565
    post-mortem revelation 298
Puritanism
    architecture 325

arts 318
covenant obedience 581–2
empirical role 338–9
ethics 697
scientific understanding 435
purity laws, Hebrew Bible 38–9
purusa 629
Pyrrhonian scepticism 370, 371, 377
Pythagoras 503

qal vahomer 34
Quakers
human nature 465
natural theology 395
pacifism 721
spirituality 678
Quantra Cura 610
quantum theory 446
quest
God 541–2
spirituality 512, 513
quietism 586, 647, 762
Qumran 29, 32, 33, 43
Qu'ran *see* Koran

rabbinic communities 33–4, 35–6
racial eqality 788–9
racism
black theology 655–6, 908
concept of God 497
missionaries 296
oppression 660
spirituality 526
Radical Reformation 240, 242–3, 693, 694
radical theology
definition 278–80
language 277
radicalism
Christianity 649, 651–2
evangelical 658–9
natural religion 253–6
Rahner, Karl
bioethics 826
Christology 930–1
doctrine of God 947–8
dogmatics 979
embryo experimentation 827
fundamental theology 981–2
inclusivism 299–302
monotheism 950
morality 708
sacramentality 612–13

spirituality 521, 522, 532
theological position 280
totality 996
Trinity doctrine 941, 948
Räisänen, Heikki 879
Ramsey, Bishop Ian 356, 840
Ramsey, Michael 651, 652, 670
Ramsey, Paul
agape 696
assisted reproduction 825–6
child experimentation 834–5
duties towards the dying 829, 832
ethics 697, 700, 837
inviolability of human life 819
medical research 840
Rashdall, Hastings 400
rationalism
classical theism 353
concept of God 351, 352
concept of reason 371
Enlightenment 457, 458
modern theology 331
Old Testament interpretation 67–9, 73
rise of 248–9
theological role 338
rationality
see also reason
feminism 491
gender 502
individualism 464
Rauschenbusch, Walker 699
Ray, John 396
reader-response criticism 128, 129
realism
just war 722–4
mythic 995
rebellion 731
scientific understanding 441
terminism 234
theism 276
warfare 716
Reality 630
reason
see also rationality
autonomy 436, 439
Cambridge Platonists 395
corrupt nature 717, 718
empirical 368
ethics 698, 699
faith 367–87
feminism 492, 494
human nature 453, 454

Ideas 630
just war 720
love 794
natural theology 391–2, 397, 405
objectivity 856–61
post Enlightenment 273–4
pre-Descartes interpretations 367–70
psychology 796
religious foundation 594
revelation 350–2, 717, 718, 734–5
scientific understanding 447
sociobiology 466
systematic theology 988
understanding distinction 70–1
rebellion
adolescents 803–4
just war 730–5
reciprocal altruism, sociobiology 465, 468
Reckitt, Maurice 645
Red Cross/Crescent 730
redaction criticism
experience-reinterpretation 136
Gospels 122
limitations 117
parables 119
redemption
feminist account 610
nineteenth century thinking 72
social politics 470
reductionism 68, 421, 457, 466
reference, problem of 413, 429–30
reflexivity, human nature 459
Reformation 239–46
biblical interpretation 108–10
Catholic 584–91
causes 225–7
concept of God 350
definition 240–1
grace and the Law 58
natural theology 393–4
Protestant 578–84
scholasticism 236
theological credibility 981
Reformed Churches
Anabaptism 242–3
Calvinism 241–2
covenant obedience 580
definition 240
Reformers
communion 671
grace 611
spirituality 647–8

Vulgate translation 157
regression, infinite 394
Reimarus, Hermann Samuel 259, 260
reincarnation, post-mortem revelation 298
relationality 910–12, 914–15
relationships
business 772–3
community 749–50
creation stories 748–9
fidelity 756
to God 811–13
to others 813–15
to self 810–11
relativism
feminism 496
historical 871–84
human nature 340–1
relativity theory 440, 446, 900
relics, cult of 563, 567
religious experience
see also mysticism; numinous feeling
aesthetic variety 324–6
eighteenth century attitudes 256–7
epistemology 629–37
era of reform 576–93
evaluation 523–5
feminism 494–5, 504
Goddess 500–1
individualism 596–7
interpretation 880
language 620–41
personal 1021
psychological interpretation 602–3
spirituality 520–3, 524
theological touchstone 1021
transcendence 600
typology 621–9
Religious Studies 892
remarriage, Greek Christianity 209
Rembrandt 323
Renaissance
historical perspective 230
humanism 236–9
post-Reformation 246–9
scholasticism 236
Rendtorff, Trutz 704
repression, God 942
reproduction
see also procreation
anatomy 502
assisted 823, 825–8
dualism 504

feminism 492
research, human experimentation 819, 825, 827, 833–5
resistance, Christian 651, 654–5
resources, non-renewable 845
responsibility
  human nature 341, 469–70
  individualism 464
  personhood 503
  wealth 765–7
Restoration 255
resurrection
  belief in 175, 177–8
  Christ as God 196–7
  dead 132, 134
  death and suffering 822, 831–2
  eschatology 924–5
  ethics 708–9
  health 823
  Hebrew Bible 40–1
  human nature 454–5
  Marxist view 1031
  redundant concept 596
  self-acceptance 809
  understanding of 179
Reuchlin, J. 48
revealed theology 374, 407–8
revelation
  concept of reason 373, 374, 375, 376
  defence of 378
  divine truth 794
  eighteenth century 261–3
  feminism 494–5
  healing 818–19, 820
  hermeneutics 527
  historical–critical exegesis 125
  lightness 544
  limits of reason 350–2
  minimalist theodicy 486
  Montanism 542
  narrative theology 968
  natural theology 389, 391
  Pelagius 553
  post-mortem 298
  reality 74
  reason 70, 717, 718, 734–5
  scepticism 594
  scientific understanding 435
  Scripture 105
  secularization 922–3
  spirituality 519
  systematic theology 982

theocentricism 294
triune God 948
Word of God 920
Revelation of John
  apocalyptic writing 88–9
  eschatology 133
  evangelists 111
  letters 97
revolution
  liberation theology 790–1, 1006
  rebellion 734
  Third World theology 1027
rhetoric 52–3, 582–3
rhetorical criticism 119, 128
Richard of St Victor 62, 202–3, 517, 951–2
Ricoeur, Paul 152, 498, 966
righteousness, liberation theology 80
rigorism 739, 752, 754–5
Ritschl, Albrecht 137, 274, 902, 980
ritual, first century Judaism 38–9
Robinson, John
  Body of Christ 650
  Christology 929–30
  ethics 700
  liturgy 652
  prayer 653
Rolle, Richard 570
Roman Catholic Church
  see also Church; papacy
  authoritarian figure 812–13
  Breviary 675
  Christ and culture 710
  Christology 930–3
  confession 795
  Enlightenment 890
  ethics 697–8
  evolution 932
  grace 801
  incarnation 764
  inclusivism 299
  inviolability of human life 819
  liturgical renewal 652
  mystical experience 630–2
  parity between religions 877
  Pharisee comparison 158
  politics 777
  primitive church 875–6
  Protestantism relationship 66–7
  Pyrrhonic scepticism 377
  Quakers 678
  revelation 794
  sin 795

spirituality 530–1, 610–15, 643–5
tradition role 3
Trinity doctrine 941, 944, 948
universal theology 1025
Roman Empire
conversion 207
law 435
pacifism 716
persecution of Christians 668–9
Romanticism
Coleridge 945–6
concept of God 353–5
cult of the artist 327
feelings 620
God as being of beings 903–4
Old Testament interpretation 67–9
pantheism 945–6
religious influence 597–602
systematic theology 979
theology and aesthetics 330
Romer, J. 150–1
Roosevelt, President Franklin D. 725
Rorty, Richard 405, 457
rosary 566, 583
Rose, Ann 600–1
Rousseau, Jean Jacques 254–5, 267–8, 351
Rowland, Christopher 133–4
Ruether, Rosemary 495, 498, 504, 660, 907–8
Rule of Faith 105, 109
Rule of St Basil 554, 674
Rule of St Benedict 527, 529, 553, 644, 674
Rule of Truth see Rule of Faith
Rupert of Deutz 55
Russell, Bertrand 361, 401, 429, 605
Russian Orthodox Church 561
see also Eastern Orthodox Church
Ruysbroeck, Jan van 569, 625, 645
Ryle, Gilbert 744

Sabatier, A. 989, 994
Sabellianism 187–8, 944
sacra pagina 102
sacralization, historical narrative 9
sacramental ethics 708
sacramentalism
candles 680
immanence 326
sacred images 330–1
sacraments
see also baptism; Eucharist; marriage

confession 611
embodiment 747–8
liturgical component 681
matrimony 239
medieval devotion 564
New Testament 537
penance 239, 795
Quakers 678
Reformation 244–5
Roman Catholic Church 612–13
Romantic influence 602
subordination of prayer 669
sacrifice
animals 179–80, 863
feminist view 886
Judaism 179–80, 881
Old Testament 75
temples 881
sadism 858
saeculum 923
Sahlins, M. 863
Said, E. 307
saints, cult of 112, 565, 576
Saiving, Valerie 501
Sales, Francis de, devotion 516
salon mysticism 516
salvation
Church 876
devotion 563
exclusivism 297
feminism 498–9
gender 502, 503
God-consciousness 595–6
grace and the Law 58–9
healing 837
human nature 461
individual 877
liberation theology 80
New Testament contradictions 124
non-Christians 297, 298, 299, 993
sacraments 613
scientific understanding 435, 439
unifying theme 102
salvation history 73, 103
Samartha, S. J. 127
Samuel 8, 18–19, 28–9
sanctification, Calvinism 581, 584
Sands, Kathleen 503
sannyasin 862
Sartre, Jean-Paul 359
Satan 53, 62, 644
Saudreau, August 630, 632

saviour-figures 934
Sayings of the Desert Fathers 538
scepticism
  Enlightenment 512
  fideism 373, 377–8, 380
  Hume 262–3
  Pyrrhonian 370, 371, 377
  types 368
Scharlemmann, R. P. 912
Schelling, F. W. J. von 599
Schillebeeckx, Edward 613, 888, 931
schism
  Acacian 207
  East and West 949
  Great 206, 225–6
Schiwy, G. 1021–2
Schleiermacher, Friedrich Daniel Ernst
  concept of God 353
  culture 315
  dependence 274, 282, 615
  feelings 620
  historical Jesus 274
  natural theology 399
  relation of individual to divine 902
  religious consciousness 269
  religious experience 595–7, 602
  systematic theology 979, 980, 982, 989,
    994
  theological credibility 981
  trinitarian theology 187, 904, 937, 943–4
Schlick, Moritz 355, 414
Schlink, Edmund 950
Schmemann, Alexander 665, 670, 674
Schoenberg, Arnold 325
scholasticism
  definition 232–3
  late medieval 232–6
  Period of Orthodoxy 249
  post-Reformation 246–7
  spirituality 515–16
  types 233
  universities 213–14
Scholes, Robert 963–4
Schüller, Bruno 698
Schweitzer, Albert 924
science
  certainty 252
  concept of reason 372, 373, 374
  creation 812
  discourse 423
  dualism 456–7, 458
  environment 853, 1014

feminism 492
foundations of 340
Hexaemeron 61
miracles 920
models 428
objectivity 856–61
renunciation of 901–2
supreme being 895, 899–900
theology 518–19
understanding 433–52
warfare 725
scientific humanism 890, 891
Scotus, Duns 233, 234, 235, 392, 426
scribes 22, 23
Scripture *see* Bible; canon; Hebrew Bible;
  New Testament; Old Testament
Second Coming 863
Second Temple period 28
sectarianism 584, 762
secular Christianity 922–4
secular theology 276–7, 1023
secularization
  contemporary theology 888–91, 922–4
  history of 888–91
  nature 1014
  symbolism 276
  systematic theology 980, 988
Sedgwick, Timothy 708
Segal, Lynne 657
Segundo, Juan Luis 1026
self
  see also personhood
  dualism 456–8
  God 902
  love of 798
  relationship to 810–11
  responsibility 470
self-consciousness 595, 606
self-denial, spirituality 809–10
self-determination of peoples 734
self-revelation, creation 530
self-sacrifice, *agape* 696
self-transcendence, spirituality 521
self-will, surrender 75
Semler, Johann Salomon 259, 260, 265–6
Seneca 577
sense-perception 370, 372
senses
  perception 631, 632, 635
  spiritual 539
sensibility, dissociation of 532
sentence literature 11

separatism, feminism 492
Sephoris 173
Septuagint
  apocryphal texts 29
  Christian Old Testament source 30
  Palestinian use 151
  Wisdom 190–1, 194
Sermon on the Mount, virtues 692
sexism
  see also feminist theology; patriarchy
  creation stories 747
  employment 1013
  spirituality 657
sexual assault 503
sexuality
  Christian attitude 642–3
  creation stories 760–1
  dualism 504
  emotional development of 802–3
  ethics 738–58, 778, 779–90
  feminist theology 504, 657–8
  homosexuality 808
  issues 661
  love 807
  original sin 748
  personhood 503
  pleasure 739
  spirituality 525, 657–8
  traditional view 739–40
Shaftesbury, A. 256–7
shamanism, indigenization 909
Shange, Ntozake 500
Shanks, Andrew 945
shareholder ethics 766–7, 773
Shelley, P. B. 154–5, 156
Shema 188, 195–6
Sheol 39
Shepherd of Hermas 188
Shinto, pantheism 844
Sifra 34
Sifre 34
Sikhs, statistics 291
simony 211–12, 213
sin
  see also original sin
  Calvinism 647
  confession 795
  disobedience 704–6
  disorientation of desires 701–3
  feminist theology 501–2, 657
  gender 503
  Gnostics 543
  grace and the Law 57–9
  human nature 463
  injustice 717
  loci of sin 701–7
  New Testament 692
  parental 818
  psychology of 796
  responsibility 469
  social structures 706–7
  spirituality 530
  unfaith 703–4
  warfare 716–17
  wealth 759, 762–4
  will 794–5
single mothers, oppression 660–1
single people 807–8
Sinn Fein 732–3, 734
Sisinnios II, Patriarch 209
sisterhood, feminism 494–5
Skinner, Quentin 231
Smart, Ninian 625, 878, 892
Smith, John 395
Smith, Ronald Gregor 923–4
Smith, Wilfred Cantwell 283, 878
Smith, William Robertson 76–7
Sobrino, Jon 926–7
Social Darwinism 718
Social Gospel 902
social justice
  completion doctrine 762
  praxis 1001
  state enforcement 787
  wealth 767–71
social sciences 340–1, 458–60, 466
socialism
  Church support 783–4, 788
  liberation theology 1006, 1008–9
socialization, gender 502
society
  evil 1005
  human nature 458–9, 460
  liberation theology 1005–6
  liberationist transformation 1008
  sociobiology 467, 470
  spirituality 647–50
  structural sin 706–7
Society of Friends *see* Quakers
Society of Jesus 249, 584, 586, 590
Socinus 937
sociobiology 465–9
sociology
  Israel 79

liberation theology 285, 1008
natural theology 404
New Testament texts 91
religion 76–7
spirituality 511
theology 136
Sojourners Community 658–9
sola fide 296, 297, 299
sola scriptura 242–3, 244
solidarity
 feminism 495
 humanity 767, 769–70
 liberation spirituality 661
 with poor 1009
solipsism 371, 744, 750, 850
Sölle, Dorothee
 divine relationality 912
 feminine characteristics of God 885–6,
  887
 radicalism 905
 types of theology 278–80
 vulnerable God 499–500
Solomon 17, 18–19
solus Christus 293–4, 299, 300, 301
Son of God
 divinity of 195, 938
 equality with Father 938
 Gospels 176
 Holy Spirit 199–200, 949
 homoousion 938
 meaning of term 201
 status 197–200
 Word of God 191–2
Son of man 176
Song of Songs 24, 559–60
songs, secular 24, 25
Sorley, William Ritchie 399, 400
Soskice, Janet 428, 498, 499
soteriocentricism 295
soul
 dualism 503
 growth 587–8
 human nature 454
 love 794
 mysticism 623–4
 patristic spirituality 549–50
 predestination 581
 separation 646
 twentieth century view 738–9
source criticism 25, 117, 122
sources
 biblical interpretations 48

Gospel texts 123
New Testament 114, 116
Old Testament 149, 150–1, 155–6
South Africa 651, 788–9, 969–70
South African Council of Churches 1027
Soviet Union 860–1
'Spaceship Earth' 851
Spain, Catholic Reformation 584–5
speculative theodicy 474–8, 485–6
Spence, T. 154
Spiegel, Yorick 1021
Spinoza, Baruch
 biblical exegesis 257
 concept of God 353, 596
 concept of reason 373, 375
 deism 351
 Hegelian interpretation 354
spirit
 dualism 442, 504
 feminism 491, 492
 Manicheism 475–6
Spirit, Holy *see* Holy Spirit
Spiritual Gospel *see* Gospel of John
spiritual senses 539
spiritual theology 517–19, 532
spirituality 514–35
 academic discipline 512, 515–16
 AIDS effect 661
 art 326–7
 black-led churches 656
 Calvinism 581
 community 650, 650–1, 659
 compassion 609
 contemporary 519–23
 decline 645–6
 definition 514, 515–16
 deinstitutionalization 609
 disjuncture 606
 domestic 677
 emotional development 809
 ethics 707–9
 eucharistic 652
 female religious communities 217
 feminist 657
 Gregory of Nyssa 643–4
 Hesychast 222
 Israel 81–2
 Jesuit 586
 liberation 659–62
 liturgical 665–76
 marriage 807
 materialism relationship 643

modern life 288, 1003–4
Native American 909
non–liturgical 677–9
patristic 536–57
Protestantism 647–8
psychology 809–10
Reformation 576–93
Roman Catholicism 610–15
Romantic influence 601
self–denial 809–10
terminological history 515–16
theological interface 523–32, 555–6
twentieth century 607–10
typologies 529–32
Spirituals 221
Spretnak, Charlene 610
Stace, Walter T. 622–4, 629, 633, 637–8
stakeholders, business 770, 772
Staniloe, Dumitru 702
star wars 499
state
    armed rebellion 730
    Church 207, 777–9
    just war 721, 724
    personal morality 778, 779, 781
    power 777–93
    terrorism 735
Steiner, George 320
stewardship
    business 773
    Calvinism 581
    environmental ethics 866
    personal possessions 765
    world 770
stigmata, Francis of Assisi 563
Stoics 577, 854, 856
story, definition 962
story-tellers 959–60, 961
Stout, J. 985
Strauss, D. F. 920, 960
Strauss, Leo 252
Stringfellow, William 649
Stroup, George 968, 970–1
structural sin 706–7
structuralism 128, 965–7, 1021–4
Stuhlmacher, P. 125, 1020
Suarez, just war 719
subjectivity
    experience 138–9, 633
    knowledge 273–4, 276
substance, transubstantiation 612
Succession Narrative 8–9

suffering
    animals 849
    Christ 563
    divine 822, 904, 911–12, 950–1, 954
    eradication of 830
    euthanasia 831
    faith 589
    feminist theology 500, 886
    Jewish people 1009
    redemptive value 179–80
Suger, Abbot 324
Sugirtharajah, R. S. 126–7
suicide, adolescents 804
supernaturalism 920–5
superstition 252–3, 897
Surin, Kenneth 302–3, 487
surrogacy, procreation 826
survival, human nature 454–6
Sutherland, Stewart 340, 430, 431
Swinburne, Richard 417, 634–7
Sykes, Stephen 288–9, 989–90
Syllabus of Errors 610
symbolism
    biblical reinterpretation 136–7
    cognitive status of doctrine 994–5
    feminist theology 907
    structuralism 1023
syncretism 1027–9
synergism, patristic spirituality 550, 552
Synoptics see Gospels
Syreeni, K., narrative worlds 129
systematic theology 976–98
    see also doctrine; dogmatics
    Anglicanism 977
    Apologists 981
    credibility 981–3
    critical criteria 983–4
    discipline of the given 988–9
    ecumenical concensus 998
    historicism 887–9
    inter-faith dialogue 992–3
    method 985–7
    model 984–91
    reason 988
    secular influences 980, 988
    sources 987
    theology of religions 308

taboos
    food 38–9
    menstruation 500
Talmud 37

Tanak 29
Tanquerey, A. A. 519
targumim 31, 151
Tarnas, Richard 601
Tatian 111
Tauler, John 569, 578, 624, 646
Tawney, R. H. 784
taxation 765
Taylor, Alfred Edward 399, 400
Taylor, Charles 616
technocracy 857
Teilhard de Chardin, Pierre
    cosmogenesis 901
    divine as omega point 901, 913
    ecology 615
    environmental ethics 855
    evolution 932
    humanism 1022
    medical ethics 827
    The Phenomenon of Man 932
teleological argument, natural theology 400
temple
    religious focus 45
    sacrifice 881
Temple, William 399, 643, 977
temporality 440, 912–15
temptation, wealth 759
Ten Commandments 10, 58
Tennant, Frederick Robert 400
Teresa of Avila, St
    Catholic Reformation 584
    Christian discipleship 646
    devotion to Christ 538
    mysticism 624
    spirituality 518, 586–88
    Trinity vision 624, 627
terminism 234
terrorism 735
    see also Palestine Liberation
        Organization; Provisional IRA
Tertullian of Carthage
    anti-philosophical thought 350
    Christ and culture 316
    Christ as illuminator 50
    economy 195
    Gnostics 543
    Lord's Prayer 537
    matter and spirituality 642
    triune God 190, 194
    Word of God 192
testimony
    apostolic 104, 109

New Testament writers 95–6, 100
text
    commentaries 559
    hermeneutics 966–7
    interpretation 526–9
    spirituality 526–9
textual criticism, New Testament 116–17
Thatcher, Margaret 843
theism
    classical framework 898–899
    feminism 497
    human nature 453
    mysticism 623–6
    post-modernism 996–7
    post-theistic options 903–6
    prudential 378–9
    revisions 900–903
    rise and fall 899–900
Theissen, Gerd 125
theocentrism
    New Testament 538
    patristic spirituality 539–41
    pluralism 293–6
    Trinity 952
theodicy
    bioethics 822
    black theology 908
    causation 899
    cosmological horizon 901
    dogmatics 992
    Holocaust 950–1
    limitations 484–5
    minimalist 486
    practical 486, 487–8
    process theology 900
    relatedness of divine 911
    secularization 890
    speculative 474–8
    types 473–4
Theodore of Mopsuestia 107, 672
Theodotian 30
Theological Enquirer 154
Theosis 702–3, 711
Theotokos 680
Thielecke, Helmut 823
Third Reich, power 499–500
Third World
    business ethics 771
    Exodus 1001–2
    liberation theology 789, 1001–2,
        1009–10
    nationalism 788

New Testament interpretation 126–7
radical movements 783
World Council of Churches 1028
Third World theology
critical theology 1025
revolution 1027
Thirty Years War 249
Thirty-Nine Articles *see* Church of
England
Thomas à Kempis
Christ as God 195–6
The Imitation of Christ 226, 569, 577,
645–6
Thomas Aquinas, St *see* Aquinas, St
Thomas
Thomas Becket, St *see* Becket, St
Thomas
Thomism
see also Aquinas, St Thomas
Catholic Reformation 248–9
laity 223
nature of God 363, 364, 365
Tillich, Paul
Christ and culture 318–20
concept of God 353, 356–7, 360, 904
creativity 907
ethics 700
existentialism 921–2
expressionist art 326
health 823
sin 703
systematic theology 979, 980, 981
theologians 682
theology and philosophy 281
time
see also temporality
concept of God 345
God 901, 912–13
narrative 962, 968, 973
scientific understanding 446
Timothy, epistles 98
Tindal, Matthew 253, 256, 316, 375
Titus, epistle 98
Toland, John 235, 256, 259, 375
tolerance, eighteenth century 255, 264, 268
Tolkien, J. R. R., eucatastrophe 964–5
Torah
see also Pentateuch
authoritative text 28, 29
food laws 38
history 15
legal code 22–3

oral form 34
Paul's interpretation 125, 130
resources 848
Scriptural component 144–5
Torrance, T. F. 440, 947
Torres, Camilo 1006
torture, objectivication 858
totalitarianism 996
Toulmin, Professor Stephen 252
Toynbee, Arnold 844
Tracy, David 281, 524
tradition
Christian 163–374
contemporary interpretation 278
continuity 163–5
divine truth 794
doctrines 875
ethics 693, 697
feminism 494
oppression of women 740
personal ethics 739–40
postmodernism 607
psychological approach 1021
spirituality 513, 521, 524
systematic theology 987
versus Scripture 3, 108–9
traditionalism
backlash against 754
celibacy 751
gender 741
marriage 751, 752–3
personalism 742
sexual ethics 752
tragedy, Aristotle 962, 964
transcendence
dualism 504, 944–5
experiential knowledge 522
God 898
immanent 325–6
negative 324–5
patristic period 180
proximate 325
radical 325
word 1023
transcendental method 521–2
transcendentalism 600–1, 902
transference, counselling 814–15
transformation, personal and social 126
translation
Bible versions 114, 149–52, 648
Hebrew Bible 30–2
Koran 149–50

New Testament 114
Old Testament 80–1
reinterpretation 147
Scriptures, twentieth century 648
translationes 53
transsignification 245
transubstantiation 612, 614
tremendum, numinous feeling 621
Trent, Council of 231, 240, 243, 611, 612, 976
triadic formulae, New Testament 115
tribal religions, statistics 291
Trigg, Roger 340–1, 453–71
trinitarian theology 937–55
  classical 898
  post-theistic 904–5
  relationality 911–12
Trinity 187–205, 937–56
  baptism 950
  Christology 919
  classical view 898
  community 942, 951–2
  concept of God 343–4
  contemporary views 937–57
  creation 953
  creational purpose 73, 74
  democracy 951
  divinity of Christ 937
  doctrine 115
  Eastern Orthodox Church 940
  economic 941, 948
  feminist theology 952
  Gospel 949
  Hegelian interpretation 354
  historicization 878
  human fellowship with 74
  immanence 941, 948
  marriage 751
  plurality-in-unity 946
  polytheistic influence 189
  post-theistic view 904–5
  protest atheism 950–1
  relatedness 911–12, 939
  Rousseau 268
  social model 279
Trito-Isaiah 14
triumphalism, Christianity 127
Troeltsch, Ernst
  essence of Christianity 989
  ethics 694
  historicism 879–80
  inter-faith dialogue 992–3

  systematic theology 978, 997
  universal religion 231, 275, 276
tropes 53
tropological interpretation 52
'Truce of God' 211
Truman, Vice-President 725–6
trust
  emotional development 799, 804–5
  faith 804
  hope 799–800
  language 801
truth
  biblical theology 67
  concepts 603–4
  dialectic 113
  encounter with God 606
  Kierkegaard's teaching 359
  liberation theology 358
  objectivism 858
  post-modernism 992, 995, 997–8
  Rahner's view 613
  reality 607
  Scriptural content 123
  self-evident 608
  stories 968
Tyconius the Donatist 52
Tyndale, W. 157–8

Ugaritic epics, Old Testament stories 150–1
'ugly ditch' 67, 71, 78
UN *see* United Nations
understanding
  human 594
  reason distinction 70–1
unemployment, liberation theology 1012–13
unfaith, sin 703–4
union, mystical experience 622–5, 632, 634
Unitarians 902
United Nations
  creation 725–6
  Gulf War 727–8
  nuclear proliferation 727
  rebellions 731
  Secretary General 729
  war crimes tribunal 736
unity-in-plurality 751
universality, ethics 688
universally human 698, 699
universities
  academic theology 891–3

Canon Law 213
  dominance by friars 217
  growth 213–14
  medieval arts 329
univocity 426
Urban, Pope, pilgrimage 568
Urban II, Pope, crusades 210
utopia, liberation theology 1006

Vaisnavas 626
Valentius, grace and freedom 551
Valla, Lorenzo 238–9
Van Buren, Paul 923
Van Harvey, A. 883
Vatican Council, Second
  Christology 930–3
  church sacramentality 612–13
  controversy 164
  Guidelines on Religious Relations with the Jews 877
  inclusivism 299
  laity 604
  marriage 749
  Mary 681
  'People of God' 614
  The Relation of the Church to Nonchristian Religions 877
  'sign of the times' 526
  tradition 278
Vatke, W. 71–2, 77
Vaux, Kenneth, medical ethics 839
veridicality, spiritual perception 628, 635
verification principle
  logical positivism 414–16
  natural theology 405
Vernunft 70
Verstand 70
Vienna Circle 355, 414, 422
Vietnam War, concientious objectors 736
violence
  ethics 716–37
  liberation theology 791, 1006
  as sin 707
Virgin Mary *see* Mary, Virgin
virginity, patristic spirituality 542
virtue
  emotional development 800
  New Testament 691–2
vision 702, 707–8
visionaries 569
Vitoria, just war 719
vocation, work ethic 774–5

Volney, Constantin-François de 153–5, 156, 157
Voltaire
  biblical criticism 259, 260
  Deism 351
  free-will defence 481
  intolerence 252
  Meslier 259
  spirituality 516
voluntarism 235, 942
von Rad, G. 78–9
Vulgate Bible 152, 157, 231, 238–9, 558–9

Wainwright, Geoffrey 950, 952–3, 953
Wainwright, William J. 513
Wakefield, Gordon 513
Waldensians 215, 216, 217, 645
Wallis, Jim 658
Walter, Nikolaus 134
Ward, Keith 339, 342–66, 430
warfare
  Christian soldiers 564
  ethics 716–37
  feminism 492
Watt, James 863
wealth
  bibilical theologies 759–61
  creation 761–5, 767–9, 774
  distribution 760, 764, 765, 771
  divine gift 760
  doctrine 761–5
  ghettos 1012
  gratitude to God 760
  Hebrew Scriptures 1009
  responsibilities 765–7
  spiritual risk 774
Weber, Jans-Ruedi 1026
Weiss, J. 137, 924
Welch, Claud 955
Welch, Sharon 496, 497, 499, 500, 506
welfare, morality 787
Wellhausen, J. 77
Wendebourg, Dorothea 940
Wesley, Charles 168, 531
Wesley, John
  ecstasies 257
  hymns 667–8
  nineteenth century images of Christ 255
  perfection 516
  Psalms 676
Wesleyanism
  biblical criticism 260–1

holiness movement 268
  spirituality and social justice 648
West, Cornel 656
Westcott, Brooke 877
Westphalia, Peace of 249
Wetzel, James 486, 487
Wheaton Declaration 658
Whitehead, A. N.
  concept of God 361–3
  natural theology 399, 402
  process theology 361, 900
Wicca, feminist theology 907
Wiebe, D. 448–9
Wiles, Maurice 137, 275–6, 277–8, 282,
    882–3
will
  see also free will; self-will
  belief 604–5, 606
  creation 953
  emotional development 800
  limits 607
  locus of moral fault 701
  psychology 796
  sin 794–5
William of Ockham
  concept of God 349
  creation 953
  natural theology 392
  nominalism 223, 234
  prophecy 56
  scholasticism 232
  Unitarianism 941
  via moderna 233
William of Rubruck 218
Williams, Daniel Day 696
Williams, Robert 595
Williams, Rowan 520, 609
Wilmore, Gayraud 656
Wilson, E.O. 465, 466
Winch, Peter 423
Windesheim Congregation 215, 226
Wink, Walter 125–6, 1019–20
Winter, Colin 655
Winter, Paul 326
Winward, Stephen, Office 675
wisdom
  as divine agent 190–1
  life of Christ 194
  Paul's Jesus 169
Wisdom, J. 417, 419
wisdom literature
  canonization 16, 19

development 11–12
  origins 23–4
Wisdom of Solomon 12, 19
witchcraft 500–1, 864
witness, pacifism 721
Wittenberg, University of 240, 241
Wittgenstein, Ludwig
  human nature 460–1
  language 422–3, 903
  personalism 744
  Positivism 355
  post-foundationalism 379–80
  predication 424, 426
  religious language 430
  sociobiology 468
Wolf, Herbert 606–7
Wollaston, William 388
Wollstonecraft, Mary 491
Wolterstorff, N. 436
women
  see also feminist theology; sexism
  communication 806
  devotion 572
  divine metaphors 907
  early church role 885
  gender roles 740
  Jesus' attitude 885
  knowledge 859–60
  Old Testament subordination 80
  oppression 740
  ordination of 499, 876, 883, 986
  pleasure 739
  religious communities 217
  spirituality 523
Woolman, John 648
Woolston, Thomas 253, 259
Wooman, John, Quakerism 678
Word of God
  see also Logos
  embodiment 747–8
  Gospel of John 169
  independent existence 191–2
  Lord's Prayer 537
  patristic spirituality 540
  revelation 920
  secularization 923
  Son of God 192
  systematic theology 980, 982
Wordsworth, William 326, 598–9, 751–2
World Bank 769, 773
World Council of Churches
  British dominance 1028

ecumenical theology 1024
formation 877
membership 1028
Seventh Assembly 287
world religions
academic theology 892
Christianity today 872, 873
inter-faith dialogue 291–2, 992–3
statistics 291
World War I 720, 725, 918
World War II 725
worship
see also liturgy
corporate 652
early church 665–6
importance 288
liturgy 666–76
Psalms 12
Quaker 678
Wren, Christopher 324
writing prophets 13, 25
Writings, Hebrew Bible 145

Wycliffe, John 56–7, 108, 227, 568
Wynn, Mark 339, 413–32

Yahweh, concept of God 342
Yavneh 29
Yoder, J. Y. 720
Yoder, John Howard 650
Christian community 659
ethics 694–5, 697
Yogins 625, 626, 628–9

Zaehner, Robert Charles 623–5, 629
Zen tradition, Thomas Merton 654
Zizioulas, John 280, 949
Zoroastrianism 151, 845
Zurich, Reformation 240, 241–2
Zwingli, Huldrych
Anabaptism 242
Calvinism 242
divine causation 899
Reformation 239–40
sacraments 245
transsignification 245